HIGHWAYS

THE ISLANDS

MAJOR ATTRACTIONS

MAJOR CITIES

GENERAL INFORMATION

Northwest Mileposts®

Fourth Edition

Publisher, Peter L. Green
General Manager, Gary C. Tranter
Publishing/Production Director,
  Kathleen M. Gammon

Managing Editor, Kris Valencia
Copy Editors: Fay Bartels, Carolyn Smith
Editorial Assistance: Camilla Deux, Brita
  Gilthvedt, Billie Greenhalgh
Contributing Editors: Barry and Hilda
  Anderson, Tom Barr, Liz Bryan, Ted
  Dethlefs, Robert Graef, George Hein

Art Director, Kate Thompson
Designers: Alice Merrill Brown, Alyson
  Hallberg
Visuals Editor, Carrie Seglin

Production Manager, Nancy Deahl
Production Supervisor, Louise Helmick
Production Staff: David Berger, Amy Hines,
  Brenda Mooyman, David Ranta,
  Karen G. Smith

Fulfillment Manager, Cherryl Benson
Fulfillment Supervisor, Georgia Boyd

ISBN: 0-88240-278-1
Key title: Northwest Mileposts

PRINTED IN U.S.A.

Alaska Northwest Books™
A division of GTE Discovery Publications, Inc.

22026 20th Avenue S.E., Bothell, WA 98021

Publishers of: *The MILEPOST®*
  The ALASKA WILDERNESS MILEPOST®
Books about the North Country

Photography credits (pages 12-14): Salish
figure and basket, The Burke Museum;
Whittlesey portrait, Mercer Girls, miniature
portraits and gold miner, Museum of History
& Industry; train, Montana Historical Society;
Chief Joseph, F. Haynes, Special Collections,
University of Washington.

Cover: *Following the blacktop to Mount Adams.*
(Pat O'Hara)

Balsamroot and lupine under basalt cliffs in Columbia River Gorge   (© John Barger)

Field Editor Report

Between the time of our field editors'
surveys and the time of our reader's trip,
changes may take place along the highway
routes covered in *NORTHWEST MILEPOSTS®*.
A sincere effort is made to give you a complete,
accurate and up-to-date guidebook, but
travelers may nonetheless find changes in
hours of operation, prices, road conditions,
and services and facilities available. In all
such cases the publisher will not be held
responsible.

We would appreciate hearing from you,
our reader, about any inaccuracies or changes
that have taken place which need to be
corrected or included in the next edition of
NORTHWEST MILEPOSTS®. We would also like
to hear about new attractions, or old attractions we may have missed, that you wish to
see included in *NORTHWEST MILEPOSTS®*,
and any suggestions you may have on how we
can improve or expand our coverage of the
Northwest.

Please use the Field Editor Report form
on page 328 to let us know what you
discover while traveling the Northwest with
NORTHWEST MILEPOSTS®. Or drop us a letter
anytime in care of The Editor, *NORTHWEST
MILEPOSTS®*, P.O. Box 3007, Bothell, WA
98041-3007.

Photo Contribution

NORTHWEST MILEPOSTS® invites Northwest travelers and residents to submit photographs for consideration in future editions.
Copies of photo submission guidelines must
be requested before submitting photos. Send
request and a postpaid return envelope to
Visuals Editor, *NORTHWEST MILEPOSTS®*,
P.O. Box 3007, Bothell, WA 98041-3007. GTE
Discovery Publications, Inc. assumes no
responsibility for unsolicited materials.

Thanks

The editors of *NORTHWEST MILEPOSTS®*
would like to acknowledge their appreci-
ation to the many staff members of the U.S.
National Park Service, the U.S. Forest Service,
and other federal agencies; the state and
provincial divisions of tourism, parks, fish
and game, fish and wildlife, and transportation; and the many local chambers of
commerce, tourist bureaus, and countless individuals who have contributed
information and ideas to *NORTHWEST
MILEPOSTS®*.

The MILEPOST® Family

The northern companion publication to
NORTHWEST MILEPOSTS® is *The MILEPOST®*
All-the-North Travel Guide®, which picks up
where *NORTHWEST MILEPOSTS®* leaves off.
The MILEPOST® covers all highways in Alaska
and Yukon Territory; the Mackenzie Highway
system in Northwest Territories; and highways north from and including Yellowhead
Highway 16 in British Columbia and Alberta.
The MILEPOST® has been guiding travelers to
and from Alaska since 1949, and it continues
to serve as the leading travel guide to the
North.

Highways cover only about a third of Alaska;
the rest of the state is accessible only by air or
water. The third member of the MILEPOST
family, *The ALASKA WILDERNESS MILEPOST®*,
provides detailed information on Bush communities and off-the-road attractions in
Alaska.

Alaska Northwest Books™, A divison of
GTE Discovery Publications, Inc., also
publishes a wide array of regional and general interest books. A free catalog is available
on request; write GTE Discovery Publications,
Inc., P.O. Box 3007, Bothell, WA 98041-
3007; or phone 1-800-343-4567.

Key to Highways in NORTHWEST MILEPOSTS®

→ Indicates direction
highway is logged

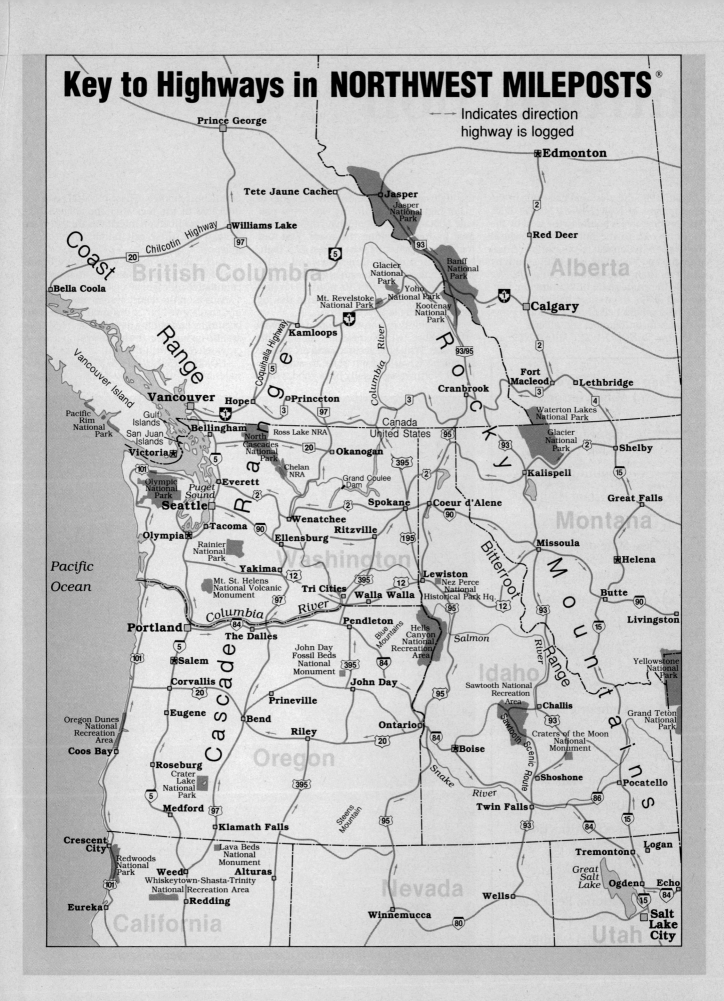

Introduction

Political boundaries were cast aside in the development of *NORTHWEST MILEPOSTS*®. Our coverage area is bound to the west by the Pacific Ocean; to the north by Yellowhead Highway 16 in Canada; to the east by central Montana and Wyoming; and to the south by northern Utah, Nevada and California. We include the entire states of Washington, Oregon and Idaho, the western half of Montana, and the southern half of the Canadian provinces of British Columbia and Alberta.

Central to *NORTHWEST MILEPOSTS*® are the highway logs. These mile-by-mile logs of major highway routes in the Northwest provide a detailed account of what you will see — mile by mile — along the roads. East-west routes are logged either east to west (U.S. highways) or west to east (interstates). All south-north routes (both interstates and U.S. highways) are logged south to north. Travelers headed in the opposite direction of the log should read the log back to front.

The highway logs are based upon the physical mileposts which measure our nation's highways. While the accuracy and prevalence of mileposts varies from state to state, the Pacific Northwest generally has a good system of milepost markers. These physical posts are indicated in the logs after the abbreviation MP. Exit numbers on interstates are also given in logs, and these exit numbers reflect the milepost.

Each highway that is logged has a beginning destination and ending destination, with cumulative mileages given for both. (Because Canada is on the metric system, highway logs in Canada give both miles and kilometers for beginning and ending destinations.) Mileages are also included on the highway strip maps to cross-reference with the text.

NORTHWEST MILEPOSTS® logs all interstates and most U.S. highways that cross the

Map and Text Symbols and Abbreviations

▬▬ — Highway described in log

─── — Adjoining Highways

⬭ — Interstate Highways

⬠ — U.S. Highways

▭ — State or Provincial and Secondary Routes

)(— Mountain Pass

▲ — Mountain

○ — Point of Interest/ Park

〜 — Rivers/Waterways

▲ — Campground

🐟 — Fishing

🜋 — Picnic Area

🚶 — Hiking Trail

⛷ — Alpine Ski Area

★ — Special Attraction

FS — Forest Service

MP — Milepost

NRA — National Recreation Area

NWR — National Wildlife Refuge

Monkeyflowers and arnica along a stream in Glacier National Park.   (© John Barger)

northwestern United States, plus 2 highway scenic routes. In Canada, we log the major provincial highways, trans-Canada routes and 2 scenic highways. See the Key to Highways map on page 3 and the Contents page for a detailed look at our coverage.

A major destination in the Pacific Northwest for residents and visitors alike are the islands of the region. The San Juan Islands, Whidbey Island, Vancouver Island, the Gulf Islands and Queen Charlotte Islands are covered in THE ISLANDS section. Included is information on the U.S. and Canadian ferry systems serving them.

Nine metropolitan areas are featured in the MAJOR CITIES section. The city descriptions offer travelers historical background and a list of attractions not to be missed.

Both U.S. and Canadian national parks are covered in the MAJOR ATTRACTIONS section. Also under Major Attractions are the National Monuments and National Recreation Areas of the Northwest.

See the GENERAL INFORMATION section for just that — general information. Helpful information, such as legal holidays in the U.S. and Canada, is included along with fun facts to know, such as what is Washington's state flower and how to pronounce Ucluelet.

And finally, use the INDEX in the back of the book to reference specific place-names throughout *NORTHWEST MILEPOSTS®*.

(© John Barger)

Moose and other large game thrive in remote Glacier National Park.

(© John Barger)

Broken Top peak in Deschutes National Forest in the Oregon Cascades.

Welcome to the Northwest

Welcome to the Northwest! There's more to be seen and experienced here than any other corner of the country.

The Northwest was the birthplace of the National Park System, and rightfully so. The towering, glaciated peaks of the Rocky and Cascade mountains contain the most beautiful natural treasures on earth. From the rolling plains of Montana, through the mountain spine of the Continental Divide, the high deserts of the Great Basin, mysterious rain forests of the Olympic Peninsula, unspoiled beauty of the thunderous coastline and the isolated serenity of the islands, the Northwest is diverse, exciting and unparalleled in beauty.

Yet the topography is only a part of what makes the Northwest spectacular. Ethnically, economically, politically and historically, the Northwest offers a wide range of lifestyles and stories. Here, Indians and Indonesians, Basques and Doukhobors, Hmongs and Hispanics, and dozens of other nationalities add their special flavor to the melting pot of the Northwest.

While the plentiful natural resources are a source of pride for Northwesterners, high-tech industries have taken a prominent position in the Northwest's economy, alongside forest products, mining and agriculture. The Idaho Nuclear Engineering Laboratory is located in the lava beds of southcentral Idaho. The Boeing Co., one of the world's largest leaders in aerospace, is headquartered in Seattle. Morton Thiokol, the world's largest producer of rocket motors, is located in the desert of northern Utah. The Hanford Nuclear Reservation, birthplace of the atomic bomb, is located on the high plateaus of the Columbia River Basin in Washington.

The Northwest also has its share of legends and myths. It is home to Sasquatch, the apelike creature that reportedly roams the Cascade mountain range, and the aquatic monster of Flathead Lake, the Northwest's answer to the Loch Ness Monster.

And just when you think you've seen it all, it all changes. Such was the case on May 18, 1980, when Mount St. Helens exploded in a violent eruption, dramatically changing the surrounding terrain, and the lives of many Northwesterners.

To describe the Northwest as an angler's paradise would be an understatement. Thousands of lakes and streams carry hundreds of species of fish including salmon, steelhead, trout, bass and char. The culture of the Northwest Indians was based largely on the ample supply of salmon.

Wildlife is still abundant here. The southernmost herd of caribou in North America make their home in the Selkirk Mountains of the Northwest. This region is the range of the North American King of Beasts, the grizzly bear, the largest land predator on the continent. Gray wolves, nearly eradicated in the rest of the country, still roam the upper reaches of the Rocky Mountains.

Storm waves pound the coast at Shore Acres State Park in Oregon.

(© John Barger)

Similkameen valley vineyards. *(L.Linkhart)*

British Columbia

Population: 2,889,207
Capital City: Victoria
Total Area: 365,950 square miles

British Columbia is Canada's most westerly province, stretching 813 miles from its southern border with the United States to its northern border with Yukon Territory. It is 438 miles wide, bounded on the east by Alberta and on the west by the Pacific Ocean. Victoria, the capital city, is located on Vancouver Island. Vancouver, the province's largest city, is on the west coast of the province. Vancouver is covered in the MAJOR CITIES section, while information on Victoria and Vancouver Island, including a log of the island's main highway, is included in THE ISLANDS section.

NORTHWEST MILEPOSTS® logs several highways in British Columbia. TRANS-CANADA HIGHWAY 1 descends from the Canadian Rockies into British Columbia and ends in Vancouver. It is a major east-west travel route. CROWSNEST HIGHWAY 3 also crosses the Rockies from Alberta into British Columbia, winding along the U.S. border west to Hope. It is a slower route than Trans-Canada Highway 1.

CANADA HIGHWAY 93 is the major access route to the Canadian Rockies for U.S. visitors and southern British Columbia residents from west of the Rockies. It also takes motorists past the headwaters of one of the Northwest's most important rivers — the Columbia.

CANADA HIGHWAY 97 begins at the U.S. border and travels north through the Okanagan-Similkameen and Cariboo Chilcotin country to Prince George on the Yellowhead Highway. This is a major south-north route which provides access to several of the province's large Interior communities. The CHILCOTIN HIGHWAY, which junctions with Highway 97 at Williams Lake, offers a look at the wilder side of the Cariboo Chilcotin on its way west to Bella Coola.

The COQUIHALLA HIGHWAY, British Columbia's newest highway, makes accessible to motorists some spectacular country in the Coquihalla River canyon. By combining YELLOWHEAD HIGHWAY 5 with the Coquihalla Highway, motorists have another south-north route, less populated but just as scenic as Highway 97.

Alberta

Population: 2,365,764
Capital City: Edmonton
Total Area: 255,290 square miles

The province of Alberta is known for its great geographical diversity, from the Canadian Rockies which mark the western border of the province to the vast wilderness region of lakes, rivers and forests of the northern half of the province. Rolling prairie and grainfields stretch from the U.S. border north to the capital city of Edmonton.

CANADA HIGHWAYS 4, 3 and 2 cross the agricultural heartland of Alberta, bisecting the province south to north. CANADA HIGHWAY 93 begins in British Columbia, but its most scenic stretch — the Icefields Parkway — is located within Alberta. TRANS-CANADA HIGHWAY 1 and CROWSNEST HIGHWAY 3 cut across Alberta from east to west. Crowsnest Highway 3 hugs the U.S. border, winding across the Rockies at Crowsnest Pass, while Trans-Canada Highway 1 cuts west from Calgary, crossing the Rockies at Kicking Horse Pass.

Canada's Rocky Mountain National Parks are covered in the MAJOR ATTRACTIONS section; Jasper, Banff and Waterton are located in Alberta. Alberta's 2 population centers — Edmonton and Calgary — are featured in the MAJOR CITIES section.

Mt. Hardisty and Horseshoe Lake, Jasper National Park. *(L.Linkhart)*

Glacier park's Lake McDonald. *(Paul Fugleberg)*

Idaho
The Gem State

Population: 1,036,500
Capital City: Boise
Total Area: 83,557 square miles

Wedged between Washington and Oregon to the west, and Montana and Wyoming to the east, Idaho has been in the path of westward migration since Lewis and Clark. (In southern Idaho, visitors can still see the ruts left by Conestoga wagons.) Today, all major east-west highways in the Northwest cross Idaho.

NORTHWEST MILEPOSTS® follows 4 of these east-west routes through Idaho: U.S. HIGHWAY 2, INTERSTATE 90 and U.S. HIGHWAY 12, all of which cut across the narrow, thickly forested panhandle that is northern Idaho; and INTERSTATE 84, which swings across the sagebrush-covered desert, agricultural lands (this is where the famous Idaho potatoes come from), and lava lands of southern Idaho. *NORTHWEST MILEPOSTS®* also logs INTERSTATE 86, a 63-mile connector route.

The 3 south-north routes logged in *NORTHWEST MILEPOSTS®* are: INTERSTATE 15, U.S. HIGHWAY 93 and U.S. HIGHWAY 95. Interstate 15 skirts Utah's Wasatch Mountains and enters the dry southeastern corner of Idaho, before continuing north over the Continental Divide into Montana. This interstate passes through Pocatello, eastern Idaho's largest city. U.S. Highway 93 cuts through the lava lands of central Idaho and climbs into the rugged Rocky Mountain range. U.S. Highway 95 winds up the western edge of the state, passing farming and ranching country before entering the evergreen forests of Idaho's panhandle.

NORTHWEST MILEPOSTS® also includes a log of Idaho Highway 75, known as the SAWTOOTH SCENIC ROUTE. This highway provides access to Sun Valley and to the magnificent Sawtooth National Recreation Area (see MAJOR ATTRACTIONS).

Montana
The Treasure State

Population: 824,000
Capital City: Helena
Total area: 147,138 square miles

NORTHWEST MILEPOSTS® covers western Montana, which is the more populous half of the Northwest's least populated state. The western half of Montana also offers some of the state's most spectacular scenery, a wealth of outdoor recreation, and interesting historic sites. Two major interstate routes and 2 U.S. highways now crisscross the land where once only explorers and Indians walked.

U.S. HIGHWAY 2 crosses the plains of eastern and central Montana before climbing into the jagged peaks of the Rocky Mountains at Glacier National Park (see MAJOR ATTRACTIONS). Along the way, stop in Browning to see the excellent Museum of the Plains Indian.

Our second east-west route through Montana is INTERSTATE 90, a heavily traveled freeway and the northernmost western arterial in the federal interstate highway system. Interstate 90 provides access to Bozeman, site of Montana State University (largest campus in the state), and Missoula, home of the University of Montana. Travelers along Interstate 90 will also get a glimpse of the Treasure State's mining history, still thriving in towns like Anaconda and Butte, and in the ghost towns and old mining areas tucked back in the hills.

INTERSTATE 15 crosses some rugged and lonely mountain country in Montana's southwest corner, before dropping down into Helena, the state capital (see MAJOR CITIES section). Fishermen can sample some of the state's famous world-class trout fishing along Interstate 15. The highway goes through the oil fields and grainfields north of Great Falls, Montana's second-largest city, and ends at the Canadian border.

More rugged and lonely mountain country can be found along U.S. HIGHWAY 93, which crosses into Montana near Big Hole National Battlefield, a monument commemorating the Nez Perce War and one of several historic sites along this route. U.S. Highway 93 leads north up the west side of the Rocky Mountains, providing access to the National Bison Range and huge Flathead Lake.

NORTHWEST MILEPOSTS® begins its log of U.S. HIGHWAY 12 in Missoula, following the trail of Lewis and Clark through Idaho and Washington.

Snake River at Twin Falls, ID. *(L.Linkhart)*

Oregon
The Beaver State

Population: 2,674,000
Capital City: Salem
Total Area: 96,981 square miles

Oregon was a magic word that originally stood for the mythical river flowing to the West which explorers hoped would be the gateway to the Orient. Later, it came to mean the territory between the Rocky Mountains and the Pacific, which lay north of California and south of Alaska.

It was further defined in the 1840s (as thousands of settlers headed for the "New Eden") as all of the land west of the Rockies between the 42nd and the 49th parallels. That Oregon Territory eventually became 3 states: Oregon (1859), Washington (1889), and Idaho (1890).

Oregon state is bounded to the north by the Columbia River; to the west by the Pacific; to the northeast by Hells Canyon and the Snake River; to the southeast by high desert plateau; and to the southwest by the Siskiyou Mountains.

Within these natural boundaries the state divides itself further into 7 distinct regions: the Willamette Valley, Oregon Coast, Columbia River area, Southern, Central, Northeastern and Southeastern Oregon. *NORTHWEST MILEPOSTS®* logs 5 south-north routes and 2 east-west routes which encompass all these regions.

INTERSTATE 84 follows the scenic Columbia River east from Portland, Oregon's major metropolitan area (see MAJOR CITIES section), and travels through the beautiful Columbia Gorge on its way to Idaho. U.S. HIGHWAY 20 cuts through the lonely high desert country of central Oregon, across the Cascade mountains, and down to the scenic Oregon coast.

U.S. HIGHWAY 101 stretches along the Oregon coast from the California border to the Washington border. There's probably more scenery and recreation mile for mile along the Coast highway than any other major route in the Northwest.

Less scenic, but the most important south-north route on the West Coast, is INTERSTATE 5, which cuts through southern Oregon and the Willamette Valley to Portland. U.S. HIGHWAY 97 is a pleasant alternative to Interstate 5 for south-north travelers, offering 2-lanes instead of 6, and towns instead of cities. It runs the length of Oregon, hugging the eastern side of the Cascade Range, and also provides access to Crater Lake National Park (see MAJOR ATTRACTIONS section).

U.S. HIGHWAY 395 and U.S. HIGHWAY 95 cross the wide open high desert plateau of southeastern Oregon, where the state's 3 largest — and least populated — counties are located. (They are Harney, Lake and Malheur counties.) U.S. Highway 395 also provides access to John Day Fossil Beds National Monument (see the MAJOR ATTRACTIONS section) and crosses the historic Oregon Trail at Pendleton.

Mount Shuksan reflected in Highwood Lake in the North Cascades. (© John Barger)

Washington
The Evergreen State

Population: 4,302,000
Capital City: Olympia
Total Area: 68,192 square miles

Like other Northwestern states, Washington has a striking dichotomy of climate, terrain and population: the western half is green, wet and populous; the eastern half is drier and flatter and a little bit lonelier.

Five major Northwest highway routes end in Washington. U.S. HIGHWAY 101 continues north from the Oregon border, winding up the coast of Washington and around the Olympic Peninsula to end at Olympia on Puget Sound. U.S. Highway 101 provides access to Olympic National Park (see MAJOR ATTRACTIONS section). INTERSTATE 5 also continues north from the Oregon border, past the major metropolitan areas of Tacoma and Seattle (see MAJOR CITIES), right to the Canadian border. U.S. HIGHWAY 395 crosses the Columbia River into eastern Washington, providing access to Spokane (see MAJOR CITIES) and the Canadian border.

The east-west routes in Washington that are logged in *NORTHWEST MILEPOSTS®* are U.S HIGHWAY 2, INTERSTATE 90 and the NORTH CASCADES HIGHWAY. U.S. Highway 2 crosses into Washington from Idaho just north of Spokane, capital of the Inland Empire (see MAJOR CITIES section), then crests the Cascades at Stevens Pass before junctioning with Interstate 5 near Everett. Interstate 90 counts Mile 0 from Interstate 5 in Seattle, then cuts across the Cascades at Snoqualmie Pass and through central Washington to Spokane, where it crosses into Idaho. The portion of Washington Highway 20 called the North Cascades Highway provides access to magnificent North Cascades National Park.

The not-to-be-missed parks of the Cascades are included in the MAJOR ATTRACTIONS section. These are North Cascades National Park, Rainier National Park, and Mount St. Helens National Volcanic Monument. Also covered are Ross Lake and Lake Chelan national recreation areas in the North Cascades.

U.S. HIGHWAY 97 is a south-north route that travels from California, through Oregon and Washington, right on into Canada, where it becomes B.C. Highway 97. A slower paced route than Interstate 5, U.S. Highway 97 passes much of Washington's agricultural land, including orchards of apples, perhaps the state's most well-known product.

Calendar of Events

Following are some of the annual events celebrated throughout the Northwest. Including one or several of these festivals in one's plans will greatly enhance your vacation. The exact dates are not given, but the approximate time period is noted as follows: Early – 1-10, Mid – 11-23, Late – 24-31. Check with the respective chambers of commerce or visitors bureaus for exact dates of events.

JANUARY

Alberta: *Mid* — Winter Carnival, Canmore. *Late* — Men's Open Bonspiel, Canmore; Snowarama, provincewide.

British Columbia: *Early* — Shoofest, Revelstoke.

Idaho: *Late* — Winter Carnival, Sandpoint.

Washington: *Mid* — Oak Harbor Yacht Club Salmon Derby. *Late* — Dogsled Races, Winthrop.

Cross-country skiing in Sawtooth National Recreation Area. (L.Linkhart)

FEBRUARY

Alberta: *Early* — Banff/Lake Louise Winter Festival, Banff. *Mid* — Ladies' Open Bonspiel, Canmore. Numerous Winter Carnivals throughout the province.

Fishing the McKenzie River near Eugene, OR. (L. Linkhart)

Idaho: *Early* — Mardi Gras, Sandpoint; Winter Carnival, McCall. *Mid* — Boulder Mountain Cross-Country Ski Tour and Race, Ketchum.

Oregon: *Mid* — Mardi Gras, Salem. *Late* — Newport Seafood & Wine Festival, South Beach.

Washington: *Mid* — Smelt Derby, LaConner.

MARCH

Alberta: *Mid* — International Indian Pow-Wow, Lethbridge; Annual Ice Show, Innisfail. Late—Superodeo, Edmonton.

Idaho: *Early* — Dogsled Days Celebration, McCall. *Mid* — Frontier Rodeo, Pocatello.

Oregon: *Early* — Indian-Style Salmon Bake, Oregon City; Mid-Winter Swiss Festival, Tillamook; Northwest Cup Giant Slalom, Bend. *Mid* — Fiddler's Jamboree, Roseburg; Bay Area Festival of Myrtle Trees, Coos Bay/North Bend/Charleston; Beachcomber Festival, Brookings.

Washington: *Early* — Wine Fair & Mardi Gras, Pasco. *Late* — Puyallup Valley Daffodil Festival, Tacoma and surrounding communities.

APRIL

Alberta: *Mid* — Arts & Crafts Show, Carstairs.

Idaho: *Late* — Apple Blossom Festival, Payette.

Montana: *Early* — Figure Skating Championships, Great Falls; University of Montana Indoor Rodeo, Missoula. *Late* — Libby Arts Festival.

Oregon: *Early* — Early Rhododendron Show, Florence; Spring Festival, Reedsport. *Mid* — Pear Blossom Festival, Medford. *Late* — Blossom Festival, Hoodsport.

Washington: *Early* — Skagit Valley Tulip Festival, Mount Vernon. *Late* — Washington State Apple Blossom Festival, Wenatchee; Opening Day Boat Parade, Oak Harbor; Columbia River Rowing Regatta, Tri-Cities.

MAY

Alberta: *Mid* — Air Show, Edmonton; Little Britches Rodeo, High River.

Idaho: *Mid* — Lake Coeur d'Alene Days Festival; Firefly Air Show and Firearms Championships, Bonners Ferry; Arts and Crafts Festival, Idaho Falls.

Montana: *Early* — Cherry Blossom Festival, Yellow Bay, Flathead Lake. *Mid*—Territorial Prison Break Run, Deer Lodge; Art Show, Butte.

Oregon: *Early* — Loyalty Days & Sea Fair Festival, Newport. *Mid* — Springfest, Springfield; Oregon Wine Festival, Lincoln City. *Late* — Boatnik Festival, Grants Pass; Azalea Festival, Brookings.

Washington: Apple Blossom Festival continues, Wenatchee. *Early* — Blessing of Fishing Fleet, Anacortes. Historic Home Tours, Port Townsend; Lilac Festival, Spokane. *Mid* — Rhododendron Festival, Port Townsend; Ski to Sea Festival, Bellingham. *Late* — Spring Festival, Moses Lake; Folk Life Festival, Seattle.

JUNE

Alberta: *Early* — Wooperee Daze, Warner; Bathtub Race, Sylvan Lake. *Mid* — Couttsgrass Rodeo, Coutts; Deer Run, Red Deer. *Late* — Ponoka Stampede, Ponoka; Midnight Days, Fort Macleod.

British Columbia: *Early* — Adams Lake Indian Band Rodeo, Chase. *Mid* — Elks Rodeo, Revelstoke; Stampede, Ashcroft. *Late* — Kamloops International Folkfest; Funfest, Salmon Arm; Sicamous Horse Club Draught Horse & Pony Show; Rodeo, Williams Lake.

Idaho: *Mid* — Frontier Days, Smelterville; Cherry Festival, Emmett; Arts and Crafts Festival, Idaho City; Old-time Fiddlers Contest, Weiser; Twin Falls Western Days; Summerfest, Hagerman; Jefferson County Stampede, Mud Lake.

Montana: *Early* — Governor's Cup Marathon, Helena. *Mid* — Libby Logger Days; College National Finals Rodeo, Bozeman. *Late* — Jazz Festival, Helena.

Oregon: *Early* — Strawberry Festival, Lebanon; Portland Rose Festival; NRA Professional Rodeo, Umatilla. *Mid* — Timber Festival, LaGrande. *Late* — Sandcastle Contest, Cannon Beach. *Continuing till late October* — Oregon Shakespearean Festival, Ashland.

Washington: *Early* — Salty Sea Days, Everett; Wine Festival, Spokane. *Mid* — Strawberry Festival, Marysville. *Late* — Timberbowl Rodeo, Darrington; Air Fair, Yakima; Hot Air Fair, Chehalis.

JULY

Alberta: Canada Day celebrations throughout the province. *Early* — Calgary Exhibition & Stampede. *Mid* — Klondike Days Exposition, Edmonton. *Late* — Whoop-up Days, Lethbridge.

British Columbia: *Early* — Anahim Lake Stampede, Chilcotin; Strawberry Festival, Clearwater; Shuswap Summer Showdown (10K run), Scotch Creek. *Mid* — Pow Wow, Squilax; Billie Barker Days, Quesnel. *Late* — Shuswap Festival of the Arts, Sorrento.

Idaho: *Early* — Fourth of July celebrations throughout the state. Little Britches Rodeo, Caldwell; Old-Time Western BBQ, Arimo. *Mid* — Kootenai River Days, Bonners Ferry; Snake River Stampede and Festival, Nampa; Arts & Crafts Fair, Twin Falls; Sun Dance, Fort Hall.

Montana: *Early* — Fourth of July celebrations throughout the state, many including rodeos. *Early* — Livingston Roundup; Choteau Rodeo. *Late* — Last Chance Stampede and Fair, Helena; Montana State Fiddlers Championships, Polson; State Fair, Great Falls.

Oregon: *Early* — Fourth of July parades and celebrations throughout the state; World Championship Timber Carnival, Albany. *Mid* — Miss Oregon Pageant, Seaside; Outdoor Summer Theatre Festival, Eugene; Salem Art Fair & Festival; Willamette Midsummer Jazzfest, Albany.

Washington: *Early* — Fourth of July celebrations in many communities; Lake Chelan Rodeo, Chelan; Loggerodeo, Sedro Woolley. *Mid* — 1990 Goodwill Games, Seattle, Tacoma, Spokane and other venues around the state; Seafair, Seattle; Lakefair Air Show, Olympia; Bellevue Jazz Festival; Darrington Bluegrass Festival; Tri-Cities Water Follies. *Late* — Port Townsend Jazz Festival; San Juan Islands Jazz Festival; Sand Castle Contest, Long Beach.

Sailing regatta on Alturas Lake in Sawtooth National Recreation Area. (L.Linkhart)

Folk Festival; Spitzee Days, High River; Folk Music Festival, Edmonton. *Late* — Agricultural Fair & Rodeo, Cardston.

British Columbia: *Early* — Fishing Derby, Kamloops; Moose Mouse Days, Sicamous. *Mid* — Summer Fair, Kamloops; Annual Slow Pitch Tournament, Clearwater. *Late* — Pacific National Exhibition, Vancouver.

Idaho: *Early* — Art on the Green, Coeur d'Alene; Air Show, Idaho Falls; Warbonnet Roundup, Idaho Falls. *Mid* — Snake River Run and Jamboree, Hagerman; Shoshone-Bannock Indian Festival, Fort Hall. *Late* — Jazz Festival, Coeur d'Alene; Western Idaho State Fair, Boise; Pocatello Air Show.

Montana: *Early* — Sweet Pea Festival, Bozeman; Ethnic Festival, Butte. *Late* — Western Montana Fair, Missoula.

Oregon: *Early* — Many fairs offered throughout the state; Outdoor Summer Theatre Festival, Eugene; Salem Celebration Summer Festival; Mount Hood Festival of Jazz, Gresham. *Mid* — Scandinavian Festival, Junction City; Astoria Regatta; Blue Grass Festival, Klamath Falls; Folklife Festival, Corvallis; Sea Sculpture, Rockaway State Park.

Washington: *Early* — Arts & Crafts Festival, Anacortes; Omak Stampede & Suicide Race. *Mid* — Highland Scottish Games, Everett; Coupeville Arts & Crafts Festival & Sailing Regatta, Oak Harbor; Washington International Kite Festival, Long Beach.

AUGUST

Alberta: *Early* — Heritage Day celebrations throughout the province. *Mid* — Calgary

---

SEPTEMBER

Alberta: *Mid* — Terry Fox Run, Red Deer. *Late* — World of Wheels, Lethbridge.

British Columbia: *Early* — Rodeo & Fall Fair, Merritt. *Mid* — Fall Fair, Ashcroft; Fall Fair, Salmon Arm; Fall Fair, Revelstoke.

Idaho: *Early* — Bunyan Days, St. Maries; Art in the Park, Boise; Southeast Idaho Fair, Blackfoot. *Mid* — Wallace Roundup.

Montana: *Mid* — Kalispell Art Show and Auction; State Draft Horse Show, Bozeman.

Oregon: *Early* — Numerous fairs throughout the state. Harvest Fair Folk Festival, Eugene; Oregon State Fair, Salem; Umatilla Watermelon Festival. *Mid* — Pendleton Round-Up; Oregon Hazelnut Festival, Hillsboro. *Late* — Oktoberfest, Baker; Fall Festival, Corvallis.

Washington: *Early* — Ellensburg Rodeo; Bumbershoot Festival, Seattle; Wooden Boat Festival, Port Townsend; Western Washington Fair, Puyallup; Lake Chelan Harvest Festival; Loggers Play Day, Hoquiam. *Mid* — Sausage Festival and Sailing Regatta, Everett; Interstate Fair, Spokane; Sausage Festival, Vancouver. *Late* — Historical Homes Tour, Port Townsend; Sunfair, Yakima; Autumn Leaf Festival, Leavenworth.

OCTOBER

Alberta: Numerous Rodeos and Octoberfest festivals throughout the province. *Late* — Round-up, Calgary.

Idaho: *Early* — Air Show, Twin Falls. *Mid* — Octoberfest, Coeur d'Alene; Basque Carnival and Bazaar, Boise.

Oregon: *Early*—Octoberfest, Bend; Oregon Dixieland Jubilee Jazz Festival, Seaside, Astoria and Gearhart. *Mid* — Octoberfest, Springfield.

Washington: Oktoberfest celebrations in Eastsound, Leavenworth and other communities. *Early* — Harvest Days, Centralia; Harvest Festival, Bellingham; Salmon Days, Issaquah.

NOVEMBER

Alberta: *Early* — Farm Fair, Edmonton; Art Fair, Edmonton; Arts & Crafts Show, Carstairs.

British Columbia: *Mid* — Arts & Crafts Fair, Valemount.

Idaho: *Late* — Holiday Parade, Boise.

Oregon: *Mid* — Salem Arts & Crafts Show.

Washington: *Mid* — Dixieland Jazz Festival, Ocean Shores; Holiday Fairs, Christmas parades and celebrations throughout the state.

DECEMBER

Alberta: *Early* — Santa Claus Parade, Fort Macleod; Annual Christmas Craft Sales, Leduc.

British Columbia: *Mid*—Larch Hills Marathon (cross-country skiing), Salmon Arm.

Idaho: *Mid* — Traditional Basque Sheepherders Ball, Boise.

Oregon: Christmas Fairs and Parades in many communities throughout the state.

Washington: Town Christmas Lighting, Leavenworth; Christmas Parade of Boats in Des Moines, Seattle, Tri-Cities, Anacortes and Bellingham.

A Chronology of Northwest History

The Pacific Northwest was one of the last major areas of the American West to be explored and developed. The first prehistoric inhabitants of the Northwest lived here some 10,000 years ago, but recorded history of the region begins with Spanish explorer Bartolome Ferello in 1543.

The following chronology of significant events in the history of the Northwest is intended to give a brief overview of this region's rich and diverse heritage.

1543 – Spanish explorer Bartolome Ferello sails north along the coast of modern day Oregon.

1592 – Apostolos Valerianos (Juan de Fuca) claims discovery of the legendary Strait of Anian, the Northwest Passage.

1741 – Vitus Bering reaches the Alaskan mainland.

1765 – First known use of the name Oregon, spelled Ouragon.

1774 – Juan Perez explores the coast for Spain; he sights Mount Olympus and reports the existence of Nootka Sound.

1778 – The last voyage of Capt. James Cook, during which he explores much of the Northwest coast between California and Alaska.

1787 – Charles W. Barkley finds and names the Strait of Juan de Fuca, after its presumed discoverer.

1792 – Captain Robert Gray, an American, discovers and names the Columbia River.

1793 – Alexander Mackenzie completes the first overland crossing of the North American continent to the Pacific Ocean.

1803 – Thomas Jefferson engineers the Louisiana Purchase. For $15 million, the United States buys Louisiana Territory from France, which includes all of the land west of the Mississippi drained by it and its tributaries.

1804-06 – Meriwether Lewis and William Clark explore the Louisiana Territory and the Northwest, from St. Louis to the mouth of the Columbia River.

1810 – Spokane House (9 miles from present-day Spokane) is established by the North West Co.

1811 – Astoria is founded at the mouth of the Columbia River by John Jacob Astor's Pacific Fur Co. The Astorians explore the Snake River region on their way west, and discover the Boise Valley. Fort Okanogan is established.

1812 – War of 1812. Fur posts established at Fort Spokane and Lewiston. A Pacific Fur Co. trader discovers South Pass through the Rocky Mountains, the route followed by the Oregon Trail.

1813 – North West Co. buys out interests of the Pacific Fur Co. in the Columbia River valley.

1818 – Fort Nez Perce (Fort Walla Walla) is constructed by the North West Co. Treaty is signed by United States and Great Britain agreeing that the Northwest will remain under the joint control of both nations, pending the final settlement

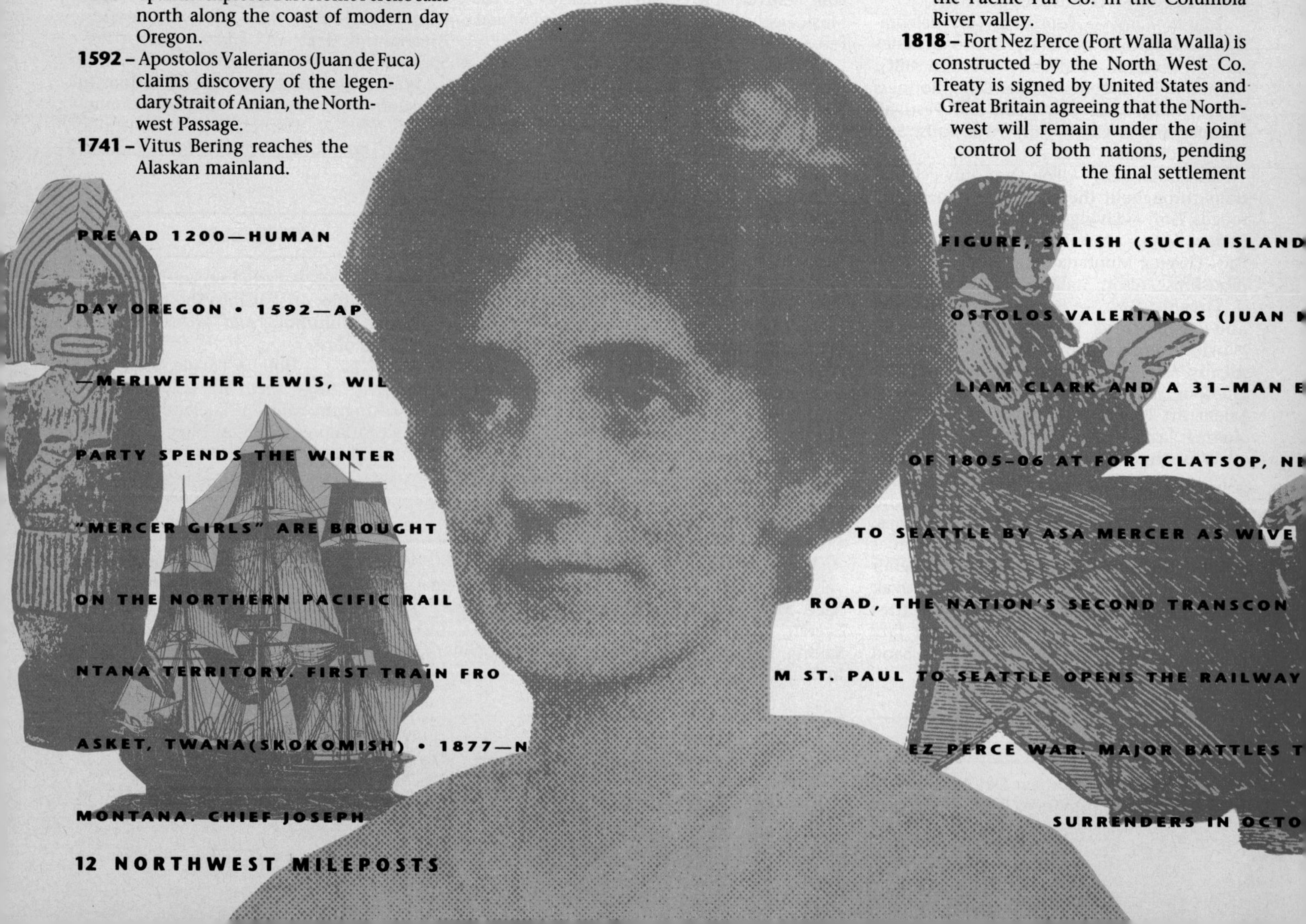

PRE AD 1200—HUMAN

FIGURE, SALISH (SUCIA ISLAND

DAY OREGON • 1592—AP

OSTOLOS VALERIANOS (JUAN

—MERIWETHER LEWIS, WIL

LIAM CLARK AND A 31—MAN

PARTY SPENDS THE WINTER

OF 1805–06 AT FORT CLATSOP, NI

"MERCER GIRLS" ARE BROUGHT

TO SEATTLE BY ASA MERCER AS WIVE

ON THE NORTHERN PACIFIC RAIL

ROAD, THE NATION'S SECOND TRANSCON

NTANA TERRITORY. FIRST TRAIN FRO

M ST. PAUL TO SEATTLE OPENS THE RAILWAY

ASKET, TWANA(SKOKOMISH) • 1877—N

EZ PERCE WAR. MAJOR BATTLES T

MONTANA. CHIEF JOSEPH

SURRENDERS IN OCTO

of the question of sovereignty.

1821 – North West Co. and Hudson's Bay Co. unite under the name of Hudson's Bay Co.

1824 – Hudson's Bay Co. establishes Fort Vancouver on the north bank of the Columbia River.

1832 – First crossing of the Rocky Mountains in covered wagons by Captain B.L.E. Bonneville, leading 110 men to Fort Walla Walla and Fort Vancouver.

1833 – First school in the Pacific Northwest is founded at Fort Vancouver. Fort Nisqually, the first trading post on Puget Sound, is established.

1836 – Missionaries Marcus Whitman and H.H. Spalding establish a mission near Fort Walla Walla, and the *Beaver*, the first steam boat on the Pacific Ocean, arrives at Fort Vancouver.

1839 – The first printing press in the Northwest is brought from Hawaii to Lapwai in Idaho. The missionaries use it to produce a Nez Perce primer, the first book published in the Pacific Northwest.

1841 – The Wilkes Expedition lands in the Northwest, explores Puget Sound and makes surveys inland as far as Fort Colville.

1842 – Willamette University, the first university located west of the Mississippi River, is established at Salem.

1843 – Beginning of heavy migration on the Oregon Trail.

1844 – The national election hinges on the slogan, "Fifty-four Forty or Fight." The Democratic party (which nominated James K. Polk) made this their slogan, signifying that they wished the United States to take control from the British of the entire Northwest up to the southern boundary of Russian America (Alaska) at 54°40'.

1845 – First American settlers on Puget Sound reach Tumwater.

1846 – The United States and Great Britain agree that the boundary between the U.S. and Canada will be at 49°N latitude. The first newspaper in the Oregon country, the *Oregon Spectator*, is published in Oregon City.

1847 – The Whitman massacre at Waiilatpu Mission near Walla Walla.

1848 – Oregon Territory is created by an Act of Congress on Aug. 14. The territory includes the present-day states of Oregon and Washington and most of Idaho. Abraham Lincoln is asked to be the first governor of the Oregon Territory, but he declines.

1849 – Many immigrants cross through southeastern Idaho on their way to the California goldfields. Fort Steilacoom is established by the U.S. Army.

1851 – The city of Portland (named for Portland, Maine) is incorporated. The name is chosen by a coin flip, to decide between the names Boston and Portland. On Puget Sound, the schooner *Exact* brings the first members of the Denny Party to Alki Point, in present-day Seattle.

1852 – Washington Territory is created north of the Columbia River. The territory includes the present-day state of Washington and most of present-day Idaho. The first survey for a railroad across the Cascade Range is begun by Isaac Stevens, who is appointed the first governor of Washington Territory.

1855 – Yakima Indian War begins.

1859 – Oregon becomes the 33rd state in the Union. The Fraser River gold rush begins in present-day British Columbia, and gold strikes are made in eastern Washington and Idaho. Construction begins on the Mullan

Road from Fort Walla Walla in Washington, to Fort Benton in Montana.

1860 – Franklin, one of the oldest towns in Idaho, is founded north of the Utah border on April 14. Daily stagecoach service is initiated between Portland and Seattle.

1861 – Lewiston is established as a distribution center for local mining camps and the town has the first newspaper to be published in the present-day state of Idaho, the *Golden Age*. In Seattle the Territorial University, now the University of Washington, opens its doors.

1863 – Alder Gulch strike in Montana, which leads to the founding of Virginia City and Nevada City. The Territory of Idaho is created out of parts of Washington, Nebraska and the Dakota territories, and includes all of present-day Idaho, Montana and much of Wyoming. Lewiston is the first capital.

1864 – Montana Territory is created. Other suggestions were that it be called Jefferson, Douglas, Shoshone and Abyssinia. The first "Mercer Girls" are brought to Seattle by Asa Mercer, to supply wives for the local unmarried men. Salem is made the capital of Oregon. The first transcontinental telegraph lines are completed.

1865 – Boise is made the capital of Idaho Territory.

1866 – The Idaho Legislature proposes that Congress should establish the state of Columbia, which would include western Montana, northern Idaho and eastern Oregon.

1867 – The United States purchases Alaska from Russia for $7.2 million.

1869 – The first transcontinental railroad is

543—EXPLORER BARTO LOME FERELLO SAILS NORTH ALONG THE COAST OF MODERN CA) CLAIMS DISCOVERY OF THE STRAIT OF ANIAN, THE NORTHWEST PASSAGE • 1805 ITION DEPART FORT MANDA N, NORTH DAKOTA, FOR THE PACIFIC NORTHWEST. THE AR PRESENT–DAY ASTORIA, OREGON • 1864—THE FIRST S FOR T HE LOCAL BACHELORS • 1883—LAST SPIKE TINENTAL LINE, IS DRIVEN AT GOLD CREEK, MO LINE • LATE 19TH CENTURY—TWINED B PLACE IN IDAHO AND 1897–98—KLONDIKE GO

CHRONOLOGY

completed, with the driving of the golden spike at Promontory Summit in Utah on May 10.

1871 – British Columbia enters the Confederation of Canada.

1872 – Congress establishes Yellowstone as first national park.

1875 – Helena becomes the capital of Montana Territory.

1876 – George Armstrong Custer and his men are killed at the Battle of the Little Big Horn.

1877 – Nez Perce Indian War.

1878 – Bannock Indian War.

1879 – Sheepeater Indian War.

1880 – Population of Oregon — 174,768; Washington Territory — 75,116; Idaho Territory — 32,619; Montana Territory — 39,159. A 16-year-old cowboy named Charles Russell arrives in Montana.

1883 – Completion of the Northern Pacific Railroad.

1889 – Montana is admitted as the 41st state into the Union and Washington is admitted as the 42nd state.

1890 – Idaho is admitted as the 43rd state into the Union. Population of Oregon — 317,704; Washington — 337,232; Idaho — 88,548; Montana — 142,924.

1893 – Great Northern Railway reaches Seattle.

1895 – The bitterroot is selected as the state flower of Montana.

1897-98 – Klondike gold rush begins.

1899 – Mount Rainier National Park is created.

1900 – Population of Oregon — 413,536; Washington — 518,103; Idaho — 161,772; Montana — 243,329.

1905 – Lewis and Clark Centennial Exposition held in Portland. Alberta enters the Dominion of Canada.

1909 – Alaska-Yukon-Pacific Exposition held in Seattle.

1910 – Population of Oregon — 672,765; Washington — 1,141,990; Idaho — 325,594; Montana — 376,053. Glacier National Park is created.

1912 – Women's suffrage enacted in Oregon.

1916 – First transcontinental telephone service to Seattle. The "Everett Massacre" of 5 Wobblies takes place on November 5 in Everett, Washington. Wobblies were members of the IWW (Industrial Workers of the World) which formed in 1905.

1917 – Representative Jeannette Rankin of Montana, the first woman to serve in the U.S. Congress, votes against U.S. entry into WWI.

1921 – First airplane service between Seattle and Vancouver, B.C.

1922 – Radio station KGW, the first commercial broadcasting station in Oregon, goes on the air. In Montana, the *Great Falls Tribune* opens station KDYS, the first officially licensed radio station in the state. Only 15 people in Great Falls have sets to receive its signal.

1927 – *Oregon, My Oregon* is adopted as the official Oregon state song.

1931 – *Here We Have Idaho* is adopted as the official Idaho state song.

1933 – The Tillamook Burn, one of the worst forest fires in recorded history, destroys hundreds of thousands of acres in Oregon.

1940 – Tacoma Narrows Bridge "Galloping Gertie" collapses in windstorm within four months of its completion.

1941 – Grand Coulee Dam is completed. Called the "eighth wonder of the world," it is the largest concrete dam in the world.

1942 – Farragut Naval Training Station is established at Lake Pend Oreille as part of the war effort.

1947 – A.B. Guthrie's classic novel of mountain men during the fur trade era, *The Big Sky*, is published.

1948 – Tragic Memorial Day flood destroys Vanport, Oregon.

1955 – First public test flight of the Boeing 707 jet aircraft in Seattle.

1962 – "Century 21," Seattle World's Fair.

1966 – Official completion of Interstate 5 between Washington and California.

1971 – Oregon's "Bottle Bill" is passed, first such legislation in the U.S.

1974 – Spokane hosts EXPO 74 world exposition.

1980 – Eruption of Mount St. Helens.

1986 – Vancouver, BC, is site of EXPO 86 world exposition.

LD RUSH BEGINS • 1909—SEATTLE HOSTS THE ALASKA-YUKON-PACIFIC EXPOSITION ON THE UNIVERSITY OF WASHINGTON CAMPUS. PRESIDENT TAFT, HENRY FORD AND RAILROAD BUILDER JAMES J. HILL ARE AMONG THE FAIRGOERS • 1962— SEATTLE HOSTS THE WORLD'S FAIR. BUILT FOR THE CENTURY 21 WORLD'S FAIR. BUILT FOR THE FAIR ARE THE SPACE NEEDLE, THE MONORAIL AND SEATTLE CENTER • 1980—ERUPTION OF MOUNT ST. HELENS

Trans-Canada Highway 1

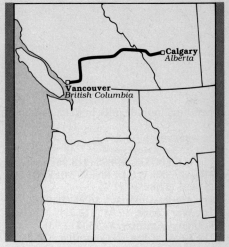

See map pages 17, 21 and 25

Trans-Canada Highway 1 is the world's longest national highway, stretching nearly 5,000 miles/8047 km from St. Johns, NF, on the Atlantic Coast, to Victoria, BC, on Vancouver Island on the Pacific Coast.

NORTHWEST MILEPOSTS® logs Trans-Canada Highway 1 west from Calgary, AB, across the Rocky Mountains to Vancouver, BC, perhaps the most scenic 600 miles in all of Canada. The highway crosses the flat prairies of Alberta, then climbs through the Rocky, Selkirk and Purcell mountains, crossing British Columbia to the Coast Mountains and then the flatlands of the Fraser River.

Trans-Canada Highway 1 Log

Distance in miles from Calgary, AB, is followed by distance in miles from Vancouver, BC. Equivalent distances in kilometers are indicated by Km.

Mile 0 (637) Km 0 (1025): **CALGARY** western city limits; access to Calgary city centre via 16th Avenue. For more information on Calgary, see the MAJOR CITIES section.

Mile 10.5 (626.5) Km 17 (1008): Junction with Highway 22 North to **COCHRANE**, Highway 22 South to Bragg Creek. Cochrane was the center of early ranching ventures in 1881. Cochrane Ranche Historic Site, watched over by a giant statue of a cowboy on a horse, preserves original ranch property and locations of buildings. The visitor centre displays ranching relics and offers slide shows. Picnic tables are available and admission is free. Summer hours to the park are 8 a.m. to 8 p.m. and the centre is open from 10 a.m. until 8 p.m. The city of Cochrane is noted for its ice creamery. ⊼

Mile 21.5 (616) Km 34.5 (990.5): Junction with Highway 68, which leads south 9 miles/15 km to Sibbald Lake Provincial Park with 134 campsites, beach, canoe launch, interpretative programs and trails. Fee is $3. ⋀▲

Mile 23.5 (613.5) Km 38 (987): Boundary of Stoney Indian Reserve.

Mile 29 (608) Km 46.5 (978.5): Access road to **MORLEY** on Highway 1A. The Rev. George McDougall and his 2 sons established a mission here in 1873. The mission school, church and homestead became a centre for nomadic Stoney Indians who chose to make Morley the center of their reserve. The church, built in 1875, has been restored as a historic site.

Mile 33 (604) Km 53 (972): Peigan Post historical stop of interest commemorates the site of a Hudson's Bay Co. trading post built in 1832 across the river. Blood Indians threatened to burn the post, so the traders retreated.

Mile 37 (600) Km 59.5 (965.5): Junction with Highway 40, which leads south along the Kananaskis River about 35 miles to Highwood Pass (elev. 7,204 feet/2,206m), the highest highway pass in Canada (open only in summer). Access to Nakiska, site of the 1988 Winter Olympics alpine events on Mount Allan, 15 miles/24 km south on Highway 40. Visitors can ride the Olympic Chair to the mid-mountain lodge with its Olympic displays and videos of events. Kananaskis village at the ski area has all services.

Peter Lougheed Provincial Park, about 31 miles/50 km south on Highway 40, has a total of 496 campsites in 6 locations on Kananaskis Lakes.

Mile 39.5 (597.5) Km 63.5 (961.5): Junction with Highway 1A North to Seebee and Exshaw communities. Access to Bow Valley Provincial Park just north of Highway 1; 246 campsites, sani-station, showers, fishing and interpretative trails. ⋀⇌▲

Mile 44.5 (592) Km 72 (953): Access road north to Lac des Arcs Provincial Park; 29 campsites, fishing and hiking trails. Camping fee is $3. ⋀⇌▲

Mile 46 (590.5) Km 74.5 (950.5): Gravel turnout (westbound traffic only) and stop of interest sign about the limestone across the river. Limestone quarries on Mount Exshaw, still in operation, provide one of the raw materials for Portland cement and have been in operation since 1906.

Mile 49.5 (587.5) Km 79.5 (945.5): Viewpoint for Mount Lougheed, named after a Calgary pioneer and senator. This is also the turnoff to Deadman Flats and Three Sisters Campground; 32 sites, fishing, picnicking. ⊼⇌▲

Mile 52.5 (584.5) Km 84.5 (940.5): Access to Spray Lakes Provincial Park; 50 campsites, boat launch, hiking. Access to Canmore Nordic Center (Winter Olympics of 1988) for summer hiking and mountain biking. ⋀▲

Mile 53.5 (583) Km 86.5 (938.5): Junction with Highway 1A to Exshaw and Calgary via the north side of the Bow River.

Mile 56.5 (580.5) Km 91 (934): Exit to **CANMORE**, year-round resort community with full tourist facilities. Travel Alberta information office; drinking water and picnic tables are available. Canmore was founded as a coal mining centre in 1888, but tunnels were flooded in 1900 and the mine closed. Today the community caters to a variety of mountain sports and it is also a centre for arts and crafts. Visit the Northwest Mounted Police barracks and the 1890 United Church. ⊼

Mile 60.5 (576.5) Km 97.5 (927.5): Carrot Creek bridge and eastern gateway to Banff National Park. Motor vehicle license sticker required for all visitors using facilities in Rocky Mountain national parks. Permit fees: 1 day, $3; 4 days, $6; annual permit, $20. Fishermen *NOTE:* National park fishing license is required. For more information on Banff National Park, see the MAJOR ATTRACTIONS section.

Mile 67 (570) Km 108 (917): Junction with Lake Minnewanka loop road (8.5 miles/13.5 km long) and campgrounds at Two Jack Lake with a total of 460 campsites. Scenic Lake Minnewanka offers lake cruises, fishing, boating and picnicking. ⊼⇌▲

Mile 68.5 (568.5) Km 110 (915): Access for westbound traffic only to Buffalo Paddock. A 1-mile/1.6-km road leads through an enclosure where a herd of wood buffalo, a species that once ran wild in the mountain meadows, is kept. The best time to see these animals is early morning or at dusk. Good view from highway of Cascade Mountain (elev. 9,836 feet/2,998m), the highest in the Banff region.

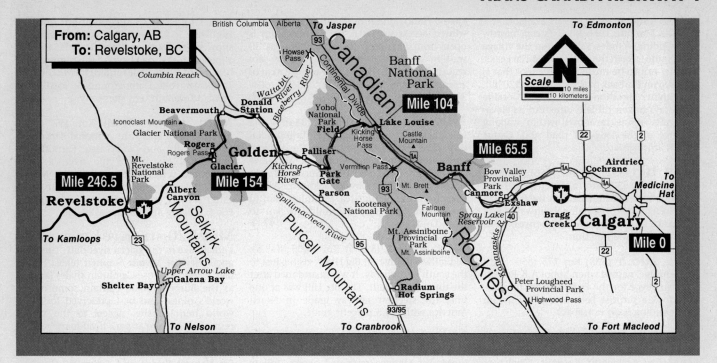

From: Calgary, AB
To: Revelstoke, BC

Columbia Reach · British Columbia · Alberta · To Jasper · To Edmonton

Canadian · Banff National Park · Mile 104

Scale — 10 miles / 10 kilometers · N

Howse Pass · Continental Divide · Lake Louise · Castle Mountain · Mile 65.5

Donald Station · Wattabit River · Blueberry River · Yoho National Park Field · Kicking Horse Pass

Beavermouth · Iconoclast Mountain · Glacier National Park · Rogers · Rogers Pass · Golden · Palliser · Vermilion Pass · Banff · Bow Valley Provincial Park · Airdrie · Cochrane

Mt. Revelstoke National Park · Glacier · Mile 154 · Kicking Horse River · Park Gate · Parson · Mt. Brett · Canmore · Exshaw · Bragg Creek · Calgary

Mile 246.5 · Albert Canyon · Selkirk Mountains · Spillimacheen River · Kootenay National Park · Fatique Mountain · Spray Lake Reservoir · Mile 0

Revelstoke · To Medicine Hat · To Kamloops

Purcell Mountains · Mt. Assiniboine Provincial Park · Mt. Assiniboine · Rockies · Kananaskis · Peter Lougheed Provincial Park · Highwood Pass

Upper Arrow Lake · Shelter Bay · Galena Bay · Radium Hot Springs · 93/95

To Nelson · To Cranbrook · To Fort Macleod

Mile 69.5 (567.5) Km 112 (913): Exit south to Banff townsite and Vermilion Lakes scenic drive (descriptions follow). Exit north for Mount Norquay scenic drive and cable car ride to the summit of Mount Norquay (elev. 7,005 feet/2,135m) for spectacular vistas of Banff and Mount Rundle. The lift is open daily, mid-June to September.

BANFF (pop. 5,200) townsite is the headquarters of Banff National Park and offers accommodations of all types, restaurants and shopping. This scenic resort attracts more than 2.5 million visitors annually, in summer for the scenery, and in winter for the skiing.

The area was first set aside for the public because of the hot springs which bubble out from the base of Sulphur Mountain and the springs are still a leading attraction today. There are 2 springs: the Upper Hot Springs Pool and the older Cave and Basin. Other attractions include a summer gondola ride to the summit of Sulphur Mountain; the Luxton Museum for Canadian Indian artifacts and wildlife; the Victoria-era Banff Museum; the Whyte Museum of the Canadian Rockies; and the grand old Banff Springs Hotel.

Vermilion Lakes, between Highway 1 and the Banff townsite, are accessed by a 6.8-mile/11-km round-trip drive from Banff. Marshland habitat is a good spot to observe wildlife.

National park campgrounds are located at 3 locations on Tunnel Mountain Road, providing a total of nearly 1,200 campsites; all have showers, sani-stations, covered picnic sites and hiking trails.

Mile 71.5 (565.5) Km 115 (910): Viewpoint across Vermilion Lakes to Mount Rundle. During the early morning and evening, watch for moose in the lake. Rocky mountain bighorn sheep cross the highway frequently in this area.

Mile 73 (564) Km 117.5 (907.5): Junction with Highway 1A (Bow Valley Parkway), a scenic alternate route to Lake Louise with access to Johnston Canyon Campground, open mid-May to mid-September; 140 campsites and sani-station. Dramatic Johnston Canyon has been made accessible to visitors by means of a suspended walkway built out over the rock walls. Catwalk leads to falls.

Mile 75 (562) Km 120.5 (904.5): Junction with road to Sunshine Village (downhill) Ski Area. Summer gondola rides to alpine meadows for nature walks are available daily from the end of June to the beginning of September.

Mile 77.5 (559.5) Km 124.5 (900.5): Wolverine Creek and picnic area.

Mile 81.5 (555) Km 131.5 (893.5): Picnic area and trail up Red Earth Creek to Shadow and Egypt lakes; cross-country ski area.

Mile 82.5 (554.5) Km 133 (892): Castle Mountain viewpoint. The mountain, a block of turreted crags, is aptly named Castle, although for several years it was known as Eisenhower Mountain.

Mile 87 (550) Km 140 (885): Copper Lake picnic site beside the Bow River. A short distance west, hidden in the trees, is small Copper Lake, named after the nearby mines.

Mile 88 (548.5) Km 142 (883): Altrude Creek picnic site.

Mile 88.5 (548.5) Km 142.5 (882.5): Castle Junction. Turn south on Highway 93 for Radium Hot Springs (see **Mile 205** in CANADA HIGHWAY 93 section). Highways 1 and 93 share a common alignment between Castle Junction and Lake Louise. Turn north on Highway 1A (Bow Valley Parkway) for alter-

nate access route to Lake Louise and Banff along the north bank of the Bow River. Highway 1A provides access to Castle Mountain Campground with 44 campsites.

Mile 93 (543.5) Km 150 (875): Taylor Creek picnic area and trail to Taylor Lake.

Mile 99 (538) Km 159.5 (865.5): Rest area by the Bow River. View of glacier-crowned Mount Temple (elev. 11,627 feet/3,544m) to west, highest mountain in the Bow Range.

Mile 100 (537) Km 161 (864): Lake Louise overflow campsite. Banff National Park is so popular with tourists that campgrounds often are full. Arrive early in the day to find a spot.

Mile 104 (533) Km 167.5 (857.5): Exit to Lake Louise village and visitor information office. Access to Highway 1A and Protection Mountain Campground; 89 campsites.

LAKE LOUISE village (pop. 700) is a popular destination resort, with all tourist facilities, including a shopping mall. The historic Post Hotel is located on the Pipestone River. South of the village are 2 national park campgrounds with all facilities and a total of 400 campsites. Lake Louise ski resort, with 9 lifts and 30 miles/50 km of cross-country trails, is located north of the highway. The gondola at the resort operates in summer and from the top visitors get uninterrupted views of Lake Louise, the Victoria Glacier, Mount Temple and other peaks of the Bow Range.

From the village, a road leads 2.5 miles/4 km across the Bow River to Lake Louise itself. This much photographed alpine lake is brilliantly colored and surrounded by the glaciers of Mounts Victoria and Lefroy. On the lakeshore is the baronial Chateau Lake Louise (dining and lodging available). Hiking trail from the Chateau to the plain of the Six

Glaciers teahouse. Boat rentals available.

Take Moraine Lake Road (steep, narrow and winding) 8 miles/14 km from the village to Moraine Lake in the valley of the Ten Peaks, another not-to-be-missed beauty spot that is pictured on the back of the Canadian $20 bill. At a higher elevation than Louise, Moraine Lake stays frozen till late June, but its elevation puts alpine meadows within walking distance of the lodge at road end. Canoe rentals at lodge.

Mile 105 (532) Km 169 (856): Junction with Highway 93 North to Jasper via Icefields Parkway; turn to **Mile 222.5** in the CANADA HIGHWAY 93 section for log. Highways 1 and 93 share a common alignment between Lake Louise and Castle Junction.

Mile 108.5 (528) Km 175 (850): Bath Creek bridge, named when Major A.B. Rogers, chief surveyor for the Canadian Pacific Railway, took a surprise bath in this icy stream while fording it on horseback.

Mile 109.5 (527.5) Km 176 (849): Kicking Horse Pass (elev. 5,333 feet/1,625m) lies just below viewpoint turnout. The pass marks the boundary between Alberta and British Columbia and between Banff and Yoho national parks. In 1881, railway surveyors chose this route over the Continental Divide for Canada's first transcontinental railway, the Canadian Pacific.

Mile 110 (527) Km 177 (848): Sink Lake picnic area. The lake has no visible outlet; it is believed to drain underground, perhaps into the Kicking Horse River.

Mile 111 (526) Km 178.5 (846.5): Junction with Highway 1A to Lake Louise. Great Divide picnic area and limited access road to

Lake O'Hara Campground and lodge (open in winter, access by skis). The campground is open from late June to September, has 30 walk-in campsites and reservations are required. Fee is $5. Hikers may use the road or arrange transportation by bus; phone (604) 343-6324.

Mile 112.5 (524.5) Km 181 (844): Wapta Lake picnic area, lodge and gas station adjacent. The lake is the source of the Kicking Horse River which was named by Sir James Hector of the 1857-60 Palliser Survey Expedition, who was killed by a packhorse. A trail leads from the picnic area 1.8 miles/3 km to Sherbrooke Lake and 2.2 miles/3.6 km to Paget Lookout.

Mile 113.5 (523.5) Km 182.5 (842.5): Old railway bridge on Big Hill is visible just to the south of highway. It was abandoned after the tunnel was built. The Big Hill was at one time the steepest railway grade in North America with a 4.5 percent grade.

Mile 114.5 (522.5) Km 184.5 (840.5): Viewpoint of the Lower Spiral railway tunnel in Mount Ogden (restricted access, follow signs). A display explains the history and present operation of the 2 tunnels (the other is in Cathedral Mountain to the south).

Mile 116 (521) Km 186.5 (838.5): Viewpoint, Mount Stephen and old tunnel entrance to abandoned lead, zinc and silver mine on the mountain slope. To find the tunnel, look below and to the right of the hanging glacier.

Mile 117 (520) Km 188.5 (836.5): Junction with Yoho Valley Road north 10 miles/16 km to spectacular Takakkaw Falls, which drop 1,248 feet/380m from a limestone cliff. Access

to Kicking Horse Campground just north of Highway 1; 92 campsites, kitchen shelters, showers and sani-station. Trailers are not allowed on the road beyond the campground because of steep grades and tight switchbacks. Takakkaw Falls Campground at road's end offers 35 walk-in tent sites only.

Mile 119.5 (517.5) Km 192 (833): Alberta Travel and Yoho National Park information office and picnic area. Turnoff here for **FIELD**, east across the river, a small settlement under the shadow of Mount Stephen. Field began as a railway construction camp and is still a railway division plant. Food, lodging and gas are available.

Mile 120 (517) Km 193 (832): Rest area by a small lake in the glacial river flats. There is a good view of Mount Stephen (elev. 10,495 feet/3,199m) whose Cambrian shales (known as the Burgess Shale) contain some of the world's oldest and best preserved fossils. A world heritage site. Access to the site is restricted; inquire at park headquarters.

Mile 121 (516) Km 194.5 (830.5): Turnoff for Natural Bridge and Emerald Lake. The Kicking Horse River gouged the natural bridge out of the rocks. The road also goes to animal salt licks frequented by moose. Hiking trails to Burgess and Yoho passes and Hamilton Lake Falls. There are tourist facilities at Emerald Lake, including a lodge and tearoom. Horses and boats are available for hire.

Mile 127 (510) Km 204.5 (820.5): Valley of the Kicking Horse viewpoint and picnic area. Heavily braided river formations are due to heavy silts carried by the glacially-fed river and its tributaries.

Mile 130 (507) Km 209 (816): Finn Creek picnic area.

Mile 130.5 (506.5) Km 210 (815): Misko lookout over the valley to the peaks of Vaux, Hunter and King. Sign explains effect of glaciation. Look at the rocks on the west side of the road for glacial scratches.

Mile 132.5 (504.5) Km 213 (812): Picnic area; avalanche nature trail leads through the forest to the edge of a large avalanche slope on the side of Mount Vaux.

Mile 133 (504) Km 214 (811): Hoodoo Creek Campground, open late June to Labor Day; 106 campsites, 4 kitchens, sani-station. Short steep trail to the hoodoos, which are eroded towers of boulder clay topped by harder rocks. Beaver Pond nature trail; Deerlodge trail to the first warden cabin; and trail access to Beaverfoot Valley and Ice River, where the largest outcropping of igneous rock in the Rockies contains veins of blue sodalite.

Mile 134.5 (502.5) Km 216.5 (808.5): Turnoff to Chancellor Peak campground, open May to October; 64 campsites, kitchen shelters.

Mile 135 (502) Km 217.5 (807.5): Wapta

Historic Post Hotel on Pipestone River; turnoff at Mile 104.   (Liz Bryan)

Falls Road leads south 1.5 miles/2.5 km to parking area and 2.5 miles/4 km south to trailhead for falls. The falls are 200 feet/60m wide and more than 90 feet/27m high.

On the north side of the highway a trail takes off for Mount Hunter Lookout (2.2 miles/3.5 km) which provides a grand panoramic view of the mountains.

Mile 135.5 (501.5) Km 218 (807): Picnic area and viewpoint for Mount Vaux (elev. 10,892 feet/3,320m). Watch for elk crossing the highway.

Mile 137 (500) Km 220.5 (804.5): Park information office, picnic tables and route map of road through Yoho Park. Sign identifies Mount Hunter (elev. 8,661 feet/2,640m).

Mile 137.5 (499.5) Km 221.5 (803.5): Western entrance to Yoho National Park.

Mile 139 (498) Km 224 (801): Viewpoint with picnic tables.

Mile 145.5 (491.5) Km 234 (791): Park Bridge over Kicking Horse Canyon; railway below.

Mile 146 (491) Km 235 (790): Yoho rest area.

Mile 153.5 (483.5) Km 247 (778): Viewpoint to south with stop of interest sign about the town of Golden. This is a good view over the Rocky Mountain Trench, the geological fault line which divides the Rocky Mountains on the east from the Columbia Mountains on the west. The Kicking Horse River cuts a canyon far below the road. Nearby is a wildlife museum.

Mile 154 (483) Km 247.5 (777.5): Junction with Highway 95 South to Radium Hot Springs (62 miles/100 km) on Highway 93.

Entering **GOLDEN** (pop. 3,500), all visitor facilities. Golden began life as a Canadian Pacific Railway construction camp and boomed when the railway came through. Golden became primarily a logging community in the 1880s. Around the turn of the century, when the railway began advertising the alpine charms of Glacier National Park, Swiss guides were brought here to lead the tourists. The guides were housed in the Swiss-style chalets of Edelweiss Village northeast of town.

Today, white-water rafting on the Kicking Horse and Blaeberry rivers is gaining popularity here.

Mile 162 (475) Km 260.5 (764.5): Stop of interest marker commemorates Walter Moberly, the first surveyor of the railway route through the mountains. To the west lies Moberly Marsh, a wildlife preserve donated to British Columbia by pioneers Burges and James Gadsden. Look for muskrat lodges, osprey and bald eagles. The marsh is accessible from the old Moberly railway station just south through dense bush. Dyke trail leads along the river-bank for about 2.2 miles/3.5 km.

Park Bridge crosses the Kicking Horse River at Mile 145.5.　(Liz Bryan)

Mile 163.5 (473.5) Km 263.5 (761.5): Blaeberry River bridge. The river was named by explorer David Thompson who crossed the Rockies via Howse Pass in 1807 and followed the river down to the Columbia Valley where he founded Kootenae House, a fur-trapping post beside Lake Windermere (see CANADA HIGHWAY 93). The river is turbulent and discharges much silt and gravel into the Columbia; its delta is a maze of sloughs and marshy ponds. Blaeberry School Road follows the river upstream for nearly 30 miles/50 km. Past Mummery Creek Forestry Recreation Area follow signs to trail which leads 3 miles/5 km up to the toe of the Mummery Glacier. At road end a hiking trail continues over Howse Pass across the Continental Divide to Banff. This is the route of a proposed new highway link, one that is being opposed by conservationist groups.

Mile 166 (471) Km 267 (758): Doyle Creek rest area; picnic tables under the trees.

Mile 169.5 (467.5) Km 273 (752): Small community of **DONALD STATION** just off highway; no services. Old Big Bend Highway to north, once the only auto route through the rugged Columbia Mountains, provides access to Columbia Reach, Bush Arm and Kinbasket Lake.

Highway 23 North

Highway 23 North leads up the eastern shore of Lake Revelstoke to Revelstoke and Mica dams.

Mile 0 Km 0: Junction of Highway 1 and Highway 23 North.

Mile 2.5 Km 4: Canada's highest concrete dam, Revelstoke Dam rises 575 feet/175m above the canyon floor. Year-round tours include elevator to the dam crest lookout and views of the main powerhouse gallery, tailrace and control room. Open 8 a.m. to 8 p.m., mid-June to mid-September; 9 a.m. to 5 p.m. rest of year. Tours are free, self-guided, though tour guides are on hand. Just below the dam is Columbia View Provincial Park picnic area and playground.

Mile 10 Km 16: Martha Creek Provincial Park; 26 campsites, swimming beach and boat launch. Trail to Martha Lakes (5 hours round-trip).

Mile 17 Km 27: Lake Revelstoke Resort on La Forme Creek; camping, boat launch. Lake access also at Carnes and Mars Creek, to the north.

Mile 49 Km 65: Downie Creek Provincial Park on a sheltered bay which is the drowned lower section of the creek; 22 campsites, picnic shelter, boat ramp. Good view of nearby glaciers.

Mile 52 Km 85: Gravel road east to the Noranda Mine and access to a popular canoe route on the Goldstream River.

Mile 71 Km 115: Lake access at the mouth of Bigmouth Creek.

Mile 80 Km 130: Pitt Creek Forestry Recreation Site; 18 campsites, maintained June 1 to September 30.

Mile 83.5 Km 135: **Mica Village,** home base for dam workers. Store with basic supplies and gas (no propane or diesel). Just north is a hiking trail up Fred Laing Ridge, 1.6 miles round-trip (great views).

Nearby is the drowned historic site of Boat Encampment where explorer David Thompson built canoes to carry him and his party down the Columbia to the Pacific. An important depot of the fur-brigade, goods traveled up the Columbia in boats, were transferred here to packhorses for the journey over Athabasca Pass.

Mile 88 Km 142: Mica Dam, North America's largest earth-filled dam, more than 800 feet/250m high. Daily 90-minute guided tours 11 a.m. and 2 p.m., mid-June to early September. North lies one of the arms of sprawling Kinbasket Lake reservoir and a forestry campsite and boat launch at the mouth of Potlatch Creek. The road is unpaved and used by logging trucks: Drive with caution.

WARNING: Boaters on both Revelstoke and Kinbasket lakes are warned of sudden gusting winds, icy water, unstable shoreline and the presence of debris and deadheads. Night boating is not advised. Boaters on Revelstoke Lake just south of the Mica Dam are advised to keep well away from the spillway and racehouse.

Mile 171 (466) Km 275.5 (749.5): Highway and railway cross the Columbia River.

Mile 177.5 (459.5) Km 286 (739): Picnic areas on both sides of the road. 🛆

Mile 192 (445) Km 309 (716): Heather Hill lookout and mountain panorama, with signposts.

Mile 192.5 (444.5) Km 309.5 (715.5): East boundary of Glacier National Park. Mountain-Pacific time zone change: eastbound travelers move watches ahead 1 hour, westbound travelers set watches back 1 hour.

Mile 193.5 (443.5) Km 311.5 (713.5): Mountain Creek Campground; 306 campsites, kitchen shelters. Trestle hiking trail, a 20-minute walk up to the modern rail bridge which replaced the wooden trestle bridge over Mountain Creek. 🚶🚶▲

Mile 194.5 (442.5) Km 313 (712): East entrance to Glacier National Park. Travelers who plan to stop overnight in any of the mountain national parks are required to buy auto permits: $3 for 1 day; $6 for 4 days; $20 for 1 year, good in all national parks in Canada.

Mile 196 (441) Km 315.5 (709.5): Picnic area. 🛆

Mile 197 (440) Km 317 (708): Viewpoint over Beaver Valley.

Mile 198 (439) Km 319 (706): East entrance to Rogers Pass, viewpoint and rest area.

Mile 198.5 (438.4) Km 320 (705): East end of the first of 3 snowsheds westbound. WARNING: Obscured vision, speed 35 mph/60 kmph in tunnel. Near here the Canadian Pacific Railway enters the long Connaught Tunnel, which bypasses its earlier route over the pass and most of the avalanche hazards, and the recently completed Mount MacDonald Tunnel, the longest rail tunnel in North America (more than 9 miles/14.7 km).

Mile 202 (437) Km 323 (702): Avalanche

Defence viewpoint at the west end of the third snowshed westbound. Picnic area with exhibit explaining avalanche control. Travelers can see several active avalanche paths, a gun emplacement (for triggering avalanches), and an old railway snowshed. A short 1 mile/1.6 km walk along the Sir Donald Trail leads to an avalanche path strewn with the debris from a 1972 avalanche. *WARNING:* Obscured vision, speed limit of 35 mph/60 kmph, in tunnel. 🛆

Mile 203 (434) Km 326.5 (698.5): ROGERS PASS tourist service area; lodge with restaurant, store and gas station. Park headquarters south side of highway. Just west of the lodge is the Rogers Pass Information Centre, built of massive timbers to resemble an old-time railway snowshed, complete with sod roof.

From the center a 0.5-mile/1.2-km trail traces the abandoned railway route through the pass, leading to abandoned snowsheds.

Mile 204 (433) Km 328 (697): Rogers Pass Summit (elev. 4,347 feet/1,325m) marker arch. Turnouts on both sides of the highway. The views are great, particularly of Mounts Rogers and Sir Donald. The pass was named for its discoverer, Major A.B. Rogers, a railway engineer in charge of the Canadian Pacific Railway route-finding expedition in 1882.

Mile 205.5 (431.5) Km 331 (694): Access road to Illecillewaet Campground; 59 campsites, kitchen shelters, open July to mid-September. Trail from campground to the site of Glacier House, a major Canadian Pacific Railway hotel at the turn of the century. Also trailheads here for several strenuous day hikes up to some of the glaciers.

Westbound travelers watch for the eastern portal of the Connaught Tunnel north of the highway. 🚶🚶▲

Mile 207 (430) Km 333 (692): Loop Brook Campground; open mid-July to mid-September, 20 campsites, kitchen shelter. Just east along the highway is a large turnout and viewpoint of the mammoth stone pillars (60 feet/18m high) that once carried the railway across the creek, bypassing an earlier long loop. A scenic 1-mile/1.6-km trail follows the abandoned railway loop back to the campground. From the trail there are stunning views of the north face of Mount Bonney, hung with glaciers. 🚶🚶▲

Mile 208 (429) Km 334.5 (690.5): Illecillewaet River bridge; picnic tables and viewpoint of Mount Sir Donald (elev. 10,817 feet/3,297m), the park's highest peak. 🛆

Mile 209.5 (427.5) Km 337.5 (687.5): Large turnout. South of highway look for west portal of the Mount MacDonald rail tunnel.

Mile 216 (421) Km 347.5 (677.5): Bostock Creek bridge and the west gateway of Glacier National Park. Picnic tables are located on the north side of the highway. Westbound Highway 1 goes through 3 avalanche sheds. 🛆

Mile 218 (419) Km 351 (674): An ava-

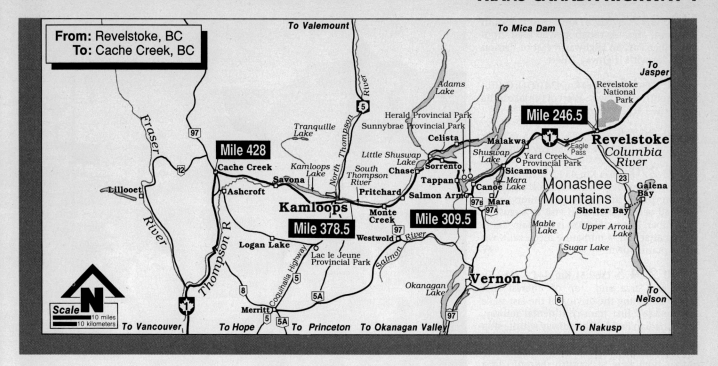

From: Revelstoke, BC
To: Cache Creek, BC

lanche shed (visible from the road) was built to protect the highway. Heavy snowfall and steep mountain terrain make this one of the most active avalanche areas in the world.

Mile 224.5 (412.5) Km 361.5 (663.5): ALBERT CANYON road to Canyon Hot Springs; campground, restaurant, store; hot pool and cooler swimming pool; trails to Albert Canyon ghost town, trail rides.

Mile 227.5 (409.5) Km 366.5 (658.5): Woolsey Creek. Eastern boundary of Mount Revelstoke National Park.

Mile 228.5 (408.5) Km 367.5 (657.5): Giant Cedars picnic area. Short interpretative trail along a boardwalk through Interior rain forest typical of wet valley bottoms in the Columbia Mountains.

Mile 230 (407) Km 370 (655): Skunk Cabbage picnic area and 1/2-hour nature trail along a boardwalk through Illecillewaet River swamplands. Good bird-watching; watch for dippers in trailhead creek.

Mile 235 (402) Km 378 (647): West boundary, Mount Revelstoke National Park. Only the northeast corner of the park is accessible along Trans-Canada Highway 1. The major portion is accessed at **Mile 246.**

Mile 237 (399.5) Km 382 (643): Illecillewaet rest area with cairn commemorating the opening of the Rogers Pass Highway in 1962. This route over the Selkirks was pioneered by the railway builders of the Canadian Pacific Railway (CPR) in the 1800s.

Mile 245 (392) Km 395 (630): Secondary access road to Revelstoke city center: good view southwest to snowy Mount Begbie which overlooks the city. The mountain was named for Judge Begbie, known throughout British

Columbia at the time of the Cariboo gold rush as the Hanging Judge.

CAUTION: Signs along the highway warn of the danger of feeding bears. Black bears are numerous in the mountains, regular pests in camp and picnic sites and often stroll down the highway. Stop at safe distances only, with windows closed. Do not feed the bears! Stay in your vehicle!

Mile 246 (391) Km 396 (629): Junction with scenic Summit Road, which leads north into Mount Revelstoke National Park. Open from late June to early September, this well-maintained gravel road switchbacks 16 miles/ 26 km up to high alpine lakes and meadows. The Mountain Meadows Interpretive Trail (a 0.5-mile/1-km round-trip) begins at Heather Lake parking lot at road's end and is highly recommended. An easily accessible spectacular mountain area not to be missed!

Mile 246.5 (390.5) Km 396.5 (628.5): Main entrance to city of Revelstoke (to south) and junction with Highway 23 north to Revelstoke and Mica Creek dams (see feature this section).

REVELSTOKE (pop. 8,500) lies at the confluence of the Illecillewaet and Columbia rivers. Originally an Indian trading centre, the city saw fur trading and gold rush activities, though the main impetus for its growth was the construction of the Canadian Pacific Railway. Later, highway construction and the building of 2 large dams on the Columbia added to its importance.

Today, tourism is playing an increasingly important part in the city's economy, both in summer (hiking, boating, fishing, swimming) and in winter (alpine and cross-country skiing, snow-cat and heli-skiing, plus ice-fishing, snowmobiling). The city's downtown core has recently been revitalized, with restoration of all the major heritage buildings and shop fronts and the construction of Grizzly Plaza, a

pedestrian area with huge sculptures of grizzly bears and a bandstand. Full tourist facilities.

Hydroelectric dams on the Columbia have created Lake Revelstoke, above the Revelstoke Dam; Kinbasket above the Mica Dam; and the Arrow Lakes above the Hugh Keenleyside Dam near Castlegar. All of these provide good fishing for rainbow, ling, Dolly Varden and mountain whitefish.

Mile 247 (390) Km 397.5 (627.5): Columbia River bridge. The river was named by David Thompson, first man to map the river, after the ship of Robert Gray, the first independent trader on the north Pacific coast.

Just west of the bridge, Trans-Canada Highway 1 junctions with Highway 23 south to Shelter Bay (30 miles/50 km) on Arrow Lakes for Galena Bay ferry. From Galena Bay, Highways 23 and 6 continue south beside Arrow and Kootenay lakes to Crowsnest Highway 3 at Castlegar. The ferry runs on the half hour from Shelter Bay and makes 20-minute runs.

Mile 254.5 (382.5) Km 409.5 (615.5): Summit Lake, the divide between the Fraser and Columbia watersheds. Good view of rail tunnels.

Mile 255.5 (381.5) Km 411.5 (613.5): Provincial park picnic area by Victor Lake; good swimming. Stop of interest sign describes how railway surveyor Walter Moberly found Eagle Pass through the Monashee Mountains (the route of the highway) by watching flying eagles.

Mile 258 (379) Km 415.5 (609.5): THREE VALLEY GAP at the eastern end of Three Valley Lake. Resort motel adjacent to an excellent relocated ghost town village with heritage buildings brought in from outlying areas. Restaurant and gas station. Note avalanche shed protecting railway on the steep north bank of the lake.

Mile 259.5 (377.5) Km 418 (607): South Pass rest area. A rough gravel road from Monashee Pass on Highway 6 east of Vernon junctions with Highway 1 here.

Mile 263.5 (373.5) Km 424 (601): Griffin Lake, south of highway. West of the lake is the Enchanted Forest tourist attraction.

Mile 267.5 (369.5) Km 430.5 (594.5): Rest area; short shady walk to Kay Falls.

Mile 270 (367) Km 434.5 (590.5): Eagle River Fish Hatchery raises chinook and coho salmon; picnic area, self-guided tours, open daily all year. Best time to visit is August to November. Just to the west is Beardale Castle tourist attaction, a miniature medieval town and a prairie town. ⛏

Mile 274.5 (362.5) Km 441.5 (583.5): Large rest area and stop of interest sign commemorating the driving of the last spike on Canada's first trans-continental railway, the Canadian Pacific. The railway whistle stop here is Craigellachie, part of the battle cry of the Grant clan. (Most of the CPR hierarchy at that time were of Scottish descent.) In a historic telegram from London in 1884, "Stand fast, Craigellachie!" was used as a code signifying the successful completion of a loan that guaranteed the railway's completion. Information cabin and gift shop open in summer.

Mile 276.5 (360.5) Km 445 (580): Eagle River bridge. The Eagle River offers good family canoeing and fishing for Dolly Varden and rainbow trout and char. 🐟

Mile 279.5 (357.5) Km 450 (575): Access road to small community of **MALAKWA**; limited services.

Mile 281 (356) Km 452.5 (572.5): Yard Creek Provincial Park, one of the most popular stopping places on the Trans-Canada Highway; 90 campsites in the rain forest with sani-station; fishing in the creek, mushrooms in fall. ▲

Mile 283 (354) Km 456 (569): Access road to small communities of Solsqua and Cambie.

Mile 290 (347) Km 467 (558): Junction with Highway 97A to Enderby, Vernon and the Okanagan Valley. Access to the "D" Dutchman's Dairy which features fresh dairy products of all kinds, including homemade cheese and incredibly good ice cream. Free children's zoo with exotic petting animals, including llamas and camels. It is well worth a stop. ★

Mile 296.5 (340.5) Km 477 (548): Western boundary of **SICAMOUS** (pop. 3,000), all tourist services. Originally a railway construction depot, Sicamous is now primarily a resort community strategically located on a narrow neck of water separating Shuswap and Mara lakes. It calls itself the "Houseboat Capital of Canada" because of the number of houseboats (more than 300) available for rent here.

Grizzly Plaza in downtown Revelstoke, Mile 246.5. (Liz Bryan)

From Sicamous public dock (turn south just east of the river bridge), the Shuswap Lake ferry provides service to the northern reaches of enormous Shuswap Lake, its final destination the old gold camp at the head of Seymour Arm. Mail run round-trip sailings Monday, Wednesday and Friday in summer, twice weekly in winter. Ferry maintains 2 boats — the MV *Phoebe Ann* is a stern-wheeler with snack bar and room for 40 passengers and is also used for lake cruises. The MV *Stephanie* is the lake workhorse, a steel tug which pushes a barge, accommodates 9 cars and 18 passengers, plus freight. From the docks, where many houseboats are moored, you can walk under the highway bridge to Finlayson Park for swimming, sunning and boating in Shuswap Lake.

Mile 297.5 (339.5) Km 479 (546): Rest area with stop of interest marker about Shuswap Lake and the local Shuswap Indians. The lake is huge, with 190 miles/300 km of shoreline, and it's popular with sailors and windsurfers because of its high winds.

Mile 301 (336) Km 484 (541): Junction with road north to small community of **CANOE** and public beach and boat launch.

Mile 305 (332) Km 491 (534): Eastern city limits of Salmon Arm.

Mile 307 (330) Km 494 (531): Junction of Highway 97B which connects with Highway 97A South to the Okanagan Valley.

Mile 308 (329) Km 495.5 (529.5): Turnoff south to Salmon Arm airport, Bird Zoo and community swimming pool.

Mile 309.5 (327.5) Km 498 (527): **SALMON ARM** (pop. 11,900) lies at the southern tip of the southeastern arm of Shuswap Lake. It takes its name from the salmon in nearby Salmon River that were once so prolific at spawning time that pioneer farmers shoveled them onto the fields for fertilizer. Today the city is a busy supply center for surrounding farms where fruit, berries and dairy products are the mainstay. The wood industry and tourism are also important to the economy. Highway 1 goes beside McGuire Lake, the city's main park.

The city provides full tourist services. Visitor information office at the junction of Highway 1 and Hudson Street. Main summer activities centre around the lake for swimming, boating and fishing. There is a new waterfront marina with moorings for houseboats and other craft and plans are afoot for a new harborfront village. Lakefront east of the government wharf is a winter refuge and spring nesting area for waterfowl.

Mile 311.5 (325.5) Km 501.5 (523.5): Silver Creek Road south to Gort's Gouda Farm for flavored gouda and quark. Salmon River back road here connects with Highway 97 near Falkland.

Mile 314.5 (322) Km 506.5 (518.5): Western city limits of Salmon Arm.

Mile 315 (322) Km 507 (518): Small community of TAPPEN; gas and groceries available.

Mile 316 (321) Km 509 (516): Turnoff north to Sunnybrae (3.5 miles/6 km distance) and Herald (7 miles/12 km), both provincial parks on the lakeshore. Sunnybrae has lakeside picnic areas, swimming beaches and fishing. Herald has 51 campsites, picnicking, swimming and a boat launch. A short trail leads from Herald park to Margaret Falls on Reinecker Creek. West of the creek are circular depressions, the remains of Indian kekuli, which were circular, semi-underground winter homes up to 30 feet in diameter. Also in the park are remains of the pioneer Herald family farm buildings.

Mile 319 (318) Km 513 (512): Turnoff to Little White and White Lake; excellent rainbow fishing by fly or troll.

Mile 321 (316) Km 517 (508): Balmoral general store and road south to old railway settlement of Notch Hill. Notch Hill Road follows the railway and returns to Highway 1 at Sorrento, 10 miles/16 km west.

Mile 324 (313) Km 521.5 (503.5): Turnoff north to lakeshore communities of Blind Bay and Eagle Bay.

Mile 329.5 (307.5) Km 530 (495): SORRENTO, a resort community with motels, store, restaurants, gas; tourist information on Notch Hill Road. The community is known for its Arts Festival held in July.

Mile 331.5 (305.5) Km 533.5 (491.5): Turnout with viewpoint of Shuswap Lake.

Mile 336 (301) Km 540.5 (484.5): Small community of SQUILAX (Indian word for "bear"), at the junction with road north to Adams River, Lake Adams and Shuswap Lake Provincial Park.

The whole of the lower Adams River has been set aside as the Roderick Haig-Brown Conservation Area, named after the famous conservationist. Adams River sockeye salmon spawn along here in October and it is a great tourist spectacle. The runs peak every 4 years: 1990 is the next peak. Roderick Haig-Brown Park, 3 miles/5 km north of Highway 1, has interpretative trails and viewing platforms.

Shuswap Lake Provincial Park, 12 miles/20 km north of Highway 1, has 260 campsites, a sani-station, swimming, boat launch, visitor center, interpretative programs, and fishing for large lake and rainbow trout, kokanee and whitefish. Camping fee May to September is $10.

Mile 340 (297) Km 547.5 (477.5): Jade Mountain lookout with a good view of Little Shuswap Lake, headwaters of the South Thompson River, and Chase Indian village. The short stretch of water between Shuswap and Little Shuswap lakes is known as Little River. It offers excellent trout fishing in February, March and October.

Mile 341.5 (295.5) Km 549.5 (475.5): Chase Creek rest area. Watch for bighorn sheep on the bluffs south of the highway. A small band of sheep, brought in from Banff, lives on nearby Squilax Mountain and often come to the lake for water.

Mile 342 (295) Km 550.5 (474.5): Junction with a loop road to CHASE (pop. 1,850), a small village dependent on the lumber industry, situated on the western end of Little Shuswap Lake. Fishing for rainbow, lake trout, Dolly Varden and kokanee. All visitor facilities. Watch for osprey nests in snags overlooking the river. There is a boat launch at the government wharf and picnic areas in the community parks.

Chase bridge crosses the Thompson River and provides access to Niskonlith Lake Provincial Recreation Area, 5 miles/8 km north, which has 50 campsites and good fishing for large rainbows. In May and June, the spring flower displays here are wonderful.

Mile 345.5 (291.5) Km 556 (469): Gravel road south up Chase Creek to Pillar Lake and Falkland on Highway 97. Pillar is an 82-foot/25-m tower of glacial conglomerate topped by a giant boulder. Pillar Lake has rainbows to 3 pounds.

Mile 353.5 (283.5) Km 569 (456): Turnoff to PRITCHARD, a small community on the South Thompson River. Good fishing for spring salmon here. Bridge crosses river at Pritchard to a network of good gravel roads leading along the north bank of the Thompson to Kamloops and Chase and back into the hills to several good fishing lakes.

Near north side of bridge at Gore Creek, archaeologists recently discovered the earliest human remains in British Columbia, that of a man believed to have been trapped and drowned in a mud flow some 8,500 years ago.

Mile 356 (281) Km 573 (452): Good view of high clay banks on the north side of the river, remnants of glacial lake beaches eroded into hoodoos.

Mile 359.5 (277) Km 579 (446): MONTE CREEK, store and gas station at junction with Highway 97 South to Vernon and the Okanagan Valley (see **Mile 165** in the CANADA HIGHWAY 97 section for log of that route.) Highways 1 and 97 share a common alignment west from here to Cache Creek.

On the north side of the railway tracks west of here is an interesting antique shop, while a road south of the highway leads steeply up to tiny St. Peter's Church, built in 1926.

Mile 364 (273) Km 585.5 (439.5): Stop of interest on a gravel turnout on north side of the highway, near Monte Creek railway station, explains the "Great Train Robbery." The robbery took place near here in 1906. Bill Miner and his gang held up a Canadian Pacific Railway express but netted only $15. He was successfully tracked by a mounted police posse and sent to jail for life. His story was made into a movie, *The Grey Fox.*

Mile 364.5 (272.5) Km 586.5 (438.5): Kamloops city limits, B.C. Livestock Auction yards.

Mile 365.5 (271.5) Km 588.5 (436.5): Wildlife park and museum. More than 60 species of birds and animals inhabit the park. There is a petting farm for youngsters, hiking trails, miniature railway, picnic areas and playground. The park is open daily in summer from 8 a.m. until 6 p.m. Waterslide and RV park adjacent.

Mile 376 (261) Km 605 (420): Westbound exit for Kamloops and exit for Yellowhead Highway 5 North to Tete Jaune Cache (turn to the YELLOWHEAD HIGHWAY 5 section for log).

Mile 378.5 (258.5) Km 609.5 (415.5): Eastbound exit for city of KAMLOOPS (pop. 67,000), established by fur traders as Fort Kamloops in 1811, at the confluence of the North and South Thompson rivers. In 1862, the Overlanders, a group of immigrants who had set out from the prairies to travel to the goldfields by land, rafted down the North Thompson from Tete Jaune Cache. They arrived at Fort Kamloops in time for the only woman among them, Catherine Schuman, to deliver the first white girl born in the British Columbia Interior. Several of the Overlanders settled in Kamloops. One of them, William Fortune, built British Columbia's first flour mill.

Kamloops boomed with the arrival of the Canadian Pacific Railway in 1885. Today it is British Columbia's fourth-largest settlement, a bustling city with excellent shopping and tourist facilities at the crossroads of 2 major tourist routes: Trans-Canada Highway 1 and Highway 5. Travel information centre at 10 10th Avenue is open daily June to September; phone 374-3377.

Its economy is based on primary and secondary manufacturing, with a copper smelter, 2 plywood plants and a pulp mill. The tall stack of Weyerhauser Canada's mill carries effluent (and odor) high above the city. Only rarely do climatic conditions force it down. Daily tours of the mill available May to September. Cattle ranching continues to be a mainstay along with mining and tourism.

Attractions include Riverside Park, with its replica of old Fort Kamloops. There are 2-hour river cruises on the paddle-wheeler MV *Wanda Sue,* which depart from the river dock near the Travel Information Centre, May to September. The 200 lakes around Kamloops make the city a magnet for fishermen. Local rainbow trout, known as Kamloops trout, have a reputation as wily fighters; 5- to 6-pounders are not uncommon.

Mile 379.5 (257.5) Km 610.5 (414.5): Junction of Highway 5A South to Merritt and Princeton. This is now one of the least traveled highways in southern British Columbia having been supplanted by the new Coquihalla Highway.

Mile 382 (255) Km 615 (410): Paved road leads south 18 miles/29 km to Lac le Jeune Provincial Park; 144 campsites, swimming and fishing.

Mile 382.5 (254.5) Km 615.5 (409.5): Junction with Highway 5, the Coquihalla Highway to Merritt and Hope (see COQUIHALLA HIGHWAY section). Kamloops western city limits.

Mile 387 (250) Km 622.5 (402.5): Tailings of the Afton copper mine are visible on the south side of the highway. Mining operations are spread for some distance along the highway. On the north side of the highway, notice the range rehabilitation project in which sagebrush semidesert has been cultivated and seeded to grass.

Mile 388.5 (248.5) Km 625 (400): Greenstone Mountain Road leads to several high fishing lakes.

Mile 392 (245) Km 631 (394): Cherry Creek ranch, one of the pioneer ranches in the area.

Mile 398.5 (238.5) Km 641 (384): Rest area and viewpoint. A trailer usually parked here in summer sells ice cream and snacks. Stop of interest sign here recalls the days of lake steamboats, and a display board illustrates the types of Indian shelters on the interior Plateau. Sign identifies the different types of noxious knapweed, which in areas of British Columbia are taking over the rangeland.

Across the lake are Battle Bluffs, their red color attributed to legendary blood stains from an Indian battle fought on top.

Mile 401 (236) Km 645.5 (379.5): Turnout and viewpoint over Kamloops Lake (a widening of the Thompson River). Geologists believe that the lake may be an ancient volcanic crater, the source of the area's lava outcrops.

Mile 403 (234) Km 648.5 (376.5): Turnoff north to Savona Provincial Park for swimming and picnicking. **SAVONA** is a small trading community at the narrow west end of Kamloops Lake; limited facilities. Access south

to Logan Lake mining community and fishing lakes.

Mile 406 (231) Km 653.5 (371.5): Steel-decked bridge over the Thompson River. Explorer David Thompson never saw the river that bears his name. It was named for him by Simon Fraser. *CAUTION:* Bridge deck is slippery.

Mile 408 (229) Km 656.5 (368.5): Bridge over Deadman River. Pacific salmon spawn here in the fall. The river was named for an early Hudson's Bay Co. trader who was found murdered here.

Mile 409 (228) Km 658 (367): Turnoff on gravel road north to Deadman River valley, an attractive ranch valley with a spectacular multicolored volcanic canyon (good rockhounding for agates and petrified wood) and rock hoodoos (ask for permission and directions at Deadman Creek Ranch).

Mile 414 (223) Km 666 (359): Turnoff south to a bridge over the Thompson River and the small community of **WALHACHIN.** When nearby orchards flourished, so did Walhachin; today a desert of prickly pear cactus and sagebrush has ousted the fruit trees and the settlement is almost a ghost town. No services available.

Mile 415.5 (221.5) Km 668.5 (356.5): Remains of an irrigation flume are visible on the north side of the highway.

Mile 418 (219) Km 672.5 (352.5): Stop of interest sign commemorates the orchard settlement of Walhachin. On the river flats east of here pioneers planted apple orchards, building dams in the hills and miles of irrigation flumes to bring water. By 1913, these dry benches were covered with sturdy young trees. But when all but 10 of the eligible males of the area enlisted for service in WWI, the irrigation flumes were breached by floods and landslides and the thirsty orchards shriveled. Today there are still a few phantom trees among the sagebrush and cactus. The flumes are merely rotting streaks of wood along the hillsides.

The climate, too dry for orchards, is ideal for cattle but few are to be seen from June to September because they are sent to the high forested hills to graze. There are huge cattle-feeding stations just east of Cache Creek.

Mile 428 (209) Km 689 (336): Junction of Trans-Canada Highway 1 and Highway 97 at **CACHE CREEK** (pop. 3,000). Travel Information Centre just north of highway intersection. The settlement grew up around the confluence of the creek (named after a reputed cache of gold) and the Bonaparte River. The Hudson's Bay Co. opened a store to benefit from trade at the intersection of trails east and north. Cache Creek became a major supply point on the Cariboo Wagon Road. Today, the junction is still very much a traveler's way station. Gas stations, motels and restaurants line both sides of the highway. The area is famous for jade (nephrite). Visit the Cariboo Jade Shop to see this stone being cut and polished.

Highways 1 and 97 share a common alignment between Cache Creek and Monte Creek to the east. Travelers continuing north on Highway 97 turn to **Mile 232.5** in the CANADA HIGHWAY 97 section for log of that route. Trans-Canada Highway 1 swings south from Cache Creek for Vancouver-bound travelers.

Mile 428.5 (208.5) Km 689.5 (335.5): Bonaparte River bridge. The river flows into the Thompson River at Ashcroft.

Mile 429 (208) Km 690 (335): Junction with road to **ASHCROFT**, a small village with full tourist facilities just east of the highway, and to the mining community of Logan

Historic Ashcroft Manor, Mile 434.5, offers a shady oasis.   (Liz Bryan)

Lake and open-pit copper mines of Highland Valley.

Mile 434.5 (202.5) Km 699 (326):
Stop of interest sign describes Ashcroft Manor and roadhouses built in 1864 by the 2 Cornwall brothers, Clement and Henry, who brought fox hunting and horse racing to the Canadian frontier. The manor burned in 1943 but the roadhouse remains, one of the few left on the Cariboo Wagon Road. Today it houses several shops selling antiques, memorabilia and British Columbia crafts. Behind the manor a cedar building houses an English-style tearoom which serves afternoon tea and cakes as well as lunches and dinners. Well worth a stop. ★

Mile 438 (199) Km 704.5 (320.5):
Turnoff for Cornwall Forestry Lookout, 12 miles/19 km west. The road is narrow and rough and the climb to the lookout is steep, but alpine meadows and the view are worth the trip.

Mile 439 (198) Km 706.5 (318.5):
Rest area on the east side of the highway beneath Red Hill. A side road 2 miles/3 km south turns west to Venables Valley. Up this narrow, winding road 1.5 miles/3 km are 3 mineral lakes, heavily encrusted with white salts of magnesium sulphate, which were mined sporadically for epsom salts. An interesting excursion.

Mile 446 (191) Km 717.5 (307.5):
Excellent viewpoint of the Thompson River valley. The broad river benches are evidence of temporary lakes created during periods of glaciation. Stop of interest sign commemorates the driving of the last spike in 1915 of Canada's third transcontinental railway, the Canadian Northern Pacific, now the Canadian National Railway.

Mile 453 (184) Km 729 (296):
Watch for bighorn sheep on the road. A small band of sheep live on the rocky bluffs west of the highway and they come down to the river for water. They are fed in winter beside the highway. On the east side of the river is a huge talus or scree slope. This feature was noted on early maps as "the great rock slide."

Mile 454.5 (182.5) Km 731.5 (293.5):
Side road down to the river at the Canadian Pacific Railway flagstop of Spatsum. The name is derived from Indian spep-sum, meaning "place where milkweed grows." Milkweed is abundant in the dry interior of British Columbia along with the monarch butterfly, whose larvae feed on the leaves. This is the northern extremity of the monarch's range. The sand beach at Spatsum is a good place for picnics; rafts for river float trips are often put into the water here. Across the river lies the tiny Indian settlement of Spatsum with its wooden church.

Mile 456.5 (180.5) Km 735 (290):
North access road to Spences Bridge and Highway 8 to Merritt. SPENCES BRIDGE (pop. 300) lies at the confluence of the Nicola and Thompson rivers. The first settlement was known as

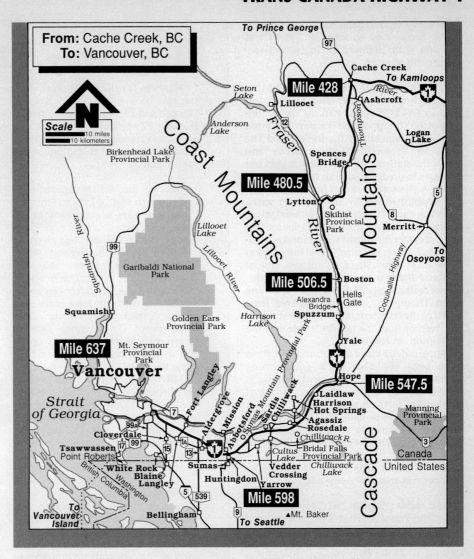

From: Cache Creek, BC
To: Vancouver, BC

Cook's Ferry because of the ferry crossing here, but the name was changed in 1864 when Thomas Spence built a toll bridge. An important stop on the Cariboo Road, Spences Bridge used to be known for some of the best steelhead fishing in British Columbia, but today the Thompson River is subject to intense regulation.

Mile 457.5 (179.5) Km 736.5 (288.5):
Junction with Highway 8 East to Merritt along the Nicola River. This is also the south access to the community of Spences Bridge. A stop of interest sign commemorates the great mudslide of 1905 which dammed the Thompson River for 5 hours. Across the river, Murray Creek Falls tumble over the lip of a narrow canyon into an inviting pool, a popular rest stop for white-water rafters.

Mile 464.5 (172.5) Km 747.5 (277.5):
Goldpan Provincial Park is located on the narrow flats beside the river; 14 campsites, picnic area, fishing. The park is usually full from mid-October to December with steelhead fishermen. Gold can be panned from the river gravels here. ⛽🚣▲

Mile 465 (172) Km 748 (277):
Shaw Springs, a resort on the river bench where

once mule and oxen teams pastured overnight.

Mile 466.5 (170.5) Km 750.5 (274.5):
Highway winds along river level on steel retaining walls; this section of road cost $1 million a mile to build. Good close-up view of river rapids and migrating salmon in the fall. Excellent fishing spot during low water when trout may be taken on a fly. 🐟

Mile 469.5 (167.5) Km 755.5 (269.5):
Little Hells Gate rapids on the Thompson River, a good place to watch spawning salmon in the fall. The rapids are also one of the thrills of a ride downriver in an inflatable raft. There are several companies operating on the river, with trips from a few hours to several days.

Mile 475 (162) Km 764.5 (260.5):
Skihist Provincial Park. Picnic area on west side of highway provides spectacular view over the Thompson River canyon; good place to watch the trains go by. (Both Canadian Pacific and Canadian National rail lines pass through the canyon.) On the east side of the highway are 68 shaded campsites, sani-station and hiking trails. Fee from June to September. Keep a lookout for elk: an introduced herd thrives in this dry belt country. 🚶‍♂️⛽▲

Mile 478.5 (158.5) Km 770.5 (254.5): North access road to town of Lytton and junction with Highway 12 to Lillooet (see feature this section).

Mile 480.5 (156.5) Km 773.5 (251.5): Lytton pioneer cemetery and south access road to **LYTTON** (pop. 400). At the confluence of the Thompson and Fraser rivers, Lytton was called Camchin by the Indians and The Forks by explorers. Sandbars above and below the settlement yielded much gold but attempts to dredge gold from submerged bars failed. A Hudson's Bay Co. post, Fort Dallas, was established nearby and the later settlement was named for Sir Edward Bulwer Lytton, secretary of state for the British Colonies. The town provides full tourist services and is headquarters for river raft trips. Travel information office is on Fraser Street, downtown. One of the local sights is the confluence of the turbulent coffee-colored Fraser and the sparkling green Thompson. It is best observed from south of the ferry terminal on the west side of the river, or from the railway bridge over the Thompson on Highway 12.

Three miles/5 km of river frontage in Lytton have been set aside as a gold-panning recreational reserve. Only hand-panning is permitted. Ask for directions at the travel office. An Environment Canada weather station is located here and tours can be arranged. Lytton has recorded the highest temperature in British Columbia (111°F/44°C).

Mile 483.5 (153.5) Km 778.5 (246.5): Skupper rest area and viewpoint.

Mile 486 (151) Km 782 (243): Viewpoint down the Fraser River at Siska where 2 rail bridges cross. The Canadian Pacific Railway reached here first and crossed here by choice, seeking the easiest route through the canyon. Thirty years later, the Canadian National also came this way and was forced to cross here because there wasn't room for 2 tracks on the same side of the river.

Mile 488.5 (148.5) Km 786.5 (238.5): **KANAKA BAR**, with gas station and restaurant, and tunnel of the same name. The river bar below was worked by Kanakas, natives of Hawaii, who were probably brought over from the Hudson's Bay Co. post in Honolulu.

Mile 491.5 (145.5) Km 791 (234): The highway climbs up and over Jackass Mountain, the steepest hill on the old wagon road, so named because many mules slipped to their deaths on the narrow, tortuous track. Viewpoint and stop of interest plaque on west side of highway.

Mile 496.5 (140.5) Km 799 (226): An Indian cemetery is visible on the hillside. Both sides of the canyon are sprinkled with small Indian reserves. The Salish population was large at one time, but the Indians succumbed quickly to the diseases of the white pioneers. Just to the south, a steep road leads eastward onto a forested shelf where Blue Lake resort provides boating, swimming, horseback riding, meals and accommodations.

Highway 12 to Lillooet

Highway 12 winds it way north along the east bank of the Fraser River to Lillooet and beyond to junction with Highway 97 north of Cache Creek. One of the less traveled highway routes of British Columbia, it is also one of the most scenic.

Mile 0 Km 0: Thompson River bridge, north edge of Lytton. From the bridge you have a good view of the Fraser/Thompson confluence, the Fraser muddy, the Thompson clear green.

Mile 1 Km 1.5: Road west to Lytton-Westside ferry, a reaction cable ferry across the Fraser River. The free ferry carries 2 vehicles, 20 passengers and is operated solely by the force of the river current. A stout cable prevents it from being swept downstream. One of several reaction ferries still in operation on the Fraser, this one has been going since 1894.

Mile 24 Km 38.5: Ginseng farm on river bench. The soil and climate here were found to be favorable for the growth of this oriental specialty prized for its medicinal root. The plants are grown under huge tarpaulins of black plastic.

Mile 27 Km 43.5: Section of rough narrow road along steep canyon wall, subject to washout.

Mile 40 Km 64: Junction with road west to Lillooet across the Fraser. There are 2 bridges: the old narrow suspension bridge upstream (closed to traffic), and a more recent construction, known as the Bridge of the 23 Camels. (Bactrian camels were once used as beasts of burden on the Cariboo Wagon Road.)

LILLOOET (pop. 1,800) stands on the confluence of the Fraser and Bridge rivers and Cayoosh Creek. The Hudson's Bay Co. built Fort Berens across the Fraser in 1846 but it wasn't until the gold rush almost 20 years later that the town was established. On the northern end of the Harrison-Lillooet trail from the coast (a route that pre-dated the Fraser Canyon road), Lillooet became a boisterous supply center for miners

View of Fraser River benches on Highway 12. (Liz Bryan)

headed north on the Cariboo Wagon Road from here.

Lillooet's importance declined with the opening of the road up the Fraser Canyon which went up the Thompson River from Lytton (the route of today's Highway 1) but mileposts along the Wagon Road still denote original distances from Lillooet, a fact that confuses many travelers. Today, the town provides full tourist services. It has an interesting main street, with many historical points of interest including the Mile 0 cairn and the Miyazaki heritage house. The tourist information centre is in the former old Anglican church. Summer activities include fishing (giant sturgeon are caught in the Fraser here) and rockhounding (agates and jade). Just north of the old suspension bridge, local Indians can be seen catching salmon from the river in dip nets and stringing the fish out to dry under covered cedar racks. The local golf course on Texas Creek Road is called Sheep Pasture: the greens are nibbled close by 4-footed mowers.

Highway 12 continues 46 miles/74 km to junction with Highway 97 north at Cache Creek.

Mile 498 (139) Km 801.5 (223.5): Boston Bar airstrip.

Mile 501.5 (135.5) Km 807 (218): Turnout for view over canyon.

Mile 506.5 (130.5) Km 815 (210): **BOSTON BAR** (pop. 1,000) named for the many Americans (called Boston Men by the Indians) who came to seek gold in the Fraser River gravel bars. Unique aerial car ferry to North Bend on the river's west bank was replaced by a bridge in the spring of 1986. The

old cable cage is on display at the bridge's north side. The main industry here is logging and a large sawmill operation occupies one of the river benches. All services are available. Boston Bar/North Bend's annual May Day celebrations are among the province's oldest. They include old-fashioned English Maypole dancing.

NORTH BEND is a fascinating old railroad community, complete with storage sheds and roundhouse and a picturesque station-cum-hotel. Today it is still a Canadian Pacific divisional point, but acts mainly as a dormitory community for Boston Bar.

Mile 508 (129) Km 812 (213): Anderson Creek bridge.

Mile 512 (125) Km 824 (201): China Bar Tunnel, almost 2,300 feet/700m long, one of the longest in North America. The tunnel curves and should be driven with extreme care. A stop of interest sign at the south end of the tunnel quotes from the writings of Simon Fraser, the first white man to descend the river that now bears his name: "We could scarcely make our way . . . we had to pass where no human being should venture."

Mile 513 (124) Km 826 (199): Entrance to Hells Gate for southbound travelers.

Mile 514 (123) Km 827 (198): Entrance for northbound traffic to parking lot and pedestrian overpass to Hells Gate. Here, where the Fraser River is at its narrowest, are fish ladders built in 1913-14 by the International Fisheries Commission to enable spawning salmon to overcome a blockage in the river caused by railway construction. Two 28-passenger aerial trams take tourists 500 feet/153m down across the river to a restaurant, shops and other attractions. Footbridge across the river provides view of fish ladders and access to fisheries displays. Trams operate daily, April to November.

If you want some exercise, there is a trail down to the fish ladders. It starts from the southern end of the river viewpoint. The trail is steep. Allow about an hour for the return trip.

Hells Gate was well named. Construction of the railways through this narrow gap was hazardous and many workers lost their lives here. To haul supplies for the railway upstream of Hells Gate, railroad builder Andrew Onderdonk ordered a stern-wheeler steamer to be built at Yale. The gallant little *Skuzzy* miraculously made its way upstream through the terrifying waters of Hells Gate in 1882, hauled by ropes attached to the canyon walls by bolts. Estimated speed of the river through Hells Gate is 17 mph/28 kmph. 🚶★

Mile 515.5 (121.5) Km 829.5 (195.5): Hells Gate and Ferrabee tunnels.

Mile 517 (120) Km 832 (193): Rest area by Copper Creek, a leafy grotto, east of highway.

Mile 518 (119) Km 833.5 (191.5): Alexandra Tunnel.

Mile 520 (117) Km 836.5 (188.5): Historic Alexandra Lodge, still in business as a restaurant (famous for its cinnamon buns), and bed-and-breakfast establishment. Just north of the lodge a section of the 1848 Hudson's Bay Co. trail from Yale to Kamloops leads east to a high valley above the river. The 8-mile/13-km hike ends at a small lake where the brigade once camped. 🚶

Mile 520.5 (116.5) Km 837.5 (187.5): Alexandra Bridge Provincial Park picnic area with interpretative displays on both sides of

the highway. Good view of the river and bridges. Just north of the park you can walk the old wagon road alignment across the rail tracks to the now-abandoned suspension bridge, built in 1926 on the same abutments of an earlier structure built in 1863. 🚻

Mile 521 (116) Km 838.5 (186.5): Stop of interest at the south end of the Alexandra Bridge, built in 1962, more than 1,640 feet/500m long, the second-largest fixed arch span in the world. A marker commemorates the building of the first suspension bridge in 1863 and its 1926 replacement.

Mile 523.5 (113.5) Km 842.5 (182.5): SPUZZUM, a small community with gas and food. The Hudson's Bay Co. maintained a fur depot here and it was a toll station on the wagon road. Before the building of the Alexandra Bridge, a ferry took travelers across the river here.

Mile 525.5 (111.5) Km 846 (179): Sailor Bar Tunnel.

Mile 529.5 (107.5) Km 852.5 (172.5): Saddle Rock Tunnel, named after a saddle-shaped rock in the river, an early landmark.

Mile 530.5 (106.5) Km 854 (171): Turn-out and stop of interest sign for the Cariboo Wagon Road, built by Royal Engineers from England in 1861-63. Up this 20-foot-/6-m-wide road hacked out of the wilderness came men and supplies bound for the gold rush boom towns of the Cariboo.

From Cache Creek to Yale, Highway 1 follows the general route of the old wagon road, much of which was destroyed by the building of the Canadian Pacific Railway, although several well-preserved sections can still be seen.

Mile 533 (104) Km 857.5 (167.5): Yale Tunnel. The huge dark rock in the river north of the tunnel was named after the wife of arctic explorer Sir John Franklin, who disappeared while searching for the Northwest Passage in 1845. Lady Franklin, refusing to believe her husband was dead, came to British Columbia in search of him.

Mile 533.5 (103.5) Km 858.5 (166.5): YALE (pop. 500), a small community on the river bench. Founded in 1847 as a fur-trading post of the Hudson's Bay Co., the fort was named after trader James Yale.

The discovery of gold in the Fraser catapulted the small settlement into a boom town with 3,000 miners eager to spend their pokes of gold dust in the saloons and dance halls. Yale was head of navigation on the Fraser and paddle-steamers arrived almost daily from the coast during gold rush days. When gold was discovered upriver in the creeks of the Cariboo, Yale became the southern terminus of a wagon road. It experienced a second boom with the construction of the Canadian Pacific Railway but today it is a quiet little place, dependent on lumber, mining and tourism. All services are available.

Yale is the home of the St. John of the

Divine Church, built in 1859, the oldest Anglican church in British Columbia still on its original site. It is just east of the highway in the town center. Beside it is the museum, housed in an 1868 heritage house; open daily June to September. Visit the pioneer cemetery with gravestones dating back to 1850 and Foreshore Park where you can pan for gold. On Front Street there are monuments to the Cariboo Wagon Road and to Barnard's Express.

Mile 535.5 (101.5) Km 862 (163): Trail to Spirit Cave starts on the east side of the highway and climbs steeply up the mountain to the cave mouth. It is a 4-hour hike, not for the novice. On the river side of the highway near here is Yale Pioneer Cemetery. 🚶

Mile 538 (99) Km 865.5 (159.5): Turnoff for Emory Creek Provincial Park with 34 shaded campsites; gold panning and fishing in the creek mouth. Camping fee May to October.

The gold rush settlement of Emoryville grew into a lusty town with 9 saloons, a brewery and the mainland's first newspaper. When the gold on the river bars was gone, the town was abandoned. A nearby stop of interest sign commemorates Chinese immigrants who came with the gold rush and stayed on to help build the Cariboo Wagon Road, then the railway. ▲

Mile 541 (96) Km 871 (154): Texas Creek bridge. Road west to B.C. Nickel Mine.

Mile 545 (92) Km 877 (148): Lake of the Woods (officially Schkam Lake) rest area; good swimming and fair fishing for cutthroat and rainbow trout. Restaurant and motel at north end of lake. *NOTE:* Northbound travelers have no direct access to the rest area. To use the site, turn around at the motel entrance. 🐟

Mile 546.5 (90.5) Km 879.5 (145.5): Junction with Highway 7, a more leisurely route to the coast along the north side of the Fraser River to Agassiz, the resort town of Harrison Hot Springs, and Mission to Vancouver. Highway 1 between Hope and Vancouver is a 4-lane freeway.

Mile 547.5 (89.5) Km 881 (144): Two-lane double-deck bridge over the Fraser River. The upper deck (metal surface) carries the road and the lower deck used to carry the track of the now defunct Kettle Valley Railway. Park at the large turnout on the north side of the bridge if you want to cross the bridge on the pedestrian footpath for a close-up view of the churning river beneath.

South of the bridge is the town of HOPE (pop. 4,000), at the confluence of the Fraser and Coquihalla rivers. At Hope, the Fraser River leaves the rugged confines of the canyon and becomes wide, flat and pastoral. Hope is overlooked by the Coast Range mountains on the north and the Cascade Mountains to the south and east. In 1848, the Hudson's Bay Co. built a fur-trading post here. When 10 years later gold was discovered on the river bars, 30,000 miners converged on the tiny settlement. Royal Engineers surveyed a townsite in

1859. When gold was discovered in the Cariboo, Hope was bypassed as a supply centre in favor of Yale, farther upriver.

Today, Hope is a bustling little town strategically located at the junction of several travel routes: Highways 1, 3, 5 and 7. All services are available. Tourist Information Office is on Water Street (beside the highway as its skirts the town along the riverbank), sharing premises with the museum. Outside the museum is the impressive, fully restored gold mill concentrator from the Home Gold Mining Co.'s Pipestem Mine in the Coquihalla area. Inside, the museum presents 6 displays of pioneer life. Open 8 a.m. to 8 p.m., June to September.

Tourist highlight of the town is Coquihalla Canyon Provincial Recreation Area where you can walk the abandoned tracks of the Kettle Valley Railway through 3 of the famous Quintette tunnels and cross a bridge over the foaming river. (See also COQUIHALLA HIGHWAY section.) To reach the tunnels, take Kawkawa Lake Road north from town.

Just across Coquihalla River bridge on Kawkawa Lake road are Kawkawa Creek Fish Spawning Channels with boardwalk trails and a viewing area. Chum salmon spawn here in late September, coho in late October. In odd-numbered years, heavy runs of pink salmon also clog the channels. Municipal campgrounds nearby provide full facilities and space for 95 RVs and 22 tents. Farther along the road is Kawkawa Lake itself with a provincial park at its southern end, a popular spot for swimming, fishing, picnics and boating (no camping).

If Hope and Coquihalla Canyon seem vaguely familiar, you have seen them before in the movies, including *First Blood*, *Rambo* and *Fire with Fire*. ★ ⅂ ▲

Mile 548.5 (88.5) Km 882.5 (142.5):
Freeway overpass; junction with Highway 3 and access to Flood/Hope Road. Travelers heading east on Highway 3 turn to the end of the CROWSNEST HIGHWAY 3 section and read log back to front. Junction with Coquihalla Highway 5 lies a short distance to the east. Highway 1 westbound enters the freeway at the junction. At the junction, a 1914 railway station has been restored as a teahouse and centre for local arts and crafts. The freeway westbound is 4 lanes, maximum speed 65 mph/110 kmph.

Mile 550 (87) Km 885 (140): Silverhope Creek exit for eastbound travelers. EXIT 168

Mile 553 (84) Km 890 (135): Exit to Flood/Hope Road, business route to Hope for eastbound travelers and access to Hope airport. Gliders enjoy mountain thermals and soar high above the river. They can be seen here most weekends. Mount Hope is visible to the east. EXIT 165

Mile 555.5 (81.5) Km 894 (131): Hunter Creek rest area, public phone and summer Tourist Information trailer. EXIT 160

Mile 558 (79) Km 898 (127): Exit to small community of **LAIDLAW** and road to Jones Lake (officially Wahleach Lake), 7 miles/11

km of rough road; fishing for rainbow, kokanee and cutthroat in glacially fed hydro reservoir. Near Laidlaw is the F.H. Barber Provincial Park; picnic tables and trails beside the Fraser; fishing for Dolly Varden and coho. Also The Remember When antique doll museum. Highway runs beside the Fraser River; good views; watch for bald eagles in trees in the winter; also for remains of gold dredge, visible at low water. 🎣⅂► EXIT 153

Mile 564 (73) Km 907 (117.5): Exit for Herrling Island. EXIT 146

Mile 570.5 (66.5) Km 918 (107): Exit to Popkum Road for Bridal Veil Falls Provincial Park, the small community of **POPKUM** and various roadside highway attractions, including waterslide, Sandstone Gallery rock and gem museum, Flintstones amusement park, restaurant, motel and gas station. The provincial park provides excellent picnic facilities in meadows at the base of aptly named Bridal Veil Falls, an exquisite tumble of water 200 feet/60m high. Short trail leads to base of falls. ⅂ EXIT 138

Mile 571 (66) Km 918.5 (106.5): Exit to Highway 9 east for Rosedale, Agassiz, Harrison Hot Springs and alternate route Highway 7 to Hope and Vancouver; this is the recommended route for eastbound travelers on Highway 1 who wish to bypass Hope. This is also the west exit for Bridal Veil Falls.

On Highway 9 at the intersection is Minter Gardens, which rivals Victoria's famous Butchart Gardens for beauty. It features seasonal floral displays, trails, topiary, a maze, fountains, streams, gazebos, a restaurant and gift shop. Gardens are open daily mid-June to mid-September; weekends only late May to mid-June. ★ EXIT 135

Mile 579.5 (57.5) Km 932.5 (92.5): Prest Road exit north to Rosedale, south to the small mountain community of Ryder Lake. EXIT 123

Mile 580 (57) Km 933.5 (91.5): Field of hop vines on the north side of the highway and on the south 2.5 miles/4 km west. The Fraser Valley is British Columbia's biggest producer of hops, used in the brewing of beer. Good view to the south of Mount Slesse, a giant sawtooth, and Mount Tomahoy, a snowy ridgeback tent.

Mile 580.5 (56.5) Km 934 (91): Vedder Road exit south to Sardis and Vedder Crossing, north to Chilliwack and Chilliwack airport. **SARDIS** is the center of a hop-growing industry and home of the native Salish weavers who spin and weave traditional Indian baskets. **VEDDER CROSSING** is the site of the Canadian Forces Base Camp and Royal Engineers Military Museum. (Kids will love the outdoor displays of tanks and a bailey bridge.)

Access to Cultus Lake resort area (10 miles/16 km south) which has full tourist facilities, including a giant waterslide and a provincial park with 300 campsites. Continue southeast 27 miles/44 km via rough road for

Chilliwack Lake Provincial Park; 100 campsites, picnicking, swimming, fishing and boating.

CHILLIWACK (pop. 41,300) is a large city, primarily a trading center for the surrounding dairy farmers and vegetable growers. Excellent tourist facilities. It is an old community which began life as a busy steamboat landing and transshipment point during the gold rush era of the 1880s and grew to city stature in 1908. Many heritage buildings remain, including the old city hall, now a national historic site and used as the city museum. 🎣⅂►▲ EXIT 119

Mile 583.5 (53.5) Km 939 (86): Lickman Road exit; access to tourist information centre, open daily in summer, weekdays the rest of the year. Behind the Infocentre is Chilliwack Antique Powerland where old farm machinery, including steam-driven tractors, are restored and displayed in a working museum, complete with busy blacksmith. Annual old-time threshing bee is held here in early August and plowing match in April. EXIT 116

Mile 587 (50) Km 945 (80): Vedder Canal, built in 1920 to drain Sumas Lake and reclaim large areas of floodlands for agriculture.

Mile 590.5 (46.5) Km 950 (75): Exit south to **YARROW**, a small farming community founded by Mennonites. Access to Cultus Lake and Chilliwack Lake provincial parks for eastbound travelers (see **Mile 580.5**). EXIT 104

Mile 594 (43) Km 956 (69): Rest area beside Sumas River. Stop of interest marker tells of the reclamation of 33,000 acres from shallow Sumas Lake in 1924 by a system of stream diversions, dams, dikes, canals and pumps. EXIT 99

Mile 595 (42) Km 957.5 (67.5): Exit to Whatcom Road and rest area (see **Mile 594**). Access to Sumas Mountain Provincial Park. No camping but there are hiking trails with great views. 🎣 EXIT 95

Mile 596.5 (40.5) Km 960 (65): The Lucky Four group of mountains is visible to eastbound travelers.

Mile 598 (39) Km 962 (63): Exit for Highway 11 South to Huntingdon-Sumas border crossing (open 24 hours a day) and highway north to **ABBOTSFORD** (pop. 60,400), all services, and bridge over the Fraser River to Mission and Highway 7 to Harrison Hot Springs. Major attraction at **MISSION** (pop. 28,800), located on the Fraser River, is the Westminster Abbey, a Benedictine monastery built in 1861.

South on Highway 11 is the Fraser Valley Trout Hatchery, British Columbia's largest, which raises rainbow, cutthroat and steelhead. One entire floor of the building is allocated to public displays, viewing walkways and a theatre. The garden area around outdoor rearing ponds provides excellent views of Mount Baker and the valley. EXIT 90

Old Alexandra Bridge is a short walk from highway at Mile 520.5.   (Liz Bryan)

Mile 601 (36) Km 967 (58): Exit to **CLEARBROOK**, a fruit and vegetable processing community and center of a raspberry growing area. Some raspberry fields are visible to the south.   EXIT 87

Mile 603.5 (33.5) Km 971 (54): Exit for Highway 1A, Mount Lehman Road to Aldergrove and Abbotsford airport. Abbotsford International Air Show, largest in Canada, is held here every August. The 3-day event attracts 100,000 spectators. Around Mount Lehman, fields are planted with daffodils and the community of Bradner holds an annual Daffodil Festival and flower show every April.   EXIT 83

Mile 605 (32) Km 974 (51): A good view (best eastbound) of Mount Baker and the other snowcapped peaks of the Cascade Range in Washington. Mount Baker (elev. 10,778 feet/3,285m) is a dormant volcano; it last erupted in 1881 and still belches sulfurous fumes.

Mile 606.5 (30.5) Km 976 (49): Exit westbound traffic only to rest area and Tourism B.C. visitor center.

Mile 607 (30) Km 977 (48): Good view north of Mount Judge Howay.

Mile 609 (27.5) Km 980.5 (44.5): Exit to Highway 13 South to the U.S.-Canada customs at Aldergrove, open 8 a.m. to midnight, and the Vancouver Game Farm. The game farm houses more than 60 species of animals from all parts of the world in large paddocks. The site may be toured by car or on foot. There are picnic areas, a gift shop and food available.   EXIT 73

Mile 614 (23) Km 988.5 (36.5): Exit to Highway 10 to **CLOVERDALE**, known for its annual Victoria Day Rodeo (end of May) and for harness racing (October through April). Historic Transportation Centre, south on Highway 10, displays more than 100 antique cars, trucks and planes. Open daily in summer; Tuesday to Saturday rest of year.   EXIT 66

Mile 615.5 (21.5) Km 990.5 (34.5): Good view of Mount Baker.

Mile 618 (19) Km 995 (30): Exit on 200th Street to **LANGLEY** (pop. 15,200) and **FORT LANGLEY** (pop. 10,000). The fort at Fort Langley is a national historic park. A Hudson's Bay Co. fur-trading post was built here in 1827 just downstream and was rebuilt at its present location in 1840. It served for many years as the fur company's headquarters on the West Coast. In 1868 the mainland of British Columbia was declared a crown colony here and Sir James Douglas was proclaimed the colony's first governor. To commemorate this event, the British Columbia Cabinet meets here every Nov. 19.

Langley is a fast-growing trading center of the lower Fraser Valley and provides good shopping and full tourist facilities.   EXIT 58

Mile 621.5 (15.5) Km 1000 (25): Exit to Highway 15 South to the U.S. border at Douglas (customs open 24 hours); north to Barnston Island. Barnston Island (follow 176th Street until it hits 104th Avenue, then turn north) is accessible by a free ferry; its encircling dike makes a bracing 2- to 3-hour walk.   EXIT 53

Mile 625 (12) Km 1006 (19.5): Exit for municipality of **SURREY** (pop. 168,000), which includes the communities of Whalley,

South Surrey, Cloverdale, Newton and Guildford. Tourist Information Center on 105th Avenue is open year-round.   EXIT 48

Mile 626 (11) Km 1007.5 (17.5): Port Mann Bridge over the Fraser River.

Mile 627 (10) Km 1009 (16): Exit for Highway 7 which goes east along the north side of the Fraser River through Maple Ridge and Mission to Harrison Hot Springs and Hope. Also exit here for the Greater Vancouver suburbs of Coquitlam and Port Coquitlam.   EXIT 44

Mile 627.5 (9.5) Km 1010 (15): Brunette River, a tributary of the Fraser. The river water is dark because of peat deposits.

Mile 629.5 (7.5) Km 1013 (12): Exit to New Westminster, Coquitlam and Maillardville. The highway parallels the Canadian National Railway. **NEW WESTMINSTER** (pop. 40,000) was designed to be the capital of British Columbia. Its site was chosen and surveyed in 1858 and Queen Victoria bestowed its name in 1859, but the capital later went to Victoria, for mostly political reasons.

The city has some colorful traditions, including a 100-year-old May Day celebration and the Hyack Anvil Battery which fires a 21-gun salute in honor of the queen each May 24, using blacksmith anvils and gunpowder instead of cannons.

New Westminster is presently the eastern terminus for Greater Vancouver's rapid transit system, Skytrain, introduced in 1986. Electrically powered, computer driven trains run mostly on elevated tracks (tunnels in the downtown area) from New Westminster 8th Street Station to Vancouver harborfront. Service is continuous, and the total trip takes less than 30 minutes. The Rail is being extended out across the Fraser to Surrey; due for completion by 1990.

Mile 632.5 (4.5) Km 1018 (7): Cariboo Road exit.   EXIT 37

Mile 634 (3) Km 1020 (5): Exit on Kensington Avenue South for Deer Lake Park, Burnaby, New Westminster and Highway 99A which crosses the Fraser on Pattullo Bridge and connects to Highway 99 South, Highway 1A East. Visit Burnaby Village Museum, 30 buildings depicting pioneer life; Simon Fraser University atop Burnaby Mountain for spectacular architecture and views and excellent Museum of Archaeology.   EXIT 33

Mile 634.5 (2.5) Km 1021 (4): Exit to the visitor information centre, Sprott Street and Sperling Avenue, in Burnaby. Go north on Sprott, then east to Burnaby Lake Regional Park; hiking trails, canoeing.   EXIT 32

Mile 636.5 (0.5) Km 1024 (1): Willingdon Road exit.   EXIT 29

Mile 637 (0) Km 1025 (0): **VANCOUVER** city boundary at Grandview Highway. For more information on Greater Vancouver, see the MAJOR CITIES section.   EXIT 28

U.S. Highway 2

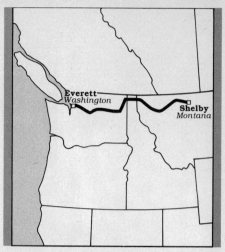

See map pages 31, 34 and 36

Highway 2 is the last of the U.S. transcontinental highways, a thin ribbon of road, often 2-lane, crossing the northern tier of the country from the Atlantic to the Pacific. *NORTHWEST MILEPOSTS®* logs Highway 2 from Shelby, MT, at the junction of Interstate 15, west to Interstate 5 at Everett, WA.

The route is rich with history, scenery, wildlife and, for those who want it, adventure. There is much to see and it's advisable to allow ample travel time for spontaneous side trips. Some of the most prominent attractions along Highway 2 include the modern Museum of the Plains Indians at Browning; magnificent Waterton/Glacier International Peace Park (a slow drive along the Going-to-the-Sun Road through spectacular Logan Pass is a must); and the world's largest hydroelectric dam at Grand Coulee.

Travel on this highway is much slower and decidedly more scenic than in the fast lane of the east-west interstate highways. Travelers should be prepared for ice and snow in fall and winter. Some of the higher mountain passes are occasionally closed by avalanches and it is not unusual for chains to be required for mountain travel during the snow season. As a rule, however, the highway is a well-maintained all-season route. Gas stations, modern motels and the usual highway service facilities are numerous and convenient.

Physical mileposts along U.S. Highway 2 in Montana indicate distance from the Idaho-Montana border. In Idaho, mileposts on U.S. 2 indicate distance from the Washington-Idaho border, except for a 37-mile section between Sandpoint and Bonners Ferry, where U.S. 2 shares a common alignment with U.S. 95 and mileposts reflect distance from the Washington-Idaho border via U.S. 95. Mileposts in Washington reflect distance from the U.S. Highway 2 junction with I-5 at Everett.

U.S. Highway 2 Log

Distance from Shelby, MT, is followed by distance from Everett, WA.

Mile 0 (698.5): The mileage log begins at the junction of U.S. Highway 2 and Interstate 15 on the western outskirts of **SHELBY** (pop. 3,000), a ranching community on the edge of the Sweetgrass Hills. The land is mostly flat, buffeted by prairie winds, checkered with large folds of irrigated farm fields and arid grasslands. Small fenced tracts housing underground Minuteman rocket silos are visible from the highway. The community was built in 1891 as a railroad town and is still a major grain shipping station. Jack Dempsey and Tommy Gibbons waged a heavyweight boxing championship fight here in 1923. (It was Dempsey in 15 rounds!) In 1921 oil was discovered just north of Shelby in an area now called Oilmont where pumps continue to tap the oil deposits today.

Gold Butte, one of several ghost towns to explore along this route, is located just north of Shelby.

Camping with complete hookups is available at Lake Shel-oole Park just 1 mile north of Shelby. ▲

Mile 12.5 (686): **ETHRIDGE.** Gas and food available.

Mile 23.5 (674.5): **CUT BANK** (pop. 3,750; elev. 3,751 feet), a farm and ranch community at the junction of U.S. 2 and County Highway 213. All services and several motels are available. In the winter Cut Bank frequently receives national exposure as one of the coldest spots in the nation. The town is named for the way the stream has eroded the bank soil.

On the western edge of town, travelers cross Cut Bank Creek, heavily fished for rainbow, brook, cutthroat and brown trout, and enter the 2,400-square-mile Blackfeet Indian Reservation. Tribal sportsmen permits must be purchased to fish, hunt, boat, snowmobile or cross-country ski on the reservation. Permits and tribal regulations are available at most general stores on the reservation or at tribal headquarters in Browning.
🐟▲ MP 255

Mile 25.5 (673): Junction with Montana Highway 358. Airport. MP 253

Mile 29.5 (669): Private RV campground. ▲

Mile 43.5 (655): Junction with County Highway 444 leading north 26 miles to the Alberta border at Port of Del Bonita. MP 235

Mile 45.5 (653): Camp Disappointment Historical Marker and Monument. The northernmost point reached by the Lewis and Clark expedition, July 23, 1806. Captain Lewis hoped to tell President Jefferson that the headwaters of the Marias River rose north of the 49th parallel. If this were true, the boundaries of the Louisiana Purchase would have extended farther into English territory. From this point, Lewis could see clearly that the river rose to the west rather than the north as he had hoped. Thus, Camp Disappointment.

From Shelby to west of Browning the landscape is treeless and fairly flat. The few trees visible along this route mark ranch or farm yards. MP 233

Mile 50 (648.5): **BLACKFOOT.** Small Indian community near Kipps Lake. MP 230

Mile 54 (644.5): Junction with U.S. Highway 89 South to Great Falls.

Mile 55.5 (643): Junction at Browning (description follows) with U.S. Highway 89 North to the Canadian border. Highway 89 also provides access to the St. Mary entrance to Glacier National Park, the Many Glacier area of the park, and junctions with Chief Mountain Road to Waterton Lakes National Park. (See national park descriptions in the MAJOR ATTRACTIONS section.)

BROWNING (pop. 1,280) is agency headquarters for the Blackfeet Indian Reservation and the largest town on the reservation. All services available, including motels and RV camping. The free Museum of the Plains Indian exhibits the crafts, history, dress, culture and art of the Plains tribes. Colorful tepees are erected on the museum grounds during the summer. The annual Indian Days festival, held in July, is one of the largest gatherings of U.S. and Canadian tribes. The festival features traditional drumming, singing, dancing and feasting, and spectators are welcome.

Museum of Montana Wildlife, owned by sculptor Bob Scriver, is open daily June to September; admission charged. It is located near the Indian museum at the junction of Highways 2 and 89.

Eastbound, Highway 2 from Browning on into North Dakota is known as "The Highline." During the era of big cattle drives, cowboys could drive herds of cattle from here to North Dakota without cutting a fence.

Westbound, the flat, nearly desolate plains begin to give way to rolling hills and forested mountains. ▲MP 224

Mile 70.5 (628): Two Medicine River bridge. Outlet of Two Medicine Lake in Glacier National Park. Heavily fished near roads and bridges for pan-sized rainbow and a few brook trout. Tribal fishing permit required. 🐟 MP 211

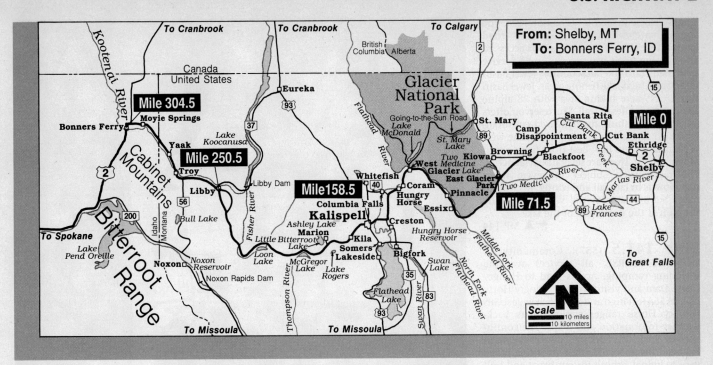

Mile 71.5 (627): EAST GLACIER PARK, all services available. This small community dramatically marks the western border of the great plains region and the sudden geographic upheaval into the Rocky Mountains.

Junction with Montana Highway 49, which leads north 0.5 mile to Glacier Park Lodge, 11 miles to Two Medicine Lake in Glacier National Park, and 12 miles to Kiowa on U.S. Highway 89.

Westbound, Highway 2 follows the south boundary of Glacier National Park.

Mile 74 (624.5): Gravel Road to Heart Butte, 23 miles south.

Mile 75.5 (623): Boundary of Blackfeet Indian Reservation and Lewis and Clark National Forest. RV camping. ▲

Mile 83.5 (615): Marias Pass (elev. 5,216 feet) and Continental Divide. Marias Pass is the lowest U.S. pass through the American Rockies. A bronze statue commemorates John F. Stevens, who discovered the pass for the railroad in 1889. Look for moose and beaver in the sloughs beside the road. The Forest Service campground at the summit offers drinking water, RV spaces and restrooms. The Theodore Roosevelt Monument here, shaped like a miniature Washington Monument, marks the boundary between the Flathead and Lewis and Clark national forests.
MP 197

Mile 90.5 (608): Private campground.
▲

Mile 91.5 (607): Chain-up area for westbound travelers. MP 192

Mile 93.5 (605): Devil Creek National Forest Campground, 12 tent sites, water, stock ramp, trailhead into Great Bear Wilderness Area. Guest ranch, motel and gasoline are available. Devil's Stairway, a multileveled waterfall, can be seen from the campground. To the north is Mount Snowslip (elev. 7,290 feet). 🥾▲ MP 190

Mile 98.5 (600): Trailhead of Trail 155 into Great Bear Wilderness along Middle Fork Flathead River. The Middle Fork is often acclaimed as "Montana's Wildest River," and is famous for its white-water rafting and fishing inside the wilderness area. Some camping at trailhead. 🥾 MP 185

Mile 99.5 (599): Boundary of Glacier National Park: Middle Fork Flathead River bridge.

Mile 101 (597.5): Goat Lick Mountain. Wild mountain goats can sometimes be seen here licking minerals from river rocks.

Mile 102.5 (596): Glacier National Park, Walton entrance. Walton USFS ranger station, picnic area. Backcountry hiking permits available here. This is the trailhead hub for several hiking routes. 🥾⛲ MP 181

Mile 103.5 (595): ESSEX, small community with food, lodging and train depot. Chain-up area.

Mile 107.5 (591): Paola Creek; river access to the Middle Fork Flathead River.

Mile 109 (589.5): Motel, gas and food facilities.

Mile 113 (585.5): Lodge, camping, rental cabins, 1.5-mile hiking trail to Stanton Lake. Usually poor fishing. 🥾▲ MP 170

Mile 122.5 (576): Moccasin Creek river access.

Mile 124.5 (574): Highway parallels Middle Fork Flathead River for approximately 40 miles westbound. This area, known as the John F. Stevens Canyon, is bordered on the north by Glacier National Park and on the south by the Great Bear Wilderness Area. Fishing is generally poor to fair for cutthroat trout near the road, good in less accessible areas. The Middle Fork is an excellent cutthroat and bull trout fishery in the wilderness area before it reaches Highway 2. Most of the creeks along the north bank are closed to protect spawning bull trout. 🐟

Mile 130.5 (568): WEST GLACIER, a small resort community with full facilities, including post office, grocery, motels, river rafting companies, restaurants, gas and train depot. This is the Glacier National Park headquarters and west entrance to the park via Apgar and Going-to-the-Sun Road over Logan Pass. (See Glacier National Park description in MAJOR ATTRACTIONS section.) Camping facilities near town. ▲ MP 153

Mile 134 (564.5): Motel, RV camping, Middle Fork boat access area, popular take-out point for white-water rafters and launch site for downstream float fishing trips. ▲

Mile 131.5 (567): Campground.
▲ MP 152

Mile 132.5 (566): KOA Campground.
▲ MP 151

Mile 133.5 (565): Campground to north of highway. Entrance to Lake Five, which has camping. ▲ MP 150

Mile 136.5 (562): CORAM, a small community with all services available, including camping. ▲

Mile 139.5 (559): MARTIN CITY. All services available. Easternmost access road to

Hungry Horse Reservoir Recreation Area. The approximately 115-mile-long loop road around the 34-mile-long lake offers access to 10 camping areas, numerous Forest Service spur roads into the backcountry, Jewel Basin hiking and high lake fishing areas. Jewel Basin is a 15,349-acre hiking area with 28 alpine lakes and 35 miles of trail. The reservoir offers fair to good fishing for pan-sized cutthroat, whitefish and a few grayling along the west bank near Graves Bay. Best trout fishing is in May and June. There are several boat launches. The reservoir is subject to severe water drawdowns in late fall and winter. Recreation maps are available at the visitor center by the dam at the north end of the lake.

🐟▲ MP 144

Mile 141.5 (557): Community of **HUNGRY HORSE**, all services available including camping. Access road to Hungry Horse Dam and visitor center. Hungry Horse Dam is 564 feet high and 2,115 feet wide. USFS Hungry Horse ranger station offers backcountry information and maps. The confluence of the South Fork here creates the main Flathead River, a cold, clear river that offers very marginal fishing for cutthroat and bull trout.

🐟▲ MP 142

Mile 143 (555.5): Shepard Memorial Fountain, a roadside spring, provides cold, sweet drinking water at a turnout on the south side of the road. There is also a historical marker describing a local battle between Blackfeet and Kalispell Indian tribes.

MP 140

Mile 145.5 (553): House of Mystery, motel and restaurant facilities.

Mile 146 (552.5): Junction with Montana Highway 206, which leads south to the west side of Flathead Lake and town of Bigfork. All services available, including RV camping, at junction. Resort facilities available at the lake.

▲ MP 138

Mile 147.5 (551): **COLUMBIA FALLS** (pop. 3,380). All services available. A lumber, aluminum mill and agricultural town with a strong recreational industry, Columbia Falls is the first major town west of Glacier National Park. ARCO Aluminum Co. dominates employment. Columbia Falls does not have a waterfall. According to local legend the name was bestowed in 1889 by the wife of the area's postmaster. After the U.S. Postal Service rejected the name of Columbia, fearing confusion with the existing Montana city of Columbus, she reportedly told her husband to add the word falls to the name.

Junction with Montana Highway 486, which follows the North Fork Flathead River north to the remote northwest corner of Glacier National Park, and crosses into Canada at Port of Trail Creek (where the custom station is solar-powered).

The main Flathead River is best fished by boat and produces best between Columbia Falls and Kalispell for west slope cutthroat and bull trout. Local sporting goods stores provide good fishing and hunting recreation. 🐟

Craftwork at the Museum of the Plains Indians in Browning, Mile 55.5. *(Tom Barr)*

Mile 148.5 (550): Western city limits of Columbia Falls. Golf course. MP 136

Mile 150.5 (548): Junction with Montana Highway 40, which provides a 4.5-mile link with U.S. Highway 93. Highway 93 leads north to Whitefish and Big Mountain Ski Area. For details, turn to **Mile 640** in the U.S. HIGHWAY 93 section.

Highway 2 becomes 4-lane as it turns south toward Kalispell. Begin 2-lane road eastbound.

Mile 155.5 (543): Glacier International Airport. Regularly scheduled commercial flights available. MP 129

Mile 157 (541.5): Junction with Montana 35 to Bigfork and east shore of Flathead Lake.

Mile 158.5 (540): Western city limits of **KALISPELL** (pop. 11,890), the seat of Flathead County and the largest city in northwestern Montana. All services available. The town has been called several names since the mid-1800s, including Gregg's Landing, Greggsville, Scooptown and Demersville. The town of Demersville was located 4 miles south of the present city of Kalispell and when the Great Northern Railway was completed in 1891, the city moved and the name was changed.

Kalispell is a word taken from the Pend Oreille (pon-do-RAY) Indians meaning either "camas" or "the prairie above the lake," depending on who is doing the translating.

Recreation is a major industry in Kalispell. It is a gateway to Glacier National Park (30 miles to the east), a base for skiers enjoying the popular Big Mountain Ski Area (17 miles north) and a home port for those enjoying the facilities at Flathead Lake (7 miles south).

The Conrad Mansion, completed in 1895, is one of the most beautiful examples of turn-of-the-century architecture in the Northwest. It was donated to the city of Kalispell in 1975 and the building has been completely restored. The furnishings in the home are also original, giving visitors an authentic taste of 19th century Montana. The home was originally built for Charles E. Conrad who made his fortune in the water commerce on the Missouri River from 1868 to 1891. The home is open daily for guided tours. Admission fee.

Woodland Park is a favorite location in Kalispell for picnicking. It is located off Woodland Avenue and Conrad Drive.

Lone Pine State Park, located on a ridgetop just west of Kalispell, has a picnic area and nature trail. Take 5th Street west from Main Street and turn left on Meridian Road. Continue to the right as Meridian turns into Foy Lake Road and goes up the hill 3 miles to the lake. Lone Pine Park appears 0.5 mile past the lake on your left. Foy Lake offers public swimming and boating.

Mile 159.5 (539): Junction with U.S. Highway 93. (Turn to **Mile 627** in the U.S. HIGHWAY 93 section for log of that highway.)

Mile 170.5 (528): Junction with Kila Road which leads to a fishing access on Mount Creek to the south and goes to the community of **KILA** and Smith Lake, then joins Montana Highway 28 near Nirada. Smith Lake is 300 acres, extremely marshy, with a public access site on the south side. Small boats are needed to reach the 10-inch yellow perch and small largemouth bass population. ⚓ MP 110

Mile 172.5 (526): Small picnic turnout beneath a sheer cliff with views of a beautiful ranch valley. 🌲

Mile 175.5 (523): Junction with 13-mile gravel road north to Ashley Lake State Recreation Area; 12 campsites, picnic area and boat launch. Ashley Lake is just under 5 miles long, about 2 miles wide, more than 200 feet deep, and most famous for producing the state-record rainbow-cutthroat hybrid; a 30-pound, 4-ounce trophy caught in 1982. That same year Ashley also produced the state-record pygmy whitefish which weighed only 2.6 ounces. Also kokanee fishing, big yellow perch, and pan-sized cutthroat with a few hybrids between 10 and 15 pounds caught each year. 🌲⚓▲ MP 105

Mile 179.5 (519): Junction with gravel side road which leads 5 miles north to Bitterroot Lake State Recreation Area; 20 campsites, boat launch and picnic area on the north end of the lake, and another boat launch on the south end. There are also 2 resorts and a good fishery for pan-sized cutthroat, kokanee salmon and rainbow. Phone, gas and cabins are available in **MARION**. 🌲⚓▲

Mile 180.5 (518): Lions Recreation Area.

Mile 181.5 (517): Private campground with gas, diesel, propane, and laundry. ▲ MP 100

Mile 185.5 (513): Little Bitterroot River crossing. This small stream is heavily tapped for irrigation water and affords generally fair fishing for small cutthroat, rainbow and brookies. ⚓

Mile 192.5 (506): Motel. MP 89

Mile 193.5 (505): McGregor Lake is along the south side of the highway. Camping, cabins, stores and cafe along the lake. McGregor is 5 miles long and provides good fishing for rainbow, cutthroat, kokanee, perch and lake (mackinaw) trout. ⚓▲

Mile 198.5 (500): McGregor Lake National Forest Recreation Area at the western end of the lake. Forest Service campground with 15 sites, water, picnic area and a boat launch. MP 85.5

Mile 207.5 (491): Logan State Park; 50 campsites, picnic area, swimming beach, dump station and boat ramp. Dedicated to memory of Sidney M. Logan, author and lawyer. 🌲▲ MP77

Mile 209.5 (489): Thompson River Road, good gravel, strikes south from Highway 2 and follows the Thompson River for 45 miles to Montana Highway 200 near the town of Thompson Falls.

Mile 210.5 (488): Lower, Middle and Upper Thompson lakes south of highway.

Another chain of lakes, Crystal, Horseshoe and Loon, extend west along the highway from the end of Upper Thompson. Lower Thompson is good for small largemouth bass, fair for kokanee salmon, cutthroat and rainbow and the shoreline is rich with small pumpkinseed bluegills. Logan State Recreation Area on Middle Thompson Lake offers 30 campsites, a boat launch, swimming area, drinking water, boat rental and a reputation for excellent catches of kokanee, largemouth bass, cutthroat to 7 pounds, mackinaw and perch. The Upper Thompson is fished for cutthroat, perch and good numbers of fair-sized largemouth bass. Crystal Lake is stocked with kokanee, rainbow trout and perch. A tiny landstrip separates Crystal from Horseshoe Lake, generally poor angling. ⚓▲MP 74

Mile 212 (486.5): Small resort settlement, with grocery store and restaurants. Pleasant Valley Road leads north to Libby Dam. (Main access to dam is via Highway 37 from Libby at **Mile 250.5**.) MP 72

Mile 215 (483.5): Remnants of the Houghton Creek fire that started Aug. 27, 1984, and burned some 12,000 acres in about a week, are seen on both sides of the highway for about 9 miles westbound.

Mile 217 (481.5): Junction of McKillop Road, northbound to intersect with the Fisher River Road.

Mile 219 (479.5): Crystal Creek Road to hiking trailheads in the Kenelty Mountain (elev. 5,931 feet) area, a popular deer and elk hunting region crisscrossed with streams and springs. 🚶

Mile 215 (483.5): Loon Lake; good small and largemouth bass, pansized rainbow, and some brook trout. ⚓ MP 69

Mile 220.5 (478): Raven Work Center Forest Service ranger station and information office for the Kootenai National Forest and Cabinet Mountains Wilderness Area. The 7,000-foot Cabinet Mountains may be seen to the west. From U.S. Highway 2, access to the Cabinet Wilderness Area via gravel roads following Fisher Creek, Libby Creek and Cherry Creek. MP 63.5

Mile 223.5 (475): Houghton Creek Road leads south to Monicke Community Church and Silver Creek Road. MP 61

Mile 227.5 (471): Libby Creek, a poor to fair producer of rainbow and cutthroat thanks to pollution seeping into the water from mining operations, enters Fisher River here. Junction with Miller Creek Road. ⚓ MP 56

Mile 228.5 (470): Junction with Old Fisher River Road. Fisher River is small, followed by gravel roads, and channelized into a ditch in the lower 5 miles. Above the ditch, the stream winds through a wooded valley and is a fair producer of cutthroat, rainbow and whitefish. ⚓

Mile 231.5 (467): Junction with Tepee Creek Road.

Mile 239.5 (459): Libby Creek Campground; 20 primitive sites. MP 44

Mile 242.5 (456): Junction with Libby Creek Road. Junction with Highway 482 to Libby. MP41

Mile 247 (451.5): Airfield, a 4,200-foot lighted landing strip. No scheduled flights. MP 36

Mile 247.5 (451): The St. Regis tree farm grows ponderosa pine.

Mile 250.5 (448): **LIBBY** (pop. 2,530). All services available. Logging is the major industry with mining and tourism almost equally important. Libby Heritage Museum displays Montana wildlife, mining equipment, Indian relics, photography and toys. Outside are old cabins, machinery, and a Shay locomotive. Open daily.

The major tourist attraction here is Libby Dam, 17 miles east of town via Highway 37, with the 90-mile-long Lake Koocanusa (impounded in 1972) providing water sports, a boat launch, picnic area, tent sites, hiking trails, and excellent fishing for kokanee salmon. The word Koocanusa is derived from the first 3 letters in the names of the 3 geographic areas involved: *Koo*tenai, *Can*ada and *USA*. ⚓▲ MP30

Mile 262.5 (436): Kootenai Falls viewpoint and picnic table just off highway. Historical marker explains that Kootenai means "deer robes" in Blackfeet Indian language, and the Blackfeet Indians were the main enemies of the trappers who first entered the area in 1809. The only white sturgeon found in Montana live below these falls, and they are protected by state law.

If you enjoy stream fishing take the time to try a few sections of the Kootenai. It's worth the effort. Inquire locally about the availability of guided float trips. ⚓

Mile 265.5 (433): Junction with Montana Highway 56 which leads south to Montana Highway 200. Access to Bull Lake (camping and fishing) and Ross Creek Cedar Grove, a 1-mile nature trail through 150-foot-tall western red cedar, hemlock, white pine and spruce. ⚓▲ MP 17

Mile 268.5 (430): TROY (pop. 1,200), all services available. Troy once had the world's largest silver mine and enormous gold mines. The ASARCO silver mine south of town is still one of the major employers, along with the Forest Service.

Callahan Creek flows into the Kootenai River at Troy, the only stream in Montana with a native rainbow trout population. ⚓

Mile 269.5 (429): Troy Forest Service Ranger Station. MP 12.5

Mile 271.5 (427): KOA campground near bridge across Kootenai River. ▲ MP 11

Mile 272.5 (426): Access to lakes.
MP 10

Mile 273.5 (425): Art gallery.

Mile 276.5 (422): Yaak River bridge. Forest Service campground with 43 primitive sites at the confluence of the Yaak and Kootenai rivers. The mouth of the Yaak River is an excellent spot to find a spring concentration of trophy-sized rainbow.

Mile 279.5 (419): Junction with Montana Highway 508 to Yaak. Yaak Falls and Forest Service campground with 7 sites are located 7 miles north of Highway 2 on this gravel road. The Yaak River is popular with fly-fishermen and white-water rafters. Best fishing between the Kootenai River and Yaak Falls. MP 4

Mile 281.5 (417): Kootenai National Forest boundary. MP 1

Mile 282 (416.5): Montana-Idaho state border. Mountain-Pacific time zone line. Pacific time is 1 hour earlier than Mountain. Restaurant, bingo parlor, gas, and phone.
MP 80

Mile 286.5 (412): Side road to Herman Lake in Kanisku National Forest. There is a resort on Herman Lake with rental boats, swimming area and an excellent largemouth bass potential. This is moose county and the largest of North America's deer family are frequently visible from the road.

Mile 293.5 (405): MOYIE SPRINGS (pop. 370) Limited services. An overlook on the outskirts of town has a view down into a deep gorge and the town. Moyie River Road (gravel) leads north along the Moyie River to the spectacular Moyie Falls and dam and also campgrounds. The Moyie is a white-water stream with a local reputation for rafting thrills and producing pan-sized trout when fly-fishing. MP 70

Mile 299.5 (399): Junction of U.S. Highway 2 with U.S. Highway 95; turn to **Mile 699** in the U.S. HIGHWAY 95 section for log of that route. (Highways 2 and 95 share a common alignment south to Sandpoint.)

County airport and several service stations are located at this intersection.

Mile 300.5 (398): Historical marker commemorating David Thompson's passage. The famous map maker and trader for the North West Co. explored this area in 1808.

Mile 302.5 (396): Start of 1.5 miles of 6 percent downhill grade westbound to the Kootenai River.

Mile 304.5 (394): BONNERS FERRY (pop. 1,900) and Kootenai River bridge. This is the county seat of Boundary County and its economy is dependent on farming and lumber. Tree farming and nursery stock has become a major new industry here. Visitor

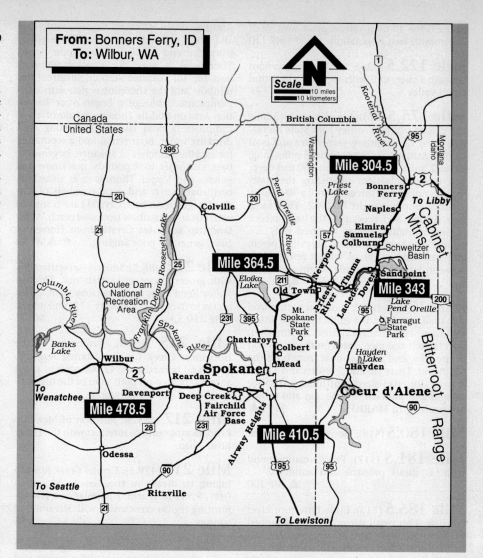

From: Bonners Ferry, ID
To: Wilbur, WA

services are limited and hunting and fishing are the major recreational opportunities. Bonners Ferry ranger station has information and maps on Kanisku National Forest.

Bonners Ferry is a mecca for wildlife photographers and wildlife viewing. Kootenai National Wildlife Refuge is 3 miles from the Kootenai River bridge. There is a loop auto tour along the refuge's dike system for viewing mallards, pintails, Canada geese, swans, great blue herons, sandpipers and other marsh and shorebirds. MP 506

Mile 305.5 (393): Geologic and historic site. Parts of 1864-65 gold rush trail can be seen. Sign explains glacial lake formation during ice age. MP 504

Mile 307.5 (391): Start of 6 percent downgrade for next 2 miles westbound.

Mile 308.5 (390): Pleasant Valley.

Mile 311.5 (387): Blue Lake private campground. Winter snowmobile recreation area trailhead 3 miles west.

Mile 312.5 (386): NAPLES is a small community with a general store and gasoline pumps.

Mile 316 (382.5): Sportsman's access to Kanisku National Forest, Kootenai National Wildlife Refuge and McArthur Lake Game Management Area. The highway runs the eastern edge of the popular bass, perch and crappie lake. MP 496

Mile 319.5 (379): Small town of ELMIRA. Gas and food available. MP 490

Mile 323.5 (375): Small community of SAMUELS. No services. MP 486

Mile 324.5 (374): Bridge crosses the Pack River, a major tributary of giant Lake Pend Oreille. Above the bridge the Pack is small and fair to good for trout fishing with light tackle and is accessible from a gravel Forest Service road. Downstream of Highway 2 the Pack is broad, slow and not a significant contributor to the regional fishery.

Mile 326.5 (372): COLBURN. Service station, groceries, bar and cafe. MP 483

Mile 333.5 (365): The northern edge of Sandpoint and the junction with road to Schweitzer Basin Ski Area, 11 miles; 7 chair lifts, stunning view of Lake Pend Oreille. Lifts are open in summer. Also access to Bonner County Fairgrounds.

Mile 334 (364.5): Junction with Idaho Highway 200.

Mile 334.5 (364): Chamber of Commerce information center. The friendly and helpful staff here provide maps and travel information.

Mile 336.5 (362): SANDPOINT (pop. 5,370), has all tourist facilities, including some top hotels and restaurants along Lake Pend Oreille. Of interest is the Cedar Street bridge shopping center, a 2-story, rough-lumber-and-glass series of boutiques. The Vintage Wheel Museum, on U.S. 2, displays carriages, steam engines, and automobiles dating from early 1900s to a 1962 Rolls Royce Silver Cloud 2; admission charge.

Sandpoint is situated on Lake Pend Oreille which is 43.2 miles long, 6.3 miles wide, has a shoreline of 111 miles, and is up to 1,150 feet deep. It is one of the most popular fishing lakes in the state. Guides and rental boats are available along with first-class boat ramps and moorage facilities. Fishing is concentrated on kokanee salmon and kamloops rainbow, and is celebrated with Kamloops and Kokanee Days early in May each year. This lake is large, confusing and can be overwhelming for the newcomer. Sporting goods stores in Sandpoint are excellent sources for fishing maps of the lake, current catch conditions and guide service.

U.S. Highway 2 junctions with U.S. Highway 95 at Sandpoint and the 2 highways follow a common alignment north to Bonners Ferry. See **Mile 663** in the U.S. HIGHWAY 95 section for log of that highway.

Westbound, U.S. Highway 2 follows the Pend Oreille River to the Idaho-Washington border.

Mile 338.5 (360): DOVER, unincorporated.   MP 25

Mile 348.5 (350): Historic marker commemorating ancient Indian crossing and camp.   MP 15

Mile 349.5 (349): LACLEDE. A small community with a tavern and store. Riley Creek Recreation Area is a mile south; 68 campsites, 45 picnic tables, swim beach, boat launch and drinking water. One of the nicest campsites along the river. The river here is part of the Hoodoo Game Management Unit.   ▲ MP 14

Mile 357 (341.5): Priest River Recreation Area; 17 campsites, water, swim beach, boat launch, and picnic shelter.   ⊼▲ MP 7

Mile 357.5 (341): Junction with Highway 57 which leads 25 miles north to Priest Lake, known for watersports, fishing, resorts and camping. (See feature this section.) ★

Mile 358.5 (340): PRIEST RIVER (pop. 1,840), gateway to Priest Lake, has most services, including public and private camp-

grounds. The town is at the junction of the Pend Oreille and Priest rivers, and was built by workers on the Great Northern Railroad during the early part of the 1890s. Fishermen will find boat launches at the city park and city dock, boat rentals, a marina and commercial outfitters. Local sporting goods outlets can provide current hunting and fishing information.   ⚓▲ MP 5

Mile 360.5 (338): Public golf course.   MP 4

Mile 362.5 (336): Albeni Dam Visitor Center and viewpoint. Albeni Cove Campground; 13 sites, picnic facilities, boat launch and swim beach.   ⊼▲ MP 2

Mile 364.5 (334): OLD TOWN, ID (pop. 340), and NEWPORT, WA. These towns straddle the state borderline and the Pend Oreille River. The towns have modest tourist facilities, most of which are on the Washington side. Junction with Washington Highway 20.

Mile 373.5 (325): DIAMOND LAKE resort area has a popular cutthroat trout fishing lake, boat launch, rentals and gas station.   ⚓

Mile 376.5 (322): Junction with Washington Highway 211, which goes due north to join Highway 20 at Usk. Access to Kalispell Indian Reservation, Pend Oreille River Recreation Area and Mateline Falls.

Mile 380.5 (318): A 6-mile stretch of 4-lane highway begins southbound. Access to Sacheen Lake and Pend Oreille County Park, which has a trailer park, hiking, and horseback riding.   🚶‍♀️▲

Mile 384.5 (314): Turnoff west for gravel road to Eloika Lake, which has camping, service stations and is one of the best largemouth bass and crappie lakes in this region. There are resort facilities, boat rentals and boat launches at the lake. Good duck and white-tailed deer hunting in the fall.   ⚓▲

Mile 388.5 (310): Community of RIVERSIDE.

Mile 390 (308.5): Junction with all-weather road west to Deer Park on U.S. Highway 395.

Mile 396 (302.5): CHATTAROY, an unincorporated town with limited services. The road bridges the Little Spokane River,

Priest Lake

Often called "a sapphire set in emerald," Priest Lake is one of the Northwest's most visited year-round destinations. Demand is so great at resorts that summer accommodations sometimes require reservations a year in advance. The town of Priest River on U.S. Highway 2 (see **Mile 358.5**) is the gateway to the Priest Lake Recreation Area. The lake is 25 miles north of Priest River via Idaho Highway 57 (turnoff at **Mile 357.5**).

Despite its popularity, Priest Lake exudes solitude. It is still a place where deer cross front lawns and moose feed in shoreline shallows. Known for its clear waters, 19-mile-long Priest Lake is connected to Upper Priest Lake (2.5 miles long) by a 2-mile channel. Upper Priest Lake is not accessible by road.

Except for a small town and a golf course, Priest Lake and its facilities are completely hidden from Highway 57. Along the shores are condominiums, waterfront resorts, bed-and-breakfasts, 14 campgrounds and several marinas. Water-skiers and the bright sails of windsurfers often decorate the lake's surface.

In summer, these lakes offer some of Idaho's best trout fishing. Anglers use everything from surface, leaded, and steel line for jig and fly-fishing.

Hiking trails provide good opportunities to see wildlife as well as enjoy the pine-scented outdoors. Hanna Flats Nature Trail, off Highway 57 at Priest Lake, is an easy 0.5-mile walk by various species of flora. Other summer lakeside activities are tennis, horseshoes, volleyball, and swimming in heated pools. Several northshore beaches are favorites of sunbathers. Virtually any and all sport equipment may be rented locally.

Many visitors elect to experience Priest Lake from an island campsite. Kalispell Island's 400 campsites and large, sandy beaches are often filled with swimmers and sunbathers. Bartoo Island has primitive camping areas and is also known for its large beaches. Four Mile and Eight Mile Island make up in solitude and scenery what they lack in beach area.

In winter, it is usually either sunny or snowing at Priest Lake. With over 400 miles of groomed trails, winter brings droves of snowmobilers along with ice skaters and ice fishermen. Winter festivals center around snow sculpture contests, guided winter photo tours, and the Snowlympics held on President's Day. Another Priest Lake tradition is the annual Snowshoe Softball tournament. It is held in conjunction with the U.S. Pacific Coast International Sled Dog Racing Championships. The 2-day event attracts about 75 teams annually from the western states and Alaska.

which flows mostly through private ranch property, but can provide fair trout fishing for rainbow and brookies if you ask permission. There is a small campground, 4 sites, 4 miles northeast of Chattaroy accessible from Bruce Road.

Mile 401.5 (297): Junction with Highway 206 which leads east about 20 miles to Mount Spokane State Park (14 tent sites) and the downhill ski area. Mount Spokane (elev. 5,878 feet) rises abuptly on the eastern horizon.

Mile 410.5 (288): SPOKANE (pop. 172,700) city limits. See the MAJOR CITIES section for detailed information on Spokane.

Mile 411.5 (287): Junction of U.S. Highway 395/Interstate 90 and U.S. Highway 2. The highways merge to become Division Street. Travelers continuing on Interstate 90 in either direction turn to .Mile 281 in the INTERSTATE 90 section for log.

Mile 415.5 (283): Junction with Interstate 90.

Mile 425.5 (273): Junction with Highway 902 South to Medical Lake.

Mile 426.5 (272): Community of DEEP CREEK.

Mile 433.5 (265): Junction with road which leads south 8 miles to Waukon.
MP 265.5

Mile 435.5 (263): REARDAN (pop. 485). This small incorporated town is at the intersection of U.S. Highway 2 and Washington Highway 231.
MP 262

Mile 448.5 (250): DAVENPORT (pop. 1,600) is the county seat of Lincoln County,

and the intersection of U.S. Highway 2 and Washington Highways 28 and 25. Highway 28 leads to Harrington. Highway 25 leads north to Coulee Dam National Recreation Area, following Roosevelt Lake north to the Canadian border. Roosevelt Lake impounds the Columbia River behind Grand Coulee Dam.

Coulee Dam National Recreation Area campgrounds are located 20 miles north of Davenport at Porcupine Bay (29 campsites, swimming, boating and picnic facilities), and 23 miles north at Fort Spokane (62 campsites, swimming, boating and picnic facilities). Established in 1880 at the confluence of the Spokane and Columbia rivers, Fort Spokane was the last of the frontier Army posts to be established in the Pacific Northwest. A visitor center at the fort is open 9 a.m. to 6 p.m. daily, May through September. ▲

Mile 461.5 (237): Rest area on the south side of the highway. This part of the region is notable for the number of lava outcroppings seen along the highway, which makes farming difficult because they can't be easily and cheaply moved, so equipment has to be driven around them. This area is generally known as the Big Bend because the Columbia River takes a big southward swing to the west well beyond Grand Coulee Dam. ᴦ

Mile 466.5 (232): Junction with north road to Fort Spokane (18 miles) and Kettle Falls (76 miles).

Mile 469.5 (229): CRESTON, a small town (pop. 310) that is famous for the arrival of Harry Tracy in August 1902. He was a hard-case criminal who had escaped from an Oregon penitentiary with another prisoner and they went through Washington robbing and shooting. Tracy was cornered in a field near town, but he committed suicide rather than surrender.
MP 230

Mile 473.5 (225): Access road north to Sherman (5 miles).
MP 225

Mile 477.5 (221): Access north to Wilbur Museum. Highway 21 South to Lind and Odessa.

Mile 478.5 (220): WILBUR (pop. 1,070) is a major intersection with the east-west Highway 2 being principal and Highway 21 running north-south from Interstate 90 across the Columbia River and into the Colville Indian Reservation. Also, Highway 174 leads northwest from Wilbur to Grand Coulee Dam.

Wilbur was named for Samuel Wilbur Condit, the first homesteader in the area. He was known as "Wild Goose Bill" because he once shot into what he thought was a flock of wild geese and downed a tame goose belonging to a settler. Thus, until it was platted in 1889, the community was called Goosetown. Highway 21 North from Wilbur leads to a tiny auto ferry christened the *Martha S* that crosses Lake Roosevelt. The crossing is free and quite an experience.
MP 222

Mile 483.5 (215): Road to the community of GOVAN, 1 mile off the highway.

Mile 489.5 (209): ALMIRA (pop. 330) is mainly an agricultural community. Gas, food, and lodging.
MP 210

Mile 498.5 (200): HARTLINE (pop. 175) is another incorporated farming town. Many towns in this area were established first as railroad sidings with elevators built by the railroads to stimulate business.
MP 202

Mile 506.5 (192): COULEE CITY (pop. 618), just west of the junction of U.S. Highway 2 and Washington Highway 155. Highway 155 follows the east shore of Banks Lake north to Grand Coulee Dam (see Grand Coulee Side Trip this section.) Coulee City has all services. Camping at Coulee City Park on Banks Lake and 16 miles north on Highway 155 at Steamboat Rock State Park. Coulee City is one of a trio of towns with names that confuse visitors, the other two being Coulee Dam and Grand Coulee some 25 miles north. Banks Lake is a major recreation area for boaters and fishermen.　　⬤▲★ MP 192

Mile 509.5 (189): Junction with Highway 17, which leads south 2 miles to Dry Falls State Park, a spectacular ancient waterfall, and 4 miles to Sun Lakes State Park, a popular camping and watersports area. (See Grand Coulee Side Trip this section.)　　⬤▲★

Mile 526.5 (172): Winding descent westbound to the floor of Moses Coulee. This is one of the longest of the coulees in the region, running from Grimes and Jameson lakes to the north, southwest to the Columbia River a few miles downstream from Wenatchee. Most of the coulee floor is irrigated farming now, and less than a mile south of Highway 2 is a unique suspended irrigation system. The basalt walls are fairly narrow here and sheer, so the farmer strung steel cables back and forth between the walls and hung irrigation sprinklers from them, making it unnecessary to move the sprinklers.

There are resorts on Jameson Lake, which in the spring is considered one of the best rainbow trout producers in the state. Grimes Lake is a highly alkaline lake that has been stocked with Lahontan cutthroat, imported from Nevada's Pyramid Lake and growing to 10 or 12 pounds. No facilities on Grimes, but boat rentals can be arranged at Jameson Lake Resort. Turnoff for Jameson Lake to north.⬤

Mile 527.5 (171): Road leads 8 miles south to Rimrock.

Mile 535.5 (163): Washington Highway 172 leads north to Mansfield (pop. 380).

Mile 545.5 (153): DOUGLAS, former county seat of Douglas County before they lost it to Waterville, is a tiny but picturesque village in a small coulee.　　MP 153

Mile 548.5 (150): WATERVILLE (pop. 955) is the county seat of Douglas County. Limited services. The town has a small museum that contains a large rock collection and some pioneer relics.　　MP 150

Mile 556.5 (142): The highway drops rapidly westbound, from the 2,800-foot Waterville plateau down the picturesque Pine Canyon to the Columbia River valley, which is 700 feet above sea level here. A small ski area has been developed in the canyon.

Mile 558.5 (140): ORONDO is a small town at the junction with Highway 97, which heads north upriver 25 miles to Chelan. It was named for Indians of the same name who worked the copper mines near Lake Superior. It is a major orchard town and you will see thousands of trees — apple, cherry, peach, etc., — along the roadside, stands selling the fresh fruit and fresh vegetables in season, and

Grand Coulee Side Trip

Two interesting side trips from U.S. Highway 2, one 30 miles north on Washington Highway 155, and the other 20 miles south on Highway 17, offer an introduction to Grand Coulee country.

Following are logs of both these routes, showing distance measured from the junction with U.S. Highway 2.

HIGHWAY 155

Mile 0: Highway 155 junctions with U.S. 2 just east of Coulee City, **Mile 506.5.** This route parallels 27-mile-long Banks Lake which was formed by Grand Coulee Dam and is used as a reservoir for irrigation water. Along the first 10 miles there are many dirt roads leading from the highway to the water's edge; trailers and motorhomes cluster at the lakeside for tailgate fishing, picnicking and informal camping.

Mile 15.7: Steamboat Rock State Park. Steamboat Butte rises 700 feet above Banks Lake, and was used as a reference point by Indians and pioneers. It's still used as a visual reference by pilots. A hiking trail leads to the top, where there are panoramic views of the surrounding area. Situated on a peninsula in Banks Lake, Steamboat Rock attracts fishermen drawn to the lake's walleye, crappie and rainbow trout. Many largemouth and small-mouth bass tournaments are held here. The park has over 100 full hookup campsites, tent areas, boat launch and concessions.

Mile 18: Historical marker tells of Indians, fur traders, military expeditions and settlers who traveled this route.

Mile 19.1: Steamboat Rock rest area and boat launch. Informal camping.

Mile 24.9: Electric City (pop. 995) is primarily a residential community for Grand Coulee Dam employees. All services available, including airport.

Mile 28.2: Grand Coulee Dam Visitor Center. Grand Coulee Dam is the world's largest concrete structure. Visitor center displays highlight the project's history and technology. A self-guided tour brochure covers the visitor center, pump-generator plant, spillway and power plants. From Memorial Day through Labor Day, Grand Coulee tops off the evening with an after dark laser light show. Visitor Center hours are 8:30 a.m. to 10 p.m.

HIGHWAY 17

Mile 0: Highway 17 junctions with U.S. Highway 2 at **Mile 509.5.**

Mile 2.1: Dry Falls Visitor Center. Centuries ago, Dry Falls was the largest

waterfall on earth. It equaled 5 Niagaras in width, was 2^{1}/$_{2}$ times its height, and 100 times more powerful. The wall of water dropped 400 feet over a double crescent 3 miles wide. In the visitor center are geologic time charts and relief maps which interpret the formation of Grand Coulee County and Dry Falls. A path leads 400 feet down to the falls base and a small cave. On the floor of the falls are Deep Lake, Perch Lake and Dry Falls Lake. All are accessible by car from Sun Lakes State Park.

Mile 4.2: Sun Lakes State Park sprawls over 4,000 acres of desert with most of it sandwiched between 400- to 800-foot cliffs. Inside are 10 small lakes, several natural springs, 17 miles of trails and 12 miles of equestrian trails. It also has a 9-hole golf course, heated swimming pool, environmental learning center and 4 boat launches. From opening day of fishing season to Labor Day, the lakes are prime fishing spots for rainbow, eastern brook and German brown trout. Sunbathers, boaters and swimmers take over during July and August when temperatures soar into the 90s and 100s. Sun Lakes has 181 campsites.

Mile 14: Blue Lake Resort and historical marker at site of an ancient Indian campground and Caribou Cattle Trail Crossing. Blue Lake is an excellent rainbow fishery.

Mile 17.5: Access to Lake Lenore Caves via a 0.4-mile good gravel road. A moderately steep 0.7-mile hiking trail leads from the parking area to the shelters.

Mile 18: Lake Lenore produced Washington's record Lahontan cutthroat trout. Fish taken from here average 16 to 20 inches. The lake is open year-round to artificial flies and lures and single pointed barbless hooks only. Catch limit is 1 fish daily.

Mile 20.8: Soap Lake (pop. 1,295). Indians camped at Soap Lake for centuries and used its healing waters. Cowboys and settlers learned of the healthlike quality from Indians. White men named it Soap Lake because of the soapy feel of the water and the "suds" that formed along the shore.

The lake's water contains 17 minerals and an ishthyol-like oil. Visitors have claimed its waters have helped relieve arthritis, psoriasis, acne and Buergers disease. A city park on the lakeshore has a campground with playground equipment. The lake is used by windsurfers, water-skiers and swimmers.

From Soap Lake, travelers have the option of backtracking to U.S. Highway 2 or continuing south to Interstate 90.

mountains of picking bins. The rugged hill to the east of the highway is Badger Mountain (elev. 3,500 feet), a landmark for the Wenatchee area.   MP 140

Mile 567.5 (131): Lincoln Rock State Park with 27 campsites and full hookups. Adjacent the park is Rocky Reach Dam (main entrance on Highway 97). Excellent museum on west side of the river. Also a fish viewing area, gardens, playground and picnic areas.   ▲

Mile 578.5 (120): Junction with Washington Highway 28 (Sunset Highway), which leads south 4 miles to East Wenatchee. Access to central Wenatchee via Columbia River bridge from East Wenatchee. Continue west on Highway 2 to bypass city.

Mile 580.5 (118): Junction with U.S. Highway 97. Highways 2 and 97 share a common alignment the next 15 miles westbound via a 4-lane stretch of highway through the Wenatchee River valley. Access south to Wenatchee. Motel at junction.

Travelers continuing north on U.S. Highway 97 turn to **Mile 543** in the U.S. HIGHWAY 97 section for log of that route.

WENATCHEE (pop. 17,980) is the center of the fruit growing industry in central Washington, and its name is synonymous with apples. The major event each year is the Apple Blossom Festival in April. Shopping at Valley North Mall at the north end of town, downtown and in East Wenatchee. Major motels are located along Wenatchee Avenue. All visitor services are available.

A major attraction here is Ohme Gardens, located north of town off Highway 97. The North Central Washington Museum, featuring historical room settings, is downtown at 127 South Mission. South of town 13 miles is Mission Ridge, a popular ski resort with 4 double-chair lifts and 33 groomed ski runs. Near Mission Ridge is Squilchuck Recreation Area with 20 campsites.   ⚞▲

Mile 582.5 (116): Small town of MONITOR. Camping at Wenatchee River County Park south of highway along the river; some RV sites, restrooms, picnic tables and shelter. Nice view of the Wenatchee River, which is fished in summer for trout and in the fall and early winter for steelhead and salmon.   ⛱⚞▲

Mile 586.5 (112): CASHMERE (pop. 2,325) was named for the scenery that its founders believed was similar to that of a region of India. Cashmere is probably best known as the home of Aplets and Cotlets, a confection which has been described as a sweetmeat flavored with apple or apricot juice and enriched with walnuts and spices. The Chelan County Museum and Pioneer Village here is noted for the quality reconstruction of the village buildings and the Indian artifact collection. The Chelan County fairgrounds are also in the town. Cashmere has a motel and 9 restaurants.   MP 111

Mile 591 (107.5): DRYDEN is a small

Icicle Creek campsite in the eastern Cascades, accessible at Mile 599.

fruit town with gas, food and groceries available.

Mile 591.5 (107): Crossing the Wenatchee River.

Mile 592.5 (106): Junction with U.S. Highway 97, which leads south over Blewett Pass (actually named Swauk Pass, but engraved in all Northwesterners' memories as Blewett, the original tortuous pass that was abandoned in favor of the lower and straighter Swauk Pass), to Interstate 90, a distance of 50 miles. For Highway 97 log south from here, turn to **Mile 523** in the U.S. HIGHWAY 97 section and read that log back to front.

Mile 593.5 (105): PESHASTIN, unincorporated, is primarily a sawmill town just across the Wenatchee River from the highway. This is one of the favorite steelheading areas during late fall. There is a rough boat launch near Peshastin.   ⚞

Mile 598.5 (100): Entering LEAVENWORTH (pop. 1,565), all visitor facilities available including numerous motels, restaurants and gift shops. Leavenworth was one of America's first theme towns, and it decided to become a Bavarian village in the 1960s when its lumber business was failing and the town was in danger of becoming a ghost town. The town has frequent festivals, such as the Autumn Leaf Festival, and others celebrating Spring, plus a Christmas Lighting ceremony. Throughout the summer, arts and crafts events are held, and it is popular with cross-country skiers during the winter.   ⚞★MP 100

Mile 599 (99.5): Icicle Creek Road west of town leads southwest to hiking trails and Forest Service campgrounds up Icicle Canyon, a popular rock climbing practice area. Icicle Creek is also a popular rainbow trout stream.   ⚞▲ MP 99

Mile 600.5 (98): East end of Tumwater Canyon, one of the prettiest drives in Washington that goes 10 miles west from here along the Wenatchee River through a sheer canyon with lots of waterfalls and rapids. The canyon is famous for its fall colors and tour companies run dozens of buses over to Leavenworth with an emphasis on the canyon. The Wenatchee River heads near the west end of the canyon at Lake Wenatchee and flows east to join the Columbia River at the town of Wenatchee. It is one of the best rivers for river runners in the Washington Cascades although the Tumwater Canyon section of the river is generally considered unrunnable. Commercial raft trips on the Wenatchee are run from Leavenworth to Cashmere or Monitor. Inquire in Leavenworth. The Wenatchee is a rough, complicated river and should not be attempted by novice floaters. In summer this area is heavily stocked with fat rainbow and fishing can be good with bait, flies or spinners.   ⚞⚞

Mile 605.5 (93): Swiftwater Forest Service campground, with 76 sites, tables. This is one of the very few places in the narrow canyon where you can safely pull off the highway. The river near the campground is stocked during the summer with rainbow trout.   ⚞▲ MP 93

Mile 607 (91.5): Tumwater Forest Service campground and Wenatchee River bridge at the head of the canyon. Access to state fish hatchery.   ▲

Mile 613 (85.5): Coles Corner; restaurants and service stations. Junction with Highway 207 which leads to Lake Wenatchee State Park (3 miles north) and Fish Lake. Lake Wenatchee is 2,445 acres and 5 miles long. The state park campground is one of the most popular in the state, with 199 sites and swim beach. Several resorts also service the lake, the largest of which is the Cougar Inn on the lake's northwest shore. Anglers troll for rainbow, cutthroat, kokanee and sometimes, depending on seasonal restrictions, Dolly Varden and sockeye salmon.

Additional and more primitive camping can be found in several Wenatchee National Forest campgrounds above the lake by following roads up the Little Wenatchee River, which also offers fair to good light spin and fly-fishing action for rainbow and brook trout. Fish Lake, 1 mile north of Lake Wenatchee, has resort facilities with boat rentals, and is a good rainbow and brown trout fishery, with excellent yellow perch catches reported.

Trailheads take off from the Little Wenatchee to Pacific Crest Trail hiking areas and alpine fishing lakes, with backpack access to the Glacier Peak Wilderness Area, dominated by 10,541-foot Glacier Peak, visible from Glacier View Forest Service campground on the lake's south side. There is a ranger station on Highway 207 where maps and local mountain information is available. ⚞⚞▲ MP 86

Mile 614.5 (82): Nason Creek Campground; 76 sites, tables, stocked rainbow trout in the stream.   ⚞▲

Mile 617.5 (81): Highway rest area; the last one westbound for many miles.

Mile 618.5 (80): MERRITT, a one-store town, and a road leading to a Forest Service campground and trailheads. This is a chain-up area for pass traffic.

Mile 619.5 (79): White Pine Road and Cascade Meadows.

Mile 621.5 (77): Mount Lake Trail.
MP 70

Mile 627.7 (70.8): Sno-Park parking south of highway.

Mile 633.5 (65): Summit of Stevens Pass (elev. 4,061 feet). It has a popular ski area and a crossing of the Pacific Crest Trail. Several cross-country ski areas are on the eastern slope. Much of the mountain country south of the pass almost to Interstate 90 is part of the Alpine Lakes Wilderness Area.

Mile 639.5 (59): The western portal of the railroad tunnel beneath Stevens Pass. At 7.8 miles long, it is one of the longest in the world. It is not unusual to spot the creamy-white form of mountain goats on the surrounding peaks, and black-tailed deer are frequently seen from the highway.

Mile 640 (58.5): Winter chain-up area for eastbound travelers.

Mile 641.5 (57): Deception Falls south of highway. Picnic area and nature trail north of highway.

Mile 647 (51.5): Tye River.

Mile 648 (50.5): Skykomish ranger station with a small store and gas pumps nearby. Recreational maps of the Mount Baker/Snoqualmie National Forest and Skykomish Ranger District are available here. Beckler River Forest Service campground 1 mile north.
▲ MP 50

Mile 649.5 (49): SKYKOMISH (pop. 226) city limits. All services are available on the highway. This is primarily a logging town built right on the Skykomish (nicknamed the "Sky") River to the south of the highway. Many river runners put their kayaks and inflatable rafts in the river at Skykomish to drift the upper portions well above the waterfalls and Class VI rapids that characterize much of the Skykomish farther west. In this area the Skykomish and a major tributary, the Beckler River, are fished primarily for resident rainbow and cutthroat trout. Downstream the Skykomish is one of the most productive Puget Sound salmon and steelhead streams.

Mile 652.5 (46): Money Creek Forest Service campground with 20 sites. Miller River campground, 3.5 miles south, has 18 sites.
▲ MP 46

Mile 657.5 (41): GROTTO, unincorpo-

rated, was formerly a town built around a cement plant. Snohomish/King County line.
MP 41

Mile 660.5 (38): BARING was named for the nearby mountain of the same name. Limited services. The prominent peak to the southwest is Mount Index (elev. 5,979 feet) and due north is Gunn Peak (elev. 6,245 feet).

Mile 661 (37.5): Mount Baker/Snoqualmie National Forest boundary.

Mile 662.5 (36): Junction with road to INDEX (pop. 148), a small town 1 mile north on the North Fork Skykomish River with restaurants, a small hotel and a hardware store. Mount Index looms over the town and the whole area. Its north face is one of the great challenges for rock climbers in the region, and a favorite with photographers.

The high bridge carrying Highway 2 across the Skykomish River marks the beginning of the most popular steelhead and salmon fishing waters. Upstream from the bridge the river is extremely dangerous for float fishermen, and not recommended for novice boatmen.

Mile 667.5 (31): Public fishing access.

Mile 670.5 (28): GOLD BAR (pop. 770) is an incorporated town named by an early prospector who found promising "colors" in the river here. It has all visitor services. Just east of town is the road leading to Wallace Falls State Park, 2 miles away, which offers 6 tent sites. At the foot of the falls is a trail that leads 2.5 miles to the summit with an excellent view from the 250-foot-high falls.

Mile 671.5 (27): State salmon hatchery; in the fall you can sometimes see the biologists taking eggs from the salmon.

Mile 673 (25.5): STARTUP, unincorporated, has all services. It originally was named Wallace but after its mail kept going to Wallace, ID, it was renamed in honor of a local sawmill manager named George S. Startup (not, as some suggest, because it is where you start up the mountains). The Wallace River joins the Skykomish River near here.

Mile 673.5 (25): Covered picnic area on riverbank south of highway.

Mile 675.5 (23): Covered picnic area with 1,000-year-old Douglas fir. Lodging.

Mile 676.5 (22): Private campground.

Mile 677 (21.5): SULTAN (pop. 1,850) began as a rip-snorting frontier mining town, but over the years calmed down to a pleasant little town where the Sultan and Skykomish rivers join. There is a pleasant little park near

the Sultan River confluence where steelheaders frequently launch McKenzie-style drift boats and there are tables for picnicking. A road runs north along to the Sultan/Pilchuck Multiple Use Area, 62,000 acres of recreation land, which includes numerous small trout lakes, hiking trails, stream fishing access sites and campgrounds.

Mile 677.5 (21): Wayside chapel.

Mile 683 (15.5): Access north to Monroe public golf course. Crossing Woods Creek.

Mile 683.5 (15): Junction with Highway 203 south to Duvall (10 miles) and Fall City (25 miles).

Mile 684 (14.5): Junction with Highway 522 south to Interstate 405 (13 miles).

Mile 684.5 (14): MONROE (pop. 3,125) is probably best known as the home of the state reformatory, but it is also well known as the home of the Evergreen Fairgrounds, located at the west end of town, site of the Evergreen State Fair (held the last week of August through Labor Day).

Washington Highway 203 runs south from Monroe, crossing the Skykomish River at the Lewis Street bridge (one of the most popular steelhead and salmon fishing areas on the river), through the scenic Snoqualmie River valley to join Interstate 90 at North Bend (33 miles).

Mile 688 (10.5): Rest area.   MP 10

Mile 690.5 (8): Access north to Snohomish public golf course and south to Snohomish.

Mile 692.5 (6): Pilchuck River.

Mile 693.5 (5): Junction with Highway 9 north to Arlington (17 miles) and south to Highway 522 to Bothell (17 miles).   MP 4

Mile 695 (3.5): Junction with access road to SNOHOMISH (pop. 5,790), one of the most historic towns in the region with much of the original Victorian architecture surviving. The town was founded in 1854. Once a shipping center on the Snohomish River, it now is best known for its antique shopping center. Follow signs for historic district (0.5 mile from exit), which is where most of the antique shops are located.   MP 3

Mile 696.5 (2): Junction with Highway 204 north to Lake Stevens. Start of the 2-mile-long Snohomish River bridge and causeway that protects the highway from the annual floods that are part of life in the flood plain.

Mile 698.5 (0): Junction of U.S. Highway 2 and Interstate 5. End of U.S. Highway 2 log. Turn to **Mile 622** in the INTERSTATE 5 section for log of that highway.

Canada Highways 4, 3 & 2

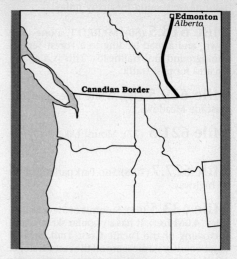

See map pages 41 and 44

This highway section of *NORTHWEST MILEPOSTS®* links 3 Canadian highways, which together form the most direct route from Interstate 15 in Montana to Calgary and Edmonton in Alberta.

This route is logged from south to north, beginning at the U.S.-Canada border at Coutts, AB. The highway log follows Alberta Highway 4 north to Lethbridge, then Crowsnest Highway 3 west to Fort Macleod, and finally Alberta Highway 2 north to Calgary and Edmonton.

Driving this route, motorists will cross the great grainfields of southern Alberta into the parklands of central Alberta. Visitor services are readily available at communities along the highways.

Alberta Highway 4 Log

Distance in miles from Canadian border is followed by distance in miles from Edmonton, AB. Equivalent distances in kilometres are indicated by Km.

Mile 0 (382) Km 0 (615): U.S.-Canada border, between the communities of Sweet Grass, MT, and Coutts, AB. A 24-hour customs station and duty-free shop are located at the boundary. On the Alberta side of the border, **COUTTS** (pop. 400) provides all services.

Secondary Road 500 leads east to the small community of Aden, near Port of Whitlash border crossing (open 9 a.m. to 5 p.m., weekdays).

Mile 2.5 (379.5) Km 4 (611): End 4-lane divided highway, begin 2-lane highway, northbound. Colorfully painted grain elevators dot the flat wheat field countryside. This is the heart of one of the richest wheat producing areas in North America.

Mile 4 (378) Km 6.5 (608.5): Red Creek bridge. The creek is a tributary of Milk River.

Mile 7.5 (374.5) Km 12 (603): Gold Springs Park County campground; 35 campsites, canoeing on creek.   ▲

Mile 10.5 (371.5) Km 17 (598): Junction with Secondary Road 501 west to Del Bonita border crossing (open 9 a.m. to 9 p.m. daily, June to Sept. 15; 9 a.m. to 6 p.m. the rest of the year).

Mile 13 (369) Km 21 (594): Milk River bridge; southern limits of community of **MILK RIVER** (pop. 900); Travel Alberta information centre and free campground with 6 sites.

The Milk River Interpretative Centre, just north of the bridge, has displays and information on recent finds of dinosaur nests and eggs in Devil's Coulee, southwest of Warner. Information on Writing-on-Stone Provincial Park is also available. The centre is open daily from June to September.

The 8 flags flying over the cairn in front of the information centre represent the 7 countries, and the Hudson's Bay Co., each of which had dominion over this area at one time. The countries were France, Spain, the United States, Great Britain and the Dominion of Canada (Canada flew 2 flags: The Red Ensign and, after 1965, the Maple Leaf).

Milk River community has food, gas, stores and tourist accommodations. Riverside golf course has public dining in the clubhouse. Grain elevators line the west side of the highway; services are on the east.   ▲

Mile 13.5 (368.5) Km 21.5 (593.5): Junction with Secondary Road 501 east to Writing-on-Stone Provincial Park, 26 miles/42 km; 75 campsites, fishing and swimming in Milk River, hiking trails and guided tours. The park received its name from the abundant Indian petroglyphs which cover the sandstone cliffs along this stretch of the Milk River (see feature page 42.)   ⚞⊶▲★

Mile 16 (366) Km 26 (589): Stop of interest marker pointing out the Milk River Ridge, the height of land between the Saskatchewan and Missouri rivers drainage systems. This elevated dome-shaped area is on the western horizon. Look for whitetails, mule deer and pronghorn.

Mile 24.5 (357.5) Km 39 (576): Junction with Secondary Road 504 to community of **WARNER**, just off highway to the west. There are grain elevators, store, gas and restaurant.

West of Warner is Devil's Coulee, the site of recent dinosaur nest finds.

Junction with Highway 36 north to Taber, 37 miles/60 km, center of Alberta's sugar beet industry.

Mile 25 (357) Km 40 (575): Junction with Secondary Road 504 east.

Mile 27.5 (354.5) Km 44 (571): Northbound, the highway descends Middle Coulee, a glacial meltwater stream. Junction with Secondary Road 506 west to grain elevator. Access to Ridge Reservoir, an excellent place for observing waterfowl and shorebirds. Also access to Park Ridge Campground (15.5 miles/25 km west); 12 sites, fishing, swimming and boating in the reservoir.   ⊶▲

Mile 29 (353) Km 46.5 (568.5): Junction with short road east to Tyrrell Lake. To the south, good views of the Sweetgrass Hills in Montana.

Mile 31.5 (350.5) Km 50.5 (564.5): Historical point of interest marker about Jerry Potts, famous guide, fighter and buffalo hunter who helped the Mounted Police in their dealings with the local Indians.

Mile 36.5 (345.5) Km 59 (556): Small community of **NEW DAYTON**; 3 elevators, 2 churches and a hotel.

Mile 41.5 (340.5) Km 66.5 (548.5): Junction at Craddock with Highway 52 west to Raymond (10 miles/16 km), Magrath (20 miles/32 km), Cardston (46 miles/74 km), and Waterton National Park (74 miles/119 km).

Waterton National Park forms an International Peace Park with Glacier National Park, MT. For more information see Canadian National Parks in the MAJOR ATTRACTIONS section.

Mile 46 (336) Km 74 (541): Secondary Road 846 west to small community of Stirling; grain elevators and rail yards west of highway.

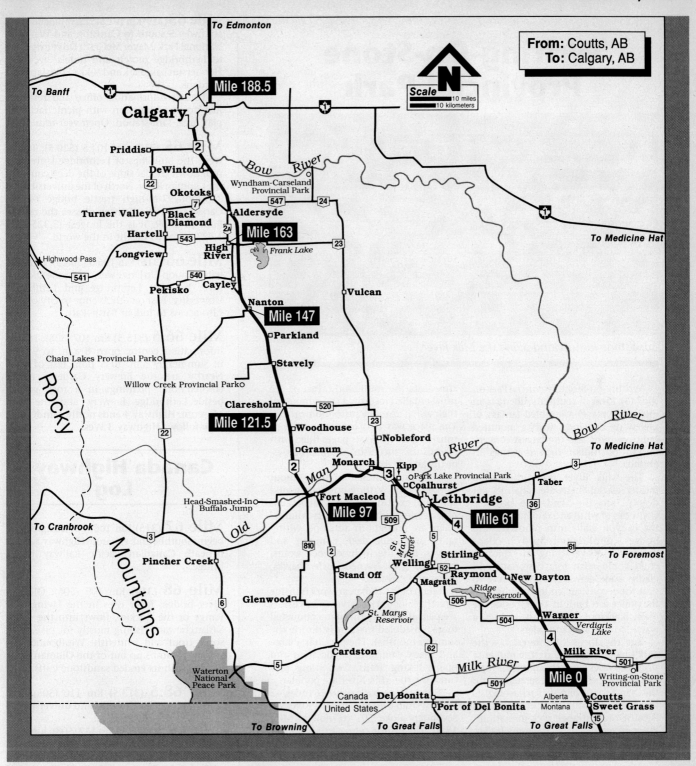

Mile 46.5 (335.5) Km 75 (540): Highway 61 east to Foremost (91 miles/147 km), and the Cypress Hills. This is the Red Coat Trail from Fort Walsh, SK, the route the North West Mounted Police (later the RCMP) followed on their trek west to found Fort Macleod. Highway 4 crosses Etzikom Coulee north of the junction.

Mile 54.5 (327.5) Km 88 (527): Grain elevators of Wilson; junction with Secondary Road 845 south to Raymond (8.5 miles/14 km), and north to Coaldale (10 miles/16 km).

Mile 57 (325) Km 92 (523): Stop of interest describing how large-scale irrigation began in the area in 1901 to make the arid plain suitable for agriculture. Today, the waters from 3 rivers spread over 840,000 acres for the growing of alfalfa, grains and specialty crops.

Mile 60 (322) Km 965 (518.5): Road to Lethbridge airport.

Mile 61 (321) Km 98.5 (516.5): LETHBRIDGE (pop. 60,000) city limits. The third largest of Alberta's cities, Lethbridge provides complete tourist facilities. The city was founded in 1870 on the wealth of nearby coal mines; its original name was Coalbanks. Its economy today is based upon grain, livestock, sugar beets, oil and gas. It is home to Canada's largest agricultural research station.

A major attraction here is Indian Battle Park (take scenic drive west to park signs), site of the last great Indian battle of the Canadian plains, fought here in 1870 between the Blackfoot and the Crees; picnic facilities and fitness trails. In the park under the high trestle of the Canadian Pacific Railway, is a replica of

Writing-On-Stone Provincial Park

Sandstone fantasyland along the Milk River.   (Jack Bryan)

Writing-on-Stone Provincial Park on the Milk River in southern Alberta is an intriguing place, a jumbled fantasy of sandstone badlands, with a mounted police outpost and the largest concentration of Indian rock drawings in Canada.

The Milk River flows through a former glacial meltwater channel cut deeply into the sandstone bedrock. Centuries of wind and rain have eroded the canyon walls into pinnacles and bridges, mushroom-topped hoodoos and caves — everything an exploring child could wish for. Historians will gladly wade across the Milk River to visit the reconstructed log buildings of the police fort built in 1889, beside the main Blackfoot Trail south, to keep a watch out for whisky traders.

But the focus of interest, as the park's name suggests, are the immense stone canvases where hundreds of years of Indian experiences are scratched into the sandstone bluffs. Archaeologists think that the Milk River area, perhaps because of its strange rock formations, was a sacred place where young Indian men came on vision quests to seek guidance from the spirit world. Part of the ritual entailed recording the symbols of their vision onto the surrounding rocks. The place was also used as a kind of tribal history book, its pages filled with records of successful hunts, battles, births and deaths.

Without its Indian art and without its police fort, Writing-on-Stone would still be an exciting place to visit because of its eerie landscape and its wildlife. There are pronghorn antelope, white-tailed and mule deer, marmots and beaver. Bird life includes rock wrens, vultures, great-horned owls, hawks, doves and catbirds.

Much of the Indian artwork is inside an archaeological preserve where visitors are permitted only through conducted tours (scheduled frequently during the summer months). The park has a large and shady campsite, picnic areas and many hiking trails. Swimming and canoeing the Milk River are popular.

To reach the park, drive 26 miles/42 km east from the town of Milk River via Secondary Road 501 (turnoff at **Mile 13.5**). The visitor center in Milk River also has information on the park.

Fort Whoop-Up, one of the whiskey-trading posts which were instrumental in bringing out the North West Mounted Police to establish law and order. Open daily 10 a.m. to 8 p.m., mid-May to September; free. The Fort Whoop-Up wagon train provides tours of the river valley and historical points; 50 cents.

During the first week in August, Lethbridge celebrates Whoop-Up Days, including rodeo, horse show, casino, midway, livestock show and exhibits. Exhibition grounds are east of Henderson Park.

Camping at Henderson Lake Park (exit on Mayor McGrath Drive): picnic area, tent and full hookup campsites, playground, outdoor pool, lake fishing and boating. Nikka Yuko Japanese Gardens, at west end of Henderson Lake, has authentic Oriental gardens. 🚻▲

Mile 61.5 (320.5) Km 99 (516): House on east side has long "fence" of old wagons.

Mile 62 (320) Km 100 (515): Access route to Crowsnest Highway 3 east.

Mile 63 (319) Km 101.5 (513.5): Junction with Highway 5 south to Cardston and Waterton National Park. Mayor McGrath Drive exit north to Lethbridge motels and hotels; access to Henderson Lake Park and Nikka Yuko Japanese Gardens.

Tourist information office and rest area just north of junction with picnic facilities, play area, sani-station. Open year-round. 🚻

Mile 65 (317) Km 104.5 (510.5): To the west, the buildings of Lethbridge University spill down the far slope of the deep coulee of the Oldman River. North of the university, the 318-foot-/97-m-high trestle bridge of the Canadian Pacific Railway crosses the ravine. Built in 1909, it is the longest (5,325 feet/1,623m) for its height in the world.

Mile 66 (316) Km 106.5 (508.5): Junction with Whoop-Up Drive west across the Oldman River to West Lethbridge and Lethbridge University. East on 6th Avenue to city center. Also access to Indian Battle Park.

Mile 66.5 (315.5) Km 107 (508): Tourist information centre; open 8 a.m. to 9 p.m. in summer, 9 a.m. to 5 p.m. rest of year. Nearby are the Brewery Gardens, multi-colored floral plantings in a rock garden beside Lethbridge Brewery and the Galt Museum. Highway 4 ends northbound; route now follows Highway 3 West.

Canada Highway 3 Log

Mile 67 (315) Km 108 (507): Highway 4 begins southbound: exit from Highway 3 passes beneath Canadian Pacific Railway trestle bridge.

Mile 68 (314) Km 109 (506): Oldman River bridge. River rises in the Livingstone Range of the Rockies, flows into the south Saskatchewan. Fishing mostly for pike, with some trout and whitefish. Westbound, the highway climbs up out of the Oldman River Coulee with its eroded sandstone cliffs. 🐟

Mile 68.5 (313.5) Km 110 (505): Exit south for West Lethbridge and university.

Mile 69.5 (312.5) Km 112 (503): Junction with Highway 25 north to Picture Butte; Highway 25 south to West Lethbridge. Access to Park Lake Provincial Park, 9 miles/14 km north; 53 campsites, swimming, boat launch, fishing, playground. 🐟▲

Mile 72 (310) Km 116 (499): **COALHURST** community (1 elevator) just north of highway; gas station.

Mile 73.5 (308.5) Km 118.5 (496.5): Canadian Pacific Railway overpass and huge marshaling yards at **KIPP**. Nearby was the site of a whiskey-trading post, Fort Kipp.

Junction with Secondary Road 509 which goes south across the Blood Indian

Reserve to community of Stand Off on Highway 2.

Mile 78 (304) Km 125 (490): Belly River flows in from the south to join the Oldman. The Belly and the Oldman rivers form the northern boundary of the Blood Indian Reserve, the largest in Canada (some 69,000 acres, mostly rangeland). The Bloods are members of the Blackfoot Confederacy and hold their Indian Days celebrations at Stand Off, a small community on Highway 2 south of Fort Macleod, in the third week of July.

Mile 80 (302) Km 129 (486): Junction with Highway 23 North to Vulcan.

Mile 81.5 (300.5) Km 131 (484): Community of **MONARCH**; hotel, gas.

Mile 82 (300) Km 132 (483): Road descends westbound into Oldman Valley. River has steep yellow clay banks and loops through stands of cottonwoods.

Mile 83 (299) Km 133 (482): Oldman River bridge.

Mile 89.5 (292.5) Km 144 (471): Good view (west) of Rockies on a clear day.

Mile 93 (289) Km 150 (465): Grain elevators of Fort Macleod to the west. Low dark hills to the north are the Porcupines.

Mile 96 (286) Km 155 (460): Junction with Highway 2 to Cardston.

Mile 96.5 (285.5) Km 156 (459): Turn south for tourist services and stores in **FORT MACLEOD** (pop. 3,100) town centre. Fort Macleod, site of the first North West Mounted Police fort in western Canada, has several tourist motels and restaurants. Chief attractions are the reconstructed fort (see description next milepost) and the turn-of-the-century architecture.

Mile 97 (285) Km 156 (459): Junction with Secondary Road 811 north. Fort Macleod business centre is to the south, replica of Fort Macleod is to the north. Chamber of commerce tourist information office adjacent fort.

The original fort, named for Colonel J.F. Macleod, was built in 1874 by North West Mounted Police who rode west to rout out the whiskey traders who were fomenting unrest with local Indian tribes. Fort buildings contain museums depicting Indian, pioneer and NWMP life. Outside the fort are full-size replicas of Plains Indian tepees. There are 4 corner blockhouses; connecting the 2 to the north is a catwalk which provides a good view of the Old Man River. The British Union Jack flies over the fort. A special feature is the RCMP mounted patrol ride held daily at 10 a.m., 11:30 a.m., 2 p.m. and 3:30 p.m. during July and August. The fort is open the beginning of May to the beginning of September, 9 a.m. to 5 p.m. (after mid-June, hours are extended until 7 p.m.). Admission fee.

The Red Coat Trail from Fort Walsh, SK, ends here.

Mile 98 (284) Km 158 (457): Midnight Rodeo Grounds, named after a champion bucking horse.

Mile 98.5 (283.5) Km 159 (456): Secondary Road 810 south to Glenwood.

Mile 99 (283) Km 160 (455): Junction with Highway 2 North to Calgary and Edmonton. At west side of junction is a Travel Alberta information office, open late May to September. The *NORTHWEST MILEPOSTS®* route now follows Highway 2 north through some of Alberta's finest ranch lands.

Travelers continuing west on Highway 3 turn to the CROWSNEST HIGHWAY 3 section for highway log.

Alberta Highway 2 Log

Mile 100 (282) Km 161 (454): Oldman River bridge. Alberta Transportation free campground on southwest side of bridge; 10 campsites, sani-station, playground; fishing and swimming. North of the river is the largest turkey farm in Alberta. ▲

Mile 100.5 (281.5) Km 161.5 (453.5): Junction with Secondary Road 785 west to Head-Smashed-In Buffalo Jump, 10 miles/16 km. The jump site, where Indians for 6,000 years stampeded buffalo over sandstone cliffs to their deaths, is a World Heritage Site. The interpretive centre, built into the cliff, contains first-class displays re-creating the drama of the hunt. Facilities include a cafeteria and gift shop. Guided walks through the site pass archaeologists at work. Open daily 9 a.m. to 8 p.m. from the end of May to the beginning of September, 9 a.m. to 5 p.m. the rest of the year. Admission free.

Mile 105 (277) Km 169 (446): Road west to Mud Lake, an alkali flat in summer.

Mile 106.5 (275.5) Km 171 (444): Willow Creek bridge.

Mile 111 (271) Km 179 (436): Secondary Road 519 East to **GRANUM** (Latin for "grain"), an appropriate name for a small settlement dominated by elevators. Granview Recreation Park in town has 41 campsites. ▲

Mile 116 (266) Km 187 (428): **WOOD-HOUSE** community.

Mile 121.5 (260.5) Km 195 (420): Southern limits of **CLARESHOLM** (pop. 3,500), a prosperous ranching centre with all tourist facilities. The old railway station, on the east side of the highway in town, houses the town museum. For horse fans, the Appaloosa Horse Club of Canada also maintains a small museum about this breed which was developed by the Nez Perce Indians of Idaho and Montana. Camping in Centennial Park; 16 sites, sani-station, playground.

Junction with Secondary Road 520 west. A scenic back road, this leads through ranch lands over the forested Porcupine Hills to Highway 22, a north-south connection between Calgary and Lundbreck, on Highway 3. ▲

Mile 125.5 (256.5) Km 202 (413): Stop of interest sign commemorating the location, 4 miles west, of the stopping place called The Leavings, built in 1870 along the Fort Macleod-Calgary trail. Nearby are the remains of a

Replica of historic Fort Macleod at Mile 97.

(Liz Bryan)

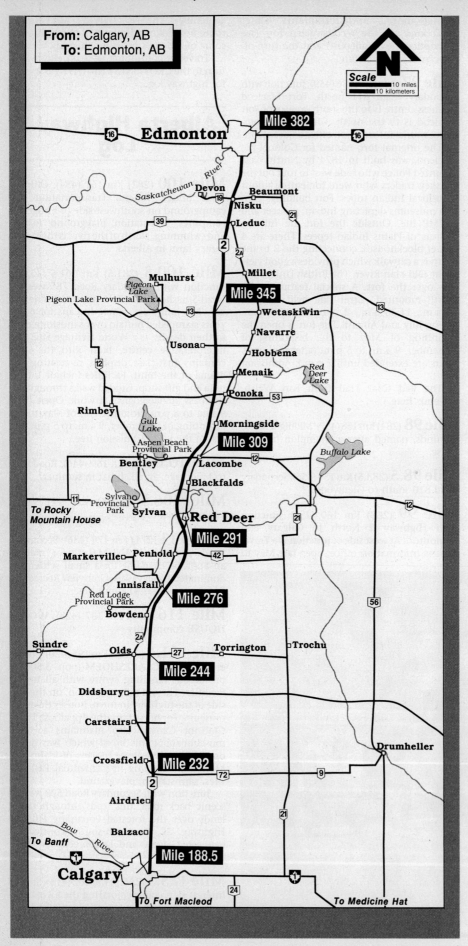

From: Calgary, AB
To: Edmonton, AB

Scale
10 miles
10 kilometers

Mile 382

Edmonton

Devon
Beaumont
Nisku
Leduc

Mulhurst
Millet

Mile 345

Pigeon Lake
Pigeon Lake Provincial Park

Wetaskiwin

Navarre
Usona
Hobbema
Menaik
Red Deer Lake
Ponoka

Rimbey

Gull Lake
Morningside

Mile 309

Aspen Beach Provincial Park
Bentley
Lacombe
Buffalo Lake
Blackfalds

To Rocky Mountain House
Sylvan Provincial Park
Sylvan

Red Deer

Mile 291

Markerville
Penhold

Innisfail
Red Lodge Provincial Park

Mile 276

Bowden

Sundre
Olds
Torrington
Trochu

Mile 244

Didsbury

Carstairs

Drumheller

Crossfield

Mile 232

Airdrie

To Banff
Bow River

Balzac

Mile 188.5

Calgary

To Fort Macleod
To Medicine Hat

police outpost, established in 1886. Grain elevators mark the community of Pulteney.

Mile 131 (251) Km 211 (404): Community of **STAVELY**, little more than grain elevators, to the east.

Mile 132 (250) Km 212.5 (402.5): Secondary Road 527 leads 8.5 miles/14 km west to Willow Creek Provincial Park; 150 campsites, swimming and fishing (cutthroat and rainbow trout).

Mile 138 (244) Km 222 (393): Secondary Road 529 east to Champion.

Mile 138.5 (243.5) Km 223 (392): The grain elevators of **PARKLAND**; the tiny settlement was once promoted as the site of a health resort.

Mile 146 (236) Km 235 (380): Nanton free campground (20 sites) at junction with Secondary Road 533 west to Chain Lakes Provincial Park and Highway 22.

Mile 147 (235) Km 236 (379): Community of **NANTON** (pop. 1,700). All services are available. Nanton is famous for the spring-water which is piped from the Big Spring in the Porcupine Hills, 6 miles/10 km west, to a large tap in town center. The tap is turned on in mid-May and turned off the beginning of September. The mineral water is bottled and sold commercially. Centennial Park displays a WWII Lancaster bomber, one of only 16 still in existence.

North of Nanton, Highway 2 is a 4-lane divided highway.

Mile 151 (231) Km 243 (372): South junction with Highway 2A, which parallels Highway 2 north to Aldersyde. Highway 2A, the old road to Calgary, is less direct than the newer one, but it is quieter and more scenic.

Mile 155 (227) Km 249.5 (365.5): Side road west to small ranch community of Cayley on Highway 2A.

Mile 157 (225) Km 252.5 (362.5): Secondary Road 540 west to Pekisko and Highway 22.

Mile 161 (221) Km 260 (355): Junction with Highway 23 east. Access to Frank Lake for good bird-watching.

Mile 163 (219) Km 262 (353): Junction with Highway 23 west to the town of **HIGH RIVER** (pop. 5,000) on Highway 2A. All services available. Once the centre of a harness-making industry, High River has elegant sandstone buildings and the Museum of the Highwood. The museum is housed in the 1911 Canadian Pacific Railway station, with displays of Indian, police, settlers, ranchers and natural history. Open 10 a.m. to 5 p.m. daily mid-May to beginning of September; admission fee. Next to the museum is the tourist information centre, housed in a train caboose; open 9 a.m. to 9 p.m. mid-May to September. The city park is a memorial to pioneer rancher George Lane, one of the founders of the Calgary Stampede. It features a campground (59 sites), picnicking, playground and trails.

Twenty-one miles/34 km west of High River on Secondary Road 543 is the historic E.P. Ranch (the initials stand for Edward Prince), owned by HRH Edward VIII for 42 years. Open for visitors, guests can see memorabilia and photos, enjoy lunch or afternoon tea and take a ride in a horse-drawn buggy. Open May to September; phone 395-2418 for reservations.

Mile 164 (218) Km 264 (351): Stop of interest commemorating the site of Spitzee Post. Another of the whiskey-trading posts, this one was built in 1869 by "Liver-Eating" Johnson and Dave Akers. Abandoned, it was destroyed by the Blackfoot Indians, rebuilt and abandoned again when the Mounties came West in 1874.

Mile 170 (212) Km 273.5 (341.5): Stop of interest sign about cattle brands. Some pioneer brands of the area are displayed.

Highwood River bridge. Secondary Road 541 leads west to Longview on Highway 22 and follows the river over Highwood Pass (elev. 7,336 feet/2,253m), the highest drivable pass in Canada. Pass is usually open June 15 to Nov. 30, depending on snow conditions. Road 541 connects with Highway 40, which goes north through the Kananaskis Valley to join Trans-Canada Highway 1.

Mile 171.5 (210.5) Km 276 (339): Junction at Aldersyde with Highway 2A and Highway 7 to Okotoks, Black Diamond and Turner Valley (18.5 miles/30 km). Stop of interest at junction commemorates the Turner Valley oil fields. The Dingman Discovery well tapped the first major gas and oil field in the British Commonwealth. It blew in May 1914; in 1936 new rotary drills brought in the first crude well and Calgary became Oil Capital of Canada. Two of the oil wells in Turner Valley are open for tours.

Six miles/10 km west of Okotoks is one of the largest erratic rocks found in North America. Carried to the Turner Valley by glacial movement, the 18,000-ton rock has the same composition as that found at Mount Edith Cavell near Jasper.

Mile 172 (210) Km 277 (338): Secondary Road 547 east to Wyndham-Carseland Provincial Park (176 campsites) on the Bow River. ▲

Mile 173 (209) Km 279 (336): Sheep Creek bridge; fishing for trout and whitefish. Sheep Creek Provincial Park, picnic area, playground, swimming, fishing and hiking.

Mile 180 (202) Km 290 (325): Junction with Highway 2A south to Okotoks.

Mile 183.5 (198.5) Km 295 (320): Road west to small community of De Winton.

Mile 187.5 (194.5) Km 301.5 (313.5):

Lord Strathcona's Horse Ceremonial Troop at Heritage Park in Calgary. (L. Linkhart)

Junction with Highway 22X West to Priddis.

Mile 188.5 (193.5) Km 303.5 (311.5): CALGARY (pop. 620,000) city limits. A vigorous, enterprising city, the white Stetson hat is worn here as a proud symbol of a frontier cow town past. Today, the economy focuses more on gas and oil than cattle and the city has mushroomed in the past decade into a sophisticated metropolis, complete with large shopping malls, theaters, nightclubs, restaurants and a wide variety of hotel and motel accommodations. The city sprawls across the prairies and climbs into the grassy foothills, but it is easy to find your way via a series of ring-road freeways called Trails. Highway 2 leads directly downtown. For more information on Calgary, see the MAJOR CITIES section.

Mile 190 (192) Km 305.5 (309.5): Exit east to Fish Creek Provincial Park day-use area off Bow Bottom Trail. The first irrigation project in the Canadian prairies was established on the creek in the 1870s. Two historic churches, an Anglican (1894) and a Roman Catholic (1904), stand almost side by side on the east side of the highway.

Mile 192 (190) Km 309 (303): Anderson Road connection east to Highway 2 North via Deerfoot Trail. Continue north on Macleod Trail for downtown Calgary; Highway 2 bypasses the city centre on the east side. Tourist information office, open summer only, at intersection.

Deerfoot Trail is reached 2.5 miles/4 km along Anderson Road and is a 4-lane freeway. No gas or services on freeway route.

Mile 196.5 (185.5) Km 316.5 (298.5): Exit for Glenmore Trail, the southwest bypass route that connects with Highway 1 west. Travelers headed west on Trans-Canada Highway 1 turn to the TRANS-CANADA HIGHWAY 1 section for log.

Mile 200.5 (181.5) Km 323 (292): Calf Robe bridge over Bow River. Exit for Blackfoot Trail and Calgary city center.

Mile 203.5 (178.5) Km 327.5 (287.5): Exit for Highway 1 east.

Mile 205 (177) Km 330 (285): Exit to McKnight Boulevard for Calgary International Airport.

Mile 211 (171) Km 340 (275): Northern limits, Calgary.

The highway from Calgary to Edmonton is a relatively new freeway and as such bypasses all settlements. Except for a few service centres built specially for freeway traffic, motorists must leave the freeway and go to one of the communities for gas, food or accommodations.

Mile 214 (168) Km 345 (270): Secondary Road 566 west to Balzac, east to Kathryn. Balzac is a 3-elevator settlement just west of highway.

Mile 218 (164) Km 350.5 (264.5): Service road west to AIRDRIE (pop. 10,500). All services available. Tourist information office at junction in summer.

Mile 219 (163) Km 352.5 (262.5): Airdrie exit.

Mile 220 (162) Km 354.5 (260.5): Exit, Airdrie tourist facilities and Secondary Road 567 east to small community of Irricana, named for the many irrigation canals in the area.

Mile 225 (157) Km 362.5 (252.5): Dickson-Stephensson Stopping House on old Calgary Trail. Rest area, trails, tourist information.

Mile 232 (150) Km 373.5 (241.5): Junction with Highway 2A west to Crossfield and

The Badlands

The Tyrrell Museum of Paleontology in Alberta's badlands. (Liz Bryan)

Alberta's Badlands on the Red Deer River are famous as one of the best places in the world to recover the fossilized remains of dinosaurs. The first dinosaur fossil found here was that of an *Albertosaurus* (a slightly smaller version of the *Tyrannosaurus*), unearthed in 1884 by Joseph Burr Tyrrell, just east of today's city of Drumheller. His find sparked the "Great Canadian Dinosaur Rush," as famous fossil hunters Barnum Brown, Joseph Sternberg, and others vied for trophies. Dinosaur finds are still taking place in the Red Deer River badlands, both around Drumheller, where the world-famous Tyrrell Museum of Paleontology is located, and downstream at Dinosaur Provincial Park (accessed from Trans-Canada Highway 1).

The Badlands and the Tyrrell Museum are sights no visitor to Alberta should miss. Highways 72 and 9 east from the Highway 2 junction at **Mile 232/Km 373.5** provide the most direct route to Drumheller from Calgary. It is 60 miles/97 km from Highway 2 to Drumheller.

The Tyrrell Museum of Paleontology, located in Midland Provincial Park just outside Drumheller city limits, is probably one of the very best in the world from a presentation point of view, and its fossil collection is outstanding. Perhaps the most stunning displays are the dinosaurs presented in a huge walk-through diorama exhibit. A tropical plant conservatory at the museum simulates the botanical world of the dinosaurs. Children and adults alike will enjoy the interactive displays, videos and computer games. Park rangers lead

visitors on 90-minute interpretative hikes into the badlands around the museum, and there are special programs for children. The museum has a restaurant and gift shop. Summer hours are 9 a.m. to 9 p.m. daily. Admission is free.

The Dinosaur Trail is a loop drive northwest from Drumheller along the west side of the Red Deer River to Bleriot Ferry, returning via Secondary Road 838 east of the river. Along the Dinosaur Trail are the Dinosaur Burial Grounds; the Homestead Antique Museum; the West Drumheller Oil Field; Horsethief Canyon; Bleriot Ferry, one of the last remaining cable ferries in Alberta; and Midland Mine office in Midland Provincial Park.

The East Coulee Drive follows the Red Deer River southeast from Drumheller to East Coulee via Highway 10, looping back via Secondary Road 569 and Highway 56. Highlights along East Coulee Drive include the much-photographed hoodoos; the swinging bridge at Rosedale, once access to the Star Coal Mine across the river; East Coulee School Museum and tearoom; the wooden trestle bridge built in 1936, now open for foot traffic only; and the Atlas Coal Mine, in operation from 1928 until 1979, the last of its kind in Canada.

If you can, allow a full day to visit the Badlands. You may tour the museum in the morning, then drive the Dinosaur Trail and the East Coulee Drive loops along the river in the afternoon. Overnight accommodations are readily available in Drumheller, and there are campgrounds at nearby Bleriot Ferry and Rosedale.

Highway 72 east to Drumheller, 60 miles/97 km, site of Alberta's Badlands (see feature this page). ★

Mile 232.5 (149.5) Km 374.5 (240.5): Stop of interest sign about the buffalo which once darkened the prairies in huge herds and by the 1880s were almost gone, killed not for sustenance but for hides. Gas and restaurant at turnout. View of Rockies to the west on a fine day.

Mile 235 (147) Km 378 (237): Exit to CROSSFIELD; gas, hotel, food.

Mile 237.5 (144.5) Km 382 (233): Exit for Highway 2A west.

Mile 243 (139) Km 391 (224): Junction with Secondary Road 581 west to CARSTAIRS (pop. 1,725), a farm and service community with all visitor facilities including a full-service campground (28 campsites) and tourist information centre. Road 581 east to farm community of Acme. ▲

Mile 244 (138) Km 393 (222): Highway sign warning about wind gusts as the road dips and rises through Rosebud River coulee.

Mile 252.5 (129.5) Km 406.5 (208.5): Junction with Highway 27 west to OLDS (pop. 4,888), all services including 2 campgrounds.

Mile 268.5 (113.5) Km 432.5 (182.5): Junction with Highway 587 west to BOWDEN (pop. 1,000) and Red Lodge Provincial Park (8.5 miles/14 km); 110 campsites, playground, fishing and swimming in the Little Red Deer River. Rest area at junction has tourist information booth. ⊷▲

Mile 269.5 (112.5) Km 433.5 (181.5): Shell refinery, west side.

Mile 271 (111) Km 436.5 (178.5): Access road to Bowden Institution.

Mile 276 (106) Km 444 (171): Junction with Highway 54 west to Innisfail and Dickson Dam on the Red Deer River; Highway 2A north to Penhold; Secondary Road 590 east.

INNISFAIL (pop. 5,500) provides all services. Anthony Henday Campground in town has 34 sites, playground and trails. At the fairgrounds is a re-created pioneer village housing artifacts from the mid-1800s to the 1930s. Afternoon tea served Friday 2-4 p.m. Admission to village is free. Open mid-May to beginning of September.

South of Innisfail 3 miles/5 km is the RCMP Dog Training Centre, the only one in Canada. Open to the public year-round, daily from 9 a.m. to 4 p.m.

West of Innisfail 18 miles/30 km on Highway 54 is the turnoff to Markerville (on Secondary Road 781), a small community settled by Icelandic immigrants and now home to a cottage industry specializing in hand-crafted traditional toys. Nearby is the home of Stephan Stephansson, Iceland's national poet, who settled here in 1889. Guided tours through his restored and refurnished farmhouse are available and traditional Icelandic crafts, such as spinning and knitting, are demonstrated. Open mid-May to beginning of September, 10 a.m. to 6 p.m. daily; admission free. The farmhouse is in an idyllic country setting and there are picnic facilities.

Mile 279 (103) Km 448.5 (166.5): Stop of interest sign for explorer Anthony Henday who came this way in 1754 and caught his first glimpse of the Rocky Mountains from the top of Antler Hill near this spot. The mountains are distant and only visible on a very clear day.

Mile 285.5 (96.5) Km 459.5 (155.5): Junction with Highway 42 west to Penhold, a service community for nearby air force base, and the Stephansson House Historic Site (see **Mile 276**); Highway 42 east to summer resort community of Pine Lake on Ghost Pine Lake, reputedly haunted by a headless horseman.

Mile 287.5 (94.5) Km 463 (152): Canadian Forces Base Penhold, west; 43 Radar Squadron, east.

Mile 289 (93) Km 465 (150): Several small marshy lakes on west side here have goose nesting platforms provided by Red Deer Fish and Game Club.

Mile 290 (92) Km 467 (148): Tourist service area with gas stations, restaurants.

Mile 290.5 (91.5) Km 467.5 (147.5): Tourist information booth.

Mile 291 (91) Km 469 (146): Junction with Highway 2A east to city of **RED DEER** (pop. 55,000). In the center of a rich cattle ranching and grain growing area, Red Deer also has an oil and gas industry and nearby ethylene plants. Alberta's fourth-largest city, Red Deer provides all tourist facilities. Camping at Lions Municipal Campground on Riverside Drive; 62 sites, sani-station, laundry facilities, picnic areas, playground, hiking, fishing in river. Waskasoo Park along the Red Deer River has hiking trails and a golf course. Worth seeing is the architecturally impressive St. Mary's Catholic Church on McMillan Avenue. Built in 1908, it was designed by Metis architect Douglas Cardinal.

Mile 293 (89) Km 472 (143): C&E Trail West to replica of Fort Normandeau, one of the forts constructed during the Riel Rebellion and Indian uprising of 1885.

Mile 295 (87) Km 474.5 (140.5): Red Deer River bridge.

Mile 296 (86) Km 477 (138): Exit east to Red Deer and west to Secondary Road 596.

Mile 298 (84) Km 480 (135): Junction with Highway 11 (David Thompson Highway) which leads west to resort community of Sylvan Lake and on to Rocky Mountain House (51 miles/82 km) and the Icefields Parkway

(Highway 93). Sylvan Lake Provincial Park has picnicking and swimming. Private campgrounds and waterslide nearby.

Rocky Mountain House is the site of a historic fur-trading post, now a national historic park.

Mile 301 (81) Km 485 (130): Blind Man River bridge. North of Red Deer the landscape becomes more hilly and more forested as it enters the aspen parklands.

Mile 302.5 (79.5) Km 487 (128): Access road east to community of **BLACKFALDS** (pop. 1,500). Tourist services and accommodations available.

Mile 309 (73) Km 497.5 (117.5): Junction with Highway 12. Turnoff east for **LACOMBE** (pop. 6,000), which was named for early missionary Father Albert Lacombe. All services available. Camping at Michener Park; 21 sites. The Federal Agricultural Research Station here is famous for its cattle breeding projects, crop protection programs and swine research. Open to the public Monday to Friday, 8 a.m. to 4:30 p.m.; free admission.

Turnoff west on Highway 12 for resorts, fishing and swimming at Gull Lake, 6 miles/10km west of Highway 2. Aspen Beach Provincial Park on the lake has 572 campsites, sani-station, showers, playground, swimming, fishing, boat launch.

Mile 314.5 (67.5) Km 506 (109): Junction with Highway 2A south to Lacombe.

Mile 318 (64) Km 511.5 (103.5): Junction with Highway 2A north to **PONOKA** (pop. 5,000). Ponoka is the Blackfoot word for "elk." All services available; information booth adjacent to Stampede Park. Stampede, July 1 weekend, rivals Calgary's. Camping at Ponoka Stampede Trailer Park in town (200 sites, showers, sani-dump) and at Nelson Lake Campground (15 sites, free). Fort Ostell Museum in Centennial Park has exhibits and photographs of pioneer and Indian life. The fort was established to protect local settlers during the Riel Rebellion in 1885. Open May to August.

Mile 319.5 (62.5) Km 514 (101): Access to community of Morningside.

Mile 324.5 (57.5) Km 522.5 (92.5): Battle River bridge.

Mile 326 (56) Km 524.5 (90.5): Junction with Highway 53 east to Ponoka, west to Rimbey.

Mile 329 (53) Km 530 (85): Turnout with emergency phone for northbound traffic.

Mile 333.5 (48.5) Km 536.5 (78.5): Access to community of Menaik on Highway 2A.

Mile 337 (45) Km 542.5 (72.5): Junction with Highway 611 east to Hobbema, west to Usona.

Mile 340.5 (41.5) Km 548 (67):

Wetaskiwin Rest Centre (access for northbound traffic only), with picnic area and Travel Alberta information centre, open mid-May to September.

Mile 345 (37) Km 555.5 (59.5): Junction with Highway 13 east to **WETASKIWIN** (pop. 10,000), a city in the middle of oil and gas fields. Its name means "peace hills" in Cree. All services available. Site of Fort Ethier, another fort built during the Riel Rebellion. Reynolds Museum at 4118-57 St., houses one of North America's largest collections of antique and classic cars, trucks, fire engines and airplanes. Open daily, June to September, 10 a.m. to 5 p.m. Admission fee.

Highway 13 west leads to resort community and provincial parks at Ma-Me-O Beach and Pigeon Lake. Pigeon Lake campground has 300 sites, good fishing.

Mile 352.5 (29.5) Km 567.5 (47.5): Pipestone River bridge.

Mile 354.5 (27.5) Km 571 (44): Junction with Highway 616 east to Millet, west to Mulhurst.

Mile 363.5 (18.5) Km 584.5 (30.5): Roadside view of oil well and its "nodding donkey" pump.

Mile 366 (16) Km 589 (26): **LEDUC** (pop. 12,500) is a city founded on oil and named for an oil well, the Leduc No. 1, which blew in on Feb. 13, 1947, and continued to pump oil for 26 years. The oil field which it tapped contained some 200 million barrels of recoverable oil — one of the largest in North America. All services available.

Mile 366.5 (15.5) Km 590 (25): Highway 39 east to Leduc, west to Drayton Valley.

Mile 370 (12) Km 595.5 (19.5): Access road west to Edmonton International Airport.

Mile 372 (10) Km 598.5 (16.5): Junction with Highway 19 west to community of Devon and University of Alberta Devonian Botanic Gardens (12 miles/20 km). Highway 625 east to Nisku, Beaumont and Rabbit Hill Ski Area.

Mile 372.5 (9.5) Km 599 (16): Highway sign reads: 25 km/15 miles to Edmonton city centre.

Mile 375 (7) Km 603.5 (11.5): Blackmud Creek bridge.

Mile 376.5 (5.5) Km 605.5 (9.5): **EDMONTON** city limits. Alberta's capital and largest city. For a description of Edmonton see the MAJOR CITIES section.

Mile 382 (0) Km 615 (0): Whitemud Drive; turn east for Highway 16 east, west for Highway 16 west. Keep north for Edmonton city centre, approximately 5.5 miles/9 km.

Yellowhead Highway 16 west to Prince George and Prince Rupert, BC, is logged in *The MILEPOST® All-the-North Travel Guide®*.

Crowsnest Highway 3

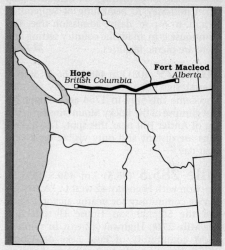

See map pages 49 and 53

Crowsnest Highway 3 is a scenic route that snakes its way west from Medicine Hat, AB, to Hope, BC. *NORTHWEST MILEPOSTS*® logs Highway 3 from its junction with Alberta Highway 2 near Fort Macleod, AB, to Hope.

Highway 3 crosses historic Crowsnest Pass, from which it derives its name, in the Rocky Mountains. Continuing west, the highway crosses 3 other high mountain passes — through the Selkirks, Monashees and Cascades — before dropping into the Fraser River valley at Hope. From Cranbrook to Hope, the highway follows the Dewdney Trail, forced through the wilderness in the 1800s by Edgar Dewdney to provide access to the gold diggings of the southern Interior of British Columbia.

Crowsnest Highway 3 Log

Distance in miles from Fort Macleod, AB, is followed by distance in miles from Hope, BC. Equivalent distances in kilometres are indicated by Km.

Mile 0 (599.5) Km 0 (965): Junction with Alberta Highway 2 north to Calgary just west of Fort Macleod (see description at **Mile 99** in CANADA HIGHWAYS 4, 3 & 2 section). Travel Alberta information office located at junction.

Mile 4.5 (595) Km 7.5 (957.5): Entering Peigan Indian Reserve westbound. The Peigans are members of the Blackfoot Confederacy. To the north are the Porcupine Hills.

Mile 18.5 (581) Km 29.5 (935): Settlement of BROKET. Peigans hold an annual 3-day celebration, Indian Days, during the first weekend in August. Indian craft shop on the highway by the church sells locally made leather, beadwork, and sweetgrass and birchbark baskets.

Mile 20.5 (579) Km 33 (931.5): Bridge over Pincher Creek.

Mile 21.5 (578) Km 35 (930): Junction with Secondary Road 785. Access to Head-Smashed-In Buffalo Jump; excellent interpretative center, open daily 9 a.m. to 8 p.m. in summer. (See **Mile 100.5** in CANADA HIGHWAYS 4, 3 & 2 section.)

Mile 22.5 (577) Km 36.5 (928.5): Road north to damsite on Oldman River, one of Alberta's last wild rivers; viewpoint.

Mile 27.5 (572) Km 44 (921): Hamlet of **PINCHER STATION** at junction with Highway 6 south to Pincher Creek (2.5 miles/4 km) and Waterton National Park (30 miles/48 km). At the junction is a miniature village made from glass electrical insulators.

PINCHER CREEK (pop. 3,800) is a center for ranching, oil and natural gas. All tourist facilities. Free municipal campground with 20 sites and sani-station. Visit Lebel Mansion, a historic house now containing an art gallery and gift shop. Kootenai Brown Historical Park and Museum has several log cabins, including one belonging to the famous Indian guide and trapper, Kootenai Brown, dating to 1889. ▲

Mile 28.5 (571) Km 46 (919): Road south to Castle River Recreation Area (3.5 miles/6 km) with 25 campsites; no fee. Fishing in the river. ➴▲

Mile 31 (568.5) Km 50 (915): Bridge over Castle River.

Mile 33.5 (565) Km 54 (911): Massacre Butte viewpoint and historic marker. The prominent hill less than 3 miles/5 km north is the site where an immigrant train of 12 men, women and children were massacred by Blood Indians. The group was part of Captain Fiske's westbound expedition from Minnesota in 1867.

Mile 34 (565.5) Km 54.5 (910.5): Community of COWLEY (pop. 304). Its small airstrip just west of town is a popular launch site for gliders.

Mile 35 (564.5) Km 56.5 (908.5): Toil & Peaceful Life historical marker recounts the story of the first settlement of 300 Doukhobors near here in 1915. The Doukhobors are members of a religious sect who immigrated to Canada from Russia.

Mile 39 (560.5) Km 62.5 (902): Community of LUNDBRECK (pop. 244); limited accommodations, gas and food.

Mile 40 (559.5) Km 64.5 (900.5): Junction with Highway 3A south to Lundbreck Falls Provincial Recreation Area; 83 campsites, swimming and fishing. No camping fee. The falls, on the Crowsnest River, are 40 feet/12m high. The access road loops around to rejoin Highway 3.

Mile 40.5 (559) Km 65 (899.5): Junction with Highway 22, an unpaved but scenic alternate route to Calgary (109 miles/177 km) which also provides access to Chain Lakes Provincial Park.

Mile 44.5 (555) Km 71.5 (893): Settlement of BURMIS and junction with Secondary Road 507 south to Lees Lake, old mining town of Beaver Mines and Beauvais Lake Provincial Park; 85 campsites, sani-station, swimming, fishing, boat launch, playground, hiking trails, interpretative programs. Camping fee. 🚶➴▲

Mile 47 (552.5) Km 75.5 (889): Leitch Collieries Historical Site and Interpretative Center. The stabilized ruins, including a stone powerhouse, manager's house and long row of brick coking ovens, give visitors some idea of a typical coal mining operation of the early 1900s. The area is known as Police Flats, for in 1881, North West Mounted Police set up a temporary post to combat cattle rustling. Picnic area. Guided tours available from late May to September, 10 a.m. to 6 p.m. daily. 🌲

Mile 50.5 (549) Km 81 (883.5): Exit north for town of Bellevue (description follows) and south for Secondary Road 774 to Hillcrest Mines, scene of Canada's worst mine disaster. In 1914, an explosion killed 236 men in the nearby mines. Road continues south 12 miles/20 km to Lynx Creek (30 campsites) and 18 miles/30 km to Beaver Mines Lake Forestry Campground (107 sites, swimming, fishing, canoeing, equestrian and hiking trails).

BELLEVUE (pop. 1,050) is part of the larger CROWSNEST MUNICIPALITY (pop. 7,600) which extends for 21.5 miles/35 km along Highway 3 and is an amalgamation of the old mining towns of Bellevue, Blairmore, Coleman and Franke. In Bellevue is Alberta's oldest Chinese restaurant, built in 1915 and still in operation. Bellcrest Businessmen's Camp-

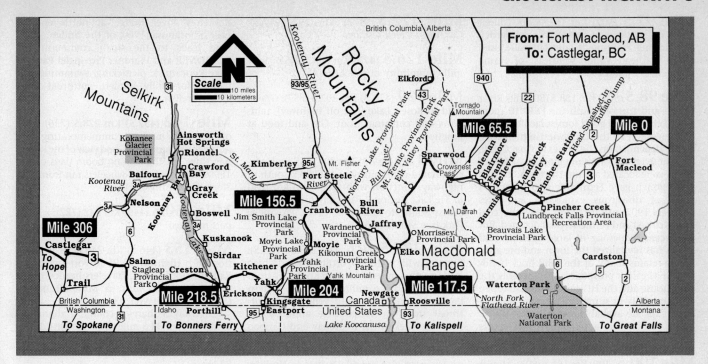

From: Fort Macleod, AB
To: Castlegar, BC

ground, at highway intersection, has 16 sites. Small chapel on grounds is a local landmark. Summer tourist office adjacent campground. 🚶🎣🛶▲

Mile 51.5 (548) Km 83 (882): Frank; slide sign and viewpoint (see description next milepost).

Mile 52.5 (547) Km 84.5 (880): Frank Slide Interpretive Center. In April 1903, 90 million tons of limestone fell from the slopes of Turtle Mountain onto the valley below, killing 70 people, engulfing most of the coal mining town of Frank and spreading debris for more than a mile. The centre gives the story of the Crowsnest Pass coal mining industry as well as details of the disaster. It provides magnificent views and is open daily 10 a.m. to 4 p.m. (to 8 p.m. in summer).

Mile 53.5 (546) Km 86.5 (878.5): Access road to **BLAIRMORE** (pop. 2,250); full tourist facilities.

Mile 54.5 (545) Km 87.5 (877): Road south for Powderkeg Ski Area. ⛷

Mile 57 (542.5) Km 91.5 (873): Junction with Secondary Road 940, known as the Kananaskis or Forestry Trunk Road, a scenic, unpaved route which leads north 69.5 miles/ 112 km to junction with Highway 40.

Mile 59.5 (540) Km 95.5 (869): Access to town of **COLEMAN** (pop. 2,600); full tourist facilities. Worth a visit because of its early 1900s architecture and the Crowsnest Museum, housed in the old high school; open daily in summer, 10 a.m. to 5 p.m.

Mile 60.5 (539) Km 97.5 (867.5): Turnout with geological point of interest sign. Volcanic outcrops in this area, the only major occurrence in Alberta, are of ash and cinders

with some large blocks of pumice, and are 100 million years old, far older than the Rocky Mountains.

Mile 61.5 (538) Km 99 (866): Allison Creek Road leads north to trout hatchery (1.2 miles/2 km) and Alberta Forestry Service Chinook Lake Campground (2.5 miles/4 km) with 74 sites, boat launch, fishing, swimming and hiking; cross-country skiing in winter. Eggs of brook, brown and cutthroat trout are procured at the Allison Creek trout station. Self-guided tours, picnic area. Open year-round 9:30 a.m. to noon and 1-3:30 p.m. 🏕▲

Mile 63 (536.5) Km 101.5 (863.5): Travel Alberta information centre, open daily, mid-May to September; picnic tables, drinking water. Excellent view north of Crowsnest Mountain (elev. 9,114 feet/2,778m) and west to Crowsnest Ridge. 🏕

Mile 63.5 (536) Km 102 (862.5): Summit Lime Works. The mountains here are predominantly limestone.

Mile 64 (535.5) Km 103 (861.5): Alberta Transportation Campground with 35 sites, picnic area, boat launch, fishing and hiking. 🚶🏕🛶▲

Mile 65.5 (534) Km 105.5 (859.5): Viewpoint and stop of interest, Crowsnest Pass, one of the lowest passes in the Rockies (elev. 4,534 feet/1,382m). Below lies Crowsnest Lake. The old railway community on the lake has a thriving pub. The pass marks the boundary between British Columbia and Alberta.

Mile 68 (531.5) Km 109.5 (855.5): Crowsnest Provincial Park; overnight parking for 25 vehicles, picnic tables, interpretative display. 🏕

Mile 72.5 (527) Km 116.5 (848): Road

south to Byron Creek collieries.

Mile 76 (523.5) Km 122.5 (842.5): Michel Hotel, still in operation, is the only building left of the towns of Michel and Natal. Residents of both communities moved into the new towns when strip mining operations began.

Mile 78.5 (521) Km 126.5 (838.5): Road passes through Westar coal mining operations.

Mile 80 (519.5) Km 129 (836): Junction with Highway 43 which leads north 8 miles/ 13 km to Crowsnest Resources Line Creek open-pit coal mine and 22 miles/35 km to community of **ELKFORD** (pop. 3,000), one of the new mining towns built near 2 large metallurgical coal operations—Fording Coal and Westar/Greenhills.

Mile 80.5 (519) Km 129.5 (835.5): Access north to **SPARWOOD** (pop. 4,000); all tourist facilities. Sparwood was built in 1968 when Kaiser Resources opened its open-pit coal mine on Harmer Ridge. The mine was bought by the BC government in 1980 and operates today as Westar. Daily tours of the world's largest coal mine, Balmer, in July and August; visitors can watch the 350-ton Titan Terex truck in action. For tour information, contact the Tourist Information booth on Highway 3 (look for statue of coal miner in front).

Mile 87.5 (512) Km 141 (824): Elk Valley Provincial Park picnic area. 🏕

Mile 88.5 (511) Km 142.5 (822.5): Olson rest area. 🏕

Mile 92 (507.5) Km 148 (816.5): All that is left of the once thriving mine settlement of Hasmer is the big old Elk River Inn, still in operation.

Mile 97.5 (502) Km 157 (808): Tourist office on outskirts of Fernie. The oil derrick and drilling eqiupment adjacent were used in the Flathead Valley southeast of Fernie between 1914 and 1920.

Mile 98.5 (501) Km 158.5 (806): Elk River bridge and turnoff south for **FERNIE** (pop. 6,000) city centre; good tourist facilities. One of the earliest of the Crowsnest settlements, Fernie depended on the mines at Coal Creek. Coking ovens, at one time more than 400 of them, were located around the town. But the mine which gave Fernie life also brought a series of disastrous explosions and fires between 1902 and 1917. In 1957 the coal mines closed and Fernie seemed doomed. But the recent reopening of large open-pit coal mines has revitalized the town and the area. Fernie retains many of the solid brick buildings of its earlier prosperity, most notably the courthouse and the Historical Museum (open 1-5 p.m. daily in summer). Heritage walking tour maps are available at the tourist office. Today the city is a popular winter sports centre.

Mile 100.5 (499) Km 161.5 (803): Mount Fernie Provincial Park; 38 campsites, camping fee, picnic area. Fishing in the Elk River for cutthroat, Dolly Varden and brook trout. ◄▲

Mile 102 (497.5) Km 164 (800.5): Junction with the road to Snow Valley Ski Area.

Mile 107.5 (492) Km 173 (791.5): Morrissey Provincial Park beside Elk River offers shaded picnic areas and fishing. ⊼◄

Mile 117.5 (482) Km 189 (775.5): Community of **ELKO**, named for the Elk River on which it is situated. Limited services available.

Mile 118.5 (481) Km 190.5 (774): Junction with Highway 93, which leads south 25 miles/40.5 km to the U.S. border and customs post at Roosville (open 8 a.m. to midnight daily).

Travelers headed south on Highway 93 turn to the end of the U.S. HIGHWAY 93 section and read the log back to front.

Highways 3 and 93 share a common alignment the next 34.5 miles/55.5 km westbound.

Mile 119.5 (480) Km 192.5 (772.5): Road south to Baynes Lake (2.5 miles/4 km); fishing for eastern brook trout. The road also goes to Kikomun Creek Provincial Park (7 miles/11 km) on the east shore of Lake Koocanusa, a large reservoir formed by the Libby dam on the Kootenai River in Montana; 74 campsites, camping fee, sani-station, picnicking, swimming, fishing and boat launch. Within the park are 2 small lakes, Surveyor's and Hidden (no powerboats). Fishing in Koocanusa for cutthroat, Dolly Varden and whitefish; Surveyor's Lake for eastern brook, rainbow, Dolly Varden, and kokanee in September. One of the largest concentrations of turtles in North America occurs here. Badgers are also abundant. ◄▲

Mile 122.5 (477) Km 197 (767.5): Caithness Creek rest area.

Mile 126.5 (473) Km 203.5 (761): Sawmill community of **GALLOWAY**.

Mile 129 (470.5) Km 207.5 (757): Gravel road to Rosen Lake (just off highway); rainbows and cutthroat trout. Gas and food at junction. ◄

Mile 130 (469.5) Km 209 (755.5): Unincorporated community of **JAFFRAY** south of highway. Junction with 2.5-mile/4-km road to Tie Lake Regional Park; day-use only. Also access south to Kikomun Creek Provincial Park (see **Mile 119.5**).

Mile 136.5 (463) Km 219.5 (745.5): Junction with Wardner-Fort Steele Road which leads north 4 miles/6.5 km to Kootenay trout hatchery. About 6 million rainbow, eastern brook, kokanee, lake and yellowstone cutthroat trout are raised here annually for stocking lakes in the Kootenay and Cariboo region. An aquarium features local fishes. Open 8:30 a.m. to 4:30 p.m. year-round.

The road also provides access to Norbury Lake Provincial Park, 10 miles/16 km north; 46 campsites, picnic area, fishing, swimming, boat launch (no power boats) and interpretative display.

The side road continues north to junction with Highways 93/95 at Fort Steele. ⊼◄▲

Mile 137 (462.5) Km 220.5 (744.5): Kootenay River bridge at north end of Lake Koocanusa. West of the bridge a side road leads to the small community of **WARDNER** and Wardner Provincial Park on Lake Koocanusa; picnicking, swimming and fishing for Dolly Varden, cutthroat trout and whitefish. ⊼◄

Mile 142 (457.5) Km 228.5 (736): Stop of interest marker commemorating the Kootenay steamboats. Good view of the Kootenay River. In the mining boom days of the 1890s, a fleet of stern-wheelers ran from Fort Steele to Jennings, MT.

Mile 150.5 (449) Km 242 (722.5): Rampart rest area.

Mile 153 (446.5) Km 246 (718.5): Junction with Highway 93/95 to Fort Steele and Radium Hot Springs. Travelers headed north on Highway 93 turn to **Mile 60** in the CANADA HIGHWAY 93 section.

Highway 3 shares a common alignment eastbound for 34.5 miles/55.5 km with Highway 93, and a common alignment with Highway 95 westbound for the next 51 miles/82 km.

Mile 156.5 (443) Km 252 (713): Junction with Highway 95A for Kimberley (see feature this section) and eastern city limits of **CRANBROOK** (pop. 16,000). Highway 3 bypasses the downtown area. Tourist information office on highway is open all year. The main shopping and distribution centre for

Kimberley

From Cranbrook, **Mile 156.5** on Crowsnest Highway 3, travelers may head north via Highway 95A to the old mining town of Kimberley, now nicely revamped in Bavarian style. It is 20.5 miles/31 km to Kimberley from Cranbrook.

In 1892, 3 tremendous deposits of galena (silver/lead) were staked in the mountains near Kimberley. One of these became the famous North Star Mine, whose ores were shipped down the Kootenay River to a smelter at Jennings, MT. While the ores were rich, the quantity was limited, and the North Star was soon played out. But the 2 other deposits—Shylock and Hamlet—eventually became the Sullivan mine. Put into production in 1909, the Sullivan became one of the largest lead-zinc mines in the world. Still in operation today, it employs more than 1,000 men in its underground and open-pit operations. Ore from the mine is processed in smelters at Trail. Check with the tourist office in Kimberley about mine tours.

Though Kimberley was founded and sustained on mining, the settlement today presents a startling new face as a Bavarian alpine village. The town centre has become the Platzl, an L-shaped pedestrian area with tiled walkways, streams, fountains, trees and flower beds, and the world's largest cuckoo clock (it yodels on the hour). The shops and open-air restaurants have Black Forest facades, with window boxes, steeply gabled roofs and hand-painted murals. In summer, a wandering minstrel plays the accordian.

Attractions include the Bavarian City Mining Railway, a train that once hauled ore underground and now takes visitors on a scenic parkland loop. The ski area chairlift operates in summer for great views of the area. There are also thrills on the alpine bob slide and wet bumper boats.

Events in Kimberley include an accordian championship in July and alpine folk dance festival in September. In winter, Kimberley comes into its own as a destination ski resort on the slopes of North Star Mountain.

For travelers continuing north from Kimberley to Highway 93/95, it is 16.5 miles/27 km to the junction.

the East Kootenays, Cranbrook is a thriving city well endowed with tourist facilities. Settled in 1885, Cranbrook was located between the rich gold mines of Moyie to the west and Wildhorse to the east. When the Canadian Pacific Railway's Crowsnest line came through in 1888, it stimulated an instant boom. But unlike many other towns that rose to glory in the 19th century, Cranbrook has retained its ascendancy, though the mines are played out. Several outstanding heritage homes and buildings are in the downtown area. Ask at the visitor centre or Railway Museum for tour maps.

The Railway Museum is not to be missed. Located on Van Horne Street (bypass route), it comprises 6 restored cars of the Trans-Canada Limited, one of the great trains of the Canadian Pacific Railway's heyday of the 1920s. Open daily 9 a.m. to 8 p.m. June to August; afternoons only the rest of the year. Admission is free. ★

Mile 160 (439.5) Km 257.5 (707): Western city limits of Cranbrook. Visitor information office (open May to September) on south side of highway by Elizabeth Lake Wildlife Sanctuary. The lake has nesting islands for waterfowl, hiking trails and picnic tables.

Just west of Elizabeth Lake, a side road leads north 2.5 miles/4 km to Jim Smith Lake Provincial Park; 28 campsites, camping fee, picnic area, fishing, boat launch (no powerboats), swimming.

Mile 169.5 (430) Km 272.5 (692): Moyie Lake Provincial Park with 104 campsites, camping fee, picnic area, fishing, hiking, swimming, boat launch and sani-station. Sailing and windsurfing are popular here.

Mile 179.5 (420) Km 289 (676): Viewpoint over Moyie Lake. Sign commemorates David Thompson, the first white man to find this route through the Purcell Mountains.

Mile 180 (419.5) Km 289.5 (675): Community of **MOYIE**, notable for its elegant Roman Catholic church and picturesque wooden fire hall which date from the turn of the century. Gas, general store and pub.

Mile 180.5 (419) Km 290.5 (674): Stop of interest sign near the site of the St. Eugene Mine, once the largest silver/lead mine in Canada. The deposits were discovered by Pierre, a Kootenai Indian from Father Coccola's St. Eugene mission near Fort Steele.

Mile 192 (407.5) Km 309 (655.5): Pacific-Mountain time zone line. Westbound travelers set their watches back 1 hour; ahead 1 hour for eastbound travelers.

Mile 196.5 (403) Km 316 (648.5): Ryan rest area.

Mile 200.5 (399) Km 322.5 (642): Small community of **YAHK** (pop. 170) with a general store, motels and gas station. A pub operates in the grand old hotel here. Yahk was a major supplier of railway ties for the Canadian

Old steam train at Fort Steele Historical Park; turnoff at Mile 153. (L. Linkhart)

Pacific Railway until the 1940s. The mill still operates, but today produces mainly pine fence posts. The name Yahk is a Kootenai Indian word meaning "bow," and was given to the curving Kootenay River near here.

Mile 201.5 (398) Km 324 (640.5): Yahk Provincial Park with 24 campsites and picnic tables on Moyie River. Camping fee. Good fall fishing for rainbow and cutthroat trout.

CAUTION: Watch for deer.

Mile 204 (395.5) Km 328 (636.5): Junction with Highway 95, which leads south 7.5 miles/12 km to the border crossing at Kingsgate, BC (open 24 hours a day). Travelers headed south on U.S. Highway 95 turn to the end of the U.S. HIGHWAY 95 section and read log back to front.

Eastbound, Highway 3 shares a common alignment with Highway 95 for 51 miles/82 km.

Mile 206.5 (393) Km 332.5 (632.5): Kidd rest area.

Mile 209.5 (390) Km 337 (628): Meadow Creek bridge. Side road south to small community of **KITCHENER**; store, pub, restaurant.

Mile 213 (386.5) Km 343 (622): Goat River bridge. **ERICKSON**, a farm community surrounded by orchards; many fruit stands. Visit Wayside Gardens and Arboretum, open May to October; roses, rhododendrons and 200 other species of trees and shrubs are featured.

Mile 218.5 (381) Km 351.5 (613): Junction at Creston with Highway 21 south to U.S. border at Rykerts and Porthill, ID. Customs open daily 7 a.m. to 11 p.m., late April to late October; 8 a.m. to midnight the rest of the year.

CRESTON (pop. 4,200) is primarily a farming town surrounded by fruit orchards and grain and hay fields. The highway east of town is lined with fruit stands, open most of the summer starting with strawberries in June through to apples in the fall. Creston also has several large sawmills and Columbia Brewing Co. (tours available in summer). Tourism is becoming increasingly important. Look for the log cabin Tourist Information Centre on the south side of the highway near town centre. Creston has a wide variety of tourist accommodations.

Attractions include the Creston Valley Museum on Devon Road, open 10 a.m. to 4 p.m., which features animated, speaking mannequins of pioneer residents.

The Kootenay Candle Factory, just off Highway 3 south of the junction with Highway 3A, is known for its beeswax creations. Tours Monday to Saturday, 9 a.m. to 5 p.m., from May 15 to Oct. 15.

Mile 222.5 (377) Km 358 (606.5): Junction with Highway 3A which loops north along the east side of Kootenay Lake to ferry crossing and back to Highway 3 at Castlegar. See feature this section. ★

Mile 225 (374.5) Km 362 (602.5): Road to Creston Valley Wildlife Interpretation Centre, open May 1 to Oct. 31, from 9 a.m. to 5 p.m. (extended hours July and August); weekdays only the rest of the year. The centre, where bird books and binoculars may be borrowed, is built on stilts in the middle of Corn Creek marsh, with several self-guided nature trails around. Naturalists also lead nature walks in the marsh or along nearby mountainsides and conduct canoe trips. Wildlife ranges from the moose to the tiny Calliope hummingbird, though the emphasis is on water birds and marsh life. An osprey nest is in view on the mountainside behind the centre.

Highway 3A Loop

Creston to Castlegar

This slow and scenic alternate route between Creston and Castlegar is only 12 miles/19 km longer than Highway 3, but much longer in terms of time. The road is narrow, winding along the shore of giant Kootenay Lake, and there's a 40-minute ferry crossing (the longest free ferry ride in North America). However, it leads through some interesting old mining towns.

Mile 0 Km 0: Junction with Highway 3 just west of Creston. The Kootenay Lake ferry schedule is posted here.

Mile 2 Km 3: Large viewpoint with picnic shelter overlooking the Kootenay Valley. Stop of interest marker describes 1880s reclamation efforts.

Mile 3 Km 5: Grain elevator at small community of **WYNNDEL**.

Mile 8 Km 12.5: Gravel turnout by Washout Creek. Below the highway is shallow Duck Lake, part of Creston Valley Wildlife Management Area. There are gravel roads and dikes for walking and bird-watching.

Mile 10.5 Km 17: Small community of **SIRDAR**, once the site of an old B.C. Southern Railway roundhouse and turntable. A visit to the Sirdar store and post office, built in 1913, is well worthwhile. Nextdoor is the Sirdar Pub. Access to Duck Lake boat launch.

Mile 12.5 Km 20: Access to Duck Lake and Creston Valley Wildlife Area trails.

Mile 14 Km 23: South end of Kootenay Lake.

Mile 15 Km 24: Kuskanook rest area with picnic tables and boat launch on the site of railway roundhouse. The art gallery beside the road occupies the 1903 station house.

Mile 19 Km 30.5: Twin Bays loop road to public beach.

Mile 21.5 Km 35: Sanca Creek and small resort community of Sanca, once the mining town of Granite Creek, destroyed by fire in 1900.

Mile 24 Km 38.5: Community of **BOSWELL**, known for its Glass House, a private home constructed from 500,000 square glass bottles that once held embalming fluid. (The builder was a retired mortician.) Open to the public, admission fee.

Mile 26 Km 42: Good viewpoint of lake. Destiny Bay, a private resort, is to the north. Store, post office and gas station beside highway.

Elegant turn-of-the-century architecture at Nelson. (Liz Bryan)

Mile 28.5 Km 66.5: Boat launch.

Mile 29 Km 47: Road west to Lewis Bay, a public pebble beach.

Mile 32 Km 51.5: Lockhart Creek Provincial Park; 18 campsites, picnic tables, beach, boat launch, fishing. Trail leads up Lockhart Creek 8 miles/12 km to Baker Lake, a popular fishing hole. Private marina, resort and restaurant nearby.

Mile 33 Km 53.5: La France Creek. Several resorts, restaurants, marina, RV campground and residential area.

Mile 35.5 Km 57.5: Public lake access with small beach.

Mile 37 Km 69: **GRAY CREEK**, a thriving resort community overlooking Crawford Bay. The old-fashioned general store has been in business since 1913 and the hand-hewn log community hall, built in 1912, still stands. All tourist services; public beach.

Mile 43.5 Km 70: **CRAWFORD BAY** (pop. 200) is the largest community on Kootenay Lake's eastern shore. Cottage industries here include Crawford Bay Clothing, the North Woven Broom Co. and Kootenay Forge. All tourist services are available. Of interest architecturally is the Wedgwood Manor, a bed-and-breakfast originally built as a private home by a British naval commander.

Mile 47.5 Km 76.5: Stop of interst sign about the Bluebell Mine at Riondel. The village of Riondel is mostly a retirement community today.

Mile 48 Km 77.5: Kootenay Lake ferry terminal at **KOOTENAY BAY**, a small community with a post office, bank, accommodations and restaurant. Rest area and tourist information office by the ferry terminal. Two boats operate on this crossing: the MV *Balfour* and the MV *Anscomb*.

Pilot Bay road leads south 3 miles/5 km from Kootenay Bay to historic Pilot Point lighthouse (reached by a short trail). The lighthouse, built in 1905, is a federal park and is open to the public. Great views from the top of the tower.

Mile 48 Km 77.5: Kootenay Lake ferry terminal at **BALFOUR**, on the west side of Kootenay Lake, a resort community with all tourist services. Pleasant beachside rest area.

Junction with Highway 31, which provides access to Ainsworth Hot Springs Resort (9 miles/14.5 km), Cody Caves Provincial Park (20.5 miles/33 km) and the historic old mining town of Kaslo (22 miles/35.5 km), site of the SS *Moyie*, the last stern-wheeler to ply the Kootenay.

Mile 52 Km 84: Small 10-car cable ferry to Procter and Harrop.

Mile 56 Km 90: Kokanee Creek Provincial Park; 112 campsites, picnic areas, beaches, boat launch, playground, visitor center.

Mile 65 Km 104.5: Upper saloon and wheelhouse of old stern-wheeler, the MV *Nasookin*, now a private house on the west side of road.

Mile 66.5 Km 107.5: Bridge across Kootenay Lake to city of **NELSON** (pop. 8,000), an old mining city with a considerable heritage of elegant turn-of-the century architecture. The Steve Martin movie *Roxanne* was filmed here. A thriving commercial and lumbering centre. Full tourist facilities.

Mile 72.5 Km 117: Grohman Narrows Provincial Park; picnicking, hiking trail.

Mile 74.5 Km 119.5: Kootenay River bridge and the community of Taghum.

Mile 79 Km 127.5: Viewpoint of the Kootenay River. Five hydro dams owned by West Kootenay Power make use of the 360-foot/200-m drop between Kootenay Lake and the Columbia River.

Mile 81 Km 130: Viewpoint of Bonnington Falls and stop of interest marker about West Kootenay Power. The first hydroelectric plant was built at the falls here in 1898 to generate power for the mines at Rossland.

Mile 87.5 Km 141: Small community of Tarrys.

Mile 91.5 Km 147.5 Brilliant rest area.

Mile 92 Km 148: Viewpoint of Lower Bonnington Dam.

Mile 93 Km 149.5: Viewpoint of Brilliant Dam just north of Kootenay River bridge at Brilliant. Access to Hugh Keenleyside Dam.

Mile 95 Km 153: Junction with Highway 3 just east of Castlegar, **Mile 306.**

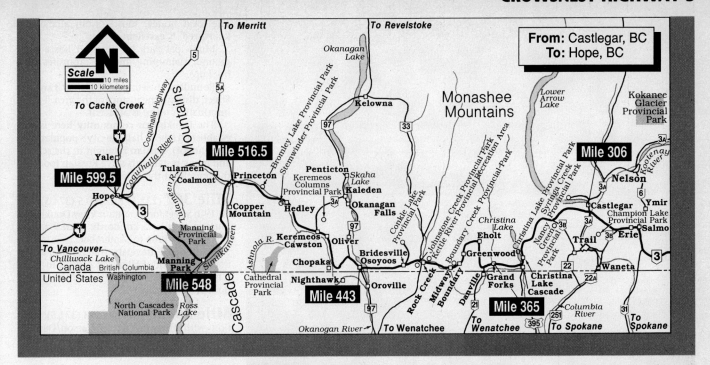

From: Castlegar, BC
To: Hope, BC

Best times are mid-March for spring migration; October for fall migration.

Mile 226.5 (373) Km 364.5 (600): Creston Valley Wildlife Management Area Summit Creek Campground; camping (July and August only, fee charged), picnicking, children's play area, nature programs and walks.

Pedestrian suspension bridge crosses Summit Creek to connect with a restored section of the Dewdney Trail.

Mile 235 (364.5) Km 378 (586.5): Rest area.

Mile 250 (349.5) Km 402.5 (562.5): Kootenay Pass, also known as Stagleap Summit (elev. 5,823 feet/1,775m). Stagleap Provincial Park on Bridal Lake; hiking and picnicking.

Mile 263 (336.5) Km 423.5 (541.5): Lost Creek rest area.

Mile 264 (335.5) Km 425 (540): Junction with Highway 6 south to border crossing at Nelway (open daily 8 a.m. to midnight).

Highways 3 and 6 share a common alignment for the next 9 miles/14.5 km westbound.

Mile 271.5 (328) Km 437 (528): Junction with road to Salmo Ski Hill.

Mile 273 (326.5) Km 439.5 (525.5): SALMO (pop. 1,000), at the junction with Highway 6 north to Nelson, was named for the fish in the Salmo River, a tributary of the Columbia River. (Columbia dams ruined the salmon runs.) Full tourist facilities. An old mining town, today forestry and sawmills support this tidy little town with its 1930s architecture. The local golf course is also the airport; locals call it a golfport. Visitor information office on Highway 3 is open daily May to September.

Mile 275.5 (324) Km 443.5 (521.5): Erie Lake rest area.

Mile 290 (309.5) Km 466.5 (498): Junction with Highway 3B to Trail.

Mile 302.5 (297) Km 487 (478): Rest area and viewpoint over Columbia River.

Mile 305 (294.5) Km 491 (474): Junction with Highway 3A to Nelson and Kootenay Lake communities (see feature this section). Turn here for airport and access to Doukhobor Historic Village (opposite the airport). A model communal settlement, it was built to show the way of life of the early Russian settlers. A large portion of the village was destroyed by fire in 1985, but much of interest remains. Adjacent is the Cultural Education Centre which serves authentic Doukhobor foods.

Mile 305 (294.5) Km 491 (473.5): Columbia River bridge.

Mile 306 (293.5) Km 492.5 (472.5): Exit north for city of CASTLEGAR (pop. 7,500), at the confluence of the Kootenay and Columbia rivers; full tourist facilities. It's a thriving community whose livelihood is largely based on lumber and a big pulp mill. Many residents work at nearby Trail's big lead-zinc smelter.

Visit Zuckerberg Island Heritage Park, once home to Doukhobor teacher Alexander Zuckerberg, who built Chapel House there in 1931. The park is accessible by a pedestrian suspension bridge. Just outside of town on the road to Robson is the tomb of Peter Verigin, the Doukhobor's spiritual leader who led his people here from Russia in 1908.

West of town is Syringa Creek Provincial Park, with 60 campsites, picnic tables, boat launch, sani-station, swimming, boating and fishing. Camping fee.

North of the town is the Hugh Keenleyside Dam. Built in 1965, the 164 foot/50m high earthfill and concrete structure impounds the waters of Arrow Lakes reservoir (the Columbia River).

Mile 322.5 (277) Km 519.5 (445.5): Junction with Highway 3B south to Rossland (description follows). In summer, a small tourist information trailer is parked here. Also at the junction is Nancy Greene Provincial Park with 12 campsites, picnic area, swimming, fishing and nature trails. Camping fee. The lake was named in honor of Rossland resident Nancy Greene, who won Canada a gold medal for alpine skiing in the 1968 Olympics.

ROSSLAND (pop. 3,400), an old mining town 17 miles/28 km south from the junction, is well worth a visit, particularly if you have children. Here you can tour the only hard-rock gold mine in Canada that's open to the public, the famous Le Roi mine. Guided tours (with hard hats) from mid-May to mid-September. Gold panning outside mine entrance. Museum and tearoom adjacent. Tourist information at museum. The town itself, in a dramatic alpine setting, has 30 heritage buildings, full tourist facilities and a well-known alpine ski area.

Mile 326 (273.5) Km 525 (440): Rest area at Sheep Creek, north of the highway. Side road leads south to a cross-country ski area.

Mile 329.5 (270) Km 530.5 (434.5): Bonanza Pass (elev. 5,036 feet/1,535m).

Mile 332.5 (267) Km 535 (429.5): Walker Creek rest area.

Mile 336 (263.5) Km 540.5 (424): Paulson bridge over deep McRae Canyon. The suspension bridge is 295 feet/90m high with an arch span of 590 feet/180m.

Mile 337.5 (262) Km 543.5 (521.5): McRae Creek rest area.

Christina Lake flows into the Kettle River east of Grand Forks.   (L. Linkhart)

Mile 343.5 (256) Km 553.5 (411.5): Rest area. Highway descends westbound to Christina Lake.

Mile 345.5 (254) Km 556.5 (408.5): Exit for Texas Creek Provincial Park on Christina Lake; 10 campsites, camping fee, fishing, picnicking, boat launch, sandy beach.

Mile 347.5 (252) Km 559 (405.5): CHRISTINA LAKE (pop. 1,500) resort community with full tourist facilities. This 12-mile-/19-km-long lake is clear, shallow and warm, offering good fishing and swimming. It is a popular sailing and windsurfing spot. Christina Lake Provincial Park, at the south end of the lake, has an extensive beach, change rooms, picnic tables, children's play area and boat launch.

Mile 350.5 (248.5) Km 564 (401): *CAUTION:* Watch for mountain sheep on road.

Mile 353.5 (246) Km 569 (396): Junction with Highway 395 south to border crossing at Cascade, open daily 8 a.m. to midnight. (Just south of this junction there is a good viewpoint of the Cascade River gorge.)

Travelers heading south on U.S. Highway 395 turn to the end of the U.S. HIGHWAY 395 section and read log back to front.

Mile 365 (234.5) Km 587.5 (377.5): Bridge over Granby River. Pleasant, well-preserved city of **GRAND FORKS** (pop. 3,500), incorporated in 1897. A road near the bridge leads north to the site of the famous Granby copper smelter, at one time the second largest in the world, which operated from 1900 to 1919. Today, Grand Forks is known for its potatoes.

The local honey, mostly from alfalfa and knapweed, is excellent.

Municipal park by the river has a playground, swimming and 28 campsites with hookups.

Boundary Museum, on Highway 3 and 5th Street, displays the history of the area. Tourist information office is adjacent.

The Doukhobor community here is well established (about half the city's population is Doukhobor). Russian is taught in the schools and many restaurants serve Russian food. Try the borscht at the Yale Hotel. ▲

Mile 367 (232.5) Km 390.5 (374.5): Exit on 19th Street for Mountain View Doukhobor Museum 3 miles/5 km north; open 9 a.m. to 7 p.m. daily June to September.

Westbound travelers watch for pioneer flour mill south of Highway 3. Built in 1915, it is still in operation. Its "Pride of the Valley" flour is sold locally.

Mile 368.5 (231) Km 593 (371.5): Junction with Highway 41 to Carson/Danville border crossing, open daily 8 a.m. to midnight.

Mile 375.5 (224) Km 604 (360.5): Road to Phoenix Mountain Ski Area and site of once booming city of Phoenix, destroyed by huge open-pit copper mine.

Mile 382 (217.5) Km 614.5 (350): Rest area beside small Wilgress Lake.

Mile 389.5 (210) Km 627 (338): Boundary Creek Road and junction with road to Jewel Lake fishing camp (private) and provincial park day-use area; swimming and fishing for rainbows.

Mile 390.5 (209) Km 628.5 (336.5): GREENWOOD (pop. 1,000) offers motels, restaurants, several stores and a pleasant creekside municipal campground. Greenwood was incorporated in 1899 when it was the center of a rich mining area with a population of 2,500. When the ore bodies diminished in the 1920s, the smelters closed and Greenwood's population dwindled. It now is one of Canada's smallest cities. However, it still boasts a magnificent courthouse, gothic-spired Catholic church and 20 heritage buildings. Greenwood Museum contains excellent memorabilia of the city's mining days; tourist office adajcent. And not to be missed is a visit to the smelter site in Lotzgar Park. At the western edge of the city is a stop of interest marker for Greenwood smelter. ▲

Mile 395.5 (204) Km 636.5 (328): Boundary Creek Provincial Park with 18 campsites and fishing. Camping fee.

Mile 396.5 (203) Km 638 (327): Boundary Creek bridge and marker commemorating the building of the Dewdney Trail from Hope to the Kootenays in 1865.

Mile 400.5 (199) Km 644.5 (320): MIDWAY (pop. 650). All services available. The road through the village leads south to the border crossing of Midway (open daily 9 a.m. to 5 p.m.).

When Midway was founded, settlers believed it to be in Washington state. When the boundary was resurveyed in 1861, the settlement was found to be just north of the boundary line. Indians living north of the line were given a choice; to remain in Canada or move south to Colville. Most chose to move south but before they went, one of them twined 2 sapling pines as a symbol of the continuing unity of the divided tribe. These entwined trees, today a larger symbol of the friendship between the United States and Canada, grow in the park beside the museum. There are several picnic tables in the park.

Midway Museum is open May through September, 10 a.m. to 4 p.m. daily. The Canadian Pacific Railway caboose is the children's favorite. The Midway courthouse has memorabilia of the B.C. Provincial Police Force.

Municipal park in town beside the Kettle River provides 12 campsites. Good place for a swim. ▲

Mile 401 (198.5) Km 645.5 (319.5): Stop of interest sign at restored Midway railway station, built in 1900, on the history of the Kettle Valley Railway.

Mile 403 (196.5) Km 648.5 (316): Pope and Talbot sawmill, major employer of the area.

Mile 406.5 (193) Km 654 (310.5): Bridge over the Kettle River. West of the bridge is a war memorial cairn.

Mile 412 (187.5) Km 663 (301.5): Bridge over Kettle River. Community of **ROCK CREEK** has a general store and post office, medical clinic, 2 gas stations, a motel and the oldest continuously operating hotel in British Columbia.

In Olsen Park, east of the bridge, a stop of interest sign commemorates the finding of gold in the creek in 1859. The ensuing gold rush led to the building of the Dewdney Trail.

Junction with Highway 33 to Kelowna. Kettle River Provincial Recreation Area, 3 miles/5 km north on Highway 33, is an attractive riverside spot with 49 campsites, picnicking, fishing, swimming and hiking. Camping fee. A popular summer pursuit is floating downriver to the Rock Creek bridge on air mattresses or inner tubes. 🏊🏕️🐟▲

Mile 416.5 (183) Km 670 (294.5): Johnstone Creek Provincial Park with 16 campsites; camping fee. ▲

Mile 417.4 (182) Km 671.5 (293): Rough gravel road (not suitable for trailers) leads north 16 miles/26 km to Conkle Lake Provincial Park. The park has 24 campsites, a picnic area, a boat launch, swimming and fishing for rainbows. Camping fee. Alternate park access via Highway 33. 🐟▲

Mile 420.5 (179) Km 676.5 (288): Bridge over Rock Creek canyon, 328 feet/100m above the river. Junction with gravel road to Mount Baldy Ski Area and site of Camp McKinney gold mining ghost town. ⛷️

Mile 421.5 (178) Km 678.5 (286.5): **BRIDESVILLE**, limited services. Town was named for David McBride who cornered the local market on land when the Vancouver, Victoria and Eastern Railway built here and agreed to sell only if the town was named after him. He built a hotel here in 1910 and in it he installed the mahogany bar from Camp McKinney's Bucket of Blood Saloon.

Mile 424 (175.5) Km 682.5 (282.5): Anarchist Summit (elev. 4,435 feet/1,352m). The mountain was named for Richard Sidley who settled here in 1889 and lost his job as local justice of the peace because of his extremist political views.

Good gravel turnouts on both sides of highway. Excellent view west of the Cascade Mountains in Cathedral Park.

Mile 433 (166.5) Km 697 (268): Anarchist Mountain rest area in yellow pine forest. A good spot to watch for the rare white-headed woodpecker.

CAUTION: Steep downgrades and hairpin turns.

Mile 436.5 (163) Km 703 (262): Viewpoint for westbound travelers of Osoyoos Lake and the town of Osoyoos.

At the next hairpin turn eastbound, there is a large viewpoint at Eddy's Point, with a stop of interest sign about Southern Crossroads.

Mile 443 (156.5) Km 713 (252): **OSOYOOS** (3,000) has an annual precipitation of less than 8 inches and summer temperatures as high as 111°F/44°C. Surrounding it is an arid biotic zone, though much of the semi-desert has been transformed by irrigation into orchards and vineyards. There is even a banana farm, the only one in Canada.

Lake Osoyoos, which straddles the international boundary, is Canada's warmest freshwater lake and its sandy beaches make it a popular summer playground. Watersports are the chief attraction in this desert hotspot.

The town architecture has been renovated in a Spanish motif. The co-op fruit packing shed has been decorated with murals by artist Jack Campbell. Osoyoos has full tourist facilities.

Just east of the town center is Canada's only fully operational Dutch windmill, a faithful replica of an 1816 building where the owners live and grind flour the old-fashioned way. Stone-ground whole-wheat bread and flour are for sale in the bakery. Open for tours daily early May to late September, Monday to Saturday only the rest of the year.

Mile 444 (155.5) Km 714.5 (250): Junction with Highway 97, which leads 2.5 miles/4.5 km south to border crossing at Oroville, WA (open 24 hours a day), and north to Oliver and Penticton. B.C. government information trailer at intersection open mid-May to mid-September.

Travelers headed north on Highway 97 turn to CANADA HIGHWAY 97 section for log. If southbound on Highway 97, turn to the end of the U.S. HIGHWAY 97 section and read log back to front.

Mile 447.5 (152) Km 720 (244.5): Viewpoints of south end of Okanagan Valley and Osoyoos Lake. Stop of interest sign about irrigation.

Mile 449.5 (150) Km 723.5 (241.5): Spotted Lake (private property). High concentrations of magnesium and sodium create white spots on this alkali lake, although in years of high rainfall the water is relatively clear. Indians used the lake water for its curative properties.

Mile 452 (147.5) Km 727.5 (237.5): Richter Pass summit (elev. 2,231 feet/680m). The road leads north to the site of a proposed observatory on top of Mount Kobau. Construction was suspended because of high costs. The road gives access to alpine meadows.

The highway at Keremeos, Mile 474, is lined with fruit stands.   (Liz Bryan)

Mile 458.5 (141) Km 738 (227): Large turnout at junction with road south to U.S. border crossing near Nighthawk, WA (open 9 a.m. to 5 p.m. daily).

Mile 461.5 (138) Km 742.5 (222.5): Dankoe silver mine, still in operation, was originally worked in 1901 as the Horn mine.

Mile 462.5 (137) Km 744.5 (220.5): Bridge over Similkameen leads to Indian village of Chopaka and border crossing (open 9 a.m. to 5 p.m. daily).

Mile 470.5 (129) Km 757 (208): CAWSTON, a small fruit-growing community with packing plant. Site of Hudson's Bay Co. store in 1860. First homesteaded in 1865 by Frank Richter who wintered cattle here. There are many fruit stands in season along the highway here.

Mile 471 (128.5) Km 758 (207): Becks Road leads north 2.5 miles/4 km to restored Keremeos gristmill built in 1877.

Mile 472 (127.5) Km 760 (205): St. Laszlo Vineyard Estate Winery. Tasting room and store open 9 a.m. to 9 p.m. daily year-round.

Mile 473.5 (126) Km 762 (203): Junction with Highway 3A to Penticton. This road passes close to Keremeos Columns Provincial Park, with its cliffs of gigantic basaltic columns; no road access, hike in.

Mile 474 (125.5) Km 763 (202): KEREMEOS (pop. 850), a small supply center for surrounding orchardists and ranchers. All services available. Public campgrounds are located by the river. Tourist information office in the park on main street.

The grassy river benches of the Similkameen River are covered with fruit trees, mostly early ripening apricots, cherries and peaches. The highway on both sides of town is lined with fruit stands.

On Keremeos Creek just north of town centre is British Columbia's only fully operational water-powered gristmill, still with its original machinery. Built in 1877, the mill has been fully restored as a provincial historic site. The grounds are open year-round. The mill is open from mid-May to mid-September, 9 a.m. to 4 p.m. Guided tours. A great place for a picnic.

Mile 476.5 (123) Km 767 (198): Gravel side road crosses Similkameen River (covered railway bridge) and follows the Ashnola River 13.5 miles/22 km southwest to Cathedral Provincial Park boundary. Park access is on foot or by prearranged 4-wheel-drive transport to private lodge in park centre. The heart of Cathedral Park is a ring of 7,000-foot/2,100-m alpine lakes.

Mile 477 (122.5) Km 767.5 (197): Rest area and picnic site beside river. Stop of interest sign about the covered railway bridges built by the Vancouver, Victoria and Eastern Railway which serviced the mines at Hedley and Princeton. ⊼

Mile 478.5 (121) Km 770 (194.5): Standing Rock, a prominent glacial erratic on the north side of the highway, is an ancient Indian trail marker and pictograph rock.

Mile 480 (119.5) Km 772.5 (192.5): Large turnout and viewpoint with sign about California bighorn sheep transplanted to this area.

Mile 487.5 (112) Km 784.5 (180): Watch for Indian grave marked by pickets in the middle of field south of the highway. Park off highway near here for a short walk to Indian pictographs. (Climb steep road embankment north of highway then head northwest across pine-clad bench to base of white cliffs.) Pictographs are in good condition, painted in red and black.

Mile 489.5 (110) Km 787.5 (177): St. Ann's Catholic Church, built of logs on a glacial ridge above the river, and the nearby Indian village of Snazaist in the Chuchuawaa Indian Reserve. "Corkscrew Road" (4-wheel drive only) to Nickel Plate townsite turns north off highway opposite Indian village.

Mile 492 (107.5) Km 791.5 (173): HEDLEY village lies just to the north of the highway in the valley of 20 Mile Creek. Named after the man who had grubstaked many of the prospectors, Hedley flourished with the mines, but faded when the mines closed. Fires in 1956 and 1957 destroyed much of the old town. Visit Heritage House, a modern building displaying Hedley's past in photographs. Service station, restaurants, bed-and-breakfast accommodation in town; private campgrounds on highway.

Rock cliff to the west of the Hedley townsite shows good examples of deeply folded rock strata. The Indians called this the Striped Rock, or Snazaist.

Stop of interest sign west of town commemorates the rich gold finds above the town of Hedley. From 1903 to 1955, over $47 million in gold was taken out of the mountain and brought down by aerial tramway to a reduction mill. Old mine buildings are visible on the rock ridge high above town. Recently, gold mining activity has begun again at Hedley, with the Candorado Mine in operation. ▲

Mile 495.5 (104) Km 797.5 (167.5): Stemwinder Provincial Park on riverbank with 23 campsites and picnic tables. Camping fee. The park is named for the stemwinder snake. The Similkameen River flows swiftly here; recommended for very strong swimmers only. Indian pithouse depression inside park. Watch for poison ivy. ⊼▲

Mile 496.5 (103) Km 799.5 (165.5): Highway crosses Similkameen River. Old Hedley Road follows river's north bank to Princeton.

Mile 502.5 (97) Km 808.5 (156): Bromley Rock Provincial Park with 17 campsites, picnic area, swimming and fishing.

Camping fee. The river here forms a large deep pool overhung by Bromley Rock, an excellent summer swimming hole with small sandy beaches. Fishing for rainbow trout. ⊼⊷▲

Mile 514 (85.5) Km 827 (137.5): Road south to Amber Ski Hill. The road continues to open pit mines on Copper Mountain (restricted access). ⊼

Mile 516 (83.5) Km 830.5 (134.5): Bridge over Similkameen River. Junction with Highway 5A north to Merritt. Access to Princeton Airport, home of the Princeton Cadet Glider School.

Mile 516.5 (83) Km 831 (133.5): PRINCETON (pop. 4,000); all services available. Princeton is located at the confluence of the Similkameen and Tulameen rivers. Tulameen is the local Indian name for "red earth" and refers to the nearby bluffs of red ochre. The first white settlement here in the 1850s was known as Vermilion Forks, but in 1860 when the Royal Engineers surveyed the road through the valley, a townsite was laid out and renamed after Edward, Prince of Wales, who was visiting eastern Canada.

Princeton was an important centre for coal mining, which reached its peak here in the 1920s. The hills are riddled with old workings. Today the town is a supply centre for surrounding ranches, the nearby copper mine and lumber companies.

Tourist information in the old rail caboose on Vermilion Avenue; museum adjacent. Fishing in the rivers and many small lakes in the surrounding hills is the main recreational attraction here. Also rockhounding and exploring the back roads and ghost towns of the mining areas. Take the back road northwest of Princeton up the Tulameen River to the coal mining towns of Coalmont and Tulameen, and the old gold camp of Granite Creek.

Mile 524 (75.5) Km 843 (121.5): Bridge over Whipsaw Creek and stop of interest sign for yellow or Ponderosa Pine Ecological Reserve. Old Hope Trail (1861), which follows the creek, has been restored as a hiking and horse trail. It extends 16 miles/26 km into Manning Provincial Park. *CAUTION:* 8 percent downgrade for westbound traffic, trucks use lower gear. Watch for hairpin turn and narrow bridge over Copper Creek at bottom of hill. ⫯

Mile 526 (73.5) Km 846.5 (118): Similco Mine. Copper ores are mined in open pits across the valley, concentrated here for shipment.

Mile 534 (65.5) Km 859.5 (105.5): Large gravel turnout and brake testing area for eastbound traffic. Map shows hairpin turns and steep downgrades.

Mile 537.5 (62) Km 865 (99.5): Sunday Summit (elev. 4,596 feet/1,401m). The mountains nearby are covered with lodgepole pine, the first evergreen to grow back after a forest fire.

West entrance to Manning Provincial Park at Mile 583.5.
(Liz Bryan)

Mile 541.5 (58) Km 871.5 (93.5): Copper Creek rest areas.

Mile 545 (54.5) Km 877 (87.5): View south to Similkameen Falls; limited parking at bend in highway east of falls.

Mile 548 (51.5) Km 882 (83): **MANNING PARK**, east gate of Manning Provincial Park; gas station, small store, restaurant and motel. The big carved wooden bear by the sign is a popular background for family photos. (Bears are common in the park.)

Mile 549 (50.5) Km 883.5 (81): McDiarmid Meadows picnic area. 🏕

Mile 552 (47.5) Km 888.5 (76.5): Mule Deer Campground with 34 sites (some on river). Camping fee. Mule deer are common on the east side of the Cascades, black-tailed deer on the west side. ▲

Mile 555 (44.5) Km 893 (71.5): Blow-down picnic area beside river. On the opposite side of the highway is Hampton Campground with 80 sites. Camping fee. 🏕▲

Mile 555.5 (44) Km 894 (71): Castle Creek Trail to Monument 78 on Canada-U.S. boundary, the start of the Pacific Crest Trail. Also trail to Monument 83. 🚶

Mile 557 (42.5) Km 896.5 (68.5): Road south to parking lot for Beaver Pond nature trail. Several varieties of birds can be seen here, as well as beaver, muskrat and mule deer. Windy Joe Mountain trailhead. 🚶

Mile 557.5 (42) Km 897 (67.5): Manning Provincial Park Visitor Center; sani-station.

Mile 558 (41.5) Km 898 (66.5): Road south to Manning Park Lodge, trail rides, Gibson Pass Ski Area, Lightning Lakes and Strawberry Flats. Road north to Cascade Lookout and alpine meadows.

Mile 559.5 (40) Km 900.5 (64.5): Cold-spring Campground with 67 sites and picnic tables beside the Similkameen River. Camping fee. Nature trail. 🚶🏕▲

Mile 562 (37.5) Km 904.5 (60.5): Cambie Creek Cross-country Ski Area. ⛷

Mile 563.5 (36) Km 907 (58): Summit of Allison Pass (elev. 4,403 feet/1,342m). The pass was named for John Fall Allison, Princeton's first settler, who pioneered this route through the mountains. Near the summit, B.C. Highways has a road maintenance depot; emergency phone. West of the pass, Highway 3 follows the Skagit River.

Mile 568 (31.5) Km 914 (50.5): Remains of old forest fire. In 1945 fire swept through area, destroying nearly 1.2 million acres of forest. Hillsides still bear scars despite reforestation.

Mile 573 (26.5) Km 922 (42.5): Cayuse Flats rest area. Beginning of Hope Pass horse trail which goes north up Skaist Creek.

Mile 576.5 (23) Km 927.5 (37): Snass Creek (Indian word for "rain"). Just east of the bridge, a stop of interest sign describes the Dewdney Trail, built from Hope to Rock Creek in 1860-61 and completed to the Kootenays 4 years later.

Mile 577.5 (22) Km 929.5 (35.5): Rhododendron Flats rest area and nature trail. Here is one of the few places where the red rhododendron grows wild on the British Columbia mainland. The shrubs provide a colorful display in June. The red rhododendron is protected: do not pick or uproot.

Mile 578.5 (21) Km 931 (33.5): Sumallo Grove picnic area. The Whatcom Trail follows the Skagit River southwest from here to Hope. A good, easy hike, but long (9 miles/15 km). 🚶🏕

Mile 579 (20.5) Km 931.5 (33): Old buildings of former Foundation Mines to east.

Mile 581.5 (18) Km 936 (29): Stop of interest. In 1860, a platoon of 80 Royal Engineers from England replaced the Dewdney Trail with a wagon road. They completed 34 miles/55 km from Hope but were called off the job because of more urgent work in the Cariboo where a gold rush was in full swing. A well-preserved section of the old road lies just north of the highway.

Mile 583.5 (16) Km 939 (25.5): West gate of Manning Provincial Park is marked by large carving of a hoary marmot. Rest area, picnic tables and short loop trail to section of Engineer's Road. Just outside the park gates is a lodge with restaurant and gas station. 🏕

Mile 585.5 (14) Km 942 (22.5): Small vacation community of **SUNSHINE VALLEY** beside the Sumallo River. On nearby Trites Ranch property was Tashme Camp where some 3,500 Japanese were interned during WWII.

Mile 589 (10.5) Km 948 (17): Rest area and viewpoint of Hope Slide. In January 1965 a minor earthquake triggered a gigantic rockfall. Tons of rock, earth and snow slid from Johnson's Peak north of the highway, killing 4 people and burying the road and adjacent Outram Lake.
CAUTION: 7 percent downgrade westbound, trucks stop here to check brakes.

Mile 593 (6.5) Km 954.5 (10.5): Nicolum River Provincial Park; 9 campsites, picnic area. 🏕▲

Mile 594 (5.5) Km 956.5 (9.5): Junction with Coquihalla Highway 5 to Merritt and Kamloops. See the COQUIHALLA HIGHWAY section.

Mile 598 (1.5) Km 962.5 (2.5): Exit to Hope business route. Hope has all visitor services. See description of Hope in the TRANS-CANADA HIGHWAY 1 section.   EXIT 171

Mile 599.5 (0) Km 964.5 (0): Exit to Hope town centre and junction with Trans-Canada Highway 1. Turn to **Mile 548.5** in the TRANS-CANADA HIGHWAY 1 section.   EXIT 170

Interstate 5

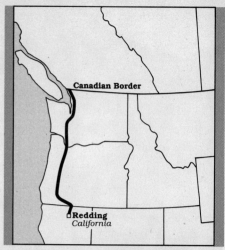

See maps pages 59, 61, 66 and 73

Interstate 5 is a 4- to 6-lane divided highway that cuts an almost straight line from the southern to the northern border of the United States. In the Northwest it passes through California, Oregon and Washington. It's the most important north-south shipping and travel route on the West Coast, heavily traveled day and night, especially in the metropolitan areas.

While not generally regarded as a scenic route, Interstate 5 climbs through the steep green canyons of the Siskiyou Mountains, divides agricultural farms in the Willamette Valley and crosses the historically rich Columbia River (10th-longest river in the country at 1,214 miles). It skirts the western edge of the Cascade Range and the eastern shore of sprawling Puget Sound. It passes next to vast fields of tulips and daffodils in the Skagit Valley and enters Canada in the beautifully landscaped flower gardens at the Peace Arch Park in Blaine, WA.

There are many attractions along the interstate easily accessible to motorists who take the time to pull off the highway for an hour or more. Food, gas and lodging are readily available, with major hotels, restaurants and gas stations at most major exits. Travelers overnighting along the way are advised to call ahead for motel accommodations in summer. Well-maintained highway rest areas, with restrooms and pay phones, are located along the interstate.

Exit numbers and physical mileposts along Interstate 5 in Oregon reflect distance from the California-Oregon border. Mileposts and exit numbers in Washington reflect distance from the Oregon-Washington border. The NORTHWEST MILEPOSTS® log reflects cumulative mileages from Redding, CA, to the Canadian border.

Interstate 5 Log

Distance from Redding, CA, is followed by distance from the Canadian border.

Mile 0 (704.5): Junction with California Highways 44 and 299, central Redding. Easy access to all services both east and west of Interstate 5. Highway 44 extends east 48 miles to Lassen Volcanic National Park. Highway 299 leads west 0.5 mile to Redding and continues through the Trinity National Forest to junction with U.S. Highway 101 (139 miles).

REDDING (pop. 53,000) has all visitor services. The Central Pacific Railroad established a terminus here in 1872. Originally called Poverty Flat, it was renamed in honor of railroad executive B.B. Redding. Redding's elevation is 560 feet.

Its major industries are timber and wood products, recreation and tourism. Millions come annually to fish, hunt, sail, camp, water and snow ski.

Redding is the gateway to Whiskeytown-Shasta-Trinity National Recreation Area. This area encompasses 3 separate lakes: Clair Engle Lake in the Trinity Unit; Shasta Lake; and Whiskeytown Lake. Smallest of the 3 units, Whiskeytown Lake is located 8 miles west of Redding via Highway 299.

Also west of Redding 3 miles via Highway 299 is Shasta State Historic Park. In its heyday, the "queen city" of California gold rush towns shipped over $100,000 in gold per week. All roads north of San Francisco teminated at Shasta. The state park includes 14 buildings, sites and ruins. A courthouse built in 1855 houses a museum of paintings, mining artifacts and the original courtroom. The park also has farm and mining machinery, a restored store and one of the state's oldest Masonic lodges.

Mile 2 (702.5): Exit to Highway 299 east to Burney and Alturas. Access to Shasta College and Lake Boulevard.

Mile 2.5 (702): Exit to Twinview Boulevard with easy access to services.

Mile 4 (700.5): Exit to Oasis Road with easy access to gas, food and camper park.

Mile 5 (699.5): Northern Redding city limits.

Mile 5.5 (699): Exit to Pine Grove Avenue.

Mile 6.5 (698): Exit to Central Valley, Project City and Shasta Dam. All services are available. To reach Shasta Dam, go west through Project City. Follow road 7.3 miles to the dam. A roadside viewpoint 0.5 mile south of the dam provides an outstanding view of the dam, Lake Shasta and Mount Shasta. Visitor center at the dam with an observation theater overlooking the spillway. Historic photos and a 28-minute film explain the history and operations. Gift shop and snack bar.

Built between 1938 and 1945, Shasta Dam is the nation's second-largest concrete gravity dam. The dam was built by the Bureau of Reclamation to store water for use in the Sacramento and San Joaquin valleys. It is one of California's largest power plants with a capacity of 456,000 kilowatts. Waters of the McCloud, Pit and Sacramento rivers, plus Squaw Creek, are backed up by the dam.

Mile 8.5 (696): Exit to Mountain Gate

(pop. 700) Wonderland Boulevard area. Access to Shasta Lake ranger station; visitor information.

Mile 11 (693.5): Exit to Fawndale Road, Wonderland Boulevard. Easy access to RV parks and lodging. ▲

Mile 11.5 (693): Entering (northbound) the Shasta Lake Unit of the Whiskeytown-Shasta-Trinity National Recreation Area. Shasta Lake has 365 miles of shoreline and is the largest man-made reservoir in California. The recreation area was created in 1965, to recognize the many recreational opportunities provided by the reservoirs developed by the Bureau of Reclamation's Central Valley Project. Shasta and Trinity units are administered by the U.S. Forest Service, and Whiskeytown by the National Park Service.

Mile 12.5 (692): Exit to Bridge Bay Road and Resort. Food, lodging, boat ramp. Highway crosses Pit River bridge. Good view northbound of the Sacramento arm of Lake Shasta to the west of Interstate 5 and McCloud arm to the east.

Mile 14 (690.5): Exit to Turntable Bay Road. This exit allows southbound travelers access to Interstate 5 northbound and vice versa.

Mile 16 (688.5): Exit to rest area and Packers Bay Road. Boat marina and launch at Packers Bay. Southbound travelers begin 6 percent downgrade.

Mile 17 (687.5): Exit to Shasta Caverns Road and O'Brien. Access to Forest Service campgrounds at Bailey Cove and Wyntoon. Also access to private resorts with camping and boating. To reach Lake Shasta Caverns, follow road east approximately 2 miles to parking lot. The caverns are privately owned. See feature this section. ▲★

Mile 20.5 (684): Exit to Salt Creek Road

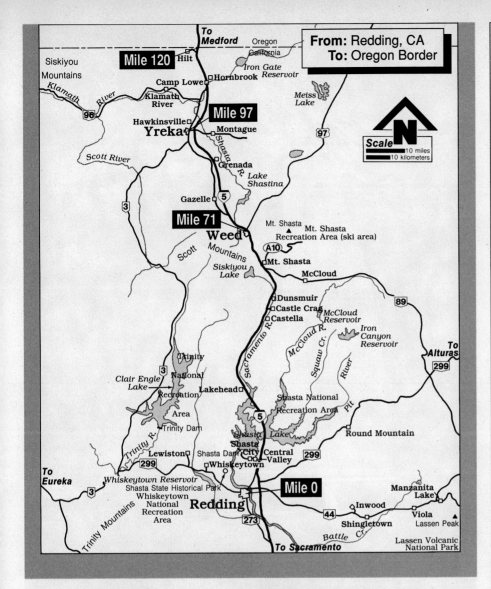

From: Redding, CA
To: Oregon Border

Lake Shasta Caverns

In a 2-hour tour of Lake Shasta Caverns, you can see virtually all the formations found in any cave; take a bus ride up a spiraling mountain road; and enjoy a catamaran cruise across the placid waters of the McCloud arm of Lake Shasta.

Lake Shasta Caverns is located 15 miles north of Redding, CA. From Interstate 5, take the O'Brien exit (**Mile 17**) and travel east on a paved road 2 miles to the reception center.

Since the reception center is on the west side of the lake and the caverns are on the eastern shore, you start and conclude with a 15-minute catamaran cruise across the McCloud arm of Lake Shasta. On the eastern shore, you're transferred to a bus for a rousing ride of 2 miles and an 800-foot gain in elevation to the cave's entrance. With rocks in the roadbed, steep grades, and hairpin turns, you'll be glad you had to leave your vehicle in the parking lot. Caveside facilities include restrooms and snack bar, plus a boat launch.

Cave passageways have been improved with paved walkways and stairs. Temperatures are a constant, comfortable 58°F inside.

The cave tour begins with the Discovery Room. It is 200 feet long, 40 feet wide, and 20 to 45 feet high. In it are virtually every formation found in any cave: helictites, tiger tooth crystals and lacy "peanut brittle." The caverns have their share of stalactites hanging from the ceiling, stalagmites growing on the ground, and the 2 joining to form columns. Flowstone — formed by mineral-bearing waters — are seen in a variety of shapes and colors.

A climb of 111 fairly easy steps leads to a room partially filled with white crystals, and so vast parts are still awaiting exploration. In the Basement Room are prime examples of first-stage cave development plus a 45-foot-deep natural chimney. The Popcorn Room contains outstanding examples of cave coral which resembles sea coral but is formed from inert matter rather than living organisms. The tour concludes in the Cathedral Room. It is the largest, most spectacular, and measures 20 feet long, 70 feet wide, and 100 feet high. A drapation stretches over 60 feet high and 60 feet wide.

On exiting the cave, you pass a viewpoint from which you can see the junction of the Pitt and McCloud arms of Lake Shasta. The view also includes Pitt River Bridge which is the world's tallest double-decked bridge.

---

and Gilman Road. Easy access to food, lodging, marina and camper sites. ▲

Mile 22.5 (682): Northbound travelers begin a 6 percent downgrade for 1 mile. As you continue north, you are climbing with elevations varying between 2,000 and 3,000 feet above sea level. Deer are frequently seen between here and the Oregon border.

Mile 24.5 (680): Exit to Lakeshore Drive and Antlers Road. Easy access to food, gas, lodging and camping. ▲

Mile 26 (678.5): Exit to Lakehead and River View Drive. Access to food, gas, lodging and camping. ▲

Mile 27 (677.5): Southbound travelers enter the Shasta Lake Unit of Whiskeytown-Shasta-Trinity National Recreation Area.

Mile 28 (676.5): Exit to rest area (southbound only).

Mile 30 (674.5): Dog Creek Road exits to the west of Interstate 5 and Delta Road to the east.

Mile 33 (671.5): Exit west to La Moines Road for northbound travelers and begin 6 percent downgrade for southbound travelers.

Mile 34.5 (670): Exit to Pollard Flat. Diesel; food.

Mile 37 (667.5): Exit to Gibson Road, westbound.

Mile 40 (664.5): Exit to Shotgun Creek Road. Diesel, food.

Mile 41.5 (663): Exit to Sims Road and easy access to trailer camp.

Mile 43.5 (661): Exit to Flume Creek Road.

Mile 45 (659.5): Exit to Conant Road.

Mile 46 (658.5): Exit to Sweetbrier Avenue.

Mile 46.5 (658): Vista Point (northbound only) with excellent view of Mount Shasta to the northeast and the Castle Crags to the northwest of the highway.

Mile 48 (656.5): Exit to Castella and Castle Crags State Park. Turn west and take freeway underpass 1 mile to park entrance. Castle Crags' soaring spires are 170,000-year-old granite which was formed deep within the earth. Gradually they were pushed to the surface and their current elevation of 6,000 feet. For best views of the crags and Mount Shasta, take a 2-mile narrow, winding road to the park's Vista Point. The state park has 64 campsites, hiking trails, fishing and picnic areas. Fee: $10, no hookups; seniors, $8.

Mile 49.5 (655): Exit to Soda Creek Road and Pacific Crest Trail. Soda Creek is one of many streams and springs which are known for their mineral waters. During the 1890s, several resorts were built around these supposedly therapeutic waters.

Mile 50.5 (654): Exit to Crag View Drive. Access to Railroad Park Resort, which features accommodations in railroad cars or more traditional cabins. The resort also has an RV campground and a railroad museum. The museum has a gear-driven logging engine and 1893 Wells Fargo car, a wooden snowplow and flanger. ▲

Mile 52 (652.5): Dunsmuir Avenue. Gas, food and lodging.

Mile 53.5 (651): Exit to central DUNSMUIR (pop. 2,300) and crossing the Sacramento River. (For easy access to services, exit at **Mile 56**.) During the 1890s, Shasta Springs Resort was located north of Dunsmuir. The spring waters were bottled and sold as Shasta Mineral Water. The resort site and picturesque Mossbrae Falls can be seen by walking north along the railroad tracks.

Mile 56 (648.5): Exit to Dunsmuir Avenue and Siskiyou Avenue. Easy access to gas, diesel, food, lodging and campgrounds. ▲

Mile 57 (647.5): Southbound travelers begin 7 percent downgrade for next 3 miles.

Mile 57.5 (647): Exit to Mott Road, Dunsmuir Avenue and airport.

Mile 59 (645.5): Exit to inspection and weigh station.

Mile 60 (644.5): Exit to California Highway 89 which leads southeast to McCloud, Burney Falls State Park and Lassen Volcanic National Park. Lodging.

Mile 61.5 (643): MOUNT SHASTA (pop. 3,300) is the service center for the hikers, rock collectors, and winter sports enthusiasts who come to enjoy Mount Shasta. The Mount Shasta ski park has 15 groomed runs, a day lodge, ski school, and 2 triple-chair lifts. Access is via Highway 89 or County Road A10.

Mile 62 (642.5): Exit to central Mount Shasta and Lake Siskiyou. Trailer parks and RV campgrounds, tourist information center,

Lake Siskiyou provides recreation in the shadow of Mount Shasta, Mile 62. (L. Linkhart)

lodging and family restaurants are readily accessible. ▲

Mile 64.5 (640): Exit to Abrams Lake Road. Camping. ▲

Mile 66 (638.5): Black Butte Summit (elev. 3,912 feet). Black Butte (elev. 6,325 feet) is east of the interstate. This volcanic cone of hornblende andesite was formed about 10,000 years ago. A 2.5-mile trail, built by the Civilian Conservation Corps, can be hiked in a half day. The climb is strenuous due to the rocky terrain, steepness and heat. Bring water as none is available at the site. Snake kits are advisable. Total vertical climb is 1,845 feet.

Mile 67 (637.5): Exit to Summit Drive and truck village which has food, gas and diesel.

Mile 69 (635.5): Exit to South Weed Boulevard and College of the Siskiyous. Trailer camping. Gas, diesel, fast food and family restaurants. ▲

Mile 71 (633.5): Exit to central Weed and U.S. Highway 97. Visitor information, lodging.

WEED (pop. 3,000) was named in honor of settler Abner Weed. Italian immigrants settled in the early 1900s, and left as their legacy many of the city's street names, including Lombardi, Genoa, Camino and Florence avenues. Weed's economy is based on timber, education and as a centrally located service center for skiers, fishermen and hunters.

U.S. Highway 97 leads north through Oregon and Washington into Canada. Turn to the U.S. HIGHWAY 97 section for log of this route.

Mile 71.5 (633): Exit to N. Weed Boulevard (northbound only).

Mile 72.5 (632): Entering Shasta-Trinity National Forest.

Mile 73.5 (631): Crossing Shasta River which is fished for trout, and exit to Elgenwood, Gazelle and Stewart Springs Road (southbound only). ►

Mile 76 (628.5): Exit to Weed airport and rest area.

Mile 81.5 (623): Exit to Louie Road.

Mile 89 (615.5): Exit to Grenada and southbound to Gazelle. Northbound to Montague.

Mile 93 (611.5): Exit to Easy Street and Shamrock Road. Although it may seem like you are traveling on a valley floor, the elevation is 3,000 feet above sea level. The next 40 miles are often subject to gusty winds.

Mile 96.5 (608): Exit to California Highway 3 which meanders southwest for 109 miles through the Scott Valley to Trinity Lakes. Fort Jones, 15 miles south of Interstate 5 on Highway 3, was the site of an 1852-58 U.S. Army post. Ranger station, fast-food restaurants, truck stops.

Mile 97 (607.5): YREKA (pop. 5,900) is the Siskiyou County seat and the center of an agricultural area that produces dairy products, cattle, grain and alfalfa. In 1851, Abraham Thompson supposedly found his pack mules pulling up flecks of gold in the roots of grass they were eating. Yreka was born. The name is anglicized from an Indian word meaning "white mountain."

Many of the Victorian homes and buildings constructed from 1850-80s are preserved as part of the Yreka Historical District. They can be toured with a self-guiding map. The district is accessible from Interstate 5 by turning at the central Yreka exit and continuing west on Minor Street. Major-chain motel, major-chain 24-hour restaurant, gas, diesel, campground, hospital. ▲

Mile 98 (606.5): Exit to Yreka airport and Montague. All services available. Lodging, family restaurants.

Mile 101 (603.5): Crossing the Shasta River.

Mile 102.5 (602): Vista Point accessible only to southbound travelers. Outstanding view of Mount Shasta.

Mile 103.5 (601): Anderson Grade Summit (elev. 3,067 feet). Northbound

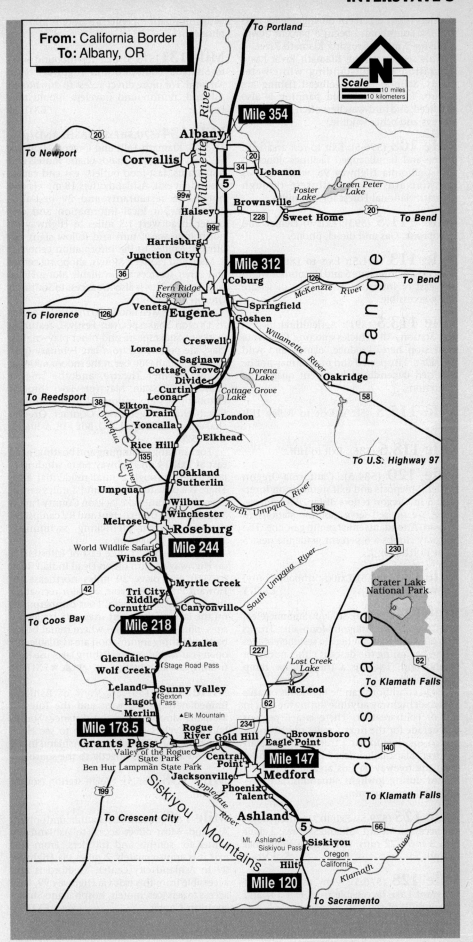

From: California Border
To: Albany, OR

travelers begin 6 percent downgrade for next 4 miles. Southbound begin 5 percent downgrade for 3 miles. Crossing Klamath River.

This section of the Klamath River has a reputation for outstanding white-water rapids. Salmon and steelhead fishing are superb. Recreational gold panning is also practiced, and bird-watchers often spot eagles, ospreys and other wildlife.

Mile 108 (596.5): Exit to rest area with phone and handicapped facilities. Junction with California Highway 96, which follows the Klamath River southwest through Klamath National Forest for 153 miles.

Mile 111.5 (593): Exit to Henley and Hornbrook. Gas and diesel, phone.

Mile 113 (591.5): Exit to Ditch Creek Road west of Interstate 5 and Hornbrook Highway east of Interstate 5. Gas and diesel are easily accessible.

Mile 113.5 (591): Agricultural Inspection Station. All vehicles entering California must stop here. Produce, plants, and wild animals are inspected and may or may not be admitted depending on current quarantine restrictions.

Mile 115.5 (589): Exit to Bailey Hill Road.

Mile 118.5 (586): Exit to Hilt.

Mile 120 (584.5): California-Oregon border. Mileposts and exit numbers on Interstate 5 in Oregon reflect distance from here. There are no self-serve gasoline stations in Oregon. Attendants must pump gasoline. The highway climbs a 6 percent grade the next 5 miles northbound.

Mile 121 (583.5): Exit (northbound only) Siskiyou Summit. EXIT 1

Mile 124.5 (580): Siskiyou Summit (elev. 4,310 feet) in the Siskiyou Mountains. Trucks turn off at the road cut here to test their brakes before beginning the descent either north- or southbound. There is a truck escape ramp northbound.

Road conditions can be hazardous on this stretch of highway anytime during the year in wet or cold weather. There is a 6 percent downgrade for the next 7 miles northbound. Watch for slow-moving trucks, and be alert for deer. Black-tailed deer frequently wander onto the freeway in this area and can be a hazard during lowlight situations, late evening and early morning.

Mile 125 (579.5): Exit to Mount Ashland and access to Mount Ashland Ski Area: 2 chair lifts, 3 tows, 22 runs, skiing from November to April. EXIT 5

Mile 128 (576.5): View to the east of Emigrant Lake (accessible from Exit 14) and the foothills of the Cascade Range.

Mile 130 (574.5): Rest area (northbound)

with information center, restrooms and pay phones.

Mile 131 (573.5): Exit (northbound only) to Siskiyou Boulevard and Highway 99 in Ashland. For more direct access to downtown Ashland, northbound travelers should take Exit 14. EXIT 11

Mile 134 (570.5): Exit to ASHLAND (pop. 16,310), Klamath Falls and Oregon Highway 66. Easy access to major-chain motels and restaurants, fast-food outlets, gas and campgrounds at exit. Ashland offers 18 motels and hotels, 56 restaurants and 29 bed-and-breakfasts. For local information and city center, head west 1.3 miles to Highway 99 north (one way); turn and follow signs another 1.7 miles to the information center at E. Main and Pioneer. Motels, shopping center and other services are available along Highway 66 west. This is also the access to Southern Oregon State College.

Ashland is well known to theater lovers for its Oregon Shakespearean Festival, featuring works of Shakespeare and other playwrights. Plays are performed from late February (previews) through October at the indoor 600-seat Angus Bowmer Theatre, and the smaller indoor Black Swan. May (preview) through October plays are performed in the outdoor Elizabethan Stagehouse. Contact Oregon Shakespearean Festival, P.O. Box 158, Ashland, OR 97520.

For camping, swimming and boating, head east at Exit 14 on Highway 66 (a winding 2-lane road) through a rural residential area. There is a private campground 3 miles east of Exit 14. Emigrant Lake Jackson County Park is 3.5 miles from the exit; tent and RV campsites, day-use area for picnicking, swimming, showers and boat ramp.

Approximately 1 mile east of Interstate 5 on Highway 66 turn off on Dead Indian Road (paved) and drive 20 miles northeast for Howard Prairie Reservoir, a major recreation site for the Ashland area. Four campgrounds on the lake offer 84 tent sites, 195 trailer/RV sites, plus resort facilities where rental boats, bait and fishing information are available. It's open year-round; a good fishing lake, use flies, trolling tackle or bait. EXIT 14

Mile 137 (567.5): View of Ashland immediately to the west and the forested Klamath Mountains in the distance. Southbound travelers should be able to see Horn Peak behind 7,523-foot Mount Ashland in the Siskiyou Mountains directly to the south.

Mile 138 (566.5): Weigh station (southbound).

Mile 139 (565.5): Exit (southbound only) to Ashland. Most direct access to Ashland city center for southbound travelers. From this exit it is approximately 2 miles via Highway 99 to Ashland city center. Medford is also accessible from this exit via Highway 99. Easy access to services, motels, hospital and Shakespearean Center. EXIT 19

Mile 141 (563.5): Exit to Talent (pop.

2,660), a residential area. There is an RV park on the west side of the interstate. EXIT 21

Mile 142.5 (562): Rest area (southbound) and Bear Creek. A tributary of the Rogue River, Bear Creek flows through the city of Medford and meanders across the interstate 4 times during the next 9 miles. Orchards seen on either side of the interstate produce pears, this area's primary fruit crop.

Mile 144 (560.5): Exit to PHOENIX (pop. 2,950). Motel, family restaurants, gas, truck stop with diesel and an RV park on the west side of the highway. EXIT 24

Mile 147 (557.5): Exit to Medford, Jacksonville National Historic Landmark, Barnett Road. Easy access to food, gas and lodging at this exit; shopping center just east of exit. There is the northbound access to Medford city center and riverside motels. Travelers may note the large building on the hill to the east: It is a retirement home.

MEDFORD (pop. 41,975) is a sprawling service center for this area's agriculture and tourism industry, with 27 motels (including major chains), family restaurants and fast-food establishments, gas, diesel, and other facilities.

The historic town of Jacksonville (pop. 1,990) is 5 miles west of Medford and accessible from several exits on Interstate 5. A boom town in 1852, this former mining settlement is now a National Historic Landmark District with many restored buildings from the 1800s. The museum on 5th Street offers guided tours of the town. Jacksonville hosts the Peter Britt Festivals — a program of outdoor concerts — late July through August. Contact Peter Britt Festivals, P.O. Box 1124, Medford, OR 97501. MP 28 EXIT 27

Mile 150 (554.5): Exit to Medford, Crater Lake, Oregon Highway 62, Rogue Valley Mall, and Klamath Falls. Easy access to food, gas and lodging at this exit; 24-hour restaurant and truck stop with diesel. This is the southbound access to Medford's city center and riverside major-chain motels, northbound access to Medford airport. Highway 62 provides the most direct access to Crater Lake National Park for northbound Interstate 5 motorists. Crater Lake is approximately 75 miles from Medford via this route. There are several campgrounds along Highway 62. (See description of Crater Lake in the MAJOR ATTRACTIONS section.) MP 31 EXIT 30

Mile 152 (552.5): Exit for northbound access to CENTRAL POINT (pop. 7,200), Medford airport and Jackson County Exposition Park. Easy access to gas stations with diesel and family restaurant at this exit. MP 33 EXIT 32

Mile 153 (551.5): Northeast of the highway is distinctive Table Rock. On a clear day, travelers may see the top of cone-shaped Mount McLoughlin (elev. 9,495 feet) in the distance directly to the east.

Northbound, the highway leaves the flat valley and enters the mountains. It is a

The Rogue River is well known for its river rafting opportunities.

(L. Linkhart)

winding road with steep grades from here to Canyonville (next 70 miles).

Mile 155 (549.5): Exit for northbound access to Blackwell Road, southbound access to Highway 99, Central Point, North Medford, Medford airport and Jackson County Exposition Park. Restaurants and gas stations are at this exit.   EXIT 35

Mile 160 (544.5): Exit to Gold Hill, Jacksonville, Highways 99 and 234. Access to Ben Hur Lampman State Park, on the northeast side of the interstate (follow signs), a day-use area on the Rogue River with picnicking and swimming.

The community of **GOLD HILL** (pop. 960) is about a mile northeast from the interstate. All services available including gas, groceries, deli and campground. This is the location of the Oregon Vortex, a natural phenomenon of magnetic forces which affects the perception of height, among other things. Follow the signs from the interstate approximately 5 miles for House of Mystery/Oregon Vortex.

Gold Hill, originally on the south bank of the Rogue River opposite the current townsite, was the location of an early gold discovery in Oregon. The Old Oregon Historical Museum, on the road to the Oregon Vortex, has an excellent gun and Indian artifacts collection.   ⊼▲ EXIT 40

Mile 163 (541.5): Exit for Rogue River Route (Oregon Highway 99) to Rock Point and Highway 234 to Gold Hill and Crater Lake Highway (Highway 62).   MP 44 EXIT 43

Mile 165 (539.5): Exit 45A Rogue River Route (Oregon Highway 99), Savage Rapids Dam with fish ladders; steelhead and salmon

viewing in season. There is a gas station with diesel east off the exit.

Highway 99 follows the Rogue River to junction with U.S. Highway 199 (Redwood Highway) just west of Grants Pass. The Rogue River heads in the Cascade Range and flows west into the Pacific Ocean at Gold Beach. It is well known throughout the country for its fishing and white-water rafting. It was named for the fierce Indians in the area, which the French called *Les Coquins*, "the rogues."

Exit 45B, just north , is the access to Valley of the Rogue State Park Campground and highway rest area, both located just off the interstate to the west. Restrooms and pay phones at rest area. Paved loop road through shaded camping area along Rogue River; 22 tent and 100 RV sites, full hookups, dump station and showers.   ▲ MP46 EXIT 45

Mile 168 (536.5): Exit to **ROGUE RIVER** (pop. 1,850) and South Grants Pass via Highway 99. All services are available. Easy access to gas, diesel east off this exit. The town was originally called Woodville, but changed its name to that of the river in 1912. Western author Zane Grey (1875-1939), who had a cabin along the Rogue, helped popularize the river in his novels.   MP 49 EXIT 48

Mile 175 (529.5): Exit to East Grants Pass, U.S. Highway 199 (Redwood Highway) to Crescent City, CA. Highway 199 leads southwest approximately 35 miles to Cave Junction, gateway to Oregon Caves National Monument.   EXIT 55

Mile 178.5 (526): Exit to Grants Pass, Highway 99 and U.S. Highway 199, Oregon caves, and Redwood Highway. Easy access to

major-chain lodging, 24-hour major-chain restaurants, fast-food outlets, gas, diesel, hospital and state police at this exit. Grants Pass city center is to the south.

GRANTS PASS (pop. 16,200) is headquarters for Rogue River outfitters. For information contact the U.S. Forest Service office in Grants Pass or the Grants Pass Visitors Bureau at 1439 NE 6th St. The visitors bureau can also offer directions to campgrounds and scenic overlooks along the Rogue River on roads west of town.

The Rogue River above Grants Pass is heavily fished during the summer for rainbow with seasonal runs of chinook to 40 pounds, steelhead and fall salmon. Numerous boat launches, guide services, parks and fishing resorts are available. Sporting goods stores in Grants Pass are good sources of current fishing conditions and guide trip information.   ⇜▲ EXIT 58

Mile 181 (523.5): Exit to Merlin (unincorporated), which has a gas station with diesel. Access to airport.   EXIT 61

Mile 182.5 (522): Rest area.   MP 63

Mile 185 (519.5): Jump-off Joe Creek.

Mile 186 (518.5): Exit to Hugo (unincorporated). Lodging and RV park.   ▲ EXIT 66

Mile 189 (515.5): Summit of Sexton Mountain Pass (elev. 1,960 feet) and beginning of 6 percent downgrade for 3 miles.

Mile 191 (513.5): Exit to Sunny Valley (unincorporated) and LeLand. This village used to go by the name Grave Creek, but the locals thought the name was too morbid, so they selected the name Sunny Valley because the area is often free of the low fogs which hang in adjacent valleys. Motel, food, gas, campground.   ▲ MP 72 EXIT 71

Mile 194 (510.5): Smith Hill Summit (elev. 1,730 feet).   MP 74

Mile 196 (508.5): Exit to **WOLF CREEK** (unincorporated); food, gas, lodging and camping available. Easy on-off access to this small community and historic Wolf Creek Tavern, 0.5 mile west of interstate.

Wolf Creek Tavern was one of 60 stage stops on the Portland-Sacramento stage route where travelers could get a night's rest and meals and where new horses and drivers took over. It remained in almost continual operation between 1868 and 1873. Wolf Creek Tavern was restored in 1979 and today offers food and lodging as it did in the 1800s and it is well worth a stop. There is a general store across the street and a family restaurant and gas station with diesel nearby. Drive to the end of Main Street (follow signs) for Wolf Creek Josephine County Park; 18 tent/RV campsites.   ▲ MP 77 EXIT 76

Mile 198 (506.5): Exit (southbound only) to Speaker Road.   EXIT 78

Mile 199.5 (505): Summit of Stage Road Pass (elev. 1,830 feet).   MP 80

Mile 200.5 (504): Leaving Josephine County, entering Douglas County, northbound. Douglas County produces more sheep than any other county in Oregon. Lumbering and sawmilling are the principal industries.

Mile 201 (503.5): Exit to Glendale (pop. 712), family restaurant, drive-in.   EXIT 80

Mile 202 (502.5): Rest area with pay phones and restrooms.   MP 82

Mile 203 (501.5): Exit to Barton Road (northbound only).   EXIT 83

Mile 206 (498.5): Exit to Quines Creek Road and Barton Road. There is a gas station with diesel and convenience store east of this exit; also a 24-hour cafe and a RV park.   ▲ EXIT 86

Mile 208 (496.5): Exit to Azalea (unincorporated); gas available. The town was named for the abundance of azalea plants which grow in the area.   EXIT 88

Mile 210 (494.5): Summit of Canyon Creek Pass (elev. 2,020 feet).

Mile 215 (489.5): Exit to Canyon Creek. North to Roseburg, Interstate 5 is roughly paralleled by the South Fork Umpqua River, a fine fishing stream.   ⬅ MP 96 EXIT 95

Mile 218 (486.5): Exit to Canyonville and Days Creek and Oregon Highway 227. Highway 227 junctions with Highway 62 to Crater Lake. Easy access to food and gas at this exit. CANYONVILLE (pop. 1,350) has all services available.

Canyonville is situated at the north end of Canyon Creek canyon, the area which offered so much trouble for immigrants en route to the Willamette Valley in 1846. The total descent from the pass at the head of Canyon Creek to Canyonville is nearly 1,300 feet.   EXIT 98

Mile 219 (485.5): Exit to North Canyonville. Southbound to Crater Lake and Highway 227. Easy access to lodging and truck stop with diesel at this exit. Information center. Northbound access to Charles V. Stanton Douglas County Park on the east side of the interstate (follow signs); 40 tent/RV campsites, picnic tables, restrooms and showers.   ▲ MP 100 EXIT 99

Mile 220.5 (484): South Umpqua River.

Mile 221 (483.5): Exit for junction with Highway 99 west to Riddle, site of the Hanna Nickel Mine. Southbound access for county park campground. See **Mile 219**.   EXIT 101

Mile 221.5 (483): South Umpqua River. Interstate 5 parallels the South Umpqua north to Roseburg, where it meets the North Umpqua at River Forks.

Mile 222 (482.5): Exit to Gazley Road. RV park.   ▲ EXIT 102

Mile 222.5 (482): Wide gravel turnout (southbound only) next to the Umpqua River.   MP 103

Mile 223 (481.5): Exit to Tri City and Highway 99 to Riddle. Easy access to gas stations, diesel, restaurant and fast-food outlet at this exit.   MP 104 EXIT 103

A zebra grazes in the Africa section of Wildlife Safari, Mile 239.   (Tom Barr)

Mile 225.5 (479): South Umpqua River.

Mile 226 (478.5): Exit to Weaver Road.   MP 107 EXIT 106

Mile 228 (476.5): Exit for junction with Highway 99 to MYRTLE CREEK (pop. 3,225). All services available. The town, established in 1854, was named for the groves of Oregon myrtle which grow in the area.   MP 109 EXIT 108

Mile 230 (474.5): Exit to Boomer Hill Road.   MP 111 EXIT 110

Mile 231 (473.5): Weigh station (northbound).

Mile 231.5 (473): Rest area (southbound access).   MP 112

Mile 232 (472.5): Rest area (northbound access) and junction with Highway 99 to Dillard and Winston (see **Mile 239**) and Highway 42 to Coos Bay.   EXIT 112

Mile 232.5 (472): South Umpqua River.

Mile 233 (471.5): Exit to Round Prairie and Clarks Branch Road. Motel.   EXIT 113

Mile 239 (465.5): Exit for junction with Highways 99 south and 42 west to Winston (4 miles) and Coos Bay (75 miles). This is the access to the 600-acre Wildlife Safari reserve, a drive-through wild animal park, located a few miles west of the interstate; open year-round.

See feature this section.   ▲★ MP 120 EXIT 119

Mile 240 (464.5): Exit for junction with Highway 99 north to the Green District, Roseburg. For Roseburg city center, use Exit 124. Lodging and camping.   ▲ EXIT 120

Mile 240.5 (464): South Umpqua River.

Mile 241 (463.5): Exit to McLain Avenue in Roseburg.   MP 122 EXIT 121

Mile 243 (461.5): Exit to Umpqua Park, Douglas County Fairgrounds and museum in Roseburg. Camping.   ▲ EXIT 123

Mile 244 (460.5): Exit to Roseburg city center and the junction with Oregon Highway 138 (North Umpqua Highway). Food and gas are available at this exit. ROSEBURG (pop. 16,240) city center is to the east; all services available with 15 motels and 70 restaurants including major-chain 24-hour restaurants and fast-food outlets. Information center.

Aaron Rose chose this location to settle in 1851, after filing for land under the Land Claim Act of 1850. Rose donated land for a public school and gave free lots to several persons wishing to establish commercial outlets. Rose wanted his city to be selected as the county seat and generously extended the hospitality of his tavern for outlying settlers who wished to stop by and vote. His generosity worked and the town became the county seat. Rose donated land for the courthouse.

The Rogue River Indian Wars of 1855-56 brought hundreds of soldiers into the area, which helped the local businesses prosper. In 1857, the town was renamed Roseburg in honor of Aaron Rose.

Roseburg touts itself as the "Timber Capital of the World," and the community offers historical displays, excellent fishing and hunting and wineries.

Highway 138 follows the North Umpqua River east. This is a scenic route to Crater Lake National Park (approximately 100 miles) and Diamond Lake. The North Fork Umpqua is one of the finest fishing streams in Oregon. Sporting goods dealers in Roseburg can provide current fishing information   ⬅ EXIT 124

Mile 245 (459.5): Exit to Roseburg, Garden Valley Boulevard. Easy access to restaurants and fast-food outlets, major-chain lodging, gas and diesel. Airport to east of freeway. Roseburg city center is approximately 2 miles east (follow signs).

Private campground and River Forks Park are located 6.5 miles west from this exit. Head west on Garden Valley Road (follow signs for camping) 4.6 miles; turn left at llama farm and continue 1.9 miles for private campground and River Forks Douglas County Park. River Forks Park has picnicking and a playground; no dogs allowed May to September. It was named for the spectacular meeting of the North and South Umpqua rivers here.   ▲ EXIT 125

Mile 248.5 (456): North Umpqua River.

Wildlife Safari

The rhino stood a few feet from the edge of the road and stared at the motorhome brought to a halt by the ostriches. One ostrich was in the middle of the road, inches from the front bumper. The other was face-to-face with the driver, separated only by the vehicle's window.

This is Wildlife Safari, where 550 birds and animals — 116 species — roam over 600 acres. Motorists on the 1½-hour auto tour will travel through the Asian section, filled with cheetahs and tigers, past ape and elephant islands to the North American compound, where Roosevelt elk, desert bighorn sheep, pronghorn antelope and bison roam. In the African section are hippo ponds, lions, white bearded gnus and zebras.

Southern Oregon's climate is moderate and closely resembles many habitats and areas of Africa. With plenty of open space and a hospitable environment, Wildlife Safari has become a prime breeding ground for many animals. (The endangered cheetahs have reproduced 97 cubs here.) Unlike many zoos and wild animal parks where species are represented by 1 or 2 animals, herds of animals roam here, increasing the possibility of reproduction.

In addition to the auto tour, there is Safari Village, where attractions include flamingo ponds, bear and timber wolf compounds, and a walk-in zoo. There are elephant and camel rides, or visitors may board a narrow-gauge train for a short ride by the bear exhibit. Birds of prey demonstration is presented several times daily, and there are trained animal shows and a wildlife theater. Visitor facilities include a restaurant, gift shop, RV park for self-contained vehicles, picnic area, and pet kennels (pets are not allowed on the auto tour).

Wildlife Safari is located 6 miles south of Roseburg, OR, and 4 miles west of Exit 119 on Interstate 5 (**Mile 239**). It is open year-round. Summer hours are: 8:30 a.m. to 8 p.m., daily. Admission is $1 per vehicle plus $7.50 adults; $6 over 65 years; $5.25 ages 4 to 12; 3 and under, free. Admission includes 2 drive-throughs on the same date, plus Safari Village attractions. Safari Village-only admission: $2 adults, $1 children.

Mile 249 (455.5): Exit to Winchester, North Roseburg and Highway 99 to Wilbur. This is the access to Umpqua Community College and Amacher Park. Amacher Douglas County Park has 30 tent/RV campsites, full hookups, restrooms and showers. The campground is located 0.5 mile south of Winchester on Highway 99.

WINCHESTER is the town that paid the price of Roseburg's success. It had been the county seat and a prospering community until Aaron Rose promoted Roseburg. The town was named after the Winchester brothers, who were part of a San Francisco exploring expedition on the Umpqua River in the 1850s. ▲ EXIT 129

Mile 250 (454.5): Weigh station (southbound) with phone. MP 150

Mile 255 (449.5): Exit to WILBUR and northbound access to Sutherlin (pop. 4,500). Wilbur was named for James H. Wilbur, D.D., known as Father Wilbur, who was one of Oregon's best-known Methodist ministers and who founded several educational institutions. EXIT 135

Mile 256 (448.5): Exit to SUTHERLIN (pop. 4,500) and ELKTON (pop. 175) via Highway 138. Access to Oregon beaches. Gas, fast-food outlets, restaurants, lodging and camping. Information center. Sutherlin has all services available. ▲ EXIT 136

Mile 257 (447.5): Crossing Calpulia Creek.

Mile 258 (446.5): Northbound exit to Oakland Historic District, an easy and worthwhile side trip. Head east on paved 2-lane winding road through a rural area and follow signs 1.6 miles to OAKLAND (pop. 850). Food service available.

Settled in the 1850s, Oakland prospered first as a trading center and mail point for the surrounding area; then as a shipping center on the railroad between Portland and San Francisco; and finally as a turkey ranching and shipping center in the 1900s. The present-day economy is based on farming, cattle and sheep ranching. Many of the town's early structures remain and house local businesses. The area is noted for its covered bridges.

Follow north-south signs from Oakland to continue on the interstate. ★ EXIT 138

Mile 260.5 (444): Southbound exit to Oakland Historic District (see **Mile 258**). EXIT 138

Mile 262 (442.5): Exit to Metz Hill. EXIT 142

Mile 262.5 (442): Rest area with restrooms and pay phone.

Mile 266 (438.5): Exit to Rice Valley and northbound access to Rice Hill (food, gas, diesel, lodging). Rice Hill was named for I.F. Rice who settled here in 1850, and the hill which presented a problem for pioneer travelers and railroad construction crews. EXIT 146

Mile 268 (436.5): Exit to Rice Hill (southbound only), easy access to food, gas, diesel and lodging east of the interstate. MP 149 EXIT 148

Mile 270 (434.5): Exit to YONCALLA (pop. 870), Drain and Red Hill; Highway 99 heads north to junction with Highway 38 to Reedsport. Yoncalla is an Indian word meaning "home of the eagles," and refers to the mountain near this town.

DRAIN (pop. 1,070) was named for a pioneer settler, Charles Drain, who donated 60 acres to the railroad for a total sum of $1, "in consideration of establishing a station and laying out a town to be called Drain." He and his son, J.C. Drain, served terms on the Oregon legislature and the younger Drain became speaker of the house. A Queen Anne-style house here, built in 1893, is on the National Register of Historic Places. RV park, motel. ▲ EXIT 150

Mile 274 (430.5): Exit to Scotts Valley, Yoncalla and Elkhead. EXIT 154

Mile 279 (425.5): Exit to Elk Creek and Cox Road. EXIT 159

Mile 280 (424.5): Exit to Salt Springs Road. MP 160 EXIT 160

Mile 281 (423.5): Exit (northbound only) to Anlauf and Lorane, both were railroad towns during their founding. EXIT 161

Mile 282 (422.5): Exit to Drain and Elkton; Highway 99 heads south to junction with Highway 38 to Reedsport. EXIT 162

Mile 283 (421.5): Exit to Curtin and Lorane. There are gas stations, diesel, truck stop, a motel and a 24-hour restaurant at this exit. EXIT 163

Mile 290 (414.5): Exit for junction with Highway 99 to London Road and Cottage Grove Lake. EXIT 170

Mile 291.5 (413): Coast Fork Willamette River. Northbound travelers may note the change in vegetation as the interstate enters the Willamette River valley.

Mile 294 (410.5): Exit to COTTAGE GROVE (pop. 6,915) and Dorena Lake. All services available including motels, restaurants, fast-food outlets and information center.

There is access to Baker Bay Lane County Park on Dorena Lake, 8 miles east on a county road; swimming, boating, fishing and camping. ▲ EXIT 174

Mile 296 (408.5): Exit to Saginaw, named after the town in Michigan. Vehicles with loads over 12 feet wide must use this exit. EXIT 176

Mile 298 (406.5): Rest area with restrooms, phones and travel information.

Mile 300 (404.5): Coast Fork Willamette

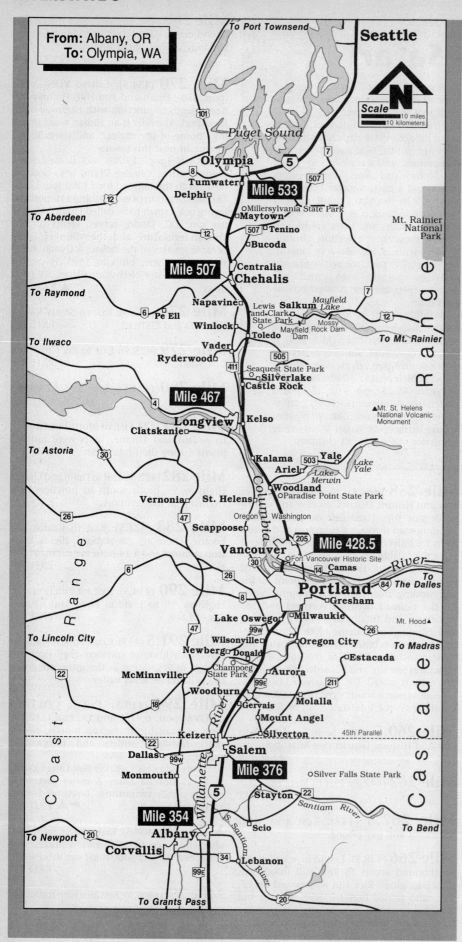

From: Albany, OR
To: Olympia, WA

Scale
10 miles
10 kilometers

To Port Townsend

Seattle

Puget Sound

Olympia

Mile 533

Tumwater

Delphi

To Aberdeen

Millersylvania State Park

Maytown

Tenino

Bucoda

Mt. Rainier National Park

Mile 507

Centralia
Chehalis

To Raymond

Napavine

Pe Ell

Salkum

Mayfield Lake

Lewis and Clark State Park

Mayfield Rock Dam

Mossy Rock Dam

To Mt. Rainier

Winlock

Toledo

To Ilwaco

Vader

Ryderwood

Seaquest State Park

Silverlake

Castle Rock

Mile 467

Longview

Kelso

Mt. St. Helens National Volcanic Monument

Clatskanie

To Astoria

Kalama

Ariel

Yale

Lake Yale

Lake Merwin

Woodland

Paradise Point State Park

Vernonia

St. Helens

Scappoose

Oregon / Washington

Columbia River

Mile 428.5

Vancouver

Fort Vancouver Historic Site

Camas

To The Dalles

Portland

Gresham

Lake Oswego

Milwaukie

Mt. Hood

To Lincoln City

Wilsonville

Oregon City

To Madras

Newberg

Donald

McMinnville

Champoeg State Park

Aurora

Estacada

Woodburn

Gervais

Molalla

Mount Angel

Keizer

Silverton

45th Parallel

Dallas

Salem

Mile 376

Monmouth

Silver Falls State Park

Stayton

Santiam River

Mile 354

Scio

To Bend

Albany

Corvallis

To Newport

Lebanon

S. Santiam River

To Grants Pass

Coast Range

Cascade Range

Willamette River

River. Northbound, the highway cuts a flat, straight line up the Willamette Valley. The Coast Range is to the west and the Cascade Range is to the east. MP 180

Mile 302 (402.5): Exit to **CRESWELL** (pop. 1,975), easy access to gas, diesel, fast-food outlets, motel, campground, information center, west off the exit. ▲ EXIT 182

Mile 303.5 (401): Creswell airstrip to the east.

Mile 305.5 (399): Exit (northbound only) to Goshen. EXIT 186

Mile 308 (396.5): Exit 188A is the junction with Oregon Highway 58 (Willamette Highway) to Oakridge, Klamath Falls and Highway 99 to Goshen. Exit 188B is the junction with Highway 99 south to Goshen. EXIT 188

Mile 309 (395.5): Exit to 30th Avenue in Eugene, access to Lane Community College and South Eugene. Camping. ▲ EXIT 189

Mile 311 (393.5): Exit to Glenwood, Springfield and East Eugene. Easy access to food, gas and major-chain lodging west off this exit. EXIT 191

Mile 312 (392.5): Exit for junction with Highway 99 to Eugene and northbound access to the city center via Highways 99/126 (Franklin Boulevard).

EUGENE (pop. 108,770) is a major wood products center and site of the University of Oregon, which serves some 16,000 students. All services are available. Special events are held at the Hult Center for the Performing Arts, located downtown adjacent the hotel-conference complex. The Fifth Street Public Market offers unique shopping opportunities. Eugene has an extensive system of bicycle and jogging trails and has more than 70 parks.

The town was named after pioneer Eugene F. Skinner, whose wife was the first white woman to live in Lane County and whose daughter was the first white child born in the county. EXIT 192

Mile 313 (391.5): Willamette River. The Willamette is a long, slow powerful river with literally dozens of sport fish species. Fishing regulations vary on this major Columbia River tributary and state pamphlets should be consulted before tackling it.

Mile 314 (390.5): Exit to junction of Highway 126 and Interstate 105 to Eugene and Springfield. Exit 194A is access to Springfield east, and McKenzie River. Southbound Exit 194B permits access to University of Oregon, city center and Valley River Center (the largest shopping center in the southern Willamette Valley) located off Interstate 105.

SPRINGFIELD (pop. 41,080), east of Interstate 5, is the fourth-largest city in Oregon; all services available.

Access to the McKenzie River via Highway 126 east. The McKenzie is almost 90 miles long, and is where the McKenzie-style river drift boat originated. The double-ended, rocker-bottomed craft, built to float on just an inch or so of water yet safely ride out the wildest white water, is the standard for river fishing craft throughout the West. Now known as drift boats, the craft were originally called McKenzies after this river.

The McKenzie River is best known as a trout stream, generously endowed with camp-sites, boat launches and access areas. Local tackle shops can recommend fishing and white-water guides.

Twelve miles west on Highway 126 is Fern Ridge Reservoir, the most popular water recreation area near Eugene. The Long Tom River impoundment has 6 launch ramps, several picnic sites and a commercial camp-ground. The lake is good for waterskiing and fishing. It's open year-round. No boat rentals. ⚓●▲ EXIT 194

Mile 315 (389.5): Exit 195 is the north-bound access to Florence, North Springfield, Junction and Eugene airport. Southbound Exit 195A provides access to Springfield and Exit 195B leads to Santa Clara and Florence. There is easy access to family and fast-food restau-rants, diesel and gas, and major-chain lodging at these exits. Armitage State Park, with 32 campsites, is located on Coburg Road to the west. ▲ EXIT 195

Mile 319 (385.5): Exit to COBURG (pop. 665), a national historic district. Easy access to food, lodging, gas and diesel at this exit. Campground. ▲ MP 200 EXIT 199

Mile 326 (378.5): Rest area with restrooms and phone.

Mile 329 (375.5): Exit to Harrisburg and Junction City. There is easy access to gas at the exit. RV park. ▲ EXIT 209

Mile 334 (370.5): After the long, flat drive through the Willamette Valley, southbound travelers will notice the hump-shaped Coburg Hills to the east.

Mile 336 (368.5): Exit to Halsey and Highway 228 to Brownsville. This is the access to the Linn County Historical Museum. Food, gas, diesel, lodging and market are available east off this exit. EXIT 216

Mile 337 (367.5): Crossing Calapooya River.

Mile 348 (356.5): Exit for junction with Highway 34 to Corvallis, Lebanon and Sweet Home. There is easy access to gas, diesel, campground and a 24-hour restaurant at this exit. Corvallis, about 10 miles west, is the site of Oregon State University. ▲ EXIT 228

Mile 353 (351.5): Exit for junction with U.S. Highway 20 (Santiam Highway) to Albany, Lebanon and Sweet Home. North-bound access to Albany city center via Highway 20 west and Pacific Boulevard. Family restaurants, lodging, gas, diesel. EXIT 233

Mile 354 (350.5): Exit 234A east to municipal airport and Knox Butte. Exit 234B is the junction with Highway 99 east to Albany. Easy access to restaurants, fast-food outlets, gas, diesel and lodging at this exit. Information center. Just west of the interstate exit is Waverly Lake Park where there is a small lake stocked with panfish and restricted to anglers under 18 years old.

Drive west 2 miles on Highway 99 east/Pacific Boulevard for downtown ALBANY (pop. 28,020) and historic district (follow signs). Fast-food outlets, shopping and gas stations are located along Highway 99 east/Pacific Boulevard. Albany offers 9 motels and 71 restaurants.

Albany's historic districts (Hackleman, Monteith and downtown) are well known for the varied architectural styles of their build-ings, constructed between the 1840s and 1920s. The buildings are detailed in a guide available from the Albany Chamber of Commerce, 435 W. 1st, P.O. Box 548, Albany, OR 97321.

Albany was named after Albany, NY, by its founders who purchased the land for the city for $400 and a horse. Some 500 Chinese workers who had been brought to the valley to work on the railroad, dug the Santiam Canal, bringing water and hydropower to the city.

Albany is the retail center of the mid-Willamette Valley and touts itself as the "Ryegrass Capital of the World." It is the center of the world's foremost grass seed regions. EXIT 234

Mile 355 (349.5): Exit to Viewcrest and MILLERSBURG (pop. 550), site of 2 wood processing plants, which sometimes give off a noxious odor. MP 236 EXIT 235

Mile 355.5 (349): Southbound exit to Viewcrest. EXIT 237

Mile 358 (346.5): Exit to Scio (pop. 590) and Jefferson. EXIT 238

Mile 359 (345.5): Exit to Dever and Conner. EXIT 239

Mile 360 (344.5): Exit to Hoefer Road. Gas and diesel available. MP 240 EXIT 240

Mile 360.5 (344): Santiam River. The North and South forks of the Santiam meet a few miles north of Albany and create one of the most productive fishing streams in the state. The North Fork is paralleled by Highway 22 and the South Fork by Highway 20. ⚓

Mile 361 (343.5): Rest area with restrooms and pay phone.

Mile 362 (342.5): Exit to Talbot Road. MP 242 EXIT 242

Mile 363 (341.5): Exit to Ankeny Hill. No services, but easy access to Ankeny National Wildlife Refuge; a good opportunity for bird-watching and to see area farms (follow signs). MP 244 EXIT 243

Mile 364 (340.5): Exit to Jefferson. EXIT 244

Mile 368 (336.5): Exit to Sunnyside and Turner. There is a gas station with diesel west of the exit. This is the access to the Enchanted Forest theme park and RV park east of the interstate. Major-chain fast-food outlets. ▲ MP 249 EXIT 248

Mile 369 (335.5): Exit (northbound only) to Salem, Western Oregon State College and museum via Highway 99. EXIT 249

Mile 373 (331.5): Exit for junction with Oregon Highway 22 (North Santiam Highway) east to Stayton and Detroit Lake, and west (via Mission Street) to the airport, downtown Sa-lem and Willamette University. Major-chain motels, family restaurant, campground.

Stayton, 17 miles east via Highway 22, is the site of a historic woolen mill (still oper-ating).

Silver Falls State Park, 25 miles east via Highways 22 and 214, offers 10 waterfalls, riding and hiking trails, and 52 campsites. A scenic park, worth the drive. ▲ EXIT 253

Mile 376 (328.5): Exit to Market Street, access to downtown SALEM (pop. 96,830), shopping mall and state fairgrounds. Easy access to gas, major-chain lodging, family and 24-hour restaurants, fast-food outlets at this exit. Salem is the capital of Oregon and the site of Willamette University. Scheduled tours of the capitol building weekdays in summer. Salem offers 17 motels and 195 restaurants.

Salem is the third-largest city in Oregon and is the center of the fertile Willamette Valley between Portland and Eugene. The 4 biggest industries in Salem are government, food processing, light manufacturing and wood products. Boise Cascade has a fine paper and container plant here.

Salem offers several parks: Mission Mill Village on Mill Street SE is a 4.5-acre park featuring a visitor center, the Thomas Kay Woolen Mill, Marion Museum, John D. Boone House and Jason Lee House; Deepwood Estate on Mission Street SE (Highway 22) is a Queen Anne-style home located in a 6-acre garden; and Bush House, located in the 89-acre Pasture Park on Mission Street SE, was built in 1877. The state capitol on Court Street also has extensive grounds. MP 256 EXIT 256

Mile 378 (326.5): Exit (northbound only) for junction with Highway 99 east (Salem Parkway) to Salem and access to Chemeketa Community College plus Salem historic museums, fairgrounds and state capitol. Gas and lodging available. MP 259 EXIT 258

Mile 379.5 (325): Northbound access to Keizer (unincorporated).

Southbound Exit 260A leads to the Salem Parkway; Exit 260B to Keizer, Chemawa Road and Western Oregon State College. Fast-food restaurant. EXIT 260

Mile 380 (324.5): Sign marks the 45th parallel, halfway between the equator and the North Pole. MP 260

Mile 382.5 (322): Commercial flower fields either side of highway.

Mile 383 (321.5): Exit to Brooks (unincorporated), a small farming community, and access to Gervais (pop. 745). There is a truck stop with diesel west of the exit. Drive west approximately 6 miles to Maud Williamson and Willamette Mission state parks (day use only) and Wheatland ferry.   EXIT 263

Mile 391 (313.5): Exit to Woodburn, Silverton and Oregon Highway 214 to St. Paul, Hubbard and Mount Angel; and Oregon Highway 219 west to Newberg. Family restaurants and fast-food outlets, motels, gas, diesel and RV park are available.

Commercial flower crops grow north of Salem, OR.   (L. Linkhart)

MOUNT ANGEL (pop. 2,970) is the home of the Benedictine Mount Angel Abbey. Mount Angel's Oktoberfest, held in September, is a popular annual event.

The abbey is a monastery of Benedictine monks founded by Fr. Adelelm Odermatt and a group of monks from the Abbey of Engelberg in Switzerland. The main work of the abbey for the last 100 years has been the education of young men for the Catholic priesthood. The church, retreat house and library are open to guests and visitors daily. For further information, write Mount Angel Abbey/Seminary, St. Benedict, OR 97373.

WOODBURN (pop. 12,080) was named after a large fire which grew out of control. The railroad right-of-way passed through a grove of fir trees and the trees were felled to provide room for the tracks. The crews waited until winter to burn the slash and dead trees, but the fire went out of control and destroyed the standing timber as well as the felled trees.

Woodburn is now a busy agricultural community with all services available.
▲ EXIT 271

Mile 394 (310.5): Southbound weigh station.

Mile 398 (306.5): Exit to DONALD (pop. 275) and Aurora. There is a truck stop with diesel on the west side of this exit, an RV park on the east side.

AURORA (pop. 535), located 3 miles east of the interstate, is a National Historic Landmark District. Founded as a religious colony in the 1850s and named after the daughter of the founder, Dr. William Keil, many of the original buildings of the Aurora Colony now house antique stores. Arts and crafts are preserved at the Ox Barn Museum.

Drive 6 miles west on a winding 2-lane road through farming area for Champoeg State Park (follow signs). The park has a visitor center, museum, large picnic area on the Willamette River and a 48-site campground. Champoeg was the site of the first Hudson's Bay Co. warehouse and was later a shipping point for Willamette Valley wheat. A provincial government was established at Champoeg in 1843 but the town was destroyed by a flood in 1861. An outdoor historical pageant is presented Friday, Saturday and Sunday nights in July.

The town of NEWBERG (pop. 11,630), site of Herbert Hoover's boyhood home, is 7 miles northwest of Champoeg. Hoover was the only president to have lived in Oregon. Newberg was settled by Quakers. ▲ MP 279 EXIT 278

Mile 401.5 (303): Rest area and travel information center.

Mile 403 (301.5): Exit to the Charbonneau District and CANBY (pop. 7,750). Canby has 15 restaurants and a motel.

Southbound Exit 282A is the access to Canby and Hubbard; Exit 282B to the Charbonneau District and Aurora, family restaurants.   EXIT 282

Mile 403.5 (301): Willamette River. Exit to WILSONVILLE (pop. 5,025). Easy access to family restaurants, fast-food outlets, major-chain motel, gas stations, hospital and information center.   MP 283 EXIT 283

Mile 406 (298.5): Exit to Stafford, North Wilsonville and Boones Ferry Road. Hotels, major-chain restaurants, gas, diesel.
EXIT 286

Mile 408 (296.5): Exit for junction with Interstate 205 to WEST LINN (pop. 14,020), Oregon City and Interstate 84 to Portland International Airport.

OREGON CITY (pop. 15,030) was the first incorporated city west of the Mississippi River. It was the end of the Oregon Trail and the first territorial capital of Oregon. It is a city of firsts: It had the West's first government, newspaper, library, Protestant church, mint, water-powered industry, Catholic archdioces, Masonic lodge and first court of record.

The End of the Oregon Trail interpretative center, located at 5th and Washington Street, is one of several historical information centers. Admission fee.

Interstate 205 is a 4- to 6-lane divided highway which bypasses downtown Portland and rejoins Interstate 5 at **Mile 435** in Washington. This 37-mile route is somewhat longer than Interstate 5, but may be less congested during peak traffic times. (See Alternate Route Interstate 205 log this section.)   EXIT 288

Mile 409 (295.5): Exit to TUALATIN (pop. 12,160) and SHERWOOD (pop. 2,990). Major-chain motels and restaurants, gas, trailer park available.   ▲ MP 289 EXIT 289

Mile 409.5 (295): Tualatin River.

Mile 410 (294.5): Exit to Durham (pop. 790) and Lake Oswego. Family restaurants and fast-food outlets, gas and diesel available at this exit.   EXIT 290

Mile 411 (293.5): Exit to Carman Drive, King City (pop. 2,010) and access to Oregon Business Park with all services available.
EXIT 291

Mile 412 (292.5): Exit for junction with Highway 217 to LAKE OSWEGO (pop. 28,360), a suburb of Portland, Beaverton and the Sunset Highway.   EXIT 292

Mile 413 (291.5): Exit to Haines Street, Portland Community College and Silvania.
EXIT 293

Mile 414 (290.5): Exit to TIGARD (pop. 25,510), Newberg and Highway 99 west. All services available. This is the access to Highway 18 to McMinnville and Lincoln City. Northbound access to Barbur Boulevard. Motels and fast-food outlets.   EXIT 294

Mile 415 (289.5): Exit to Capitol Highway and access to food, gas, lodging, Sylvania, Portland Community College and Taylor's Ferry Road.   EXIT 295

Mile 416 (288.5): Exit 296A (southbound only) to Barbur Boulevard; all services available. Just north is Exit 296B (southbound only) to Multnomah Boulevard.   EXIT 296

Mile 417 (287.5): Exit to Terwilliger Boulevard S. and access to Lewis and Clark College, Oregon Health Science University. This exit is closed to trucks over 15 tons.   EXIT 297

Mile 418.5 (286): Exit to Corbett Avenue and John's Landing (northbound only).
EXIT 298

Mile 419 (285.5): Exit to Lake Oswego via Highway 43 (SW Macadam Street). Ross Island Bridge.   EXIT 299A

Mile 419.5 (286): Northbound exit on west side of freeway to city center, Beaverton, Interstate 405 and U.S. Highway 26.
EXIT 299B

Mile 420 (284.5): Exit to Portland city center, U.S. Highways 26 and 99 east to Oregon City and **MILWAUKIE** (pop. 19,045). Exit 300B northbound is access to Water Avenue.   EXIT 300B

Mile 420.5 (284): The Marquam Bridge spans the Willamette River. **PORTLAND** (pop. 429,410) lies on either side of the Willamette River. The city center is on the west side. (See Portland in the MAJOR CITIES section.)

Mile 421 (283.5): Exit for junction with Interstate 84 and U.S. Highway 30 to Mount Hood and Gresham. Interstate 84 is the scenic route east up the Columbia River gorge. Turn to the INTERSTATE 84 section for log.
EXIT 301

Mile 422 (282.5): Exit 302A is access to Portland city center and Broadway Bridge, the Coliseum and Lloyd Center (shopping).

Just north is Exit 302B, the junctions of Interstate 405 and U.S. Highway 30 to Beaverton, Oregon beaches and St. Helens (pop. 7,525). Exit 302C northbound is to Swan Island.   EXIT 302

Mile 423 (281.5): Exit to Alberta Street and Swan Island, Killingsworth, Interstate Avenue Hospital.   EXIT 303

Mile 424 (280.5): Exit to Portland Boulevard, access to University of Portland.
EXIT 304

Mile 424.5 (280): Exit 305A to Lombard Street east; U.S. Highway 30 bypass, and Portland International Airport (northbound only); Exit 305B (northbound only) to U.S. Highway 30 bypass and Lombard Street west.
EXIT 305

Mile 426 (278.5): Exit 306B southbound to Interstate Avenue, U.S. Highway 30 bypass, Delta Park and Lombard Street. It is also the access to Portland Meadows, Portland International Raceway and Multnomah Kennel Club's greyhound race track, the only greyhound race track in the Northwest. Major-chain pancake restaurant and fast-food outlets. Exit 306A northbound is to Columbia Boulevard. Exit 306B northbound is access to Delta Park and Expo Center.   EXIT 306

Mile 427 (277.5): Exit to Union Avenue, Marine Drive, the Rivergate area, shipping terminals T4, T5 and T6 and the junction with Highway 99 east. Truck stop.   EXIT 307

Mile 428 (276.5): Exit to turnoff for Jantzen Beach. All services available. PUC permits. Major-chain motel, fast-food outlets, gas.   EXIT 308

Alternate Route Interstate 205

Travelers passing through Portland, OR, on their way south or north may wish to avoid the heavy traffic of Interstate 5 by taking Interstate 205.

This short highway log is an alternate route through Portland which leaves Interstate 5 at **Mile 408** and rejoins the main highway at **Mile 435** in Washington.

In terms of distance, the route is longer, but it may be quicker during heavy traffic hours and is a thoroughfare for north-south travelers passing through Portland. It also provides easier access to travelers intending to use Interstate 84 east.

This log begins at **Mile 408** and continues north 37 miles to the junction with Interstate 5 in Washington.

Mile 0 (37): South junction with Interstate 5.

Mile 3 (34): Exit 3 to Stafford Road and access to Lake Oswego.

Mile 4 (33): Tualatin River.

Mile 6 (31): Exit 6 to 10th Street.

Mile 7 (30): Viewpoint (northbound) of snowcapped Mount Hood (elev. 11,235 feet), Oregon's only active volcano.

Mile 8 (29): Exit 9 is the junction with Highway 99 east to Oregon City, Gladstone and access to McLoughlin House Historic Site.

Mile 10 (27): Exit 10 to Oregon City and access to Oregon Trail Visitor Center.

Mile 11 (26): Exit 11 to Gladstone.

Mile 12 (25): Exit 12 to Estacada, Mount Hood, Oregon Highways 212 and 224 east; all services available.

Mile 13 (24): Exit 13 to 82nd Avenue, Milwaukie and access to Clackamas city center. All services available.

Mile 17 (20): Exit 17 to Foster Road.

Mile 19 (18): Exit 19 to Highway 26, Powell Boulevard W., and Division Street E.

Mile 20 (17): Exit 20 to Washington Street, Stark Street and shopping mall.

Mile 21 (16): Exit 21 to Glisan Street.

Mile 22 (15): Exit 22 to Interstate 84, U.S. Highway 30 and The Dalles. Travelers headed east on Interstate 84 should take this exit and turn to the INTERSTATE 84 highway log.

Mile 23 (14): Exit 23A to U.S. Highway 30 east bypass and Sandy Boulevard.

Just north is Exit 23B to U.S. Highway 30 west and Columbia Boulevard.

Mile 24 (13): Exit 24A to the Portland airport. Just north is Exit 24B to 122nd Avenue.

Mile 25 (12): Columbia River crossing via Glenn Jackson Bridge marks the border between Oregon and Washington.

Mile 27 (10): Exit 27 to Vancouver, Camas and Washington Highway 14.

Mile 28 (9): Exit 28 to Mill Plain Road.

Mile 30 (7): Exit 30 to Orchards, Vancouver and Washington Highway 500.

Mile 32 (5): Exit 32 to NE 83rd Street, Andresen Road and access to Battle Ground.

Mile 36 (1): Exit 36 to NE 134th Street and NE 20th Avenue.

Mile 37 (0): North junction with Interstate 5 at **Mile 435.**

Mile 428.5 (276): Columbia River, the border between Oregon and Washington. Northbound travelers are entering Vancouver, WA.

Mile 429 (275.5): Exit 1A is the junction with Washington Highway 14 east to Camas. Just north is Exit 1B to Fort Vancouver National Historic Site, Clark College, city center, Mill Plain Boulevard and 4th Plain Boulevard. Exit 1C is southbound exit to Fort Vancouver and Mill Plain Boulevard. North of this exit is Exit 1D which is to E. 4th Plain Boulevard, west to Fort Vancouver, and the junction with Highway 501.

Highway 14 parallels the north bank of the Columbia River through the famed Columbia Gorge and junctions with Interstate 82 180 miles east from here.

VANCOUVER (pop. 43,290) is the oldest continuous settlement in the Northwest. Today, it is an important navigation center as the terminus of the Columbia channel at the Pacific Ocean. It is the gateway for ocean-going vessels headed to ports in Washington, Oregon and Idaho via the Columbia and Snake rivers.

Among the many attractions in Vancouver is the Clark County Historical Museum, located at 1511 Main St.; the Fort Vancouver barracks located at 1106 E. Evergreen St.; the Grist Mill on Cedar Creek, north of Vancouver (believed to be the only remaining 19th century grist mill in the state) and Fort Vancouver National Historical Site, located at 1501 E. Evergreen Blvd.   EXIT 1

Mile 430 (274.5): Exit for junction with Washington Highway 500 east to Orchards and 39th Street, northbound.   MP 2 EXIT 2

Mile 431 (273.5): Exit to Main Street and access to hospital facilities. This is the northbound access to Hazel Dell and NE 99th Street.   EXIT 3

Mile 432 (272.5): Exit to NE 78th Street. Easy access on either side of this exit to motels, major-chain 24-hour restaurants, fast-food outlets and gas.   EXIT 4

Mile 435 (269.5): Exit for junction with Interstate 205 (see **Mile 408** and Alternate Route Interstate 205 log this section). It also leads to Highway 14, Interstate 84 and north to NE 134th Street and Hazel Dell. Motels, fast-food outlets and RV park.   ▲ EXIT 7

Mile 437 (267.5): Exit to NE 179th Street, Clark County Fairgrounds and Washington Highway 502 to Battle Ground State Park; 56 developed campsites and numerous primitive spots, showers, swimming beach and boat launch on lake. Battle Ground Lake is stocked with trout and heavily fished. Gas, diesel, 24-hour family restaurant, and pizza parlor at exit.   ➤▲ EXIT 9

Mile 439 (265.5): Rest area (northbound) with restrooms and dump station.   MP 11

Mile 441 (263.5): Rest area (southbound) with restrooms and dump station.

Mile 442 (262.5): Exit to NW 269th Street, Ridgefield, Washington Highway 501 west; southbound access to Battle Ground and Battle Ground Lake State Park. There are gas stations and a restaurant at this exit.
                                ▲ MP 14 EXIT 14

Mile 443 (261.5): Weigh station with pay phone (northbound).   MP 15

Mile 444 (260.5): Exit to NW 319th Street and **LaCENTER** (pop. 380). Gas, food, 24-hour food mart, phone and diesel 2 miles east of exit. Access to Paradise Point State Park. For the state park, follow signs 1.1 miles north to entrance; 70 sites in grassy area on east side of Interstate 5. Ranger in residence. There is a small day-use area 0.7 mile from the park entrance (follow signs) with a dirt turnaround and some picnic tables beside the East Fork Lewis River underneath the highway bridge.
                                ⛺▲ EXIT 16

Mile 446.5 (258): The East Fork Lewis River is one of Washington's premier steelhead and salmon streams with year-round runs.   ➤

Mile 448 (256.5): The North Fork Lewis River is not as productive as the East Fork, but does offer steelhead and salmon summer and winter.   ➤ MP 20

Mile 449 (255.5): Exit to **WOODLAND** (pop. 2,510) and the junction with Washington Highway 503 east to Cougar and Mount St. Helens. Motels, fast-food outlets, deli and 24-hour restaurant, gas, diesel and RV park at this exit. This is the access to Hulda Klager Lilac Gardens (0.5 mile west) and visitor

information. Highway 503 leads east to the Yale Information Station at the southwest corner of Mount St. Helens National Volcanic Monument. (For more information on Mount St. Helens National Volcanic Monument, see the MAJOR ATTRACTIONS section.)

Highway 503 also provides access to the 3-lake chain of Merwin, Yale and Swift Creek reservoirs on the North Fork Lewis River. Good for rainbow and kokanee with a few stray cutthroat and Dolly Varden.
                                ➤▲ EXIT 21

Mile 450 (254.5): Exit to Dike Access Road. RV park.   ▲ MP 23 EXIT 22

Mile 453 (251.5): View of Columbia River to the west. Logs are often stockpiled along the river here, bound for the shipping docks at Longview. Excellent bass fishing near log rafts and pilings and some sturgeon fishing.   ➤

Mile 455 (249.5): Exit to Todd Road, access to Port of Kalama.   EXIT 27

Mile 458 (246.5): Exit to **KALAMA** (pop. 1,120). All services available. 24-hour cafe, family restaurant and food mart; motel, gas.
                                MP 31 EXIT 30

Mile 458.5 (246): Kalama River.

Mile 460 (244.5): Exit to Kalama River Road. There is an RV park and small gas station east of this exit. The Kalama River is a premium steelhead river. The river road parallels the water upstream, leading to several boat launches and access points. Camp Kalama Campground is just above the Interstate 5 bridge.   ➤▲ MP 32 EXIT 32

Mile 464 (240.5): Exit for junction with Highway 432 west to Cowlitz County Fairgrounds, the Kelso-Longview industrial area and Oregon Highway 433 to U.S. Highway 30, which parallels the Columbia River west to Astoria and south to Portland. The odor in this area comes from the pulp and paper mills, visible to the west. Exit here for the Trojan Nuclear Power Plant; follow signs to Lewis and Clark Bridge across the Columbia River. Head east on Highway 30 for 7 miles to Trojan power plant. The visitor center is open Wednesday through Sunday, 9:30 a.m. to 5 p.m.; phone (503) 556-3751 or 226-8510. Trailer and RV park this exit.   ▲ EXIT 36

Mile 466.5 (238): Highway crosses Coweeman River, excellent August to November producer of sea-run cutthroat; winter steel-heading.   ➤

Mile 467 (237.5): Exit for junction with Washington Highway 4 west to **KELSO** (pop. 10,880) and the Long Beach Peninsula. This is also the access to Lower Columbia College, Mount St. Helens Volcano Center, city center and the Cowlitz County Museum. Easy access on the east side of the highway to major-chain motels, fast-food outlets, family restaurants and gas.

Highway 4 parallels the north bank of the lower Columbia and provides access to coastal

highways. Good sturgeon, salmon and steel-head fishing from the sandbars near Stella, Cathlamet and Megler. Kelso was named by Peter Crawford for his home town in Scotland and this Scottish heritage is shown during the Kelso Hilander Summer Festival held during the last weekend in June. Because of the commercial fishery, Kelso touts itself as the "Smelt Capital of the World."   ➤ EXIT 39

Mile 468 (236.5): Exit to N. Kelso Avenue, Highway 431 and access to **LONGVIEW** (pop. 29,560) via the Cowlitz River bridge. Longview is the first planned city in the Northwest, named for its founder, R.A. Long. The Port of Longview is the third largest in Washington and the seventh largest on the West Coast. Access south to Kelso and Long Beach via Highways 4 and 431. Gas, food, lodging and hospital.   EXIT 40

Mile 470 (234.5): Exit to Ostrander Road and Pleasant Hill Road.   MP 42 EXIT 42

Mile 472 (232.5): Weigh station and phone (southbound).

Mile 474 (230.5): Exit to Headquarters Road. Pleasant Hill Road. Campground.
                                ▲ EXIT 46

Mile 476 (228.5): Exit to **CASTLE ROCK** (pop. 2,100) city center, 1.5 miles west, Huntington Avenue.   EXIT 48

Mile 477 (227.5): Exit to Castle Rock and Washington Highway 504 to Mount St. Helens National Volcanic Monument Visitor Center and Seaquest State Park. Follow Highway 504 east 5 miles for Seaquest State Park; 54 tent sites, 6 RV sites with hookups. Highway 504 parallels the Toutle River east for 27 miles and ends at Mount St. Helens National Volcanic Monument.

Access to Castle Rock visitor information, motels, family restaurants, deli, fast-food outlet, food mart and gas. ▲ MP 50 EXIT 49

Mile 480 (224.5): The Toutle River. Dredging operations continue on the Toutle River and there is quite a deposit of volcanic ash along its banks. The river, once a premier steelhead and salmon fishing stream was completely washed out by the 1980 eruption of Mount St. Helens. The gray ash being dredged out here originated on the volcano and was washed down by torrential floods unleashed by the melting glacier and the collapse of Spirit Lake on the flanks of the volcano.

Incredibly, steelhead and salmon are again returning to the silt-laden Toutle and some spawning is taking place in upstream tributaries.

Mile 480.5 (224): Exit to Barnes Drive and Toutle Park Road. Gas, phone and campground.   ▲ EXIT 52

Mile 482.5 (222): Toutle River rest areas with restrooms.

Mile 485 (219.5): Exit to the Jackson

Washington's 14,410-foot Mount Rainier is visible to Interstate 5 travelers.

(Ray Weisgerber)

Highway and Barnes Drive. Truck stop.
MP 57 EXIT 57

Mile 487 (217.5): Crossing the Cowlitz River. Exit to **VADER** (pop. 395), Ryderwood and Washington Highway 506. Northbound-only access to an RV park, gas station, diesel, mini market and fast-food outlet on the east side of the highway. Southbound-only access to a gas station and cafe on the west side of the highway. ▲ MP 59 EXIT 59

Mile 488 (216.5): Exit to **TOLEDO** (pop. 570) on Highway 505, which junctions with Highway 504 13 miles east of Toledo.
MP 61 EXIT 60

Mile 491 (213.5): Exit to **WINLOCK** (pop. 1,050), access to Toledo and junction with Washington Highway 603. Motel and RV park.
▲ MP 63 EXIT 63

Mile 496 (208.5): Exit for junction with U.S. Highway 12 east to Mossy Rock and Yakima; access to Mount Rainier National Park. See U.S. HIGHWAY 12 section. RV park, 24-hour gas, diesel, family restaurant at exit.

For an interesting side trip, drive 2 miles east on U.S. Highway 12, then turn south on the Jackson Highway, which parallels the old Oregon Trail. One mile south of the U.S. Highway 12 junction is the John R. Jackson House. Built in 1848, this renovated log cabin was the first American pioneer home north of the Columbia River. Directly south of the cabin is Lewis and Clark State Park with 25 campsites, a marked nature trail and juvenile fishing for stocked trout. A good viewpoint for Mount St. Helens is 600 feet south of the park. 👫▲ MP 68 EXIT 68

Mile 499 (205.5): Exit to **NAPAVINE** (pop. 740) to the west and Washington Highway 508 east to Onalaska. There are a gas station, truck stop and store, diesel, and a family restaurant east of the exit. EXIT 71

Mile 499.5 (205): Newaukum River. Fly-fishermen like this small brushy stream for steelhead, cutthroat and rainbow. ◂►

Mile 500 (204.5): Exit to Rush Road and Napavine. Family restaurant, drive-in, and gas and diesel east of exit. EXIT 72

Mile 504 (200.5): Exit to 13th Street, Chehalis industrial area. Major-chain 24-hour restaurant, gas, mini market and major-chain lodging east of this exit. RV park and hospital access. ▲ MP 76 EXIT 76

Mile 505 (199.5): Exit for junction with Washington Highway 6 west to Pe Ell (pop. 585) and Raymond (pop. 2,970). Easy access to gas station, drive-in, food mart and lodging at this exit. MP 78 EXIT 77

Mile 507 (197.5): Exit to National Avenue, Chehalis city center and access to Lewis County museum and fairgrounds. **CHEHALIS** (pop. 6,250) is the seat of Lewis County and located halfway between Portland and Seattle. It is the home of the Claquato Church, one of the oldest territorial churches still standing. All services available. MP 79 EXIT 79

Mile 508 (196.5): Salzer Creek.

Mile 509 (195.5): Exit to Centralia, junction with Washington Highway 507 to Bucoda (pop. 535) and access to Centralia College. Easy access to motel, family restaurants, gas, RV park and hospital east of the exit. **CENTRALIA** (pop. 11,850) was founded in 1875 by George Washington, a black man born into slavery 50 years before the end of the Civil War. He was adopted by a white family and moved West in 1852. It is the home of the largest coal-burning plant in the West, the Centralia Steam-Electric Plant. In spite of the vast amounts of coal burned, you won't see a sign of emission from either of the 400-foot stacks. Tours of the facility are available.

The Fort Borst Blockhouse in Centralia was constructed in the 1850s as a defense against hostile natives. The natives weren't hostile and the fort was used only to store grain.

All services are available. ▲ EXIT 81

Mile 509.5 (195): Skookumchuck River, a small river fished primarily for winter steelhead in March and April. MP 82

Mile 510 (194.5): Exit to Centralia and access to Centralia College. Easy access to major-chain motel, fast-food outlets, cafe and family restaurants, RV park. ▲ EXIT 82

Mile 516 (188.5): Exit 88B is the junction with U.S. Highway 12 west to Rochester and Aberdeen. All services available. Just north is Exit 88A, the junction of Highway 507 east to **TENINO** (pop. 1,285) and access to the Olympia-Tenino Speedway. EXIT 88

Mile 518 (186.5): Rest area (northbound) with restrooms.

Mile 521.5 (183): Rest area (southbound) with restrooms.

Mile 523 (181.5): Exit to Little Rock, Maytown and junction with Washington Highway 121. Access to Millersylvania State Park: Follow signs east 2.4 miles on 2-lane paved road; turn left on Tilley Road and continue 0.5 mile to the state park entrance. Millersylvania has 135 tent sites, 52 RV sites with hookups, all shaded; good swimming beach and restrooms. Boat rentals are available from Deep Lake Resort adjacent the state park. Deep Lake is stocked each spring with rainbow. There is a Game Department boat launch. Fast-food drive-in west of exit.
◅▲ MP95 EXIT 95

Mile 527 (177.5): Exit to 93rd Avenue, Scott Lake. Southbound access to Tenino. Campground, RV park, family restaurant, truck stop and gas. ▲ MP 99 EXIT 99

Mile 529 (179.5): Exit to Airdustrial Way and Olympia airport. MP 101 EXIT 101

Mile 530 (174.5): Exit to South Tumwater, Black Lake, Trosper Road and access to the Olympia airport. Major-chain motel, fast-food outlets and gas are available at this exit. Black Lake is an outstanding year-round lake with rental boats and resorts, providing rainbow, cutthroat, largemouth bass, bluegills, perch, crappie and bullhead catfish.
◅ EXIT 102

Mile 531 (173.5): Exit to **TUMWATER** (pop. 8,100), Deschutes Parkway, 2nd Avenue, and access to the courthouse and Olympia Brewing Co. (guided tours available daily 8 a.m. to 4:30 p.m.). This exit also leads to Evergreen State College, South Puget Sound Community College, and the historic area. The Deschutes River, visible between the freeway and the brewery, is fished for winter steelhead in December, January and February. Above the brewery it is stocked with rainbow and supports a native cutthroat population.
CAUTION: Road construction in this area has narrowed the highway and creates heavy traffic congestion. ◅ EXIT 103

Mile 532 (172.5): Exit to Capitol Mall and West Olympia. Visitor information; hospital. Junction with U.S. Highway 101 to Shelton, Aberdeen and Port Angeles. Travelers headed north on U.S. Highway 101 turn to the end of the U.S. HIGHWAY 101 section and read log back to front. EXIT 104

Mile 533 (171.5): Exit to OLYMPIA (pop. 30,270) is the northbound access to Henderson Boulevard, city center, the state capitol and museum and Port of Olympia. The capitol building is visible from the highway. Olympia offers 16 motels and numerous restaurants.
Washington was made a territory in 1853. Olympia was designated the state capital in 1854 and the capitol building was completed in 1928.

In 1853 a bed of tiny oysters was found in Budd Inlet, and the Olympia oysters, still grown in this area, are considered one of the world's rarest delicacies.
Olympia's largest industry is known worldwide: Olympia Brewing Co., now Pabst Brewing Co. Oyster farming, mushroom growing and dairying along with logging and timber production are important economic mainstays in Olympia. MP 105 EXIT 105

Mile 533.5 (171): Southbound Exit 105A leads to the capitol and museum; Exit 105B to Plum Street and the Port of Olympia. Major-chain motels and 24-hour gas are available at this exit. EXIT 105

Washington's stately capitol building is in Olympia, Mile 533. (L. Linkhart)

Mile 535 (169.5): Exit to Pacific Avenue. Family restaurants, fast-food outlets, 24-hour gas, diesel, food mart and hospital at this exit. EXIT 107

Mile 536 (168.5): Exit to Sleater-Kinney Road, College Street, and Sound Center. Food, gas and shopping are available at this exit. EXIT 108

Mile 537 (167.5): Exit to Martin Way, St. Martins College, **LACEY** (pop. 16,380) city center and access to Thurston County Fairgrounds. Motels, major-chain fast-food outlets, family restaurants at this exit. EXIT 109

Mile 539 (165.5): Exit for junction with Washington Highway 510 to Yelm and Marvin Road. Family restaurants, deli cafe, pizza, 24-hour gas and RV park are available at this exit.

Access to Tolmie State Park, a day-use area with underwater park for divers.
▲ EXIT 111

Mile 542 (162.5): Exit to **NISQUALLY** and Old Nisqually. Gas, RV park and fast-food outlet are available on the east side of the highway. View to the west of the tide flats on Puget Sound that are part of Nisqually National Wildlife Refuge. An interpretative trail helps visitors learn about the refuge and resident animals. 🚶▲ Exit 114

Mile 543 (161.5): Nisqually River.

Mile 544 (160.5): Exit to Mounts Road and Old Nisqually. MP 117 EXIT 116

Mile 545 (159.5): Weigh station and phone.

Mile 547 (157.5): Exit to **Du PONT** (pop. 595), Steilacoom and access to Fort Lewis Military Museum. Interstate 5 passes through Fort Lewis Military Reservation between **Mile 544** and **Mile 555** (Exits 116 to 127). The Fort Lewis Military Museum catalogs the military history of the Pacific Northwest from the Lewis and Clark expedition of 1803 to present-day Fort Lewis. The military museum, which can be seen on the west side of the highway, is open to the public Tuesday through Sunday, noon to 4 p.m.; phone (206) 967-7206.
STEILACOOM (pop. 5,290), pronounced still-a-come, is one of the oldest settlements in the state. Founded in 1854, several historic structures are preserved there. Many buildings are listed on the National Register of Historic Places. The original volumes in Washington Territory's first library are a prized collection at the Steilacoom Historical Museum.
A ferry leaves Steilacoom for McNeil Island in Puget Sound, home of a Washington state correctional facility. The McNeil Island facility, formerly a federal penitentiary, is the only island prison still operating in the United States. EXIT 119

Mile 548 (156.5): Exit to Fort Lewis, North Fort Lewis and Fort Lewis Military Museum. No services available. Tourist information center. MP 120 EXIT 120

Mile 550 (154.5): Exit to Madigan Hospital and Camp Murray. Gas and fast-food outlets available at this exit.
MP 123 EXIT 122

Mile 551 (153.5): Exit to Thorne Road in Tillicum and access to American Lake, a favorite fishing, waterskiing and general recreation lake for the Tacoma area. Boathouses, rental boats, bait are available. There are also good free boat launches.
◅ EXIT 123

Mile 552 (152.5): Exit to Gravelly Lake Drive and access to Ponders, VA Hospital and Pierce College. EXIT 124

Mile 553 (151.5): Exit to Lakewood and McChord AFB. Easy access to major-chain fast-food outlets. Hospital; visitor information, gas and diesel at this exit. The McChord Air Museum offers vintage aircraft and aviation memorabilia.   MP 126 EXIT 125

Mile 555 (149.5): Exit for junction with Washington Highway 512 east to Puyallup. This is the access to S. Tacoma Way and Pacific Lutheran University, Northwest Trek and Mount Rainier.

PUYALLUP (pop. 20,840), pronounced pew-AL-up, offers 7 motels and 18 family and fast-food restaurants, an RV park and all visitor services. Puyallup was founded in 1877 by Oregon Trail pioneer Ezra Meeker. The Meeker Mansion, built in 1890, was a showplace for social and political events. It is a national historic landmark and is open to the public Sunday from 1-5 p.m. It is located at 321 Pioneer Ave.

Puyallup is also the home of the Pettinger-Guiley Astronomical Observatory, the largest amateur-owned and operated observatory in western Washington. It is open for the public to view the night sky at no charge.

In April, Puyallup celebrates the coming of spring with the third-largest floral parade in the U.S. and makes use of the thousands of bulb flowers grown in the valley.

In September, Puyallup welcomes more than 1.3 million visitors to the Western Washington State Fair (1 of the 10th largest in U.S.).

Northwest Trek, a 600-acre wildlife park, 6 miles east on Washington Highway 512, where guided tram tours offer viewing of North American animals in their natural habitat. Spring is a favorite visiting time to view newborn animals and special events are held throughout the summer. ★ EXIT 127

Mile 556 (148.5): Exit to S. 84th Street (northbound only). All services available at this exit including major-chain and 24-hour family restaurants, gas and diesel. EXIT 128

Mile 557 (147.5): Exit to S. 72nd Street, southbound access to S. 84th Street. Food and lodging on the east side of the highway including major-chain motels and fast-food outlets, pancake restaurant.   EXIT 129

Mile 558 (146.5): Exit to S. 56th Street and access to Tacoma Mall shopping center.   EXIT 130

Mile 560 (144.5): Exit to S. 38th Street, junction with Highway 16 west to Gig Harbor and Bremerton via Tacoma Narrows Bridge. Access to Fircrest-Ruston, Point Defiance Park, South Tacoma, Tacoma Mall, University of Puget Sound and city center, family restaurants, hospital.

The Tacoma Narrows Bridge is one of the world's largest suspension bridges. The existing structure replaced "Galloping Gertie," the original suspension bridge which collapsed in high winds some 4 months after construction in 1940. The Narrows are treacherous for boaters and the current literally races through this bottleneck during a tide change.

Point Defiance Park contains an excellent zoo and aquarium, outdoor forest industry museum, Fort Nisqually, and also hiking trails,

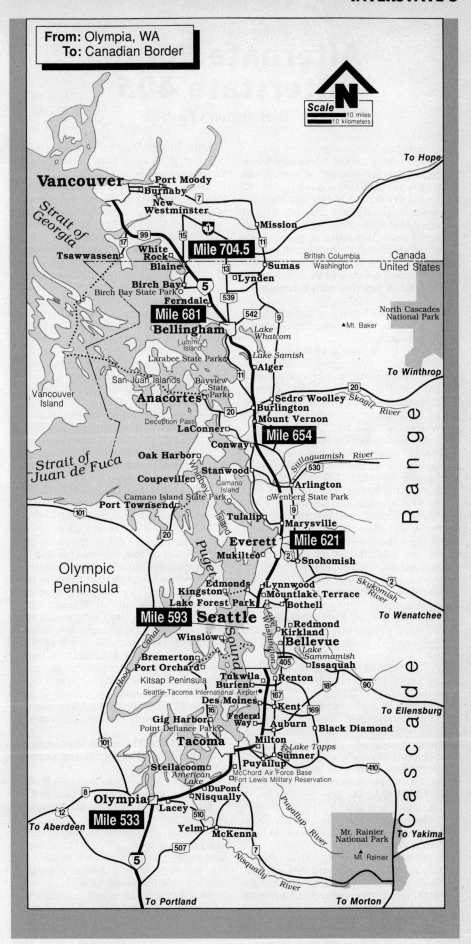

From: Olympia, WA
To: Canadian Border

Alternate Route Interstate 405

Lake Washington's Eastside

Interstate 405 provides access to communities along the east side of Lake Washington. It joins Interstate 5 at its south end at **Mile 582** (Exit 154) and at its north end at **Mile 610** (Exit 182). Ongoing construction at the south end of Interstate 405 and heavy commuter traffic to east side businesses make this route as heavily congested as Interstate 5 during rush hours. **Distance from the south junction with Interstate 5 is followed by distance from north junction with Interstate 5.**

Mile 0 (30): South junction with Interstate 5 (Exit 154). Southcenter shopping mall to south.

Mile 1 (29): Exit 1 to Tukwila, West Valley Road, Washington Highway 181 south. Major motel south off exit. Access to Southcenter shopping mall. Also access to Longacres Racetrack (follow signs), noted for its attractive grounds as well as its horse racing (April into October).

Mile 2 (28): Exit 2 to Washington Highway 167 south to Kent and Auburn, and Rainier Avenue and Renton. Major motel south off exit. **RENTON** (pop. 36,940) is home to the Boeing Co. plant which does the final assembly of 737s and 757s, the smaller commercial airplanes. (Larger planes are assembled in Everett.) Flight testing is also done here, although the jets can only take off from the Renton municipal airport; the airfield is too small for them to land. No tours are available; tours are offered at the Everett Boeing plant.

Mile 4 (26): Exit 4A and B to Renton, Maple Valley Road, Washington Highway 169 south to Enumclaw, and Washington Highway 900. Food, gas and lodging off exit.

CAUTION: In traffic reports, this winding section of Interstate 405 is referred to as the "S-curves." Drive carefully.

Mile 5 (25): Exit 5 to Sunset Boulevard NE and Washington Highway 900 east to Issaquah. Access to the Renton Boeing Plant. Also access to Renton's Coulon Beach Park on Lake Washington; pavilion, good beach, swimming, picnicking, boat launch and playground.

Mile 6 (24): Exit 6 to NE 30th Street; gas station west off exit.

Mile 7 (23): Exit 7 to NE 44th Street. Major motel and fast-food outlet, 24-hour restaurant, at exit.

Mile 9 (21): Exit 9 to 112th Avenue SE, Lake Washington Boulevard. Park and Ride. Access to Newcastle Beach Park on Lake Washington; dock, swimming, bathhouse with showers.

Mile 10 (20): Exit 10 to Coal Creek Parkway, SE Newport Way. Access to the Factoria Square shopping mall.

Mile 11 (19): Exit 11 is junction with Interstate 90 west to Seattle via Mercer Island Floating Bridge and east to Spokane.

Mile 12.5 (17.5): Exit 12 to SE 8th Street. Food, gas and lodging.

Mile 13 (17): Exit 13A and B to NE 4th and NE 8th to downtown Bellevue. **BELLEVUE** (pop. 86,350), the Eastside's remarkably fast-growing metropolis, has all visitor services including a number of major motels. The big attraction here for shoppers is glittering Bellevue Square (Bell Square for short), west off this exit, a very popular 2-story mall of top shops.

Mile 14 (16): Exit 14 to Washington Highway 520 west to Seattle via the Evergreen Point Floating Bridge and east to Redmond. **REDMOND** (pop. 27,500) has all facilities. The downtown area is also accessible via Washington Highway 908 west from Exit 18. Access this exit to Marymoor Park, which has picnicking, playfields, and the Northwest's only velodrome; follow Highway 520 east several miles.

Mile 17 (13): Exit 17 to NE 70th Place, which becomes NE 72nd west to Kirkland. Gas and convenience stores 0.5 mile west.

Mile 18 (12): Exit 18 to Highway 908 east to Redmond, Central Way west to Kirkland. Gas stations, convenience stores, fast-food outlets and other services east off exit. Kirkland Parkplace mall 1 mile west. **KIRKLAND** (pop. 36,620) towncenter, at the bottom of the hill, has shopping and other services. The city's long stretch of public waterfront has several public parks.

Mile 20 (10): Exit 20A and B to NE 116th and 124th. Major chain motels, fast-food outlets, 24-hour restaurant and gas stations off these exits. Totem Lake shopping mall east off exit.

Mile 22 (8): Exit 22 to NE 160th Street, Juanita-Woodinville Way NE. Gas station east off exit.

Mile 23 (7): Exit 23 to Washington Highway 522 west to Bothell, and east to Woodinville.

Mile 25 (5): Exit 25 to Beardslee Blvd. Access to major motel and business park.

Mile 26 (4): Exit 26 to Washington Highway 527 (Bothell-Everett Highway). Supermarket, gas stations, fast-food outlet and shopping south off exit. Major fast-food outlet and business park north off exit. Follow Highway 527 south approximately 1 mile for private RV park.

Mile 30 (0): Junction with Interstate 5. Turn to **Mile 610** INTERSTATE 5 section.

picnic facilities, boat rentals, scenic drives, a short line ride on a steam locomotive, playgrounds and public beach areas.

The waters near Point Defiance are popular fishing grounds for salmon and bottom fish, and rental boats and tackle are available at the boathouse on the far north side of the park. There is a public fishing pier east of the park extending into Commencement Bay.

🚶🏕🐟 EXIT 132

Mile 561 (143.5): Exit to **TACOMA** (pop. 161,400) city center. Access to Tacoma Dome, Washington State Museum, north to Highway 705, south to Highway 7 and Mount Rainier. Tacoma has all visitor facilities including major-chain motels. For more information, see the MAJOR CITIES section.

CAUTION: Winding road, heavy traffic congestion.   MP 134 EXIT 133

Mile 562 (142.5): Exit to Portland Avenue (northbound only) and AMTRAK.

EXIT 134

Mile 563 (141.5): Exit for junction with Washington Highway 167 (River Road) to Puyallup. Southbound access to Portland Avenue via Bay Street and the Tacoma Dome.

Crossing the Puyallup River, a major steelhead and salmon river, heavily fished by commercial Indian nets and sportsmen. The Puyallup originates on Mount Rainier and is discolored by glacial silt during the summer. In the winter, when the glaciers refreeze, the river clears. Fishing areas can be reached by traveling east on the river road.

🐟 MP 135 EXIT 135

Mile 564 (140.5): Exit to the Port of Tacoma and 20th Street E. Northbound Exit 136A is access to 20th Street E., and Exit 136B is to Port of Tacoma. Major-chain motels are available this exit.   MP 136 EXIT 136

Mile 565 (139.5): Exit for junction with Highway 99 to **FIFE** (pop. 2,405) and **MILTON** (pop. 2,860). Gas stations are east of the exit; fast-food, a 24-hour restaurant and major-chain motels are west of the exit.

EXIT 137

Mile 568 (136.5): Weigh station and rest area.

Mile 570 (134.5): Exit 142A to **AUBURN** (pop. 30,790), and Washington Highways 18 east and 167. Access to Seattle International Raceway. Highway 18 joins Interstate 90 east of Issaquah, bypassing the downtown Seattle corridor. Travelers planning on driving east on Interstate 90, turn to the INTERSTATE 90 section.

Exit 142B for junction with Highway 161 to Puyallup and Mount Rainier. Access to Enchanted Village children's amusement park and water slide via Federal Way/Route 99. Major-chain motels and major-chain 24-hour family restaurant, fast-food outlets, hospital access from this exit.   EXIT 142

Mile 571 (133.5): Exit to **FEDERAL WAY** (pop. 56,000) and S. 320th Street and SeaTac

Mall. Access to major-chain motels, shopping facilities, gas, diesel, major-chain restaurants and fast-food outlets west of exit.   EXIT 143

Mile 575 (129.5): Exit to S. 272nd Street.   EXIT 147

Mile 577 (127.5): Exit is the southbound junction with Highway 516 east to **KENT** (pop. 32,350) offering 4 motels and numerous restaurants. Also access to Midway and Highline Community College, motels and major-chain fast-food outlets, restaurants.

Northbound Exit 149A is access to Kent and Washington Highway 516 east. Just north is Exit 149B, the junction with Highway 516 west to Des Moines (pop. 14,120). Food, gas and lodging west off exit.   EXIT 149

Mile 579 (125.5): Exit to S. 200th Street and Military Road. Access to gas, food and major-chain lodging.   MP 152 EXIT 151

Mile 580 (124.5): Exit to Orillia Road and S. 188th Street. This is the northbound access to Seattle-Tacoma (Sea-Tac) International Airport via Highway 99; all services available. Three miles east on Orillia Road is the Boeing Co. Kent (Boeing Space Center) plant where the vehicle that was driven and abandoned on the moon was manufactured. Campground, gas, major-chain motels, fast-food outlets at this exit.   ▲ EXIT 152

Mile 581 (123.5): Exit (northbound only) to **TUKWILA** (pop. 4,760), Southcenter Parkway and Interstate 405. Tukwila calls itself the Northwest's "Crossroads of Commerce," where Interstate 405 and Interstate 5 meet. Attractions include Southcenter shopping mall, featuring 4 major department stores and more than 100 retail, dining and service facilities; Parkway Plaza — the West's largest concentration of home furnishing outlets; and The Pavilion outlet center, the Northwest's first factory outlet mall. Other attractions are Foster Municipal Golf Course, Fort Dente Park and the Christensen Trail near the Green River.   EXIT 153

Mile 582 (122.5): Exit to Seattle-Tacoma International Airport and **BURIEN** (pop. 23,189) via Washington Highway 518 west, Southcenter shopping mall, Longacres horse racing track, and Interstate 405 east to Renton and Bellevue.

Interstate 405 goes up the east side of Lake Washington and intersects with Interstate 90 between Bellevue and Renton. It junctions with Interstate 5 north of Lynnwood at **Mile 610**. See Alternate Route Interstate 405 log this section.   EXIT 154

Mile 584 (120.5): Exit to Tukwila, W. Marginal Way, Interurban Avenue and Highway 599. Major-chain 24-hour restaurant and gas stations are available to the west. Good view northbound of city of Seattle.   EXIT 156

Mile 585 (119.5): Exit for junction with Highway 900 west, Martin Luther King Way, Empire Way and Renton.   EXIT 157

Mile 586 (118.5): Exit to Pacific Avenue, Airport Way, E. Marginal Way and access to Boeing Field and the Museum of Flight. The premier aviation museum on the West Coast, the Museum of Flight features dozens of planes in the 4-story Great Gallery, an impressive glass structure. Exhibits are also housed in the Red Barn, the original Boeing manufacturing plant. A full-size theater presents films on flight. Open daily, 10 a.m. to 5 p.m.; Thursday and Friday until 9 p.m. Admission fee. Phone (206) 764-5720.
   ★ EXIT 158

Mile 588 (116.5): View of Boeing Development Center and Boeing Field to the west.

Mile 589 (115.5): Exit to Swift Avenue, Albro Place and access to the VA Medical Center. View to the west of the Port of Seattle.   EXIT 161

Mile 590 (114.5): Exit to Corson Avenue, Michigan Street (center lane exit northbound) and access to South Seattle Community College.   EXIT 162

Mile 591 (113.5): Exit 163A is the southbound exit to Spokane Street, Columbia Way and access to the Kingdome, West Seattle and cross-sound ferries to Bremerton and Winslow. Good view northbound of the city of Seattle, the Kingdome and Port of Seattle.

Exit 163B is a southbound exit to 6th Avenue S. and Forest Street. Exit 163 is northbound access to these points.   EXIT 163

Mile 592 (112.5): Exit for junction with Interstate 90 east to Ellensburg, James Street, Madison Street and access to Seattle University and Seattle Central Community College. It is also the southbound access to the Kingdome, Dearborn Street and Airport Way. Interstate 90 east crosses Lake Washington via the Lacey V. Murrow Floating Bridge (locally referred to as the Mercer Island bridge).

Travelers headed east on Interstate 90 should take this exit and turn to the INTERSTATE 90 section for highway log.
   MP 164 EXIT 164

Mile 592.5 (112): Express lane northbound entrance (center lane). The reversible express lanes bypass most downtown Seattle exits and end at about Exit 173, where traffic rejoins Interstate 5. The lanes are generally open for southbound traffic in the morning and northbound traffic in the evening.

Mile 593 (111.5): Exit 165 is a northbound access to Seneca Street and to downtown **SEATTLE** (pop. 495,900). Exit 165A is southbound access to Columbia and James streets; Exit 165B to Union Street and 7th Avenue. For description of Seattle, see the MAJOR CITIES section.   EXIT 165

Mile 594 (110.5): Exit to Olive Way, Denny Way and Stewart Street.
   MP 167 EXIT 166

Mile 595 (109.5): Exit to Mercer Street and Fairview Avenue. Center lane exit (northbound) for the Seattle Center and the Space Needle.   EXIT 167

Mile 596 (108.5): Exit to Lakeview Boulevard, Roanoke Street and Boylston Avenue.

Just north is Exit 168B to Bellevue, Kirkland and Interstate 405 via Highway 520 east over the Evergreen Point Floating Bridge across Lake Washington.

Northbound, the highway crosses the Ship Canal. View of University of Washington to the northeast. Lake Union is to the west.
   MP 168 EXIT 168

Mile 597 (107.5): Exit to NE 45th Street and NE 50th Street. This is the access to the University of Washington campus and the University District to the east via NE 45th Street. Access to Seattle Pacific University and Woodland Park Zoological Gardens to the west.   MP 169 EXIT 169

Mile 598 (106.5): Exit to Ravenna Boulevard and NE 65th Street.
   MP 170 EXIT 170

Mile 599 (105.5): Exit to **BOTHELL** (pop. 9,850), Highway 522, Lake City Way, NE 71st Street and NE 65th Street.   EXIT 171

Mile 600 (104.5): Exit to N. 85th Street, NE 80th Street, Aurora Avenue N. (Highway 99) and access to North Seattle Community College.   MP 172 EXIT 172

Mile 600.5 (104): Express lane southbound entrance (center lane).

Mile 601 (103.5): Exit to Northgate Way, 1st Avenue NE. Access east to hospitals and Northgate shopping center (the first developed shopping mall in the U.S.).

Southbound: On a clear day, you can see 14,410-foot Mount Rainier.   EXIT 173

Mile 601.5 (103): Express lane northbound exit.

Mile 602 (102.5): Exit (northbound only) to NE 130th Street, Roosevelt Way and hospital.   EXIT 174

Mile 603 (101.5): Exit to NE 145th Street and 5th Avenue NE.   MP 175 EXIT 175

Mile 604 (100.5): Exit to NE 175th Street and Aurora Avenue N. (Highway 99) and Shoreline Community College.   EXIT 176

Mile 605 (99.5): Exit to **LAKE FOREST PARK** (pop. 2,770), Edmonds, Kingston ferry and northbound access to **MOUNTLAKE TERRACE** (pop. 16,290). Follow Washington Highway 104 west 4.5 miles for Edmonds-Kingston ferry and connections west to the Olympic Peninsula. Gas available east and west of the exit.

EDMONDS (pop. 28,500) is a quiet, bedroom community for Seattle, located about 10 miles north of Seattle city limits and about 15 miles south of Everett. It sits on the edge of Puget Sound with a dramatic view of the

Olympic Mountains on the peninsula to the west. The town prides itself on the slow lifestyle and beautiful, flower-lined streets. Old Milltown is a renovated shopping mall in the downtown area which offers a unique blend of pioneer artifacts, local history and small retail shops. The Edmonds Museum, which served as a library and city hall, is listed on the National Register of Historic Places. All services available.   MP 177 EXIT 177

Mile 606.5 (98): Exit to 220th Street SW and Mountlake Terrace.   EXIT 179

Mile 609 (95.5): Exit to 44th Avenue W., Lynnwood, Washington Highway 524, and access to **BRIER** (pop. 4,790) and Edmonds Community College. **LYNNWOOD** (pop. 25,420) has all visitor and shopping facilities.   MP 182 EXIT 181

Mile 610 (94.5): Exit for junction with Interstate 405 south to Bellevue and Renton and Washington Highway 525 north to Highway 99. Access west to Alderwood shopping mall (largest covered shopping mall in the Northwest), food and gas. This is the northbound access to U.S. Highway 2 to Stevens Pass and Wenatchee via Interstate 405 and Washington Highway 522. (See Alternate Route Interstate 405 log page 74.)   MP 183 EXIT 182

Mile 611 (93.5): Exit to 164th Street SW (Martha Lake Road), Washington Highway 525 to Highway 99, Alderwood Boulevard and **MILL CREEK** (pop. 5,262). Mill Creek is one of Washington's newest communities offering motels, family restaurants and gas stations (visitor center at top of eastbound freeway ramp). It was incorporated Sept. 30, 1983.   EXIT 183

Mile 614 (90.5): Exit to 128th Street SW and Post Road west to Paine Field. Motels, major-chain 24-hour restaurant, fast-food outlets and gas stations west of exit. Motel and gas station east of exit.   MP 187 EXIT 186

Mile 616 (88.5): Weigh station (northbound).

Mile 617 (87.5): Exit to Washington Highways 526 west and 527 south, 99S, and Broadway Street, Everett Mall Way and access via Highway 526 west to the Boeing Co.'s Everett plant and the Mukilteo-Whidbey Island ferry. Motels, restaurants and fast-food outlets available at this exit. View to east of the Snohomish River Valley and the Cascade Range.

The Boeing Co.'s main assembly building for 747s, 757s and 767s is 11 stories tall and covers 62 acres. By volume, it is the world's largest building. Eight 747s and 8 767s can be on the final assembly line at one time. Material and parts for the airplanes are moved to the factory along a 3-mile railroad spur which climbs 600 feet from the main track — the second steepest standard-gauge rail line in the U.S. Over 900 planes have been built at this facility since 1968. A 90-minute free tour of the assembly bay and a film are offered several times daily. Children under 12

are not allowed on the tour. To reach the center, go west 3 miles on Highway 516 and follow signs to tour center parking lot. For schedules and information call (206) 342-4801.   ★ EXIT 189

Mile 620 (84.5): Exit to Washington Highway 529 north, Broadway Street and Everett city center (center lane exit northbound). Major-chain motels and major-chain fast-food outlets at this exit. MP 192 EXIT 192

Mile 621 (83.5): Exit to Pacific Avenue and **EVERETT** (pop. 60,920) city center. Access to hospital. All services are available including 15 motels and numerous restaurants including major-chain 24-hour family restaurant at this exit.

Everett, "Great Little City by the Bay," dates from the 1890s when Eastern industrialists Charles Colby, principal owner of the Wisconsin Central Railroad, Walter Oakes of the Northern Pacific, and John D. Rockefeller were contacted by their friend Henry Hewitt Jr. about establishing industrial plants in an ideal western location. With the additional help of timber barons, lumberjacks, mariners and prospectors, Everett (named for Colby's son) became a boom town with a strong industrial base. In 1893, the last spike was driven completing the first transcontinental railroad into Everett.

Built on Port Gardiner Bay, many of its industries and pleasure centers are on the waterfront. The Everett Marina Village offers food items from ice cream and muffins to fine-dining on steaks and seafood in the many restaurants. There are gift shops, souvenirs, fishing charters and sightseeing cruises on the sound. Strolling the promenade deck and enjoying the sea lions offshore are some of the pleasures of the waterfront. The historic schooner *Equator* is also at the Marina Village.

Everett is proud of the Everett Giants, its Class A professional baseball team, an affiliate of the San Francisco Giants. They play other major league affiliate teams in the Memorial Stadium.

A major transportation hub on Puget Sound, Everett has 2 transcontinental railroads, AMTRAK, 10 auto freight lines, ocean shipping facilities at the Port of Everett, Snohomish County Airfield at Paine Field and the Everett plant of the Boeing Co. where construction of 767s and 747s provide transportation to the world.   MP 193 EXIT 193

Mile 622 (82.5): Exit for junction with U.S. Highway 2 east to Snohomish, Stevens Pass and Wenatchee. Watch for fog in the river valley. Also access to Lake Stevens and Granite Falls via Washington Highway 92. Travelers headed east on U.S. Highway 2 turn to the U.S. HIGHWAY 2 section for log.

The city of **SNOHOMISH** (pop. 5,790) was founded in 1854 and is situated on the Snohomish River 6 miles east of Everett. All services are available including 3 bed-and-breakfast facilities and 17 restaurants. Antique shops are a major attraction here: Follow signs for historic district. Snohomish is named after the local Indian tribe. Notice that several place names of Indian origin end in "ish." The suffix means "people."   MP 195 EXIT 194

Mile 623 (81.5): Exit (northbound only) to the Port of Everett (see **Mile 626.5**), Marine View Drive, Everett Community College and state patrol.   EXIT 195

Mile 624 (80.5): Snohomish River. Union Slough.   MP 197

Mile 626 (78.5): Steamboat Slough.   MP 198

The Edmonds ferry docks as the sun sets behind the Olympic Mountains.   (© David Shott)

Mile 626.5 (78): Southbound exit to North Broadway, the Port of Everett and Washington Highway 529 south. Portside attractions include Marina Village shops and waterfront restaurants. The hulk of Robert Louis Stevenson's *Equator* is on display with an interpretative center. Everett Marina, adjacent to the village, has all marine services and is second in size only to Marina Del Ray, CA. EXIT 198

Mile 627 (77.5): Exit to MARYSVILLE (pop. 7,726), the Tulalip (too-LAY-lip) Indian Reservation and Washington Highway 528 east. Easy access to gas stations, family and fast-food restaurants on either side of the freeway. Marysville has 2 motels and 13 restaurants. For an interesting side trip through the reservation and resort lakes turn west onto Tulalip/Marine Drive.

The Tribal Entertainment Center, featuring bingo, is 0.3 mile west. A fish hatchery which breeds 4 species of salmon can be seen via a 2.5-mile-long dirt road which leaves the main drive at approximately **Mile 5**. Kayak Point County Park, with public boat launch, pier fishing and Puget Sound beaches, is at **Mile 13.5**. Across the road is 18-hole Kayak Point public golf course.

Several lakes are accessible via Lake Goodwin Road which junctions with Tulalip/Marine Drive. They are Martha, Howard, Crab Apple, Goodwin, Ki and Glissberg Twin lakes. Fishing is fair to good in most for cutthroat and stocked rainbows. Access to Wenberg State Park on Lake Goodwin with tent and camper sites. The total loop is 25 miles and can be taken in reverse by southbound travelers by taking Exit 206 west at Smokey Point.
MP 200 EXIT 199

Mile 630 (74.5): Exit to 116th Street NE. Truck stop, gas. MP 202 EXIT 202

Mile 634 (70.5): Exit to Lakewood, Smokey Point and Wenberg State Park (7 miles west) which offers 65 tent sites and 10 RV sites with hookups. This is also the exit to Arlington airport, gas, diesel, family restaurants, fast-food outlets and motor inn.
MP 206 EXIT 206

Mile 635 (69.5): Rest area (northbound). A large, hollow tree is on display that is large enough for several people to stand inside. Free coffee is frequently dispersed by volunteers at this stop. MP 207

Mile 636 (68.5): Exit to Silvana, Arlington and access to North Cascades Highway (Washington Highway 20) via Washington Highway 530. There is a gas station east off this exit. Highway 530 is a scenic alternative for travelers heading east on Highway 20, winding through sparsely settled river valleys on the apron of the North Cascade Mountains. It intersects with Highway 20 at Rockport and is a pleasant, shorter alternative to the freeway hum. Motor inn, restaurant and gas at this exit. MP 208 EXIT 208

Mile 637.5 (67): Stillaguamish River (a popular fishing destination) offers cutthroat trout, king and coho salmon and steelhead. Summer fly-fishing only. Check state regulations before tackling this river.

Mile 638 (66.5): Exit to 236th Street NE. MP 210 EXIT 210

Mile 640 (64.5): Exit to Washington Highway 532 west, Stanwood, Camano Island. Access to Camano Island State Park, located 19 miles west with 93 sites, showers, boat launch. EXIT 212

Mile 643 (61.5): Exit to 300th Street NW. Gas station to the west. MP 215 EXIT 215

Mile 646 (58.5): Exit to Starbird Road. MP 218 EXIT 218

Mile 647 (57.5): Good view of Skagit River Valley northbound.

Mile 649 (55.5): Exit to Washington Highways 530 west and 534 east, Conway and Lake McMurray with rainbow fishing and resort facilities. There is a gas station east of this exit.

La CONNER (pop. 665) is located 11 miles northwest of the exit. Good opportunity to see Skagit Valley flowers in the spring. The valley is famous for producing tulip and daffodil flower bulbs which are grown in large fields and in the spring create a blanket of color on the valley floor. The town of La Conner, on the national historic register, has several museums and historic buildings.

Also access this exit to Skagit Wildlife Area, used by hunters from October to January, and by bird-watchers the rest of the year. A trail from the parking area leads out to Skagit Flats, where thousands of snow geese and swans stop in winter and spring. Exit west off the interstate and follow Fir Island Road to first major side road south (watch for easy-to-miss sign). MP 221 EXIT 221

Mile 652 (52.5): Exit to South Mount Vernon. Airfield to west just south of exit. Food, gas, diesel. MP 224 EXIT 224

Mile 653 (51.5): Exit to Anderson Road. Food, gas, diesel. MP 225 EXIT 225

Mile 654 (50.5): Exit to Washington Highway 536 west, Kincaid Street and access to Mount Vernon city center and hospital. MOUNT VERNON (pop. 14,590) is county seat and trade center for Skagit County; all services available. It is well known for its flowers, with thousands of visitors coming to view the daffodil, tulip and iris fields in the spring. Best access to the flower fields is off the road to La Conner (Exit 221) or from this exit follow Highway 536 (Memorial Highway) west across the Skagit River to McLean Road. A number of country roads cross McLean and lead to more flower fields. MP 226 EXIT 226

Mile 655 (49.5): Exit to College Way, Washington Highway 538 east and access to Clear Lake, Skagit Valley College and state patrol. Easy access to gas, 24-hour restaurant, motel and shopping mall east of this exit; fast-food outlets, restaurant and gas west of this exit. EXIT 227

Mile 656.5 (48): Skagit River, the largest drainage into Puget Sound with 2,989 named tributary streams. Fishing guides work the river and in the fall and winter the river hosts large numbers of bald eagles attracted by the thousands of salmon carcasses washed ashore in the wake of the spawning run. The river offers fishing every month of the year. Check with sporting goods dealers in Mount Vernon to see what's biting where.

Mile 657 (47.5): Exit to George Hopper Road. MP 229 EXIT 229

Mile 658 (46.5): Exit for junction with Washington Highway 20 east to BURLINGTON (pop. 3,890), Sedro Woolley and North Cascades Highway, and west to La Conner, Anacortes and Whidbey Island. Travelers headed for the San Juan Islands or ferry connections to Canada should take this exit and travel to Anacortes. Gas, diesel, food and lodging on both sides of highway. See Washington Highway 20 West feature this section.

The North Cascades Highway (Washington Highway 20 east) traverses the spectacular North Cascades National Park. The highway is closed in winter. See description of North Cascades National Park in the MAJOR ATTRACTIONS section. Travelers headed east on Washington Highway 20 turn to NORTH CASCADES HIGHWAY section for log of that route. EXIT 230

Mile 659 (45.5): Exit to Highway 11 north (Chuckanut Drive), Bow-Edison and access to Bay View State Park.

Washington Highway 11 is a scenic 2-lane roadway that winds north along the shoreline of Samish Bay, provides access to Larrabee State Park (61 tent sites, 26 RV sites and boat launch), and rejoins Interstate 5 approximately 21 miles distance at Exit 250. This drive is winding and narrow in places and is not recommended for oversized vehicles. EXIT 231

Mile 660 (44.5): Exit 232 to Cook Road and access to Sedro Woolley. Access to campground and hospital. EXIT 232

Mile 662 (42.5): Northbound, the highway leaves the Skagit River valley and enters the hills.

Mile 664 (40.5): Exit to southbound access to Bow Edison and Bow Hill Road. Restaurant. EXIT 236

Mile 665.5 (39): Rest area (northbound). MP 238

Mile 669 (35.5): Exit to Alger. The northbound interstate begins winding through the Lookout Mountains. Lodge and gas. EXIT 240

Mile 670 (34.5): Exit to Nulle Road and South Lake Samish. EXIT 242

Washington Highway 20 West

Interstate 5 to Anacortes

For an interesting side trip, leave Interstate 5 at Exit 230 and travel west on Washington Highway 20. The 16-mile one-way trip takes you through the flower fields of the Skagit Valley within 4 to 13 miles of a historic channel port and a natural preserve, and to the port city of Anacortes.

Distance from Interstate 5 is followed by distance from Anacortes.

Sunset Beach Park offers picnicking, boating, playground and camping.
(Tom Barr)

Mile 0 (16): Western Burlington (pop. 3,890). Gas, food and other services are available at this exit.

Mile 3.5 (12.5): Port of Skagit Regional Airport and Bay View business and industrial park. MP 56

Mile 4 (12): Junction with Washington Highway 536 which leads southeast to Mount Vernon. MP 55

Mile 6 (10): Junction with Washington Highway 237 which leads 4 miles north to Bay View State Park and 5.1 miles to Padilla Bay National Estuarine Sanctuary. Access to La Conner, 4 miles south, via paved county road. Family restaurant at junction.

Bay View State Park has 90 campsites, 9 full hookups, 30 picnic sites, group camping, hot showers and shoreline picnic facilities. With 1,300 feet of saltwater frontage, it is a popular beachcombing, kite flying and bird-watching area.

Through displays and saltwater aquarium, Padilla Bay National Estuarine Sanctuary's visitor center interprets birds, mammals, aquatic life and the variety of environments found in the bay. A 0.8-mile upland nature trail identifies trees, plants, and examples of glacial action. The center has maps and information on where wildlife may be seen during the year. Free. Open Wednesday through Sunday, 10 a.m. to 5 p.m.

La Conner has many buildings dating back to the late 1800s and early 1900s and the town is on the national historic register. The waterfront is lined with unique shops and a variety of restaurants.

Mile 7 (9): South of Highway 20 are some of Skagit County's famed flower fields. Constant temperatures, together with rich soil and rainfall, create a climate ideal for growing tulips, daffodils and irises. April and May are prime viewing months, and fields are a riot of purples, pinks, reds and yellows. The Skagit Valley

Tulip Festival in April draws thousands of visitors to the area.

Mile 7.5 (8.5): Swinomish Channel boat launch at the eastern end of Berentson Bridge is an easily accessible area for viewing wildlife. Channel marshes are stopovers for mallard ducks, herons, winter snow geese and swans.

Mile 8.5 (7.5): Northbound access road to Swinomish Indian Reservation and combination store/Indian gift shop.

Mile 11 (5): Restaurant and lounge with food, gas and diesel.

Mile 11.5 (4.5): Junction. Highway 20 spur continues west to Anacortes while Highway 20 heads southwest to the spectacular Deception Pass bridge, Deception Pass State Park and Whidbey Island. The view of Puget Sound from Deception Pass bridge is one of the most photographed sites in the state. (See description of Whidbey Island in THE ISLANDS section.)

Mile 13 (5): Viewpoint of Swinomish Channel with restrooms and picnic tables. A cross section of a Douglas fir log taken from Olympic National Forest is on display. The tree was 970 years old, 242 feet tall, and contained 51,000 board feet of lumber. Texaco and Shell oil refineries and Mount Baker can be seen across the channel.

Mile 14 (2): Access to Anacortes waterfront, port and marina. Bulk cargoes of logs, lumber, sulfur and petroleum coke are shipped over the port's deep-water docks. The marina serves both commercial and pleasure boaters. MP 50

Mile 16 (0): ANACORTES (pop. 10,320) is situated on Fidalgo Island, southernmost of the San Juan Islands. (Best view of the area is from Mount Erie.) Surrounded on 3 sides by Puget Sound, it is Skagit County's primary industrial and shipping center. All services available.

Anacortes is the gateway to the 170

islands in the San Juan archipelago and the Gulf Islands of Canada. Known as one of the world's most beautiful boating areas, the San Juans can be experienced either by Washington State ferry or private boat. (The Washington State Ferry Terminal is west of town via Oakes Avenue; follow signs.)

Anacortes marine facilities include: fuel, service and repair shops; boat building, charters, supplies and equipment. The annual Blessing of the Fleet takes place in Anacortes in April. The fleet of fishing vessels then heads for Alaska and northern fishing grounds.

The Railway Depot, built in 1911, is on the National Register of Historic Places. It is home for an arts center and the departure point for the Anacortes Railway. On summer weekends, this authentically scaled 0-4-4 coal/wood-burning steam locomotive pulls 3 passenger cars on a 0.7-mile run. Fee: 75¢ per person.

The *W.T. Preston,* a 163-foot wooden stern-wheeler, is docked next to the depot. It is open for touring Thursday through Monday, noon to 5 p.m. Fee: Adults, $1; children under 18, 50¢.

Anacortes Museum, on 12th Street, features traveling exhibits and Skagit County memorabilia. An outside water fountain has separate drinking levels for cats, dogs, horses and people.

Causland Memorial Park was built in 1919 to honor WWI servicemen. The beautiful design by French architect John LePage was realized through the work of volunteers who set thousands of colored rocks brought from nearby islands.

Washington Park, past the ferry terminal, sits on the shores of Puget Sound. The park's Sunset Beach offers beautiful island vistas, playground equipment, spacious lawns, and a year-round boat ramp. It has 46 campsites with water and electricity, 29 tent sites, restrooms, showers, laundry, dump station, and 3 covered picnic shelters.

Mile 671 (33.5): Lake Samish to the west, popular with water-skiers and windsurfers during the summer. Summer fishery for silvers, crappie, largemouth bass and perch. There are resort facilities and a public boat launch. Several years ago a mudslide washed down from Interstate 5 and into the lake, blocking traffic and badly discoloring and silting the lake. ⤙ MP 245

Mile 674 (30.5): Exit to North Lake Samish and access to Lake Padden Recreation Area, a Bellingham community park (day use only). Lake Padden offers fair fishing. ⤙ MP 246 EXIT 246

Mile 678.5 (26): Exit to Highway 11 south (Chuckanut Drive), Valley Parkway, Fairhaven Historical Site and Larrabee State Park. There are gas stations and services to the west. Scenic Highway 11 leads south along Samish Bay and rejoins Interstate 5 at Exit 231. Driving distance is 21 miles. (See **Mile 659.**) Restaurants, drive-in and coffee shop available here.

Fairhaven Historical Site encompasses 10 historic sites and buildings spread over an 8-block area, including a residential section of Victorian homes. The district preserves what remains from one of the Northwest's great booms in 1889. Picnic grounds and 12-acre rose garden at Fairhaven Park.

Access to Alaska Ferry Fairhaven Terminal. The Alaska Marine Highway moved its southern terminus from Seattle to Bellingham in October 1989. The Alaska state ferries sail year-round to mainline ports in Southeast Alaska. 🛪 MP 251 EXIT 250

Mile 680 (24.5): Exit to Samish Way, College Park Way and access to Western Washington University. Gas, diesel, motels, pizza, fast-food outlets available at this exit. MP 252 EXIT 252

Mile 680.5 (22.5): Exit to Lakeway Drive and city center. Major-chain motels, pizza, cafe, fast-food outlets and gas stations available. MP 253 EXIT 253

Mile 681 (23.5): Exit to State Street, Iowa Street and Bellingham city center. **BELLINGHAM** (pop. 46,610) has a large port and also relies on forestry and agriculture. Downtown shopping area includes historic Fairhaven district (see **Mile 678.5** Exit 250). All services available.

The Whatcom Museum of History and Art is on the National Register of Historic Places as an outstanding example of Victorian art. Originally the city hall, its 3 floors include permanent exhibits on Northwest birds, the logging industry, Northwest coastal Indians and Eskimos. Collections range from 30,000 photographic prints and negatives to Eskimo, Aleut and Northwest Indian artifacts, plus contemporary regional art. It is open noon to 5 p.m., closed Monday. For information write the Whatcom Museum of History and Art, 121 Prospect St., Bellingham, WA 98225 or call (206) 675-6981. Gas and fast-food outlets at this exit. MP 254 EXIT 254

Mile 683 (21.5): Exit to Sunset Drive and Washington Highway 542 east to Mount Baker. Impressive cone-shaped Mount Baker (elev. 10,778 feet) can be seen from many directions in northwestern Washington. Mount Baker Ski Area is 60 miles northeast from here via Highway 542, a winding road (up to 2 hours' drive); limited facilities along the road. Good spring skiing. 🎿 MP 255 EXIT 255

Mile 684 (20.5): Exit to Meridian Street, Bellis Fair Mall Parkway and Washington Highway 539 to Lynden. Easy access to food, gas, lodging and shopping east off exit. Access to Sumas and Canada border crossing via Washington Highways 539, 546 and 9. Inns, motels, major-chain 24-hour restaurant and fast-food outlets available at this exit. EXIT 256

Mile 685 (19.5): Exit to Northwest Avenue and access to Whatcom Community College. Access to motels. EXIT 257

Mile 686 (18.5): Exit to Bakerview Road and Bellingham airport. Southbound access to Bellis Fair Mall Parkway, Whatcom County Sports Arena, gas, diesel, truck stop. MP 258 EXIT 258

Mile 688 (16.5): Exit to Slater Road and Washington Highway 540 west to Lummi Indian Reservation and Lummi Island. Food available. MP 260 EXIT 260

Mile 688.5 (16): Highway crosses the flat Nooksack River valley northbound. Good view to east of Cascade Range and to the north the Coast Range in Canada.

Mile 690 (14.5): Exit to **FERNDALE** (pop. 4,750) and Axton Road. There is a truck stop with gas and a fast-food outlet to east and a motel to west of exit.

The lumbering, fishing and agriculture which were once mainstays of Ferndale's economy have been joined by 2 major oil refineries and an aluminum plant.

Pioneer Park has several old cabins which were moved here and preserved as an early village.

Hovander Homestead, 5299 Nielsen Road, is a National Historic Register farmhouse built in 1901-03. The complex includes early furniture, artifacts and farm animals. The house is open weekends, June 1 to Aug. 30. Next to Hovander is Tennent Lake Natural History Interpretative Center. A trail system and bird-watching tower overlooks 200 acres of marsh near the banks of the Nooksack River. 🚶 EXIT 262

Mile 691 (13.5): Nooksack River. Exit to Portal Way, southbound exit to Ferndale. Gas stations with diesel to east. Access to Blaine via Portal Way. The Nooksack is a marginal fishing stream, often discolored by silt sloughing off glaciers in the headwaters. Camping. ▲ EXIT 263

Mile 694 (10.5): Exit to Custer and Grandview Road; northbound access to Birch Bay. For Birch Bay State Park, follow Grandview

Road west to Jackson Road; turn north on Jackson to Helweg Road and state park entrance. The state park has 147 tent sites, 20 RV sites with hookups, hot showers and a picnic area on the beach. 🛪▲ MP 266 EXIT 266

Mile 695.5 (9): Rest area; restrooms.

Mile 698 (6.5): Exit to Lynden and **BIRCH BAY**. Birch Bay resort area has water sports and a giant water slide. Follow Birch Bay-Lynden Road west. Access to back entrance to Birch Bay State Park via Birch Bay Drive along the water. Camping and lodging available.

LYNDEN (pop. 4,780) is the home of the Northwest Washington Fair and the annual Tractor Pull Contest held in August. All visitor services. A major stop on the way to or from the Sumas border crossing. Lynden Pioneer Museum features restored buggies and wagons, antique autos and Indian artifacts. ▲ EXIT 270

Mile 702 (2.5): Exit to Blaine via Loomis Trail Road and Blaine Road. Food, gas, lodging and camping available. ▲ MP 274 EXIT 274

Mile 703 (1.5): Exit for junction with Washington Highway 543 north to the Canada (truck) customs and access to Highway 15 north to Trans-Canada Highway 1 via Cloverdale. (See TRANS-CANADA HIGHWAY 1 section for log of that route.) Gas and diesel available. EXIT 275

Mile 704 (0.5): Exit to Blaine city center and Peace Arch Park. *THIS IS THE LAST EXIT BEFORE BORDER.* There are a restaurant, gas station, visitor information and lodging available at this exit.

BLAINE (pop. 2,420), just west of Interstate 5, has all services available. Good view from main street of Drayton Harbor and Semiahmoo Spit. Semiahmoo Spit is the site of the Alaska Packers Assn. cannery, the largest salmon cannery in the Northwest. The restored cannery buildings are open to the public.

The recently developed Semiahmoo Resort encompasses nearly 5 miles of the spit's shoreline. The 200-room convention hotel centers around a golf course designed by Arnold Palmer.

For access to Semiahmoo Spit and Drayton Harbor, follow Portal Way south of town to Blaine Road; turn right on Blaine Road for Drayton Harbor Road. From Blaine Road, there is also access to Birch Bay resort area and Birch Bay State Park (follow signs). Blaine offers 6 hotels and motels and 26 restaurants. The town's nearby resort area, Birch Bay, offers 7 hotels and motels and 11 restaurants. MP 276 EXIT 276

Mile 704.5 (0): U.S.-Canada international border. Customs and immigration open 24 hours a day. (See Customs Requirements in the GENERAL INFORMATION section.) If you are headed to Vancouver, BC, continue straight on Highway 99.

Yellowhead Highway 5

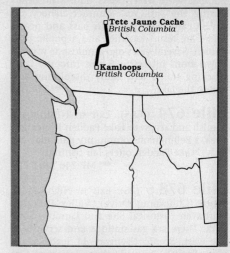

See map opposite page

British Columbia's 208-mile/335-km Yellowhead Highway 5 connects 2 major east-west routes: Trans-Canada Highway 1 and Yellowhead Highway 16. Yellowhead Highway 5 is logged south to north, from Kamloops to Tete Jaune Cache. The route is not a particularly scenic one, but it gives access to one of British Columbia's largest and most attractive wilderness parks, Wells Gray.

Yellowhead Highway 5 begins in dry belt country, with ponderosa pine parklands and sagebrush, but it very soon passes into the Interior wet zone and runs through thick forests most of the way north. In places, the forest has been cleared for the hay fields of cattle ranches and, in the area around Vavenby, for some of the largest sheep farms in the Interior.

Yellowhead Highway 5 Log

Distance in miles from Kamloops is followed by distance in miles from Tete Jaune Cache. Equivalent distances in kilometres are indicated by Km.

Mile 0 (208) Km 0 (335): Junction with Highway 1 at Kamloops (see description at **Mile 378.5** in the TRANS-CANADA HIGHWAY 1 section). Yellowhead Highway 5 crosses the South Thompson River bridge.

Mile 0.5 (207.5) Km 1 (334): Kamloops Indian residential school (opened in 1890) now houses the Secwepemc Museum of the Shuswap Nation's Kamloops Indian band, and serves as an Indian Education Centre; displays of historical and archaeological artifacts and old photos. Nearby St. Joseph's Church dates from 1870. Junction with road east along the north shore of the South Thompson River to Chase on Highway 1.

Mile 2 (206) Km 3 (332): Truck weigh scale.

Mile 3 (205) Km 5 (330): Junction with road east to Harper Mountain Ski Area and Paul Lake Provincial Park (11 miles/18 km). Park has 111 campsites, camping fee, sani-station, picnic area, swimming, fishing (rainbows to 9 pounds) and hiking. Also access to Pinantan Lake (another 4 miles/6.5 km); fly-fishing and trolling for rainbow. Accommodations and boats at lake. ⛺🛶▲

Mile 8 (200) Km 13 (322): Northern boundary of the Kamloops Indian Reserve. To the east lie the Dome Hills.

Mile 9 (199) Km 14 (321): Kamloops suburb of Aspen Park; store.

Mile 12 (196) Km 19.5 (315.5): Sign for southbound travelers: 22 km to Kamloops city centre.

Mile 13 (195) Km 21 (314): Heffley Creek sawmill.

Mile 14 (194) Km 23 (312): Small settlement of **HEFFLEY CREEK**. Tod Mountain Road leads east to Big and Little Heffley lakes (11.5 miles/19 km) with cabins, boats, camping and fishing for rainbows. Also access to Tod Mountain Ski Resort (16.5 miles/27 km); bed-and-breakfast accommodations. 🐟🛶▲

Mile 27 (181) Km 43 (292): Road west to the free ferry across the Thompson River to Westside Road, which goes south back to Kamloops or north to meet Highway 5 at Barriere. The ferry is on call between 7 a.m. and 7 p.m. and has room for 2 cars and 10 passengers. Ferry does not operate in high water (early to late June) and during freezeup.

Mile 30 (178) Km 48 (287): Small community of **McLURE**; coffee shop and campground.

Just north of McLure, the Fish Trap rest area overlooks Fishtrap Rapids, where Indians used to trap spawning salmon. ▲

Mile 34.5 (173.5) Km 55.5 (279.5): Thompson River overlook. The North Thompson River rises in the Cariboo Mountains and flows southward to meet the South Thompson at Kamloops. The route was made famous by a small group of Overlanders, led by Thomas McMicking, who turned south at Tete Jaune Cache and headed for Fort Kamloops on their way to the Cariboo goldfields in 1862. (The rest of the Overlanders went down the Fraser.) It took the McMicking group (a party of 32 men, a pregnant woman and her 3 small children) almost a month to reach the civilization of the fort, where the following day, Mrs. Catherine Schubert was delivered of her fourth child, Rose, the first white girl born in the British Columbia Interior. The story of their trip is one of incredible privation and courage.

Every year, a raft race on the Thompson from Clearwater to Kamloops, the quieter section of the river, honours the bravery of the Overlanders, many of whom settled in the Kamloops area.

Mile 35.5 (172.5) Km 57.5 (277.5): Louis Creek bridge.

Mile 36.5 (171.5) Km 59 (276): Small community of **LOUIS CREEK** (unincorporated) is supported by a large lumbermill. Gas and food are available. A road leads southeast from here to Forest Lake (13.5 miles/22 km) and Johnson Lake (25 miles/40 km). Both lakes have rainbows; boats and accommodations on Johnson. Road continues to Agate Bay on Adams Lake (north of Squilax on Highway 1). 🐟

Mile 38.5 (169.5) Km 62 (273): Tourist information booth and gas station at south end of loop road to community of **BARRIERE** (area pop. 5,000). Full tourist facilities, small museum in town centre. Large sawmill at north edge of town.

Roads from Barriere lead northeast to Barriere Lakes (North Barriere Lake 13.5 miles/ 22 km; East Barriere Lake 20 miles/32 km) and north to Chu Chua and Dunn and Halamore lakes via east side of Thompson River, rejoining Highway 5 at Clearwater.

Mile 39 (169) Km 63 (272): Barriere River bridge.

Mile 39.5 (168.5) Km 64 (271): North end of loop road to Barriere.

Mile 40 (168) Km 64.5 (270.5): Thompson River bridge.

Mile 40.5 (167.5) Km 65 (270): Access to Westside Road which leads down the west side of the Thompson River to Kamloops.

Mile 41.5 (166.5) Km 66.5 (268.5): Boulder Mountain Road, south end of loop that climbs into the hills, returning to Yellowhead Highway 5. The road gives rough access to Bonaparte Lake, which is more easily reached from 70 Mile House on Highway 97.

Mile 42 (166) Km 67.5 (267.5): Chinook Cove rest area; pleasantly shaded picnic area. **CHINOOK COVE** is a small community by the river. 🏕

Mile 44.5 (163.5) Km 72 (263): Rest area with picnic tables on the east side of the road. Drinking water is piped from a spring. 🏕

Mile 51.5 (156.5) Km 83 (252): Unincorporated community of **DARFIELD**, with a sawmill and cluster of old buildings. The valley is irrigated for corn and hay.

Mile 57 (151) Km 92 (243): Community of **LITTLE FORT** (pop. less than 200) takes its name from a Hudson's Bay Co. fur-trading post that was located here. Food, gas, accommodations available.

Junction with Highway 24 which leads west 60 miles/96.5 km to Highway 97 near 100 Mile House. This road gives access to great rainbow fishing in many lakes, including Bridge and Sheridan lakes.

A free ferry connects Little Fort with the road up the east side of the Thompson River to Blackpool.

Mile 66 (142) Km 106 (229): Highway parallels the North Thompson River, with several turnouts and fishing spots among the cottonwoods. Rainbow, Dolly Varden and whitefish are caught here. 🐟

Mile 70.5 (137.5) Km 113.5 (221.5): Gas and store at the junction with Old North Thompson Road.

Mile 72.5 (135.5) Km 117 (218): North Thompson River Provincial Park, 61 campsites, sani-station, picnic area and fishing at the mouth of the Clearwater River. Camping fee. This was once the site of a Shuswap Indian camp and many kekuli holes (remains of semisubterranean dwellings) can still be found. 🏕🐟▲

Mile 73.5 (134.5) Km 118.5 (216.5): Clearwater River bridge. The Overlanders named this river because its crystal-clear waters contrasted strongly with the muddy Thompson. The Clearwater rises in the glaciated Cariboo Mountains at the north end of Wells Gray Provincial Park.

Mile 75 (133) Km 121 (214): Junction with access road to village of **CLEARWATER** (pop. 2,500). A tourist information office is located at the junction. This striking wood building also serves as the information centre for Wells Gray Provincial Park. Turn west for tourist facilities (motels, RV parks, restaurants, gas stations, shopping centre), Dutch Lake public beach, airstrip, Star and Lolo lakes. Fishing is good for rainbow and Dolly Varden in both lakes and Clearwater River. Turn east for old village centre and bridge over the Thompson River to connect with road along the east side to Blackpool, Dunn and Halamore lakes and the ferry to Little Fort. 🐟▲

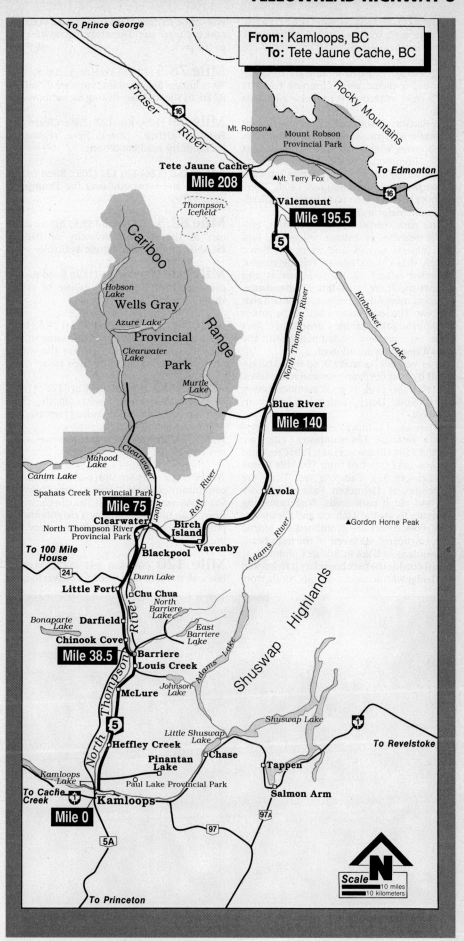

Mile 75.5 (132.5) Km 121.5 (213.5): Junction with road west to Spahats Creek Provincial Park (10 miles/16 km) and Wells Gray Provincial Park (25 miles/40 km).

At Spahats Creek Park there are 20 campsites and a picnic area. Camping fee. The park's chief attraction is impressive Spahats Falls.

Wells Gray Provincial Park is a magnificent mountain wilderness containing 5 large lakes and 3 rivers which, on their steep descent to the Thompson, cascade over many spectacular waterfalls, including Helmcken Falls on the Murtle River at 460 feet/140m. There are more than a dozen trails in the park leading to the major scenic attractions.

The park contains such interesting geological features as extinct volcanoes, lava beds, mineral springs and warm gas flows, though it is chiefly known for the rugged, unspoiled beauty of its lakes, rivers and mountains. There is wildlife in abundance, including moose, deer, caribou, mountain goat and bear. The southeastern half of the park is the Murtle Lake Nature Conservancy Area where no roads and no tampering with the natural resources are allowed.

It is possible to make a 63-mile/102-km circuit by boat of Clearwater and Azure lakes. The lakes also provide good summer fishing for rainbows, Dolly Varden and mountain whitefish.

There are 4 campgrounds in Wells Gray, with a total of 154 campsites. They are Dawson Falls, Clearwater Lake, Falls Creek and Mahood Lake (reached from 100 Mile House on Highway 97). Camping fee. There are picnic sites at Helmcken Falls, Clearwater Lake and along park roads. Boat launching ramps are located at Mahood and Clearwater lakes. Powerboats are prohibited on Murtle Lake, considered to be one of the most beautiful wilderness lakes in British Columbia.

Just outside the park boundary is Helmcken Falls Lodge with accommodations, meals, store and canoe rentals. Make sure you fill your gas tank in Clearwater: There is no gas on the road to the park.

Mile 78.5 (129.5) Km 126.5 (208.5): Raft River bridge. Side road leads upriver 22 miles/37 km to Silence Lake; fishing for rainbows.

Mile 79 (129) Km 127 (208): Clearwater Forestry Office. Check here regarding backcountry road conditions.

Mile 82 (126) Km 132 (203): Birch Island rest area and viewpoint over the Thompson River valley.

Mile 82.5 (125.5) Km 132.5 (202.5): Road east to the small community of **BIRCH ISLAND**; store, public phone available.

Mile 91 (117) Km 146 (189): Road east to community of **VAVENBY**, centre of valley sheep farming.

Mile 99.5 (108.5) Km 160.5 (174.5): Mad River bridge. The river gives its name to the rapids in the river below, where the weary Overlanders had to portage their rafts.

Mile 106.5 (101.5) Km 171 (164): McMurphy rest area to west. On the cliffs south of picnic tables are Indian pictographs.

Mile 108 (100) Km 174 (161): Wire Cache rest area beside Thompson River.

Mile 117 (91) Km 188 (147): Road west to community of **AVOLA**, named after a town in Sicily. All services available. In the centre of town is an old log inn, now a neighborhood pub, and a small log schoolhouse, now the library.

Mile 120 (88) Km 193 (142): Marshy lakes, west side of road. Look for beaver lodges.

Mile 120.5 (87.5) Km 194 (141): Tum Tum Creek.

Mile 126.5 (81.5) Km 203.5 (131.5): Rest area beside Finn Creek at the south end of the bridge.

Mile 128 (80) Km 206 (129): Messiter Summit (elev. 2,411 feet/735m) with view south of the U-shaped Thompson River valley with the Monashee Mountains to the east, the Cariboo Mountains to the west. The old highway is visible on the canyon side across the river.

Mile 129 (79) Km 208 (127): Porte d'Enfer or Hells Gate canyon below the highway. The river turns abruptly through a narrow canyon and emerges south into tempestuous whirlpools. Here the Overlanders had to abandon their rafts (after a member of the party and all the horses were drowned) and go around the rapids on foot. It took them 3 days to make the 8.5-mile/14-km walk.

Mile 134.5 (73.5) Km 216.5 (118.5): Thompson River bridge.

Mile 140 (68) Km 225.5 (109.5): Community of **BLUE RIVER** (pop. 1,000). Begun as a divisional point on the Canadian National Railway, today Blue River is also supported by logging and tourism. Blue River is a jumping-off point for helicopter skiing in the Monashee Mountains. All services are available.

Mile 141.5 (66.5) Km 227.5 (107.5): Junction with road east to Blue River and 15-mile/24-km gravel road west into the Murtle Lake Nature Conservancy of Wells Gray Provincial Park.

Mile 142 (66) Km 229 (106): Blue River airport to east.

Mile 143 (65) Km 230 (105): Mud Lake Forestry Road. Fishing is good for rainbows in Mud Lake, a short distance east from the highway.

Mile 147 (61) Km 236 (99): Whitewater Creek.

Mile 150 (58) Km 241.5 (93.5): Rest area by Thunder River, a tributary of the Thompson River.

Mile 159 (49) Km 256 (79): Pyramid Falls, east side of valley, drains from lake on Mount Cheadle.

Mile 168 (40) Km 270.5 (64.5): Thompson River bridge. The highway leaves the valley of the Thompson, which turns west, and follows the Albreda River north almost to its source. The Thompson River rises in the Cariboo Range of the Columbia Mountains, its headwater streams draining the Rausch Glacier.

Mile 183.5 (24.5) Km 295.5 (39.5): Good view southbound of Albreda Glacier. Northbound, the highway enters the Rocky Mountain Trench.

Helmcken Falls, in Wells Gray Provincial Park, plunges 460 feet/140m. (L. Linkhart)

Gray Jay, also called a Canada Jay, is common in northern boreal forests.

(L. Linkhart)

Mile 188.5 (19.5) Km 303.5 (31.5): Camp Creek rest area and stop of interest with sign telling about British Columbia's first tourists, Viscount Milton and Doctor Cheadle, who came this way the year after the Overlanders and had an equally terrifying time.

Mile 189 (19) Km 304 (31): Camp Creek bridge. One of the headwater streams of the Canoe River, the creek was named for an 1871 survey party which wintered here.

Mile 191 (17) Km 307.5 (27.5): Canoe River bridge. At the confluence of this river and the Columbia, explorer David Thompson built canoes for his travels downriver. East of here is the northern tip of long Kinbasket Lake, impounded behind giant Mica Dam on the Columbia north of Revelstoke. Boat launch; good fishing for rainbows, Dolly Varden, freshwater ling and whitefish, mainly by troll.

Mile 192.5 (15.5) Km 310 (25): Railway underpass.

Mile 194.5 (13.5) Km 313 (22): Cranberry Marsh, Robert W. Starratt Wildlife Sanctuary. The diked reserve has nesting islands for migrant birds and trails for bird-watchers. The marshes, remnant of a prehistoric flat-bottomed lake, are in the Rocky Mountain Trench migration corridor where the Thompson and Columbia valleys meet.

It is prime habitat for waterfowl, beaver, muskrat and moose.

Mile 195.5 (12.5) Km 315 (20): Tourist information office at the south entrance to village of **VALEMOUNT** (pop. 1,200). Village is well named, for it is indeed in a wide valley surrounded by high mountains, the Selwyn Range of the Rockies to the east, the Premier Group of the Cariboo Mountains to the west. Heavily dependent on tourism, the community has excellent facilities. It is the nearest centre for Mount Robson, the highest mountain in the Canadian Rockies and its provincial park, east along Highway 16 from Tete Jaune Cache.

Mile 196 (12) Km 316 (19): North entrance to Valemount; village centre to east. Junction with road west to George Hicks Park, where chinook salmon spawn in Swift Creek in August. Access to spawning grounds is on foot and there is a footbridge for viewing the salmon.

Mile 196.5 (11.5) Km 316.5 (18.5): Swift Creek bridge.

Mile 197 (11) Km 317.5 (17.5): North limits of Valemount; road east to airport. Peak directly south is Canoe Mountain.

Mile 200.5 (7.5) Km 322.5 (12.5): Mount Terry Fox viewpoint and rest area. The peak

and nearby undeveloped provincial park were named for the young Canadian who started an epic run across Canada on one leg to raise funds for cancer research. A recurrence of cancer took his life midway through the run. In 1985, another young Canadian, Steve Fonyo, who had also lost a leg to cancer, completed a cross-Canada run.

Mile 204.5 (3.5) Km 329 (6): Jackman Flats Cross-country Ski Area to east.

Mile 207.5 (0.5) Km 334.5 (0.5): Turnoff east to small community of **TETE JAUNE CACHE** (pronounced Tee John Cash). *Tete Jaune* is French for "yellow head." Reputedly, a fair-haired trapper regularly cached his furs here in the 18th century. During construction of the Canadian Northern Railway (now the Canadian National), Tete Jaune was a brawling camp, supplied by river steamer from Prince George. Today, it has a store, gas and limited accommodations. The main CNR north line junctions with the east-west line here.

Mile 208 (0) Km 335 (0): Fraser River bridge and junction with Yellowhead Highway 16.

To travel northern Canada and Alaska highways, travelers should obtain a copy of *The MILEPOST®*, All-the-NorthTravel Guide®, the northern companion guide of *NORTHWEST MILEPOSTS®*.

U.S. Highway 12

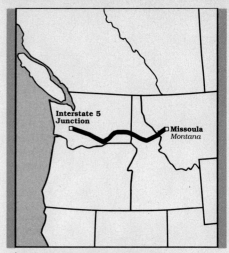

See map pages 85, 88 and 91

U.S. Highway 12, between Missoula, MT, and its junction with Interstate 5 just south of Centralia, WA, is one of the most historically rich and scenically diverse routes in the Pacific Northwest.

It follows the historic path across Lolo Pass and down the valley of the Lochsa and Clearwater rivers taken by the Lewis and Clark expedition heading for the Pacific in 1805 and returning to the Missouri River in 1806. It touches the land of the Nez Perce and parallels the tragic route of retreat of Chief Joseph and his band in 1877.

In Idaho and southeastern Washington, U.S. Highway 12 winds through the hills and small towns of the Palouse, the richest wheat growing region in the U.S. From Walla Walla through the Yakima Valley, vineyards dot the hillsides and roadside stands offer a bounty of fruits and vegetables. The route climbs the east side of the Cascades, crosses White Pass and descends through logging country to the lush green valleys of western Washington.

U.S. Highway 12 Log

Distance from Missoula, MT, is followed by distance from the Interstate 5 junction.

Mile 0 (583): Crossing the Clark Fork River in Missoula. See **Mile 504.5** in the U.S. HIGHWAY 93 section for description of Missoula. U.S. Highways 12 and 93 share a common alignment south to Lolo; mileposts on this stretch of highway reflect distance from Montana-Idaho border via U.S. Highway 93.   MP 94

Mile 10.5 (572.5): LOLO, junction of U.S. Highways 12 and 93. Turn west on U.S. 12. Mileposts reflect distance from Montana-Idaho border via U.S. Highway 12. This small town has gas stations, restaurant, goceries and a private campground.   ▲

Mile 11 (572): Turnout and information sign about Lolo Trail. This route over Lolo Pass was an Indian trail used for at least 200 years before Lewis and Clark passed this way in 1805. The Nez Perce Indians came east to reach the buffalo country east of the Continental Divide and the Flathead Indians used it to reach the salmon and steelhead fishing grounds along the Clearwater River. The present highway across the Bitterroot Mountains was completed in 1961.

Mile 14 (569): Cattle ranch on north side of highway raises Texas longhorn cattle. Stream to south is Lolo Creek; trees adjacent to the creek are cottonwoods with pines growing on the drier hillsides.   MP 31

Mile 14.5 (568.5): Gas and food to south.

Mile 17 (566): Fort Fizzle. Lolo National Forest picnic area with shaded tables and wheelchair accessible pit toilets. Fort Fizzle was a log fort constructed on the hillside by the Army's 7th Infantry regiment in an aborted attempt to stop the flight of Chief Joseph and Nez Perce in 1877. The Indians detoured around the fort without firing a shot, thus the name.   ⊼ MP 28

Mile 19 (564): Grocery store.   MP 26

Mile 20 (563): Anderson Gulch. Lewis and Clark camped here on Sept. 11, 1805. Cattle ranches line both sides of the valley.

Mile 26 (557): Narrow winding road westbound.   MP 19

Mile 28 (555): Lewis and Clark Campground, Lolo National Forest; open May to September, 17 sites, trout fishing in adjacent Lolo Creek.   ◄▲ MP 17

Mile 29 (554): Graves Creek Road. Gravel road leads 1.5 miles north to restaurant, phone, private campground with 10 sites.   ▲

Mile 36 (547): Historical marker. Lewis and Clark camped here on Sept. 12, 1805. "Party and horses much fatigued."

Mile 38 (545): LOLO HOT SPRINGS. Lewis and Clark stopped here in 1805 and 1806. They soaked in the hot springs on both occasions, noting in their journals that the Indians steamed themselves in the springs, then plunged into the icy waters of Lolo Creek. Facilities today include a private campground (open April to November), grocery, restaurant, gas, and indoor and outoor pools fed by thermal springs at 140°F.   ▲

Mile 39 (544): Lee Creek Campground, Lolo National Forest, open May to September, 22 sites and will accommodate trailers up to 22 feet.   ▲ MP 6

Mile 40.5 (542.5): Chain-up area.

Mile 42 (541): Highway twists and climbs steeply westbound with deep ravines on the south side. Clumps of white beargrass, the Montana state flower, are visible in early summer.   MP 3

Mile 45 (538): Lolo Summit (elev. 5,233 feet) marks the Montana-Idaho border and the division between Mountain and Pacific time zones. Set watches back 1 hour westbound, forward 1 hour eastbound.

Lolo Pass Visitor Center, operated by the Forest Service is open 9 a.m. to noon and 1-4 p.m. (Pacific time), daily, Memorial Day to Labor Day, weekdays in winter. The chinked log cabin has interpretive displays, maps, brochures and guidebooks for sale. There are picnic tables and pit toilets adjacent. A gravel road leads 1 mile south to Packer Meadows, where blooming camas give the meadows the appearance of a blue lake in summer. The camas root, much like an onion, was a staple of the Indian diet. Lewis and Clark camped near here on Sept. 13, 1805.

From the pass west, U.S. 12 parallels the route of Lewis and Clark. Some parts of the original trail are no longer intact, but you can follow remnants of it as it descends the western slope to the north of U.S. 12. The Lolo Motorway (Forest Road 500) was constructed in the 1930s by the Civilian Conservation Corps on or adjacent to much of the original trail. Normally snowbound from October to late July, in August and September the trail can be driven by 4-wheel-drive vehicles and some cars with high clearance. Check with the ranger at the Lolo Pass Visitor Center for current road conditions and specific directions on this route.   ⊼

Mile 45.5 (537.5): Westbound, the highway drops steeply down a 6 percent grade with sweeping views of the Lochsa Valley and the snowcapped Bitterroots. Mileposts reflect distance from Idaho-Washington border.
          MP 174

Mile 48.5 (534.5): Historical marker. Site of the Lolo Trail crossing. Lewis and Clark camped here June 29, 1806. In fall the larch (tamarack) on the sides of this steep canyon turn brilliant gold against a background of evergreens. The larch is the only deciduous conifer in the Northwest.

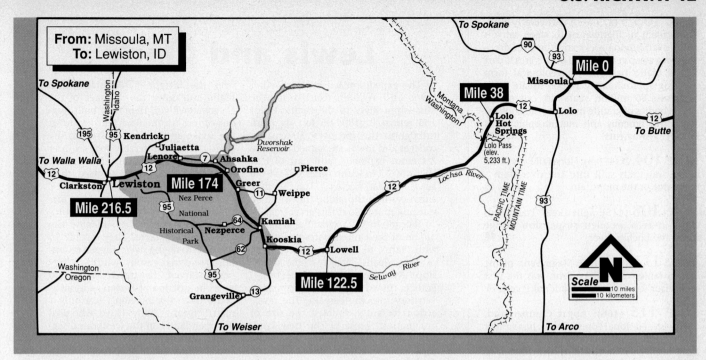

From: Missoula, MT
To: Lewiston, ID

Mile 50 (533): Highway crosses Crooked Fork Creek.

Mile 51 (532): Turnout to south. Lochsa River flows beside highway.

Mile 52.5 (530.5): Highway passes through stands of old-growth cedar. Few specimens as good as these are left anywhere in the Northwest. This entire route through Idaho has been designated a Wild and Scenic River Corridor.   MP 167

Mile 54.5 (528.5): Bernard De Voto Memorial Grove. De Voto (1897-1955) was a prominent conservationist, author and historian, winner of the Pulitzer Prize and National Book Award, who camped in this grove of old-growth Western red cedar while studying the journals of Lewis and Clark. His ashes were scattered here in 1955 and the grove was dedicated in 1962. Pit toilets, campground directory showing current status and large-scale recreation map of the entire Lewis and Clark Highway are located on the north side of the road.   MP 165

Mile 58 (525): Powell Junction. Powell ranger station (open 8 a.m. to 4:30 p.m., weekdays) is 0.6 mile south on paved road. Access to Powell Campground, Clearwater National Forest, with 29 sites, and White Sand Campground with 6 sites.
   Rustic Lochsa Lodge, just south of the highway, has been a landmark on this route since it was built in 1929 by Andrew Erickson as a commercial hunting lodge for sportsmen who braved the primitive road from Missoula and Kooskia, ID. The lodge makes a good stopping place for a cup of coffee or a meal in a dining room decorated with goat, moose, fox, bear and other animal trophies. It's open every day of the year; meals served 6 a.m. to 9 p.m. There are 7 cabins and 5 motel units available; gas, groceries and playground.

Forest Service maintains 35 miles of cross-country ski trails and 83 miles of snowmobile trails in the area. The next gas station westbound is 64 miles. Winding road next 66 miles westbound.   ▲★

Mile 60.5 (622.5): Papoose Creek.

Mile 61.5 (521.5): Whitehorse Campground, Clearwater National Forest; 13 campsites, 3 picnic tables.   ⛱▲

Mile 62 (521): Wendover Campground, Clearwater National Forest; 27 campsites, 3 picnic tables.   ⛱▲

Mile 69 (514): The highway and Lochsa River share a narrow, twisting canyon with massive rock face on the north side. A footbridge crosses the river on the south side of the highway to a mile-long trail that leads up Warm Springs Creek to Jerry Johnson Hot Springs (thermal pools).   🚶MP 151

Mile 69.5 (513.5): Jerry Johnson Campground, Clearwater National Forest; 15 sites. Jerry Johnson was a Prussian who, with a partner, built a cabin and prospected along the river in 1893.   ▲

Mile 71.5 (511.5): Point of interest: Colgate Licks Elk Trail on north side of road. A 0.6-mile loop trail climbs from the parking lot to warm springs where salt and other mineral deposits attract deer, elk and sheep. The spot is named for George Colgate, the cook of an ill-fated hunting party, who died near here during the winter of 1893. Parking, pit toilets.   🚶 MP 148

Mile 73 (510): Historical marker describes the meaning of Lochsa as "rough water." This is a popular river for rafters. The floating season normally extends from May to August. Professional boatmen consider the Lochsa a hazardous river requiring heavy equipment and technical knowledge. In the section of the river between Powell ranger station and Lowell, about 65 miles, there are 63 named rapids, the majority of them Class IV.

Mile 76.5 (506.5): Wooden suspension bridge to south.

Mile 84 (499): Wooden bridge to south. Clouds of white syringa, the Idaho state flower, along the road in early summer.

Mile 85.5 (497.5): For the next mile the river presents a particularly dramatic series of rapids; pullouts provide good vantage points for watching rafters.   MP 134

Mile 91.5 (491.5): The forest on both sides of the road is typical of second growth with trees tightly spaced and of nearly uniform size.   MP 128

Mile 97 (486): Wilderness Gateway Campground; 89 sites, playground, amphitheater, summer campfire programs, facilities for trail stock. One of the primary gateways to the Selway-Bitterroot Wilderness to the south.▲

Mile 98 (485): Lochsa Historical Ranger Station (open daily 9 a.m. to 5 p.m., Memorial Day to Labor Day) dates from the 1920s; the first road reached the station in 1952. The site consists of 8 stops on a self-guided walking tour including 2 ranger dwellings, woodshed, root cellar, Boulder Creek station, barn and corral and other buildings. The small museum is probably the finest exhibit on the Forest Service in the Northwest.   ★

Mile 99.5 (483.5): Fish Creek trailhead to north.   🚶

Mile 102 (481): Point of interest. View into Selway-Bitterroot Wilderness.

Mile 103.5 (479.5): A particularly beautiful stretch of highway with steep canyon walls, overhanging rocks and the river dropping on a steep gradient. All of this area is part of the Idaho batholith, a geological form covering approximately 14,000 square miles of granite 80 million years old, one of the largest bodies of granite in the world. Look for distinctive igneous and metamorphic rocks in the highway cuts.   MP 116

Mile 104.5 (478.5): Horsetail Falls Creek where waterfalls spill into the river from a rocky slot in the mountain.   MP 115

Mile 108 (475): Split Creek Trail heads south over a wooden suspension bridge across the Lochsa River.

Mile 111.5 (471.5): Major Fenn picnic area; 5 tables, pit toilets. Fenn was the first supervisor for Clearwater National Forest.

Mile 115 (468): Apgar Campground, Clearwater National Forest; 7 sites. Just west of here the U.S. government established a prison work camp in 1935 to aid in construction of the highway. In 1943, Japanese were relocated from the West Coast and interned here. ▲

Mile 122.5 (460.5): Turnoff for LOWELL (pop. 30), at the confluence of the Lochsa and Selway rivers, which now form the Middle Fork Clearwater. Two bridges cross the river into town. Gas, groceries, motel and cafe available. Float and horse pack trips depart from here. Resort and private campground offers cabins, 55 campsites and RV hookups.

Forest Service Road 223 heads south along the Selway River for 19 miles to Selway Falls. Eight Forest Service campgrounds along this road have a total of 67 campsites. Steelhead trout and chinook salmon hatch in the Lochsa and Selway rivers and their tributaries and migrate to the ocean 550 miles downstream. They return to spawn after 2 years weighing as much as 30 pounds. The Selway is also known as an outstanding cutthroat trout fishery.   ◄▲ MP 97

Mile 124 (459): Wild Goose Campground, Clearwater National Forest; 6 campsites, 2 picnic tables.   ▲

Mile 125 (458): Three Devils picnic area; 7 tables, water.

Mile 129.5 (453.5): SYRINGA; gas, cafe, groceries and private RV campground with 35 sites. Westbound the river broadens and the highway levels out beyond Syringa.▲ MP90

Mile 132 (451): Leaving Clearwater National Forest westbound.

Mile 134.5 (448.5): Resort lodge. Small ranches and homes on the north side of the highway; Clearwater River to south.

Mile 140 (443): Dramatic cliffs of columnar basalt from an ancient lava flow. U.S. Highway 12 enters Nez Perce Indian Reservation westbound.   MP 79

Lewis and Clark

The expedition led by Meriwether Lewis and William Clark from the Mississippi River to the Pacific Coast and return in 1804-06 left its mark throughout the Northwest. State parks, colleges and towns are named after the 2 famous explorers, and part of U.S. Highway 12 in Idaho is designated the Lewis and Clark Highway. Travelers may enhance their trip along this route by learning more about this great trek.

It began in 1803 when the fledgling nation of the United States negotiated with France to buy the strategic port of New Orleans, gateway to the Mississippi River system. Unexpectedly, France tossed the entire Louisiana Territory into the bargain. The transaction instantly doubled the size of our nation. Most of the new land, especially those portions west of the Mississippi, was unexplored territory. Then President Thomas Jefferson commissioned a young Army officer, Meriwether Lewis, to organize and carry out an expedition of exploration to the Pacific Coast. His mission was to map the new territory and to gather as much information as possible about its flora, fauna, mineral wealth, animal species, weather patterns and Indian inhabitants.

Making his way westward with co-leader and former Army comrade, William Clark, Lewis wintered at St. Louis and gathered supplies for the hard push up the Missouri River during the summer of 1804. The Corps of Discovery, now whittled to a lean, tough 31 men, 1 woman, 1 infant and Lewis' Newfoundland dog, Seaman, departed Fort Mandan (North Dakota) in 2 pirogues and 6 dugout canoes, for the arduous trek to the Pacific in April 1805.

They made their way up the Missouri to Great Falls, then on to the river's source. Overland by foot and horseback through western Montana, over the Bitterroot Mountains into Idaho and down the drainage of the Clearwater River. Here they built dugout canoes for the final journey down the Snake and Columbia rivers to the Pacific. After a miserably soggy winter spent in Fort Clatsop (near present-day Astoria), the company retraced their route in 1806.

Driving the route in the air-conditioned comfort of a modern automobile, it's difficult to imagine the incredible obstacles they faced. In addition to raging rivers, rugged mountains and dangerous wildlife, they nearly starved. They traveled over 8,000 miles in a period of 2 years, 4 months and 9 days, yet incredibly lost only 1 man, Sergeant Charles Floyd, who died of appendicitis on the westbound segment. Also remarkable is that 2 men could share leadership of such an expedition and retain their friendship and respect for one another. As one writer put it, "Their relationship ranks high in the realm of notable human associations."

Many romantic stories have grown up around these 2 young explorers (Lewis was just 29; Clark 4 years older when they began the trek from Fort Mandan). The Indian woman, Sacajawea, has been portrayed as a heroine; her knowledge of the trails and her ability to negotiate with Indians was invaluable to the success of the expedition. She was a Shoshoni, wife of the fur trader, Toussaint Charbonneau, and the mother of an infant son, Jean Baptiste, who accompanied the expedition all the way.

Interpretative signs along U.S. Highway 12 tell parts of the Lewis and Clark story as do exhibits at Nez Perce National Historical Park Visitor Center in Spalding. For a thorough understanding of the event, travelers may wish to obtain a copy of the very readable Lewis and Clark Journals.

Mile 143 (440): Historic site. In the Nez Perce War of 1877, General Howard's infantry attacked Chief Looking Glass' band here even though the Indians had said they were not warlike and wanted to live peacefully. Subsequently, Looking Glass and his followers, formerly neutral, joined Chief Joseph and the other Nez Perce fleeing to Montana.   MP 76

Mile 144 (439): KOOSKIA (pop. 830) city center is south of the highway across the Clearwater River. The town sprawls across the valley and has a frontier Western appearance with false-front buildings, small sawmill and other photogenic structures. Limited visitor services include gas, several cafes and 1 motel. Kooskia ranger station is open 8 a.m. to 4 p.m., weekdays. Kooskia National Fish Hatchery, 2 miles southeast (turn left at south end of bridge into town), raises chinook salmon; self-guiding tour daily, 7:30 a.m. to 4 p.m.

Junction with Idaho Highway 13 from Grangeville joins U.S. 12 here. Together with U.S. 95 the highways form a loop of about 400 miles that stitches together the 24 sites of Nez Perce National Historical Park. Most of the park sites involve the Lewis and Clark expedition, the Nez Perce Indians or early missionaries and pioneers in central Idaho.

The nearest site on Highway 13 is Clearwater Battlefield, about 7 miles south of Kooskia. Here, on Oct. 11, 1877, Army troops met the Nez Perce in battle with inconclusive results and the Indians withdrawing to the east.

Mile 148 (435): Gas station.   MP 71

Mile 149 (434): Handsome gray and yellow Indian Presbyterian Church, founded in 1871, stands on the north side of the highway. Historic graveyard adjacent.

Mile 150 (433): Nez Perce National Park site, Heart of the Monster, legendary birthplace of the Nez Perce tribe and "comparable to the Garden of Eden as a place of reverence, respect and awe." Here, Coyote slew a great monster. The Nez Perce and other tribes came forth from the parts of the monster that fell to the ground. An interpretative exhibit explains the tale and a 0.2-mile trail leads to the basaltic formation that is the heart. Restrooms. Private full-service RV park on north side of highway.   ▲

Mile 151 (432): **KAMIAH** (pop. 1,300). Bridge crosses Clearwater into town; gas, restaurants, motels. Junction with Idaho Highways 62 and 64.

Mile 153 (430): National Park historic site. Lewis and Clark's Long Camp, where for 6 weeks in 1806 they waited for the snow to melt in the Bitterroots, one of the longest stops on their journey. Nearby is the site of the Asa Smith Mission established in April 1839 and abandoned 2 years later.   MP 65

Mile 156 (427): The highway hugs the south bank of the Clearwater, flowing broad and flat between treeless foothills. The Camas Prairie Railroad runs along the north side. The Charles Bronson movie *Breakheart Pass* was filmed along another portion of this same railroad near Grangeville.

Mile 166.5 (416.5): **GREER** at junction with Idaho Highway 11; limited visitor services. Highway 11 leads 18 miles through the hills to Weippe Prairie and another 17.5 miles to Pierce. Weippe Prairie is the location of the first meeting between Lewis and Clark and the Nez Perce on Sept. 20, 1805. During the 1877 War, the Nez Perce came here after the Battle of the Clearwater and held a council to decide what to do.

In the fall of 1860 E.D. Pierce, an Irish immigrant and the first man to have climbed California's Mount Shasta, discovered gold at what is now Pierce. The brief gold rush that followed lasted little more than 2 years, but Pierce managed to survive on subsequent lumbering activities and the branch line of the Camas Prairie Railroad that now runs through town. Photogenic old buildings remain including the Pierce courthouse, Idaho's oldest public building, several pioneer stores and cabins and a Chinese cemetery.

Mile 174 (409): U.S. Highway 12 widens to 4 lanes at **OROFINO** (pop. 3,800), full tourist services including automobile repair,

several restaurants, motels and 2 RV campgrounds. Orofino is a lumber, cattle and farming center for Orofino Creek where it enters the Middle Fork Clearwater River. The town has the distinction of recording Idaho's highest temperature, 118°F on July 8, 1934. The Clearwater County Museum (open 1-4 p.m., Tuesday through Saturday) has some pioneer displays of mining, lumbering history.

Junction with Idaho Highway 7. Follow Highway 7 for 0.5 mile to the Clearwater National Forest office; a tree section imprinted with Chinese ideograms, found in 1939, is on display in the lobby. Three miles from Orofino on Highway 7 is the Dworshak National Fish Hatchery, at the confluence of the North Fork and Middle Fork Clearwater rivers. The largest steelhead trout hatchery in the world, it offers self-guiding tours of the rearing ponds, fish ladder and other facilities that produce annually about 3 million steelhead, 1.5 million rainbow trout and 1 million chinook salmon. Open daily 7:30 a.m. to 4 p.m.

Nearby Dworshak Dam, one of the highest straight-axis-concrete gravity dams in the world, has a visitor center and guided tours of the dam daily, 10 a.m. to 6 p.m., from mid-May to September; Saturday and Sunday, 8 a.m. to 5 p.m., the rest of the year. Dworshak Reservoir extends 54 miles behind the dam providing 6 campgrounds, boat launching ramps, fishing, hiking trails, picnic facilities and water recreation. Marinas offers houseboat and powerboat rentals. Dworshak State Park, Idaho's newest, opened in May 1989 and features 1,000 acres of wooded land along the shore of the reservoir with 101 campsites. It's located 26 miles northwest of Orofino.
    🚶🏕️🎣▲ MP 44

Mile 178 (405): National Park Historic Site, Canoe Camp, north side of highway. Lewis and Clark camped here beside the Clearwater from Sept. 26 to Oct. 7, 1805, while constructing 5 canoes for the remainder of their journey down the Snake and Columbia rivers to the Pacific. A motel and RV campground are located here. The highway follows the south bank of the Clearwater for the next several miles westbound, twisting and turning with each bend in the river.   ▲ MP 40

Mile 190 (393): Historical site and rest area with sheltered picnic tables, barbecue grills and toilets. This was the location of Slaterville, a steamboat port on the Clearwater supplying the gold rush that began at Pierce in 1860. Tricky boat handling conditions here above Big Eddy caused the steamship company to relocate their landing at the confluence of the Clearwater and Snake rivers, establishing Lewiston and leading to the collapse of Slaterville.

Indians have lived here next to good fishing for at least 10,000 years. Archaeological digs at the Lenore site uncovered oval pit houses occupied from about 900 B.C. to about 1300 A.D. as well as evidence this was an important gathering place as early as 8000 B.C. This is one of the oldest prehistoric sites in the Northwest.   🏕️

Mile 202.5 (380.5): Junction with Idaho Highway 3 to Juliaetta and Kendrick. The Potlatch River empties into the Clearwater here.

Mile 207 (376): National Park historic site. Indian legend of the ant and the yellowjacket relates how Coyote tried to settle an argument between them and when they refused to be pacified, he turned them to stone,

View of Helena looking east from the Continental Divide.   (L. Linkhart)

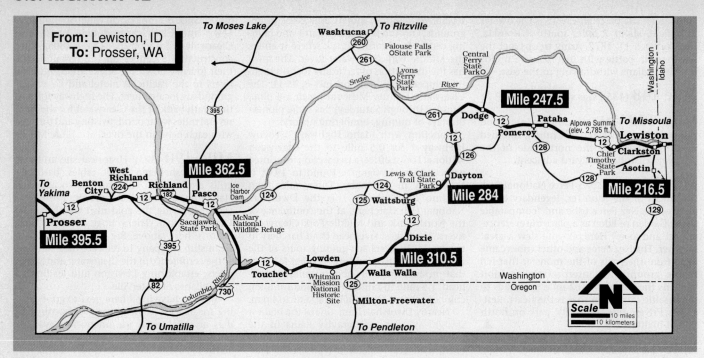

From: Lewiston, ID
To: Prosser, WA

To Moses Lake · Washtucna · To Ritzville
260 · 261 · Palouse Falls State Park · Lyons Ferry State Park · Snake · River · Central Ferry State Park · Washington Idaho

395 · 261 · Dodge · 12 · Pomeroy · Pataha · Alpowa Summit (elev. 2,785 ft.) · To Missoula · Lewiston

Mile 247.5 · 12 · 126 · 128 · 12 · Chief Timothy State Park · Clarkston · Asotin

West Richland · 224 · Richland · 182 · Pasco · Ice Harbor Dam · Lewis & Clark Trail State Park · Dayton · 128 · **Mile 216.5**

To Yakima · Benton City · 12 · 124 · 125 · Waitsburg · 129

Mile 362.5 · McNary National Wildlife Refuge · U.S. 12 · **Mile 284**

Prosser · Sacajawea State Park · Dixie

Mile 395.5 · 395 · 12 · Touchet · Lowden · **Mile 310.5** · Washington Oregon

82 · 730 · Columbia River · Whitman Mission National Historic Site · Walla Walla · 125 · Milton-Freewater · Scale N 10 miles / 10 kilometers

To Umatilla · To Pendleton

---

which is the large basalt formation visible on the south hillside.   MP 11

Mile 207.5 (375.5): Junction of U.S. Highway 12 and U.S. Highway 95 (turn to **Mile 503.5** in the U.S. HIGHWAY 95 section). Turn south on U.S. Highway 95 to reach the Nez Perce National Historical Park Visitor Center, 1.5 miles from here. Perched atop a knoll, the center has an excellent small museum devoted to Indian culture, several audio-visual programs, literature and interpretative walks and programs. During the summer, Nez Perce men and women demonstrate pitching a tepee, weaving, beadwork and other skills. Indian arts and crafts are for sale. The center is open daily 8 a.m. to 6 p.m., June to Labor Day; 8 a.m. to 4:30 p.m. the rest of the year.   MP 8

Mile 210 (373): National Park historical marker. Another of the Nez Perce tales of the all-powerful Coyote relates an encounter with a bear while fishing. The Coyote threw both bear and fishnet high on the hillsides on opposite sides of the river and turned them to stone. Both are visible from this marker. Clearly visible downstream and across the river is the large pulp and sawmill complex of the Potlatch Corporation.

Mile 216 (367): Junction with U.S. Highway 95 north and U.S Highway 195. (Turn to **Mile 510** in the U.S. HIGHWAY 95 section.)

Mile 216.5 (366.5): LEWISTON (pop. 27,730), named for Meriwether Lewis; complete visitors facilities including 14 motels and 85 restaurants. (U.S. Highway 12 detours the downtown area, routing noisy truck traffic away from the town's lodgings, most of which are situated in the heart of downtown.) This bustling town at the confuence of the Clearwater and Snake rivers is Idaho's only seaport.

Attractions include the Luna Museum which features Indian and pioneer exhibits (9 a.m. to 5 p.m., Tuesday to Saturday). Hells Gate State Park, 4 miles south on Snake River Avenue, has a marina open all year; trout, bass and steelhead fishing; swimming; sheltered picnic tables; 93 campsites, hookups for RVs, hot showers and flush toilets. The marina is the departure point for jet boat trips that go up the Snake River into Hells Canyon, the deepest gorge in North America. Passengers are welcome on the Hells Canyon mailboat which departs on Wednesdays to deliver the U.S. mail to isolated ranches as far as the head of navigation, 90 miles upstream from Lewiston. The trip takes 2 days with an overnight at a comfortable cabin camp in the canyon.   ⛺ ⛵ ▲ ★

Mile 218 (365): Idaho-Washington border. Crossing the Snake River.

Mile 218.5 (364.5): CLARKSTON (pop. 6,903); complete visitor facilities including 14 motels, 27 restaurants. Junction with Washington Highway 129 to Asotin and Oregon border. The Snake River upstream from Clarkston has a reputation for excellent sturgeon fishing.   ⛵ MP 434

Mile 220.5 (362.5): Highway parallels Snake River on south bank past Port of Whitman (north side) where barges are often being loaded at the grain terminal. For several miles steep basalt bluffs hem the highway to the south. The waters of the Snake are placid in Lower Granite Lake, an impoundment of Lower Granite Dam. Big day-glo red triangles at water's edge are navigation markers for tugs.   MP 432

Mile 226.5 (356.5): Silcott Road. Turn north across bridge for Alpowai Interpretative Center (open 1-5 p.m., Wednesday to Sunday) and Chief Timothy State Park. The

center details local Indian history and that of the town of Silcott that existed here from the late 1880s until the 1920s. Nez Perce chiefs Timothy (the first man to be baptized by Reverend Spalding) and Red Wolf lived here in the 1860s. The state park has 33 hookup campsites, 17 pull-through sites, 16 tent sites, boat launch, playground, swimming beach, bathhouse, concession stand, picnic shelters and barbecue grills.   ⛺ ▲

Mile 239 (344): Alpowa Summit (elev. 2,785 feet). Rest area with toilets, picnic tables and sweeping view of Garfield County to the west.   ⛺

Mile 243 (340): Historical marker. Three Forks Indian trails; Lewis and Clark camped near here May 3, 1806.

Mile 246 (337): Pataha (meaning Indian brush, also briefly named Waterstown and Favorsburg) is a tiny settlement with cafe.

Mile 247.5 (335.5): POMEROY (pop. 1,675) is the county seat of Garfield County. It was named for Joseph M. Pomeroy, who platted the town in 1878. Big grain elevators shoulder against Villard Street (U.S. Highway 12) in this long, narrow town squeezed down between hills on either side. Visitor services include 1 motel, several restaurants and gas stations. The handsome white county courthouse with its statue of Justice holding her scales is particularly photogenic. There is a small pioneer museum at the Umatilla National Forest ranger station. Junction with Washington Highway 128 that makes a loop south into the Blue Mountain foothills before returning to Clarkston (partially gravel).   MP 405

Mile 254.5 (328.5): Junction with Washington Highway 126. This route rejoins U.S. Highway 12 5 miles north of Dayton. High-

way 126 is steep, narrow and winding, with about 5 miles unpaved. U.S. 12 continues to follow the valley lush with fields of grain and an abandoned 1-room schoolhouse surrounded by tall stands of wheat. Wheat harvest generally begins here in mid-July when you may see the combines specially designed for these hills at work cutting the wheat. It's wise to be especially alert when driving these winding roads through the Palouse; you're likely to encounter slow-moving farm vehicles around the next bend.

Mile 261.5 (321.5): Tiny cluster of buildings known as Dodge used to be a major stagecoach transfer point on the route to Lewiston. Junction with Washington Highway 127. Central Ferry State Park is located on the Snake River 10 miles north. The park has a beach, boat launching, picnic shelters, 60 campsites with hookups and wheelchair accessible restrooms. Excellent fishing here for smallmouth bass, channel catfish and summer run steelhead.

Mile 270 (313): Junction with Washington Highway 261 to Starbuck and Washtucna. Lyons Ferry State Park, 15 miles northwest at the confluence of Palouse and Snake rivers, has 50 campsites, swimming beach, marina, boat launch, fishing, picnic facilities and wheelchair accessible restrooms. Six miles beyond Lyons Ferry is Palouse Falls State Park, where the Palouse River plunges over the rim of the plateau to thunder 190 feet into a rocky basin in a spectacular display of spray and rainbows. A primitive state park with picnic tables, but no other facilities, perches on a promontory overlooking the falls.

Mile 270.5 (312.5): Private campground.

Mile 271 (312): Cafe.   MP 381

Mile 271.5 (311.5): Crossing the Tucannon River, Nez Perce for "break root creek."

Mile 276 (307): Pasture land with grazing cattle punctuates fields of grains. The highway is following the old Walla Walla-Colville wagon trail, over which thousands of settlers and miners traveled when land north of the Snake River was opened to development in 1858.   MP 376

Mile 279 (304): Highway crests top of hill for sweeping views in all directions.   MP 373

Mile 279.5 (303.5): Junction with Washington Highway 126 which rejoins U.S. Highway 12 east of Dodge.

Mile 284 (299): DAYTON (pop. 2,630); motel, cafe, grocery, gas, limited services. The county seat of Columbia County and a busy agricultural center, Dayton sits at the end of a Union Pacific Railroad spur line that formerly ran as far as Pomeroy. Fruit and vegetable packing houses here keep the railroad busy. The restored Victorian depot (circa 1881)

that now houses the chamber of commerce and a modest museum is a real charmer in butterscotch with chocolate brown trim. The depot and the county courthouse are reputed to be the oldest in the state.   MP 368

Mile 289.5 (293.5): The big propellers on both sides of the highway are activated during cold weather to keep the air moving and prevent the orchards from freezing.

Mile 290 (293): Lewis and Clark Trail State Park has 30 campsites nestled in a grove of big trees, firepits, picnic tables and summer campfire programs relating to the Lewis and Clark expedition. Campsites are on the north side of the road, picnic area on south side.   MP 362

Mile 291.5 (291.5): Airfield north side of highway.

Mile 294 (289): WAITSBURG (pop. 1,060); gas stations, restaurants, 1 motel. One of the most picturesque towns in the Palouse, Waitsburg was settled in 1859 around a flour mill built by Sylvester M. Wait. The town retains much of its 19th century character. Detour off U.S. 12 to residential streets (especially Main Street) shaded by huge overhanging trees and lined with gingerbread Victorian homes and turn-of-the-century brick business buildings. Bruce Memorial Museum, in one of the vintage homes, displays historical memorabilia and is open 1-4 p.m., Friday and Saturday. Vistas of Oregon's Blue Mountains on the horizon to the south.

Palouse Falls is 21 miles north of U.S. Highway 12 via Highway 261.   (Tom Barr)

Mile 304.5 (278.5): Dixie; gas and groceries available. Settled in the 1860s by 3 Kershaw brothers who were known for their dancing and singing performances and especially the tune Dixie, thus the name. Turn south at Biscuit Ridge Road and drive 0.8 mile through vineyards to Biscuit Ridge Winery, open for tasting, daily 10 a.m. to 5 p.m.   MP 348

Mile 310.5 (272.5): Business exit Walla Walla; Isaacs Avenue to Walla Walla Community College, Dietrich Dome.

WALLA WALLA (pop. 25,600) has complete visitor services including 10 motels and 36 restaurants. It is the primary city in the Walla Walla Valley. Local wags like to say this is the city they liked so much they named it twice. As an agricultural center it is important in the growing and marketing of wheat, alfalfa, wool, potatoes, dry peas and lentils, asparagus, apples, peaches, pears and the Walla Walla sweet onion for which the valley is famous.

The site of the city has always been an important crossroads in the affairs of the Pacific Northwest. In prehistoric times it lay astride an important Indian trail and gathering place. In 1836 Marcus and Narcissa Whitman arrived to set up a mission (see **Mile 322**). The Indian wars of 1855-58 resulted in Fort Walla Walla being built here, an important garrison for military establishments in other parts of the territory and, later, the terminus of the Mullan Military Road from Fort Benton, head of navigation on the Missouri River.

The Fort Walla Walla Museum Complex features 14 pioneer buildings. It is the largest horse-drawn era agricultural museum in the West. Open Tuesday through Sunday, 1-5 p.m., in July and August; 1-5 p.m., Saturday and Sunday in May, June and September. Old Fort Walla Walla is now the Veterans Medical Center with many of the buildings intact. See also the lovely campus of Whitman College on the north side of town.

Mile 311.5 (271.5): Walla Walla airport exit.

Mile 313.5 (269.5): Wilbur Avenue exit; access to major chain fast-food and restaurants.

Mile 314.5 (268.5): Exit to Waitsburg Road and Clinton Street.

Mile 315 (268): Exit to Rees Avenue, Whitman College.

Mile 315.5 (267.5): Walla Walla city center, fairgrounds exit; access to major-chain motel at exit.

Mile 317 (266): Freeway ends westbound. Junction with Washington Highway 125 to Prescott, Pendleton and Milton-Freewater, OR.

Mile 318 (265): College Place; Walla Walla College.

Mile 322 (261): Gose Road; Waiilatpu (means "place of the people of the rye grass") historical marker describing Whitman Mission. A short distance west of the marker, turn south 0.5 mile for Whitman Mission National Historic Site. In 1836, the American Board of Commissioners of Foreign Missions (representing Congregational, Presbyterian and Dutch Reformed churches) sent Reverend H.H. Spalding and Dr. Marcus Whitman to establish missions in the region. Against the advice of Dr. John McLoughlin, Hudson's Bay Factor at Fort Vancouver and the most important and experienced leader in the area, Spalding went to Lapwai and Whitman settled here west of present-day Walla Walla. Whitman and his wife Narcissa, a former New York teacher, established their mission and an Indian school.

Pioneer wagon at Whitman Mission historic site.   (Tom Barr)

During the following years the mission became relatively prosperous with fields of cultivated vegetables, wheat, corn and potatoes, cattle and other domestic animals surrounding several wood and adobe buildings adjacent to Mill Creek. Gradually the differences between the Whitmans and the Indians led to distrust and hostility. The Indians blamed a devastating outbreak of measles on the white intruders and in 1847 killed the Whitmans and 11 others.

The visitor center, shaded by large trees and surrounded by a split rail fence, details the missionary period in Northwest history, the mission itself and pioneer immigration along the Oregon Trail. In summer there are demonstrations of pioneer skills and interpretative programs. A mile-long trail leads to mission sites and the hilltop memorial monument. Picnic tables. Open daily 8 a.m. to 6 p.m., June to August; 8 a.m. to 4:30 p.m. other months. Admission $1.   ⛱★

Mile 323 (260): McDonald Road. Turn south 2.5 miles for Waterbrook Winery, open by appointment (phone 522-1918).   MP 329

Mile 324 (259): Stone marker commemorates the site of St. Rose Mission (1850-1900) and the location of an 1855 Indian skirmish.   MP 328

Mile 327.5 (255.5): Little settlement of Lowden, named for pioneer Francis M. Lowden and one of the first farm communities in the Walla Walla Valley. No services. Woodward Canyon Winery, just west of Lowden, is a small family-owned winery specializing in Cabernet Sauvignon, Chardonnay and Riesling; open for tasting.

Mile 331.5 (251.5): Touchet, at the confluence of the Walla Walla and Touchet rivers; no services.

Mile 340 (243): Highway leaves cultivated farmlands and begins to wind through sagebrush covered hills westbound. Remnants of the old Walla Walla & Columbia Railroad, one of the first in the Washington Territory, are visible.   MP 312

Mile 344.5 (238.5): Junction with U.S. Highways 730 and 395 to Pasco and Umatilla; gas and cafe. U.S. 12 turns north beside the Columbia River. The area is known as the Big Bend of the Columbia or just Big Bend. Visible immediately to the south is Columbia Gap, also known as Wallula Gap, where the Columbia has sliced through the hills flanking the river creating dramatic palisades of rock.

Mile 347.5 (235.5): Boise Cascade's Wallula pulp and paper mill to west. The long strings of railroad cars arrive on the Union Pacific from Spokane and Oregon points and on the Burlington Northern from western Washington and Spokane loaded with wood chips to be converted into pulp. Freight cars depart loaded with corrugated paperboard and corrugated containers. The unpleasant odor is typical of these plants and is caused by chemicals used in the pulping process.

Mile 352 (231): McNary Pool, a good spot to observe pelicans, cranes, geese and other waterfowl.   MP 300

Mile 356 (227): McNary National Wildlife Refuge.

Mile 357 (226): Junction with Washington Highway 124. Ice Harbor Dam and Locks on the Snake River (tours available) lie 5 miles east via Highway 124 then 3 miles north. Chateau Gallant Winery lies at the end of Gallant Road, 1 mile east off Highway 124. The winery specializes in Chardonnay and Sauvignon Blanc and is open for tasting noon to 5 p.m., Monday through Saturday. Hood Park on the Snake River has 69 campsites, electrical hookups, swimming beach, boat dock, fishing and playground.   ⤚▲

Mile 358 (225): The Snake River. Turn

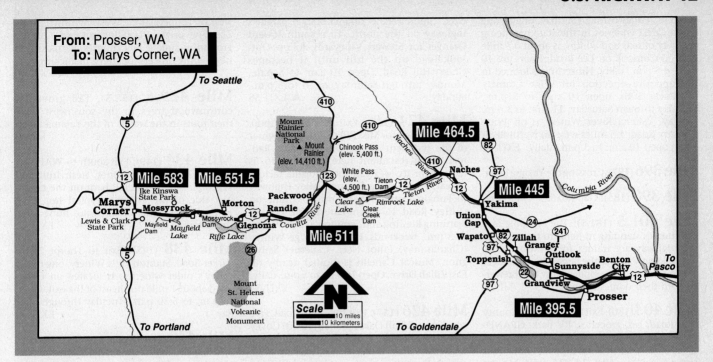

From: Prosser, WA
To: Marys Corner, WA

south 2 miles for Sacajawea State Park, interpretative center on Lewis and Clark expedition, water sports, swimming, fishing, picnic area and snack food concession.

Mile 359.5 (223.5): Lewis Street.
MP 293

Mile 361.5 (221.5): Junction with U.S. Highway 395 north (turn to **Mile 458** in the U.S. HIGHWAY 395 section). All services available. EXIT 14

Mile 362 (221): U.S. Highway 12 merges with Interstate 182 for 14 miles westbound. Burlington Northern Railroad yards.

Mile 362.5 (220.5): Exit to Pasco city center, 4th Avenue. PASCO (pop. 19,100), has all services. According to *Washington State Place Names*, Pasco was named by railroad surveyors who, "suffering from the flatland heat, named it in contrast after Cerro de Pasco, a mining town in the cool atmosphere of a 15,000-foot-high mountain in Peru." Annual Northwest Wine Festival, held in mid-July, is a major event in the city. Sightseeing includes the Franklin County Historical Museum. EXIT 13

Mile 363 (220): Exit 20th Avenue, Columbia Basin College, Tri-Cities Airport.
MP 13 EXIT 128

Mile 364 (219): Exit for U.S. Highway 395 south to Kennewick and Umatilla. (Turn to **Mile 448** in the U.S. HIGHWAY 395 section.) Interstate 182 becomes 6-lane divided highway. EXIT 12A

Mile 367 (216): Exit to Road 68; no services. EXIT 9

Mile 368.5 (214.5): Exit to Road 100; no services. EXIT 7

Mile 370 (213): Crossing the Yakima River.

Mile 371 (212): Exit to Richland city center, hospital. Major-chain motels, restaurants and gas stations at exit. RICHLAND (pop. 33,100) was 1 of 4 primary sites for the development of the atomic bomb in WWII and, until recently, has been a major facility for the development of atomic energy at its Hanford plant. A science center operated by the U.S. Dept. of Energy has hands-on exhibits, computer games and interpretative films. Open 8 a.m. to 5 p.m., weekdays, 9 a.m. to 5 p.m., Saturday and noon to 5 p.m. on Sunday. EXIT 5B

Mile 371.5 (211.5): Exit for Washington Highway 240 east to Kennewick.
MP 5 EXIT 5A

Mile 372.5 (210.5): Exit for Washington 240 north to Wellsian Way and Vantage. No services. EXIT 4

Mile 373 (210): Crossing the Yakima River.

Mile 373.5 (209.5): Keene Road and Columbia Drive. No services. EXIT 3

Mile 376.5 (206.5): U.S. Highway 12 merges with Interstate 82 sharing a common alignment westbound to Yakima. MP 102

Mile 381.5 (201.5): Exit for Washington Highway 224 to Benton City and West Richland. BENTON CITY (pop. 1,880) was originally named Giezentanner after the town's first postmaster. There are a family restaurant and private RV park. Fishing in the Yakima River is fair to good for large- and smallmouth bass, crappie and channel catfish.

Three wineries lie east of Benton City off

Highway 224. Oakwood Cellars is located 0.5 mile east, then north 1 mile on Demoss Road. Tasting room open noon to 6 p.m. weekends. Turn north on Sunset Road 1 mile to Kiona Vineyards and Blackwood Canyon Vintners. Both are open 10 a.m. to 6 p.m. weekends.
EXIT 96

Mile 384.5 (198.5): Yakitat Road exit; no services. EXIT 93

Mile 389.5 (193.5): Gibbon Road exit; no services. EXIT 88

Mile 395.5 (187.5): Exit to Mabton and Patterson via Washington Highways 22 and 221, and Prosser. Motel, 2 restaurants, Benton County Historical Museum adjoining the city park (picnic tables) and hospital. PROSSER (pop. 4,150) was named for Col. William Prosser who established a trading post here in 1882. Prosser has the largest concentration of wineries in the Yakima Valley. The Yakima Valley is the richest fruit and vegetable producing region in the Pacific Northwest and grows substantial quantities of everything from apples to zucchini. A detailed list of the crops, when they are harvested and where to get them, is available from the Yakima Valley Convention and Visitors Bureau, P.O. Box 124, Yakima, WA 98907 or by writing Farm Products Map, 1731 Beam Road, Granger, WA 98932.

Washington State University's Irrigated Agriculture Research and Extension Center here is open to the public and a fine source of information for home gardeners on growing techniques.

Chinook Winery, Hogue Cellars, Hinzerline Vineyards and Yakima River Winery are located off Exit 82. Turn east onto Wine Country Road then south onto Wittkopf Road for Chinook, a small winery that specializes in Sauvignon Blanc, Chardonnay, Merlot and sparkling Riesling, open for tasting noon to 5 p.m., Friday through Sunday. Hogue, one of the larest wineries in the state producing a variety of reds and whites, is about 0.5 mile beyond Chinook on Lee Road; hours are 10 a.m. to 5 p.m., daily. Hinzerling is located in the opposite direction off Wine Country Road near 10th, open 10 a.m. to 5 p.m., Monday through Saturday, 11 a.m. to 3 p.m. Sunday. Yakima River Winery is off Wine Country Road, 1.5 miles west on North River Road; open 10 a.m. to 5 p.m., daily. EXIT 82

Mile 396 (187): Crossing the Yakima River.

Mile 398 (185): Gap Road.   EXIT 80

Mile 401.5 (181.5): The tall pole and wire frames standing in fields to the north of the highway are frames for growing hops. The Yakima Valley is the largest hop producer in the country and supplies most U.S. breweries with their domestic hops.   MP 77

Mile 403 (180): Exit to Grandview County Line Road; gas, groceries, RV park. **GRANDVIEW** (pop. 6,300) is named for the splendid views from here of snowcapped 12,307-foot Mount Adams and 14,411-foot Mount Rainier. Chateau Ste. Michelle's Grandview winery is located at West 5th and Avenue B, 1 mile west. This is the state's oldest operating winery and it specializes in reds such as Merlot and Cabernet Sauvignon. Open 10 a.m. to 4:30 p.m. daily.

A map and directions for touring all these Yakima Valley wineries is available from the Yakima Valley Wine Growers Assoc., P.O. Box 39, Grandview, WA 98930.   EXIT 75

Mile 405.5 (177.5): Stover Road exit; cafe. Vineyards on both sides of the highway. Tucker Cellars, featuring Riesling, Gewurztraminer, Chenin Blanc, Chardonnay, Muscat Canelli and Pinot Noir, is located on Ray Road off Wine Country Road, 1.5 miles west. Winery and tasting room are combined with a fresh fruit market. Open 9 a.m. to 6 p.m. daily.   MP 73 EXIT 73

Mile 409.5 (173.5): Exit for Washington Highway 241 to Sunnyside and Mabton. Several major-chain fast-food restaurants, motels and gas at the exit. Note the large fruit packing shed north of the highway.
      EXIT 69

Mile 411.5 (171.5): Midvale Road exit. Go south to Alexander Road, then east, for the Yakima Valley Cheese Co. specializing in Gouda, Edam, cumin and Havarti cheese. Tours, viewing and sales room open 9:30 a.m. to 5 p.m., Monday through Saturday. Exit north for **SUNNYSIDE** (pop. 9,700), known for its asparagus crop. Sightseeing includes pioneer Ben Snipes' cabin (circa 1859) and the Sunnyside Wildlife Refuge for waterfowl.
      EXIT 67

Mile 414.5 (168.5): Exit for the small settlement of Outlook.   MP 64 EXIT 63

Mile 419.5 (163.5): Exit for Washington Highway 223 south to Granger. Gas and RV

park. Union Pacific Yakima branch parallels highway on the north. Turn south toward Granger for Stewart Vineyards; follow Outlook Road up the hill until it becomes Cherry Hill Road. Open 10 a.m. to 5 p.m., Monday through Saturday, noon to 5 p.m., Sunday.   ▲ EXIT 58

Mile 424 (159): Exit to ZILLAH (pop. 1,800), named for Miss Zillah Oakes, daughter of the president of the Union Pacific Railroad. Local restaurant here, El Ranchito, is famous for its Mexican food; tortilla factory in rear. Turn east on Yakima Valley Highway to Punkin Corner, then north 0.5 mile on Gurley Road to reach Eaton Hill Winery featuring Riesling and Semillon. Open 10 a.m. to 5 pm., weekends. Horizon's Edge Winery (Chardonnay, Pinot Noir, Cabernet Sauvignon, Muscat Canelli) is located nearby on East Zillah Drive. Open 10 a.m. to 5 pm., daily.
      EXIT 54

Mile 426 (157): Exit for Zillah Road. Five wineries — Zillah Oakes, Bonair, Hyatt, Covey Run and Portteus — are located north of the highway. Zillah Oakes is immediately adjacent to the exit.   EXIT 52

Mile 428 (155): Exit to Washington Highway 22 south to **TOPPENISH** (pop. 6,500); all services. This is headquarters for the vast million-acre Yakima Indian Nation that stretches westward as far as the summit of Mount Adams. The Yakima Pow Wow, in late June and early July and again in September, features ceremonial dancing, stick games and story telling. The cultural center here has excellent dioramas and exhibits of Yakima culture. Fort Simcoe State Park, a preserved frontier military post of the 1850s, is 27 miles

west of Toppenish via Washington Highway 220. Five original buildings around a parade ground include 2 blockhouses, barracks and neat, white officers' quarters; picnicking.
      ⊼ EXIT 50

Mile 429.5 (153.5): Tall groves of cottonwood trees to the southwest have their roots in the waters of the Yakima River.
      MP 49

Mile 434 (149): Exit south to **WAPATO** (pop. 3,310); gas, groceries, fresh fruit and vegetable stand. The tall barn on the northeast side of the exit is a typical hop barn where long strands of hops are hung from the rafters to dry.   EXIT 44

Mile 438 (145): Exit to Thorpe Road, Parker Road. Stanton Hills Winery, one of the valley's older wineries, is located on Gangi Road about 1 mile northeast of the exit. Open 11 a.m. to 5:30 p.m., Tuesday through Sunday.   EXIT 40

Mile 440 (143): Exit to **UNION GAP** (pop. 3,120), formerly Yakima City, named for the obvious gap between segments of Ahtanum Ridge. Except for the stubborness of local landholders back in the 1880s, Union Gap might well be the major city in the valley instead of Yakima. When the Northern Pacific Railroad built through here on its way over Stampede Pass to Tacoma, Union Gap landholders refused to provide concessions to the railroad for yards, station and other facilities thinking they'd hold out for large profits. The railroad created a new town, North Yakima (now Yakima), 4 miles north, and offered Yakima City residents free property and to move their buildings to the new location.

View of Mount Adams near Toppenish; hay stacks in foreground.   (© Ray T. Weisgerber)

Elk winter on the Oak Creek Game Range near Naches. (© John Barger)

During the winter and spring of 1884-85, more than 100 buildings were moved to the new town. EXIT 38

Mile 442 (141): Exit to Union Gap, Valley Mall Boulevard, Yakima air terminal, state patrol offices, Perry Technical Institute. 24-hour gas station, numerous restaurants and chain motels at exit. EXIT 36

Mile 443.5 (139.5): Exit to the Yakima County Fairgrounds, Yakima Valley Community College and Washington Highway 24 to Moxee City. Go east on Highway 24 for 1 mile to Keyes Road, then north for private campground on the Yakima River. Just beyond is Yakima Sportsman State Park with 28 tent sites, 36 hookup sites, swimming, fishing and picnic shelters. ⛩🐟▲ MP 35 EXIT 34

Mile 445 (138): Exit for business route, historical district, Yakima Avenue and Mall, convention center, Terrace Heights and city center. YAKIMA (pop. 48,900), the largest and most important city in central Washington, is a transportation and market center for the surrounding agricultural lands. Complete visitor services available, with about 40 motels and 150 restaurants. Downtown features the Capitol Theatre, an original vaudeville house built in the 1920s and faithfully refurbished in 1977. Track 29, also in the city's core, is a unique shopping center housed in 21 train cars transformed into a gallery of shops. Adjoining this shopping center is the Yakima Depot, where the Spirit of Yakima Dinner Train departs for 4-hour trips that include dinner or brunch. The Spirit Train includes 5 beautifully restored 1937 aluminum passenger cars that chug along the Yakima River. On the outskirts of town is the Yakima Valley Museum, with the country's most comprehensive collection of horse-drawn vehicles and a tribute to former Supreme Court Justice William O. Douglas, a longtime Yakima resident. EXIT 33

Mile 446.5 (136.5): Exit here for U.S. Highway 12 west to Naches and White Pass, N. 1st Street, Chinook Pass. Numerous motels, restaurants along N. 1st Street, large RV park. ▲ EXIT 31

Mile 447.5 (135.5): Exit to 16th Avenue, Yakima Valley Community College, Yakima Valley Museum, Perry Technical Institute.

Food, gas and lodging. Highways crosses Washington Central Railroad and Yakima Trolley line.

Mile 449 (134): N. 40th Avenue, Fruitvale Boulevard. Gas, market, cafe, Yakima airport.

Mile 451 (132): Naches River Valley, heart of the Yakima apple country, highway lined with apple packing sheds. Twin bridges cross Naches River. Highway changes to 4-lane divided with local access westbound. Note the columnar basalt cliffs. The flume high up on the cliff is used to carry water to orchards.

Mile 451.5 (131.5): Selah Road, Old Naches Highway. Gas, market, restaurant, fruit stands. MP 198

Mile 456 (127): Highway narrows to 2 lanes westbound and is flanked by Umtanum and Cleman mountains.

Mile 456.5 (126.5): NACHES (pop. 645), an Indian name meaning "plenty of water." Wenatchee National Forest ranger station. Gas, groceries, numerous fruit stands on both sides of the highway. NOTE: Next gas westbound is 58 miles from here.

Mile 464.5 (118.5): Junction with Washington Highway 410, which leads 51 miles west to 5,440-foot Chinook Pass (closed in winter) and the east entrance to Mount Rainier National Park. U.S. 12 turns west to follow the Tieton River.

Mile 465 (118): Sign on north side marks Oak Creek Game Range, 94,718 acres between the Tieton River and the Wenas Valley, bisected by the Naches River. This is elk winter range with elk, deer, chukar patridge and grouse along 28 miles of streambank. Established in 1939.

Mile 466 (117): Examples of columnar basalt on the south side of the river. This type of formation, common to eastern Washington, occurs when molten lava cools in huge crystals, the facets of which form regular columns that look like giant pillars. MP 184

Mile 466.5 (116.5): Elk viewing area and small exhibit area. During the winter months motorists can often view elk here that have come to this lower elevation to feed. The highway climbs gradually westbound. There are frequent slow vehicle turnouts to accommodate slow-moving trucks, RVs and sightseers and not impede traffic. The Tieton River is a prime fishing stream all the way from its origin at Rimrock Lake to its confluence with the Naches River. The Washington Dept. of Game stocks the river with rainbow trout. 🐟

Mile 471 (112): Highway enters Wenatchee National Forest. Pine trees are beginning to appear on the hillsides as the road gains elevation. MP 179

Mile 472.5 (110.5): Windy Point Forest

A familiar sight to Northwesterners is magnificent Mount Rainier.

(© John Barger)

Service campground has 15 sites, pit toilets. Open April to November. ▲

Mile 477 (106): Lodge and motel beside the river, cafe and groceries. MP 173

Mile 479.5 (103.5): Willows Forest Service campground; 16 sites, pit toilets, open mid-May to mid-September. ▲

Mile 480 (103): Wild Rose Forest Service campground; 9 sites, pit toilets, open mid-May to mid-September.

Most of the pines are lodgepoles (needles in pairs and asymmetric cones). The large red-barked pines are Ponderosas. ▲

Mile 481 (102): River Bend Forest Service campground; 8 sites, pit toilets, open mid-May to mid-September. ▲

Mile 481.5 (101.5): Haus Creek Forest Service campground; 42 sites, pit toilets, nature trails, open mid-May to mid-November. 🚶‍♂️▲

Mile 482 (101): Highway crosses Tieton Creek. MP 16

Mile 484.5 (98.5): Tieton Dam to south. This earth-fill dam is 220 feet high and dams the Tieton River and its tributaries to form 6-mile-wide Rimrock Lake, used primarily for irrigation storage. A spur road branches south from U.S. 12 and leads around the southern shore of the lake. Three resorts, boat launches, campgrounds and other recreation facilities ring this popular lake. Fishing is excellent for large kokanee from mid-May through the fall. 🐟▲

Mile 486 (97): Silver Cove resort, restaurant.

Mile 487.5 (95.5): Restaurant, recreation facilities, RV park. ▲

Mile 490 (93): Silver Beach lake resort, marina, restaurant, RV campground, groceries, swimming, boat rentals, fishing and hiking trails. Splendid views southwest across the lake into the rugged Goat Rocks Wilderness.

Just west of the resort is Indian Creek Forest Service campground with 39 sites, pit toilets, groceries, swimming, rental boats, fishing and boat ramp. 🚶‍♂️🐟▲

Mile 490.5 (92.5): Indian Creek Corral offers trail rides, pack trips. MP 159

Mile 491 (92): Tieton Road circles the lake on the south shore. Mixed forest of fir, hemlock and cedar here is an excellent example of second-growth timber. Note uniform size of the trees and dense branching nearly to the ground.

Mile 493.5 (89.5): Westbound, the highway climbs and twists along the mountainside on its way to White Pass. Magnificent views across the valley to the south with numerous talus slopes of loose rock. Note the paths of avalanches down the mountainsides that have swept all of the trees from steep, narrow chutes. MP 156

Mile 496 (87): Turnout to south with view of Clear Creek Falls.

Mile 496.5 (86.5): Road to Clear Lake 2 miles south and west; Forest Service campground with 26 sites, pit toilets, boat ramp and fishing for rainbow and brook trout. 🐟▲

Mile 497 (86): Dog Lake to north offers

some fishing for rainbows and brook trout early in the summer. Forest Service campground with 9 sites, pit toilets and boat launch.

Mile 498 (85): White Pass (elev. 4,500 feet).

Mile 498.5 (84.5): White Pass winter-recreation complex, lodging, groceries, restaurants, gas. Visitor facilities are open year-round.

The ski area has 4 chair lifts, 1 poma and 1 rope tow, rentals and a ski school. One of the chairs operates during the summer for mountaintop sightseeing. There are 12 kilometers of groomed cross-country trails, rentals and lessons. The world and Olympic champion ski twins, Phil and Steve Mahre, train on these slopes. Highway begins a 6 percent downgrade westbound.   MP 151

Mile 501.5 (81.5): For the next several miles westbound the south slope of 14,411-foot Mount Rainier is visible from time to time looming above and to the north. In its winding descent the highway hugs the mountainside and passes through several groves with magnificent examples of old-growth fir towering more than 150 feet in the air.
MP 148

Mile 508.5 (74.5): Scenic viewpoint on south side of road of Palisades Rock Formation, another excellent example of columnar basalt. From mid-September, vine maple, willow, big leaf maple and other trees provide splendid autumn color along this section of road.   MP 141

Mile 511 (72): Junction with Washington Highway 123. This route leads north to the south entrance to Mount Rainier National Park, 5,440-foot Chinook Pass and 4,630-foot Cayuse Pass. There is an information bulletin board at the intersection that provides current information on camping, trail and road conditions in the national park. It is 2.5 miles north from here to the park entrance and Ohanapecosh, location of a visitor center, nature trails, interpretative programs and a 205-site campground. (See also Rainier National Park in the MAJOR ATTRACTIONS section.)

Mile 511.5 (71.5): La Wis Wis Forest Service campground has 100 sites, flush toilets, fishing and nature trails.

Highway descends westbound. The Cowlitz River is visible to the north. The Washington Game Dept. plants this river with rainbow.   MP 138

Mile 514.5 (68.5): Gas station and groceries.   MP 135

Mile 517.5 (65.5): PACKWOOD was named for pioneer settler William Packwood. It's a logging town and the primary supply and jumping-off spot for backpackers, anglers, campers and outdoor recreationists heading into Gifford Pinchot National Forest, Mount Rainier National Park, Mount St.

Helens National Volcanic Park or the Goat Rocks Wilderness. Complete visitor services including several motels and an RV park. Several outfitters and guides operate out of Packwood.   ▲ MP 132

Mile 522.5 (60.5): Christmas tree farm, one of many in this area.

Mile 524 (59): Motel.

Mile 526.5 (56.5): Bridge over Cowlitz River. The broad Cowlitz Valley opens up on either side of the highway and leads past stump ranches and patches of woodland.

The "stump" ranch is a phenomenon peculiar to western Washington and Oregon. Typically it denotes a relatively small subsistence-type of farm where the trees have been felled and removed, but the stumps remain. The land between the stumps has not been cultivated and is usually used for grazing. Historically, the landowner paid less tax on land that had not been cleared than on land under cultivation.

Mile 532.5 (50.5): RANDLE is another small logging town and one of the access points to Mount St. Helens National Volcanic Monument. Gas, groceries, restaurants and 4 motels are available. Gifford Pinchot National Forest ranger station in the middle of town on U.S. Highway 12 has information on Mount St. Helens. Turn south on Cispus Road for Mount St. Helens and large full-service private RV campground 0.3 mile south. Access road to Mount St. Helens has 7 Forest Service campgrounds with a total of 210 sites.   ▲

Mile 538 (45): Restaurant, gas station.

Mile 542.5 (40.5): GLENOMA; groceries, 9-hole golf course, gas and RV park.   ▲

Mile 544.5 (38.5): Road to Riffe Lake, the impoundment behind Mossy Rock Dam. The lake is 23 miles long and is excellent for rainbow trout fishing. Boat launches.   ➤

Mile 546.5 (36.5): Access road south to Riffe Lake Recreation Area.   MP 103

Mile 551.5 (31.5): MORTON (pop. 1,220) is a typical logging town where the main street is often lined with big logging trucks. There's a chain saw sculpture of a logger at the entrance to town. Complete visitor services including several motels and restaurants. This is the southern terminus of the Mount Rainier Scenic Railroad steam train excursions that operate during the summer from the little town of Elbe, to the north on Washington Highway 7.

The town's big celebration of the year is the Morton Logger's Jubilee, held in mid-August. In addition to the traditional lumberjack competitions — tree topping, speed chopping, ax throwing, chain saw and hand saw bucking and log rolling — the celebration features an unusual contest: riding lawnmower races. It's a zany event.

Mile 553 (30): Morton airport.

Mile 555 (28): Mount St. Helens viewpoint atop Hopkins Hill. The mountain is about 25 miles south from here.   MP 94

Mile 556.5 (26.5): Viewpoint of Mount St. Helens and Cowlitz Valley.

Mile 559 (24): Viewpoint of Mossyrock Dam.   MP 90

Mile 561 (22): Highway crosses Mayfield Lake.   MP 88

Mile 561.5 (21.5): MOSSYROCK (pop. 460). Gas, restaurant, groceries and motels.

Mile 562 (21): Turnoff to Mossyrock Dam. Ike Kinswa State Park, 4 miles north on Mayfield Lake, offers 101 campsites, 41 hookups, concession stand for groceries, camping and fishing supplies, fishing, swimming and boat launch. There are 2 private full-service RV resorts on the lake. The 13-mile-long lake has excellent fishing for rainbow and cutthroat trout, crappie and bass. Blueberry picking in summer.   ➤▲ MP 87

Mile 563.5 (19.5): Mossyrock Trout Hatchery; open 9 a.m. to 5 p.m., weekdays.

Mile 565.5 (17.5): Mayfield Lake County Park, boating, picnicking, fishing.   ⛫➤

Mile 566 (17): Gas station.

Mile 566.5 (16.5): Road to south leads to lakeside resort with 138 campsites, 100 hookups, showers, grocery, swimming, fishing, boat rentals.   ➤▲

Mile 567 (16): Highway crosses Mayfield Lake.

Mile 568.5 (14.5): Silver Creek Road to Mayfield Dam; gas, restaurant, motel.

Mile 571 (12): Cowlitz Salmon Hatchery to south; open 9 a.m. to 5 p.m., weekdays.

Mile 575.5 (7.5): Gas and groceries.

Mile 576 (7): Small town of Ethel. Cowlitz Trout Hatchery Road.

Mile 576.5 (6.5): County road leads south to Toledo.

Mile 580.5 (2.5): Mary's Corner; groceries. County road leads south 0.2 mile to Jackson House Historic Site. This old log cabin (circa 1844) pioneer home was also used as a courthouse. Open 2-4 p.m., daily. Lewis and Clark State Park is 1.5 miles south along this road. The park has 25 campsites, an old-growth forest exhibit, nature trails and structures built by the Civilian Conservation Corps (1933-42). There's a restaurant near the park entrance.   ⛺▲

Mile 583 (0): Junction with Interstate 5. Gas, restaurant, fruit stand. Turn to **Mile 496** in the INTERSTATE 5 section.

Interstate 15

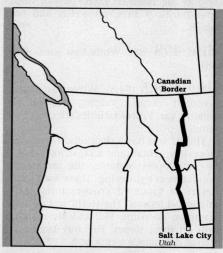

Canadian Border

Salt Lake City
Utah

See map pages 97 and 104

Interstate 15 is the easternmost north-south route logged in *NORTHWEST MILEPOSTS®*. And when combined with the Canada Highways 4, 3 and 2 route, which junctions with Interstate 15 at the Canadian border, it is also one of the longest.

The Interstate 15 log begins in South Salt Lake City at the eastern junction with Interstate 80. Heading north, the highway crosses the parched desert of southeastern Idaho, skirting the great lava beds of the Snake River Plain. In Montana, Interstate 15 crosses the Continental Divide 3 times. North of the Rocky Mountains, the highway straightens out for a long, flat drive through the oil fields and grainfields of northern Montana to the international border crossing at Sweetgrass.

This highway crosses some very remote and lonesome country and is not as well endowed with travelers' facilities as many Northwest highways. Overnight accommodations, restaurants and gasoline stations tend to be clustered near urban areas, and roadside campgrounds are also farther apart than on most roads.

Interstate 15 Log

Distance in miles from Salt Lake City, UT, is followed by distance in miles from the Canadian border.

Mile 0 (690): South Salt Lake City. Junction with Interstate 80 east to Laramie and Cheyenne, WY.

SALT LAKE CITY (pop. 168,000) has all services. The city was settled on July 24, 1847, by Brigham Young, leader of the Mormon Church. Young's 148 followers platted the town and their basic layout still exists. With Temple Square as the point of origin, streets run in increments of 100. They are 132 feet wide so that oxen teams could turn around without having to back up.

Salt Lake City became the capital of the Mormon settlement and later, of the state. The California gold rush and transcontinental railroad brought prosperity and made it the "Crossroads of the West."

Almost half of Utah's 1,461,000 people live in the Salt Lake Valley. Often called the "City of Saints," it is known for its ecclesiastical architecture. As a cultural center it offers dance, theater, opera and symphony.

Recreation includes a professional basketball team (the Utah Jazz), ice hockey and college sports. Shoppers have a choice between Cottonwood Mall, ZCMI Center, and several other malls. Trolley Square features a marketplace in historical trolley car barns.

Within 40 minutes of Salt Lake City are 7 world-class ski resorts.

A self-guided, walking-driving tour, available from the Visitor Information Center at 180 SW Temple, covers 50 sites. Some of the most popular are:

Walled Temple Square encloses the Mormon Temple and Salt Lake Tabernacle. Tours, noon organ recitals (Monday through Friday and at 4 p.m. on Saturday and Sunday), Mormon Tabernacle Choir rehearsals Thursday at 8 p.m., and live radio broadcasts Sunday at 9:30 a.m. are available free of charge. Temple Square hours are 8 a.m. to 10 p.m. The Brigham Young Monument, Eagle Gate and Beehive House (the entrance and residence of Brigham Young), are nearby.

The Family History Library, 35 NW Temple, contains the world's largest genealogical library. Resources are available free of charge. Hours: Monday, 7:30 a.m. to 6 p.m.; Tuesday-Friday, 7:30 a.m. to 10 p.m.; and Saturday, 7:30 a.m. to 5 p.m. Closed Sunday.

Pioneer Trail State Park, 2601 E. Sunnyside Ave., features the "This is the Place Monument." Old Deseret Village includes Brigham Young's forest farmhouse plus several pioneer homes, cabins and a social hall. The visitor center has audiovisual programs and books for sale. Summer hours: 8 a.m. to 8 p.m. daily. Adults, $1; ages 6-15, 50¢.　★ EXIT 307

Mile 1 (689): Access to 13th S. Street and 21st S. Street.　EXIT 309

Mile 2 (688): City center via 6th Street S. and Visitor Information Center at 180 SW Temple. Hours: Monday-Friday, 8 a.m. to 5:30 p.m.; Saturday, 9 a.m. to 6 p.m.; Sunday, 10 a.m. to 4 p.m.　MP 309 EXIT 310

Mile 2.5 (687.5): Salt Lake International Airport, Interstate 80 west to Reno, NV.　EXIT 311

Mile 3 (687): Temple Square, city center, 6th N. Street east and westbound.　EXIT 312

Mile 4 (686): 19th and Rose Park area.　EXIT 313

Mile 5 (685): Redwood Road and northbound access to Beck Street. MP 314 EXIT 314

Mile 7.5 (682.5): North Salt Lake, Beck Street, and U.S. 89 north/south.　EXIT 315

Mile 8 (682): Southbound access to Salt Lake International Airport and Interstate 215 west.　EXIT 316

Mile 8.5 (681.5): Southbound access to Cudahy Lane.　MP 317 EXIT 317

Mile 9 (681): North Salt Lake, Utah Highway 93, and the Woods Cross area. Family and fast-food restaurants east of freeway. Major-chain fast-food outlets, pizza this exit.　EXIT 318

Mile 11 (679): Exit to Bountiful, Woods Cross and Utah Highway 68. BOUNTIFUL (pop. 38,000) is the gateway to the spectacular 21-mile Bountiful Peak Scenic Drive which travels through the Wasatch National Forest to 7,500-foot elevations for panoramic views of the Great Salt Lake and surrounding countryside. All services are available including hospital.　MP 319 EXIT 320

Mile 11.5 (667.5): Exit to Bountiful, 400 North, U.S. 89 south, and Utah Highway 131.　MP 321 EXIT 321

Mile 13.5 (676.5): CENTERVILLE (pop. 11,000). Settled in 1847, the town received its name because of its location which is between Salt Lake and Ogden. Fast-food outlets east of freeway.　EXIT 322

Mile 16 (674): Northbound access to Farmington, Lagoon Drive, and Utah Highway 27. Lagoon Amusement Park at FARMINGTON (pop. 7,800) is the largest amusement park between St. Louis and the Pacific Coast. Highlights are a 2,500-foot-long roller coaster, an 85-foot dragon fire ride, arcade games, fountains, gardens, a Victorian restaurant and an opera house featuring name entertainment and Broadway musicals. The 100-year-old park's Pioneer Village buildings (many were brought here and reassembled stone-by-stone) house outstanding collections of antique guns, dolls and Ute Indian beadwork. Admission varies with attractions. Open daily Memorial Day through Labor Day and on weekends in April, May and September.

Utah Botanical Gardens, 1817 N. Main St., has flowers, shrubs and trees used in residential landscaping. It is a Utah State University research and demonstration station and is open to visitors from daylight to dark.

Farmington Bay Waterfowl Management Area, 3 miles west of Lagoon, is frequented by a variety of ducks, shore and diving birds. The 24,000-acre refuge is open daily. Tours by prearrangement are operated by the Utah State Division of Wildlife Resources. ★ EXIT 325

Mile 17 (673): Southern access by Ogden Valley Recreation Area and Webber State College. WSC is known for its allied health sciences, education, technology, and business programs. The first college-built satellite sent into space was built here. All Utah paramedics are trained at WSC, and the state's only teaching crime lab is in the School of Social Sciences. EXIT 326

Mile 19 (671): Southbound access to Lagoon Drive, Farmington and Utah Highway 225. EXIT 327

Mile 23 (667): Exit to KAYSVILLE (pop. 13,000) and Utah Highway 273. Cherry Hill, 1325 S. Main, is a combination recreation park and campground. Situated in a cherry orchard, it has an 18-hole miniature golf course, 2 waterslides, and a 6-station batting range. U-pick cherries are free during the season. Other facilities include a restaurant, service station, convenience store, and 250 RV or tent spaces with 143 drive-throughs. ▲ MP 333 EXIT 331

Mile 24 (666): Northbound access to Layton and Utah Highway 126. Valley View Golf Course in LAYTON (pop. 41,539) is rated among the nation's top 75 municipal courses. Fast-food outlet and 24-hour convenience store near highway. EXIT 332

Mile 25 (665): Layton and Utah Highway 232, Utah Highway 126, and Main Gate Hill Air Force Base. The base is Utah's largest employer with over 20,000 civilians and military personnel, and an annual payroll of $586 million. Ogden Air Logistics Center has worldwide management and support responsibilities for Minuteman and Peacekeeper missiles and the Emergency Rocket Communications System. EXIT 334

Mile 26 (664): Exit to Freeport Center and SYRACUSE (pop. 5,000), which means "City of Salt," offers easy access to Great Salt Lake. The lake is approximately 70 miles long, 30 miles wide, and has an average depth of 13 feet. Since the lake has no outlet, water level and salt content depend on precipitation. Percentages of salt have been as high as 27 percent which is 8 times saltier than the ocean. The salt provides buoyancy and allows swimmers to float like a cork without sinking. The lake's Antelope Island State Park is accessible by boat only. It has resident herds of buffalo, mule deer, coyotes and bobcats. A 2-lane road, inundated by a 1989 flooding, is scheduled to reopen when the water recedes. Family restaurant east of freeway. Hospital. EXIT 335

Mile 27 (663): Exit to Clearfield, Freeport Center, Hill Air Force Base, Utah Highway 93 and Truck Route. CLEARFIELD (pop. 23,000) is a Hill Air Force Base residential area. Free-

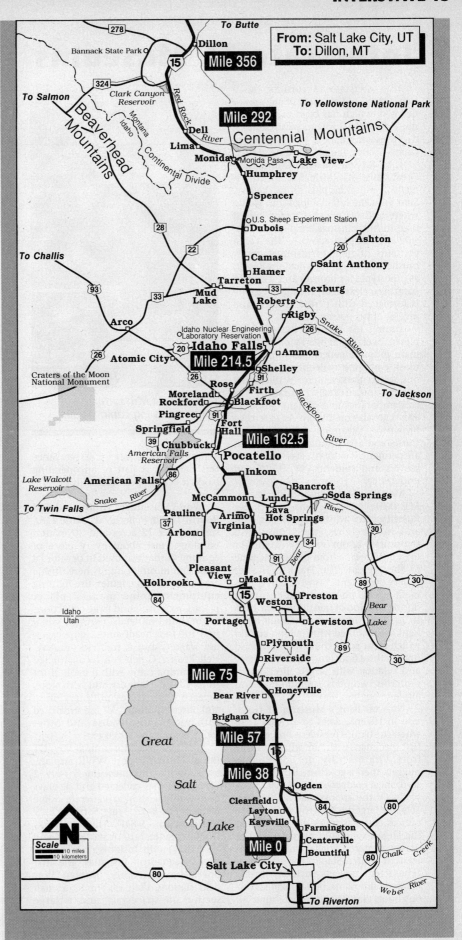

From: Salt Lake City, UT
To: Dillon, MT

Interstate 15 Museums

The Interstate 15 corridor has a rich history and a variety of cultures — much of which has been preserved in museums. Like the history and cultures, the museums appeal to a variety of tastes. Among the outstanding are:

C.M. Russell Museum Complex in Great Falls, MT (**Mile 572.5**). This is really 2 museums plus an art gallery. Start with the original log cabin studio where artifacts which Charles Russell used in his paintings are displayed beside the finished artwork. The cabin contains original furnishings, tools, brushes and clay models made by Russell as prototypes for bronzes and scenes in paintings. Next door, the Russell home is furnished with period artifacts and several of his possessions.

During his lifetime, Russell completed over 4,500 works of art. The main museum/gallery has the world's most complete collection of Russell oils, watercolors, sculptures, illustrated letters, and artifacts. Works by his contemporaries and current Montana artists are also on display. An extensive Browning Weapons collection and Curtis and Sharp Indian photographs are permanent exhibits. Fee: Adults, $3; seniors and students, $1.50, 12 and under, free.

Montana State Museum, in Helena, MT (**Mile 485**), also has a Charles Russell gallery with over 30 oils, pen and ink sketches, watercolors and sculptures. Major exhibits highlight man in Montana from prehistoric time to the present. The Frank J. Haynes gallery documents his work and equipment as he photographed the West during a period of transition from 1876 to 1916. For many, the museum highlight is the stuffed white albino buffalo which is the sole exhibit on the second floor. A third floor is devoted to military and aviation with large collections of uniforms, weapons, ammunition and airplane engines. Free.

Norwest Bank's **Museum of Gold,** also in Helena, dates to at least 1898 when the bank's president brought the first specimens with him when he came from Virginia City. In addition to nuggets, there is gold in quartz, pumpkin seed, sheet gold, crystallized, flakes and scads. Of the approximately 700 nuggets, the largest has a Troy weight of 46 ounces and was found in Alaska. It is the largest solid gold nugget found in Alaska, western Canada, and the northwestern United States. The section of "character" nuggets includes Jimmy Durante, dinosaurs, buffalo skulls, cowboy boots and other unusual forms. All of this fits into 3 display cases which are

C.M. Russell Museum contains his log cabin studio. (Tom Barr)

approximately 4 feet by 4 feet. Since this museum is part of an operating bank, it is not open weekends or holidays.

World Museum of Mining and **Hell Roarin' Gulch** in Butte, MT (**Mile 415**), sprawls over 12 acres and 30 exhibit buildings. Just about every piece of equipment that was used in or out of a mine and mining camp is here. Inside are Stanley steam engines, fire-fighting equipment, mine models, player pianos, rock drills and large collections of rocks and minerals. Outside, you'll find 100-foot headframes, mine cages, ore wagons and a train locomotive. Hell Roarin' Gulch is a reconstructed 1900 mining camp with a bank, print shop, Chinese laundry and herb store, tobacco store, ladies millinery shop and other buildings. All are furnished with tools, merchandise and other artifacts from the 1900s era.

Hill Air Force Museum, at Roy, UT (**Mile 33**), is for post WWII airplane buffs. While this museum is only 2 years old, it has collected and displays 28 now-vintage military aircraft. Some of them are: B-17 Flying Fortress; B-29 Superfortress; F-84F Thunderstreak; F-86L Sabre Jet; F-104A Starfighter; and a C-47B Skytrain. Inside is a large collection of squadron insignias, the first operating helicopter, Korean War field stations, Vietnam bombs, a small section on spacecraft, and a large collection of model airplanes.

port Center, a 2-square-mile industrial park, was once the largest inland naval base in the nation. MP 336 EXIT 336

Mile 28 (662): Exit to Sunset, West Point, Hill Air Force Base, Clearfield and Utah Highway 103. **SUNSET** (pop. 6,700) is famous for the beautiful Great Salt Lake sunsets. **WEST POINT** (pop, 3,600) was settled in 1885 and originally called Muskrat Springs. Fast-food outlets at this exit. MP 338 EXIT 338

Mile 33 (657): Exit to Roy, Sunset, Utah Highway 97 and Hill Air Force Museum. **ROY** (pop. 26,000) was named for the founder's son. Hill Air Force Museum displays 28 vintage aircraft including a B-29 Superfortress, Sabre Jets and Starfighters along with missiles and bombs, model aircraft, uniforms and insignia. Free. Hours: Tuesday-Friday, 9 a.m. to 3 p.m.; Saturday, 9 a.m. to 5 p.m.; and Sunday, 11 a.m. to 5 p.m. Major-chain restaurant and fast-food outlets here.
★MP 342 EXIT 341

Mile 34 (656): Northbound access to junction with Interstate 84 east and Riverdale (pop. 7,000). EXIT 342

Mile 35.5 (654.5): Southbound access to Riverdale and Interstate 84 east. EXIT 343

Mile 37 (653): Southbound access to Webber State College. Hospital. EXIT 344A

Mile 37.5 (652.5): Southbound access to Ogden airport, 31st Street and Utah Highway 79. MP 345 EXIT 344B

Mile 38 (652): Northbound access to Ogden city center via 24th Street and Highway 53. **OGDEN** (pop. 69,000) was named in honor of explorer/trapper Peter Skeen Ogden. The city was designed by Brigham Young and is characterized by broad straight streets lined with poplar, box elder and elm trees. The completion of the transcontinental railroad made this an important railroad hub.

Memorabilia of John M. and Mathew Browning (pioneer gunsmiths born in Ogden) and railroad history are preserved at the restored Union Station, 2501 Wall Ave. The complex also houses the Browning-Kimball car collection, a theater, the Myra Powell Gallery, and Golden Spike Empire visitor information offices. Monday-Saturday, 10 a.m. to 6 p.m. Inclusive admission: Adults, $2; over 62, $1.50; ages 3-12, $1.

Fort Buenaventura State Park, 2450 A Ave., is a reconstruction of the 1834-37 fort built by Miles Goodyear. It was the first permanent white settlement in the Great Basin. The 32-acre park has a stockade, cabin replicas, working craftsmen and a canoeing pond. Open 8 a.m. to dusk. $3 per car.

Goodyear's cabin in Tabernacle Square is the first permanent home built in Utah and one of the state's oldest buildings. The Daughter's of Utah Pioneer Museum, adjacent to the cabin, contains furnishings reminiscent of the pioneer era. Free. Monday-Saturday, 9 a.m. to 5 p.m. June 10 through Sept. 10.
MP 347 EXIT 345

Mile 39 (651): Southbound access to Ogden city center via 21st Street, Wilson Lane and Utah Highway 104.   EXIT 346

Mile 40.5 (649.5): Exit to Ogden via 12th Street and Utah Highway 12. This is also the access to Ogden Canyon and Pineview Reservoir, prime ski and recreation areas.

Pineview Reservoir attracts boaters, water-skiers, trout fishermen and campers from May 15 to Sept. 15. Facilities include 2 boat ramps, a public beach and 7 campgrounds. Nordic Valley Ski Area, near the reservoir, has 2 ski lifts primarily for weekend and night skiing.

Snow Basin, 19 miles east of Ogden, has produced national champion freestylers. Altitudes range from 6,600 to 9,200 feet; 1 double and 4 triple chair lifts.

Powder Mountain, near Huntsville, boasts unsurpassed powder snow for cross-country, downhill, and day and night skiing. It offers 2 lodges, 1 triple chair lift, 2 double chair lifts and 3 surface tows.

Mount Ben Lomond (elev. 9,717 feet) is a favorite of climbers. The last 800 feet are so steep that poles must be used for stability. The mountain supposedly served as the inspiration for Paramount Pictures' logo.
                        ⟲▲ EXIT 347

Mile 42 (648): Defense Depot and Harrisville (pop. 2,050), fairgrounds.
                        MP 350 EXIT 349

Mile 45 (645): North Ogden, Utah Highway 134, Farr West, Plain City and northbound access to Pleasant View. Farr West (pop. 1,905) was named for pioneers Lorin Farr and Chauncey West. Plain City (pop. 2,700) is a major producer of asparagus. Pleasant View (pop. 4,570) was a favorite of Indian tribes who came to bathe in area hot springs.   MP 352 EXIT 352

Mile 47.5 (642.5): Southbound access to Pleasant View, Utah Highway 126 and U.S. 89. Southern marina of Willard Bay State Park is open April through November. Willard Bay yields good catches of walleye, crappie, bluegill and catfish; 3 boat ramps, 40 primitive campsites, small-boat rentals and concessions with food, camping and boating supplies.
                        ⛵▲ MP 355 EXIT 354

Mile 53 (637): Willard Bay State Park and northern marina. Water-skiers, sunbathers, swimmers and bird-watchers frequent the park. Over 200 bird species have been sighted — Western grebes, white pelicans, great blue herons, snow egrets, bald and golden eagles. Gas, concessions, sandy beaches, 77 campsites and seasonal/transient boat slip rentals are available at the north marina. Open year-round. Camping fee.   ▲ MP 361 EXIT 360

Mile 54 (636): Port of Entry. Trucks over 10,000 GDW and unlicensed dealers must stop here.   MP 362

Mile 56 (634): Northbound visitor center with public phone, drinking water, covered picnic tables, restrooms and information booths.   🏕 MP 363

Mile 57 (633): Exit to Brigham City, north to Barry and Logan on U.S. Hwy 91. **BRIGHAM CITY** (pop. 20,000) lies 2 miles east of the freeway and has all services including hospital. Area fields produce bumper crops of apricots, cherries and peaches. Fruit stands line the 18-mile-long Golden Spike Fruitway section of Utah Highway 89 from mid-July to September.

The city was originally called Box Elder, then Youngsville. In 1856, it was renamed in honor of Brigham Young who personally selected the site for the Box Elder Tabernacle at the corner of Main and 2nd streets. It is one of Utah's most photographed buildings. Constructed in Roman Gothic Doric design, both interior and exterior are masterpieces of workmanship. Free tours are available 9 a.m. to 9 p.m., April through October. Camping in area.   ▲ EXIT 364

Mile 61 (629): Exit to Brigham City, Corinne (pop. 605) and Golden Spike National Historic Site via Utah Highway 13 west. Corinne Railroad Museum has a collection of equipment, historic buildings, artifacts and photos. Open 2-5 p.m. daily during summer.

At Promontory Point on May 10, 1869, the driving of a golden spike completed the first transcontinental railroad in the U.S. Golden Spike National Historic Site (32 miles west of Brigham City) has working replicas of the original 1869 Jupiter and 119 engines. An auto-guide brochure covers 9 miles of the historic railroad grade. Remains of Central Pacific's Big Fill and Union Pacific's Big Trestle can be seen. Replicas of 4 ceremonial spikes, historic photos and audiovisual programs are available at the visitor center. $3 per vehicle. Hours: 8 a.m. to 6 p.m. Memorial Day through Labor Day, and 8 a.m. to 4 p.m. during winter.   ★ EXIT 368

Mile 62 (628): Southbound rest area. Staffed visitor center has maps and brochures on Utah travel destinations and recreation. Picnic tables and drinking water. Audiovisual program.   🏕

Mile 68 (622): Exit to **HONEYVILLE** (pop. 1,100), **BEAR RIVER** (pop. 600), Crystal Springs Campground and Utah Highways 13 and 240. Crystal Hot Springs is a year-round resort with 6 campsites. Resort facilities are a large freshwater pool, 4 hot mineral pools, 2 waterslides, steamroom and a restaurant.
                        ▲ MP 375 EXIT 375

Mile 72 (618): Junction of Interstate 15 and Interstate 84.   MP 379 EXIT 379

Mile 75 (615): **TREMONTON** (pop. 4,128), all services available. The town is situated on the Malad River at the northern tip of the Wasatch Mountains.

Tremonton was named by early settlers of German descent after their hometown of Tremont, IL.

Major employers in the Tremonton area are Morton Thiokol, which produces rocket motors for military missiles and the Space Shuttle; La-Z-Boy® chair factory, which

employs some 500 to 600 residents; and Nucor Steel Co. near Plymouth, which manufactures mill trusses and other construction steel products.

Mile 76.5 (613.5): Malad River.

Mile 80 (610): Junction with Utah Highway 82 and **RIVERSIDE**, a small agricultural community on the banks of the Malad River. All services available. This is also the junction of Utah Highway 30 to Logan and Bear Lake and Highway 129 east.

Mile 81.5 (608.5): Turnoff to **FIELDING**, another small agricultural community, with gas, groceries and phone available.

Mile 83.5 (606.5): Malad River.

Mile 86 (603.5): **PLYMOUTH** (pop. 260), a small unincorporated village with gas, phone and groceries available. Plymouth was originally called Squaretown because of the Mormon-inspired layout of the town which had streets and blocks situated north-south and east-west in a square, symmetrical format. The term Mormon refers to a member of the Church of Jesus Christ of Latter-Day Saints (LDS). Belmont Springs Camping Area (0.5 mile west of highway) has a RV park, golf course and mineral pools.   ▲

Mile 87.5 (602.5): Turnoff to **WASHAKIE**, a small railroad stop named after Shoshoni Indian Chief Washakie, who never lived here. The ground was owned by the Mormon Church, but donated to the Shoshoni Indians for their use. About 20 years ago, the tribal members began moving to more lucrative areas for jobs and the land was leased to a cattle company. Recently, some of the Shoshoni have returned to claim their property.

Mile 92 (598): Interstate 15 becomes a 4-lane highway and continues with multiple lanes from here north to the Canadian border, except in areas still under construction.
                        MP 56

Mile 93.5 (596.5): Exit to Portage, a small village with phone and gas available. Portage is situated at the mouth of North and South canyons. Many of the small towns in this area are agriculturally supported. MP 402 EXIT 402

Mile 95 (595): Idaho-Utah state border.

Mile 98 (592): Exit to the small communities of Woodruff and Samaria, more a collection of farms and ranches than towns. Woodruff was settled by Mormon immigrants and is believed named for Wilford Woodruff, an early president of the Mormon Church. Samaria was named after the ancient biblical city of the same name in the Jordan region.
                        MP 3 EXIT 3

Mile 108.5 (581.5): Exit for junction with Idaho Highway 38 and access west to **MALAD CITY** (pop. 2,020), the seat of Oneida County. Malad is French for "sick."

Apparently some early trappers suffered from food poisoning in this area. The city has a rich Mormon history and was once a major stage and freight station for the Mormon Road. David Evans, Sr., was a prominent business-man in Malad and served terms on the territorial and state legislatures at the turn of the century. His grandson, John Evans, served 2 terms as governor of Idaho. Facilities include gas, diesel, dump station, motel and hospital.

West on Highway 38 approximately 25 miles is Curlew National Grasslands, a 150,000-acre range rehabilitation project.

Stone Reservoir on the Curlew National Grasslands offers fair to good fishing for rainbows to 14 inches and during the spring, bass and perch fishing is occasionally hot. Part of Crowthers Reservoir lies within the Malad city limits and offers good fishing for bass, perch, cutthroat and rainbows up to 20 inches.
EXIT 13

Mile 112 (578): Exit to Deep Creek Road, heads to Deep Creek Reservoir, Weston Creek Reservoir, the town of Weston and Idaho Highway 36. Deep Creek Reservoir is always an excellent fish producer for rainbows up to 16 inches. Some of the largest brook trout in the state are pulled from these waters. Native cutthroat, which spawn in the headwaters of Deep Creek, often run 3 to 5 pounds. Weston Creek Reservoir offers rainbow, cutthroat and occasionally bass to 3 pounds. Ice fishing for perch is popular at Weston Creek. Food outlet.
MP 17 EXIT 17

Mile 117 (573): Exit to Devil Creek Reservoir, a stockholder-owned irrigation reservoir and campground offers rainbows to 16 inches and cutthroat to 12 pounds. Most of the cutthroat run up to 3 or 4 pounds.
MP 22 EXIT 22

Mile 119 (571): Malad Summit (elev. 5,574 feet).

Mile 120 (570): Rest area for southbound traffic only. Handicapped accessible, phone.

Mile 125.5 (564.5): Marsh Creek.

Mile 126.5 (563.5): Exit to Downey and Preston and the junction with Idaho Highway 40 connecting with U.S. Highway 91. All services available including cafe, store, motel, gas and diesel, east of highway.   EXIT 31

Mile 131 (559): Exit to VIRGINIA, a small agricultural community with no services available.   MP 36 EXIT 36

Mile 136 (554): Exit east to ARIMO (pop. 340), an unincorporated village with gas and food available. The Portneuf Mountain Range is on the east side of the highway, which runs through the eastern edge of Marsh Valley.
EXIT 40

Mile 139.5 (550.5): Exit to Jensen Road is the Interstate 15 business route through McCAMMON (pop. 910). Gas and food available. Exit 47 is a quicker route to McCammon since the town is located just off the highway

on the way to Lava Hot Springs and Soda Springs.   EXIT 44

Mile 142.5 (547.5): Exit to McCammon and the junction with U.S. Highway 30 to LAVA HOT SPRINGS (pop. 420), a resort-recreation community 12 miles east of the interstate and Soda Springs, 32 miles east. The premier attraction is Lava Hot Springs Resort, which attracts some 200,000 visitors each year. This beautiful resort offers an Olympic-size swimming pool, natural hot pools and a 17-acre park. (See feature this section.) All services are available including 24-hour diesel fuel stop. Interstate trip permits. Restaurant 0.2 mile east of exit.   ★EXIT 47

Mile 151.5 (538.5): Portneuf River.

Mile 152 (538): Exit (northbound only) is the interstate business loop through the town of Inkom and the turnoff to Pebble Creek Ski Area.   EXIT 57

Mile 153 (537): Exit (southbound only) through INKOM (pop. 1,090), a small incorporated community with gas and food available. It was named for an Indian word which means "red" or "red rock," referring to a large red rock near town that resembles a rabbit. Pebble Creek Ski Area, east of Inkom, is accessible from this exit.

The biggest employer in Inkom is Ash Grove Cement West, Inc., western division of Ash Grove Cement based in Kansas, which operates the only cement manufacturing plant in Idaho. They employ 75 Inkom-area residents and produce some 240,000 tons of cement each year. They own 3 cement manufacturing plants in the Northwest including the Inkom plant (built in the late 1920s), the Durkee, OR, plant and the Seattle, WA, plant.

As a cement manufacturer, the plant quarries limestone and silica, crushes and mixes the powder and burns the mixture in a kiln. The product is crushed again into a fine powder and additives are mixed with it to produce the cement. Cement should not be confused with concrete. Cement is the fine powder used to make concrete. Concrete is a mixture of cement, gravel, sand and water used to make sidewalks, patios, etc.
MP 58 EXIT 58

Mile 154.5 (535.5): Weigh station, rest area and historical site. Through this canyon, the wood-burning locomotives of the narrow-gauge Utah Northern Railroad once operated. Construction of the railroad, undertaken by a Mormon cooperative, came northward from a junction with the first transcontinental line, but stopped in 1874 at Franklin on the Utah-Idaho border. Jay Gould, famous financier of the Union Pacific Railroad, took over in 1877. Trains were passing through here the next summer and the rails reached Montana in 1880.

Mile 158 (532): Exit to the Portneuf area. The turnoff parallels the Portneuf River and continues to Pocatello. The Pocatello Mountain Range is north of the highway and the Bannock Range is southeast. MP 63 EXIT 63

Mile 160 (530): Pocatello's Highway Pond is located on the east side of the road. Local fishermen often try their luck here and scuba divers also use the pond for practice.

Mile 162.5 (527.5): Exit to 65th Street and the junction with U.S. Highway 91, U.S. Highway 30 and the interstate business loop through POCATELLO (pop. 44,420). This is also the turnoff to the Old Fort Hall Historic Site. Major-chain motel and fast-food outlets at this exit.

Pocatello is the largest city in eastern Idaho and the economic and political hub for the southeast corner of the state. Home of Idaho State University and the huge Quonset hut-style Mini Dome, which houses the athletic and entertainment events for the university and community. Pocatello is the seat of Bannock County and produces chemicals, flour, cement, fertilizer and dairy products.

Pocatello was named by the builders of the Union Pacific Railroad for an Indian chief who helped secure tribal consent for the transfer of land, right-of-way and building sites to the railroad. Union Pacific is still an important employer in Pocatello. Other major employers in Pocatello are American Micro Systems, FMC Corp., Kraft Foods, the Pocatello Assembly Facilities Co. (PAFCO) and Simplot.

The replica of Old Fort Hall, one of Pocatello's major tourist attractions, is a realistic reproduction of the original trading post established in 1834. The fort is open Tuesday through Saturday, 11 a.m. to 3 p.m. from April 1 to May 31 and daily from 9 a.m. to 8 p.m. from June 1 to Sept. 15. There is a small admission charge.

The Bannock County Historical Museum, located at Center and Garfield streets, is open without charge from 2-5 p.m. Tuesday through Saturday.

Pocatello is often referred to as the "Gate City," because when first established, it was the gateway to the Pacific Northwest.
EXIT 67

Mile 165 (525): Exit to Clark Street, Idaho State University and the Idaho Museum of Natural History. City center is 1 mile west of exit. The Mini Dome is visible to the west and the Pocatello Regional Medical Center is visible to the east. Two hospitals.   EXIT 69

Mile 166.5 (523.5): Exit to Pocatello Creek Road which winds its way west through the Pocatello Mountains to the Silver Sage Girl Scout Camp and to the Caribou Ski Area. Major-chain motels, family and fast-food restaurants, campground and hospital all within 0.2 mile of exit.   EXIT 71

Mile 168 (522): Exit to the Pocatello Air Terminal, Chubbuck and the junction with Interstate 86 to Twin Falls and Boise. Travelers headed west on Interstate 86 should refer to the INTERSTATE 86 section for highway log.
EXIT 72

Mile 171.5 (518.5): Boundary of the Fort Hall Indian Reservation. Nontribal hunters and fishermen must acquire tribal permits here.

Mile 175.5 (514.5): Exit to FORT HALL, the headquarters of the Shoshoni-Bannock Indian Reservation. Fort Hall was established by Nathaniel Wyeth in 1834 and named for Henry Hall, the oldest member of the New England-based financial group who sponsored the post.   MP 80 EXIT 80

Mile 185 (505): Exit for junction with Idaho Highway 91 to Blackfoot, Shelley and Idaho Falls on the south side of the Snake River, and the interstate business loop through the community of **BLACKFOOT** (pop. 10,080), the seat of Bingham County. Blackfoot is the home of the Eastern Idaho State Fair which begins on Labor Day and runs through the following weekend.

The town is located at the confluence of the Blackfoot and Snake rivers and was originally called Grove City. It later was named for the river (which was named by McKenzie for the tribe of Blackfeet Indians he met here).

In 1885 Blackfoot was named the Bingham County seat. The same year, the Idaho legislature approved the construction of Idaho's first mental health facility at Blackfoot. It is now called State Hospital South and is still in operation.

The famous Idaho potato, the russet Burbank species, was developed by Luther Burbank in Blackfoot in 1872. After further development, the potato, which is larger than most, formed a netted skin resistant to blight. Idaho's climate, elevation and soil conditions produce what many believe is the world's highest quality potato. Idaho is the nation's top producer of potatoes.

The stately Southern Plantation House at 190 N. Shilling in Blackfoot is the home of the Bingham County Historical Museum. The design and architecture of the building is Victorian and is itself, a relic. The museum, which displays guns, dolls and other artifacts, is open from 1-5 p.m., Wednesday through Friday.

The Blackfoot River is a favorite for cutthroat fishing. A 3-fish limit is in effect to protect brood stock.   ◄ EXIT 89

Mile 186 (504): Blackfoot River.

Mile 189 (501): Exit for junction of U.S. Highway 26 and Idaho Highway 39 to Blackfoot, Arco and Craters of the Moon National Monument. For information on Craters of the Moon, see National Monuments in the MAJOR ATTRACTIONS section. Gas, lodging, fast-food outlet and hospital to east of highway.   EXIT 93

Mile 191 (499): Snake River.

Mile 194 (496): Exit to ROSE and FIRTH (pop. 470), 2 small agricultural communities with limited services.   EXIT 98

Mile 197.5 (492.5): Rest area and Hells Half Acre Lava Flow Area and geological site. Molten lava has been forced up through the earth's crust and continued pressure has made great cracks in the contorted surface. This area is characteristic of the central Idaho's lava fields and is similar in appearance to the

Lava Hot Springs

Geologists estimate that eastern Idaho's Lava Hot Springs have remained at a constant 110°F for at least 50 million years. Centuries ago, the Bannock and Shoshone tribes set the mineral springs aside as neutral ground to be used for curative and recreational purposes.

By 1863, they had become a major stopover on the Oregon Trail. In the 1890s, the Indians gave over 20 springs and 178 acres to the United States. The government, in turn, deeded it to Idaho for "health and recreational facilities with comfortable and aesthetic surroundings for enjoyment of all."

Over 250,000 people per year visit Lava Hot Springs, 12 miles east of **Mile 142.5** Interstate 15 log, Idaho's Exit 47. The mineral waters are still the heart of the resort. Motel signboards advertise mineral baths, and bed-and-breakfasts announce that mineral waters are piped into the rooms. While some use the hot pools as therapy for arthritis and other ailments, most come to enjoy the variety of recreation in the pools and surrounding area.

Set at the base of a towering cliff, the main resort complex has 4 pools (2 with whirlpools) and a masseur. The small pools have a constant temperature of 104°F and the main one is 110°F. Those closer to the source are 112°F. A short distance away are the Lava Hot Springs swimming pools. The Olympic-sized pool contains 1 million gallons of water at 86°F. It won a gold medal for design. The other is 50 meters with 5 diving

boards including one which is 33 feet high.

The Portneuf River is separated from the main resort by a park and the main street. It attracts swimmers and picnickers and is a premier trout stream.

Between the pools are 17 acres of parks with tennis courts, firepits and covered group picnic shelters. A favorite sightseeing attraction is Lava Sunken Gardens where flowers grow in the terrace of an extinct volcano. The town golf course is a picturesque but challenging 9 holes situated in the undulating hills of Thunder Canyon.

Lava Hot Springs also attracts scores of hunters, hikers and winter sports enthusiasts. Surrounding mountains — some of which are 10,000 feet in elevation — are known for deer, elk and moose hunting. River valleys are open for grouse, chukar and waterfowl. Hiking is popular for the landscape varies with spring wildflowers, summer grasses and the russets of Indian summer.

During winter, the mountains, valleys and pools are filled with cross-country skiers. The Alpine Ski Resort of Pebble Creek on 9,271-foot Mount Bonneville is less than an hour's ride away. Scenic, groomed snowmobile trails lead in all directions, loop through farmlands and valleys, and by the base of mountains. At the end of the day, many retire to the outdoor hot pools where, despite the cold of winter, the water temperature is always a constant 110°F.

Craters of the Moon National Monument. Eventually, windblown soil and vegetation will cover these lava outcroppings and the area will resemble the surrounding plains.

Mile 204.5 (485.5): Exit to Shelley and Firth area. SHELLEY (pop. 3,680) is a small agricultural community on the south side of the Snake River. Gas and food available.   EXIT 108

Mile 210 (480): Exit to Shelley, junction with U.S. Highway 26 to Jackson, WY, and Grand Teton National Park. This is also the interstate business loop through the city of Idaho Falls, the last large city between here and Butte, MT. Interstate trucks can secure trip permits at Yellowstone truck stop.   EXIT 113

Mile 214.5 (475.5): Exit for junction with U.S. Highway 20 west to Arco, Craters of the Moon National Monument (see MAJOR ATTRACTIONS section), the Idaho National Engineering Laboratory and Broadway Street access to Idaho Falls.

IDAHO FALLS (pop. 42,830) offers all visitor services. Harry Rickets established a ferry crossing the Snake River at the site of Idaho Falls in 1864 to accommodate the miners headed to the goldfields. The following year, a toll bridge was constructed across the Snake by J.M. "Matt" Taylor. The area was first called Taylor's Crossing and later Eagle Rock before receiving its final name in 1891. It is named after the scenic falls on the river.

Idaho Falls serves as the major economic center for eastern Idaho north of Blackfoot and is surrounded by various small agricultural communities. Crops include wheat, barley and sugar beets. Idaho's largest stockyards are located in Idaho Falls. The U.S. Dept. of Energy's Idaho Operations Office, which administers the Idaho National Engineering Laboratory (INEL) west of town, is located here. (See **Mile 223.5** in the U.S. HIGHWAY 93 section.)

Idaho Falls is the home of the Eastern Idaho Vocational Technical School and University Place, which offers classes from the University of Idaho, Idaho State University and Ricks College.   EXIT 118

Mile 215 (475): Exit for junction with U.S. Highway 20 to the Idaho Falls Air Terminal, Rexburg, St. Anthony, West Yellowstone and Yellowstone National Park. Major-chain motels, family restaurants, pancake house, pizza and campground available at this exit. ▲ EXIT 119

Mile 223.5 (466.5): Exit to the Osgood area, a rural farming and residential area. No services but gas, diesel and propane are available. EXIT 128

Mile 230.5 (459.5): Exit for junction of Idaho Highway 48 to the village of **ROBERTS**, a small, unincorporated farming community. Interstate trip permits available at Texaco station. Gas, food and camping available. ▲ MP 135 EXIT 135

Mile 237 (453): Rest area. This area has a sign that warns travelers to watch for snakes. Watch for rattlesnakes not only here, but at any wayside in the desert. Rest areas often provide water, shade and amenities favorable to desert-dwelling wildlife, including reptiles. The western diamondback rattlesnake inhabits much of Idaho. Trailer dump station, historic marker on Market Lake.

Mile 238 (452): Exit for junction of Idaho Highways 28 and 33. The 2 highways share the same alignment for nearly 15 miles until Highway 33 heads for Arco and Highway 28 branches off through the Lemhi Valley to Salmon. East on Highway 33 is Rexburg, about 20 miles. EXIT 143

Mile 245 (445): Exit to the small agricultural community of **HAMER** (pop. 120). Just northwest of this community is the Camas National Wildlife Refuge, a 10,000-acre refuge inhabited by migrating geese and ducks, cranes, herons, egrets, swans and several birds of prey. Wildlife include pronghorns, mule deer, beaver and muskrat. The best time to visit the refuge is during the spring and fall, when the birds are nesting and migrating. EXIT 150

Mile 246 (444): Divided highway ends; 2-way traffic begins northbound and continues to the Montana border, about 45 miles from here.

Mile 263 (427): Exit for junction with Idaho Highway 22 to the community of **DUBOIS** (pop. 360), pronounced DEW-boyce, a small farming and ranching community. Limited services. Access to Arco and Craters of the Moon National Monument (see MAJOR ATTRACTIONS section). MP 168 EXIT 167

Mile 268 (422): Exit to the U.S. Sheep Experimental Station. This is the only governmental-funded sheep research center in the nation. Established in 1916, it comprises 93,000 acres and 5,000 sheep. Experiments are performed here on new breeds of sheep, disease control and predator control.

Coyotes have for centuries been a bane to the sheep industry and millions of dollars are lost annually due to coyote predation on sheep bands. The U.S. Sheep Experimental

There are 5,000 sheep at the U.S. Sheep Experimental Station at Mile 268. (Tom Barr)

Station researchers have been testing several breeds of guard dogs bred to protect sheep on the open range. Among the breeds being tested is the Komondor, an exotic Hungarian breed which has been guarding flocks of sheep for ages. The dogs are being developed in response to protectionist groups which oppose lethal coyote control programs. EXIT 172

Mile 273.5 (416.5): Fences on the east side of the highway are designed to keep snow from drifting over the highway during blizzard conditions. Travelers should check with state police before attempting to cross Monida Pass (**Mile 292**) during severe winter weather.

Mile 276.5 (413.5): Exit to **SPENCER** (pop. 20). Gas, phone and food available. Near Spencer are commercial fire opal mines where visitors may dig their own fire opals. The mines are privately owned and those wishing to dig must secure a permit in Spencer. MP 180 EXIT 180

Mile 277 (413): Entering Targhee National Forest northbound. Travelers may notice several areas of dead or dying trees, victims of the mountain pine bark beetle which infested the area around 1960.

The Targhee National Forest contains some 1,873,000 acres. The name is that of a Bannock Indian leader at Fort Hall during the 1850s and 1860s. Targhee was the chief of the Bannocks in 1867 when Fort Hall Reservation was established.

In honor of Chief Targhee, the lands where he roamed received his name, the Targhee National Forest. The mountain pass the Bannocks used to reach their buffalo hunting grounds (now on U.S. Highway 20 east of West Yellowstone) is also called Targhee Pass.

Mile 281 (409): Exit to Stoddard Creek

Campground (elev. 6,200 feet) with 14 campsites, picnic tables, toilets, grills, water and garbage bins. This is a fee campground. ▲ EXIT 184

Mile 284.5 (405.5): Targhee National Forest boundary.

Mile 286 (404): Exit to **HUMPHREY**, a small village with no services available. The impressive spires of the Centennial Mountains are on the east and the Beaverhead Mountains are on the west. The Centennials form a massive 10,000-foot-high border between Idaho and Montana. MP 190 EXIT 190

Mile 290 (400): Exit 195.

Mile 291 (399): Turnout. MP 196

Mile 292 (398): Exit to **MONIDA**, a small community with all services available. Two-lane highway ends, 4-lane divided highway begins, northbound. This is the Idaho-Montana state border and the summit of Monida Pass (elev. 6,823 feet) and the crest of the Continental Divide.

Turnoff here for Red Rock Lakes National Wildlife Refuge, 28 miles east. The road to the refuge is good gravel and crosses the 7,000-foot-high Centennial Valley, a high mountain sage bowl where you are likely to spot pronghorns in the sage.

The Red Rock Lakes National Wildlife Refuge is home to one-third of the North America trumpeter swan population and is credited with bringing the trumpeters back from the brink of extinction — one of the most striking and rare birds in the country. Up to 350 trumpeters nest on this 40,000-acre refuge. Birds from this flock have been used to reestablish trumpeters in Oregon, Washington, Nevada, South Dakota, Nebraska and Minnesota. Unlike Alaskan trumpeters, Red

Rock's swan population does not migrate south during the winter.

Mile 301 (389): Exit to the community of Snowline. No services available.　　EXIT 9

Mile 307 (383): Exit to the small community of **LIMA** (pop. 360). All services available. Originally a railroad stop, Lima has held the names Allerdice and Spring Hill before eventually being named after Lima, WI.　EXIT 15

Mile 313 (377): The Tendoy Mountains are visible on the west side of the highway.

Mile 314 (376): Turnoff to unincorporated community of **DELL**. All services available.　　　　　　　　MP 24 EXIT 23

Mile 322 (368): Turnoff to unincorporated community of Kidd. No services available.　　　　　　　　　　EXIT 29

Mile 325 (365): Rest area.　　MP 34

Mile 329 (361): Turnoff to Red Rock, small unincorporated community. No services available.　　　　EXIT 37

Mile 328 (362): Red Rock River. Good fly-fishing for cutthroat and rainbows. Rain that falls into Hellroaring Creek on the Continental Divide between Reas Mountain and Mount Jefferson, headwaters of the Red Rock River, runs more than 4,000 miles to the Gulf of Mexico, reported to be the third-longest river system in the world.　　　　　　　　　●━

Mile 334 (356): Exit for junction with Montana Highway 324 west to Clark Canyon Dam, Reservoir and Recreation Area. Camp Fortune overlook on reservoir. North shore details Lewis and Clark encampment which marked transition from water to overland travel.

Four-lane divided highway ends, 2-lane highway begins, northbound.

Clark Canyon Recreation Area offers 12 campgrounds with a total of 57 campsites, 69 picnic areas, trailer spaces, drinking water, toilets, boat launches and fishing access. RV spaces, full service, rented by season, month, week or day.

Considered one of the best lakes in southern Montana for trophy-sized trout, Clark Canyon Reservoir offers fishing for browns to 10 pounds, stocked rainbow to 7 pounds, whitefish and ling. Spring, fall, and winter ice fishing is good but summer fishing can be slow. The lake is a Bureau of Reclamation project. Rental boats are available from a resort on the lake.　●━▲ MP 42 EXIT 44

Mile 335 (355): Beaverhead River, the headwaters of which are at Clark Canyon Dam. Fly-fishermen are very successful in pulling in rainbows and browns in large numbers. Brush is thick along the banks, inhibiting shore fishing and the swift current and depth make it a tough river to wade. Best way to fish the Beaverhead is to float it in a boat. There are several bridge crossing access points.　　　　　　　　　●━ MP 355

Mile 339 (351): Pipe Organ Bridge crosses the Beaverhead River. Below here bank access improves, but the tremendously large trout found below the reservoir are fewer and farther apart. Below Barretts, bank fishing is the best way to tackle this stream.

Mile 343 (347): Exit to Frontage Road.　　　　　　　　　　　　　　EXIT 51

Mile 343.5 (346.5): Exit to Grasshopper Road. No services.　　　　EXIT 52

Mile 346 (344): Two-lane highway ends, 4-lane divided highway begins, northbound.

Mile 346.5 (343.5): Rest area, southbound only. Picnic tables, restrooms, and information.　　　　　　　　　　🛉

Mile 347 (343): Exit to Barretts. The Barretts Talc Mills, owned by Pfizer, Inc., is visible to the east of the highway. Notice the trail of talc left by the trucks hauling the material from the plant.

Talc, aside from its use as talcum powder, is used in the manufacture of paper, Corningware dishes, plastics, pharmaceutical and cosmetic products. It is also present in rice to keep the moisture content down and prevent the grains of rice from sticking together.　　　　　　　　　　　　　EXIT 56

Mile 350.5 (339.5): Exit 59 is the junction of Montana Highway 278 to Jackson, Wisdom, Bannack State Park and Maverick Ski Area.

Bannack State Park, 21 miles west, is the site of the first major gold discovery in Montana. In July 1862, a small party of miners discovered gold on Grasshopper Creek and the town of Bannack was born.

Law and order were scarce in the boom town and the sheriff, Henry Plummer, played both sides of the fence. He served as sheriff and was leader of an outlaw gang which became known as the Plummer gang. He and his band of road agents killed and robbed hundreds of prospectors and residents before meeting their fate at the end of a hangman's noose provided by the Montana Vigilantes at Yankee Flat outside of Bannack.

Bannack was the first territorial capital of Montana and the first legislature met there in 1864. The territorial seat was moved to Virginia City, following the gold rush the next year.

Self-guided tours of the ghost town of Bannack are available and brochures describe the town and each of the buildings. Fire is an ever-present danger to historic relics of this kind and smoking is prohibited. It is also illegal to remove or deface any objects or features here.　　　　★ MP 60 EXIT 59

Mile 353.5 (336.5): Beaverhead River.

Mile 356 (334): Exit 62 is the interstate business loop through **DILLON** (pop. 4,090) and access to the Western Montana College. All services are available in Dillon.

Dillon is the seat of Beaverhead County and was named after the president of the

Union Pacific Railroad, Sidney Dillon. The Beaverhead County Museum has an excellent collection of historic artifacts.　　　　　　　　　　MP 63 EXIT 62

Mile 357 (333): Exit for junction with Montana Highway 41 north to Beaverhead Rock State Monument and the town of Twin Bridges. Beaverhead Rock was named by Lewis and Clark because it appeared to them to resemble a beaver's head. The Beaverhead River is located just north of the junction.　　　　　　　　　MP 64 EXIT 63

Mile 368 (322): Exit to small community of Apex (no services) and access west 9 miles to a day-use area with 5 picnic sites, drinking water, toilets and fishing access.　　　　　　　　🛉 ●━ EXIT 74

Mile 377 (313): Exit to small community of Glen, 3 miles east of the highway. Phone and gas available.

East of this junction about 5 miles is Brownes Lake and campground. The campground offers 8 campsites, 6 picnic sites, trailer space, toilets and fishing access. Brownes Lake offers fair to poor catches of pan-sized brook and rainbow trout. Above Brownes Lake is Lake Agnes, offering an excellent grayling fishery from 9 to 13 inches. 🛉●━▲ EXIT 85

Mile 377.5 (312.5): Big Hole River offers one of the most prominent trophy trout waters in southwestern Montana. Each spring giant orange salmon flies attract fly-fishermen from around the world. Guide boats regularly work the river.　　　　　　●━

Mile 385 (305): Exit to **MELROSE**, a small community famous for the trout fishing in the nearby Big Hole River. All services available including diesel, camping 1 mile west of highway.　　　　　　　●━▲ EXIT 93

Mile 391 (299): Exit to Moose Creek Road.　　　　　　　　MP 100 EXIT 99

Mile 394 (296): Exit for junction with Montana Highway 43 to Divide, Wisdom and the Big Hole National Battlefield. Phone and gas are available at Divide. The Humbug Spires Primitive Area is visible to the east.

Located approximately 60 miles west of this junction via Highway 43, Big Hole National Battlefield is an excellent park which dramatizes the battle between the U.S. Army and Chief Joseph's band during the Nez Perce War. A visitors center provides a narrated slide show and a walking tour through the battleground. This is one of the finest attractions in the Northwest and well worth the visit.　　　　　　　　　★ EXIT 102

Mile 399.5 (290.5): Rest area. Picnic shelter, restrooms.　　🛉 MP 109

Mile 403 (287): Exit to Feely. No services available.　　　　　　EXIT 111

Mile 403.5 (286.5): Crossing the Continental Divide at Deer Lodge Pass (elev. 5,879 feet).　　　　　　　MP 112

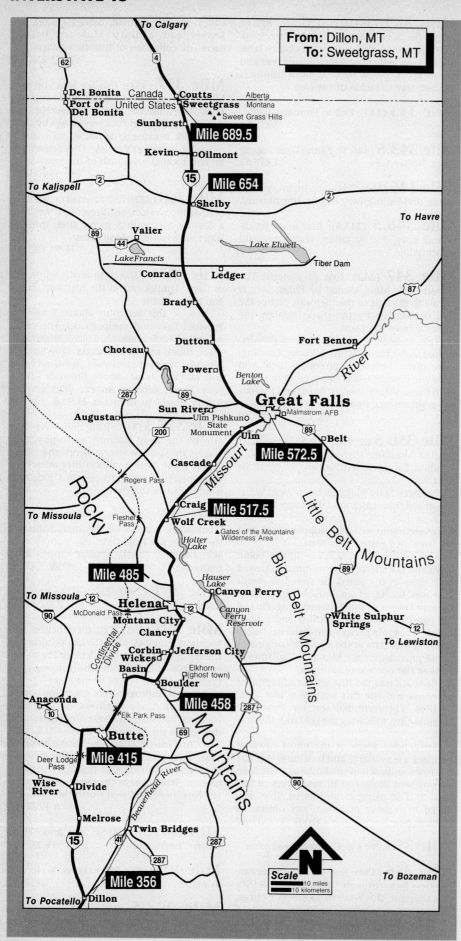

From: Dillon, MT
To: Sweetgrass, MT

Mile 689.5

Mile 654

Mile 572.5

Mile 517.5

Mile 485

Mile 458

Mile 415

Mile 356

Del Bonita Canada Coutts Alberta
Port of United States Sweetgrass Montana
Del Bonita ▲ ▲ Sweet Grass Hills
Sunburst
Kevin Oilmont
Shelby
To Kalispell
Valier
Lake Elwell
To Havre
Lake Francis Tiber Dam
Conrad Ledger
Brady
Dutton Fort Benton
Choteau River
Power
Benton Lake
Great Falls
Sun River Malmstrom AFB
Augusta Ulm Pishkun State Monument
Ulm Belt
Cascade
Missouri
Craig
Wolf Creek
To Missoula Fleshers Pass
Holter Lake ▲ Gates of the Mountains Wilderness Area
Hauser Lake
To Missoula Helena
McDonald Pass
Montana City Canyon Ferry
Clancy Canyon Ferry Reservoir
Corbin Jefferson City
Wickes Elkhorn (ghost town) White Sulphur Springs
Basin
Boulder To Lewiston
Anaconda
Elk Park Pass
Butte
Deer Lodge Pass
Wise River Divide
Beaverhead River
Melrose
Twin Bridges To Bozeman
To Pocatello Dillon
Rocky Mountains
Big Belt Mountains
Little Belt Mountains
Continental Divide
Scale 10 miles 10 kilometers N

Mile 408 (282): Exit to the small, unincorporated community of Buxton. No services available. EXIT 116

Mile 411.5 (278.5): Exit for junction with Montana Highway 423 to Silver Bow. No services available. MP 120 EXIT 119

Mile 413 (277): Junction of Interstate 15 and Interstate 90. The 2 interstates share a common alignment for the next 8 miles eastbound.

Travelers headed west on Interstate 90 turn to **Mile 594.5** in the INTERSTATE 90 section for log.

Mile 414 (276): Exit to ROCKER, a bedroom community for the city of Butte. All services available. EXIT 122

Mile 415 (275): Exit for junction with business route Interstate 15 through Butte city center.

BUTTE (pop. 33,380) has all services. The town also has a rich mining history, evidence of which is carved into the surrounding hillsides heavily eroded by mine workings and haul roads. Many of the dwellings here originated as company housing for mine workers.

The Berkeley Pit, at one time the largest of all open-pit mines in the world, is located on E. Park Street and is open during daylight hours. There is no admission charge.

At the Mineral Museum at Montana College of Mineral Science and Technology, more than 1,000 mineral specimens are on display. The museum is open from 8 a.m. until 5 p.m. daily, June through Labor Day; and winter hours are 8 a.m. to 5 p.m. weekdays. There is no admission charge.

The "Copper King" Mansion, located at 219 W. Granite St., was built by Senator William Clark. The 32-room mansion, complete with a 60-foot-long ballroom, is available for tours daily from 9 a.m. until 9 p.m. at a minimal admission charge.

The Community Arts Center and Museum, originally the Charles Clark Mansion, built in 1898, is a national historic site with changing art exhibits. Admission is free. It is located at 321 W. Broadway. ★ EXIT 124

Mile 418 (272): Exit to Montana Street and Montana Tech. Hospital exit. EXIT 126

Mile 418.5 (271.5): Exit 127A to Harrison Avenue S. and the Butte airport. Traffic information is available by tuning your radio to 1610 AM. Exit 127B heads to Harrison Avenue N. in Butte. MP 128 EXIT 127

Mile 420 (270): Junctions of Interstate 15 and 90 at the eastern edge of Butte. The 2 interstates share a common alignment for 8 miles westbound. A scenic overlook at the exit has a historical sign commemorating Butte's mining history and Meaderville, which contained the "richest hill on earth." Continue north on Interstate 15 for Helena.

Travelers headed east or west on Interstate 90 turn to **Mile 603** in the INTERSTATE 90 section for log. MP 130 EXIT 129

Mile 428 (262): Exit to Woodville, ranch land access only, no services are offered at this exit. Northbound travelers now find Interstate 15 entering an area of sweeping green valleys, open timbered slopes and clear spring creeks. Deer are often seen from the highway. Sometimes elk are visible from the roadside.
MP 135 EXIT 134

Mile 433 (257): Elk Park Pass (elev. 6,638 feet), on the Continental Divide, the third and final crossing of the divide for northbound travelers. North of Elk Park the divide follows the backbone of the peaks visible to the west. Elk Park Pass is only slightly higher than the elevation of the highway north and south of this point and the crossing is not dramatic. There are no services at this exit, but a few primitive Forest Service campsites are available. Bison Creek, paralleling the highway, offers fair fishing for brookies and rainbow.
MP 139 EXIT 138

Mile 435 (255): Boulder River bridge. There are 2 Boulder rivers in Montana. The most prominent is the Yellowstone River tributary flowing from high in the Absaroka Mountains south of Livingston to the Yellowstone at Big Timber on Interstate 90. The other Boulder River, which you are now crossing, is creeklike in its upper reaches. The tailings and slag heaps of old gold and ore mines are occasionally spotted spilling down the hillsides on either side of the valley.

Mile 438 (252): Chain removal area.
MP 144

Mile 442 (248): Chain-up area for southbound travelers.
MP 148

Mile 444 (246): Exit to Berice. No services available. Picnic area. MP 152 EXIT 151

Mile 447.5 (242.5): Crossing Boulder River.

Mile 448 (242): Deerlodge National Forest boundary.

Mile 450 (240): Exit to BASIN, once a thriving mining community, now offering limited services, and enjoying an international reputation for its "health mines." The best known is the Merry Widow Mine where low levels of radon gas fumes, a colorless, odorless element is reported to relieve the pain of arthritis, sinusitis, eczema, asthma, migraine, hay fever, psoriasis, diabetes and general allergies. Tours of the mine are offered for a fee. In the 1800s, the hills surrounding Basin offered some of the richest gold, silver, copper and lead strikes ever made in the West. The strikes are mostly played out now but antiques, abandoned mines and local history make this an interesting stop.

Primitive Forest Service campgrounds are located in the hills about 4 miles west of Basin off the highway in Deerlodge National Forest. Mormon Gulch has 16 sites and Lady Smith has 5 sites. The campgrounds are open from Memorial Day through mid-September, and are located in excellent deer and elk country.

Four miles northwest of Basin on Forest Service Road 172, Basin Canyon Campground offers an additional 12 sites and is open from June 1 to mid-September.
MP 157 EXIT 156

Mile 453.5 (236.5): Exit to High Ore Road. No services available. EXIT 160

Mile 458 (232): Exit to Montana Highway 69, Boulder, and the cutoff to Elkhorn.

Elkhorn is a ghost town complete with picturesque pioneer-era buildings and folklore. In the 1870s mines at Elkhorn produced a reported $32 million in silver and gold from the shadow of 9,381-foot Elkhorn Peak.

BOULDER (pop. 1,550), is the county seat of Jefferson County, with an economic base of logging, mining and ranching. Travelers will find full services in Boulder, including private RV campgrounds and motels.

The town was a stage depot on the Fort Benton to Virginia City run during the gold rush. The town is best known as the site of the Montana Boulder School and Hospital for the Handicapped and Boulder Hot Springs, now a commercial resort known as Diamond S Ranchotel. Water in the hot springs is believed by many to have healing properties for physical afflictions. Gold was discovered here in 1862, and in the 1880s Boulder made a bid to become Montana's state capital, losing to Helena.

South of Boulder, 2-lane Montana Highway 69 swings south through the scenic Boulder River valley to intersect with Interstate 90 near Cardwell. MP 165 EXIT 164

Mile 460.5 (229.5): Turnout, chain-up area for winter travel restrictions. MP 175

Mile 463 (227): Unnamed pass; can be difficult to negotiate during winter snows.

Mile 469 (221): Exit to JEFFERSON CITY, home of the famed 120-year-old Ting's Bar. Gasoline and groceries are available in this small one-time mining community. A road leads west out of Jefferson City to gold and silver mines at Corbin, Wickes and Comet, which at one time produced millions of dollars in gold and silver. Mining claims are still being worked in this area.
MP 176 EXIT 176

Mile 470 (220): Rest area accessible from the northbound lanes, with picnic tables and drinking water. Be aware that strong winds frequently rip through the canyon in this area.

Mile 471 (219): Rest area accessible from the southbound lanes of Interstate 15, with drinking water and picnic tables. MP 179

Mile 475 (215): Exit to CLANCY, a historically rich town now serving as a residential community of Helena. Food and gas are available here. Overnight accommodations are found near Helena. Clancy got its start as a mining camp with a silver mine that produced $1.5 million of incredibly high-grade silver ore, material so valuable that it

was freighted out of the area on mules and laboriously transported to Swansea, Wales, for processing. The Clancy store is a pioneer structure, where you can see structural cracks caused by a powerful earthquake in 1935.
MP 183 EXIT 182

Mile 481 (209): Exit to MONTANA CITY and the junction of Montana Highway 518, a connector bypass route to U.S. Highway 12 southeast of Helena. Food and gas are available at this exit. Montana City was founded as a mining town in 1864, but is now largely a residential area for Helena commerce.
MP 188 EXIT 187

Mile 485 (205): Exit to HELENA (pop. 24,670), state capitol, and the junctions with U.S. Highway 12 and Montana Highway 287.

Founded as a gold strike boom town in 1864, Helena became the capital of Montana in 1898. The gold strike that led to the capital city's creation was unearthed by 4 Georgia prospectors, down on their luck and bound for home after failing to strike it rich in the rugged Montana goldfields. According to Helena historians, the prospectors took one last chance on a promising "show" in the bottom of a creek gulch and struck a lode that produced $16 million worth of gold in an era when gold brought only $20 an ounce. Today, Last Chance Gulch, where the strike occurred, is producing gold of a different sort: It's the site of a shopping mall.

A mini train and London-style bus provide narrated daily tours of the city, beginning at the Montana Historical Society Museum. Museum hours in summer: Monday-Friday, 8 a.m. to 6 p.m.; Saturday, Sunday and holidays, 9 a.m. to 5 p.m. Free.

For further information on Helena and surrounding attractions, see the MAJOR CITIES section. EXIT 192

Mile 486 (204): Exit to Cedar Street in Helena, business route, access to airport and Carroll College. Northbound travelers leave the rolling green of the mountains and drop into the broad flats of the Missouri River valley, well developed with extensive farms and ranches. MP 194 EXIT 193

Mile 492.5 (197.5): Exit leads to the junctions of Montana Highways 279 and 453. All services are available at this exit. Highway 279 leads north to the small community of Canyon Creek and eventually intersects with Montana Highway 200 after crossing the Continental Divide at 6,130-foot Flesher Pass.

Highway 453 leads southeast to the vast recreational complexes created by large impounded Missouri River lakes, including Hauser Lake, Lake Helena and the north end of 25-mile-long Canyon Ferry Reservoir, recognized as the most popular recreation area in Montana. (The most popular route to Canyon Ferry Reservoir from Helena is via U.S. Highway 12 eastbound.)

Canyon Ferry was built in 1954 and boasts 8 public campgrounds and recreation areas plus several private campgrounds, marinas and public hunting areas. Recreation is year-round at Canyon Ferry, including summer boating, fishing, waterskiing, camping, sailing, and winter ice fishing, skating and hunting for birds. ◀▲ EXIT 200

Mile 501.5 (188.5): Exit is the main access road to the north end of Upper Holter Lake, and the jumping-off point to the 29,000-acre Gates of the Mountains Wilderness Area. The side road winds through valley ranch land to Hilger Landing, a restaurant/marina complex featuring a 90-passenger excursion boat cruise to the spectacular 1,200-foot sheer white cliffs of the Gates of the Mountains, discovered on July 19, 1805, by the Lewis and Clark expedition. The 1³/₄-hour cruise follows the Missouri River into a vertical canyon where it cuts through a solid rock wall nearly 6 miles long with jogs where the cliffs appear to close like gates across the river. The excursion boat stops at Meriwether picnic ground where travelers sometimes go ashore and catch a later boat back to the marina. Cruises every hour during July and August. Adults, $5.50; seniors, $4.50; children to 16, $2.50; under 3 free.

There is a boat launch at the marina which serves as headquarters for much of the Upper Holter waterskiing, boating and fishing recreation. The Upper Holter offers fair fishing for rainbow, brown trout and yellow perch. ⅞◀★ EXIT 209

Mile 509 (181): Exit to Sieben Ranch. No services. EXIT 216

Mile 511.5 (178.5): Exit to the Spring Creek Recreation Road. No services. Rugged red rock cliffs appear on both sides of the highway, providing scenic relief after the pastoral valley near Helena. The weathered rocks date back to the age of dinosaurs and appear to bear the indented impressions of ancient water ripples. EXIT 219

Mile 517 (173): Rest areas are accessible along both sides of the highway, with picnic tables, restrooms and water. ⅞

Mile 517.5 (172.5): Exit leads to the small town of **WOLF CREEK**, the junction with Montana Highway 434 and is a major recreational access road to Holter Lake, one of the most popular impoundments on the Missouri River. Full services available at exit. Wolf Creek is the southern terminus of the Missouri River Recreation Road, a scenic, winding alternative to the interstate, paralleling the interstate and the river. Primitive camp spots, rough boat launches and picnic sites that can't be reached from the freeway are accessible from the river road.

Camping, boating, picnic and fishing 5 miles east of the junction at Holter Lake. Holter is an outstanding spring, fall and winter fishing lake, producing excellent catches of rainbow, brown trout and perch, plus summer camping and waterskiing. Public fee campgrounds are scattered along the east shore of the lake, and include Holter Lake Campground, 28 spaces, boat launch; Juniper Bay, 6 sites, cartop boat access; Log Gulch, 40 sites, boat launch, swimming beach, wooded; Departure Point, 6 primitive sites, cartop boat access. ◀▲ EXIT 226

Mile 519.5 (170.5): Exit for junction with U.S. Highway 287 to Augusta and Choteau. MP 229 EXIT 228

Mile 525.5 (164.5): Exit to CRAIG, a small community best known for its access to Missouri River recreation, including Recreation Road to Holter Lake (see description at **Mile 517.5**). Full services are available in Craig, including camping. ▲ EXIT 234

A labyrinth of vertical canyon walls at Gates of the Mountains. (Tom Barr)

Mile 527 (163): Interstate 15 crosses the Missouri River. MP 236

Mile 528 (162): Stickney Creek.

Mile 531 (159): Rest areas with picnic facilities on both sides of the freeway. ⅞

Mile 531.5 (158.5): Exit provides access to the Dearborn River, which heads near 9,180-foot Scapegoat Mountain. A small river, the Dearborn is heavily used for irrigation water. Between Montana Highway 287 and the Interstate 15 rest area, the river eases through a steeply walled canyon where float fishermen probe deep pools for brown and rainbow trout up to 5 pounds. By late summer, low water can make this float difficult. ◀ MP 240 EXIT 240

Mile 535.5 (154.5): Exit to Missouri River Recreation Road. Food, phone, camping and boat access to the river are at this exit. ▲ MP 244 EXIT 244

Mile 537.5 (152.5): Scenic overview turnoff and historic marker commemorating St. Peter's Mission, approximately 10 miles northwest of here, southbound only.

Mile 539 (151): Exit to Hardy Creek and the Missouri River Recreation Road. Food, phone, camping 2 miles west of highway. ▲ MP 248 EXIT 247

Mile 541.5 (148.5): Exit is a local access road. No services available. EXIT 250

Mile 547 (143): Exit to the town of CASCADE (pop. 830) which, although small, provides full services. This is the northern terminus of the Missouri River Recreation Road which begins at Wolf Creek (see description at **Mile 517.5**). Northbound, the Missouri now flows continuously on the east side of the freeway, and the countryside becomes flatter, more arid, with ranches in the valleys. Secondary roads run northwest and northeast from Cascade providing access to valley ranches. MP 255 EXIT 254

Mile 549 (141): Exit to Cascade and Montana Highway 68. Food, phone, gas and lodging available. MP 257 EXIT 256

Mile 563 (127): Exit to the tiny community of **ULM** which offers a restaurant, gasoline and phone service and is the jumping-off point for Ulm Pishkun State Monument, 4 miles west. Junction with Montana Highway 330. The monument is a complex cliff and cave area where Indians once stampeded herds of buffalo over a mile-long, 50-foot-high cliff, indented with small caves. Indian cliff paintings are visible throughout the area and the remains of buffalo can be found below the cliffs. A large prairie dog town is also located here. The area is closed during the winter. Square Butte (elev. 4,793 feet), visible to the west of Ulm, was the prominent backdrop in numerous Charles Russell prairie paintings. MP 271 EXIT 270

Mile 570.5 (119.5): Exit to Great Falls International Airport and the Montana Air National Guard. MP 278 EXIT 277

Mile 571 (119): Exit to U.S. Highway 89 which combines with eastbound U.S. Highway 87. This is also the exit for College of Great Falls, hospital, and Malmstrom Air Force Base, site of the 341st Strategic Missile Wing, a headquarters base for intercontinental missiles. EXIT 278

Mile 572 (118): Sun River. MP 280

Mile 572.5 (117.5): Exit for junction with U.S. Highway 87 and the city center of **GREAT FALLS** (pop. 57,310), second-largest city in Montana, named for a series of dramatic waterfalls that halted upriver shipping and travel on the Missouri River. U.S. Highway 87 continues northeast through Great Falls.

Great Falls is located at the confluence of the Sun and Missouri rivers, a pleasant mixture of parklike greenery, stately old homes, modern glass-fronted office buildings, high-rise convention centers and Old West legacies. Platted in 1883 near the end of the famous Montana gold rush era, Great Falls is surrounded by treeless prairies, vast wheat fields, cattle ranches and river breaks. Seasonal temperature swings are dramatic, with summer highs and winter lows among the most extreme in the country. This city is the economic heart of northcentral Montana, and has earned the nickname "Electric City" because of the 5 dams and attendant power plants harnessing the energy of the Missouri River falls.

A self-guided city circle tour links 9 points of interest including famous Western artist Charles M. Russell's original studio and museum. Russell's paintings of Montana in the 1800s and the Plains Indians are world famous with many pieces included in the museum's permanent collection, along with glass-enclosed displays of Russell's collection of cowboy and Indian artifacts. Summer hours: Monday-Saturday, 9 a.m. to 6 p.m. Sunday, 1-5 p.m. Oct. 1-April 30: Tuesday-Saturday, 10 a.m. to 5 p.m. Sunday, 1-5 p.m. Closed Monday. Adults, $3; seniors and students, $1.50, under 12 free. The museum complex is at 400 13th St. N. From Exit 280 travel 3.3 miles to 13th Street and turn north to 4th.

Other attractions include the Mehmke Steam Museum, largest private collection of steam engines in the world; Montana Cowboys Assoc. Museum; Riverside Park; and the Montana State Fair held the last week of July and first week of August. A visitors information center is at 46th Street S. and 10th Avenue S.

One of the most refreshing stops is at Giant Springs State Park on the north edge of the city along River Drive. Flowing at the rate of 316,300,000 gallons per hour, the springs are one of the largest in the world, a sparkling clear pool spilling over a rock wall into the Missouri River. The Roe River, which flows out of the springs, is 201 feet long and is recognized by the Guiness Book of Records as the world's shortest river. Here, sports anglers cast flies, spinners and spoons for whitefish, big brown and rainbow trout. A state fish hatchery is open for tours and weeping willow trees shelter grassy picnic areas.

Two of the most prominent "great falls" are on the route: Black Eagle Falls and Dam named in 1805 by the Lewis and Clark expedition, and dammed in 1889 to provide power for a smelter; and Rainbow Falls and Dam, completed in 1910. Overlooks provide prominent views of both falls. Visible downstream from Rainbow Falls overlook, but inaccessible from the road, are Horseshoe and Crooked falls. ⊼☞★ MP 281 EXIT 280

Mile 575 (115): Exit to Great Falls. U.S. 87 north (NW bypass), weigh station, fairgrounds. All trucks and commercial vehicles must use this exit. MP 283 EXIT 282

Mile 579 (111): Exit runs east to Benton Lake National Wildlife Refuge, a watery oasis in a dry prairie land. Camping and picnic facilities are not provided. Primarily a waterfowl production area, Benton Lake hosts up to 100,000 ducks, 40,000 snow geese, 4,500 whistling swans and 1,000 Canada geese. A tour route through the refuge offers excellent spring, summer and fall photographic opportunities, and a hunting program is provided during the fall waterfowl season. EXIT 286

Mile 583 (107): Exit to Vaughn and to the junctions of U.S. Highway 89 to Choteau and Montana Highway 200 to Missoula via Rogers

Pass (elev. 5,610 feet). Food, phone, gas and diesel 2 miles from exit. EXIT 290

Mile 590.5 (99.5): Exit to Gorden. No services; ranch access only. MP 298 EXIT 297

Mile 595.5 (94.5): Exit to the railroad siding community of Power, 1 mile west of highway, and Montana Highway 431. No services. Ahead is Teton Ridge which offers an excellent view of the vast prairie land, wheat fields and creek breaks. EXIT 302

Mile 606 (84): Exit to full services at the farming community of DUTTON. Junction: Montana Highway 221 runs west 24 miles to Choteau and Montana Highway 379 east to ranching areas.

Mile 610.5 (79.5): Teton River.

Mile 611 (79): Rest areas on both sides of the interstate near the Teton River bridge. Be aware that during summer signs warning of potential rattlesnake problems are frequently posted at this rest stop.

The Teton affords fair fishing for brookies and rainbow trout in the upper reaches toward Choteau, while downstream the water warms during the summer and anglers work for sauger, northern pike, burbot and channel catfish. MP 319

Mile 613 (77): Exit to Collins Road, 5 miles west. No services available. Highway is extremely rough. EXIT 321

Mile 619.5 (70.5): Exit to the farm and railroad stop community of BRADY marked by the dominating towers of grain storage elevators near the railroad. Junction with Montana Highway 365. Gasoline and restaurant facilities. EXIT 328

Mile 627 (63): Exit to Midway Road, a local access road. No services. EXIT 335

Mile 631 (59): Exit to CONRAD (pop. 3,074), a farming community in the center of the wheat belt, offering all services, hospital, camping. ▲ EXIT 339

Mile 638 (52): Exit for junction with Montana Highway 366 and the crossroads community of Ledger. No services available.

Highway 366 leads 42 miles to Tiber Dam and 30-mile-long Lake Elwell. Originally built as an irrigation reservoir, the lake is now used primarily for recreation. Several boat launches and a campground are located at the dam, plus several primitive campsites along the lakeshore. Fishing for perch, walleye, northern pike and catfish, with dwindling catches of rainbow. ☞▲ EXIT 345

Mile 641 (49): Exit for junction with Montana Highway 44 which leads 15 miles west to the small community of VALIER (pop. 640), all services available, and Lake Frances Recreation Area. Lake Frances has a boat ramp, picnic area, and good population of northern pike, walleye, yellow perch, ling, rainbow and kokanee salmon. ⊼☞ EXIT 348

Mile 646 (44): Exit to Bullhead Road and Marias River picnic area. No services. ⊼ EXIT 352

Mile 649.5 (40.5): Crossing the Marias River, marked by dramatic breaks, rugged coulees and brushy canyons. The river provides a refreshing break in the harsh prairie landscape. MP 559

Mile 651.5 (38.5): Exit to the Marias Valley Road and camping. ▲ MP 359 EXIT 358

Mile 654 (36): Exit to SHELBY (pop. 3,000), and junction with U.S. Highway 2 to Cut Bank and Glacier National Park. 24-hour gas station. Town Pump is combination store/restaurant/self-service gas station. All services available.

For more information on Shelby, see Mile 0 in the U.S. HIGHWAY 2 section. EXIT 363

Mile 656 (34): Exit to Shelby. Campground, food, gas, lodging, hospital and phone at this exit. ▲ MP 365 EXIT 364

Mile 658 (32): Weigh station. All commercial vehicles must stop here.

Mile 661 (29): Exit to Bronken Road. No services available. EXIT 369

Mile 665 (25): Exit to Potter Road. No services available. EXIT 373

Mile 671 (19): Exit to Montana Highway 215 running west to the crossroad community of Kevin and Montana Highway 343 eastbound to Oilmont, where in 1921 oil was discovered, setting off a major oil boom in the prairie and ranch country. Dozens of working oil pumps are visible from the freeway. The pool is one of the most northerly oil fields in the contiguous United States. Services 0.5 mile east of freeway and gas west of highway. MP 379 EXIT 379

Mile 682 (8): Exit to SUNBURST (pop. 520). All services are available in this wheat and ranch town just south of the Alberta, Canada, border. Fifteen miles to the east, the rolling prairie is interrupted by the towers of the Sweetgrass Hills, dominated by Gold Butte (elev. 6,512 feet); West Butte (elev. 6,983 feet) and in the distance Mount Brown (elev. 6,958 feet). EXIT 389

Mile 686.5 (3.5): Exit is a ranch access. No services. MP 394 EXIT 394

Mile 689.5 (0.5): Exit to a rest area at SWEETGRASS, just south of the U.S.-Canada international border. Food, phone, gas and lodging available. At the border, there is a 24-hour customs station and duty-free shop. MP 398 EXIT 397

Mile 690 (0): Montana-Canada border.

Turn to CANADA HIGHWAYS 4, 3 and 2 section for continuation of highway log north to Calgary and Edmonton, AB.

U.S. Highway 20

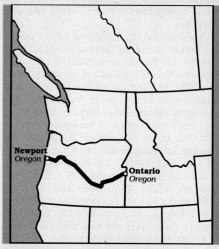

See maps page 109 and 113

U.S. Highway 20 is one of the few highways which span the breadth of the United States. It is also a major east-west, border-to-border route through Central Oregon. Cross-state motorists using U.S. 20 will experience the contrasting environment of deserts, mountains, and sea coast, as the highway travels from the wide open spaces, sagebrush, high buttes, and dry washes of Eastern Oregon, to the Alpine lakes, thick forests, meandering rivers, and quiet farmlands of Western Oregon.

Indians once chipped arrowheads from a mountain of glass on this route. Fur traders, wagon trains, cattle barons, and sheepmen also left their mark, recorded for modern travelers by roadside plaques and gravesites. There is also much history to be found in small communities and way stations on U.S. 20, many of which began as stagecoach stops.

The *NORTHWEST MILEPOSTS*® log of U.S. 20 starts at Ontario on Interstate 84 and follows Highway 201 south to begin U.S. 20 at Cairo Junction, continuing west 442 miles to Newport on the Oregon coast. There are 5 sets of highway mileposts along U.S. 20. They begin at Newport, Corvallis, Albany, Sisters and Bend. With the exception of mountain passes, where it widens to 3 lanes, U.S. 20 is a 2-lane highway. From Ontario to Sisters, it is straight with long flat stretches. Slow for winding road through the Cascades, Willamette Valley and Coast Range.

U.S. Highway 20 Log

Distance from Ontario, OR, is followed by distance from Newport, OR.

Mile 0 (445): ONTARIO (pop. 9,750) located at the junction of Interstate 84 and Oregon Highway 201. Follow Highway 201 south 3 miles for U.S. Highway 20. Ontario is the eastern gateway to Oregon and the largest city in Malheur County. All visitor facilities available. Ontario began as a cattle shipping center named for the Canadian province where one of its founders was born. With the construction of reservoirs plus an extensive pipeline and canal network, the city and county became Oregon's major row crop producer.

Ontario is the major agricultural retail center for 7 Oregon and Idaho counties. Local companies store, sort, package, and ship cattle, potatoes, sugar beets, peppermint, and an assortment of seeds. Ontario ships more fresh onions than any place in the nation.

The Snake River, 0.5 mile east of Ontario, contains largemouth and smallmouth bass, croppie and bluegills, plus catfish weighing up to 35 pounds. The Malheur River, at the town's edge, is a popular channel catfishing spot.

Mile 3 (442): CAIRO JUNCTION. Junction of U.S. Highway 20 and Highway 201 which leads north 3 miles to Ontario, and south 8 miles to Nyssa (description follows).

NYSSA (pop. 2,820) was chosen by the Oregon Short Line in 1883 because it was a convenient point to establish a railroad station. Sugar beets, introduced in 1906, are the mainstay of a diversified agricultural economy. Amalgamated Sugar Co., processors of White Satin Sugar, is the largest employer.

Nyssa is the "thunder egg capital of Oregon" and a rock hounder's hot spot. Succor Creek State Recreation Area, approximately 35 miles south of Nyssa via Highway 20 and Succor Creek Road, is known for its abundance of thunder eggs plus petrified wood, agates and jasper. Succor Creek State Park has 19 primitive campsites and a picnic area.

Leslie Gulch and Painted Canyon, south and west of Succor Creek, offer moss agates, jasper, and quartz crystal plus spectacular scenery. Area roads are rough clay dirt and should be avoided following heavy rains. Four-wheel drives and high-centered vehicles are recommended as many roads are deeply rutted. Inquire locally for directions.

Lake Owyhee, 33 miles southwest of Nyssa, fills 53 miles of canyon forming Oregon's largest reservoir lake. Often called the "most overstocked and underfished lake in America," it yields excellent catches of croppie and bass. Lake Owyhee State Park has 10 RV sites with hookups, 30 tent sites, picnicking, boating and a dump station. The reservoir's 310 miles of shoreline includes lakeside resorts, a marina, cabin rentals, and boat rentals. Before forming the state's largest reservoir, the Owyhee River runs through a 1,000-foot-deep canyon. It is a prime spring white-water rafting destination. 🏕🛶▲

Mile 4 (441): Oregon State University's Malheur Experiment Station researches weed control, sugar beets, onions, soybeans, spearmint, sweet corn and dry beans. Fields producing some of these crops line the highway between the Experiment Station and Vale.

Mile 5 (440): Potatoes grow south of the highway, sugar beets and onions to the north. Ore-Ida and Simplet are the largest potato contractors here. MP 256

Mile 7 (438): North of the highway is Malheur Butte, the neck of an extinct volcano. Indians once used it as a lookout. MP 254

Mile 8 (437): Storage sheds for bagged and crated onions. MP 253

Mile 9 (436): Nevada Ditch. This irrigation channel was dug by hand in 1881 and continues to serve local residents. Onions and alfalfa grow north of the highway. To the south are grain and sugar beets. MP 252

Mile 10.5 (434.5): Bean fields north of the highway and sugar beets to the south.

Mile 12.5 (432.5): Weigh station south side of highway. MP 248

Mile 14.5 (430.5): VALE (pop. 1,590) is the Harney County seat. Malheur Crossing, at the town's eastern edge, was an important stop on the Oregon Trail. Here, immigrants bathed and laundered in the hot springs which empty into the river. Original wagon ruts, an Oregon Trail exhibit, and pioneer grave can be seen on Lytle Boulevard south of town.

In 1854, Stephen Meek led a wagon train west from here in search of a shortcut to the Willamette Valley. They became lost in a maze of ridges and canyons. Over 70 people perished. Survivor Ezra Meeker retraced the route in 1906 placing markers at significant points. Several are in Vale. Today, water from Vale's hot springs is used to grow 3.5 million pounds of mushrooms plus heat greenhouses, a corn drying operation, and a slaughterhouse. There is a RV park 4 blocks north of the highway. ▲ MP 247

Mile 16 (429): Western city limits of Vale.

Mile 17 (428): Bully Creek Road. Bully Creek reservoir, approximately 8 miles west of Vale, is popular with swimmers and waterskiers. Good fishing for crappie, bass, trout and perch. 🛶

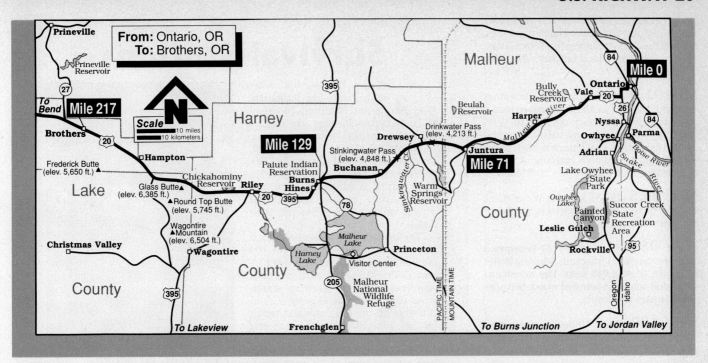

From: Ontario, OR
To: Brothers, OR

Mile 18.5 (426.5): Forty miles of dirt road ends at Dry Creek, which empties into Lake Owyhee.

Mile 22 (423): Access to Bully Creek Reservoir.

Mile 23 (422): Crossing the Malheur River, which heads in the Strawberry Mountains and flows 165 miles east to the Snake River at Ontario. Peter Skene Ogden and a group of French fur trappers named the river in 1826. Ogden's party left a cache of furs hidden on the banks. When they returned, the pelts had been stolen. Ogden christened it "Riviere Au Malheur," which translates as "unfortunate" or "unlucky river." The section of river paralleling U.S. 20 between Vale and Juntura is unlucky for sportsmen, as it contains mostly trash fish.

Westbound from Vale, the landscape changes from flat, fertile fields to rolling hills of sagebrush unbroken save for isolated juniper trees.

Mile 30.5 (414.5): LITTLE VALLEY is an unincorporated community with an estimated area population of 150 people. Combination store and gas station with informal campsites, no hookups, water available, $4 fee. Local farms and ranches grow corn, radishes and dill seed. Excellent hunting for pheasant; good for chukar, quail, deer and antelope. ▲

Mile 34 (411): Cottonwood Creek, good early spring trout stream. ◄●

Mile 38.5 (406.5): Harper Junction. HARPER, 1 mile north of the junction, was named for the Pacific Livestock Co.'s Harper Ranch. The service station here has the last gas westbound for 34 miles. No accommodations.

Mile 40.5 (404.5): Crossing the Malheur River.

Mile 44 (401): Crossing Squaw Creek, a tributary of the Malheur River. Turnout with drinking water. The highway meanders through 1.5 miles of switchbacks created by rolling ravines. *CAUTION:* Gusty winds.
MP 458

Mile 52.5 (392.5): Pass Gold Creek.

Mile 60.5 (384.5): Turnout with trash cans.

Mile 61.5 (383.5): Pass Pole Creek.

Mile 64.5 (380.5): Turnouts south of highway with good views of the Malheur River. At this point, the Malheur is a shallow, slow moving stream separated into 2 channels by several small islands.

Mile 69.5 (375.5): Historical marker south side of highway tells of Peter Skene Ogden's Oct. 10, 1828, encampment. This was Ogden's fifth and final expedition into the Snake River country. From here he journeyed south to the Humboldt River and east to the Great Salt Lake. The highway crosses the North Fork Malheur River just west of historical marker.

Mile 71 (374): JUNTURA (pop. 55) has a combination gas station/restaurant, 22-site campground (hookups and hot showers), and a 9-unit motel. Last gas westbound for 35 miles. The name Juntura is derived from a Spanish word meaning "to join," and was applied to this area because the North and South forks of the Malheur River merge here. From the turn of the century into the 1930s, Juntura was a trade and shipping center for cattle and sheep. Its decline came with the passage of the Taylor Grazing Act, which prohibited driving sheep over federal lands and shipping them in trucks.

Area rockhounding digs yield agates, and poor quality but plentiful quantities of petrified wood. Beulah Reservoir, 15 miles north, is fished for croppie and rainbow natives, best in May, June and October. The Malheur River and Butte Reservoir offer trout, perch, and catfish. ◄●▲ MP 189

Mile 72 (373): Tent camping and a boat launch 0.5 mile south of highway. ▲

Mile 79 (366): Kingsbury Gulch.

Mile 80 (365): Burns District Bureau of Land Management headquarters north of highway.

Mile 81 (364): Malheur/Harney County Line and crossing the mountains — Pacific time zone. Westward motorists set watches back 1 hour.

With 10,228 square miles of land, Harney County is the largest in Oregon and the third largest county in the nation. It exceeds the combined size of Massachusetts and Rhode Island. Created Feb. 25, 1889, it was named for William S. Harney, a veteran of Indian, Mexican, and Civil wars. The county's economy centers around lumbering and ranching. A short growing season combined with the possibility of frost in any given month inhibits crop production. Average snowfall is 37 inches and precipitation averages 8 inches per year.

Despite its size, Harney County has less than 8,000 people. MP 180

Mile 83.5 (361.5): Drinkwater Pass Summit (elev. 4,212 feet). Turnout. Start of a 3-mile-long 6 percent downgrade.

Mile 87 (358): Malheur River.

Mile 90 (355): Drewsey Junction. DREWSEY, 0.5 mile north, has a service station and post office. This ranching community was originally called Gouge Eye (after a popular frontier method of settling arguments) and attracted cattlemen, outlaws, gamblers and miners during its 1880s heyday. The name honors a local rancher's daughter, Drewsey Miller. MP 174

Mile 91 (354): Access road to Warm Springs Reservoir, 15 miles south. The unpaved road is not maintained. The reservoir, built in 1919, is used by water-skiers, and bass, catfish and croppie fishermen. Boat launch is often under water in spring. Random camping. A variety of agates are found here. MP 171

Mile 93.5 (351.5): Stinking Water Creek and the Stinking Water Mountains; named for the area's hot springs.

Mile 95 (350): Highway 20 becomes 3 lanes westbound as it ascends Stinking Water Mountain (elev. 4,948 feet). The mountains are a good source of petrified wood, belvadee jasper, agates and fossils.

Mile 100 (345): Unpaved access road leads 28 miles south to Warm Springs Reservoir.

Mile 106 (339): Roadside marker defines this point as the farthest northern edge of The Great Basin. From mid-February to late April, bald eagles are often seen along the highway between Buchanan and Riley. Between Buchanan and Burns, sagebrush fades into lowland meadows.

Mile 106.5 (338.5): BUCHANAN is a combination store and gas station with repair service and 24-hour towing. Free museum with excellent small collection of Indian artifacts, crystal and firearms. Named for settler Thomas Buchanan, this was originally a stagecoach stop. MP 153

Mile 117 (328): Historical marker on south side of highway recounts the history of Fort Harney, from its establishment on Aug. 10, 1867, to March 2, 1889, when the last 320 acres were restored to the public domain. The fort, named after General William S. Harney who commanded the Oregon Military Department, was located 2.5 miles north of the marker. MP 136

Mile 127 (318): Junction with U.S. Highway 395, major south-north route which extends from California to the Canadian border. U.S. Highway 20 and U.S. Highway 395 share a common alignment from here west 27 miles to Riley. Turn to **Mile 197** in the U.S. HIGHWAY 395 section for log.

Mile 128 (317): Weigh station.

Mile 129 (316): BURNS (pop. 2,765), all visitor facilities available. The Harney County seat, Burns was named for poet Robert Burns. It became the administrative headquarters and the modern livestock center of Oregon with the passage of the Taylor Grazing Act in 1936.

The Burns-Hines communities form a transportation hub and business center for

Survival Stations

On road maps they are the names in small print. Places like Buchanan, Riley, Juntura and Hampton. Too small to be incorporated, they are skipped when the census is taken.

Spaced out along U.S. Highway 20, they are survival stations on the 260-mile stretch between Ontario and Bend. Many started as stagecoach stops, and most have a unique recreational activity which brings outsiders to their area.

The last time anyone counted, which was years ago, there were about 100 families living in the **LITTLE VALLEY** area **(Mile 30.5)**. The total increases significantly during hunting season when throngs of upland game hunters converge on the dill fields and radish patches. Some of eastern Oregon's best pheasant hunting is in Little Valley.

JUNTURA (Mile 71) draws elk and deer hunters from as far as Portland, Coos Bay, OR, and Redding, CA. "I've got 22 RV spaces and 9 motel units," said the manager of the Oasis Motel. "During hunting season, I've had 37 rigs a night stacked up here."

With a Model T Roadster and a freight wagon perched atop the roof, you know that **BUCHANAN (Mile 106.5)** is not going to be a routine gas stop. Inside, a large collection of Paiute Indian cradle boards hang from the walls along with antique rifles, bullet displays and a spinning wheel suspended from the ceiling. A small room at the end is a museum. There are small but excellent collections of blue plate, crystal, Indian artifacts, grandfather clocks, and a piano made in London between 1780 and 1820. In the gift shop/store, you can buy turquoise Indian jewelry, arrowheads and an assortment of Oregon polished rocks.

RILEY (Mile 153) also has a gift shop selling everything from cedar postcards to Riley kitchen magnets. On the practical side, there's an assortment of auto parts plus 24-hour towing. With Riley sitting at the junction of U.S. 20 and U.S. 395 and representing the only gas in the 60-mile stretch between Hines and Hampton, it also offers brakes, muffler and tune-up services.

Look around in all 4 directions at Riley and chances are you won't see a living soul or sign of civilization. But hidden among the rolling hills and dry washes are enough ranches to support the community's only other business — an insurance office. It stands on the other side of U.S. 20 right across from the combination store/deli/gift shop/garage, and a 5-site RV park.

(Tom Barr)

U.S. Highway 20 crosses some lonely country.

HAMPTON (Mile 196) offers the basics of food and gas to hang glider fliers, rock hounds, and deer and antelope hunters. For local ranchers and anyone else who cares to enter, Hampton stages an annual rattlesnake contest that starts in June and ends in October. Bring in a dead rattler, which has to be either a Western or Great Basin species, and you get a point plus 2 more for weight and length. First prize is a silver belt buckle; second, $75; and third, a camping stove.

BROTHERS (Mile 217) started as a stage stop. Like the other stops, it serves area ranchers when not catering to the needs of travelers. In the Brothers area, there are about 100 families. Across the highway from the store/restaurant/bar/gift shop is one of the few remaining Little Red Schoolhouses. Its 1 room accommodates kindergarten through the 8th grade.

There were hang gliders soaring off the buttes and into the valley at **MILLICAN (Mile 235)**. Some participants had come from as far away as Switzerland and Australia. On another day, it might have been dirt bike or 4-wheel drag races for these are bread-and-butter sports for Millican's store. Behind the combination store/gas/campground and 1-unit motel, stand the kind of dilapidated line shacks which photographers find irresistible. A For Sale sign is tacked to the store's front door. "It's been there for over 30 years," said the owner, who bought the store 4 years ago. "Don't see any need to take it down now."

Harney County. Recreation centers around bird-watching, hunting and rock collecting, much of it taking place at Malheur National Wildlife Refuge south of Burns. Malheur Lake, one of the state's largest bodies of water during high water, is the center-piece of the 183,000-acre refuge, a major feeding stop on the Pacific flyway. Spring migrations bring waterfowl, shorebirds and songbirds and usually peak during mid-March to mid-April. To reach the refuge visitor center from Burns, drive east 2 miles on Oregon Highway 78, then south 25 miles on Oregon Highway 205, then east 9 miles on county road (gravel). The refuge visitor center is on the south shore of Malheur Lake; open 8 a.m. to 4:30 p.m. weekdays. The refuge museum located at the visitor center is open 6 a.m. to 9 p.m. daily. Refuge roads extend south from the visitor center about 35 miles to **FRENCHGLEN**; camping and historic motel. Frenchglen is 60 miles south of Burns via Highway 205. Facilities at the refuge include concealment blinds for photographers and bird-watchers. Other activities are boat-ing, canoeing, hiking, cross-county skiing and cave exploration. During fall, the refuge has 8,000 acres open to waterfowl and upland game hunting. For rock hounds, refuge grounds yield good petrified wood, bog agates, arrowheads and opalite. There are no services within the refuge; carry gas and water. For more information write: Malheur NWR, P.O. Box 245, Princeton, OR 97721; phone (503) 493-2612.

Mile 129.5 (315.5): Junction with access road which leads 1 mile north to **PAIUTE INDIAN RESERVATION** (pop. 160). The reservation is governed by a Tribal Council and maintains its own police department. The tribe operates a processing plant which freeze-dries onion rings. Burns City Park, located at the junction, has picnic tables and playground equipment.

Mile 130 (315): Harney County Histori-cal Museum and Visitor Information Center. The museum building and grounds have served as a brewery, laundry and wrecking yard. It has an extensive photo collection, women's gowns, thunder eggs, arrowheads, gun, saddles, and a waterfowl exhibit. Open June through September, 9 a.m. to 5 p.m., Tuesday-Friday, 9 a.m. to noon on Saturday. Admission fee.

Mile 131 (314): **HINES** (pop. 1,445), developed by the Edward Hines Timber Co., is designed around an oval park from which most streets extend. The police reserve sponsors an annual Obsidian Days gem and mineral show which attracts dealers from Washington, Idaho, California, and Arizona. Snow Mountain Pine, one of the state's largest ponderosa pine sawmilling operations, is located here.

Mile 131.5 (313.5): Valley Golf Club Road leads north to a public 9-hole course.

Mile 132 (313): Ochoco National Forest Ranger Station.

Mile 133 (312): Access to Delintment Lake, 58 miles northwest of Hines, in Ochoco National Forest.

Mile 134 (311): Western city limits of Hines. Westbound motorists enter Oregon's high desert country, a land of sagebrush flats, dry alkali lake beds and creek bottoms. In spring, the landscape is brightened by wild-flowers and green grass.

Mile 135 (310): Bureau of Land Manage-ment Wild Horse Corrals. This is the major facility for managing wild horses on Oregon public lands. Since 1974 when the program was started, BLM has processed over 9,000 wild horses placing 75 percent with private in-dividuals. Wild horse herds increase an aver-age of 20 percent per year. Tours are available by prior arrangement.

Mile 143 (302): Rest area with covered picnic tables, water and nature trail. The 0.5-mile Sage Hen Nature Trail takes you through sagebrush and western juniper to scenic view-points. Self-guiding brochure is available at the trailhead.

Mile 153 (292): Junction with U.S. High-way 395 south at **RILEY** (est. pop. 4), which has a combination grocery/deli, 5 RV sites, and gas station with tow truck. Last gas for 43 miles westbound. Named for rancher Amos W. Riley, first post office was established in Riley in 1880.

U.S. Highway 395 leads south from here to Klamath Falls, Lake View, and Reno, NV. Southbound travelers turn to **Mile 167** in the U.S. HIGHWAY 395 section for log.

Mile 155 (290): Historic marker tells of a Bannock, Snake and Paiute uprising in 1878 in protest of white occupation of treaty lands. They were defeated by the First U.S. Cavalry in a battle at nearby Silver Creek.

Mile 159 (286): Chickahominy Reservoir is stocked with trout and is a popular fishing spot and sometime windsurfing area. Boat ramp, dock and informal camping (water, $3 camping fee).

Mile 164 (281): Turnoff to north for Silver Valley.

Mile 167.5 (277.5): Squaw Butte-Harney Valley Livestock Experimental Station 5 miles south of highway. The station was built in 1935 by the Civilian Conservation Corps. Its 16,000 acres of federal, state and county owned land represents plants native to Central Oregon, Nevada, Idaho, Utah and California. Research centers on forage man-agement, revegetation and food additives.

Mile 175 (270): Lake County boundary.

Mile 182 (263): The best access road to Glass Buttes rockhounding area, 6 miles south. See feature next page. ★ MP 77

Mile 184 (261): Dirt road north of high-way leads to Buck Creek and G.I. Ranch.

Rough dirt road south to Glass Buttes has deep ruts and should be attempted only by 4-wheel drive or heavy-duty high-suspension vehicle.
MP 75

Mile 184.5 (260.5): Glass Buttes (elev. 6,385 feet), a mountain of volcanic glass beneath a sagebrush and juniper cover.
MP 74

Mile 188 (257): An extremely rough dirt road winds south 35 miles around the slopes of Round Top Butte (elev. 5,745 feet) and Wagontire Mountain (elev. 6,504 feet) to junction with an all-weather road which leads to U.S. Highway 395 and west to Christ-mas Valley. For 4-wheel drive and high-suspension vehicles only.

Mile 190 (255): Entering Deschutes County westbound.

Mile 196 (249): HAMPTON (est. pop. 9), named for Hampton Butte (elev. 6,333 feet), has a cafe, store, RV hookups and gas station. This is the only gas between Riley, 43 miles east, and Brothers, 21 miles west. ▲

Mile 207 (238): All-weather road leads 21 miles north to Camp Creek which empties into the Crooked River.

Mile 210 (235): Dirt road leads south 18 miles to Frederick Butte (elev. 5,650 feet) and Benjamin Lake. MP 50

Mile 217 (228): BROTHERS has gas, bar, cafe, and store. The area has been a center for ranching since 1873. Several fraternal family groups settled here, and the community was named for the many homesteading brothers. Rest area east of the store has 5 covered picnic shelters, drinking water and restrooms.
MP 43

Mile 224 (221): Junction with Oregon Highway 27 which leads north to Prineville Reservoir. MP 36

Mile 234 (211): Pine Mountain Observa-tory, 9 miles south on graded dirt road, has received worldwide recognition as a major astronomical facility. Open Friday and Satur-day, viewing begins at dusk. Special tours Thursday and Sunday by appoinment.

Mile 235 (210): MILLICAN is often called the "one-man town." It has a store and is the last gas stop westbound before Bend. There are 5 RV sites with full hookups and a 1-unit motel. ▲

Mile 240 (205): Limited-use road south to Millican Valley, closed in winter.

Mile 240.5 (204.5): Summit of Horse Ridge (elev. 4,292 feet).

Mile 241 (204): Geologic marker tells of a large prehistoric river which drained an ice-age lake. The lake's escaping water cut through lava, creating a rocky gap called Dry River which flowed north into Crooked River.

Glass Buttes

Approximately 4,900,000 years ago, Eastern Oregon rumbled and shook with volcanic activity. Rhyolite, with a high silica content, spewed from one of the vents. The thick flow cooled very quickly, and instead of spreading over the bedrock in a thin layer, it formed a mountain around the vent. When the volcanism subsided, Glass Butte had risen 2,000 feet above the surrounding countryside to an elevation of 6,385 feet. It is literally a mountain of glass, and may be the world's largest obsidian outcropping.

Indians discovered the Glass Buttes and turned it into a virtual factory for production of spear points, arrowheads, skin scrapers, axes and chisels. An implement made of Glass Buttes obsidian was a prized possession, as well as a prime trading commodity. Some have been found as far east as the mounds of Ohio.

Today, Glass Buttes obsidian is much sought after by rock hounds, who come from all over to dig in the valley between Glass Butte and its neighbor, Round Butte, which together comprise Glass Buttes. The total rockhounding area covers approximately 7,000 acres.

While most obsidian is jet black, Glass Buttes has a distinctive iridescence and comes in a variety of colors: gold, silver, rainbow, red, and brown. Fire obsidian is also found here. Rock shops in Burns (**Mile 129**) have maps of the area which pinpoint where the different varieties have been found.

Recreational rock hounds may take 25 pounds of obsidian out of Glass Buttes per day up to a total of 250 pounds per year. To make digging easier, bring shovels, picks, rock hammers and crowbars. Explosives and power equipment are not permitted.

While highway signs point to Glass Buttes, access roads are not marked. The only access road which should be attempted with the family car lies about 30 feet west of Milepost 77 (see **Mile 182**). It is in reasonably good condition, and leads south 3 miles to the start of the digging areas, where there is also an open space for informal camping and a natural reservoir that serves as a waterhole for cattle from surrounding ranches. Several more miles of dirt road continue through the prime rockhounding sites.

There are other unmaintained dirt roads leading from U.S. 20 to the diggings. An occasional muffler, exhaust pipe and other auto parts offer silent testimony to the inadvisability of trying them with anything except a 4-wheel drive or high-centered vehicle.

There are no facilities at Glass Buttes. Bring water and food as the nearest services are at Hampton, 9 miles west (**Mile 196**). Although there are no developed sites, overnight camping is permitted.

Glass Buttes is administered by the Bureau of Land Management for amateur and recreational rockhounding.

Mile 242 (203): Viewpoint with good view of the Cascades to the west.

Mile 247.5 (197.5): Turnouts on both sides of highway.

Mile 248 (197): Large turnouts; parking for 10 vehicles.

Mile 255 (190): County road leads north 3 miles to Bend Airport, 18 miles to Powell Butte and 30 miles north to Prineville.

Mile 257 (188): Access to 27th Street, golf course and hospital.

Mile 258 (187): Deschutes National Forest headquarters south of highway.

Mile 259 (186): Pilot Butte State Park and Bend city limits. A 1-mile paved road spirals to the top of Pilot Butte (elev. 3,400 feet). Visible from the summit are: Mount Hood (elev. 11,205 feet), Mount Jefferson (elev. 10,495 feet), Three Fingered Jack (elev. 7,848 feet), Mount Washington (elev. 7,802 feet), Middle Sister (elev. 10,053 feet), Broken Top (elev.

9,165 feet) and Mount Bachelor (elev. 9,075 feet).

Mile 261 (184): South junction of U.S. 20 and U.S. Highway 97, both of which become 3rd Street from downtown to northern city limits.

BEND (pop. 18,700) is the county seat of Deschutes County and a center for year-round outdoor recreation, in particular skiing in winter and golf in summer.

Mount Bachelor, 22 miles west of town via Cascade Lakes Highway is known for its powder skiing. Ski season begins in November and can run into July. The summit chair lift operates in summer for sightseers. There are several major motels in Bend and resort lodging at Mount Bachelor.

The High Desert Museum, 6 miles south on U.S. Highway 97, is a participation-oriented facility with indoor and outdoor exhibits on art, history, nature and science. Interpretative talks and demonstrations. A "walk through time" depicts the opening of the American West. Hours: April 1-Sept. 30, 9 a.m. to 5 p.m.; Oct. 1-March 31, 9 a.m. to 4 p.m. except Thanksgiving, Christmas and New Years. Fee.

Lava Butte and Lava Lands Visitor Center, 11 miles south on U.S. Highway 97, has displays, paved road to top provides outstanding view of Cascades, a slide show, interpretative trails and naturalist talks. Open daily, mid-March to October.

Lava Cast Forest, 14 miles south of Bend via U.S. Highway 97, has the world's largest lava mold trees. Self-guided nature trail.
★ 林★MP 0

Mile 265.5 (179.5): North junction of U.S. Highways 20 and 97. Highway 20 continues northwest to Sisters, and Highway 97 north to Redmond (see **Mile 210** in the U.S. HIGHWAY 97 section for log).

Mile 266 (179): Deschutes River. The Deschutes heads in the Cascades and flows 240 miles north and northeast to empty into the Columbia River 12 miles east of The Dalles. North of Bend, it is fished for brown, rainbow and some brook trout, best in June.
➤ MP 18

Mile 267.5 (177.5): Access south to Tumalo State Park on the Deschutes River; 20 RV sites with hookups, 68 tent sites and group picnic shelter. **▲MP 17**

Mile 280 (165): Sisters rodeo grounds and private campground. **▲**

Mile 282 (163): Sisters city park picnic area, playground, and Squaw Creek. The creek has fair fishing for native rainbow and cutthroat, best May through June. **⊼➤**

Mile 282.5 (162.5): SISTERS (pop. 730) was established in 1885 as an outpost for Company A of the First Oregon Volunteers. Its economy is based on small business, wood products and tourism. Sisters also has the largest llama breeding ranch in the world. Fishermen use Sisters as a base for angling the McKenzie, Deschutes, Metolius and Crooked rivers. Mule deer hunters, hikers and skiers find it convenient for excursions into the pasturelands and Cascades. All visitor facilities. Last gas westbound for 50 miles.

Mile 283 (162): Junction with Oregon Highway 242 to McKenzie Lava Beds, McKenzie Pass (elev. 5,324 feet), and Oregon Highway 126 to Eugene and Springfield. Dee Wright Memorial, 24 miles west on Highway 242 at McKenzie Pass offers a spectacular view of the Cascades. A 0.5-mile nature trail leads through portions of the 8-mile-long lava flow at the lava beds. Highway 242 is open late June to October, closed in winter. Not recommended for trailers or motorhomes; combinations of over 50 feet prohibited. Travelers can rejoin U.S. 20 by continuing west on Oregon Highway 242 to **Mile 37** and north on Highway 126 for 18 miles. **林★ MP 100**

Mile 283.5 (161.5): Entering Deschutes National Forest westbound.

Mile 287 (158): Cold Springs cutoff and west access to Graham Carroll.

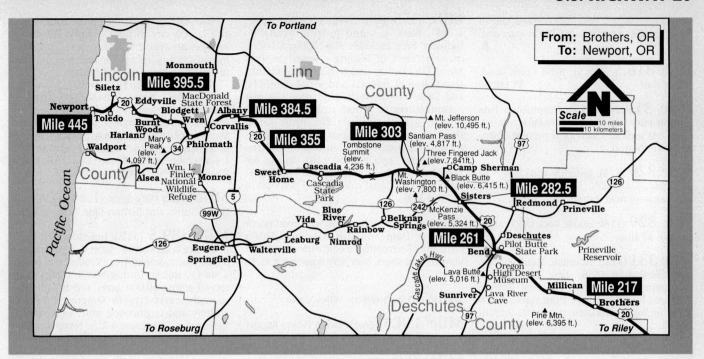

Mile 288 (157): Indian Ford Road, Green Ridge Road, Indian Ford Campground, and High Cascades Riding Stables. Indian Ford USFS campground with 24 sites. High Cascades Stables operates hourly, half-day, all-day, and overnight wilderness pack trips. Riders of all ages and skill levels welcome.

▲

Mile 290.5 (154.5): Camp Sherman junction and access to Metolius River headwaters, 5 miles north of junction via paved Forest Service Road 14. The Metolius flows from huge underground springs and empties into the Deschutes River. Some 35,000 fish are planted annually in the Metolius. The first 9 miles of the river are limited to fly-fishing with barbless hooks and a wildfish throw-back system. Wildfish populations include brook, browns, rainbow, Dolly Varden, kokanee and whitefish. Whitefish are so plentiful that there is no bag limit. Hiking trails, restrooms, observation point and marked trail. There are several Forest Service campgrounds north of Camp Sherman store.

CAMP SHERMAN, 5 miles north of junction, is a resort community of approximately 300 people. Visitors have a choice of 7 resorts, motels, RV parks, riverside cabins, lakeside lodges, bed-and-breakfasts, or kitchenettes. Gas, store, and stables.

Mile 291.5 (153.5): Jefferson County/ Deschutes County line.

Mile 294 (151): Scaling station and access to Camp Tamerack, Santiam Pass Winter Recreation Area, and westbound chain-up area. The Santiam Pass Winter Recreation Area extends west to Highway 126 and the Mount Jefferson Wilderness, and south to the Mount Washington Wilderness. It contains over 70 miles of snowmobile and Nordic trails.

Mile 294.5 (150.5): Junction with Forest

Service Road 12 to Mount Jefferson Wilderness Trail Headquarters and Jack Lake Road. Access to Jack Creek picnic area which features a self-guiding nature trail.

Mile 295.5 (149.5): Access to Blue Lake Resort, 3 miles south of highway. This 300-foot-deep lake is stocked with rainbow trout and also holds kokanee, German brown and brook trout. Link Creek, which empties Blue Lake into Suttle Lake, is a spawning stream that is off limits to fishing. Best fishing is May through June. Resorts at Blue Lake offer a full range of accommodations and campgrounds. There are also a restaurant, store, marina, boat launches, hiking trails, stables, a Nordic ski center, and playgrounds for children.

Mile 296 (149): Turnoff for Suttle Lake. Marina, Forest Service campgrounds, lakeside resort, store and coffee shop located at lake. Good fishing for rainbow, German brown, eastern brook, whitefish and kokanee.

Mile 297.5 (147.5): Mount Washington viewpoint, one of several along the south side of the highway.   MP 84

Mile 300 (145): Access to Elliott R. Corbett Memorial State Park, 1.3 miles south and Corbett Sno-Park to the north. The state funded winter parking areas require a Sno-Park permit in season. Permits may be purchased locally. Corbett State Park is for day use only with picnicking and a 0.5-mile hiking trail.

Mile 303 (142): Santiam Pass Summit (elev. 4,817 feet), Jefferson/Linn County line and Willamette, Deschutes National Forest boundaries. Approximately 10 percent of all timber cut in national forests comes from the 1.6-million-acre Willamette National Forest.

Mile 303.5 (141.5): Turnoff south for

Hoodoo Ski Area, Ray Benson Sno-Park, and Big Lake Road. Santiam Sno-Park to north and access to Pacific Crest Trail. Hoodoo Ski Bowl has 3 lifts and rope tows in the alpine area, plus a separate Nordic center with groomed trails operated in conjuction with the Forest Service. Full-service lodge with bar. Warming huts at Benson Sno-Park area and access to snowmobile trails.

The Pacific Crest Trail winds north-south along the length of Santiam Pass. A portion marked for winter travel starts here and ends 3.2 miles south.

Mile 304 (141): Brake check area and start of 4-mile steep downgrade westbound.

Mile 307 (138): Lost Lake lies in a lava basin surrounded by meadows. Nearby are craters and lava fields of the McKenzie flow. It is fished for stocked rainbows and native brown trout.

Mile 308.5 (136.5): Junction with Oregon Highway 22 northwest to Salem. U.S. 20 shares a common alignment with Oregon Highway 126 from here east to Sisters.

Mile 312 (133): Junction of U.S. 20 and Oregon Highway 126 which leads southwest to Springfield (75 miles) and Eugene (78 miles).

For the next 16 miles westbound on U.S. 20 a series of small creeks tumble out of the Cascades, flow under the highway, and empty into the Santiam River. Most hold native brook trout and offer good fishing during June and July. The creeks are: Toad, Speckle, Echo, Slide, Snow, Ram, Sheep, and Easy Creek.

MP 72

Mile 316 (129): Historical marker tells of naming Lost Prairie in 1859. Some expedition members felt the group was lost. To prove they were not, leader Andrew Wiley climbed a tree and by doing so became the first white man to see Santiam Pass from the west side of the mountains. Lost Prairie USFS Campground.

▲

Mile 316.5 (128.5): Echo Creek Road, hiking trail. 🚶🚶 MP 66

Mile 319.5 (125.5): Tombstone Pass Summit (elev. 4,236 feet); Sno-Park parking. Brake test area and start of 6 percent downgrade westbound.

Mile 320 (125): Junction with Jump Off Joe Road. *CAUTION:* Slides next 7 miles, winding road next 3 miles westbound.

Mile 329 (116): House Rock USFS campground; 17 sites. ▲

Mile 331 (114): Mountain House Restaurant. Starting in 1868, there have been 4 Mountain Houses here. The first 2 were destroyed by fire, and the third stands south of the highway. The current one was built in 1940.

Mile 332 (113): Fernview USFS campground; 10 sites. ▲

Mile 335 (110): Turnout trailhead and Trout Creek USFS campground (21 sites). The Santiam River parallels the highway westbound. 🚶🚶▲

Mile 337.5 (107.5): Crossing the South Santiam River. Steelhead in spring and fall, some salmon in summer, rainbow and cutthroat; May through June. 🐟

Mile 339 (106): Turnout to north.

Mile 340.5 (104.5): Western boundary of Willamette National Forest.

Mile 343 (102): Canyon Creek.

Mile 343.5 (101.5): Wolf Creek.

Mile 344.5 (100.5): Cascadia State Park; 26 campsites, group picnic shelter, soda water spring, 2-mile trail to Soda Creek Falls, and fishing in Santiam River. 🚶🚶⛱🐟▲

Mile 345 (100): CASCADIA. During the 1930s, this area attracted large numbers of vacationers because of its mineral springs. Today it has a store, post office and gas.

Mile 346 (99): A covered bridge, built in 1945, spans the Santiam River just off the highway.

Mile 353 (92): Junction with road north to Foster Lake and Green Peter Lake reservoirs managed by the U.S. Army Corps of Engineers; fishing, boating, swimming, camping and picnicking. Quartzille Road to Green Peter Lake also provides access to the Quartzille Recreation Corridor. The Quartzille Mining District has been the site of both hardrock and placer mining for gold since the mid-1800s. ⛱▲

Mile 355 (90): SWEET HOME (pop. 6,745), food, gas and lodging available. Industry here includes Slip-N-Snip Scissors, manufacturers of folding scissors; White's Metal Electronics, which makes the world's largest line of mineral and metal detectors; and Sweet Home, Inc., the nation's largest manufacturer of wood stoves, are headquartered here. White's Electronic Metal Detector museum is open weekdays from 8 a.m. to 5 p.m. Rock hounds will find the Sweet Home area a good place to dig for petrified wood. The Quartzille Mining is open to recreational mining (see description at **Mile 353**).

Mile 356 (89): Junction with road north to Foster Dam and fish hatchery; Foster Dam Site. Restrooms, scenic viewpoint, fish viewing and tours. Hatchery is open 8 a.m. to 5 p.m.

Mile 356.5 (88.5): Wiley Creek.

Mile 358.5 (86.5): Sweet Home Ranger Station, Willamette National Forest.

Mile 360 (85): Junction with Oregon Highway 228 West to Brownsville and Halsey.

Mile 360.5 (84.5): Access to McDowell County Park, 8 miles east; 2 waterfalls and picnic area.

Mile 369 (76): Access to Waterloo County Park; hiking and nature trails, boat ramp and playground. 🚶🚶

Mile 369.5 (75.5): Pineway public golf course; 9 holes, driving range, restaurant and lounge.

Mile 371 (74): Turnoff for Mountain Home and Sodaville.

Mile 371.5 (73.5): LEBANON (pop. 10,265) is a center for lumber and agriculture. Food, gas and lodging available. The area is rich in agates, petrified wood, jasper, opals and thunder eggs. Seven covered bridges are situated northeast of the city, and can be toured with a self-driving map available from the Lebanon Chamber of Commerce, 1040 Park St.

Mile 378 (67): Junction with Oregon Highway 226 North to Crabtree, Scio and Lyons.

Mile 382.5 (62.5): Timber Linn Memorial Park site of the annual Albany Timber Carnival held July 4 weekend. The carnival features championship and amateur competition in ax throwing, log chopping and other events, drawing contestants from throughout the Pacific Northwest.

Mile 384.5 (60.5): U.S. 20 passes over Interstate 5 and through Albany city center to Milepost 0 at the junction with Oregon Highway 99E. After merging with Highway 99, U.S. 20 goes north, across the Willamette River, then turns west.

ALBANY (pop. 28,060) is the county seat and largest city in Linn County. All visitor facilities are available. Albany is an important manufacturing center for rare metals, food processing, grass seed and timber.

The town dates to 1848, and was named for the founder's home, Albany, NY. The 350 homes in the historic district feature every major architectural style popular in the United States since 1850. Self-guiding tour brochures of the historic district and 10 covered bridges are available at the Albany Convention and Visitor's Bureau, 434 W. 1st Ave.

Mile 386 (59): Spring Hill Road, Albany Golf Course, and Benton-Linn County line.

Mile 389.5 (55.5): Junction with Independence Road north to Adair Village (4 miles), Game Management Area (5 miles) and Buena Vista (10 miles). During WWII, Camp Adair spread across 50,000 acres and became the second-largest city in Oregon. Infantry, artillery and engineering units were trained here. Later, it became a U.S. Naval hospital and a prisoner of war camp for Italians and Germans.

Mile 395 (50): Crossing the Willamette River.

Mile 395.5 (49.5): CORVALLIS (pop. 41,800) means "heart of the valley." All visitor facilities are available. Oregon State University and Hewlett Packard Corp. are major employers. Agriculture, electronics, engineering and wood products anchor the economy's base.

Over 30 buildings, dating from the late 1850s to 1917, are covered in a self-tour brochure available from the chamber of commerce.

Mile 396 (49): Oregon State University and junction with Oregon Highway 99 West to Monmouth and Junction City. The University was founded in 1858 as Corvallis College and is Oregon's oldest state-supported institution of higher education. As one of 28 land and sea grant universities in the nation, it is Oregon's major institution for basic research in forestry, agriculture, fisheries, engineering, electronics and other sciences.

Horner Museum, near the University, highlights natural sciences, history and world culture. Open year-round.

Peavy Arboretum, 8 miles north on Highway 99 West, is maintained by the university. The 40-acre site has 2 interpretative hiking trails and a picnic area. Nearby McDonald State Forest is popular with hikers, bird-watchers, and horseback and bicycle riders.

William L. Finley National Wildlife Refuge, 11 miles south on Highway 99 West, is a stopover for ducks, geese, ruffed grouse, ring-necked pheasants and California quail. Self-guiding trail; hunting from late August to mid-January.

Area wineries situated along the Highway 99 West corridor include Arlie Winery, Alpine Vineyards, Serendipity Cellars and Tyee Wine Cellars.

Yaquina Bay Lighthouse was built in 1871; it's open in summer. (Tom Barr)

Mile 397 (48): Turnoff to north for Western Stadium-OSU Coliseum, Horner Museum and junction with Highway 99 West south to Junction City and Eugene.

Mile 397.5 (47.5): Access to Oregon State University's Parker Stadium.

Mile 399.5 (45.5): 53rd Street and fairgrounds north of highway.

Mile 400 (45): PHILOMATH (pop. 2,675) means "love of learning," and was derived from 2 Greek words. The United Bretheran Church chartered a coeducational liberal arts and ministerial school in 1865. It ceased operations in 1929 and today forest, truck and tree farming are economic mainstays.

Mile 401 (44): The Philomath College Building, on the register of historic landmarks, houses the Benton County Historical Museum. Exhibits cover Camp Adair, timber, local Indians, displays of native basketry, tools and household utensils. Open Tuesday through Saturday, 10 a.m. to 4 p.m.; Sunday 1-4:40 p.m.

Mile 401.5 (43.5): Junction with Oregon Highway 34 south to Alsea and Waldport. The Alsea River is heavily fished weekends from September through November for salmon and steelhead. Services at Alsea, 18 miles south, are 2 cafes, gas, sport shop and market.

Mile 402.5 (42.5): Mary's River.

Mile 404 (41): WREN. Harris Covered Bridge, 2.5 miles west of Wren, was built in 1929 and is still in use.   MP 47

Mile 404.5 (40.5): Junction with King's Valley Highway (Oregon Highway 223). The King's Valley Community Church, 8 miles north, is representative of rural gothic style churches built locally during the late 1800s.

Mile 405 (40): Mary's River.

Mile 407 (38): Highway begins ascent westbound into Coast Range.

Mile 410 (35): BLODGETT, established in 1888 and originally called Ernerick. It was renamed after pioneer settler William Blodgett. Gas and county store.

Mile 412 (33): Old Blodgett Road.

Mile 414 (31): Lincoln County/Benton County Line.

Mile 415 (30): BURNT WOODS has a cafe with gas. A 2-lane paved road leads 8 miles south to Harlen Junction and the northern boundary of Siuslaw National Forest. MP 34

Mile 416.5 (28.5): H.D. Elmaker State Park, day-use park with picnicking and handicap facilities.   ⊼

Mile 417 (28): Cline Hill Summit (elev. 770 feet).

For the next 12 miles westbound, trees line the road's edge, forming a natural canopy over the highway. This section has a quiet beauty which can be enjoyed as sharp curves reduce speeds to 35 and 40 mph.

Mile 422 (23): Little Elk Store. Little Elk Creek meanders beside the highway and through a narrow canyon on its way to the Yaquina River.

Mile 425 (20): EDDYVILLE. Isreal Eddy was a storekeeper and grist mill operator who provided overnight accommodations for travelers. Lincoln County's oldest cemetery is located near the town. The Yaquina River, which U.S. 20 follows from Eddyville to the coast, is one of the area's best streams for salmon, steelhead, rainbow trout, native and stocked cutthroat.   ⊷

Mile 433 (12): Elk City junction. ELK CITY, 5 miles south, was platted in 1868. It was the first town in Lincoln County and became the overland stage and mail terminus. Free boat launch and dock. Elk City Store has 5 RV hookups. Camping is also available at the county park along with barbecue pits and water.   ▲

Mile 434 (11): Turnout south of highway.

Mile 435 (10): Pioneer Mountain Summit (elev. 337 feet).

Mile 437 (8): Pioneer Mountain Loop Road.

Mile 438 (7): Turnoff for business district of TOLEDO (pop. 3,200), named after Toledo, OH. The seat of Lincoln County, its economy is based on wood products and oysters. During WWI, the world's largest spruce mill was built here to supply wood for aircraft. The war ended before the plant was completed. All wood for Howard Hughes' "Spruce Goose" came from Toledo.

A pioneer blockhouse, built in 1890 for protection against Indian attacks, can be seen along with modern manufacturing complexes and a picturesque waterfront on a driving tour of local history.

Mile 438.5 (6.5): Access north to public golf course and Olalla Lake which produces good catches of cutthroat and brown trout.   ⊷

Mile 439.5 (5.5): Junction with Oregon Highway 229 which leads 8 miles north to SILETZ (pop. 1,045) and south to Toledo. The Siletz River is a top fall steelhead and good summer trout stream.   ⊷

Mile 444.5 (0.5): NEWPORT (pop. 8,455). A long sandy beach, a wealth of seafood, lively waterfront, and a mixture of scientific and historic sites make Newport a prime recreation area. The town has a wide range of accommodations available, plus private RV parks. Camping also at South Beach State Park south of town (reservations available). Picnicking at South Beach, Agate Beach and Yaquina Bay State parks. Yaquina Bay State Park is also the location of Yaquina Bay Lighthouse, built in 1871; open in summer.

Yaquina Bay is a major producer of clams, oysters and Dungeness crab. Salmon, bottom fish, perch and steelhead can be caught in season from riverbanks, shore, or charter boat. Area rivers and streams are fished for trout in summer and steelhead during winter.

In addition to equipment rentals and charters, Newport's waterfront is filled with boutiques, restaurants, specialty shops. It also has "Ripley's Believe It Or Not" Museum, the Wax Works Museum and Undersea Gardens.

Visit Hatfield Marine Science Center where displays explain the properties of the ocean and specimens of Oregon's fishes and invertebrates are on exhibit. Open daily in summer.

Lincoln County Historical Museum, 579 SW 9th, houses Siletz Reservation artifacts, plus logging, farm and maritime exhibits.   ⊼⊷▲★

Mile 445 (0): Junction with U.S. Highway 101 (South Coast Highway). Turn to **Mile 314** in the U.S. HIGHWAY 101 section for log.

Interstate 84

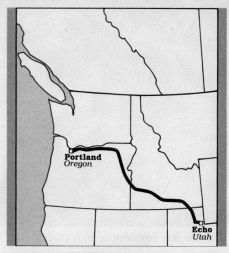

Interstate 84 is one of the most heavily used routes in the Northwest. The *NORTHWEST MILEPOSTS*® highway log starts at the junction of Interstates 205 and 84 in Portland, OR and leads 778 miles southeast to the junction with Interstate 80 near the small town of Echo in northeastern Utah.

Interstate 84 is a highway of contrasts. It travels through the historic and beautiful Columbia Gorge, past rugged vistas of the Cascade range and high desert of eastern Oregon. The highway spans the sagebrush plateaus of the Snake River valley and the alkali deserts of northern Utah on its way to the great Salt Lake .

In several areas, the interstate parallels the Oregon Trail and many of the communities have roots tied to the westward movement of the 19th century. While driving this comfortable route, consider the struggle of the immigrants of barely more than 100 years ago. Imagine the peril of traveling in Conestoga wagons across the rugged volcanic terrain, fording streams and rivers, slowly breaking trail through snowy mountain passes. Today, the 4-lane interstate allows motorists to travel across state in hours.

Interstate 84 Log

Distance from Portland, OR, is followed by distance from Echo, UT.

Mile 0 (778): Junction with Interstate 205 at Portland. Interstate 205 is an alternate route to Interstate 5 and skirts Portland city center. For further information on Portland, see the MAJOR CITIES section.

Mile 3 (775): 122nd Avenue in Portland.

Mile 6 (772): Exit 13A to U.S. Highway 26 and Exit 13B to Fairview, Gresham, 181st Street (Portland) and Blue Lake Park. The park, located at the corner of NE 233rd and Marine Drive, offers picnic sites, restrooms, play area, trails, bathhouse and concessions.   EXIT 13

Mile 9 (769): Exit to hospital, Multnomah Kennel Club, Mount Hood Community College, Gresham (pop. 36,370) and Wood Village (pop. 2,580). All traveler services available. You are in the outer perimeter of the Portland metropolitan area. EXIT 16A and B

Mile 9.5 (768.5): Exit for Marine Drive, **TROUTDALE** (pop. 7,000), and eastbound entrance to Columbia River Scenic Highway. Motel west off exit. The 24-mile-long Columbia River Scenic Highway provides access to a number of sights, including Crown Point State Park, Bridal Veil Falls and Multnomah Falls. It rejoins Interstate 84 at Exit 35. See feature on page 118.   ★ EXIT 17

Mile 10 (768): Cross Sandy River.

Mile 10.5 (767.5): Exit to Oxbow County Park and the Lewis and Clark State Park with 20 picnic sites, restrooms and a boat ramp.   ⊼ EXIT 18

Mile 14.5 (763.5): Exit to Corbett.   EXIT 22

Mile 16 (762): Crown Point Lookout visible to south above highway.

Mile 17 (761): Exit to Rooster Rock State Park on the Columbia River; 195 picnic sites, restrooms, rigging area for windsurfers, sandy beach, plenty of parking.   ⊼ EXIT 25

Mile 20.5 (757.5): Exit (eastbound only) to Bridal Veil Falls, a series of 2 falls which drop about 150 feet collectively.   EXIT 28

Mile 23.5 (754.5): Benson State Park (eastbound only). The park has 100 picnic sites, restrooms and a boat launch.   ⊼

Mile 24 (754): Exit to Multnomah Falls Historical Site and tourist information center for pedestrians. (Vehicle access via the Columbia River Scenic Highway from Exits 17 and 35). Park between the interstate lanes and walk underneath the highway via a pedestrian walkway to the Falls and the beautiful old stone Multnomah Lodge.

Multnomah Falls, the highest falls in Oregon and the fourth largest in the United States, is the most famous of the Columbia Gorge area. The top falls plunge 542 feet and the lower falls drop an additional 92 feet. A trail leads to a bridge and viewpoint over the falls.

The historical marker at the base of the falls relates the story of the Indian maiden who threw herself off the cliffs to save her lover. If you are a hopeless romantic and have a sense of imagination, legend claims that the maiden's face can be seen in the upper waterfall.

Souvenirs and food are available at the lodge.   EXIT 31

Mile 28 (750): Turnoff for Ainsworth State Park (45 trailer campsites) and westbound access to the 24-mile-long Columbia River Scenic Highway. This scenic route provides access to Multnomah Falls, Bridal Veil Falls and Crown Point State Park. It rejoins Interstate 84 at Exit 17. See Columbia River Scenic Highway on page 118.   ▲ EXIT 35

Mile 30 (748): Exit (westbound only) to Warrendale and access to scenic loop and Vista House.   EXIT 37

Mile 32 (746): Moffett Creek.

Mile 33 (745): Exit to the Bonneville Dam, fish hatchery and information center. Bonneville Dam was the first hydroelectric dam built on the Columbia River. It was completed in 1938 and a second powerhouse was added in 1981. Visitors can watch migrating fish through underwater windows at the Bonneville Regional Visitors Center or the fish viewing building on the Washington shore. The Oregon Dept. of Fish and Wildlife operates a fish hatchery on nearby Tanner Creek.   EXIT 40

Mile 35 (743): Exit to Eagle Creek Park and fish hatchery. The park offers 10 tent campsites, 5 trailer sites and 78 picnic sites.   ⊼▲ EXIT 41

Mile 37 (741): Eastbound exit to CASCADE LOCKS (pop. 815); all services. The city was named for the series of locks built in 1896, which were submerged with construction of the Bonneville Dam in 1938. Marine park with remnants of old locks, rigging area and beach for windsurfers, marina, museum and visitors center.

The sternwheeler *Columbia Gorge* operates 2-hour narrated tours from here daily from mid-June to late September. The 600-passenger boat is a replica of the sternwheelers that cruised the Columbia at the turn of the century. Well worth the trip.

The Bridge of the Gods, which spans the Columbia River at Cascade Locks, connects with Washington Highway 14, a 2-lane road connecting Interstate 5 (40 miles west) with U.S. Highway 395 (140 miles east). Access to Stevenson, WA, and Beacon Rock State Park.   EXIT 44

Mile 38.5 (739.5): Exit (westbound only) to Cascade Locks (see preceding

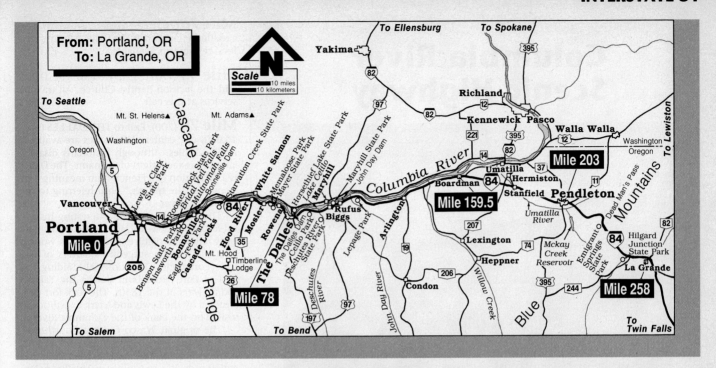

From: Portland, OR
To: La Grande, OR

milepost). **EXIT 44**

Mile 42.5 (735.5): The steep sides of the hills make this a slide area. Drive carefully.

Mile 44 (734): Exit to Wyeth. Limited services. **EXIT 51**

Mile 48 (730): Starvation Creek State Park and rest area (eastbound only); 20 picnic sites, restrooms and phone. ⊼

Mile 49.5 (728.5): Exit to Viento State Park which offers 17 tent campsites, 58 improved campsites and 28 picnic sites.
⊼▲ **EXIT 56**

Mile 55.5 (722.5): Exit to West Hood River, Westcliff Drive and the Columbia Gorge Hotel Historic Site. Major motels off exit. Tucker Park county campground (with tent sites and showers) is accessible from this exit. Follow Highway 281 to 13th Street and turn south; 13th Street becomes Tucker Road.

The elegant Columbia Gorge Hotel is a historic site. Built in 1921-22 by Simon Benson, pioneer lumberman, it sits high on the Columbia Gorge and offers unequalled views of the river, cliffs and surrounding terrain. It was built for the Roaring '20s crowd and soon became a favorite of the Jazz Age. Rudolph Valentino and Clara Bow were among the frequent guests. The hotel is restored to its original condition and makes for an elegant break from the humdrum of motel living. It is expensive, however. ▲★ **EXIT 62**

Mile 57.5 (730.5): Exit south to **HOOD RIVER** (pop. 4,500); hotel, several bed-and-breakfasts, many restaurants, 24-hour supermarket, and numerous windsurfing shops.

This formerly quiet little lumber and fruit-growing (apples, pears) town is now the mecca for the windsurfing world. The strong and steady winds that howl through the Columbia River Gorge from spring until fall, combined with the strong and opposing river current, make this one of the hottest windsurfing spots in the world. Visitors can stroll through dozens of windsurfing shops downtown to check out the gear or sign up for a lesson. For a close-up look at this sport, visit the Hood River Sailpark (see Exit 64).

The Mount Hood Railway offers scenic train rides to Odell and Parkdale from spring through fall. Phone (503) 386-3556 for reservations and information. The railway trips depart from the Hood River Depot. Take Exit 63 and turn left on Cascade.

Hood River is also known for its spring water. First tapped in 1928, the city water supply, without chlorination or filtration, has been rated third best in the nation. **EXIT 63**

Mile 58 (730): Major chain fast-food restaurants, motel and gas stations south off exit. This exit provides access to several attractions and travel routes: Oregon Highway 35 to Mount Hood; White Salmon, Bingen and Washington Highway 14; and Hood River Sailpark. (Descriptions follow.)

Oregon Highway 35 (Mt. Hood Loop Highway) leads 40 miles south to Mount Hood Ski Area and Timberline Lodge. Turnoff at Odell on to Highway 281 for access to Tucker County Park (camping).

Cross the interstate toll bridge for access north to Washington Highway 14, a good 2-lane road which connects Interstate 5 (63 miles west) and U.S. 395 (117 miles east). Across the river on Highway 14 is **BINGEN**, WA, which has an inn, bakery, and a marina with a large grassy rigging area and a long sandy beach for windsurfers.

North off this exit turn left for the Port of Hood River development which includes the Hood River County Historical Museum, Visitor Information (phone 385-2000), Port offices, and the popular Hood River Sailpark and marina. Hood River windsurfing shops hold their lessons at the sailpark, and it is a popular spot for practicing waterstarts, short board planing and jibes. (Windsurfers who venture across the river here face deep swells, strong currents, barges and sometimes end up at Bozo Beach, a steep rocky slope on the Washington side.) This is an excellent spot to view this colorful sport, which has grown so dramatically in recent years. Facilities at the sailpark include restrooms with showers, parking and food concession stands.
⊼▲★ **EXIT 64**

Mile 63 (725): Junction of U.S. Highway 30 to **MOSIER** and a 9-mile scenic loop. The loop runs from Mosier to Rowena and on a high bluff overlooking the river is the Rowena Crest viewpoint. It is adjacent to the Tom McCall Preserve, a refuge for several native plants, many of which are rare and endangered. **EXIT 69**

Mile 66 (712): Rest area and access to Memaloose State Park (westbound access only; eastbound travelers use Exit 76). Memaloose Park offer 67 tent campsites, 43 trailer sites, 18 picnic sites, drinking water and a historical site.

Memaloose Island in the Columbia River is an ancient Indian burial ground. The island was set aside by the U.S. Land Office as a burial ground for the Warm Spring Indians until Victor Trevitt, one of Oregon's early pioneers, was buried there in 1883. Before the high water of 1894, several Indian houses on the island contained the bodies of Indians with their bows, arrows, guns and other artifacts. ⊼▲

Mile 70 (708): Exit to Rowena, Memaloose State Park (eastbound access only) and Mayer State Park. Mayer Park has 36 picnic sites, water, boat ramp, restrooms, and swimming. ⊼**EXIT 76**

Columbia River Scenic Highway

Lake Bonneville on the Columbia River Gorge.

(L. Linkhart)

The Columbia River Gorge is one of our great natural treasures, a 70-mile long landscape of extraordinary drama and beauty now protected from development as a national scenic area. The first highway through the gorge was begun in 1913 and completed 2 years later. A plaque at Crown Points says of Chief Engineer Samuel C. Lancaster, "His genius overcame tremendous obstacles extending then replacing the early trail through the gorge with a highway of poetry and drama so that millions could enjoy God's spectacular creations."

The construction of Interstate 84 eliminated sections of the old highway, but one 24-mile chunk in the heart of the gorge (plus another farther east) has been preserved as Columbia River Scenic Highway. The detour is well worthwhile as it gives you a chance to savor the beauty and the subtler moods of the gorge better than you can from the interstate and it provides the best vantage points for photographs.

Eastbound, leave Interstate 84 at Exit 17 and follow the brown-and-white signs. The 2-lane road meanders through dense stands of fir and alder, crossing the Sandy River, past Dabney State Park (picnic tables) and U-pick berry farms, to Portland Women's Forum State Park, an overlook on Chanticleer Point with splendid views upriver including distinctive Crown Point. A short distance beyond you'll come to Crown Point State Park. Here, Vista House perches 733 feet above the river for a commanding 30-mile vista of the gorge. The handsome stone building, built in 1916, houses a visitor center and craft gallery in the summer.

Some of the lovely subtleties of the gorge that elude freeway travelers are the grotto-like side canyons. Carpeted with moss and ferns, they often harbor a waterfall bathed in cool green light filtering through the trees overhead. There are numerous places to pull off and explore; signed trails lead from the scenic highway into these side canyons.

Beyond Crown Point the road twists and turns through an overhanging canopy of trees. In places the old stone arched guard wall from the original highway remains, covered in a patina of rust and green moss and lichen. The road gradually descends to river level, past Latourell Falls, Shepperds Dell, Bridal Veil, Coopy, Mist and Wahkeena falls.

Multnomah Falls Lodge is nearly as well known as the gorge itself. Travelers have been stopping here for a snack or a meal since 1925. The massive stone building nestles beneath the fourth-highest waterfall in the U.S. Two separate cascades have a vertical drop of 620 feet. An easy footpath leads to a footbridge between the upper and lower falls. Beyond, the highway passes Oneonta Gorge and 176-foot Horsetail Falls before returning to Interstate 84.

Mile 76 (708): Exit to the Chenoweth area, a residential suburb of The Dalles. Gas and fast-food restaurants available.   EXIT 82

Mile 77 (701): Exit west to The Dalles and the Jackson Baptist Church. All traveler services at this exit.   EXIT 83

Mile 78 (700): Exit to THE DALLES (pop. 10,960) city center. All services are available in The Dalles. Although historians disagree about the exact origin of the name, The Dalles is a derivation of a French term meaning "the steps" or "the trough," both referring to the Columbia River.

The Dalles has several interesting historical features. The Fort Dalles Museum displays early relics and pictures of The Dalles, housed in a picturesque surgeon's quarters of historic Fort Dalles. This unusual building was part of Fort Drum built during the Yakima Indian wars of the 1850s. The rock fort constructed by the Lewis and Clark expedition is visible on the bank of the Columbia River.

The original Wasco County Courthouse, the seat of government for the largest county ever formed in the United States, still stands. Wasco County originally encompassed some 130,000 square miles from the Cascades to the Rockies, including the Grand Tetons and part of Yellowstone Park. Wasco County is significantly smaller now, but The Dalles is still the county seat.   EXIT 84

Mile 79 (699): Exit east to The Dalles, The Dalles airport and The Dalles bridge. EXIT 85

Mile 81 (697): Junction with U.S. Highway 197 north to The Dalles bridge and The Dalles Dam and south to Dufur and Bend. North on Highway 197 is Horsethief Lake State Park in Washington. The park lies on the edge of the Columbia River surrounded by huge rock formations where ancient Indian petroglyphs can be seen; 14 campsites with kitchens and tables are available. There are primitive sites for sailboaters, hikers and bikers. Horsethief Lake is a small lake separated from the river by railroad tracks. It has a swimming beach and boat launch.
▲ EXIT 87

Mile 82.5 (695.5): Exit to The Dalles Dam. The enormous 0.5-mile-long powerhouse has 22 generating units producing 1.8 million kilowatts. Two fish ladders, each 0.3 mile long, are an exciting attraction, especially during the salmon run. Visitors can take a small tour train from the visitors center on the Oregon shore to the fish ladder and powerhouse for a guided tour. Hydropower exhibits in the powerhouse explain the operation of the dam and the petroglyphs carved nearby. South of the dam on U.S. Highway 197 is the Celilo Converter, the largest converter station in the United States. Celilo converts power from The Dalles Dam for transmission over an 853-mile power line to California.   EXIT 88

Mile 91 (687): Junction with Oregon Highway 206 to Celilo Park, the Deschutes River State Park and Fulton Canyon.

Celilo Park offers 33 picnic sites, drinking water, flush toilets, boat ramp, museum, play area and a protected swim area. It is situated on the banks of Lake Celilo, the backwaters of The Dalles Dam. Celilo Falls, now inundated by the reservoir, was the site of the Ancient Indian Fishing Grounds where native Americans gathered to harvest the plentiful salmon as the fish headed upstream to spawn. The reservoir has a strong current and on-shore wind for good high-wind sailing for the experienced sailor.

Deschutes River State Park offers 34 campsites, 41 picnic sites, water, toilets and fishing. EXIT 97

Mile 94 (684): The Deschutes River is one of the world's top trout producers and native summer-run steelhead are plentiful. The Deschutes River is one of the most intensively managed rivers in the Northwest with strict catch-and-release regulations for specific species in specific areas. Before wetting your line, obtain a copy of the Oregon sportfishing regulations.

White-water enthusiasts also find the Deschutes a popular stream, and this sport is also strictly regulated. For a copy of these regulations, contact the Oregon Parks Dept., 525 Trade St. SE, Salem, OR 97310; phone (503) 378-6500.

Mile 98.5 (679.5): Junction with U.S. Highway 97 south to Biggs, and north across the Columbia River to Maryhill, WA. (Travelers heading north or south on U.S. HIGHWAY 97 turn to **Mile 349** in the U.S. HIGHWAY 97 section for log.)

Worth a side trip for Interstate 94 travelers is the Maryhill Museum, a replica of a Flemish chateau perched high on the wall of the Columbia Gorge. Built as a mansion for wealthy Sam Hill and dedicated by Queen Marie of Romania in 1926, it now is a museum featuring a large collection of antique chess pieces, Indian artifacts, Faberge eggs, and Queen Marie's throne and court gowns.

Two miles east of Maryhill is Stonehenge, a copy of the druid temple of England, also built by Sam Hill in memory of soldiers from Klickitat County who died in WWI. It is part of the Maryhill museum complex.

Maryhill State Park on the north side of the river offers 50 campsites, a swimming area, picnic areas and a boat launch.

Mile 104 (674): Exit to the John Day Dam and **RUFUS** (pop. 380); gas, food and lodging.

The John Day Lock and Dam stretches more than a mile across the Columbia River. The facilities include a navigation lock, a powerhouse, spillway and fish passage facilities. Tours are available. The John Day Dam is one of the largest producers of power in the world, producing some 2.2 million kilowatts, enough to meet the electrical needs of 2 cities the size of Seattle. Four more units are planned.

The lock on the Washington shore provides passage for more than 8 million tons of commercial traffic each year, in addition to recreation boats. One of the highest single-life locks in the world, it lifts the vessels 113 feet between Lake Celilo (the backwaters of The Dalles Dam) and Lake Umatilla. Its downstream gate is also unusual in that it opens vertically, raised by large cables extending from tall towers.

On the Oregon shore, underwater viewing of the fish ladder is provided. A guide to public recreation areas on Lake Umatilla is available at the project office and guided tours of the powerhouse may be arranged by writing or calling The Dalles-John Day Project, U.S. Army Corps of Engineers, P.O. Box 564, The Dalles, OR 97058.

The reservoir behind John Day Dam is called Lake Umatilla, and is a favorite smallmouth bass and walleye fishing area for Oregon and Washington anglers. EXIT 109

Mile 108.5 (669.5): Rest area. Exit to the John Day River Recreation Area. The John Day River crosses under the interstate at this point. LePage Park offers 71 campsites, picnic area, fishing, boating, handicap access, swimming and restrooms.

The lower portion of the John Day River below Kimberly is a major steelhead water area from August through April. Check locally for specific regulations and catch limits. EXIT 114

Mile 118 (660): Exit to Philippi Canyon. EXIT 123

Mile 124 (654): Exit to Blalock Canyon. EXIT 129

Mile 125.5 (652.5): Exit to Woelpern Road, eastbound only. EXIT 131

Mile 132.5 (645.5): Junction with Oregon Highway 19 at Arlington (pop. 450). All services are available at this exit. EXIT 137

Mile 142 (636): Junction with Oregon Highway 74 south to Ione and Heppner (pop. 1,375). All services are available at this exit. EXIT 147

Mile 146.5 (631.5): Exit to Threemile Canyon. Eastbound travelers are now leaving the Columbia Gorge. EXIT 151

Mile 154.5 (623.5): Exit to Tower Road. EXIT 159

Mile 156 (622): Rest area with phone and travel information center.

Mile 159.5 (618.5): Exit to **BOARDMAN** (pop. 1,225) with all traveler services. Boardman is on the edge of the fragmented 29,370-acre Umatilla National Wildlife Refuge, parts of which are in Oregon and Washington, flanking both sides and several islands in the Columbia River system. In the winters up to 90,000 Canada geese, and 250,000 ducks winter here, along with bald and golden eagles, peregrine falcons and hundreds of shorebirds. Mule deer, coyotes, beaver, badger, raccoons and muskrats are fairly common at the refuge. EXIT 164

Mile 160.5 (617.5): Blowing dust next 40 miles may cause hazardous driving conditions.

Mile 161 (617): Exit to the Port of Morrow. EXIT 165

Mile 163 (615): Junction with U.S. Highway 730 north to Umatilla. EXIT 168

Mile 173.5 (604.5): Exit to the Umatilla Army Depot. EXIT 177

Mile 174.5 (603.5): Exit to McNary Dam, I-82 north to Kennewick and Yakima. EXIT 179

Mile 176 (602): Exit to Westland Road, Hermiston and Umatilla. EXIT 180

Mile 178.5 (599.5): Junction with Oregon Highway 207 north to Hermiston and south to Lexington. Gas, food, campground, hospital available this exit. EXIT 182

Mile 182 (596): Rest area with phone.

Mile 184.5 (593.5): Cross Umatilla River.

Mile 185 (593): Junction with U.S. Highway 395 north to Stanfield, Hermiston, McNary Dam and the Umatilla bridge, continuing north through the Tri-Cities. Turn to **Mile 413.5** in the U.S. HIGHWAY 395 log for description of that route. Interstate 84 and U.S. Highway 395 share a common alignment here south to Pendleton. EXIT 188

Mile 189 (589): Exit to Echo Road. No services available. EXIT 193

Mile 194 (584): Exit to Lorenzen Road and McClintock Road. EXIT 198

Mile 195.5 (582.5): Exit to Stage Gulch and Yoakum Road. EXIT 199

Mile 199 (579): Exit to Barnhard Road. All services are available at this exit. EXIT 202

Mile 201 (577): Blue Mountains visible in distance as highway descends to Pendleton.

Mile 203 (575): Junction with U.S. Highway 30 to Pendleton airport, Pendleton city center and historic district, and Blue Mountain Community College. **PENDLETON** (pop. 14,150) has all services, including 13 motels and about 40 restaurants. Perhaps Pendleton's biggest claim to fame is the Pendleton Round-Up, the major Professional Rodeo Cowboy Assoc. (PRCA) sanctioned rodeo held the second full week of September. Motels and campgrounds fill to capacity as thousands of visitors converge on the seat of Umatilla County.

Another hallmark for the city of Pendleton is the Pendleton Woolen Mills, one of the most renowned woolen mills in the nation. The Pendleton Woolen Mills began using Northwest wool in Pendleton in 1909. Since that time, the company has expanded and their headquarters are now located in Portland.

Wool blankets are still produced at the Pendleton, OR, location. **EXIT 207**

Mile 205 (573): Umatilla River, a good trout and steelhead stream. The river is well stocked with rainbow. Check at Mission before fishing on the Umatilla Indian Reservation east of Pendleton. 🐟

Mile 205.5 (572.5): Junction with U.S. Highway 395 south and Oregon Highway 37 north. Travelers southbound on U.S. Highway 395 turn to **Mile 392.5** in the U.S. HIGHWAY 395 section and read log back to front.

Turnoff for McKay Creek Reservoir, a refuge area with good fishing, located 4 miles south. 🐟 **EXIT 209**

Mile 207 (571): Pendleton exit. **EXIT 210**

Mile 210 (568): Junction with Oregon Highway 11 to Pendleton, and north to Milton-Freewater and Walla Walla, WA. **EXIT 213**

Mile 212 (566): Entering Umatilla Indian Reservation.

Mile 217.5 (560.5): Viewpoint of the Pendleton Valley from Emigrant Hill.

Mile 221 (557): Poverty Flat Road and the Old Emigrant Hill Road. **EXIT 224**

Mile 225.5 (552.5): Dead Man's Pass and rest area. You are now at the top of Emigrant Hill. Anticipate a steep ascent eastbound from Pendleton as you enter the Blue Mountains. *CAUTION:* Truck traffic on this hill is heavy. Large tractor-trailer rigs travel very slowly up and down this 6 percent grade. Drive with caution. **EXIT 228**

Mile 230 (548): Exit to Emigrant Spring State Park and Meacham. Emigrant Springs State Park offers 18 full hookup campsites and 33 tent sites. Sheltered picnic sites, showers and visitor information available. 🪧▲**EXIT 234**

Mile 233.5 (544.5): Exit to Meacham and Kamela. Gas and food available. **EXIT 236**

Mile 237 (541): Summit of the Blue Mountains (elev. 4,193 feet).

Mile 239 (539): Exit to Mount Emily Road. **EXIT 243**

Mile 244 (534): Exit to Kamela and Spring Creek Road. **EXIT 248**

Mile 248 (530): Junction with Oregon Highway 244 to Ukiah. Hilgard Junction State Park here offers 18 tent sites. The park has picnic sites, fishing, handicap facilities and a dump station. 🪧🐟▲**EXIT 252**

Mile 248.5 (529.5): Five Point Creek. The Oregon Trail followed this creek west to Meacham.

Mile 252 (526): Perry, a small agricultural community. No services available. **EXIT 256**

Mile 254.5 (523.5): Crossing Grande Ronde River.

Mile 255 (523): Junction with U.S. Highway 30 to La Grande and the Eastern Oregon State College.

LA GRANDE (pop. 12,200) takes its name from the Grande Ronde River and valley. The city is the seat of Union County and is situated at the foot of the Blue Mountains where many Oregon Trail immigrants decided to settle in 1861. Today, La Grande has a diversified agricultural base. It is also the home of the Eastern Oregon State College. All services are available.

Above La Grande, the Grande Ronde River offers good trout fishing. La Grande is also the gateway to the Wallowas and Wallowa Lake. 🐟**EXIT 259**

White-water rapids on the Grande Ronde River. (L. Linkhart)

Mile 258 (520): Junction with Oregon Highway 82 to La Grande, Elgin (pop. 1,740) and Wallowa Lake; gas, food, lodging and hospital. **EXIT 261**

Mile 261 (517): Junction with Oregon Highway 203 to La Grande and Union. **EXIT 265**

Mile 264 (514): Exit to Foothill Road; campground and airport. ▲**EXIT 268**

Mile 265 (513): Rest area.

Mile 266.5 (511.5): Exit to Ladd Creek Road (eastbound only). No return to freeway eastbound. **EXIT 270**

Mile 270 (508): Exit to Ladd Canyon. **EXIT 273**

Mile 273.5 (504.5): Exit to Clover Creek Road. **EXIT 278**

Mile 280 (498): Exit to Wolf Creek Road. **EXIT 283**

Mile 282 (496): Junction with U.S. Highway 30 and Oregon Highway 237 to North Powder, Haines (pop. 395) and Anthony Lakes Ski Area; gas, food, lodging at exit.

North Powder was a stage station on the Oregon Trail. No services are available at either North Powder or Haines. Anthony Lakes Ski Area (base elev. 7,100 feet) boasts the highest chair lift in the Pacific Northwest; skiing from November to May.

The Elkhorn Mountain Range is visible on the southwest and is broken by a series of peaks (from south to north): Elkhorn Peak (elev. 8,922 feet); Rock Creek Butte (elev. 9,097 feet); Hunt Mountain (elev. 8,232 feet); Red Mountain (elev. 8,920 feet); and Twin Mountains (elev. 8,920 feet). The Wallowa Mountains are visible to the northeast. ⛷**EXIT 285**

Mile 284 (494): The 45th parallel. You are now halfway between the equator and the North Pole.

Mile 285.5 (492.5): Powder River, named for the volcanic ash which lines its banks.

Mile 291 (487): Rest area.

Mile 295 (483): Junction with Oregon Highway 203 to the Baker airport and Medical Springs, a large natural hot pool. **EXIT 298**

Mile 299 (279): Junction with Oregon Highway 86 to North Baker, Richland (pop. 180), Halfway (pop. 400) and Hells Canyon. This is also the exit to Oxbow Dam and Hells Canyon Dam along the Snake River. Food and gas are available in Halfway. **EXIT 302**

Mile 300.5 (477.5): Junction with Oregon Highway 7 south to the city center of **BAKER** (pop. 9,510). All services are available.

The city of Baker is located on the banks of the Powder River at the base of the Elkhorn Range to the west and the Wallowa Mountains to the northeast.

The Powder River is heavily stocked with rainbow for good fishing from Baker to Philips Reservoir. Philips Reservoir is also a good place to troll for rainbow and coho salmon. There are 2 campgrounds at the lake offering more than 50 sites.

If you have the time, take a 45-minute drive south of Baker to the frontier town of Sumpter in the Elkhorn Mountains along the Powder River. The drive is pleasant and the scenery is fantastic. Sumpter itself was a wild mining community in the late 1800s and many of the mining relics remain.

The Sumpter Valley Railroad is also a major attraction. The restored steam engine takes visitors on a tour through Sumpter Valley during the summer months. Those riding the train can view the mine tailings from which some $10 million was produced between 1913 and 1954. Wildlife is often visible from the

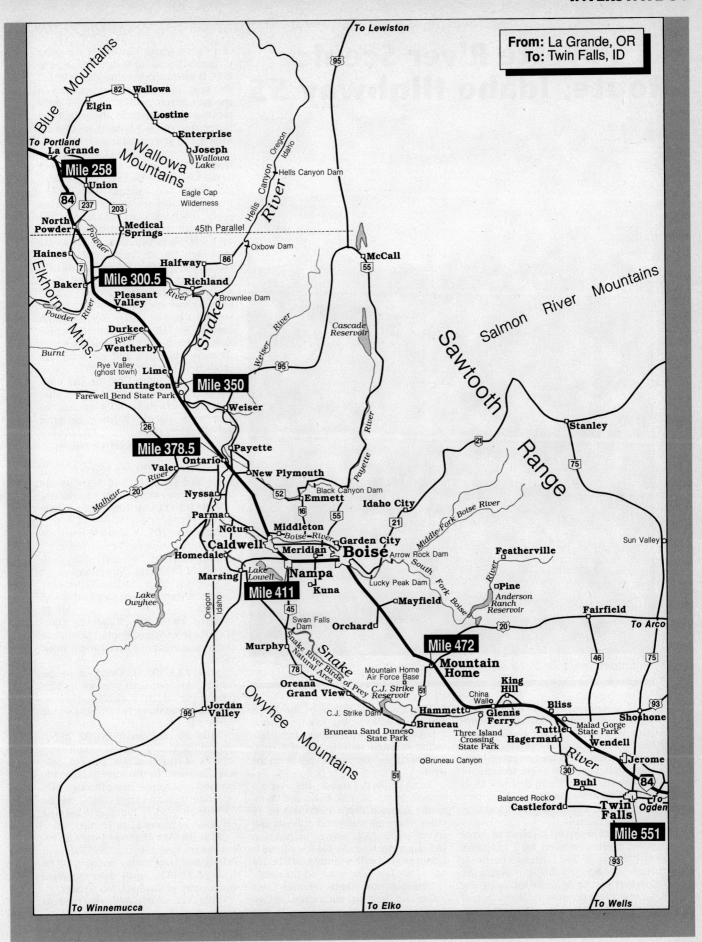

From: La Grande, OR
To: Twin Falls, ID

Payette River Scenic Route, Idaho Highway 55

Mountains and pine forest are always within sight of Highway 55. (L. Linkhart)

As you drive east on Interstate 84 through southwestern Idaho, the mountains lie always in sight to the north, distant above Caldwell and Nampa, close behind Boise. There are few paved highways that penetrate these mountains, but one that does, Idaho Highway 55, is a beautiful drive that traverses tall pine forests, roaring mountain rivers and clear mountain lakes.

The tour begins on Highway 44 out of Boise, heads northwest for a few miles to Highway 55 and continues north. At Horseshoe Bend the highway begins the loveliest part of its route following the Payette River northward. Highway and river wind between steep timbered hills to Banks, the confluence of the North and South forks of the Payette. This is a popular river with rafters from late spring through summer. Several commercial rafting companies operate on the river.

From Banks to Cascade, the river is a turmoil of rapids, sink holes and thundering spray; it drops 1,700 feet in 15 miles. There are numerous pullouts and several picnic spots where you can stop and enjoy the river. At Big Eddy there is a campground with a sandy beach beside one of the few quiet spots on the river.

The highway climbs up into Long Valley and the town of Cascade. At Cascade Reservoir the mood changes to that of a vacationland. Cascade is a popular recreational area for those who come to hike, horseback ride, camp, fish, golf, sail and boat. There are 14 campgrounds in the area, several with hookups, 1 guest ranch and 5 motels. In the winter the frozen reservoir is a favorite spot for ice fishing and snowmobiling.

McCall, one of Idaho's leading recreation and vacation towns, sits at the foot of the lovely Payette Lake. Elegant lakeside homes and resort accommodations line the southern shore. Ponderosa pines, some 500 years old and standing 150 feet tall, shade lakeside campgrounds on a 1,000-acre peninsula at Ponderosa State Park. During the summer, there is sailing, water-skiing, swimming and fishing in the many streams and lakes in the McCall area. Lakeshore Drive leads 20 miles around the lake for superb views. McCall is known for its popular winter carnival in February when the whole town turns out for snowmobile races, snowshoe baseball and ice sculpture exhibits.

The route returns to the tall evergreens of Boise National Forest and, after climbing over a short, but steep pass, the forest ends and the highway descends into the pretty Little Salmon River Valley to join Highway 95 at New Meadows.

Mile 0 (114): The trip begins at Front Street and South 15th in Boise, where Idaho Highway 44 begins, heading north.

Mile 0.5 (113.5): Turn west on State Street.

Mile 8.5 (105.5): Turnoff north on Highway 55 to Payette Scenic Route.

Mile 11 (103): Unincorporated community of Dry Creek. No services.

Mile 13 (101): Shadow Valley Golf Course. A spot of green in an otherwise dry area.   MP 49

Mile 14 (100): Roadside sign, "Payette River Scenic Route," points out and locates areas of interest and historic value.

Mile 23.5 (90.5): Overlook of the canyon downward to the north. Sign points to Bread Loaf Rock across the way. Very steep and many switchbacks on the north side.

Mile 28 (86): HORSESHOE BEND (pop. 620). Gas, groceries, food. Horseshoe Bend Historical Site. In 1862, gold was discovered in the Boise Basin to the east and gold miners came through here by saddle train and stage coach.   MP 64

Mile 28.4 (85.5): Junction to the west on Idaho Highway 52 to Emmett.

Mile 30 (84): Highway parallels Payette River along canyon floor. Frequent fishing and river rafting pullouts. MP 66

Mile 32 (82): Small unincorporated community of Gardena. No services.

Mile 33.5 (80.5): Wildlife chainsaw carvings on display.

Mile 35 (79): The Payette River is very popular for trout fishing, but even more so for river rafting. Only small rapids through here, and anyone can try it. Stream edge is thick with pines. MP 72

Mile 40 (74): Unincorporated small community of Banks. Gas, motel, restaurant, RV park.

Mile 42 (72): Boundary of Boise National Forest.

Mile 42.5 (71.5): Banks National Forest campground. Pit toilets, 5 day-use spots along the river and 7 rustic overnight spots along the steep bank above.

Mile 43 (71): Banks service station, cafe, store. River trips available.

Mile 43.5 (70.5): Crossing South Fork Payette River. At this point the North and South Forks unite to form the Payette River. North Fork has high rapids continually northward for many miles. Most guided raft trips are on the upper reaches of the South Fork. Turnoff to east along South Fork to Crouch, Garden Valley, Lowman.

Mile 44 (74): Steady climb northbound to the summit from the point, still following the North Fork of the Payette. MP 80

Mile 48.5 (65.5): Swinging Bridge National Forest Campground on side away from the river. 5 sites, water, pit toilets. Swinging bridge over the river.

Mile 53 (61): Big Eddy National Forest Campground. River sites, water, pit toilets.

Mile 54 (60): Boundary of Boise National Forest.

Mile 57 (57): SMITHS FERRY (pop. 100), a small farm and mountain community. Gas and lodging available. Turnoff west to High Valley, Sage Hen Reservoir and Ola. Sage Hen Reservoir is stocked and has Forest Service campgrounds, 2 boat ramps, tables, sanitary facilities and water.

Mile 64 (50): Private RV camp, restaurant, motel.

Mile 67 (47): Cascade airfield. No services.

Mile 68 (46): Turnoff to Cabarton Park 'n Ski Area.

Mile 70.5 (43.5): Small lumber community of **CASCADE** (pop. 1,070). All services. A popular outdoor recreation area. Boise Cascade Timber and Wood Products mill is the main industry. MP115

Mile 71 (43): Turnoff west to Cascade Lake. Historical marker.

Mile 71.5 (42.5): Crossing North Fork Payette River.

Mile 72 (42): Turnoff east to Warm Lake, Yellow Pine, Stanley. Warm Lake has public campground, boat ramp and private lodges.

Mile 75.5 (38.5): Descend into a wide, irrigated valley with Cascade Lake along its west border. The lake, 17 miles long, has nearly 50 miles of clean sandy shore,

fishing, 12 campgrounds, 8 boat ramps, restrooms and water.

Mile 85.5 (28.5): Crossing Gold Fork River.

Mile 91 (23): Small farming and lake community of **DONNELLY** (pop.210). All services. Rainbow Point Campground 4 miles west. Valley County Historical Museum 1 mile east.

Mile 98 (16): LAKE FORK (pop. 100). Groceries, RV park.

Mile 102.5 (11.5): McCall Airport. New runway construction will enable the airport to accommodate large jets. The airport is the base for the McCall unit of the elite smoke jumper corps of the U.S. Forest Service. The 7 National Forests surrounding this core base annually average 1,000 fires. Tours of their newly completed facility are welcome.

Mile 103 (11): McCALL (pop. 2,670). Resort community on beautiful Payette Lake. During summer weekends tourists come by the thousands to take advantage of the recreational opportunities on the lake. Downtown McCall has all kinds of shops for vacationers. Several marinas and a public swimming beach are close by and Ponderosa State Park is 2 miles east. The park has 170 campsites, water, hookups, fishing, boat launch, day-use area and group picnic shelter.

Mile 104 (10): Payette Lake Public Beach with restrooms. Also the turnoff to the McCall Fish Hatchery and the crossing of the North Fork Payette as it leaves the lake. MP 145

Mile 104.5 (9.5): Warren Wagon Road provides access to the west side of the lake and farther north to Upper Payette Lake. Also boundary of Payette National Forest.

Mile 105 (9): Bogus Basin Family Ski Resort.

Mile 107 (7): Turnoff to Brundage Mountain Ski Area 4 miles east.

Mile 108 (6): Steep downgrade along a narrow valley northbound. MP 151

Mile 109 (5): Last Chance National Forest campground 2 miles to the east. Dirt road. 23 sites, handicapped access. Water. MP 152

Mile 110 (4): Monument to Packer John's Cabin 0.5 mile north, built in 1862. The first Democratic Territorial Convention was held in his cabin in 1863. Now it is part of Packer John's Cabin State Park with 8 primitive sites, pit toilets. No water available. At this turnoff is Goose Creek Store and a RV park. MP 153

Mile 110 (4): Meadows, a small unincorporated community. When New Meadows was built, the town was relocated there. Colonial-style house and old brick school speak of times gone by.

Mile 114 (0): NEW MEADOWS (pop. 600). Highway ends at junction with Highway 95. MP 156

train. Also in the Sumpter Valley, on the Gagnon Ranch, is a herd of buffalo which roam the banks of Philips Lake.
◄▲EXIT 304

Mile 302.5 (475.5): Junction with Highway 30 to Baker. EXIT 306

Mile 309.5 (468.5): Turnoff to **PLEASANT VALLEY** (eastbound only), a valley named by the immigrant wagon train of 1878 that used the area as a resting place. No services are available. EXIT 315

Mile 312.5 (465.5): Alder Creek.

Mile 322 (456): Pritchard Creek.

Mile 324 (454): Exit to **DURKEE**; gas and food available. Fire opals may be found along the Burnt River near Durkee. EXIT 327

Mile 327 (451): Exit to Plano Road and Cement Plant Road. The factory on the south side of the highway is the Durkee plant for Ash Grove Cement West Co. At night, the lights on the buildings may startle the unsuspecting driver. The plant is a good distance from any major city. Ash Grove draws about 20 percent of its employees from Baker and 80 percent from the Huntington-Ontario area. EXIT 330

Mile 332.5 (445.5): Rest area and exit to Weatherby. No services available. EXIT 335

Mile 334.5 (443.5): Exit to Lookout Mountain (elev. 7,120 feet). The highway crosses the Burnt River at this point. The rugged, parched mountains in this area are the Burnt Mountains. EXIT 338

Mile 337 (441): Exit to Rye Valley, a farming and ranching valley. No services available. EXIT 340

Mile 339 (439): Exit (eastbound only) to Lime. No services available at this exit. EXIT 342

Mile 342.5 (435.5): Junction with U.S. Highway 30 to **HUNTINGTON** (pop. 550). No services available. The Oregon Trail crossed the Burnt River here and followed on top of the eastern ridges to Flagstaff Hill, east of Baker, a distance of about 40 miles. EXIT 345

Mile 348 (430): Mountain-Pacific time zone line. If you are headed east, set your watch ahead 1 hour. If headed west, turn your watch back 1 hour.

Mile 350 (428): Exit to Farewell Bend State Park and U.S. Highway 30 north to Huntington. Gas, lodging and camping available at exit. Farewell Bend gets its name from the pioneers who turned northwest from the Snake River and took a pass through the Burnt Mountains to the present site of Huntington on the Burnt River. Interstate 84 follows the same route.

Farewell Bend State Park is open year-round and offers 53 electrical campsites, 43 primitive

Idaho's state capitol building in Boise.

(L. Linkhart)

campsites, picnic tables, a dump station, camp showers, a visitor exhibit, boat launches, swimming areas and fishing.

There is another small campground at Unity Reservoir with 6 tent sites, 10 improved sites, picnic and swimming facilities. ⊼ ⬅ ▲ EXIT 353

Mile 353 (425): Exit to Weiser and junction with Oregon Highway 201. EXIT 356

Mile 359 (419): Moores Hollow Road exit. EXIT 362

Mile 368.5 (409.5): Exit to Stanton Boulevard. EXIT 371

Mile 372 (406): Junction with U.S. Highway 30 and Oregon Highway 201 to Ontario. The Malheur River crosses under the interstate at this point. EXIT 374

Mile 374 (404): Junction with U.S. Highway 30 to Ontario, OR, and Payette, ID. ONTARIO (pop. 8, 814) is an agricultural community on the banks of the Snake River offering all traveler services, including 16 motels and 35 restaurants. It is the home of the Treasure Valley Community College and has close ties to cities in the Treasure Valley: Boise, Nampa and Caldwell.

South of Ontario is Lake Owyhee, Oregon's largest lake. It is 53 miles long and has 310 miles of shoreline in the midst of the Owyhee Mountains. EXIT 376

Mile 375.5 (402.5): The Snake River marks the border of Idaho and Oregon.

Mile 376.5 (401.5): Rest area and information center.

Mile 378.5 (399.5): Junction with U.S. Highway 95 south to Parma and north to Payette and Weiser. *NORTHWEST MILEPOSTS®* travelers using Highway 95 should turn to **Mile 256** in the HIGHWAY 95 section for log of that route. EXIT 3

Mile 385 (393): Junction with U.S. Highway 30 to New Plymouth (pop. 1,186) and Idaho Highway 52 to Emmett (pop. 4,605) and Black Canyon Dam. The 183-foot-tall concrete dam backs up water for Black Canyon Reservoir, an important agricultural and recreational resource. Pumps in Black Canyon Reservoir irrigate the famous fruit-growing fields in the Emmett Irrigation District. EXIT 9

Mile 388.5 (389.5): Junction with Black Canyon Road. EXIT 13

Mile 393 (385): Exit to Sand Hollow, a small agricultural valley. No services available. EXIT 17

Mile 400.5 (377.5): Junction with Idaho Highway 44 to Middleton (pop. 1,901), named because it was located midway between Boise and Keeny's ferry on the mouth of the Boise River. Gas and food available. EXIT 25

Mile 401.5 (376.5): Junction with U.S. Highways 20 and 26 west to Notus (pop. 437) and Parma, small agricultural communities. No services available. EXIT 26

Mile 402.5 (375.5): Junction with U.S. Highway 30 and Idaho Highway 19 to Caldwell, Homedale and Wilder. The Boise River crosses below the interstate at this point.

The Boise is heavily stocked with rainbow and is a popular fishing area. ➡ EXIT 27

Mile 403.5 (374.5): 10th Avenue exit to Caldwell city center. All services available.

CALDWELL (pop. 17,699) is the seat of Canyon County and shares the agricultural distinctions of Nampa. Caldwell is the home of the College of Idaho, and among other things, Crookham Seed Co., the largest hybrid seed corn company in the world. The Caldwell Ponds are stocked with bluegill, smallmouth bass and rainbow trout.

Wineries are one of Idaho's newest agricultural industries and Caldwell boasts 3, all of which offer tours. Also in Caldwell is the Snake River mini-brewery with a tasting room. EXIT 28

Mile 404.5 (373.5): U.S. Highway 20 and U.S. Highway 26 east to Boise and Franklin Road. EXIT 29

Mile 411 (367): Junction with Idaho Highway 55 south and Nampa Boulevard to Nampa, Northwest Nazarene College, Karcher Mall and Marsing (19 miles). Karcher Mall is one of the largest shopping complexes in Idaho.

NAMPA (pop. 28,250) was named after Shoshoni Indian Chief Nampuh, a huge man whose name means "big foot." The town has all visitor facilities, including 7 motels and dozens of restaurants.

Nampa and the rest of Canyon County pride themselves on their seed crops. Idaho produces more farm crop seeds than anywhere else in America and Canyon County is the center of that production. Idaho produces 50 percent of the nation's onion and pea seed, 85 percent of the snap bean seed and 90 percent of the sweet corn seed. In addition to the quality of seed crops, Canyon County farmers produce some 80 different crops, more than any other county in America.

Nampa is the home of the Snake River Stampede, the biggest rodeo in Idaho, held the third week of July. EXIT 35

Mile 412 (366): Exit to Franklin Road. EXIT 36

Mile 414 (364): Junction with U.S. Highway 30 and Garrity Boulevard. EXIT 38

Mile 420.5 (357.5): Junction with Idaho Highway 55 north to McCall and Idaho Highway 69 south to MERIDIAN (pop. 6,658) and KUNA (pop. 1,767). Meridian is connected to Boise via Fairview Avenue, a busy commercial thoroughfare. All services are available including 1 motel and 15 restaurants.

The Kuna area features the Kuna Cave, a 1,000-foot-long lava tube discovered in 1890, and one of the area's most renowned landmarks. Also in the Kuna area is the Snake River Birds of Prey Natural Area, a reserve of nearly 500,000 acres which hosts the densest population of breeding raptors (birds of prey) in the world. EXIT 44

Mile 425.5 (352.5): Junction north with Interstate 184 to Boise city center. For more detailed information on Boise, turn to the MAJOR CITIES section. EXIT 49

Mile 426.5 (351.5): Exit to Overland Road and Cole Road. EXIT 50

Mile 428.5 (349.5): Orchard Street and the exit to Gowen Field. EXIT 52

Mile 429 (349): Exit for Vista Avenue, Boise International Airport. Vista Avenue N. passes by the historic Union Pacific Railroad Depot where it turns into Capitol Boulevard and continues straight to the capitol building. EXIT 53

Mile 431 (347): Exit for Broadway Avenue and Boise State University. EXIT 54

Mile 433 (345): Junction with Idaho Highway 21 to Idaho City and Stanley Basin, and Gowen Road. EXIT 57

Mile 438 (340): Blacks Creek rest area.

Mile 439.5 (338.5): Junction of Blacks Creek-Kuna Road. EXIT 64

Mile 447 (331): Exit to Mayfield and Orchard. Food and gas are available at the exit, but no services are available at either of the 2 communities. EXIT 71

Mile 450.5 (327.5): Junction of Simco Road, an unimproved cutoff to the Grand View Highway and C.J. Strike Reservoir. EXIT 74

Mile 467 (311): Junction with U.S. Highway 30 to Mountain Home. At the center of town, Idaho Highways 67 and 51 lead to Bruneau (limited services), Bruneau Dunes State Park and Mountain Home Air Force Base (10 miles southwest of town).

Mile 472 (306): Exit to **MOUNTAIN HOME** (pop. 8,900) and the junction with U.S. Highway 20 to Fairfield and Fun Valley. This is also the turnoff to Mountain Home Air Force Base, Bruneau, Grand View and C.J. Strike Reservoir. To the north is Anderson Ranch Dam and the popular resort community of Fun Valley along the South Fork Boise River, a popular fishing stream. Fun Valley in Sawtooth National Forest includes the communities of Pine, Paradise Resort and Featherville. Along the South Fork Boise River are remains of early mining efforts. Several ghost towns in and above Fun Valley add flavor to the area. Fly-fishing is popular here during the summer.

Mountain Home is the seat of Elmore County. Unlike most southern Idaho communities, its economy is based largely on the military, rather than agriculture.

Mountain Home was originally a "home station" for the stage route and was located 10 miles northeast of its present location. Upon completion of the railroad in 1883, the townsite was moved south to become a major shipping point for agricultural products.

In 1944, the military installation called Mountain Home Army Air Field was opened.

It was later designated Mountain Home Air Force Base and today it is the only active military installation in the state of Idaho.

South of Mountain Home is C.J. Strike Reservoir which offers sailing, powerboating, waterskiing, fishing and camping along its banks. The banks of Anderson Ranch Reservoir offer many campgrounds and resorts. Boat launches are located at several points around the reservoir which is stocked annually. ⤙▲EXIT 95

Mile 476 (302): Bennett Road exit and the junction with U.S. Highway 30 to Mountain Home. EXIT 99

Mile 488.5 (289.5): Junction with U.S. Highway 30 to **HAMMETT**, and unincorporated agricultural community where gas and food are available. At Hammett is the junction with Idaho Highway 78 to the Bruneau Dunes State Park and Bruneau Canyon, a popular spot for river rafters on the Snake River.

The Bruneau Dunes are unique in the western hemisphere in their formation and are in vivid contrast to the surrounding plateaus. Other dunes in the Americas form the edge of a natural basin; these form near the center. They include the largest single landlocked sand dune in North America, whose peak is 470 feet above the surface of a nearby desert lake. The 2 prominent dunes cover 600 acres.

Temperatures at the dunes range from 110°F/43°C in the summer to 0°F/-18°C in the winter.

The state park offers 32 campsites with electric hookups, 16 tent sites, firepits,

Bruneau Dunes State Park is south of Mountain Home. (L. Linkhart)

showers, water hookups and picnic areas. The camping fee is $9 for sites with electric hookups and $7 for tent sites. There is a $2 vehicle entrance fee for day use. ⊼▲EXIT 112

Mile 494.5 (283.5): The retention wall visible to eastbound travelers is referred to locally as the China Wall. It is 40 feet tall and nearly 4,500 feet long, holding back the steep canyon in this area called The Narrows. The China Wall is made of pre-cast concrete slabs connected with overlapped slip joints. The wall was constructed between 1977 and 1979.

Mile 497 (281): Exit to Glenns Ferry, eastbound only. EXIT 120

Mile 498 (280): Exit (eastbound only) to Glenns Ferry, King Hill and Three Island Crossing State Park. **GLENNS FERRY** (pop. 1,374), an agricultural community, has all traveler services, including groceries, gas and motel. The town was named for Gustavus Glenn who started a ferry on the Snake River in 1863. Glenns Ferry is the home of the Elmore County Fairgrounds.

Three Island Crossing State Park offers 50 campsites, water, electrical hookups, toilets, a dump station, a group picnic center and an information center. Buffalo from Montana's National Bison Range, and longhorn cattle are on display at the park. Camping fee for RVs is $9; $7 for tent sites. Non-campers pay a day-use fee of $2. ▲EXIT 121

Mile 502 (276): Snake River and exit to Paradise Valley. No services available. EXIT 125

Mile 505 (273): Exit to King Hill. Limited services. EXIT 129

Mile 510 (268): Rest area and weigh station.

Mile 514 (264): Exit to Bliss, Buhl, the Hagerman Valley and the Thousand Springs Scenic Route (U.S. Highway 30). This highway route passes by several of the fish hatcheries which have made Hagerman famous, including the Hagerman National Fish Hatchery and Research Center. Tours are available.

South of Buhl is the turnoff to **CASTLEFORD** (pop. 191), and Balanced Rock, a well-known landmark. The 40-foot-tall balloon-shaped rock is balanced on a 1-by-3-foot rock stem. In 1913, 2 Castleford residents became concerned that the tiny base could not support such a massive rock much longer, so they reinforced the base with cement. Their concern was unwarranted and the patchwork reinforcement did not strengthen the base; however, signs of the work are still visible. Visitors should be aware that Balanced Rock is 15 miles from Buhl and that the road is rough.

Castleford was named for the area where early settlers crossed Salmon Falls Creek canyon. The nearby rocks resembled castles and pioneers forded the creek at this point; hence the name Castleford.

The Hagerman Valley is the home of

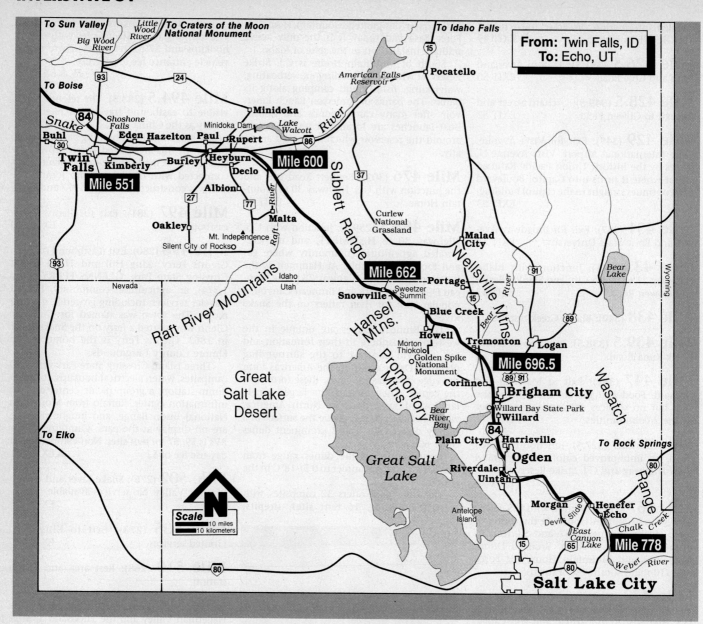

From: Twin Falls, ID
To: Echo, UT

(Map labels: To Sun Valley, Little Wood River, To Craters of the Moon National Monument, To Idaho Falls, Big Wood River, Pocatello, American Falls Reservoir, 15, To Boise, 93, 24, Snake River, Minidoka, Lake Walcott, 86, Shoshone Falls, Minidoka Dam, Eden, Hazelton, Paul, Rupert, Buhl, 30, Sublett Range, 37, Twin Falls, Kimberly, Burley, Heyburn, Declo, Mile 600, Curlew National Grassland, Albion, 27, 77, Malta, Malad City, Mile 662, Wellsville Mtns, Bear Lake, Oakley, Raft River, Mt. Independence, Silent City of Rocks, Snowville, Sweetzer Summit, Portage, 91, 93, Nevada, Idaho, Utah, Blue Creek, 15, 89, Raft River Mountains, Hansel Mtns, Howell, Tremonton, Logan, Wyoming, Morton Thiokol, Golden Spike National Monument, Mile 696.5, Promontory Mtns, Corinne, 89 91, Great Salt Lake Desert, Brigham City, Wasatch, Willard Bay State Park, Bear River Bay, Willard, 84, Great Salt Lake, Plain City, Harrisville, To Rock Springs, To Elko, Ogden, Range, Riverdale, Uintah, 80, Antelope Island, Morgan, Henefer, Echo, Devils Slide, East Canyon Lake, Chalk Creek, 65, Mile 778, 15, 80, Weber River, Salt Lake City, Scale 10 miles 10 kilometers, N)

Thousand Springs. Although not as spectacular in recent years, the springs emanating from the basalt cliffs above the Snake River offer quite a view. The water is believed to come from the Lost River in eastern Idaho. Deep-well irrigation projects have depleted the springs.

The Hagerman Valley is also famous for the archaeological finds along the Snake River. In 1928, a Hagerman rancher found and collected fossilized bones along the bluffs of the Snake River west of town. Smithsonian Institution archaeologists began excavations and discovered the remains of a horse bridging the gap between the Pliocene horse and the Equus of the Pleistocene epoch. Other discoveries included remains of a woolly mammoth, mastodon, dire wolf and several varieties of saber-toothed cats.

The Hagerman Valley also hosts the largest trout farms in the world. Both commercial and state-operated facilities line the banks of the Snake River. Inquire locally for tours. The Hagerman Wildlife Management Area also provides excellent trout fishing. ◄EXIT 137

Mile 517.5 (260.5): Exit to BLISS (pop. 208), Buhl (pop. 3,800) and Hagerman (pop. 700). All services are available in all three communities.

Mile 523.5 (254.5): Pass over Snake River and Gorge.

Mile 524 (254): Exit to TUTTLE; gas, food and groceries available, and Malad Gorge State Park. The park offers picnicking, fishing, sightseeing, photography and nature study. The gorge was named in 1824 by a troop of 37 Hudson Bay trappers led by Alexander Ross. The gorge is 2.5 miles long and 250 feet deep. The falls at Devils Washbowl is 140 feet wide and 60 feet in height.

Malad Gorge is difficult to see until you are right upon it and its obscurity made it a good hiding place for outlaws. In 1880, 3 escaped from the Boise Territorial Prison evaded law officers for a month by hiding in the gorge.

Upstream from Devils Washbowl, faint remains of the Malad Way Station can be seen. From 1869 to 1879, this way station was 1 of 19 stops along the Kelton Road, a freight wagon route from Kelton, UT, to Boise, ID. ㅠ◄EXIT 147

Mile 534 (244): Junction with Idaho 46 to WENDELL, (pop. 1,974). Gas and food available. EXIT 157

Mile 543 (235): Junction with Idaho Highway 25 to JEROME, (pop. 7,300) with all services available including 2 motels and 4 restaurants. The North Side Canal irrigation project was completed in 1909 which allowed the irrigation of thousands of acres of arid desert on the north side of the Snake River and made the settling of Jerome possible.

Mile 546 (232): Exit to Jerome. EXIT 168

Mile 549.5 (228.5): Rest area with phone for eastbound traffic only.

Mile 551 (227): Junction with U.S. Highway 93, which leads south to downtown Twin Falls and north Shoshone. For log of Highway 93, turn to **Mile 114.5** in the U.S. HIGHWAY 93 section.

TWIN FALLS (pop. 27,750) offers all traveler services, including 22 motels and numerous restaurants. It is the hub of the Magic Valley, one of the most productive agricultural areas in Idaho. Since 1905, the waters of the Snake River have been used to irrigate the arid desert of the Twin Falls area. The river is the lifeblood of the region, not only providing water for agriculture, but for fishing, boating and hunting. The Magic Valley is rich with trout lakes and is also well known for its excellent upland bird and waterfowl hunting.

One of the premier attractions of the Twin Falls area is Shoshone Falls, a 212-foot waterfall on the Snake River 5 miles east of downtown Twin Falls (follow signs along Falls Avenue). A breathtaking view of the Snake River can be seen from Perrine Memorial Bridge, site of Evil Knevel's ill-fated attempt to jump the canyon in a rocket-powered motorcyle in 1974. For additional information on the Twin Falls area, refer to **Mile 114.5** in the U.S. HIGHWAY 93 log. EXIT 173

Mile 553 (225): Rest area (westbound).

Mile 559.5 (218.5): Junction with Idaho Highway 50 north to Eden (pop. 355) and south to Kimberly (pop. 2,307). Gas and food are available in Kimberly.

East of the village of Eden, in a cave located at Wilson Butte, remains of prehistoric man were found and dated nearly 15,000 years old, which established this area as one of the earliest inhabited places in North America. EXIT 182

Mile 566 (212): Exit to HAZELTON (pop. 496) and Valley Road. Limited services in Hazelton. EXIT 188

Mile 571.5 (206.5): Exit to Ridgeway Road. EXIT 194

Mile 578.5 (199.5): Junction with Idaho Highway 25 north to Paul and Kasota Road. EXIT 201

Mile 586 (192): Junction with Idaho Highway 27 south to Burley and north to Paul. All services are available in Burley and no services are available in Paul.

BURLEY (pop. 8,761), an agricultural community, was incorporated in 1906 and is the seat of Cassia County. Burley is in the center of the Minidoka project of the U.S. Reclamation Service, containing 130,000 acres of irrigated farmland. Another 80,000 acres of privately owned land is under cultivation.

The mountain range visible to the south is the Albion Range.

Highway 27 south leads to the agricultural village of Oakley and the City of Rocks, a resting spot for immigrants on the California Trail. The "city" is a collection of rock formations covering 25 square miles and extending almost 6 miles north to south. It lies at the junction of 2 historic trails: The California Trail and the Sublett Cutoff.

Upon the eroded rock walls, cathedrals and towers is inscribed one of the largest chronicles known of transcontinental travel. The immigrants etched their names, dates and other pertinent information of their journey on the rocks as they prepared for the rest of their trip.

The City of Rocks has no tourist facilities, but does offer a look into the geology of the area and an interesting glance at the history of the westward movement. EXIT 208

Mile 589 (189): Junction with U.S. Highway 30 and Idaho Highway 24 north to RUPERT (pop. 5,476) and south to HEYBURN (pop. 2, 889). All services are available in Rupert. Limited serves in Heyburn. EXIT 211

Mile 594.5 (183.5): Crossing the Snake River.

Mile 595 (183): Junction with Idaho

Snake River waters irrigate desert land near Twin Falls. (© Ray T. Weisgerber)

Highway 25 and 77 south to Declo (pop. 276), Albion (pop. 286) and Pomerelle Ski Area. Pomerelle Ski Area is located on 9,200-foot Mount Harrison, 28 miles off Interstate 84. Skiing is generally open from late November to April. EXIT 216

Mile 600 (178): Junction with Interstate 86 and U.S. Highway 30 east to Pocatello. Travelers headed to Pocatello turn to INTERSTATE 84 section for that log.

Mile 606.5 (171.5): Junction with Idaho Highway 81 to Malta and Yale Road. EXIT 228

Mile 607.5 (170.5): Weigh station and rest area.

Mile 609.5 (168.5): Possible high winds and dust storms for the next 19 miles. Drive with caution.

Mile 613.5 (164.5): Raft River.

Mile 615.5 (162.5): Exit to Idahome Road. No services available. EXIT 237

Mile 623.5 (154.5): Exit to Sublett Road and Malta. Gas, food and camping available. ▲ EXIT 245

Mile 632.5 (145.5): Exit to Sweetzer Road. This is a winter and spring mule deer migration area. Be alert for deer crossing the highway. EXIT 254

Mile 637 (141): Sweetzer Summit (elev. 5,530 feet).

Mile 641.5 (136.5): Exit to Juniper Road. The mountains to the north are the Sublett Mountains. EXIT 263

Mile 648.5 (129.5): Rest area and Lake Bonneville Historical Site. This area was under water nearly 20,000 years ago and to the north you can see the old shore of Lake Bonneville. This was the largest lake in North America at that time with no river outlet. The water level eventually rose enough to drain into the Snake River and a climatic change caused the lake waters to recede. The Great Salt Lake and 2 other remnants are all that are left of this 20,000-square-mile lake.

Ferruginous hawks, the largest of North American hawks, are often found in this area and a sign at the rest stop explains their habits and habitat. The low, scrubby-looking trees are junipers which are found on the high desert throughout the Great Basin area.

Mile 655.5 (122.5): Utah-Idaho state border.

Mile 659.5 (118.5): Junction with U.S. Highway 30 to Park Valley (no services available and Wells, NV. EXIT 5

Mile 662 (116): Exit to SNOWVILLE, all services available. During the winter, this stretch of highway along Sweetzer Summit often experiences heavy drifting and road conditions are often hazardous. Check with state police of the highway department for road conditions. EXIT 7

Mile 667.5 (110.5): Ranch exit. No services available. EXIT 12

Mile 671 (107): Exit to Hansel Valley, an agricultural valley. No services available. EXIT 16

Mile 672.5 (105.5): This is a ranch exit. No services available. EXIT 17

Mile 676 (102): Exit to Blue Creek. No services available. EXIT 20

Mile 680 (98): Exit to Valley, a farming and ranching area. No services available. EXIT 24

Mile 682 (96): Exit to Howell and Morton Thiokol plant. No services are available in either of these locations.

Morton Thiokol is the world's largest manufacturer of solid rocket fuel propellent. At their Wasatch Division plant here in northeastern Utah, some 400 buildings are located on 19,000 acres where solid rocket propellents for Minuteman, Peacekeeper, Trident and Poseidon missiles, and the booster rockets for the Space Shuttle are manufactured. Some 6,000 persons are employed at the Wasatch Division of Morton Thiokol. The Wasatch plant is surrounded by a fence and well-marked against trespassing.

Mile 688 (90): Ranch exit with no services available. Also junction with Utah Highway 83 which heads south from here, rejoining Interstate 84 a few miles north of Brigham City. Exit Utah Highway 83 to Golden Spike National Historic Monument near the town of Promontory. The monument commemorates the driving of the golden spike which signified the completion of the nation's first transcontinental railroad in 1869. The 1,776-mile railway was completed in just 4 years with the considerable help of Chinese laborers imported by the Central Pacific Railway. At the monument, approximately 1.7 miles of track have been relaid and there are operating steam engines on site. The visitors center offers exhibits, information services and an audio-visual program. The monument is open from 8 a.m. to 8 p.m. daily from Memorial Day through Labor Day, and from 8 a.m. until 4:30 p.m. daily for the remainder of the year. The park is closed Thanksgiving and Christmas.

There are no camping facililties in the monument. The nearest motels, restaurants and camping facilities are located in Tremonton and Brigham City. EXIT 32

Mile 695.5 (82.5): Exit to Garland and Bothwell. Hospital at this exit. EXIT 39

Mile 696.5 (81.5): Exit to Tremonton; all services available. Also exit to Utah Highway 30 to Logan and Highway 102. Junction with Interstate 15 south. Interstate 15 and Interstate 84 share a common alignment from this point south to Ogden.

TREMONTON (pop. 3,350) has all traveler services. The area is a major recreation area for the Salt Lake-Ogden metropolitan area with excellent deer hunting and trout fishing. Indian caves are found in the mountains near town. Tremonton is also the home of the Box Elder County Fairgrounds. EXIT 40

Mile 701 (77): Junction with Utah Highway 13 to Bear River and access to Interstate 15 north to Pocatello, ID. Turn to the INTERSTATE 15 section for log of that route. EXIT 379

Mile 704.5 (73.5): Junction of Utah Highways 240 and 13 to Honeyville and Bear River. No services available. The Wellsville Mountains, a branch of the Wasatch Mountains, are visible to the east. EXIT 375

Mile 710.5 (67.5): Rest area with visitors center.

Mile 712 (66): Exit to Brigham City, Corinne and the Golden Spike National Historic Monument on Utah Highway 13 (see **Mile 688**). CORINNE (pop. 525) was a historic railroad community founded in 1869. Food and gas are available. EXIT 368

Mile 712.5 (65.5): Rest area.

Mile 715 (63): Exit to Perry (pop. 1,080) and Brigham City (pop. 17,525). This is also the junction of U.S. Highways 89 and 91 to Logan and Bear Lake on the Utah-Idaho border.

PERRY is located immediately south of Brigham City in the fruit-growing zone, which is famous for peaches, cherries and other fruit. Gas and food are available.

BRIGHAM CITY is the seat of Box Elder County and is the winner of several national awards for beautification efforts. Lorenzo Snow, fifth president of the LDS Church (Mormon) is buried here along with 8 of his wives.

The Golden Spike Exhibit and Pioneer Museum are located on 3rd W. and Forest Street in Brigham City and are well worth the visit. All services are available. EXIT 364

Mile 718.5 (59.5): Port of entry. The body of water to the west is Willard Bay. The mountain range to the west is the Promontory Mountains, separating Bear River Bay from the Great Salt Lake.

Mile 720 (58): Exit to WILLARD, Willard Bay State Park and the Bear River Migratory Bird Refuge (closed to the public). The refuge was established by Congress in 1928 to protect the waterfowl of the Bear River delta. Each year from 1877 to the early 1900s, some 200,000 ducks were killed by professional market hunters and sold for a few cents to elegant Eastern hotels and restaurants. Habitat was being destroyed by upstream settlements and farms, and in the early 1900s, the duck population contracted botulism which killed 50 to 70 percent of the birds who stopped to rest and feed there.

The refuge today comprises 65,000 acres of marsh, open water and mudflat, managed for migratory birds.

A Uinta ground squirrel photographed along the Snake River. (© John Barger)

In 1985, the bird refuge was subjected to flooding by the Bear River and much of the nesting habitat was destroyed. Because of the flood damage, the refuge was closed to the public. EXIT 360

Mile 725.5 (52.5): Junction with Utah Highway 126 to Pleasant View and the junction with U.S Highway 89 to Willard Bay, a man-made body of fresh water reclaimed from the salt marshes of the Great Salt Lake.

Willard Bay State Park offers a 52-unit campground, restrooms, showers, a dump station, 2 boat launches and marinas. Small-boat rentals, food, camping and boating supplies are available.

The principal activities at Willard Bay include camping, boating, waterskiing and year-round fishing. It is the home of great blue herons, sparrow hawks, red-winged blackbirds, snowy egrets, grebes, white pelicans and many other species of birds. ➛▲EXIT 354

Mile 728.5 (49.5): Exit (eastbound only) to Plain City, North Ogden and Pleasant View and the junction with Utah Highway 134. Private farmlands in this area host good numbers of wild pheasants. EXIT 352

Mile 731 (47): Exit to the Defense Depot, Slaterville and **HARRISVILLE** (pop. 4,290). Harrisville was settled in 1850 and is named in honor of Martin Harris, witness to the Book of Mormon and uncle of one of the town's first settlers. Food and gas are available. EXIT 349

Mile 733 (45): Exit to Utah 39, 12th Street and Ogden Valley Recreation Area. EXIT 347

Mile 734.5 (43.5): Exit to 21st Street, Wilson Lane and Ogden city center. This is also the junction with Utah Highway 104. The minimum speed limit in this busy section of interstate is 45 mph.

OGDEN (pop. 64,444) is the seat of Weber County and was named after Peter Skene Ogden, a trapper and explorer for the Hudson's Bay Co.

In 1841 the Mexican government assigned "all the land between the mountains and the lake" to trapper and trader Miles Goodyear. His cabin, the first permanent house built in Utah, still stands in Ogden's Temple Square. Brigham Young founded the town in 1850.

When the transcontinental railroad was completed at Promontory Summit in 1869, Ogden became the largest rail center between Omaha, NE, and the West Coast. The old train station has been converted into a museum and civic center.

Also in Ogden is Fort Buenaventura, a reconstruction of a fort established by Miles Goodyear which recalls the life and times of mountain men. EXIT 346

Mile 736.5 (36.5): Exit 344A to Ogden, 31st Street and the Ogden airport. Exit 344B heads west on 31st Street. EXIT 344

Mile 738 (40): Junction with Interstate 15 north to Brigham City and Pocatello. Inter-

Vertical cracks of sedimentary rock form Devil's Slide. (Tom Barr)

state 15 and Interstate 84 share a common alignment from this point north to Tremonton, UT. The highway crosses through the Bear River valley, a muddy flatland through which the meandering Bear River flows. The mountains to the east are the Wasatch Mountains.

Mile 739 (39): Exit to **RIVERDALE** (pop. 4,310). This is also the junction of Utah Highway 26 and Interstate 15 south to Salt Lake City. EXIT 81

Mile 742 (36): Exit to Uintah and South Weber. **UINTAH** (pop. 760) is located at the mouth of the Weber Canyon and was once the main railroad center of Utah; larger than both Ogden and Salt Lake City. The Ute Indian tribe used to summer in this area. No services available. EXIT 85

Mile 745 (33): Exit 87 (eastbound) is the junction with U.S. Highway 89 to South Ogden and Salt Lake City. Exit 87A to Hill Air Force Base and Salt Lake City on U.S. Highway 89 south. Exit 87B is the junction with U.S. Highway 89 north to Ogden. Exits 87A and 87B are for westbound traffic only. This is rather a confusing interchange, so watch the road signs carefully. EXIT 87

Mile 749 (29): Rest area (eastbound).

Mile 750 (28): Exit to Mountain Green. EXIT 92

Mile 751.5 (26.5): Rest area (westbound).

Mile 754 (24): Exit to Peterson, Stoddard and Mount Green. All are unincorporated villages. Gas and phone available. EXIT 96

Mile 761 (17): Exit to **MORGAN** (pop. 1,800) and East Canyon Recreation Area and the junction with Utah Highway 66 to Porterville. Gas, phone and food are available. Morgan is the seat of Morgan County. The mountains surrounding the city are covered with pines and quaking aspen. The city lies at the eastern edge of the Morgan Valley along the Weber River. EXIT 103

Mile 764 (14): This exit is a ranch exit. No services available. There are several ranch exits along this section of Interstate 84 which are access routes to specific ranches. In each case, no commercial services are available. EXIT 106

Mile 766 (12): Exit to **TAGGERT**. Gas and phone available. EXIT 108

Mile 769 (9): Devils Slide viewing area; narrow turnouts. The strange-looking geological formation on the south side of the interstate is Devils Slide. A disruption in the earth's crust cracked 2 sedimentary layers and turned them 90 degrees vertically. Wind and water erosion washed out the softer layer between the 2 hardpan layers, creating a curious natural sculpture.

Mile 769.5 (8.5): Exit to Croydon and Devils Slide. No services available. EXIT 111

Mile 770 (8): Thousand Mile Tree marks 1,000 miles from the start of the first transcontinental railroad in Omaha, NB.

Mile 771 (7): Exit to **HENEFER** (pop. 547), originally a settlement made by the Mormon pioneers as a supply camp where the immigrants could repair their wagons and rest before making the difficult journey over Big Mountain into the Salt Lake Valley. This is the only incorporated community in Utah along the original Mormon Trail. Gas, food, phone and lodging are available.

At Henefer, Utah Highway 65 heads south to East Canyon Reservoir and Salt Lake City. This is the route of the Donner-Reed party, led by George Donner and James Reed. Reed was banished from the group and the Donner Party eventually met with disaster in the Sierra Nevada Mountains in October 1846 in an area that is now called Donner Pass.

East Canyon Lake Recreation Area (elev. 5,700 feet) offers camping, restrooms, drinking water, boat launch for fishing and designated areas for off-road vehicles and snowmobiling. ➛▲EXIT 112

Mile 774 (4): Exit to **ECHO** (pop. 160), the vestige of the historic railroad community of Echo City. The town was settled in 1854 as a trading post along the Mormon and California trails. Gas and food available.

South of Echo on Interstate 80 is Echo Reservoir which offers good trout fishing, waterskiing and boating. Boat ramps and food services are available. There is a resort with camping. ➛▲EXIT 115

Mile 778 (0): Junction of Interstate 84 and Interstate 80.

Interstate 86

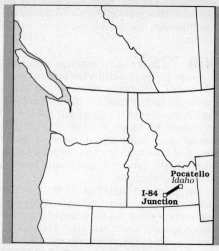

See map opposite page

Interstate 86 in southeastern Idaho connects Interstate 84 east of Burley with Interstate 15 at Pocatello. The 65-mile highway section passes through Massacre Rocks State Park and Fort Hall Indian Reservation and runs south of American Falls Reservoir, paralleling one of the most scenic portions of the Snake River.

This interstate highway is a major route for through traffic in southern Idaho connecting the capital city of Boise with Pocatello and Idaho Falls.

The terrain is primarily sagebrush-covered desert except in the Massacre Rocks area, where juniper trees dominate. Many of the farms in this area produce the world-famous Idaho potatoes. Good fishing can be enjoyed in the rivers and reservoirs along this short stretch of highway.

Interstate 86 Log

Distance from Interstate 84 junction is followed by distance from Pocatello.

Mile 0 (63): Junction of Interstate 86 and Interstate 84. Travelers headed west on Interstate 84 turn to **Mile 600** in the INTERSTATE 84 section for log.

Mile 4 (59): Rest area. Leaving the Oregon Trail at Raft River, 11 miles to the east, the California Trail headed southwest. Immigrant wagons had come nearly 1,400 miles to get here. Ahead lay the fantastic formations of the City of Rocks, the desolate wastes of Humboldt, and finally the mountain passes of the high Sierra. Forty-niners, in their rush to the California goldfields, found a more direct route south of here, but Oregon-bound travelers continued to pass this

The Snake River winds past Massacre Rocks State Park at Mile 28.5.

(L. Linkhart)

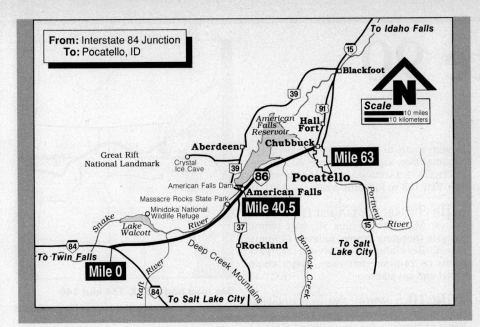

From: Interstate 84 Junction
To: Pocatello, ID

one of the best fishing lakes in the region.
EXIT 44

Mile 47 (16): Boundary of Fort Hall Indian Reservation.

Mile 49.5 (13.5): Exit to Rainbow Road.
EXIT 49

Mile 52.5 (10.5): Bannock Creek.

Mile 53 (10): Exit to the Arbon Valley, an agricultural area. EXIT 52

Mile 56 (7): Exit to the Pocatello Air Terminal. EXIT 56

Mile 58 (5): Boundary of Fort Hall Indian Reservation, home of the Shoshone-Bannock tribes. The 4-day Shoshone-Bannock Indian Festival at Fort Hall is held in mid-August and features a colorful war dance competition, Indian games, a rodeo and an art exhibit.

Mile 58.5 (4.5): Exit to West Pocatello, Food Machinery Corp. (FMC) and Simplot phosphate fertilizer plants. Both companies are major employers for the Pocatello area. The FMC plant is the largest elemental-phosphorous plant in the world. Both factories are supplied by the Gay Mine of the Fort Hall Indian Reservation. EXIT 58

Mile 59 (4): Portneuf River, a major irrigation source for southeastern Idaho farmers and an excellent trout fishing river.

Mile 61 (2): Low visibility area. Under certain cold weather conditions, the heat and humidity generated by the 2 nearby factories can produce very dense fog conditions. Driving can be hazardous.

Mile 61.5 (1.5): Exit to CHUBBUCK (pop. 7,052) and junction of U.S. Highway 91 to Blackfoot (pop. 8,000). Chubbuck, with its new shopping mall, is a rapidly growing suburb of Pocatello. Blackfoot is 25 miles north of Chubbuck. EXIT 61

Mile 63 (0): Junction with Interstate 15 in POCATELLO (pop. 46,340), the largest city in southeastern Idaho. Pocatello is the home of Idaho State University and the huge Quonset-style Mini Dome. It is the seat of Bannock County, and it produces chemicals, flour, cement, fertilizer and dairy products. Pocatello was named by the builders of the Union Pacific Railroad for a friendly Indian chief who helped secure tribal consent for the transfer of land, right-of-way and building sites to the railroad. Union Pacific is still an important employer in Pocatello. One of Pocatello's premier attractions is the replica of Old Fort Hall, a realistic reproduction of the original trading post established in 1834. The fort is open Tuesday through Saturday, 11 a.m. to 3 p.m., April 1 to May 31. It is open daily 9 a.m. to 8 p.m. from June 1 to Sept. 15. There is a small admission charge. Fort Hall replica is more easily accessible from Exit 67 on Interstate 15; turn to **Mile 168** in the INTERSTATE 15 section. EXIT 72

point forging west through the Snake River valley.

Mile 15 (48): Exit to the Raft River area. The U.S. Geological Survey has designated 30,219 acres along the Raft River as a Known Geothermal Resource Area (KGRA). The mountain range visible to the south is the Sublett Range. EXIT 15

Mile 17.5 (45.5): Boundary of Power and Cassia counties. Divided highway ends and 2-way traffic begins eastbound.

Mile 20.5 (42.5): Exit to Coldwater area. EXIT 21

Mile 28 (35): The Snake River parallels the highway on the north and there is a turnoff to a state boat ramp.

Mile 28.5 (34.5): Exit to Massacre Rock and rest area. Massacre Rocks State Park offers 52 campsites (nominal fee charged), restrooms with showers, a visitor center, guided and self-guided hiking trails, campfire programs, picnic area, horseshoe pits, fishing access, boat launch and ski docks. This park is located just upstream of Lake Wolcott Reservoir, formed by Minidoka Dam on the Snake, and is the site of the annual Mountain Man Rendezvous. "Gates of Death" and "Devil's Gate" were names given to this area during the Oregon Trail period, referring to a narrow pass through which the trail traveled. On Aug. 9 and 10, 1862, 10 immigrants died in Indian attacks on 5 separate wagon trains east of the present location of the park.

Goat Island and Beaver Island in the middle of the Snake River are visible. Pioneers on the Oregon Trail used Register Rock as a rest stop and many of the immigrants inscribed their names on the rock. The rock is now protected by a weather shelter and a picnic area surrounds it. EXIT 28

Mile 33 (30): Exit to Neeley area, an agricultural valley. EXIT 33

Mile 36.5 (26.5): Exit to Rockland and junction with Idaho Highway 37. Highway 37 runs through the Curlew National Grassland, a 150,000-acre range rehabilitation project. EXIT 36

Mile 40.5 (22.5): Exit to the city of American Falls, Aberdeen, Great Rift National Landmark, Crystal Ice Cave and the junction with Idaho Highway 39 to Aberdeen. **AMERICAN FALLS** (pop. 3,626) is the seat of Power County and a shipping point for potatoes and wheat. All services are available including 3 motels and 13 restaurants. Aberdeen, on the west side of the reservoir, is named after Aberdeen, Scotland.

Great Rift National Landmark, 46 miles long, stretches from the Craters of the Moon to 10 miles south of Crystal Ice Cave. It is a series of geological faults, through which rose much of the basalt lava of the Snake River plain some 2,100 years ago. The cracks have been explored to a depth of 800 feet, making it the longest and deepest open volcanic rift on the North American continent. Crystal Ice Cave (a private exhibit), open from May 1 to Oct. 1, is 160 feet deep and is part of the Great Rift. A gently graded, 1,200-foot tunnel leads to an ice floor where nature has sculpted ice formations through the constant seepage of water. Guided tours of the developed cave are available. The trails are wide and there are no steps. Visitors should be aware that the temperature inside the cave is 32°F and that sweaters are advised even during the summer. There is a free overnight trailer park (no hookups).

The mountains visible to the south are the Deep Creek Mountains. EXIT 40

Mile 45 (18): Exit to Seagull Bay on American Falls Reservoir. The largest reservoir on the Snake River system in Idaho, American Falls Reservoir is a popular recreational facility as well as a major irrigation and hydro-electric project. American Falls Reservoir is

Interstate 90

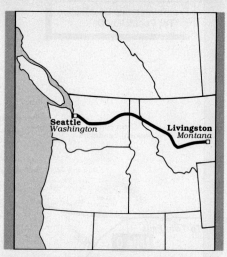

See map pages 133, 136 and 140

Interstate 90, the northernmost western arterial in the federal interstate highway system, is also a major east-west route within the Northwest. Except for a few short stretches of 2-lane road, Interstate 90 rolls across the west as a multiple-lane freeway linking nearly all of the major cities in the northern tier states.

NORTHWEST MILEPOSTS® logs the highway from Seattle, WA, east to Livingston, MT. Physical mileposts along the interstate (and corresponding exit numbers) reflect distances from the Interstate 5 junction (Milepost 0) within Washington; the Washington-Idaho border at the Spokane River, within Idaho; and the Idaho-Montana state line at Lookout Pass, within Montana.

Interstate 90 Log

Distance in miles from Seattle, WA, is followed by distance in miles from Livingston, MT.

Mile 0 (709): Junction with Interstate 5. Exit 2B to Dearborn Street. Turn to **Mile 592** in the INTERSTATE 5 section for log of that route.   EXIT 2

Mile 0.5 (708.5): Exit 3A to Rainier Avenue S. (Washington Highway 900) and Exit 3B to Rainier Avenue N.   EXIT 3

Mile 1.5 (707.5): Entering Interstate 90 tunnel eastbound. "Portal to the Pacific" is carved above the tunnel's east entrance.

Mile 2 (707): Crossing Interstate 90 floating bridge, which was built alongside the 1940 Lacey B. Murrow floating bridge. Referred to as the Mercer Island bridge in traffic reports. Twenty-mile-long Lake Washington is the largest lake in western Washington.

Mile 3.5 (705.5): Exit to W. Mercer Way.   EXIT 6

Mile 4 (705): Exit to 76th Avenue E.   EXIT 7

Mile 5.5 (703.5): Exit to E. Mercer Way.   EXIT 8

Mile 6 (703): Crossing Lake Washington via the East Channel bridge.

Mile 6.5 (702.5): Exit to Lake Washington Boulevard, Bellevue Way.   EXIT 9

Mile 7 (702): Junction with Interstate 405 north to Bellevue, Kirkland, Bothell and Everett; south to Renton, Kent, Tukwila and Tacoma. (See log of Interstate 405 in the INTERSTATE 5 section.) Exit 10A to Interstate 405, Exit 10B to Richards Road.   EXIT 10

Mile 9 (700): Exit 11A and 11B to 148th Avenue SE, 150th Avenue SE, state patrol, Eastgate shopping center, Bellevue Community College and 161st Avenue SE. Easy access to 24-hour restaurant, major chain motel and gas stations.   EXIT 11

Mile 10.5 (698.5): Exit to Washington Highway 901 north to Redmond and south to Newport Way.   EXIT 13

Mile 13 (696): Exit to Washington Highway 900 to Renton and eastbound access to Lake Sammamish State Park. Easy access to major-chain motel, fast-food oulets, 24-hour restaurant, gas station and supermarket south off exit.

Turn north at exit for Lake Sammamish State Park. After crossing interstate to stop sign by soccer fields, turn west on Lake Sammamish Parkway and drive 0.4 mile to park entrance. This popular day-use area on Lake Sammamish has a boat launch, water-skiing, swimming, picnicking, dump station and dock.   ⚠MP 13 EXIT 15

Mile 14 (695): Exit to Front Street, East Sammamish Road and Issaquah. Westbound access to Lake Sammamish State Park: Follow East Sammamish Road north 0.8 mile to second stoplight; turn west on Lake Sammamish Parkway and drive 1.1 mile to state park entrance. Gas and deli on East Sammamish Road; junction with Issaquah-Fall City Road.

Front Street leads south to **ISSAQUAH** city center (pop. 5,536). This is the home of the Edelweiss Chalet (visible from Interstate 90), makers of Boehms chocolates. The Gilman Village in Issaquah is a collection of renovated houses and buildings from the town's early days, converted into a quaint shopping center with about 40 specialty shops.   MP 17 EXIT 17

Mile 15 (694): Westbound only exit to Issaquah, E. Sunset Way.   EXIT 18

Mile 17 (692): Exit to High Point Way, access to Tiger Mountain State Forest.   EXIT 20

Mile 19 (690): Exit to Preston and Fall City on the Snoqualmie River; access to Washington Highways 202 and 203. An attraction at this exit is The Herbfarm, a nursery dedicated to herbs. The Herbfarm also offers classes, a country store, tours and special luncheons and dinners. From the exit follow Preston-Fall City Road north approximately 3 miles; turn west across the green bridge over the Raging River (SE 238th); and follow signs 0.5 mile to the Herbfarm. It is open daily in summer.

There is a gas station at Preston. Groceries and gas available in Fall City. This exit provides access to Washington Highway 203, which connects Fall City with Monroe on U.S. Highway 2 (25 miles north), and Washington Highway 202 (Redmond-Fall City Road) which connects Fall City with North Bend (9 miles) and Redmond (15 miles). These backcountry roads are scenic routes through the Snoqualmie River valley.   EXIT 22

Mile 22 (687): Junction with Washington Highway 18 west to Auburn and Tacoma. Access to Echo Glen. Highway 18 merges with Interstate 5 at Federal Way.   EXIT 25

Mile 23.5 (685.5): Short stretch of highway with 4 lanes, wide shoulders and lightposts.   MP 26

Mile 24.5 (684.5): Eastbound exit only to Snoqualmie and North Bend; access to Snoqualmie Winery and Snoqualmie.

From exit follow signs 0.5 mile uphill to Snoqualmie Winery. The winery has a tasting room open daily 10 a.m. to 4:30 p.m. Beautiful view!

To reach Snoqualmie Falls from exit, follow 4-lane paved road (SE North Bend Way) north 1 mile and turn at sign for falls; follow winding road (Washington Highway 202) approximately 2 miles to stop sign and turn west; continue about another 2 miles through the town of Snoqualmie to public parking area for Snoqualmie Falls Park. There are an overlook and gift shop at the park; food and lodging available at Salish Lodge adjacent. This magnificent waterfall is a not-to-be-missed attraction.

The community of **SNOQUALMIE** (pop. 1,400) has most visitor services. The Puget Sound and Snoqualmie Valley Railroad

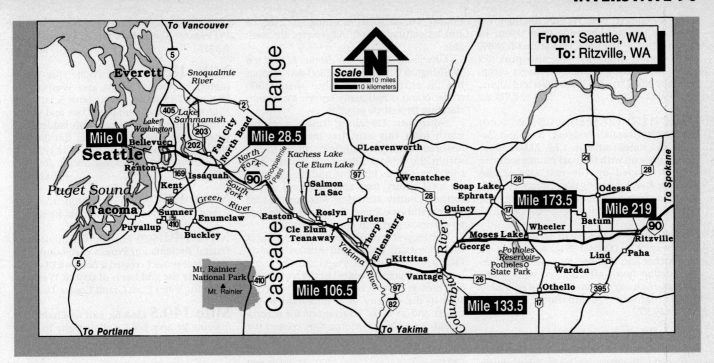

From: Seattle, WA
To: Ritzville, WA

operates from a depot on Washington Highway 202 in town. The antique train offers a 7-mile round-trip between Snoqualmie and North Bend; phone (206) 746-4025 for schedule and more information. ★EXIT 27

Mile 28.5 (680.5): Westbound exit to Snoqualmie and Snoqualmie Falls (see description at **Mile 24.5**) via Washington Highway 202 and North Bend. Major chain fast-food outlets and gas station at exit. Visitor information booth located about 0.5 mile north of interstate exit. **NORTH BEND** (pop. 1,701) has all services. The dominating monolith north of the highway is Mount Si (elev. 4,167 feet). An improved hiking trail leads up the timbered southeast side to the top. This is a popular hiking trail for Puget Sound residents. ★EXIT 31

Mile 29.5 (679.5): Exit to 436th Avenue SE, North Bend. EXIT 32

Mile 31 (678): Exit to Edgewick Road; food and gas. EXIT 34

Mile 31.5 (677.5): Distance marker shows Snoqualmie Pass 19 miles, Ellensburg 76 miles, Spokane 244 miles. MP 34

Mile 34 (675): Crossing the South Fork Snoqualmie River.

Mile 36 (673): Exit to fire training center. EXIT 38

Mile 39 (670): Exit to Tinkham Road, McClellan Butte trail. Tinkham Road leads to Tinkham Campground; 45 sites, water, camping fee. ▲EXIT 42

Mile 43 (666): Bandera airfield, Lookout Point Road, Talapus Point Trail. EXIT 45

Mile 45 (664): Denny Creek, Asahel Curtis,

Tinkham Road, chain removal area. Denny Creek campground has 32 campsites, picnic area and water. Asahel Curtis day-use area has 26 picnic sites and water. ⛺▲EXIT 47

Mile 49.5 (659.5): Exit to Alpental Road, west summit Snoqualmie Pass recreation area. EXIT 52

Mile 50 (659): Snoqualmie Pass Summit (elev. 3,022 feet). This is the lowest highway pass across Washington's Cascade Range.

Mile 50.5 (658.5): Exit to Snoqualmie Pass recreation area. Three major alpine ski resorts operate here: Alpental, Snoqualmie and Pac-West. Food, gas and phone available. Entering Kittitas County eastbound. ⛷EXIT 53

Mile 51 (658): Exit to Hyak, Rocky Run and Pacific West ski areas. Hyak is located at the east end of the Milwaukee Railroad tunnel. The 2-mile-long tunnel was built in 1914-15. ⛷EXIT 54

Mile 53 (656): West end of Keechelus Lake.

Mile 53.5 (655.5): Lighted chain-up areas both sides of highway. MP 56

Mile 55 (654): Good view across Keechelus Lake of snowsheds protecting railroad line.

Mile 58 (651): East end of Keechelus Lake and Keechelus Dam, which regulates the flow of the Yakima River. Keehcelus Lake is severely drawn down during summer for irrigation of the Kittitas and Yakima valleys.

Mile 58.5 (650.5): Snow-Park parking on north side of highway.

Mile 60 (649): Exit to Stampede Pass, Lake

Kachess and Snow-Park parking. Stampede Pass was discovered in 1881 by Virgil C. Bogue while surveying a route for the Northern Pacific Railroad across the Cascade Range. Scenic Lake Kachess, a few miles north of the interchange via a paved road, has USFS campgrounds, picnic area, swimming beaches and 2 boat ramps. Filled to capacity on summer weekends. ⛺▲EXIT 62

Mile 61 (648): Exit to Cabin Creek Road. Snow-Park parking. MP 64 EXIT 63

Mile 65.5 (643.5): Leaving Wenatchee National Forest eastbound.

Mile 67.5 (641.5): Exit to Easton, Sparks Road, Lake Easton State Park, Snow-Park parking. Food and gas available. Lake Easton has 145 campsites, hookups, dump station, picnic tables, stoves, showers, boat launch and fishing for planted rainbow; snowmobiling and cross-country skiing in winter. ⛺▲MP 70 EXIT 70

Mile 68 (641): Crossing the Yakima River.

Mile 68.5 (640.5): Exit to **EASTON**; food and gas. Access to Iron Horse State Park, John Wayne Trail. EXIT 71

Mile 71 (638): Exit to West Nelson Siding Road. EXIT 74

Mile 75 (634): Exit to East Nelson Siding Road. EXIT 78

Mile 77 (632): Weigh station (closed). Paved turnout with pay phone.

Mile 77.5 (631.5): Exit to Roslyn, Salmon la Sac and Ronald via Washington Highway 903. **ROSLYN** (pop. 900) dates back to the 1886 and has many interesting historic buildings. This Western mining town is home of the oldest operating tavern in Washington — The Brick, established in 1889. Washington Highway 903 also provides access to Wenatchee National Forest campgrounds along the Cle Elum River and Alpine Lakes Wilderness.   MP 80 EXIT 80

Mile 81.5 (627.5): Exit to Cle Elum, South Cle Elum. Hospital. Lodging, food and 24-hour gas station at exit. **CLE ELUM** (pop. 1,773) grew up with the coal mining industry that developed on the east side of the Cascade Range. Logging is a primary industry today; a chipping plant is located nearby. All services available.   EXIT 84

Mile 82.5 (626.5): Exit to Washington Highway 970 (Sunset Highway) east to Wenatchee and Highway 903 west to Roslyn. Gas station north off exit. Access to Washington Highway 10 and Teanaway Valley Road. Highway 970 junctions with U.S. Highway 97.   EXIT 85

Mile 86.5 (622.5): Indian John Hill rest areas both sides of interstate. These are large rest areas with restrooms, picnic tables, dump station and good views of the Cascade mountains on a clear day.   ㅠ MP 89

Mile 87 (622): Summit of Indian John Hill (elev. 2,141 feet).

Mile 90 (619): Summit of Elk Heights (elev. 2,359 feet).

Mile 90.5 (618.5): Exit to Elk Heights Road and Taneum Creek; no services.
                    EXIT 93

Mile 98.5 (610.5): Exit to Thorp Highway. Diesel gas south off exit. Thorp was named for Milford A. Thorp, an early settler here.   EXIT 101

Mile 100 (609): Crossing the Yakima River. The highway parallels the upper Yakima River west to Keechelus Lake, the source of the river in the Cascade Range. The Yakima River is possibly the best trout river in Washington. Best fishing in fall from inflatables or drift boats. Bait is prohibited in the Ellensburg area and upstream almost to Cle Elum.   ⮜

Mile 103.5 (605.5): Junction with U.S. Highway 97 North, exit to Ellensburg via Interstate 90 Business Loop. Motel, restaurant, gas station and fast-food outlet north off exit. This 4-mile business loop leads through west Ellensburg to town center. (Travelers heading north on U.S. Highway 97 turn to **Mile 472** in the U.S. HIGHWAY 97 section for log.)   EXIT 106

Mile 106.5 (602.5): Exit to Canyon Road, Ellensburg. Easy access to major chain motels, fast-food outlets and gas stations north off exit. Canyon Road leads south to Washington Highway 821.
ELLENSBURG (pop. 11,752) is the hub of the Kittitas Valley and the seat of Kittitas

County, a major food processing, stock raising and agricultural region. All services available.

Ellensburg is also the home of Central Washington University. The 350-acre campus has an enrollment of more than 6,000 students and is nationally known for its outstanding basketball program.

Downtown Ellensburg (easily accessible north from this exit) has many fine old restored Victorian buildings, most found within the 5-block Ellensburg Historic District. Unusual architecture and memorabilia on local history may also be found at the Kittitas County Historical Museum, E. 3rd Avenue and Pine Street. The museum also has an extensive gem and mineral collection.

The biggest annual event in Ellensburg is the Ellensburg Rodeo and Kittitas County Fair, held every Labor Day weekend. The rodeo is one of the premier rodeos in the Northwest, and each year attracts many of the top cowboys in the country. It is important to get tickets and to make reservations for accommodations early. For information, contact the Ellensburg Rodeo ticket office, P.O. Box 777, Ellensburg, WA 98926, or phone (509) 925-5381.   EXIT 109

Mile 108.5 (600.5): Junction with U.S. Highway 97 South and Interstate 82. Travelers headed south on U.S. Highway 97 turn to **Mile 466** in the U.S. HIGHWAY 97 section for log.   EXIT 110

Mile 112.5 (596.5): Exit to Kittitas; gas station with diesel fuel north off exit. Access to Olmstead Place State Park Heritage Site, where visitors may see a log cabin, farm buildings and equipment from the original homestead established in 1875. **KITTITAS** (pop. 935) is an agricultural community.
NOTE: Next exit eastbound is 21 miles.
                    EXIT 115

Mile 123.5 (585.5): Ryegrass rest area with picnic tables and restrooms at Rye Grass Summit (elev. 2,535 feet). Eastbound, the highway descends "Vantage Hill" the next 10 miles to the Columbia River.   ㅠ MP 126

Mile 133.5 (575.5): Exit to Vantage, Huntzinger Road. **VANTAGE** (pop. about 130) was one of many towns along the Columbia River that had to be moved to higher ground when the dams were built. Campground, motel and gas station.

Follow Huntzinger Road south about 3 miles for Wanapum State Park; 50 campsites, hookups, swimming, picnicking, fishing and boat launch.

One mile north of this exit is Ginkgo Petrified Forest State Park, which includes several thousand acres of fossilized trees. There are interpretive trails, a museum (open Wednesday through Sunday in summer), picnic area and boat launch.

Westbound travelers begin 10-mile ascent of the "Vantage Hill." Next exit westbound is 21 miles.   🚣 ㅠ ⮜▲ EXIT 136

Mile 134.5 (574.5): Bridge across the Columbia River. Interstate 90 crosses Wana-

pum Lake, which is in the impound area of Wanapum Dam. *CAUTION:* Strong cross winds.   MP 137

Mile 135 (574): Junction with Washington Highway 26 east and Washington Highway 243 south. Drive south 5 miles on Highway 243 for Wanapum Dam and visitor center. Self-guiding tours of fish ladders and powerhouse. The visitor center has displays and diagrams on local history. The center is open from April to October. Picnic area and restrooms.   ㅠ EXIT 137

Mile 137 (572): Eastbound access to scenic viewpoint of the Columbia River.

Mile 140 (569): Entering Columbia Basin Federal Reclamation Project eastbound. This New Deal project created a network of canals to irrigate the arid lands of central Washington using water from Grand Coulee Dam.

Mile 140.5 (568.5): Exit to Champs de Brionne Winery Road. Follow signs 10 miles for the winery, which is open daily year-round.   EXIT 143

Mile 146.5 (562.5): Exit to George and junction with Washington Highway 281 north to Quincy. **GEORGE** (pop. 265) was founded in 1957 by Charles Brown, the developer who bought the townsite from the U.S. Bureau of Reclamation and became the town's first mayor. The streets are lined with cherry trees and are named after different types of cherries. The Martha Inn in George is a popular truck stop. Gas, diesel and dump station available.   EXIT 149

Mile 148.5 (560.5): Exit to Washington Highway 281 north to Quincy and Washington Highway 283 north to Ephrata. EXIT 151

Mile 151.5 (557.5): Exit to Adams Road.
                    EXIT 154

Mile 160 (549): Winchester Wasteway rest areas with restrooms, covered picnic tables and dump station, both sides of highway. Winchester Wasteway is an irrigation canal which drains Winchester Reservoir.
                    ㅠ MP 162

Mile 161.5 (547.5): Exit to Dodson Road. This is an access road to Winchester Wasteway. Private RV park.   ▲ EXIT 164

Mile 166.5 (542.5): Exit to Hiawatha Road. Columbia Potato. Potatoes are a major product of the area, with shipping, warehousing and manufacture of potato products (granulated potatoes, french fries, hashbrowns, etc.) taking place locally.   EXIT 169

Mile 171.5 (537.5): Exit to Mae Valley Road. Access north off exit to Moses Lake State Recreation Area (day-use only) with picnic tables and swimming. Gas station with diesel at exit. Private RV park to south.
                    ㅠ ▲ EXIT 174

Mile 172 (537): Westbound-only access

Historic Andrew Carnegie Library in Ritzville.　　(Tom Barr)

Mile 187 (522): Exit to Warden and Ruff Road. **EXIT 188**

Mile 189 (520): Leaving Columbia Basin Federal Reclamation Project eastbound. In summer, the break between the irrigated fields of the Columbia Basin and the area of dryland wheat farming is sharply evident. The wheat fields in the Moses Lake-Ritzville area support one of the most dense ringneck pheasant populations in the country. MP 190

Mile 191 (518): Entering Adams County eastbound, entering Grant County westbound. MP 192

Mile 193.5 (515.5): Exit to Batum and Schrag. **EXIT 196**

Mile 195.5 (513.5): Schrag Rest Area both sides of highway with restrooms, picnic area, dump station and phone. 🍴 MP 198

Mile 205 (504): Junction with Washington Highway 21 which leads 18 miles north to Odessa and south to Lind. **EXIT 206**

Mile 212.5 (496.5): Exit to Paha and Packard. No services. **EXIT 215**

Mile 218 (491): Junction with U.S. Highway 395 south to Pasco, state patrol and Ritzville. Cafe and gas station north off exit. Travelers headed south on U.S. Highway 395 turn to **Mile 532.5** the U.S. HIGHWAY 395 section for log. Interstate 90 and U.S. Highway 395 share a common alignment east to Spokane from here. **EXIT 220**

Mile 219 (490): Exit to Ritzville and Washington Highway 261 south to Washtucna. Easy access to major-chain motel and gas station north off exit.

RITZVILLE (pop. 1,800) has all services. Ritzville is the county seat of Adams County, which ranks number one in wheat acreage in production among Washington counties. Cattle is also a major industry here. The town was named after Philip Ritz, who homesteaded here in 1878. It was predominantly cattle country until the 1890s, when local farmers realized the area's wheat farming potential.

Ritzville has several historic buildings on the National Register of Historic Places, including the Andrew Carnegie Library, the Nelson H. Green House and the Dr. Frank R. Burroughs Home. **EXIT 221**

Mile 224 (485): Exit to Coker Road (Ritzville truck access route). **EXIT 226**

Mile 229 (480): Exit to Tokio weigh station to north. Gas station with restaurant, phone and convenience store south off exit. **EXIT 231**

Mile 239.5 (469.5): Entering Lincoln County eastbound, Adams County westbound.

Mile 242 (467): Sprague Lake rest area both sides of highway with restrooms, picnic tables and dump station. 🍴 MP 242

---

to Mae Valley Road and Moses Lake state recreation area. **EXIT 175**

Mile 173.5 (535.5): Exit to **MOSES LAKE** (pop. 10,629); all services available. Major chain motels at exit. Moses Lake is the largest city in central Washington, the commercial hub of the Columbia Basin and the center of Big Bend country (so-called for its location on a bend in the Columbia River).

Travelers on Interstate 90 may be surprised to see a 747 jumbo jet with the Japan Air Lines (JAL) insignia on the tail move across the sky above Moses Lake. Moses Lake is the site of a Japan Air Lines training center, located at Grant County airport (at Exit 179), one of the largest civilian airports west of the Mississippi. The Boeing Co. also uses the airport to flight-test new planes.

The city of Moses Lake operates the Adam East Museum which contains a large collection of regional Indian artifacts. The collection originally belonged to local businessman Adam East, who left it to the city so that it would remain in the area.

Big Bend Community College (Exit 179) in Moses Lake is an accredited 2-year school which offers a variety of technical, vocational and adult education programs. It has an enrollment of about 1,800 students. The lake upon which the town lies is the third-largest natural body of water in the state of Washington. It has more than 120 miles of shoreline. Moses Lake is famous for producing giant white crappie and rainbow. Fishing from the Interstate 90 bridge, accessible from the adjoining state park. **EXIT 176**

Mile 174.5 (534.5): The interstate crosses Marsh Island in the arm of Moses Lake known as Pelican Horn. MP 177

Mile 176.5 (532.5): Exit to Moses Lake and junction with Washington Highway 17. Major-chain motel, restaurants, 24-hour gas stations with diesel and fast-food outlets north off exit. Access to Big Bend Community College and Grant County Airport. NOTE: Next services eastbound 42 miles.

Washington Highway 17 leads north 21 miles to Soap Lake and 42 miles to junction with U.S. Highway 2. Washington Highway 17 leads south 11 miles and west 7 miles to Potholes State Park on O'Sullivan Reservoir, site of the Columbia Basin Project Interpretive Center. Potholes State Park is the most popular water recreation area in the Columbia Basin region. The park has camping and picnicking. **EXIT 179**

Mile 180 (529): Exit to Wheeler, Sieler Siding. **EXIT 182**

Mile 183 (526): Exit to Peters Road, Raugust Siding. Simplot plant to south. **EXIT 184**

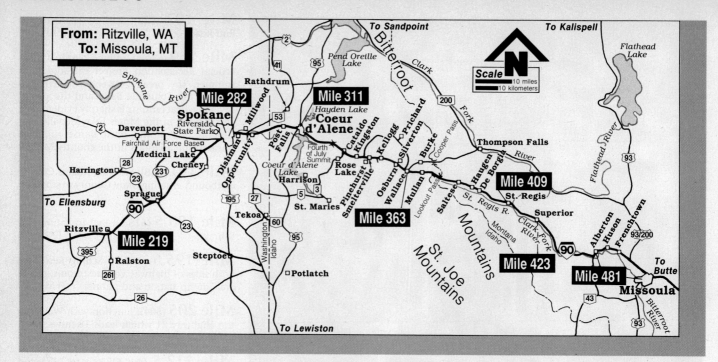

Mile 245 (464): Exit to Sprague and junction with Washington Highway 23 north to Harrington (22 miles) and south to Steptoe on U.S. Highway 195 (44 miles).

SPRAGUE (pop. 500) is located just to the south of Interstate 90; all services available. Incorporated in 1883, Sprague was named for Gen. John W. Sprague, the director of the Northern Pacific Railroad. Sprague's Roman Catholic church, Church of Mary Queen of Heaven, has a beautiful white gothic revival spire built in 1902.

Sprague Lake, visible from Interstate 90, has numerous fishing resorts. A shallow, heavily silted lake, it was poisoned in 1985 to remove an overpopulation of scrap fish. (The treatment turned up a 7-foot-long white sturgeon, much to the surprise of fish biologists.) The lake is being restocked with rainbow and brown trout, walleye, smallmouth and largemouth bass and other game fish. ☞EXIT 245

Mile 254 (455): Exit to Fishtrap Lake. Fishing in early spring, heavily stocked with rainbow. Private campground. ☞▲EXIT 254

Mile 255.5 (453.5): Entering Spokane County eastbound, Lincoln County westbound.

Mile 257 (452): Exit to Tyler, junction with Washington Highway 904 to Cheney (11 miles). Access to Turnbull National Wildlife Refuge. Also access to Badger Lake, one of the best trout lakes in the Spokane region. ☞EXIT 257

Mile 264 (455): Exit to Salnave Road, Cheney and Medical Lake. EXIT 264

Mile 270 (439): Exit to Washington Highway 904 to Four Lakes and Cheney (6 miles). CHENEY (pop. 7,630) is home of Eastern Washington University, which has

about 7,000 students enrolled. Originally known as Desert Springs, the name Cheney was adopted to cultivate the favor of Benjamin P. Cheney, a founder of the Northern Pacific Railroad. EXIT 270

Mile 272 (437): Junction with Washington Highway 902 north to Medical Lake (7 miles). The community of MEDICAL LAKE grew with the reputation of the lake's alkaline waters as a cure for rheumatism. From 1905 until the 1920s, passenger cars on the electric railway line from Spokane to Medical Lake were crowded with people seeking the cure. One of the developers of a Medical Lake health resort, Lord Stanley Hallett, built an unusual home for himself known as "The Castle" which still stands at East 623 Lake St. EXIT 272

Mile 276 (433): Exit to Geiger Field, West Spokane and Interstate 90 Business loop. Access to Worden's winery and to private RV park south off exit. ▲EXIT 276

Mile 277 (432): Junction with U.S. Highway 2 west to Fairchild Air Force Base, Garden Springs, Coulee Dam and Wenatchee. Access to Spokane Falls Community College. Fairchild AFB is a Strategic Air Command base. Travelers turning west on to U.S. Highway 2 turn to **Mile 415.5** in the U.S. HIGHWAY 2 section. EXIT 277

Mile 279 (430): Junction with U.S. Highway 195 south to Colfax and Pullman (see log on page 171). EXIT 279

Mile 280 (429): Exit to Lincoln Street, Maple Street toll bridge. EXIT 280

Mile 281 (428): Division Street exit is also the junction with U.S. Highway 2 north to Newport and U.S. Highway 395 north to Colville. (U.S. Highways 2 and 395 share a

common alignment north for several miles.) Division Street is a heavily traveled thoroughfare, lined with shopping malls and services; stay on Division Street for both highways. Access to hospital.

Travelers headed north on U.S. Highway 2 turn to **Mile 411.5** in the U.S. HIGHWAY 2 section. Travelers headed north on U.S. Highway 395 turn to **Mile 532.5** in the U.S. HIGHWAY 395 section. EXIT 281

Mile 282 (427): Exit to Trent Avenue, Hamilton Street and downtown SPOKANE, third largest metropolitan area in Washington. See description of Spokane in the MAJOR CITIES section. EXIT 282

Mile 283 (426): Exit 283A to Altamont Street; access to Playfair Race Course, which features thoroughbred racing. Exit 283B to Freya Street and Thor Street; access to Spokane Community College (drive north on Freya to Desmet, turn left on Desmet and right on Ralph Street, continue to Greene Street and Mission Avenue). EXIT 283

Mile 284 (425): Westbound-only exit to Havana Street. Spokane city limits. EXIT 283

Mile 285 (424): Exit to Sprague Avenue; access to Felt Field Municipal Airport. This busy airport caters primarily to private aircraft. Go east on Sprague to Fancher and take Fancher noth 1.5 miles to reach the airport. EXIT 285

Mile 286 (423): Exit to Broadway Avenue and access to Spokane Interstate Fairgrounds. EXIT 286

Mile 287 (422): Exit to Argonne Road. Access to community of MILLWOOD (pop. 1,717) and DISHMAN (pop. 10,169). EXIT 287

Mile 289 (420): Junction with Washington Highway 27 south to Pullman, Pines Road and the town of **OPPORTUNITY** (pop. 21,241). Valley General Hospital south off exit. EXIT 289

Mile 292 (417): Exit to Sullivan Road, Veradale, Trentwood Industrial Area and Spokane Industrial Park. Gas, food and lodging. EXIT 291

Mile 294 (415): Exit to Barker Road. Access to private campgrounds. ▲EXIT 293

Mile 295 (414): Westbound-only exit to Sprague Avenue and interstate business route. EXIT 294

Mile 296 (413): Exit to Otis Orchard and Liberty Lake; public beaches, swimming, fishing, boating and camping. ⚓▲EXIT 296

Mile 299 (410): Exit to State Line Village, Washington Port of Entry and Spokane River rest area. State visitor information center. EXIT 299

Mile 300 (409): Washington-Idaho state line, crossing the Spokane River. The Spokane River drains Lake Coeur d'Alene and flows west to the Columbia River.

Mile 302 (407): Exit to Pleasant View Road; access to dog racing track. Major chain fast-food outlet, gas station and motel at exit. EXIT 2

Mile 305 (404): Exit to Spokane Street and access to Post Falls city center. Major-chain motel and gas station at exit. **POST FALLS** (pop. 5,736) is located on the Spokane River and is named for Frederick Post, who arrived here in 1871. He purchased the site for the town from the Indian Chief Seltice of the Coeur d'Alenes, and established a sawmill here. Treaty Rock Historical Site commemorates the land exchange. It is a small city park about 1 mile off Interstate 90 toward the city.

Logging and agriculture are mainstays of the local economy. There are also 3 Washington Water Power dams at Post Falls which deliver electricity to residents of northern Idaho and eastern Washington. Jacklin Seed Co., one of the world's leading marketers of bluegrass seed, is also located here. Interstate 90 travelers may see grass fields being burned off; this helps control insects and return minerals to the soil. The Inland Empire of eastern Washington and the Idaho Panhandle are the leading producers of bluegrass seed in the United States. EXIT 5

Mile 307 (402): Junction with Idaho Highway 41 to Rathdrum and Spirit Lake. EXIT 7

Mile 308 (401): Rest area with restrooms and pay phone. MP 8

Mile 311 (398): Exit to Northwest Boulevard, Coeur d'Alene city center. Access to motels, RV park, North Idaho College and Kootenai Memorial Hospital. **COEUR**

d'ALENE (pop. 24,300) was originally the site of a fort on the old Mullan Road. General William Sherman chose the north shore of the lake for a military post in 1877, the year of the Nez Perce War. Gold, silver and lead discoveries encouraged miners to arrive in 1883-85. The town was incorporated in 1887 and steamers began plying the lake. Excursions along the lake became a favorite activity for many of the Idaho and Washington residents.

Summer cruises on Lake Coeur d'Alene are still popular for residents and visitors. Cruises depart daily from Coeur d'Alene Resort on the waterfront in downtown.

Coeur d'Alene Resort on Lake Coeur d'Alene. (Tom Barr)

Coeur d'Alene is a major recreation destination for the Inland Empire. All facilities are available. Attractions include the North Idaho Museum at 15 Northwest Boulevard, which features exhibits on mining, logging and the pioneer life of Kootenai County. The city park at Independence Point, on the lake next to the museum, provides a good view of the lake and has picnic tables. The visitor information center is located on the corner of 2nd and Sherman Avenue near the waterfront.

North Idaho College, which was founded as a private school in the early 1930s, occupies the site of old Fort Sherman, the military post built here in the late 1800s. EXIT 11

Mile 312 (397): Junction with U.S. Highway 95 north to Sandpoint and Canadian border; access to hospital and airport. Major-chain motel, fast-food outlet and gas station at exit. U.S. Highway 95 travelers turn to **Mile 623** in the U.S. HIGHWAY 95 section for log of that route. EXIT 12

Mile 313 (396): Exit to 4th Street in Coeur d'Alene. Access to 24-hour restaurant and gas stations at exit. EXIT 13

Mile 314 (395): Exit to 15th Street in Coeur d'Alene. EXIT 14

Mile 315 (394): Exit to Sherman Avenue. Gas station.

Just east of this exit travelers get a good view of Lake Coeur d'Alene, as the highway hugs the northeastern shore. The lake has more than 100 miles of shoreline and is one of the most popular resort areas in Idaho and eastern Washington for water recreation. Voted one of the 10 most beautiful lakes in the world, it is 25 miles long and has an average depth of 90 to 120 feet. EXIT 15

Mile 316 (393): Silver Beach, moorage. Gravel turnouts overlooking lake.
CAUTION: High head on collision rate this stretch of road. *Drive carefully!* MP 16

Mile 317.5 (391.5): Bennett Bay. Restaurant north side of interstate. View of the new freeway under construction to the north.

Mile 320 (389): Gravel turnout overlooking Lake Coeur d'Alene.

Mile 322 (387): Exit to Idaho Highway 97 south to Harrison and St. Maries. Highway 97 is a scenic drive along the east shore of Lake Coeur d'Alene. Access to Wolf Lodge area, private campground and to Beauty Creek Forest Service campground (2.5 miles south and 1 mile east). ▲EXIT 22

Mile 323 (386): Entering scenic Cedar Canyon for 4 miles eastbound. *CAUTION:* Watch for black ice and snow in winter. Winding road and 5 percent upgrade eastbound to Fourth of July Summit. MP 23

Mile 324.5 (384.5): Entering Idaho Panhandle National Forest eastbound.

Mile 328 (381): Fourth of July Summit (elev. 3,070 feet). Fourth of July Pass Recreation Area; snowmobiling north side of highway, cross-country skiing south of highway, in winter.

Mullan Tree Historical Site and Mullan Statue. Captain John Mullan, the builder of the Mullan Military Road from Fort Walla Walla to Fort Benton, camped near the Mullan Tree on July 4, 1861, while rerouting a 30-mile stretch of the military road along the north shore of Coeur d'Alene (approximately following the current route of Interstate 90). He and his men stopped here to rest and celebrate, marking the occasion by blazing the inscription "M.R. July 4, 1861" on the tree. Though badly weathered, the "y 4" of the inscription is still discernible. The tree was damaged by a windstorm in 1962, and all that remains is the base of the tree. EXIT 28

Mile 328.5 (380.5): Turnout eastbound, elev. 3,068 feet. *CAUTION:* Watch for black ice in winter. Winding road and 5 percent downgrade eastbound through Fourth of July Canyon.

Mile 332 (377): Weigh station (abandoned) north side of highway. The poplar trees along this stretch of highway provide a wonderful display in fall. End downgrade and winding road eastbound. *CAUTION:* Westbound travelers watch for black ice in winter. Winding road and 5 percent upgrade westbound to Fourth of July Summit.　　MP 32

Mile 334 (375): Exit to Rose Lake, St. Maries and junction with Idaho Highway 3. Gas station with diesel. Highway 3 is part of the 83-mile-long White Pine Scenic Route from Rose Lake to Potlatch which passes through one of the largest stands of white pine timber in America.　　EXIT 34

Mile 339 (370): Exit to Cataldo Mission, the oldest standing building in Idaho. Built between 1848 and 1853, it is the centerpiece of the Old Mission State Park, which includes the church and surrounding grounds. A half-mile trail walk, which takes about 25 minutes, leads past historical sites on the mission grounds. Picnic grounds and information center.　　🏕EXIT 39

Mile 340 (369): Crossing the Coeur d'Alene River. Exit to community of CATALDO; food and gas.　　EXIT 40

Mile 343 (366): Exit to KINGSTON. Access to the old mining town of Pritchard via gravel road north. (It is also accessible from Wallace.)　　EXIT 43

Mile 345 (364): Exit to PINEHURST (pop. 2,183); gas station and private campground. This community marks the western end of the Coeur d'Alene Mining District's Silver Valley. The hills in this valley, once completely denuded of vegetation by pollution from the smelters, are showing signs of recovery.　　▲EXIT 45

Mile 348 (361): Exit to SMELTERVILLE and Shoshone County airport. Visible on either side of the interstate are old mine tailings. Before modern environmental regulations were passed, the tailings (waste rock left over after the ore was mined) were dumped into the South Coeur d'Alene River. Current regulations require tailings and other mining wastes be held in impoundment areas to prevent leakage of toxic agents.　　EXIT 48

Mile 349 (360): Eastbound exit to Bunker Avenue and business route 90 through Kellogg. Rest area. To the south are the 715- and 610-foot chimneys of the Bunker Hill Co. The lead smelter, with the taller chimney, operated from 1917 to 1981. The zinc smelter operated from 1928 until 1981. Milo Gulch extends up through the mountainside behind the plant.　　EXIT 49

Mile 350 (359): Exit to KELLOGG (pop. 3,417); food, gas and lodging available. The tourist information center building, shaped like a miner's hat, is located just off the exit; restrooms and phone available.

Kellogg was originally known as Jackass. It was Noah Kellogg's jackass, according to popular legend, that discovered the Bunker Hill Mine in Milo Gulch in 1885. Historians

dispute the story of Noah and his pack animal, but however the mine was discovered, the Bunker Hill was one of the greatest lead, silver and zinc deposits ever located. The mine operated from 1885 until 1981, producing more than 35 million tons of ore, with about 130 miles of tunnels and shafts reaching almost a mile below the earth's surface.

When the mine and smelter shut down in 1981, some 2,000 men were thrown out of work. The mine was subsequently sold. The new owners continue to pump thousands of gallons of water a minute from the mine to keep the shafts from flooding, in anticipation of the mine opening again with a rise in metal prices.

Silverhorn Ski Area, 9 miles south of the interstate, is a popular winter destination.　　🎿EXIT 50

Mile 351 (358): Westbound exit to business route 90 through Kellogg; Division Street. Access to Wardner and Silverhorn Ski Area.

Wardner, an old mining town founded in 1885, is a short distance south of Kellogg. It was named for James F. Warnder, an early-day miner and one of the promoters of the Bunker Hill and Sullivan Mine.　　EXIT 51

Mile 354 (355): Exit to Big Creek Historical Site. Just off the exit ramp is the memorial that was erected in honor of the 91 men who died in the 1972 Sunshine Mine disaster. The tragedy was the worst hardrock mine accident in the United States since 1917.　　EXIT 54

Mile 357 (352): Exit to business route 90 and OSBURN (pop. 2,220), an unincorporated community and home of the valley's only

radio station, KWAL-AM 620. Gas station and private campground off exit.　　▲EXIT 57

Mile 360 (349): Exit to SILVERTON. Hospital north off exit. The U.S. Forest Service Wallace Ranger District Office, located next to the hospital, has detailed information on recreation in the region.　　EXIT 60

Mile 363 (346): Slow down as you drive through the picturesque town of WALLACE (pop. 1,736), which has all facilities, including major-chain motel, restaurants and gas station with diesel. There is no exit for Wallace because Interstate 90 runs right through the heart of the city. The stoplight in downtown Wallace is the only stoplight on Interstate 90 between Seattle and Boston. It is scheduled to be eliminated when the freeway bypass is completed (construction visible to north).

Wallace was founded by Col. W.R. Wallace, a cousin of Lew Wallace, author of the epic book, *Ben Hur.* The city grew up at a strategic trading place where five canyons meet, and became an important supply center for the mining industry. The city was incorporated in 1888 and in the 1890s, Wallace was the third-largest city in the state of Idaho. During the great forest fire of 1910, one-third of the buildings of Wallace, on the eastern edge of the city, were destroyed.

Despite the losses suffered in the fire, Wallace has numerous historic buildings, and it is well worth the time to take the 45-minute, self-guided walking tour of the city. The walking tour brochure is available from the Coeur d'Alene Mining Museum. Because of its large number of important historical structures, where whole blocks remain intact,

Coeur d'Alene Mining Museum window display.　　(Tom Barr)

the downtown as a whole is listed as a historic site on the National Register of Historic Places. Among the attractions are buildings such as the former Northern Pacific depot, which was built in 1901 out of brick imported from China, with its distinctive cupola.

The Sierra Silver Mine Tour will give you a good idea of a silver miner's life underground. The tour begins with an hour-long stop at the Coeur d'Alene District Mining Museum in downtown Wallace. (Even if you do not have time for the entire tour, a visit to the museum is a must.) A bus then takes the visitors a half mile out of town to the Sierra Silver Mine, where, after being equipped with hard hats, they are conducted by a mining student through the mine's 1,000-foot tunnel and can see how it operates. The tour departs every 20 minutes during the summer from mid-May to September; $4.50 for adults, and $3.50 for children 4-15 years and senior citizens.

On Nine Mile Canyon Road, just past the handsome old Northern Pacific depot, is the Miners' Cemetery, with the graves of many of the men who died in the mines.

Another attraction in the Wallace area is the old mining town of Burke, which is 6 miles up Idaho Highway 4 along Canyon Creek. Burke was once featured in *Ripley's Believe It or Not*, because the town was in such a narrow valley that the main street, railroad tracks and a creek all occupied the same space.   ★

Mile 364 (345): Exit to Golconda District, the site of another formerly rich mine, the Golconda Mine, which produced 300,000 tons of silver, lead and zinc ore from the late 1920s to 1950. The Golconda Mill was torn down in 1980.   EXIT 64

Mile 365 (344): Exit to the Compressor District. The name for this district came about when the Morning Mine installed a large air compressor plant at the mouth of Grouse Creek in 1900, with 3 large waterwheels turning out 1,000 horsepower.   EXIT 65

Mile 366 (343): Exit to Gold Creek.   EXIT 66

Mile 367 (342): Exit to the Morning District. The Morning Mine, near Mullan, was the second greatest all time producing mine in the Silver Valley. Since its discovery in 1884, it has yielded more than 18 million tons of lead, zinc and silver ore. Mining on the property ended in 1982.   EXIT 67

Mile 368 (341): Exit to MULLAN (pop. 1,269); all services available. This old industrial mining town has numerous historical buildings. It was named for Capt. John Mullan, who built the famous Mullan Road from Fort Walla, WA, to Fort Benton, MT, in the 1850s. An active mine in Mullan is the Lucky Friday Unit of the Hecla Mining Co. The mine was first located around the turn of the century and continues to produce silver, lead and zinc concentrates.   EXIT 68

Mile 369 (340): Exit to east Mullan.

I-90 winds through the center of historic Wallace, ID.   (Tom Barr)

Good view of headframe and mine, north side of highway.

CAUTION: Highway begins 6 mile climb with 6 percent grade eastbound to Lookout Pass. Chain-up area in winter.   EXIT 69

Mile 372.5 (336.5): Turnout. Beautiful view westbound of valley below to the north. The interstate is climbing the Bitterroot Mountains.

Mile 375.5 (333.5): Exit to Lookout Pass (elev. 4,725 feet), Idaho-Montana state line. No services available. This is a winter ski area with a Poma ski lift. Entering Lolo National Forest eastbound.

CAUTION: No center concrete divider makes winter driving hazardous on next stretch of downhill road eastbound. Truckers use low gear westbound; 6 percent downgrade next 5 miles.   EXIT 0

Mile 380 (329): Rest area and chain removal area for eastbound traffic.   MP 4

Mile 381 (328): Exit to Taft area, chain-up area for westbound traffic. Named for President William Howard Taft, Taft began as a construction camp on the Milwaukee Railroad during construction of the 8,750-foot tunnel through the mountains. When the tunnel was completed in 1909, the community disappeared.

St. Regis River to the south. Interstate 90 follows the St. Regis River east to the Clark Fork River.   EXIT 5

Mile 386 (323): Exit to SALTESE; all services available. Gas station at exit. Saltese is an old mining town on the St. Regis River, and was named for Chief Saltese of the Nez Perce Indians. The St. Regis River was named by Father DeSmet in 1842 in honor of St. Regis de Borgia.   EXIT 10

Mile 390 (319): Weigh station.

Mile 391.5 (317.5): Exit to HAUGAN; phone, food, gas and silver gift shop. The town was established as a "pusher station" for trains ascending the mountain grade. It was named for H.G. Haugan, an official with the Milwaukee Railroad.   EXIT 16

Mile 393.5 (315.5): Exit to DeBORGIA; gas, grocery and restaurant. DeBorgia was a station on the Northern Pacific Railroad.   EXIT 18

Mile 397.5 (311.5): Exit to Henderson, a logging town in the early 1900s. Fishing access to the St. Regis River. Access to Cabin City Forest Service campground, 2 miles northeast via Mullen Pass Road then north on Twelvemile Road.   ◄▲EXIT 22

Mile 401 (308): Exit to Drexel; no services.   EXIT 25

Mile 405.5 (303.5): Exit to Two Mile Road; no services. Fishing access to the St. Regis River. More of a stream than a river, the St. Regis is easily waded and fished from shore. It is heavily fished in the easy access areas, but still produces fair action for cutthroat and brookies up to 14 inches.   ◄EXIT 30

Mile 409 (300): Exit to ST. REGIS; major-chain motel, gas stations and food at exit. Junction with Montana Highway 135 to Paradise. St. Regis is a well-known shipping center for the logging and wood products industry, and is a popular truck stop. It is located at the confluence of the Clark Fork and St. Regis rivers.   EXIT 33

Mile 409.5 (299.5): Crossing the Clark Fork River. The highway crosses the Clark Fork several times from here to east of Missoula. The Clark Fork is a major fishing and recreational river, as well as one of the major drainages in western Montana. It flows west to the Columbia River. Rainbow are the dominant species for fishermen. Because of its wide breadth and meandering flow, it is a favorite for float fishing from inflatables, canoes or drift boats.   MP 34

Mile 412.5 (296.5): Exit to Sloway area; no services. Access to Sloway Forest Service campground; 19 sites; fishing.   ◄▲EXIT 37

Mile 419 (290:) Exit to Dry Creek Road; no services. Access to Sloway Forest Service campground (see preceding exit).   EXIT 43

Mile 423 (286): Exit to SUPERIOR (pop. 1,054), all services including a motel. Gas station with diesel and mini-mart at exit. Superior is the county seat of Mineral County. It was named for Superior, WI, and was once the site of numerous productive mines. This is a popular hunting and fishing area.

The Clark Fork River bisects Superior, and it is well worth a drive across the bridge on River Street to appreciate the town's setting. Downtown businesses line Mullan Road on

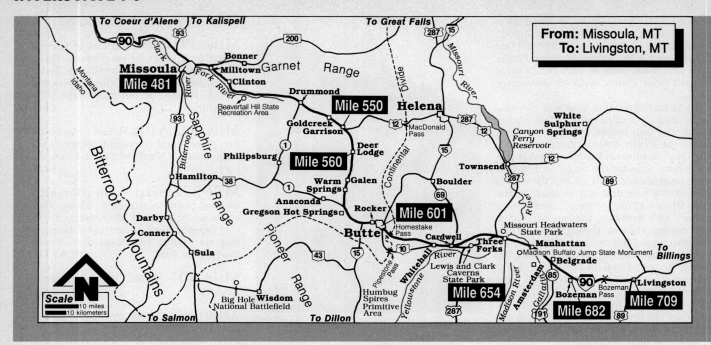

the north side of the river.

Camping at Trout Creek Forest Service campground, 7 miles south of town in Lolo National Forest; 12 sites. Trout Creek is heavily fished for cutthroat, Dolly Varden and some whitefish. Best fishing is above the falls and in the canyon below the falls.
➳▲ EXIT 47

Mile 430.5 (278.5): Exit to Lozeau; gas available. EXIT 55

Mile 433 (276): Rest area and access to campground in pine forest along interstate. Quartz Flat Forest Service campground has 52 sites, flush toilets, phone, picnic tables, drinking water and a nature trail. Access to Clark Fork for fishing.

NOTE: The next rest area westbound is 52 miles from here. ⛱➳▲

Mile 437 (272): Exit to TARKIO, the site of a station on the old Milwaukee Railroad; no services. EXIT 61

Mile 442.5 (266.5): Exit to Fish Creek Road, which leads up Fish Creek Canyon. There is a small camping and fishing spot on Fish Creek 10 miles south of the interstate; excellent fishing for cutthroat and rainbow. This is also a popular camping spot during fall hunting season. Rustic lodge, restaurant and outfitter farther up Fish Creek Canyon.
➳EXIT 66

Mile 445 (264): Exit to Cyr, formerly a station on the Northern Pacific. No services available. EXIT 70

Mile 447.5 (261.5): Rest areas both sides of highway. ⛱MP 72

Mile 450.5 (258.5): Exit to ALBERTON, an old railroad town; gas, food and camping.
▲EXIT 75

Mile 452.5 (256.5): Missoula County line. Exit to Petty Creek Road and junction with Montana Highway 507. Petty Creek is fished for small cutthroat, brookies and whitefish. Access to the Clark Fork. ➳EXIT 77

Mile 457.5 (251.5): Exit to Nine Mile Road. The settlement of Nine Mile was named for George Brown's Nine Mile Roadhouse, which was located that distance from Frenchtown. The Nine Mile ranger station, 4.5 miles north of Interstate 90, was a famous "remount station," where for 32 years Forest Service mule teams set out into the backcountry to resupply men in the field.

An exposure of silt and sediment on both sides of the interstate near here was left by glacial Lake Missoula. MP 82 EXIT 82

Mile 460.5 (248.5): Exit to HUSON, named for a Northern Pacific Railroad engineer. MP 85 EXIT 85

Mile 464.5 (244.5): Exit to FRENCHTOWN; gas station and grocery at exit. French Canadians settled here around 1864. A gold stampede brought 3,000 prospectors in 1869.
EXIT 89

Mile 468 (241): Weigh station. Travelers may note the odor of hydrogen sulfide emitted from the Champion Paper Mill to the south. The wood products industry is a leading employer in this region.

Mile 472 (237): Glacier Park exit: junction with U.S. Highway 93 North to Flathead Lake, Kalispell and Glacier National Park. A 24-hour truck stop (diesel) is located at this exit, also food and major-chain motels. Travelers headed north on U.S. Highway 93 turn to **Mile 515.5** in the U.S. HIGHWAY 93 section for log of that route. EXIT 96

Mile 477 (232): Exit to Business 90 route

(U.S. Highway 93) to Missoula. Gas station at exit, major-chain motels south off exit. Access to Reserve Street and U.S. Highway 93 South (also U.S. Highway 12); Montana Highway 430, Snow Bowl Ski Area; Smokejumpers Center and Johnson Bell (Missoula) Airport.

Travelers bound for U.S. Highway 93 South can bypass downtown Missoula by exiting here and going south on Reserve Street. Turn to **Mile 500** in the U.S. HIGHWAY 93 section for log of that route. For U.S. Highway 12 west, turn to the beginning of the U.S. HIGHWAY 12 section for log. EXIT 101

Mile 480 (229): Exit to Orange Street. Gas station at exit. Access to hospital and major-chain motels. EXIT 104

Mile 481 (228): Exit to Van Buren Street. Gas station south off exit. Access to major-chain motels, downtown Missoula (description follows), University of Montana and business loop.

MISSOULA (pop. 33,353), the seat of Missoula County, is a pleasant city at the confluence of 3 major rivers: the Clark Fork, Bitterroot and Blackfoot. Missoula has all facilities, including good shopping in the well-maintained downtown area, along with shopping centers on the city centre arterials.

Missoula is the home of the University of Montana, a 181-acre campus serving more than 9,000 students in 47 buildings. Other attractions here include the Greenough Mansion, located at 102 Ben Hogan St., built in 1897 by Thomas Greenough. It was moved from its original location and is now home of the Leisure Highlands Golf Course Clubhouse and a restaurant.

Greenough Park provides a beautiful 1-mile drive through a wooded area beside Rattlesnake Creek. The park, donated from the Greenough estate to the city of Missoula, features a landscaped picnic area and wading pool.

Fort Missoula Historical Museum, at the corner of South Avenue and Reserve Street, was established in 1877 as one of the first military posts in Montana. It now serves as the home for National Guard and Reserve units. Displays on the 28-acre reserve depict the industrial development of the West from 1880 to 1920. The Indoor Gallery has a schedule of changing exhibits. The complex is open from noon until 5 p.m. daily, except Monday.

The Memorial Rose Garden on Highway 93 was established in 1947 by the American Rose Society and maintained as a memorial to the casualties of WWII. More than 2,500 rose plants are maintained at the garden.

One of the unique facilities of Missoula is the Smokejumpers Center, located at Johnson Bell Airport, Highway 10 West. Here, smokejumpers are trained for the dangerous and difficult task of forest fire suppression. The Northern Forest Fire Laboratory is also located here. Scientists study the nature and characteristics of forest fires to better understand and help aid in the suppression of forest fires. The complex is open for visitors from May 15 through July 1, 8 a.m. to 4 p.m., weekdays; and from July 1 through the end of September, 9 a.m. until 5 p.m. daily.

The beautiful St. Francis Xavier Church, located at 420 W. Pine, was built in 1889, the year Montana became a state. It features a graceful steeple, stained glass windows and mural paintings by a Jesuit brother, Joseph Carignano, a kitchen helper, unschooled in art but later recognized as a master. Carignano also painted the 58 murals and frescoes at the famous St. Ignatius Catholic Mission south of Polson (see **Mile 547.5**).

The paintings of another muralist, Edgar Samuel Paxson, may be viewed at the Missoula County Courthouse from 8 a.m. until 5 p.m. weekdays. The artist is perhaps most famous for his painting of "Custer's Last Stand," completed in 1899. Eight murals, painted between 1912 and 1914, decorate the walls of the courthouse.   EXIT 105

Mile 483 (226): Exit to eastern Missoula and Marshall Ski Area.   EXIT 107

Mile 484 (225): Clark Fork River Bridge. The Clark Fork is one of the longest rivers in this part of the state, flowing from the Continental Divide at Butte to Lake Pend Oreille in northern Idaho.

Mile 485 (224): Exit to **BONNER** and **MILLTOWN** via Montana Highway 200. Confluence of the Blackfook and Clark Fork rivers.   EXIT 109

Mile 488.5 (220.5): Exit to Turah; store and campground.   ▲EXIT 113

Mile 495.5 (213.5): Exit to **CLINTON**; gas and groceries available.   EXIT 120

Mile 501.5 (207.5): Exit to Rock Creek Road, lodge and campgrounds. Rock Creek is one of the premier trout streams in Montana, offering excellent spin and fly-fishing for rainbow, cutthroat, brown and brook trout. Special regulations govern the fishery here; check current regulations.

Rock Creek Road leads south from Clinton through the Welcome Creek Wilderness of Lolo National Forest. There are private campgrounds just south of the interstate on Rock Creek Road. Forest Service campgrounds are located between 10 and 23 miles south of the interstate on Rock Creek Road.
          ⊶▲EXIT 126

Mile 503 (206): Rest areas on both sides of the highway.   ⊼

Mile 505.5 (203.5): Exit to Beavertail Road. Access to Beavertail Hill state recreation area with 15 campsites and fishing in the Clark Fork River.   ⊶▲EXIT 130

Mile 514 (195): Exit to the ghost towns of Bearmouth and Garnet.   EXIT 138

Mile 519 (190): Rest areas both sides of highway.   ⊼

Mile 529.5 (179.5): Exit to **DRUMMOND** (pop. 414) and junction with Montana Highway 1 south to Anaconda. Drummond is a ranching community and major cattle producing area. This is the northwestern end of the Pintler Scenic Route to Georgetown Lake (see **Mile 583.5**) and is a geographic transition area marking the line between the timber country of western Montana and the plains and grasslands of the east.   EXIT 154

Mile 537.5 (171.5): Exit to County Road; no services.   EXIT 162

Mile 541.5 (167.5): Exit to **GOLDCREEK**; no services. In 1852, Francois Finlay, a Frenchman, is believed to have panned the first gold discovered in Montana here. There is a historical marker 1 miles south of the highway.   EXIT 166

Mile 543 (166): Rest areas with picnic tables both sides of highway. Access to Clark Fork River.   ⊼

Mile 550 (159): Exit to **GARRISON** and junction with U.S. Highway 12 east to Helena. Gas and groceries available at exit.

U.S. Highway 12 shares a common alignment with Interstate 90 from here west to Missoula. U.S. Highway 12 from Missoula, MT, to its junction with Interstate 5 in Washington is logged in the U.S. HIGHWAY 12 section.   EXIT 174

Mile 554.5 (154.5): Exit to Beck Hill Road; no services.   EXIT 179

Mile 560 (149): Exit to **DEER LODGE** (pop. 4,023); all services available this exit, including major-chain motels, campground and 24-hour restaurant.

Established in the 1860s, Deer Lodge is the second oldest city in Montana. It was the jumping-off point for nearby goldfields during the gold rush of 1862. It was named after the multitude of deer attracted to the natural salt licks in the area.

Deer Lodge is best known as the site of the Montana State Prison and the former territorial prison, now the site of the Towe Antique Ford Collection, generally considered the most

(© John Barger)

Rocky Mountain (Yellowstone) elk range across western Montana, Idaho and eastern Washington.

Main house at Grant-Kohrs Cattle Ranch in Deer Lodge, at one time the largest ranch in America. (Tom Barr)

complete antique car collection in existence. Tours of the thick-walled former prison with its forbidding guard towers and antique car collection are available daily.

Deer Lodge is also home to the Powell County Museum providing a historical overview of the area including the state's first college which was located here.

An excellent attraction on the outskirts of Deer Lodge is the Grant-Kohrs Cattle Ranch, a national historic site, that was ranked as the largest ranch in America during the mid to late 1800s, and at one time covered 1 million acres. The ranch has been preserved with authentic furnishings including outbuildings, bunk houses, the blacksmith shop and the main house. ▲★EXIT 184

Mile 563 (146): Interstate 90 business loop (Highway 10) to downtown Deer Lodge. EXIT 187

Mile 570.5 (138.5): Exit to Racetrack; no services. EXIT 195

Mile 573 (136): Junction with County Road 273 to Galen; no services. EXIT 197

Mile 576.5 (132.5): Exit to **WARM SPRINGS**; all services. Site of the Montana Women's Correctional Center and Montana State Hospital. EXIT 201

Mile 583.5 (125.5): Junction with U.S. Highway 10A, which leads west 7 miles to Montana Highway 1 (Pintler Scenic Route) and Anaconda.

Originally called Copperopolis, **ANACONDA** (pop. 10,178) began in 1883 as the site of a copper smelter built by Marcus Daly, founder of Montana's copper industry. The smokestack of the smelter is one of the tallest free-standing brick structures in the world. Buildings of varying architectural styles from the 1800s still stand in Anaconda. Nearby is Discovery Basin Ski Area.

Montana Highway 1 (Pintler Scenic Route) provides access to Georgetown Lake, one of the most popular fishing lakes in western Montana. The scenic route continues north along Flint Creek to rejoin Interstate 90 at Drummond. EXIT 208

Mile 591.5 (117.5):) Exit to Ramsey; no services. EXIT 216

Mile 594.5 (114.5): Junction with Interstate 15 South to Idaho Falls. Interstate 15 and Interstate 90 share a common alignment eastbound for 8 miles. Turn to **Mile 413** in the INTERSTATE HIGHWAY 15 section for log of that route.

Mile 595.5 (113.5): Exit to **ROCKER**, a bedroom community of Butte. All services. EXIT 122

Mile 597.5 (111.5): Exit to business route Interstate 15 through Butte city center. EXIT 124

Mile 599.5 (109.5): Exit to Montana Street and Montana Tech. Access to Butte restaurants. Hospital exit. EXIT 126

Mile 601 (108): Exit to Harrison Avenue and I-90 Business Loop. Access to restaurants and motels. Also access to Butte airport.

BUTTE (pop. 33,380) has all services. The town also has a rich mining history, evidence of which is carved into the surrounding hillsides heavily eroded by mine workings and haul roads. Many of the dwellings here originated as company housing for mine workers.

The Berkeley Pit, at one time the largest of all open-pit mines in the world, is located on E. Park Street and is open during daylight hours. There is no admission charge.

At the Mineral Museum at Montana College of Mineral Science and Technology, more than 1,000 mineral specimens are on display. The museum is open from 8 a.m. until 5 p.m. daily, June through Labor Day; and winter hours are 8 a.m. to 5 p.m. weekdays. There is no admission charge.

The "Copper King" Mansion, located at 219 W. Granite St., was built by Senator William Clark. The 32-room mansion, complete with a 60-foot-long ballroom, is available for tours daily from 9 a.m. until 9 p.m. at a minimal admission charge.

The Community Arts Center and Museum, originally the Charles Clark Mansion, built in 1898, is a national historic site with changing art exhibits. Admission is free.

It is located at 321 W. Broadway.

Look for the 90-foot "Our Lady of the Rockies" statue on the East Ridge overlooking Butte. Placed there in December 1985, the concrete statue is lighted and visible at night.   MP 128 EXIT 127

Mile 603 (106): Exit to Interstate Highway 15 North to Helena. Junction of Interstate 15 and 90 at the eastern edge of Butte. The 2 interstates share a common alignment for 8 miles westbound. A scenic overlook at this exit has a historical sign commemorating Butte's mining history and Meaderville, which contained the "richest hill on earth."

Travelers headed north on Interstate 15 turn to **Mile 420** in the INTERSTATE HIGHWAY 15 section for log of that route.
MP 130 EXIT 129

Mile 609 (100): Exit to Homestake Pass (elev. 6,393 feet); access to cross-country skiing, hiking trails and hunting areas. Crossing the Continental Divide. Waters east of the divide drain into the Gulf of Mexico. Waters west of the divide flow to the Pacific Ocean.

Steep grade westbound into Butte; heavy vehicles use low gear.   EXIT 233

Mile 611 (98): Rest area with picnic tables.   ㅈ

Mile 613.5 (95.5): Boundary of Deerlodge National Forest.

Mile 616.5 (92.5): Exit to Pipestone Pass Recreation Area to south; skiing, camping and hunting available. Westbound chain-up area for Homestake Pass.   EXIT 241

Mile 625 (84): Exit to WHITEHALL (pop. 1,030), which has all services, and junction with Montana Highway 55. The sharp peaks of the Tobacco Root Range dominate the southern skyline.   EXIT 249

Mile 632 (77): Exit to CARDWELL and Montana Highway 69 North to Boulder. Access to Lewis and Clark Caverns State Park via Montana Highway 2. The largest limestone cavern in the Northwest and one of the most beautiful caves in the country, the caverns are open daily from May through September. Roundtrip through the caves covers about a mile and takes 2 hours. Camping is available at the park.   ▲★EXIT 256

Mile 650 (59): Exit to U.S. Highway 287 North to Canyon Ferry Reservoir (30 miles) and Helena, south to Ennis and West Yellowstone.   EXIT 274

Mile 654 (55): Exit to THREE FORKS (pop. 1,247), all services available. Access to Missouri Headwaters State Park, 4 miles north. The park has picnicking, 45 campsites and a boat launch. It is situated at the confluence of the Jefferson, Madison and Gallatin rivers, which create the Missouri River. The spot was a campsite for the Lewis and Clark expedition, and an important Indian cultural area. Scenic overlook, historical exhibits,

river access and hiking trails available.
㕮ㅈ▲EXIT 278

Mile 658.5 (50.5): Exit to small communities of Trident and Logan. Access to Madison Buffalo Jump State Monument, 7 miles south via gravel road. Plains Indian tribes once stampeded herds of buffalo over cliffs at this site. Picnic tables, restrooms and an interpretative center.   ㅈEXIT 283

Mile 664 (45): Exit south to Amsterdam, north to MANHATTAN (pop. 998), all services available.   EXIT 288

Mile 673.5 (35.5): Exit to BELGRADE and junction with Montana Highway 85/U.S. Highway 191 to West Yellowstone.
EXIT 298

Mile 682 (27): Exit to BOZEMAN (pop. 29,000), access to major-chain motels south off exit. Bozeman is the gateway to Yellowstone National Park and one of the state's most important agricultural areas. It is also the home of Montana State University, the largest college campus in the state.

The excellent Museum of the Rockies on the MSU campus features historic and cultural displays and artifacts on Montana dating back to the era of dinosaurs, including major Western and Indian exhibits. The museum also features a planetarium. It is open daily year-round; closed major holidays. Admission fee charged. The College National Rodeo Finals are also held on the MSU campus in June.

Bozeman was named after John Bozeman, a wagon master who brought the first group of Easterners through the Gallatin Valley in 1863. Lewis and Clark passed through the

Toston Dam on the Missouri River north of Three Forks. (L. Linkhart)

valley, called "Valley of Flowers" by the Indians, in 1806 on their return from the Pacific Ocean.

Winter and summer recreation is a major industry with excellent ski resorts, hot springs, hiking, fishing, hunting, camping and resorts. Numerous guest ranches and recreational facilities are located throughout the area.

The Gallatin River, which passes through town, is a blue-ribbon-class trout stream (brown and rainbow) and is one of the three headwaters of the Missouri River.
➻★ EXIT 306

Mile 685 (24): Exit to Bozeman. Access to hospital, food, gas and lodging. EXIT 309

Mile 689 (20): Exit to Bear Creek Canyon Road.   EXIT 313

Mile 702.5 (6.5): Chain-up area for Bozeman Pass (elev. 5,760 feet). This low pass divides the Gallatin Mountains to the south and the Bridger Range to the north. Severe winds are common in this area and occasionally will force highway traffic to stop. The Absaroka Mountains dominate the southern skyline.

Mile 709 (0): Exit to LIVINGSTON (pop. 6,994) All services including motels and restaurants.

Livingston was founded as a railroad town and was named for the director of the Northern Pacific Railroad, Johnston Livingston. The railroad built the depot of bricks imported from China in 1902; it was known as "the original entrance to Yellowstone National Park."

Livingston is now supported largely by tourism, recreation, small industries and ranching and is a center of hunting and fishing activity in the Yellowstone and Gallatin country with numerous sports shops, guides and outfitters available.

In recent years more than 20 buildings in the downtown area have been restored using old photographs as a guide to restore the original look.

The Livingston Wind Corridor blows through town with an average annual wind speed of 15 mph and gusts to 90 mph. The flats southeast of town are a testing ground for wind-generated electricity.

July 2-4 is rodeo time in Livingston each year. The Yellowstone River boat float is held the middle of July for a 107-mile float to Laurel. Park County Museum, open during the summer, features pioneer and Indian cultures.

Junction with U.S. Highway 89 South, which parallels the Yellowstone River southbound for 50 miles to the Mammoth entrance of Yellowstone National Park at Gardiner.

The Yellowstone River in the Livingston area is one of the most famous trout streams in America. The Yellowstone cutthroat, rainbow and brown trout can be found throughout the river. Bank fishing can be productive, but anglers working from a boat are usually most successful.   ➻EXIT 333

U.S. Highway 93

See map pages 145 and 148

U.S. Highway 93 enters the Northwest at Wells, NV, and winds through Idaho and Montana to the U.S.-Canada border. The highway traverses the Snake River plain, passes the volcanic wasteland of central Idaho, climbs the Rocky Mountains and runs below the jagged peaks of the Bitterroot Range.

Take along your trout rod, camera and binoculars because Highway 93 touches some fine fishing holes, big game areas and scenic mountain country. North of Twin Falls, ID, it follows the Little Wood River, an excellent trout stream, then north along the headwaters of the famous Salmon River — legendary "River of No Return" — and through the Lost River Mountains, home to mule deer, elk and bighorn sheep. It crosses into Montana over the backbone of the beautiful Bitterroot Mountains, moving north along another excellent trout and float fishing river, the Bitterroot.

North of Missoula, the highway arrows up the center of the Flathead Valley, then skirts the edge of the National Bison Range, a must stop for wildlife enthusiasts. A 2-hour self-guided auto tour usually provides close-up encounters with bison, elk, bighorn sheep, deer and pronghorn.

North of the bison range, Highway 93 curves along the west shore of 28-mile-long Flathead Lake, passes near Glacier National Park and crosses into British Columbia.

Because of the mountainous terrain, Highway 93 can often be hazardous to travel in the winter. Be sure to carry snow tires and/ or tire chains. It's also wise to carry a few blankets during the cold season in the event you become stranded by snow and have to spend some time in your vehicle before help arrives.

Even during the balmy nights of summer, the weather can be a bit brisk at the higher elevations. Prepare for the trip accordingly and plan to take your time as you travel along one of the most scenic routes in the Northwest.

U.S. Highway 93 Log

Distance from Wells, NV, is followed by distance from the Canadian border.

Mile 0 (702.5): Junction of Highway 93 with Interstate 80 just south of Wells, NV.

Mile 1 (701.5): WELLS (pop. 5,630), situated at the base of Hole in the Mountain Peak (elev. 11,276 feet), is a small desert community with all traveler services.

Wells was established as a shipping point for cattle when the railroad was completed through the area in 1869. North of Wells, near Bishop Creek Reservoir (also called Metropolis Reservoir), is the ghost town of Metropolis which once boasted a population of 7,500 people. The town was founded on dreams of agricultural wealth, but when a legal battle for water rights eliminated the possiblity of irrigating the 40,000 acres under cultivation, the town was abandoned. The beautiful Metropolis Hotel, opened in 1911, was one of the grandest stops between Ogden and Reno, but 2 years later the city collapsed. The railroad was abandoned in 1925 and in 1936, the magnificent Metropolis Hotel burned to the ground.

Today, nothing remains of Metropolis except a small cemetery located north of Wells.

Mile 14.5 (688): Turnoff to Willow Creek and Hunter Draw.

Mile 20 (682.5): H.D. Summit (elev. 6,274 feet). The mountain to the east is Antelope Peak (elev. 8,762 feet).

Mile 43 (659.5): Turnoff to Knoll Creek and Trout Creek, which have their source on Knoll Mountain (elev. 8,758 feet) just to the west.

Mile 50.5 (652): Salmon Falls Creek, which flows north to Idaho to drain into the Snake River.

Mile 52 (650.5): Contact, a small agricultural area. No services available.

Mile 56.5 (646): Turnoff to Mahogany Basin.

Mile 64.5 (638): Rest area with picnic tables. Little Salmon River crosses the highway here. ⊼

Mile 65 (637.5): Turnoff to Goose Creek and the settlement of Delaplain. No services available.

Mile 67 (635.5): Crossing the Mountain-Pacific time zone line. Turn your watches ahead 1 hour if you are headed north; back 1 hour for southbound travelers.

Mile 67.5 (635): JACKPOT, the last legal gambling resort community on Highway 93 for northbound travelers, has all services. The community is perched on the Nevada-Idaho border and is used extensively by Idaho gamblers. The casino at Jackpot regularly offers top-name performers. Conventions held in the Twin Falls area (just 50 miles away) often offer side trips to Jackpot.

The town was unimaginatively called "Unincorporated Town No. 1" until April 7, 1959, when the Elko County Commissioners officially named the community Jackpot.

Mile 68.5 (634): Nevada-Idaho border.

Mile 73 (629.5): Rabbit Spring rest area.

Mile 76 (626.5): Turnoff to Norton Bay on Salmon Falls Creek Reservoir. This reservoir, located 4 miles west, is 1 of only 2 waters in Idaho stocked with walleye. Boat launching and camping facilities are at the lake. ⊷▲

Mile 78 (624.5): Turnoff to Grey's Landing on Salmon Falls Creek Reservoir.

Mile 86 (616.5): Turnoff to Salmon Falls Creek Reservoir and the community of ROGERSON which has gas, food and lodging.

Mile 87 (615.5): Turnoff to Shoshone Basin Road.

Mile 92 (610.5): Private museum of Indian artifacts and Idaho big game animals.

Mile 94.5 (608): Weigh station and travel information.

Mile 95 (607.5): Junction with Nat Soo Pah Road which goes to Nat Soo Pah Hot Springs. Nat Soo Pah is an Indian phrase meaning "living" or "life-giving waters" and the hot springs are a popular place for camping, picnicking and swimming. ⊼▲

Mile 95.5 (607): HOLLISTER (pop. 167). Limited services. MP 27

Mile 103.5 (599): Small community of BERGER. Limited services.

Mile 106.5 (596): Junction with Idaho

Highway 74 to Twin Falls where it rejoins U.S. Highway 93 at **Mile 114.**

Mile 110 (592.5): Junction with U.S. Highway 30 (Thousand Springs Scenic Route) through Buhl and Hagerman. Springs pouring from the basalt cliffs of the Snake River canyon in the Hagerman area, known as Thousand Springs, offer quite a view. Their source is believed to be the Lost River which flows underground in the lava fields of central Idaho.

The area around Buhl is known as the "trout capital of the world" because 90 percent of the commercial trout sold in the U.S. is raised here. Visitors may tour state, federal or private hatcheries.

Mile 111 (591.5): Twin Falls County Museum.

Mile 113.5 (589): Rock Creek Park with covered picnic tables and restrooms. ⊼

Mile 114 (588.5): Junction with Idaho Highway 74.

Mile 114.5 (588): TWIN FALLS (pop. 26,209) offers all traveler services. It is the hub of the Magic Valley, one of the most productive agricultural areas in Idaho. Since 1905, the waters of the Snake River have been used to irrigate the arid desert of southcentral Idaho, and wildlife and recreational opportunities abound on the lakes and reservoirs around Twin Falls. It is a land of curious rock formations and lava flows, rich in history.

Among the attractions of the Twin Falls area are Shoshone Falls, Balanced Rock, the City of Rocks and the Snake River canyon.

For additional information on the Twin Falls area refer to **Mile 551** in the INTERSTATE 84 highway log.

Mile 117 (585.5): Turnoff to Shoshone Falls, 52 feet higher than the famous Niagara Falls. It is best to see the falls in spring, when the Snake River waters are high.

Mile 118.5 (584): Scenic overlook of the Snake River canyon and historical site. This is the Perrine Memorial Bridge, 1,500 feet long and 480 feet above the Snake River. It is the longest span bridge in America.

At the north end of the bridge is a road which leads east to the site of stunt man Evel Knieval's ill-fated attempt to jump the Snake River Canyon on a jet-powered motorcycle in the fall of 1974. MP 50

Mile 121.5 (581): Junction with Interstate 84 west to Boise and east to Ogden and Pocatello, via Interstate 86. Travelers intending to travel Interstate 84 should turn to **Mile 551** in the INTERSTATE 84 section for the log of that route.

Mile 127 (575.5): Junction with Idaho Highway 25 to **JEROME** (pop. 6,891). All services available.

Mile 140 (562.5): Notch Butte fire lookout.

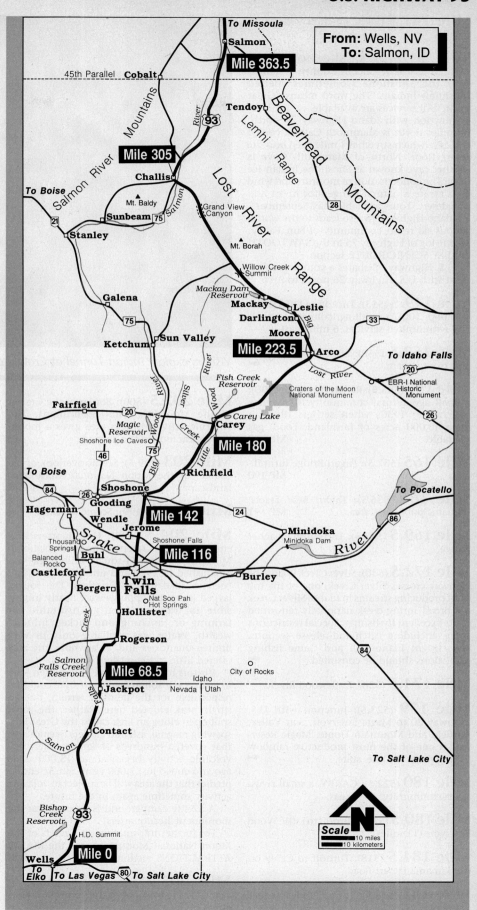

Mile 141.5 (561): Junction with Highway 24.

Mile 142 (560.5): SHOSHONE (pop. 1,242), the seat of Lincoln County, is named after the Shoshone (sometimes spelled Shoshoni) Indians. The word means "Great Spirit." All services are available.

Junction with Idaho Highway 75 north. Six miles north is Mammoth Cave, a cooled lava cave which stretches 1 mile deep into the desert floor. North of Mammoth Cave is another cave known as Shoshone Indian Ice Cave. The condensation of moisture and wind draft create a natural refrigerator in an arid lava desert. Tours available May-September.

Idaho Highway 75 also leads to the world-famous ski resort community of Sun Valley. See the log of Highway 75 in the SAWTOOTH VALLEY SCENIC ROUTE section.

U.S. Highway 93 shares a common alignment with U.S. Highway 26 north to Arco.

Mile 149.5 (553): Turnoff to DIETRICH (est. pop. 100), a small agricultural community with limited services, 6 miles east.

Mile 152.5 (550): Little Wood River, a nice trout stream. ⬲

Mile 157 (545.5): RICHFIELD (pop. 290), a small agricultural community. Its heyday was in the 1930s when settlers filed on some 40,000 acres of farmland. Food, gas available.   MP 182

Mile 165 (537.5): Pagari Bridge turnoff.
MP 190

Mile 166 (536.5): Taylor Bear Tracts, Williams public-use area.   MP 191

Mile 169.5 (533.5): Turnoff to Preacher Bridge.

Mile 172.5 (530): Silver Creek Road. The highway crosses Silver Creek, one of the top trout producing streams in Idaho. Silver Creek is a broad spring creek nationally renowned for its excellent fly-fishing. Special restrictions apply, including catch-and-release sections, and current Idaho Fish and Game fishing regulations should be consulted. ⬲

Mile 174.5 (528): Littlewood River.

Mile 179 (523.5): Junction with U.S. Highway 20 to Magic Reservoir, Sun Valley, Fairfield and Mountain Home. Magic Reservoir is one of the most productive rainbow fishing lakes in the state. ⬲

Mile 180 (522.5): CAREY, a small crossroads community. Food, gas.

Mile 180.5 (522): Turnoff to Little Wood Reservoir (11 miles).

Mile 184.5 (518): Turnoff to Carey on the Kimama Desert Road.

Mile 187 (515.5): Turnoff to Fish Creek Reservoir.

Visitors explore Indian Tunnel at Craters of the Moon National Monument. (L. Linkhart)

Mile 202.5 (500): Border of the Craters of the Moon National Monument. The volcanic activity in this area gives a moon-like appearance to the ground.

Mile 203 (499.5): Scenic overlook of the Craters of the Moon National Monument landscape.   MP 228

Mile 203.5 (499): Scenic overlook.

Mile 204.5 (498): Headquarters and entrance to the Craters of the Moon National Monument. The 83-square-mile park was established in 1924 and until that time had been avoided by early settlers. The rough, jagged lava outcroppings were nearly impossible to traverse, totally unsuitable for farming or ranching and lacked mineral wealth. Water was available only in very limited quantities and, as a whole, the area offered little to the settlers.

Visitors to Craters of the Moon often look in vain for a solitary volcano that could be responsible for the desolate terrain, but no single peak erupted here. Rather, the earth split open along an area called the Great Rift, spewing magma, ash and cinders over an area that covered hundreds of square miles. The volcanic activity began about 15,000 years ago and ended just 2,000 years ago. Scientists predict that the area will be subject to volcanic activity sometime again in the future.

A 52-site campground is located near the monument headquarters.

For further information on Craters of the Moon National Monument, see the MAJOR ATTRACTIONS section.   ▲★

Mile 205 (497.5): Scenic overlook. An easy 0.2-mile walk out to the point provides a much better view.

Mile 206 (496.5): Northern border of the Craters of the Moon National Monument.

Mile 209 (493.5): Turnoff to Blizzard Mountain Ski Area. Blizzard Mountain is one of several popular ski areas in central Idaho. ⛷

Mile 221 (481.5): Airport. No services.

Mile 222 (480.5): Big Lost River. This river flows along the surface, then disappears among the volcanic crevices at Big Lost River Sink east of Howe. The river is believed to reappear at the Snake River canyon near Hagerman in what is called Thousand Springs. The Big Lost is a favorite with trout fishermen during the summer. Good access. ⬲

Mile 223 (479.5): Atoms for Peace Historical Site describes the first peaceful use of atomic energy. On July 17, 1955, during an experimental project by the Atomic Energy Commission, Arco became the first town in the free world to be served by electrical energy developed from the atom. The energy was produced at the National Reactor Testing Station, now the Idaho Nuclear Engineering Laboratory (INEL), 23 miles east of Arco (see next milepost).

Mile 223.5 (479): ARCO (pop. 1,241) is a small agricultural community named (depending on who is telling the story) after a town in Austria; a Count Arco who was visiting in Washington, D.C., at the time; or an early resident, Arco Smith. It is the seat of Butte County and all services are available.

Junction with U.S. Highways 20/26. Access to the Idaho Nuclear Engineering Laboratory (INEL), 23 miles southeast via Highways 20/26.

Located at INEL is the Experimental Breeder Reactor No. 1. The first atomic reactor to produce usable amounts of electricity, EBR-1 opened in December of 1951. It is now a national historic landmark.

Tours of EBR-1 are available 7 days a week, 8 a.m. to 4 p.m., from Memorial Day weekend through Labor Day weekend. Guided and self-guided tours, movies and demonstrations. Fifty-two nuclear reactors have been built at INEL; 13 reactors are still operational.

Mile 231 (471.5): Big Lost River.

Mile 232 (470.5): MOORE (pop. 210). Gas and food available.

Mile 235.5 (467): Turnoff to Antelope Road.

Mile 238 (464.5): DARLINGTON, a small agricultural community. Food, gas available.

Mile 240.5 (462): Big Lost River. In springtime, flooding often occurs, so travelers may need to watch for detours in case of road washouts.

Mile 243 (459.5): Leslie, unincorporated village. No services available.

Mile 251 (451.5): MACKAY (pop. 541). All services available. This beautiful subalpine community is the destination for many outdoor enthusiasts and tourists. It is located between the Lost River Range to the north and the White Knob Mountains to the south. Mackay is a base for many deer and elk hunters in the fall heading into the Lost River Mountains, and the Sawtooth National Recreation Area at the headwaters of the Salmon River. MP 109

Mile 255 (447.5): Turnoff to Mackay Dam.

Mile 255.5 (447): Turnoff to Mackay Dam Reservoir and campground. Pit toilets, covered picnic tables, boat launch. Good summer fishing. ⊼ ⛵ ▲

Mile 256.5 (446): Turnoff to Mackay Reservoir and Battle Ground cemetery.

Mile 257 (445.5): Upper Cedar Creek Road. Sportsman access to Mackay Reservoir. MP 115

Mile 260.5 (442): Historical marker describes the discovery of the Lost River. Called Goddin's River after the fur trapper who explored the river in 1819-20, the Lost River was renamed by settlers because it sinks into the lava rocks of the desert area west of Idaho Falls. Also turnoff to Mackay Fish Hatchery 5 miles west.

Mile 262 (440.5): Lone Cedar Road.

Mile 266.5 (436): Trail Creek Road.

Mile 271.5 (431): Turnoff to Mount Borah (elev. 12,655 feet), the highest mountain peak in Idaho. The peak was named in honor of Idaho's popular Republican Sen. William Borah, "Lion of Idaho," who served as senator from 1907 until his death in 1940.

Mile 273 (429.5): Mount Borah Historical Marker and junction of a paved/gravel road to Stanley, the Sawtooth National Recreation Area and Sun Valley; Mount Borah is visible to the east.

According to geologists, as many as 12 inland seas once covered this area. The sea life is revealed in a layer of bones, shells, coral and limestone thousands of feet thick. The Lost River Range, of which Mount Borah is a part, is the result of an upward thrust in the earth's crust, exposing the sea floor and the fossils within it.

Mile 274 (428.5): Turnoff to May and Patterson.

Mile 278 (424.5): Sage Creek turnoff.

Mile 280.5 (422): Willow Creek Summit (elev. 7,161 feet).

Mile 283.5 (419): Turnoffs to Sheep Creek and Broken Wagon Creek.

Mile 286 (416.5): Turnoff on Spar Canyon Road to the East Fork Salmon River, a small, high-country cutthroat stream spilling from the Sawtooth National Recreation Area.

Mile 291 (411.5): Highway 93 passes through a small but beautiful gorge called Grand View Canyon.

Mile 297 (405.5): Lime Creek Road.

Mile 301 (401.5): Turnoff to Challis Hot Springs private campground on the Salmon River. ▲MP 159

Mile 302 (400.5): Salmon River. MP 160

Mile 302.5 (400): Junction with Highway 75 to Stanley, the Sawtooth National Recreation Area, the Sawtooth Wilderness Area and Sun Valley. See the SAWTOOTH VALLEY SCENIC ROUTE section.

Mile 305 (397.5): Turnoff to CHALLIS (pop. 1,290) city center. All services available. Challis was a trading center for the mining communities of the Stanley Basin and Salmon River, but as the mines petered out, ranching became the major economic base for Challis.

In the mid-1960s, Challis experienced another boom with the discovery of the mineral molybdenum (an alloy in the manufacturing of steel) southwest of the city. Cyprus Mines Corp. operates the mine and is the major employer in the area.

Challis is a major hunting, fishing and river rafting center for the Salmon River headwaters, Idaho Primitive Area and Lost River Range. The primitive road to Sunbeam from Challis, around 10,313-foot Bald Mountain, makes a scenic summer side trip that is likely to be interrupted with big game and scenery viewing stops. The Stanley/Challis area is tailored for the outdoorsman. who should allow plenty of time for stream and lake fishing, day hikes and big game photography. Check locally for current conditions.

Mile 310 (392.5): Challis Creek.

Mile 313.5 (389): Morgan Road, turnoff to Cobalt, Blackbird and Leesburg on a gravel road. All 3 were mining communities and none offer services to today's visitor. Cobalt and Blackbird were producers of the mineral cobalt, used as a high-temperature alloy for steel. Leesburg, established in 1866, was a gold mining camp which hosted as many as 7,000 miners. By the time the gold rush ended in 1870, Leesburg and two other towns, Smithville and Summit City, had produced an estimated $16 million in gold.

Mile 319 (383.5): Shotgun Road.

Mile 320 (382.5): Cottonwood recreation area. Picnic tables, restrooms. ⊼

Mile 322.5 (380): Community of Ellis, no services available. Ellis is located at the mouth of the Pahsimeroi River where it joins the Salmon River. This is also a turnoff to May and Patterson.

Mile 332.5 (370): McKim Creek Road.

Mile 341.5 (361): Community of Elk Bend. You are now in the Salmon River gorge. Food, gas, restaurant, motel and campground. The Lemhi Mountain Range is visible on the east and the Salmon River Mountain Range is on the west.

The Salmon River was first explored by the Lewis and Clark expedition in 1805. The Shoshoni Indians, who were recruited to help the explorers, referred to the stream as "The River of No Return," and warned the explorers that the river was not navigable. Only after attempting to travel downstream did the explorers decide the Indians were right.

Today the Salmon River offers some of the best white-water rafting in the nation, with world-class rapids attracting thousands of boaters each year. Contact the Salmon Chamber of Commerce for a list of outfitters for day trips and extended trips on the Middle Fork and main Salmon River.

The river offers some of the best salmon and steelhead fishing in Idaho. The early Indians called the river Tom-Agip-Paw, "Big Fish Waters," and today the name still holds true.

The Salmon River valley, including the Middle Fork, comprises one of the most celebrated sportsmen's destinations in the Northwest, and the largest and most remote roadless wilderness in the Lower 48, the Frank Church River of No Return Wilderness Area. ▲

Mile 344.5 (357): Turnoff to Rattlesnake Creek. MP 286

Mile 350 (352.5): Crossing the 45th parallel, halfway between the Equator and the North Pole.

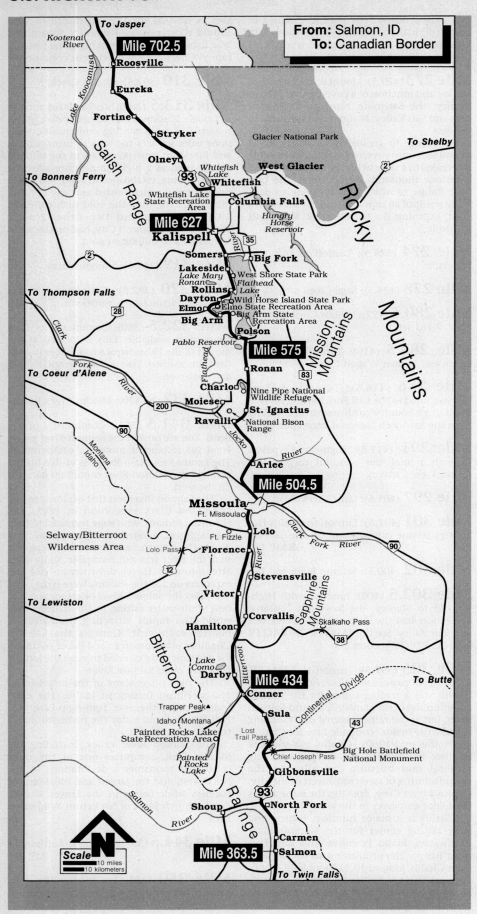

From: Salmon, ID
To: Canadian Border

Mile 358 (344.5): Turnoff to Williams Lake, Cobalt and the Shoupe Bridge Recreation Site. Williams Lake (elev. 4,500 feet) is 15 miles from the town of Salmon and is open from June to September. Food, lodging and boat rentals available. Campground with picnic tables, drinking water and a boat launch.

Mile 363 (339.5): Junction with Idaho Highway 28 to Leadore and Idaho Falls through the scenic Lemhi Valley.

Mile 363.5 (339): SALMON (pop. 3,308), the headquarters for many guides and outfitters and the recreational hub for the River of No Return area. All visitor services are available in Salmon. Salmon is a year-round recreation town offering hunting and fishing, white-water rafting, mountain climbing, snowmobiling and skiing. Steelhead fishing is very good in this area and incredibly popular. Local sporting goods stores provide solid information. Salmon thrives on its tourism industry, but ranching, logging and mining also have a significant impact on the community.

The Lemhi County Museum in Salmon has an extensive collection of Indian and early settler items. Some belonged to Chief Tendoy of the Lemhi Indians and others to Sacajawea's family. Tourist information is available at both ends of the business district.

Mile 367.5 (335): Highway crosses the Salmon River. Lemhi County Fair and Rodeo Grounds.   MP 309

Mile 368.5 (334): Unincorporated community of CARMEN has limited services. Highway crosses Carmen Creek. A historical marker here describes Fort Bonneville. On Sept. 26, 1832, Capt. B.L.E. Bonneville established a winter fur trading post in a grove of cottonwoods across the river. Flathead and Nez Perce Indians regularly camped near the fort.

Mile 374.5 (328): Highway crosses Tower Creek.

Mile 379.5 (323): Turnoff to Fourth of July Creek Campground.

Mile 380.5 (322): Entering Salmon National Forest.

Mile 383 (319.5): Wagonhammer Springs day-use area (elev. 3,700 feet) on the banks of the Salmon River is open from March to November. Picnic sites, drinking water, restrooms and fishing.

Mile 386 (316.5): Crossing the North Fork Salmon River. U.S. Forest Service information station and entering the unincorporated village of NORTH FORK. All services available. Lewis and Clark historical marker recalls the expedition's attempt to float the churning Salmon River in 1805.

Mile 387 (315.5): North Fork Salmon River.

Mile 389.5 (313): Box Springs Loop Road and turnoff to Indian Peak (elev. 7,763 feet) and Cummins Lake.

Mile 390.5 (312): Turnoff to Hughes Creek.

Mile 391.5 (311): Hughes Creek Field Station for the Salmon National Forest.

Mile 392.5 (310): Turnoff to Sheep Creek toward Stein Mountain (elev. 8,555 feet). Nearly all of these small creeks offer fair to excellent fishing for native trout. 🐟

Mile 395 (307.5): Turnoff to Granite Mountain (elev. 6,354 feet).

Mile 396.5 (306): Crossing Dahlonga Creek and entering the village of **GIBBONSVILLE**, an old gold mining camp established in 1877 and named after Col. John Gibbon, the man who led the ill-fated attack on Chief Joseph's band of Nez Perce Indians on the Big Hole River in Montana during the Nez Perce War.

Gibbonsville is now an unincorporated village with phone, gas, groceries and campground available. ▲MP 337

Mile 400.5 (302): Deep Creek Historic Site. Lewis and Clark's passage through the canyon from Idaho to Montana is recounted.

Mile 402 (300.5): North Fork Salmon River and turnoff to Twin Creek Campground (elev. 5,100 feet) which has 46 campsites, picnic areas, drinking water, fishing and hunting access. The campground is located on the historic Lewis and Clark Trail and is open from June to September. 🧺🐟▲

Mile 410.5 (292): Crossing the Idaho-Montana border and passing through Lost Trail Pass (elev. 6,995 feet) and the turnoff to the Lost Trail Ski Area. This is the junction with Montana Highway 43 east to the Big Hole National Battlefield, an impressive national monument which recalls that portion of the Nez Perce War. The Big Hole National Battlefield is approximately 15 miles east, and it is one of the best roadside attractions of its kind in the Northwest. If you're not pressed for time, make a point to visit it. On the way there, you will cross Chief Joseph Pass (elev. 7,241 feet).

You are now at the southern end of the Bitterroot Valley, passing between the Bitterroot Mountains to the west, the Beaverhead Mountains to the southeast and the Anaconda Range to the northeast.

The name Bitterroot refers to a plant which, as one might suspect, has a bitter-tasting root. The Flathead Indians (also called Salish Indians) had discovered that the plant grew in abundance along the Bitterroot River and called the stream Spet-Im-Seulko, or "the water of the bitter-root." Lewis and Clark also encountered the plants and gave the name Bitterroot to the mountain range, valley and river. ★MP 351

Mile 411.5 (291): The skeleton trees on

the west side of the highway are the victim of the mountain pine beetle. The beetles killed approximately 57 million trees on more than 1.3 million acres in the Big Hole Valley and surrounding area between 1926-38. To avoid infestations now, the Forest Service acts promptly when the insects are discovered and all overmature trees are harvested as quickly as possible.   MP 1

Mile 417.5 (285): Turnoff to Indian Trees Campground on the Camp Creek Road. The campground has 18 campsites, trailer spaces, drinking water and toilets. ▲

The Blackfoot and Bitterroot rivers meet the Clark Fork River at Missoula. (L. Linkhart)

Mile 420.5 (282): Ross Hole Historic Site and Recreation Area. On March 12, 1824, Alexander Ross of the Hudson's Bay Co. brought 55 Indian and white trappers, 89 women and children and 392 horses to camp near this spot en route from the Spokane House to the Snake River country. The group camped nearly a month here while attempting to break through the deep snow to the Big Hole, and because of their hardships, Ross called this basin, "The Valley of Troubles."

Entering the town of **SULA**; food, gas, campground. This area is best known as the spot where the Lewis and Clark expedition met the Shoshone Indians. ▲

Mile 421.5 (281): Sula Creek ranger station, Bitterroot National Forest. Junction with Reimel Creek Road.   MP 11

Mile 426 (276.5): East Fork Bitterroot River and the turnoff to Spring Gulch Forest Service Campground with 9 campsites, trailer spaces, drinking water and toilets. Southwest of the highway via a side road are Warm Springs and Crazy Creek Forest Service campgrounds, each with about 12 campsites, drinking water and toilets. Lewis and Clark historical marker here.

Private campground at the junction. ▲

Mile 428.5 (274): Highway crosses the east fork of the Bitterroot River.

Mile 431 (271.5): A 400-year-old ponderosa pine tree on the curve of the river has been the subject of an Indian legend which indicates that the tree is a Medicine Tree. A historical marker relates the story.

Mile 434 (268.5): Junction with road west to **CONNER** (a small community with all services available), Boulder Creek Forest Service Campground and the Painted Rocks State Recreation Area. Boulder Creek Campground, 13 miles southwest of Conner, has 11 campsites, a picnic area, trailer space, toilets and fishing access.

Painted Rocks State Recreation Area, 20 miles southwest, is located on Painted Rocks Lake. The Slate Creek Campground there has 28 campsites, picnic areas, trailer space, drinking water, boat launch, swimming and fishing access.

Painted Rocks Lake, also called the West Fork Bitterroot Reservoir, was drawn almost dry in 1973, but the fishery is reviving and several thousand cutthroat trout have been planted in recent years.

Private campground is also at the junction. 🏊🧺🐟▲

Mile 436.5 (266): Rye Creek.

Just north of Rye Creek is the turnoff for Hannon Memorial fishing access on the Bitterroot River. There are several public fishing access points along the Bitterroot River in this stretch of highway. The West Fork Bitterroot River joins the main Bitterroot just north of Conner.   🐟MP 26

Mile 437 (265.5): Junction with road southwest to Painted Rocks State Recreation Area (see **Mile 434**). Trapper Peak Conservation Corps Center and West Fork Road. Highway crosses the Bitterroot River.

Mile 438 (264.5): Trapper Peak (elev. 10,157 feet) is visible to the west. It is the highest peak in the Selway-Bitterroot Wilderness Area.

Mile 441 (261.5): **DARBY** (pop. 581), a small resort/ranching community on the banks of the Bitterroot River. All services are available. Darby was established as the terminus of the Northern Pacific Railroad and named after postmaster James Darby in 1889.

Darby has survived 3 fires that destroyed its main street. One of the premier attractions of this small, friendly community is the Darby Pioneer Memorial Museum in Council Park which shows the early settlement of Darby from 1800 to 1888.

Mile 446 (256.5): Turnoff to Lake Como, about 3 miles to west; 12 campsites, 2 picnic sites, trailer spaces, drinking water, toilets, boat launches and fishing for rainbows. Before the irrigation season Lake Como is one of the most pristine lakes in Montana. At the end of the summer, it is an ugly victim of drawdown, mud flats and turbidity. Wally Crawford fishing access to east. 🐟▲

Mile 446.5 (256): Durland Park (day-use area) on Lick Creek.　🖾

Mile 448 (254.5): Lick Creek Campground.　▲

Mile 448.5 (254): Lost Horse Creek.

Mile 454 (248.5): Junction with Montana Highway 531 West to several cross-country ski trails, Lost Horse Creek, Twin Lakes, Mud Lake.

Bear Creek Pass Campground, 18 miles west, offers 7 campsites and toilets.　▲

Mile 454.5 (248): Bitterroot River. U.S. Highway 93 crosses the Bitterroot several times on its way to Missoula.

Mile 455 (247.5): Turnoff to Anaconda via Montana Highway 38 over Skalkaho Pass. This becomes a narrow, winding gravel road and, although scenic, is not a major thoroughfare.

Mile 455.5 (247): Skalkaho Creek.

Mile 458 (244.5): Junction of Montana Highways 269 and 531 to several ranches and **HAMILTON** (pop. 2,661). Hamilton is the county seat of Ravalli County; a beautiful little town that serves as the business center for the Bitterroot Valley. All services are available including 9 motels and 25 restaurants.

The "Copper King," Marcus Daly, who was responsible for the development of much of western Montana, was also responsible for the development of Hamilton. He built a mansion, complete with a swimming pool and a stocked lake. The stables he constructed were called Tammany Stables after one of his race horses. The mansion is still privately owned and not available for public tours. Daly was instrumental in having the county seat moved from Stevensville to Hamilton.

The architecturally unique courthouse now houses the Ravalli County Museum with 2 floors of excellent Indian and mining exhibits, along with many of Daly's personal holdings on display.

Hamilton is the home of the Rocky Mountain U.S Public Health Laboratory, the facility which developed the vaccine for Rocky Mountain spotted fever, and is currently working on AIDS research.

Another research facility, the Ribi Immuno Chem Research Center, a privately funded cancer research facility, is also located here.

Mile 460 (242.5): Bitterroot River.

Mile 461 (241.5): Roadside tables, no water.　🖾

Mile 462.5 (240): Junction with Montana Highway 373 to **CORVALLIS**, a small, rural farming community. Corvallis was originally settled a few miles from its present site by Elija and Margaret Chaffin who came to the Bitterroot Valley in 1864. They wintered here then moved to Oregon, but returned in 1866 to the present townsite and named the community Corvallis, which means "center of the valley."　MP 52

Mile 466.5 (236): Tucker Crossing fishing access.　MP 56

Mile 470 (232.5): **VICTOR**, a small community with gas, food and campground. Originally named Garfield, after the president, it was renamed for Chief Victor of the Salish tribe. The town was first settled in the mid-1860s.　▲

Mile 471.5 (231): Junction with Montana Highway 370 which leads to a rural area east of Victor, and fishing access to Big Creek and the Bitterroot River.　🐟

Mile 472 (230.5): Bell Crossing fishing access to east.　🐟

Mile 477 (225.5): Junction with Montana Highway 269 to **STEVENSVILLE** (pop. 1,207), St. Marys Mission, Montana's first Christian mission (founded by Father DeSmet), and Fort Owen State Monument. All services in Stevensville. Metcalf National Wildlife Refuge is located east of town.

Mile 478 (224.5): Kootenai Creek trail which leads to North, Middle and South Kootenai lakes (a 12-mile walk on a good trail). Fishing for brook trout in South Kootenai Lake; rainbows in North Kootenai.　🐟

Mile 480 (222.5): Dr. Charles Waters Recreation Area, named in honor of the man who studied the life history and control of forest tree diseases on this site.

The recreation area, 2 miles west of the highway, includes Charles Waters Memorial Campground, with 17 sites, and the Larry Creek day-use area, with 10 picnic sites. Fishing in Larry Creek is fair for small rainbow and cutthroat trout.　🖾🐟▲

Mile 482 (220.5): Poker Joe fishing access to the Bitterroot River on the north end of the Lee Metcalf Wildlife Refuge. The refuge has nesting osprey and Canada geese as well as mallards, wigeon, teal, redheads, scaup and wood ducks. Marsh birds, including the great blue heron, are common during the summer. Wildlife includes deer, muskrat, fox, mink, beaver, raccoon, skunk and an occasional bear and moose.

Fishing is not permitted within the boundaries of the reserve, but hunting is permitted in portions of the reserve, subject to federal and state regulations. Hunters are required to check in and out at hunter check stations.

Mile 485 (217.5): Entering the village of **FLORENCE**; food, gas, restaurant. The highway is flanked by the Bitterroot Mountains to the west and the Sapphire Mountains to the east.

Junction with Montana Highway 203 across the Florence bridge spanning the Bitterroot River.

Mile 487 (215.5): Chief Looking Glass fishing access to the Bitterroot River and Recreation Area offering 3 picnic areas, drinking water and toilets.　🖾🐟

Mile 493 (209.5): Travelers Rest Historical Site. This is the site of the Lewis and Clark expedition's camp on Sept. 9-10, 1805, where they prepared to cross the Bitterroot Mountains via Lolo Pass. As they secured venison for the trip, the explorers were told of an Indian road up Hells Gate leading to the buffalo country east of the main Rocky Mountain Range.

On their return trip, they again camped here from June 30 to July 3, 1806, and Lewis decided to take the Indian "Road to the Buffalo," while Clark and his men headed east via the Big Hole, Beaverhead, Jefferson and

White-water enthusiasts float down the Blackfoot River.　(L. Linkhart)

Gallatin valleys and the Yellowstone River. The two parties reached their rendezvous at the mouth of the Yellowstone within 9 days of each other.

Mile 494 (208.5): Junction with U.S. Highway 12 at **LOLO**. All services available. U.S. Highways 12 and 93 share a common alignment to Missoula. (See U.S. HIGHWAY 12 section for log).

Mile 500 (202.5): Crossing the Bitterroot River.

Northbound travelers may turn on Reserve Street to bypass downtown Missoula. Reserve junctions with Highway 93 near the airport.

Mile 504.5 (194): Crossing the Clark Fork River in **MISSOULA** (pop. 33,353), the seat of Missoula County, with all services available.

Missoula is a pleasant city located at the confluence of 3 major rivers: the Clark Fork, Bitterroot and Blackfoot. It is the home of the University of Montana, a 181-acre campus serving more than 9,000 students in 47 buildings.

Other attractions in Missoula include the Greenough Mansion, located at 102 Ben Hogan St., built in 1897 by Thomas Greenough. It was moved from its original location and is now the home of the Leisure Highlands Golf Course Clubhouse and a restaurant. The house is constructed of tamarack, native to Montana.

Greenough Park provides a beautiful 1-mile drive through a wooded area beside Rattlesnake Creek. The park, donated from the Greenough estate to the city of Missoula, features a landscaped picnic area and wading pool.

Fort Missoula Historical Museum, at the corner of South Avenue and Reserve Street, was established in 1877 as one of the first military posts in Montana. It now serves as the home for National Guard and Reserve units. Displays on the 28-acre reserve depict the industrial development of the West from 1880 to 1920. The Indoor Gallery has a schedule of changing exhibits. The complex is open from noon until 5 p.m. daily, except Monday.

The Memorial Rose Garden on Highway 93 was established in 1947 by the American Rose Society and maintained as a memorial to the casualties of WWII. More than 2,500 rose plants are maintained at the garden.

One of the unique facilities of Missoula is the Smokejumpers Center, located at Johnson Bell Airport on U.S. Highway 93. Here, smokejumpers are trained for the dangerous and difficult task of forest fire suppression. The Northern Forest Fire Laboratory is also located here. Scientists study the nature and characteristics of forest fires to better understand and help aid in the suppression of forest fires. The complex is open for visitors from May 15 through July 1, 8 a.m. to 4 p.m., weekdays; and from July 1 through the end of September, 9 a.m. until 5 p.m. daily.

The beautiful St. Francis Xavier Church, located at 420 W. Pine, was built in 1889, the year Montana became a state. It features a graceful steeple, stained-glass windows and

The University of Montana at Missoula opened in 1895. *(L. Linkhart)*

mural paintings by a Jesuit brother, Joseph Carignano, a kitchen helper, unschooled in art but later recognized as a master. Carignano also painted the 58 murals and frescoes at the famous St. Ignatius Catholic Mission south of Polson (see **Mile 547.5**).

The paintings of another muralist, Edgar Samuel Paxson, may be viewed at the Missoula County Courthouse from 8 a.m. until 5 p.m. weekdays. The artist is perhaps most famous for his painting of "Custer's Last Stand," completed in 1899. Eight murals, painted between 1912 and 1914, decorate the walls of the courthouse.

After crossing the Clark Fork River, northbound travelers turn west on Broadway for continuation of Highway 93. (Travelers may also access Interstate 90 west via Orange Street or Reserve Street and take Exit 96 for continuation of U.S. Highway 93 north.)   MP 94

Mile 511 (191.5): Missoula airport and Missoula city limits.

Mile 512.5 (190): Northern Fire Laboratory, U.S. Forest Service Regional Fire Depot and Smokejumper School (see **Mile 504.5**).

Mile 515.5 (187): Junction with Interstate 90 West to Spokane, WA, and Interstate 90 East to Missoula. Travelers headed east or west on the interstate, turn to **Mile 472** in the INTERSTATE 90 section for log of that route.   MP 0

Mile 516 (186): Junction with the Frenchtown Frontage Road.

Mile 522.5 (180): Southern border of the Flathead Indian Reservation. Fishermen should secure a tribal fishing permit from the Tribal Fish and Game Dept.   MP 7

Mile 532 (170.5): Junction with Montana Highway 559.

Mile 533 (169.5): Turnoff to the Jocko

Montana's National Bison Range

The National Bison Range, located off Montana Highway 200 near Ravalli at **Mile 542.5**, was originally set aside as a conservation and redevelopment area for American bison, commonly called buffalo. The area has been instrumental in the comeback of the magnificent animals which can be viewed in a natural habitat throughout the area. Many of the buffalo now found throughout the West originated from buffalo stock at this preserve.

The hilly, arid rangeland also provides excellent photographic and view opportunities for elk, mule and white-tailed deer, pronghorns and bighorn sheep. Forty mammal species and 187 bird species inhabit the vast range. Mountaintops on the range were once islands in ancient Lake Missoula, an ice-age lake that once covered 3,300 square miles in Montana and Idaho.

In these steep hills and narrow canyons live some 300 to 500 bison, remnants of the huge herds that once thundered over the plains of the Midwest.

In addition to the bison, some 75 to 100 elk, 100 to 200 mule deer, 100 to 200 white-tailed deer, 100 bighorn sheep and between 50 to 100 pronghorn (antelope) inhabit this reserve.

Visitors to the National Bison Range may take the self-guided auto tour to see and photograph the animals in their native habitat. If you choose to take the tour, remember that buffalo are unpredictable and dangerous. Remain in your car at all times.

One of the annual highlights of the bison range is the October bison roundup when excess animals are separated. In September the bulls, engorged with the rutting instinct, engage in terrific, spectacular battles, and in late September to early October the massive bull elk make the hills ring with their bugling challenges and massive antlers clash in combat for herd domination.

During the heat of the summer months, the best viewing will be shortly after dawn before the big game animals retreat to the protection of their trees, brush and creek wallows. Anytime, however, you are likely to enjoy a close-up look at some of North America's most magnificent big game animals.

Be aware that travelers are encouraged to remain near their vehicles for protection and that the area is heavily populated by rattlesnakes. Caution and common sense will make this trip memorable, however.

For further information on the National Bison Range, write Range Manager, National Bison Range, Moiese, MT 59824 or call (406) 644-2211.

(Paul Fugleberg)

One of the largest remaining herds of American buffalo is at the National Bison Range, accessible from Mile 542.5.

River trout hatchery and entering the village of Arlee, an unincorporated town that serves as a trading center for people of the Jocko Valley.

Mile 534.5 (168): Jocko River, named in honor of Jacques "Jocko" Raphael Finley who was a trapper and trader for the North West Co. and the Hudson's Bay Fur Co. in the mid-1800s. The Jocko River offers good fishing for rainbow. Private campground.   ⌐▲

Mile 542.5 (160): Community of **RAVALLI**, and the junction with Montana Highway 200 to Thompson Falls. Ravalli is a small, unincorporated village with limited services.

Highway 200 is also the southern turnoff to the National Bison Range, visible in the hills to the northwest. The bison range includes a staffed visitors center and an excellent gravel road 19-mile (self-guided) loop tour of the vast wildlife area.

Mile 546.5 (156): Mission Valley Historical Marker explains the history of this area. The Pend Oreille tribe inhabited the area before the white settlers came, and the valley is now a reservation for the combined Pend Oreille, Flathead and Kootenai tribes. MP 31

Mile 547.5 (155): Turnoff to St. Ignatius Mission National Historic Site. The mission was established by Jesuit missionaries in 1854. Although plain brick on the outside, the mission is brilliantly appointed inside with 58 wall murals and frescoes painted by Joseph Carignano in 1901-02. The artist was a cook at the mission and painted the critically acclaimed murals in his spare time. He was untrained in art or painting, but his works are considered among the finest religious murals in the West, and bear striking resemblances to the famous murals appearing in European cathedrals.

Mile 548 (154.5): Entering the town of **ST. IGNATIUS** (est. pop. 1,000). All services available. Private Indian museum and trading post.

Mile 554 (148.5): Fort Connah scenic turnout. The fort was built by the Hudson's Bay Co. as a trading and trapping post in 1847, the last trading post built by Hudson's Bay in the U.S.

Mile 555.5 (147): Crossing Ninepipe National Wildlife Refuge. The refuge was established in 1921 and includes one of the premier bass fishing and waterfowl rearing areas in western Montana. The refuge is divided into 2 segments, the Ninepipe Refuge and the Pablo Refuge, about 15 miles to the north. Both are maintained as federal wetlands for waterfowl and marsh birds and both refuges are closed to hunting. Fishing is allowed (all floating vehicles are banned) on Ninepipe for bass and perch, Pablo Lake for rainbow.

A Flathead tribal permit is required to fish either lake, but photography, picnicking and bird-watching are free. A picnic area is

(Paul Fugleberg)

A houseboat is one way to enjoy popular Flathead Lake; Mile 575.

provided at the north end of Ninepipe Reservoir. Additional information, including a bird list, is available by contacting the Range Manager, National Bison Range, Moiese, MT 59824.   ⛌ ⊶ MP 41

Mile 556.5 (146): Junction with Montana Highway 212 to Charlo, Moiese, the National Bison Range and access to Ninepipe National Wildlife Refuge. Flathead tribal recreation permits (required to hunt and fish on tribal lands, including Ninepipe and Pablo refuges) are available in Charlo and Moiese.

Mile 558.5 (143): Mission Mountains scenic turnout. The dramatic Mission Mountain Range, located in the 73,877-acre Mission Mountains Wilderness Area, dominates the eastern horizon. A sign at the turnout identifies the individual peaks and their elevations. Roadside picnic tables are available. The wilderness area offers excellent backpacking, alpine lake fishing and is home to a good population of grizzly bears.

Mile 561.5 (141): Junction with Montana Highway 211 and entering the town of **RONAN** (pop. 1,530). The Garden of the Rockies Museum, operated by the Mission Mountain Heritage Assoc., is located in Ronan. All services are available.   MP 47

Mile 564.5 (138): Private campground.
                                 ▲

Mile 565.5 (137): Turnoff to **PABLO**

(est. pop. 300) and the headquarters for the Flathead Indian Reservation. Food, gas.

Mile 572 (130.5): Scenic turnout.

Mile 573.5 (129): Junction with Montana Highway 35 to Big Fork on the northern bank of Flathead Lake.   MP 59

Mile 575 (127.5): **POLSON** (pop. 2,798), the county seat for Lake County and recreational hub for southern Flathead Lake. During the summer, Polson's population swells as vacationers and part-time residents return to enjoy the beauty and bounty of Flathead Lake. All services available.

Flathead Lake, the single biggest tourist attraction in the area, is 28 miles long and 15 miles wide. It is the largest body of fresh water between the Mississippi River and the Pacific Ocean. Sailing, canoeing and waterskiing are popular summer activities, but the lake is renowned for its fishing opportunities. Twenty-six species of fish have been documented in Flathead Lake, 11 naturally occurring and 17 introduced or exotic. The target of most fishermen are kokanee, bull trout, cutthroat and mackinaw. More than 300,000 fish are pulled from the waters of Flathead Lake each year.

Wild Horse Island north of Polson is Montana's newest state park, complete with a resident herd of bighorn sheep. Other wildlife on the island include deer, songbirds, waterfowl, eagles, falcons, mink and coyotes. The park makes for excellent hiking and

picnicking. This is a day-use area only, accessible only by boat. Rental boats are available at commercial marinas on Flathead Lake.

For more than a century people have reported seeing a large creature, similar to the Loch Ness Monster in Flathead Lake. In 1982, the "monster" was sighted 3 times within 4 days. The existence of the Flathead Lake Monster cannot be verified, so it is placed in the same category as the Sasquatch, which allegedly roams the Cascade Range.

Kerr Dam, completed in 1938, is a spectacular structure 54 feet higher than Niagara Falls. It is situated on the Flathead River 2 miles downstream and helps stabilize the water level of Flathead Lake.

Mile 585 (117.5): Melita Island Road.

Mile 586 (116.5): Turnoff to Walstad Memorial State Recreation Area and LaBella Lane. The recreation area is primarily an access point to the lake. There is a parking lot and boat ramp and this is one of the easiest places to launch a boat for Wild Horse Island. The recreation area is a day-use area only with drinking water, toilets, a boat launch and fishing access.

Mile 588 (114.5): Community of **BIG ARM**. This is a small community comprised of residences and resorts on the west bank of the Flathead. No services available.

Mile 589 (113.5): Big Arm State Recreation Area offers 35 campsites with trailer spaces, toilets, drinking water, swimming area, fishing access and boat launch. There is a fee. ⌒▲

Mile 591.5 (111): Small community of ELMO; gas and food.

Mile 592 (110.5): Junction with Montana Highway 28 to Hot Springs (30 miles), a small, natural hot springs resort community southwest of Flathead Lake.

Mile 593 (109.5): Turnoff to Elmo State Recreation Area which offers 35 campsites with trailer spaces, toilets, boat launch and fishing access. ⌒▲

Mile 594 (108.5): Northern border of the Flathead Indian Reservation.

Mile 597.5 (105): Small community of DAYTON (no services) and turnoff to Lake Mary Ronan, Lambeth Memorial State Recrea-

tion Area and community of Proctor.

Lambeth Memorial State Recreation Area, on the banks of Lake Mary Ronan, is 7 miles west from Highway 93. The recreation area offers 20 campsites with trailer spaces, toilets and fishing access.

Lake Mary Ronan, in heavily timbered hill country, hosts a state campground, 2 resorts and a handful of private homes. The lake offers excellent fishing for kokanee, rainbows and largemouth bass. ⌒▲

Mile 602 (100.5): ROLLINS, a small community on the west bank of Flathead Lake. Limited services.

Mile 607 (95.5): Turnoff to West Shore State Park which has 30 campsites with trailer spaces, drinking water, toilets, a boat launch and fishing access. Fee. ⌒▲

Mile 613 (89.5): Community of LAKE-SIDE (pop. about 600), another small resort

community on Flathead Lake. All services available. Lakeside has 3 motels and 2 RV parks. ▲

Mile 618 (84.5): Turnoff to SOMERS (pop. about 300). No services.

Mile 619 (83.5): Turnoff on Highway 82 which connects with Montana Highway 35 south to Big Fork and access to the eastern side of Flathead Lake.

Mile 624.5 (78): Junction with Montana Highway 317. The Flathead Range is visible east of the highway and the Swan Range is just southwest of the Flatheads.

Mile 625.5 (77): Junction with Montana Highways 503 and 93.

Mile 627 (75.5): KALISPELL (pop. 10,648) is the largest community between Missoula and the Canadian border. It is also the seat of Flathead County. All services available.

The town has been called several names since the mid-1800s, including Gregg's Landing, Greggsville, Scooptown and Demersville. Demersville was located 4 miles south of the present city of Kalispell and when the Great Northern Railway was complete in 1891, the city moved and the name was changed.

Kalispell is a word taken from the Pend Oreille (pon-doe-RAY) Indians meaning either "camas" or "the prairie above the lake," depending on who is doing the translating.

Recreation is a major industry in Kalispell. It is a gateway to Glacier National Park (30 miles to the east), a base for skiers enjoying the popular Big Mountain Ski Area (17 miles north) and a home port for those enjoying the facilities at Flathead Lake (7 miles south).

The Conrad Mansion, completed in 1895, is one of the most beautiful examples of turn-of-the-century architecture in the Northwest. It was donated to the city of Kalispell in 1975 and the building has been completely restored. The furnishings in the home are also original, giving visitors an authentic taste of 19th century Montana. The home was originally built for Charles E. Conrad who made his fortune in the water commerce on the Missouri River from 1868 to 1891. The home is open daily for guided tours. Admission is $4 for adults and $1 for children.

Woodland Park is a favorite location in Kalispell for picnicking among the beds of flowers and the lagoon. It is located off Woodland Avenue and Conrad Drive.

Junction with U.S. Highway 2 west to Libby and U.S. Highway 2 east to Glacier National Park. Travelers exiting onto U.S. Highway 2 should refer to **Mile 159.5** in the U.S. HIGHWAY 2 section.

Mile 630.5 (72): Junction with Montana Highway 548.

Mile 631 (71.5): Stillwater River, previously a poor fishing stream, has been restored. It is now good to fair fishing for cutthroat and some northern pike. ⌒

Mile 640 (62.5): Junction with Montana

Ptarmigan Wall and icebergs in Iceberg Lake at Glacier National Park. (© John Barger)

Highway 40, which provides a 4.5-mile connection with Highway 2. U.S. Highway 2 leads east to Columbia Falls and West Glacier, the resort community at the entrance to Glacier National Park. For details, turn to **Mile 150.5** in the U.S. HIGHWAY 2 section.

Mile 642 (60.2): Turnoff to Big Mountain Ski Area, Whitefish Lake and the community of Whitefish on Montana Highway 487.

WHITEFISH (pop. 3,749) is a resort community with an ideal location as a base for tourists and vacationers. Big Mountain Ski Area, 8 miles north, is one of the largest and most popular ski resorts in Montana with more than 25 miles of ski runs, 3 triple chair lifts, 2 double chair lifts, a T-bar and platter lift, ski rental shop and instructors. It is open from late November through April.

Seven-mile-long Whitefish Lake offers fishing, swimming and boating.

Whitefish got its start as a division point on the Great Northern Railway.

Mile 643 (59.5): Grouse Mountain Lodge, golf course and Logan's Bar and Grill.

Mile 644 (58.5): Whitefish Lake State Recreation Area and the Tally Lake ranger station for the Flathead National Forest. The recreation area offers 25 campsites with trailer spaces, drinking water, toilets, a swimming area, fishing access and a boat launch. Fee.

Whitefish Lake is one of the nation's best mackinaw (lake) trout producers. The lake also offers some whitefish, cutthroat, bull trout, brook trout and a few largemouth bass.

Mile 646 (56.5): Skyles Lake, fishing access. Fishing here is moderately good for rainbows and cutthroats.

Mile 647 (55.5): Tally Lake, 15 miles west of Highway 93 on Forest Service Road 113, has a Forest Service campground with 36 campsites and trailer spaces, toilets, drinking water, fishing access, swimming and a boat launch. The lake is the deepest in the state at nearly 500 feet. Fishing is generally poor.

Mile 655 (47.5): Border of the Stillwater State Forest.

Mile 659 (43.5): Good Creek and turnoff to Westana Girl Scout Camp and Lower Stillwater Lake. Lower Stillwater was polluted by a lumbermill and offers poor fishing.

Mile 660 (42.5): Headquarters of the Stillwater State Forest.

Mile 660.5 (42): Community of OLNEY (0.5 mile west), Old Fort Steele Road and Whitefish Road. Olney is a small community with food and gas. You are between the Whitefish Mountain Range to the east and the Salish Range to the west.

Mile 665.5 (37): Ewing Fish Lake Road.

Mile 672 (30.5): Border of the Stillwater State Forest.

Bighorn sheep and other wildlife are often seen in Glacier National Park. (© John Barger)

Mile 673.5 (29): Community of STRYKER (no services) and border of the Kootenai National Forest (Kootenai, spelled Kootenay in Canada, is an Indian word meaning "deer robes"). Turnoff to Fish Lake, also called Stryker Lake, which is a small, deep lake excellent for brook trout.

This is also the turnoff to South Dickey Lake Campground; 2 campsites, 5 picnic areas, drinking water, toilets, boat launch, swimming and fishing access. Don't be surprised to spot a moose along the roadside anywhere in the Kootenai.

Mile 678 (24.5): Scenic overlook and turnoff to North Dickey Lake Campground with 16 campsites, 5 picnic areas, drinking water, toilets, boat launch, swimming and fishing access. MP 163

Mile 680 (22.5): Murphy Lake ranger station. Murphy Lake, a small, swampy lake, difficult to fish, produces some 8- to 10-inch rainbows and brookies. MP 165

Mile 682.5 (20): Deep Creek Road and turnoff to FORTINE and Meadow Creek Road. Fortine is a small community with limited services.

Mile 685.5 (17): Grave Creek Road to Big and Little Therriault lakes. Big Therriault Lake has a Forest Service campground with 11 campsites with trailer space, a boat launch, fishing access and trails. The Forest Service campground at Little Therriault Lake has 6 campsites with trailer space, toilets, fishing access and trails. Fishing at both lakes is fair.

Mile 690 (12.5): Glen Lake Road.

Mile 692 (10.5): Sinclair Creek Road to Glen Lake. Although the little Glen Lake hosts hordes of suckers, it's still good for rainbows and kokanee.

Mile 692.5 (10): Tobacco Plains Historic Site. Canadian and British fur-trapping agencies established posts along the Kootenai River during the late 19th century. Tobacco Plains was named for the Indians who planted tobacco for religious reasons.

Mile 694 (8.5): Outskirts of the town of EUREKA (pop. 1,119). All services available. Visitor information located at south end of town.

The town was originally called Deweyville, but was changed to Eureka in 1909. Formerly a sawmill town, Eureka has expanded its economy to include farming and the production of Christmas trees. The town hosts the Tobacco Valley Historical Village and Museum, an interesting look at turn-of-the-century Montana. At the south end of town is the first cabin built in Eureka in 1890. One of the main attractions of Eureka is Libby Dam and Lake Koocanusa (see **Mile 696**).

Mile 694.5 (8): Roadside tables, no restrooms.

Mile 696 (6.5): Junction with Montana Highway 37 to Libby Dam and Lake Koocanusa. You are 6.5 miles south of the U.S.-Canada international border. Restaurants, gas, motel at junction.

Lake Koocanusa's name is derived from KOOtenai-CANada-USA and is the backwaters of Libby Dam. The 90-mile-long lake offers good to excellent fishing for rainbow and cutthroat.

Mile 702.5 (0): United States-Canada international boundary and crossing the Pacific-Mountain time zone line. Turn your watches back one hour if you are headed north; forward one hour if you are headed south. *NORTHWEST MILEPOSTS*® travelers headed north on Canada Highway 93 should turn to the CANADA HIGHWAY 93 section for log.

Canada Highway 93

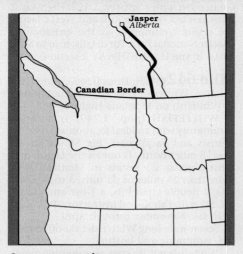

See map opposite page.

Canada Highway 93 takes travelers through some of the most spectacular scenery on the continent. From the headwaters of the Northwest's mighty Columbia River, the highway climbs into the Canadian Rockies, famous for picture-postcard views of ruggedly beautiful scenery.

The stretch of Highway 93 between Lake Louise and Jasper is known as the Icefields Parkway. This scenic 140 miles/225 km of road traverses Banff and Jasper national parks in the central Canadian Rockies.

Canada Highway 93 begins at the U.S.-Canada border near Roosville, where U.S. Highway 93 ends. (Turn to the U.S. HIGHWAY 93 section for log of that route.)

Canada Highway 93 Log

Distance in miles from the Canadian border is followed by distance in miles from Jasper, AB. Equivalent distances in kilometers are indicated by Km.

Mile 0 (362) Km 0 (582.5): United States-Canada international border and crossing the Pacific-Mountain time zone line. Turn your watch back one hour if you are headed north; forward one hour if you are headed south.

For details on crossing the border, see Customs Requirements in the GENERAL INFORMATION section.

Mile 4.5 (357.5) Km 7 (575.5): Community of ROOSVILLE. All services available.

Mile 9 (353) Km 14.5 (568): GRASMERE, a small agricultural and timber center. Limited services.

Mile 14.5 (347.5) Km 23 (559.5): Elk River bridge near the river's mouth on Lake Koocanusa.

Mile 25 (337) Km 40.5 (542): Junction with Highway 3 just west of the community of Elko (limited services).

BC Highway 93 and Crowsnest Highway 3 share a common alignment the next 35 miles/55 km westbound to the junction with BC Highway 95 at **Mile 60**.

Travelers heading east on Highway 3 turn to **Mile 118.5** in the CROWSNEST HIGHWAY 3 section for log of that route.

Mile 26.5 (335.5) Km 42.5 (540): Road south to Baynes Lake (2.5 miles/4 km); fishing for eastern brook trout; also access to Kikomun Creek Provincial Park (7 miles/11 km) on Lake Koocanusa, a man-made lake created by the building of the Libby Dam across the Kootenai River in Montana. The provincial park has 74 campsites, sani-station, picnic area, swimming, fishing, hiking trails and boat launch. 🏕 🛶 ▲

Mile 29 (333) Km 47 (535.5): Caithness Creek rest area.

Mile 33 (329) Km 53.5 (529): Canadian Pacific Railway station and sawmill at community of GALLOWAY.

Mile 35.5 (326.5) Km 57 (525.5): Gravel road north to Rosen Lake (just off highway); rainbows and cutthroat trout. Gas and food at junction. 🛶

Mile 37 (325) Km 59.5 (523): Unincorporated community of JAFFRAY, south of highway. Road to Tie Lake Regional Park, 2.5 miles/4 km; day use only. Also access south to Kikomun Creek Provincial Park (see description **Mile 26.5**).

Mile 42.5 (319.5) Km 68.5 (514): Wardner-Fort Steele Road leads 4 miles/6.5 km north to Kootenay trout hatchery. Station raises rainbow, eastern brook, kokanee, lake and cutthroat trout for stocking lakes throughout the Kootenay and Cariboo areas. Aquarium displays of native fish. Open year-round, 8 a.m. to 4 p.m.

This road also provides access to Norbury Lake Provincial Park, 10 miles/16 km; 46 campsites, picnic area, fishing, swimming, boat launch (no powerboats). Hiking trails to spectacular views of The Steeples, serrated rock peaks of the Hughes Range. Interpretive display explains the Sun Dance of the Kootenai Indians. Fee charged, May to September.

This side road continues north to junction with Highways 93/95 at Fort Steele (see **Mile 63.5**). 🏕 🛶 ▲

Mile 43.5 (318.5) Km 70 (512.5): Kootenay River bridge at the north end of Lake Koocanusa. West of the bridge, a side road leads to the small community of WARDNER, a boom town during construction of the CPR's Crowsnest Pass line. Its benefactor, James Wardner, also established a town in Idaho.

Also access to Wardner Provincial Park on the west side of Lake Koocanusa; picnicking, swimming, and fishing for Dolly Varden, cutthroat and whitefish. A nearby commercial campground provides lake and river cruises. 🏕 🛶 ▲

Mile 48 (314) Km 78 (504.5): Turnout and stop of interest marker describes the days of steamboating on the Kootenay River between Fort Steele and Jennings, MT.

Westbound, the highway climbs out of the Kootenay Valley.

Mile 57 (305) Km 91.5 (491): Rampart rest area.

Mile 60 (302) Km 95.5 (487): Junction with Highways 95 and 3. Highway 93 shares a common alignment with Highway 95 north to Radium Hot Springs and with Highway 3 the next 35 miles/55 km eastbound. Highway 3 (Crowsnest) leads west to Hope. Westbound travelers turn to **Mile 153** in the CROWSNEST HIGHWAY 3 section for log of that route.

Mile 63.5 (298.5) Km 102 (480.5): Kootenay River bridge. Ahead, old waterwheel marks location of Fort Steele. Junction with Wardner-Fort Steele Road and access west to FORT STEELE PROVINCIAL PARK, a restored and reconstructed turn-of-the-century mining town and North West Mounted Police post. The park is open dawn to dusk, daily year-round, but park activities are scheduled only during summer months. From June to September, park staff wear period dress and visitors may watch them baking, spinning, weaving, and blacksmithing, among other skills. There is a musuem and tea room, theater with live vaudeville, and stagecoach and steam train rides. Admission fee ($5 adults) charged in summer. ★

Mile 66 (296) Km 106.5 (476): Rest area by small lake.

Mile 69.5 (292.5) Km 111.5 (471): Gravel turnout with litter bins provides good viewpoint over the Kootenay River valley and nearby marshes. Mountains in the background are the Purcells.

Mile 74 (288) Km 119 (463.5): Wasa Slough Provincial Bird Sanctuary.

Mile 75 (287) Km 121 (461.5): Road east to community of **WASA** (gas, food and lodging) and to Wasa Provincial Park on the east side of Wasa Lake. Park has 104 campsites, sanistation, picnic area, excellent beaches, swimming, waterskiing, fishing and boat launch.

Mile 77 (285) Km 123.5 (459): North road to Wasa Lake.

Mile 78 (284) Km 126 (456.5): Kootenay River bridge. North of the bridge is the junction with Highway 95A south to Kimberley and Cranbrook. To the east, the ragged peaks of the Rockies.

Mile 79 (283) Km 127.5 (455): Wasa rest area beside the Kootenay River.

Mile 83 (279) Km 134 (448.5): Road west to pulp mill at Skookumchuk. This road also goes to Tamarac Lake; rainbows to 3½ pounds (artificial flies only).

Mile 86 (276) Km 138.5 (444): Kootenay River bridge.

Mile 86.5 (275.5) Km 139 (443.5): Settlement and railway station of **SKOOKUM-CHUCK** on river of same name. Skookumchuck is Chinook jargon for "strong water." Good fishing here for cutthroat and Dolly Varden, best late summer to fall. Road east to Premier Lake Provincial Park, 8.5 miles/14 km in the Hughes Range of the Rocky Mountains. Good place to see Rocky Mountain bighorn sheep, elk and deer. The provincial park has 41 campsites, picnic area, boating, fishing, boat launch (no waterskiing). Premier Lake and 3 others within the park have a good reputation for rainbow and eastern brook trout. Eggs from Premier Lake fish are collected for the Kootenay fish hatchery near Wardner; an interpretative display near fish trap explains the procedure.

Mile 87 (275) Km 140 (442.5): Gravel turnout to north with good view of pulp mill.

Mile 87.5 (274.5) Km 141 (441.5): North access to Premier Lakes Road.

Mile 98.5 (263.5) Km 158.5 (424): Gravel turnout to north side with litter bins. Stretch of old highway nearby is a good place to walk dogs or kids.

Mile 100 (262) Km 161.5 (421): Road east to Whiteswan Lake Provincial Park, 13.5 miles/ 22 km, and Top of the World Provincial Park, 34 miles/55 km. Road is rough, used by logging trucks; extreme caution is advised.

Whiteswan Lake park has 100 campsites, picnic areas, fishing, swimming, boat launch. Camping fee. Both Alces and Whiteswan lakes are kept well-stocked with rainbow trout. (Alces

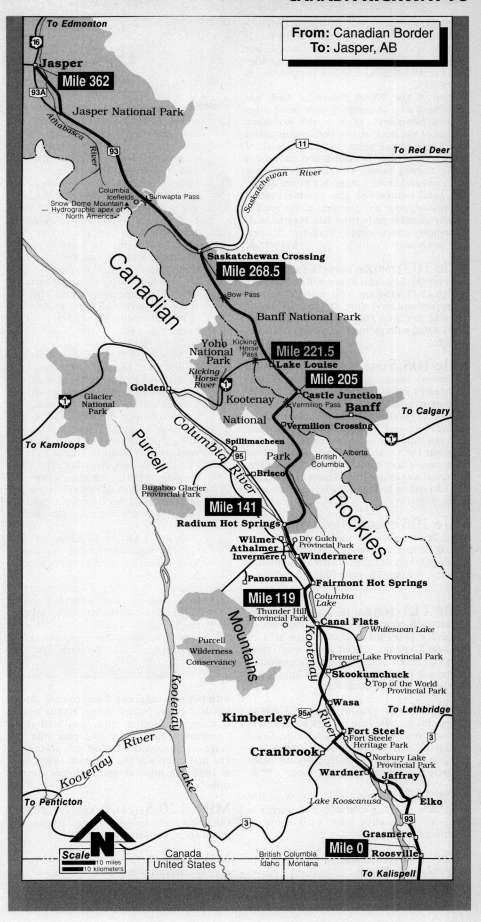

From: Canadian Border
To: Jasper, AB

Lake, no powerboats and fly-fishing only.)

Lussier Hot Springs is located at the park's western end. Springs are undeveloped, but rated as excellent, with a pool built from logs and a small bathhouse. Water temperature is 109°F/43°C.

Top of the World Provincial Park has wilderness walk-in camping only (road stops at park boundary). High in the Kootenay Ranges of the Rockies, the park encompasses superlative alpine areas, with a network of trails to the high meadows and mountain peaks. Fishing in well-stocked Fish Lake for cutthroat and Dolly Varden is a prime attraction. Small cabin at Fish Lake provides limited accommodation; fee charged. Access road is usually passable only from late May to mid-November; check locally. Park hut is open May to October. 🚶🏕⛺▲

Mile 103 (259) Km 166 (416.5): Kootenay River bridge. Road east to sawmill community of CANAL FLATS (pop. 825), with gas station, restaurant and food store. On the east side of the lake is Canal Flats Provincial Park, 2.5 miles/4 km, with picnic area, swimming, boat launch. 🏕

Mile 105.5 (256.5) Km 169.5 (413): Stop of interest marker commemorating Baillie-Grohman's canal. In 1886 William Baillie-Grohman conceived a grand scheme to connect the Kootenay and Columbia rivers by means of a canal. The canal and 1 lock were built but only 2 ships made the passage. Not only was the canal too narrow and shallow, but it caused flooding of the Columbia Valley. The canal was abandoned. Traces of it and the lock can still be found in the scrub brush west of the highway.

Mile 106 (256) Km 170.5 (412): Findlay Creek Road leads west to Thunder Hill Provincial Park; 23 campsites on hillside overlooking Columbia Lake. Nearby are remnants of tramway to the Thunder Hill lead and silver mine.

Mile 113 (249) Km 181.5 (401): Rest area to east with picnic tables and good view of Columbia Lake. Interpretive sign tells of the East Kootenay Colonization Road, built from Fort Steele to Golden in anticipation of settlement on Baillie-Grohman's land holdings beside the Kootenay River. 🏕

Mile 116.5 (245.5) Km 187.5 (395): Narrow bridge over Dutch Creek by spectacular hoodoo cliffs of yellow sandstone. Good fishing in Dutch Creek for Dolly Varden, cutthroat, rainbow and whitefish. Tourist facilities here include camping, gas, food. 🍴▲

Mile 117 (245) Km 188.5 (394): West Side Road takes off along west side of Windermere Lake, an alternative back road route to Invermere.

Mile 118.5 (243.5) Km 190.5 (392): Columbia River bridge.

Mile 119 (243) Km 191.5 (391): FAIRMONT HOT SPRINGS, a resort community

B.C. Highway 95
Radium to Golden

Highway 95 splits off Highway 93 at the Radium Junction (**Mile 141.5**) and continues north through the Rocky Mountain Trench to Golden on Trans-Canada Highway 1. Bird-watchers will love this route. The Columbia River valley is a major migration flyway and the unspoiled wetlands provide nesting grounds for many kinds of water birds. There are probably more osprey here than anywhere else in the province, and eagles are fairly common. Nesting platforms have been built for geese and there are colonies of great blue herons. Deer, elk and moose are most often seen in spring and fall and there are beaver and muskrat. Best way to see the wildlife is to travel down the river by canoe.

Mile 0 Km 0: Junction of Highways 93 and 95 at Radium Hot Springs.

Mile 6.5 Km 11: Junction with road to Edgewater, a small community with accommodations, food, gas, pub.

Mile 8.5 Km 14: Luxor Creek, also crossed on embankment. Near the mouth of the creek is Luxor whistle-stop on the Canadian Pacific Railway. Paddle-steamers provided the only transportation through the valley from the CPR line at Golden south to the end of Columbia Lake. The first steamboat to navigate this route was the *Duchess* in 1886.

Mile 11 Km 18: Deadman's Creek. Northbound, watch for the "Cauliflower Tree," a Douglas fir distorted by witches broom virus.

Mile 15.5 Km 25: Community of Brisco; general store. Access to Bugaboo Creek forestry road (rough; logging trucks) which leads 28 miles/45 km west to Bugaboo Glacier Provincial Park and Alpine Recreation Area. The park

is undeveloped. Strenuous hike in. A favorite for rock climbers.

Mile 18 Km 29: In a meadow to the east is tiny log church of St. Mark, built in 1896.

Mile 22 Km 36: Small settlement of SPILLIMACHEEN; post office, gas, store. Access to Bugaboo Park and West Side Road to Invermere.

Mile 28.5 Km 46.5: Community of HARROGATE; general store, gas station.

Mile 32 Km 52: CASTLEDALE community under the slopes of Castle Mountain.

Mile 34 Km 55: Large turnout with good view of Columbia Valley. Notice the nesting boxes erected on stilts above the water to keep Canada goose nests safe from predators. Bed-and-breakfast accommodations nearby.

Mile 40.5 Km 65.5: PARSON, a sawmill and logging community; gas, store, community hall. Gold-panning in Canyon Creek is said to be worthwhile.

Mile 55.5 Km 89.5: Loop road to community of NICHOLSON, today mostly a suburb of Golden.

Mile 61 Km 98.5: Columbia River bridge; south of the bridge is Golden Tourist Office in the red train caboose. Golden is an important junction point for the Canadian Pacific Railway: its main east/west line is joined by a north/south line up the Columbia from the Crownest area of the Kootenays. The Crownest cars carry coal from the open-pit mines. As many as 20 long coal trains a day lumber through Golden on their way to the deep sea coal ports at Roberts Bank, south of Vancouver.

Mile 62 Km 100: Junction with Highway 1. For information on Golden, see **Mile 154** in the TRANS-CANADA HIGHWAY 1 section.

with hot mineral pools, 2 golf courses, downhill and cross-country skiing, tennis courts, airplane sightseeing trips, and trail rides. Community has an RV site, plus villa and lodge accommodations, food, gas, post office. The first resort was the Fairmont Hotel, built in 1888. The mineral springs do not contain sulfur. 🍴▲

Mile 120.5 (241.5) Km 194 (388.5): Columbia Lake Indian Reserve. Indians are members of the Kootenai tribe.

Mile 125 (237) Km 201 (381.5): To the east, Indian mission church.

Mile 129 (233) Km 208 (374.5): Junction with loop road to WINDERMERE (pop. 580),

a resort settlement on the east shore of Lake Windermere. Settlement dates from about 1887, the steamboat era. Kokanee spawn in Windermere Creek in September and October, a feast for hordes of bald eagles.

Mile 131 (231) Km 210.5 (372): A llama ranch, east side of road.

Mile 133.5 (228.5) Km 214.5 (368): Chamber of commerce tourist information chalet, open May to September. Junction with road west around north end of Windermere Lake to communities of Athalmer, Wilmer and Invermere. (Opposite the junction is a fine example of Tyrolean architecture: the Black Forest Restaurant.)

ATHALMER was known to local Indians as

"Salmon Beds" because of the spawning salmon; later it became an important port of call for steamboats. Today it is site of Athalmer Beach Provincial Park on the lakeshore, with picnic tables and a fine beach for swimming and water sports.

WILMER was a mining town, riding the fortunes of the rich Parridice Mine. Today, there is bed-and-breakfast accommodations at Delphine Lodge. This restored turn-of-the-century hotel is famous for its home cooking and the country teas served in the garden.

North of Wilmer up Toby Creek Road is the year-round resort community of PANORAMA, with accommodations, ski hill, helicopter skiing, cross-country skiing, tennis, trail riding and white-water rafting.

INVERMERE (pop. 2,000) is a summer resort community, with public beaches at Dorothy Lake Park and Kinsmen Beach. Full tourist facilities; good shopping, food and services.

The first fur-trading post west of the Rockies was established on Lake Windermere by David Thompson in 1807. Known as Kootenae House, it was located at the mouth of Toby Creek between Invermere and Wilmer. A stone cairn and commemorative tablet mark the spot.

Hikers may wish to drive 20 miles/32 km up Toby Creek Road to the start of the historic Earl Grey Pass Trail in the Purcell Wilderness Conservancy. The trail follows Itamill Creek to Kootenay Lake south of Avgenta. Trail climbs to 7,400 feet. Hike takes about 3 days.

Mile 135 (227) Km 217 (365.5): Shuswap Indian Band Office, east side. Higher up the hillside is Father de Smet's church. The Belgian missionary, first in the area, came up the Columbia in the 1840s, crossing the Rockies on foot. He called this area the Plain of the Nativity and erected a large wooden cross near the church.

Mile 138.5 (223.5) Km 223 (359.5): Road east to Dry Gulch Provincial Park; 25 campsites on the lower slopes of the Stanford Range of the Rockies. Landscape is generally arid but despite its name, there is a creek in Dry Gulch. Rocky Mountain bighorn sheep winter in the park and surrounding area. ▲

Mile 140 (222) Km 225 (357.5): Stop of interest sign commemorating James Sinclair who led 200 Red River settlers from Fort Garry (today's Winnipeg) across the Rockies and down the Columbia to Oregon in an attempt to hold the territory for Great Britain in 1841. Good view of Rocky Mountain Trench and Columbia River.

Mile 140.5 (221.5) Km 226 (357): One of 3 viewpoints over Columbia River valley and its rich sloughs. Notice the white silt deposits eroded into hoodoo formations along the hillsides.

NOTE: All viewpoints are on the west side of the road. Safer access is for southbound traffic.

Mile 141 (221) Km 227 (355.5): RADIUM HOT SPRINGS (area pop. 1,000). This unincorporated resort community spreads out alongside the highway; full tourist services. Hot mineral pools are a chief attraction and there is also a luxury golf resort (open April to October), river rafting on the Kootenay and Kicking Horse rivers, a water slide and a children's playland. On the hillside, the Queen of Peace Shrine attracts many visitors.

Mile 141.5 (220.5) Km 227.5 (355): RADIUM JUNCTION, tourist facilities including gas, food and accommodations and tourist information kiosk. Highway 95 continues north along the Rocky Mountain Trench to Golden, Highway 93 goes east into the Rockies. (Highway 93 travelers continue with

The golden mantle ground squirrel emerges in spring. (L. Linkhart)

this log. (See feature on BC Highway 95 between Radium Junction and Golden in this section.) Road east to Redstreak Campground in Kootenay National Park. Camp has 242 sites, 7 kitchen shelters, showers, sani-station. Hiking trails (one goes directly to the hot springs aquacourt) and nature programs in summer months. ▲

Mile 142 (220) Km 228.5 (354): Kootenay National Park gate. Visitors planning to stay overnight in any of the national parks should have a permit, $3 for one day; $6 for four days; $20 all year. Park information office and restrooms are just east of the gate.

Turnout north side and beginning of Juniper trail, a 2-mile/3-km walk leading through Sinclair Canyon and on to the hot springs. Park here and walk up the road to photograph Sinclair Canyon.

Mile 142.5 (219.5) Km 229 (353.5): Sinclair Canyon. Highway passes through narrow cleft in high, vertical limestone walls.

Gap was cut by action of gushing Sinclair Creek. There are viewpoints north and south of the canyon; best time for photos is late afternoon.

Mile 143 (219) Km 230.5 (352): Resort facilities on both sides of the road, with 2 outdoor hot mineral pools, steam rooms, plunge baths, changing rooms and adjacent restaurant. This section of road is full of pedestrians in summer: Drive with care.

Springs gushing from the Redwall Fault at the base of Redstreak Mountain daily pour mineral water at temperatures between 95°F/35°C and 116°F/47°C into the pools. The water contains calcium, sodium, magnesium, potassium and other minerals. The springs were originally called Sinclair but were changed to Radium in 1915 because of the water's relatively high radioactivity.

Mile 143.5 (218.5) Km 231 (351.5): Large parking area opposite cliffs of limestone and dolomite breccia stained red by iron oxides in the mineral water. In spring and fall, bighorn sheep are often seen on the north side of the canyon here. Trails to aquacourt and Redstreak Creek, a short hike along the creek's canyon. Northbound the highway goes through a short tunnel known as the Iron Gates then follows fast-flowing Sinclair Creek up to the pass.

Mile 146.5 (215.5) Km 236 (346.5): Kimpton Creek trail, 2.8-mile/4.8-km hike through the forest providing good views of avalanche slides.

Mile 147.5 (214.5) Km 237.5 (345): Picnic area beside Sinclair Creek.

Mile 148.5 (213.5) Km 239 (343.5): Kindersley Pass trail leads west to the divide on the Brisco Range and on through high alpine meadows to connect with Sinclair Creek trail, a 7-hour circuit.

Mile 149 (213) Km 239.5 (343): Sinclair Creek trail up into alpine meadows. Picnic area by well-named Olive Lake.

Mile 149.5 (212.5) Km 240.5 (342): Sinclair Pass Summit (elev. 4,875 feet/1,486m). Brisco Range to the west, Stanford Range to the east.

Mile 151 (211) Km 243 (339.5): Cobb Lake trail. Fishing for eastern brook, cutthroat and rainbow trout. Fishermen should obtain a fishing permit and a copy of national parks regulations.

Mile 151.5 (210.5) Km 243.5 (339): Viewpoint overlooking the Kootenay River valley and the long ridge of the Mitchell Range with its prominent horizontal strata. The highway here turns abruptly north and begins a long descent to the Kootenay River. *WARNING:* Trucks use low gear.

Mile 154 (208) Km 247.5 (335): Settler's Road southeast to park boundary; connects with forest road which continues down the

Kootenay River to Canal Flats. This is the route by which pioneer priest Father Jean de Smet is believed to have crossed the Rockies on his way east to missionary work among Alberta's Blackfoot Indians. Logging trucks exit this way; drive with care.

Mile 156 (206) Km 251 (331.5): Kootenay River picnic site. Good views of Mitchell and Vermilion ranges to the east; Brisco Range to west. Nixon Creek trail, an easy hike to small forest lake.

Mile 158 (204) Km 254 (328.5): McLeod Meadows picnic area; good place for observing Columbia ground squirrels (usually known as prairie dogs). Trail to Dog Lake, 1.5 miles/2.4 km, across river begins here.

Mile 158.5 (203.5) Km 255 (327.5): McLeod Meadows campsite; 98 sites, 5 kitchen shelters, sani-station, nature program in summer months.

Mile 159 (203) Km 256 (326.5): Viewpoint of Mount Harkin. Mountain is the most prominent in the Mitchell Range to the east and was named for the first commissioner of national parks. Columbia ground squirrels have a colony here.

Keep a sharp lookout for elk along this stretch of the Kootenay River valley. An estimated 300 of the large animals range in Kootenay National Park throughout the year; they are most often at river level in spring and fall.

Mile 163.5 (198.5) Km 263.5 (319): Dolly Varden picnic area with rustic kitchen shelters. Dolly Varden River joins the Kootenay near here.

Mile 168 (194) Km 270 (312.5): Roadside turnout with signs commemorating the opening of the first road from Banff to Windermere in 1923.

Mile 168.5 (193.5) Km 271.5 (311): Kootenay River bridge and Kootenay Pond picnic area to the north. Small lake here is believed to be a kettle, formed by a stranded block of glacial ice buried in the gravels. When the ice block melted, gravels slumped to form deep-sided pond. Highway turns into the Vermilion River valley for its climb up to Vermilion Pass.

Mile 170 (192) Km 274 (308.5): Hector Gorge viewpoint. Turnout provides splendid view into the gorge of the Vermilion River, with the Mitchell Range on the east, the Vermilion Range to the west. The gorge was named for Dr. James Hector, a geologist who explored the area in 1858.

Mile 171 (191) Km 275 (307.5): Rocky Mountain goats are often seen just above the highway here on the lower slopes of Mount Wardle. Their white coats make identification easy. River beside road is milky green with glacial sediment.

Mile 171.5 (190.5) Km 276 (306.5): Hector Gorge picnic area.

Snowmobile tours of Athabasca Glacier are available at Mile 299.5.   (© John Barger)

Mile 174 (188) Km 280.5 (302): Wardle Creek picnic area.

Mile 175 (187) Km 282 (300.5): Roadside turnout with drinking water from a major freshwater spring.

Mile 175.5 (186.5) Km 282.5 (300): Animal lick. Moose, elk and deer come down to the river here for mineral salts from the river's mud banks. Best times for viewing are early morning and evening.

Mile 176 (186) Km 283.5 (299): Monument to George Simpson, governor of the Hudson's Bay Co., who came down the Simpson and Vermilion rivers in 1841 searching for a better, more southerly route for his fur traders to cross the Rockies. He found the way impractical for the brigades.

Mile 177 (185) Km 284.5 (298): Viewpoint. Bridge across river leads to the Mount Shanks fire lookout and Simpson River trail. The Simpson River trail provides access to isolated Mount Assiniboine Provincial Park.

Mile 179 (183) Km 288 (294.5): If the weather is clear, you might catch a glimpse of Mount Assiniboine, known as the Matterhorn of the Rockies, from this viewpoint. Look southeast; at 11,870 feet/3,618m, it is one of the highest peaks in the Rockies.

Mile 180 (182) Km 290 (292.5): Community of **VERMILION CROSSING**; lodge, gas, groceries, food. Picnic area near river bridge. Start of Verdant and Verendrye Creek trails.

Mile 181 (181) Km 291 (291.5): Viewpoint of Mount Verendrye (elev. 10,124 feet/3,086m), and the craggy cliffs of the Rockwall.

Mile 185 (177) Km 298 (284.5): Trails to Floe Lake, 6 miles/10 km west, and Hawk Creek to Ball Pass, east. Floe Lake is named for the small blocks of ice which break off from Floe Glacier and float on the lake like small icebergs.

Mile 190 (172) Km 306 (276.5): Access road west across the river to Numa picnic area and trail up Numa Creek. North of the bridge, Vermilion River tumbles into picturesque falls.

Mile 193 (169) Km 311 (271.5): Paint Pots nature trail crosses river to area of brightly colored earth along Ochre Creek. Here red and yellow clays have been stained by deposits of iron from cold mineral springs. Indians from both sides of the Rockies used to come here to collect the ochre clay for body paint and for pictographs. Later, the ochre was mined and shipped to Calgary for use as a paint base. Traces of mining activity remain.

Mile 194.5 (167.5) Km 313 (269.5): Marble Canyon Park warden station. Stop here for information or to register for trails. Trails to Tumbling Glacier and Ottertail Pass begin at bridge.

Mile 195 (167) Km 313.5 (269): Marble Creek Campground; 62 sites, 2 kitchen shelters, sani-station. Start of 1-mile/2-km return hike along rim of Marble Canyon, a deep gorge worn by Tokumm Creek into the gray-and-white limestone rock. In several places, the limestone has been changed by pressure into marble, best seen at the upper end of the canyon where the waterfall gushes over a marble slab.

Mile 197 (165) Km 317 (265.5): Trail to Stanley Glacier, 3 miles/4.8 km. The 4-hour hike leads to a spectacular hanging valley and alpine glacier.

The highway north from here leads through the site of the Vermilion Pass forest fire started by a lightning strike in 1968. Notice the young lodgepole pines, the first to return after the fire. 🚶🚶

Mile 199 (163) Km 320 (262.5): Vermilion Pass (elev. 5,382 feet/1,640m) on the Great Divide of the Rocky Mountains. Waters east flow into the Bow River and thence to Hudson Bay; waters west flow into the Columbia River and the Pacific Ocean. The pass is boundary between British Columbia and Alberta, and Kootenay and Banff national parks.

Fireweed nature trail leads in a short loop through a section of the burn area, providing a good chance to see forest self-regeneration at work. Wildflowers here are excellent.

Mile 200 (162) Km 322 (260.5): Vista Lake viewpoint. Good views of Storm Mountain (elev. 10,370 feet/3,161m) to the south, and Vista Lake in the valley. Trail starts from the viewpoint down to Vista Lake, a 1-hour hike and up the flanks of Storm Mountain to Arnica Lake, 3.3 miles/5.3 km and Twin Lakes, 4.7 miles/7.6 km. East from the viewpoint are Castle Mountain and the Sawback Range. 🚶🚶

Mile 200.5 (161.5) Km 323 (260): Boom Creek picnic area in a stand of spruce/fir forest which escaped the big fire. Trail to Boom Lake, 3.1 miles/5.1 km, begins here. 🚶🚶🏕

Mile 202 (160) Km 325 (257.5): Storm Mountain Lodge, built in 1923 as a Canadian Pacific Railway hostelry. Sold to private interests and modernized, it retains much of the rustic charm of earlier times. Excellent views of Castle Mountain and the Vermilion Pass burn may be had from the viewpoint across the road. Highway northbound begins steep descent into the Bow River valley; trucks use low gear.

Mile 205 (157) Km 330 (252.5): Castle Junction. Junction with Trans-Canada Highway 1. Highways 1 and 93 share a common alignment between Castle Junction and Lake Louise. Turn north on Highway 93 for Lake Louise and Icefields Parkway. Turn south on Trans-Canada Highway 1 for Calgary (see **Mile 88.5** in the TRANS-CANADA HIGHWAY 1 section for log).

Also access at this junction to Highway 1A, a scenic alternate route between Lake Louise and Banff which also provides access to Johnston Canyon, Castle Mountain and Protection Mountain campgrounds.

Mile 210.5 (151.5) Km 338.5 (244): Taylor Creek picnic area and trail to Taylor Lake, 3.9 miles/6.3 km. The highway is bordered by dense, even stands of lodgepole pines, trees that grow first after a forest fire. West of the picnic area, the original spruce forest remains. 🚶🚶🏕

Mile 216.5 (145.5) Km 348.5 (231): Rest area by the Bow River.

Mile 217.5 (144.5) Km 350 (232.5): Lake Louise overflow campsite. ▲

Mile 219.5 (142.5) Km 353 (229.5): Bow River bridge.

Mile 221.5 (140.5) Km 356.5 (226): Exit to **LAKE LOUISE** village and visitor information office. Access to Highway 1A and Protection Mountain Campground; 89 campsites. See description of Lake Louise village at **Mile 104** in the TRANS-CANADA HIGHWAY 1 section.▲

Mile 222 (140) Km 357.5 (225): Hiking trail up Pipestone River. 🚶🚶

Mile 222.5 (139.5) Km 358 (224.5): Junction with Trans-Canada Highway 1. Highways 1 and 93 share a common alignment between Lake Louise and Castle Junction. Jasper-bound travelers turn north on Highway 93. Turn to **Mile 105** in the TRANS-CANADA HIGHWAY 1 section.

The slab of reddish slate at the junction is among the park's oldest formations, dating from 600 million years ago.

This stretch of Highway 93 is known as the Icefields Parkway and is perhaps the most scenic and certainly the most varied of all the roads in the Canadian Rockies. Keeping just to the east of the Great Divide, the highway climbs 2 passes, Bow Summit and Sunwapta, to take motorists to the edge of alpine terrain. The parkway is well-named for more than 100 glacial remnants of the last ice age are visible along its route.

NOTE: There is no gas along this route for the next 49 miles/78 km northbound.

Mile 224 (138) Km 360.5 (222): Herbert Lake, with picnic area at north end. Surrounding forest is lodgepole pine. Good views south from the lakeshore of Mounts Temple, St. Piran, Niblock and Whyte. The lake is known as a "sink" because it has no visible outlet. Unlike other mountain lakes it warms in summer to reasonable temperatures and is popular for swimming. 🏕

Mile 230.5 (131.5) Km 371 (211.5): Hector Lake viewpoint, named for Dr. James Hector, geologist of the Palliser expedition, who was the first white man up this valley in 1858. Above the lake is the Waputik Range (Indian for "white goat") with its glacier mantle. Pulpit Peak (elev. 8,940 feet/2,725m), which rises above the lake's north end, is forested with alpine larch, the most northerly stand of this deciduous conifer in the Rockies. Look for glacially carved cirques (bowl-shaped depressions) high on the mountains' flanks.

Mile 231.5 (130) Km 373 (209.5): Hector Lake trail down to a ford across the Bow River and on to the lake. 🚶🚶

Mile 233 (129) Km 375 (207.5): Mosquito Creek Campground; 32 sites, kitchen shelter and a youth hostel. Across the Bow River can be seen the sandstone cliffs of Bow Peak (elev. 9,409 feet/2,868m); Mount Hector (elev. 11,135 feet/3,394m) is to the southeast. Across the highway from the campsite, Mosquito Creek trail leads up to Molar Pass, 6.2 miles/10 km. 🚶🚶▲

Mile 241 (121) Km 388 (194.5): Dark green rock beside the road is part of the formation known as the Crowfoot Dike, the only known occurrence of igneous rock in Banff National Park. The dike was formed by molten lava forcing its way up through the sedimentary rock.

This is the Crowfoot Glacier viewpoint. To the west, Crowfoot Mountain is hung with blue ice. At the turn of the century, this glacier had 3 tongues or toes, hence its name. Today, only 2 remain as the glacier retreats. Park panorama points out the mountains within view. Across the highway, trailhead for Helen Lake (good wildflowers in July), 3.7 miles/6 km; Katherine Lake, 5 miles/8 km; and Dolomite Pass, 5.5 miles/8.9 km, where Banff's only woodland caribou can sometimes be seen. 🚶🚶

Mile 241.5 (120) Km 389 (193.5): Bow Lake viewpoint and picnic area. Bow Lake, in summer a brilliant turquoise, is headwater for the Bow River; it is ice-covered until June. At the far end of the lake is red-roofed Num-ti-jah Lodge, built in the 1920s by pioneer guide Jimmy Simpson. The mountain above the lake was named after him. 🏕

Mile 243.5 (118.5) Km 392 (190.5): Road to Num-ti-jah Lodge, which provides meals and accommodations year-round. Good view of the icefalls of the Bow Glacier at the head of the valley. Trail starts here to the lodge and on to Bow Glacier Falls, 3 miles/5 km, which tumble 492 feet/150m over a wall of sandstone below the foot of the glacier. Packhorse trips from the lodge into the mountains are operated by Peyto Tours. 🚶🚶

Mile 245.5 (116.5) Km 395 (187.5): Bow Summit (elev. 6,788 feet/2,069m). Junction with short road west to Peyto Lake viewpoint. The glacial meltwater lake, a brilliant turquoise from suspended glacial sediments pouring in from Peyto Glacier, lies some 787 feet/240m below viewpoint. Short but steep trail leads from viewpoint to lakeshore. Mistaya Valley north of the lake is U-shaped, scoured by ancient glaciers. The highway follows this valley until the river flows into the North Saskatchewan River.

Mile 249 (113) Km 400.5 (182): Peyto Glacier viewpoint. To the southwest, the tongue of the Peyto Glacier falls from the Wapata Icefield, flanked by Mount Thompson and Peyto Peak. Trail leads down to Peyto Lake from opposite side of road. Signs explain the formation of cirques.

Mile 250.5 (111.5) Km 403 (179.5): To the west, Snowbird Glacier tumbles down the face of Mount Patterson. Notice the prominent morainal ridges, marking the glacier's former limits.

Mile 253 (109) Km 407 (175.5): Silver Horn Creek overflow campsite. ▲

Mile 255.5 (106.5) Km 411 (171.5): Viewpoint, Upper Waterfowl Lake; Mount Chephren (elev. 10,715 feet/3,266m), the abrupt pyramid to the north, and Howse Peak (elev. 10,794 feet/3,290m). Notice the 2 very prominent cirques in the rock wall of the Great Divide. Watch for moose in the braided river marshes at the lake's southern end.

Mile 256 (106) Km 412 (170.5): Waterfowl Lakes Campground; 116 sites, 7 kitchen shelters, sani-station, amphitheater. Trail to Cirque and Chephren lakes in the glacially carved cirques above, starts at the rear of the campsite.

The highway runs beside Lower Waterfowl Lake and there are several good turnouts for photography and wildlife observation. 🚶🚶▲

Mile 264.5 (97.5) Km 426 (156.5): Viewpoint with mountain markers for the 3 Kaufmann peaks, Mount Murchison (elev. 10,935 feet/3,333m) and Mount Wilson (elev. 10,630 feet/3,240m). Turnout and trail to Mistaya Canyon. Here the river has worn a deep, twisting gorge into the limestone bedrock and tumbling boulders have eroded round potholes. Bridge crosses gorge and trail continues to Howse Pass, 16 miles/26 km. David Thompson of the North West Co. crossed the Rockies this way in 1807 to set up a trading post west of the mountains (near today's Invermere). The pass was the main fur-trading route across the Rockies for 5 years until blockaded by Peigan Indians. Pass was named after Thompson's rival, Joseph Howse, who later came this way for the Hudson's Bay Co. 🚶🚶

Mile 266.5 (95.5) Km 429 (153.5): Saskatchewan River Park warden station.

Mile 268 (94) Km 431 (151.5): Viewpoint over the Mistaya and Howse River valleys. Both rivers flow into the Saskatchewan near here.

Mile 268.5 (93.5) Km 432 (150.5): SASKATCHEWAN CROSSING; all services available (some only in summer). Junction with Highway 11, which follows the North Saskatchewan River east through the mountains to Rocky Mountain House (112 miles/180 km) and Red Deer (160 miles/257 km).

Mile 269 (93) Km 433 (149.5): Trail to Glacier Lake, 5.5 miles/9 km. 🚶🚶

Mile 275 (86.5) Km 443 (139.5): Rampart Creek Campground; 50 sites, 4 kitchen shelters and a youth hostel. The highway follows the North Saskatchewan River. Watch for moose. ▲

Mile 276.5 (85.5) Km 445 (137.5): Viewpoint of Mount Amery (elev. 10,941 feet/3,335m), Mount Saskatchewan (elev. 10,964 feet/3,342m) and tiny Cleopatra's Needle on the ridge. The needle, also known as the Lighthouse Tower, is a dolomite pinnacle.

Mile 278.5 (83.5) Km 448 (134.5): Trailhead to Sunset Pass and Sunset lookout. 🚶🚶

Mile 279 (83) Km 449.5 (133): Viewpoint of the Castelets, well-named cluster of small castle crags on the western horizon.

Mile 283.5 (78.5) Km 456 (126.5): Viewpoint of the North Saskatchewan River as it flows through a narrow gorge.

Mile 284.5 (77.5) Km 458 (124.5): Cirrus Mountain Campground; 16 sites, kitchen shelter. ▲

Mile 286 (76) Km 460 (122.5): Weeping Wall viewpoint. Water from melting snowfields high above the Cirrus Mountain cliffs finds its way through cracks in the wall to emerge as a series of graceful waterfalls. Even in midsummer the wall is dark with water; in winter, it is coated with ice. To the northwest, a good example of synclinal folds in the strata of Nigel Peak.

Mile 288 (74) Km 465 (117.5): Nigel Creek canyon. Turnout by highway bridge over gorge cut into dolomite bedrock by Nigel Creek.

To the west, a short trail leads to tumbling waterfalls, about a half-hour hike. Branch trail follows old gravel road to foot of Saskatchewan Glacier, source of the Saskatchewan River, about 2 hours. 🚶🚶

Mile 289 (73) Km 465.5 (117): CAUTION: Hairpin bend and steep climb northbound up the "Big Hill." Drive with care.

Mile 289.5 (72.5) Km 466 (116.5): Viewpoint, North Saskatchewan River canyon and the Castle Mountain syncline, a giant U-shaped bend in the strata which runs from Banff to Jasper. Cliffs to the east form base of Cirrus Mountain. Breathtaking view of mountain scenery and highway snaking south. Good view of Bridal Veil Falls.

Mile 291 (71) Km 468.5 (114): Viewpoint, Cirrus Mountain and short trail to Panther Falls. 🚶🚶

Mile 291.5 (70.5) Km 469 (113.5): Viewpoint, Nigel Peak (elev. 10,535 feet/3,211m) to the northwest with its synclinal (downfolded) strata and the Nigel Creek trail which follows the river up to Nigel Pass and down into the Brazeau River.

Mile 292.5 (69.5) Km 470.5 (112): Highway warning sign for possible poor visibility: There is often fog and clouds at this high elevation.

Mile 293 (68.5) Km 472 (110.5): Parker Ridge viewpoint and trail, 1.8 miles/3 km round-trip, through the subalpine forest into alpine tundra. A short distance along the trail is a fossilized coral reef with fossils of mollusks and large-coiled cephapods. The alpine flowers in mid-June and July are splendid. Trail crosses the ridge to reach a grand viewpoint of the Saskatchewan Glacier, source of the river. Stay on the trail. Alpine terrain is delicate and should not be disturbed. 🚶🚶

Mile 294 (68) Km 473 (109.5): Hilda Creek youth hostel.

Mile 296.5 (65.5) Km 477 (105.5):

Sunwapta Pass (elev. 6,676 feet/2,035m). This high point on the Icefields Parkway is the divide between North Saskatchewan waters flowing south and east to Hudson Bay and the Athabasca River flowing north to the Arctic Ocean. The pass is also the boundary between Banff and Jasper national parks.

Sunwapta is Stoney Indian for "turbulent river." The Sunwapta River drains from the Athabasca Glacier and flows into the Athabasca River some 36 miles/50 km north. Highway 93 follows the river valley.

Mile 297.5 (64.5) Km 479 (103.5): Wilcox Creek Campground; 46 sites, sani-station, interpretive events. Good views of Mount Athabasca (elev. 11,453 feet/3,491m) and Nigel Peak. Hiking trail leads to good viewpoint of the Columbia Icefields. 🚶🚶▲

Mile 298 (63.5) Km 480 (102.5): Columbia Icefield Campground; 33 sites. ▲

Mile 299.5 (62.5) Km 482 (100.5): Columbia Icefield Chalet provides accommodations, food and gas. Good views from parking lot of Dome and Athabasca glaciers. Across the road from the chalet, a road leads west to a parking lot beside Sunwapta Lake and the toe of Athabasca Glacier; short trail leads on to glacier snout. Along this road are markers showing the extent of the retreating glacier in previous years. In 1890, the glacier was almost beside the highway.

Private road which climbs right onto the glacier is access road for snowmobile tours. Tours leave chalet by bus, cost $10 for adults, $5 for children 5 to 12 and operate from mid-May through September. CAUTION: Watch out for very tame bighorn sheep panhandling in the parking lots. (Do not feed them!)

Parks Canada Icefield Information Center, open 9 a.m. to 5 p.m., late May to first week in October; to 7 p.m. from mid-June to September. The center has good view windows with markers, an audiovisual presentation on glacier formation and a scale model of the Columbia Icefield area.

The glaciers visible from the road are merely fingers of the giant Columbia Icefield which covers 241 square miles/389 square km at an average elevation of 8,497 feet/2,590m. Mount Athabasca (elev. 11,453 feet/3,491m) and Mount Kitchener (elev. 11,397 feet/3,474m) are the dominant peaks. ★

Mile 301.5 (60.5) Km 485 (97.5): Sunwapta Canyon viewpoint. From the viewpoint, the highway descends steeply northbound to the river valley, with sharp corners signposted for 30 mph/50 kmph. Watch for Rocky Mountain bighorn sheep. They are used to people and will approach quite close. Do not feed them: Human food is bad for them.

Mile 302 (60) Km 486 (96.5): Tangle Creek. Small roadside picnic area and view of Tangle Falls, tumbling over limestone cliffs. ⛱

Mile 304.5 (57.5) Km 490 (92.5): Picnic area and viewpoint of Stutfield Glacier

and its twin icefalls tumbling down Stutfield Peak. 🏕

Mile 310 (52) Km 499 (83.5): Beauty Creek youth hostel.

Mile 310.5 (51.5) Km 500 (82.5): Roadside turnout with mountain markers for Mushroom and Diadem Peak and Tangle Ridge.

Mile 315.5 (46.5) Km 508 (74.5): Jonas Creek Campground; 37 campsites. ▲

Mile 317 (45) Km 510 (72.5): Bright pink boulders beside the road are quartz sandstone fallen from the high ridge to the east.

Mile 318.5 (43) Km 513 (69.5): Poboktan Creek Park warden station and trail into the Brazeau Lake wilderness region. 🚶🚶

Mile 326 (35.5) Km 525 (57.5): Bubbling Springs picnic site. 🏕

Mile 329.5 (32.5) Km 530 (52.5): Short access road to parking lot at Sunwapta Falls where the river changes course abruptly from northwest to southwest and has eroded a deep, smooth canyon with 30-foot/9-m falls. Short trail from parking lot. Accommodations, food and gas nearby in summer.

Mile 330.5 (31.5) Km 532 (50.5): Short access road east to Buck and Osprey Lakes.

Mile 332 (30) Km 534 (48.5): Honeymoon Lake Campground by shore of lake; 36 sites, interpretive events. Across lake is a good view of the Endless Chain Ridge. ▲

Mile 332.5 (29.5) Km 535 (47.5): Viewpoint with mountain signposts for the Winston Churchill Range and an excellent view of the Athabasca Valley and its ancient moraines.

Mile 333.5 (28.5) Km 536.5 (46): Range Creek bridge.

Mile 334.5 (27.5) Km 538 (44.5): Viewpoint, Mount Christie (elev. 10,180 feet/3,103m) and Athabasca River which here makes a tight horseshoe loop.

Mile 337.5 (24.5) Km 543 (39.5): Mount Christie picnic area beside the river. 🏕

Mile 340 (22) Km 547 (35.5): Picnic area and viewpoint by popular animal lick. Finely ground glacial deposits here contain mineral salts which attract mountain goats, sheep and other animals. Fantastic view down the Athabasca Valley and its panorama of high peaks. North of the gap created by the Whirlpool River is the snowy crest of Mount Edith Cavell (elev. 11,033 feet/3,363m), one of the highest in the Rockies. 🏕

Mile 341.5 (20) Km 550 (32.5): Mount Kerkeslin Campground; 42 sites. Watch for Canada geese on the river flats. ▲

Mile 343.5 (18.5) Km 553 (29.5): Jasper Park warden station. Youth hostel nearby.

Mile 344 (17.5) Km 554 (28.5): Junction with Highway 93A, alternate route north for 15 miles/24 km on west side of Athabasca River. A short way along this road is a viewpoint for magnificent Athabasca Falls (a must stop) which drop 40 feet/12m from a sandstone lip to thunder down a short, narrow canyon. Road continues to Wabasso Campground; 238 sites, 6 walk-in sites, sani-station, playground and interpretative events. Also access to Cavell Lake at the base of Mount Edith Cavell and the Angel Glacier; trailhead for the famous Tonquin Valley. Also on Highway 93A is Marmot Basin, Jasper's downhill ski area. 🎿🚶🏕★

Mile 346 (16) Km 557 (25.5): Turnout and parking for short trail to Horseshoe Lake under the cliffs of Mount Hardisty.

Mile 348 (14) Km 560 (22.5): Viewpoint, Mount Edith Cavell. Between this peak and Whirlpool Peak to the south lies the valley of the Whirlpool River. Early fur brigades left the Athabasca River and followed the Whirlpool up to Athabasca Pass.

Mile 355 (7) Km 571 (11.5): Trail to Wabasso Lake and on to Shovel Pass and the Maligne Valley. 🚶🚶

Mile 357 (4.5) Km 575 (7.5): Trail to Valley of the Five Lakes. 🚶🚶

Mile 359 (3) Km 578 (4.5): Athabasca River bridge. Highway 93A rejoins route just north of bridge.

Mile 360 (2) Km 581 (1.5): Wapiti Campground; 345 trailer sites (40 with electrical hookup), sani-station, hot showers, interpretative events. Wapiti winter campground has 28 trailer sites and 10 walk-in sites. Wapiti is another name for elk which frequent this valley in fall and winter, often feeding on the bark of the aspen trees. ▲

Mile 361 (1) Km 583 (0.5): Junction west to Whistler Campground; 758 sites (77 with full hookups, 43 with electricity only), 24 walk-in sites, sani-station, hot showers, playground and interpretative events. Road continues to the Jasper Tramway which whisks tourists up Whistler Mountain to the 7,496-foot/2,285-m level. Open late March to mid-October. At the top of lift is a restaurant, an interpretative area describing life in the alpine zone, and a trail to Whistler Summit. Whistler is the local name for the hoary marmot. ▲

Mile 362 (0) Km 584 (0): Junction with Highway 16 at west end of **JASPER** (pop. 4,000) townsite, park headquarters for Jasper National Park. All facilities available, with accommodations ranging from bungalows to luxury lodges. A popular ski area in winter, Jasper also offers a variety of summer attractions, including fishing, hiking, boat excursions on Maligne Lake, sky tram rides for aerial views of the park, and river raft trips.

   NORTHWEST MILEPOSTS® travelers using Yellowhead Highway 16 refer to *The MILEPOST*® All-The-North Travel Guide® which covers highways to and in Alaska.

Mountain peaks rise abruptly from the shores of Lake Maligne.   (L. Linkhart)

U.S. Highway 95

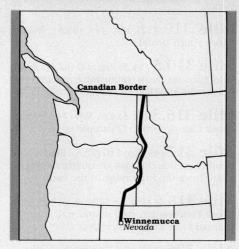

Canadian Border

Winnemucca
Nevada

See map pages 165, 167 and 169

U.S. Highway 95 enters the Northwest at Winnemucca, NV, and continues to the junction with Highway 93 near Cranbrook, BC. Beginning in the sagebrush-covered desert of northern Nevada, the highway passes through rich farming and ranching territory, runs parallel to the Hells Canyon National Recreation Area, and winds through the ever-green forests of northern Idaho and British Columbia. Antelope, mule and white-tailed deer, bighorn sheep and elk inhabit the wooded country and rolling sagebrush regions. The highway crosses numerous good fishing streams plus several major rivers including the Snake, Salmon and Clearwater.

There are many historical points of interest along Highway 95 which reveal the colorful events leading to the settlement of the West. Before attempting to take Highway 95 in the winter, contact the state police or transportation department for road conditions. Towns are few and far between, particularly in the southern section, so be sure to check your gas gauge as you pass through the communities.

U.S. Highway 95 Log

Distance from Winnemucca, NV, is followed by distance from the Canadian border.

Mile 0 (727): The highway log begins at the intersection of Winnemucca Boulevard and Kelarney Street in **WINNEMUCCA** (pop. 4,140), the Humboldt County seat and the area's agricultural, ranching and commercial center.

Named in the mid-1800s after Paiute Indian Chief Winnemucca, the town was a major stop for wagon trains traveling the Emigrant Trail. Winnemucca achieved notoriety in September 1900, when Butch Cassidy and his gang robbed the First National Bank of more than $32,000 in gold coin. Cassidy later sent a note of thanks to the bank president, along with a photo of himself and his gang.

Today, Winnemucca retains much of its Western flavor and vestiges of the frontier. There are several casinos and taverns — and a colorful nightlife — to remind today's visitor of its wild past. The Basque people have made their mark on this northern Nevada town, as one motel and several restaurants carry the Basque slogan and motif. There are several Basque restaurants in town offering home-style cooking. Each June residents and visitors join in a week-long festival to celebrate Basque heritage.

Mile 0.5 (726.5): Jungo, Sulfur Mountain Road turnoff and crossing the Humboldt River. On the west side of the highway is Pioneer Memorial Park with shady picnic tables, restrooms and the Humboldt County Museum and Thrift Shop. The mountain peak to the south is Sonoma Peak (elev. 9,395 feet), a part of the Sonoma Range. ⅋

Mile 2 (725): Little Humboldt River meanders on the east side of the highway for several miles.

Mile 8 (719): Sand dunes parallel the highway for a few miles.

Mile 11 (716): Sand Pass Road junction.

Mile 13.5 (713.5): Dutch Flat Road junction.

Mile 15 (712): Bloody Run Peak (elev. 7,835 feet) is visible on the west side of the highway.

Mile 20 (707): Paradise Rancho Drive junction.

Mile 21.5 (705.5): **PARADISE HILL**, a small unincorporated community at the junction with Nevada Highway 290. This secondary road leads northeast to Paradise Valley with tavern and RV park. Beyond Paradise Valley, a gravel Forest Service road leads into Humboldt National Forest via 7,865-foot Hinkey Summit.

Mile 22 (705): Hinkey Summit and Lye Creek campground to east. ▲

Mile 31 (696): Junction with Nevada Highway 140 (also called the Winnemucca to the Sea Highway and the Veteran's Memorial Highway). The highway starts in Winnemucca and runs to Crescent City, CA. From this point on Highway 95, the Santa Rosa Mountain Range is east of the highway.

Mile 35 (692): Androna Creek.

Mile 35.5 (691.5): Junction with Buffalo Canyon Road east.

Mile 42 (685): Rest area. Picnic tables and garbage cans are available, but there are no toilet facilities. The monument at the rest area is dedicated to 5 men who were killed fighting a range fire 3 miles east of this point in 1939. The McConnell Creek Road exits into the Santa Rosa Mountains from this rest area. ⅋

Mile 43.5 (683.5): **OROVADA**, unincorporated community (elev. 4,337 feet). Gas,

food, lodging available. Highway junction west to Kings River. Rugged-looking Sawtooth Mountain is visible on the east side of the highway.

Mile 58 (669): Rock Creek Road junction.

Mile 60 (667): Buckskin Canyon Road junction.

Mile 70 (657): Fort McDermitt Indian Reservation. Historical marker describes Fort McDermitt, named for Col. Charles McDermitt who, in 1865, established a camp intended to protect travelers headed to Boise, Star City and Virginia City. McDermitt was later killed in an Indian ambush and the camp was subsequently named Fort McDermitt.

Mile 74 (653): **McDERMITT**, the last stop between Nevada and the Oregon border and the last chance to play the slot machines if you're headed north on Highway 95. The town in fact straddles the border. No sales tax on the Oregon side. McDermitt Mine, the largest mercury-producing mine in the Western Hemisphere, is located southwest of town.

Mile 74.5 (652.5): Nevada-Oregon state border.

Mile 92.5 (634.5): Snow zone begins (northbound). Blue Mountain Pass lies ahead. During winter months it is advisable to check with the Oregon or Nevada State Patrol before attempting to cross this pass.   MP 103

Mile 95.5 (631.5): Blue Mountain (elev. 7,439 feet) is visible to the west.   MP 100

Mile 97 (630): Summit of Blue Mountain Pass (elev. 5,293 feet).

Mile 103.5 (623.5): Entering **BASQUE**. No services available.   MP 92

Mile 108 (619): Junction with

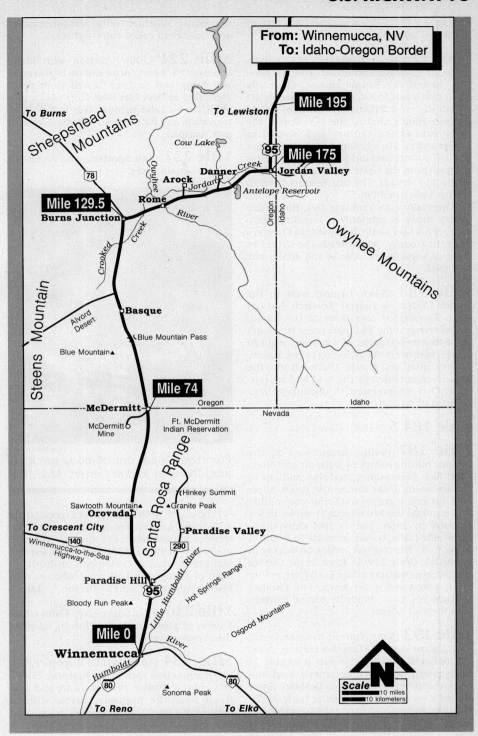

Whitehorse Ranch Road. Steens Mountain is visible to the west and is home for pronghorn antelope, bighorn sheep and mule deer. Also popular chukar and Hungarian partridge areas.

Mile 117 (610): Pacific-Mountain time zone. Set your watches ahead one hour if you're headed north, back one hour if you're headed south.

Mile 122.5 (604.5): Crooked Creek.
MP 73

Mile 129.5 (597.5): BURNS JUNCTION; gas, food.
MP 66

Mile 130 (597): Burns Junction Guard Station.

Mile 135 (592): Rest area with picnic tables and drinking water. Historical marker tells of the last major Indian uprising in the Pacific Northwest, the Bannock War of 1878.

Mile 136 (591): Crooked Creek.

Mile 142.5 (584.5): Crossing the Owyhee Canyon at ROME; food, gas available. The town derived its name from the sandstone formations along the Owyhee River just north of the highway which resemble the columns of Rome. The Owyhee River flows more than 200 miles from the Owyhee Mountains of Nevada through the scabland of Idaho and Oregon. Popular float fishing and white-water rafting area with Class 4 rapids. Downstream from Rome the river is classified as a scenic waterway. Rafting and fishing guides are available locally. BLM boat launch site just south of the crossing; pit toilets, picnic tables, barbecue.
MP 53

Mile 143.5 (583.5): Geological monument describes the Owyhee River and surrounding terrain.
MP 52

Mile 148.5 (578.5): Turnoff north 3 miles to AROCK (pop. 35), a small farming community.
MP 47

Mile 156.5 (570.5): Rock Creek.

Mile 158.5 (568.5): Turnoff north to DANNER, Charbonneau Historical Marker, Cow Lakes and Inskip Station, a hostel on Skinner's Toll Road, founded in 1863. The fortified dwelling often served as refuge during Indian raids. This is also the burial place for Jean Baptiste Charbonneau, the youngest member of the Lewis and Clark expedition, born to Sacajawea and Toussaint Charbonneau in 1805. Baptiste was educated in Europe and returned to the West to become a mountain man, magistrate, interpreter and '49er for nearly 4 decades. He died of pneumonia at this spot on May 16, 1866, en route to a new gold strike in Montana.

Only Upper Cow Lake offers any sportfishing with a fair population of brown bullhead catfish and crappie. Best fishing is near the west end lava beds which has a BLM

campground and boat launch.

Mile 159.5 (567.5): Turnoff south to Indian Canyon and Three Forks. Popular Owyhee River access and launch at Three Forks.
MP 36

Mile 161 (566): In 1960, under the authority of the Taylor Grazing Act, the Bureau of Land Management began an experimental program of rehabilitating 4.5 million acres of desert rangeland in this area. Called the Vale Project, the program was intended to

test new concepts in rangeland rehabilitation and restore the land to productive use. The project was a success and now some 220 livestock operators graze 82,000 cattle and 6,000 sheep on the project area.

Mile 162.5 (564.5): Jack Creek.

Mile 163 (564): Turnoff to Antelope Reservoir which offers good rainbow trout fishing, plus a BLM campground. This is also the turnoff to Antelope School and the Charbonneau Historical Marker.

Mile 170 (557): Jordan Creek and turnoff north to Cow Lake.

Mile 175 (552): JORDAN VALLEY (pop. 360). All services are available. This is a good area to test the Basque cuisine. Originally from northwest Spain, the Basque people are culturally and ethnically unique. Many Basques immigrated to the U.S. during the early part of the century and worked as sheepherders. They brought with them their ancient culture and unique lifestyle which is prominent in the Great Basin area of Oregon, Idaho and Nevada. The first Basques came to Jordan Valley in 1898.

Originally a gold mining area, the Jordan Valley today is primarily a ranching community for beef cattle. It lies within Oregon's Malheur County, which leads the nation in acres of sugar beets, onions and alfalfa hay and seed.

Mile 183 (544): Turnoff west to the Jordon Craters, a Federal Research Natural Area. The rugged lava flows of the Jordan Craters cover some 36 square miles which are inhabited by 60 species of waterfowl and 120 species of other birds, including eagles, hawks, falcons, quail and grouse. The roads into the area are maintained by the BLM and are purposely left undeveloped to discourage large influxes of visitors.

Mile 184.5 (542.5): Cow Creek. MP 11

Mile 187 (540): Turnoff east to the historic mining camps of Delamar and Silver City. Rich silver mines produced millions of dollars worth of ore during the 1860s. Silver City became a major territorial community and acquired the first telegraph service in the territory in 1866. Idaho's first daily newspaper, the *Idaho Avalanche*, made its home in Silver City. The original press is on display in Homedale (**Mile 229**) in front of the *Owyhee Avalanche* newspaper office. Today, Silver City is an unrestored ghost town. The Owyhee Cattlemen's Assoc. holds its annual convention there in August.

Mile 193 (534): Turnoff to Leslie Gulch and Succor Creek State Recreation Area. Succor Creek crossing. The park is located 25 miles north on this unimproved road and offers camping and picnicking facilities. There is also a viewpoint with hiking trails. Leslie Gulch provides access to 40-mile-long Owyhee Reservoir, often rated as the premier fishing lake in southeastern Oregon. (Best access to Owyhee Lake is via Oregon Highway 201 and Lake Owyhee Road south from Nyssa.) 🏕🏞🐟▲ MP2

Mile 195 (532): Oregon-Idaho state border. Historical marker.

Mile 209 (518): Scenic overlook and historical marker. You are in Owyhee Country, a misspelling of the word Hawaii. In 1818, Donald MacKenzie brought a brigade of Hawaiian fur hunters to this area to trap. He sent several Hawaiians to the Snake River valley. They never returned. Since that time, the county, mountain range and surrounding area have been called the Owyhees.

Mile 221 (506): Junction with Idaho Highway 55. A short drive east on Highway 55 will bring you to Lake Lowell (sometimes identified as Deer Flat Reservoir) which provides fair to good fishing. This is a popular recreation area for residents of Boise, Caldwell and Nampa. 🐟

Mile 227 (500): Sportsman access east 12 miles to Snake River.

(Ray Weisgerber)
Ptarmigan is just one of many species of birds found at Jordan Craters, Mile 183.

Mile 229 (498): HOMEDALE (pop. 2,078), a farming and ranching community. All services are available. On the way through town, stop to see the printing press for the first Idaho territorial daily newspaper on display in front of the *Owyhee Avalanche*. Junction with Idaho Highway 19 west to Oregon. MP 34

Mile 230 (497): Snake River. Dams create a series of giant, productive fishing lakes on this famous river.

Mile 234 (493): WILDER (pop. 1,350) and the junction with Idaho Highway 19 east to Caldwell. Notice the vineyards and hop fields near the highway. Idaho wine is becoming a significant economic resource in this area. MP 39

Mile 239 (488): Boise River. Stocked with rainbow trout, plus good for whitefish. 🐟

Mile 240 (487): South junction with U.S. Highways 20 and 26. (See U.S. HIGHWAY 20 section.)

Mile 241.5 (485.5): Old Fort Boise Historical Marker. Two miles west of this point, on the bank of the Snake River, an important Hudson's Bay Co. fur-trading post was established in 1834.

Mile 242 (485): PARMA (pop. 1,910), a small ranching and farming community. All traveler services available. This is the home of the Old Fort Boise State Park. A replica of Old Fort Boise is located in the park; open afternoons Wednesday to Saturday during the summer. The state park also has a RV park, picnic tables and restrooms. 🛌▲

Mile 242.5 (484.5): Turnoff west to Roswell, a small farming community.

Mile 246 (481): North junction with U.S. Highways 20 and 26; access to Nyssa, OR. (See U.S. HIGHWAY 20 section.)

Mile 256 (471): U.S. Highway 95 crosses Interstate 84. Travelers heading east or west on Interstate 84 turn to **Mile 378.5** in the INTERSTATE 84 section for log of that route.

Mile 257 (470): Junction with U.S. Highway 30 to New Plymouth. MP 62

Mile 259 (468): FRUITLAND (pop. 2,559). All services available.

Mile 260 (467): Junction with U.S. Highway 30 to Ontario. MP 65

Mile 261 (466): Payette River. Annually stocked with trout, the river also offers native and warm-water fish. 🐟

Mile 263.5 (463.5): Highway 95 business route passes through the town of PAYETTE (pop. 5,780) while main Highway 95 goes around the town. They join north of the city. Payette offers motels, restaurants and all traveler services. Payette is named after Francois Payette, a fur trader and the first postmaster at Old Fort Boise. The town boasts Killebrew Stadium, a large sports complex located at the high school, that was named in honor of Payette native and Baseball Hall of Fame member, Harmon Killebrew.

Junction with Idaho Highway 52 to Emmett. When traveling in these rural farming communities, be cautious when approaching slow-moving farm vehicles on the highway.

Mile 277 (450): WEISER (pop. 4,771) and the Weiser River. Weiser (Wee-zer) is billed as the "Gateway to Hells Canyon," the deepest gorge in North America. It is the home of the National Old-Time Fiddlers Contest, held the third full week of June each year. The town and river were named after Peter Weiser, a Revolutionary War veteran and later a sergeant, cook and hunter for the Lewis and Clark expedition of 1804-06. One of the interesting landmarks of Weiser is the Pythian Castle, a nearly perfect replica of a castle that still exists in Wales. Weiser River and its forks are planted with trout each spring.

Mile 288 (439): Mann's Creek. Road leads northwest to Mann's Creek Reservoir. Campground and fishing. 🐟▲

Mile 290 (437): Chain-up area and turnout.

Mile 292 (435): Midvale Summit (elev. 3,326 feet).

Mile 296 (431): Rest area and historical marker explaining the prehistoric rock quarry where natives fashioned a variety of stone tools some 3,000 to 5,000 years ago. Restrooms, covered picnic tables and a beautiful overlook to the north of the Weiser River Valley below.   ⊼ MP 101

Mile 301 (426): MIDVALE (pop. 205), a small farming and ranching community. Limited services.   MP 105

Mile 302.5 (424.5): The scenic Weiser River valley parallels the highway to the east.

Mile 309 (418): CAMBRIDGE (pop. 428), a small farming and ranching community. Most services. Turnoff to Brownlee Dam, Hells Canyon.   MP 113

Mile 310 (417): Weiser River.

Mile 320 (407): Turnoff east to Indian Valley.

Mile 324 (403): Middle Fork Weiser River, stocked with rainbow.   ⟨fish⟩

Mile 329 (398): COUNCIL (pop. 917). Early Indians held periodic councils at an area near the present location of the town. National Forest information center located there.   MP 134

Mile 331.5 (395.5): Chain-up area and turnout.

Mile 335 (392): Turnoff west to Fruitvale. No services.

Mile 339 (388): Payette National Forest boundary.

Mile 340 (387): Weiser River. This area is a beautiful thickly-wooded drive. Use the slow-vehicle turnouts if 3 or more vehicles are behind you.

Mile 341 (386): Pin Creek.

Mile 342.5 (384.5): Railroad Creek.

Mile 343 (384): Rest area with picnic tables.   ⊼

Mile 343.5 (383.5): Evergreen Forest Service campground. The campground (elev. 3,800 feet) has 12 campsites and is open between June and October.   ▲ MP 149

Mile 345 (382): Payette National Forest boundary.

Mile 346 (381): Lost Valley Reservoir road.

Mile 347 (380): TAMARACK, a small unincorporated village. No services available.

Mile 354 (373): NEW MEADOWS (pop.

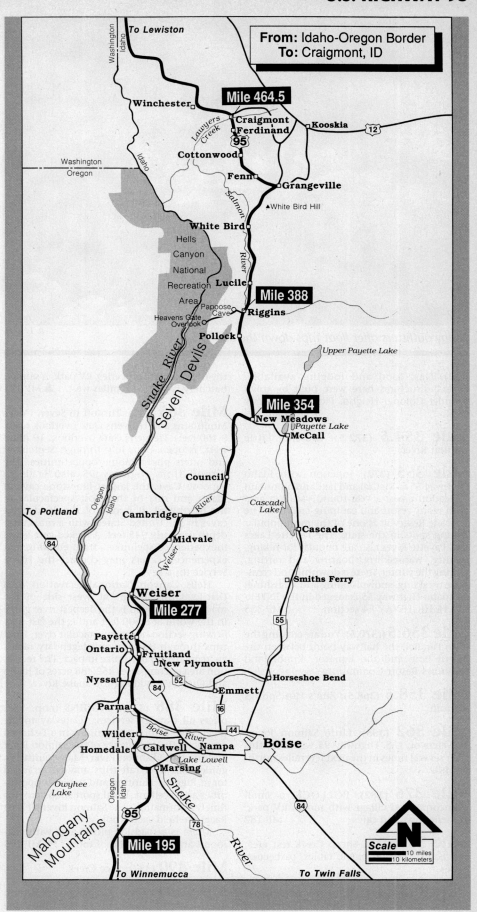

Many outfitters offer float trips down the Salmon River.
(L. Linkhart)

600). Gas, food and lodging available. Several structures here were built by town founder Colonel Heigho. Picnicking at city park. ⊼MP 159

Mile 354.5 (372.5): Crossing Little Salmon River.

Mile 355 (372): Junction with Idaho Highway 55 to McCall and lake and mountain recreation areas; a year-round vacation area with many resort and camping facilities. The Cascade Reservoir is one of the most popular fishing spots in the state. The Payette Lakes and Payette River also are popular for hiking, fishing, waterskiing, boating and rafting. During the winter, there is downhill and cross-country skiing, snowmobiling and ice fishing.

Idaho Highway 55 is logged in the INTERSTATE HIGHWAY 84 section. MP 355

Mile 356.5 ((370.5): You are crossing the 45th Parallel, the halfway point between the North Pole and the Equator. Kimberland Meadows Resort Community.

Mile 358.5 (368.5): Zim's Hot Springs turnoff.

Mile 362 (365): Little Salmon River. Travelers on U.S. Highway 95 will cross this river several times in the next few miles northbound.

Mile 376 (182): POLLOCK, a small unincorporated village with motel, RV park, groceries, gas and cafe. MP 182

Mile 382 (345): Sheep Creek rest area; restrooms, covered picnic tables, barbecues, water. ⊼

Mile 383.5 (343.5): Crossing the Rapid River at RAPID RIVER, a tiny community in the river canyon; groceries, RV park. A salmon hatchery is located 3 miles west. ▲MP 191

Mile 385 (342): Turnoff to Seven Devils Mountains and Heavens Gate overlook (elev. 8,400 feet). Heavens Gate overlook, 19 miles west, is open from July through September and offers photographic opportunities. The turnoff from Highway 95 also leads to Papoose Cave, the largest limestone cave in Idaho and one of the most spectacular in the Northwest. It is one of the 10 deepest caves in the United States, with a maximum depth of nearly 945 feet. A locked gate keeps inexperienced spelunkers from entering, but experienced cavers may contact the Forest Service for a key.

Hells Canyon National Recreation Area District Office is on the west side of the road. Hells Canyon is the deepest river gorge in the world at 6,600 feet and is the last free-flowing section of this spectacular river. Float trips through the canyon's legendary rapids are regulated to minimize impact. The recreation area encompasses 652,488 acres of Idaho and Oregon straddling the Snake River.

Mile 388 (339): RIGGINS (pop. 527) offers all traveler services. "Gateway to the River of No Return," Riggins lies in a T-shaped canyon at the confluence of the Salmon River and the Little Salmon River. Many outfitters, guides and river raft trips may be arranged for in Riggins. Hunting and fishing opportunities are excellent. Local sport shops provide timely information. The Salmon River Jet Boat Races are held each April.

There is a roadside picnic area with restrooms at the north end of town. ➤ MP 195

Mile 390 (337): Race Creek.

Mile 391 (336): Crossing the Salmon River and the Mountain-Pacific time zone line. Turn your watches ahead 1 hour if you are headed north, back 1 hour if you are headed south. Gold dredges mounted on floating rafts in the river are sometimes visible working the riverbed.

Mile 392.5 (334.5): Lightning Creek.

Mile 393.5 (333.5): Chair Creek.

Mile 394 (333): Fiddle Creek. MP 200

Mile 398 (329): Lucile Recreation site; boat launch.

Mile 399 (328): LUCILE, a small unincorporated village. Food available.

Mile 400 (327): Hilo Creek. Historical marker explains the city of Florence, a gold mining town 14 air miles east of this point which produced millions of dollars in gold during a 1-year period.

Mile 401.5 (325.5): John Day Creek.

Mile 404 (323): Salmon River canyon geological site.

Mile 408 (319): Slate Creek ranger station and Slate Creek. No services.

Mile 408.5 (318.5): Slate Creek Recreation area; boat launch.

Mile 409 (318): Rest area. MP 215

Mile 412 (315): Sportsman access. MP 218

Mile 412.5 (314.5): Skookumchuck Creek and roadside rest area; restrooms, picnic tables. ⊼MP 219

Mile 414 (313): Hammer Creek Recreation Area. MP 222

Mile 417 (310): White Bird Junction and White Bird Creek. The small town of WHITE BIRD has all services available. You are about to ascend White Bird Hill.

Mile 421 (306): Nez Perce War Historic Site and valley overlook. Near the base of White Bird Hill is a battleground where the Nez Perce soundly defeated a much larger force of cavalry soldiers on June 17, 1877. That marked the beginning of the Nez Perce War. MP 228

Mile 424 (303): Historical marker about the Salmon River.

Mile 425 (302): Summit of White Bird Hill (elev. 4,245 feet). This highway, completed in 1975, replaced the treacherous 16- to 18-foot-wide highway that wound its way up the hill. The old highway had so many switchbacks that a car would make the equivalent of 37 complete circles in 22 miles. The new highway cut the driving distance in half.

Mile 429 (298): Camas Prairie Historical

Site. The Camas Prairie is named after the camas plant, the root of which was a staple in the Indian diet. In this area, the Nez Perce Indians met to hunt, fish and gather camas roots for the winter.

Mile 432 (295): GRANGEVILLE (pop. 3,470), Idaho County seat, largest county in Idaho at 5.4 million acres. Logging, mining and agriculture are the major industries in this area. Wild scenic rivers, forest wilderness and ski areas nearby. All services available.

Junction with Idaho Highway 13 to U.S. Highway 12 at Kooskia (26 miles). See U.S. HIGHWAY 12 section.　MP 240

Mile 434 (293): Junction with road to Nezperce. Limited services available. MP 242

Mile 438 (289): Lawyer Creek.　MP 246

Mile 439 (288): The small, unincorporated village of FENN. Groceries available.

Mile 444.5 (282.5): Turnoff to the ancient Weis rock shelter (7 miles off the highway) and a historical marker (0.5 mile north) which explains the old Native dwelling. Roadside tables are available.

Mile 446.5 (280.5): Turnoff to COTTONWOOD (pop. 941) and the Priory of St. Gertrude. The historic convent, established in 1919, is the only "motherhouse" in the Idaho Catholic diocese. St. Gertrude's Museum is a fascinating study of Western history and is well worth the visit. Cottonwood is also the home of the North Idaho Correctional Institution.

Mile 448 (279): Cottonwood Butte Ski Area turnoff.

Mile 450 (277): Nez Perce Indian Reservation boundary.

Mile 456 (268): FERDINAND (pop. 160). Cafe.　MP 264

Mile 464.5 (262.5): CRAIGMONT (pop. 600) named after the first permanent white settler in Idaho, Col. William Craig. All services. This is also the junction of Idaho Highway 62 to Nezperce.

Mile 470 (257): Turnoff to Winchester Lake State Park and city of WINCHESTER. Winchester Lake State Park is a forested campground on a small trout lake. No gas motors are allowed on the lake. Boats with electric motors, kayaks, canoes, etc., are permitted. The 418-acre park is open year-round and offers picnic sites, water, toilets, fishing, trails and a boat ramp. Sixty campsites are available and a fee of $6 per night is required (Idaho resident senior citizens receive a $3 discount). Winter activities include ice skating, ice fishing, sledding and cross-country skiing.　MP 278

Mile 478 (249): Lapwai Creek.　MP 286

Mile 483 (244): Turnoff to the small unin-

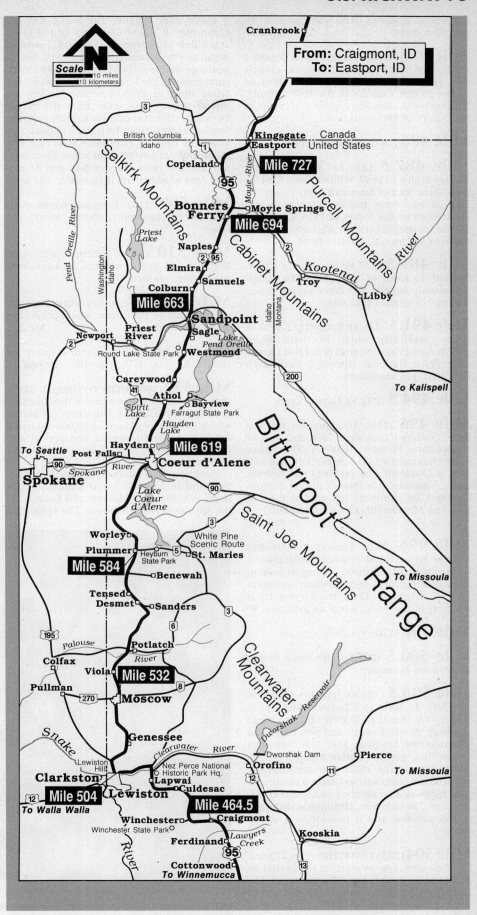

corporated village of **CULDESAC** (pop. 262); groceries, bank. MP 291

Mile 485 (242): Turnoff to St. Joseph's Mission (4 miles west). This restored church was built in 1874 under the direction of Father Joseph Cataldo as the first Catholic mission for the Nez Perce Indians. It is part of the Nez Perce Historical Park.

Mile 486 (241): Mission Creek.

Mile 487.5 (239.5): William Craig Historical Site. In 1850, William Craig filed for a 640-acre tract of farmland here. When the original Nez Perce Indian Reservation was established by the Treaty of 1855, Craig was allowed to keep his acreage after requests were made by his friends, the Nez Perce.

Mile 489.5 (237.5): Sweetwater Creek. Turnoff to town of **SWEETWATER**, small community on the Nez Perce Indian Reservation. No services available.

Mile 491.5 (236.5): Turnoff to **LAPWAI** (pop. 1,043) city center, Northern Idaho Indian Agency and grounds of old Fort Lapwai (Nez Perce National Historical Park Site). Groceries, gas, restaurant.

Mile 494.5 (232.5): Lapwai Creek.

Mile 495 (232): Headquarters for Nez Perce National Historical Park and site of the Spalding Mission (1838-47). The visitor center has exhibits on Nez Perce Indian culture, a 23-minute film on Nez Perce history, and a 5-minute slide show. Cultural demonstrations in summer. Self-guided tour of Spalding Mission site. Open year-round. MP 303

Mile 496 (231): Turnoff to Lewiston Wildlife Preserve and crossing the Clearwater River. Excellent steelhead fishing in season. Dworshak National Fish Hatchery upstream on U.S. Highway 12 is the largest trout hatchery in the world. Tours are available. ✦

Mile 497 (230): Sportsman access.

Mile 500.5 (227.5): Nez Perce Indian Reservation boundary.

Mile 503.5 (223.5): Junction with U.S. Highway 12 west to Clarkston and Walla Walla, WA. (See U.S. HIGHWAY 12 section.) Highway 95 veers north and you begin the ascent of the Lewiston Hill. The "Lewiston Grade" is 6 percent. Potlatch paper mill to the southeast. The route you are traveling replaced the old Lewiston Grade, a twisting 2-lane highway that climbed nearly 2,000 vertical feet. The old route, although in disrepair, is still passable and is considered a scenic drive. MP 312

Mile 504 (223): **LEWISTON** (pop. 27,986). All services are available in Lewiston including 16 motels and 71 restaurants. The Lewiston-Clarkston Valley, ancestral home of the Nez Perce Indians, is at the confluence of

2 major river systems, the Snake and the Clearwater. It was also a camp for the Lewis and Clark expedition of 1804-06. Lewiston began as a steamboat landing in 1861. Steamboats operated from Lewiston until 1940. With completion of the Lower Granite Dam on the Snake River in 1975, Lewiston became an inland seaport, 464 miles from the Pacific Ocean. It is the river gateway to Hells Canyon. Numerous outfitters offer jet boat or float trips down the canyon. Hells Gate State Park is 4 miles south of Lewiston on Snake River Avenue and the Hells Canyon National Recreation Area headquarters is located in the park.

Mile 509 (218): Dramatic scenic overlook of Lewiston and Clarkston. Worth the stop. ★

Mile 510 (217): Junction with U.S. Highway 195 to Pullman and Spokane, WA. See feature this section.

Mile 511 (216): Entering Palouse country, one of the largest wheat-producing areas in the U.S. MP 320

Mile 518 (209): Turnoff east to **GENESSEE** (pop. 170); groceries, cafe, gas.

Mile 532 (195): **MOSCOW** (pop. 17,080), pronounced mos-coe, was first settled in 1871. It is the home of the University of Idaho, which has an enrollment of 10,000 students. It is a commercial, service and agricultural center. (Bumper stickers here read "wear wool, eat lamb.")

Junction with Idaho Highway 8 east to Troy and Highway 270 west 8 miles to Pullman, WA. Between Moscow and Pullman is the Appaloosa Horse Museum. The Appaloosa

was indigenous to the Nez Perce Indians; its name is derived from "a Palouse horse." More than 250,000 horses are registered at the museum, which contains a number of excellent Nez Perce artifacts.

Mile 539 (188): Fourmile Creek. Large grain elevators to west.

Mile 542 (185): Fourmile Creek. Turnoff to **VIOLA**.

Mile 549 (178): Turnoff to Palouse, junction with Idaho Highway 66. MP 358

Mile 550.5 (176.5): Palouse River. Brown and rainbow trout fishing. Junction with Idaho Highway 6 west to Palouse and Colfax, WA. ✦

Mile 554 (173): Crossing Deep Creek. Junction with Idaho Highway 6 east to Potlatch and St. Maries and the White Pine Scenic Route. The 83-mile scenic route from Potlatch to Rose Lake via Highways 6 and 3 brings you near the largest stand of white pine timber in America. The highway intersects Interstate 90 east of Coeur d'Alene.

Mile 558.5 (168.5): Rest area with restrooms and phone.

Mile 559.5 (167.5): Coeur d'Alene Indian Reservation boundary.

Mile 566.5 (160.5): Sheep Creek.

Mile 569 (158): Hangman Creek and turnoff to **DESMET**. The Desmet Mission was the third of the Sacred Heart Missions established by Father Pierre De Smet in the

Scenic Clearwater River east of Lewiston, ID. (L. Linkhart)

1800s. The new homes built next to the mission buildings are tribal housing for the Indian reservation. No services.   MP 381

Mile 570 (157): TENSED (pop. 113), gas and food available.

Mile 575 (152): Junction with Idaho Highway 16 to Tekoa, WA.

Mile 576 (151): Moctileme Creek.

Mile 577.5 (149.5): Turnoff to Minaloosa Valley.

Mile 584 (143): PLUMMER (pop. 634), a lumber town; gas and food. Junction with Idaho Highway 5 east to St. Maries, west to Fairfield, WA. Heyburn State Park, the Pacific Northwest's oldest state park, is located off Highway 5 east on the south shore of Lake Coeur d'Alene. Camping, hiking, picnicking, boating.

Mile 587 (140): Rock Creek.

Mile 590 (137): WORLEY (pop. 206), named after the Coeur d'Alene Indian Agency superintendent in 1909. All services available.   MP 402

Mile 594 (133): Junction with Idaho Highway 58 east to Rockford and Spokane, WA.

Mile 595 (132): Small community of SETTERS. No services available.

Mile 598 (129): Lake Creek.

Mile 601 (126): Turnoff to Windy Bay and Sun Up Bay on Lake Coeur d'Alene. Popular boating and fishing access areas to this big recreational lake.

Mile 603.5 (123.5): Fighting Creek and boundary of Coeur d'Alene Indian Reservation.

Mile 604.5 (122.5): Turnoff to Rockford Bay on Lake Coeur d'Alene.

Mile 610 (116): Mica Creek.

Mile 610.5 (116.5): Turnoff to Mica Bay on Lake Coeur d'Alene.

Mile 612.5 (114.5): Turnoff to Kidd Island Bay on Lake Coeur d'Alene.

Mile 616 (111): Cougar Creek.

Mile 618 (109): Turnoff to Harbor Island and Green Ferry.   MP 430

Mile 619 (108): Crossing the Spokane River and entering the city of COEUR d'ALENE (pop. 20,054). The Interstate 90 business route loops through the city. Coeur d'Alene (CORR-duh-LANE) is the largest city in Idaho's panhandle and is a popular resort town with motels, restaurants and shops. The city has been described as "an Outdoor

U.S. Highway 195
Lewiston to Spokane

U.S. Highway 195 is a 96-mile stretch of mostly 2-lane highway through the scenic Palouse country of Eastern Washington. A vaguely defined area measuring roughly 85 by 100 miles, the rolling wheatfields of the Palouse straddle the Washington-Idaho border. U.S. Highway 195 is an important north-south connector route between U.S. Highways 95 and 12 at Lewiston, ID, and Interstate 90 at Spokane, WA.

Mile 0 (96): Idaho-Washington state line, approximately a half-mile west of the U.S. Highway 95 junction. Physical mileposts on U.S. Highway 195 reflect distance from here.

Mile 2 (94): Northbound travelers get their first glimpse of Palouse country. The term "palouse" is derived from a French word early settlers used to describe the distinctive rolling hills of the area. Today, this corner of Washington is a prime producer of soft wheat, which is used in crackers, cookies and other pastry items. (Bread requires hard wheat.) Much of this soft wheat is shipped to the Orient for use in noodles.

Planting of the wheat is done in October. Harvesting takes place in August. Watch for huge combines working the fields well into the night during harvest time.

Mile 5 (91): UNIONTOWN; market and gas station. There's a charming little St. Boniface church here with handsome twin wooden bell towers and stained glass windows.

Mile 8.5 (87.5): COLTON; market, liquor store and post office.

Mile 20 (76): Junction with Washington Highway 27 (Grand Ave.) to PULLMAN (pop. 23,579), the largest city in Whitman County, offering several hotels and motels, an RV park and numerous restaurants. The town was named Pullman in 1881 after George Pullman, the Chicago industrialist who invented the Pullman sleeping car.

Pullman's economy revolves around agriculture and Washington State University. Established as a land-grant college in 1890, the university today has about 17,000 students. It is home to the Cougar football team. WSU offers free campus tours on weekdays. Ferdinand's Dairy Bar is the retail outlet for the college's dairy operations and serves "real" ice cream and Cougar Gold cheddar cheese.

Mile 22.5 (73.5): Junction with Washington Highway 270 (Davis Way)

east to Pullman and Moscow, ID. See description previous milepost.

Mile 31 (65): Turnoff for Klemgard County Park, a grassy day-use area on Union Flat Creek; interpretative trails, playground, picnic sites.

Mile 38 (58): COLFAX (pop. 2,500); 2 motels, RV park, restaurants and shopping. This compact and bustling community was first settled in the late 1860s. It became county seat for Whitman County in 1871. Whitman County is the nation's leading producer of soft wheat, dry peas and lentils. It is also one of the state's largest cattle and swine producing regions.

Junction with Washington Highway 272 to Palouse.

Mile 38.5 (57.5): Junction with Washington Highway 26 to Washtucna.

Mile 45 (51): Turnoff for Steptoe Butte State Park picnic area. A winding drive leads to the top of Steptoe Butte (elev. 3,612 feet) and a panoramic view of surrounding farmlands. Steptoe is a geological term for an islandlike area in a lava flow.

Mile 49 (47): Steptoe Butte historical marker and junction with Washington Highway 23 to St. John. Steptoe Butte was named after Lt. Col. E.J. Steptoe of the U.S. Cavalry.

Mile 60.5 (35.5): Rest area.

Mile 62.5 (33.5): Junction with Washington Highway 271 to Oakesdale. Access to Steptoe Butte State Park (see **Mile 45**).

Mile 65.5 (30.5): Turnoff for ROSALIA (pop. 650), which has a main street with a gas station, cafe, 2 banks and shops. There's also a classic old street clock that dates from the 1905 Lewis and Clark Exposition in Portland, the turreted Howard House, and the Harthill Clock Museum.

Mile 66.5 (29.5): Leaving Whitman County, entering Spokane County, northbound. Whitman County was named in honor of Dr. Marcus Whitman, who established a mission near present-day Walla Walla in 1836. Whitman, his wife Narcissa, and 11 others were killed by Indians in 1847.

Mile 71 (25): Turnoff for Plaza.

Mile 79 (17): Turnoff for SPANGLE; gas and food. North of here U.S. Highway 195 becomes a free freeway.

Mile 96 (0): U.S. Highway 195 (Inland Empire Way) junctions with Interstate 90 on the western edge of Spokane. (See description of Spokane in the MAJOR CITIES section; turn to **Mile 279** in the INTERSTATE 90 section for log of that route.)

Paradise" and was named as one of the 10 best places to live in the U.S. by *U.S. News and World Report* in 1982. It is located on the north shore of Coeur d'Alene Lake with over 100 miles of forested shoreline. Boating, sailing and fishing are especially popular and there are nearly 30 resorts, campgrounds and public docks available to campers, boaters and fishermen. Hunting, backpacking and skiing facilities are also available.

Idaho's oldest building, the Cataldo Mission, is east of the city on Interstate 90 at Exit 39. The Coeur d'Alene Mining District features an underground tour at the Sierra Silver Mine.

Mile 623 (104): Junction with Interstate 90 East to Kellogg, Mullan and Lookout Pass Ski Area on Montana border. Westbound on Interstate 90 to Spokane.

Travelers turning on to Interstate 90 refer to **Mile 312** in the INTERSTATE 90 section for log of that route.

Mile 626 (101): HAYDEN (pop. 2,586); gas, food, store. The town was named for Matt Heyden who in 1878 won the right to name the lake during a poker game. The spelling eventually was corrupted. Turnoff to city center and to Hayden Lake, a popular fishing lake, plus water sports and recreational facilities. ⬥

Mile 631 (96): Junction with Idaho Highway 53 west to Rathdrum.

Mile 632 (95): GARWOOD, a small community with limited services. RV park.
▲MP 440

Mile 636.5 (90.5): Small community of **CHILCO**, site of a large sawmill; no services available.

Mile 639 (88): Silverwood Theme Park re-creates a turn-of-the-century mining town with period buildings and furnishings. A 3.2-mile narrow-gauge steam train ride, Norton Antique Aircraft Museum, children's zoo, and carriage rides are featured attractions. Restaurant, RV park, coffee shop. ▲★

Vintage aircraft fly over Silverwood Theme Park at Mile 639. (Paul Fugleberg)

Mile 641 (86): ATHOL (pop. 312); gas, restaurant, RV park. The town's name is reportedly that of an Indian leader. At Athol is the junction with Idaho Highway 54 west to Spirit Lake and Twin Lakes resort areas and east to Bayview and Farragut State Park on Lake Pend Oreille (pon-doe-RAY). Pend Oreille is a corruption of the name *pen d'orielle,* a name given to the lake by French mountain men which means "shape of the ear."

Farragut, formerly a Naval Training Station, was the site of the 1967 World Boy Scout Jamboree and since that time has hosted more than 130,000 Boy and Girl Scouts.

Farragut State Park, 4 miles east, offers campgrounds for both tents and trailers, restrooms, showers, a visitors center and park museum, picnic areas, swimming (lifeguard on duty), hiking trails, bicycle routes, a boat launch and dock, rifle range, fishing and

horseback riding. During the winter, snow-mobiling, sledding, snowshoeing and cross-country skiing on groomed trails are popular. 🎿🍴🛥️▲

Mile 644 (83): Rest area. Turnoff to Granite Lake and Kelso Lake, offering fair trout fishing.

Mile 648 (79): CAREYWOOD; food and gas. Turnoff to Cape Horn and Bayview (7 miles from the highway). MP 456

Mile 648.5 (78.5): Cocolalla Creek.

Mile 651 (76): Cocolalla Lake is on the west side of the highway. MP 462

Mile 655 (72): Small community of WESTMOND and turnoff to Talache. Food and gas.

Mile 656.5 (70.5): Turnoff to Round Lake State Park, 2 miles west. The 142-acre park, which surrounds a small lake, has 53 campsites. Facilities include picnic sites, water, toilets, swimming, fishing, trails, a boat ramp, central water, a dump station, vault toilets and restrooms with showers. The area is open for ice skating, ice fishing, sledding and cross-country skiing. An information center is available and interpretative programs are scheduled. 🎿🍴🛥️▲

Mile 658 (69): Small community of SAGLE; restaurant, gas, RV park. Turnoff to Garfield Bay recreation area on Lake Pend Oreille (8 miles east); campgrounds, resort, boat launch. ▲.

Mile 659.5 (67.5): Turnoff to Bottle Bay on Lake Pend Oreille. This giant natural lake is a major recreational attraction. Fishing available. Kamloops and kokanee are the prime attractions. Surrounding area is excellent white-tailed deer and elk areas with moose and black bear occasionally spotted. Fishing guides and rental boats are available at nearly all developed areas.

Mile 660 (67): Turnoff to Springy Point Recreation Area just south of bridge across Lake Pend Oreille at the osprey nest viewpoint. Osprey often nest on the southwest shore of Lake Pend Oreille. Springy Point has 36 campsites, picnic facilities and boat launch.

The bridge is the fourth one built at this crossing. The first bridge, constructed on 1,540 cedar pilings, was nearly 2 miles long, which made it the longest wooden bridge in the world when it was built in 1910. ⛱▲

Mile 663 (64): SANDPOINT (pop. 4,460); all services, 2 information centers (south and north ends of town). Originally a fur-trading camp and later a mining camp, Sandpoint is now a popular resort community on the shores of Lake Pend Oreille. The first week of October brings the International Draft Horse Competition and a month-long music festival is held each summer.

Junction of U.S. Highway 95 with U.S. Highway 2; turn to **Mile 336.5** in the U.S. HIGHWAY 2 section for log of that route. Highways 95 and 2 share a common alignment from here north to Bonners Ferry.

Mile 664 (63): Excellent well-stocked information center, north end of town.

Mile 664.5 (62.5): Junction with Idaho Highway 200.

Mile 665 (62): Turnoff to Bonner County Fairgrounds and Schweitzer Basin Ski Area with 7 double chair lifts and over 40 runs. Lifts are open during the summer. 🎿

Mile 672.5 (54.5): Small community of COLBURN. Food, gas and motel available.

Mile 674 (52.5): Pack River. Good fly and light tackle trout fishing. ➤

Mile 675 (52): Small community of SAMUELS. No services available.

Mile 678.5 (48.5): Small town of ELMIRA. Gas and food available. MP 490

Mile 680.5 (46.5): McArthur Lake is on the west side of the road. Sportsman's access. A scenic wildlife refuge for nesting Canadian geese and other birds. Fishing. ➤ MP 492

Mile 683.5 (43.5): Kootenai National Wildlife Refuge to west.

Mile 684 (43): NAPLES, so-named for the Italian workers who labored vigorously on the railroad here. Gas and food available.

Mile 685 (42): Blue Lake private campground.

Mile 690.5 (36.5): Geologic marker explains

Osprey nest on Lake Coeur d'Alene. *(L. Linkhart)*

the glacial action which formed this valley, Lake Pend Oreille and Lake Coeur d'Alene. A second marker tells of the thousands of miners who came through this valley on the way to the gold fields at Wild Horse, B.C., in 1864-65.

Mile 694 (33): BONNER'S FERRY (pop. 1,906), named after Edwin Bonner who, in 1864, operated a ferry boat transporting miners and their pack animals across the Kootenai River. All services available. One of the world's largest lumber mills, Bonners Ferry Lumber Co., is located here.

There is a visitor center at the south end of Kootenai River bridge. The Kootenai National Wildlife Refuge is nearby in a wetlands area. Take Riverside Street near the Kootenai River bridge to reach the refuge. MP 506

Mile 698 (29): Historical marker commemorating David Thompson's passage. The famous map maker and trader for the Northwest Co. explored this area in 1808.

Mile 699 (28): Junction with U.S. Highway 2 east; turn to **Mile 299.5** in the U.S. HIGHWAY 2 section for log of that route. Highways 95 and 2 share a common alignment from here south to Sandpoint.

Mile 701 (26): Side road to Smith and Dawson lakes. Camping. ▲

Mile 711 (16): Small community of COPELAND and junction with Idaho Highway 1, which follows the Kootenai River

northwest to the Canadian border along the river's east side. West Side Road goes up the west shore and provides the best access to the Selkirk Mountains. The Selkirks host the only herd of woodland caribou remaining in the Lower 48.

Near the junction of Highways 1 and 95, Brush Lake is heavily stocked with kokanee and trout. ➤

Mile 715 (12): Round Prairie Creek. Numerous small creeks drain this region and offer fair to surprisingly good fishing. ➤

Mile 718 (7): Hell Roaring Creek.

Mile 721 (6): Robinson Lake Campground. Boating. ▲

Mile 722.5 (4.5): Private campground. ▲

Mile 723 (4): Meadow Creek Forest Service Campground 10 miles south via a gravel road. ▲

Mile 726 (1): Moyie River. Copper Creek Forest Service Campground. ▲

Mile 727 (0): EASTPORT (pop. 64; elev. 2,580 feet). United States-Canada international boundary at Kingsgate. Canadian customs. Read through the GENERAL INFORMATION section for details on travel in Canada. Use of seat belts is compulsory in British Columbia. Seven miles north is the junction of Crowsnest Highway 3. Turn to **Mile 204** in the CROWSNEST HIGHWAY 3 section.

U.S. Highway 97

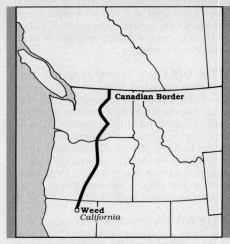

Canadian Border

Weed
California

See map pages 175, 177 and 180

U.S. Highway 97 begins in Weed, CA, and passes through some of the Northwest's most dramatic desert, ranching and orchard scenery. It runs the length of Oregon and Washington, hugging the eastern foothills of the Cascade Range after crossing it in a low spot north of Weed. Then it crosses into British Columbia to run the full length of the province (see CANADA HIGHWAY 97 section for log of that portion). It is a 2-lane blacktop all the way except for an occasional 4-lane section near a city.

Highway 97 offers the traveler a pleasant and very scenic alternative to the interstate system. You will go through towns instead of cities, past farms instead of shopping centers, along rivers with many scenic turnouts, and pass lakes of all sizes, from the vast Upper Klamath Lake to small ponds.

U.S. Highway 97 Log

Distance from Weed, CA, is followed by distance from the Canadian border.

Mile 0 (682): The highway begins on the northern edge of **WEED** (pop. 3,000), 55 miles south of the Oregon state border. Weed offers all visitor facilities including 6 motels, 12 restaurants and 2 RV parks. It is in a hilly setting with the massive Mount Shasta (elev. 14,162 feet) looming on the eastern horizon a short distance from town. Weed, incorporated in 1961, is essentially a logging town with some agriculture.

The highway begins climbing immediately upon leaving town and climbs for 30-odd miles, seldom very steep but always upward. The route isn't mountainous, and you won't be aware that you are crossing the Cascade Range because the topography is mainly jumbled basalt deposited over the centuries by eruptions from the active, but now dormant, Mount Shasta.

Mile 5 (677): Exit to Big Springs Road and Lake Shastina. Lake Shastina is a planned community catering to seniors. Facilities include golf courses, lakeside campsites, vacation homes which are rented when not in use; townhouses, and time-share condominiums. Hiking, cave exploring, swimming, fishing and golf are popular.

Mile 12 (670): Junction with California Highway A12 west to Grenada, Yreka and Interstate 5. Elevation is 4,000 feet.

Mile 13 (669): Roadside marker stating that this was part of the emigrant trail system that led from the California spur of the Oregon Trail into southern Oregon.

Mile 14.5 (667.5): Private lodge. Services and lodging available.

Mile 19 (663): Vista Point on west side of highway with good view of Mount Shasta.

Mile 20 (662): Grass Lake Summit (elev. 5,101 feet).

Mile 21 (661): Forest Service ranger station.

Mile 22 (660): Rest area in a grove of trees on west side of highway.

Mile 28 (654): Bray and Tenant Road to east. No services.

Mile 30 (652): Mount Hebron and summit of Cascade Range (elev. 5,200 feet).

Mile 36 (646): Butte Valley is a broad, flat valley with extensive irrigated row crops and hay fields. A small airplane landing strip is at the southern edge of the valley.

Mile 38 (644): Klamath National Forest Goosenest ranger station.

Mile 39.5 (642.5): Juanita Lake Campground 7 miles west.

Mile 40 (642): **MACDOEL**, unincorporated, is a collection of a few houses surrounding a store. Butte Valley Wildlife Refuge on west side of highway.

Mile 45 (637): Butte Valley airport is on the west side of the highway. No scheduled service.

Mile 50 (632): **DORRIS**, a small community along the railroad at the north end of Butte Valley. Most services are available. Gravel road leads east to Lower Klamath Lake and Tule Lake wildlife refuges. The refuges are among the most important on the West Coast for waterfowl, with thousands of geese and ducks wintering here, and regulated hunting allowed in season. An excellent summer side trip for nature photographers.

Mile 54 (628): Another intersection with paved road east to Lower Klamath Lake and Tule Lake, 23 miles east of the highway. Tule Lake was a well-known "relocation camp" during WWII when Japanese-American citizens within 100 miles of the West Coast were packed up and moved inland following the attack on Pearl Harbor in 1941.

Mile 55 (627): Oregon-California state border.

Mile 56.5 (625.5): Exit to Keno, 8 miles west of the highway, and Ashland.

Mile 58.5 (623.5): **WORDEN**, a railroad siding, and a paved road that cuts off several miles for travelers headed west on Oregon Highway 66 between Klamath Falls and Ashland.

Mile 63.5 (618.5): Rest area with restrooms near the small town of Midland. Groceries and gas available in Midland.

Mile 64.5 (617.5): Oregon Highways 66 and 140 west to Keno and Ashland and Medford at Interstate 5. Highway 140 east connects with Oregon Highway 39 to California Highway 139 to Lava Beds National Monument.

Mile 66.5 (615.5): Vast log pond owned by Columbia Plywood Corp. These ponds are holding areas for logs en route to the sawmill. Most have been replaced by the so-called "dry" sorting lots where logs are stored on the ground and sorted by large forklifts and other machinery. Logs can float for years before they finally sink. All along the slow rivers and in backwaters of dams you will see logs tied together in booms, some so old that weeds and willow brush have started growing on them.

Mile 71 (611): **KLAMATH FALLS** (pop. 17,350) offers all visitor services including 22 motels and numerous restaurants. It is the business and recreational center of southcentral Oregon. The town has a beautiful setting with the vast Upper Klamath Lake serving as its western boundary, and to the west of the lake is the dramatic Mountain Lakes Wilderness recently carved out of the Rogue River National Forest. The city is at a relatively high elevation, 4,100 feet, which gives credence to the catchall description of eastern Oregon as high desert country.

Klamath Falls has a number of visitor attractions, including an old-time trolley that operates in the downtown area during the summer months. There are also several successful museums in town, including the Favell Museum of Western Art and Indian Artifacts, one of the best privately owned museums of its kind. Because the lake is right at the door, several marinas and RV parks are available.

Junction with Oregon Highways 140 and 39. MP 270

Mile 74 (608): Oregon Institute of Technology. MP 267

Mile 77 (605): Hagelstein County park with camping, boat launch, fishing and restrooms available. ⊶▲MP 264

Mile 80 (602): Klamath Lake Historical Marker on west side of highway. MP 261

Mile 88 (594): A beautiful viewpoint that shows the mountains across the lake, dominated by Mount McLoughlin (elev. 9,495 feet) and Pelican Butte (elev. 8,036 feet).

Upper Klamath Lake is the largest lake in Oregon; shallow with an average depth of less than 25 feet and prone to developing vicious winds and dangerous wave action. It is a popular fishing lake. The upper end of Upper Klamath Lake is in the federal refuge system and attracts thousands of waterfowl, including bald eagles and white pelicans.

A natural canal connects Upper Klamath Lake with Agency Lake, a brown and rainbow trout-producing lake. ⊶

Mile 89 (593): MODOC POINT, no services, but an intersection for a lake access road. The highway swings away from the lake here. MP 258

Mile 92 (590): Turnout with sign pointing out Mount McLoughlin across the lake. The 9,495-foot peak dominates the Cascade Range in this area. MP 255

Mile 94 (588): Williamson River and the town of Williamson. Restaurant, motel and gas available. MP 252

Mile 96 (586): Crater Lake junction with Oregon Highway 62. It is 37 miles to Crater Lake National Park from here. For more information on Crater Lake National Park see the MAJOR ATTRACTIONS section.

Mile 98.5 (583.5): Chiloquin airport. Limited services.

Mile 99 (583): Exit to CHILOQUIN (pop. 770), a farm and ranching town about 3 miles east off the highway. Limited services (6 motels); Forest Service campground and ranger station north of town. ▲

Mile 100 (582): Chiloquin exit. Access to Oregon Highway 61 and Fort Klamath. MP 248

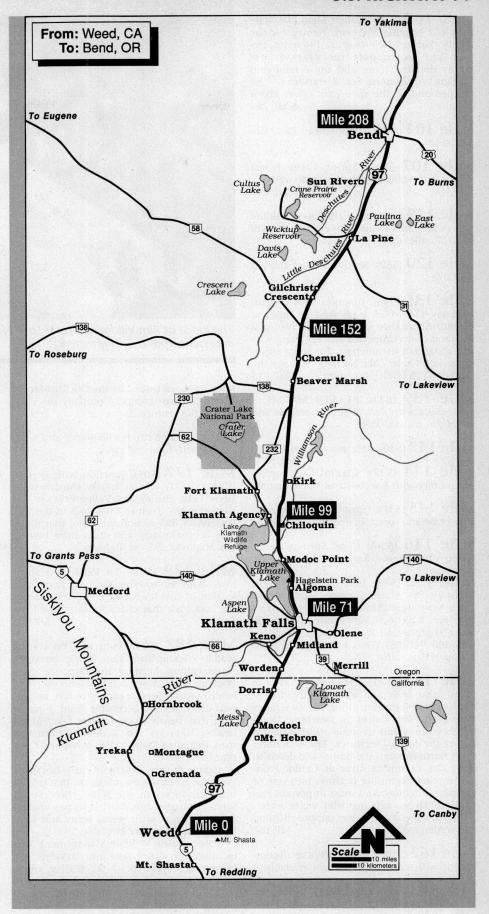

From: Weed, CA
To: Bend, OR

Mile 103 (579): Collier Memorial State Park and Logging Museum. Named for the family that gave the original 146 acres, the park has grown over the years as the family donated more and more land and logging equipment for a museum. The campground at the state park offers about 150 sites. ▲MP 244

Mile 104 (578): Thunderbeast Park. Gas available.

Mile 107 (575): Spring Creek Forest Service campground with 48 sites to west. ▲ MP 243

Mile 119 (563): Klamath Forest Wildlife Refuge is 9 miles east. Silver Lake, a small town 52 miles east.

Mile 120 (562): Sandlake. Store and gas available.

Mile 136 (546): Junction with Oregon Highway 138 which leads west 15 miles to the north entrance to Crater Lake National Park and on to Umpquah and Roseburg. Gas and restaurant at junction. For more information on Crater Lake National Park see the MAJOR ATTRACTIONS section. MP 213

Mile 139 (543): BEAVER MARSH, a community with a small airport, market and motel. No gas available.

Mile 142 (540): Rest area with restrooms.

Mile 144 (538): CHEMULT, a small community with 8 motels and 5 restaurants.

Mile 145 (537): Turnoff west 12 miles to Miller Lake and Forest Service campground.▲

Mile 146 (536): Coral Springs Forest Service campground; 5 sites. ▲

Mile 152 (530): Junction with Oregon Highway 58. A scenic drive, Highway 58 heads northwest through the mountains to Oakridge, Eugene and Interstate 5. Travelers using Highway 58 to Interstate 5 turn to **Mile 308** INTERSTATE 5 section for continuation of that route.

Mile 161 (521): Deschutes National Forest land ends and almost immediately housing developments along the Deschutes River begin. This fork of the Deschutes headwaters is small and streamlike and is identified as the Little Deschutes. The Deschutes flows north through the timber and desert to enter the Columbia River at Celilo. From this modest beginning it grows into one of Oregon's mightiest and most important recreational rivers, offering wild white water, quality steelhead and native rainbow fishing, and wilderness float trips. MP 187

Mile 162 (520): CRESCENT, a small community with store, motel and gas available.

Mile 163 (519): GILCHRIST. Reputed to be the "last company town in America," the

The lodge at Rim Village in Crater Lake National Park. The park is accessible from U.S. Highway 97. *(L. Linkhart)*

town has been owned by the Gilchrist family of the Gilchrist Lumber Company since the turn of the century.

Mile 172 (510): Public phone and mini-market with food and gas.

Mile 177 (505): Junction with Oregon Highway 31, which heads southeast to Silver Lake, Paisley and Valley Falls on U.S. Highway 395. Turn to **Mile 76.5** in the U.S. HIGHWAY 395 section for log of that route. It is approximately 120 miles from here to U.S. Highway 395 via Highway 31.

Mile 179 (503): La PINE is a small town with all traveler services. There is a local road that leads east to ice caves out in the lava beds that characterize most of the region. MP 167

Mile 182 (500): Turn west on county road to Wickiup and Crane Prairie reservoirs, major fishing, hunting and camping areas. Wickiup is a shallow, rich lake with excellent fishing. Forest Service campgrounds, resorts, boat launches are accessible from a paved road that nearly encircles the lake. Many smaller lakes are also accessible from this road, including Twin, Odell, Davis and Crescent lakes.

Crane Prairie Reservoir, just north of Wickiup, is considered one of the best trophy trout producers in the state. Three Forest Service campgrounds, boat launches and an excellent resort with rental boats and local fishing know-how are available.

Crane Prairie Wildlife Management Area includes the entire lake and travelers can expect to see elk, black-tailed deer, otter, ospreys, bald eagles, geese and ducks and possibly a sandhill crane. This is an extremely popular recreational area. ◄▲MP 165

Mile 185 (497): Turnoff on county road to Newberry Volcano Recreation Area, 12 miles east. The crater, measuring 5 miles across, is an ancient caldera of a vast volcano that collapsed into itself. The crater area offers beautiful scenery, Forest Service campgrounds and cold-water lakes. Remnants of the volcano rumblings are visible throughout the area, with lava cones and basalt boulders littering the steep hillsides.

Two of Oregon's finest fishing lakes, East Lake and Paulina Lake, fill the twin craters of an extinct volcano. Both lakes are over 6,000 feet in elevation, and you can expect to encounter snow into June. There's a resort with excellent fishing information, boats and supplies on East Lake. Paulina Lake is a fishing lake with 3 Forest Service campgrounds, Little Crater, Paulina and Chief Paulina, on the lakeshore. There are 2 boat launches, a resort with rental cabins and a restaurant. ◄▲MP 162

Mile 186 (496): La Pine State Recreation Area 4 miles west of the highway has 165 campsites and is a major outdoor recreation area straddling the Deschutes River in an area with good rainbow and brook trout fishing. ◄▲MP 160

Mile 191 (491): Junction to Fall River, which is 13 miles west of the highway.

Mile 194 (488): SUNRIVER, a resort development, has a mixture of permanent residents, condominiums owned by time-sharing organizations, many private homes, all the amenities of a first-class resort, and a good transportation system to Mount Bachelor, the nearby mecca for skiers.

Across the highway from the Sunriver entrance is a 9-mile-long dirt road that leads to the lava cast forest. It is the largest forest of lava cast trees in the world. MP 153

Mile 196.5 (485.5): Lava River Caves State Park contains a lava tube nearly a mile long that was formed when flowing lava cooled on top to form a crust while the lava continued flowing beneath the surface until it left the tube. The tunnel, discovered in 1889, is 20 to 35 feet wide and about the same height. No overnight camping facilities.

Mile 197.5 (484.5): Lava Lands Visitor Center. The center is your best introduction to the history of volcanism and the geology of the area. The complex includes interpretative displays, 3 short trails, 1 of which leads to nearby Lava Butte, the site of 2 volcano spouts and a magnificent view of the surrounding area.

Mile 202 (480): Oregon High Desert Museum, on 20 acres with trails throughout, is one of the best natural history museums in the region. In addition to the static exhibits the staff and volunteers bring in desert wildlife, such as owls, rattlesnakes and other wildlife to show visitors what life is like on the desert. ★MP 145

Mile 208 (474): BEND (pop. 18,000) is the major city in the central Oregon desert, and one of the fastest growing. It was discovered several years ago by Hollywood as an excellent place for movie-making because of its clean air and dramatic scenery. Bend has all services including 37 motels, 2 RV parks and 54 restaurants.

Until recreation became such a big factor in its economy, Bend was primarily a ranching and farming town. Today it is a mecca for artists and writers, skiers, backpackers and real estate investors taking advantage of the area's rapid growth.

This is also the jumping-off point to the Mount Bachelor Ski Area and the scenic Cascade Lakes. Access is via either Division Street at the north end of the city or Franklin Avenue in south Bend.

There are several parks in the area, including 2 state parks. Pilot Butte is located within Bend's city limits and offers a view of the surrounding area; and Tumalo State Park, 5 miles northwest of town on U.S. Highway 20, has 88 campsites. ⚓▲MP 137

Mile 210 (472): Northern city limits. MP 135

Mile 213 (469): Junction with U.S. Highway 20, a major cross-state highway that connects Newport on the Oregon coast with Corvallis, Albany, Lebanon, Bend and Burns. It joins U.S. Highway 395 at Riley and Interstate 84 at Ontario. Turn to **Mile 265.5** in the U.S. HIGHWAY 20 section for log. MP 133

Mile 217 (465): Tumalo junction, a local road that leads west to the town and Tumalo State Park. ▲

Mile 219 (463): Redmond Airport Road and Redmond Air Center. U.S. Forest Service fire suppression, management and smoke jumper center for Oregon and Washington is located here. MP 123

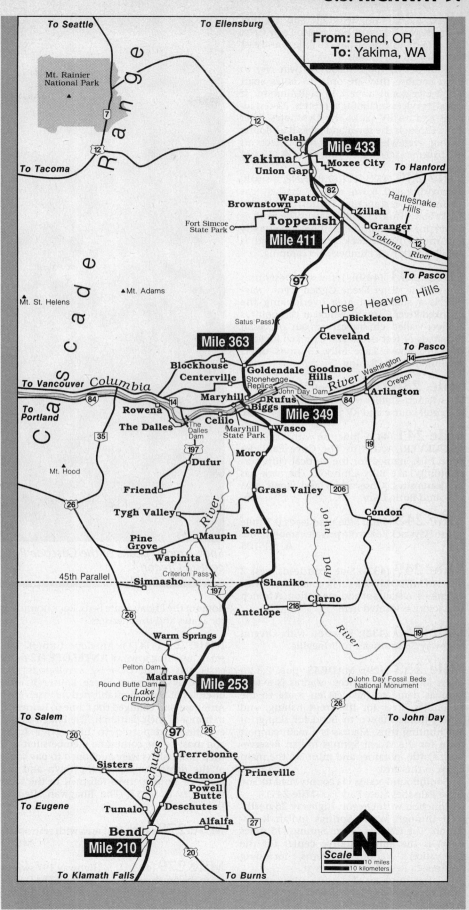

From: Bend, OR
To: Yakima, WA

Mile 224 (458): Redmond and junction with Oregon Highway 126 west to Eagle Crest Resort (5 miles) and Sisters (20 miles), and east to Prineville (20 miles).

REDMOND (pop. 6,830), a twin city to Bend because they are only 15 miles apart and the regional airport is in Redmond. It has all services including 6 motels, 22 restaurants and an RV park. The Deschutes River flows through the town and gives it a cooling feeling, even when the desert heat reflects off the pavement back into your face. ▲MP 124

Mile 230 (452): TERREBONNE, a small, unincorporated town with a market, gas station and restaurant. Turnoff for Smith Rocks State Park (3 miles east). The park is noted for its beautiful canyon topography and multicolored rock formations and is popular with rock climbers. No camping.

Mile 233 (449): Jefferson/Deschutes county line. Peter Skene Ogden scenic wayside is a small rest area overlooking the Crooked River Canyon, which at this point is a sheer-walled chasm carved out of basalt hundreds of feet deep. The Crooked River in this area above Lake Billy Chinook offers smallmouth bass fishing. ⌒

Mile 236 (446): Turnoff for Crooked River Ranch, 7 miles west, a resort community with golf course and RV park. ▲

Mile 241 (441): Junction with road west to CULVER. Access to The Cove Palisades State Park, named for the vertical cliffs surrounding Lake Billy Chinook. The park has 272 campsites. Observatory and picnic area at Round Butte Dam. ▲

Mile 242 (440): Side road leads 0.5 mile east to Haystack Reservoir; private campground. ▲ MP 105

Mile 249 (433): Side road leads west 2 miles to METOLIUS, a small community with 2 markets, restaurant and gas station. A french fry factory is located here.

Mile 250 (432): Junction with Oregon Highway 26 southeast to Prineville.

Mile 253 (429): MADRAS (pop. 2,320) offers all traveler services. Madras is a very familiar name to travelers en route to the Deschutes River for the trout fishing, and others headed down to Bend for skiing, or fall hunting trips. Madras is a main support town for the Warm Springs Indian Reservation. Cattle, potatoes and mint are the main crops in this area.

Southbound access via county road to The Cove Palisades State Park (see **Mile 241**).

Junction with Oregon Highway 26 northwest through Warm Springs Indian Reservation. The town of Warm Springs (15 miles west) is the administrative center for the reservation's various concerns, including Kah-nee-ta Resort north of town.

Mile 257 (425): Turnoff to east for Richardson's Recreational Ranch (3 miles),

Snowcapped peaks of the Cascade Range rise above the lava fields of central Oregon. (© John Barger)

home of the Priday Agate Beds. Rock hounding for agates and thundereggs.

Mile 271 (411): Antelope turnoff. The small ranching town of ANTELOPE (12 miles east) was taken over by a religious sect headed by Bhagwan Shree Rajneesh. The disciples of the cult established themselves in Antelope and changed the name to Rajneesh, in honor of their patriarch. The Bhagwan was eventually deported to his native India and most of the commune members left and their possessions were auctioned to pay some of the debts. Control of the town and the name of Antelope was returned to the local residents in 1987. The Bhagwan died in January 1990.

Mile 278 (404): Rest area with restrooms. MP 69

Mile 279 (403): U.S. Highway 197 swings off to the northwest to Maupin and The Dalles. It can easily be an alternate route to the Columbia River since it emerges at the river

about 20 miles west of Highway 97's crossing at Biggs. Maupin sits high above the Deschutes River and is a favorite place for river rafters to put in to shoot the rapids all the way to the Columbia.

Mile 286 (396): A snowcap identifier is on the west side of the highway. This is a round concrete slab with brass nameplates and photo-engravings showing the major, snowcapped mountain peaks of the Cascade Range that can be seen from this site on clear days.

Mile 288 (394): 45th parallel line, the point where you are halfway between the equator and the North Pole.

Mile 290 (392): SHANIKO (pop. 25), at the junction with Oregon Highway 218 to Antelope (see Mile 271) and John Day Fossil Beds National Monument (see MAJOR ATTRACTIONS section). This is one of the most photographed ghost towns in the Northwest because it is on a busy highway that goes through the center of town. It was founded as a railroad siding and named for August Scherneckau (the local Indians pronounced his name Shaniko), and was a construction headquarters when two opposing railroad companies were racing each other up opposite sides of the Deschutes Canyon. It was also an important station on the stagecoach line that went through the desert. But hard times came when the railroad was completed and the stagecoaches abandoned. Services now include a refurbished hotel, minimarket and gas station.

Mile 306 (376): Kent is mainly a grain elevator and a few houses. No services.

Mile 319 (363): Junction with Oregon Highway 216 to Sherars Bridge (22 miles) and Tygh Valley, 29 miles to the west. Junction is just south of the town of GRASS VALLEY (pop. 175). Excellent fly-fishing in the Deschutes throughout this area. Inquire at local tackle dealers for current fishing information.

Mile 329 (353): MORO (pop. 328) is the county seat of Sherman County and a typical grain and cattle country small town with a motel, 2 restaurants, market, hardware store and a nice park with a stream running through it. No gas available. Sherman County Museum is located here.

Mile 334.5 (347.5): DeMOSS SPRINGS and county park. The townsite was named for a family of that name who were local entertainers and called themselves the Lyric Bards. They performed when their services weren't required on the wheat farms. They also operated an amusement park on the site of the present park. MP 14

Mile 339 (343): A roadside marker pointing out Oregon's Mount Hood (elev. 11,245 feet), almost due west, and Mount Adams (elev. 12,307 feet) across the river to the west-northwest in Washington.

Mile 340 (342): Junction with Oregon Highway 206 to WASCO (pop. 445), 1 mile east. Wasco has a market and restaurant. No gas available. MP 9

Mile 349 (333): Junction with Interstate 84, U.S. Highways 30 and 97 at BIGGS on the Columbia River. Most services available in Biggs. The highway crosses the Columbia River into Washington. The slackwater here is Lake Celilo behind The Dalles Dam. Upstream a short distance is the John Day Dam with the Lake Umatilla slackwater. This area of the Columbia River is generally regarded as the best trophy walleye water in Washington and Oregon. Information is available in Biggs and guides can be arranged.

Travelers headed west to Portland or east to Pendleton on Interstate 84 turn to **Mile 98.5** in INTERSTATE 84 section for log.

Mile 350 (332): Washington-Oregon border.

Mile 351 (331): Maryhill State Park, a large park on the river with 50 campsites, all with electrical and water hookups. The topography along the river is largely columnar basalt, often looking as though it were cast in hexagonal forms and stacked against the cliffs. Lava often cooled and hardened into these forms that are common along the Columbia River east of the Cascades. ▲

Mile 353 (329): Junction with Washington Highway 14, west to Vancouver and east to Kennewick. One mile east on Highway 14 is the access road to Stonehenge replica built by the famous Sam Hill as a memorial to those from Klickitat County killed in WWII. It is part of the Maryhill Museum complex. Two miles west on Highway 14 is the Maryhill Museum. This is one of the most eccentric sites in the Northwest and one of the most dramatic buildings along the Columbia River. Built as a mansion for wealthy Sam Hill, it was dedicated by Queen Marie of Rumania in 1926 and now houses a large collection of antique chess pieces, one of the largest collections of Rodin sculpture, several Faberge eggs, Queen Marie's throne and court gowns, and several display cases of Indian artifacts. A modest admission is charged. A free picnic area complete with peacocks is available.

Mile 358 (324): From the west side of the highway you have a view of several of the Northwest's most prominent mountain peaks. Their distances and elevations are: Mount Hood (elev. 11,235 feet) 50 miles; Mount St. Helens (elev. 8,365 feet) 70 miles; Mount Adams (elev. 12,307 feet) 45 miles; and Mount Rainier (elev. 14,408 feet) 85 miles.

Mile 363 (319): GOLDENDALE (pop.

3,730) is the county seat of Klickitat County. It has all services, including bed-and-breakfast in a historic home, and a good county museum in a Victorian home. The highway bypasses the town. Before leaving Goldendale northbound, check your gas as there are no services for 38 miles.

Above Goldendale on a high hill is the Goldendale Park Observatory, with the world's largest public telescope. It is open year-round and has facilities to handle up to 25 guests. Along with the telescopes, the observatory offers complete darkroom facilities and a science library. Special programs are offered as well as lectures and tours. For further information, write to the Goldendale Park Observatory, Route 1, Box 67, Goldendale, WA 98620.

For a really different experience, visit the tiny rural community of Bickleton, about 30 miles northeast of Goldendale via dirt road. It is the "Bluebird Capital of America," with some 2,000 birdhouses erected by residents.

Mile 365 (317): The Little Klickitat River borders the highway north of Goldendale and is a fair light-tackle stream for pan-sized rainbow.

Mile 376 (306): Brooks Memorial State Park, with 45 campsites. This is in a forested area along the Klickitat River and near Satus Pass only a short distance along the road. The pass (elev. 3,149 feet) is the crest of the Horse Heaven Hills and has limited skiing in the winter. The Yakima Indian Reservation's southern border is on the north side of the pass. All hunting and fishing on the reservation requires tribal permits. ▲

Mile 377 (305): Satus Pass summit, elevation 3,107 feet. MP 27

(Tom Barr)

Maryhill Museum, west of Mile 353, is one of the Northwest's most eccentric sites.

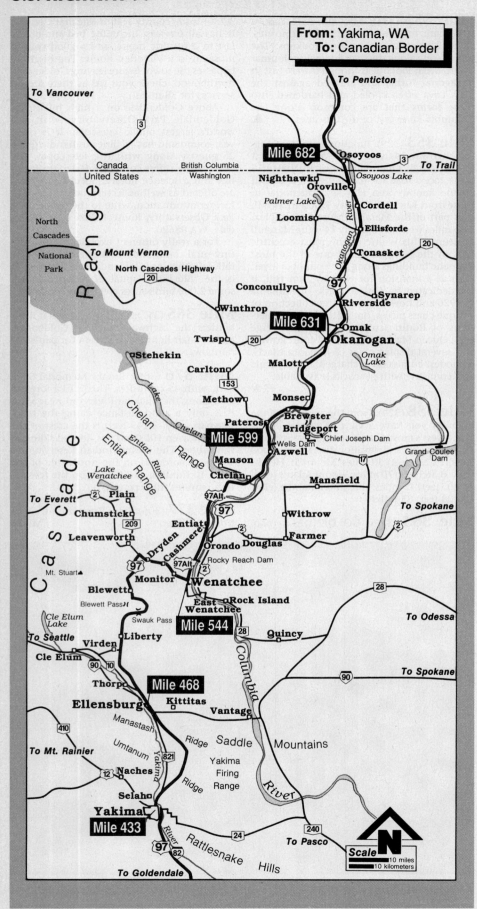

From: Yakima, WA
To: Canadian Border

Mile 404 (278): The 8-mile-long down-grade into the fertile Yakima Valley begins northbound.   MP 54

Mile 411 (271): TOPPENISH (pop. 6,550) is an agricultural center known for its crops of apples and other produce. All services available. No more services for 38 miles southbound. Intersection with Washington Highway 22, which goes east to Prosser and west to Wapato and Yakima.   MP 61

Mile 414 (268): Junction with Washington Highway 220 to White Swan (21 miles) and the Yakima Nation Cultural Center. The cultural center is a combination museum, library, meeting hall and restaurant established by the Yakima tribe.

Highway 220 West leads 27 miles to Fort Simcoe State Historical Park. From 1856-59, the fort was a U.S. Infantry Advance Post. Original officers' homes, reconstructed and original block houses, a small museum and picnic facilities are available. Open year-round.   ⚡MP 62

Mile 421 (261): WAPATO (pop. 3,310) is one of the many towns that grew up along the Yakima River and the highway as irrigated agriculture developed in the valley. All services available.

Mile 424 (258): Parker.   MP 70

Mile 425.5 (256.5): Lateral A — southbound only — leads south 11 miles to junction with Washington Highway 220.

Mile 427 (255): Southbound only. Yakima Indian War Historical Marker and southbound entrance to Yakima Indian Reservation.   MP 75

Mile 428 (254): Yakima and Union Gap exits. UNION GAP (pop. 3,160) is a suburb of Yakima with all services available.

Mile 431 (251): Union Gap exit. Here Interstate 82 and U.S. Highway 97 merge with U.S. Highway 12 south to Prosser and the Tri-Cities area.

Mile 432 (250): Exit to Fairgrounds, Yakima Valley Museum.   EXIT 34

Mile 433 (249): Exit to Yakima business district, Convention Center.

YAKIMA (pop. 49,670) is a major city in southcentral Washington with a thriving downtown core, strong arts and cultural offerings, and abundant produce and fruit. The Yakima appellation is located here, one of 3 distinct wine-growing regions in Washington. Most of the 20 local wineries offer tours and tastings of the varietal wines including Reisling, Chardonnay, Cabernet Sauvignon and Merlot. Downtown features the Capitol Theatre, an original vaudeville house built in the 1920s and faithfully refurbished in 1977. Track 29, also in the city's core, is a unique shopping center housed in 21 train cars transformed into a gallery of shops. Adjoining this shopping center is the Yakima

Depot, where the Spirit of Yakima Dinner Train departs for 4-hour trips that include dinner or brunch. The Spirit Train includes 5 beautifully restored 1937 aluminum passenger cars that chug along the Yakima River. On the outskirts of town is the Yakima Valley Museum, with the country's most comprehensive collection of horse-drawn vehicles and a tribute to former Supreme Court Justice William O. Douglas, a longtime Yakima resident. Exit 33

Mile 435 (247): Junction with U.S. Highway 12 west, which leads west to Naches, then across White Pass to White Pass Ski Area and Mount Rainier National Park.

For more information on Mount Rainier National Park turn to the MAJOR ATTRACTIONS section. EXIT 31

Mile 436 (246): Exit to Selah, a small agricultural community. EXIT 30

Mile 443 (239): Fred G. Redmond Memorial Bridge. Note the windsock that flies there to remind drivers of the strength of the side wind coming across the bridge. This is a long, steep grade and vehicles low on coolant fluid are prone to overheat on the climb. A rest area is at the south end of the bridge for southbound traffic; on the north end for northbound. MP 24

Mile 446 (236): Summit of South Umptanum Ridge (elev. 2,265 feet). MP 21

Mile 450 (232): Summit of North Umptanum Ridge (elev. 2,315 feet). Watch for mule deer and occasional desert bighorn sheep in the sagebrush west of the highway.

Mile 456 (226): Entering the military reservation, which includes the Yakima Firing Range. Admission prohibited. EXIT 11

Mile 460 (222): Viewpoint of the Kittitas Valley far below. At night the view of the valley is spectacular. Crossing the summit of Manastash Ridge (elev. 2,672 feet).

Mile 466 (216): Junction with Interstate 90. U.S. Highway 97 shares a common alignment with Interstate 90 westbound for next 5 miles. Travelers headed east to Spokane, turn to **Mile 108.5** in the INTERSTATE 90 section for log.

Mile 468 (214): Exit to Canyon Road, Ellensburg. Easy access to major chain motels, fast-food outlets and gas stations north off exit.

ELLENSBURG (pop. 11,752) is the hub of the Kittitas Valley and the seat of Kittitas County, a major food processing, stock raising and agricultural region. All services are available. It is also the home of Central Washington University. The 350-acre campus has an enrollment of more than 6,000 students and is nationally known for its outstanding basketball program.

Downtown Ellensburg (easily accessible north from this exit) has many fine old restored Victorian buildings, most found within the 5-block Ellensburg Historic District. Unusual architecture and memorabilia on local history may also be found at the Kittitas County Historical Museum, E. 3rd Avenue and Pine Street. The museum also has an extensive gem and mineral collection.

The biggest annual event in Ellensburg is the Ellensburg Rodeo and Kittitas County Fair, held every Labor Day weekend. The rodeo is one of the premier rodeos in the Northwest. For information, contact the

(Tom Barr)

Officers Row at Fort Simcoe, a state historical park 27 miles west of Toppenish.

Ellensburg Rodeo ticket office, P.O. Box 777, Ellensburg, WA 98926, or phone (509) 925-5381. EXIT 109

Mile 472 (210): U.S. Highway 97 north leaves Interstate 90 and makes a series of turns before joining Washington Highway 10 for a short distance. Travelers headed west to Seattle turn to **Mile 103.5** in the INTERSTATE 90 section for log. EXIT 106

Mile 487 (195): The first of a series of pretty views northbound across the Teanaway Valley as the highway climbs into the foothills. On the northwest side of the Teanaway Valley are the sharp spires of the Stuart Range. Tallest peak is Mount Stuart (elev. 9,415 feet). MP 147

Mile 489 (193): Intersection with Washington Highway 970 to Cle Elum.

Mile 492 (190): Liberty Road intersection. LIBERTY (pop. 130) is 2 miles off the main highway and is a ghostly remnant of the gold rushes that brought people to the area over the decades. When the price of gold shot up in the 1970s, Liberty became repopulated and the old claims are being worked again. Mines are visible from the Liberty Road and it makes an interesting side trip. MP 152

Mile 496 (186): Mineral Springs Road and Forest Service campground. There is a nice, lodge-style restaurant and local recreation information available here. Mule deer and elk are frequently spotted from the highway. Cross-country skiing is popular in the Swakane Range east of Mineral Springs. ▲

Mile 499 (183): Chain-up area at base of Swauk Pass. MP 159

Mile 500 (182): Old Blewett Pass Road intersection. This road, slightly maintained by the Forest Service for its historical value, is one of the most beautiful drives in the region and offers a glimpse back into the early days of motoring when cars were slow and the curves steep and extremely sharp. This route is a nice alternative to whizzing over the pass at top speed. It rejoins U.S. Highway 97 at **Mile 513** near the old Mining Arrastra rest area.

Mile 504.5 (177.5): Summit of Swauk Pass (elev. 4,102 feet). This is also a Snow-Park area for cross-country skiers. MP 164

Mile 505.5 (176.5): Tronsen Creek Forest Service campground with 12 sites. ▲MP 165

Mile 509.5 (172.5): Bonanza Forest Service campground with 5 sites. ▲MP 169

Mile 513 (169): Intersection with Old Blewett Pass Road.

Mile 514.5 (167.5): Mining Arrastra historic site. This relic of the mining days is a stone grinding wheel used to pulverize ore and was used from 1861 to 1880.

Mile 523 (159): Junction with U.S. Highway 2. Highways 97 and 2 share a common alignment eastbound via a 4-lane stretch of highway through the Wenatchee River valley.

Travelers continuing west on U.S. Highway 2 turn to **Mile 592.5** in the U.S. HIGHWAY 2 section. MP 185

Mile 525 (157): **DRYDEN** is a small fruit town with gas, food and groceries available.

Mile 525.5 (156.5): Private lodge and RV park.

Mile 530 (152): **CASHMERE** (pop. 2,295) has 1 motel and 9 restaurants. It is probably best known as the home of Aplets and Cotlets, a confection made with apples, apricots and walnuts. The Chelan County Museum here is noted for its pioneer village with 19 restored buildings and Indian artifacts collection. MP 111

Mile 534 (148): Small town of **MONITOR**. MP 114

Mile 535 (147): Wenatchee River County Park. Beautiful setting between river and highway with 40 full hookups, 24 with water and electric. Picnic shelter, play areas and restrooms available. ⛏▲MP 115

Mile 543 (139): Access to city of Wenatchee to south; complete visitor facilities available. Travelers continuing east on Highway 2 turn to **Mile 580.5** in the U.S. HIGHWAY 2 section for log of that route and description of Wenatchee.

Junction with Highway 97 Alternate route which follows the west side of Lake Entiat north to Chelan. Highway 97 continues its common alignment with U.S. Highway 2 from Wenatchee north to Orondo on the east side of Lake Entiat, rejoining 97A at Chelan.

Log follows Highway 97 Alternate and rejoins Highway 97 at **Mile 582**. MP 119

Mile 545 (137): Exit to Ohme Gardens, a popular alpine garden built high on rock outcroppings with pools, high altitude ground coverings and views of the surrounding countryside.

Mile 548.5 (133.5): Rocky Reach Dam, museum and picnic grounds. There is a glass-enclosed fish ladder in the dam where runs of salmon, steelhead and trout can be watched during migration.

Mile 559 (123): Entiat River.

Stehekin docks on Lake Chelan, one of the state's most popular recreation areas. (Tom Barr)

Mile 562 (120): **ENTIAT** (pop. 492). Gas and food available.

Mile 564 (118): Earthquake Historical Marker.

Mile 571 (111): Chelan Recreation Area exit.

Mile 579 (103): **CHELAN** (pop. 3,000), a popular recreation area on one of the state's most beautiful and most heavily used lakes, Lake Chelan, the largest natural lake in Washington. The city offers 22 motels, 3 bed-and-breakfast facilities, 3 uplake resorts, 6 campgrounds and 27 restaurants. The narrow lake is 50 miles long and runs northwest deep into the North Cascades National Park. At its far end is the isolated town of Stehekin, a popular resort area for people who want to get away for awhile. No roads lead in; a daily boat from Chelan brings in passengers and freight. The south end of Lake Chelan is a very popular spot for waterskiing and windsurfing. There is an excellent campground on the southwest shore.

Lake Chelan Recreation Area has 163 campsites, showers and a boat launch. This has been called the most popular campground in Washington, so expect a crowd. A second state campground, Twentyfive Mile Camp, provides 85 sites, a boat launch and a swimming beach. A private facility also offers camping. (See also Lake Chelan Recreation Area in the MAJOR ATTRACTIONS section.) ▲★MP 233

Mile 582 (100): Highway 97 Alternate rejoins Highway 97. Southbound travelers cross the Columbia River and follow the eastern banks south to U.S. Highway 2 at Orondo, or continue on 97A via Entiat. MP 235

Mile 585 (97): Chelan airport. No scheduled flights.

Mile 589 (93): Town of Azwell and Wells Dam. Visitor facilities, exhibits, fish viewing, and fish hatchery are open to the public. Indian pictographs are located at the vista point overlooking Wells Dam.

Mile 598.5 (83.5): Washington Highway 153. The road follows the beautiful Methow River valley northwest to Twisp and Highway 20 (31 miles), the popular North Cascades Highway (see NORTH CASCADES HIGHWAY section for log). Another popular drive is the "Loup Loup" Highway, following Highway 153 from Pateros to Twisp, then Highway 20 from Twisp to Okanogan. A scenic loop for U.S. Highway 97 travelers.

The road to Alta Lake State Park is located 3 miles north on Highway 153. A very scenic spot, the lake is popular for boating and swimming and has 164 tent sites, 16 full hookup sites. A private lodge is on the north end of the lake. ▲★

Mile 599 (83): **PATEROS** (pop. 540). Gas, lodging and food available.

Mile 605 (77): **BREWSTER** (pop. 1,360) and Washington Highway 173 to Bridgeport (pop. 1,045) and Chief Joseph Dam on the Columbia River. All services available in this orchard community. Brewster was built at the confluence of the Okanogan and Columbia rivers and was for decades a transfer point between the 2 rivers when river navigation was the major system.

Mile 608.5 (73.5): Brewster airport. No scheduled service.

Mile 610 (72): Junction with Washington Highway 17 south to Chief Joseph Dam, Bridgeport, Fort Okanogan Interpretative Center, Bridgeport State Park and on to Grand Coulee Dam.

Mile 612.5 (69.5): MONSE junction, an unincorporated community across the Okanogan River west of the highway. No services available. The Okanogan River is lightly fished, but can provide fair small-mouth bass and trout fishing. ◄

Mile 623 (59): MALOTT junction, an unincorporated community on west side of the river with 2 markets, restaurant and gas station. This was the home of Johnny Appleseed.

Mile 627 (55): Cariboo Trail Historical Marker. Picnic tables, no water available.

Mile 630.5 (51.5): Junction with Washington Highway 20, the North Cascades Highway, to North Cascades National Park. If you are heading west on Highway 20, see **Mile 174.5** in the NORTH CASCADES HIGHWAY section. For more information on the North Cascades National Park, turn to the MAJOR ATTRACTIONS section.

Mile 631 (51): OKANOGAN (pop. 2,340) is the county seat of the county with the same name, and is close by Omak, its twin city. Okanogan offers all traveler services including 10 restaurants, 4 motels and 3 campgrounds. Okanogan began as a trading post on the Okanogan River, and only barely survived until the advent of orchards just after the turn of this century. Both Okanogan and Omak are on the edge of the vast Colville Indian Reservation. The Okanogan airport has no scheduled service. ▲

Mile 632 (50): Omak Lake Road, a local gravel road to the popular fishing areas. Fishing and hunting privileges on the reservation are controlled by the Colville tribe and permits are required. Inquire in Omak.

Mile 635.5 (46.5): Omak exit and junction with Washington Highway 155. OMAK (pop. 3,910) is a bit larger than Okanogan and has more services as a result. Omak offers 7 motels, 1 campground and 17 restaurants. It is best known for the annual rodeo called the Omak Stampede. The controversial suicide race is its main event, and involves racing horses down a very steep hill into and across the Okanogan River. The suicide course is visible from the highway,

View of Okanogan country near Oroville. (Ray T. Weisgerber)

looking west across the river, appearing like a washed-out slash in the hillside. Highway 155 goes through the heart of the Colville Indian Reservation to Nespelem and Grand Coulee Dam.

Mile 637.5 (44.5): Omak airport road. No scheduled services.

Mile 644 (38): RIVERSIDE (pop. 240), a small agricultural community with grocery and cafe. Turnoff to Conconully State Park, 15 miles west. Located between 2 lakes, the park is popular with swimmers, boaters and fishermen. Facilities include 0.5 mile nature trail, 65 tent sites, 10 hookups with water and 6 primitive sites; boat launch. ◄▲MP 299

Mile 649.5 (32.5): Cross South Pine Creek and pass turnoff to Fish Lake.

Mile 655.5 (26.5): Crossing Okanogan River.

Mile 660 (28): TONASKET (pop. 1,060) has food, gas, motel and hospital available. Junction with Washington Highway 20 east through the famed Okanogan Highlands to Wauconda, Republic and Kettle Falls. The Okanogan Highlands are pine forests and granite mountains that are more heavily forested than much of eastern Washington but not nearly as much as the Cascades. The region has numerous lakes, streams and wildlife. The Republic area is a longtime gold mining area, and as with most mining areas, ghost towns are spotted throughout the mountains. Turnoff from Tonasket east 15 miles to Sitzmark ski area at Havillah for

downhill and cross-country skiing. ◄ MP 315

Mile 665 (17): ELLISFORDE has gas, food and overnight hookups available. Turnoff to Many Lakes Recreation Area which has fishing, tents, camping and lodging.

Old Okanogan Mission Historical Marker and Indian cemetery are located behind Ellisforde's church. The site also includes the original church bell and headstones which date to the 1880s. ◄▲

Mile 675.5 (6.5): Okanogan River.

Mile 677 (5): OROVILLE (pop. 1,480). Mostly an orchard town, Oroville is the last town before entering Canada and is at the south end of Osoyoos Lake, which straddles the international border. Oroville has all traveler services. Osoyoos is an excellent smallmouth bass lake. The Osoyoos Lake Recreation Area is on the south end of the lake and provides 86 campsites, showers, swimming beach and a boat launch. The lake is a major wintering area for geese and ducks. The area is also heavily mined, and the amount of mining conducted at any given time is almost directly related to the price of gold. ◄▲

Mile 682 (0): U.S.-Canada international border. Open 24 hours daily. The highway mileage ends for the southern section of U.S. Highway 97 and begins anew at the international border. Northbound travelers should turn to CANADA HIGHWAY 97 section for log of that route. For details on crossing the border, see Customs Requirements in the GENERAL INFORMATION section.

Canada Highway 97

See map pages 185 and 190

Canada Highway 97 is an extension of U.S. Highway 97, running from the international boundary between Osoyoos, BC, and Oroville, WA, to Prince George, BC.

Travelers along this route will sample 2 of British Columbia's prime vacation areas: the Okanagan and the Cariboo. The Okanagan Valley, with its string of long lakes, is in the Interior dry belt and enjoys more than 2,000 hours of sunshine a year. It is Canada's premier fruit-growing area; orchards stretch from Osoyoos in the south to Vernon in the north, making the valley a tourist destination from spring blossomtime through fall harvest. Water recreation plays a large part in an Okanagan holiday because of the warm waters and sandy beaches.

The Cariboo is far less populated than the Okanagan. It is also rougher and wilder, home to cattle ranchers rather than orchardists. Here visitors will find dude ranches, excellent fishing and gold rush history. No visitor will want to miss a side excursion from Quesnel along B.C. Highway 26 to the restored gold rush town of Barkerville.

Canada Highway 97 Log

Distance in miles from the Canadian border is followed by distance in miles from Prince George, BC. Equivalent distance in kilometers are indicated by Km.

Mile 0 (504) Km 0 (811.5): U.S.-Canada border; customs open 24 hours.

Mile 1 (503) Km 1.5 (810): Haynes Point Provincial Park, situated on a sandspit jutting into Osoyoos Lake. Day-use area for swimming, waterskiing and fishing (bass and rainbows); 36 campsites, boat launch. A park naturalist program is offered during July and August. Camping fee. A very popular campground in summer.

Throughout the Okanagan Valley, motorists will see signs urging control of Eurasian milfoil, a weed that is growing out of control and gradually choking the lakes in the area. Boaters should remove all weeds from their boats before and after launching. ➤▲

Mile 1.5 (502.5) Km 2 (809.5): Access road east to **OSOYOOS** (pop. 3,000) offering all traveler services. (For more information on

Osoyoos, see **Mile 443** in the CROWSNEST HIGHWAY 3 section.)

Mile 2.5 (501.5) Km 4.5 (807): Junction with Crowsnest Highway 3 (see CROWSNEST HIGHWAY 3 section). British Columbia government information trailer at junction is open mid-May to mid-Sept.

Mile 5.5 (498.5) Km 8.5 (803): Side loop road east to site of first customs house, built in 1861 with John Haynes in charge. A Canadian government historic site cairn marks the spot. During the Cariboo gold rush, miners traveled up the Okanagan on the Fur Brigade trail from Oroville, WA.

Mile 6 (498) Km 10 (801.5): Good bird-watching at end of lake marshes. Watch for osprey nests.

Mile 7.5 (496.5) Km 12 (799.5): Road 22 leads east across meadows and crosses Okanagan River to desert. Road branches beyond bridge: turn left (north) for road through vineyards to Oliver, right for dusty road through Inkaneep Indian Reserve to Inkaneep churches (see feature page 186). ★

Mile 8 (496) Km 13 (798.5): Rest area at Desert Oasis Picnic Park beside south end of Deadman Lake. The lake is a glacial pothole, home to nesting Canada geese. ⇧

Mile 11.5 (492.5) Km 19 (792.5): Okanagan Vineyard Winery to west.

Mile 12 (492) Km 19.5 (792): Divino and Gehringer Bros. estate wineries to west.

Mile 12.5 (491.5) Km 20 (791.5): View to the east of Mount Baldy, a local ski hill.

Mile 14 (490) Km 22.5 (789): **OLIVER** (pop. 1,970) with all traveler services. The town was named for Premier John Oliver, who encouraged a soldier settlement and irrigation scheme here in 1919 that turned the dry sagebrush slopes into rich orchards. Oliver museum and archives are located on 6th Street. Turn east on 7th Avenue for Tuc-el-Nuit Lake; swimming, camping and boating (no motors). Also available here is a hiking and biking trail, 8.5 miles/14 km long, that is part of the new International Peace Park. The trail will ultimately wind 185 miles/300 km through Washington's Okanogan and British Columbia's Okanagan. 👫▲

Mile 16 (488) Km 25.5 (786): Quarry above road to west is a silica mine.

Mile 19 (485) Km 30.5 (781): Okanagan River bridge. Today mostly canalized for flood control and irrigation, the Okanagan River is a tributary of the Columbia River. Access to Bright's Winery and Inkaneep Provincial Park at north end of bridge. The park has 7 campsites and fishing. Camping fee May to October. ➤▲

Mile 19.5 (484.5) Km 31 (780.5): Gallagher Lake, east of highway but hidden by trees, has a resort, private campground and swimming. Opposite is Ye Olde Welcome Inn, an authentic English pub. ▲

Mile 20 (484) Km 31.5 (780): McIntyre Creek, named for an early settler. The highway passes under McIntyre Bluffs, vertical cliffs which rise 820 feet/250m high, site of an Indian battle between the Shuswaps and Okanagans. A small herd of California bighorn sheep makes its home in the rocky hills. They often come down to the lake for water in the evenings and early mornings, and in winter are fed in roadside fields.

Mile 22 (482) Km 35 (776.5): South end of Vaseux Lake; resort and beach.

The highway north of here is narrow and very winding along the lake. Recommended speed is 25 mph/40 kmph.

Mile 23 (481) Km 37 (774.5): Rock shop west of road advertises jade and fossils.

Mile 23.5 (480.5) Km 37.5 (774): Vaseux Lake Provincial Park; 9 campsites, swimming and fishing (largemouth bass, rainbow, perch and whitefish). No motors allowed on the lake. Camping fee May to September. ➤▲

Mile 24 (480) Km 38 (773.5): Vaseux Wildlife Center; interpretative panels, trails and bird blind. Excellent waterfowl watching.

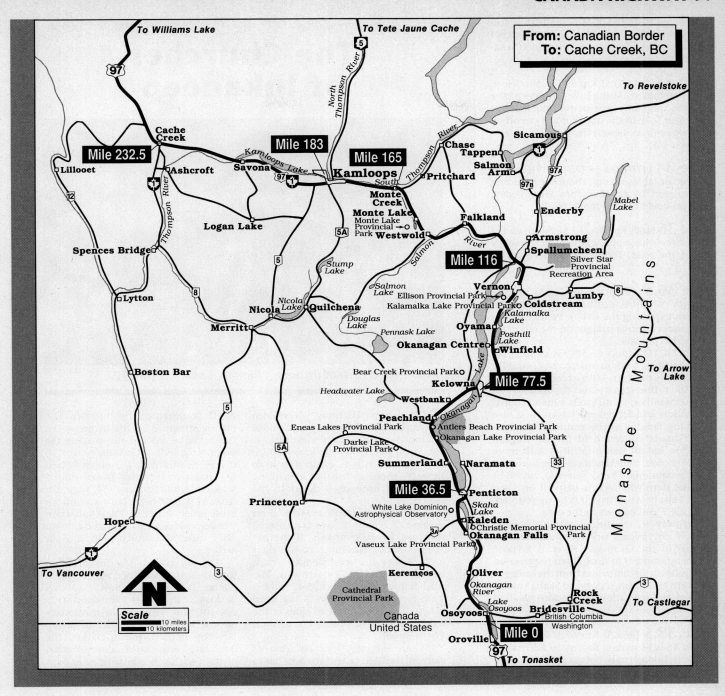

Cliffs to east are home to Canada's largest colony of white-throated swifts.

Mile 24.5 (479.5) Km 39 (772.5): Oliver Ranch Road. Alternate route to Okanagan Falls.

Mile 27 (477) Km 43.5 (768): **OKANAGAN FALLS** (pop. 1,200), a small resort community at the south end of Skaha Lake which has recently become known for its 2 flea markets. All services available. Heritage Bassett House (1909), at the south end of town, is worth a visit.

Mile 27.5 (476.5) Km 44.5 (767): Christie Memorial Provincial Park on Skaha Lake;

picnic area, swimming and fishing for rainbows and kokanee.

Mile 28 (476) Km 45 (766.5): Okanagan River bridge. Original falls south of bridge have been dammed for irrigation purposes. Turn south on Green Lake Road for Okanagan Falls Provincial Park; 20 campsites in the trees by the river. The park is known for its variety and number of bats. Le Comte Estate Winery in converted historic log ranch is 3 miles/ 5 km south on road. ▲

Mile 30.5 (473.5) Km 49.5 (762): Road west to St. Andrews by the Lake golf course and White Lake Dominion Astrophysical Observatory (4 miles/7 km). The observatory

visitor center is open year-round with displays and explanations. Guided tours are given Sunday afternoons from 2-5 p.m. in July and August only. NOTE: Automobiles must be parked at the gate, enter on foot only.

Mile 31 (473) Km 50 (761.5): Junction with Highway 3A to Keremeos, a shortcut to Crowsnest Highway 3 for westbound travelers.

Mile 32 (472) Km 51 (760.5): Steep side road east to lakeshore community of **KALEDEN**; resort facility, food, gas.

Mile 32.5 (471.5) Km 52 (759.5): Okanagan Game Farm to the west. Drive or walk to see 130 species of native and exotic animals. Open year-round, 8 a.m. to dusk, except December and January. Late afternoon feeding time is best.

Mile 33.5 (470.5) Km 53.5 (758): Viewpoint overlooking Skaha Lake. This deep blue lake was originally part of the much larger Okanagan Lake to the north; it was cut off by build-up of delta deposits from creeks on east and west side.

Mile 34 (470) Km 55 (756.5): Viewpoint with picnic table and sign about the founding of Penticton by rancher Tom Ellis. Today, orchards cover the old ranch lands. 🏕

Mile 36 (468) Km 58 (753.5): North end of Skaha Lake with a public beach on the south side of the road. Penticton airport road to north.

Mile 36.5 (467.5) Km 59 (752.5): Canada Highway 97 turns north for Kelowna and Vernon, bypassing the city of Penticton. For city center continue straight on the old highway beside the lake.

PENTICTON (pop. 25,500) is a center for fruit packing and canning, but equally important is tourism. With excellent beaches on 2 lakes, fine scenery and dependable hot summer weather, Penticton is a major tourist destination and retirement haven. It is also becoming famous as the venue of the Iron Man Canada contest held in late August. Penticton has all visitor facilities with more than 70 hotels, motels and campgrounds and many restaurants. The SS *Sicamous*, largest of the lake stern-wheelers, is berthed on Okanagan Lake beach, where it is being restored. There are 7 golf courses in the area.

Highway 97 continues along Channel Parkway city bypass which runs beside the channel of the Okanagan River. A favorite summer pastime is to float down the river on inner tubes or air mattresses from the bridge at the north end of town down to Skaha Lake, 2 hours of cool relaxation. A bike path parallels the channel.

Mile 38.5 (465.5) Km 62 (749.5): Road west to Apex Mountain Provincial Recreation Area with hiking trails, but no other facilities. Downhill and cross-country skiing at nearby resort. ⛷🎿

Mile 39.5 (464.5) Km 63.5 (748): Junction with old highway connecting Canada Highway 97 with Penticton city center. Access to lakeshore resorts and services.

Mile 40 (464) Km 64.5 (747): Okanagan River bridge. Put-in point for rafters floating down to Skaha Lake (2 hours).

Northbound the highway runs beside Okanagan Lake. Prominent features of this area are the high clay banks, eroded into miniature hoodoos.

Mile 41 (463) Km 66 (744.5): Travel information to west.

Mile 42.5 (461.5) Km 68.5 (743): View-

The Churches of Inkaneep

Historic old church at Inkaneep; turnoff at Mile 7.5 (Km 12). (Liz Bryan)

Travelers on Highway 97 between Osoyoos and Oliver usually miss one of the province's oldest and most historic churches, located on the Inkaneep Indian reserve. This side trip also leads through some of the last remaining stretches of untouched desert in the region.

Turn off Highway 97 at **Mile 7.5** on to Road 22. Follow this west to a fork in the road where remnants of the old Haynes Ranch remain; take the right fork. Where the road divides again, branch left and head northwest. The road follows Inkaneep Creek, hidden from view at the bottom of the steep canyon. The land on both sides of the road is Indian reserve and trespassing is not allowed.

Where the creek emerges from its canyon, the high valley broadens out to reveal Inkaneep village—an abandoned schoolhouse, a few houses. The road rounds a corner and on the little hill ahead is the Inkaneep church, a tidy, steepled affair painted in blue and white, dominating the horizon. The old log structure by the cemetery on the opposite side of the road is the original church of Inkaneep, one of the oldest in British Columbia. When the Okanagan Historical Society undertook its restoration in 1964, they discovered it had been built around an even older structure that had been smaller, windowless and sod-roofed. They dated this structure to 1860 or earlier.

The old church was first built of logs, then later sheathed with wooden planks. It is deserted now. Swallows nest under its roof and the doorway is open to the elements. In missionary days it was known as the Inkaneep Division church, for it marked the boundary between the administration of the Oblates, headquartered at Mission in the Fraser Valley, and the Jesuits at Colville, WA.

The road continues through Indian ranchlands to Oliver, where travelers rejoin Highway 97.

point over Okanagan Lake, which stretches 67 miles/112 km from Penticton to north of Vernon. Across the lake are the orchard benches and resort community of Naramata.

Mile 43 (461) Km 69.5 (742): Kickininee Provincial Park; 14 picnic sites. Kickininee is the local name for kokanee, a species of landlocked salmon abundant in the lake. 🏕

Mile 43.5 (460.5) Km 70 (741.5): Soorimpt picnic area; 10 sites, boat launch. 🏕

Mile 44 (460) Km 71 (740.5): Pyramid picnic area; 16 sites. The highway here has cut through several ridges in the white silt cliffs forming prominent pyramids. 🏕

Mile 45 (459) Km 72.5 (739): Sun-Oka Beach picnic area with one of the best swimming beaches in the Okanagan. Site of summer sand castle contests and the Jan. 1 Polar Bear Swim. 🏕★

Mile 45.5 (458.5) Km 73 (738.5):

Summerland Agricultural Research Station, 1.2 miles/2 km west, open to the public for tours in July and August. Gardens are open daily for picnics from 7:30 a.m. to 8:30 p.m., May 1 to Oct. 31. ⅂

Mile 46 (458) Km 73.5 (738): Prairie Valley Road west to Giant's Head Park for picnics, walks and great views (summit is 3,000 feet/900m). The large Tudor-style building about halfway up, built in 1916 as a Baptist College, is now a resort. Access to Darke Lake (10 miles/16 km gravel) and Eneas Lakes (12 miles/20 km rough gravel) provincial parks; 5 campsites at Darke, none at Eneas, but good fishing for rainbow and brook trout. ⅂◀▲

Mile 47.5 (456.5) Km 76.5 (735): Turnoff east to lower Summerland, lakeshore. Peach Orchard Municipal Campground, 90 sites. ▲

Mile 48.5 (455.5) Km 78.5 (733): Turnoff west for **SUMMERLAND** (pop. 8,000); all services available. The first commercial orchard in the Okanagan was planted here in 1890 and Summerland, a small but busy village, is still dominated by the fruit industry.

Visit Summerland fish hatchery, which raises rainbow and eastern brook trout for stocking Okanagan lakes and streams; open year-round.

Tour Summerland Sweets on Canyonview Road which manufactures fruit candy, jams and syrups. Tours 9:30 a.m. to 4 p.m., weekdays only in July and August.

Mile 50 (454) Km 81(730.5): Sumac Ridge Estate Winery, golf course and restaurant.

Mile 51.5 (452.5) Km 83 (728.5): Viewpoint with sign commemorating J.M. Robinson, who is considered the father of the fruit industry here, having founded orchards in Peachland, Summerland and Naramata.

Mile 55.5 (448.5) Km 89.5 (722): Okanagan Lake Provincial Park offers 156 campsites, picnic tables, sani-station, fishing, swimming and boat launch. A shady oasis. Camping fee April to Oct. Across the lake is Okanagan Mountain Provincial Park, a wilderness area accessible only on foot. ⅂◀▲

Mile 59 (445) Km 95 (716.5): Viewpoint with sign pointing out the legendary home of Ogopogo, the Okanagan's resident lake monster, on Squally Point on the opposite shore. Below the point is Rattlesnake Island.

Mile 60 (444) Km 96.5 (715): Antlers Beach Provincial Park; picnicking, fishing, swimming. Just north of the park the highway crosses Deep Creek bridge. A good trail leads up the creek 15 minutes to Hardy Falls. In late September and early October the creek is crimson with spawning kokanee. ⚲⅂◀

Mile 62.5 (441.5) Km 100.5 (711): Picnic tables with small swimming beach. Junction with road to **PEACHLAND** (area pop. 3,200), a small fruit-growing settlement founded by J.M. Robinson in 1898. The community grew with the opening of the Brenda molybdenum and copper mine in the hill behind. All services available.

Visit United Church (1916); March house (a 1907 log cabin) on Trepanier Bench Road; Greata fruit packing house (1920); and the library and museum, housed in old octagonal-shaped Baptist church.

Turn west (uphill) for Silver Lake Forestry Centre, an open-air museum of the logging industry (10 miles/16 km), and Headwaters Lake fishing camp (17 miles/27 km). Road also provides access to Pennask Lake Provincial Recreation Area (34 miles/55 km rough gravel); no park facilities but excellent fishing. ◀

Mile 64 (440) Km 102.5 (709): North entrance to Peachland.

Mile 64.5 (439.5) Km 103.5 (708): Highway crosses Trepanier Creek and junctions with Trepanier Bench Road, west to Chateau St. Claire Estate Winery.

Mile 68.5 (435.5) Km 110 (701.5): Glenrosa Road leads west to Last Mountain and Telemark downhill and cross-country ski areas. ⌇

Mile 69.5 (434.5) Km 111.5 (700): Next 4 exits northbound for **WESTBANK** (pop. 6,100), a small shopping community with all services available, including several beachside resorts. A cairn marks the old Hudson's Bay Co. Fur Brigade trail which passed through the Okanagan Valley on the west side of Okanagan Lake. Much of the land in the area is Tsinstikeptum Indian Reserve.

Mile 70 (434) Km 112.5 (699): Exit east for lakeshore resorts and Boucherie Road scenic drive which leads to Mission Hill Vineyards.

Mile 75.5 (428.5) Km 121.5 (690): Junction with Westside Road which goes up the west side of Okanagan Lake to north of Vernon (49.5 miles/80 km). Bear Creek Provincial Park, 4 miles/7 km from junction, has 80 campsites, picnic tables, sani-station, swimming, fishing and hiking. ⚲⅂◀▲

Mile 76 (428) Km 122.5 (689): The highway starts down long hill to 3-lane floating bridge which crosses Okanagan Lake at Siwash Point, site of an ancient Indian settlement. The bridge, opened in 1958 by Princess Margaret, is the only one of its kind in Canada. The center portion is made from floating concrete pontoons anchored to the lake bottom. A section of the span can be lifted to allow large boats through. The center lane is reversible for traffic control. Shelter Bay marina is at the south end of the bridge.

Mile 77.5 (426.5) Km 124.5 (687): **KELOWNA** (pop. 63,000), the largest of the Okanagan communities, has 20 miles/32 km of lake frontage. With a backdrop of rugged hills and orchard-covered benches, Kelowna provides much in the way of tourist attractions. Its central business area is compact, sandwiched between Highway 97 and the lakeshore, but its suburbs sprawl pleasantly to the north and east. It offers excellent accommodations — from luxury resorts to campgrounds — many restaurants and good shopping. Tourist information center on Highway 97 (Harvey Ave.).

Settlement started here in 1859 when Oblate missionaries, Father Charles Pandosy, Father Richard and Brother Sorel founded a mission on a creek at L'Anse au Sable (Sandy Bay). The priests built a tiny church and a school and planted apple trees and vines.

Apart from a few pack trails, settlers depended on the lakes for transportation and shipment of supplies. With the completion of the Canadian Pacific Railway to Kamloops in 1885 and its later spur line to Okanagan Landing near today's Vernon, lake steamer service grew in efficiency and importance. When a townsite was surveyed at L'Anse au Sable in 1892, it planted its feet firmly beside the lake, not back in Mission Valley, and the new town was called Kelowna after the Indian word for "grizzly bear."

Today its economy is based on fruit-growing (one-third of Canada's fruit exports come from this area) and manufacturing (Crown Forests plywood plant, Western Star tractor trucks).

Kelowna has 10 golf courses and more than 60 parks, one of them the focus of the downtown waterfront. Visit the city park (a blaze of flowers at the foot of Bernard Avenue) downtown to swim at Hotsands Beach, rent paddleboats and windsurfers, play tennis, and go lawn bowling. Or dine at the MV *Fintry Queen*, an authentic lake paddle-wheeler, now a cruise ship and floating restaurant. Nearby are the soaring white sails of a 40-foot-/12-m-high fiberglass sculpture and a reminder of the Kelowna Regatta, held each August. Nearby, the real sails at the boat harbor emphasize the water sport possibilities of this resort city. There's also a statue of the legendary lake monster, Ogopogo.

Drive up Knox Mountain Nature Park (north on Ellis Street at east end of bridge) for easy hiking trails and bird's-eye view of city.

Tour the Sun-Rype fruit processing plant at Ethel Street and Vaughan Avenue; tours Monday to Friday, 9 a.m. to 3 p.m., summer months only. Also visit Calona Winery on Richter Street, the valley's oldest and biggest winery.

Turn east on Richter Street and follow signs for Okanagan Mission to reach Father Pandosy's mission at Benvoulin and Casorso roads. This newly designated provincial heritage site includes hand-hewn log buildings that served as mission chapel, living quarters and school, plus 2 pioneer homes that have been moved to the site. Outdoor display of early farm implements and picnic tables under the willows make this a good family spot. Nearby is the recently rediscovered mission cemetery where Father Pandosy was buried. Mission is open from 8 a.m. to dusk; no admission charge. ⅂

Mile 81.5 (422.5) Km 131 (680.5): Junction with B.C. Highway 33 south to communities of Rutland, Beaverdell and Rock Creek on Crowsnest Highway 3. Access to Big White ski area. ⌇

Mile 86 (418) Km 138.5 (673): Kelowna airport.

Mile 87.5 (416.5) Km 141 (670.5): Road east to Postill Lake (9.5 miles/16 km); accommodations, boat launch and camping. Good fishing for rainbows. Good cross-country skiing in winter.

Mile 88.5 (415.5) Km 142 (669.5): South end of Duck Lake, warm and shallow, good spot for waterskiing. There are several turnouts along the lake with trash bins.

Mile 91 (413) Km 146.5 (665): Community of **WINFIELD**. Junction with road west to **OKANAGAN CENTRE**, an orchard community on Okanagan Lake, and east on Beaver Lake Road to Hiram Walker Distillery, second largest in Canada. Tours are given year-round on weekdays. No children under 12.

Mile 91.5 (412.5) Km 147.5 (664): Junction with Berry Road west for Gray Monk Winery.

Mile 92.5 (411.5) Km 149 (662.5): South end of Wood Lake. Turn east for lakeside resorts.

Mile 94 (410) Km 151.5 (660): Viewpoint overlooking Wood Lake. Several turnouts along lake to the north. Fishing for rainbow and kokanee is good.

Mile 97.5 (406.5) Km 157 (654.5): **OYAMA**, a small resort and fruit-packing community on the isthmus between Wood and Kalamalka lakes. Gas is available at the junction.

Mile 101 (403) Km 162 (649.5): Viewpoint of Kalamalka Lake, named after the son of an early settler from Hawaii who later became chief of the Okanagan Indians. The lake is noted for its brilliant colors, ranging from green in the shallows to deep blue. There are several viewpoints and turnouts north along the highway.

Mile 107 (397) Km 172.5 (639): Viewpoint overlooking Coldstream Valley across the lake. Homesteaded in 1864 by Forbes and Charles Vernon (after whom the city of Vernon, just to the north, is named), the ranch was later subdivided into orchards, a move which helped foster fruit-growing in the Okanagan.

The mountains to the east are the Monashees. Across the lake is Cosens Bay and the ranchlands of Coldstream Valley.

Mile 108 (396) Km 173.5 (638): Turn-off east at head of lake to Coldstream and Kalamalka Lake Provincial Park; swimming, hiking, picnicking. *CAUTION:* Watch for rattlesnakes.

Mile 108.5 (395.5) Km 174.5 (637): To the west is a weather station; to the east, a government forest research station.

Mile 109 (395) Km 175.5 (636): Dept. of National Defence Camp Vernon, on Mission Hill. A visitor information booth is open in summer.

Mile 109.5 (394.5) Km 176 (635.5): Stop of interest sign about Camp Vernon; gravel turnaround on west side. The Okanagan Cavalry first mustered here in 1908 and the site grew into the largest military camp in British Columbia where soldiers received basic training for 2 world wars. Today, only summer cadets train here.

Mile 110 (394) Km 177 (634.5): **VERNON** (pop. 22,000) is situated between Kalamalka and Okanagan lakes, with beach frontage and parks on both. The city, with its parks and recreation facilities and its emphasis on cultural events, is a popular tourist destination. It offers a wide range of tourist facilities and shopping.

Incorporated in 1892, Vernon is the Okanagan's oldest city, settled in 1867 by Luc Girouard, who became the area's first postmaster. His original cabin is preserved in Polson Park. As head of the Okanagan Lake paddlewheeler service, Vernon grew in importance with the construction of a branch line of the Canadian Pacific Railway. Later, irrigation made commercial agriculture possible, with orchards, vegetable farming and dairying being added to the area's cattle ranching and forestry base.

Visit Polson Park, on the east as you enter town, a green oasis lined with weeping willows and with a unique floral clock. See the historic turn-of-the-century courthouse now surrounded by a flowery courtyard and waterfalls.

Swim at Kalamalka Lake public beach or Kinsmen beach on Okanagan Lake. Drive to Silver Star Provincial Park and ride the chair lift to the alpine meadows. Great views and hiking trails.

At the first intersection when you enter Vernon from the south, turn east on Highway 6 to Lumby and the Arrow Lakes; turn west for Okanagan Lake, Okanagan Landing and Ellison Provincial Park (9.6 miles/16 km). Ellison Provincial Park has 54 campsites, picnicking, swimming and hiking trails. It also has British Columbia's only freshwater marine diving park for scuba and snorkeling.

Mile 112 (392) Km 180 (631.5): Junction with road east to Silver Star Provincial Recreation Area, primarily a ski resort but the chair lift operates in summer for sightseers. Accommodation on the mountain year-round in "Wild West" village. Also access to Cedar Hot Springs, with 4 mineral pools and camping.

Mile 112.5 (391.5) Km 181 (630.5): Tourist information center near the south end of Swan Lake, bordered by marshes. Fishing for rainbow, eastern brook trout and ling; boat launch (no motors).

Mile 116 (388) Km 187 (624.5): Junction with B.C. Highway 97A to Armstrong (7 miles/12 km) and Sicamous on Trans-Canada Highway 1 (39 miles/65 km). Attractions in **ARMSTRONG** (pop. 2,700) include the Olde Schoolhouse (1884), now a teahouse; Armstrong Cheese Factory, open Monday to Saturday; Canoga Carriage Co., where visitors can watch the restoration of horse-drawn carriages; and Rogers Flour Mills, open for tours in summer, where visitors bag their own flour in the old-fashioned mill store.

Canada Highway 97 turns west for Kamloops and heads across the north end of

Okanagan Lake and orchards in bloom. (Jack Bryan)

Swan Lake. Travelers headed north on B.C. Highway 97A to Trans-Canada Highway 1 turn to **Mile 290** in the TRANS-CANADA HIGHWAY 1 section for log of that route.

Mile 116.5 (387.5) Km 187.5 (624): Old Vernon Road goes south to Vernon along western side of Swan Lake.

Mile 119 (385) Km 191.5 (620): Spallumcheen golf course and O'Keefe Ranch, heritage site and stop of interest. One of the earliest cattle empires in British Columbia, this spread was staked in 1867. Soon the ranch grew into a regular village, complete with store, blacksmith's shop, flour and sawmills, church and manor house.

Several of the ranch buildings, including St. Anne's Church which dates from 1886, the original log cabin and a fascinating general store, have been restored and are open to the public daily, May to October. Restaurant, gift shop and picnic facilities. ⛤

Mile 119.5 (384.5) Km 192.5 (619): Junction with Westside Road which goes south on the west side of Okanagan Lake to Westbank.

Mile 125.5 (378.5) Km 202 (609.5): Round Lake, east of highway.

Mile 127.5 (376.5) Km 205 (606.5): Salmon River, which flows north into Shuswap Lake at Salmon Arm. Junction with Salmon River Road, a quiet backroad route to Armstrong, Enderby and Salmon Arm.

Mile 131 (373) Km 211 (600.5): Rest area.

Mile 136 (368) Km 218.5 (593): Spanish Lake Ranch.

Mile 137 (367) Km 220.5 (591): Road east to Bolean, Spa and Arthur lakes; rainbow trout, on fly or by troll. Public campground and fishing camp with full facilities are at Bolean Lake, 6.5 miles/11 km. The lakes are high, so summer fishing is good. 🐟▲

Mile 137.5 (366.5) Km 221 (590.5): FALKLAND (pop. 500), small ranching community. All services available. There is an old gypsum mine on the hill above. Falkland is home to a 2-day stampede each Victoria Day weekend (around May 24) when its population swells to nearly 10,000.

Mile 138 (366) Km 222 (589.5): Junction with road north to Pillar Lake, 6.5 miles/11 km, Paxton Valley and Trans-Canada Highway 1 near Chase. Pillar Lake takes its name from a rock hoodoo capped by a giant boulder. Resorts, camping and boat launch are available and fishing for rainbows is good. 🐟▲

Mile 144 (360) Km 231.5 (580): Road west to Pinaus, Ladyking and Square lakes, 6.6 miles/11 km. Accommodations and boats on Pinaus; good fly-fishing for rainbows. 🐟

Mile 146.5 (357.5) Km 235.5 (576):

Okanagan Landing, accessible in Vernon.   (Jack Bryan)

WESTWOLD, a small farm community, with food and gas available. The wide valley, first called Grande Prairie by French Canadian fur traders, was changed by the post office to avoid confusion with the Alberta town.

The highway crosses the Salmon River bridge and junctions with a gravel road southwest to Salmon Lake (25 miles/42 km), Douglas Lake and on to B.C. Highway 5A at Quilchena.

Mile 151.5 (352.5) Km 244 (567.5): South end of Monte Lake. The highway runs along the eastern shore, hemmed in by basalt cliffs. Rock hounds find agates in basaltic outcrops here. There are resort facilities along the lake. Monte Lake Provincial Park has 7 campsites, picnicking, swimming and fishing for rainbows. **MONTE LAKE** community has a rock and gem store, gas and food. ⛤🐟▲

Mile 154 (350) Km 248 (563.5): Road east to Paxton Valley.

Mile 159 (345) Km 256 (555.5): Rest area with travel information board. Road east to Barnhardtvale.

Mile 165 (339) Km 266 (545.5): Junction with Trans-Canada Highway 1 at **MONTE CREEK**; store and gas station. Canada Highway 97 shares a common alignment with Trans-Canada Highway 1 West to Cache Creek.

Travelers headed east to Revelstoke, Banff and Jasper national parks, turn to **Mile 359.5** in the TRANS-CANADA HIGHWAY 1 section and read log back to front.

Mile 169 (335) Km 272 (539.5): Stop of interest on a gravel turnout on the north side of the highway near Monte Creek railway station explains the "Great Train Robbery." The robbery took place near here in 1906. Bill Miner and his gang held up a Canadian Pacific Railway express but netted only $15. He was

successfully tracked by a mounted police posse and sent to jail for life. His story was made into a movie, *The Grey Fox*.

Mile 169.5 (334.5) Km 273 (538.5): Kamloops city limits.

Mile 171 (333) Km 275 (536.5): Wildlife park and museum with petting farm and picnic areas; open in summer. Waterslide and RV park adjacent. ⛤▲

Mile 181 (323) Km 291.5 (520): Exit for Yellowhead Highway 5 north to Tete Jaune Cache on Yellowhead Highway 16. Travelers headed north on Yellowhead Highway 5 turn to **Mile 0** in the YELLOWHEAD HIGHWAY 5 section for log of that route.

Mile 183 (321) Km 294.5 (517): Eastbound exit for city of **KAMLOOPS** (pop. 67,000), established by fur traders as Fort Kamloops in 1811, at the confluence of the North and South Thompson rivers. In 1862, the Overlanders, a group of immigrants who had set out from the prairies to travel to the goldfields by land, rafted down the North Thompson from Tete Jaune Cache. They arrived at Fort Kamloops in time for the only woman among them, Catherine Schuman, to deliver the first white girl born in the British Columbia Interior. Several of the Overlanders settled in Kamloops. One of them, William Fortune, built British Columbia's first flour mill.

Kamloops boomed with the arrival of the Canadian Pacific Railway in 1885. Today it is British Columbia's fourth-largest settlement, a bustling city with excellent shopping and tourist facilities at the crossroads of 2 major tourist routes: Trans-Canada Highway 1 and Highway 5. Travel information center at 10 10th Avenue is open daily June to September; phone 374-3377.

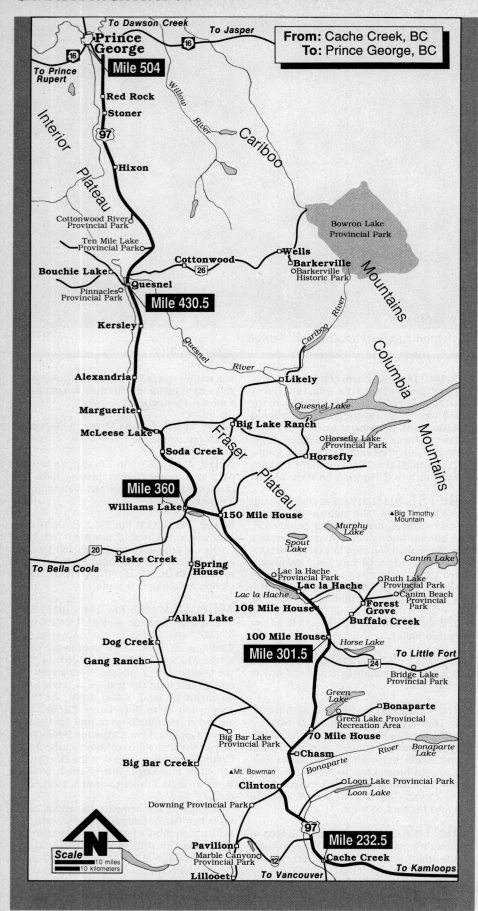

From: Cache Creek, BC
To: Prince George, BC

To Dawson Creek
To Jasper
16
Prince George
16
To Prince Rupert
Mile 504
Red Rock
Stoner
97
Hixon
Willow River
Cariboo
Cottonwood River Provincial Park
Ten Mile Lake Provincial Park
Bouchie Lake
Cottonwood
26
Wells
Barkerville
Barkerville Historic Park
Bowron Lake Provincial Park
Quesnel
Mile 430.5
Pinnacles Provincial Park
Kersley
Quesnel River
Cariboo River
Columbia Mountains
Alexandria
River
Likely
Quesnel Lake
Marguerite
Big Lake Ranch
McLeese Lake
Horsefly Lake Provincial Park
Soda Creek
Horsefly
Fraser Plateau
Mountains
Mile 360
Williams Lake
150 Mile House
Big Timothy Mountain
Murphy Lake
20
Riske Creek
Spout Lake
Canim Lake
To Bella Coola
Spring House
Lac la Hache Provincial Park
Ruth Lake Provincial Park
Lac la Hache
Canim Beach Provincial Park
Lac la Hache
108 Mile House
Forest Grove
Alkali Lake
Buffalo Creek
100 Mile House
Horse Lake
Dog Creek
Mile 301.5
To Little Fort
Gang Ranch
24
Bridge Lake Provincial Park
Green Lake
Bonaparte
Green Lake Provincial Recreation Area
Big Bar Lake Provincial Park
70 Mile House
Big Bar Creek
Chasm
Bonaparte River
Bonaparte Lake
Mt. Bowman
Bonaparte
Loon Lake Provincial Park
Clinton
Loon Lake
Downing Provincial Park
97
Mile 232.5
N
Scale
Pavilion
10 miles
Marble Canyon Provincial Park
12
10 kilometers
Cache Creek
Lillooet
To Vancouver
To Kamloops

Its economy is based on primary and secondary manufacturing, with a copper smelter, 2 plywood plants and a pulp mill. The tall stack of Weyerhauser Canada's mill carries effluent (and odor) high above the city. Only rarely do climatic conditions force it down. Daily tours of the mill available May to September. Cattle ranching continues to be a mainstay along with mining and tourism.

Attractions include Riverside Park, with its replica of old Fort Kamloops. There are 2-hour river cruises on the paddle-wheeler MV *Wanda Sue,* which depart from the river dock near the Travel Information Center, May to September. The 200 lakes around Kamloops make the city a magnet for fishermen. Local rainbow trout, known as Kamloops trout, have a reputation as wily fighters; 5- to 6-pounders are not uncommon.

Mile 184.5 (319.5) Km 297 (514.5): Junction with B.C. Highway 5 south to Merritt and Princeton. This is now one of the least traveled highways in southern British Columbia, having been supplanted by the new Coquihalla Highway.

Mile 187 (317) Km 301 (510.5): Paved road leads south 18 miles/29 km to Lac le Jeune Provincial Park; 144 campsites, excellent swimming and fishing for medium rainbow trout.

Mile 192 (312) Km 309 (502.5): Tailings of the Afton copper mine are visible on the south side of the highway. Mining operations are spread for some distance along the highway. On the north side of the highway, notice the range rehabilitaton project in which sagebrush semidesert has been cultivated and seeded to grass.

Mile 194 (310) Km 312 (499.5): Greenstone Mountain Road leads to several high fishing lakes.

Mile 197 (307) Km 317 (494.5): Cherry Creek Ranch, one of the pioneer ranches in the area.

Mile 203.5 (300.5) Km 327.5 (484): Viewpoint and rest area with picnic tables. A trailer usually parked here in summer sells ice cream and snacks. A stop of interest sign recalls the days of lake steamboats, and display board illustrates the types of Indian shelters on the interior plateau. Sign identifies the different types of noxious knapweed, which in some areas of British Columbia are taking over the rangeland.

Across the lake are Battle Bluffs, their red color attributed to legendary blood stains from an Indian battle fought on top.

Mile 205.5 (298.5) Km 331 (480.5): Turnout and viewpoint over Kamloops Lake (a widening of the Thompson River). Geologists believe that the lake may be an ancient volcanic crater, the source of the area's lava outcrops.

Mile 207.5 (296.5) Km 334 (477.5): Turnoff north to Savona Provincial Park for swimming and picnics. **SAVONA** is a small trading community at the narrow west end of Kamloops Lake; limited facilities. Access south to Logan Lake mining community and fishing lakes.

Mile 210.5 (293.5) Km 339 (472.5): Steel-decked bridge over the Thompson River. *CAUTION:* Bridge deck is slippery. Explorer David Thompson never saw the river that bears his name. It was named for him by Simon Fraser.

Mile 213 (291) Km 342.5 (469): Bridge over Deadman River. Pacific salmon spawn here in the fall. The river was named for an early Hudson's Bay Co. trader who was found murdered here.

Mile 213.5 (290.5) Km 344 (467.5): Turnoff on gravel road north to Deadman River valley, an attractive ranch valley with a spectacular multicolored volcanic canyon (good rockhounding for agates and petrified wood) and rock hoodoos (ask for permission and directions at Deadman Creek Ranch).

Mile 218.5 (285.5) Km 352 (459.5): Turnoff south to a bridge over the Thompson River and the small community of **WAL-HACHIN**. When nearby orchards flourished, so did Walhachin; today a desert of prickly pear cactus and sagebrush has ousted the fruit trees and the settlement is almost a ghost town. No services available.

Mile 220 (284) Km 354 (457.5): Remains of an irrigation flume are visible on the north side of the highway.

Mile 223 (281) Km 358.5 (453): Stop of interest sign commemorates the orchard settlement of Walhachin. On the river flats east of here pioneers planted apple orchards, building dams in the hills and miles of irrigation flumes to bring water. By 1913, these dry benches were covered with sturdy young trees. But when all but 10 of the eligible males of the area enlisted for service in WWI, the irrigation flumes were breached by floods and landslides and the thirsty orchards shriveled. Today there are still a few phantom trees among the sagebrush and cactus. The flumes are merely rotting streaks of wood along the hillsides.

The climate, too dry for orchards, is ideal for cattle, but few are to be seen from June to September because they are sent to the forested hills to graze. There are huge cattle-feeding stations just east of Cache Creek.

Mile 232.5 (271.5) Km 374.5 (437): Junction of Highway 97 and Trans-Canada Highway 1 at **CACHE CREEK** (pop. 3,000). Travel information center just north of highway junction. All visitor services offered. Gas stations, motels and restaurants line both sides of the highway. The settlement grew up around the confluence of the creek (named after a reputed cache of gold) and the Bonaparte River. The Hudson's Bay Co. opened a store to benefit from trade at the intersection of trails east and north. Cache Creek became

a major supply point on the Cariboo Wagon Road. Today, the junction is still very much a traveler's way station. The area is famous for jade; visit the Cariboo Jade Shop to see stone being cut and polished.

Travelers continuing on Trans-Canada Highway 1 to Hope, turn to **Mile 428** in the TRANS-CANADA HIGHWAY 1 section for log of that route.

Mile 235.5 (268.5) Km 379 (432.5): Indian village of Bonaparte with its lumber-covered log church dating from 1894 and impressive cemetery gates.

Mile 236.5 (267.5) Km 380.5 (431): Bonaparte River bridge.

Mile 238.5 (265.5) Km 384 (427.5): Good view west across fields to Hat Creek House (see description next entry).

Mile 239.5 (264.5) Km 384.5 (427): Junction with Highway 12 to Lillooet (46.5 miles/75 km) and Lytton (86 miles/138 km) on Trans-Canada Highway 1. A short distance west on Highway 12 is Hat Creek House, one of the last of the Cariboo trail roadhouses, and a section of the original trail. The roadhouse and farm buildings are undergoing restoration as a provincial heritage site.

Marble Canyon Provincial Park is 17.5 miles/28 km west on Highway 12. The park includes well-named Turquoise Lake and Crown Lake, where there is a swimming beach. There are 34 campsites, picnic tables, and a hiking trail to a waterfall and the Teapot, an interesting rock formation.

PAVILION, 26 miles/42 km west on Highway 12, is an Indian village with a fine Catholic church. The post office and a general store are located at nearby Pavilion Lodge. Resort accommodations and fishing at south end of Pavilion Lake. 🚶‍♂️🐟▲

Mile 242 (262) Km 389.5 (422): Gravel turnout with sign commemorating the "BX," the British Columbia Express Co. stage line founded by Francis Barnard, which linked the goldfields of the Cariboo with the outside world for nearly 50 years. Starting point was originally Yale, then Ashcroft and the red-and-yellow stagecoaches made the 270-mile/450-km journey in 4 days.

Across the valley to the west brilliant orange and yellow sulfur stained cliffs mark the location of the Maggie Mine, founded in 1885, which yielded $500,000 worth of gold.

Mile 246 (258) Km 396 (415.5): Junction with Loon Lake Road which leads east to Loon Creek fish hatchery and Loon Lake Provincial Park (15.5 miles/26 km); 14 campsites, rainbow fishing. 🐟▲

Mile 246.5 (257.5) Km 397 (414.5): Maiden Creek bridge.

Mile 251 (253) Km 403.5 (408): Several shallow alkaline lakes along the highway for the next 5 miles/8 km, including Four Mile and Five Mile lakes; gravel turnouts, fair fishing for rainbow and eastern brook trout. 🐟

Mile 256 (248) Km 412.5 (399): Junction with road west to Pavilion via Kelly Lake at south edge of Clinton. Built in 1861 from Lillooet, this road was the first Cariboo Wagon Road. A stone cairn marks the junction of this route with the later one from Yale in the Fraser Canyon. From Kelly Lake another road goes north to Jesmond, Dog Creek and Alkali Lake, the original River Trail to the Cariboo.

Downing Provincial Park on Kelly Lake (11 miles/18 km west), has 25 campsites, picnicking, swimming and fishing for rainbows.

The village of **CLINTON** (pop. 900) has all services. It was originally the site of the 47 Mile Roadhouse (mileage was calculated from Lillooet), a supply settlement at the junction of the 2 gold rush trails. It was later renamed Clinton in honor of the Colonial Secretary and was the center for freighting on the Cariboo Road.

Traces of gold rush days still to be found include Robertson's General Store (1864), with its wagon-wheel veranda; the museum, housed in a red building that served as the first school (1892), then as a courthouse; and the pioneer cemetery. The present Cariboo Lodge, built of logs, is on the site of the famous old Clinton Hotel, which dated from the 1860s and burned in 1958. The Clinton Ball, held yearly in May, is the oldest continuous annual celebration in British Columbia. It began in 1868 and usually lasted for several days, nonstop. 🪧🐟▲

Mile 257.5 (246.5) Km 414.5 (397): Pioneer cemetery to east.

Mile 263 (241) Km 423 (388.5): Junction with a gravel road west to Big Bar Lake Provincial Park (21 miles/34 km), 33 campsites, picnicking, swimming, boat launch and fishing for rainbows. Rest area along the highway just north of this junction. 🪧🐟▲

Mile 266.5 (237.5) Km 429 (382.5): Junction with loop road east to Painted Chasm (3 miles/5 km) and marker explaining its geology. The box canyon, some 984 feet/300m deep, was cut into volcanic bedrock by the eroding action of a glacial meltwater stream. The canyon walls are striped with the multicolored layers of different lava flows. A provincial picnic area is on the canyon lip. Chasm road rejoins Highway 97 3.5 miles/5.5 km north of here. 🪧

Mile 267.5 (236.5) Km 430.5 (381): Junction with gravel road east to Meadow Lake, Canoe Creek and Cariboo River Trail back road. Roads are rough but drivable by ordinary automobiles.

Mile 276.5 (227.5) Km 444.5 (367): **70 MILE HOUSE** settlement, site of a Cariboo roadhouse built in 1862. Junction with road east to Green Lake Provincial Recreation Area (7.5 miles/12 km), 121 campsites at 5 separate locations, picnic area, sani-station, swimming, boat launch and fishing for rainbows. Accommodations, boats and services are available on lake. Green Lake is named for its color, attributed to algae growth.

Green Lake Road provides access to several

other fishing lakes, including Tin Cup, Round, Little Green and Watch and connects with B.C. Highway 24 to Little Fort north of Kamloops.

Mile 278 (226) Km 447 (364.5): Loch Lomond, the largest of several lakes along the highway.

Mile 287.5 (216.5) Km 463 (348.5): 83 Mile Creek, site of 83 Mile House, built in 1862 and later owned by the BX Co. which kept horses here. Road goes up creek 7 miles/11 km to Green Lake.

Mile 289 (215) Km 465 (346.5): Lookout Road to forestry tower on summit of Mount Begbie (elev. 4,186 feet/1,276m).

Mile 297 (207) Km 478 (333.5): Junction with B.C. Highway 24 east to Bridge Lake and Little Fort on Yellowhead Highway 5 north of Kamloops. Bridge Lake Provincial Park (30 miles/50 km) has camping, swimming, boat launch and fishing. Many resorts and dude ranches are in the area.

Mile 300.5 (203.5) Km 483.5 (328): Road east to 99 Mile Hill cross-country ski area.

Mile 301.5 (202.5) Km 485.5 (326): South edge of **100 MILE HOUSE** (pop. 1,900), a thriving town in the center of ranching and lumbering activities. All tourist facilities are available, including dude ranches in the area.

The first building here was Bridge Creek House which predated the gold rush, catering to fur traders and early ranchers. The settlement turned out to be exactly 100 miles from Mile 0 on the Cariboo Road at Lillooet, so the roadhouse changed its name and its clientele from ranchers to miners. Bridge Creek Ranch was bought by the Marquis of Exeter in 1912 and the family still owns the holdings. Little remains of the old days except for one of the stagecoaches in the parking lot of the Red Coach Inn, built on the site of the first roadhouse, and the barn across the road where stage line horses were kept.

Local special events include the 30-mile/50-km Cariboo Cross-Country Ski Marathon, the first Saturday of February, and the Great Cariboo Ride, a 6- to 8-day trail ride across the Fraser plateau in August.

Mile 302 (202) Km 486.5 (325): Junction with gravel road east to Horse Lake, restocked with kokanee, and other fishing lakes of the high plateau.

Mile 302.5 (201.5) Km 487 (324.5): Tourist information log cabin by 100 Mile House Marsh, a bird sanctuary. The 39-foot-/12-m-long skis beside the cabin are a reminder of 100 Mile House's place as an important cross-country ski center.

Mile 303 (201) Km 488 (323.5): Road west to Exeter Station on B.C. Railway. Access to Moose Valley lakes; canoeing.

Mile 304.5 (199.5) Km 489.5(322): Side road east to Ruth, Canim and Mahood lakes, all endowed with resorts and famous for fishing. Ruth Lake Provincial Park (18 miles/30 km), has picnicking, swimming and a boat launch. Canim Lake (21 miles/35 km), 22 miles/37 km long, has lake trout, rainbow and kokanee fishing. Canim Beach Provincial Park (26 miles/43 km) has 16 campsites, swimming and fishing.

Between Canim and Mahood lakes is spectacular Canim Falls. From Canim Lake, gravel road leads to community of Hendrix Lake, built by Noranda for the workers at its Boss Mountain molybdenum mine.

Mile 309 (195) Km 498 (313.5): 108 MILE RANCH, now a recreational community with health spa, cabins, golf course, tennis courts, riding stables, hiking and cross-country ski trails, lodge and restaurant.

Mile 310.5 (193.5) Km 500 (311.5): 108 Mile airstrip.

Mile 311 (193) Km 501 (310.5): Rest area beside 108 Mile House Lake. Alongside is Heritage Center, with some of the original log buildings from 108 Ranch and others relocated from 105 Mile.

Mile 314 (190) Km 505.5 (306): Road east to Spring and Dempsey lakes by 111 Mile Creek.

Mile 318 (186) Km 512 (299.5): South entrance to **LAC LA HACHE** (pop. 800), a small community on a lake of the same name, so-called because a French Canadian settler lost his ax here while chopping a waterhole in the ice. Small museum and information center in log schoolhouse beside highway. Lakeside resorts offer full tourist facilities and camping.

The lake is 11.5 miles/19 km long; good fishing for rainbow, kokanee, large lake trout. Excellent ice fishing in winter.

Mile 318.5 (185.5) Km 513 (298.5): Road east to Timothy, Spout, Murphy and other fishing lakes.

Mile 327 (177) Km 526 (285.5): Lac La Hache Provincial Park offers 83 campsites, picnic area, sani-station, swimming, hiking trail, fishing and boat launch.

Mile 329.5 (174.5) Km 530.5 (281): San Jose River to west.

Mile 335 (169) Km 539.5 (272): Stop of interest sign commemorating the miners, traders and adventurers who came this way to the Cariboo goldfields in the 1860s.

Mile 340 (164) Km 547.5 (264): 140 Mile House (unincorporated).

Mile 341 (163) Km 549 (262.5): Highway warning: Strong crosswinds in this area.

Mile 341.5 (162.5) Km 549.5 (262): Knife Creek Road to Spout and Murphy lakes.

Old gold mining camp Quesnel Forks is now a ghost town. (Liz Bryan)

Mile 346 (158) Km 557 (254.5): Mission Road leads west to St. Joseph's Mission, founded in 1867 by Oblate Father James McGuckin who built a chapel, residence and school and started a cattle ranch whose OMI brand was the first registered brand in the Cariboo.

Mile 349.5 (154.5) Km 562 (249.5): **150 MILE HOUSE**, once an important roadhouse and junction on the Cariboo Road, now a small service community.

Mile 350 (154) Km 563 (248.5): Road northeast to Quesnel and Horsefly lakes and to communities of Likely (50 miles/80 km) and Horsefly (35 miles/56 km). Provincial park campground at Horsefly Lake. ▲

Mile 353.5 (150.5) Km 569 (242.5): South end of Williams Lake; good rainbow fishing. Named for Chief William of the nearby Sugar Cane Reserve. Scenic back road through the reserve rejoins the highway at **Mile 346**. ✔

Mile 360 (144) Km 579 (232.5): **WILLIAMS LAKE** (pop. 10,000). Tourist information and a museum are located at the junction of Highways 97 and 20. All services available.

Virtually bypassed by the Cariboo gold rush, Williams Lake was originally an overnight camp for the Hudson's Bay Co. fur brigade. It later became a farming community. Later it became a center for ranchers working the Chilcotin country. The advent of the Pacific Great Eastern Railway (now the B.C. Railway) in 1919 made the town the cattle marketing and shipping center for the whole Cariboo-Chilcotin. Today the city has the largest and most active cattleyards in the province. Lumber and mining for copper-molybdenum are the mainstays of the economy.

Williams Lake is famous for its rip-roaring 4-day stampede held in July.

At the south end of town is the junction with B.C. Highway 20 which goes west across the Chilcotin to Bella Coola on the coast (see the CHILCOTIN HIGHWAY section for log of Highway 20).

Visit Scout Island Nature Center (accessible off Highway 20), located on 2 small islands at the west end of the lake; interpretative center, nature trails, picnic area, boat launch and beach.

Cariboo Friendship Center on South Third Avenue, has native crafts for sale. Local arts and crafts are also on display at the Stationhouse Gallery in the historic train station on Oliver Street. ⅊

Mile 372.5 (131.5) Km 599.5 (212): Mountain House Road to Likely Road and 150 Mile House.

Mile 378.5 (125.5) Km 609.5 (202): Side road leads west 2.5 miles/4.5 km to settlement of **SODA CREEK** on the banks of the Fraser. The original wagon road to the goldfields ended here and miners went the rest of the way to Quesnel by river steamboats. Soda Creek became an important transfer point for

men and supplies until the railway went through in 1920. Soda Creek was so named because the creek bed is carbonate of lime and the water bubbles like soda water.

Mile 381 (123) Km 613.5 (198): Marshy lake to east has a muskrat house.

Mile 382.5 (121.5) Km 615.5 (196):

High bluffs line the shore of the Fraser River near Mile 360 (Km 579). *(Liz Bryan)*

Osprey nest in the tree snag on the east side of the highway.

Mile 385.5 (118.5) Km 620.5 (191): **McLEESE LAKE**; gas, food, stores, motel and a private campground. Junction with road east to Gibraltar Mines open-pit copper molybdenum mine and road to Beaver Lake. Public tours of the mine site are given at 1 p.m. Wednesday, June to September. No children under 6.

There is a picnic area on the highway by McLeese Lake, just north of the junction. Fishing is good for small to medium rainbows. There are resorts around the lake. ⅊ ✔ ▲

Mile 390 (114) Km 628 (183.5): Large gravel turnout and stop of interest sign about the paddle-wheelers which provided transport on the Fraser for 390 miles/650 km north of Soda Creek. Good view of river.

Mile 390.5 (113.5) Km 629 (182.5): B.C. Railway overpass.

Mile 391 (113) Km 629.5 (182): Road west to McAlister and Soda Creek.

Mile 396.5 (107.5) Km 638.5 (173): Marguerite reaction cable ferry across Fraser. Ferry crossing takes 10 minutes; 2 cars and 10 passengers can be accommodated. On the far side of the river is a gravel road which goes north to Quesnel, south to meet B.C. Highway 20 near Riske Creek.

Mile 398.5 (105.5) Km 641 (170.5): East of highway an outcropping of basalt columns creates a formation known as the Devils Palisades.

Mile 399 (105) Km 642.5 (169): Stone cairn commemorates Fort Alexandria, the last North West Co. fur-trading post established west of the Rockies, built in 1821. The actual site of the fort is across the river. Cairn also marks the approximate farthest point reached by Alexander Mackenzie in his descent of the Fraser in 1793.

Mile 400.5 (103.5) Km 645 (166.5): Old barn, house and assorted buildings of Lansdowne Farm, run by the Moffats in the gold rush era.

Mile 404 (100) Km 650.5 (161): Notice prominent clay cliffs along the river, remnants of glacial deposits.

Mile 409.5 (94.5) Km 659 (152.5): Rest area.

Mile 417 (87) Km 671 (140.5): Small community of **KERSLEY**, Kersley Creek and pioneer ranch.

Mile 424.5 (79.5) Km 683 (128.5): Loop road east to Dragon Lake; rainbow fishing. ✔

Mile 430.5 (73.5) Km 693 (118.5): Loop road east to Dragon Lake along Quesnel River to old mining center of Hydraulic and to Beavermouth Forestry Recreation Area; swimming, picnicking, boat launch.

South edge of **QUESNEL** (pop. 8,200). The city provides good shopping and full tourist facilities. At the confluence of the Quesnel and Fraser rivers, the town was originally called Quesnelle Mouth to distinguish it from the gold camp of Quesnelle Forks upriver. (The river was named by Simon Fraser in 1808 for his lieutenant, Jules Quesnelle.) From a small fur-trading outpost, Quesnel burgeoned during the Cariboo gold rush, when paddle wheel boats from Soda Creek brought in men and supplies. Other gold rush towns have faded away but Quesnel grew to become the commercial hub of the North Cariboo, its economy centered on the forest industry, with sawmills, a plywood plant and 2 pulpmills.

Downtown beside the river is a Cornish waterwheel used in the gold mines and a stone cairn commemorating the building of the Collins Overland telegraph, an ambitious scheme to link America with Asia across the Bering Strait. The scheme was abandoned when a trans-Atlantic cable was successfully laid from Ireland to Newfoundland.

The old road bridge (now a pedestrian bridge) across the Fraser here has been replaced by a modern one downstream. Across the street from the waterwheel is the restored Hudson's Bay Co. store, built in 1867. The museum in LeBourdais Park displays old gold mining equipment; tourist information office is adjacent. Gold panning is permitted at the confluence of the Fraser and Quesnel rivers.

Highway 97 swings north along Front Street (turn east for downtown shops) and crosses

B.C. Highway 26 to Barkerville

The 50-mile/80-km road from Quesnel to Barkerville is the most historic in British Columbia, for it was here in the 1850s that the gold rush miners converged, on foot, on horseback, by wagon and stage, lured by the promise of riches from the Cariboo creeks. At road's end was Barkerville, the largest and lustiest of all the gold camps, in its hectic heyday the biggest city west of Chicago and north of San Francisco.

Barkerville is today a provincial historic park, its buildings and boardwalks faithfully restored or reconstructed in period style. The shops and restaurants are open; there are performances at the opera house; and horse-drawn carriages rattle down the main streets.

Today's Highway 26 follows the route of the original wagon road, built in 1865. No travelers on Highway 97 should miss this side trip into history.

Mile 0 Km 0: Junction with Highway 97, at **Mile 434.5** near Quesnel. Highway 26 climbs steeply up through the jackpine forests of Mouse Mountain, then descends to the Cottonwood River.

Mile 9.5 Km 15: Good example of Cariboo bull or snake fence, on the west side.

Mile 16 Km 25.5: Cottonwood House, one of the original roadhouses on the Cariboo Road, is now a provincial historic park. The log house, built in 1864, has been faithfully restored and furnished, along with surrounding barns and outbuildings. The former chicken shed is a small museum and interpretive center. From the end of May until September there are guides in period costume and stagecoach rides along an original stretch of wagon road. Picnic tables are available.

The John Boyd family operated the roadhouse for more than 50 years and the account books and diaries (34 volumes) are priceless historical records.

Mile 19.5 Km 31: Coldspring Creek.
Mile 20 Km 32: Swift River Forestry Road, south.
Mile 21 Km 34: Viewpoint to south.
Mile 24.5 Km 39.5: Highway descends steep hill into valley of Lightning Creek. Wingdam, a small gold rush settlement beside Lightning Creek, has a small cabin and an old bridge. The huge piles of gravel are the remains of fairly recent hydraulic operations, which used huge water jets to wash the creek gravels for gold.

Mile 26 Km 42: Rest area, north side.
Mile 26.5 Km 43: Historical stop of interest marker for Blessing's grave. Charles Morgan Blessing from Ohio was murdered on his way to Barkerville in 1866. His killer was caught when he gave Blessing's keepsake gold nugget stickpin, in the shape of an angel, to a Barkerville dance hall girl. Blessing was buried here. His grave, surrounded by a white picket fence, is in the trees to the north. His murderer, John Barry, was the only white man hanged in the Cariboo during the gold rush.

Mile 27 Km 43.5: Troll's Ski Resort; cross-country and downhill.
Mile 31 Km 50: Ketchum Creek Forestry Road, north.
Mile 35 Km 56.5: Jawbone Creek.
Mile 36.5 Km 59: Stanley Road, north. Site of the gold rush camps of Stanley and Van Winkle. The only relic remaining from the gold rush days is the cemetery on Stanley Road. Buried here are Capt. John Evans, leader of a group of 36 Welsh miners, and 9 men named Jones.
Mile 39.5 Km 63.5: Gravel turnout at start of Devil's Canyon, a narrow winding stretch of road high above Chisholm Creek, one of the many rich creeks of the Cariboo.
Mile 42 Km 67.5: Rest area at Slough Creek.
Mile 44 Km 70.5: Highway traverses northern shore of Jack of Clubs Lake.

Fishing for rainbows, lake trout and Dolly Varden. Picnic tables and boat launch.

Mile 45 Km 73: WELLS (pop. 300) offers full tourist facilities. A museum with displays of local mining history is open daily from June to September. Wells is a gold rush town, too, but of a different vintage. It dates to the 1930s when the Cariboo Gold Quartz Mine, promoted and developed by Fred Wells, lured hundreds of workers again to this lonely valley. The gold mine closed in 1967 and Wells depends for survival mostly on the tourists who flock to Barkerville.

Mile 47 Km 75.5: South boundary, Barkerville Historic Park.

(Liz Bryan)

Once an 1800s gold rush town, Barkerville has been faithfully restored.

Mile 48.5 Km 78: Forest Rose Campground to north, Lowhee Campground to south, 2 of the 3 Barkerville provincial park campgrounds available; total of 170 campsites, picnic areas and sani-stations.

Mile 49 Km 79: Gravel road leads north 11 miles/18 km to Bowron Lakes Provincial Park, a wilderness park in the rugged Cariboo Mountains. It is noted for its interconnecting chain of lakes which form an almost perfect diamond, making possible a 72-mile/116-km canoe circuit which takes from 7 to 10 days to complete. The park is a wildlife sanctuary and closed to hunting.

Visitor information is available at the registration center next to the main parking lot where canoeists must register and pay fees. Groups are limited to 6 people. Circuit fees are: $25 full circuit, $15 west side only. The lakes are patrolled by park wardens. *CAUTION:* Watch for bears.

At the north end of the lake are 2 private lodges with restaurants which can provide canoes and supplies; a campground with 25 sites; a boat launch; and park headquarters.

In the lakes are rainbow, Dolly Varden, lake trout, Rocky Mountain whitefish and kokanee, with fishing ranging from poor to excellent.

Mile 49.5 Km 80: Road to Barkerville cemetery connects to Government Hill provincial campgrounds.

Mile 50 Km 80.5: Parking lot by Barkerville museum; information centre.

BARKERVILLE was named for stubborn Cornish miner Billy Barker, who persisted in staking a claim on Williams Creek below the canyon, where no trace of gold had ever been found. Above the canyon, 4,000 miners were hard at work mining the rich placer gold and the gold camp of Richfield was in full swing.

Barker dug down 52 feet/16m to the former creek bed where the gold lay thick. His claim yielded more than $600,000. Men abandoned the diggings at Richfield and scrambled to locate claims near Barker's. A new town, Barkerville, crowded about the creek banks, little more than a single street, crammed with saloons and gambling dens, dance halls and miners' shanties.

Born in 1862, Barkerville grew and dazzled for 6 years until wiped out by a disastrous fire. The town rebuilt the next day, bigger and bolder than ever, but the glory and most of the gold was gone. The town lingered on for another 20 years, its fortunes ebbing and surging with the price of gold but it was virtually a ghost town when the province of British Columbia started restoration in 1958.

Today, long years of labor have re-created Barkerville in its heyday. You can walk the wooden sidewalks of the narrow street, ride a stagecoach, eat lunch at Wake-Up-Jake's or the Lung Duck Tong Chinese restaurant; guzzle a root beer in the saloon; buy goods at the bakery, including miner's bannock, and at Mason & Daly General Store. You can pan for gold at the Eldorado Shafthouse, take in a performance at the Theatre Royal (shows daily from mid-June to mid-September); watch the blacksmith at work in his forge or the printer working the hand presses at the newspaper office. You can attend Sunday service at St. Saviour's Church, or peer through the windows of the gold commissioner's office, into the dentist's, the barber's, the front parlors and bedrooms and imagine just what life was like here so long ago.

Beyond the long main street of Barkerville, the Cariboo Wagon Road leads on (for pedestrians only) to Richfield, 1.5 miles/2 km, to the courthouse where "Hanging" Judge Begbie still holds court.

the Fraser to West Quesnel and junctions with road west to Nazko (60 miles/96 km). Access to Puntchesakut Lake Provincial Park (21 miles/35 km); picnicking, swimming, boat launch.

Pinnacles Provincial Park, 5 miles/8 km west from Highway 97, has picnic areas and hiking trails among distinctive eroded sandstone pillars.

Quesnel is trailhead for the Alexander Mackenzie Heritage Trail to Bella Coola. The trail is presently being restored; it can be hiked in sections. The complete 260-mile/420-km route takes about 3 weeks. Contact the B.C. Parks office at 640 Borland Street for more information.

Mile 434.5 (69.5) Km 699 (112.5): Junction with B.C. Highway 26 to Wells and historic Barkerville. See feature this section. ★

Mile 438.5 (65.5) Km 706 (105.5): Ten Mile Lake Provincial Park; 142 campsites, picnic area, sani-station, hiking trails, swimming, fishing for rainbows and boat launch. Cross-country skiing in winter.

Mile 442.5 (61.5) Km 712 (99.5): Cottonwood River bridge; at the south end, a gravel turnout and stop of interest sign describes the railway bridge seen upriver. This high trestle was built in 1952. The deep canyon of the Cottonwood presented such difficulties for the Pacific Great Eastern Railway (now B.C. Rail) in the 1920s that rail construction halted here for more than 20 years.

Mile 446.5 (57.5) Km 719 (92.5): Hush Lake rest area; boat launch for canoes and rowboats, fishing for rainbow and brook trout.

Mile 452.5 (51.5) Km 728 (83.5): Side road leads west 4 miles/7 km to Cottonwood River Provincial Park; 15 campsites and fishing.

Mile 457.5 (46.5) Km 736.5 (75): Strathnaver (unincorporated); no facilities.

Mile 459 (45) Km 739 (72.5): CAUTION: Steep 7 percent downgrade for northbound traffic.

Mile 467.5 (36.5) Km 752 (59.5): Small community of **HIXON**; all services.

Mile 468.5 (35.5) Km 753.5 (58): Canyon Creek bridge.

Mile 469 (35) Km 754.5 (57): Hixon Creek bridge.

Mile 474 (30) Km 763 (48.5): Woodpecker rest area with picnic tables. To the north is a road to Woodpecker Landing, one of the old paddle-wheeler docks on the Fraser River.

Mile 477.5 (26.5) Km 769 (42.5): Sign for southbound travelers: Entering the Cariboo.

Mile 483 (21) Km 777.5 (34): Stone Creek forestry road, east.

Mile 483.5 (20.5) Km 778 (33.5): Stoner (unincorporated), no services.

Mile 488 (16) Km 785.5 (26): Red Rock (unincorporated), no services.

Mile 494 (10) Km 795 (16.5): Road to Buckhorn and St. Marys lakes. Buckhorn Lake is a bird sanctuary with a Forest Service campsite and fishing for small rainbow. St. Marys also has small rainbow and a campsite.

Mile 494.5 (9.5) Km 796 (15.5): Honey farm on the east side of the road.

Mile 495.5 (8.5) Km 797.5 (14): Tabor Creek.

Mile 500 (4) Km 804.5 (7): Road east to Prince George airport.

Mile 503 (1) Km 810 (1.5): Fraser River bridge. At the north end, Queensway leads east to Prince George city center.

Mile 504 (0) Km 811.5 (0): Junction with Yellowhead Highway 16 at **PRINCE GEORGE** (pop. 67,000), third largest city in British Columbia. All visitor facilities are available.

In the early 1800s, Simon Fraser of the North West Trading Co. erected a fur-trading post here at the confluence of the Nechako and Fraser rivers. He named it Fort George in honor of the reigning English monarch. In 1906, survey parties for the transcontinental Grand Trunk Pacific Railway (later Canadian National Railways) passed through the area, and with the building of the railroad a great land boom took place. The city was incorporated in 1915 under the name Prince George. Old Fort George is now a park and picnic spot and the site of Fort George Museum.

Visitors can walk the 6-mile/10-km Heritage River Trail along the Fraser and Nechako Rivers; visit the Cottonwood Island Nature Park; ride a narrow-gauge steam train in Fort George Park; or drive up to Connaught Hill for views of the city.

The Railway Museum here includes a station and rolling stock from the days of steam trains. The Regional Museum tells the story of transportation from Indian dugouts to railways. The Native Art Gallery has Indian arts and crafts for sale.

Prince George is primarily an industrial center, fairly dependent on the lumber industry, with 3 pulp mills, sawmills, planers, dry kilns, a plywood plant and 2 chemical plants to serve the pulp mills. Oil refining, mining and heavy construction are other major area industries. The Prince George Forest Region is the largest in the province.

Prince George is roughly the geographical heart of British Columbia. It is also the hub of major highways (Highway 97 and Yellowhead Highway 16) and railways (B.C. Rail and Canadian National Railways).

Yellowhead Highway 16 and other northern highways are logged in *The MILEPOST*, available in bookstores or from GTE Discovery Publications (phone 1-800-331-3510).

U.S. Highway 101

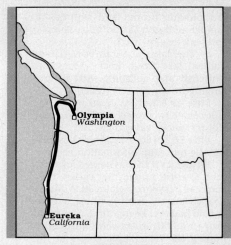

See map pages 197, 200, 205, 207, 212

U.S. Highway 101 is one of the world's most popular vacation roads, a 2-lane trail curving through cathedrals of California redwoods, Oregon's mountainous sand dunes, black cliffs and white beaches and winding through the soft green cushion of Washington's Olympic Peninsula rain forest.

Highway 101 weaves through 3 states, several national parks and recreation areas, innumerable historic sites and scenic areas of international fame. Visitor centers in each community provide a wealth of informational pamphlets. Motels, resorts, campgrounds and other facilities are plentiful along all but 1 section of the highway. North of Aberdeen, WA, to Crescent Lake, where Highway 101 winds inland, there are numerous campgrounds and turnouts, but resorts and motels are scattered and may be filled to capacity during the summer tourist season.

Allow more time than you think you'll need to travel this route, drive slowly and stop often.

U.S. Highway 101 Log

Distance from Eureka, CA, is followed by distance from the U.S. Highway 101 junction with Interstate 5 at Olympia, WA.

Mile 0 (817): The highway log begins at the Eureka Slough bridge in **EUREKA**, CA (pop. 24,337), at the northern city limit sign. Eureka is one of the largest towns on the logged highway, offering all visitor services. Located on Humboldt Bay, Eureka is a historic city. The fine brick work and restored Victorian-era homes of Old Town Square, plus the famous and architecturally unique Carson Mansion built in 1885 are points of interest. Others are the Clarke Memorial Museum of the Indian and pioneer era, Indian Art Gallery, Humboldt Cultural Center and Fort Humboldt. The Arcata Marsh and Wildlife Sanctuary gives good opportunities for birdwatching and photography. The Woodley Island Marina has mooring for both commercial and pleasure craft and also is home for the Fisherman's Memorial Statue and Table Bluff Lighthouse. Humboldt Bay's fleet of fishing boats and its processing plants supply nearly one-half of California's retail fish.

Mile 2 (815): Arcata Redwood Co. mill, producing redwood boards for construction and industry.

Mile 4.5 (812.5): Campground. ▲

Mile 5.5 (811.5): **ARCATA** (pop. 12,850) is located on the north end of Humboldt Bay and is the home of Humboldt State University. All visitor services are available. Founded in 1850, Arcata is a picturesque community with a central plaza and several fine examples of Victorian and Revival architecture. Junction with California Highway 255.

Mile 8.5 (808.5): Junction with California Highway 299 to Redding and Interstate 5. Highway 299 leads east to the Whiskeytown-Shasta-Trinity Recreation Area.

Mile 10 (807): **McKINLEYVILLE** (pop. 8,000), on the bank of the Mad River. All services available. McKinleyville has 2 notable distinctions: the world's tallest totem pole (160 feet high) and the nation's foggiest airport. Blind approach systems have been researched here, representing the worst possible conditions. The Mad River offers fall fishing for steelhead and salmon; excellent trout fishing in the upstream reaches. ➤

Mile 13 (804): Murray Road exit. Tourist information available.

Mile 14.5 (802.5): McKinleyville overlook of Clam Beach County Park, on the west shoulder of the road (southbound only).

Mile 15.5 (801.5): Clam Beach County Park offers 4-wheel-drive beach driving access, camping, restrooms, water and razor clam digging. No swimming is permitted because of a dangerous undertow. ▲

Mile 17 (800): Little River bridge and turnoff to the Little River State Beach access, a small recreation area with estuary and marsh. The road access also continues south to Clam Beach.

Mile 19 (798): Community of **WESTHAVEN**. Take the overpass to Moonstone County Beach. The scenic drive takes you north to Trinidad.

Mile 21 (796): **TRINIDAD** (pop. 432) is a vacation and resort area. Memorial Lighthouse overlooks a picturesque bay and, although 196 feet above sea level, the light was doused in 1914 by a giant ocean wave. This site also marks the first landing by Europeans on the Northwest coast. On Trinity Sunday 1775, a Spanish expedition led by Don Bruno de Heceta and Capt. Juan Bodega came ashore, making Trinidad one of the oldest California towns. The natural harbor once supported a substantial whaling fleet.

Trinidad Head State Park offers camping and a rail boat launch along the cliff face. Excellent salmon and bottom fishing area. Charter boats are available. ➤▲

Mile 23.5 (793.5): Rest area (southbound only). Wildflowers line the roadside in May and June.

Mile 25.5 (791.5): Trinidad rest area (northbound only). Picnic tables and water available. ⛱

Mile 26 (791): Patrick's Point State Park with 123 campsites. A museum offers exhibits on natural features and Indian life. There are picnic areas and hiking trails along the coast. The Agate Beach area, just north of the point, is excellent for finding agates and driftwood. Famous Wedding Rock sea stack and cliff are visible. There is good fishing from the rocks below the cliffs for assorted rockfish and lingcod. This area can be crowded during the peak travel periods. 🚶⛱➤▲

Mile 28 (789): Big Lagoon County Park has primitive campsites. There is good surf fishing on the ocean side of the lengthy sand spit. This is an excellent salt marsh, estuary observation area. ▲

Mile 29.5 (788): Big Lagoon bridge. Visible to the east is the giant Louisiana Coastal Division mill where tours may be arranged. Redwood groves, numerous spur logging roads and turnouts are along the highway. Heavy logging truck traffic transports redwoods to mill operations in this area.

Mile 34 (783): Dry Lagoon State Park with 20 primitive campsites and picnic area. No water is available. Surf fishing is good along with trout in nearby ponds and creeks. The bright red 1-room Stone Lagoon schoolhouse, now used as a free museum, is accessible through adjacent Idlewood Redwood Trails Family Campground. ⛱▲

Mile 35 (782): Humboldt Lagoon State Park Visitor Center adjacent to the highway.

Mile 35.5 (781.5): Stone Lagoon environmental campsites are located on the far side of lagoon and are accessible by boat only. A fair boat ramp provides access to the estuary.

Mile 37.5 (779.5): Stone Lagoon Primitive Area and coastal beach access.

Mile 38 (779): A freshwater lagoon is located on the east and a saltwater beach is on the west. This is a unique turnout area where fresh- and saltwater areas are separated only by a thread of sand and U.S. Highway 101. Although there are no camping facilities, many self-contained campers park along the west road shoulder. Beach access, razor clams and surf fishing are available. Stocked rainbow trout in freshwater lagoon.

Mile 39 (778): The Redwood National Park information center is on the western sand spit, opposite the northern end of the freshwater lagoon. Register here for several local campgrounds. Numerous informational pamphlets are available on the Redwood National Forest, coastal trails, self-guided tours and recreational maps. A 24-hour phone number, (707) 464-6101, gives information about the park.

Mile 40.5 (776.5): ORICK (pop.650) is the southern gateway to Redwood National Park. All services available including motels and trailer parks. The world's tallest tree, the Howard A. Libbey Tree, a 367.8-foot coast redwood, is located just southeast of Orick on Redwood Creek. The giant redwood is accessible by a hiking trail or shuttle bus. Tours are available for Arcata Lumber Co. mill. Horseback trips into the redwoods are popular. Redwood burls, myrtlewood and chain saw sculptures are plentiful. There is an access road to coastal beaches.

Mile 44 (773): Lady Bird Johnson Dedicated Redwood Grove features giant 600-year-old trees, a 1-mile self-guided nature trail and interpretative exhibits on old-growth redwood habitat.

Mile 44.5 (772.5): Prairie Creek fish hatchery. More than 1.5 million salmon are raised annually at this facility. A weathered giant redwood sculpture, "The Indomitable Salmon," stands at the gate. Visitors are welcome.

Mile 48 (769): Prairie Creek Redwoods State Park encompasses 2 separate areas. Elk Prairie Campground, where a herd of 200 wild Roosevelt elk are frequently visible near the roadside, offers 75 developed campsites, 24 trailer sites, and 27 camper sites, as well as picnic facilities and hiking trails. Gold Bluffs Beach Campground, 6.5 miles west via narrow and unpaved Davison Road (closed to trailers), has 25 campsites. Davison Road continues 1.5 miles west to Fern Canyon, a beautiful fern-covered gorge.

The visitors center at Elk Prairie Creek

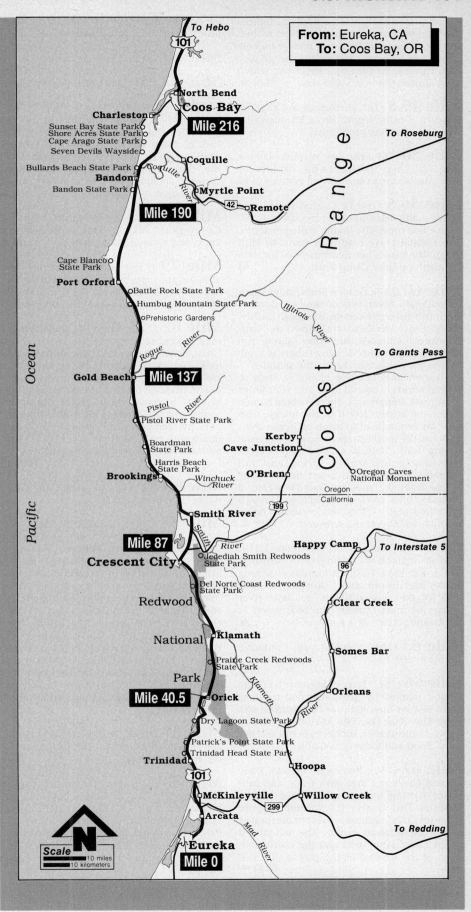

includes informational pamphlets, lighted displays, history and natural oddities including the antlers and skull of a mature bull elk encased in a stump. Apparently the elk died with its head wedged in a small tree which grew around the horns and skull. 🚶🏕️▲

Mile 49.5 (767.5): Turnoff to Cal-Barrel Road, a 3-mile scenic drive through the redwoods. Trailers prohibited.

Mile 50 (767): Big Tree Wayside day-use area. Trail leads 50 yards to the 304-foot Big Tree; also access to several trail systems. 🚶

Mile 56.5 (760.5): Coastal hiking trail access point. Sections of the trail are passable at low tide only. The hiking trail goes south. The Coastal Drive road goes north to Flint Ridge. The road is not recommended for trailers north of Alder Camp Road. 🚶

Mile 60 (757): Golden Bears bridge spans the Klamath River, one of the best summer steelhead fishing rivers in the area. Locally, the summer steelhead are known as "half-pounders." Chinook and coho salmon run the river and a smelt dipping fishery is available in the ocean surf during the summer.

Turnoff at south end of bridge leads to several resorts, a coastal drive and Flint Ridge Primitive Campground. There is a boat launch below the bridge. North of the bridge, turn west on Requa Road to reach an ocean overlook and the southern trailhead of the Coastal hiking trail. This is a good gray whale-watching point during spring and fall migration period. A drive just north of the bridge leads 0.2 mile to Tour-Thru-Tree, a private exhibit where the road leads through an 8-foot-high, 15-foot-wide tunnel hewn through a 700-year-old redwood. 🚶🐟▲

Mile 61 (756): KLAMATH (pop. 1,419) townsite replaces the original town destroyed by flood in 1964. Tourist information, fishing guides and information, shopping, motels and RV park are available. Jet boat river cruises 64 miles upriver. The boat leaves at 9 a.m. and returns at 3 p.m. ▲

Mile 63 (754): Junction with California Highway 169.

Mile 66 (751): Trees of Mystery, a private exhibit marked by giant redwood carvings and a 50-foot-high statue of Paul Bunyan and Babe The Blue Ox. The exhibit includes a redwood shrine tour, Indian museum and gift shop. Food and lodging available.

Mile 67 (750): Redwood National Park, Lagoon Creek rest area with fresh- and salt-water fishing access, picnic and hiking facilities. This is also the turnoff to False Klamath Cove beach area. Exhibits are located at the information center. The self-guided Yurok Loop nature trail and the north trailhead of the Coastal hiking trail are located here. 🚶🏕️🐟

Mile 68 (749): Viewpoint overlooking ocean. From here north to Crescent City there are numerous small viewpoints and overlooks off the west shoulder of the road.

Mile 69.5 (747.5): Slide area.

Mile 73 (744): Start of 6 percent downgrade, southbound.

Mile 75.5 (741.5): The Mill Creek Campground of Del Norte Coast Redwoods State Park (2 miles east of Highway 101), open April 1 to Oct. 31. It is considered to be the "Gateway to the California Redwood Empire." Included are 145 campsites and a dump station. No hookups. ▲

Mile 77.5 (739.5): DeMartin (primitive) Campground; hiking access to the Footsteps Rocks and Coastal hiking trail. 🚶▲

Mile 79 (738): Look for 2 osprey nests visible in the snags on the west side of the road just south of Vista Point. As you make the turn, it is straight ahead to the northwest.

Mile 82 (735): Turnoff to Enderts Beach road, access to Crescent Beach, Del Norte Coast, Enderts Beach and Crescent Beach overlook. Picnicking, beachcombing and hiking are available at Crescent Beach and Enderts Beach. Crescent Beach overlook is a good spot to view migrating gray whales during the spring and fall. There is a 0.5-mile hike to 5 primitive campsites without water at Enderts Beach with good seashore access and 2-hour narrated tidepool walks during summer. 🚶🏕️▲

Mile 83.5 (733.5): RV park, Coast Guard station and boat launch. ▲

Mile 87 (730): CRESCENT CITY (pop. 3,105), the largest resort city in northern California. All services available. The headquarters of the Redwood National Park is located at the corner of 2nd and K streets and offers exhibits, interpretative publications and coastal maps. A 24-hour phone number, (707) 464-6101, gives information about the park. Other attractions include the Battery Point Lighthouse and the Citizens Dock at City Harbor, the home of a large fleet of commercial and charter boats fishing for salmon, crab and shrimp. Launching facilities and boat rentals are available. The Undersea Gardens of marine life, fish, octopus, sharks and wolf eels is worth seeing.

Mile 87.5 (729.5): Private campground and Florence Keller Park which has tent camping and picnicking. 🏕️▲

Mile 88 (729): Junction with California Highway 199 east to Grants Pass, OR, and Interstate 5. Access via Highway 199 to scenic canyon drive along the West Fork Smith River (fair trout fishing), Jedediah Smith Redwoods State Park, Hiouchi Area ranger station, picnicking, camping, fishing and the Oregon Caves.

Mile 89 (728): Border of Six Rivers National Forest.

Mile 92 (725): Kings Valley Road to Camp Lincoln Army Campground.

Mile 94 (723): Smith River bridge and boat launch; restaurant and gas. This is an excellent fishing area. The Smith has produced the last 2 California record steelhead. Fishing guides and information are available at several local tackle shops and resorts. 🐟

Mile 97 (720): Town of SMITH RIVER, "Easter Lily Capital of the World." Beachcombing is popular. This is the northern border of the redwood groves. The Rowdy Creek steelhead and salmon fish hatchery is located here.

Mile 100 (717): Ship Ashore Resort and gift shop, built from a landlocked 160-foot luxury yacht once used by the U.S. Navy. Salmon fishing from the pier is good, and the area offers resorts, groceries, tackle shops, fishing guides and RV hookups.

Mount Emily, the only place in the contiguous 48 states ever bombed by a foreign power, is near here. During WWII, a seaplane took off from a Japanese submarine and dropped bombs on Mount Emily, hoping to start forest fires that would burn out the whole area. The fires were easily extinguished. The pilot made it back to the submarine safely. 🐟▲

Mile 100.5 (716.5): Road to mouth of the Smith River, which leads to a picturesque overlook where the river meets the sea, 0.5 mile from U.S. Highway 101.

Mile 102 (715): Clifford Kampf Memorial Park, with ocean overlook and beach access.

Mile 104 (713): Oregon-California border. California agricultural inspections are in the southbound lanes.

Mile 105 (712): Crossing the Winchuck River. A myrtlewood factory is located here. Private campground. ▲

Mile 106 (711): Largest Monterey Cypress in U.S., Chetco Museum. MP 362

Mile 107.5 (709.5): Information center, private RV parks, shopping center and gas station. ▲

Mile 108 (709): Loeb State Park, 8 miles to the northeast, has 53 campsites and 21 RV sites. ▲

Mile 109 (708): BROOKINGS (pop. 4,185) is a major recreational area famous for fishing, hunting, beaches and fields of hybrid lilies and azaleas. Resorts, motels and restaurants are available. The area is noted for its sheep and wool. Ninety percent of all wool sold to the papermaking industry comes from Curry County because of the wool's special "felting quality."

In May, Azalea State Park is a blaze of color. Facilities include picnic sites, a boat launch, Coast Guard marina, rentals, fishing charters and tackle shops. Guides are available. This is a favorite coastal area for small-boaters. Beaches offer good clamming while the harbor is good for crabs and shrimp.

A picturesque bridge spans the Chetco River, which offers good access to salt- and freshwater fishing. Gray whales are often visible offshore in the spring and fall.

🐟 MP 357

Mile 110 (707): Harris Beach State Park offers exceptionally scenic sea stacks, cliffs and beach. A state visitor center here provides phones for making campground reservations. The Goat Island Bird Preserve offshore is the southernmost part of the Oregon Islands National Wildlife Refuge. Camping and picnicking sites are available. ⛺▲

Mile 111 (706): The west shoulder of U.S. Highway 101 affords 11 named viewpoints in the next 8 miles, providing often-spectacular views of cliffs, sea stacks and beach access. The viewpoints are included in 11-mile-long Boardman State Park, a network of day-use areas which includes hiking trails, beach access and picnic areas. One of the viewpoints, Thomas Creek Bridge, is the highest bridge in Oregon at 530 feet, spanning 970 feet. Viewpoints include (from south to north) Rainbow Rock, Lone Ranch Beach, Cape Ferrelo, House Rock, Whalehead, Indian Sands Trail, Thomas Creek Bridge, Natural Bridge, Spruce Creek and Arch Rock. 🚶⛺

Mile 115.5 (701.5): Whalehead Beach.
MP 349

Mile 122.5 (694.5): Northern boundary of Samuel H. Boardman State Park. Day-use area with picnicking, fishing, viewpoints, beach access, swimming and handicapped facilities. Hiking on Oregon Coast Trail. 🚶⛺🐟

Mile 128 (688): Pistol River State Park with beach access. The river mouth is often sand-bound during the summer. There are no nearby camping facilities. Battle of Pistol River Historical Site from the Rogue Indian War of 1856. Good beachcombing.

Mile 130.5 (686.5): Cape Sebastian viewpoint. This point was discovered and named by the Spanish explorer Sebastian Vizciano in 1603.

Mile 135 (682): Hunter Creek Beach area. Good year-round fishing. The best salmon action is in tidewater and lower river near U.S. Highway 101 bridge. 🐟

Mile 137 (680): GOLD BEACH (pop. 1,585) at the mouth of the Rogue River. A USFS ranger station and visitor center is located here as well as camping and all travelers services. Fishing guides and resorts are available. White-water jet boat trips upriver 64 and 104 miles are available. Agates are found on the beach areas. There is excellent salt- and freshwater salmon and steelhead fishing in the Rogue River and offshore from the protective jetties that offer easy access to the ocean for small-boat fishermen. Jetty

Wide beaches and scenic sea stacks at Harris Beach State Park. (L. Linkhart)

Myrtlewood

Southwestern Oregon and Northern California are the heart of myrtlewood country. Every city, town and hamlet has gift shops filled with myrtlewood salt and pepper shakers, chip and dip bowls, clocks, boxes and cutting boards. Along U.S. 101, myrtlewood factories stand in isolation manufacturing an assortment of bowls, plaques, goblets, napkin holders and other souvenirs.

While pioneers used myrtlewood for furniture and oxen yokes, the souvenir industry dates only to the 1930s. During the Depression, woodworkers who had lost their jobs survived by making figurines, jewelry boxes and bowls.

Colors of the hard, fine-grained wood vary with each tree. Shades of white, yellow, brown and black are often mottled. Each piece is unique and cannot be duplicated. The widely-held belief that myrtlewood grows only near the Oregon/California border adds to its appeal as a momento unique to the area.

The Oregon myrtlewood tree is actually a California laurel. It grows between Coos County, OR, and Baja, CA, and from the Pacific Coast to the Sierra Nevada Mountains.

It takes about 100 years for a tree to grow 100 feet tall and 14 to 16 inches in diameter. Each souvenir requires 15 to 17 steps and an average of 3 months processing time from start to finish. Approximately 6 weeks are spent in drying the wood which has a 40 percent water content. The process cannot be hurried, for myrtlewood which is not dried properly will crack and warp. Without rooms of 85°-100°F circulating heat and dehumidifiers, the drying would take from 1 to 3 years. Because of the processing time, products are fairly expensive. A plain, 10-inch bowl retails for around $50. Button-sized earrings cost $5 to $10.

The assortment of souvenirs in the typical myrtlewood gift shop are the products of many craftsmen. Most are specialists who operate out of their homes or backyard shops. The products they make are dictated by the machinery required to manufacture them.

Most jewelry is made in San Francisco by a company with equipment to manufacture small beads and marble-sized balls. A factory in Grants Pass, OR, mass produces flying seagulls, and another near Roseburg specializes in bear figurines. Bowls, goblets and round trays come from lathe-equipped shops.

Myrtlewood's unique properties are limiting. Because of its tendency to buckle, a huge demand for myrtlewood mantles remains unfilled. Several yo-yo makers have tried in vain to balance the wood and fill another void. Its hardness makes ornamentation difficult, time consuming and costly. Very few souvenirs are intricately detailed.

Meanwhile, the myrtlewood industry is doing just fine, thanks to the growing numbers of travelers who are more than happy with the handsome wood and the simple design. For them, it is enough to have an attractive souvenir which is clearly identified with an area in which they had bought it.

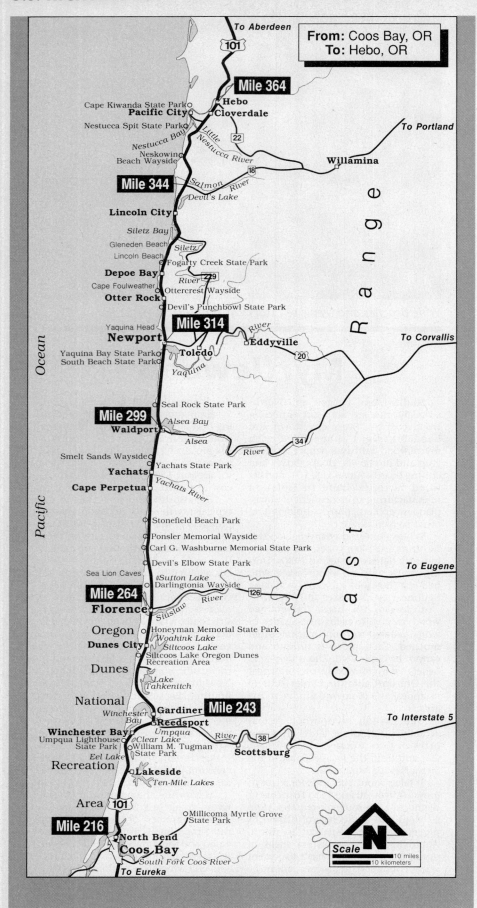

From: Coos Bay, OR
To: Hebo, OR

fishing for salmon is popular during the summer. Flood tides bring chinook into the bay to feed during August.

Mile 139 (678): Rogue River viewpoint (westbound) and Rogue River Beach road (eastbound).

Mile 144 (673): Giesel (Ge-sell) Monument, commemorating the Indian massacre of the Giesel family in 1856.

Mile 145 (672): Nesika (Ness-ih-ka) Beach wayside offers camping, beachcombing, agate hunting and picnicking. Gas, food and RV park.

Mile 147 (670): Honey Bear Beach access and rest area. Surf fishing, beach walking and travel information are available.

Mile 153.5 (663.5): Prehistoric Gardens, a private exhibit featuring life-size replicas of dinosaurs and other prehistoric animals. The arboretum is also worth visiting.

Mile 160 (657): Humbug Mountain State Park has 30 campsites with full hookups, 75 tent campsites, camp showers and picnic sites. The primary feature is Humbug Mountain which rises 1,750 feet shear above the ocean. Food, lodging available. Access to excellent beach is under the highway. MP 308

Mile 163 (654): Garrison Lake public boat landing.

Mile 164 (653): PORT ORFORD (pop. 1,065) has the distinction of being the oldest townsite on the Oregon coast (established in 1851) and the westernmost incorporated city in the Lower 48 states. All services are available. There are 2 fish buying stations and an urchin processing plant on the pier. Port Orford provides an excellent "barless" boat harbor for fishing for salmon and bottom fish during August, September and October just offshore. There are no charter or rental boats available. In late summer, cartop boats are used to fish the protected waters and the ocean during windless periods. A few commercial fishing boats work from the public dock. A heavy-duty hoist lifts both recreational and commercial vessels from dock to ocean. It is the only Oregon port where commercial fishing vessels are hauled out of the water and stored on trailers each night. Port Orford Head offers whale watching in the spring and fall migration seasons. Battle Rock State Park Historic Site with beach access is a day-use only area.

Mile 169 (648): Cape Blanco State Park has 58 campsites and dump station. The lighthouse on the cape is the farthest western point that a vehicle may be driven in the Lower 48 states. The cape was discovered on Jan. 19, 1603, by Spanish explorer Martin De Augilar. Scenic cliffs and a waterfall are visible. Secluded campsites and picnic areas offer beautiful ocean views. Blanco reef and Orford reef are both part of the Oregon Islands National Wildlife Refuge.

Mile 169.5 (647.5): Sixes River bridge.

Mile 173.5 (643.5): Private campground and RV park. ▲

Mile 175 (642): Floras Lake Road, public boat landing.

Mile 177 (640): Town of LANGLOIS. Originally called Dairyville, it was confused with a town in Ohio, so they named it after the postmaster, a Frenchman named Langlois. RV park, food and gas available. ▲

Mile 183.5 (633.5): Westcoast Game Park, private exhibit featuring walk-through wildlife safari. There are many myrtlewood shops found in the next few miles northbound. MP 282

offers 128 full hookup spaces for RVs, 64 improved sites, showers, picnic facilities, viewpoint, boat ramp, beach access and swimming area. Fishing in the river is open year-round. Information is available at sporting goods stores in Bandon. ⊼⋖▲

Mile 194.5 (622.5): Seven Devils Wayside viewpoint with picnicking, beach access, beachcombing for agates and driftwood, and surf fishing at Whiskey Run Beach. ⊼⋖

Mile 199 (618): Westbound turnoff to Charleston area recreation facilities. These include Seven Devils Wayside, a day-use only area; Cape Arago State Park day-use area with picnicking, hiking, fishing, viewpoint and sea lions; Shore Acres State Park day-use area for picnics, canoe launch, interpretative

Oregon coast. Fishing charter boats available daily from Coos Bay at nearby Charleston.

Coos River is a major striped bass fishing area. Clamming is good at low tide in the boat basin at Charleston and nearby beaches. Most recreational features are found in nearby Charleston, including state parks, charter boats, boat ramps and bait and tackle stores. The local fishing situation varies seasonally. Check with local fishermen for latest conditions and where-to-go information. ⋖

Mile 219.5 (597.5): NORTH BEND (pop. 8,850) is a major commercial shipping port. The 3-city complex of Coos Bay, Charleston and North Bend forms the metropolitan center serving the central Oregon coast and has all services. There is a visitor information center at the north city limits for local tour and fishing information. Coos County Historical Society Museum is located here.

Mile 220.5 (596.5): C.B. McCullough Bridge across the Coos River.

Mile 221 (596): Southern boundary of Oregon Dunes National Recreation Area in the Siuslaw (sigh-OOS-law) National Forest. For more information on the Oregon Dunes National Recreation Area see the MAJOR ATTRACTIONS section.

Mile 222 (595): West access road to 4 camping areas including Bluebill Campground, ORV area, water, hiking, fishing and dune access. One camping area provides horse corral at each site. A hiking trail leads to Sandpoint and Horsefall lakes. 大⋖▲

Mile 223 (594): Hauser area; Beale Lakes access.

Mile 227 (590): Saunders and Butterfield lakes are adjacent to highway.

Mile 230 (587): Spinreel Campground access road to a boat ramp, fishing and ORV access. ORV rentals are available. ⋖▲MP224

Mile 231 (586): LAKESIDE (pop. 1,425) offers resort facilities, access to Camp Easter Seal, South Eel campgrounds and Ten-Mile Lakes Recreation Area. Fee camping at South Eel (no beach driving is permitted). Ten-Mile Lakes area is 2 major lakes, North and South Ten-Mile, offering some of the finest largemouth bass fishing in Oregon. North Lake Resort on North Ten-Mile Lake offers the only camping facilities, plus a boat launch, boat rentals, RV hookups and access to both lakes. ⋖▲

Mile 233 (584): Eel Lake and William M. Tugman State Park on the southwest end of the lake. Tugman includes 115 tent/RV sites, dump station, picnicking, swimming beach, fishing and a boat ramp on Eel Lake. ⊼⋖▲

Mile 235.5 (581.5): Clear Lake is closed to fishing and recreational use. This lake is the water supply for Reedsport.

Mile 237.5 (579.5): Umpqua Lighthouse

Beautifully landscaped gardens at Shore Acres State Park; Mile 199 turnoff. (L. Linkhart)

Mile 187.5 (629.5): Scenic Beach Loop Drive, a 3.6-mile drive following the coastline and Bandon State Park. This is for day use only, no restrooms. There is good beach access, scenic overlooks of brilliant yellow gorse fields, picnicking, beachcombing and surf fishing for perch. ⊼⋖ MP 274

Mile 190 (627): BANDON (pop. 2,770) has all visitor services. The self-proclaimed "Cranberry Capital of Oregon," Bandon has a picturesque harbor and fishing village atmosphere. The area offers excellent river, bay and ocean fishing as well as cranberry bogs, myrtlewood factories and the Bandon cranberry festival in September. ⋖ MP 261

Mile 191.5 (625.5): Face Rock viewpoint with wayside facilities. Good photo opportunities.

Mile 192.5 (624.5): Bandon Beach Lighthouse, Coquille River bridge and Bullards Beach State Park. The park, open year-round,

center, summer workshop information, hiking, photography and fishing. There is exceptional landscaping and Oriental gardens on the former estate of lumber baron Louis J. Simpson. Sunset Bay State Park provides overnight camping for 108 tents and 29 RVs, hookups, showers, picnicking, hiking, swimming, fishing on rocks, viewpoints and striking natural rock carvings. 大⊼⋖▲

Mile 208.5 (608.5): Public boat ramp.

Mile 210 (607): Junction with Oregon Highway 42 to Coquille, Roseburg and Interstate 5.

Mile 216 (601): COOS BAY (pop. 14,220), world's largest lumber shipping port. Coos Bay has all visitor services including 20 motels and 70 restaurants. This is a major recreation area with numerous state parks, beach access, bay and river fishing, crabbing and clamming, House of Myrtlewood factory tours, and one of the largest Coast Guard stations on the

State Park; 22 RV hookup sites, 41 tent sites, fishing, boating, hiking trails and dune access. The picturesque lighthouse marks the mouth of the Umpqua River and was rebuilt in 1892 on the bluff, replacing a beach lighthouse destroyed by flood in 1857. 🚶‍♀️🐟▲

Mile 239 (578): WINCHESTER BAY, a small commercial sportfishing community at the mouth of the Umpqua River, has the largest sportfishing marina on the Oregon coast at Salmon Harbor. Winchester Bay has most traveler services including restaurants and gift shops. A favorite destination for scuba divers. Viewed from sea, the lighthouse guarding the mouth of Winchester Bay is the only one on the Oregon coast with a red light beam. Salmon fishing charter boat facilities usually close for the season in late September. This is a large harbor with marina docking area, boat launch, RV camping and cannery services. Crabbing is done in the harbor and ring traps are available for rent.

Windy Cove County Campground is accessible from marina area on County Road 251 and has beach and dune access. 🐟▲ MP 216

Mile 243 (574): REEDSPORT (pop. 5,000), at the junction with Oregon Highway 38; all services available. Headquarters for Oregon Dunes National Recreation Area is located here (see MAJOR ATTRACTIONS section). The region at the confluence of the Smith and Umpqua rivers was first mentioned in 1578 in the account of Sir Francis Drake's exploration in the North Pacific seeking the mythical Strait of Anian. There are boat ramps onto the Umpqua River and Scholfield Creek, a major tributary. The Roosevelt Elk Preserve is located here.

Mile 243.5 (573.5): Bridge spans the Umpqua River near the Smith River confluence. The Umpqua is the second-largest river on the Oregon Pacific coast, behind the Columbia, and is a major sportfishing attraction. Some type of fishing is available all year, but run peaks vary seasonally. Many sporting goods stores, guides and charter facilities provide local seasonal fishing information. 🐟

Mile 244 (573): Jedediah Smith Historical Marker, commemorating the massacre of his companions and his narrow escape.

Mile 245 (572): GARDINER, founded in 1841 by the shipwrecked crew of a Boston fur-trading company, is located at the mouth of the Smith River. There is a public boat ramp and gas station. Clamming is excellent.

Mile 247 (570): Threemile Road 247 corridor to beach. This is recommended for 4-wheel-drive units only.

Mile 249 (568): Elbow Lake.

Mile 251 (566): Lake Tahkenitch offers swimming, water sports, boating and year-round fishing. The brushy shoreline requires a boat. The lake is stocked with rainbow trout annually. There is a boat launch and camping at Tahkenitch Campground. Hiking and dune access (dunes are closed to vehicles in this area year-round). The resort offers rental boats and a boat ramp. This is a very popular summer recreation area. 🚶‍♀️🐟▲ MP 203

Roosevelt Elk Preserve is in Reedsport; Mile 243.   (L. Linkhart)

Mile 254.5 (562.5): Oregon Dunes overlook with access to the ocean beach and dunes trail system. Drinking water and dunes information are available.

Mile 256 (561): East Carter Lake Campground has a boat ramp, fishing, hiking and drinking water. 🚶‍♀️🐟▲ MP 199

Mile 256.5 (560.5): Siltcoos Lake Oregon Dunes National Recreation Area (see MAJOR ATTRACTIONS section). Access road to Driftwood II and Lagoon campgrounds, drinking water, hiking trails, beach access. Small freshwater lagoons and ponds provide fishing. Siltcoos Lake adjoins U.S. Highway 101 on the east. This lake is rated as one of the most productive fishing lakes in Oregon. There are 2 resorts on the lake near U.S. Highway 101 with boat launches, rental boats, bait, tackle and fishing information. 🚶‍♀️🐟▲

Mile 258 (559): West Lake Campground. Oregon Dunes National Recreation Area. ▲

Mile 259 (558): DUNES CITY (pop. 1,180) and Woahink Lake. There are 2 boat ramps, RV parks, and state park campground. Fishing, waterskiing and water sports are popular here. 🐟▲

Mile 260 (557): Sand Dunes Frontier, a private exhibit offering the only commercial sightseeing trips into the Oregon Dunes National Recreation Area on giant custom-built dune buggies. They also have ATV rentals for dune riding, trout pond, miniature golf and a gift shop.

Mile 261 (556): Honeyman State Park has camping with 66 full hookups, 75 electrical only, 241 tent sites, a dump station, picnic facilities, hiking trail, swimming, fishing, boating at Cleawox Lake, beach and dune access. 🚶‍♀️🏕🐟▲

Mile 262.5 (554.5): South Jetty Road west to jetty at the mouth of the Siuslaw River; also Siuslaw Vista, Goose Pasture and South Jetty ORV areas. A crabbing and fishing dock is located at the end of the road.

Mile 263 (554): GLENADA; restaurant.

Mile 263.5 (553.5): Crossing the Siuslaw River bridge. This is a major sportfishing area. There are no charter boat operations, however, rental boats are available at marinas and a few fishing guides work the river. Boat launches are located on the north side of the bridge and at several upriver points off Oregon Highway 126 which leads to Mapleton and Eugene. Gas, food, lodging available. 🐟

Mile 264 (553): FLORENCE (pop. 5,020) is a recreational resort town, midway on the Oregon coast, and is the northern boundary of the Oregon Dunes National Recreation Area (see MAJOR ATTRACTIONS section). All services available. It has a Coast Guard station, the pioneer museum and a rhododendron festival in May. MP 188

Mile 267 (550): Heceta (Ha-SEE-ta) Beach road access area. There is a scenic loop, motels and resorts.   MP 187

Mile 268 (549): Indian Forest, private exhibit walk-through of an Indian village replica, live buffalo and deer and a trading post.

Mile 269 (548): Sutton Lake is stocked with rainbow trout and panfish. Forest Service campground on the lake, and another on Sutton Creek, a few hundred yards west. ◀▲

Mile 269.5 (547.5): USFS Sutton public boat launch.

Mile 270 (547): The Darlingtonia Botanical Wayside and its rare cobralike insect-eating plants.   MP 185

Mile 271 (546): Alder Dune Campground at Buck Lake; camping, picnicking and hiking.   ⅄⅄⅄ ▲

Mile 271.5 (545.5): Cliffside turnouts for ocean viewpoint and photos. Motel.

Mile 275 (542): Sea Lion Caves, private exhibit featuring one of the world's largest sea caves and the only mainland home of the Steller sea lion. Hundreds of sea lions can be seen inside a massive sea cave (accessible by elevator to a viewing area) and lounging on rocks near cormorant nesting areas. The Sea Lion Caves are a must stop for travelers on U.S. Highway 101. Viewpoint of picturesque Heceta Head Lighthouse.   ★ MP 179

Mile 276 (541): Devil's Elbow State Park is a day-use area only, with beach access. Heceta Head picnic area, the lighthouse and marine gardens are attractions.   ⅄⅄

Mile 278 (539): Southern boundary of Carl G. Washburne Memorial State Park which offers 58 full RV hookups, 8 tent sites, showers, a picnic area, fishing, hiking trails and beach access.   ⅄⅄⅄⅄◀▲

Mile 279 (538): Ponsler Memorial Wayside day-use area. Water is available.

Mile 280 (537): USFS Rock Creek Campground. Lodging available.   ▲

Mile 283 (534): Ragan Art Gallery and Stonefield Beach Park, day use only.

Mile 286.5 (530.5): Neptune State Park with day-use area, picnicking and restrooms.   ⅄⅄

Mile 287.5 (529.5): Cape Perpetua Visitors Center has a movie relating the history of the Oregon coast, and offers a self-guided auto tour and hiking trails to the beach and forest. Excellent viewpoint from this 800-foot tower named by English explorer James Cook on March 7, 1778.   ⅄⅄⅄

Mile 288 (529): Devil's Churn viewpoint, a trough carved into rock where the tides

Devil's Punchbowl fills at high tide; Mile 322.   (Ray Weisgerber)

churn; picnicking, hiking trails (including Trail of the Restless Water) and tidepools.   ⅄⅄⅄

Mile 290 (527): YACHATS (pop. 620), a resort town at the mouth of the Yachats (Ya-HOTS) River, is famous for the July to September run of smelt that triggers the annual July Smelt Fry Festival. Smelt are caught at night with seines, nets and mesh-framed rakes between Yachats and Beachside State Park about 4 miles north. The area also offers agate hunting beaches, surf fishing, swimming, clam digging and beach walking. Motel and gas station.

The Yachats Ocean Wayside offers access to the beach on the southern edge of town, and another wayside overlooks the river mouth from the north.

Mile 291 (526): Smelt Sands Wayside (day use only). Smelt dipping is popular during late summer.

Mile 294 (523): USFS Tillicum Beach Campground with 7 tent and 40 RV sites.   ▲ MP 160

Mile 295 (522): Beachside Campground with 60 tent and 20 RV sites.   ▲

Mile 297 (520): Governor I.L. Patterson State Park, day-use area with beach access, picnicking and restrooms.   ⅄⅄

Mile 298 (519): Junction with Oregon Highway 34 to Corvallis and Interstate 5.

Mile 299 (518): WALDPORT (pop. 1,670), a resort town at the mouth of the Alsea River has all services and a ranger station. Waldport was settled in the late 1870s by Germans (wald meaning "forest" in German). David Ruble was the first to establish a permanent community, laying out streets and

establishing a townsite. The townsite is an old Indian burial ground and Chief Yaquina John of the Alsea tribe is buried just south of town. Although commercial fishing has had an impact on the community, its mainstay is still logging. Two of the town's biggest celebrations are Beachcomber Days held each June, and an annual salmon derby held the first part of October during the fall salmon run on the Alsea River.

Mile 301 (516): Driftwood State Park, with beach access, picnicking and restrooms.   ⅄⅄

Mile 304 (513): Seal Rock State Park offers beach access, surf fishing and picnic tables.   ⅄⅄ ◀ MP 151

Mile 304.5 (512.5): Sea Gulch, a private exhibit built around an Old West town populated with humorous, life-sized chain saw sculptures and carvings.

Mile 306 (511): Ona Beach State Park, with beach access, picnicking, restrooms.   ⅄⅄ MP 149

Mile 307.5 (509.5): Lost Creek State Park with beach access, picnicking, restrooms. ⅄⅄

Mile 311.5 (505.5): South Beach State Park Campground, 257 sites all with electrical hookups, showers, picnic areas, beach access, hiking trails and fishing.   ⅄⅄⅄⅄◀▲

Mile 313 (504): Oregon State Marine Science Center features aquariums and marine pool displays. The center attracts some 250,000 visitors each year. Hours: 9:30 a.m. to 6:00 p.m. Free.

Mile 314 (503): NEWPORT (pop. 8,685) offers all services including excellent hotels, motels and restaurants. Newport is the largest port on the central Oregon coast and is famous for shrimp, crab and sport fisheries. More bottom fish are caught from Newport boats than from any other Oregon port. There is excellent jetty and boat fishing in Yaquina Bay. Numerous fishing charter boats are available. Oyster farms, scuba diving, surfing and agate beds are located here.

Other attractions include the Yaquina (Ya-kwin-a) Bay Coast Guard Station, Undersea Gardens and the Lincoln County Historical Society Museum. Yaquina Bay State Park offers picnicking, fishing, beach access and a lighthouse museum. U.S. Highway 101 junctions with U.S. Highway 20 to Corvallis and Interstate 5. (See U.S. HIGHWAY 20 section.)   ⅄⅄ ◀ MP 140

Mile 319 (498): Moolack Beach area.

Mile 320.5 (496.5): Beverly Beach State Park, one of the more popular oceanside parks. It offers camping, with 52 full hookups, 75 electrical, 152 tent sites and showers. There are also trails, picnicking, fishing and beach access by way of an underpass.   ⅄⅄⅄⅄◀▲

Mile 322 (495): Otter Rock, Otter Crest

day-use and resort area, with beach tidal pools. Devil's Punchbowl State Park has picnicking and restrooms and features a remnant of a collapsed sea cave that creates the Devil's Punchbowl.

Mile 324 (493): Cape Foulweather overlook, Otter Crest Wayside, perched 500 feet above the sea offers an excellent view of Otter Crest and the beach area. A small gift shop is available. Sea lions, cormorants, murres and other seabirds abound. Migrating whales are often spotted during fall and spring. Cape Foulweather was named by Capt. James Cook in 1778.

Mile 325.5 (491.5): Northern end of Otter Crest Loop Road. Also Rocky Creek State Park, with beach access, picnicking and restrooms.

Mile 326 (491): Whale Cove. Whales have been seen inside this small bay.

Mile 327 (490): DEPOE BAY (pop. 865); cafe, lodging and RV park. Depoe Bay has the world's smallest boat harbor, a 6-acre lagoon accessible by a narrow (less than 50 feet wide) natural opening through a rock wall. Depoe Bay has all services and offers charter boat fishing for salmon and bottom fish, whale-watching, ocean-front resorts and a mid-September Indian salmon bake. Depoe Bay is the site where actor Jack Nicholson was filmed stealing a charter boat in the acclaimed movie, *One Flew Over the Cuckoo's Nest.*
▲MP 127

Mile 328.5 (488.5): Boiler Bay Wayside, named for a steam boiler which exploded and sank the boat *J. Marhoffer* here in 1910. It is sometimes visible at low tide. Fogarty Creek State Park (day use only) offers picnic sites. Food, gas and lodging available. ⊼ MP 125

Mile 330 (487): Lincoln Beach offers surf fishing and swimming. ⬷

Mile 332 (485): Gleneden Beach area has picnic sites, fishing, swimming and a golf course. ⊼⬷

Mile 333.5 (483.5): Salishan Lodge Resort. The only 5-star and 5-diamond AAA-rated resort in the Pacific Northwest. It has 150 rooms, 18-hole golf course, tennis courts both inside and out, beach access, conference rooms and a nearby airport.

Mile 334 (483): Junction with Immonen Road. Drive east 0.5 mile to Mossey Creek Pottery Co. and Art Gallery. Alder House glassblowing, one of the oldest glassblowing operations in the Northwest, is located here and visitors are welcome. MP 121

Mile 335 (482): Siletz River and junction with Oregon Highway 229 southeast to Kernville. Fishing for surfperch; boat launch at bridge. RV park. ▲

Mile 339 (478): LINCOLN CITY (pop. 6,340). All traveler services available. South-

Rugged coastline at Cape Foulweather overlook; Mile 324. (Tom Barr)

ernmost city in Oregon's famous 20 Miracle Miles area of art galleries and craft shops. This is a major recreational area with beaches, clamming, crabbing, fishing and resorts. A resident population of sea lions is visible on sandbars at the mouth of Siletz River. Other attractions include kite flying and a wayside at the "world's shortest river," the D River (approximately 200 yards long), which is actually the mouth of Devils Lake. ⬷

Mile 341 (476): East Devils Lake Road encircles Devils Lake, a narrow, 5-mile-long weedy lake where many world boating speed records have been set. There is a state park campground with 32 full hookups and 68 tent sites, and a boat ramp at south end of lake. Sand Point County Park is a day-use area. The Roads End Wayside, Honeywood Winery and Oregon wine tasting room at D River bridge are additional attractions. ▲ MP 112

Mile 342 (475): 45th parallel, marking the halfway point between the equator and the North Pole.

Mile 344 (473): Junction with Oregon Highway 18 to Portland and Interstate 5 and crossing the Salmon River bridge. Although small, the Salmon River is an excellent fall and winter salmon and steelhead producer. The fish are unusually large and bank access is plentiful from roads along both banks. ⬷

Mile 347 (470): Siuslaw National Forest boundary.

Mile 348 (469): Siuslaw National Forest boundary and hiking trailhead. 🏃

Mile 350 (467): Junction with Slab Creek Road scenic drive. Neskowin Beach Wayside day-use area has fishing, beach access and resorts with horse rentals. RV park and campground. ⬷▲ MP 99

Mile 357 (460): Little Nestucca River. October chinook and coho fishing and December to February steelheading is good.⬷

Mile 358.5 (458.5): Junction with Brooten Road, a 34-mile scenic drive to the resort and fishing community of **PACIFIC CITY**, Cape Kiwanda State Park and recreation area, the community of Oceanside and Three Capes Scenic Loop Road.

Pacific City's famous fleet of fishing dories launches from the hard-packed sand beach at Cape Kiwanda, inside Haystack Rock, just north of Pacific City. Spectacular views, sandstone cliffs and beautiful beach make Cape Kiwanda a popular day-use area for beachcombing. Hang gliders launch from the cape headland.

The road continues north along the coast to Cape Lookout and then to Cape Meares on the southern point of Tillamook Bay. Several public beaches, dune buggy riding areas and nature trails are available.

Camping facilities are available at Sandbeach, Cape Lookout State Park, Happy Camp Resort, Bay Shore and Island County Park.

Three Arches Rock, a National Wildlife Refuge, is located off Oceanside. Thousands of birds nest on the rocks offshore and sea lions and seals can be seen playing in the surf much of the year.

Cape Meares has a lighthouse which is open to the public. A photo museum features Oregon lighthouses and their histories and the Octopus Tree, an oddly-shaped giant Sitka spruce measuring 50 feet around, are attractions here. 🏃⬷▲★

Mile 361 (456): CLOVERDALE, a small farming community. Food, gas.

Mile 364 (453): Community of HEBO. Junction with Oregon Highway 22 to Salem and crossing the Nestucca River bridge. This is a large river (heavily stocked with cutthroat).

There is good fishing from boat or bank, several boat launches and a riverside camping area. RV park, food, gas, showers and laundry facilities also available.　　　⬦▲ MP 85

Mile 369 (448): Town of BEAVER; grocery, deli and gas stations.

Mile 371.5 (445.5): Access to Cape Kiwanda State Park with sand dunes, fishing, marina, hiking, scenic viewpoints, tide pools and wave-sculptured sandstone cliffs. 🚶🚶⬦

Mile 374 (443): Trask River has good seasonal fishing. It is stocked heavily in spring with hatchery trout.　　　⬦

Mile 378 (439): Turnoff to Munson Creek Falls County Park, about 9 miles east.

Mile 380 (437): Oregon highway rest area.

Mile 383 (434): TILLAMOOK (pop. 3,770), famous for its cheese. All traveler services available. Free daily tours of the largest cheese factory in the West are available at Tillamook Cheese Factory (Hours: 8 a.m. to 8 p.m.) on the northern edge of city along U.S. Highway 101. Junction with Oregon Highway 6 to Portland and Interstate 5. Northern access to Three Capes Scenic Route. Tillamook Bay, the largest bay on the Oregon coast, is fed by 9 major rivers and offers fishing, clamming and crabbing. Local sporting goods stores provide current information.

Mile 387.5 (429.5): Kilchis River Junction and public golf course.　　MP 61

Mile 389 (428): BAY CITY (pop. 1,100) offering full services.　　MP 60

Mile 390.5 (426.5): Historical marker on Captain Robert Gray.

Mile 393 (424): GARIBALDI (pop. 1,055) has all tourist services. It is a major fishing port, offering charters for salmon and bottom fish. A county park is located north of the bayfront. Jetty fishing, Fisherman's Wharf, launch ramps, fresh seafood stands, tours of fish and shrimp processing plants and oyster shucking are attractions.　　⬦

Mile 395.5 (421.5): Barview Jetty County Park and viewpoint of the often stormy entrance to Tillamook Bay. Camping and beach access are available. Gas and food. ▲ MP 53

Mile 399 (418): ROCKAWAY BEACH (pop. 1,330) with beach access, surfperch fishing, and adjacent Twin Rocks resort area. Gas, lodging, RV park.　　⬦▲ MP 51

Mile 400.5 (416.5): Manhattan Beach Wayside with beach access. Lake Lytle offers boating, fishing, waterskiing and windsurfing. It is connected to Crescent Lake, a trout and bass lake surrounded by sand dunes. ⬦

Mile 406 (411): WHEELER (pop. 350) has a public dock, motel, restaurant and gas.

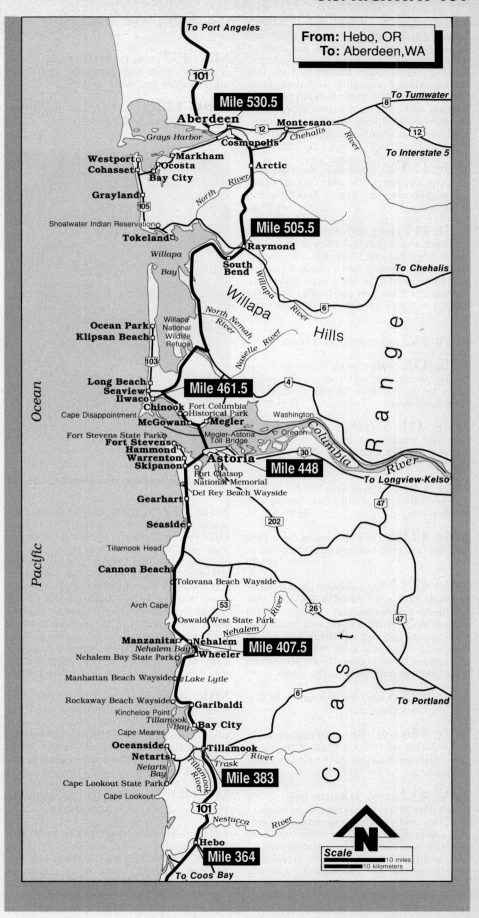

Mile 407.5 (409.5): Junction with Oregon Highway 53 North to U.S. Highway 26 to Portland and Interstate 5. The town of **NEHALEM** (pop. 240) has shops and galleries. Tours of Nehalem Bay Winery and the Old Fishing Village available. Nehalem River bridge and bay. This area offers fall coho and chinook salmon runs, winter steelhead, cutthroat, numerous boat launches, clamming, crabbing areas, resorts and fishing guides.
MP 45

Mile 410 (407): Nehalem Bay State Park has 292 campsites, showers, ocean beach access, clamming, surf fishing, boat ramp and picnic areas.

Mile 411 (406): **MANZANITA** (pop. 555) is a resort area featuring 7 miles of open sand beach, Neah-Kah-Nie Mountain, a 1,700-foot mountain viewpoint, and a wrecked Spanish galleon believed to be the source of beeswax occasionally found on the beach. There are legends of buried Spanish treasure here.
MP 43

Mile 412 (405): Public golf course.

Mile 415 (402): Oswald State Park offers fishing, picnic area, beach access, clamming. There are 35 primitive hike-in campsites at Short Sand Beach.

Mile 419.5 (397.5): Cannon Beach Historical Marker, and cannon that washed ashore here from a Columbia River bar shipwreck in 1846.

Mile 420.5 (396.5): Hug Point State Park (day use only) has picnic sites, fishing and beach access.
MP 33

Mile 421.5 (395.5): Arcadia State Park (day use only) has picnic sites and fishing.

Mile 423 (394): Tolovana Loop Road to Tolovana Park and **CANNON BEACH** (pop. 1,270). All traveler services. The area has 9 miles of sandy beach, a resort area, music and art programs, galleries, kite flying, fishing and clamming. Haystack Rock Wildlife Refuge offshore is 235 feet high and is one of the most photographed monoliths in the world.

Mile 423.5 (393.5): Junction with U.S. Highway 26 to Portland.

Mile 426 (391): Historical marker. Ecola is the site where William Clark of the Lewis and Clark expedition bought whale meat from the Indians.
MP 28

Mile 432 (385): **SEASIDE** (pop. 5,735) has all traveler services. Seaside is the home of the Lewis and Clark Trail turnaround. Lewis and Clark stopped here to make salt from seawater, now a historical site open to visitors. Seaside offers a 2-mile concrete promenade with swimming, beach resorts and the Seaside Aquarium, one of the few places where visitors can feed seals. This is a very popular spot, especially for youngsters. Seaside is the largest beach resort city in the Pacific Northwest.
MP 12

Mile 437 (380): **GEARHART** (pop. 1,100) is a resort town with clamming and swimming beaches and some services.

Mile 439.5 (377.5): Del Rey Beach Wayside (day-use beach area). No facilities are available.

Astoria Column, a memorial to Lewis and Clark, in Astoria; Mile 448. (L. Linkhart)

Mile 442.5 (374.5): **SKIPANON** and the junction with side road to Fort Stevens State Park (5 miles northwest) which is the largest state park and one of the most popular recreational areas in Oregon. Fort Stevens has 603 sites, full facilities, beaches, freshwater and saltwater fishing and access to Columbia River beaches. It was built on the site of historic Fort Stevens, constructed in 1864, to guard the entrance to the Columbia River. Gun emplacements and underground tunnels still exist. The fort was fired upon by a Japanese submarine in 1942. Wreck of the ship *Peter Iredale* is visible on the beach.

Mile 443.5 (373.5): Fort Clatsop. A reconstructed fort in which Lewis and Clark spent the winter of 1805-06. The area is administered by the National Park Service, and includes a visitor center, the fort, trails, and examples of the equipment used by the party.

Mile 445 (372): Turnoff for **WARREN-TON** (pop. 2,535) with most services.

Mile 448 (369): **ASTORIA** (pop. 10,180) has all major tourist services including motels, bed-and-breakfast facilities and restaurants. Astoria is the first permanent American settlement on the Pacific Coast, established in 1811 as a fur-trading post. The Megler-Astoria Bridge (toll) across the Columbia River is the longest continuous truss bridge in the world (1,232 feet long). The Astoria Column, built in 1926, is 125 feet high and has 166 steps to the top.

Junction with U.S. Highway 30 east to Longview, WA, and Portland, OR.

Mile 452 (365): Washington-Oregon state border at midspan on Megler-Astoria Bridge (toll) across the Columbia River.

Mile 453 (364): North end of bridge, junction with Washington Highway 401 to Longview via Washington Highway 4.

Mile 453.5 (363.5): Historical marker commemorating the discovery of the Columbia River by Capt. Robert Gray in 1792. RV park.
MP 1

Mile 454.5 (362.5): Fort Columbia Historical State Park and viewpoint. Picnic area and interpretive center. Gun battery emplacements are visible.
MP 3

Mile 458 (359): Lewis and Clark historical campsite, community of **CHINOOK**, a county park with camping, beach access, picnicking and restrooms, a Port of Chinook boat launch and most tourist facilities are available here.

Mile 461.5 (355.5): Junction with bypass to U.S. Highway 101 and Raymond. Continue west 1.5 miles to **ILWACO**, a fishing town for commercial and charter boat fleets working the Columbia and offshore waters. North Head, Cape Disappointment Lighthouse, and Coast Guard station. Fort Canby State Park has 250 campsites, beach access, fishing, boat launch and the Lewis and Clark Interpretive Center. Washington Highway 103 leads north up the Long Beach Peninsula to 28 miles of sandy beaches, oyster farms, campgrounds and wildlife refuges. This is a popular vacation area. The peninsula creates Willapa Bay.

Mile 466.5 (350.5): Willapa Bay with famous oyster farming areas, tours available. Good waterfowl hunting, crabbing and perch fishing.

Mile 470.5 (346.5): Willapa National Wildlife Refuge.

Mile 472.5 (344.5): Bridge across Willapa Bay backwater lagoon.

Mile 475.5 (341.5): Junction Washington Highway 4 to Longview-Kelso and Interstate 5.

Mile 481.5 (335.5): North Nemah Road, turn east to see the state salmon hatchery. Cafe.

Mile 487.5 (329.5): Bush Pioneer County Park offers camping and picnicking on Willapa Bay. Palix River has spring and fall fishing.

Mile 489.5 (327.5): Willapa River.

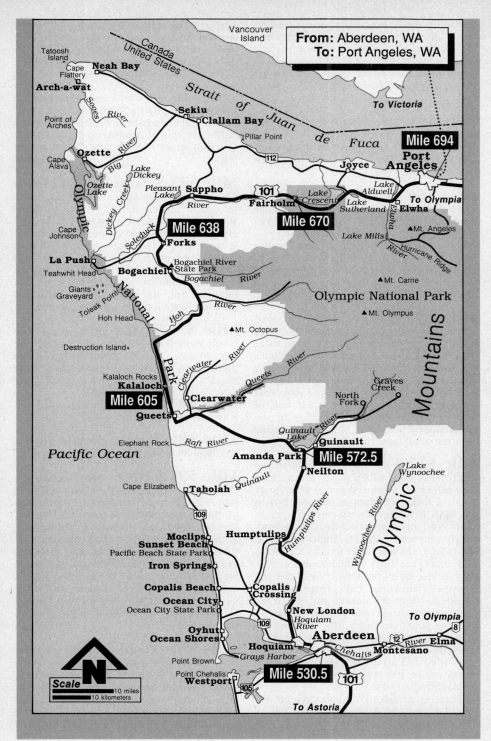

From: Aberdeen, WA
To: Port Angeles, WA

Mile 504.5 (312.5): Port of Willapa Harbor. MP 57

Mile 505 (312): Golf course and south fork of Willapa River. MP 58

Mile 505.5 (311.5): RAYMOND (pop. 2,870) is a logging community with mill operations. All services available. Junction with Washington Highway 6 east to Chehalis and Interstate 5.

Mile 506.5 (310.5): Junction with Washington Highway 105 west to Westport, Grayland and coastal camping, razor clam beaches and recreation areas.

Mile 511 (306): Battle Creek picnic area. ⚲

Mile 516 (301): Heavily forested area. Watch clear-cuts for deer, elk and black bear. *CAUTION:* Winding road, 40 mph.

Mile 519.5 (297.5): North River bridge, community of ARCTIC. Excellent sea-run cutthroat fishing, fair steelhead, salmon. This is a popular deer hunting area. RV park and restaurant. ⚓▲

Mile 523.5 (293.5): Junction with Washington Highway 107 to Montesano (Monta-say-no).

Mile 529.5 (287.5): COSMOPOLIS (pop. 1,545) has all services and a lumbermill. Good sturgeon and salmon fishing in Chehalis River. There is a launch ramp at the Weyerhauser mill. ⚓

Mile 530.5 (286.5): ABERDEEN (pop. 17,130) has all major tourist facilities. Aberdeen received its name from Scottish settlers who gave the name of their home town, Aberdeen, Scotland, to this new area. It is appropriate since Aberdeen is the Gaelic word meaning "the meeting of 2 rivers." Many present residents of Aberdeen are descendents of the original immigrants who came to log the greatest stand of Douglas fir trees in the Pacific Northwest. Today the town thrives on lumbering, fishing and related industries. Junction with U.S. Highway 12 east to Olympia.

Mile 534.5 (282.5): HOQUIAM (HO-Kwee-um) (pop. 9,050) is the twin city of Aberdeen. The communities share geographical and political ties. All services are available. This deep-water port of Grays Harbor is heavily used in transporting lumber and related products. This is one of the gateways to the spectacular Olympic Peninsula, Olympic National Forest and Olympic National Park. An attraction of particular interest is Hoquiam's Castle, a 20-room mansion built in 1897 by lumber tycoon Robert Lytle.

Junction with Washington Highway 109, a 2-lane highway leading west 20 miles to OCEAN SHORES (pop. 2,179), a resort area with several motels and restaurants and south to Point Brown; then north along the coast to OCEAN CITY (with 1 resort), COPALIS

Mile 490.5 (326.5): Historical marker on Bruce Port. The deserted site is 1 mile north at Willapa Bay and was once the county seat. The crew of the oyster schooner, *Robert Bruce*, settled here in December 1851 after their ship burned. They built cabins and named the settlement Bruceville. This site recalls the oyster industry of 1851-80 when enormous quantities of oysters were gathered and shipped to San Francisco.

Mile 492.5 (324.5): Bruce Port County Park and public fishing. Hiking, camping. Free

coffee is served from 7 a.m. to 7 p.m. 🚶‍♂️⚓▲

Mile 500.5 (316.5): Pacific County Historic Courthouse and Museum.

Mile 501 (316): Public park with picnicking and restrooms. ⚲

Mile 501.5 (315.5): SOUTH BEND (pop. 1,605), the "Oyster Capital of the World," has most traveler services. Oyster processing plants and excellent steelhead fishing on the Willapa River.

BEACH (1 resort), **MOCLIPS** (2 resorts) and Cape Elizabeth. Highway 109 ends at the south border of the Quinault Indian Reservation, where restrictions and special travel regulations are required for nontribal travelers. Highway 109 offers more direct ocean beach access than any other section of U.S. Highway 101 in Washington with numerous beachfront resorts.

The coastal shoreline here is dominated by wide, sandy beaches, low brush and small fir trees.

Ocean City State Park, located 2 miles north of Ocean Shores, has 149 tent sites, 29 RV sites, full hookups, swimming beach and surf fishing.

One of the most popular destinations is Pacific Beach State Park with 118 tent sites, 20 RV sites, full hookups and swimming beach. Fee campground. These beaches are very popular for razor clam digging and surfperch fishing during peak seasons. Check locally for razor clam digging regulations. 🎣◄▲

Mile 538.5 (278.5): Little Hoquiam River bridge. This is a small tidal stream with brushy roadside access and minimal recreational opportunities.

Mile 541 (276): Bernard Creek bridge, cafe. Junction with 2-lane road leading west to Copalis Beach and coastal resort areas. Washington Highway 109 at **Mile 534.5** junction provides better access to the same area.
MP 92

Mile 543.5 (273.5): West fork of the Hoquiam River parallels and crosses below the highway. The alder, Douglas fir and Sitka spruce forests are heavily clear-cut in this area and early morning or evening travelers frequently spot black-tailed deer.

Mile 547.5 (269.5): Failor Lake Road leads west to Failor Lake, a Dept. of Game access area with a boat launch. It is a popular rainbow trout fishing water, especially during early May and June. ◄

Mile 556.5 (260.5): The highway crosses the Humptulips River, a major steelhead, sea-run cutthroat and salmon producing river, at the crossroads community of **HUMPTULIPS**. Motel, camping and gas are available at the bridge crossing. Identified as the Humptulips Recreation Area, several boat launches are available on the East Fork Road along the south bank of the river. North bank launches are found west of town along the Humptulips Road which also leads to Copalis Crossing, the ocean beaches and the Copalis National Wildlife Refuge in the Washington Islands Wilderness Area. The refuge and wilderness area extends north along the Quinault Indian Reservation. This is a very popular winter steelhead fishing area with most of the action concentrated below the highway. Current fishing information is available at the store in Humptulips. There is also a salmon hatchery nearby. ◄▲ MP 109

Mile 559.5 (257.5): Donkey Creek rest area, along the west side of the highway, offers restrooms, shelter house, shaded picnic tables and a small pond. This scenic little area also includes an antique steam locomotive and steam donkey on display. Nearby Donkey Creek Road leads to the Humptulips ranger station and Promised Land Recreation Area. 🛉

Mile 565 (252): Burnt Hill lookout and Newbury Creek Road. The state lookout is accessible via a rough road branching south off the Newbury Creek Road about 1 mile east of U.S. Highway 101.

Mile 566 (251): Boundary of Olympic National Forest and turnoff to Quinault Ridge Road and Neilton Point. MP 118

Mile 568 (249): Junction with Moclips Road which leads 20 miles southwest to Moclips and ocean beaches. Four miles west of the junction is the Quinault national fish hatchery.

Mile 571 (246): **NEILTON**, a small community with gas and groceries. This area is the heart of the Olympic Peninsula cedar shake industry, and many small working mills are along the highway, marked by a prominent drying kiln. The kilns provide the intense heat required to cure and dry cedar shakes. The shakes are split from large bolts of wood which are often carried out of the mountains by helicopter. Most of these shake mills are small family-owned businesses.

Mile 572.5 (244.5): Junction with the South Shore Road which winds around Lake Quinault in the southwest corner of Olympic National Park. (See Olympic National Park in the MAJOR ATTRACTIONS section.) South Shore Road junctions with North Shore Road, which connects with U.S. Highway 101 at **Mile 572.5**. The loop drive around the lake is 27.5 miles, mostly well-maintained gravel. One of the most impressive lakes on the Olympic Peninsula, Lake Quinault is a favorite vacation destination, and one of the world's wettest areas with approximately 200 inches of rainfall annually. The road hugs the south shore which supports most of the lake's development. Lake Quinault is 4 miles long, 2 miles wide and up to 300 feet deep. Recreational use of the lake is regulated by the Quinault Indian tribe.

There is a walk-in campground on the North Shore Road at July Creek that has 31 primitive sites. Two USFS campgrounds, Falls Creek and Willaby, are on the South Shore Road. Both restrict trailer lengths to 16 feet and offer picnicking, drinking water, restrooms, hiking trails, self-guided nature tours and boat launches. There are also some very pleasant lakeside picnic areas. Several resorts, restaurants and mercantiles can be found about midlake at **QUINAULT** where a ranger station and tribal office are also located.

Beyond the lake the South Shore Road becomes gravel and winds up the Quinault Valley along the upper river to the Quinault segment of the famous rain forest, ending at Graves Creek USFS ranger station and campground, 45 sites with a 21-foot maximum length. No fee at this campground, which also serves as a trailhead to the Enchanted Valley region of the Olympic National Park, a 21-mile hike along the East Fork Quinault River. A few miles before Graves Creek the road forks and the left turn bridges the Quinault River to connect with the North Shore Road which provides access to the North Fork USFS ranger station and campground, 8 sites, no fee and a trailhead for hikers heading up the North Fork Quinault River trail to Low Divide ranger station. 🎣🛉▲★

Mile 573.5 (243.5): **AMANDA PARK** at the outlet of Lake Quinault; gas, food and lodging. U.S. Highway 101 bridges the Quinault River and turns west toward the coast and except for a 1-mile section near Prairie Creek, is bordered on both sides by the Quinault Indian Reservation. All recreational land and water use in this area is regulated by the Quinault Indian Council and permits are required. Inquire at the general store in Amanda Park for permits and regulations.

Mile 575.5 (241.5): Junction with the North Shore Road (see **Mile 572.5**). Over the next 20 miles, the full-grown firs border the highway so closely, their branches almost touch.

Mile 581.5 (235.5): Olympic National Forest boundary.

Mile 582.5 (234.5): ITT Rayonier mill and Boulder Creek.

Mile 591.5 (225.5): Junction with the Queets Valley Recreation Area Road to Queets rain forest. The road parallels the south bank of the Queets River, an excellent winter/summer steelhead, sea-run cutthroat and salmon fishing river outside of the tribal jurisdiction. A ranger station and primitive campground (26 sites, no services, unsuitable for trailers) are located 14 miles upriver in the rain forest area. The Queets rain forest is the middle of the 3 official rain forest areas, flanked by the Quinault to the south and the Hoh to the north. ◄ MP 145

Mile 594 (223): Junction with Clearwater River Recreation Area Road (gravel) which follows the Clearwater River upstream. A rough boat launch and 3 primitive campgrounds are along the river. A pretty river that offers fair steelhead fishing in December and January and cutthroat fishing from July through October, plus hiking access into Olympic National Park. 🎣◄▲

Mile 599 (218): **QUEETS**, a small tribal town located on the Queets River has limited services. The bridge here can often be a good place to watch Indian fishermen setting gill nets across the river to harvest steelhead and salmon.

Mile 601 (216): Northern boundary of Quinault Indian Reservation and southern coastal segment of Olympic National Park. South Beach camping area is a graveled parking lot-style area best suited for RVs,

Olympic Rain Forests

The Hoh, Quinault and Queets River rain forests sit side by side in the southwest corner of Olympic National Park. They are part of one of the world's few temperate rain forests.

It covers roughly one-third of the park's 900,000 acres. Here, mild temperatures and an annual precipitation of over 140 inches combine to create giant coniferous trees, moss-draped maples and a forest floor covered with ferns. Most of the rain falls during winter leaving a comparatively dry summer with many clear and sunny days.

The 3 river valleys were formed by glacial action some 2,000 years ago. Broad and flat, they gain only 600 feet in elevation in 20 miles and are about a mile wide. Virtually every square inch of ground is covered by vegetation, ranging from tiny mosses to giant 300-foot spruce trees. There are over 300 species of plants, 71 mosses, 30 different liverworts and 70 separate lichens.

Sitka spruce and western hemlock dominate an environment characterized by large numbers of giant trees. Douglas fir, western red cedar, big-leaf maple and vine maple are second-class citizens. The varied wildlife ranges from the often-seen Roosevelt elk and black-tailed deer to the reclusive black bear and cougar. Bobcats, coyotes, beaver and otter inhabit forests and riverbanks.

While virtually interchangeable in plants and topography, the 3 forests are diverse in terms of services and facilities.

The Hoh is the most famous and easily accessible. A 19-mile paved road leads east from **Mile 625** Highway 101 to a visitor center, evening campfire programs, guided walks and campground.

A 0.25-mile trail is easily walked by children and accessible to the handicapped. Signs explain "lower story" plants, moss-draped boughs, the giant Douglas fir, Sitka spruce and hemlock.

The "Hall of Mosses" is the most photographed and popular of all rain forest interpretative trails. Less than a mile long, it is lined with dramatic draperies of club moss and the largest old-growth trees. The 1-mile Spruce Trail meanders through a variety of vegetation and topography, including the present Hoh riverbank and former streambeds. For an extended hike, there is the 17-mile Hoh River Trail. It starts at the visitor center, winds through the river valley and ends with Blue Glacier and the park's highest peak, Mount Olympus (elev. 7,965 feet).

For $5 per night, visitors can camp beside the Hoh River. It is a premier fishing stream for winter steelhead, mid-summer chinook salmon, and fall runs of salmon, steelhead and trout.

Quinault is often called the most beautiful of the rain forests. Situated on the shores of Lake Quinault, it offers a choice of accommodations in a lodge, private resort and several campgrounds.

The rain forest can be seen from cars on a 25-mile loop road that includes the scenic lake, farms and views of the Olympic Mountains. Seasonal attractions are Roosevelt elk, flocks of swans, spring rhododendrons and azaleas. Several trails begin at the lake. They range from short rain forest hikes to paths leading to remote areas and distant park borders.

Lake Quinault is frequented by swimmers, boaters and fishermen seeking Dolly Varden, steelhead, cutthroat, rainbow and salmon. Fishing is regulated by the Quinault Indian Nation.

Quinault Lodge was built during the 1920s. It contains most of the original furnishings and has one of the largest private collections of Indian art and baskets in the Northwest. The full-menu dining room is open during summer along with rooms in the main lodge, annex and cabins. A heated indoor pool, saunas and therapy spa are available to guests.

At Rain Forest Resort Village, cabins are set along a creek and on the lakefront. The full service restaurant and lounge specializes in local seafoods and Washington wines. To reach Lake Quinault, leave U.S. 101 at **Mile 572.5** and travel 3 miles northeast to the lake, lodge and campgrounds.

The Queets River rain forest is for those who want to get away from people and are content with a minimum of services. Facilities are limited to a boat ramp and 26-unit, no fee campground situated on the riverbank. A ranger is on duty during the summer.

For most of the year, hiking is limited to the 3-mile-long Sam's River Loop Trail. It starts at the campground, winds along the river and through beautiful fern and moss displays. Because Queets attracts fewer people, elk frequently feed in 2 meadows along the loop.

During low water months, hikers ford the stream and take the 16-mile-long Queets River Trail. Highlights are one of the park's largest Douglas fir trees, abandoned fields and buildings. The latter are relics from the 1880s to the 1940s when the valley was heavily homesteaded by Europeans. A generator house, settlers cabin and classic barn still stand.

From December to April, the Queets River is heavily fished for steelhead. It is known for its runs of wild salmon, fall chinook and summer Dolly Varden. Floaters, rafters and boaters use the river during spring and summer. Potential hazards are log jams and sweepers — trees which have fallen into the river and are too low to get under and too high to go over.

Queets access is via 14 miles of good dirt road from **Mile 591.5** Highway 101.

Moss-draped trees and lush vegetation of the Olympic rain forests. (L. Linkhart)

although some beachcombers pitch small tents in primitive spots on nearby bluffs or along the beach. No drinking water, but restrooms are available. Very popular RV area with excellent beach access and acres of giant driftwood logs. Some surf fishing for perch and swimming for those tough enough to brave the cold ocean waters. Ashenbrenner picnic day-use area adjoins the camping stretch on the south on a brushy, picturesque bluff overlooking miles of sandy beach. A fine place to stop for a travel break. ⛱ ◄▲ MP 154

Mile 603 (214): Beach access. MP 156

Mile 605 (212): KALALOCH (Ka-Lay-Lock) is comprised of the Kalaloch ranger station, Kalaloch Lodge, and Kalaloch Campground. The ranger station has maps and current information on Olympic National Park facilities. Kalaloch Lodge is a private resort with rental cabins and beach access. The lodge also has a small grocery store, restaurant, gas station and gift shop.

Kalaloch Campground, within Olympic National Park, is the largest coastal beach campground on the Olympic Peninsula. It has 179 campsites, full hookups, picnicking and hiking. A popular camping area, likely to be full during peak summer travel periods. Excellent beach access, with a view to the northwest of Destruction Island. ⛱⛱▲ MP 158

Mile 607.5 (209.5): Beachfront picnic and day-use area. Beach access. ⛱

Mile 609.5 (207.5): Big Cedar Road leads east to the site of a giant cedar tree. Once thought to be the world's largest western red cedar, was later found to be slightly smaller than the 183-foot-high record holder located a little north of here in the Hoh River valley. A pleasant beach access area is about 200 yards north on the west side of the road. MP 162

Mile 610.5 (206.5): Destruction Island Historical Marker, commemorating the slaughter of 13 sailors. In 1775 Spanish explorer Bodega y Quadra anchored in the lee of the island and sent 7 sailors ashore for wood and water. They were killed by Indians and Quadra named the island Isla de Delores, "the island of sorrow." In 1787, a Captain Barkley also anchored in the protection of the island and sent 6 sailors ashore for supplies. They too were killed by Indians and the captain named the nearby river Destruction River. Later the name was given to the island and the river returned to its native title of Hoh.

Mile 611.5 (205.5): Ruby Beach day-use area; excellent beach trails, picnicking and restrooms. Offshore rock is named Abbey Island and is part of the Quillayute Needles National Wildlife Refuge set aside as a reserve in 1907 by President Theodore Roosevelt. In 1970 the refuge was made part of the Washington Islands Wilderness Area, which extends 100 miles and includes some 870 islands, rocks and reefs between Copalis Beach and Cape Flattery at the entrance to the Strait of Juan de Fuca. Only the islands have refuge status and are important sanctuaries for sea lions, harbor and fur seals, shorebirds, waterfowl and land birds.

The main purpose of this refuge is to provide protection for nesting seabirds, including common murres, cormorants, Cassin's and rhinocerous auklets, tufted puffins, Leach's and fork-tailed petrels, and gulls. These birds nest in large colonies on the high cliffs of predator-free coastal islands. The islands are closed to the public to protect these nesting birds from human disturbance. During peak periods an estimated 1 million birds use the area. The area is frequented by porpoises, piked whales, Pacific right whales, gray whales, humpback whales and sometimes sea lions and otters. Highway 101 leaves the coast at this point and swings east through the lower Hoh River valley. ⛱⛱⛱

Mile 613.5 (203.5): Olympic National Park boundary.

Mile 614 (203): Hoh Tribal Center. This is both the smallest reservation and the smallest tribe on the Olympic Peninsula. The reservation is only 1 mile square. MP 168

Mile 622 (195): Hoh River Recreation Area boundary, rental cabins, RV camping, gasoline. ▲

Mile 623 (194): Hoh River bridge and Hoh Oxbow Recreation Area which includes 7 primitive campsites, no water and rough boat launch to the river. The Hoh is the largest and best known of the Olympic Peninsula steelhead and salmon fishing rivers, flowing from the flanks of Mount Olympus to the Pacific

Canoeing on the deep waters of Quinault Lake; Mile 572.5. (L. Linkhart)

Ocean. Guided trips can be arranged at many of the local resorts, tackle or grocery stores. The river is famed for its large salmon and steelhead. There are numerous access points and boat launches on this glacial river. Upriver sites are reached via paved road to the Hoh rain forest, while downstream sites are along the Oil City Road.

Mile 624 (193): Turnoff to the Cottonwood Recreation Area and the Oil City Road leading downstream to Hoh River areas. The Cottonwood campground offers 9 campsites, a boat launch and picnic area. 🏕▲ MP 177

Mile 625 (192): Junction with Hoh River Road which runs east 17 miles along the river to the Hoh rain forest, and Olympic National Park Hoh Rain Forest Visitor Center. A small drive-in and general store-fruit stand combination are located a few miles down the road before entering Olympic National Park, but despite an informational sign at the highway, there is no resort lodging along this road. The primary campground is at the visitor center near the river and offers 95 excellent sites for RVs and tents. The visitor center is the hub for numerous hiking trails through the rain forest ranging from less than a mile to more than 26 miles to Mount Olympus.

One of the most popular short hikes is the Hall of Mosses 0.8-mile walk through a cathedral of towering Sitka spruce and broad-leaved maples draped with cloaks of club moss. An interpretive center, amphitheater and narrated nature walks operate seasonally. This is one of the most well-known areas of the peninsula rain forests and a picturesque campground. Be warned, the Hoh registers more than 180 inches of rainfall a year. For more information on Olympic National Park turn to the MAJOR ATTRACTIONS section. 🏃🏕▲★ MP 179

Mile 632 (185): Bogachiel River State Park and resort. The state park has 42 campsites, a beach area and river fishing, and is a popular camping spot for summer vacationers and winter steelhead fishermen. Rental cabins and a general store are available at the bridge. 🐟▲ MP 186

Mile 638 (179): Southern city limits of FORKS (pop. 2,860), largest town on the western side of the peninsula, providing a full complement of services and outdoor recreational facilities. Timber, sportfishing and tourism are the major economic influences on this colorful community, which lies within a few miles of 6 major steelhead and salmon rivers, in a thickly timbered cedar and spruce woods that nearly destroyed the town in 1951. A forest fire roared down the Calawah River valley and forced the evacuation of the town. Thirty-two buildings were destroyed in Forks along with 30,275 acres before the fire was controlled.

Logging and the timber industry are still major, although somewhat depressed, economic factors here and the heritage of this industry is interestingly displayed at the Forks Timber Museum adjacent to Tillicum Park.

Forks is the hub for the Olympic Peninsula's world-famous steelhead and salmon fishing rivers, and is in prime elk, black-tailed deer, black bear and grouse country. Dozens of fishing and hunting guides are based here during the seasons. The river guides fish from McKenzie-style drift boats, a high-sided rocker-bottomed craft specifically designed for the white water.

One of the most prominent landmarks is the Sol Duc Shake Co., a mill manufacturing cedar shakes on the north edge of town, and a salmonoid fish hatchery on the south edge. MP 192

Mile 640.5 (176.5): Junction with La Push Road, which leads west about 15 miles to Pacific Coast Beach Area 14, Quillayute Indian Reservation and the town of LA PUSH. Accommodations are available in La Push, which also has charter services for saltwater fishing and a great beach. Camping at Rialto Beach-Mora Campground; 91 sites. La Push is also the trailhead for hiking trails to remote wilderness beaches within Olympic National Park.

The La Push Road also gives access to Leyendecker County Park (picnic area, boat launch); fishing at the confluence of the Sol Duc, Bogachiel and Quillayute rivers; and the popular Second Beach 0.5-mile trail and Third Beach 3-mile round-trip trail. 🏃▲ MP 193

Mile 641.5 (175.5): Sol Duc River bridge. The Sol Duc (more commonly spelled Soleduck) is an excellent summer and winter steelhead and fall salmon fishing river and because it is followed much of the way by U.S. Highway 101 there is abundant bank access. Drift boats float fishermen down the river in winter, but it takes an experienced hand on the oars to navigate the treacherous boulder drops and rock gardens. 🐟

Mile 642.5 (174.5): Olympic National Forest and National Park ranger station. A good source for maps of the national forest and national park. An information specialist is on duty during the day. (See the MAJOR ATTRACTIONS section for more information on Olympic National Park.) MP 196

Mile 645.5 (171.5): Private RV campground. ▲MP 200

Mile 646.5 (170.5): Junction with access road to Pleasant Lake; boat launch. A small grocery store, plus gas and restaurant are at the junction.

Mile 648 (169): Junction to Lake Ozette-Pacific Coast section of Olympic National Park. Salmon hatchery, interpretive center and rest area. Crossing Soleduck River.

Mile 649 (168): The small community of SAPPHO. Turn southeast on Clark Road and drive 1.7 miles for Soleduck salmon hatchery; interpretive center, boat launch.

Junction with 10-mile connector road to Washington Highway 112, which leads to SEKIU, CLALLAM BAY and NEAH BAY — all popular sportfishing areas with food, gas,

lodging, camping, boat rentals and fishing charters. Neah Bay is an Indian village and the site of the Makah Cultural and Research Center museum, where one of the finest collections of Indian art in the Northwest is on display. At road end west of Neah Bay, a 0.5-mile walk leads to Cape Flattery, the most northwestern point of the continental United States.

West of Sekiu Washington Highway 112 junctions with the 19-mile Hoku River Road to Lake Ozette; camping, resort cabins, fishing, hiking trails and archaeological digs.

Washington Highway 112 rejoins U.S. Highway 101 at **Mile 694.**

Mile 652.5 (164.5): Bear Creek-Albin Wahlgreen Washington Dept. of Natural Resources Recreation Site. Free camping with 10 sites, no hookups, but nice forested picnic areas and good water. This site is on the Soleduck River, but the bank is high and steep and there is no boat access. 🏕▲

Mile 656.5 (160.5): Boundary of Olympic National Forest.

Mile 659.5 (157.5): USFS Klahowya Campground and boat launch open May 15 to Nov. 10 with 43 campsites, no hookups. There are picnic tables and hiking trails with fishing access to the Soleduck River. 🏃🏕🐟▲ MP 212

Mile 664.5 (152.5): Junction with Southeast Sol Duc River Road.

Mile 668 (149): Junction with Soleduck Valley Road which winds nearly 12 miles through forested hills to Sol Duc Hot Springs, resort and campground. The hot springs are incorporated into the resort which includes 3 mineral and a freshwater swimming pools, motels, cabins, trailer park, restaurant facilities and a grocery store. This is also the trailhead for the Seven Lakes Basin Area of Olympic National Park. The resort is adjacent to Sol Duc Hot Springs National Park Service Campground providing 84 campsites, amphitheater, trailers up to 21 feet, nature trails. There is a camping fee. An interesting stop is at Cascades Falls on the Soleduck River where in September you can watch a rare run of summer coho salmon climb the white water. 🏃▲

Mile 669 (148): Campground; boat launch. ▲

Mile 670 (147): Lake Crescent Campground and store at FAIRHOLM on the western end of Lake Crescent, the largest lake in Olympic National Park. Campers will find 87 sites at Fairholm, plus a boat launch, dock, store and amphitheater. Daily camp fee.

U.S. Highway 101 follows the twisting shoreline of 9-mile-long Lake Crescent providing excellent views of 3,000-foot Pyramid Mountain on the north shore at the elbow in the lake and the jagged 4-peak summit of 4,500-foot Mount Storm King down lake. Lake Crescent has numerous resorts, boat rentals and launches, and its clear 624-foot-deep waters are home to Crescenti cutthroat and

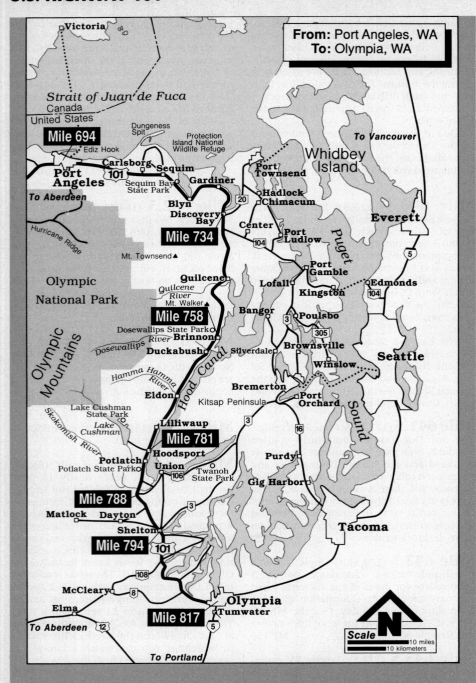

From: Port Angeles, WA
To: Olympia, WA

Strait of Juan de Fuca
Canada
United States

Victoria

Dungeness Spit

Protection Island National Wildlife Refuge

To Vancouver

Whidbey Island

Mile 694

Ediz Hook

Carlsborg

Sequim

Port Angeles

101

Gardiner

Sequim Bay State Park

To Aberdeen

Blyn

Discovery Bay

Port Townsend

Hadlock
Chimacum

Everett

Mile 734

20

Center

104

Port Ludlow

Mt. Townsend▲

Hurricane Ridge

Olympic National Park

Quilcene

Quilcene River
Mt. Walker

Port Gamble

Lofall

Kingston

Edmonds

104

Mile 758

Bangor

3

Poulsbo

305

Dosewallips State Park
River
Brinnon

Duckabush

Dosewallips

Silverdale

Brownsville

Seattle

Olympic Mountains

Hamma Hamma River

Eldon

Hood Canal

Kitsap Peninsula

Bremerton

Port Orchard

Winslow

Puget Sound

Lake Cushman State Park

Lake Cushman

Skokomish River

Lilliwaup

Mile 781

Hoodsport
Union

106

Twanoh State Park

3

Purdy

16

Gig Harbor

Tacoma

Potlatch
Potlatch State Park

Mile 788

Matlock   Dayton

3

Shelton

Mile 794   101

108

McCleary

8

Elma

To Aberdeen   12

Mile 817

Tumwater

5

Olympia

N

Scale
10 miles
10 kilometers

To Portland

Beardslee rainbow trout (very rare sub-species), plus Montana black spot cutthroat, steelhead and landlocked silver salmon. The lake is entirely within the Olympic National Park and a fishing license is not required.

CAUTION: The highway is narrow, twists from one curve to the next along the lake and carries a heavy load of logging truck and vacation trailer traffic, a hazardous combination that demands attention.

Mile 672.5 (144.5): La Poel picnic area with 590 feet of lakeshore. The access road is narrow with sharp bends unsuitable for trailers. There are pleasant picnic sites, water and restrooms.

Mile 677 (140): Barnes Point is the peninsular location of one of the lake's major developed recreation areas, including Olympic National Park ranger station, boat launch (steep and unsuited for large boats), Lake Crescent Lodge (open May to September) and 0.8-mile hiking path leads to 90-foot Mary-mere Falls. Picnic tables are near the visitor center. The resort offers 30 cottages or lodge rooms, 20 motel units, a dining room specializing in seafood, boat rentals and craft shops.

Mile 681.5 (135.5): Turnoff to north to East Beach-Piedmont Recreation Area, resort, camping, picnic and boat launch area. The resort is open year-round, located 3.5 miles

---

north of the highway and offers cabins, campground with full hookups, showers, laundromat, dining room, rental boats, launch ramp, groceries and swimming beach. Nearby the Park Service maintains a picnic area with restrooms, 600 feet of lakefront fishing and swimming area.

Mile 683 (134): Restaurant, store and resort with food and camping.

Mile 685 (132): Access road turns southwest off U.S. Highway 101 to Lake Sutherland, where unusually warm summer temperatures attract heavy waterskiing, swimming and boating pressure. A couple of resorts offer restaurants, RV park, camping, cabins, swimming pool, grocery store and tackle. The lake reportedly holds some of the largest cutthroat in Washington, with 5-pounders not uncommon, for fishermen trolling small plugs. Most of the fishing effort is directed at kokanee salmon. Several local resorts provide current fishing information and boat rental. The road parallels the residentially developed south shore of the lake. A free public boat launch is provided by the Dept. of Game.

Mile 686 (131): Motel and cafe. MP 235

Mile 690 (127): ELWHA. Entering the Indian Creek Recreation Area providing access to Lake Aldwell and the upper Elwha River Recreation Area and trailhead. There is a Dept. of Game boat launch and primitive camping area on Lake Aldwell, an undeveloped impoundment on the Elwha River that can provide some very satisfying light spin and fly-fishing. A resort located at the bridge on Highway 101 provides rustic cabins, RV sites, tackle, groceries, current fishing information and can book raft trips on the river.

A road runs south from the highway, paralleling the Elwha River for 3 miles to the Elwha Campground, 41 campsites, picnic, shelter, water, restrooms, naturalist program and hiking trail access. The river is a fine fly-fishing stream. One mile south of Elwha Campground is the Altaire Campground with 29 campsites, picnic area, water, restrooms and trails. Both campgrounds have a fee. The road forks at Altaire, the west fork going 12 miles up Boulder Creek. The east fork runs south along the shoreline of 2-mile-long Lake Mills. Public boat launch near the dam, fishing for brookies, Dolly Varden and a few rainbow and cutthroat. The best fishing is found in the upper lake near the canyon walls of the Elwha River during late summer and fall. A few primitive campsites are at the upper end of the lake.   MP 240

Mile 694 (123): Junction with Washington Highway 112 which runs west along the Strait of Juan de Fuca through Joyce, Clallam Bay, Sekiu and Neah Bay ending on the Makah Indian Reservation. Travelers leaving U.S. Highway 101 to follow this loop road west can rejoin Highway 101 at Sappho. (See **Mile 649.**) Many of the best salmon and bottom fish fishing areas along the strait are located along Highway 112.

Mile 696 (121): Fairchild International Airport.

Mile 698 (119): Western city limits of **PORT ANGELES** (pop. 17,350) largest city on the peninsula north of Aberdeen/Hoquiam, headquarters of Olympic National Park and a major summer vacation area. All major traveler services are offered. Protected by the natural curved peninsula of Ediz Hook, the harbor is a major shipping port for wood products bound for the Orient and protects a large commercial sportfishing fleet, with year-round salmon and bottom fishing action, including charter operations. Black Ball Transport, Inc., provides daily ferry service to Victoria, BC, from downtown Port Angeles. Tours of Victoria and Butchart Gardens originate here in cooperation with the ferry system, and local motels provide overnight lodging. During the summer months the chamber of commerce mans a visitor information booth at the ferry terminal.

The Clallam County Museum, in the old courthouse building at the intersection of Lincoln and 4th, is an interesting source of regional history and artifacts. The Marine Laboratory on the city pier has an excellent collection of marine life and exhibits. Marine Drive on the west end of downtown's Front Street passes through the giant Crown Zellerbach mill and runs along the narrow backbone of Ediz Hook to a Coast Guard station and a public boat launch on the tip of the peninsula. The view of the Olympic Mountains and the salmon fleet from the end of the hook can be exceptional on a clear day.

Port Angeles is also the northern portal to Olympic National Park and spectacular Hurricane Ridge. Overlooks on the road to Hurricane Ridge offer dramatic views of the Strait of Juan de Fuca, Dungeness Spit and Vancouver Island. From U.S. Highway 101 turn south on Race Street and continue to the Olympic National Park Visitor Center at the park boundary. Heart O' The Hills Campground has 105 sites, nature trail, amphitheater and fishing in small lake Dawn. The road to the ridge is paved and follows the contour of the mountains up to 5,200-foot elevation to a visitors center, lodge and interpretative area with a spectacular view of the jagged snow-capped Olympic peaks, including glacier-bound Mount Carrie (elev. 6,995 feet) and Mount Olympus (elev. 7,965 feet), the glaciated centerpiece of the park beyond. For more information about Olympic National Park turn to the MAJOR ATTRACTIONS section. ▲★

Mile 705.5 (111.5): Junction with Deer Park Road which leads 17 miles south to Deer Park Campground, a small site with only 18 campsites and no trailer facilities. A ranger station is manned from June through September, and several hiking trails originate here. The road is very scenic and passes through mountain alpine country but is not safe for motorhomes, trailers or campers. 🥾▲

Mile 706 (111): Private campground 0.5 mile east. ▲MP 255

Mile 712.5 (104.5): Boundary of the Dungeness Recreation Area, an extremely popular camping and recreational destination adjacent to Dungeness National Wildlife Refuge, commonly called Dungeness Spit, a 7-mile-long, curving peninsula that has been designated as the world's longest natural sand spit. Dungeness Recreation Campground is located on the bluffs overlooking the spit and offers 65 sites with water, full service restrooms, showers, playground and kitchen facilities. The daily fee is $6 for noncounty residents, $4 for residents.

A lighthouse, built in 1857 and open to the public, marks the tip of Dungeness Spit. The strip of sand is maintained in a roadless wilderness state, with excellent winter clamming on the beaches, tossed rows of salt-seasoned driftwood sculptures, shells and agates, and more than 275 species of birds including black brant that winter on the vast eelgrass beds and were the reason the area was first designated as a wildlife sanctuary in 1915.

Hiking, boating, fishing, clamming, wildlife observation and horseback riding are available. No fires, camping, pets or hunting are allowed on the spit. Open daily, daylight use only. The spit forms a 556-acre bay bisected by a finger of sand known as Graveyard Spit, once the site of an Indian massacre and now used as a picnic area. Steep bluffs overlook the spit. A boat launch ramp is provided on Marine Drive, near Cline Spit. Black-tailed deer, elephant and harbor seals are frequently spotted, plus there is good crabbing and salmon fishing in the area around the spit. (NOTE: No established picnic areas, tables, water, etc., exist on the refuge. There is a trail for handicapped from the joint recreation/refuge parking lot to the bluff on the refuge for a scenic overlook of the spit.) 🥾🐟▲

Snowcapped peaks of the Olympic Mountains from Deer Park, Mile 705.5. (David Shott)

Mile 714 (103): Sequim Valley Center, a small shopping area providing food, gas, RV park and lodging near the Dungeness River bridge. The river provides some seasonal fishing (check state regulations for restrictions). There is a state fish hatchery upstream, and a primitive USFS campground with 9 sites 4.5 miles south on County Road 9537 and 3 miles southwest on Forest Service Road 2958. Four more miles brings you to a second USFS 9-site campground. No fees. 🐟▲

Mile 715 (102): Large, red-barked Pacific madrone trees begin to appear at roadside, the only broad-leaved evergreen tree growing in any numbers north of the Oregon border. These curious trees only grow in mild oceanic areas, preferably rocky, and shed their thin bark annually revealing a smooth reddish covering. The largest known madrone, also called madrona, is 10 feet thick with a crown spread of 126 feet.

Mile 716 (101): SEQUIM (pop. 3,330), a popular community for retirees because of its proximity to the mountains, salt water and most importantly its lack of rainfall. Full services are available in Sequim including nearby waterfront resorts on the Strait of Juan de Fuca.

Sequim (Skwim) is in a unique belt of sunshine so dry that in pioneer days cactus plants flourished, and even today irrigation is required for farming, within sight of the famous rain forest, less than 30 miles away. The phenomenon is created by the Olympic Mountains which obstruct Pacific rain squalls moving in from the southwest dropping up to 200 inches of rain in the Hoh and Queets river valleys, producing an umbrella effect that shelters the downslope northeast of the mountains. Some years Sequim gets as little as 10 inches of rain, aridity comparable to San Diego.

The Sequim-Dungeness Museum, 175 W. Cedar, exhibits cultural artifacts of the area and displays of 19th century living.

West Sequim Bay Recreation Area, east of town, includes the John Wayne Marina on property donated to the public by the famous western movie star, who often anchored his yacht in Sequim Bay. Picnic facilities, boat launch, fishing charter boats, showers and RV sites are at the marina. Private resort facilities are located near the marina.

The Olympic Game Farm, located on Ward Road (follow signs from Sequim), offers tours through wildlife areas that include tigers, wolves, grizzly bears, cougars, lions and other exotic animals. Many of these animals are movie stars, appearing in Hollywood and Walt Disney productions. Perhaps the best-known resident is the grizzly bear that played Gentle Ben in the popular television serial "Grizzly Adams."

Mile 718 (99): Access to John Wayne Marina east 0.5 mile. MP 267

Mile 720 (97): Sequim Bay State Park provides 26 RV campsites with full hookups and 60 tent sites. There are 3 kitchen areas, plus showers, tennis courts, environmental

Port Townsend

Historically rich Port Townsend (pop. 6,067) has a wealth of see-and-do attractions. Visitors may take a self-guided tour of Victorian homes; wander through the downtown area of 19th-century brick and stone buildings, or the restored military encampment of Fort Worden (now a state park); or visit the busy waterfront. Port Townsend offers 4 motels, 5 hotels, 9 bed-and-breakfast facilities and 31 restaurants.

The first log cabin was built in Port Townsend in 1851. As the town's importance as a shipping capital grew the population rose to 7,000. Hopes of Port Townsend becoming the terminus for the railroad were never realized and the town struggled along until the 1920s when Crown Zellerbach opened a kraft paper mill and the economy stabilized.

Today, a kraft paper mill, marine-oriented businesses and tourism are the mainstays of Port Townsend.

A recommended first stop for visitors is the Port Townsend Chamber of Commerce at 2437 Sims Way, on the southwest edge of the business district. Free maps are available locating the points of interest, including a self-guided auto tour of Victorian home sites, some providing tours, and others offering bed-and-breakfast overnight facilities, including the Manresa Castle, built in 1892 as a Jesuit seminary patterned after castles built along Germany's Rhine River.

The Rothschild House, a New England style house, was built in 1867 by one of the town's first merchants. It is one of the smallest state parks at just 50 by 200 feet, and has daily tours of the 1867 architecture including the neatly kept rose and herb garden. It is located on Taylor between Jefferson and Franklin streets. Many of the homes and nearly all of the downtown buildings are registered historical landmarks.

The Jefferson County Historical Museum is in City Hall between Madison and Monroe streets. It features nautical artifacts, an antique hearse and fire engine, glassware, machinery and Victorian clothing, plus thousands of photographs are on display. Among the many more items it also offers Indian baskets, an antique button collection and bound editions of the local weekly newspapers since 1891.

The Jefferson County Courthouse, built in 1891, is one of the oldest jails in the state. On the first floor is the Hall of Honor which pays tribute to early

Victorian-era commercial buildings in downtown Port Townsend. (David A. Shott)

pioneers. It is sponsored by the historical society and is located on Jefferson and Cass streets.

An annual spring home tour is held in early May and again in September when several of the privately owned restored homes are opened for inspection. A popular event is the Rhododendron Festival held in mid-May when the many activities include an air fair, bed races and a grand parade. Other events include a jazz festival and in September a wooden boat festival (the only one of its kind in the nation).

In this nautical city a good place to visit is the Port Townsend Yacht Club where sailboat races are regularly scheduled from April to November plus holiday races in the winter.

The starch-white buildings at Fort Worden, at the foot of Point Wilson, are where *An Officer And A Gentleman* was filmed in 1980. The fort, along with Fort Flagler at Marrowstone Point and Fort Casey on Whidbey Island, was con-

structed between 1897 and 1911 around a battery of cannons designed to defend against enemy naval invasion through the Strait of Juan de Fuca to cities farther down Puget Sound. The buildings have been restored, the grounds neatly manicured and a self-guided loop path marked through the historical barracks, gun emplacements, parade grounds and officers' housing areas.

The fort is owned by the State Parks Commission and includes a campground with 53 sites, showers, concrete boat ramp, beach access, an underwater scuba diving park and beachfront picnic areas. This is an excellent salmon fishing and crabbing area, with late summer developing a beach-casting fishery for chinook salmon at the lighthouse.

Campers will find a 43-site campground 3 miles south of Port Townsend at Old Fort Townsend Recreation Area. There are also showers, tables, beach access, buoy moorage and the remnants of an 1859 fort.

learning center and a lodge area. Sequim Bay Marina has 43 RV sites with hookups and 50 without, plus showers. ▲

Mile 722 (95): Junction with access road to the South Sequim Bay Recreation Area, state park and marina. Tent and trailer camping, trailer dump station. Tribal center. ▲

Mile 723.5 (91.5): The small crossroads community of **BLYN**. No facilities are available.

Mile 727 (90): Access road to Diamond Point at the head of Discovery Bay. Just offshore, at the mouth of Discovery Bay, is Protection Island National Wildlife Refuge and a major nesting area for eagles and seabirds (21,000 pairs, roughly 70 percent of all the nesting seabirds in the Puget Sound area nest here). They share the island with up to 300 harbor seals and approximately one-half of the rhinoceros auklet breeding population in the U.S. The 400-acre island is 1.8 miles long and is closed to public entry. Boats are required to stay at least 200 yards offshore. The island was named by the explorer Capt. George Vancouver and was given refuge status in 1982.

Mile 728 (89): **GARDINER**, a small recreational community where travelers will find gasoline, grocery store, RV park and a public boat launch to Discovery Bay. A historical marker at roadside denotes the May 2, 1792, exploration of the bay by English explorer, Capt. George Vancouver during his legendary search for the Northwest Passage. Vancouver named the bay in honor of his sailing sloop, *Discovery*.

Mile 734 (83): The small community of **DISCOVERY BAY** is located at the scenic southern end of the inlet, marked by an abandoned mill and the junction with Washington Highway 20. Food, gas and lodging available. Highway 20 runs 12 miles north along the east bank of Discovery Bay to Port Townsend and Fort Worden (see feature this section), where a Washington state ferry links Highway 20 to Whidbey Island. It eventually merges with Interstate 5 at Mount Vernon.

Mile 737 (80): Junction with Washington Highway 104, the primary arterial between the northern Olympic Peninsula region and Puget Sound's metropolitan regions of Seattle-Tacoma-Bremerton. Highway 104 crosses Hood Canal on a floating bridge, merges with Washington Highway 3 on the east bank with direct access to cross-sound ferries from Kingston and Bremerton. The bridge earned national notoriety in the late 1970s when it broke apart and was partially sunk by an exceptionally savage storm. The Kingston ferry lands at Edmonds between Everett and Seattle while the Bremerton ferries provide service to downtown Seattle. A public clamming and crabbing beach is open on the west shore of Bywater Bay just north of the bridge's west end. On the east side there is a public boat ramp at Salsbury Point County Park.

Mile 739 (78): Crocker Lake borders the east shoulder of the highway. There is a boat launch and portable restroom.

Mile 741 (76): Access road to Lake Leland leads to a county park, small campground and public boat launch. ▲MP 289

Mile 746 (71): Full services are provided in the quaint community of **QUILCENE**, a town famous for its oyster production and seafood. A side trip down Linger Longer Road leads to the marina at Quilcene Bay and a close-up view of oyster farming and commercial clam harvesting. A shop of chain saw wood sculptures is also in this area. Quilcene ranger station office for the Olympic National Forest provides maps and information on current recreational opportunities in the park.

Mile 748.5 (68.5): Bridge crosses the Quilcene River. The Quilcene national fish hatchery is just west on Fish Hatchery Road.

Mile 750 (67): Boundary of the Olympic National Forest and the turnoff to Falls View Campground, a wooded 35-site camp overlooking the Quilcene River gorge and a falls. The site is open from May through October only. There is a nightly fee, 30 RV units and 5 tent sites. ▲MP 298

Mile 751.5 (65.5): Turnoff, on the east side of the road, to a gravel road that leads 5 miles into the woods to the Mount Walker viewpoint (elev. 2,750 feet) with Hood Canal, Puget Sound, Seattle, the Cascade Mountains and the Trident nuclear submarine base at Bangor to the east and the Olympic Mountains to the west. This view is worth the drive.

Mile 754 (63): Southbound travelers will find the highway leaves the Douglas fir and rhododendron forest for the shoreline of Hood Canal's Dabob Bay. The Point Whitney Shellfish Research Laboratory and Camp Parsons Boy Scout Camp are accessible from the 2-lane road intersecting from the east. Dabob Bay is an extremely productive shellfish area, rich with oysters, clams, shrimp and Dungeness crab. A small beach, adjacent to the lab, is open to clam digging and oyster-gathering. A boat launch at the shellfish lab provides boat access to 2 public shellfish beaches: a Dept. of Fisheries beach north of the lab and a Dept. of Natural Resources beach just inside Pulali Point near Camp Parsons. Both beaches are accessible by water only. A tour through the shellfish lab is an interesting side trip.

Mile 757 (60): Seal Rock Campground, adjacent to the highway, offers 35 campsites and is open from early April until mid-October. Camp fee is $6 with 19 tent and 16 RV sites. There is 100 feet of beachfront with swimming, fishing, picnicking and restrooms. The beach can yield good clam digging and oyster gathering. For those with boats excellent shrimping is available just offshore from Seal Rock during the spring season. Salmon and bottom fishing is also productive in this area throughout the year. ⛱◀▲

Mile 757.5 (59.5): Dosewallips State Park offers 142 standard campsites at $6 per night and 40 with full hookups at $8.50 per night. The park is on both sides of the highway, giving campers access to fresh water in the

Blue grouse in Olympic National Park.   (John Barger)

Dosewallips River and salt water on Hood Canal. ▲ MP 307

Mile 758 (59): The small resort, timber and fishing community of **BRINNON** has all visitor services and is the access point for the Dosewallips Recreation Area.

Mile 762 (55): Duckabush Recreation Area and Pleasant Harbor State Park day-use area. The Duckabush River is paralleled by a road along the north shore and has a reputation for providing fair steelheading in the summer, good fall sea-run cutthroat action and fair winter steelhead. There is a small USFS campground 2 miles from the end of the river road often used by fishermen and deer and elk hunters. The Duckabush delta area is good for shrimp and crab pots. ⛵▲MP 310

Mile 766.5 (50.5): Triton Cove is located inside Triton Head and hosts a private RV park and boat launch into Hood Canal. Oyster farm. ▲

Mile 770 (47): Olympic National Forest Hamma Hamma Recreation Area, 6.5 miles west on the Hamma Hamma River, provides fishing, camping and hiking, and private resort facilities. Hamma Hamma is an Indian word meaning "stinking fish." 🏃🐟▲

Mile 771 (46): At **ELDON**, near the Hamma Hamma River bridge, a cafe, gas station and small grocery store serve the tiny community.

Mile 772 (45): Crossing Hamma Hamma River. Seafood store and oyster farm. Picnic area. Gas station. 🛆MP 320

Mile 778.5 (39): Eagle Creek Recreational Tidelands public beach access, open to clamming and crabbing during season.

Mile 779 (38): Lilliwaup Recreational Tidelands, just north of Lilliwaup Bay, is open to public harvest of oysters and shellfish and just offshore you will find good shrimp and crab trapping. The highway crosses the back of the bay in a sharp switchback. Motel, grocery, gasoline and private resort campground south of the bay. Lilliwaup (Lily-wop) is an Indian word meaning "inlet." ▲

Mile 781 (36): **HOODSPORT** is the largest community on the west side of Hood Canal and unofficial headquarter community for outdoor recreation in the southern Hood Canal area. Full tourist services include motels, restaurants overlooking the canal, gift shops, sporting goods stores, beach access, winery, public docks and the Finch Creek-Hood Canal salmon hatchery, the only state hatchery equipped for both salt- and fresh-water fish. Near the mouth of Sund Creek is a marina, RV campground and private boat launch.

Both Olympic National Park and Forest maintain a year-round ranger and information station in Hoodsport, at the junction of the Lake Cushman Road. For more information on Olympic National Park turn to the MAJOR ATTRACTIONS section.

Lake Cushman, an 8.5-mile-long impoundment on the Skokomish River, is a major recreational and camping area. The lake is developed only on the east bank where a full-service resort, vacation cabins and a large public campground look cross-lake at the Prospect Ridge mountains or north to the 6,000-foot peaks inside Olympic National Park.

Lake Cushman State Park is at midlake providing 82 campsites, 30 with full hookups, showers, a boat launch, trailheads for the Olympic hiking system, There is a daily fee and the camp is open year-round. At the north end of the lake, literally at the base of the Olympic Mountains, is Staircase Campground, open from May to September only, with 63 standard sites but no hookups or showers, $5 per night. The Staircase area is a popular base for fishing the upper Skokomish River and jumping-off point for Olympic National Park

Crab pots attest to the productive waters of Puget Sound. (Ray Weisgerber)

Puget Sound sunset.   (David A. Shott)

trails. Cartop boats can be launched here, but there is no developed ramp.

Lake Cushman offers anglers a big variety of catches. Boat rentals and launches are available at the resort on the southeast end of the lake, along with current fishing conditions. 🚶‍♂️🐟▲

Mile 785 (32): POTLATCH, a small residential community, with gas service. Potlatch is a Skokomish Indian word meaning "to bestow valuable gifts and feast," and the town is on the site of an ancient tribal house.
MP 334

Mile 786 (31): Tacoma City Light sponsored day-use area is on the east side of the highway, providing an extremely steep boat ramp into Hood Canal, swimming, picnicking and fishing. There are crabs and shrimp to be trapped offshore. On the west side of the highway, enormous water pipes carry water from Lake Cushman (see **Mile 781**) to the Tacoma City Light electrical generating plant at the highway. Cafe. 🏕️🐟

Mile 786.5 (30.5): Potlatch State Park encompasses both sides of the highway, covering 57 acres with 37 campsites, including 18 RV sites with hookups, showers, picnic tables, boat moorage buoys and a beach for shellfishing and swimming. Fees are $6 for standard sites and $8.50 for hookups. This neat, well-maintained state park is popular during the summer. Private marina and RV park adjacent. 🏕️▲

Mile 788 (29): Junction with Washington Highway 106, which swings east to parallel the southern shore of Hood Canal, while U.S. Highway 101 continues south and inland. Highway 106 leads, via intersecting highways, to Bremerton and the only bridge crossing Puget Sound at the Tacoma Narrows. Twanoh State Park is adjacent to Highway

106 (about 7 miles east of junction) and includes 182 acres with 49 campsites, 9 with full hookups, showers, moorage buoys, a boat launch, shelter house, tables, hiking trails and shellfish beaches for clams, crabs and oysters. There is also a boat launch and small beach area in the community of Union. 🏊🏕️▲

Mile 789.5 (28): The Skokomish Indian Tribal Center office and reservation administration offices. Store. Recreational opportunities on the reservation, plus cultural and tribal information is available here. Much of the nearby Skokomish River is on tribal land.

The Great Bend Area of Hood Canal is famed for crabbing on the Skokomish delta flats in Annas Bay, shrimping in the deeper water, plus fishing for salmon, sea-run cutthroat near shore and bottom fish from Ayres Point north to Dewatto Bay. 🐟MP 339

Mile 790 (27): The Skokomish River bridge crosses the largest Hood Canal river, a prolific producer of salmon, steelhead and sea-run cutthroat trout. Although heavily netted by tribal fishermen, the Skokomish is a good producer for sportfishermen. A tribal fishing permit is required. Access to Olympic National Forest Skokomish River Recreation Area with tenting, fishing and hiking and state salmon and trout hatcheries, 4 miles west of the highway. 🐟

Mile 794 (23): SHELTON (pop. 7,530) the only incorporated city in Mason County, nationally known as Christmastown in recognition of its burgeoning Christmas tree industry. All services are available. Shelton draws its economic base from the shellfish, fishing and timber industry. One of the community highlights is the Washington State Oyster Shucking and Seafood Festival held the first weekend of October. The city is located on the westernmost inlet of Puget Sound and provides access to state parks on

Squaxin Island and Jarrell Cove on Hartstene Island. Among Shelton's attractions are the Grisdale House, a turn-of-the-century mansion owned by a timber baron and a steam engine listed on the National Historic Register and 3 city parks. The regional ranger district of the Olympic National Forest is also located here and can provide maps and information of the nearby forest.

Mile 794.5 (22.5): Port of Shelton Entry Industrial park; airport, county fairgrounds, motel, RV park and hospital.

Junction with Washington Highway 102 west to the community of Dayton and on to Nahwatzel Lake Recreation Area. Excellent waterskiing and fishing. There is a public boat ramp on the lake and a resort with restaurant, cabins and RV hookups. 🐟▲

Mile 798 (19): Access to National Historic sites at Shelton and Matlock. Motel and visitor information.

Mile 800 (17): Junction with Washington Highway 3 to Bremerton. Motels, RV park, fast food and 24-hour gas station.   MP 351

Mile 803 (14): Junction with 2-lane Washington Highway 108 west to McCleary and Aberdeen, coastal beach and resort areas, and Squaxin Island Tribal Center. Cafe.
MP 354

Mile 809.5 (7.5): Gas and grocery at junction with road to Steamboat Island and Hunter Point.   MP 360

Mile 811 (6): Junction with Washington Highway 8, a multiple-lane freeway that is the main arterial between Interstate 5 and the ocean beaches at Aberdeen. U.S. Highway 101 shares a common alignment with Highway 8 eastbound to Olympia.

Mile 813.5 (4.5): Access to Evergreen State College.   MP 364

Mile 815 (2): Exit to the residential area of West Olympia and the recreational area at Black Lake, providing good rainbow trout, largemouth bass, panfish and catfish. Waterskiing is popular and there are resort facilities for boat rentals. A free boat launch is located at midlake on the east side. Full services are available at this exit. 🐟 MP 366

Mile 817 (0): U.S. Highway 101 ends with the cloverleaf junction to Interstate 5 south of Olympia near TUMWATER (pop. 8,100), the southernmost reach of Puget Sound and the terminus of the Oregon Trail. Near this junction the first American community was established on Puget Sound, a sparse encampment known as New Market. The Deschutes River tumbles down a picturesque waterfall into Budd Inlet within sight of the junction.

Travelers joining Interstate 5 at this junction turn to **Mile 532** in the INTERSTATE 5 section and continue with that log if northbound for Seattle, or read log back to front if southbound to Portland.

U.S. Highway 395

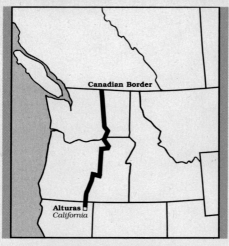

Canadian Border

Alturas
California

See map pages 219, 222 and 225

U.S. Highway 395 is one of the original Three Flags Routes, so designated because they ran from Mexico, north across the United States and into Canada. Highway 395 originally started at the Mexican border near Tijuana. From San Bernardino it heads north through the desert to Bishop, on the east side of Yosemite National Park, into Nevada to Reno before heading back north through California to junction with Canada's Crowsnest Highway 3 at the international border northwest of Spokane, WA.

NORTHWEST MILEPOSTS® logs U.S. Highway 395 from Alturas, CA, to the Canadian border. Physical mileposts along U.S. 395 in Washington are very straightforward: they reflect distance from the Oregon-Washington border. However, in Oregon there are several sets of mileposts along U.S. 395 reflecting distance from various points too confusing to explain or be of much help to the motorist.

U.S. Highway 395 Log

Distance from Alturas, CA, is followed by distance from the Canadian border.

Mile 0 (704.5): North edge of ALTURAS (pop. about 3,000) at the intersection of U.S. Highway 395 and California Highway 299 to Redding. Alturas is a farming and ranching town 35 miles south of the Oregon border and offers all services for travelers, including 2 large service stations located at the junction.

The Alturas area is rolling ranch land with nearly all flat valleys given over to irrigated crops, primarily alfalfa, although some row crops can be seen from the highway. Because there are so many farm trucks in this area, be prepared for slow going on crooked roads and up hills.

Mile 4 (700.5): California State Agricultural Inspection Station. Incoming (southbound) traffic must stop.

Mile 5.5 (699): Junction with California Highway 299 east to Cedarville.

Mile 7 (697.5): Historical marker on history of Chimney Rock. A dirt road leads 4 miles west to the rock.

Mile 20 (684.5): DAVIS CREEK has a combination service station, grocery store/deli, and few homes. Approximately 90 people live in the surrounding valley.

Road access to the south end of 30-mile long Goose Lake, which straddles the California-Oregon border. Like a lot of features named by practical pioneers, this one came about after seeing the thousands and thousands of wild geese which live here. It is a favorite fall waterfowl hunting area.

Mile 27 (677.5): The elevation is marked on a bluff just above the lake at 5,000 feet.

Mile 29 (675.5): Goose Lake map at turnout west of highway. When full, 29-mile-long Goose Lake has 82 miles of shoreline. Maximum width is 10 miles and average depth is 8 feet, with its deepest point 24 feet. Cranes, pelicans, ducks, geese and gulls may be seen here.

Mile 34 (670.5): Side road to Willow Ranch.

Mile 38 (666.5): Wild Plum Winery. It has a free tasting room open daily. This vineyard and winery is the only commercial establishment along Goose Lake.

Mile 38.5 (666): NEW PINE CREEK (pop. 260) straddles the border with half in California and part in Oregon.

Mile 39 (665.5): Turnoff for Goose Lake State Park; 48 sites with electrical hookups, picnicking and lake access. 🏕▲

Mile 46 (658.5): North end of Goose Lake. Like many Northwest desert lakes, its level has been fluctuating a great deal during the past few years so the shoreline changes. The lake was dry in the summer of 1926 and 1929 through 1934.

Mile 52 (652.5): LAKEVIEW (pop. 2,750) has all traveler services. This attractive small town is the county seat of Lake County, one of those enormous eastern Oregon counties with a lot of scenery and very few people. At 4,800 feet, it is one of Oregon's highest towns. It is a busy town for its size, not only from the recreational traffic but because it is the only town of any size in an area larger than most New England states.

Oregon Highway 140 from Klamath Falls junctions with U.S. Highway 395 in Lakeview. It shares a common alignment northbound with U.S. Highway 395 for a short distance.
MP 145

Mile 53.5 (651): Schminck Memorial Museum. Collections include quilts, American pressed glass goblets, china head and bisque dolls, pipes, personalized shaving mugs and gold watches. Open Tuesday through Saturday, 1-5 p.m.

Mile 55.5 (649): Lakeview Ranger District offices.

Mile 56 (648.5): Hunter Hot Springs; motor inn, restaurant, lounge, RV park and Oregon's only geyser. "Old Perpetua" erupts every 60 seconds and sometimes reaches a height of 40 feet. ▲

Mile 58.5 (646): Junction with Oregon Highway 140 east to Adel. Highway 140 provides access to Hart Mountain National Antelope Refuge, established in 1936 to preserve pronghorn (antelope) rangeland.

Mile 71 (633.5): Chandler Wayside, a small rest area with picnic tables. 🏕

Mile 73.5 (631): Chandler Station Historic Ranch.
MP 124

Mile 75.5 (629): Wildlife viewing area.
MP 122

Mile 76.5 (628): VALLEY FALLS, a 1-store town with a gas station at the junction with Oregon Highway 31, which heads northwest to La Pine on U.S. Highway 97. The town was named for some low falls nearby on the Chewaucan River, which is rated as one of the finest trout rivers, as well as the largest, in Fremont National Forest. The stream is heavily stocked with rainbow trout, especially in the upper reaches near Bly. The lower river is fished for catfish. 🐟

Mile 80 (624.5): South end of Lake Abert, one of Oregon's largest lakes, with an average area of 60 square miles. The water is unusually salty. The lake was first chronicled by the John Work party in 1832 and he called it Salt Lake, but when John C. Fremont came through in 1843, he named it for his chief, Col. J.J. Abert of the U.S. Topographical Engineers.

Mile 86 (618.5): Abert Rim roadside sign. The rim, seen along the highway, is 2,500 feet above the valley floor and is one of the highest fault scarps in the U.S. It was formed when the lava that covered the region was fractured, then tilted by forces in the earth. Abert Rim is the western edge of one, while the lake lies atop another one.   MP 89

Mile 97 (607.5): North end of Lake Abert is a broad expanse of salt flats.

Mile 104 (600.5): Hogback Summit (elev. 5,033 feet). Juniper Mountain (elev. 6,630 feet) is straight ahead northbound.

Mile 106 (598.5): Rest area.   MP 61

Mile 117 (587.5): Alkali Lake. A small cafe, gas station (24-hour diesel) and highway department maintenance station. Next gas northbound 22 miles, southbound 39 miles.

Mile 126 (578.5): A small airfield, mostly for emergency use, is just off the highway.

Mile 130 (574.5): Junction with county road that leads to Christmas Valley off to the west. Travelers are in the middle of the great eastern Oregon high desert with virtually no population and where ranches are measured in thousands of square miles.

Mile 131 (573.5): Highway leaves Lake County northbound and enters Harney County, at 10,132 square miles the largest county in Oregon, and one of the largest counties in America. It was named for William Selby Harney, who was in command of the Dept. of Oregon of the U.S. Army.

Mile 139 (565.5): WAGONTIRE. A sign painted on the store gives the population 2; elev. 4,725 feet. A 16-unit motel, trailer park (10 sites, full hookups), cafe/store, and landing strip make up the town. There are probably few towns as small, known by so many people, in part because it is so remote that hardly anything else shows on the map, and also because of its unusual name. It came by the name because for many years an old wagon tire lay beside the road up Wagontire Mountain. The mountain lies a short distance to the northwest and is 6,510 feet high.   ▲ MP 28

Mile 157 (547.5): Squaw Butte/Harney Valley Livestock Experimental Station. The station was built in 1935 by the Civilian Conservation Corps. It includes 16,000 acres of land, and is located here because vegetation is representative of plants from central Oregon to Nevada, Idaho, Utah and California. Five to 6 different species of sagebrush grow here which are typical of those in the Great Basin region. Research centers on forage management, revegetation and food additives.

Mile 167 (537.5): RILEY, limited services. Junction with U.S. Highway 20, one of the major east-west routes across Oregon (see U.S. HIGHWAY 20 section for log.) U.S. Highway 395 shares a common alignment with U.S. Highway 20 for the next 27 miles east.   MP 105

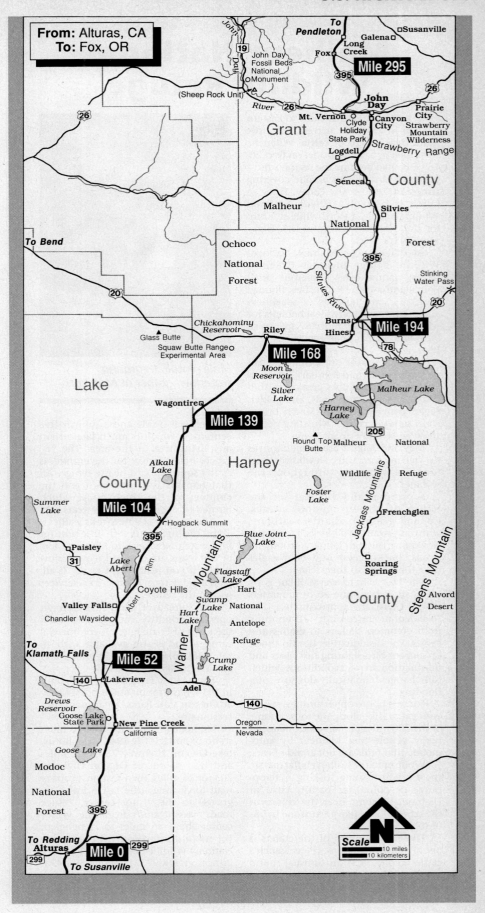

Malheur National Wildlife Refuge

When Peter French came to Eastern Oregon in 1872, he arrived with little more than a herd of cattle. When he was killed by a homesteader on Dec. 26, 1897, he had become the region's most powerful rancher, his empire covering almost 200,000 acres. Today, French's ranch is part of Malheur National Wildlife Refuge, a worthwhile side trip for U.S. Highway 395 (and U.S. Highway 20) travelers.

At 183,000 acres, Malheur National Wildlife Refuge includes Oregon's largest natural lake, numerous small ponds and a river. Bullrushes, flooded meadows, and uplands of sagebrush and prairie grasses are ideal habitats for nesting birds. A total of 287 species of birds and 58 mammals have been seen here.

It is a stopover on spring and fall migrations. In mid-February, concentrations of pintail ducks, greater sandhill cranes, great horned owls, and golden eagles congregate here. March brings lesser sandhill cranes, whistling swans, snow geese and Canada geese.

May and August are prime months for viewing songbirds. Newborn waterfowl are common throughout the summer.

September and October see the return of greater sandhill cranes, Canada geese, mallards, warblers, whistling swans and hawks. From mid-November through January, trumpeter swans, ducks, geese and bald eagles have the refuge to themselves.

The best way to see Malheur is by car. Start at the museum headquarters where there are approximately 200 species of mounted birds — everything from common flickers to cranes and eagles. The headquarters has tip sheets on current bird sighting hot spots and information on road conditions (which can change dramatically due to winter flooding).

For best photo opportunities, stay in your car or hike along the tops of some of the 200 miles of man-made dikes. So many people tour Malheur by automobile that birds are not afraid of cars.

While much of Malheur is flat marsh, there are also some striking outcroppings of columnar basalt. Lava at Diamond Craters, near the center of the refuge, looks like great stone bands of rope.

Three miles north of the craters is one of the last remnants of Peter French's cattle empire. It is an unusual round barn built in the 1800s. The barn has a

Male pintail. Migrating waterfowl gather at Malheur. *(Ray Weisgerber)*

stone corral inside and a juniper tree centerpost which is much larger than any living tree in the area. The "P" ranch, headquarters for the empire, is at the southern end of the refuge. All that remains is a long barn and the chimney of the ranch house which burned to the ground many years ago.

Allow plenty of time to tour Malheur. To hit the highlights with little time for bird-watching takes 3 to 5 hours. Most of the roads are dirt and require slow travel. If you really want to see it all, plan a 2-day tour. There are no services within the refuge.

The Bureau of Land Management operates primitive campgrounds near the town of Frenchglen. A commercial campground is also available with 46 full hookup spaces and 51 with water and electricity.

The historic Frenchglen Hotel, built in 1914, has 8 rooms and is operated by an Oregon State Parks Department concessionaire.

Malheur's headquarters is 40 miles south of Burns (**Mile 194**). From Burns, take Oregon Highway 78 east 2 miles and turn south on Oregon Highway 205 for 25 miles, then east on a county road for 9 miles (the last 6 miles are gravel) to the visitor center. Refuge roads extend south from the visitor center about 35 miles to Frenchglen. For more information write: Malheur National Wildlife Refuge, P.O. Box 245, Princeton, OR 97721; phone 503/493-2612.

Mile 176.5 (528): Rest area with covered picnic tables and water. The 0.5-mile Sage Hen Nature Trail here takes you through sagebrush and western juniper to viewpoints. Self-guiding brochure at trailhead.

Mile 184 (520.5): Burns District Bureau of Land Management Wild Horse Corrals, a major facility for managing wild horses on Oregon public lands. Since 1974, when the program was started, BLM has processed over 9,000 wild horses placing 75 percent with private individuals. Wild horse herds increase at an average of 20 percent per year. Tours are available by prior arrangement.

Mile 191 (513.5): HINES (pop. 1,445), which is a sawmill town named for Edward Hines, who owned the lumber sawmill and logging railroad. Private campground with full hookups. ▲

Mile 192 (512.5): Valley golf course.

Mile 194 (510.5): BURNS (pop. 2,835). All traveler services. This desert town (elev. 4,148 feet) is very well known for such a small town. It is the county seat of the vast Harney County. It was named in 1883 for the Scottish poet, Robert Burns, by George McGowan, the founder who was a merchant.

Burns is the gateway to most of Harney County's attractions, such as the Malheur National Wildlife Refuge, at 183,000 acres one of the largest wildlife refuges in the nation. See feature this section. ★

Mile 194.5 (510): Burns City Park with picnic tables and playground. Access to **PAIUTE INDIAN RESERVATION** (pop. 160), 1 mile north. The tribe operates a processing plant which freeze-dries onion rings. 卅

Mile 196 (508.5): Weigh station and 24-hour deli and gas.

Mile 197 (507.5): Junction with U.S. Highway 20 which heads east to Ontario. U.S. Highway 395 continues north. See U.S. HIGHWAY 20 section for log of that route.
MP 134

Mile 208.5 (496): This is the first and/or last of several boundaries U.S 395 crosses of the 1,457,457-acre Malheur National Forest.

Mile 211 (493.5): Idlewild Forest Service campground; 25 sites. ▲ MP 53

Mile 211.5 (493): Devine Ridge Summit (elev. 5,340 feet).

Mile 217 (487.5): Malheur National Forest boundary. MP 48

Mile 225 (479.5): Entering Grant County, leaving Harney County, northbound.

Mile 228.5 (476): SILVIES is a 1-building town set in a wide valley. There is a store and gas. The Silvies post office was founded in 1892. The Silvies River parallels the highway northbound. MP 35

Mile 229.5 (475): Rock Springs Forest Service campground 6 miles east of highway. ▲

Mile 240 (464.5): SENECA (pop. 290) is an unincorporated former sawmill town with a store, tavern, church and a few dwellings.

Mile 246 (458.5): Malheur National Forest boundary.

Mile 248 (456.5): Junction with road that leads west to Izee (24 miles), Paulina (55 miles).

Mile 249 (455.5): Starr Forest Service campground (elev. 5,152 feet); 14 sites. ▲

Mile 254 (450.5): Rest area.

Mile 254.5 (450): Malheur National Forest boundary.

Mile 261 (443.5): CANYON CITY (pop. 675) city limits, services include gas and food. Airport west of highway. The town is well named because it sits in a narrow canyon between steep walls. It was built during the 1862 gold rush to Whiskey Flat, 0.5 mile north of town toward John Day. It was the site of clashes between Oregon miners and Californians who were sympathetic to the Confederate cause during the Civil War, and Rebel Hill above town was the site of a battle when the Californians raised the Rebel flag. The Oregonians stormed the hill and tore it down. A special cemetery on the rimrocks was set aside for "bad men."

Mile 263 (441.5): Grant County Oliver Historical Museum. Joachin Miller's cabin stands beside the museum. Miller, the self-proclaimed poet of the Sierras, was the first judge of Grant County (formed in 1864).

Mile 265 (439.5): JOHN DAY (pop. 2,130) has all services, and the Malheur National Forest office is in the middle of town. John Day was named for a member of John Jacob Astor's overland expedition to Astoria in 1811. For reasons not completely clear, his name has been left all over the region — the town, 2 rivers, more recently a dam, and one of the most interesting of the national monuments in the Northwest.

Of special interest is the Kam Wah Chung & Co. museum in the city park. It pays tribute to the Chinese laborers who were brought to the area during the gold rush of 1862-64. The central portion of the building went up in 1867 and it was alternately a herb doctor's office, an assay office, a store and social club. There is a 20-minute narrated tour. Open May 1 to Oct. 31, 9 a.m. to noon and 1-5 p.m. Monday through Thursday; 1-5 p.m. weekends. Admission fee. From John Day, Highway 395 shares a common alignment with U.S. Highway 26 for about 10 miles west along the John Day River to Mount Vernon. U.S. Highway 26 continues west 30 miles to the Sheep Rock Unit of John Day Fossil Beds National Monument. (See MAJOR ATTRACTIONS section.) ★

Mile 267.5 (437): Mountain View Country Club and Golf Course. MP 160

Mile 273 (431.5): Clyde Holliday State Park and John Day River. Holliday Park has 30 sites with electrical hookups, tent sites, dump station. ▲ MP 155

Mile 273.5 (431): MOUNT VERNON (pop. 620), a small town at the junction with U.S. Highway 26, set in a pretty valley beside the John Day River. Limited services. From Mount Vernon north, the highway begins climbing through pine forests. MP 120

Mile 283.5 (421): Malheur National Forest boundary.

Mile 289 (415.5): Beech Creek Forest Service campground; 5 tent sites. ▲

Mile 289.5 (415): Malheur National Forest boundary.

Mile 291 (413.5): Beach Creek Summit (elev. 4,687 feet) is at the top of a long, winding climb through timber. The summit has some abandoned buildings in the rocky clearing.

Mile 295 (409.5): FOX (unincorporated) is a small, picturesque town on the high plains with a church, grocery, tavern and cluster of houses. From the hill north of town it looks almost like a Western movie set. Fox Creek flows through and feeds into the John Day River.

Mile 298 (406.5): Malheur National Forest boundary.

Mile 300 (404.5): Long Creek Summit (elev. 5,101 feet) offers great views as you descend northbound.

Mile 300.5 (404): A primitive rest area on a sharp curve on the east side of the highway.

Mile 303 (401.5): LONG CREEK (pop. 265) was named for the creek that flows through. At one time locals believed the creek was the longest in the state, but the claim has been modified to the longest in the general area. The town has a pretty church, a cafe, pool hall, service station, grocery store and sawmill.

Mile 313 (391.5): Begin steep 4-mile downgrade northbound. MP 81

Mile 316.5 (388): Middle Fork John Day River. Access road to Ritter Hot Springs, 10 miles west of highway.

Mile 322 (382.5): Umatilla National Forest boundary.

Mile 324 (380.5): Meadow Brook Summit (elev. 4,127 feet) has great views in both directions, and a dirt road leads off to the northwest to Ritter on the Middle Fork John Day River. Store, gas and RV park. ▲

Mile 329 (375.5): DALE (unincorporated). A small logging town with service station, cafe, laundromat, etc. It is on the North Fork John Day River, and also right on the Umatilla County line. MP 66

Mile 330 (374.5): Junction with road east to Live Lake (89 miles).

Mile 331.5 (373): 45th parallel line marker, which is the halfway point between the equator and the Arctic Circle.

Mile 343 (361.5): Ukiah Dale Forest Wayside with camping sites. ▲ MP 51

Eroded mudslides at Clarno Unit of John Day Fossil Beds. (Linda J. Moore)

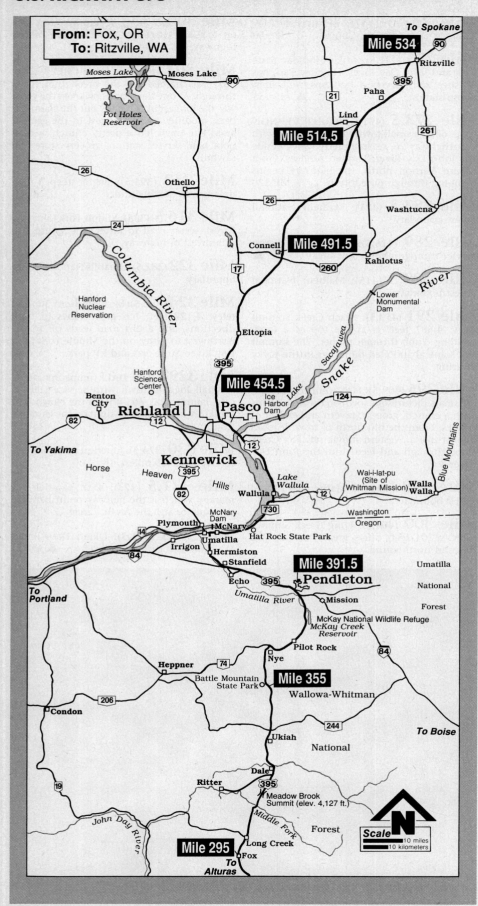

From: Fox, OR
To: Ritzville, WA

Mile 344.5 (360): Junction with Oregon Highway 244 which goes east to La Grande. UKIAH (unincorporated) is a short distance east on Highway 244; no services. It was named for the town in California. MP 50

Mile 352 (352.5): Junction with road east to Albee (6 miles). MP 42

Mile 354 (350.5): Summit of Battle Mountain (elev. 4,270 feet). The name commemorates a battle in 1878 between whites and Indians that is said to be the last such fight in the region. It occurred when Gen. O.O. Howard out of Fort Vancouver defeated Chief Egan and his Paiute band by chasing them down the Malheur River and out of Oregon.

Mile 355 (349.5): Battle Mountain State Park, day use only. The park has one of the grandest views of the region with the towns and farms and ranches laid out below almost as though you are in a small plane. ⛱

Mile 370.5 (334): Junction with Oregon Highway 74 west to Heppner (37 miles) and Condon (81 miles).

Mile 378 (326.5): PILOT ROCK (pop. 1,605) is a sawmill and agricultural town. An enormous community bulletin board kind of sign on the south end of town lists coming events. The town was named for a basalt butte above town. MP 16

Mile 385.5 (319): Pendleton golf and country club.

Mile 387.5 (317): McKay Creek Reservoir and McKay National Wildlife Refuge, established in 1927. Bird sightings here include bald eagles, great blue and black crowned night herons, long-billed curlews and American avocets. Waterfowl and game bird hunting in season. A near record bass was caught in the reservoir along with Oregon's record catfish, which weighed 36$\frac{1}{2}$ pounds. Perch also thrive here. Two boat ramps. Closed from the first Monday after waterfowl season until March 1. ➤

Mile 391.5 (313): PENDLETON (pop. 14,610) has all major traveler services including motels and numerous restaurants. Pendleton owes its name to the Democratic contender for vice-president in 1864, George Hunt Pendleton of Ohio.

The famous Pendleton Round-Up, a major professional Rodeo Cowboy Assn. sanctioned rodeo is held the second full week of September. Pendleton is also the location of the famed Pendleton Woolen Mills, begun in 1909.

Mile 392.5 (312): Junction with Interstate 84 in Pendleton. U.S. Highway 395 shares a common alignment with Interstate 84 west for the next 20 miles. Turn to **Mile 205.5** in the INTERSTATE 84 section.

Mile 394 (310.5): Exit to airport, west Pendleton and Blue Mountain Community College. MP 208 EXIT 207

Boat launch at Hat Rock State Park. Turn off at Mile 426.5 for this day-use area.   (Tom Barr)

Mile 399 (305.5): Sign warns of blowing dust for the next 40 miles westbound.

Mile 400 (304.5): Exit to Stage Gulch and Barnhart Road. Cafe, motel and truck stop.
MP 203 EXIT 202

Mile 402 (302.5): Exit to Yaokum Road.
MP 200 EXIT 199

Mile 403.5 (301): Exit to Lorenzen Road and McClintock.   MP 198 EXIT 198

Mile 408.5 (296): Exit to Echo and Lexington. Original trail ruts can be seen at Echo, 2 miles south of the highway, along with many buildings erected prior to 1915. The Echo Museum is on the National Register of Historic Places and contains pioneer and Indian artifacts.   MP 194 EXIT 193

Mile 413.5 (291): Exit here for continuation of U.S. 395 north to Stanfield and Hermiston. Interstate 84 continues west. Turn to **Mile 185** in the INTERSTATE 84 section for log of that route.   EXIT 188

Mile 414.5 (290): STANFIELD (pop. 1,620) is a farming town with grain elevators and most visitor services.   MP 189

Mile 418 (286.5): HERMISTON (pop. 9,855) is one of the major towns in agricultural Umatilla County. The area is noted for pioneer "wind farms," where windmills have been tested for electrical power generation, and the nearby Army depot where chemicals have been stored in concrete bunkers. Hermiston has 5 motels and numerous restaurants.

Mile 419 (285.5): Hermiston municipal airport.

Mile 422.5 (282): Doll and Toy Museum on U.S. 395 at 1315 N. 1st, Hermiston. Housed in a railroad car, this museum documents dolls and toys from the 1850s to the 1980s. Included is the first ever patented doll in America (1853). Open May to October, 10 a.m. to noon and 1-5 p.m. Admission fee.

Mile 424.5 (280): Power City Wildlife Management Area.

Mile 425.5 (279): Power City.

Mile 426.5 (278): Junction with U.S. Highway 730 west to Umatilla, and east 7 miles to Hat Rock State Park, a day-use area on Lake Wallula, the backwaters of the Columbia River formed by McNary Dam.

Mile 427 (277.5): U.S. 395 merges with Interstate 82 North to Yakima and Kennewick.

Mile 427.5 (277): The Columbia River, Oregon-Washington state line.

Mile 428.5 (276): Exit 131 junction with Washington Highway 14 west to Plymouth and Vancouver. Easy access east to McNary Dam. The dam is named for Senator Charles L. McNary of Oregon, who spearheaded efforts to construct it. Construction began in 1947 and was completed in 1953. Visitor facilities include interpretative displays, fish viewing rooms, and powerhouse galleries. Open daily, April to September, 8 a.m. to 5 p.m. Guided tours for groups and organizations by prior arrangements. Free.

Washington Highway 14 is a good 2-lane road, almost empty of traffic, which leads west from Plymouth 180 miles to junction with Interstate 5 at Vancouver. It is a useful route for westbound motorists.

U.S. 395 shares a common alignment with Interstate 82 north through the Horse Heaven Hills, so named because in an earlier era this was a natural grazing area for roving bands of wild horses.   EXIT 131

Mile 429.5 (275): Weigh station.
MP 131

Mile 437.5 (267): Exit to Coffin Road.
MP 123 EXIT 122

Mile 446 (258.5): Exit to Locust Grove Road.   MP 115 EXIT 114

Mile 448 (256.5): Exit here for continuation of U.S. 395 North, Kennewick and Pasco. 24-hour restaurant and gas stations at exit. Kennewick, Pasco, and Richland comprise the

Tri-Cities area. With a regional population of approximately 150,000 people, this is Washington's fourth-largest metropolitan area.

The region's development came in 3 stages. In 1880, the Northern Pacific Railroad reached Pasco, which became an important railway maintenance and division point. In 1892, the Northern Pacific Irrigation Co. plotted the Kennewick townsite and later imported settlers from the Midwest. In 1942, the completion of Grand Coulee Dam greatly expanded the agricultural potential of the area. Grand Coulee's vast supplies of hydroelectric power and cold water also led to the building of Hanford Atomic Energy Plant and the booming of Richland.

Long growing seasons and fertile soil return over $300 million annually from crops of apples, asparagus, alfalfa, hay, dry beans, wheat, corn, cherries, onions, potatoes and a variety of seed crops. Climate and land have also made the Tri-Cities the heartland of Washington's wine county. Over 30 wineries are situated within a 50-mile radius of the Tri-Cities.   EXIT 113

Mile 449 (255.5): KENNEWICK (pop. 37,180) is derived from an Indian word meaning "winter paradise." Its sunny climate and proximity to the Columbia and Snake rivers make it the departure point for a variety of water-based activities. Oasis Waterworks, at 6321 W. Canal, has a 5,000-square-foot swimming pool and 11 waterslides; open mid-May through Labor Day.

RICHLAND (pop. 30,140), 10 miles north via Highway 240 West, was an irrigation boomtown until 1943, when it became "Atomic City" with the building of Hanford, the first plant to produce plutonium for the world's first nuclear weapons. Hanford plutonium was used in the world's first nuclear detonation at Alamogordo, NM. Of interest here is the Hanford Science Center in the Federal Building at 825 Jadwin, which features

displays on Hanford programs, a public document room and hands-on exhibits. Films on energy are shown on request. Free, open daily.

The Fast Flux Test Facility (FFTX), 11 miles north of Richland, is a sodium-cooled 400-megawatt thermal reactor which tests fuels and materials for fast breeder reactors. A visitor center overlooking the facility has models and audiovisual presentations explaining the process. Free, open Wednesday through Sunday, 10 a.m. to 4 p.m.

Mile 454 (250.5): Highway crosses the Columbia River via the Intercity Bridge. It is America's longest cable-stayed bridge and has a continuous concrete girder of 1,794 feet.

Mile 454.5 (250): PASCO (pop. 18,430) is the Franklin County seat. It was named by a railroad surveyor because heat, rust, and sandstorms reminded him of the Peruvian city of Cerro de Pasco. Major employers include Burlington Northern, Green Giant and Universal Frozen Foods.

Sacajawea State Park, 3 miles southeast of Pasco on U.S. Highway 12, was an important Indian meeting place. An artifacts room features a large collection of Indian implements found along the riverbanks. Exhibits emphasize the role of Sacajawea in the Lewis and Clark Expedition, which camped here on October 1805. Boat launch, mooring buoys, docks, picnic tables and stoves.   ⊼

Mile 458 (246.5): Exit here for U.S. 395 North to Ritzville and Spokane.   EXIT 14

Mile 460 (244.5): Bookwalter Winery, at 2708 Commercial Ave., produces award-winning Chardonnay, Cabernet Sauvignon, plus other wines and champagne. Tasting room open daily 10 a.m. to 5 p.m.

Quarry Lake Vinters, 2520 Commercial Ave., has been a Washington winemaker for

2 decades. Wines made from grapes grown here have received top honors. Open Friday through Monday, noon to 5 p.m.

Mile 464 (240.5): Turnoff to east for Preston Wine Cellars, cafe at junction. Washington's largest family-operated winery. Tasting room open daily 10 a.m. to 5:30 p.m.
                                              MP 28

Mile 469 (235.5): Weigh station.

Mile 474.5 (230): ELTOPIA. A grain elevator beside the railroad track.

Mile 482.5 (222): Junction with Washington Highway 17, which leads north to Mesa and Moses Lake (45 miles). This agricultural area was created by the Columbia Basin irrigation project. It is mostly wheat farming country.   MP 46

Mile 491.5 (213): CONNELL (pop. 2,060) is an agricultural center serving both the Columbia Basin irrigation farms, and those still farming without irrigation (dryland farming). Connell has all services and a restaurant near the highway that serves enormous country breakfasts. It is also the junction with Washington Highway 260, which leads east to Washtucna.   MP 55

Mile 496.5 (208): The Milepost 60 cafe; deli/mart and truck stop with gas.   MP 60

Mile 503.5 (201): Junction with Washington Highway 26, which runs from Vantage across the wheat country to Colfax. This is the favorite route for students and families between the coast and Washington State University in Pullman. There is a modern rest area at this intersection.   MP 67

Mile 514.5 (190): Exit to LIND, a farming town about 4 miles to the west. A welcoming sign invited: "Drop in. Mount St. Helens did," a reference to the load of ash the southwestern Washington volcano dropped on this area at the eruption in 1980, which for some reason was worse here than anywhere else. Grayish traces of the ash fall can still be seen beside the road and on barren, uncultivated hillsides.

Mile 518 (186.5): Junction with Highway 21 South to Kahlotus.   MP 82

Mile 519 (185.5): Junction with Highway 21 to Lind.   MP 83

Mile 519.5 (185): PAHA, another town that appears on most maps but is only a grain elevator.

Mile 532.5 (172): Junction with Interstate 90 at Ritzville; cafes and lodging at intersection. Interstate 90 and U.S. 395 share a common alignment east to Spokane. Travelers headed west on Interstate 90 turn to **Mile 218** in the INTERSTATE 90 section.

Mile 534 (170.5): Exit to Washington Highway 261 to Washtucna (27 miles) and

Preston Wine Cellars at Mile 464 has a tasting room open daily.   (Tom Barr)

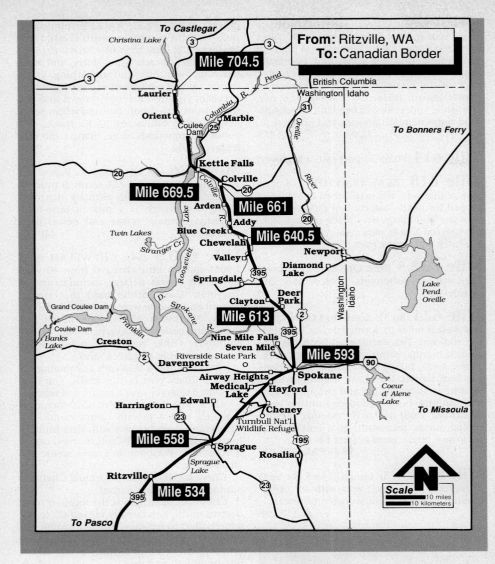

From: Ritzville, WA
To: Canadian Border

Mile 704.5
Mile 669.5
Mile 661
Mile 640.5
Mile 613
Mile 593
Mile 558
Mile 534

To Castlegar
Christina Lake
Laurier
Orient
Marble
Coulee Dam
Kettle Falls
Colville
Arden
Addy
Blue Creek
Chewelah
Valley
Springdale
Clayton
Deer Park
Nine Mile Falls
Seven Mile
Riverside State Park
Davenport
Creston
Airway Heights
Medical Lake
Hayford
Spokane
Harrington
Edwall
Cheney
Turnbull Nat'l. Wildlife Refuge
Sprague
Rosalia
Ritzville
To Pasco
To Bonners Ferry
Newport
Diamond Lake
Lake Pend Oreille
Coeur d' Alene Lake
To Missoula
British Columbia
Washington / Idaho
Twin Lakes
Stranger Cr.
Grand Coulee Dam
Coulee Dam
Banks Lake
Franklin D.
Roosevelt Lake
Spokane R.
Colville R.
Pend Oreille R.

Scale: 10 miles / 10 kilometers N

RITZVILLE (pop. 1,845); 2 restaurants, 2 motels and a RV park. Ritzville dates to 1878, when Philip Ritz staked the first claim near here. He secured a subcontract from the Northern Pacific Railroad, the town was platted, and by 1882 numbered about 150 people. Wheat was planted in 1879, but played a secondary role to cattle ranching, until bumper crops in 1897 and 1898 established the dominance which continues today. Ritzville's Carnegie Library was one of 33 funded by the Carnegie Institute in Washington State. It is thought to be the third-oldest Carnegie building still used as a library in the state. ▲ EXIT 221

Mile 538.5 (166): Exit to Coker Road. EXIT 226

Mile 543.5 (161): Exit to Tokie weigh station, food and lodging. EXIT 231

Mile 551.5 (153): RV campground with all services. ▲ MP 239

Mile 554.5 (150): Rest area on bluff overlooking Sprague Lake. The 6-mile-long lake is a popular fishing hole which yields trout, croppie and bass. Following a 1985 poisoning to remove trash fish, the 1,800-acre lake was restocked with rainbow, brown trout, walleye, smallmouth and largemouth bass. ◂ MP 241

Mile 558 (146.5): Exit north for Washington Highway 23 and 231, exit south for SPRAGUE (pop. 462), named for General John W. Sprague, director of the Northern Pacific Railway. There are 2 motels, a RV park and 2 drive-ins.

Sprague is situated in basalt "seablands" which are unique to the area. The geological phenomena was created by flood waters from Lake Missoula leaving a landscape of canyons, deep ravines, towering mesas and rock formations. ▲ MP 245 EXIT 245

Mile 566.5 (138): Exit to Fish Trap. MP 253 EXIT 254

Mile 570.5 (134): Exit to Tyler and east 10 miles via Washington Highway 904 to CHENEY (pop. 7,550), home of Eastern Washington University. Cheney has a motel and RV park. Its agricultural-based economy produces multimillion dollar annual wheat crops. Peas, oats, barley, beef and dairy products are also marketed. Trout and bass fishing are enjoyed on "50 lakes within 50 miles."

Turnbull National Wildlife Refuge, southwest of Cheney, is a stopover for migrating ducks and geese. As many as 50,000 can be seen during fall. Redheads, diving ducks, and Canadian geese nest here. ▲ EXIT 257

Mile 577 (127.5): Exit south to Cheney and north to MEDICAL LAKE (pop. 3,760). The salty waters of the lake were thought to have medicinal value, hence the name of the town. It was once a lively resort with trains bringing vacationers from Spokane to dance halls and shoreline camps. MP 264 EXIT 264

Mile 583.5 (121): Exit south to Four Lakes and Washington Highway 904 to Cheney; gas and motels. Four Lakes was the site of the Battle of Four Lakes, fought Sept. 1, 1858, by 700 U.S. Army troops and 5,000 Indians. MP 270 EXIT 270

Mile 585.5 (119): Exit north for Washington Highway 902 to Medical Lake. RV camping. ▲MP 272 EXIT 272

Mile 589 (115.5): Exit to Interstate 90 business loop, Spokane and Geiger Field; gas station, diesel. Access to Warden's Winery, open noon to 5 p.m. daily for free tastings. A free 20-minute tour explains the compressor, wine crushing machines, oak barrel rooms and bottling plant. MP 276 EXIT 276

Mile 590 (114.5): Exit 277A to Garden Springs, Spokane Falls and Community College. Exit 277B to junction with U.S. Highway 2 West, Spokane Airport and Fairchild Airforce Base. MP 277 EXIT 277

Mile 591 (113.5): Spokane city limits.

Mile 591.5 (113): Exit to U.S. Highway 195 South to Colfax and Pullman. MP 279 EXIT 279

Mile 592 (112.5): Exit to Maple Toll Bridge, Lincoln Street and Spokane city center. MP 280 EXIT 280

Mile 593 (111.5): Exit here for continuation of U.S. 395 North, which shares a common alignment with U.S. Highway 2 through Spokane where they become Division Street. Interstate 90 continues east into Idaho and Montana. This is also the exit to Whitworth College, Gonzaga University, Riverside Park, The Museum of Native American Cultures and city center. (See Spokane in the MAJOR CITIES section.) MP 281 EXIT 281

Mile 594 (110.5): Crossing the Spokane River. View of Riverside Park, built for the 1974 World's Fair. The park includes a carousel, spacious lawns, an IMAX theater, an opera house and railroad station clock tower. Restaurants, fast food and restrooms.

Mile 594.5 (110): Access east to Gonzaga University. Gonzaga's library was a gift from its 1924 alumnus, Bing Crosby. The Crosby-ana Room contains his Oscar for "Going My Way."

Mile 596.5 (108): Junction with Washington Highway 291 to Nine Mile Falls; access to Riverside State Park on the Spokane River. Spokane House Interpretive Center at the park has exhibits on the fur-trading post established here in 1810. Hiking trails at the park lead to Deep Creek Canyon's fossil beds, Indian rock paintings, and to volcanic outcroppings which form the "bowl and pitcher" on the river. The park also offers equestrian trails, horse rentals, a 600-acre ORV area, 100 campsites, fishing, boat launch and beach access.

Mile 597.5 (107): Junction of U.S. 395 with U.S. 2, which continues northeast to Idaho. Turn to **Mile 411.5** in the U.S. HIGHWAY 2 section for log of that route.

Mile 599 (105.5): Access west to Whitworth College. Rated among the West's best small universities, Whitworth has approximately 2,000 students.

Mile 600 (104.5): Pine Acres golf course.

Mile 601 (103.5): Wandermeer public golf course, lounge and restaurant.

Mile 601.5 (103): Little Spokane River.

Mile 608.5 (96): Dragoon Creek Campground, west of the highway; 22 campsites, 5 picnic sites, water and restrooms.

Mile 613 (91.5): DEER PARK (pop. 2,350) is 0.5 mile east of the highway. The Great Northern Railroad constructed a branch line from Spokane to this area in 1884. Large deposits of clay, kaolin and mineral pigment were found near the town and eventually lumber companies and settlers cut the timber back to the mountains. Deer Park's annual winter festival features a frostbite fun run, snowshoe volleyball and baseball. Motel, fast-food restaurant, fairgrounds and hospital.

MP 179

Mile 614 (90.5): Airport east of highway.

Mile 618 (86.5): CLAYTON, 0.5 mile west of highway, was established in 1889 and named for nearby deposits of clay. Many of Spokane's buildings were made of brick from the Clayton area as were ceramics, terra cotta, fire brick and flower pots.

Mile 622.5 (82): One-mile-long Loon Lake attracts fishermen, boaters and sailboarders.

Mile 624 (80.5): Access to **LOON LAKE** and west 6 miles to Springdale via Washington Highway 292. Facilities at Loon Lake include a marina, resort, public campgrounds, picnic areas, hiking trails, store, restaurants and boat rentals. Deer Lake, 4 miles east, is a favorite summer fishing and swimming spot and autumn duck and deer hunting area. Mackinaw trout reach 30 pounds. Resort, campgrounds, restaurant, boat rentals, boat ramp and picnic areas at Deer Lake.

MP 190

Mile 631.5 (73): Jump Off Joe Lake, west of highway, is a resort area with RV campgrounds, showers, boat launch and rentals.

▲ MP 198

Mile 632 (72.5): VALLEY (unincorporated) at the junction with Washington Highway 232 West to Waitts Lake Recreation Area. Waitts attracts water-skiers, and has a beach for swimming and sunbathing. Washington's largest rainbow trout was caught here. Excellent fishing for brook, brown and cutthroat trout, largemouth bass and yellow perch. Resort with 6 cabins and 55 RV spaces, also public campgrounds, store, marina and boat rentals at lake.

Mile 636 (68.5): Access to Valley and Washington Highway 231 south 8 miles to Springdale. A 1908 fire virtually destroyed Springdale, which is a mix of false-front buildings, vintage frame and newer brick structures.

MP 202

Mile 640.5 (64): CHEWELAH (pop. 1,965) appears little changed from 40 years ago when it was a large manufacturer of Thermax Board. Stone used in terrazzo, cement and stucco were also quarried here. Today, Northwest Alloys, Inc., which produces magnesium products, is the largest employer. Other resources include wood products, marble and silica sand.

Chewelah was a Hudson's Bay trading site and a military post in the 1860s. The local museum preserves over a century of relics.

All visitor services available, including 2 motels and a private campground. The Chewelah area is popular with deer hunters. In town, the community golf course is one of northeastern Washington's most scenic and challenging.

Chewelah also hosts an annual Chataqua outdoor summer arts festival.

Chewelah Mountain is the location of 49 degrees north, a nationally ranked ski resort, which caters to families. Situated 9 miles east of town, it offers day and night skiing from mid-November to mid-April, a day lodge, restaurant and rentals.

Mile 645.5 (59): BLUE CREEK was once a logging and mining area and a shipping point for farm products, copper and dolomite.

Mile 647 (57.5): ADDY is a small farming community, just west of the highway. Services on U.S. 395 include the Rainbow Cafe and Old Schoolhouse Trading Post and Emporium.

MP 216

Mile 656.5 (48): ARDEN. A scattering of homes and small business stretches along 2 to 3 miles of U.S. 395. RV park, gas and food.

▲ MP 228

Mile 661 (43.5): COLVILLE (pop. 4,470) is the Stevens County seat and largest town. Its primary industries are agriculture, manufacturing, timber and tourism.

David Thompson of the Northwest Fur Co. explored the area in 1911. Within a year, 11,000 pounds of furs were shipped from here and by 1840 the number grew to 18,000 annually.

In 1859, Fort Colville was built. Four companies of United States Infantry were stationed here. When the fort was abandoned

Duncan Gardens in Spokane's Manito Park; take Exit 281. (L. Linkhart)

Kettle Falls Bridge crosses upper Lake Roosevelt at Mile 673.

(L. Linkhart)

in 1882, the town was founded. During the 1890s gold rush, Colville became a wide open frontier town with more than its share of brawling, robberies, and murders.

U.S. 395 forms Colville's main street. Other streets are unusually wide, and were originally designed to allow 16 horse teams to turn around wagons loaded with logs.

Recreation in the Colville area includes camping, horseback riding, swimming, boating and hunting the state's largest population of white-tailed deer. The local fish hatchery, which produces trout, is open for tours.

Mile 661.5 (43): Junction with Washington Highway 20 East. From Colville to the Columbia River, U.S. 395 and Highway 20 share a common alignment. Access to Keller House and Stevens County Historical Society Museum. Situated at Keller Historical Park, 700 N. Wynne, exhibits cover Indians, guns, the Hudson's Bay Co., prominent pioneers and founding fathers. Open May through September.

Keller House is an example of early 20th century architecture and the Craftsmen Movement in interior design. Open 1-4 p.m., Wednesday through Saturday.

Mile 663 (41.5): Williams Lake Drive leads north 16 miles to Williams Lake campground; 8 campsites, 2 picnic sites and drinking water.

Mile 669.5 (35): KETTLE FALLS (pop. 1,224). Prior to 1941, Kettle Falls was situated 4 miles west on the banks of the Columbia River, and the present town was called Meyers Falls. With the building of Grand Coulee Dam, Kettle Falls was one of several towns which were submerged by the backwaters or moved.

French trappers called the area Los Chaudieres, meaning "The Kettles," when they saw water churning in holes ground in rock along the Columbia's shores. The original town and the falls lie buried under the waters of Roosevelt Lake. During spring drawdown, the streets and remains of the original town are above water and can be visited.

The falls were an important meeting, trading and fishing spot for Indians. It was settled in 1826 when Fort Colville was built by the Hudson's Bay Co.

Logging, wood products, farming orchards and tourism are major industries. All visitor services are available, including motels and campgrounds.

Mile 670.5 (34): Junction with Washington Highway 25 south to Davenport and north to Northport.

Mile 672.5 (32): Kettle Falls Campground; 89 campsites, picnic areas, swimming beach, amphitheater programs, drinking water, boat dock, ramp and fuel.

East of the highway is St. Paul's Mission. It was built in 1845 by Father Anthony Raville and was made of hand-hewn logs and wooden pegs. In 1951, it was restored and given to Washington State as a memorial park. Interpretative center details the importance of the falls as an Indian meeting place.

Mile 673 (31.5): Kettle Falls Bridge over the Columbia River. Backed up by Grand Coulee Dam, the Columbia forms 150-mile-long Lake Roosevelt. The Coulee Dam National Recreation Area includes approximately 75 percent of the reservoir and shoreline. The remaining area is part of the Colville and Spokane Indian reservations.

Mile 674.5 (30): Northbound, U.S. 395 and Highway 20 common alignment ends. Highway 20 continues west to Tonasket and Whidbey Island. Continue north on U.S. Highway 395.

Mile 678.5 (26): East of highway is Kamloops Island, Coulee Dam National Recreation Area Campground; 14 campsites, picnic area, boat dock and water. MP 245

Mile 680 (24.5): Private RV park with laundromat, showers and full hookups.

Mile 681.5 (23): Kettle River Coulee Dam National Recreation Area campground; 20 sites, boat dock, picnic area and water. MP 248

Mile 686.5 (18): Kerry Hill Lake.

Mile 690.5 (14): Begin 1 mile of sharp switchbacks northbound. MP 257

Mile 693.5 (11): ORIENT started as a mining camp in 1902 and was originally called Morgan. It was renamed for a local mine, and when the price of gold increased in 1935 enjoyed a second boom. Medical clinic, store and restaurant.

Mile 703.5 (1): Pierre Lake Forest Service campground; 15 campsites, 10 picnic sites, water, fishing, boating and hiking.

Mile 704 (0.5): LAURIER is largely a residential and service community for customs personnel. During the 1890s gold rush, it was a stopping point for wagon and pack trains. At its peak, it had a population of over 2,000 people.

Mile 704.5 (0): United States-Canada border. Turn to **Mile 353.5** in the CROWSNEST HIGHWAY 3 section.

Chilcotin Highway

(BC Highway 20)

See map opposite page.

BC Highway 20, known as the Chilcotin Highway, is one of only 3 roads that reach the British Columbia coast. The road west to the coastal settlement of Bella Coola from the town of Williams Lake, on BC Highway 97 (Gold Rush Trail), is a long and lonely road, one that used to be a test of endurance because nearly all of its 287.5 miles/448.5 km was rough gravel — in summer a maelstrom of choking dust, with potholes as big as tank traps. Even optimistic travelers carried more than one spare tire, and the cautious took with them extra fan belts, canteens of water and extra gas, for the settlements were tiny, few and far between.

But the bad times on Highway 20 are all gone — or nearly so. Today 160 miles (sections at both ends) are paved and the middle gravel section is usually well-maintained. There are just enough settlements so that gas, supplies and even accommodations en route are in good supply. However, if you make the drive through on a Sunday, don't depend on settlements en route for gas. Several service stations (and general stores) are open on weekdays only. The scenery is superb, from the grasslands of the rolling Chilcotin country, through the mountain wilderness of Tweedsmuir Provincial Park to the rain forests and pastoral valleys of the coast.

There is still "The Hill," a nerve-wracking switchback descent from the top of Heckman Pass (elev. 5,000 feet/1,524m) down to the forests of the Bella Coola Valley at just above sea level. This enormous drop is engineered in just 12 miles/19 km of narrow, mostly 1-way track, much of it at 18 percent grade. This section of the route is not for timid drivers, and autos should be in good repair, particularly brakes. Trailers and large RVs will have difficulty negotiating some of the hairpin bends.

The drive DOWN the big hill will be exhilarating to say the least — and remember, since Bella Coola is a dead end with no ferry connections out, after your stay you will have to drive UP it. Engines can quickly overheat on the steep grades. The locals know the highway as Freedom Road, as it is their only road connection with the rest of the world. Buses navigate the road from Williams Lake twice a week.

A Forest Service Recreation Sites map of the Cariboo Region which details roads, lakes and campsites can be obtained from Forest Service offices at Williams Lake, 100 Mile House and Alexis Creek, as well as tourist information outlets.

Chilcotin Highway Log

Distance in miles from Williams Lake is followed by distance in miles from Bella Coola. Equivalent distances in kilometres are indicated by Km.

Mile 0 (287.5) Km 0 (448.5): Junction of Highways 20 and 97 at Williams Lake (see description of Williams Lake at **Mile 360** in the CANADA HIGHWAY 97 section).

Mile 1.5 (277) Km 2.5 (446): Road south to Alkali Lake, Dog Creek and south via old Goldrush River Trail to Pavilion and Lillooet.

Westbound, Highway 20 climbs high onto plateau, then drops steeply down to the Fraser River.

Mile 15 (263.5) Km 24.5 (424): Viewpoint at the eastern end of Sheep Creek bridge over Fraser River. Begin steep 6 percent grade westbound up to plateau level.

Mile 16 (262.5) Km 25.5 (423): Top of river trench. Eastbound: Begin steep downgrade; watch for slow-moving loaded logging trucks. The great Fraser Plateau spreads to the west, with snowcapped peaks of the distant Coast Range visible on the horizon. The country west of the Fraser is known as the Chilcotin, taking its name from the river which cuts through the plateau. The country is chiefly rangeland for cattle, though forestry is also important.

Mile 20.5 (258) Km 33 (415.5) Gravel road north to Forest Service picnic area on McIntyre Lake, the small community of Meldrum Creek and on to Quesnel along the west side of the Fraser River. Sweeping grasslands here are known as Becher's Prairie. Notice the nesting boxes set up at regular intervals along the fences here. Boxes are sited in pairs; this allows bluebirds to nest in one box, the far more numerous tree swallows in the other. Both bluebirds and swallows are encouraged because they eat vast quantities of mosquitoes. ⼍

Mile 21.5 (257) Km 34.5 (414): Canadian Coastguard Service loran-C tower, part of long range navigation system shared by British Columbia, Alaska and Washington. Tours by reservation preferred; drop-in tours from 9 a.m. to 4 p.m.

Mile 27.5 (251) Km 44 (404.5): Gravel road south to the Indian village of Toosey, Farwell Canyon on the Chilcotin River and on to the ranch community of Big Creek. A side-trip down the sinuous road into the canyon (10 miles/16 km) is recommended. River cliffs have been eroded into statuesque hoodoos and pinnacles; area east of the river has been set aside as a reserve for a band of 400 California bighorn sheep. Road can be driven as a 30-mile/50-km loop, returning to Highway 20 at Lee's Corner at **Mile 55.3.**

Mile 29 (249.5) Km 46.5 (402): Small community of **RISKE CREEK**. Gas, food, accommodations. Note old log cabins painted bright yellow behind gas pumps. Historic Chilcotin Lodge, a capacious log structure, can be seen just north of the highway.

Mile 30 (248.5) Km 48 (400.5): Forest Service Recreation Area at Becher Pond; fishing for small rainbow; picnic tables. Highway here is flanked by lodgepole pines and aspens. ⼍⟜

Mile 50.5 (228) Km 81 (367.5): Rest area south of highway and start of 9 percent downgrade westbound. Historic marker commemorates the epic and ill-fated Yukon cattle drive of Norman Lee, a local pioneer rancher, who drove 200 head of cattle 1,500 miles through the mountain wilderness in an attempt to get beef to the Klondike goldfields in 1898.

Mile 35.5 (243) Km 57 (391.5): Riske Creek recreation complex, including rodeo grounds. Stampede held in mid-June.

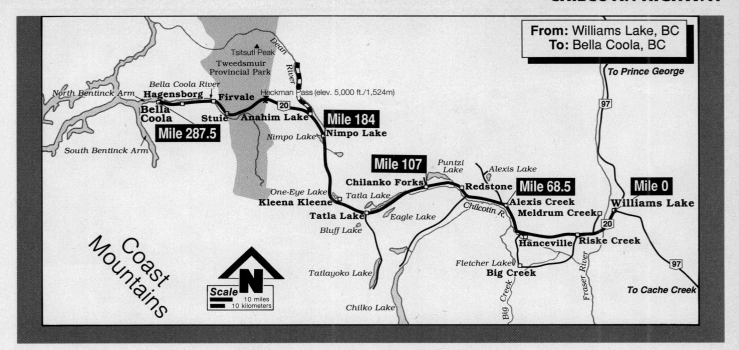

From: Williams Lake, BC
To: Bella Coola, BC

Mile 41.5 (237) Km 67 (381.5): Gravel road north to Forest Service recreation area on Ravel Lake; fishing; boat launch.

Mile 44.5 (234) Km 72 (376.5): Good stretch of snake fence. Farther west, example of Russell fence, 2 of several traditional Cariboo designs.

Mile 55.5 (223) Km 89 (359.5): Lee's Corner, on site of Norman Lee's ranch house (see **Mile 50.5**) and Hanceville post office. Gas, groceries and food. Turnoff south for old settlement of Hanceville, named for Tom Hance, the original settler, and the TH guest ranch.

This side road continues south, crossing the Chilcotin River, to Fletcher Lake Forest Service Recreation Area for canoeing and fishing and the community of Big Creek. (Road loops back to the highway at **Mile 27.5**.) The Chilcotin country is laced with a network of backcountry roads leading to lakes and rivers for marvelous fishing — lake, rainbow and Dolly Varden trout, kokanee and burbot.

Mile 62 (216.5) Km 99.5 (349): Steepled church and houses of Anahim Reserve, the largest of 6 Indian reserves in the Chilcotin. Highway follows the Chilcotin River but the river (to the south) is deeply entrenched and out of sight.

Mile 68.5 (210) Km 110.5 (338): Village of **ALEXIS CREEK** (pop. 1,200), largest settlement of the east Chilcotin. Gas, groceries, accommodations, outpost hospital and administrative office for forestry, fish and wildlife, and highways departments. Pigeon's General Store is a link with pioneer days.

Stum Lake Road leads northwest to network of cross-country ski trails and on to forestry recreation areas at McKill and Palmer lakes for fishing and boating. (Final access to

McKill is on foot only.) In the area is White Pelican Provincial Park, a sanctuary for white pelicans. It is the only known pelican nesting area in British Columbia. Visitors wishing access must contact the B.C. Parks Cariboo office, RR 1, Lac La Hache, BC, V0K 1T0.

Mile 72.5 (206) Km 116.5 (332): Westbound, road goes steeply downhill; view of Chilcotin River and rock cliffs.

Mile 74 (204.5) Km 119 (329.5): Bull Canyon Provincial Recreation Area; picnic tables and 25 campsites in aspen forest beside Chilcotin River. No fee. River is turbulent and colored a bright gray-green from glacial silt. Kayaking and rafting are popular. Explore canyon walls for caves.

Mile 76.5 (202) Km 123 (325.5): Gravel road north up Alexis Creek to forestry recreation areas on Two and Alexis lakes (16.5 miles/ 27 km).

Mile 82 (196.5) Km 132 (316.5): Rough road leads deep into the Chilcotin wilderness; follow Chilko River valley south to Chilko Lake, one of the largest in the area; recreation sites at the junction of the Chilko and Taseko rivers; at Tsuniah and Choelquoit lakes and at Chilko Lake itself. Motorboats are allowed on Chilko Lake. *WARNING:* Boaters, beware of sudden high winds. The Chilko River is a famous white-water stream popular with kayakers and rafters.

Mile 87.5 (191) Km 141 (307.5): Chilcotin River bridge; gravel road north to tiny ranch settlement of Chezacut (30 miles/48 km). Just to the west is the scattered community of Redstone at the confluence of the Chilcotin and Chilanko rivers. Highway west follows the Chilanko River southwest; Chilcotin River comes in from the northwest.

Mile 102 (176.5) Km 164 (284.5): Redstone Indian cemetery, crammed with white-painted picket fences and crosses. Indians west of the Fraser are Carrier and Chilcotin tribes, members of the northern Dene nation. Beyond the cemetery the river lies in a deep trench.

Mile 103 (175.5) Km 165.5 (283): Indian village of **REDSTONE**, its steepled church painted bright blue; general store, gas.

Mile 104 (174.5) Km 167.5 (281): Stunning view west of snowcapped Coast Mountains.

Mile 107 (171.5) Km 172 (276.5): Community of **CHILANKO FORKS**; gas, store, accommodations.

Mile 107.5 (171) Km 173 (275.5): Road north to Puntzi Lake (4.5 miles7 km), well stocked with rainbow and kokanee. Five resorts and private campground.

Mile 112.5 (166) Km 181 (267.5): Gravel road south to Pyper Lake Forest Service Recreation Area with picnic tables and fishing.

Pavement ends; all-weather gravel road continues. Use headlights in dusty conditions.

Mile 115 (163.5) Km 185 (263.5): Gravel turnout and viewpoint north to the long, deep valley of Tatla Lake.

Mile 129 (149.5) Km 208 (240.5): Pollywog rest area with picnic tables beside small lake.

Mile 130.5 (148) Km 210 (238.5): Gravel road north to Tatla Lake Forest Service Recreation Area; fishing (kokanee to 2 pounds); boat launching (motors allowed). To the west,

View looking west of Bella Coola harbor.

(Liz Bryan)

road leads south to Eagle Lake.

Mile 133 (145.5) Km 214.5 (234): Road south to Pinto Lake Forest Service Recreation Area with picnic tables and boating.

Mile 136 (142.5) Km 219 (229.5): Road junction. Highway 20 goes north to community of Tatla Lake. Road leads south over the divide to Tatlayoko Lake in the Homathco Valley (21.5 miles/35 km), jumping-off point for expeditions to Mount Waddington (elev. 13,100 feet/2,994m), the highest peak in the Coast Range. Resort on lake, plus Forest Service recreation area for fishing, hiking, boating (powerboats allowed). Road branches to Sapeye, Horn and Bluff lakes, all popular fishing spots.

Mile 137 (141.5) Km 220.5 (228): Community of **TATLA LAKE** on north shore of small lake with a magnificent view south toward the mountains. Old Graham Hotel (food, accommodations) commemorates the name of first settlers, Robert and Margaret Graham. Settlement has gas, store, restaurant, motel, post office and clinic.

Mile 146.5 (132) Km 236 (212.6): Klinaklini River bridge. River is closed to fishing April 1 to June 30.

Mile 153 (125.5) Km 246 (202.5): Road north to Forestry Service recreation area on One Eye Lake; fishing, boating.

Mile 156.5 (122) Km 252 (196.5): Tiny community of **KLEENA KLEENE**, with general store and post office. Highway now goes almost due north.

Mile 158.5 (120) Km 255.5 (193): Road south to Clearwater Lake Forest Service Recreation Area with picnic tables, fishing and boating.

Mile 163 (115.5) Km 262 (186.5): Bridge over McClinchie Creek, Dean River tributary.

Mile 177.5 (101) Km 286 (162.5): Road south to Charlotte Lake (12 miles/20 km), rainbows to 4 pounds. Near here is one of the very few Indian pictograph sites in the Chilcotin painted on a single block of granite. One glyph clearly depicts the horns of a big-horn sheep. Ask for directions at Kleena Kleene or Nimpo Lake.

Mile 184 (94.5) Km 296 (152.5): **NIMPO LAKE** community marked by a stretch of paved road. All basic services and several fishing resorts. The area is often quite noisy with

floatplanes taxiing on the 7.5-mile/12-km lake which lies just to the west of the settlement. Lake contains choice rainbows, also cross-bred trout with both rainbow and cutthroat characteristics.

From Nimpo Lake to Anahim Lake Highway 20 follows the upper reaches of the Dean River, famous for its fishing. The river is managed as a special fishery and a permit is needed to fish certain sections. Check British Columbia fishing regulations.

Mile 187 (91.5) Km 301 (147.5): Bridge over Dean River; Forest Service recreation site; canoeing and fly-fishing. Historical marker on west side of bridge commemorates the Chilcotin War that prompted the abandonment of Waddington's Road to the goldfields. The road was pioneered by Victoria merchant Alfred Waddington as a shortcut to the Cariboo gold rush. The marker is about 65 miles/104 km north of where the incident took place in 1864, but apparently the Indian war party also killed members of a pack train here at the river crossing known as The Fishtrap, spreading terror throughout the Chilcotin.

Mile 191.5 (87) Km 308 (140.5): Huge planer mill, a cultural shock after so many miles without a sign of industry.

Mile 195 (83.5) Km 313.5 (135): ANAHIM LAKE community, home of a large and boisterous stampede in mid-July. Settlement grew in size in 1940 when scattered communities of Ulkatcho Indians relocated here. All major services located on north loop road. Airstrip with daily connections to Vancouver and Bella Coola. Above lake is the ancient volcanic plug of Anahim Peak. Paved road around village is due to be linked up with the pavement at Nimpo Lake in the fall of 1989.

From Anahim Lake, a gravel road leads north along the Dean River valley for 20 miles/32 km. Access to abandoned Indian villages of Iluak and Ulkatcho and to the mountains of the Rainbow Range. Also access to the Alexander Mackenzie Heritage Trail (see **Mile 249.5**). Highway leaves the Dean Valley west of the lake and heads up to Heckman Pass. The climb west is easy and effortless.

Mile 197.5 (81) Km 318 (130.5): Little Anahim Lake Forestry Recreation Area with picnic tables, swimming and boating. 🎋

Mile 215 (63.5) Km 346.5 (103): Road closure gate and bridge over Tsulko River, a tributary of the Dean. Road climbs more steeply, with a good view to the north of the Rainbow Range, fragmented shield volcanoes, stained purple, yellow and red with minerals. The highest is Tsitsutl Peak (elev. 8,200 feet/2,500m), site of prehistoric obsidian quarries. Natives used the rock to make spear points and arrowheads.

Mile 217 (61.5) Km 349 (99.5): Eastern entrance to Tweedsmuir Provincial Park and summit of Heckman Pass (elev. 5,000 feet/1,524m). Park is a huge expanse of pristine wilderness, much of it inaccessible except on foot, on horseback or by floatplane onto remote lakes. Along Highway 20, the park has 5 picnic sites and 2 campgrounds with a total of 42 campsites, and a sani-station. Prime attractions are hiking and fishing. 🎋🏕🛶▲

Mile 221 (57.5) Km 355.5 (93): Rainbow Range trailhead and East Branch picnic site. 🎋

Mile 221.5 (57) Km 357 (91.5): Brake check area. Beginning of the notorious descent to the Bella Coola Valley. Hill, much of which is at 18 percent grade, descends in 2 stages, with switchbacks around steeply falling Young Creek, which the road crosses twice. It is difficult to take your eyes off the road to view the scenery as the road is narrow (in places single track) and traverses unstable rock slopes.

Mile 225 (53.5) Km 362 (86.5): One-lane plank bridge over Young Creek. Space at the creek to pull off and take a break. Highway west climbs up again before final descent.

Mile 227 (51.5) Km 365 (83.5): Beginning of 5.5-mile/9-km steep descent, requiring very cautious driving. *WARNING:* The mountainside is steep, the road very narrow and there are no guard rails. Watch for rock slides and extremely tight hairpin bends. Use low gear to prevent brakes overheating.

Mile 232 (46.5) Km 374 (74.5): Road closure gate. Suddenly the road is bordered with coastal cedar and hemlock.

Mile 233 (45.5) Km 374.5 (74): Young Creek bridge and park picnic ground; trailhead south to the upper Atnarko River valley and the Turner Lakes chain, a subalpine canoe route and spectacular Hunlet Falls (18 miles/29 km), which drops 853 feet/260m in a single cascade. Trails also lead to Ptarmigan Lake and the Monarch Icefield. Begin paved road; in summer there's a roadside sign with information about park services and warning of grizzly bears that frequent the rivers, particularly in spring and fall, around the salmon hatcheries farther downstream. 🏕🎋

Mile 233.5 (45) Km 376 (72.5): Atnarko River Campground (fee); 28 campsites just east of the park headquarters; sani-station. The Atnarko and Bella Coola rivers are famous around the world for their fish: steelhead, cutthroat, Dolly Varden and 5 varieties of salmon. Conservation regulations are in effect — both rivers have "special" status and are subject to special regulations and closures. Check with the B.C. Freshwater Fishing Regulations Synopsis, or with park officials. 🎣▲

Mile 240.5 (38) Km 387 (61.5): Big Rock picnic area in the tall cedars. Rock is a giant fallen boulder. Across the road a 1-hour loop trail circles Kettle Pond. 🎋

Mile 241.5 (37) Km 388.5 (60): Atnarko River Spawning Channels in former bed of river. Center provides spawning channels for 50,000 pink salmon and also rearing channels for chinook salmon for Snootli Creek Hatchery downstream (see **Mile 271**). In 1988, 2 million juvenile chinooks were released. A good system of trails lead along the banks of the old river channel and beside spawning and rearing beds. Best time to see the pinks spawn is August and September. Grizzly bears have discovered the easy fishing of the spawning beds and often the trails will be closed because of bear danger.

Mile 242.5 (36) Km 390 (58.5): Small resort community of STUIE. Nearby, ancient Indian burial ground and smokehouse.

Mile 243.5 (35) Km 392 (56.5): Fisheries Pool Campground; 14 campsites, fee, boat launch and picnic area beside Atnarko River. 🎋▲

Mile 246.5 (32) Km 397 (51.5): Horsetail Falls Creek. Falls drop from high overhanging cliffs to provide a long gush of water like a horse's flowing tail. Best view from the highway, just west of bridge.

Mile 249.5 (29) Km 401.5 (47): Burnt Bridge trailhead and picnic area. Two-hour loop trail leads to good viewpoint of river and Stupendous Mountain (elev. 8,800 feet/2,700m).

West of bridge sign commemorates the Alexander Mackenzie Heritage Trail. Explorer Mackenzie of the North West Co. was the first white man to cross the North American continent. In 1793 he and his party left Lake Athabaska to find a trade route to the Pacific, a 72-day trek through 1,200 miles/2,000 km of unmapped territory. The 260-mile/420-km trail from Quesnel has been retraced and is being restored in a joint federal, provincial and regional project. The land trail terminates at the Burnt Creek bridge where Mackenzie first came into contact with the coastal Natives. He went the rest of the way to the Pacific by canoe.

Mile 254 (24.5) Km 409 (39.5): Small settlement of FIRVALE; gas available.

Mile 258.5 (20) Km 416 (32.5): Bridge across Bella Coola River.

Mile 269 (9.5) Km 433 (15.5): Community of HAGENSBORG, settled by Norwegians from Minnesota who found the country similar to the fjords of their home country. The valley floor here is flat and fertile, the mountains high and sheer. All basic services.

Mile 270.5 (8) Km 435.5 (13): Road to airport.

Mile 271.5 (7) Km 437 (11.5): Snootli Creek Fish Hatchery. Each September, eggs from Atnarko chinook salmon are brought here for fertilization and incubation; fry are raised here for 8 to 10 weeks, then transferred to the Atnarko rearing channels. (See **Mile 241.5**.)

Mile 275 (3.5) Km 443 (5.5): Road south up Thorsen Creek. Up this road lies a large and important Indian petroglyph site with more than 100 glyphs. Ask locally for directions.

Mile 276 (2.5) Km 444.5 (4): Bella Coola school, constructed of cedar with Indian graphic designs and carvings.

Mile 287.5 (0) Km 448.5 (0): Junction at entrance to town of **BELLA COOLA** (area pop. 2,500). All tourist services. Town is home to the Bella Coola Band of the Nuxalk Nation; Look for totems outside the band office and the traditional house replica next to the church. Alexander Mackenzie was the first white man to visit this settlement at the head of Bentinck Arm in 1793. The Hudson's Bay Co. established a trading post here in 1869 (the factor's house by the river still remains). The museum is in a schoolhouse that dates from the 1800s and displays Hudson's Bay Co. relics and items brought by Norwegian settlers. Attractions include charter flights, fishing charters and boat trips to Alexander Mackenzie Historic Park in Dean Channel where the explorer left a record of his momentous journey "From Canada by Land, 22nd July, 1793" inscribed on a rock.

Paved road continues around the tidewater flats at the head of the inlet for 1.2 miles/2 km to the government wharf and the fishing harbor. No scheduled ferry.

Coquihalla Highway

(BC Highway 5)

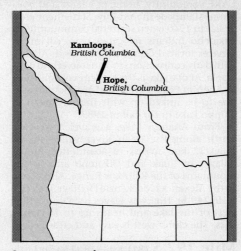

See map opposite page.

British Columbia's newest highway, the Coquihalla connects Hope at the junction of Highways 1 and 3 with Kamloops on Trans-Canada Highway 1. As an alternate route to the Interior of the province (and to points east and north), it is shorter and faster than Highway 1 because it bypasses the older, twisting Fraser Canyon section. The new road is a marvel of modern road-building: 4 lanes, with extra passing lanes for trucks, carved through the Cascade Mountains and Nicola Plateau. Beginning close to sea level at the confluence of the Coquihalla and Fraser rivers at Hope, the road was built in 2 stages: the first 70 miles/112 km up the Coquihalla River and Boston Bar Creek valleys, then down the Coldwater River drainage to the town of Merritt. This first stage was completed in a rush for Expo 86 and it is one of the most scenic stretches of highway in southern British Columbia.

The second stage of the highway north from Merritt climbs even higher onto the shoulders of the Nicola Plateau before plunging again into the Thompson River Valley at Kamloops. While the second part of the highway lacks the alpine grandeur of the first, it compensates by providing easy access to some of the high-country lakes south of Kamloops famous for their fighting rainbow trout.

The Coquihalla has a history of use as a transportation corridor. The ruggedness of the river canyon deterred early fur traders but Nicola Valley ranchers determinedly scraped out a cattle trail over the mountains to the coast in 1876. This Hope-Nicola Trail saw good use until 1913 when it was supplanted by a railway. The Kettle Valley Railway was a prodigious undertaking, requiring great engineering skills — the Coquihalla River section alone required 43 bridges, 13 tunnels and 16 snowsheds—and tremendous upkeep expenses for the constant removal of rock slides and snowfall. Its importance as an economic lifeline to the Interior was diminished by the opening of the Hope-Princeton Highway (Highway 3) in 1949 and when a massive rock slide wiped out a major bridge in 1959, the railway decided to close for good.

Residents of Hope and Merritt used the rough pipeline access road, known familiarly as "The Coke," to find their favorite fishing holes along the river canyon and beyond to the Coquihalla Lakes.

The new Coquihalla Highway was built to relieve pressure on the Fraser Canyon route from Hope to Kamloops, the most-used stretch of highway in western Canada, and one that in winter is subject to closure because of rock slides. The highway follows the Kettle Valley route as far as the old railway station of Portia, but then leaves the narrow Upper Coquihalla Canyon in favor of a route up the wide flat Boston Bar Creek valley to the summit above the lakes. This valley, however, is prone to avalanches: here, highway engineers had to design foolproof protection against 67 active avalanche tracks. These protections include trenches and rock dams to deflect and stop the snow; mounds to slow it down, basins to trap it before it reaches the highway and, most expensive of all, a huge snowshed, nearly 1,000 feet/300m long, in the track of the potentially most dangerous avalanche. There are 2 tramways and 12 gun emplacements, where nitrogen-fired missiles are used to shoot down potential avalanches.

Because it is a new road and traverses for the most part a delicate alpine terrain where growth is slow, the highway still tends to look a bit raw and tourist facilities are sparse. There are no gas stations or restaurants along the way except at Hope, Merritt and near Kamloops. There are several picnic areas, rest stops and new provincial parks; the only provincial campsites are near the Merritt/Kamloops summit; no recreational facilities apart from fishing and wilderness hiking.

The Coquihalla Highway is British Columbia's only toll road. The 1 central toll booth is located near the summit of the Hope-Merritt section and fees are $10 for passenger cars, light trucks and campers, more for oversize and commercial vehicles. Tolls are payable in cash or by VISA and MasterCard. Permitted driving speed is 65 mph/110 kmph, the highest in the province. It is a limited access freeway; no U-turns except where indicated.

Coquihalla Highway Log

Distance in miles from Hope is followed by distance in miles from Kamloops. Equivalent distances in kilometres are indicated by Km.

Mile 0 (118) Km 0 (190): Junction of Highways 3 and 1, just east of Hope. (For information on Hope see TRANS-CANADA HIGHWAY 1 section at **Mile 547.5/Km 881**.) Highways 5 and 3 follow the same alignment eastbound for several miles.

Mile 4.5 (113.5) Km 7 (193): Highway 5 strikes north across Nicolum River bridge, one of the engineering wonders of the new road. A 5-lane, 4-span bridge with 240-foot-/71-m-long steel box beams, passes 160 feet/48m above the river channel. Just beyond the bridge, the road swings north into the Coquihalla River valley; the river is west of the highway.

Mile 7.5 (110.5) Km 12 (178): Othello Road exit to Kawkawa Lake and Coquihalla Canyon Provincial Recreation Area. Here the focus of interest is the abandoned Kettle Valley Railway which forced a route through the tortuous canyon by means of 5 rock tunnels linked by bridges over the river. This stretch of railway has been restored as a walking trail, through 3 of the tunnels and across bridges, with spectacular views of the high canyon walls and the rushing water. Restrooms and an information shelter are located at the parking lot near the old station of Othello. Farther along the road is Kawkawa Lake, a great place for family picnics, swimming, boating; commercial and Hope municipal campgrounds nearby. Peers bridge across the Coquihalla just to the north was named for Hudson's Bay Co. clerk Henry Newsham Peers who in 1847 laid out the Brigade Trail up Peers and Sowaqua creeks over Hope Pass, and a year later built the first Fort Hope.

Mile 9.5 (108.5) Km 15.5 (174.5): Orange-and-white checkered buildings mark the start of aerial tramway to microwave station on Mount Jarvis, to the east.

Mile 11 (107) Km 18 (172): Ten Mile Creek bridge.

Mile 11.5 (106.5) Km 18.5 (171.5): Deneau Creek bridge.

Mile 12.5 (105.5) Km 19.5 (170.5): Large turnout by Coquihalla River, east side of highway, well used by fishermen. The river offers Dolly Varden in spring and fall, coho in fall, and steelhead in the upper reaches in summer, lower reaches in winter. Fly-fishing only; river closures, catch and bait restrictions are posted here. There are several river turnouts north of here, accessible by northbound traffic only. One at **Mile 15.5/Km 25** has picnic tables.

Mile 13 (105) Km 21 (169): Coquihalla River bridge at Sowaqua Creek near the Kettle Valley station of Jessica.

Mile 16 (102) Km 25.5 (164.5): Dewdney Creek; exit via Carolyn Mines (an operating gold mine) Road. Northbound travelers make U-turn to Coquihalla River Provincial Recreation Area located southwest of the highway. Access is easier for southbound traffic. Recreation area has picnic tables, fishing and hiking. In winter, watch for road closure barriers as highway crews remove potential avalanche and rock fall dangers.

Mile 17 (101) Km 27.5 (172.5): Ladner Creek bridge, a gently curving 6-span structure 840 feet/257m long and 130 feet/40m high. Old railway right-of-way loops to cross creek high upstream.

Mile 18 (100) Km 29 (161): Shylock Road overpass (to gravel pit) and U-turn route for southbound traffic. Nearby is a stop of interest marker about the Kettle Valley Railway. This marks the approximate location of the station of Portia; highway leaves the Coquihalla River and veers northwest into the valley of its tributary, Boston Bar Creek, looping around Needle Peak. Immediately one can notice a difference in topography: The highway begins a steep climb, with rock faces to the west of highway carrying a series of waterfalls. Old pipeline access road follows the railway up Coquihalla Canyon; a private road, but accessible to the public, it is a rough, narrow track.

Mile 20 (98) Km 32 (158): Chain-up area for northbound vehicles; snow lingers on the slopes here well into June.

Mile 21 (97) Km 34 (156): Portia bridge over Boston Bar Creek.

Mile 22 (96) Km 35 (156): Road closure barrier. Start of avalanche protection devices, including earthworks and the first of 12 gun emplacements. Nitrogen-propelled missile launches are used to prematurely trigger avalanches while highway is closed to traffic.

Mile 22.5 (95.5) Km 36 (154): Cassio-Miranda avalanche control ropeway, one of 2 in the area. The other is just north of the Great Bear avalanche track and snowshed. Ropeways deliver explosive charges to avalanche trigger zones; charges are detonated by remote control.

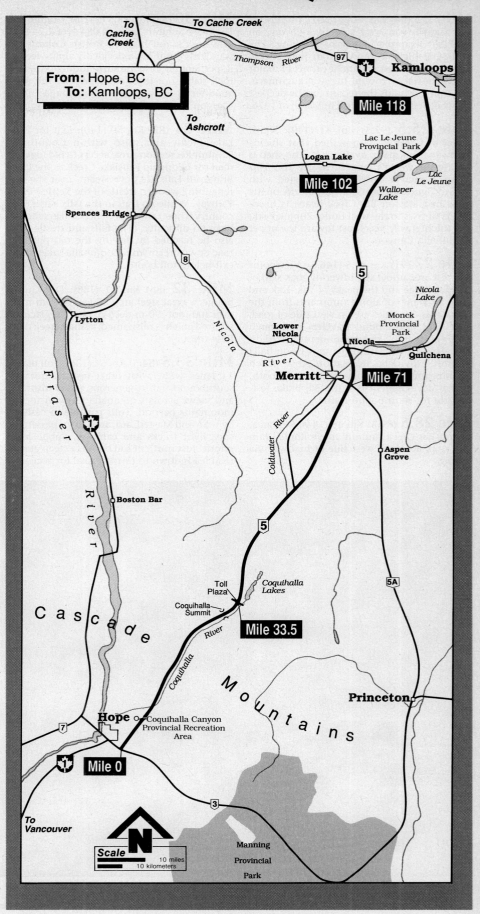

COQUIHALLA HIGHWAY

Mile 24 (94) Km 38.5 (151.1): Impressive Box Canyon on west side of highway, an excellent example of glacial scouring. The stretch of highway north from here to the summit is the most avalanche prone; 11 major avalanche tracks cross the highway alignment. Box Canyon holds the record for the deepest snowfall of the route: 15 feet in March of 1976.

Mile 25.5 (92.5) Km 41 (149): South portal of Great Bear snowshed that shields highway from major avalanches. The shed is among the world's longest: nearly 100 feet/300m. Concrete lintels are decorated with incised figures of bears. A mile north of the snowshed, Boston Bar Creek nears its headwaters (it rises to the west under Zupjok Peak) and the highway veers east toward the upper Coquihalla Canyon.

Mile 27 (91) Km 43.5 (146.5): Viewpoint and rest area under the towering rock slab of Zopkios Ridge and the peaks of Yak, Nak and Thar, all names of alpine ruminants from the Himalayas. Facilities are on west side of road. Access for northbound travelers is through steel "armadillo" culvert underneath highway. This area is within the new Coquihalla Summit Provincial Recreation Area which extends north to just beyond the toll booth; further development is expected. Brake testing area for southbound traffic.

Mile 28.5 (89.5) Km 46 (144): Rest area, Boston Bar Creek summit above Romeo railway stop; access to west side of highway via tunnel.

Mile 30 (88) Km 48.5 (141.5): Coquihalla Highway Summit (elev. 4,084 feet/1,244m). This pass is not high by British Columbia's standards but it has a decidedly alpine feel to it, perhaps because the surrounding peaks are rock slabs, not forested slopes. To the east, good views out across the Coquihalla Upper Canyon.

Mile 31 (87) Km 50 (140): Exit for Falls Lake picnic area, also within Coquihalla Summit Recreation Area; access to old logging road for hiking up Fallslake Creek to the lake; Bridalveil Falls are downsteam, near the last remaining wooden trestle of the Kettle Valley Railway. While no trail to the falls exists, the country is open and experienced hikers should have no difficulty. (The falls and trestle may also be reached by driving the old pipeline road downstream from Coquihalla Lakes.) Last exit before toll booth.

Mile 32 (86) Km 51 (138): Dry Gulch bridge, a great steel arch 580 feet/175m high over 300-foot-/90-m-deep gulch. (The glacially scoured gulch is misnamed: a small creek does flow through it.)

Mile 33.5 (84.5) Km 54 (136): Toll plaza; 14 lanes wide, with brake-testing area for southbound traffic, generous gravel turnouts and views across Coquihalla Canyon to the mountains beyond. Tolls payable in cash or by VISA and MasterCard, are $10 for passenger cars, light trucks and campers. Public telephone. Just north of toll booth, a steep gravel road leads down to canyon road for access to Coquihalla Lakes resort area; better access farther north.

Mile 35 (83) Km 56.5 (133.5): Exit for Britton Creek rest area and picnic tables in trees north of Coquihalla Lakes, headwaters of the Coquihalla River. Access to lakes south along Coldwater Road; resort provides cabin rentals, boat launching and camping. The lakes are stocked with rainbow trout to 2¼ pounds; fly-fish or troll. Coldwater Road continues south down the Coldwater River to Merritt, a good condition forestry road.

Mile 35.5 (82.5) Km 57 (133): Coldwater River bridge. The Coldwater, a tributary of the Nicola River, rises just to the north of Zopkios Ridge. The highway north crosses the Coldwater several times in the next 10 miles/16 km.

Mile 41.5 (76.5) Km 66.5 (123.5): Bridge over Juliet Creek; exit north of bridge for Coldwater River Provincial Recreation Area; fishing and picnicking beside the river. Coldwater has small rainbow and Dolly Varden to 5½ pounds, best fishing July to November. The country is now in the Interior dry belt; the trees are lodgepole pines.

Mile 48 (70) Km 78.5 (44.5): Larson Hill exit, forestry access.

Mile 49.5 (68.5) Km 79.5 (110.5): Begin 6 percent downhill grade northbound. Despite the ruggedness of the terrain, high-

Camping, fishing and swimming are offered at Lac Le Jeune; turnoff at Mile 102.

(Liz Bryan)

way engineers were able to maintain a steady grade, with 6 percent being the steepest incline.

Mile 51 (67) Km 82.5 (107.7): Exit Coldwater Road, alternate backcountry route north to Merritt and southeast to the old railway settlement of Brookmere.

Mile 54 (64) Km 87 (103): Exit to Gillis Lake and the Kane Valley Road, a well-maintained backcountry route to Highway 5A south of Merritt. Excellent cross-country ski trails.

Mile 66.5 (51.5) Km 107 (83): Good view to the north of the city of Merritt and the Nicola Valley, some of British Columbia's best ranchland.

Mile 71 (47) Km 114 (76): Exit to Merritt; rest area by tourist information office in grand log chalet. Also exit to Highway 5A South.

MERRITT (pop. 6,500) has all visitor services, including campgrounds, motels, restaurants and shops. Logging and mining are the major industries here and the city is also at the center of 3 large, historic cattle ranches: the Nicola Ranch, the Quilchena Cattle Co. and the famous Douglas Lake Cattle Co., Canada's largest. Tourism has become more important to Merritt because of the Coquihalla Highway and efforts are under way to restore the city's heritage core. An excellent example is the renovated 1908 Coldwater Hotel with its veranda and 4-story turret crowned by a red cupola. Nicola Valley museum on Jackson Avenue features the human history of the area, including the native Indians, mining and ranching; open daily.

Merritt is surrounded by hills dotted with lakes, many with resorts, most of a rustic nature. The fishing for rainbow trout (known locally as Kamloops trout) is exceptionally good.

Mile 72.5 (45.5) Km 116.5 (73.5): Nicola River bridge. The Nicola rises in Douglas Lake cattle country, flows through Nicola Lake and empties into the Fraser at Spences Bridge on Highway 1. River is fished for rainbow and Dolly Varden trout, whitefish, steelhead and salmon; river is closed below Nicola Lake March through May, above lake January through June. Check restrictions. The valley here is semiarid: notice the sagebrush and yellow pines.

Mile 73 (45) Km 117.5 (72.5): North exit for Merritt; also exit for Highway 5A North to Nicola, Quilchena, Monck Provincial Park, and Kamloops and for Highway 8 which follows the Nicola River northwest to Spences Bridge.

The town of NICOLA was once the supply center of the valley; still has an impressive courthouse, a Victorian mansion and a jaunty little church. Several miles north of Nicola is the Quilchena Hotel, built in 1908 and still providing accommodations in elegant guest rooms, restaurant and bar, tennis courts, boats, riding stables and golf course. Store and gas station adjacent. Across Nicola Lake is Monck

Picturesque church in the town of Nicola at Mile 73.   (Liz Bryan)

Provincial Park; 71 campsites, fishing, swimming, boating. Indian paintings are nearby. Nicola Lake has whitefish, kokanee, burbot and rainbow. *WARNING:* Boaters be prepared for sudden winds.

Mile 76 (42) Km 122.5 (67.5): Chain-up area; highway north starts a long, steady climb up Clapperton Creek into the high forests of the Nicola Plateau. Good view northeast toward the blue twinkle of Nicola Lake.

Mile 85.5 (32.5) Km 135.5 (54.5): Summit (elev. 4,741 feet/1,445m).

Mile 89 (29) Km 143.5 (46.5): Helmer Road exit to Helmer Lake.

Mile 92.5 (25.5) Km 148.5 (41.5): Tiny Quaint Lake tucked into the forest.

Mile 96.5 (21.5) Km 155.5 (34.5): Begin 6 percent downhill grade for next 3 miles/4.5 km northbound.

Mile 102 (16) Km 164.5 (25.5): Meadow Creek Road exit; westbound to Logan Lake and Ashcroft; eastbound to string of fishing lakes, including Walloper, Lac Le Jeune, Stake and McConnell.

LOGAN LAKE (pop. 1,880) lies 9 miles/15 km west, a service center for mine workers in the Highland Valley known for its rich copper deposits. Highland Valley Copper, North America's largest open-pit copper mine is open for tours May through August. Check at

tourist offices in Merritt or downtown Logan Lake. Full tourist facilities.

Walloper Lake and Lac Le Jeune provincial parks and Stake/McConnell Lakes provincial recreation areas all provide excellent fishing for rainbow trout; Lac Le Jeune provides 144 campsites (fee), beach, boat launch and visitor programs. Private resort on lake provides meals, accommodations, boat rentals and a small store with some groceries and fishing tackle. In winter the resort is famous for its cross-country ski trails and also runs a small alpine ski area. There is also an extensive network of ski trails at Stake/McConnell.

For a more leisurely and prettier route north, keep on the Le Jeune road all the way to Kamloops. It joins Highway 1 just east of the Highway 5 junction.

Mile 107.5 (10.5) Km 173 (17): Highway north begins its descent from the plateau into the Thompson Valley; 6 percent downgrade; brake check area.

Mile 113.5 (4.5) Km 183 (7): Exit for Inks Lake; U-turn route.

Mile 117 (1) Km 188 (2): Kamloops city limits.

Mile 118 (0) Km 190 (0): Junction with Trans-Canada Highway 1 (also Canada Highway 97) at Kamloops, B.C.'s fourth-largest city, offering all tourist facilities. Turn to **Mile 379** in the TRANS-CANADA HIGHWAY section for log of that route.

North Cascades Highway

(Washington Highway 20)

See map opposite page.

Efforts to build a highway across the rugged North Cascade mountains began as early as 1893, when Washington State appropriated $20,000 for 200 miles of road. A year later, construction crews were defeated by the seemingly impenetrable mountains. Travelers waited through the first half of the 20th century before construction was started again in 1960. When the project was completed in 1972, Washington Highway 20 spanned the state from Anacortes in Puget Sound to Newport on the Idaho border.

The *NORTHWEST MILEPOSTS*® log begins on the edge of the Skagit Valley at Interstate 5 and Burlington. It proceeds east through the highest and wildest mountains in Washington on a route that has been called one of America's great drives. After winding through the Methow Valley recreation area, it ends in the fruit country of Okanogan, near the site of the first permanent settlement in Washington Territory.

The North Cascades Highway is closed in winter between Colonial Creek Campground (**Mile 70**) on the west side of the Cascades and Mazama (**Mile 120**) on the east side. The highway is open from about mid-April through November, depending on snow conditions. Chains or traction devices are sometimes required. Travelers should check with ranger stations or the State Patrol. In Washington, motorists may call 1-976-7623 for winter pass conditions.

North Cascades Highway Log

Distance in miles from Burlington is followed by miles from Okanogan.

Mile 0 (174.5): Junction with Interstate 5 at Exit 230 to **BURLINGTON** (pop. 3,890). Scenic Chuckanut Drive to Bellingham begins in northern Burlington (see **Mile 659** INTERSTATE 5 section). All services are available in Burlington, including several family restaurants, drive-ins, campground, gas and hospital. The city's 3-day celebration in June features 2 local products (strawberries and dairy) at the annual Berry-Dairy Days.

Although a logging camp was established in 1882, Burlington was not platted until 1890.

With the arrival of the Great Northern Railroad in 1891, the community became the hub of an extensive rail system. Today, its economy is linked to field crops, dairy farming, boat building and chemical manufacturing. MP 60

Mile 4.5 (170): Sedro-Woolley western city limits.

Mile 5 (169.5): Junction with Washington Highway 9 which leads south 21 miles to Arlington and north to Wickersham, Acme and Deming.

The Lake Whatcom Railway to Acme operates a 1-hour scenic trip in antique Northern Pacific passenger cars pulled by an early 20th century steam engine. The ride through the countryside includes picturesque Lake Whatcom. 11 a.m. to 1 p.m. Fee: Adults, $6; juniors 17 and under, $3. MP 65

Mile 5.5 (169): **SEDRO-WOOLLEY** (6,330) city center, park and pool. Sedro (Spanish for cedar) was founded by Mortimer Cook in 1884. In 1889, P.A. Woolley started a community at the Great Northern and Northern Pacific railroad crossing junction nearby and gave it his name. The 2 rival towns eventually merged in 1898 to become 1 town. Downtown buildings display murals depicting Sedro-Woolley's past. The Loggerodeo, held July 4 weekend, celebrates its timber heritage with tree rigging and topping, wood splitting, ax throws and other events. In addition to logging, the economy is based on manufacturing and wood production.

Sedro-Woolley is the gateway to the North Cascades. A visitor information center, the offices of Mount Baker-Snoqualmie National Forest and North Cascades National Park are located on Highway 20 near the western city limits.

Mile 6 (168.5): Sedro-Woolley eastern city limits. MP 66

Mile 6.5 (168): Rodeo grounds.

Mile 7 (167.5): Gateway golf course, 18-hole, north of the highway. MP 67

Mile 7.5 (167): Crossing Haven Creek, which is a protected salmon spawning stream.

Mile 10 (164.5): Crossing Coal Creek, a protected salmon stream.

Mile 10.5 (164): Wiseman Creek.

Mile 13 (161.5): An Indian art museum and gift shop features collector-quality soapstone sculptures, jewelry, rugs and artifacts. Open Friday through Monday. MP 73

Mile 14 (160.5): Access to **LYMAN** (pop. 310) via a side road south of the main highway. Platted in 1884, Lyman was once a busy railroad town. Anticipated industrial growth never materialized. A reroute of Highway 20 and business closures turned Lyman and its neighbor Hamilton into ghostlike towns.

Some of the early buildings still stand. The Birdsey Minkler House, built in 1891, is on the National Register of Historic Places. MP 74

Mile 17.5 (157): **HAMILTON** (pop. 220) was settled around the homestead of William Hamilton. It grew to 1,500 people, 4 saloons, a general store, bank, newspaper, large hotels and a school. The town was plagued with economic problems and floods. During high water, merchants wired wooden sidewalks to hitching posts to keep them from floating away. Both Hamilton and Lyman are still incorporated and have town councils and mayors. In addition to a lumber mill, Hamilton has a store, tavern and a bed-and-breakfast. MP 77

Mile 22.5 (152): Baker Lake Road is a paved Forest Service road which leads 22 miles north to the Baker Lakes Recreation Area. See feature page 238.

Mile 23 (151.5): Birdsview is an unincorporated area linked to agriculture and timber. It offers an inn, grocery and fast-food outlet.

Mile 25 (149.5): Private RV park.

▲ MP 84

Mile 27.5 (147): Shopping center with

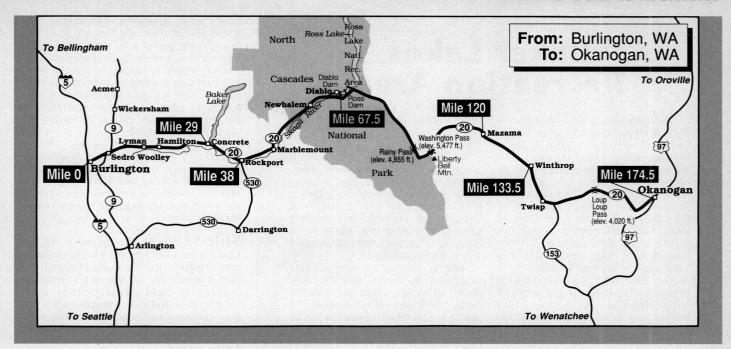

From: Burlington, WA
To: Okanogan, WA

groceries, family restaurant, motel. Delacorte's Restaurant is filled with antique firearms, tools and other collectibles.

Mile 29 (145.5): CONCRETE (pop. 620)
western city limits and airport road. All services are offered including several restaurants, cafes, gas stations, motel and medical clinic. Situated near the banks of the Skagit and Baker rivers, Concrete attracts steelhead, salmon and trout fishermen. A public boat launch is located at the mouth of the Baker River.

From the early 1900s to 1968, a Portland Cement plant was the dominant industry. Following several devastating fires prior to the early 1920s, most subsequent structures were made of concrete. Visitor information office offers a self-guiding brochure covering 15 dams, bridges and buildings dating from 1906 to 1925.

Concrete Municipal Airport with a 2,600-foot runway is used by glider, experimental and antique airplane clubs for fly-ins. There is no fee for using the facility.

Mile 29.5 (145): Crossing Baker River. A
unique fish transfer operation can be seen directly east of the bridge. Migrating salmon are diverted into holding tanks, and a 1,000-gallon tank truck "fish taxi" transports them to Baker Lake spawning grounds. A visitor center features a large topographical map of the Mount Baker area, displays and mounted fish. Open weekdays 8 a.m. to 4:30 p.m. Fish-holding tanks are open to the public 24 hours a day.

Mile 30 (144.5): Concrete eastern city limits.

Mile 33.5 (141): Access south to public fishing on the Skagit River. The Concrete to Rockport section of the Skagit is a popular rafting route known for its gentle rapids and riverbank scenery.

Mile 37 (137.5): Rockport State Park
(purchased from a timber company in 1935 for $1); 50 full hookups, 12 walk-in tent sites and sleeping shelters with bunk beds, group camp, large picnic area, firepits, showers and handicapped facilities. Opportunities for steelhead fishing. Some 5 miles of trails lead through stands of timber (some trees are 300 feet tall and several hundred years old) and marshy bogs to sunlit viewpoints. Stands of old-growth Douglas fir and hemlock are maintained as a natural forest. MP 95

Mile 37.5 (137): ROCKPORT, a small
community 0.2 mile south of the highway, was named for the rocky shores of the Skagit River where boats docked. Limited services are available.

Rockport was overshadowed for several years by rival Sauk City. With the decline of Monte Cristo Mining and panic of 1893, Sauk City became a ghost town, but Rockport survived when the general store was moved across the river to serve several shingle mills. Rockport became a railroad terminus and in 1928 Seattle City Light chose it as a departure point for overnight trips to Newhalem and Diablo Dam.

Mile 38 (136.5): Junction with Washington Highway 530 which leads south to Howard Miller Steelhead Park and Darrington (20 miles). Howard Miller park includes an 1881 restored cabin, Indian dugout canoe, and the Rockport ferry which transported passengers across the Skagit until 1981. The 13-acre park has RV hookups, showers, play area and a boat launch.

The Nature Conservancy's Skagit River Bald Eagle Natural Area is a 1,500-acre preserve. Most of it borders the riverbanks between Howard Miller park and 10 miles east to Marblemount. In winter, large populations of bald eagles gather along the streams to feed on chum salmon. Scenic float trips from

Marblemount to the park are scheduled during the eagle-watching season. ▲MP 98

Mile 40.5 (134): Rest area, south of the highway, is one of the best places to watch bald eagles. During the peak months of January and February, approximately 500 eagles congregate on the Skagit and the Nooksack rivers. MP 100

Mile 43 (131.5): Crossing Corkendale Creek. RV park and motel. ▲MP 102

Mile 44 (130.5): River cabins, 35-unit RV park with hookups, drive-in and museum here. ▲

Mile 45.5 (129): North Cascades National Park ranger station is 1 mile north of the highway. Travel information and free backcountry permits are available here.
MP 105

Mile 47.5 (127): MARBLEMOUNT.
Check your gas gauge as this is the last available gas until you reach Mazama on the east side of the mountains 75.5 miles from here. Gas is available there only during daytime hours and may not be available evenings, Sundays or holidays. The next available gas is 13.5 miles farther at Winthrop, some 90 miles away. Likewise, be prepared to wait for food as there are no restaurants available until Mazama or Winthrop. (Gas and food are available at Diablo Resort for limited time periods.)

Marblemount got its name from its proximity to nearby Marble Mountain and the talc and marble in the area. The Log House Inn, built in 1890, has a restaurant and lounge and 5 rooms which rent for $20 to $24 per night. Gas and RV park available.

The Cascade River joins the Skagit River in Marblemount and is a base for river rafters to launch their craft for float trips; inquire

Baker Lakes Recreation Area

The construction of 2 dams on the Baker River has created a prime recreation area offering hiking, fishing, boating, sailing, swimming and camping in one of the most beautiful regions of Washington state. Lake Shannon, with views of Mount Baker and Mount Shuksan, backs up for 10 miles behind the Lower Baker Dam (completed in 1925). The Upper Baker Dam, built farther upstream and completed in 1959, created Baker Lake, which stretches northward for another 10 miles.

The Baker Lake Road junctions off Highway 20 at Concrete and heads 22 miles north into the Baker Lakes Recreation Area. En route to the Mount Baker-Snoqualmie National Forest and Baker Lakes, the road passes Grandy Creek and Lake, Vogler Lake, Tyee Lake and Lake Shannon. Three miles inside the forest boundary is Koma Kulshan Guard Station and Forest Service fire crews headquarter here. From the Baker Lake Road several Forest Service side roads offer many opportunities for picnicking, hiking and photo stops. Watch for logging trucks on weekdays.

Access to Lake Shannon is difficult. Stumps and submerged logs make powerboating and waterskiing hazardous. Major activities are canoeing, fishing, and watching Washington's largest flock of ospreys. Biologists are studying the ospreys, sometimes called fish hawks, when they return from Mexico and points south each spring to nest on Lake Shannon and Baker Lake. As many as 11 active nests are found in the area representing about 22 adult osprey. The nests are built of sticks on top of snags surrounding the lakes, and biologists have installed additional bowl-shaped nesting sites on tall poles in hopes of encouraging the osprey to nest.

Fishing: Each year Baker Lake is stocked with 50,000 rainbow trout. Whitefish, landlocked king salmon, steelhead, silver trout and Dolly Varden to 10 pounds are caught here. Boat launches are available at Horseshoe Cove Campground near Upper Baker Dam, near Shannon Creek Campground and at Baker Lake Resort.

Hiking: Hikes range from 0.2 mile to several-day backcountry trips and climbs of Mount Baker (elev. 10,778 feet). "The Shadow of the Sentinels," a nature trail, interprets plant life (on 38 metal photosigns) in the surrounding forest, from seedling to giant Douglas firs. Some Douglas firs here are over 600 years old.

Area attractions accessible by trail are Baker Hot Springs, Rainbow Falls, and agate and jasper beds at Swift Creek. The Baker River trail leads through the high passes.

Adjacent to Upper Baker Dam is Glover Mountain Observation Point, offering a view of Baker Dam and nearby Lake Shannon. There is a short nature hike available here.

Camping: Baker Lake has numerous campgrounds along its shoreline and many do not require a camping fee. There are ample parking opportunities for self-contained RV vacationers. Baker Lake Resort operates 2 campgrounds with 47 hookup sites, 100 sites with water and electricity, plus modern and semimodern cabins. Other services are boat rentals, 40 moorage sites, snack bar, store, dump station and boat launches.

Snowcapped Mount Baker in the North Cascades. (Ray Weisgerber)

locally about commercial river rafting firms. A steel bridge across the Cascade River leads to a 23-mile gravel road that dead ends at Cascade Pass, a scenic drive of approximately 3 hours length. A popular hike is the 6-mile trek over Cascade Pass and into the Stehekin Valley. There is a gain in elevation of 1,800 feet in 3.5 miles. At Marblemount, Highway 20 swings sharply north, following the Skagit River eastbound. 🚶🚶▲

Mile 51 (123.5): Crossing Skagit River. The highway follows the Skagit River (designated a Wild and Scenic River) from Marblemount to Diablo Dam and travels along the power lines coming from the dam area to Seattle.

Mile 52 (122.5): The highway enters Ross Lake National Recreation Area. The recreation area divides North Cascades National Park into 2 units. Its 107,000 acres include 3 Seattle City Light power projects. Food, lodging, boat and motor rentals, tackle, and basic camper supplies can be obtained in the area.　　　　　　　　MP 111

Mile 55.5 (119): The highway crosses Damnation Creek.

Mile 57.5 (117): Exit to Thornton Creek Road and access to the Thornton Lakes trailhead. Backcountry use permits are required for camping along the trail. Wood fires are prohibited.　　　　🚶🚶MP 117

Mile 60 (114.5): Goodell Creek Campground, with 22 tent/RV sites, drinking water, pit toilets and boat launch area for river rafters. No hookups. The campground is a launching spot for white-water rafting down the Skagit to Bacon Creek. It can be safely run by experienced rafters, kayakers and white-water canoeists. The first 6 miles are Class II. The latter part is Class III.　▲ MP 119

Mile 60.5 (114): Highway crosses Goodell Creek and enters the Seattle City Light village of **NEWHALEM**. The utility and the National Park Service maintain a joint visitor center here. The visitor center has information about the area, tours, hiking trails and restroom facilities. A store is available in Newhalem for last-minute purchases. Newhalem houses City Light employees who maintain the operation of the powerhouse and dams. Also some highway and National Park Service personnel reside in Newhalem. Children are now bused to Concrete for school since the local school closed.

Entering Newhalem from the west, a turnoff to the right leads southeast across the Skagit River bridge to the Newhalem Campground, with 129 tent/RV sites (suitable for small trailers), flush toilets and dump station. No hookups. The side road continues on to the Newhalem Creek trailhead access or to Ladder Creek Falls and Rock Gardens located behind the Gorge powerhouse.　🚶🚶▲ MP 120

Mile 62.5 (112): Highway passes through a 500-foot-long tunnel.

Mile 63.5 (111): Turnoff and parking area for viewing the Gorge Creek waterfalls and Gorge Lake. Walk across the steel bridge for the best views; a spectacular sight and photo opportunity.   MP 123

Mile 64 (110.5): Highway passes through 200-foot-long tunnel.

Mile 66 (108.5): Junction with road north to Seattle City Light village of **DIABLO** and tour center for Skagit Tours. Seattle City Light, a municipal utility, has been offering tours of their Skagit River dams since 1928. The 4-hour Skagit Tour is a popular attraction with visitors. Beginning at the tour center, the guided tour includes a ride up an incline railway, a boat cruise across Diablo Lake to Ross Dam powerhouse and back, and a family-style meal at Diablo. The cost is $21 for adults, $19 for seniors over 62 years and $10 for children 6 to 11. Children 5 and under are free. Reservations are strongly advised. The tours are offered from mid-June to the beginning of September. No tours Tuesday and Wednesday. Reservations are accepted starting in mid-April. For reservations and information phone Seattle City Light's Skagit Tour desk at (206) 684-3030.

Diablo is the trailhead for the Sourdough Mountain hike, which gains 5,200 feet in 5 miles and culminates in spectacular views of the North Cascades, Mount Baker and southern Canada.   🚶🚶★ MP 126

Mile 66.5 (108): Pyramid Lake trailhead.
🚶🚶

Mile 67.5 (107): Diablo Dam Road turnoff north to Ross Lake Resort. The road ends at a parking lot where tugboats transfer passengers to the resort at 8:30 a.m. and 3 p.m. daily. The resort has 10 cabins, 3 bunkhouses built on log floats, full marina services with boat and canoe rentals, water taxi for backpackers and hikers, and boat launch.

Mile 70 (104.5): Colonial Creek Campground and trailhead for Thunder Creek trail. The campground is the largest along the highway with 162 tent/trailer sites, flush toilets, dump station and boat launch. No hookups. Docks, fish-cleaning station, nature walks. Fee: $5 per night. The main campground is often filled to capacity and additional campsites may be available in the annex located across the highway. The lake is good for swimming, canoeing, kayaking, rafting, fishing and all water-related activities. Nature programs and campfire programs are offered during the summer months. The 30-mile trail passes through a variety of vegetation, ascends Park Creek Pass (elev. 5,400 feet), and descends into the Stehekin Valley.

The highway may be closed from here east in the winter.   🚶🚶⛵▲ MP 130

Mile 71.5 (103): Diablo Lake overlook. The lake appears jade green due to rock particles, ground into dust by glaciers, which stay suspended in the water. Light reflected off the particles changes the lake's color.

Footbridge over Thunder Creek, accessible at Mile 70.   (L. Linkhart)

Numerous turnouts are available in the next 2 miles east to the Ross Lake overlook; all offer ample pulloff space and a directional photo exhibit pinpointing the mountains, valleys and highlights in the viewing area.

Mile 73 (101.5): The Ross Lake viewpoint offers the only view of Ross Lake from the highway. Ross Lake is 24 miles long, covers some 12,000 acres, and reaches north into Canada. Diablo Lake covers 910 acres. Ross Lake was named for J.D. Ross, the Seattle City Light superintendent who conceived and promoted the Skagit Project.   MP 133

Mile 74 (100.5): Ross Dam trailhead and parking for approximately 40 cars. The trail leads north for numerous hike-in camping areas along Ross Lake. There are facilities for loading and unloading stock for horseback trips into the mountains.   🚶🚶 MP 135

Mile 74.5 (100): Happy Creek Interpretative Trail is a 0.3-mile boardwalk with 13 informational panels, which leads into an old-growth forest. Wheelchair accessible. 🚶🚶

Mile 78.5 (96): Bridge over Panther Creek; large parking area for the East Bank trailhead for hiking and horses.   🚶🚶

Mile 79.5 (95): Highway enters Okanogan National Forest. Land management changes from the National Park Service to the Forest Service at this point.

Mile 80 (94.5): Okanogan Creek trailhead.   🚶🚶

Mile 81 (93.5): Eastern boundary, Ross Lake National Recreation Area.

Mile 81.5 (93): Canyon Creek trail, north of highway, connects several trails entering the Pasayten Wilderness in the Okanogan National Forest.   🚶🚶 MP 141

Mile 85 (89.5): Ample parking for East Creek trailhead.   🚶🚶 MP 144

Mile 88.5 (86): Highway passes over Granite Creek.   MP 148

Mile 91.5 (83): Easy Pass trailhead. The scenic, 24-mile hike takes about 3 days as it leads to Colonial Campground. 🚶🚶 MP 151

Mile 96 (78.5): Swamp Creek trailhead, parking area and winter chain-up area for westbound traffic.   🚶🚶

Mile 96.5 (78): Crossing Porcupine Creek. Highway eastward begins steep 0.7-mile climb.   MP 156

Mile 98 (76.5): The Pacific Crest Trail crosses the highway; summit of Rainy Pass (elev. 4,855 feet). Picnic area. ⛱ MP 158

Mile 99 (75.5): Bridge Creek trailhead. Turnout south of highway for about 10 cars.   MP 159

Mile 101 (73.5): Whistler Mountain (elev. 7,790 feet) viewpoint. A spectacular photo stop.

Mile 102 (72.5): Blue Lake trail, south of highway, and beginning eastbound of steep 3-mile grade. The trail is a gradual 3-mile slope to Blue Lake.

Mile 102.5 (72): After a steep climb, the

highway crests the more dramatic Washington Pass (elev. 5,477 feet). This is the highest point on the North Cascades Highway, and is slightly over a mile above sea level. A turnoff leads 0.2 mile to overlook access. There is ample parking, a manned visitor information booth in summer, picnic areas and restroom facilities. The nearby overlook (handicap accessible) provides a breathtaking view of the rugged Cascades and 7,550-foot Liberty Bell Mountain. Also visible from here are the Early Winter Spires (elev. 7,808 feet) and the highway's hairpin curves below. Excellent photo opportunities. Picnic area.

In the next couple of miles eastbound the highway descends the east side of the Cascades in hairpin curves as it follows the mountainsides. Notice the snow avalanche chutes that are the cause for closure of the highway pass in the winter months. ⊼ MP 162

Mile 106.5 (68): Turnout south of highway with excellent views of Silver Star Mountain. MP 164

Mile 107.5 (67): Cutthroat Creek Road, trailhead and small campground with hitching rack, truck parking and water for stock. The 1.7-mile trek to Cutthroat Lake is considered an easy day-hike. 🏃‍♂️▲

Mile 109 (65.5): Lone Fir Campground, an Okanogan National Forest campground with pit toilets, firepits and rustic campsites. ▲ MP 168

Mile 111 (63.5): Silver Star Creek turnout area.

Mile 114.5 (60): Steep descent for trucks and large RVs next 1.5 miles.

Mile 116 (58.5): Klipchuck Forest Service Campground; 6 tent sites, 40 tent/RV sites, water. Fee: $5 per night. Fishing and hiking trails. 🏃‍♂️🐟▲ MP 175

Mile 116.5 (58): Cedar Creek trailhead access. A gentle hiker and horse trail leads 2 miles to Cedar Falls and 6 miles to Cedar Creek Basin. 🏃‍♂️

Mile 118 (56.5): Okanogan National Forest boundary. Early Winters Creek and western unit of Early Winters Campground are south of the highway. ▲

Mile 118.5 (56): National Park Service/ Forest Service Early Winters Visitor Center has information, maps, brochures, and hiking trail information. Closed in winter. The Mazama unit of Early Winters Campground, south of the highway, has water available, but no hookups. Fee: $5 per night. ▲

Mile 120 (54.5): **MAZAMA** offers a motel, restaurant, phone, gas and a small store. Rental horses for trail rides are available. It is also a base for heli-skiing operators.

Mile 124.5 (50): Rocking Horse Ranch operates trail rides and overnight pack trips. Private campground with 12 full hookups for trailer/tents. ▲ MP 184

Mile 133.5 (41): Crossing Chewack River and entering **WINTHROP** (pop. 400), offering all services including gas, family restaurants, fast-food outlets, lodging and campgrounds. The Western-style town of Winthrop is well worth a stop to investigate. It is a good chance to stretch your legs, enjoy a meal or snack, visit one of the many local businesses or stop in at the visitor center. The visitor center offers publications, brochures, hand-outs, and information on the Methow Valley, Lake Chelan, Grand Coulee Dam and other travel destinations.

In 1891, Guy Waring opened a store and post office at the forks of the Methow and Chewack rivers. He named it after Colonial Governor John Winthrop of Massachusetts. His friend, Owen Wister, visited in 1898 and may have been inspired by the town and setting for parts of his novel, *The Virginian.* Winthrop's false-front buildings and Western theme date to 1972 and were a conscious effort to attract visitors. Original buildings include The Last Trading Post, which was the first trading post, and a post office. Waring's Duck Brand Saloon has been a restaurant, pool hall, school, church and hospital. It is currently a community hall. Waring's log cabin is the Shafer Museum and is on the National Register of Historic Sites.

With over 300 days of sunshine per year, Winthrop is frequented by campers, photographers, hikers, fishermen and water sports enthusiasts. Seventeen campgrounds are situated within 8 miles of town. Pearrygin Lake State Park, 5 miles northeast, has 30 full hookups, 27 water only, and 26 standard units. Reservations required. Open for snowmobiling, cross-country skiing, fishing, boating and hiking. The Methow Valley is a top Washington snowmobiling and Nordic ski area.

Check with the Winthrop Ranger Station for highway conditions, hiking trails, and information on secondary roads to area streams and lakes. A sign advises westbound travelers that services and sanitary facilities are limited for the next 86 miles. 🏃‍♂️🐟▲★ MP 193

Mile 134 (40.5): Access to smoke jumper base and private golf course with open play guest policy.

Frontier-style storefronts in Winthrop, Mile 133.5. (Ray Weisgerber)

Mile 135 (39.5): Private campground on riverbank. ▲ MP 194

Mile 136.5 (38): Access to Sun Mountain Lodge, Twin Lakes and Patterson Lake. Sun Mountain Lodge, 8 miles north of the highway, has 50 rooms, 2 heated pools, tennis courts, a golf course, trout fishing and over 50 miles of hiking trails and cross-country skiing. ⛷🚶➤ MP 196

Mile 141.5 (33): TWISP (pop. 885), name derived from an Indian word for "yellow jacket." Since its founding in 1899, Twisp's fortunes have rested on mining, ranching and agriculture. It has survived several fires, floods and freezing cold which destroyed fruit crops. The coldest temperature ever recorded in Washington state was at Twisp in 1968 when the thermometer plunged to -48°. Between 2 and 2¹/₂ feet of snowfall can be expected in the Twisp area in winter. Twisp offers all traveler services including gas stations with towing and repair service, restaurants, motels, 2 medical clinics, private RV parks, ranger station and headquarters for the Twisp Recreation Area. Recreation encompasses fishing, hiking, horseback riding, rafting, snowmobiling and cross-country skiing. Washington's largest mule deer herd winters here. Over 100 birds are indigenous to the area. 🚶➤▲ MP 200

Mile 143 (31.5): Golf course.

Mile 143.5 (31): Twisp eastern city limits. The section of the highway between Twisp and Okanogan is called the Loup Loup Highway.

Mile 145 (29.5): Junction with Washington Highway 153 which heads south 31 miles to join U.S. Highway 97 at Pateros. Airport road is to the north of the highway. MP 204

Mile 148 (26.5): Campbell Loop and Beaver Creek turnoff.

Mile 151 (23.5): Okanogan National Forest boundary. Established in 1897, the Okanogan is one of the nation's oldest national forests. It spreads from here to the Okanogan-Ferry county line, and from the Canadian border to the Methow-Chelan divide. Okanogan is an Indian word meaning "rendezvous." MP 210

Mile 155 (19.5): Junior Campground; 5 tent/RV sites, water. $4 per night. MP 214

Mile 155.5 (19): Loup Loup Pass Summit (elev. 4,020 feet) and Summit Road.

Mile 156 (18.5): Loup Loup Ski Bowl, north of highway, offers 4 primary runs and a vertical drop of 1,200 feet, 2 lifts and 2 rope tows. A day lodge, snack bar, equipment rentals, snowmobiling and cross-country and telemark lessons are available. Tent/trailer camping. 🚶▲ MP 215

Mile 163.5 (11): Loup Loup Creek. Campground near the creek has 11 picnic

Threadlike waterfall tumbles down the steep slopes of the North Cascades. (L. Linkhart)

sites, 20 tent/RV sites and water. $4 per night. 🏕▲ MP 222

Mile 164 (10.5): Rock Creek Campground with 6 sites, group shelters. ▲

Mile 164.5 (10): Little Loup Creek and campground. ▲

Mile 165.5 (9): Leader Lake Campground; 16 sites, boat launch and fishing. ➤▲ MP 224

Mile 169 (5.5): Historical marker commemorates confrontation between cattlemen and sheepmen near here in the early 1900s.

Mile 172 (2.5): Junction with road leading south to Malott and Brewster.

Mile 174 (0.5): Junction with Washington Highway 215, U.S. 97 business loop, museum and visitor information center.

Mile 174.5 (0): OKANOGAN (pop. 2,340) is located approximately 20 miles west of the first American settlement in Washington, Old Fort Okanogan. The present town began as a trading post in 1886. It includes the former settlements of Alma and Pogue. Until 1906, when an irrigation system was built, Okanogan was little more than a river landing and general store. Local orchards grow cherries, apricots, peaches, pears and apples. Okanogan is the county seat and headquarters for Okanogan National Forest, plus several other government agencies and county offices. Okanogan offers motels, gas, restaurants and most facilities, while its sister city, Omak, 4 miles north, serves the area as the commercial center and offers all visitor services.

At Okanogan, Washington Highway 20 merges with U.S. Highway 97. They continue as a joint highway north to Tonasket. Turn to **Mile 630.5** in the U.S. HIGHWAY 97 section for log of that route.

Sawtooth Scenic Route

(Idaho Highway 75)

See map opposite page

In its 170-mile northward journey from Shoshone to Challis, Idaho Highway 75, dubbed the Sawtooth Scenic Route, introduces the motorist to some of the finest mountain scenery and outdoor recreation in the West. This is where railroad baron Averell Harriman chose to locate America's first ski resort, Sun Valley, in the 1930s. Over the next several decades most of the big Hollywood stars managed to make at least one trip to Sun Valley to see and be seen. Sun Valley is still one of the top winter sports resorts in the country and also has an extensive summer season.

Just to the north, Sawtooth National Recreation Area (NRA) remains one of the West's last great mountain treasures to be discovered by the traveling public. Though popular with Idahoans, it is still relatively unknown as a vacation destination. Nearly the size of Yosemite National Park, it was seriously considered for national park status in the 1960s. See Sawtooth National Recreation Area description in the MAJOR ATTRACTIONS section.

Mileposts along Idaho Highway 75 reflect distance from the Idaho-Nevada border via U.S. Highway 93 South.

Sawtooth Scenic Route Log

Distance from Shoshone is followed by distance from Challis.

Mile 0 (170): SHOSHONE (pop. 1,280); has all services, including 1 motel and 6 restaurants. A railroad town and supply point on the east-west line of the Union Pacific Railroad, it was once the connecting point where transcontinental passengers boarded trains for Sun Valley. The wide main street is split by the railroad tracks and lined with old brick and false front buildings that make it look like a set from a Western movie. MP 74

Mile 4 (166): Groceries and gas available.

Mile 7.5 (162.5): Side road west to Mammoth Cave, 1.5 miles (gravel road). Mammoth Cave is a 0.2-mile-long lava tube discovered in 1902. A museum there has a large collection of mounted bird specimens. Admission is charged.

Mile 15 (155): Clear view of the distinctive shape of the Sawtooths to the north. Sparse sagebrush here barely covers broad fields of lava. View of 1,499-foot Kinzie Butte to the east. MP 89

Mile 15.5 (154.5): County road to Richfield, 16 miles east.

Mile 16 (154): Gas and cafe on east side of highway. Side road leads west to Shoshone Ice Caves, lava tubes with ice formations caused by cool air passing through. Museum has fossil exhibits; admission fee is charged. MP 90

Mile 16.5 (153.5): Highway crosses a good example of exposed lava flow. View of 1,458-foot Black Butte Crater to the northwest.

Mile 17 (153): Magic Dam historical marker. Magic Dam was completed in 1910 to store water for 89,000 acres of irrigated farms near Shoshone and Richfield. It is now a fishing and recreational area.

Mile 18 (152): Crossing Big Wood River. Side road leads west 10 miles to Magic Reservoir.

Mile 19 (151): Highway crosses Richfield Canal and begins gradual ascent into the foothills northbound.

Mile 24.5 (145.5): Side road leads west 5 miles to Magic Reservoir.

Mile 27 (143): Highway crests hill and begins descent into the Big Wood River Valley farmland northbound. MP 101

Mile 27.5 (142.5): Cafe, RV park with 35 sites and hookups available. ▲

Mile 28 (142): Rest area at junction with U.S. Highway 20, an alternate route across the Camas prairie through Fairfield to Interstate 84 at Mountain Home. Access to Magic Reservoir; good fishing for rainbow and brown trout, waterskiing, windsurfing, sailing, 1 resort and RV park with 60 sites. ⛵▲MP 102

Mile 37 (133): BELLEVUE (pop. 1,500); all services, including 1 motel and 4 restaurants. Private RV park with 31 sites, 25 with hookups, is open April through November.

Founded as a mining town when rich silver-lead deposits were discovered in the nearby hills in 1880, Bellevue now serves surrounding farms. Topographical features in this area have fascinating names dating from the mining era — Cowcatcher Ridge, Minnie Moore Gulch, Poverty Flat. In the spring and fall it is not unusual to encounter Basque shepherds driving flocks of hundreds of sheep along this road accompanied by a bread loaf-shaped wagon and a couple of skillful border collies. The railroad right-of-way on the east side of the highway is the original line that caused Sun Valley to be built. ▲

Mile 39 (131): Wood River Mines historical marker. Lead and silver strikes beginning in 1879 made this, for a time, Idaho's leading mining region. Hailey had Idaho's first phone service in 1883 and 3 daily newspapers; a Ketchum smelter pioneered electric lighting in Idaho.

Mile 41 (129): Friedman Memorial Airport, used by both private and commercial aircraft serving Sun Valley. MP 115

Mile 42 (128): HAILEY (pop. 2,920), offers all services, including 8 restaurants and 4 motels. Hailey was also a mining town and now serves primarily vacationers. The main street has been gentrified with a number of the old buildings spruced up with new paint and fixtures. Blaine County Historical Museum (N. Main and Galena) occupies an 1882 brick building and features pioneer artifacts and a collection of political campaign memorabilia. Ezra Pound was born in Hailey in the house on the northeast corner of Second Avenue and Pine Street. MP 116

Mile 48 (122): Highway crosses Big Wood River. Both the Big and Little Wood rivers, often fished by Ernest Hemingway, are excellent trout streams. Scores of elegant new homes and ranchettes on both sides of the highway reflect the major influx of affluent migrants to this valley in the last couple of years.

Mile 51 (119): Private RV park with 46 sites, 44 with hookups, showers and laundry facilities. ▲

Mile 52.5 (117.5): Highway crosses Big Wood River.

Mile 53 (117): Elkhorn Road leads 3 miles east to Elkhorn Village. RV campground beside river on west side of highway has 78 sites, 32 hookups, showers, laundry, groceries, mini-golf, recreation room and swimming pool. ▲

Mile 54 (116): KETCHUM (pop. 3,280) and SUN VALLEY (pop. 660) have 58 restaurants, 21 motels and resorts, and 3 RV parks with 125 hookups. Sun Valley/Ketchum Central Reservations handles reservations and information for the whole area: phone 1-800-635-4156.

Though the towns are actually about a mile apart, Ketchum and Sun Valley are thought of as one and restaurants and accommodations spill across the boundaries between the 2 communities. Sun Valley (and nearby Elkhorn Resort) winter sports facilities are focused on Bald Mountain and Dollar Mountain. The resort has 66 downhill runs with a vertical drop of 3,400 feet serviced by 8 double chairlifts and 8 T-bar lifts. It was here that James Curran, a Union Pacific engineer, invented the chairlift and installed the first of them on Dollar and Proctor mountains in 1936. Today the resort offers a complete range of winter activities including cross-country skiing, sleigh rides, helicopter skiing, ballooning, ice fishing, snowmobiling and snowshoeing.

Elegant old Sun Valley Lodge is worth a visit whether or not you stay there. Built in 1936 of formed concrete disguised to look like wood, the lodge sits surrounded by gardens, ponds and an ice skating rink where world champions perform in summer ice shows. Hundreds of photos of the rich and famous who have visited Sun Valley adorn a hallway wall adjacent to the lobby. Hemingway wrote *For Whom the Bell Tolls* in room 206 at the lodge. Nearby, the Sun Valley Opera House shows the Sonja Henie Film, *Sun Valley Serenade,* every day of the year.

In summer, the resort offers a host of activities including bicycling, golf, tennis, riding, fishing, trap and skeet shooting, hiking, river rafting, archery, soaring and several music and arts events. Fly fishing is superb and some area streams such as Silver Creek (pronounced "crick" by Idahoans) are world famous. Lessons and guides are available from several shops in Ketchum. ☇🏃🐟▲★

Mile 56 (114): Ernest Hemingway is buried here in the Ketchum cemetery. MP 130

Mile 56.5 (113.5): Small picnic site beside Big Wood River. 🏕

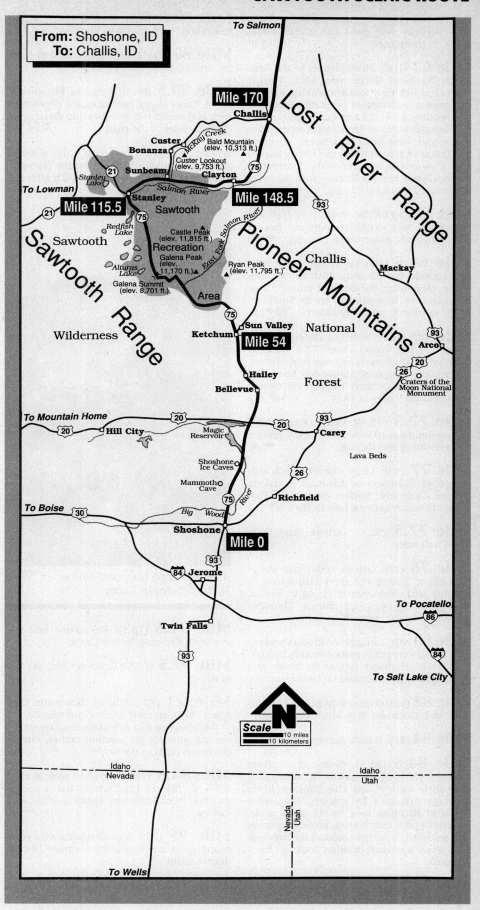

Mile 61 (109): Crossing Big Wood River. The highway will cross this river several times on this route.   MP 135

Mile 62 (108): Headquarters to the Sawtooth National Recreation Area. Visitor center has free tape tour for playing in your car, several audio-visual programs, literature and restrooms. Open 8 a.m. to 5:30 p.m. daily.

Sawtooth National Recreation Area stretches north and west from this point, covering 756,000 acres (about the size of Rhode Island) and 3 mountain ranges — the Sawtooths, White Clouds and Boulders — with 40 peaks reaching 10,000 feet or more.

Mile 62.5 (107.5): North Fork National Recreation Area (NRA) campground has 39 sites, pit toilets, groceries and fishing. ⛟▲

Mile 64.5 (105.5): Wood River NRA campground has 32 sites, flush toilets, groceries, swimming, fishing and nature trails. Mountains to the southwest are the Smokeys, to the northeast are the Boulders. 🚴⛟▲

Mile 69 (101): Note the Aspen thickets along the Big Wood River. This route is carpeted in wildflowers by early July. Historical marker explains Alexander Ross and Hudson's Bay Company trappers discovered the Sawtooth Valley in 1824.   MP 143

Mile 72.5 (97.5): Prairie Creek NRA campground has 10 sites, flush toilets, groceries, swimming and fishing. ⛟▲

Mile 77 (93): Large volcanic rock outcroppings. Road on east side leads to Galena Pioneer Cemetery. Miners made their first strike of lead ore (galena) here in 1879. MP 151

Mile 77.5 (92.5): Galena Stage Stop offers trail rides.

Mile 78 (92): Galena Lodge has horseback riding, hiking and mountain biking in summer and cross-country skiing in winter. The lodge is open for dinner Thursday through Saturday; brunch on Sunday.

Mile 80 (90): Terraces on sides of the steep hills ahead were cut to reduce erosion by grazing sheep. Highway begins its steep and winding climb northbound to Galena Summit.

Mile 82 (88): Overlook to Boulder Mountains and Alexander Ross historical marker.

Mile 84 (86): Galena Summit; 8,701 feet.

Mile 84.5 (85.5): Overlook provides splendid views of the Sawtooth Mountains, Sawtooth Valley and the Salmon River drainages. Gouged by glaciers, the valley below is 30 miles long by 15 miles wide. Dozens of pika, chipmunks, ground squirrels and bold Clark's jays live around the overlook and often approach tourists looking for a handout.

Mile 87 (83): Historical marker on the Salmon River.

Mile 88.5 (81.5): Road to south leads to headwaters of the Salmon River.

Mile 89 (91): Crossing the Salmon River for the first time northbound.

Mile 89.5 (80.5): Crossing Frenchman Creek. Large glacial moraines, the deposits of rock and debris left by retreating glaciers, lie on both sides of the road.

Mile 91 (79): Sawtooth City, a small corridor of private land within the National Recreation Area. Residents named it after the historic mining town nearby.   MP 165

A field of sego lilies and lupine in the Sawtooth Valley. (L. Linkhart)

Mile 91.5 (78.5): Restaurant and gas available. Crossing Smiley Creek.

Mile 92.5 (77.5): Groceries and gas station.

Mile 93 (77): Site of Sawtooth City (circa 1879), an early mining community.

Meadows on east side of the road are spring nesting grounds for sandhill cranes, one of the tallest birds in the world.

Mile 94.5 (75.5): Road to west leads 2 miles to Alturas Lake which has 4 campgrounds, boat launches, sandy beaches and fishing. ⛟▲

Mile 95 (75): Busterback Ranch, year-round guest ranch offering a variety of outdoor activities.

Mile 97 (73): Road leads west 1 mile to Pettit Lake, a small quiet lake with timbered

shoreline and a campground.   ▲

Mile 98.5 (71.5): Crossing the Salmon River.

Mile 100 (70): Crossing Champion Creek. The White Cloud peaks are coming into view to the east for northbound travelers. MP 174

Mile 100.5 (69.5): Fourth of July Creek.

Mile 102 (68): Fisher Creek.

Mile 104 (66): Sessions Lodge offers accommodations, cafe, gas, groceries, 16 RV spaces with hookups. Obsidian found in this area is a black, glassy volcanic rock made when lava cools quickly.   ▲

Mile 105.5 (64.5): Crossing Williams Creek.

Mile 106 (64): Idaho Rocky Mountain Ranch, another guest ranch and restaurant that offers fishing, watersports, hiking and horseback riding. The handsome log lodge, built in 1929 and said to be one of the best log structures in the West, was the former retreat of the president of Frigidaire, Winston Paul.   🚴⛟

Mile 106.5 (63.5): Crossing Gold Creek.

Mile 109.5 (60.5): Sawtooth Fish Hatchery, open 8:30 a.m. to 5 p.m.

Mile 110.5 (59.5): Highway crosses the Salmon River and slices through a glacial moraine.

Mile 111 (59): Junction with road to Redfish Lake. The largest lake in the Sawtooths, Redfish is named for the sockeye that come here to spawn. Fishing in both the lake and nearby streams is outstanding. The resort here has boats for rent, restaurant, cabins, horseback riding, swimming, sightseeing excursions on the lake, hiking trails and stunning views of the Sawtooths. Gas, groceries and 10 NRA campgrounds with 138 sites are available.

Redfish Lake Visitor Center has nature exhibits, audio-visual programs, map, interpretive programs, self-guided nature trail, guided nature walks, hiking and auto tours. Open 9 a.m. to 6 p.m., late June through Labor Day.   🚴⛟▲MP 185

Mile 113 (57): Stanley ranger station, open weekdays year-round, 8 a.m. to 5 p.m.

Mile 115.5 (54.5): STANLEY (pop. 140), offers all visitor services, including 7 motels/lodges, 5 restaurants, 1 gas station and 3 private RV campgrounds. Stanley has the unenviable reputation of being the coldest town in the state, where -50°F has been recorded. It is also one of the primary outfitting spots for rafting trips down the Salmon River, including single-day excursions from Stanley, and horsepacking and guided hiking trips into the surrounding mountains. For information on these services, contact Idaho

Float trips on the Salmon River are offered out of Stanley. (L. Linkhart)

Outfitters and Guides Association, P.O. Box 95, Boise, ID 83701; phone (208) 342-1438. Scenic flights over the Sawtooths and White Clouds are available from the Stanley airport. In winter local dealers rent snowmobiles.

The Ponderosa Pine Scenic Route, Idaho 21, enters Stanley from the west and offers the opportunity (with Interstate 84 and Idaho Highway 75) for a loop trip through this whole region from Boise. The highway follows the white water Payette River, climbs over 2 summits of more than 6,000 feet and passes through the gold rush relic town of Idaho City. From Stanley to the outskirts of Boise it is 130 miles.

Mile 116.5 (53.5): Gas, lodging, groceries and cafe. Idaho 75 is designated the Salmon River Scenic Route north from here. The highway follows the river closely as it swings almost due east for most of the way to Challis, threading through narrow canyons between the mountains.

Mile 119.5 (50.5): Salmon River NRA campground has 132 sites, pit toilets, laundry facilities and fishing.

Mile 121.5 (48.5): Riverside NRA campground offers 18 sites, pit toilets and fishing.

Mile 122 (48): Mormon Bend NRA campground has 17 sites, pit toilets and fishing.

Mile 123.5 (46.5): Basin Creek campground offers 13 sites, pit toilets, fishing. The highway and river wind along the bottom of the canyon with mountains rising nearly a thousand feet on either side. Note the thickly-wooded north-facing slopes and the open sagebrush terrain on the south slopes due to temperature and rainfall variations.

Mile 127.5 (42.5): Sunbeam Hot Springs. Hot water bubbles from the slope on both sides of the road; there is a small unused rock bathhouse and a large wooden hot tub resembling a horse trough just below the road. It was built by locals for soaking in the hot mineral waters; visitors are welcome to use it.

Mile 128.5 (41.5): SUNBEAM has gas, cafe, groceries and float trips available. The remains of Sunbeam dam jut into the river below the highway. Built in 1909-1910 to supply electricity to Sunbeam mine and mill, it is the only dam ever built on the Salmon River. In 1934, after years of controversy because it blocked the salmon and steelhead runs, the dam was dynamited.

A gravel side road leads 9 miles north to the ghost town of Bonanza, 1 mile farther to the Yankee Fork gold dredge and another 2 miles to the mining relic town of Custer and the Custer museum. The gold rush really got under way here on Yankee Fork in 1875. Both towns peaked during the late 1800s when the combined population reached about 5,000, then faded and finally folded in 1910.

A few cabins are all that remain of Bonanza; Custer is somewhat better preserved. A pioneer cemetery is situated on a hillside about a mile beyond the Bonanza Forest Service guard station. The massive Yankee Fork gold dredge operated between 1939 and 1952 and now sits beached on piles of rock waste at the mouth of Jordan Creek. It is open for tours daily, June through Labor Day, from 10 a.m. to 5 p.m. The Custer Ghost Town Museum has a collection of historic mining equipment and other pioneer memorabilia.

Mile 131 (39): Crossing Yankee Fork and Salmon River. Turnouts along here provide good vantage points for watching the many rafters and kayakers who float this river in summer.

Mile 132 (38): Crossing Warm Springs Creek.

Mile 134 (36): Crossing Peach Creek.
                                        MP 208

Mile 135 (35): Snyder Springs picnic area.

Mile 135.5 (34.5): Crossing Gardner Creek.

Mile 136.5 (33.5): Burnt Creek Inn offers cabins, RV park with 17 sites, hookups, cafe and **groceries**.

Mile 139 (31): Crossing Slate Creek.

Mile 139.5 (30.5): Highway crosses the Salmon River.

Mile 140 (30): Mill Creek.   MP 214

Mile 141 (29): Leaving Sawtooth National Recreation Area eastbound.

Mile 141.5 (28.5): Thompson Creek.

Mile 142 (28): Small, unnamed residential community with handsome old log barn on the north side of the highway.

Mile 143 (27): Yankee Fork ranger station, Challis National Forest.   MP 217

Mile 146.5 (23.5): Crossing the Salmon River. Note colorful green lichen on the rocks on the south side of the river.

Mile 148.5 (21.5): CLAYTON (pop. 43), has a cafe, groceries and gas. Clayton was founded in 1881 as the site of a smelter for nearby mines. The smelter closed in 1904. Several mines in the adjacent mountains are still active, producing primarily silver.

Mile 161.5 (8.5): Domestic buffalo graze on the south side of the highway. Valley is dotted with hay and cattle ranches.

Mile 162.5 (7.5): The ghost town of Bayhorse is located 2.5 miles up Bayhorse Creek.

Mile 163 (7): Bayhorse Recreation Site on the north side of the highway adjacent to the river, has picnic tables, pit toilets and fishing access.   MP 237

Mile 169.5 (0.5): Shoshone Indians used the steep bluff just to the north as a buffalo jump. Buffalo would be driven over the cliffs so the Indians could harvest the meat and hides.

Mile 170 (0): Junction with U.S. Highway 93. Challis is 1 mile north.

For more information on Challis, turn to **Mile 305** in the U.S. HIGHWAY 93 section.

The Islands

San Juan Islands, Whidbey Island, Vancouver Island, Gulf Islands, Queen Charlotte Islands, Ferry Systems

Land meets sea in a flurry of islands along the Northwest Coast. There, where the Pacific Ocean is anything but pacific, lies a cruiser's paradise. The scenic, sheltered waterway called the Inside Passage is "inside" of islands — countless hundreds of them — which take the brunt of the ocean surge and storms. The Northwest's islands range in size from rocks that disappear beneath the highest tides to Whidbey Island, largest in the contiguous United States, and Vancouver Island, the continent's largest on the Pacific Coast. Their total miles of shoreline outdistance the girth of the globe.

Ferries serve the major islands, putting them within easy reach. Among those with special appeal to visitors are Washington's jewel-like San Juans, historic Whidbey Island and the rural refuges of Bainbridge and Vashon. The latter 2 are only a half-hour commute from Seattle's urban heart.

Visitors to the Canadian metropolis of Vancouver (near but not on the island of the same name) are just 2 hours by ferry from Victoria. That "little bit of England" is just a sample of what Vancouver Island has available to see. Ferries zigzag between the big island, the mainland and the smaller islands in between (including the Gulf Islands, near Victoria). Most remote of the Canadian islands served by ferry are the Queen Charlottes, famed for totem poles.

A triangular route popular with motorists links Seattle, Victoria and Vancouver. Starting in Seattle, drive north to the Washington state ferry terminal at Anacortes. Cruise through the San Juans to Victoria. From there, take a British Columbia ferry through the Gulf Islands to Vancouver. A drive back to Seattle is the trip's final leg.

San Juan Islands

The first inhabitants of the San Juan Islands, the Lummi Indians, believed that human life began in a wilderness paradise on San Juan Island and that the land of the islands was truly sacred. In the 1770s and 1780s, Spanish explorers arrived to chart the waters and islands of the archipelago. A look at a map today will establish the importance of these explorers — Lopez de Haro,

View from Mount Constitution, Orcas Island.

(Ray Weisgerber)

Jacinto Caamano, Galiano, Valdez, Salvador Fidalgo, Qiumper, Juan de Guemes and others. Later, the English and the Russians began to stake claims in the islands. Finally, with the arrival of George Vancouver in the 1790s to chart the channels and bays, the Russians withdrew.

In 1841, a U.S. expedition led by Capt. John Wilkes established American claim to the islands. British and American rivalry escalated during this period of joint occupancy culminating in the infamous Pig War which ended with a border settlement in 1872. The islands were finally American.

Today, islanders probably agree with the Lummis — that the islands are a wilderness paradise. A moderate climate, friendly people, the easy-going way of life, and lack of hectic traffic make these tranquil islands an attractive haven for vacationers and sightseers. There are 172 named islands out of 400, (700 islands are counted at high tide), totaling 175 square miles. Fewer than 35 of those are inhabited and only the 4 biggest, San Juan, Orcas, Lopez and Shaw, can be reached by Washington state ferries.

By car, bicycle or on foot, travelers visit the San Juans via the Washington State Ferry System from Anacortes. Anacortes, on Fidalgo Island, is reached from Exit 230 off Interstate 5 by traveling west about 8.5 miles on Washington Highway 20. The route through Anacortes is well marked. Ferries serve Lopez, Shaw, Orcas and San Juan islands as well as Sidney, BC. The islands are a favorite vacation destination and the ferries can be very crowded during the summer. Long lines, a long wait and full campgrounds can be exasperating if you are not prepared. Make sure you arrange for overnight accommodations well in advance, arrive at the ferry terminal early and expect a wait if you are taking your vehicle on board. Be sure to check current ferry schedules or phone (206) 464-6400 for information. Not all ferries make all stops. Overnight parking is available near the Anacortes ferry terminal.

Gray Line Water Sightseeing offers narrated cruises of the San Juan Islands from May to October. Inquire locally for details or call (206) 441-1887.

Gray Line of Seattle offers daily bus service from Seattle to the Anacortes ferry terminal. Call (206) 624-5077 for details. Bicycle and car rentals are available on San Juan and Orcas (not located near the ferry docking site).

West Isle Air of Anacortes offers direct charters and several others including Lake Union Air Service, Kenmore Air and San Juan Airlines connect from major cities such as Seattle, as well as offering inter-island service.

Charters and rentals of private boats may be arranged in Seattle, Anacortes or on the islands themselves for inter-island travel.

Lopez Island

The first stop on the ferry from Anacortes is Lopez Island, a 29-square-mile island of 1,200 people. Because of its rugged shoreline and lack of good harbors, it is the least visited island among pleasure boaters, but bicyclists find it their favorite because of the rural atmosphere and the lack of tiring hills and busy traffic.

From **UPRIGHT HEAD**, where the ferry lands, it is approximately 1.3 miles to Odlin County Park where there is an old Civil War cannon and a beached boat for kids to play on. The beach is one of the best in the San Juans; great beachcombing and clamming.

The hub of activity on Lopez Island is **LOPEZ VILLAGE**, located about 4 miles from the ferry landing. There are stores, restaurants,

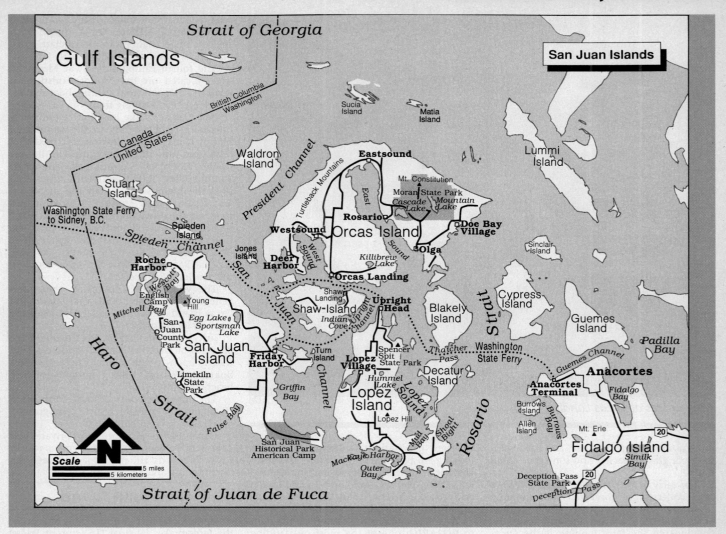

a wonderful bakery, a bank, post office, library, medical clinic and a historical museum that features artifacts and photos from Lopez Island's past.

Hummel Lake has a bicycle camp, the only one of its kind in the islands. Rental bikes are available here. It is also a great spot to fly-fish for stocked rainbow trout, picnic or swim. No gas powered boats are allowed on the lake.

The Richardson Store is an old-time general store, once a major shipping port and base for a large fishing fleet. This is a popular spot for cyclists needing an ice cream break. The old cannery still remains.

Agate Beach is a small public beach on Outer Bay at the south side of Lopez. There are picnic tables, pit toilets and a stairway descending to the beach — a great place to hunt for agates or interesting pieces of driftwood.

Spencer Spit State Park offers the visitor many attractions — clam digging, fishing, bicycling, beachcombing, swimming, camping, canoeing and marine views. Spencer Spit is an outstanding example of a sandspit surrounding a saltwater lagoon that has evolved over a long period of time by the action of the wind and surf. There is a sign at the park entrance that explains the geology and ecology of this unique lagoon.

Lopez Island has a private golf course (located near the airport) open to the public for greens fees.

Shaw Island

The second stop for ferry passengers is Shaw Island, the smallest of the major islands at 8 square miles.

First-time visitors to Shaw Island are surprised to see a nun in her Franciscan habit operating the ferry slip. The nuns also run the island's only store, post office, marina, laundromat and 2 gas pumps. The store is a remarkable old-time general store stocked not only with the usual fare but also imported cheese, beer and wine, a selection of gifts and baskets, gift wrapping and beautiful greeting cards. They also feature herbs and spices locally grown and dried from the Benedictine monastery near the middle of the island.

Shaw is a heavily wooded island with meadows, pastures and orchards. Most of the 17 miles of road are inland, with few views of the water and no access to bays. Because there are no accommodations or restaurants, Shaw gets few visitors.

In the middle of the island where Blind Bay Road intersects with Hoffman Cove Road, there is a "little red schoolhouse." The one-room schoolhouse with an enrollment of 10 students is listed on the National Register of Historic Places.

Approximately 2 miles from the ferry terminal at Indian Cove is Shaw Island County Park, the location of the only public campsites. They are large and situated above South Beach, one of the loveliest sandy beaches in the San Juans. On hot summer days the water of the bay warms enough for swimming.

Orcas Island

The third stop for Washington state ferry passengers, horseshoe-shaped Orcas Island is the largest of the group (57 square miles) though second in population to San Juan Island. The quiet, mood-setting ambience and the enchanting land and seascape of Orcas Island make this a popular destination for Northwest travelers.

Between the Turtleback Mountains to the west and Mount Constitution rising 2,400 feet to the east are green pastures with sheep and cows, picturesque split rail fences and rolling hills with forests of fir trees. The 125

Ferry arrives at Orcas Landing on Orcas Island. (Staff)

miles of shoreline feature bays and coves with sandy or gravel beaches and sometimes high bluffs.

The ferry arrives at **ORCAS LANDING**, a small collection of stores that cater primarily to tourists waiting for the ferry and pleasure boats that stop to fuel up and resupply. Overlooking the ferry landing is the Orcas Hotel, a 3-story Victorian resort built between 1900 and 1904, which is now on the National Register for Historic Places. It was extensively restored in 1985 and once again offers lodging. A bullet hole through one of the veranda posts gives testimony to the escape in the early 1900s of a bank robber who jumped to freedom over the porch railing.

An immediate left after debarking from the ferry puts you on the main road of the island, Horseshoe Highway. Follow the highway north 2.5 miles from the ferry landing and turn west on Deer Harbor Road to the community of **WEST SOUND** at the base of 1,500-foot Turtleback Mountain. There is a yacht club, marina and store. Four miles past West Sound is **DEER HARBOR**, a charming town of clapboard buildings which date from the 1890s. The marina, a favorite stopping place for pleasure boaters, provides moorage, fuel, launching, boat rentals, supplies, groceries, gift shops, restaurants, showers, laundry and a swimming pool.

EASTSOUND, the population center for the island, has been the main business community of Orcas Island since the 1880s. Some of the original buildings still exist. Outlook Inn, built in 1883, and the beautiful little Emmanuel Episcopal Church, built in 1886, are good examples. Restaurants, shops,

galleries, gas stations, a library, bank and lodging are available to the visitor. The Orcas Historical Museum, housed in 6 homestead log cabins, features island pioneer and Indian artifacts collected by Ethan Allan, the county superintendent of schools during the 1900s.

Near Eastsound is the turnoff on the right to **ROSARIO**, one of the most outstanding historical landmarks of the San Juans. The estate was built in 1904 by Robert Moran, Seattle mayor and millionaire shipbuilder. When the 47-year-old businessman was told by his doctor that he had a year to live, he sold everything and bought almost a quarter of the land on Orcas Island and built the mansion. No expense was spared. An organ with 1,972 pipes, installed by Moran, is still used regularly and visitors can admire the intricate parquet floors, rare hardwood paneling, solid mahogany doors and the imported stained glass window. All of the original buildings of Rosario are on the National Register of Historic Places. Moran didn't die immediately, and in 1921 he donated 3,600 acres of his land to the state of Washington to be used as a park.

Moran State Park is considered one of the finest parks in the state. The park, encompassing nearly 5,000 acres of forest, features 4 campgrounds, 1,800 feet of saltwater shoreline, 5 freshwater lakes, almost 30 miles of hiking trails, 4 waterfalls and the highest peak in the San Juans, Mount Constitution (elev. 2,409 feet). Moran is a popular campground. Write ahead for reservations: Moran State Park, Star Route Box 22, Eastsound, WA 98245.

Three of the campgrounds are located at Cascade Lake. The lake offers swimming, a

boat launch, boat rentals, fishing and windsurfing rentals. There are a picnic area, shelter, ranger station, an interpretative display and a number of hiking trails.

The fourth campground is at Mountain Lake, located off the Mount Constitution Road. It has good trout fishing, boat rentals, boat launch and hiking trails.

Past Cascade Lake less than a mile, a 6-mile-long road ascends to the summit of Mount Constitution. The road is closed after dusk from June through August. On the way to the summit is Summit Lake and Little Summit (elev. 2,032 feet) with views that rival the main summit. On top of Mount Constitution is a stone fire lookout and observation tower, built in 1936, which is a replica of a 12th century Russian fort. The tower provides spectacular 360-degree views of Canada, the Olympic Mountains, the Cascade Range, the Strait of Juan de Fuca and the San Juan archipelago.

The village of **OLGA** offers the oldest general store on the island, a restaurant and Orcas Island Artworks Cooperative featuring work by local artists.

Just south of Olga is Obstruction Pass, 80 acres of Dept. of Natural Resources land that is open to the public. The park offers boating, fishing, hiking, picnicking and beachcombing.

The tiny village of **DOE BAY**, northeast of Olga, offers a private resort, campground, beach and mineral baths.

Orcas Island also offers a private golf course, open to the public for greens fees in Crow Valley, on the main road between the ferry landing and Eastsound.

San Juan Island

Approximately 1½ hours from Anacortes, the ferry makes its final U.S. stop at Friday Harbor on San Juan Island before sailing on to Sidney, BC, on Vancouver Island. San Juan Island is the most populated and the "busiest" island in the archipelago. It is an island of forests, meadows, orchards and farmlands that gently slope down to the sea and in some places drop off abruptly from bluffs pounded by the surf.

Friday Harbor, the county seat and the largest and only incorporated town in the San Juan Islands, is a picturesque business community of grocery stores, arts and crafts galleries, gift shops, real estate offices, bookstores, fine restaurants, a movie theater and more. The marina, which has doubled in size in the past couple years, hosts thousands of transient boats each summer from the United States and Canada. In July, the island hosts a 3-day dixieland jazz festival. There are a number of inns and resorts around the town.

FRIDAY HARBOR is also the home of the University of Washington Oceanographic Laboratories, established in 1903. Scientists from all over the world visit the labs to research marine life in the underwater environment of the islands. The labs are open to the public for tours during July and August. The labs also operate a 200-acre biological preserve located on False Bay which is open to the public for walking and beach observation.

There are 2 museums in Friday Harbor. The San Juan Historical Museum is located on Price Street off Spring Street in an 1890s homestead. It features artifacts from pioneer days and the famous Pig War incident. The Whale Museum (62 First Street N.) is the only museum in the U.S. strictly devoted to whales. It features a life-size model of an infant humpback and a scale model of an Orca skeleton. There is also a special room for children's activities.

San Juan Island National Historical Park was established to commemorate the settlement of the border dispute between the United States and England in 1872 which was started in 1859 by a shot that killed a pig. It is really 2 separate parks in 2 locations, English Camp and American Camp. Picnic areas and drinking water are available at both camps. There are no campgrounds at either site.

English Camp (429 acres) lies in the tree-sheltered cove known as Garrison Bay, 10 miles northwest of Friday Harbor. The park contains a historic display, a small formal garden and 4 original buildings — barracks, guardhouse, hospital and commissary. Near the barracks is a 300-year-old big-leaf maple, one of the world's largest. A hiking trail starts at the camp and winds up Young Hill past a tiny cemetery where 4 British soldiers are buried. The 680-foot summit provides wonderful views of Haro Strait, Vancouver Island, the Olympic Mountains, the Canadian Gulf Islands, Mount Baker and the Cascade Range.

American Camp (1,222 acres) is on the barren, windswept southeast tip of the island, about 5 miles from Friday Harbor. Two original buildings, an officers' quarters and a laundress' quarters, survive. There is a 0.7-mile interpretive trail starting near the information center that provides a self-guided tour with signs portraying the Pig War history and other features of the park. On some summer weekends there are slide shows and actors recreate the lives of the soldiers and settlers who lived at the time.

One phenomenon at the park is the extremely large population of rabbits. The loose glacial soil of sand and gravel is ideal for tunneling and entrances can be seen everywhere. Use caution when walking to avoid stepping into one. Along the interpretative trail the soil has been cut away to reveal the intricate network of tunnels that comprise a rabbit warren. The rabbits, protected from hunting and trapping, are a major food source for the bald eagles, golden eagles, great horned owls and other predatory birds that live on the island.

The only sand dune area in the San Juan Islands is located at Cattle Point. The Department of Natural Resources has almost 7 acres with facilities that include toilets, garbage cans, parking lot, and picnic shelter with tables and stove. The Cattle Point Light, a white concrete tower, is perched on the dunes 80 feet above the beach.

ROCHE HARBOR, the one-time site of a Hudson's Bay Co. trading post and the largest

English Camp is 10 miles northwest of Friday Harbor on San Juan Island. *(Staff)*

lime producing company west of the Mississippi River, was turned into a first-class resort and marina in the 1950s. One of the largest private pleasure boating marinas in Washington north of Seattle, Roche Harbor attracts thousands of boaters from Canada and the U.S. The Hotel de Haro, on the National Register of Historic Sites, hosted many famous people including Presidents Teddy Roosevelt and William Howard Taft. Other points of interest at Roche Harbor include the beautiful formal gardens of the hotel; Our Lady of Good Voyage Catholic Church, the only privately owned Catholic church north of Mexico; the Afterglow Vista Mausoleum; the old lime kilns and lime quarry; and the company store which is still in operation. At sunset, there is a traditional flag-lowering ceremony when Canadians and Americans join together to honor their countries.

San Juan Island County Park is located on the west side of the island, 12 miles from Friday Harbor at Smallpox Bay, the site of an Indian village wiped out by smallpox many years ago. The popular 12-acre park is at the head of the bay, with magnificent evening views across Haro Strait to the lights of Vancouver Island. The park has 11 campsites. A tiny log cabin in the campground was built in the early 1900s.

Past San Juan County Park is Lime Kiln Lighthouse, the location of the first Whale Watching Park in the country. Pods of whales passing very near to the rocky shoreline offer whale watchers incredible close-up views. The park has interpretative displays and will soon have underwater hydrophones enabling visitors to hear the whales. Whale Watch Park is a day-use park with parking, picnic tables and pit toilets.

Sportsman's Lake (4 miles from Friday Harbor) and nearby Egg Lake are open for swimming and fishing. There is a privately owned campground located at Sportsman's Lake. The marshes surrounding the lakes are ideal for bird-watching in the spring.

Whidbey Island

It's possible to tour Whidbey Island in one day, but to do so would be a shame. The largest island in the contiguous United States has much to see: beautiful parks, rich farmlands, bed and breakfast inns, shops for browsing, historical monuments, military installations and a spectacular coastline.

The island lies in the rain shadow of the Olympic range, consequently enjoying more sunshine and less of the rain for which Puget Sound is known. When Capt. George Vancouver visited the island in 1792, he found it densely populated with friendly Skagit Indians. Vancouver named the place for Joseph Whidbey, master of their ship, *Discovery.*

Two Washington state ferry routes serve Whidbey. One runs between Mukilteo (45 minutes north of Seattle) and Clinton, at the island's southern end. The other ferry runs between Port Townsend on the Olympic Peninsula and Keystone, near the island's midpoint. It is possible to tour the island without taking the scenic ferry ride by approaching the island at the north end via Deception Pass bridge on Highway 20.

The main highway that runs the length of the island has 2 designations: Washington Highway 525 between the Clinton ferry dock and the Keystone ferry turnoff (30.5 miles); and Washington Highway 20 from the Keystone ferry turnoff to the north end of the island at Deception Pass (31.5 miles). (Highway 20 begins at the junction with U.S. 101, 13 miles south of Port Townsend. From the Keystone ferry dock to the junction with Highway 525 it is 3.5 miles.) Roads off the main highway invite exploration of coves and beaches. There are several campgrounds on the island and many bed and breakfast inns around the island if you want to make more than a day trip out of a visit.

LANGLEY, at the southeast end of the

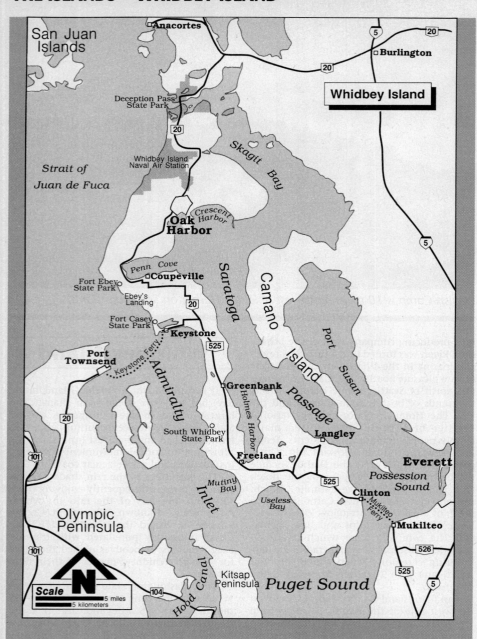

Admiralty Head Lighthouse at Fort Casey, Whidbey Island. (Tom Barr)

Perched on the shore of Penn Cove, Coupeville is one of the oldest cities in the state and home of the Island County Historical Museum. Many of the town's Victorian homes have been restored.

OAK HARBOR, the largest city on the island, has all traveler services, including a hospital. Two golf courses are open to visitors. Oak Harbor was named for the many Garry oaks which grew to great size in this area. Many sea captains and their families settled here to be within sight of the water. In the 1850s Irish settlers dominated the area, but in the 1890s Hollanders came from Michigan and the Dakotas. In 1941, the Navy arrived to build the Whidbey Island Naval Air Station. The air station, with 9,850 military and civilians and 13,600 dependants, comprises 45 percent of the island's population.

At the north tip of the island on Highway 20 is Deception Pass State Park and Deception Pass bridge. Deception Pass is a treacherous channel separating Whidbey and Fidalgo Island with tiny Pass Island in the middle of the channel. Swirling water and spectacular views of the sea and distant islands make this a favorite picnic, camping and beach-combing spot. A good vantage point is afforded by Deception Pass bridge where there is ample parking and restroom facilities. Deception Pass State Park actually spans the channel, encompassing beaches and forests on Whidbey and Fidalgo islands and with hiking trails and 2 freshwater lakes. The park has 251 campsites, picnic tables, stoves, bathhouse, dump station and seasonally operated concession stands.

North of Deception Pass a spur road off Highway 20 leads 4.5 miles to Anacortes on Fidalgo Island, departure point for Washington state ferries to the San Juan Islands. Main Highway 20 continues east 11.5 miles to junction with Interstate 5 (see **Mile 658**, Exit 230 in the INTERSTATE 5 section) at Burlington. Washington Highway 20 continues east as the North Cascades Highway (see the NORTH CASCADES HIGHWAY section).

island, is known for its small town atmosphere and upscale shops. An arts and crafts festival in July and the Island County Fair in August draw crowds, but otherwise Langley is a nice place to browse. The elegant Inn at Langley serves up gourmet dinners on Friday and Saturday nights (reservations only) in a beautiful cedar-shingled building. For those on a smaller budget, the Dog House reputedly has the best burgers on the island. Langley has several bed and breakfast inns.

Near Greenback, mid-island, are the red barns of Chateau Ste. Michelle where they grow the loganberries to make Whidbey's Liqueur.

Adjacent to the Keystone-Port Townsend ferry dock is Fort Casey State Park and the picturesque farmlands of the Ebey's Landing National Historical Reserve just beyond. The Fort Casey area, along with Ebey's Landing and prairie, the town and Coupeville and

other sites around Penn Cove (together encompassing more than 17,000 acres), make up the historical reserve. The reserve was named for Colonel Issac Ebey who was killed by Haida Indians in 1857. Today this reserve provides a living record of the 19th century exploration and settlement of Puget Sound.

Established in the 1890s, Fort Casey became one of the string of gun emplacements that guarded Puget Sound through WWII. The fortifications and underground bunkers are open for exploring. Admiralty Head Lighthouse at the park is now a small museum. From the top of the tower are sweeping views across the inlet and the Strait of Juan de Fuca.

COUPEVILLE is the most historically-rich town on the island. Some of its early character is present in the main street's wooden storefronts now filled with souvenir and antique shops, restaurants and boutiques.

Vancouver Island

Beautiful Vancouver Island lies just off the Northwest coast at the border between the United States and Canada, its southern tip extending below the 49th parallel. The rest of its 282-mile length runs northwesterly, sheltering smaller islands on the landward side.

Both ships and planes link Vancouver Island with the mainland. Connecting points in the U.S. include Seattle (for scheduled air service and summer sailings of the B.C. Stena Lines' *Vancouver Island Princess;* also Clipper Navigation's *Victoria Clipper,* a jet-propelled catamaran), Anacortes (for Washington state ferries), and Port Angeles (for Black Ball ferries). Most of these ships carry vehicles as well as foot passengers. All dock in or near Victoria. For more information, see Ferry Systems this section.

Air Canada, Canadian Airlines International, Air B.C. and Time Air fly from the mainland to Victoria. Helijet Airways schedules flights between downtown Vancouver and downtown Victoria. British Columbia ferries run between Tsawwassen (south of Vancouver) and Swartz Bay (just north of Victoria); from Horseshoe Bay (west of Vancouver) to Nanaimo; and from mainland Powell River to Comox. British Columbia ferries also run between Port Hardy (at the north end of Vancouver Island) and Prince Rupert (on the mainland farther north). Pacific Coach Lines operates buses between Vancouver and Victoria via the B.C. ferries.

Within Vancouver Island, rail, bus, air and water service connects major towns and other key points along the coast. The Esquimalt and Nanaimo Railway operates a daily passenger dayliner between Victoria and Courtenay, with 19 stops along the way. Island Coach Lines operates buses between Victoria, Nanaimo, Port Alberni, Campbell River and Port Hardy (with connections to the B.C. ferry *Queen of the North* at Bear Cove).

The backbone of the island is the Insular Mountain Range that runs the island's length. Its jagged, snowy peaks punctuate the skyline, contrasting with the greens and blues of forest and sea. The mountains are at their most impressive midway up the island at Strathcona Provincial Park.

West of the mountains the climate is stormy and the coastine rugged. The open ocean, beautiful scenery, picturesque settlements and Pacific Rim National Park are major attractions for visitors here. Settlement has gravitated toward the island's sheltered, sunnier eastern side. Most of the people live in a narrow strip along the east-facing coast, half of them clustered around Victoria. Trans-Canada Highway 1 and Provincial Highway 19 run north from Victoria to Port Hardy, linking major communities along the way (see log of these highways this page). In addition, several very good east-west roads span the island's 62-mile width.

Forestry is a major industry. Much of the land is under lease to timber companies, now harvesting a second generation of trees

Victoria Harbor is central to downtown Victoria.

(Liz Bryan)

and planting more. Agriculture, fishing and mining (of coal and even gold) were early contributors to the island's development. Farming and fishing remain important, but mining has played out. Now recreation and tourism are significant elements in the economy.

Britain's Captain Cook, who landed on the island's west shore in 1778, was the first European visitor. Fur traders followed, and Vancouver Island came under the influence of the Hudson's Bay Co. Victoria became the company's headquarters in 1842 and grew to be the economic hub of the region and eventually, capital of British Columbia.

The island today has more than 50 provincial parks; public and private campgrounds abound. A list of hotels, motels, lodges, trailer parks and campgrounds on the island is available free from Tourism British Columbia; ask for the current *Accommodations Guide.* The same agency offers a free *British Columbia Road Map and Parks Guide* which includes a summary of all provincial park facilities.

Recreational opportunities on the island range from whale watching to antique hunting, from salmon fishing to sunbathing on sandy beaches, from the most rugged backpacking to the most civilized taking of crumpets and tea.

If you look at a map of Vancouver Island, you can see why most of the settlements and the roads concentrate along the eastern shore. The western side of the island, exposed to the full brunt open Pacific, is steep, rugged and tortuous, fretted with long, deep and sinuous fjords that make land access difficult. By contrast, the eastern shore faces the sheltered waters of the Inside Passage and it is smooth and gently sloped, with miles of sandy beaches.

Trans-Canada Highway 1 and Provincial Highway 19 together provide continous access up the east coast from Victoria to Port Hardy, a distance of about 300 miles/500 km. Considered as a whole, the highway provides a stimulating contrast between the settled and domesticated south and the wilderness north. Up the island as far as Campbell River, the road threads its scenic way betwen a whole string of resort communities that are famous for recreational fishing and boating in the island-sprinkled waters of the Strait of Georgia. But north of Campbell River, the relatively new highway forges away from the coast to provide a lonely, austerely beautiful route through the forested heartland before reaching the north coast communities of Port McNeil and Port Hardy. Port Hardy is the terminus for the B.C. ferry route to Prince Rupert and points north.

Trans-Canada Highway 1/ B.C. Highway 19

Mile 0 (305) Km 0 (491): Just north of downtown Victoria, at Mayfair Shopping Centre, Highway 17 branches off to Saanich and the B.C. ferries connection to the mainland at Tsawwassen.

Mile 1 (304) Km 1.5 (489.5): Tillicum Road south; Gladstone Avenue north. Take Gladstone for an unhurried route to the Dominion Astrophysical Observatory and Butchart Gardens.

Mile 2 (303) Km 3 (488): View of Portage Inlet.

Mile 3.5 (301.5) Km 6 (486): Exit for Highway 1A to Colwood, Fort Rodd Hill, Sooke and along the West Coast Road (Highway 14) to Port Renfrew and the start of the West Coast Trail in Pacific Rim National Park.

Victoria

Victoria, the capital city of British Columbia with a population of 250,000, occupies the southeastern tip of Vancouver Island. The city's European past dates from 1843 when the Hudson's Bay Co. built a fort on the shore of Portage Inlet which today is Victoria's inner harbour. From this tiny outpost, the fur traders controlled the fur trade of the Pacific and established farms nearby to ensure availability of fresh meat and supplies. Vancouver Island became a British Crown Colony and the townsite of Victoria grew up outside the fort walls.

During the Fraser River gold rush, Victoria boomed as the major supply point, its population swelled to more than 2,000 — 10 times that of Seattle. Population dwindled when the rush was spent, but Victoria had established itself as the premier settlement; it became the capital of the new colony of British Columbia and its future growth was assured.

Today, Victoria is a gracious, friendly city. All that is left of the HBC fort are 2 mooring rings in the rocky bluffs below Wharf Street. The grand sandstone and granite parliament buildings, topped by a copper dome, have replaced the old wooden gingerbread capitol buildings known as The Birdcages. The city has grown larger and more commercial, but it has retained its colonial air.

Flower baskets embellish all the old-fashioned streetlamps; there are manicured parks and squares, specialty import shops and outdoor cafes, magnificent Victorian houses and Gothic spired churches. Under the very nose of the aristocratic Empress Hotel, across an elegant esplanade, sleek modern cruise ships fill the harbour, and horse-drawn carriages and scarlet London double-decker buses tour the city. It's picturesque and theatrical.

The Empress Hotel, Victoria's elegant dowager (modestly covered with ivy), has undergone extensive renovation without sacrificing its atmosphere of British gentility. Afternoon tea is served with the traditional finger sandwiches, crumpets, seed cakes and Earl Grey tea. Other signs of "a little bit of England" are fish and chips, dark pubs with dart boards, sweet shops, shops selling Wedgewood and Spode, Scottish tartans and Irish linens, cricket matches in Beacon Hill Park, and lots of roses and formal gardens.

Victoria is an excellent city for walking. Most of the historic places of interest are conveniently located near the inner harbour where the Parliament Buildings are lit up at night like a fairy-tale castle. Stop at Tourism Victoria at the corner of

Colorful Butchart Gardens outside Victoria. (David A. Shott)

Government and Wharf streets for maps and information on the sights. This spot is also one of the best for taking photographs of the Parliament Buildings and the inner harbour with its bobbing little boats.

The city wears a mantle of old-fashioned days, but new things are in the works. Behind the Empress, a new convention centre has mushroomed, all in glass like a crystal palace. In the heart of town, Eaton Centre has already opened phase one of a massive new shopping facility; and across the harbour on the former Songhees Indian lands, hotels, condominiums, shopping plazas and parks are taking shape. This is a major development and won't be finished for another 8 years, though some of the new hotels are already open for business.

Though shopping is a major activity for tourists in Victoria (Government Street between Humboldt and Yates streets is the place to start), don't miss the Royal British Columbia Museum (Belleville and Government streets), renowned for its innovative dioramas of British Columbia's human and natural history, Northwest Coast Indian exhibits and reconstructions of pioneer life. The museum is open daily.

The Art Gallery of Greater Victoria (1040 Moss Street) contains, among its outstanding collection of Oriental art, the only Shinto shrine in North America. Phone (604) 384-4101.

Three restored Victorian homes are open free to the public. Helmcken House, built in 1852 (phone 387-3440); Point Ellice House (phone 387-5953) dates from 1860; and the Craigflower farmhouse and school from 1856 (387-3067).

Craigdarroch Castle (phone 592-5323), with its turn-of-the-century furnishings and stained glass windows, should not be missed. Coal baron Robert Dunsmuir built this lavish sandstone mansion to

persuade a Scottish wife to come to Victoria. Open daily.

The Crystal Gardens, a lovely tropical conservatory located behind the Empress Hotel, has a songbird aviary, streams, waterfalls and tropical plantings that make a lovely setting for afternoon tea. Open daily, admission is $5.50.

Victoria has many parks and gardens. Thunderbird Park, located in the same block as the Royal British Columbia Museum, has a collection of totem poles and an authentic longhouse. During summer months you can sometimes watch Indian carvers working on new totems. Beacon Hill Park has wonderful views of the water and informal gardens.

For the unusual, there are the Royal London Wax Museum, the Pacific Undersea Gardens and the Classic Car Museum.

Outside Victoria (13 miles/27 km north), Butchart Gardens attracts thousands of visitors each year to its 50 acres of beautifully landscaped gardens. Built on a former rock quarry, the gardens are arranged in different international styles and something is in bloom no matter what time of year you visit. During the summer, however, it is best to visit the gardens in the early morning or late afternoon to miss the busloads of tourists. Open daily. Phone (604) 652-5256.

Also outside of town is Fable Cottage, a fanciful fairy-tale house set amid extensive gardens with some interesting outdoor animation. Near here is Hatley Castle, now the Royal Roads Military College, with extensive formal gardens and views.

And for "authentic" English pubs outside the downtown area, try Four Mile Roadhouse, established in 1858, on the road to Sooke; and the Prairie Inn (1859) in Saanich. Prairie Inn even brews its own ale.

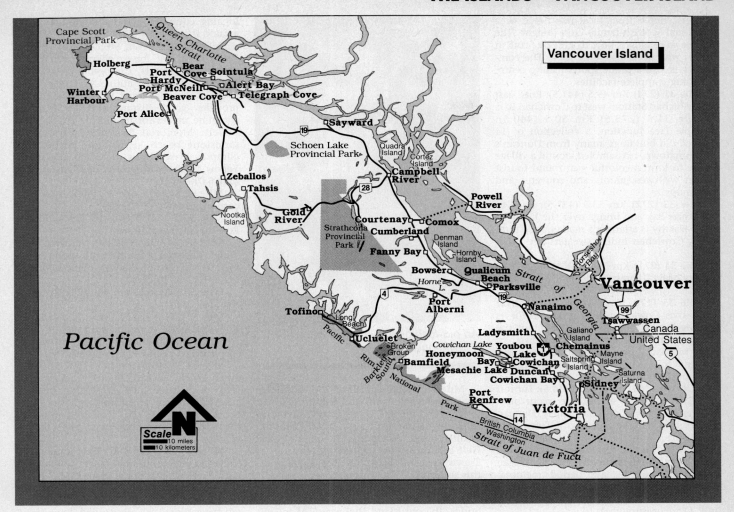

Vancouver Island

Mile 6.5 (298.5) Km 10 (481): Exit to Thetis Lake Regional Park. A large natural forest park laced with hiking trails. The horseshoe-shaped lake with sandy beaches is popular for swimming, canoeing and fishing for trout and bass.

Mile 8 (297) Km 13 (478): Tourist Information Centre beside Langford Lake.

Mile 8.5 (296.5) Km 13.5 (477.5): Sooke Lake Road to Goldstream Provincial Park with 160 vehicle/tent sites, showers, sani-station. There is a fee. Visitor Interpretative Centre has programs June through August. The forested park is named for the Goldstream River which witnessed a brief flurry of gold mining activity in 1863. Some of the park trails are old prospectors' paths and one leads to an old gold mine. The river was important to the native Coast Salish Indians and still supports a large fall salmon run. Naturalists enjoy the diversity of the forest that ranges from the dry Arbutus and Garry oaks at the higher elevations to the near rain forest conditions with 600-year-old Douglas firs and red cedars.

Mile 9 (296) Km 15 (476): South end of Malahat Drive, a scenic stretch of highway that climbs high above Saanich Inlet. This road was originally a trail cut across the bluffs to get cattle to the Victoria market. It became a wagon road in 1884 and a narrow paved highway in 1911. It is now a 4-lane super highway, but the views are still magnificent. Malahat is Indian for "the place where one gets bait."

Mile 10 (295) Km 16 (475): Trail access to Niagara Falls and canyon. To the east, a good view down to the head of Finlayson Arm.

Mile 14 (291) Km 22.5 (468.5): Dutch Latch restaurant commands excellent views.

Mile 16 (289) Km 25.5 (465.5): Turnoff for the south end of Shawnigan Lake (4.5 miles/7 km), a summer cottage area and provincial park for picnicking, swimming, fishing and waterskiing. Memory Island, accessible by boat only, has good walking trails, picnicking, and excellent bird-watching. No camping permitted.

Mile 16.5 (288.5) Km 26.5 (464.5): Exit to Spectacle Lake Provincial Park, 1.2 miles/ 2 km, with picnic tables, hiking trails, fishing for rainbow trout, swimming from small beach. You can hike around the lake in less than 1 hour.

Mile 17 (288) Km 27.5 (463.5): Malahat Summit, 1,156 ft/352m. Parking for view of Saanich Inlet and peninsula and, if it's clear, to the mountains on the mainland. The most spectacular peak is Mount Baker in Washington State.

Mile 18.5 (286.5) Km 29.5 (461.5): Arbutus rest area and viewpoint.

Mile 20 (185) Km 32.5 (458.5): Exit east to Bamberton Provincial Park overlooking Finlayson Arm. There is a developed sandy beach, 50 campsites; fee.

Mile 20.5 (284.5) Km 33.5 (457.5): Exit west to small car ferry across Saanich Inlet to Brentwood Bay. Several sailings daily.

Mile 21 (284) Km 33.5 (457.5): North end of Malahat Drive. Look for golden broom in bloom along the road in May and June, a legacy of early British settlers.

Mile 23.5 (281.5) Km 38.5 (452.5): Community of Mill Bay and a travel information centre. North access road to ferry. Distance to Victoria via ferry is given as 16 miles/26 km.

Mile 24 (281) Km 39 (452): Road to Shawnigan Lake, 3 miles/5 km east. Roads encircle the lake and connect with forestry roads to Port Renfrew, west about 40 miles/ 64 km, and south to Milne's Landing on Highway 14. Check condition and public accessibility of these roads before attempting travel, some of these roads are active logging roads.

Mile 28 (277) Km 45.5 (445.5): Junction with road west to community of Cobble Hill, founded in 1868 and known for its fall fair; and road east to Cowichan Bay and a section of the Old Island Highway, an alternate route which hugs the shore and returns to the highway at Mile 33/Km 53.5.

COWICHAN BAY (pop. 3,356) is home to the Cowichan band of the Coast Salish Indians who are famous for their hand-knit sweaters crafted from local raw fleece with traditional Scottish family crest designs. The Indians were taught how to knit by Scottish settlers who arrived here in 1862. The community is also a prime sports fishing centre providing complete facilities.

Mile 31 (274) Km 49.5 (441.5): Road east to Cowhichan Station; west to Cowichan Bay.

Mile 31.5 (273.5) Km 50.5 (440.5): Whipple Tree Junction, a collection of 14 restored old buildings, many from Duncan's old Chinatown, reassembled around a village square to form a colorful year-round tourist market with restaurants and souvenir and craft shops.

Mile 33 (272) Km 53.5 (437.5): Road to Cowichan Bay and bridge over the Koksilah River. Nearby is a farmer's market and stores selling Cowichan Indian sweaters and other crafts.

Mile 34 (271) Km 55 (436): Koksilah tree nursery of B.C. Forest Products. Duncan City limits.

Mile 35 (170) Km 56 (435): The Silver Bridge over Cowichan River is famous for its fighting brown trout. Some sections of the river are for fly-fishing only. The Cowichan River footpath provides continuous access upstream for 19 miles/31 kms. Canoeing and kayaking also on this river.

Mile 35.5 (269.5) Km 56.5 (434.5): Turnoff for **DUNCAN** (pop. 4,100), the major business centre for the Cowichan Valley. Duncan has recently become the City of Totems. At last count 23 totems stand alongside the highway and in the downtown area, all the work of local native carvers. The Cowichan Valley Museum displays period memorabilia and is open Monday to Saturday, May through September; Thursday and Friday only, October through April.

Mile 37 (268) Km 59.5 (431.5): B.C. Forest Museum. Spread throughout 100 acres of woodland and meadows beside Somenos Lake is a living history of the forest industry complete with a working sawmill and planer mill, blacksmith's shop, logging camp and heavy machinery. Visitors can ride a narrow-gauge steam train that crosses a spindly wooden trestle over the lake. Open May to September.

Mile 38 (267) Km 61.5 (429.5): Junction with Highway 18 east 17 miles/28 km to the community of **LAKE COWICHAN** (pop. 2,350). Lake Cowichan is at the eastern end of Cowichan Lake, one of the island's largest. Paved roads run north along the lake to the logging community of Youbou and south to Mesachie Lake and Honeymoon Bay. Logging roads complete the lake circuit and continue through the forest to the west coast communities of Port Renfrew and Bamfield.

Along the road to Youbou is the Teleglobe Canada Satellite Earth Station, 1 of 5 major transmission stations in Canada that pass data back and forth from space. The facility is open to the public from mid-June to early September.

Cowichan Lake offers good fishing and water sports. Gordon Bay Provincial Park along the lake's southern shore has 130 campsites (fee April to October), boat launch, and excellent swimming beach. Cowichan is the Indian word for "the warm land."

An old-fashioned watermill at Chemainus. (Staff)

Mile 42.5 (62.5) Km 68 (423): Mount Sicker Road to the pulp mill and fishing town of Crofton and the B.C. car ferry to Vesuvius on Saltspring Island. Ferries run hourly but only until 6:30 p.m. Saltspring, the largest of the Gulf Islands, is also serviced by ferries from Tsawwassen and Swartz Bay. (See Gulf Islands, this section.)

Mile 42.5 (262.5) Km 68.5 (422.5): Chemainus River bridge. Just north of the bridge, the old Island Highway (1A) follows the shore around to the town of Chemainus. The road rejoins Highway 1 just south of Ladysmith.

CHEMAINUS, (pop. 3,450), was a sawmill town until the early 1980s when the mill closed and citizens faced an uncertain future. They have succeeded in attracting tourists to their town by turning the walls of downtown buildings into an open-air art gallery. Twenty-four huge, colorful murals depict the area's history. Giant yellow footprints painted on the sidewalks provide a walking tour to the various exhibits. Art galleries, craft shops, restaurants and other tourist facilities abound.

Car ferries leave Chemainus for the tiny islands of Kuyper, a native Indian reserve, and Thetis.

Mile 51 (254) Km 82 (409): **LADYSMITH** (pop. 4,393) is a town that has the distinction of lying exactly on the 49th Parallel. Once a coal port for the mines at Nanaimo, the town has been restoring its heritage buildings. For train buffs, there are old locomotives and logging equipment at the Railway Historical Society's working museum and nearby the Tall Ships Society is restoring a historic tugboat. Beachside park offers summer swimming and picnicking.

Mile 52 (253) Km 84 (407): Highway totem marks the Museum and Arboretum of Crown Forest Industries that features early logging equipment and locomotives from around the world.

Mile 56 (249) Km 90.5 (400.5): Yellow Point Road east for excellent ocean beach access, fine resorts, campgrounds and the Crow and Gate, an authentic English pub overlook Stuart Channel. Small Quennell Lake provides good fishing and its intricate shoreline makes for interesting canoe trips. Roberts Memorial Provincial Park has a sandstone beach, perfect for picnics and glimpses of sea lions in March and April. Yellow Point Road returns to Highway 1 at Mile 63/Km 101.

Mile 56.5 (248.5) Km 91 (400): The unincorporated town of Cassidy.

Mile 57.5 (247.5) Km 93 (398): Spitfire Road to Nanaimo Airport.

Mile 58 (247) Km 94 (397): Nanaimo River bridge. The river, a favorite with sports fishermen, is the site of a government salmonid enhancement project.

Mile 58.5 (246.5) Km 94 (397): Roadside rest area.

Mile 59 (246) Km 95 (396): Exit to South Wellington and the Nanaimo Lakes.

Mile 63 (242) Km 101 (390): North end of loop road to Yellow Point and beaches.

Mile 64.5 (240.5) Km 103.5 (387.5): Petroglyph Provincial Park. Short woodland trail leads to a large area of sloping bedrock covered with native carvings believed to be about 1,000 years old. Park sign indicates location of other petroglyph sites in the vicinity.

Mile 66 (239) Km 106 (385): Junction to Nanaimo city centre and ferries to Gabriola and Newcastle Islands. **NANAIMO** (pop. 52,000), the second-largest city on Vancouver Island, was originally the site of 5 Indian villages gathered at a place called "Snenymo," which means "big strong people." The Hudson's Bay Co. established a settlement here in 1852 to work the nearby coal deposits, and soon Nanaimo became the largest coal producer on the Pacific Coast. The original Hudson's Bay Co. bastion, erected as a defence against possible Indian raids, still stands near the waterfront, and in summer months at noon every day, the Bastion Guards in 19th-century uniforms fire its old cannon.

The downtown is undergoing a massive renovation program, restoring many of its heritage buildings and completing a waterfront promenade. It is an important deep-sea port and its harbour is always a hub of activity. Sport fishing is good for salmon, cod and red snapper.

Nanaimo is well-endowed with parks, including Newcastle Island, accessible by passenger ferry. This island was the site of the first coal mines worked by the Hudson's Bay Co. and it was named for the coal mining town in England. It was later purchased by the Canadian Pacific Railway who turned it into a pleasure island, complete with teahouse, soccer field, dance pavilion and floating hotels. It was turned over to the city in 1955. Today the island is a nature reserve with abundant bird and animal life; there are 18 campsites, picnic tables, good beaches, boat anchorage and a marvellous network of walking trails. Sea caves along the north and west shores were used for ancient ritual burials.

The third Sunday in July is Nanaimo's big day, the annual Bathtub Race across the 30 miles/48 km of Georgia Strait to Vancouver, which attracts competitors from around the world.

Mile 66.5 (238.5) Km 107 (384): South exit for Departure Bay ferry. Car and passenger ferries leave hourly for Horseshoe Bay north of Vancouver on the B.C. mainland. Highway 19 begins here.

Mile 68 (237) Km 110 (381): North exit to ferry via Departure Bay Road.

Mile 71 (234) Km 114.5 (376.5): Rest area beside Long Lake; note miniature Bastion replica.

Mile 73 (232) Km 118 (373): Hammond Bay Road to Piper's Lagoon (good bird-watching) and the Pacific Biological Station, established in 1908 for researching the management of the Pacific fisheries. Visitors welcome; arrange tours in advance by calling 767-7000.

Mile 74 (231) Km 119.5 (371.5): South end of loop road to Lantzville, a small seaside community with a good sandy beach. Ada Islands offshore are wintering grounds for hundreds of sea lions.

The coastal highway from Nanaimo to Campbell River links together a string of resort communities, each with its own particular appeal. Most have facilities for fishing and boating, comfortable accommodations, including bed-and-breakfast homes and good restaurants. Another British import, the tea-house, is growing in numbers and popularity on this part of the island. All of these serve the traditional English tea of sandwiches and cakes in the afternoon, and most also serve lunches. Excellent food is also available at many of the British-style pubs along the road, though these are licensed premises and children are usually not allowed inside.

Mile 77 (228) Km 124.5 (366.5): North end of Lantzville loop road.

Mile 80.5 (224.5) Km 129.5 (361.5): Road to Schooner Cove with its large marina. The small community of Nanoose is site of the Canadian Forces Maritime Experimental and Test Ranges Base. The yellow submarine out in the bay is part of the base training grounds.

Mile 81 (224) Km 129 (362): Nanoose Creek.

Mile 84 (221) Km 136 (355): Junction with Highway 4 to Port Alberni, the west coast communities of Tofino and Ucluelet and the Pacific Rim National Park. (See Canadian National Parks in the MAJOR ATTRACTIONS section.) PORT ALBERNI, 30 miles/48.5 km west, is the home port of the MV *Lady Rose*, a steamship that makes day trips to the west coast towns of Bamfield and Ucluelet, sometimes stopping en route in the islands of the Broken Group. Also in Port Alberni is the Alberni Harbour Quay, a bustling marketplace with stalls selling fresh seafood, produce and local crafts. The Alberni Inlet is one of the best places to fish for salmon.

Mile 85 (220) Km 137 (354): Craig Heritage Park is a small collection of pioneer buildings, including a log schoolhouse that

has been moved onto this small site to provide a living museum of history. Open early June to early September.

Mile 86 (219) Km 138 (353): Access to Rathtrevor Beach Provincial Park, 1 mile/2 km east. This is a major park with 174 campsites (fee), extensive picnic and day-use area, nature displays, interpretative programs and nature house. Its chief appeal is its huge sandy beach where the shallow water is usually warm.

Mile 86.5 (218.5) Km 139 (352): English-man River bridge. Good fishing.

Mile 87.5 (217.5) Km 141 (350): Village of PARKSVILLE (pop. 5,800), a popular seaside resort and retirement community. The beach here is wide and at low tide is perfect for building sandcastles. The annual Parksville Sandcastle Contest brings entrants from all over the West. In August, the sport switches to croquet, and the championships are taken very seriously. Parksville Community Park (east on Beachside Drive) has picnicking, playground and sportsfield beside the beach.

Mile 90.5 (214.5) Km 145.5 (345.5): Road east to small community of French Creek and the Lasqueti Island ferry; foot passengers only. The island lies 10.5 miles/17 km out in the Strait and its serrated coastline, offshore islands and reefs invite exploration by canoe or kayak. The island is also popular with cyclists, though the gravel roads are better suited to mountain bikes.

Mile 91 (214) Km 146 (345): Bridge over French Creek. Good steelhead and trout fishing.

Mile 92.5 (212.5) Km 148.5 (342.5): Qualicum Airport.

Mile 93 (212) Km 150 (341): QUALICUM BEACH (pop. 3,400) is a resort and retirement community.

Mile 94 (211) Km 151.5 (339.5): Junction with Highway 4A which links to Highway 4, the route to the west coast of the island.

Mile 97 (208) Km 156 (335): Little Qualicum River.

Mile 102.5 (202.5) Km 165 (326): Horne Lake Road. This gravel road follows the route of the original Indian trail to the west coast at Alberni Inlet. The Hudson's Bay Co. came this way in 1840 and established a farm on Cherry Creek. Today, the road provides access to Spider Lake (5.5 miles/9 km) for picnicking, swimming and nonmotorized boating. Farther down the road is Horne Lake (9.5 miles/15 km), famous for its spectacular limestone caves. Four of the 6 undeveloped caves are open to the public, but anyone venturing inside must be well equipped and experienced. Guided tours are sometimes given in summer; check at Rathtrevor Beach. Both Spider Lake and the Horne Lake Caves are provincial parks, but there are no camping facilities.

Mile 103 (202) Km 166 (325): Qualicum River Fish Hatchery is just south of the Big Qualicum River bridge. More than 100,000 salmon return to spawn here every year. Visitors are welcome to tour the self-guiding trails.

Mile 105.5 (199.5) Km 169.5 (321.5): Nile Creek bridge.

Mile 106 (199) Km 170.5 (320.5): Village

of Bowser. There is a story that in the 1930s the Bowser Hotel had a dog that served beer to the customers. The village was, however, named for a premier of B.C.

Mile 111 (194) Km 179 (312): Cook Creek bridge.

Mile 112.5 (192.5) Km 181 (310): Rose-wall Creek Provincial Park has picnicking and fishing.

Mile 114 (191) Km 183.5 (307.5): Water-look Creek bridge.

Mile 115.5 (189.5) Km 185.5 (305.5): Paul Creek bridge. The highway runs along the shore of Fanny Bay, with Denman Island off to the east. The beach is shingle, scattered with heaps of oyster shells.

Mile 116.5 (188.5) Km 187.5 (303.5): The old established Fanny Bay Inn (known locally as the FBI) is still open for business near Cougar Creek.

Mile 117 (188) Km 188 (303): The former cable-laying vessel, the *Brico*, is beached and has been converted to a restaurant.

Mile 118.5 (186.5) Km 191 (300): Buckley Bay Road turnoff to the Denman Island Ferry. From Denman, a second ferry connects to Hornby Island.

Mile 120.5 (184.5) Km 194 (297): Buckley Bay rest area by the beach.

Mile 123 (182) Km 198 (293): At the Union Bay centre, the old jailhouse is now a gift shop, and the post office is in a red Victorian mansion. Union Bay was once the shipping port for the Cumberland coal mines. Now its fortunes rest with oysters. Fanny Bay oysters are considered especially tasty.

Mile 127.5 (177.5) Km 205.5 (285.5): Trent River bridge and community of Royston.

Mile 128 (176) Km 206.5 (284.5): Junction with road to Comox Lake and CUMBER-LAND (pop. 2,000), 3.5 miles/6 km west. Cumberland was an important coal mining town from the 1880s until the 1930s. Cumberland's Chinatown was the island's largest mine. Today only a few of the old buildings remain, but the museum displays relics of the mining era. Comox Lark Park, just north of the old town, has camping, picnicking, hiking, fishing and watersports.

Mile 130.5 (174.5) Km 210.5 (280.5): Puntledge River Fish Hatchery.

Mile 131 (174) Km 211.5 (279.5): Comox Valley Visitor Information Centre at the entrance to the town of COURTENAY (pop. 9,100), a logging, fishing, farming and tourist centre. Courtenay is the terminus for the Esquimalt and Nanaimo Railway that runs daily service to and from Victoria. The city is rapidly becoming the ski centre of Vancouver Island with 2 ski mountains: the older Forbidden Plateau and the newer Mount Washington. In summer the same terrain offers suberb hiking and salt- and freshwater fishing.

Mile 131.5 (173.5) Km 212 (279): Road branches east to Courtenay's twin city of COMOX (pop. 7,000), home of a Canadian Forces base. The Comox Valley is fertile and has been farmed since 1862. The old Lorne Hotel (1878) and Filberg Lodge (1890) still survive from the Victorian era. Just north of Comox, B.C. Ferries provides 4 sailings a day

Picnic shelter at Campbell River's Discovery Park is constructed to look like a longhouse.   (Liz Bryan)

for cars and passengers to Powell River on the B.C. mainland north of Vancouver.

Mile 133 (172) Km 214 (277): Junction with road east to Forbidden Plateau and connections to Mount Washington ski area.

Mile 136 (169) Km 219 (272): Carlton Sheep Farm, operating since 1886.

Mile 139 (166) Km 223.5 (267.5): Community of Merville.

Mile 143.5 (161.5) Km 231 (260): Black Creek bridge and Black Creek General Store.

Mile 145 (160) Km 234.5 (256.5): Miracle Beach Provincial Park, 1.2 miles/2 km east. This is a popular family camping spot beside a long sandy beach with 193 campsites, hiking trails, visitor centre and interpretative programs. Black Creek runs through the park and flows into the sea through a salt marsh. Lots of wildlife in the forest, marine life in tidal pools, spawning coho in the river and wildflowers all summer make this park extremely enjoyable.

Mile 148 (157) Km 238 (253): Oyster River bridge and road east to Saratoga Beach, with golf course, marina and boat launch.

Mile 149 (156) Km 240 (251): Rest area beside the beach on Oyster Bay.

Mile 154.5 (150.5) Km 248.5 (242.5): Roadside sign commemorating Captain Vancouver who first sailed up Discovery Passage and Johnstone Strait in 1792 and established that Vancouver Island was an island.

Mile 155 (150) Km 250 (241): Road to Campbell River airport which has regularly scheduled flights from Vancouver and Seattle.

Mile 157 (148) Km 252.5 (238.5): Huge glacial boulder on beach just south of the

sign for the 50th Parallel. Rocks offshore are popular perches for cormorants.

City of **CAMPBELL RIVER** (pop. 17,000) is famous as a world-class fishing centre. The turbulent waters of Discovery Passage with their strong tidal surges stir up bait from the sea bottom, attracting giant salmon. The Tyee Club of British Columbia, organized in 1924, is open to anyone who catches a salmon weighing more than 30 pounds from an open rowboat and using certain tackle. Many sportsmen come to Campbell River to take up the challenge. The Tyee record, established in 1968, is 71 pounds. The harbour is full of boats of all kinds, and there are many resorts and boat charters for the serious offshore fisherman. But one can fish successfully from 600-foot/182-metre Discovery Pier, Canada's first saltwater fishing pier, which has shelters, fish cleaning stations, lots of seats and lighting for night fishing. Admission to the pier is $1. Seniors are free.

Primarily geared to visiting sports fishermen, Campbell River is also an important centre for forestry and mining.

The Campbell River Museum and Archives (1235 Island Highway) contains a fine selection of Indian artifacts; organized nature tours available. Discovery Park along the downtown waterfront has an Indian longhouse shelter, complete with house totems and canoe.

B.C. Ferries carries autos and passengers to Quadra Islands. It leaves hourly from the terminal just north of Discovery Park for a 15-minute ride across the narrow passage.

Mile 161.5 (143.5) Km 259.5 (231.5): Highway 28 west 57 miles/92 km to Gold River, a

modern pulp mill community; and Tahsis, a small timber town.

Highway 28 is one of the few highways that cross Vancouver Island east to west. The highway provides access to Elk Falls Provincial Park with 121 campsites. The falls are spectacular in spring when water is let out of the John Hart hydroelectric dam on Lower Campbell Lake.

Highway 28 passes through Strathcona Provincial Park, British Columbia's oldest park. Strathcona has 2 campgrounds, one at Buttle Lake with 85 campsites, and one at Ralph River with 76 campsites. This huge, rugged mountain wilderness has glaciers, lakes and streams. Within the park are 3 nature conservancies which have been set aside to protect areas of outstanding scenery and natural history. At the south end of the park is Della Falls (no road access), among the world's 10 highest falls.

GOLD RIVER (pop. 2,200) was built in 1965 as an "instant town" and has full traveler services. Gold River is a centre for caving. The local Speleological Association runs regular trips to the deepest vertical cave in North America and to the scenic Upana Caves, located about 10 miles/16 km west of Gold River on the gravel road to Tahsis. Self-guided tours are possible (make sure you check in at the register) and take about 1 hour. You'll need rubber-soled shoes and a good flashlight to explore the 1,500 feet/460m of passageways.

TAHSIS, at the head of Tahsis Inlet, is 41.5 miles/67 km from Gold River. Limited accommodations are available.

Mile 161.5 (143.5) Km 260 (231): Campbell River bridge. North of Campbell River the country becomes far more wild; settlements are few and far between (fewer than 3 percent of the island's residents live on the north island), and the scenery is mostly forest. Vast stretches of timber have been clear-cut and the land is a patchwork of regrowth forest of various ages. Forest companies have provided details of the forest's history on large billboards. Watch for logging trucks and heavy machinery on the 2-lane highway.

Mile 164 (141) Km 264 (227): Elk Falls Pulp Mill on Duncan Bay.

Mile 168 (137) Km 270.5 (220.5): Rest area and Seymour Narrows Lookout. The narrow stretch of water between Quadra and Vancouver Island has tides up to 16 knots which makes navigation tricky. It used to be even more dangerous because of Ripple Rock, a shallowly submerged hazard which is claimed to have caused the demise of 2 dozen ships and more than 100 lives. In 1958, one of the largest nonatomic explosions in history blasted the double-peaked rock out of the water. Race Point Road just to the north of the rest area leads down to the cliffs above the narrows.

Mile 169.5 (135.5) Km 273 (218): Mohun Creek bridge.

Mile 171.5 (133.5) Km 276.5 (214.5): Hiking trail to vantage point above Seymour Narrows and site of Ripple Rock.

Mile 173 (132) Km 278 (213): Gravel road west 12.5 miles/20km to Morton Lake Provincial Park with 24 campsites, picnic tables, boat launch and beach. The lake is popular for windsurfing and swimming.

Mile 181 (124) Km 291 (200): Roberts Lake rest area with boat launch and fishing.

Mile 186 (119) Km 299.5 (191.5): Road east to Rock Bay and Chatham Point Light Station, about 13 miles/20 km. Just north of the road is Amor de Cosmos Creek. De Cosmos was a former premier of British Columbia, a flamboyant newspaperman who changed his name from William Smith, and in 1858 founded the *British Colonist* newspaper in Victoria, still in existence as the *Victoria Colonist*.

Mile 195 (110) Km 313.5 (177.5): Sayward Valley bee farm has honey for sale.

Mile 200 (105) Km 321.5 (169.5): Salmon River bridge.

Mile 200.5 (104.5) Km 322.5 (168.5): Road east to Sayward and Kelsey Bay, 6 miles/10 km. SAYWARD (area pop. 600) provides full tourist services. The Link and Pin Logging Museum is worth a visit. Next door, the Cable Cookhouse, constructed of tons of used steel logging cable, serves excellent pies. Just west of the Sayward junction is the Valley of a Thousand Faces where an enterprising artist has painted the faces of famous people on cedar slabs displayed in the forest.

Mile 204.5 (100.5) Km 329.5 (161.5): Bridge over Upper Elk Creek canyon.

Mile 206 (99) Km 332 (159): Rest area on Keta Lake.

Mile 212 (93) Km 341.5 (149.5): Adam River bridge.

Mile 217.5 (87.5) Km 350.5 (140.5): Rest area by Eve River.

Mile 228.5 (76.5) Km 367.5 (123.5): Tsika River bridge and entrance to the Nimpkish Valley, one of Vancouver Island's largest watersheds and richest sources of timber. Watch for herds of Roosevelt elk.

Mile 234 (71) Km 376.5 (114.5): Gravel road east to Mount Cain Regional Alpine Park and ski area and Schoen Lake Provincial Park, 7.5 miles/12 km. The road is rough and not suited to trailers. The provincial park, which has 10 campsites (no fee), is one of the best wilderness parks on the island. Hiking is superb, especially when alpine flowers are in bloom. Lots of wildlife, canoeing, fishing, swimming and mountain climbing on Mount Schoen.

Mile 236 (69) Km 380 (111): Hoomack Lake rest area and seasonal travel information centre, open late June to early September.

Mile 240.5 (64.5) Km 387.5 (103.5): Road to Woss Camp, a logging community that lies 1 mile/1.6 km to the south. In the centre is an old steam locomotive, used when railways played an important part in island logging. Gravel logging road from Woss leads south to Gold River. Check at Woss for accessibility.

Mile 241.5 (63.5) Km 288.5 (102.5): Gold Creek bridge.

Mile 244.5 (60.5) Km 393.5 (97.5): Eagles Nest rest area, with a fine view over Nimpkish valley.

Mile 253.5 (51.5) Km 408 (83): Gravel road to ZEBALLOS, 26 miles/42 km south. With a population of just over 200, Zeballos was once a gold and iron mining town. While the mines are not as active (panning for gold is now a tourist pursuit), its scenic location makes it a popular take-off point for ocean kayakers and fishing charters. Zeballos is served by the *Uchuck III* from Gold River.

A short distance down the Zeballos road from the junction with the highway, Little Hustan Lake Cave Park is an excellent place for first-time cavers. The caves are extensive and remarkable with arches, sinkholes and a huge vaulted entrance. Exercise caution, wear good shoes and carry a dependable flashlight.

Mile 259 (46) Km 417 (74): Turnoff to Nimpkish Camp at the south end of Nimpkish Lake. Gas station and store are on the highway.

Nimpkish Lake is long, narrow and windy — a popular place for sailboard enthusiasts who gather in August for the Speed Weekend competitions. The highway follows its 14-mile/22.5-km length high above its eastern shoreline. Nimpkish is the name of the local Indian tribe, named for a mythical monster halibut who is said to cause riptides near the river mouth.

Mile 262.5 (42.5) Km 423 (68): Noomas Creek.

Mile 275 (30) Km 442.5 (48.5): Road east to Beaver Cove (8 miles/13 km) and Telegraph Cove (9 miles/14.5 km). BEAVER COVE is a huge log sorting ground, with giant machinery that loads logs from railway cars and logging trucks. There's a roadside pulloff that provides a perfect bird's eye view of the hustle and bustle.

TELEGRAPH COVE provides a distinct contrast to Beaver Cove. Here, one of the last existing boardwalk communities on the coast bustles in summer with activity of a different sort. Thousands of tourists come here with canoes and kayaks to launch into the waters of Johnstone Strait to see the killer whales. Others cram into tour boats. At Robson Bight (12 miles/20 km south), the orca whales congregate to rub their bellies on the gravel in the shallow waters at the mouth of the Tsitika River, an area preserved as a government ecological reserve. During the rest of the year, Telegraph Cove is a quiet, idyllic little village, its houses on stilts above the bay and its main street a wooden boardwalk between them.

Mile 276 (29) Km 444.5 (46.5): Nimpkish River bridge.

Mile 279 (26) Km 449.5 (41.5): Junction with road to Port McNeill, 1.2 miles/2 km north.

PORT McNEILL (pop. 3,000) provides full tourist services in a neat little town that owes its livelihood to logging and fishing. From its docks, B.C. Ferries provides a triangular service between Sointula, on Malcolm Island, and Alert Bay on Cormorant Island. Sointula was originally established in 1901 as a colony by Finnish miners from Nanaimo who wanted a peaceful place to farm and fish. The colony survived and today is a fishing village of about 1,000 inhabitants.

Alert Bay is a thriving settlement with strong Kwakiutl Indian connections. All tourist services are available. Tall totems of the Nimpkish Band tower above the burial ground; the U'Mista Cultural Centre displays potlatch collections and old and contempo-

Indian longhouse at Alert Bay on Cormorant Island. (Staff)

rary Kwakiutl artifacts in an Indian-style longhouse. The museum is crammed with Indian materials and local shops sell Indian handicrafts.

The ferry from Port McNeill accommodates cars as well as passengers, but both Cormorant and Malcom islands are small so cars are not needed. Travelers can explore the 2 communities on foot, since ferries arrive and depart every 2 or 3 hours during the day.

Mile 285.5 (19.5) Km 459 (32): Cluxewe River bridge.

Mile 287 (18) Km 462.5 (28.5): Johnstone Strait viewpoint.

Mile 290 (15) Km 467 (24): Rest area by lake.

Mile 291.5 (13.5) Km 469 (22): One-way plank bridge over the Keogh River.

Mile 292 (13) Km 470 (21): Junction with road to Port Alice, 36 miles/58 km south. Located in scenic Quatsino Sound, PORT ALICE (pop. 1,340) was built in 1965, near the site of a much older townsite. A pulp mill provides the main means of livelihood although hunting, fishing and boating attract increasing numbers of travelers each year. Forestry roads lead to several good lakes for fishing and picnicking and also to incredible limestone rock formations and caves. Limited service.

Mile 301.5 (3.5) Km 485.5 (5.5): Junction with road to Prince Rupert Ferry at BEAR COVE, 3 miles/5 km. In the centre of the ferry parking lot is a huge spruce burl and a totem, the remains of an 8,000-year-old Native settlement, the oldest known on Vancouver Island. There is a picnic area beside the bay and a travel information centre. From June to September, car and passenger ferries leave Bear Cove on alternate days for the 15-hour cruise through the Inside Passage to Prince Rupert; reservations are recommended. Cabins are available for those who want to overnight on board in Prince Rupert and return the next day. In winter the ferry schedule is curtailed.

Farms and orchards dot Saltspring Island. (Staff)

Near the ferry terminus, a gravel road leads to the site of Fort Rupert, an early Hudson's Bay Co. trading post.

Mile 302.5 (2.5) Km 487 (4): Junction with road south to old whaling port of Coal Harbour (8.5 miles/14 km) on Holberg Inlet; and north to Port Hardy via Hardy Bay Road.

Mile 303 (2) Km 487.5 (3.5): Junction with unpaved road west to community of Holberg, 26 miles/42 km; Winter Harbour, 39 miles/62 km; and to Cape Scott Provincial Park at the extreme northwestern tip of Vancouver Island. The park is large, with more than 37,000 acres/15,000 hectares and is accessible only by sea or on foot along a rough trail from the end of a 10 mile/16 km forest track from Holberg. It's a magnificent, rugged wilderness of forest and shore and the site of a defeated turn-of-the-century Danish settlement of which a few relics remain. Trails, some of them historic, range in length from 1 mile/2 km to 19 miles/30 km; some sections are boardwalk. The lighthouse crew at Cape Scott and a few residents of the San Josef Valley are the only human inhabitants, but wildlife abounds.

Mile 305 (0) Km 491 (0): PORT HARDY (pop. 5,000), the main community on the north island, is situated on Hardy Bay where the town beach is ringed by parkland and a promenade. Fishing boats line the harbour. Full tourist facilities are available. Activities include fishing, scuba diving and harbour cruises.

At the north end of the waterfront promenade is Carrot Park, its name commemorating the long delay in getting the road north from Campbell River paved. As officials in Victoria kept "dangling the carrot" of paving, residents along the muddy, pot-holed road publicized their plight by holding an annual Pothole Golf Tournament.

The Southern Gulf Islands

Nestled against the southeast side of Vancouver Island, the Gulf Islands attract those who welcome a slower pace. The sheltered waters, miles of coastline, and good harbours have long been popular with pleasure craft. Much of island life is water-oriented, but farming also is a mainstay of the economy, and there are miles of rural roads to explore.

Easily reached by ferry from either the mainland or Vancouver Island, the larger islands attract day-trippers with bicycles or cars, weekenders who may stay at the few hotels or a growing number of bed-and-breakfast establishments, and vacationers who scatter to secluded resorts. Many artists and artisans make the islands their home, and a popular pastime is shopping for their wares.

Not all of the islands offer overnight accommodations, and the ferry schedule is complex. Visitors are well advised to avoid island-hopping without first determining that they can either stay on the other side or hop back.

Saltspring Island

Saltspring Island, the largest and most populous with all tourist facilities available, was the first thriving agricultural settlement in the colony of Vancouver Island. Sheep farming became important, and Saltspring lamb is an internationally known gourmet specialty.

A 40-mile trip around the island can start or end at any of the 3 ferry terminals. Ferries from the mainland dock at Long Harbour, outside Ganges, the largest village. Ferries from Swartz Bay (on Vancouver Island near Victoria) dock at Fulford Harbour. Ferries from Crofton (not far from Duncan on Vancouver Island) dock at Vesuvius Bay, near St. Mary Lake, largest body of fresh water in the Gulfs.

Attractions on Saltspring include the Farmers' Market in Ganges on Saturday mornings, arts and crafts galleries, Hastings House (a well known luxury inn), and many pleasant resorts on saltwater beaches around St. Mary's Lake. The island has many bed and breakfast establishments and several English pubs that serve good lunches and snacks. St. Paul's Church in Fulford Harbour was built around 1880, and the second oldest school in British Columbia still stands in Beaver Point Provincial Park.

One of the nicest places to sample the atmosphere of the Gulf Islands is from the meadows of Ruckle Provincial Park, a sheep farm operated by the Ruckle family who homesteaded here in 1872. The old farmhouse is being restored. Beaver Point has camping, hiking and beachcombing.

The drive up Baynes Peak in Mount Maxwell Provincial Park has great views of the islands and mainland.

Mayne Island

Mayne Island is popular with cyclists because of its quiet, paved country roads and absence of hills. There are about 19 miles of main road on the island. The ferry docks at Village Bay, but Miners Bay is the centre of activity. Named for the throngs of fortune-seekers who stopped there on the way from Victoria to the goldfields, Miners Bay welcomes visitors and pulses with life during the summer pleasure-boat season. The government wharf is a good vantage point for watching marine traffic in Active Pass, a major transportation route through turbulent waters. All tourist facilities are available.

Mayne is a mixture of old and new, with century-old mansions standing side-by-side with homes straight from modern suburbia. Many of the original farms are still in operation, including Hardscrabble Farm with its blue-roofed farmhouse, visible from Fernhill Road. Other attractions are Bennett Bay Beach (the best on this island), and turn-of-the-century buildings that include the Plumper Pass Lockup (1896), now the Mayne Island Museum, St. Mary Magdalene Church (1898) and Active Pass Lighthouse (1885).

Pender Islands

North and South Pender islands are joined by a bridge that spans a canal between Bedwell and Browning harbours. Before the federal government dredged the canal to provide access from one harbour to another, boats had to be carried across a wide neck of land called Indian Portage. A recent archaeological dig here unearthed artifacts dating back 10,000 years.

The Penders are known for their many secluded coves and beaches accessible to visitors, and for the number of artists and artisans who live here. A gallery of their work is in an old schoolhouse at the top of the hill as you leave Hope Bay on Bedwell Harbour Road. There is another craft store at Port Washington. Other attractions are the picturesque barns, turn-of-the-century mansions, and country stores. The ferry docks at Otter Bay. Camping is available at Prior Centennial Park. Other accommodations can be found at inns, resorts and bed-and-breakfast homes.

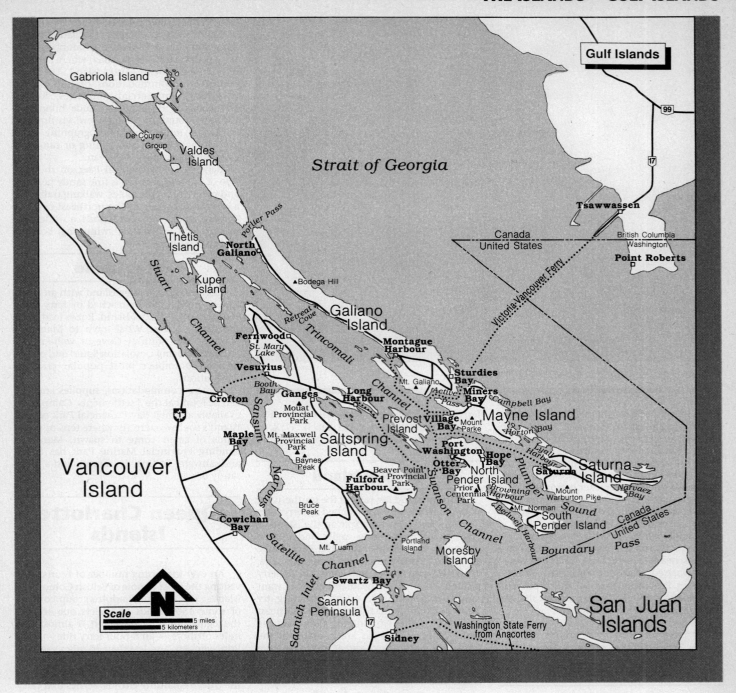

Galiano Island

Scenic Galiano Island is long and slender, sheltering many of the other islands from the winds of Georgia Strait. Nearly three-fourths of the land is a tree farm of fir and cedar. Ferries from the mainland, Vancouver Island and other Gulf Islands dock at Sturdies Bay where lodging, stores, gas and an information centre are found. Up the road from the ferry terminal at Sturdies Bay is Bluff Drive, with a good viewpoint for marine traffic in Active Pass. Two miles beyond is Active Pass Road with a small, well-kept cemetery where early settlers are buried. A few feet out from the beach is a marker on

Collision Reef where the ferry *Queen of Alberni* ran aground in 1979. Several ancient Indian village sites have been found on this island.

Saturna Island

Saturna Island, the most southerly of the Gulf Islands, is sparsely populated and accommodations are limited. The B.C. Ferry Terminal is located at Lyall Harbour and is serviced by ferries from Swartz Bay, Mayne and Galiano Islands. There is no direct connection with the mainland. Inter-island connections are infrequent, so check schedules carefully. There are no public campgrounds on the island.

Saturna Island is known for its Lamb Barbecue on the July 1 holiday weekend. An old-fashioned country fair, crafts sale, games and a beer garden keep visitors entertained until the lamb (barbecued whole over an open pit) is served in midafternoon. Other attractions include beautiful Winter Cove Provincial Park, the historic East Point Lighthouse (1888), and Mount Wharburton Pike, second-highest peak in the Gulfs.

Gabriola Island

Accessible by car and passenger ferry from downtown Nanaimo to Descanso Bay, Gabriola is the second largest of the southern Gulf Islands. It is known unofficially as Petro-

Haida-style band office at Skidegate Mission. (Tom Parkin, staff)

glyph Island because of the large number of ancient Indian stone carvings found here. The best known petroglyph, that of a killer whale, is found by the shore at Degnen Bay. At nearby Weldwood, more than 50 separate motifs have been recently discovered under a carpet of thick moss. Other petroglyph sites are at Jack Point and Lock Bay. The only sizeable community on the island is Gabriola, which has most services.

Gabriola Sands Provincial Park on the north end of the island is known for its expansive beaches; nearby are the Malaspina Galleries — wave-washed, eroded sandstone ledges. Drumbeg Provincial Park on the south end has a small sandy beach and sandstone shelves. Neither park provides camping.

The Northern Gulf Islands

Denman Island

Denman Island, separated from Vancouver Island by narrow Baynes Sound, is accessible by ferry from Buckley Bay (about midway between Qualicum Beach and Courtenay on Vancouver Island). The rural, unspoiled island is surrounded by rocky and gravel shores, good for clams, crabs and oysters. The village has a store, gas station, restaurant and guesthouses. Island artists weave, make pottery and other handicrafts.

Accessible on foot during low tides or by boat, Sandy Island Provincial Marine Park is just off the northwest coast for wilderness beach camping and beachcombing. Near the

ferry dock is Fillongley Provincial Park with 10 campsites and a good oyster beach. Walk to Boyle Point for a good view of Chrome Island lighthouse.

Hornby Island

Hornby Island lies just off the southern toe of Denman Island and is reached by ferry from Gravelly Bay to Shingle Spit on the island. A good spot for watching eagles and marine mammals is Helliwell Provincial Park. There are colonies of nesting birds along the cliffs, a 3-mile/5-km hiking trail, and huckleberry picking on forested headland. If you want sandy beaches and safe, warm swimming, try Tribune Bay Provincial Park at the southeast end of the island. No camping allowed in the parks. Supplies and gas are available at the ferry dock, Ford's Cove and at the co-op store in the island centre. Some accommodations are available in bed-and-breakfast homes.

Quadra Island

Accessible by a short ferry ride from Campbell River, Quadra Island is known for its sports fishing and for the Kwakiutl Museum in Yaculta Indian Village on the Cape Mudge Reserve. Built in the form of a sea snail, the museum houses heritage potlatch goods seized by the government when this traditional ceremony was decreed illegal and only returned to the band in the early 1980s. The totem poles, ceremonial masks and tribal costumes are truly priceless. The museum is open daily, July to September, and Tuesday to Saturday the rest of the year. Across from the museum is a small park containing petroglyph boulders moved from their original beach location to protect them

from vandalism and water erosion.

There are 2 settlements on Quadra Island: At Quathiaski Cove, where the Campbell River ferry docks; and at Heriot Bay, where another ferry connects with Cortes Island. There are plenty of accommodations on the island, including commercial campsites, lodges and cottages. Highlights include hiking up Chinese Mountain for the view; visiting the Lucky Jim mine ruins; photographing Cape Mudge Lighthouse; and fishing or canoeing on island lakes or in the ocean.

Rebecca Spit Provincial Park on the east side of Drew Harbour, has fine sandy beaches and plenty of picnic tables, walking trails and a boat launch. Just off the northeast coast of Quadra are the Octopus Islands, a wilderness marine park for fishing, swimming, boating and scuba-diving.

Cortes Island

Cortes Island, a large island with an intricate shoreline, can be reached by ferry from Heriot Bay on Quadra Island. Roads lead from the ferry dock at Whaletown to Manson's Landing and Squirrel Cove, a well-known anchorage facing Desolation South and one of British Columbia's most popular cruising destinations.

Some accommodations, supplies and gas can be found at the 3 settlements. Camping is available at Smelt Bay Provincial Park on the island's southwestern tip where tens of thousands of smelt come to spawn. Manson's Landing Provincial Marine Park has fresh- and saltwater fishing, swimming and a good sandy beach.

Queen Charlotte Islands

An ever-increasing number of tourists are visiting the most remote of British Columbia's islands. The Queen Charlotte group consists of some 150 islands and islets out beyond the regular lanes of travel. (It is almost 100 miles offshore — an 8-hour ferry ride — from Prince Rupert, and less than 30 miles south of the Alaskan border.)

The British Columbia Ferry System serves the Queen Charlotte Islands. Ferries that carry both foot passengers and vehicles operate year-round between Prince Rupert on the mainland (a 940-mile drive from Vancouver) and Skidegate on Graham Island. Scheduled air transportation includes service by Canadian Airlines between Vancouver, BC, and Sandspit, and service by Canadian Airlines or Transprovincial Airlines between Prince Rupert and the islands, and also within the Charlottes. Helicopters also run regular charters between the islands.

Fishing and logging are the Charlottes' main industries, but to most visitors, the islands mean a vibrant Indian culture and outdoor recreation in beautiful wild country. Beachcombing, fishing, clamming, crabbing, hunting, camping, hiking, boating and bird-watching opportunities abound.

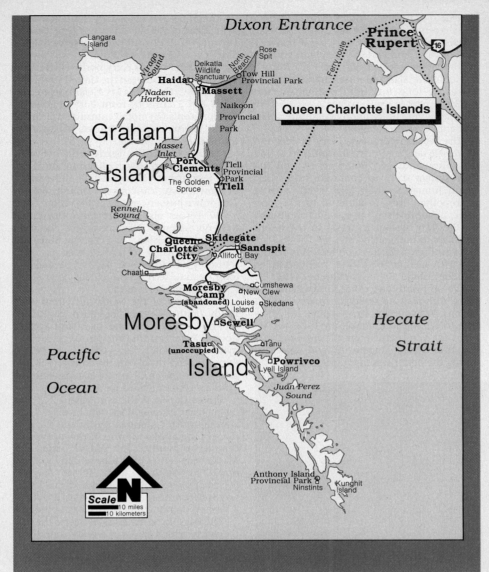

View of Dixon Entrance from Tow Hill in Naikoon Provincial Park. (Tom Parkin, staff)

The 6 major islands cluster in a triangle 156 miles long and up to 52 miles wide. Most visitors arrive on the shores of Skidegate Inlet, near the islands' midpoint. Lodging, food, transportation and information are readily available here. Communities at the hub include Queen Charlotte City, Skidegate and Skidegate Mission on Graham Island, and Sandspit on Moresby Island.

The earliest residents of the islands were the artistic, sea-oriented Haida Indians. Their population, which once numbered more than 8,000 in 17 villages, was decimated by small-pox during the 19th century. Surviving Haidas reluctantly abandoned their ancestral homes and moved into either Skidegate Mission or Old Masset (now called Haida) just before 1900. By 1915, there were only 588 of them. Now there are about 1,300 natives in the Charlottes.

The abandoned settlements, best known of which is Ninstints in Anthony Island Provincial Park, now a United Nations Heritage Site, draw visitors who wish to see the much-photographed totems and remnants of long-houses. All of the sites are on Haida land, and visitors must have permission to go there. To purchase permits, write or call the Haida Band Council in either Haida, phone (604) 626-3925 or Skidegate Mission, phone (604) 559-4496.

None of the abandoned villages can be reached by road. Visitors go there by boat, helicopter or floatplane, either private or chartered. Charters are not difficult to arrange.

There are roads only on the 2 largest islands, Graham and Moresby. A government ferry carries vehicles between the two.

A good investment for Queen Charlotte Island visitors is Neil G. Carey's *A Guide to the Queen Charlotte Islands*. The guide is available in bookstores or by mail from Alaska Northwest Books, 22026 20th Ave. S.E., P.O. Box 3007, Bothell, WA 98041-3007; cost is $9.95 ($12.95 Canadian) plus $1.50 ($2 Canadian) postage.

Graham Island

The largest island (home of 4 out of 5 islanders) is Graham. Most of its 12 major settlements are linked by black-topped roads.

Attractions include Haida artwork displayed and sold at several places; the Queen Charlotte Islands Regional Museum at Skidegate Mission; Naikoon Provincial Park with headquarters near Tlell; the unique Golden Spruce near Port Clements; the Ed Jones Haida Museum at Haida, and the Delkatla Wildlife Refuge at Masset, the Queen Charlotte Islands' largest town with a population of 2,000.

The challenging Dixon entrance golf course is east of Masset along North Beach.

Moresby Island

Moresby offers great boating, but fewer than 20 miles of public road. Few beaches are accessible to drivers or hikers.

However, Crown Forest Corp.'s 7-mile public road to Copper Bay is always open to the public, and many miles of new and old logging roads may be used after working hours and on most weekends. A pleasant day can be spent on a road known locally as the Loop Drive south from Sandspit, following the valley of the Copper River to Skidegate Lake, then returning along the Skidegate Inlet's shore. Attractions include The Willows, a popular 9-hole golf course in Sandspit; the salmon hatchery along Pallant Creek between Mosquito Lake and Moresby Camp; and Crown Forest's log dump and sorting grounds at South Bay.

The southern part of Moresby Island is in the last stages of becoming a national park reserve. This 880-square-mile area will remain, for the time being, an undeveloped wilderness with no road access. For information on the park, write: Superintendent, South Moresby National Park Reserve, P.O. Box 37, Queen Charlotte, BC, V0T 1S0 or phone (604) 559-8818.

Ferry Systems

The adventure of visiting the islands of the Northwest begins when you leave the mainland. There are only 3 ways to gain access to these popular destinations: swim, fly or float. The most popular means is the latter, via the ferry system.

The ferry ride itself is a popular pastime with Northwesterners. On the shorter routes, many walk-on passengers take a round-trip just to relax and enjoy the view in a hassle-free fashion. Whales, dolphins and other marine mammals are often sighted by ferry passengers. The ferries come in a variety of shapes and sizes, from big sleek computerized "super ferries" to small vintage craft. The waterways are endlessly fascinating, from the wide open crossing of the Strait of Juan de Fuca, to the zigzag passage through the San Juan archipelago. Visitors will find the ferry system a convenient and memorable way to explore this corner of the Northwest.

The southernmost ferry system, serving the islands in and around Puget Sound, is Washington State Ferries, whose vessels ply Puget Sound through the San Juan Islands to Canada's Vancouver Island. The Canadian coast is served by the British Columbia Ferry Corp. Its ships crisscross the passage between Vancouver Island and the mainland and sail north to remote Bella Bella and Prince Rupert. Ferries of the Alaska Marine Highway System make the long run from Bellingham and Prince Rupert to southeastern Alaska, where they forge vital links among communities in that almost roadless region.

The **Washington State Ferry System** has 22 vessels ranging in length from 150 to 440 feet. Thousands of commuters rely on the ferry system daily to commute from their island homes to their jobs in the Seattle metropolitan area. In addition to the commuters, hundreds of thousands of visitors use the ferry system to travel to the island paradises of the Northwest.

Washington ferries connect the Seattle area with such popular travel destinations as Whidbey Island, Bremerton (home of the U.S. Navy's shipyard) and other Kitsap Peninsula ports. Although no reservations are required on any Washington ferry system run, it is wise to call ahead to make sure there will be room for your vehicle on the international trips to and from Vancouver Island, especially during the busier summer months.

That run leaves twice daily from Anacortes, WA, about a 2-hour drive north of Seattle. Downtown-to-downtown bus service links Seattle and Victoria via ferry.

Two other vessels carry both vehicles and foot passengers between the United States and Victoria, BC. One is the MV *Coho*, operated by Black Ball Transport, from Port Angeles on Washington's Olympic Peninsula. B.C. Stena Lines' *Vancouver Island Princess* makes daily round trips from Seattle.

British Columbia Ferries run between Vancouver Island's Swartz Bay and the mainland terminal at Tsawwassen, 20 miles south of downtown Vancouver. Downtown-to-downtown bus service is available via the ferry.

BC Ferries also depart from Horseshoe Bay, northwest of Vancouver, for Nanaimo on Vancouver Island and for the Sunshine Coast. It's possible to take a scenic day trip, returning to Horseshoe Bay, or to make a loop by auto ferry that includes both island and mainland ports of call.

The *Queen of the North* sails from Port Hardy, on the north end of Vancouver Island, to Prince Rupert on the mainland farther north. Reservations are strongly recommended, especially for vehicles. At Prince Rupert, a ferry makes the round-trip to Skidegate, in the Queen Charlotte Islands. Reservations are recommended for that run.

Prince Rupert is the port where 2 of the major ferry systems dock side-by-side. They are the British Columbia Ferries and the segment of the **Alaska Marine Highway System** that serves southeastern Alaska ports. The Alaska state ferries offer almost daily sailings north in summer from Prince Rupert. (Another segment of the Alaska Marine Highway System serves southcentral Alaska, but the 2 systems do not connect with each other.)

The flagship of the Alaskan fleet is the MV *Columbia*, which makes a weekly round-trip between Bellingham and the major communities in southeastern Alaska. Stateroom and vehicle reservations are required. Passengers without staterooms sleep in lounge chairs or on deck.

Smaller vessels, on which reservations are not needed, run to smaller communities as well as to the connecting points along the *Columbia*'s route.

Air, bus, rail and other water connections give travelers a wide range of options in making travel plans. In each region, the ferry system is a logical starting point in exploring schedules, routes and connecting services. To obtain schedules and specific information, contact the systems at their headquarters:

Washington State Ferries, Colman Dock, Seattle, WA 98104; phone (206) 464-6400.

British Columbia Ferry Corp., 1112 Fort St., Victoria, BC, Canada V8V 4V2; phone (604) 386-3431. In Seattle phone (206) 441-6865.

Alaska Marine Highway System, P.O. Box R, Juneau, AK 99811; phone toll free 1-800-642-0066 or 1-800-526-6731.

Black Ball Transport, 106 Surrey Bldg., 10777 Main St., Bellevue, WA 98004; phone (206) 622-2222.

BC Stena Lines, Pier 48, Alaskan Way, Seattle, WA 98121; phone 1-800-962-5984 or (206) 624-6986.

(Staff)

BC Ferry Captain's Passage *sails past Beaver Point on Saltspring Island.*

Major Attractions

Canadian National Parks

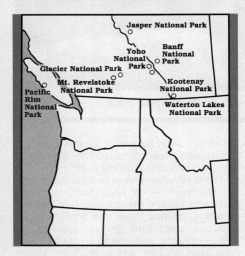

With the exception of Pacific Rim National Park, all of the national parks of British Columbia and western Alberta are in the mountains. In 1985, 4 of the major parks, Banff and Jasper national parks in Alberta, and Yoho and Kootenay in British Columbia, were given UNESCO World Heritage Site designations for their scenic beauty and unique geologic features. These 4 parks are adjacent to one another and, while still mostly wilderness, the general motoring public can easily visit these areas on an accessible highway system.

In British Columbia, 2 more mountain national parks, Glacier and Mount Revelstoke, preserve the beauty of sections of the Selkirk Mountains. Both are reached by Trans-Canada Highway 1. Pacific Rim National Park on Vancouver Island in British Columbia, a narrow strip of rugged coast and giant native trees, is the most remote and least developed of these national parks. Pacific Rim national park is accessible by ferry to Vancouver Island and B.C. Highway 4 to the north end of the park. Other areas of the park can be reached either by logging roads or by ferry from Port Alberni.

Motorists driving through the Canandian national parks on the major highways and not stopping overnight can do so free of charge; otherwise the fees are $4 a day, $9 for 4 days or $25 for a year's pass. Each permit is good in any of the parks across the country. Overnight hikers must obtain a free park-use permit designed to regulate the numbers of people using the trails and wilderness camp-sites. For safety and rescue purposes, climbers and serious backcountry hikers should register with the park warden and check back in on return. Most park lakes are closed to powerboats, though canoes and rowboats are welcome.

All the parks, with the exception of Mount Revelstoke, have campgrounds, the larger ones fully equipped for RV use. Rates vary depending on the time of year and facilities provided. Most backcountry camp-ing is free, though registration and permits are required.

To fish in the national parks, a permit is required and anglers should familiarize themselves about regulations, catch limits and closures. Details at parks information and warden offices.

All Canadian national parks are game pre-serves and as such are excellent places to view wildlife, particularly in the early morning. Canadian parks contain fairly large and stable populations of grizzly and black bear, elk, deer, moose, mountain goat, deer and big-horn sheep. Though big game may often be seen right beside the highway, remember it is dangerous and illegal to feed them.

For information, maps and brochures about any of Canada's national parks, write the Superintendent at the following addresses:

Banff National Park, Box 900, Banff, AB, TOL 0C0. Phone 762-3324.

Glacier National Park, P.O. Box 350, Revel-stoke, BC, VOE 2S0. Phone 837-5155 or 837-6274.

Jasper National Park, Box 10, Jasper, AB, TOE 1E0. Phone 852-6161.

Kootenay National Park, Box 220, Radium Hot Springs, BC, VOA 1M0. Phone 347-9615.

Mount Revelstoke National Park, P.O. Box 350, Revelstoke, BC, VOE 2S0. Phone 837-5155 or 837-6274.

Pacific Rim National Park, Box 280, Ucluelet, BC, VOR 3A0

Waterton Lakes National Park, Box 145 Waterton Park, AB, TOK 2M0. Phone 859-2624.

Yoho National Park, P.O. Box 99, Field, BC, VOA 1G0. Phone 343-6324.

Distinctive Mount Rundle dominates the skyline in the Banff area. (© John Barger)

The 4 Rocky Mountain national parks, Banff, Jasper, Kootenay and Yoho, were set aside before much destruction of the habitat from logging or mining had taken place. Today, they are magnificent wilderness areas and wildlife reserves, renowned for the textbook examples they provide of mountain formation by geologic upheaval and intense glaciation. The Rockies, in the framework of earth history, are young mountains, formed some 75 million years ago when sedimentary rocks (formed on the bottom of a vast and ancient sea some 600 million years ago) were thrust up, broken along great faults and in some places, strongly compressed.

Since their formation, the mountains and valleys have been slowly eroded by water and wind, but most dramatically by ice. Remnants of the great ice field that covered much of North America during the most recent ice age remain in the Rocky Mountains, most evidently in the huge Columbia Icefield which covers 125 square miles, feeds 6 enormous glaciers and rivers flowing to 3 oceans.

Glacial ice flowing over and down from the mountains scooped out bowl-shaped depressions called cirques, sometimes leaving knife-edged ridges and dramatic horn-shaped peaks. Carrying with it huge amounts of rock rubble, the ice scoured deep U-shaped valleys, created mountain tarns and hanging valleys where waterfalls tumble. When the glaciers retreated, piles of the rock rubble or glacial debris were left behind, choking the valleys, damming rivers and leaving ridges to mark the glaciers' former extent.

A Rocky Mountain sunset over Herbert Lake in Banff National Park. (© John Barger)

Banff National Park

Banff National Park on the eastern side of the Continental Divide is accessible by Trans-Canada Highway 1, which runs east-west through the park, or Canada Highway 93, which bisects the park on a north-south route. Canada's first national park, Banff was established in 1885 as a small preserve around the mineral hot springs that, though well known to the Indians for generations, were first recorded in 1858 by Sir James Hector. With the building of the Canadian Pacific Railway (CPR) through the area in 1883, the tourist possibilities of the mountain scenery and hot springs were realized. By 1887, the reserve was considerably enlarged to become Canada's first national park, then known as Rocky Mountains Park. Its sole access was, of course, the railway and hotels were built by the CPR at Banff and Lake Louise. Cars and buses were not permitted full access into the park until 1915, by which time the scenery of the Canadian Rockies was world famous.

Banff National Park today covers some 2,564 square miles/6,641 square kilometres of the Rockies east of the divide, encompassing the valleys of the Bow, Mistaya and North Saskatchewan Rivers. It is the most popular of the mountain national parks, hosting more than 3 million visitors a year from all over the world. Because it is so spectacularly scenic and famous, it is crowded — that is, the highways and major tourist centers and attractions are crowded. But the park is immense; hikers and backpackers only have to walk a few miles to find solitude.

There are 2 centers in the park: Banff townsite near the southeastern boundary; and Lake Louise at about the midway point, near the west junction of Highway 93 and Trans-Canada 1. Both centers have huge CPR baronial chateaux. Banff Springs Hotel is near downtown Banff. Chateau Lake Louise sits on the banks of the spectacularly scenic lake of the same name and is looked down upon by the perpetual snow and ice of the Victoria glacier. Both are built in an architectural style that is a blend of Scottish baronial and French chateau. Both are immense, stately, even luxurious, and are packed solid every summer. (A most modest room is around $85 a night to $3,000 for the Presidential Suite at Banff Springs.) Reservations are essential. Both have beautiful grounds, however, that are open to the public and several nice restaurants. Anyone can wander the lobbies of these resorts to get a taste of the interior decor.

Northbound from Lake Louise, Highway 93 follows the Bow River to its source, glacier-hung Bow Lake with historic Num-Ti-Jah lodge (built in the 1920s) at its northern end. From Bow summit and Peyto Lake, the brightest turquoise of all the Rockies lakes, the highway drops down into the valley of the Mistaya River. The North Saskatchewan River flows south here from its source in the great Columbia Icefields. At Saskatchewan Crossing, the great river turns east, cutting through the side ranges to reach the plains of Alberta. Highway 11 follows the river east to Rocky Mountain House and Red Deer.

Sunwapta Pass below the icefields is the boundary between Banff and Jasper national parks. Here, Highway 93 is known as the Icefields Parkway because of the many glaciers that it passes, especially as it comes close to the toe of the Columbia Icefield itself.

The main attraction in Banff is the mountain wilderness — the high glacially-scoured peaks and valleys, the glaciers, lakes, alpine meadows, rushing rivers and wildlife. Main activities, apart from general touring, are hiking, camping and fishing. If you are not a great hiker, an easy way to reach the alpine areas for great views is by chairlift. Mount Norquay (phone 762-4421) and Sulphur Mountain (762-5438) gondolas near Banff and the Whitehorn gondola (522-3555) at Lake Louise operate from mid-June to the beginning of September. Another way to experience the solitude is by boat. Cruise boats ply the waters of Lake Minnewanka all the way to Devil's Canyon and you can rent canoes and rowboats on Lake Louise and nearby Moraine Lake (which some say is even more beautiful than Lake Louise).

You can relax in the hot springs at Banff townsite. The historic Cave and Basin springs has a swimming pool, cave hot springs and interpretative displays. Upper Hot Springs on Mountain Avenue has hot mineral springs and a cooler swimming pool.

There are gentle hikes out from Lake Louise to the Plain of the Six Glaciers and to Lake Agnes. Both have tea houses at their destination points. Longer, more strenuous trips traverse the western shore of Moraine Lake, to Larch Valley, Eiffel Lake and Sentinel Pass. For an overnight trip without a heavy pack, you can hike (or ski in winter) 8.5 miles/14 km to Skoki Lodge, a historic old log chalet and cabins built in 1930 and still in operation. Expect rustic comfort, good food and mountain solitude. Open Christmas to April and June to September. Phone 522-3555 for information and booking.

For a less crowded automobile tour of the

park, Highway 1A between Banff and Lake Louise, the original park road, is more narrow and winding but less traveled. It passes scenic Johnston Canyon with its waterfalls and trail to the Inkpots, 7 cold water springs bubbling into pools of different colors. It passes also the site of the old copper mining town of Silver City. Many nice picnic areas, viewpoints and 2 campgrounds are along this route.

Vermillion Lakes, a chain of little swampy lakes known for their large populations of wildlife, are circumscribed by a scenic road. There are good views of Mount Rundle, the tilted mountain at the back of Banff. Beside the lakes, archaeologists have uncovered remains of early man dating 11,000 years ago.

The Buffalo Paddock, just east of Banff townsite, permits visitors to drive through a small herd of buffalo, remnant of the huge herds of buffalo that once darkened the plains.

Angel Glacier on Mt. Edith Cavell in Jasper National Park. *(© John Barger)*

Jasper National Park

Jasper National Park adjoins Banff along its northern boundary. It is the largest of the mountain parks, covering 4,200 square miles/10,878 square kilometres, and was set aside as a national park in 1907 when the Grank Trunk Pacific Railway line traversed the country. Most of its beauty and attractions are accessible from Highway 93, the Icefields Parkway, and Highway 16, the Yellowhead. The headquarters and only tourist center in the park is in Jasper, at the junction of the 2 highways, near the site of a fur-trading outpost called Jasper House.

Highway 93 north from the park boundary at Sunwapta Pass follows the Sunwapta River northeast to its confluence with the mighty Athabasca River which, like the North Saskatchewan, flows from the Columbia Icefields. The Columbia Icefields are often called the hydrographic centre of North America because streams from its melting ice feed 3 oceans — the Atlantic, Pacific and Arctic oceans. Just north of Sunwapta Pass, the highway passes close to the receding toe of the icefield and without doubt, the glacier experience, whether on foot or by snowcat tour bus, is the park's principal attraction.

Jasper National Park has but 1 center, the townsite of Jasper. Like Banff, it also has hot springs, though these, tucked away at the end of the side road up the Fiddle River just inside the park's northeast boundary, are not nearly as popular. Also like Banff, it has a grand old railway hotel, Jasper Park Lodge, built in the 1920s on scenic Lac Beauvert.

Most visitors experience Jasper's mountain grandeur from the highways. (See CANADA HIGHWAY 93 log. Yellowhead Highway 16, which traverses the park east to west, is logged in *The MILEPOST®*.)

The most popular park destination is the Columbia Icefield, a great saucer of ancient ice and snow sitting on the Continental Divide, some of which is 1,000 feet/300m deep, left over from the ice age. Surrounding this 9,000-foot-/2,700-m-high icy remnant are huge mountains. Between these peaks, the ice from the saucer spills down in tongues of glacial ice. This high ice-covered area stretches nearly 150 square miles/388 square kilometres. Only a small fraction can be seen from the road, and even the special snowcat tour buses only venture out a little way onto the nearest glacier to the highway, the Athabasca. This river of ice is today receding at an average rate of 100 feet/30m a year. A line of stakes marks its annual regression.

There's a lodge with full tourist facilities right beside the Athabasca Glacier access and also a Parks Icefield Interpretative Centre, open June to September, which will provide a far better grasp of the immensity and grandeur of the icefield than the obligatory scramble onto the glacial toe. But take a tour onto the glacier itself by Snowcoach, summers only. Phone 762-2241.

Do not miss the drive to Cavell Lake with its reflective views of Mount Edith Cavell and the Angel Glacier — it's just about as lovely as Lake Louise. Take Highway 93A, a parallel 14.5 mile/23 km alternative to the main highway. Follow the signs for another 9.5 miles/15 km up the Astoria River. A short hike will take you to the viewpoint. This is also the trailhead for the most popular of the Jasper backcountry hikes — the Tonquin Valley with its beautiful Amethyst Lake and towering Ramparts. It's a 3-day, 26 mile/42 km loop.

Highway 93A will also take you to Athabasca Falls and to Marmot Basin downhill ski area.

Another sidetrip off Highway 93, shortly before the junction with Highway 16 if you are traveling north, is Whistlers Road. This road leads a short distance to the biggest of Jasper's campgrounds (781 sites, some with full hookups) and to the Jasper Tramway up Whistlers Mountain. The Skytram was Canada's first mountain lift and it was designed as a means of access to high alpine country during the summer. From the top terminal with its breathtaking views, a network of trails and paths invite exploration.

And if you hear a whistle, it's probably one of the large colony of whistling marmots from which the mountain got its name. For Tramway times and rates call 852-3093.

Another recommended side trip is the 35 mile/56 km road to Maligne Lake which takes off east of Jasper townsite from Highway 16. This is also the access road to Jasper Park Lodge, where you can stop in for breakfast, play a few holes of golf, rent horses or boats. Plan to stop at Maligne Canyon, a deep gorge where the river falls 23m over a limestone lip. But keep going. At the end of the road is Maligne Lake, one of Jasper's premier attractions and the largest lake in the Canadian Rockies. Here the views are idyllic, especially if you take a cruise to the end of the lake, passing Spirit Island, the photogenic halfway point. Maligne Lake can also be reached by the 2-day Skyline Trail packtrip (or 3-day hike) from Jasper, with an overnight camp in the Big Shovel meadows. The trail stays above timber most of the way through magnificent wilderness scenery.

Miette Hot Springs, located east of Jasper off Highway 16, has the hottest springs in the Canadian Rockies, which are mixed with cold water to permit comfortable swimming. Miette Hot Springs has a chalet, changing facilities, restaurant, accommodations and picnic grounds.

Kootenay National Park

Kootenay National Park stretches on both sides of the Vermilion and Kootenay Rivers and adjoins Banff and Yoho national parks on the west side of the Continental Divide. It is bisected by Highway 93 which follows the main river valleys. Points of interest accessible from the highway are covered in the CANADA HIGHWAY 93 section.

The park is best known for its hot springs, first known as Kootenay, now Radium, at its southern tip. The first development of the spring took place in 1911. The area was set aside as a national park in 1919, and in 1922, the Banff-Windermere Road was completed, the first motor road across the central Canadian Rockies.

Chief focus of the park are the hot springs, which bubble up from the Redstreak breccia fault line, itself noteworthy for its towering red cliffs and pinnacles. The hot springs lie just north of a very congested tourist and commercial area outside the park at the town of Radium. All facilities are here.

Hike the trail to Floe Lake, 6 miles/10 km up the Floe River. This pretty alpine lake has miniature icebergs, chunks of ancient ice from Floe Glacier, on its waters. It is one of the very few lakes in the Rockies with this phenomenon.

If you are a sturdy hiker, take the 4-hour hike up to the Stanley Glacier through a spectacularly beautiful valley. If you're looking for more of a gentle stroll, try the Paintpots self-guiding nature trail. It's only a short and pleasant walk to ochre beds that supplied the vermilion used by Indians to paint and decorate their lodges and bodies. The ochre was once commercially mined and a few traces of the operations still remain. Another gentle walk and spectacular scenery await in Marble Canyon, with a trail along the canyon rim to the waterfall at its head.

Yoho National Park

Yoho is the Cree Indian word used to express awe and visitors tend to agree that the park is well named. Geographically, it encompasses almost the entire watershed of the Kicking Horse River, 507 square miles/1,313 square kilometres of high mountain country. It adjoins Banff Park along the Continental Divide and Kootenay Park to the southwest. The Kicking Horse rises in Wapta Lake near the Great Divide and flows all the way to Golden where it joins the Columbia River. Just about halfway through the park, the river has carved a natural bridge through the solid rock, one of the more interesting attractions.

From a scientific point of view, the most important feature of the park is the Burgess Shale site where, preserved in ancient Cambrian sedimentary layers, are more than 150 species of marine organisms that date back more than 500 million years. The shale is exceptionally fine-grained, and the fossils themselves are so well preserved that scientists can see soft appendages and even some internal organs. The site is a protected area, though sometimes guided tours are available. Check with the park headquarters in Field.

The small railroad town of Field in the center of the park has basic tourist services. There is a lodge at Wapta Lake and also at nearby Lake O'Hara, though here casual drop-ins are discouraged. Lake O'Hara lodge is at the end of a 8 mile/13 km private road that must be walked or skied, unless advanced arangements are made to be picked up in the lodge bus. Despite this, the lodge, lake, campground and trails are very popular. Campground reservations must be made at least 2 months in advance.

Emerald Lake also has a lodge. It is worth the 4.5 mile/7 km drive for the view and the hiking trails that surround the lake. Canoe rentals are available and there are stables with horses for hire. En route you will pass by the famous Natural Bridge.

Another automobile excursion is up the Yoho Valley road east of Field to Takakkaw Falls, at 1,248 feet/380m the second highest falls in British Columbia. Here water melting from the Daly Glacier and Waputik Icefield plunges over the lip of the main valley into the Yoho River. North of the falls, trails lead to 2 other impressive waterfalls, Laughing Falls and Twin Falls.

Glacier National Park

Glacier National Park lies in the Selkirk Range of the Columbia Mountains. Located on the eastern side of the great fault line, the Columbia Trench, these mountains are not sedimentary like the Rockies but made of metamorphic and igneous rocks which pushed up through older sedimentary beds. The mountains are older than the Rockies and are more resistant to erosion, though they were boldly sculpted by the glaciers of the last Ice Age.

The park is at the collision point between 2 weather systems, the moist Pacific airflow and the cold, dry Continental. This results in a tremendous amount of precipitation. In summer there is always a 50 percent chance of rainfall and in winter snow falls almost constantly. Heavy snowfalls feed large and active glaciers — there are more than 100 of them within park boundaries and more than 10 percent of the park is under perpetual ice. In winter, avalanches are common.

This was the terrain through which the Canadian Pacific Railway chose to route its railroad in 1885. Rogers Pass was the best they could find, even though it was desperately steep and plagued with avalanches. The alpine area of the pass around Mount Sir Donald was set aside as a park preserve in 1886 and the park was extended to its present size in 1930. Access for the casual visitor is limited to areas around Highway 1, which parallels the route the railroad took. In later years, however, the railway has been able to escape the worst of the Rogers Pass snowfall and avalanche hazards by tunneling under the mountains; the highway goes bravely over the top of the pass (see the TRANS-CANADA Highway 1 Section).

This is a park for mountain climbers and backpackers. The average tourist driving through can do little but stand in awe of the rock peaks and the hanging glaciers, though there are a few short hikes the beginner or a family can take and 3 of these have to do with railway history. Recommended walks include the Trestle Trail to a high bridge viewpoint; the Loop Trail which follows an abandoned loop of the original railroad grade; the Abandoned Rails Trail at the pass crest which was abandoned when the first tunnel was built; and the Meeting-of-the-Waters Trail. Details of these and other trails in Glacier and nearby Revelstoke National Park are contained in a handy little booklet called "Footloose in the Columbias," available free of charge from the Rogers Pass Visitors Center on the summit.

The center provides excellent interpretation of the park's railway history and the avalanche phenomenon. Children will be delighted by the scale model of the pass, complete with railway lines, tunnels, snowsheds and tiny moving trains. Visitors will also be

Bunchberry, or Canadian dwarf dogwood, is found in subalpine habitat.   (L. Linkhart)

intrigued to know about the gun positions along the highway which are used to shoot down potential avalanches while they are small and while the highway is closed. Shells are used and because these do not always explode on impact, hikers are warned not to pick up any strange metal object.

Mount Revelstoke National Park

Just west along Highway 1 from Glacier Park is tiny Mount Revelstoke, a 161 square mile/260 square kilometre section of rugged territory with impressive icefields and angular peaks. Like Glacier, it is in the Selkirk Range of the Columbia Mountains and enjoys heavy rain and snowfalls. Rain forests just as dank and deep as those along the coast of British Columbia occur here.

Highway 1 does not penetrate this park except for a brief few miles around its southeastern edge. But there is a road that leads right up into the high alpine plateau, to a world of sparkling mountain tarns, meadows full of flowers, groves of mountain spruce and balsam and incomparable views. The people of Revelstoke built this road up to the summit in 1910 and the park was established 4 years later. The winding gravel road is 16 miles/26 km long, but the alpine meadow is well worth the trip. There are few places in Canada where you can drive right up to an alpine meadow. Summit Road is generally open from July to early September. See the TRANS-CANADA Highway 1 section for log.

At the end of the road, a network of self-guiding nature paths and trails introduce the visitor to the sights and sounds of the high alpine, including 2 lovely little lakes. Mountain Meadows Trail begins at the summit parking lot and passes the "Icebox," a place where snow and ice linger to provide ice-cold air even in midsummer. For more serious hiking, the trail to Eva Lake takes about 2 hours. The flowers along this route are so spectacular that in mid-August each year the park organizes an Eva Lake pilgrimage hike.

Other park trails introduce visitors to the Interior Wetbelt Forest. The trailheads for Giant Cedars or the Skunk Cabbage trails begin off of Highway 1.

There are no campgrounds in Mount Revelstoke park, but full facilities are available at the nearby city of Revelstoke.

Waterton Lakes National Park

Separated from all the other Canadian mountain national parks, Waterton Lakes is at the extreme southwestern tip of the province of Alberta where it joins Glacier National Park in Montana. The 2 parks together are known as the Waterton-Glacier International Peace Park.

Waterton was set aside as a park in 1895.

Here the mountains rise abruptly from the Alberta plains without intervening foothills to soften the transition. Two very different biotic zones, mountain and prairie, adjoin each other to provide an interesting intermingling of species. Botanists love the place.

The mountains, mostly of sedimentary rocks, include some of the oldest rocks in the Canadian Rockies. These have been uplifted and displaced horizontally quite recently (in geologic time) and now lie adjacent to much younger rocks. The oldest rocks contain fossils of some of the most ancient forms of life, while the younger rocks yield fossilized shells, dating from the time when the interior of North America was a giant ocean. Waterton's landscape bears the sharp peaks, knife-edged ridges and deep valleys of past glaciation. The mountain rocks are unusually colored in shades of purple, red and green as a result of chemical changes in the mineral contents caused by climatic changes when the sedimentary deposits were being laid down.

Waterton Park is accessible via Alberta Highway 6 south from Pincher Creek, Montana Highway 17 from the south, and Alberta Highway 5 from Cardston. There are 2 other roads within the park. The Akamina Highway follows Cameron Creek from Waterton townsite to Cameron Lake; and Red Rock Canyon Parkway follows the Blakiston River to famous Red Rock Canyon. Both are very scenic drives and provide access to some of the park's hiking trails. At Cameron Lake (which straddles the 49th Parallel), there are campsites, canoe rentals, lakeshore trails and picnic sites.

The main valley in the park, a very deep glacially-dug trough, is almost filled by the Lower, Middle and Upper Waterton Lakes — really 1 large lake broken into sections by straits and narrows. Lower Waterton Lake extends down into Montana. Visitors can take a cruise on this lake; there are ports of call along the way for trailhead access. Most popular is the 2-hour return cruise. For information, call 859-2362.

Waterton townsite occupies an ancient delta of Cameron Creek at the narrows between Upper and Middle Waterton lakes. This is very much a summer-only community; in winter its population dwindles to under 100 and accommodations and services are extremely limited. At the height of the summer, however, its population swells to around 1,000. It's a popular spot with full tourist facilities and fishing, swimming, boating, windsurfing and hiking.

Waterton also has a fairy tale chateau in the Prince of Wales Hotel (859-2231), a 7-story Gothic wooden structure which was built by the Great Northern Railway in 1927. It sits on a bluff just north of town with lovely little Linnet Lake at its back. It is surely one of the most scenic locations and is open only from June to September.

Buffalo Paddock, located just inside the Highway 6 park entrance, is larger than Banff's. It is easy to imagine these great beasts roaming the prairie.

Pacific Rim National Park

There is only 1 paved road to Pacific Rim National Park. BC Highway 4 bisects Vancouver Island and leads to the beaches of the wild West Coast, where the waves roll in, uninterrupted, all the way from Japan. The national park includes the rugged and challenging West Coast Trail between Bamfield and Port Renfrew; the Broken Group of about 100 islands clustered at the mouth of Barkley Sound; and the most accessible area of the park which is around Long Beach, facing the open Pacific between Ucluelet and Tofino. (See Vancouver Island map on page 253 in THE ISLANDS section.)

Information centres for the West Coast Trail are at the head of Pachena Bay near Bamfield and at Port Renfrew. The 45-mile/73-km hike, considered one of Canada's toughest, takes veteran backpackers 5 to 6 days to complete. Nevertheless, it attracts more than 5,000 hikers each year.

This is not a route for novices. There are neither established campgrounds nor access roads along the way. All equipment and supplies must be carried.

The trail is as beautiful and wild as it is challenging. It was carved out of dense brush soon after the turn of the century to reach the rugged coast where survivors of frequent shipwrecks were cast.

Most hikers make a 1-way trip, beginning either at Port Renfrew (66 miles west of Victoria via BC Highway 14) or Bamfield (60 miles southwest of Port Alberni via a gravel logging road). Alternate transportation to Bamfield is aboard the MV *Lady Rose* from Port Alberni.

The Broken Group, accessible only by boat, is popular with kayakers and canoeists. A favorite launching place is scenic Toquart Bay, 22 miles north of Ucluelet at the head of Barkley Sound. It is reached by way of a logging road that runs west from BC Highway 4 at Kennedy Lake. Alternate access to the islands of the Broken Group is aboard the MV *Lady Rose* out of Port Alberni. Charter boats (primarily those based in Ucluelet) will drop off and pick up those who would like to spend a day playing Robinson Crusoe.

Long Beach is the section of Pacific Rim National Park that draws the overwhelming majority of visitors. Attractions there include the Wickaninnish Centre with displays and films on the ocean, trails and beaches.

Most of the trails carved out of the wilderness are surfaced with wood chips and boardwalks. They include the woodland walks to beaches, a bog walk, a trail through the rain forest, a hike along an old gold mine trail and a series of viewing platforms on a crest overlooking the sweep of Long Beach.

Public and private campgrounds accommodate visitors as do facilities in Ucluelet and Tofino. Each of these villages also has restaurants, stores and such visitor-oriented services as fishing charters, whale-watching excursions, and day trips to nearby hot springs. The West Coast Maritime Museum is in Tofino.

U. S. National Parks

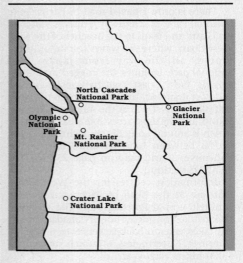

The 5 U.S. national parks featured in *NORTHWEST MILEPOSTS*® present some of the most dramatic scenery and extraordinary beauty of a land that only a few centuries ago was wilderness. Towering rain forests, pounding surf, jagged mountain peaks and alpine glaciers and lakes are home to diverse plant and animal life.

Summer is the busiest time of year to visit these parks. Campgrounds fill on a first-come, first-served basis. For more information, contact the National Park Service Regional Information Office at (206) 442-0170.

Crater Lake National Park

Crater Lake, a remote and mysterious body of water in the Cascade Range of southcentral Oregon, is situated in a huge caldera formed by the collapse of ancient Mount Mazama.

Access to Crater Lake National Park from the east is via Oregon Highway 62 (turn off at **Mile 96** U.S. Highway 97) north of Klamath Falls, OR, or Oregon Highway 138 (**Mile 136** U.S. Highway 97) south of Beaver Marsh. Access from the west is via Oregon Highway 227 (**Mile 219** Interstate 5) south to Oregon Highway 62 or via Oregon Highway 138 (**Mile 244** Interstate 5) at Roseburg, OR.

The 183,180-acre park is open year-round and winter recreation is becoming increasingly popular. For information, weather and road conditions, write to the Crater Lake National Park, P.O. Box 7, Crater Lake, OR 97604; phone (503) 594-2211. For maps and books containing information on the park, write to the Crater Lake Natural History Assoc., P.O. Box 56, Crater Lake, OR 97604.

Park Headquarters for Crater Lake National Park is located 3 miles south of Rim Village and is open daily year-round. A post office, located in the administration building, is open weekdays during the summer. Visitor services include information, first aid, backcountry permits, maps and publications sales. There is a service station near the headquarters which is open from Memorial Day to October.

History: At one time the powerful volcano, Mount Mazama, reached a height of approximately 12,000 feet. Indians in the region some 6,800 years ago who witnessed the violent eruptions believed the volcanic action was the result of a war between 2 gods. Instead of having just 1 vent at the peak of the mountain, several vents formed, spewing lava and gases, weakening the stability of the mountain. Geologists estimate that in about 4,840 B.C., the mountain collapsed in a thunderous implosion, forming a deep caldera in place of the mountain.

Archaeological evidence indicates that the Indians witnessed the collapse of the mountain. Stories conflict concerning the Indians knowledge and use of the lake following the eruptions. Some bathed in it; others avoided it. Tribal shamans in historic times forbade most Indians to view it, and the Indians offered no information about the lake to pioneers who traveled in the area for 50 years without discovering it. A small party of prospectors, among them John Wesley Hillman, accidentally stumbled upon the lake in 1853 while searching for the Lost Cabin gold mine.

Their reports of the deep blue mysterious lake, virtually void of life, prompted exploration by the government. In 1886, a U.S. Geological Survey party carried a boat which weighed nearly 1,000 pounds up to the lake to explore it. Their depth readings indicated the lake was 1,996 feet deep at its deepest point, amazingly close to the sonar reading recorded in 1959.

The man responsible for having this area dedicated as a national park was William Gladstone Steel, who as a boy read about the lake in a newspaper in which his lunch was wrapped. Upon discovering its beauty, Steel lobbied for 17 years to have the area set aside. He was successful and Crater Lake National Park was established on May 22, 1902. Today, it is Oregon's only national park.

Attractions: Crater Lake, which fills that caldera, is the deepest lake in the United States, the second deepest in the Western Hemisphere and the seventh deepest in the world. Its maximum depth is 1,932 feet.

Wizard Island, a volcanic cone which rises 764 feet above the lake surface, was formed shortly after the collapse of the mountain. When the volcanic activity subsided some 1,000 years ago, springs, snow and rain began to fill the huge caldera with water. As the lake deepened and widened, evaporation and seepage eventually balanced with the incoming flow, causing a constant lake level. The level now fluctuates no more than 3 feet each year. There are no streams into or out of Crater Lake.

Visitors at Crater Lake immediately comment on the incredible blue color of the lake. Naturalists explain that light is absorbed color by color as it passes through clear water.

Rim Drive may remain closed by snow until mid-July. (© John Barger)

The first color to be absorbed is red, then orange, yellow and then green. Absorbed last is blue and only the deepest blue reflects back to the surface from as deep as 300 feet, the natural limit of light penetration. The fact that the lake is so deep and so clear results in its deep, rich blue color. No other lake has light penetration as deep as Crater Lake. Moss grows to depths of 325 feet, the greatest known depth of any freshwater moss in the world.

Activities: Summer camp fire programs are presented at the Mazama Campground amphitheater. Topics change nightly. Snowshoe hikes are conducted between December and mid-April on weekend afternoons, with snowshoes provided for $1. For a schedule of ranger-led programs, tour information and reservations, call the park headquarters.

During the summer and fall, the visitor center at Rim Village is open daily. Park rangers provide information, assistance and backcountry permits. Services include displays, activity schedules, map and publication sales and first aid. A rock stairway at the Sinnott Memorial leads to an overlook which is open daily in the summer. Here you find an unobstructed view of the lake.

Park rangers present a short geology talk each hour. Inside are geology and historic displays.

Boat Tours: From July through early September, narrated boat tours are offered by the Crater Lake Lodge Co. and the National Park Service. The 2-hour tour circles the inside of the caldera and stops at Wizard Island, where visitors may hike or relax until the mid-afternoon return trip. The boat leaves from Cleetwood Cove on the opposite side of the lake from the lodge. Rates are $7.25 for adults and $3.75 for children under 12. Boat tours are available from June 28 to Sept. 6 (weather permitting) and reservations may be obtained at the Crater Lake Lodge front desk at Rim Village.

Rim Drive: Rim Drive, the 33-mile road which circles the lake, has excellent views of the lake and geographic formations. It is closed during the winter. From Rim Drive, a spur road leads to the volcanic spires of the Pinnacles area.

Crater Lake Lodge offers a 2-hour narrated Rim Drive Bus Tour. Contact the lodge for information, reservations and rates charged at (403) 594-2511.

Camping: Camping is allowed only at Mazama and Lost Creek campgrounds, or in the backcountry by permit. Mazama Campground has 198 wooded sites, restrooms and a dump station; Lost Creek has 12 sites, water and pit toilets. Campgrounds are open when the snow melts in early summer and are closed by snow in the fall. There are no showers or hookups and both campgrounds have a 14-day limit. Areas fill quickly. Additional camping is available on the national forest land adjacent to the park.

Lodging: Crater Lake Lodge at Rim Village offers restaurant and cafeteria facilities and cocktails with a scenic view of the lake. The lodge also offers a gift shop and, during the summer, ponderosa cottages are available. There are no lodging facilities

Summer view of Crater Lake and Wizard Island from Rim Drive. (© John Barger)

during the winter. For information, write Crater Lake Lodge Co., P.O. Box 128, Crater Lake, OR 97604; phone (503) 594-2511.

Hiking: Trails ascend Garfield Peak, The Watchman and Mount Scott, providing spectacular views of the lake and surrounding terrain. The Cleetwood Trail is the only access to the lake. The Pacific Crest Trail traverses the park and connecting trails crisscross the backcountry. Information folders, available for Godfrey Glen, Annie Creek canyon and Castle Crest wildflower trails, may be obtained from the park headquarters.

Fishing: Fish are not native to Crater Lake because of its lack of feeder streams. However, plantings have been made and though skill is required, good fishing is reported. No license is required. Check specific regulations at the park headquarters.

The lake was stocked from 1888 to 1941, and was begun by William Steel who hand-carried buckets of fish from nearby streams. The lake is no longer stocked.

The best fishing is near the surface and in shallow water, such as the Wizard Island area. No private boats are permitted on the lake so fishing must be done from the shore areas near Cleetwood Cove or from Wizard Island, which can be reached by concessionaire-operated tour boats.

Winter: During the winter, the park annually receives about 500 to 600 inches (45 feet) of snow, yet the lake rarely freezes. Heat from the summer sun, stored in this immense body of water, retards ice formation throughout the winter.

There are no lodging or camping facilities available during the winter months, however, winter activities are becoming more popular. Check with park headquarters for details.

Glacier National Park

There are nearly 10 times as many miles of trails in Glacier National Park as there are miles of roads. The park is maintained primarily as a wilderness area, a policy which is responsible for the wide diversity of wildlife and unspoiled resources within the park. At 1,600 square miles (1 million acres), Glacier is the nation's fourth-largest national park.

Access: U.S. Highway 2 follows the southern boundary of Glacier National Park from its eastern entrance at East Glacier Park (**Mile 71.5**, 15 miles west of Browning, MT, and junction with U.S. Highway 89) to the western entrance at West Glacier (approximately 35 miles east of Kalispell, MT, and its junction with U.S. Highway 93 **Mile 627**).

Going-to-the-Sun Road is still the only thoroughfare through the center of the park. The steep, narrow 2-lane road snakes its way over the Continental Divide through the center of the park, cresting at Logan Pass (elev. 6,664 feet). While Going-to-the-Sun Road is a breathtakingly beautiful drive, drivers are warned to be cautious. During July and August vehicles wider than 8 feet (including mirrors and extensions) or longer than 30 feet are prohibited from traveling the highway between Avalanche Creek and Sun Point parking area.

Trailers may be parked temporarily at Sun Point on the east side or in the regular campgrounds on either side of the park while you drive to the other side and return. However, before July 1 and after Aug. 31, vehicles with maximum length of 35 feet and a width of 8 feet may travel Going-to-the-Sun Road over Logan Pass. The road is closed due to avalanche danger from mid-October to early June.

For maps, brochures and information, write to the Park Superintendent, Glacier National Park, West Glacier, MT 59936; phone (406) 888-5441.

History: George B. Grinnell, naturalist and editor of an outdoor magazine, made the first recorded visit in 1887 into what was to become Glacier National Park. Grinnell, railroad magnate James J. Hill and Dr. Lyman B. Sperry were largely responsible for the area being set aside as a national park in 1910. Completion of the Great Northern Railroad over Maries Pass on the southern boundary of the park brought notoriety to the area.

Louis W. Hill, son of the railroad millionaire, oversaw the construction of Glacier Park Lodge, the first inn to serve Glacier's visitors. A few years later, Many Glacier Hotel was constructed to handle the load of tourists coming to witness the untarnished beauty of this glaciated range. Hill was so impressed with Glacier National Park and the wildlife that he adopted the mountain goat, a species prominent in the park, into the logo for his company.

The completion of Going-to-the-Sun Road allowed visitors access to the interior of the park and tourism boomed. Before this road was completed, most visitors toured the park on horseback or on foot.

Glacier and its Canadian counterpart, Waterton Lakes National Park, are an international peace park, a designation of friendship and cooperation between the 2 North American neighbors. Rotary clubs of both nations sponsored this proclamation, which both governments passed in 1932.

In 1974 the United Nations named the Glacier-Waterton area a World Biosphere Reserve. This designation will help assure that Glacier National Park will remain unaltered for continuing scientific research on wildlands. In addition, the 2 rivers that form the western and southern boundaries of Glacier National Park are protected under the Wild and Scenic Rivers Act. This means that strong efforts are being made to maintain water quality, protect scenery and restrict the construction of dams, bridges, commercial developments and private homes within a quarter mile of the rivers.

Activities: Though motorists can see many spectacular sights along the 76 miles of paved road within the park, to really enjoy the splendor of this unspoiled wilderness requires walking. More than 730 miles of developed trails lead to 50 glaciers, more than 200 mountain lakes, through thousands of acres of alpine valleys where grizzly bear, deer, elk, moose and countless other species live without interference.

There are 3 corrals in Glacier National Park that rent horses and sponsor pack trips. They are located at Many Glacier, Lake McDonald and at Apgar.

Boating is restricted to non-motorized craft on many of Glacier Park's lakes. Kintla, Bowman and Two Medicine lakes restrict outboards to 10 horsepower or less. Higher-powered boats are allowed on Lakes McDonald, Sherburne and St. Mary. Small-boat rentals, with or without motors, and commercially sponsored scenic cruises are available on Lakes McDonald, Sherburne, Waterton, Two Medicine and St. Mary.

A 90-minute audio cassette tape describes roadside features and can be purchased at the park's visitor centers.

Bicyclists are welcome to the park, but they are restricted from traveling Going-to-the-Sun Road during peak traffic time, 11 a.m. to 4 p.m.

Hiking: Before hiking any of the trails in the park, study the park maps and geological maps. The terrain can be difficult and strenuous, so plan accordingly. Most passes are open by mid-July for hikers and a week or so later for riders and packers. Valley trails are usually opened earlier, but snowstorms leaving a foot of snow have been known to ruin a Fourth of July weekend. Check with park officials before you begin your adventure.

Park officials pay careful attention to the preservation of the park. Stay on the trails to avoid contributing to erosion and to protect yourself from dangerous falls. Weather in Glacier National Park is generally cool and unpredictable; be sure to bring proper clothing and footwear. Many experienced hikers recommend wearing different layers of clothes, both cotton and wool. Be sure to include a warm coat and rainwear.

Horses and mules have the right-of-way on the trails. Move off the trail on the lower side and stand quietly until they pass.

Park rangers discourage hiking alone. Dangerous terrain and the possibility of bear attack dictates that you have at least one partner with you at all times.

Camping: There are 15 public campgrounds accessible by car in Glacier National Park. Most of these are large, offering up to 196 campsites. Even so, during peak periods they fill up early in the morning and campsites are available on a strict first-come, first-served basis. With the exception of the 6 campgrounds off the North Fork Road in the park's more rugged northwest corner, all of the campgrounds offer full amenities: flush toilets, spigot water faucets, trash disposal, and evening educational programs offered by the park rangers.

Overnight camping in the backcountry requires a free permit. Each campground has a limit to the number of persons which can use the area without damaging the ecosystem. Limiting numbers reduces the wear and tear on the campgrounds and provides a quality wilderness experience for the backcountry visitor. The limits may vary from 8 to 24 persons per campground, depending on the area. Permits are available at the St. Mary and Apgar visitor centers from June through mid-September.

Lodging: Seven major resorts serve visitors of Glacier National Park. The largest is Many Glacier Hotel, built in 1914, offering more than 200 rooms. The decor of Many Glacier Hotel is Swiss with plaques representing each of the Swiss cantons hanging in the lobby.

Swiftcurrent Motor Inn near Swiftcurrent Lake, offers additional motel rooms and cabin units to supplement Many Glacier Hotel.

On the west side of the park, Lake McDonald Lodge offers 101 rooms and features an Old West hunting lodge atmosphere. The hotel was built in 1913 and the lobby sports trophy heads of mountain goats, elk, moose and bighorn sheep, all harvested before the area became a national park.

The Village Inn is located north of West Glacier at the west entrance to the park at Apgar overlooking Lake McDonald. In addition to regular motel units, housekeeping units are available.

Crowfeet Mountain and Mt. Henkel rise above a meadow in Glacier. (© John Barger)

Aurora Lake reflects sunset alpenglow off Mt. Rainier.   (Linda J. Moore)

Glacier Park Lodge is located just north of East Glacier Park on Montana Highway 49. Huge timbers, some from trees more than 500 years old, were used in the construction of this 155-room lodge. The timbers were brought from Washington and Oregon on Great Northern railroad cars and inspired the Indians to call it Oom-Coo-La-Mush-Taw, "the big tree lodge." It has a golf course and pool.

Situated on the bank of St. Mary Lake is the Rising Sun Motor Inn, one of the smaller facilities of the park.

On the Canadian side, the Prince of Wales Hotel offers additional accommodations in Waterton township, an hour's drive (42 miles) along the Chief Mountain Highway from St. Mary Visitor Center.

Glacier Park, Inc. administers these lodgings and during the summer months it is best to make room reservations well in advance. Write Glacier Park, Inc., East Glacier Park, MT 59434 or phone (406) 226-5551 from June to September. From September to June, contact the company c/o Greyhound Tower, Mail Station 5185, Phoenix, AZ 85077; phone (602) 248-6000..

Backcountry Chalets: Up the trail 6.7 miles from Lake McDonald Lodge is Sperry Chalet, 1 of 2 remote inns built in 1916. The other is Granite Park Chalet, 7.5 miles from Logan Pass along the Garden Wall trail. Both are accessible only by hiking or horseback, and each offers comfortable sleeping facilities and 3 full meals each day served family style. You don't have to carry everything on your back to experience an overnight in Glacier National Park's backcountry. The chalets don't open until the snow melts from the alpine trails (usually around July 1) and they close soon after the beginning of September. Reservations must be made in advance through Belton Chalets, Inc., P.O. Box 188, West Glacier, MT 59936-0188; phone (406) 888-5511.

Fishing: More than 50 of the 200 lakes within the park offer excellent fishing for native trout. While stream fishing is generally poor due to the cold water and virtually sterile runoff, lake fishing is considered good.

Within the park, no fishing licenses are required. Copies of fishing regulations are available at all ranger stations and visitor centers.

The rivers which border the park offer excellent angling, but are regulated by the Montana Fish and Game Commission, and state licenses are required. Pick up a copy of the current fishing regulations.

Hunting: Though the park is rich in wildlife, no hunting is permitted in this or any other national park. Guns, when carried into a national park, must be disassembled or otherwise made inoperable before being permitted in the park.

Wildlife: Glacier National Park is an excellent destination for those who have never viewed wildlife in its native habitat. As many as 260 species thrive in this rugged setting and many allow themselves to be viewed.

Among the more popular species are the black and grizzly bear, bighorn sheep, Rocky Mountain goat, mule and white-tailed deer, moose, cougar, wolverine and Canada lynx. There is also a very small but growing population of gray wolves keeping mostly to the northwestern section of the park.

Visitors should not attempt to feed or in any way disturb or harass the wildlife and photographers are warned that these animals, despite their appearance, are truly wild and capable of inflicting serious injury when threatened or harassed.

There are also more than 200 species of birds, and the reigning monarch of the park's birds is undoubtedly the bald eagle. Every November as many as 600 bald eagles converge on McDonald Creek to feed on spawning kokanee salmon. Kokanee salmon are freshwater, dwarf relatives of the ocean-going sockeye salmon, and their numbers in Flathead Lake, 60 miles downstream from Glacier, have swelled since 1916 when they were first introduced. Visitors can stand on Apgar Bridge and watch the eagles soar and dive into the creek to capture the foot-long fish in their talons.

Once found in every state except Hawaii, bald eagles are now endangered in 43 states, and they are threatened in 5 others. Yet for 2 months every autumn, Glacier is home to the remaining population of our American national bird.

Winter: Though winter activities, including snowshoeing and cross-country skiing, are becoming more popular, the 3 months of summer bring fully 80 percent of the more than 2 million visitors each year. Park naturalists provide interpretative programs from mid-June through Labor Day to explain the wildlife and geology of this ruggedly remote park.

Mount Rainier National Park

Mount Rainier National Park is located southeast of the Olympia/Tacoma area in the Cascade Range of Washington.

Access: There are 4 main entrances to the park. At the southwest corner of the park is the Nisqually entrance, accessible via Washington Highways 7 and 706. The Ohanapecosh entrance at the southeast corner of the park off Highway 123 is accessible via U.S. Highway 12. The White River entrance, at the northeast corner of the park, is off Highway 410 from Enumclaw to the north, while the Chinook Pass entrance is off Highway 410 from Naches to the east. Only the Nisqually entrance and the Nisqually-Paradise Road are open in winter; all other park roads are closed in winter.

The fee to enter the park is $5 per vehicle for a 7-day visit. For those entering by commercial bus, it is $2 per person for anyone between the ages of 16 and 62. The fee is $2 for motorcycles and individuals on bikes, walking or otherwise entering the park.

For maps, brochures and further information, write to the Mount Rainier National Park, Tahoma Woods, Star Route, Ashford, WA 98304; phone (206) 569-2211.

The park's boundaries include 378 square miles and elevations from a low of 1,640 feet in the Ohanapecosh area to the summit of the glacier-covered Mount Rainier at more than 14,000 feet. More than 1.8 million visitors travel through Mount Rainier National Park each year to enjoy the misty rain forests, giant old-growth forests, subalpine meadows, glaciers and rocky outcrops, along with the wide diversity of plants and wildlife.

The towering mountain is a landmark for Puget Sound communities and the focal point of Mount Rainier National Park (established on March 2, 1899, as the nation's fifth national park).

Mount Rainier is often said to create its own weather. It reaches high into the upper atmosphere and interrupts the flow of moist maritime air masses from the Pacific Ocean.

The result is great amounts of rain and snowfall. During the winter of 1971-72, a world's record 93.5 feet (1,122 inches) of snow fell at Paradise.

Glaciers: There are approximately 75 glaciers in the park, 25 larger ones which have been named and about 50 smaller ones, all on the slopes of Mount Rainier. The glaciers are tracked and measured each year to help determine climatic changes.

A rapid retreat of the glaciers began around 1920, but since 1950, a general advance of the larger glaciers has been noted. The total retreat of the glaciers until 1950 averaged about one-quarter of their length, but some, like Paradise, retreated drastically. However, Winthrop and Carbon glaciers showed very little change. In 1980, the smaller glaciers continued to retreat.

History: Mount Rainier is the largest single-peak glacier system in the Lower 48 states and the greatest volcano in the Cascade chain. It is considered a dormant volcano which developed at a weak spot in the earth's crust between 500,000 and 1 million years ago.

Before the discovery of the area by explorers, Indians lived in the lowlands surrounding the mountain. During the summer they would move up the slopes of the mountain to hunt, collect berries, bulbs, herbs and beargrass. The native Indians called it Tahoma "the highest mountain." Captain George Vancouver was so impressed with this majestic 14,410-foot peak that in 1792, he named it for a friend, Admiral Peter Rainier.

The first recorded ascent of Mount Rainier was made in 1870 by Hazard Stevens and Philimon Beecher Van Trumph from the south side of the mountain. Their Indian guide, Sluiskin, warned them of the perils and begged them not to go. Sluiskin then waited in fear at their camp on Mazama Ridge while Stevens and Trumph completed their climb. The duo returned late the next day, having conquered the summit. Since then, thousands of people have climbed to the summit by several routes.

Climbing: Each year, more than 4,000 people stand on the summit with more people reaching that goal every year. Climbers must be in top physical condition and have experience in glacial travel, ice ax use and rescue. Climbers must register with a ranger before attempting the climb. A guide service at Paradise offers 1-day climbing schools and guided 2-day climbs to the summit.

Persons climbing above 10,000 feet or on glaciers must register with park rangers before making their trip. Day hikers should sign trail registers.

Hiking: Hiking the more than 300 miles of trails in the park is a premier attraction, drawing some 30,000 outdoor enthusiasts each year. The park headquarters offers the *Backcountry Trip Planner*, outlining the rules and regulations, a chart of trail miles and maps of the hiking trails. Hiker information centers are open daily during the summer at the Longmire and White River entrances to the park.

Self-guiding nature trails can be found at Longmire Meadows, Sourdough Ridge, Nisqually Vista, Emmons Vista, Ohanapecosh, Grove of the Patriarchs and Carbon River.

Hiking seasons generally extend from mid-July to mid-October for the park, though trails at the lower elevations are open somewhat earlier and remain open later into the fall. The weather is generally best from mid-May to mid-September, though the upper elevation trails may not open until mid-July. The number of clear days peaks in July and August, though campers should remember that the nights are cool and the weather is unpredictable. Prepare for most any weather condition.

Mount Rainier seen from Mirror Lake in summer. (Linda J. Moore)

The best type of clothing for hiking in the Pacific Northwest during the summer months is a combination of wool, cotton and outer rain wear. If the weather is warm, cotton clothing is suitable, but frequent rainstorms should be anticipated and wool clothing and rain gear, including a tent, should be carried. Leather hiking boots are recommended. Your equipment should include a pack of some kind, first-aid kit, flashlight and extra batteries. Sunglasses, a map, compass, insect repellent, a knife and extra food are also recommended.

Water is available at most backcountry sites. Hikers should carry their water as surface water is not safe to drink unless treated or boiled. Giardiasis is an intestinal condition caused by a parasite which infests some waters. (See Giardiasis in the GENERAL INFORMATION section.)

Dogs, cats and other pets are not permitted away from roads and parking lots. Pets are allowed on the Pacific Crest Trail.

Facilities: There are 5 auto camps within the park providing a total of 600 campsites. All are available on a first come, first served basis. All have toilets and water. There are no RV hookups. Sunshine Point near the Nisqually entrance is the only campground open year-round. Lodging is available year-round at the National Park Inn at Longmire and from May through early October at Paradise Inn. Food service can be found at Longmire (year-round), Paradise and Sunrise. Visitor centers are at Longmire (year-round), Paradise (daily, April through December; weekends January through March), Ohanapecosh and Sunrise (summer only).

Backcountry: Camping permits are required for all backcountry campsites. Campsites in the backcountry are on a first-come, first-served basis.

The use of firearms is prohibited and possession of firearms is prohibited unless it is unloaded and cased, or otherwise packed in such a way as to prevent its use while in the park.

Cutting of green plants, shrubs and trees is prohibited, as is collecting of wood in campgrounds and along roads. Wood can be brought in or purchased at the campgrounds.

It is important that persons using the backcountry carry out their cans, bottles, foil and other noncombustible food containers. Plastic carry-out bags may be obtained at the park's ranger stations.

Fishing: Mount Rainier is not noted for its exceptional fishery and generally only experienced anglers do well. Rangers report that anglers' success is often less than anticipated. The park waters are not stocked and depend on limited natural reproduction to replenish the fish population. Anglers are encouraged to use barbless hooks and artificial lures and to release uninjured fish. No license is required to fish within the park. The species most sought after include cutthroat, rainbow, brook and Dolly Varden.

Boating: Nonmotorized boating is permitted on all lakes, except Frozen Lake, Reflection Lakes, Ghost Lake and Tipsoo Lake.

Wildlife: Without the pressure of hunting, several big game species find Mount Rainier National Park a haven.

The largest animal to be encountered at Mount Rainier is the elk. September is the best time to listen for the male's bugling call which can be heard from most high ridges on the east side of the park. Elk are found mostly in the high meadows and subalpine forests during the summer, browsing on twigs, bark and shrubs. Some of the best places to see elk are Cowlitz and Ohanapecosh areas, Shriner Peak and Stevens Ridge. Elk are most often found on the east and north sides of the park, but have been seen in all areas.

The elk, which number about 1,500, are the number one resource management problem in the park. Introduced into the Cascades in the 1920s, the elk migrate into the park each spring and remain until very late fall. With habits like domestic cattle, they selectively over-browse forest and subalpine meadows all summer. There is no hunting and no predation, so the herds continue to grow. They threaten irreversible damage to an ecosystem not designed for elk, according to park officials.

The mountain goat is the only large mammal in the park that remains white year-round. The envy of all climbers, this large animal with its strong legs and soft hooves is specially suited to live among rocky crags. Never far from the snowline, mountain goats venture into alpine meadows to feed on grasses and flowers in the early morning and evening. They spend warm afternoons resting in the shade digesting their food. Binoculars are usually needed to spot goats high in the meadows. The best times to see goats are early in the morning (until about 10 a.m.) and late afternoon (from 6 p.m. until dark).

Black-tailed deer follow the melting snows up into the high mountains in early summer as the shrubs develop buds and leaves and huckleberries begin to ripen. In June and July, new fawns may be seen with their does. Their tan color and white spots allow them to effectively blend into their surroundings. Deer can often be seen from the road as you drive through the park in the morning or evening. If you want to watch them, choose a safe place to pull off the road so you will not create a traffic hazard.

Black bears, the only kind found in the park, are not commonly seen. When located, they are generally spotted in the backcountry and again are most visible during the morning and evening hours.

Other mammals common in Mount Rainier National Park include cougar, marten, raccoon, porcupine, beaver, snowshoe hare, hoary marmot, pika, golden mantled ground squirrel and the yellow pine chipmunk.

Birds found in the park include geese, ducks, peregrine falcons, red-tailed hawks, osprey, kestrel, golden and bald eagles, herons, gulls and countless other species.

Winter Activities: Winter is a popular season in the Paradise area of Mount Rainier National Park. Snow depth is the factor which determines the start of many winter activities at Paradise. The snowpack must be adequate to protect the fragile alpine plants from being damaged or destroyed. Thus, snow camping begins when the snow depth has reached about 3 feet and the snow play area cannot be constructed until approximately 5 feet of snow covers the ground.

One of the most popular activities at Paradise is inner-tube sliding. Due to the potential hazards of terrain and trees, sliding is permitted only on the supervised, constructed runs located north of the large parking lot near the Paradise Inn. Here, 2 long runs for adults and 1 shorter run for children are provided. For safety, sliding is permitted only on inner tubes, saucers and other soft sliding devices. Wooden toboggans, metal-runner sleds and other hard devices are not permitted. The sliding runs are usually constructed in late November or early December, depending on snow depth. They are maintained and operated on weekends and holidays only throughout the winter and are not maintained or supervised on weekdays. The operation generally closes by mid-April.

Snowshoeing is also a popular pastime at Paradise. The snow is sometimes hard and

North Cascades Highway winds across Washington Pass. (L. Linkhart)

crusty, which impairs traction, but with fresh new snow, snowshoeing is a relaxing way to enjoy the winter at a slow pace. Cameras and snowshoers go well together. Park naturalists lead snowshoe walks to introduce visitors to snowshoeing and explore winter ecology. The walks are presented from January through mid-April at 10:30 a.m., 12:30 p.m. and 2:30 p.m. weekends only. The walks are limited to 25 participants and the 12:30 p.m. walk is available for reservation by groups. Snowshoes are available for use by participants during the walks. A $1 donation is requested and is used for snowshoe maintenance. There is no charge for the naturalist-led walks if you bring your own snowshoes.

When there is sufficient snow, park rangers mark 3 trails in the Paradise area for cross-country ski touring. These trails are the Nisqually Vista Trail, the Narada Falls Trail and the trail from the Valley Road over Mazama Ridge to Reflection Lakes. A map of these trails is available at the Paradise Visitor Center. The rule is to prepare for fairly warm snow. A waxing guide has been developed and is available at the visitor center.

Both snowshoes and cross-country skis and related equipment are available for rent at Longmire. The concessionaire-operated facility is located just west of the National Park Inn. Cross-country ski lessons are available.

Regardless of the activity, prepare for cold conditions and changes in the weather. Wear wool and carry extra clothing for touring. The danger of hypothermia is ever present and a pamphlet is available at the ranger stations and at the visitor center.

Knowledge of the local avalanche danger is extremely important. When touring, climbing or camping, be sure to inquire at the visitor center or ranger station before departing. A good handout explaining the dangers of avalanches is available at the visitor center.

Tire chains are frequently required on all vehicles traveling from Longmire to Paradise. Be sure to carry them and comply with posted signs for safety. Meals and hotel rooms are available daily, year-round at the National Park Inn in Longmire. For winter reservations, call (206) 569-2275. A snack bar at the Paradise Visitor Center is open weekends throughout the winter and during the holiday season.

North Cascades National Park

The North Cascades National Park complex is located in the wild northernmost reaches of the Cascade Range in northwestern Washington. The complex is comprised of 3 adjoining areas: Ross Lake and Lake Chelan national recreation areas and the North Cascades National Park. National forest lands flank the park on the south, east and west. This remote wilderness has giant forests of red cedar, crevass-scoured glaciers, deep valleys and sheer-walled pinnacles that challenge backcountry travelers. Readily accessible areas are heavily visited, but there are areas of the park that have yet to be explored.

Access: The North Cascades Highway (Washington Highway 20) separates the north and south units of North Cascades National Park, cutting across the Cascade Range through Ross Lake National Recreation Area. Forming a large L-shape within North Cascades National Park, Ross Lake National Recreation Area encompasses Ross Lake, Diablo Lake and Gorge Lake. Lake Chelan National Recreation Area is the second recreation area within North Cascades National Park. It is accessible from U.S. Highway 97 at **Mile 571**.

From the west, Highway 20 exits Interstate 5 at Burlington (**Mile 658**); from the

Cascade Loop Drive

One of the more popular drives for motorists is the Cascade Loop, a highway route offering spectacular scenery and access to some of Washington's most quaint towns and villages. See individual highway section for road logs.

Start on the North Cascades Highway (Washington Highway 20) through Burlington, Sedro Woolley, Concrete, Marblemount, Mazama, Twisp, Carlton and Methow. This route passes through the Ross Lake National Recreation Area along the Skagit River. Each of these small communities offers most services. At Pateros, join Highway 97 along the Columbia River to just north of Wenatchee, where you join U.S. Highway 2 West. This highway through Stevens Pass includes the towns of Leavenworth, Skykomish, Goldbar, Startup, Sultan, Monroe and Snohomish, before joining Interstate 5.

You may either head north on Interstate 5 to complete the route, or continue on to Mukilteo and take the short ferry ride to Whidbey Island. Head north on Highway 525 through the communities of Clinton, Coupeville and Oak Harbor. North of Oak Harbor is Deception Park and the bridge over Deception Pass. In crossing the bridge, you leave Whidbey Island and enter Fidalgo Island, with the principal city of Anacortes. Anacortes is the jump-off point for the San Juan Islands and Vancouver Island, B.C. Washington Park near Anacortes offers a nice picnic/rest area for travelers. Continue east to rejoin the Interstate 5 and complete the route.

Among the attractions on the Cascade Loop are the beautiful spires, white-water streams, waterfalls and glaciers of the North Cascades; breath-takingly beautiful Washington Pass, the frontier village of Winthrop; the fruit producing Wenatchee Valley along the Columbia River; the quaint Bavarian-style village of Leavenworth; more beautiful alpine settings through Stevens Pass; saltwater wildlife offshore of Whidbey and Fidalgo islands; historic and present-day military installations on Puget Sound; scores of national forests, state and private campgrounds and virtually unlimited fishing and recreational opportunities.

This route may be covered in one long day, but to do that would be a waste. Spend several days on the Cascade Loop to discover the best of northwestern Washington.

east Highway 20 junctions with U.S. Highway 97 (**Mile 630.5**) at Okanogan. See the NORTH CASCADES HIGHWAY section for log.

For information, maps and brochures on North Cascades National Park or the national recreation areas, write to the Superintendent, North Cascades National Park, 800 State Street, Sedro Woolley, WA 98284 or call (206) 856-5700.

History: Exploration of the North Cascades began in 1814 when Alexander Ross crossed the present national park's southern unit. The handful of explorers who followed Ross also commented on the region's rugged, isolated nature. Miners prospected for gold, lead, zinc and platinum here from 1880 to 1910, but because of limited profits and extremely rough terrain, mining was abandoned. Some logging and homesteading occurred around 1900 and the electric potential of the Skagit River was realized, providing some development. Three dams were built on the Skagit River between 1924 and 1949 for electrical generation.

The North Cascades Highway crosses the park complex through Ross Lake Recreation Area along an old rail and truck route originally intended for building and serving Skagit River power projects. The highway was extended after the park was established and the route was dedicated in 1972. It has been called the "most scenic mountain drive in Washington." The mountains of the North Cascades have been called "the North American Alps" for the spectacular beauty of their jagged peaks, hanging glaciers, cascading waterfalls and wildflower meadows. The most visited areas of the 505,000-acre park are those accessible by automobile or requiring just a short walk.

North Cascades National Park is a beautifully diverse park, bisected by Ross Lake National Recreation Area and bordered on the south by Lake Chelan National Recreation Area. Because of the different designations, there are different regulations governing the use of the national park and the recreation areas.

After some controversy, Congress established North Cascades National Park in 1968. Some recreational uses are restricted in the park which are otherwise permitted in the national recreation areas, such as hunting. In the national park, man is a temporary visitor.

In the recreation areas, there is a continuation of private property ownership, mining, hunting and agricultural uses. The combination of the 2 separate and unique designations allows for the maximum possible enjoyment of the North Cascades.

Attractions: The Ross Lake National Recreation Area divides the North Cascades National Park into 2 units. This area encompasses 107,000 acres, all 3 of the electrical dams and provides a corridor for the scenic North Cascades Highway.

Seattle City Light has been offering tours of their Ross Dam and Diablo Lake hydro facilities since 1928. The tours are offered from mid-June to the beginning of September; reservations are advised. Phone Seattle City Light's Skagit Tour desk at (206) 684-3030.

Lake Chelan National Recreation Area is the southernmost tip of this park complex. The destination of most visitors is the wilderness community of Stehekin at the northern end of the lake. There are no roads to this wonderfully remote community and visitors must hike, boat or fly in. Many visitors take a boat from Chelan and travel 50 miles north on the lake to Stehekin. The 4-hour trip provides shoreline views of private residential and farming development on the lower lake, rugged mid-lake shorelines and national forest lands, and the lake's upper 4 miles, within the Lake Chelan National Recreation Area.

Lake Chelan is a natural lake, resting in a glacially carved trough. At 1,500 feet it is one of the deepest lakes in the nation. Its bottom lies 400 feet below sea level. A dam built at Chelan in 1927 raised the water level 21 feet to increase power production.

Hiking: Hiking the 345 miles of trails within the national park complex is one of the principal activities of the North Cascades. Permits, required for all backcountry camping, may be obtained either at the ranger station in Marblemount or Chelan.

Most hikers and backpackers enter the national park complex from trailheads along the North Cascades Highway. Several long trails traverse or loop the north and south units of the park and most have campsites spaced every 3 to 4 miles. Day hikes are more numerous in the national recreation areas.

The only road penetrating the park is the North Cascades Highway. Three other roads bring you near trailheads for hiking into the park. The Cascade River Road, a 25-mile dirt and gravel road open during the summer and fall, provides access to the Cascade Pass trailhead. The Stehekin Valley Road, accessible only by ferry from Lake Chelan, is served by a Park Service shuttle to Cottonwood Campground. The Nooksack Valley Road provides an access to the park through the Mount Baker-Snoqualmie National Forest at Hannegan Campground.

Nature trails, conducted walks and evening programs are available in the summer at Colonial Creek and Newhalem campgrounds, Hozomeen and at Stehekin. Ask a park ranger for details.

Remember that weather in the North Cascades in notoriously changeable. Unless you are taking a brief stroll, take extra clothing, water and supplies along on day hikes.

Pack animals are available for rent at several of the communities, or horsemen may bring their own. Professional guide and pack train services are available. For a list of guides, contact the park headquarters.

Both the north and south units of the national park have many high peaks to

View of the snow-clad Olympic mountains from Hurricane Ridge. (© John Barger)

challenge the mountain climber. For safety, it is recommended that parties have 3 or more climbers; be equipped with internationally recognized climbing gear; and register names of the party, destination, name of the mountain and the approximate length of stay.

Accommodations: Lodging is available at Ross Lake and Diablo Lake resorts and in Stehekin at the North Cascades Lodge. Groceries can be found outside the park at Marblemount and Newhalem.

Camping: Major campgrounds with vehicle access are along the North Cascades Highway at Newhalem, Goodell Creek and Colonial Creek. Group campsites at Goodell Creek must be reserved.

Fishing: A valid Washington fishing license is required to fish in the national park and in both national recreation areas. Besides the 2 large lakes, there are hundreds of small mountain and valley lakes with thousands of streams. Ross Lake is one of the few large lakes left in Washington that depends on its native fishery and is not artificially stocked. The principal game fish is trout, including rainbow, brookies, cutthroat and Dolly Varden.

Hunting: No hunting is permitted within the boundaries of the national park, but hunting is permitted in both recreation areas. A valid Washington hunting license is required and all state regulations apply.

Wildlife: Because of the many wilderness areas and the remote setting of the rugged North Cascades National Park, the area hosts some of the highest populations of big game animals in the state. Black-tailed deer are many, as well as black bear, elk and smaller mammals. Less numerous are the wolverine, marten, fisher and cougar. White ptarmigan, blue grouse and countless other smaller birds make their home here. During the winter, large numbers of bald eagles may be viewed feeding on the salmon of the Skagit River.

Winter: There are no developed ski areas in the North Cascade group, but cross-country skiing and snowshoeing is growing in popularity. There are well-developed areas in the national forests on all sides of the North Cascades.

Summer: Swimming and waterskiing will probably never take a big hold in Ross and Diablo lakes. The glacier-fed lakes are just too cold to permit such activities safely. Even in August, water activities are mainly confined to boating and fishing.

Olympic National Park

Perhaps no other place on earth has the diversity of terrain, climate, plant and wildlife species as the Olympic Peninsula in northwest Washington. The Olympic National Park and Olympic National Forest are located on that peninsula. The park offers year-round recreational opportunities, including skiing, hiking, boating, fishing, mountaineering and horseback riding.

Access: The peninsula is bordered on the west by the Pacific Ocean, the north by the Strait of Juan de Fuca and on the east by Hood Canal and the Puget Sound. The impressive Olympic Mountains form the backbone of the park, forest and peninsula. U.S. Highway 101 is the best access to the area as it runs the outer perimeter of the park on the west, north and east sides.

Entrance fees for Olympic National Park are collected at Heart O' the Hills, Soleduck and Hoh ranger stations from May 21 to the end of September: $3 per vehicle, good anywhere in the park; $1 per person (on foot, bicycle or bus). Permits are valid for 7 days. An annual park-specific permit is $10 per vehicle. Campgrounds are $5 per vehicle per night.

For maps, information and brochures, write to the Park Superintendent, Olympic National Park, 600 E. Park Ave., Port Angeles, WA 98362; or call (206) 452-4501.

History: Mount Olympus was named in 1788 by a British captain but the first major explorations of the area didn't happen until 1885-90 when public attention to the area began. President Cleveland set aside half the Olympic Peninsula as a forest reserve in 1897 and President Theodore Roosevelt turned 600,000 acres of the forest into a national monument, but President Franklin Roosevelt signed the bill in 1938 that created the national park. Fifty miles of ocean strip were added in 1953.

The land received national park status for 3 basic reasons: (1) to protect and preserve the native wildlife, including the Roosevelt elk, together with sufficient range to perpetuate this and other rain forest species under natural conditions; (2) to preserve a substantial remnant of the dense, virgin rain forests of the Northwest coast type which elsewhere are rapidly disappearing and; (3) to protect one of the finest scenic and wilderness areas remaining, of which the Olympic Mountains are the climax.

Scientists have separated the "life zones" into 7 distinct parts. The Olympic Peninsula has 4 of those zones, more than any other place in North America. The forest and park are noted for the marine climate, dense rain forests, rugged mountain terrain and its principal big game resident, the Roosevelt elk.

The park's mountains have been dissected by streams and living glaciers into one of the most rugged landscapes in the entire country. No mountain range in the nation of comparable height rises so near the coast. The mountain wildflowers form one of the finest displays in the country. Ten varieties, which are found nowhere else, grow in the higher mountains.

The park contains 57 miles of coastline, the longest primitive stretch of coastline remaining in the contiguous United States.

Attractions: There are 3 separate entities which bear the Olympic name. The first is the peninsula, on which the other 2 are located. The Olympic National Forest surrounds the park and contains much of the peninsula's area. Inside the boundaries of the forest is Olympic National Park. All 3 share common environmental characteristics.

Olympic is synonymous with wet. The Olympic Mountains block and catch the Pacific Ocean storm clouds, causing them to dump their heavy loads of rain on the western slopes. The wettest point in the contiguous United States is Mount Olympus (elev. 7,965 feet) with 200 inches of precipitation per year. The mountain also receives the greatest amount of snow of any place in the contiguous United States.

The park is perhaps most noted for its rain forests. Three rain forest valleys exist within the park and each receives about 145 inches of precipitation per year. The lush forest floor and towering evergreens shrouded in moss attract hundreds of thousands of visitors each year.

For visitors who want to experience the diversity of the park but have little time, Hurricane Ridge, Ruby Beach and the Hoh Rain Forests are easily accessible from Highway 101 and offer spectacular views.

Rain Forests: One of the unique environments of the park is the coastal rain forests. Three forest valleys, the Quinault, Queets and Hoh, located on the west side of the park, are noted as rain forests.

Most of the 145 inches of rain received each year falls from late fall to early spring. The summers are comparatively dry with many days of clear, sunny weather. Along with the wet weather comes mild temperatures. Temperatures rarely dip below freezing in the lower elevation valleys and summer highs rarely exceed 80°F.

The rain forest is noted for its quantity and quality of vegetation. There is hardly a square inch of soil not occupied by plants, which range in size from microscopic to giant spruces more than 300 feet tall. Sitka spruce and western hemlock are the dominant species, but Douglas fir, western red cedar, big-leaved maple, red alder, vine maple and black cottonwood also thrive in the forest.

Over a thousand varieties of ferns, mosses and fungi carpet the soggy floor of the rain forest. The rays of light shining between the thick canopy of trees upon the lush green undergrowth is a favorite subject for photographers.

Of the 3, the Hoh rain forest is the most popular among visitors. The Hoh River valley and rain forest is accessible from U.S. Highway 101 on the western side of the peninsula. The Hoh River Road exits from Highway 101 at **Mile 625** (see the U.S. HIGHWAY 101 log). The Hoh River Visitor Center offers interpretive programs, displays, exhibits and informative publications about the formation and biology of the rain forest. Two trailheads are located at the center for those wishing a closer view of the forest.

Glaciers: Glacial ice is one of the fore-most scenic and scientific values of Olympic National Park. There are nearly 60 glaciers crowning the Olympic peaks. The prominent glaciers are those on Mount Olympus, covering approximately 10 square miles. Beyond the Olympus complex are the glaciers of Mount Carrie, the Bailey Range, Mount Christie and Mount Anderson. In the company of these glaciers are perpetual snowbanks that have the superficial appearance of glacial ice.

The Olympic glaciers are slow moving in comparison to those in Alaska (where glaciers can advance up to 100 feet per day). There is no great advance of these glaciers today, but neither are they retreating. Forward surges in glacial flow often occur after a number of very heavy winters and cool summers, but such activity has been relatively infrequent with Olympic glaciers in recorded time.

The movement of glacial ice, past and present, has produced striking geological features in the Olympic Mountains. The lake basins, U-shaped valleys and jagged peaks are the products of massive glacial erosion that occurred many thousands of years ago when the year-round climate was much colder. This erosion process continues today, but on a much smaller scale.

Access to the Olympic glaciers is by trails and cross-country routes. The most visited glaciers in the park are the Blue and Anderson glaciers on Mount Olympus. From the Hoh rain forest, the upriver hiking trail leads 18 miles up to the snout of Blue Glacier. Anderson Glacier can be reached by hiking up to the Dosewallips River for 11 miles, or from the west side by the East Fork Quinault River trail for 16 miles. To visit the other glaciers requires more mountaineering skill and time.

Travel on glacial ice is a special phase of mountaineering requiring the basic use of climbing rope, ice ax, crampons and good judgment by the individual climber. The presence of snow-bridged crevasses on glaciers is a very great hazard to climbers and no one should attempt glacier travel alone. Self-evacuation from a deep, steep-walled crevasse is nearly impossible.

Camping: Nearly 20 campgrounds (some walk-in) are scattered around the perimeter of Olympic National Park. Many are accessible to vehicles and offer piped water, toilet facilities, tables and fireplaces and many will accommodate trailers. No showers or hookups are offered at park campgrounds.

Hiking: Potential Hazards — There are approximately 40 miles of rugged, picturesque beaches available to the energetic hiker. As you hike these beaches and explore the tide pools, be alert to the change in tides along this coast. There can be a difference of 10 feet between the low and high tides. Always be alert to having an escape route on an incoming tide. There are many points of land that jut into the ocean. Several of these headlands are farther around than they appear and should be crossed over rather than trying to walk around their base. If you try to round some of the points at other than the lowest (minus) tides, you may get trapped and find that you cannot continue, your retreat cut off by the rising waters of an incoming tide.

Each year some visitors are trapped on cliff faces and in some cases (most notably Taylor Point, which is particularly dangerous), have been washed from the cliffs to their deaths. Check at the visitor centers or at the coastal ranger stations for information on local hazards before attempting beach hiking.

Whenever you go on an extended hike, you should plan on the possibility of abrupt weather changes. A brilliant, warm, cloudless day can become a blinding rain or snow storm in a matter of hours. Take extra waterproof clothing, food, water and supplies.

It is always wise to travel with a companion. The park contains almost 916,136 acres, most of which are wilderness. This makes search and rescue extremely difficult and a great amount of time may be spent in just finding a missing person — time the person may not have to spare. Let someone know where you are going and when you plan to return before embarking on your trip.

Fishing: The many lakes and streams on the Olympic Peninsula, as well as the surrounding bodies of salt water offer outstanding fishing. Salmon, steelhead, cutthroat, eastern brook, Dolly Varden and rainbow trout are the most popular game fish on the peninsula. Some of the most famous salmon and steelhead rivers on the peninsula are the Hoh, Soleduck, Queets, Bogachiel and Humptulips. The Hamma Hamma is a popular stream for sea-run cutthroat and the mouth of this river is good for steamer clams and Dungeness crabs.

Two subspecies of trout offer unique fishing in Lake Crescent. The state record for the largest *Crescenti* caught in Lake Crescent is 12 pounds while the record for the largest *Beardslee* is 15 pounds, 4 ounces.

The general fishing season begins in April and extends through October, but the high lakes (over 4,000-foot elevation) generally don't begin to thaw until mid-June. The Fourth of July holiday is usually the kick-off for the season in these lakes.

No license is required within Olympic National Park, however, a punch card is needed for steelhead and salmon.

There is a large variety of shellfish on the peninsula, the most popular of which are oysters, razor clams, steamer clams, crabs and the monstrous geoducks (gooey-ducks). The Hood Canal region is popular for its oysters, steamer clams and the delicate spot shrimp (prawns).

With the exception of razor clams, no license is required to harvest the ocean-shore clams. The best time to dig these shellfish is during a minus tide. (Tide charts are available at nearly every resort and sports shop along the coast.)

Wildlife: The park hosts the largest remaining herd of Roosevelt elk in the nation (which number approximately 5,000). Black-tailed deer, black bear, cougar and other large mammals inhabit the region. The Olympic marmot is one of the several small animals which are found only in this area. Five species of sea lions, seals and whales live in the water or on the rocks just offshore.

National Monuments

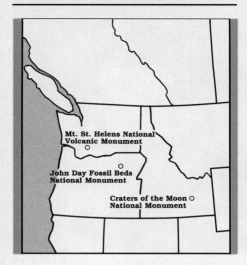

The violent, fiery volcanic eruptions of the Northwest are dramatized in 2 national monuments: Craters of the Moon National Monument in south-central Idaho and Mount St. Helens Volcanic Monument in southwestern Washington.

A third national monument, John Day Fossil Beds National Monument in central Oregon is the result of several geological changes over the centuries and today offers one of the most complete fossil records of world history known to man.

A trip to any of these monuments reminds visitors of the great natural power of the earth and its atmosphere, and helps visitors understand the land formations of the Great Northwest.

Craters of the Moon National Monument

The 83 square miles of Craters of the Moon National Monument in southcentral Idaho is covered with a thick mat of volcanic rock, ash and cinders, underlaid by miles of caves (lava tubes). For the most part, the barren, rocky surface is void of vegetation, except for sparse bunches of sagebrush, cheatgrass, limber pine and springtime floral displays.

Access: Access from the west is via U.S. Highway 93/Interstate 84 at Twin Falls, ID. U.S. Highway 93 travels through the Craters of the Moon National Monument. From the east, access is from Interstate 15 and either U.S. Highway 26 or 20 at their junctions with Interstate 15 near Idaho Falls, ID, then west to the junction with U.S. Highway 93 at Arco. See **Mile 204.5** in the U.S. HIGHWAY 93 section.

The visitor center is open year-round from 8:30 a.m. until 4:30 p.m. From June 15 to Labor Day, the visitor center has extended hours from 8 a.m. until 6 p.m. The park is most often busy during June, July and August. The 7-mile loop road is closed from Nov. 1 to April 15.

There is a fee of $3 per vehicle or $1 per bicycle to enter the park. For maps and a brochure, write to the Superintendent, Craters of the Moon National Monument, P.O. Box 29, Arco, ID 83213; phone (208) 527-3257.

History: To the onlooker, this vast, open plateau located off U.S. Highway 93 is anything but inviting. It is the result of a series of cracks in the earth's surface (The Great Rift), through which hot lava, ash and steam exploded and shot skyward nearly 15,000 years ago and continued to erupt sporadically until just 2,000 years ago.

The area was virtually unknown until 1921. Early settlers avoided it because the terrain is so difficult to cross. Farmers and ranchers ignored the inhospitable area which would not support a good growth of sagebrush, much less cattle or crops.

In the 1920s, the area was described as a "weird lunar landscape" and many scientists speculated that the surface of the moon must look much the same as this area. In 1924, 83 square miles were set aside as a national monument.

Craters of the Moon was discovered when Robert Limbert headed into the then-unknown lava beds in 1921 with W.L. Cole and a dog. For 28 miles the trio trekked the rugged lava, unable to sleep for lack of level ground. Cole's feet were blistered and the dog's were so cut to shreds that they carried it. At last they reached smoother flows, but now they lacked water as the porous lava allowed no water to remain on the surface. By following dove flights, they found snowmelt water holes within Great Rift faults. According to a pamphlet issued by the Park Service, Limbert's reports of the expedition and his photographs of the area were instrumental in securing its protection as a national monument.

Attractions: Visitors should drive the 7-mile loop road to discover spatter and cinder cones, lava flows and lava tubes. To the south of the park lies the vast Craters of the Moon Wilderness established in 1970. Check with park rangers before entering the wilderness. The area provides no natural water sources and although the spectacular volcanic features are exciting to the eye, they are hard on the feet. Backcountry permits are required for overnight stays in the wilderness.

Stop at the visitor center at the park headquarters to view a dramatic film about erupting volcanoes. The film explains how lava flowed from fissures in the earth to create the volcanic features within the park. The displays — complete with easy-to-read graphics and samples of various lava rocks — help visitors recognize the formations, wildflowers and animals of the park. Check at the visitor center for information about the conducted nature walks and talks offered during the mornings and evenings in the summer. Campfire talks, some illustrated with movies or slides, are a regular summer feature.

Water and restrooms are available at the visitor center and the nearby campground. Take advantage of them here, because water is not available anywhere else in the park. Waterless restrooms are available at the Tree Molds parking lot and at the Cave Area parking lot on the loop road and its spurs.

Park naturalists conduct nature walks in summer at Craters of the Moon. (L. Linkhart)

Loop road: Seven stops along the loop road offer a quick, graphic explanation of the phenomena which formed Craters of the Moon. A short trail at the North Crater Flow leads to a group of monoliths (crater wall fragments) transported by lava flows. This flow is one of the youngest. Here the Triple Twist Tree suggests, because of its 1,350 growth rings, that these eruptions ceased only 2,000 years ago. Two forms of lava are visible: the crumbly *aa* (ah-ah), which literally means "hard on the feet," and the *pahoehoe* (pa-hoy-hoy), meaning "ropy."

The Devils Orchard is a group of lava fragments standing like islands in a sea of cinders.

A spur road beyond the Inferno Cone leads to the Tree Molds area, Trench Mortar Flats and the Craters of the Moon Wilderness. Tree molds formed where molten lava flows encased trees and then hardened. The cylindrical molds that remained after the wood rotted away range from a few inches to just under one foot in diameter.

Camping: There is 1 campground at Craters of the Moon National Monument. Fifty campsites are available and the campground is located at the park headquarters. Drinking water and toilets are available. No hookups are available and there is a $5 fee per night. No wood fires are permitted, but a charcoal grill is located at each site. Any campers planning to stay overnight in the wilderness must secure a camping permit from the visitor center. There are commercial campgrounds with hookups, showers, dump stations and laundry facilities in Arco (located 20 miles northeast) and other nearby communities.

Hiking: One of the interesting formations in the park are the lava tubes. When molten lava flowed out of the ground, it behaved like a stream of water working its way downhill. When the surface of the lava stream cooled, it solidified, but beneath the surface the lava continued to flow. The interior lava eventually flowed out of its caselike stream leaving an empty tube which exists today. Check with park rangers before attempting to explore any lava tubes and secure a copy of *The Cave Trail*, a pamphlet describing the caves and safety guidelines for explorers.

Craters of the Moon offers a land of exploration for even the meekest hiker. Several caves are located off trails on the loop road, but a powerful flashlight or lantern is needed for all except Indian Tunnel. Visitors should wear sturdy boots or shoes and stay on the trails, because lava rocks can be sharp. Never climb on spatter cones or monoliths. Collecting rocks or any natural object is prohibited — the area is being preserved, and visitor cooperation is needed.

Flora and fauna: More than 2,000 species of insects fly, roam and crawl throughout the crevises of Craters of the Moon. In addition, there are 140 bird species, 26 mammals, 6 reptiles and 1 amphibian which survive the rugged terrain. Mule deer pick their way through the cinders in search of feed, and bobcats, great horned owls and other birds of prey hunt for smaller mammals. Although

Painted Hills is 1 of 3 units that make up John Day Fossil Beds.   (© John Barger)

vegetation is sparce, more than 300 species of plants take root in Craters of the Moon, including sagebrush, antelope bitterbrush, rabbitbrush and several wildflowers.

John Day Fossil Beds National Monument

Lying peacefully along the quiet banks of the John Day River in central Oregon is one of the most complete collections of natural history in the world, the John Day Fossil Beds National Monument.

Access: To reach John Day Fossil Beds National Monument visitor center from U.S. Highway 395 **(Mile 265)**, take U.S. Highway 26 west at John Day, OR, and continue west to the Highway 26/Oregon Highway 19 junction and travel 2 miles north on Highway 19. The center, located within the Sheep Rock Unit, is the best place to start a visit to the monument.

To reach the Painted Hills Unit, leave U.S. Highway 26 near Mitchell and follow a paved county road for 6 miles. The Clarno Unit is on Oregon Highway 218, 18 miles west of Fossil and 15 miles east of Antelope.

From U.S. Highway 97, take Oregon Highway 126 at its junction in Redmond **(Mile 224)**, then to its merger with U.S. Highway 26 at Prineville and travel to Mitchell or farther on to the Highway 19 junction. Access from the west is also from the U.S Highway 97/U.S. Highway 26 junction at Madras **(Mile 250)**.

For further information, write to the John Day Fossil Beds National Monument, 420 W. Main St., John Day, OR 97845.

History: Forty million years ago, a semitropical forest covered portions of central Oregon. Fifteen million years later, sabretoothed cats prowled the same landscape. Through the centuries, tiny 3-toed horses, camels, rhinoceroses and tapirs inhabited Oregon along with huge animals which have no counterparts in the current animal kingdom. The Oreodont was a grazing hog with a sheep's lifestyle. Creodonts were primitive meat eaters. Titanotheres evolved from the size of a hog to that of an elephant.

The record of this past life is preserved in the rocks of the 3 units of the John Day Fossil Beds National Monument. Collectively, the beds portray a total environment. Each has its unique landscape, attractions and scientific importance.

Settlers were removing fossilized bones and wood as early as the 1860s, about 40 years after pioneer explorer and trapper John Day traveled through the area. One of the first to recognize the value of this historical resource was Thomas Condon, a frontier missionary and natural history enthusiast who shared his findings with professional paleontologists and geologists.

To protect this resource, John Day Fossil Beds National Monument was created in 1974. Today it encompasses more than 14,030 acres including fossil beds and the surrounding semidesert landscape.

Attractions: The best time of the year to visit the John Day Fossil Beds is in late spring (May through June) when the trail surfaces have dried and the wildflowers are in bloom. Another good time is in the fall. Summer visitors usually prefer early morning tours of the monument to escape the summer heat.

The summers here are dry with an average monthly rainfall of less than 1 inch from July through September. Generally, the spring seasons are cold and wet with warm, drying weather not prevalent until late May. The climate in the fall is pleasant, with warm sunny days and crisp cool nights.

The park was established to preserve part of the past for present and future generations to see, study and enjoy. Scientific and educational research is allowed with appropriate permits, but individual collecting, digging and removal of fossils or other geological materials is prohibited.

Sheep Rock Unit: The Sheep Rock unit is your best introduction to John Day Fossil Beds. The Cant Ranch House Visitor Center displays fossils of many prehistoric animals. They include the entelodont, a rhinoceros, foot bones of a 3-toed horse and teeth from a sabre-toothed cat. A fossil preparation laboratory is in an 1800s cabin. There are interpretative displays on the 3 units and a history of fossil expeditions in the area.

The Cant Ranch House, built in 1917, is on the national register of historic places. Some rooms are furnished with antiques.

Sheep Rock Unit, spread in 4 sub-units along Oregon Highway 19, exposes a continuous sequence of evolutionary development spanning 8 million years. A series of short trails branch from each parking area and lead to creeks, fossil beds, a scenic amphitheater, fossil replicas and magnificent views of the John Day River and valley. Expect to see towering cliffs, rugged mountains and colors running from sulfur yellows to red rock.

Painted Hills Unit, 10 miles northwest of the town of Mitchell, is characterized by dune-like mounds with brilliant bands of chimney red and gray-green volcanic ash. Its scientific importance lies in the large numbers of plant fossils preserved in the beds. It is known for spring shows of wildflowers which peak in May. One plant, the John Day Canactus, grows only here.

Three trails, from 0.3 to 2 miles in length, lead to viewpoints of colorful hills, dunes, the open valley floor and leaf impressions in stone.

Clarno Unit, 11 miles east of Antelope, is the oldest of the 3. It dates from 60 million to 40 million years ago. Fossil seeds, nuts and fruits are preserved here, making it unique among geologic sites. Seeds of grapes, magnolia, water lily and palms have been found at Clarno.

Its most spectacular feature is the Palisades — 200-foot cliffs formed by an ancient mudslide. Fossils in their natural setting can be seen along the 0.3-mile "Trail of the Fossils." The 0.5-mile Clarno Arch Trail climbs 150 feet to a rock arch and fossil remains of trees embedded in the Palisades Cliff. Cross-country hiking is not encouraged due to sharp rocks, unstable soil and an abundance of rattlesnakes.

Camping: There are no campgrounds within the monument. State and federally operated campgrounds are available within the region, however. Check with the information center for campground locations near the monument. Lodging, food, gasoline and phones are available in the surrounding communities. These services are not available in the park.

Hiking: When hiking in areas with exposed geological formations, stay on established trails. Walking off trails or climbing rocks in these areas is dangerous and damages the fragile fossil beds.

Mount St. Helens National Volcanic Monument

For a look at more recent volcanic activity, stop at Mount St. Helens National Volcanic Monument. In a blast more powerful than an atomic bomb, Mount St. Helens erupted on May 18, 1980. Administered by the Forest Service, the monument is a graphic example of the power of nature.

Access: Mount St. Helens National Volcanic Monument is located east of Interstate 5. Northern access is via U.S. Highway 12 East from Interstate 5 (Exit 68 **Mile 496**) to Randle. Southern access is via Washington Highway 503 from Woodland (Exit 21 **Mile 449**) on Interstate 5. It is about a 2½-hour drive from either exit to Windy Ridge in the monument. Washington Highway 504 from Castle Rock (Exit 49 **Mile 477**) and Highway 505 from Toledo (Exit 60 **Mile 488**) provide access to a county viewpoint up the North Fork Toutle River valley, where the state is working on the highway and the Corps of Engineers is working on a sediment debris dam.

The Mount St. Helens Visitor Center is located next to Silver Lake, across from Seaquest State Park, 5 miles east of Interstate 5 on Highway 504. Visitors can walk under a relief model of the mountain for an inside view of a volcano in action. The center also has a 22-minute film on the eruption, seismographs, and naturalist talks and walks. Open daily, except major holidays, from 9 a.m. to 6 p.m. May to September, 9 a.m. to 5 p.m. the remainder of the year.

The Mount St. Helens National Monument Headquarters is located outside Amboy on Highway 503. For information, write Mount St. Helens Volcanic National Monument Headquarters at Route 1, Box 369, Amboy, WA 98601; phone (206) 247-5473 or 247-4038. Maps and information are also available in or near the monument at the ranger station in Randle and information stations in Pine Creek and Iron Creek (open daily from Memorial Day through Labor Day). It is important to obtain a current map of the monument for information on roads, trails and lookouts in the monument.

History: Fifty-seven persons were killed in the unexpectedly violent explosion and the cloud of ash, which reached more than 80,000 feet into the atmosphere, spread over much of the Northwestern states.

Scientists began expecting activity at Mount St. Helens on March 20, 1980, when an earthquake that registered 4 on the Richter scale shook the mountain. A week later, the first eruption of steam and ash was reported and similar explosions continued until about April 22. The mountain was quiet until the week of May 7-14, when steam and ash again belched from the mountain.

The morning of Sunday, May 18, 1980, Mount St. Helens made worldwide headlines. In a powerful, violent explosion following an earthquake, the mountain blew one cubic mile of earth into the air, clouding the skies of the Northwest with its fine, abrasive ash. The eruption was accompanied by huge landslides, flooding, heavy ash deposits and devastating mudflows which choked the Toutle River and enlarged the formerly scenic Spirit Lake.

The bodies of 31 visitors, forest workers and government researchers were later found among the debris and several more were

Ample evidence remains of Mount St. Helens' devastating eruption. (© John Barger)

reported missing. Virtually all of the campgrounds immediately adjacent to the mountain were wiped out in a matter of seconds. More than 3 billion board feet of timber was tossed about and demolished by super-heated hurricane-force winds spewing from the mouth of the volcano.

Hundreds of miles away, the ash cloud dropped like snow on hundreds of communities, blanketing fields, contaminating watersheds and destroying mechanical equipment. The ominous cloud of ash was accompanied by lightning as it rolled over Washington, Oregon, Idaho and Montana. Millions of dollars were spent cleaning up the ash and recovering from the fury of the mountain.

Attractions: Today, the land around Mount St. Helens is beginning to recover. Scattered throughout the devastated area, wildflowers are blooming and regrowth trees are reaching heights of 6 feet in some areas. Look for the bright pink of fireweed in ash deposits and along roadsides. Blue lupine can be found on rocky surfaces and on coverings of pumice. Animals which have returned include mountain bluebirds, elk and the seldom-seen pocket gopher. Although most of the recreational facilities have been destroyed, the area has been set aside as a national volcanic monument and perhaps more visitors than ever before are coming to the mountain to witness the devastation. There are few developed facilities in the monument area; no campgrounds, gas stations or food services.

During the summer interpretive naturalist talks and excursions are conducted at various points in the monument, including Windy Ridge, Lahar Viewpoint, Meta Lake, Harmony Falls and Ape Cave. For times and places, check with the visitor center or the free *Volcano Review* newspaper published by the monument.

After stopping at the visitor center, visitors may wish to continue east on Spirit Lake Highway 504. Although the highway and surrounding lands are outside the monument boundaries, the route offers close-up views of the ash-choked Toutle River and remnants of bridges, logging camps and houses which were destroyed in the May 18, 1980, mudflows. Reconstruction of Highway 504 is expected to be completed in 1992 to provide greater access to the west side of the mountain.

Road 83 Auto Tour: This tour leads through the southern section of the monument. The trip begins at the junction of Forest Service (FS) Roads 83 and 90 and continues on 83. Notice the basalt flows where lava blanketed the landscape nearly 2,000 years ago. Three miles north of the junction on FS 8303 is Apes Headquarters, offering lantern rentals, information and interpretive activites. Ape Cave, the longest lava tube in the nation, can be explored by those with good sources of light and warm clothes. Continuing up the southeast side of the mountain, visitors can see where the powerful mudflows cut through the forest. Lahar Viewpoint 4.5 miles from the crater rim provides a view of the beheaded Shoestring Glacier. Road construction is continuing on some sections of this road. Drive cautiously and be prepared for delays.

Vegetation is making a slow comeback in areas affected by the blast (© John Barger)

Trail of Two Forests: The Trail of Two Forests is located 6 miles east of Cougar on FS Road 90. Turn north on FS 83 and drive 2 miles to FS 8303 and turn west for 0.5 mile. The Trail of Two Forests is a 0.3-mile-long boardwalk through a forest that has grown on top of an old lava flow. The tree casts were formed when lava solidified around the trunks of trees; the trees burned from the intense heat and the remaining charcoal decomposed, leaving the cylindrical wells. The trail is wheelchair accessible. There are restrooms and picnic tables.

Windy Ridge Auto Tour: For face-to-face views of the destruction of Mount St. Helens, you can drive in to Windy Ridge from U.S. 12 at Randle. Randle is almost 2 hours' drive from Interstate 5. This route is usually open from June to October.

From Randle, follow FS Road 25 9 miles to its junction with FS 26. Here you have a choice of roads. The fastest, easiest route to Windy Ridge continues on FS 25 (a 2-lane paved road) another 11 miles to FS 99. Turn west on FS 99 for the remaining 17 miles to Windy Ridge Viewpoint. FS 26 is a single paved lane with pullouts for passing, but it is more scenic.

Nothing prepares you for seeing the devastation for the first time. You approach the Windy Ridge viewpoint on the north side through miles of lush green forest. Magnificent virgin timber, including 650-year-old Douglas firs, reaches up more than 200 feet. Velvety moss covers the forest floor, huge

sword ferns grow in abundance, sunlight filters through the trees. Suddenly you come around a bend in the road and confront a view that extends across the horizon — all of gray. Gray tree trunks, gray mountains, gray valley . . . a naked landscape without its deep forest cover. The crushed hulk of a miner's car caught in the blast stands beside the road near the junction of FS 99 and FS 26.

The resilience of nature is equally impressive as the land begins to recover. Tiny seedlings, pearly everlasting and fireweed are reclaiming the ashen ground.

At Windy Ridge you are within 4 miles of the crater and can see the side of the mountain that was blown away. A log and gravel path anchored by cables climbs the ridge for outstanding views of the mountain and the new Spirit Lake far below. Park rangers conduct informational talks at Windy Ridge during the summer, 11:30 a.m. to 4:30 p.m. daily.

Camping: There are no campgrounds within the national monument, but several campgrounds are located within driving distance.

Hiking: Visitors should purchase a copy of the *Recreation Opportunity Guide* from the visitor center for narrative interpretations of the trails and loops.

Cedar Flats Trail: The Cedar Flats trail is a loop through the northern parts of Cedar Flats Research Natural Area. The trail provides an opportunity to walk among magnificent western red cedar and Douglas fir trees of this natural old-growth forest.

Independence Pass Trail: This popular trail leads through downed timber to an overlook that provides a spectacular wide-angle view of Spirit Lake and Mount St. Helens and other Cascade peaks. The top of the dome may be seen with binoculars.

Meta Lake Trail: Visitors on the Meta Lake trail are surrounded by the effects of the catastrophic eruption. Trees, killed by the hurricane-force winds and heated to hundreds of degrees Fahrenheit, testify to the forcefulness of the blast. The landscape appears gray and is dotted by patches of new, regrowth trees.

Norway Pass Trail: This 2.2-mile hike takes a little under 2 hours. It features outstanding views of the crater and lava dome, logjammed Spirit Lake, blown down trees, and waterfalls. Plants which have regrown here include the colorful avalanche lily, huckleberry and mountain ash. Drinking water is available at the trailhead.

Plains of Abraham Trail: This 8-mile trail begins at Windy Ridge and terminates at Lahar off FS Road 83. It is suitable for backpackers wanting to spend an evening within the monument. Campfires are not allowed; campers must bring a cookstove.

Other Sightseeing Tours: Helicopter and sightseeing planes can be hired in nearby communities for flights over the craters. Helicopter flights are about $60 per person for a half-hour flight. In Cougar, call Bluebird Helicopters at (206) 238-5326. Two companies offer helicopter flights from Highway 504, east of the Mount St. Helens Visitor Center. Aero-West offers sightseeing plane flights out of Kelso; call (206) 423-4902.

National Recreation Areas

Recreational pursuits abound in the Northwest, but unusual opportunities exist in the region's National Recreation Areas. These areas have been set aside for their unique recreational attributes and thousands of visitors walk the trails, fish the rivers and streams, admire the wildlife and photograph the scenic wonders within the boundaries of these areas.

Administered by the U.S. Forest Service or National Park Service, NRAs in the Northwest include: Hells Canyon on the Oregon-Idaho border between Lewiston and Weiser, ID; Oregon Dunes, on the central Oregon coast between Florence and Coos Bay, OR; Ross Lake and Lake Chelan, in the Cascade Range of northern Washington; and Sawtooth National Recreation Area, 8 miles north of Sun Valley, in central Idaho.

Hells Canyon National Recreation Area

The name Hells Canyon conjures up visions of frontier ruggedness, impassable obstacles and Western romance. And well it should. Hells Canyon is all that and more. It is generally a remote and undeveloped area with few good roads. Access to the river is limited. It is a good idea to plan your trip carefully before entering the area.

For information, maps, brochures and a list of outfitters in Hells Canyon NRA, write to the Hells Canyon National Recreation Area Headquarters, Wallowa-Whitman National Forest, P.O. Box 490, Enterprise, OR 97828, phone (503) 426-3151; or to the Wallowa-Whitman National Forest, P.O. Box 907, Baker, OR 97814, phone (503) 523-6391. There are offices in Lewiston and Riggins as well. Write to the Hells Canyon NRA, 3620-B Snake River Ave., Lewiston, ID 83501; or Hells Canyon NRA, P.O. Box 832, Riggins, ID 83549.

Access: You can reach Hells Canyon Dam via the Idaho Highway 71/U.S. Highway 95 junction at Cambridge, ID, north of Weiser or turn off Interstate 84/U.S. Highway 30 (Exit 302 **Mile 299**), near Baker, OR, via Oregon Highway 86 East to Oxbow Dam. Northern access is via Interstate 84/Oregon Highway 82 junction at La Grande (Exit 261, **Mile 258**) then to Joseph and Imnaha on Oregon Highway 350.

Road and trail conditions vary due to weather, surface and the time of year. Many roads are rough and slippery and some do not open until mid-summer because of the snow. Many roads are suitable for passenger cars while some are passable only by 4-wheel-drive vehicles. There are few roads providing access to the Snake River. Boat launches are located at Hells Canyon Dam and Pittsburg Landing. Check on current road and trail conditions before entering the area.

From the town of Imnaha, located east from Oregon Highway 82, a graveled Forest Service Road 4260 runs north along the Imnaha River to Cow Creek. Near Cow Creek the road changes to a dirt surface and winds its way to Dug Bar. The road to Dug Bar is rough and not recommended for trailers, passenger cars or 2-wheel-drive vehicles during wet weather.

Going south from the town of Imnaha, the Imnaha River Road (Forest Service Road 3955) parallels the river as it meanders through rims and benches much like those along the Snake River. You can continue on this road to Indian Crossing Campground, or join the Wallowa Mountain Loop Road (Forest Service Road 39) leading either back to Joseph on Highway 82 or on to Halfway on Highway 86. All of these roads entail traveling on narrow, secondary gravel roads maintained for passenger cars and trailers. There are turnouts, but drive cautiously.

The road to Hat Point is rough and narrow and not recommended for heavy recreation vehicles or trailers.

The road to Pittsburg Landing from U.S. Highway 95 near Whitebird, ID, is single lane with turnouts and a gravel surface to the Snake River-Salmon River divide. This is a slow, crooked route with steep sections.

As the road plunges into the Snake River canyon, it becomes even rougher and steeper with sharp switchbacks and no surfacing. Passenger cars travel this road, but are not recommended beyond the divide. The route to Pittsburg Landing is not recommended for RVs or trailers.

History: It was the mild winters which attracted the first human visitors to Hells Canyon. The Native American Indians lived in much of the region, leaving traces of their camps on nearly every terrace. Rock faces are covered with Indian carvings and petroglyphs. Relics of early white settlement have also been discovered, built atop ancient Indian villages because of the lack of flat land.

The canyon formed a natural barrier against white explorers, who were time and again forced to retreat. In 1877, the swift river prevented the Army from following Chief Joseph into Idaho at the start of the Nez Perce War. Chief Joseph, on the other hand, was able to lead his people across the flooding Snake River without losing a single human, horse or cow.

In 1975, 652,488 acres were set aside as

Hells Canyon is the deepest river gorge in the world.   (Tom Barr)

View of Hell's Canyon from Hat Point Overlook. (Tom Barr)

the Hells Canyon National Recreation Area (NRA) and the river was designated a "wild and scenic river." The canyon is a sportsman's paradise and the adventurous take advantage of the white-water rafting opportunities available from local guides and outfitters.

Attractions: The canyon, formed by the erosion of the Snake River, is the deepest river gorge in the world with an average depth of 6,600 feet. This 20-mile slot along the Idaho-Oregon border from Spring Creek to Johnson Bar is flanked by the 10,000-foot peaks of the Seven Devils Range in Idaho to the east and the Wallowa Mountains of Oregon to the west. The upper 5 miles of the gorge is inundated by Hells Canyon Reservoir. Below Hells Canyon Dam, the Snake River winds north to Lewiston, a free-flowing wild and scenic river for 67.5 miles. The river drops more than 11 feet per mile as it thunders over a succession of spectacular rapids, interspersed with placid stretches.

In the springtime, Hells Canyon shows its beauty with an abundance of grasses, shrubs, trees and colorful wildflowers. As summer approaches and temperatures soar to above 100°F, the perennial grasses and flora dry and bake to form a parched, gray and brown scene. The wind within the canyon is relatively calm and even in the winter, the canyon bottom has comparatively mild temperatures.

Visitors to Hells Canyon should be aware that fire danger during the summer months is extremely high. The parched cheatgrass and sagebrush is explosively flammable. An open fire closure is in effect annually between July 1 and Sept. 15 in the river corridor.

Hat Point: The Hat Point observation site (elev. 6,982 feet) offers an excellent view of Hells Canyon and the Seven Devils Mountains. The viewpoint is accessible by car on a dirt and gravel road 24 miles from the town of Imnaha, OR. Some of the most rugged and spectacular backcountry in the state of

Oregon can be seen on the trip from Imnaha to Hat Point. It is a rough road and a one-way trip takes 2 1/2 hours. The road is not recommended for cars with low clearance and those pulling trailers.

At the end of the steep grades leading to Hat Point is Five Mile viewpoint, where the Wallowa Mountains and the scenic Imnaha River valley are visible. There are picnic facilities available at Hat Point and nearby Horse Creek viewpoint. Water, which is not available at either point, is available at Sacajawea Spring, 0.3 mile north of Hat Point along the rim trail.

Camping: The road leading to Seven Devils Campground and overlook from U.S. Highway 95 near Riggins, ID, is a single lane with turnouts and gravel surfacing. This low-speed route is traveled via automobile, but requires caution. It generally isn't clear of snow until early July.

Sacajawea Campground is 0.5 mile north of Hat Point observation site, approximately 25 miles from Imnaha, OR. Primitive overnight camping facilities are available.

Water can be scarce during dry summer months in some parts of the NRA. Plan on carrying water. Drink only water from developed systems; water from springs, lakes, ponds and streams should not be consumed without first being treated.

Hiking: Nearly 1,000 miles of trails traverse Hells Canyon NRA. Some are maintained yearly and are easy to travel; others are rarely maintained and difficult to find and use. Check on trail conditions before embarking on your trip.

Some of the hazards of cross-country hiking are snakes and poison ivy. Poison ivy is abundant along the river and side drainages. Hikers should watch side drainages where often times the trails pass through patches of these plants.

Rattlesnakes are common in the Hells Canyon area. Normally, snakes are active between May and September and generally

are not active in the heat of the day, but should be expected in the morning and late afternoon.

If rattlesnakes and poison ivy don't scare you, the parasitic insects probably won't either. Ticks are notorious in the sagebrush regions and visitors should be sure to check their clothing and each other for the insects. Aside from minor infections, ticks can spread Rocky Mountain spotted fever, and should not be taken lightly. Take precautions.

The Nee-Me-Poo National Recreation Trail is a historic trail following the steps of Chief Joseph. This 3.7-mile trail is part of the 1,800-mile trek led by Chief Joseph in 1877 just prior to the Nez Perce War. Nearly 700 Nez Perce Indians passed along this trail when they were forced to leave their fertile, lush homeland in the Wallowas. They were en route to the Lapwai Indian Reservation when their relocation movement turned to a historic flight for freedom at the beginning of the Nez Perce War. Their hope of freedom turned to tragedy when the tribe was captured just 30 miles south of the Canadian border in the Bear Paw Mountains of Montana.

The Nee-Me-Poo (means "the real people") National Recreation Trail was set aside in 1968 as a reminder of the nation's history and the tragedy of the Nez Perce people.

From the south, the trail can be reached by taking Oregon Highway 350 from Joseph, OR, to the town of Imnaha. From Imnaha, take the gravel County Road 735 north to Fence Creek. Beyond this point, the road (which is now Forest Service Road 4260) deteriorates into a steep, narrow dirt road unsuitable for vehicles pulling trailers. Passenger cars may be used during dry weather by carefully negotiating this last segment of the journey, about 10 miles.

The trail may also be entered from the north at Dug Bar on the Snake River. Dug Bar is reached by jet boating upriver from the mouth of the Grande Ronde River (about 28 miles) or by float trip downstream from Hells Canyon Dam (about 51 miles).

The Nee-Me-Poo Trail represents a wealth of Indian and pioneer history which must be preserved for future generations. Be careful not to damage or destroy artifacts and historical markings, and report those who do.

For experienced hikers, the 31.5-mile Snake River National Recreation Trail parallels the Snake River on the Idaho side. The trail begins at Granite Creek (access by boat from the Hells Canyon Dam) and ends at Pittsburg Landing. Sections of the trail may be flooded in high water.

Jet Boat, Float Trips and Scenic Flights: Numerous outfitters provide jet boat trips down the Snake River from Hells Canyon Dam and upriver from Lewiston. Float trips down the Snake are provided by licensed outfitters. Trips generally last 2 to 5 days and the usual float season is from the Friday preceding Memorial Day weekend through Sept. 15. Float reservations are required. A list of outfitters is available by contacting the Hells Canyon NRA headquarters.

Private parties floating the river are required to make reservations and secure a permit. Application forms are available from the District Ranger, Lewiston office at 3620-B Snake River Ave., Lewiston, ID 83501. For information on reservations and permits, call (208) 743-2297. Phone reservations are not accepted.

Registration by private boat owners is mandatory. Self-issuing permits are available at Pittsburg Landing, Dug Bar and at the mouth of the Salmon River. River guards are available to issue permits at the mouth of the Grande Ronde River and at Hells Canyon Dam during the season. The Forest Service maintains a boat launch site and an information station at the road end below Hells Canyon Dam. No overnight facilities are available.

Fishing Hells Canyon: Since the Snake River forms the boundary between Idaho and Oregon, fishermen securing a license from either state may fish the entire river by boat. Those fishing from the bank must secure the appropriate state's license. Smallmouth bass and crappie are the target of most anglers in the gorge. Most successful fishing is done from drift boats, rafts or floating downstream from Hells Canyon Dam and jet boats coming upstream from Lewiston.

Although the river previously produced trophy-sized trout, the fishery has suffered from nitrogen supersaturation from the dams and the numbers of trophy fish are down. Best trout fishing is in the first few miles below Hells Canyon Dam.

The most popular fish in the canyon is the smallmouth bass. Smallmouth run from 1 to 3 pounds and there are a lot of them. The farther downstream from Hells Canyon Dam you get the better the smallmouth fishing becomes.

Although they are not as popularly sought as smallmouth, crappie are plentiful in the canyon. The sturgeon fishery is a popular target for anglers, though a catch-and-release program is now in effect.

Wildlife: The distance is so great between the top and bottom of the canyon that several ecosystems exist within themselves. The canyon and mountain ranges within the NRA contain the widest varieties of wildlife species in the Northwest, including elk, mule and white-tailed deer, bear, cougar, marten, eagle, mountain goats and bighorn sheep. Many birds of prey roost and nest on the craggy cliffs of Hells Canyon and the gorge is the premier chukar hunting region in the Northwest. Blue and ruffed grouse also inhabit the canyon.

Hells Canyon Wilderness Area: The 190,000-acre Hells Canyon Wilderness Area is divided by the wild and scenic Snake River corridor into 2 distinct units. Canyon slopes ascend to the Seven Devils peaks on the Idaho side. In Oregon, the river rimrock gives way to grassy benches and timbered regions.

Congress designated this a wilderness area and all applicable restrictions should be followed. No motorized vehicles, chain saws, etc., are permitted within the boundaries of the wilderness area. Contact the NRA headquarters for other restrictions.

Oregon Dunes National Recreation Area

Of the 32,000 acres between the Coos and Siuslaw rivers on the central Oregon coast that have been set aside as the Oregon Dunes National Recreation Area, 14,000 acres are sand.

Stellar sea lions haul out along the Oregon coast.

(© John Barger)

For information, maps and brochures, write to the Area Ranger, Oregon Dunes National Recreation Area, Siuslaw National Forest, 855 Highway Ave., Reedsport, OR 97467; or Forest Supervisor, Suislaw National Forest, P.O. Box 1148, Corvallis, OR 97339.

Access: Access to the Oregon Dunes National Recreation Area is via U.S. Highway 101. From Interstate 5 take Oregon Highway 42 (**Mile 232**/Exit 112) west from Roseburg; Oregon Highway 38 junction with Interstate 5 (**Mile 282**/Exit 162) near Cottage Grove; or Oregon Highway 126 West from Eugene.

History: The dunes are the result of 60 million years of erosion on volcanic bluffs, high ocean winds and glacial movement. The wind continues to shift the sand, changing the size and location of the dunes and creating an eerie, almost mystical atmosphere.

Attractions: Visitors to the Oregon Dunes are treated to some of the most scenic stretches of coastline in the world. The sand dunes, among the largest in the world, reach up to 700 feet high and are more than a mile in length. Dunes such as these, associated with the ocean, exist nowhere else in the northern hemisphere.

The Oregon Dunes offer a wide range of activities, including camping, off-road vehicle (ORV) driving, hiking, beachcombing, fishing, horseback riding, canoeing and various hobbies using the wind, including kite flying.

Camping: Campers may choose from any of several national forest, state park, county and private campgrounds in the area.

Hiking: Oregon Dunes offers several nature trails for the hiker and the dunes themselves are a challenge. Park officials ask that hikers observe the landmarks around when you start across the open sand. Stop often and look back so that you may recognize the area when you return. Because of the nature of the sand and wind, you probably won't be able to follow your footsteps back and you can easily become disoriented in the dunes.

Also, wear lightweight shoes (such as tennis shoes) when hiking the dunes or beach. Other items you might bring along include a windbreaker (wind velocity averages 12 to 16 mph), sunglasses, hat, sunscreen, a light raincoat and a compass. Don't forget your camera. The wind can form spectacular features in the sand and the creative photographer can have a heyday in this constantly changing environment.

Although freshwater lakes can be found in the area, don't drink from them. Carry safe drinking water with you. Some of the areas are open to ORVs as well as hikers, and both parties should be aware of and respect the other's presence.

The dunes can be deceiving. The walk may be much farther than it looks and walking on sand is twice as difficult as walking on solid ground. Take your time and reserve enough energy to get back. And never turn your back on the ocean. It's unpredictable behavior could result in serious injury.

ORV Travel: More than half of the Oregon Dunes National Recreation Area is open to ORV travel. Some beaches are open year-round and some are open seasonally. Secure a map of the area before driving in the dune area.

The North Siltcoos area, in the northern portion of the recreation area, is open to ORVers between the Siltcoos Road and the South Jetty access road. There is a small closure around Honeyman State Park/Cleawox Lake area because of heavy pedestrian traffic.

Just south of Winchester Bay is the High Dunes area, in the southern portion of the recreation area. This area is open to ORVs from here to the Douglas-Coos County line, approximately 1 mile south of the last beach parking lot on the bay. The dunes are closed to motor vehicles from this point to Tenmile Creek, where the South Dunes area begins.

The most popular ORV area is in the South Dunes, between Tenmile Creek and Horsefall Road. Here, lakes and forests divide the dunes in half, providing many spots for remote camping. ORVers should be aware that there are some scattered parcels of privately owned land, and the landowners rights should be respected.

Oregon State law requires all ORVs to be equipped with lights, brakes, flags, roll bars or cages, chain guards and secure fuel tanks and seats. Specific regulations are available at the Oregon Dunes National Recreation Area headquarters.

Beachcombing: Combing the beach for natural and man-made treasures is popular with visitors. Hundreds of species of sea life or remnants of them, may be found along the beach. Sea shells, driftwood, old bottles, Japanese floats and countless other items are collected by visitors.

Beach Fires: Permits are not required for beach fires, but officials ask that fires be built from down, dead wood. Unfortunately, a good supply of such material is not always available and it is wise to bring your own fuel. Fires should be attended with care. Sand-covered embers can quickly be uncovered by the wind and the embers may spread.

Also, use common sense when building fires. Do not build fires in or near a standing pile of driftwood.

Fishing: The area in and around the Oregon Dunes NRA is one of the prime fishing spots in the Northwest. The Umpqua is the second-largest river on the Oregon coast and is a major sportfishing attraction, offering striped bass, chinook, coho and jack salmon, steelhead, green and white sturgeon, shad, smelt, perch and sea-run cutthroat.

Lake Tahkenitch is stocked annually with rainbows, but is best fished from a boat due to the brushy shoreline. Siltcoos Lake and the 2-mile-long Siltcoos River is good for anadromous cutthroat, steelhead and coho salmon. It also has a good resident population of panfish, cutthroat, rainbows, largemouth bass and brown bullhead catfish. Tahkenitch and Siltcoos are considered the best bass fishing lakes in Oregon.

The Siuslaw River and Bay offer Dungeness crab, the largest sea-run cutthroat fishery in the world, shad, chinook and coho salmon, steelhead, surf smelt, pinkfin perch, lingcod and rockfish. The harbor can be treacherous but offshore fishing is often good for salmon and bottom fish.

There are hundreds of charter fishing operations along the coastline which offer charter trips, equipment and everything necessary to fish the ocean. Inquire locally.

Ross Lake National Recreation Area

Ross Lake NRA divides the North Cascades National Park into 2 units. The 107,000-acre recreation area encompasses 3 power dams impounding 3 lakes and provides a corridor for the North Cascades Highway. Ross Lake is 24 miles long and its waters are cold. Even during hot summers, activity on Ross and Diablo lakes is confined to boating and fishing.

For information, maps and brochures, contact the North Cascades National Park, 800 State St., Sedro Woolley, WA 98284; phone (206) 855-1331.

Access: Ross Lake National Recreation Area is accessible via Washington Highway 20, the

Ross Lake is popular with boaters and fishermen, but too cold for swimming. (L.Linkhart)

North Cascades Highway (see the NORTH CASCADES HIGHWAY section for log of that route). Within the recreation area, Diablo Lake can be reached by car off the North Cascades Highway at **Mile 66.** Ross Lake is accessible by car from the north only through Canada via a 40-mile gravel road near Hope, B.C. At the south end, access to Ross Lake is limited to trail and water routes. The Diablo Lake Trail begins near Diablo Lake Resort (at **Mile 67.5** on the North Cascades Highway) and continues 3.5 miles to Ross Dam. Seattle City Light has a tugboat which runs twice daily from Diablo to Ross Dam at 8:30 a.m. to 3 p.m. Only personal gear can be carried and there is a fee. The tug makes the return trip to Diablo at 9 a.m. and 3:30 p.m.

Activities: Seattle City Light sponsors regular, scheduled tours of Diablo Lake and Ross Dam Hydro facilities. The 4-hour tour begins in Diablo with a presentation and slide show on the history of the Skagit Project and includes a ride on an antique incline railway to Diablo Dam, a boat cruise across Diablo Lake for a tour of the Ross Dam, and a family-style meal upon returning to Diablo. The tours operate mid-June through Labor Day. Reservations are required. Tickets cost $21 for adults, $19 for seniors over 62 and $10 for children 6-12, and may be purchased through the Skagit Tours Office, Seattle City Light, 1015 Third Ave., Seattle, WA 98104; phone (206) 625-3030.

If you are simply passing through the recreation area along the North Cascades Highway, be sure to stop at Washington Pass overlook (**Mile 102.5**) for breathtaking views of the Cascades and Liberty Bell Mountain. Also visible from the overlook are the Early Winter Spires and the highway's hairpin curves below.

Hiking: There are many trailheads off the North Cascades Highway. A gentle introduction to the mountain country can be found on the 1.5-mile trail to Lake Ann at Rainy Pass. Trails from Ross Lake and Colonial Creek lead into the backcountry of the recreation area.

Camping: Seventeen boat-access camping areas are located on Ross Lake, some have docking facilities, others are accessible only to kayaks and canoes. Picnic tables and pit toilets are at the campsites, but water must be carried in or treated.

From the North Cascades Highway, Colonial Creek and Goodell are developed, drive-in campgrounds. Nature trails, evening programs and conducted walks take place during the summer at Colonial Creek Campground.

Boating: The only boat launch facility on Ross Lake is located at the north end of the lake at Hozomeen. Those wishing to transport kayaks and canoes to Ross Lake can launch them at Colonial Creek Campground and portage around Ross Dam on a 1-mile trail to enter the lake. Gorge Lake has a small ramp near the town of Diablo.

Fishing: Fishing is popular on Ross Lake and in mountain lakes and streams in the recreation area. Rainbow, Dolly Varden, brook and golden trout are the principal game fish. State fishing regulations apply to fishing in the recreation area and a Washington license is required.

Accommodations: Overnight lodging can be found at Diablo and Ross lakes. Diablo Lake Resort has rooms and housekeeping units, food service, boat rentals and gasoline. Ross Lake Resort, a favorite destination for canoeists and trout anglers, has rustic (community bathrooms) and modern units, boat rentals, gasoline and a water taxi service. No food service is available.

Lake Chelan National Recreation Area

Lake Chelan National Recreation Area at the southern tip of the North Cascades National Park is a magnificent scenic wilderness inaccessible by car. The 55-mile-long lake, one of the deepest in the country at 1,500 feet, thrusts up into the North Cascade mountains. At its southern end is the resort area around the town of Chelan which, with 300 days of sunshine a year, is a favorite vacation destination for those wishing to escape the Northwest rains. Only the upper 4 miles of the lake lie in the recreation area.

For information, maps and brochures, contact the North Cascades National Park, 800 State St., Sedro Woolley, WA 98284; phone (206) 855-1331.

Access: You can fly, hike or boat in, but you can't get to Lake Chelan National Recreation Area by car. Most visitors take the *Lady of the Lake,* a commercial boat that travels 50 miles up the lake to Stehekin. The boat leaves Chelan at 10 a.m. and the 4-hour trip provides shoreline views of private residential and farming development on the lower lake and rugged mid-lake shorelines and national forest lands before reaching the wilderness area. Charter floatplane service is also available in Chelan. Chelan, in central Washington, can be reached on U.S. Highway 97 at **Mile 579.**

The shortest trail access to the national recreation area is via the Pacific Crest Trail from Rainy Pass off the North Cascades Highway.

A shuttle bus provides regular transportation to trailheads and campgrounds from Stehekin, May through October.

History: The Stehekin Valley enjoyed a short-lived fur-trapping, mining and homesteading history during the late part of the 19th century. Many of the descendents of the early homesteaders still live here year-round. The scenic valley's recreational potential was recognized early and summer cabins and resorts began to appear around the turn of the century. Today Stehekin remains isolated and residents must rely on the *Lady of the Lake* for mail and supplies.

Attractions: Hiking and exploring the beautiful remote wilderness is the prime reason for coming here. The Stehekin valley offers a wide choice of day hikes from several trailheads in Stehekin or near the campgrounds. A shuttle bus from the North Cascades Lodge provides transportation to hikers to trailheads and campgrounds, fishing holes and scenic areas along the Stehekin Valley Road. For a day trip into the recreation area, many people take a round-trip cruise on the *Lady of the Lake* from Chelan and stop for lunch at the North Cascades Lodge or a short trip to Rainbow Falls on an old open-topped bus before returning to Chelan in the afternoon.

Accommodations: Lodging, meals and

Most boating activity on Lake Chelan takes place at the south end. (Tom Barr)

basic supplies can be found at Stehekin Landing. The North Cascades Lodge overlooking the lake has rooms in the lodge, housekeeping cabins and serves all meals.

Camping: The Stehekin Valley Road begins at the boat landing in Stehekin and continues 20 miles up the valley to enter the North Cascades National Park, Cottonwood Campground and Cascade Pass Trail. There are 7 other campgrounds and numerous trailheads along the road.

Backpacking: This is a backpacker's paradise. Established trails run north into the national park and high alpine country or follow the shore of the lake. Weather can change abruptly in the Cascades so be sure to take extra clothing (wool, not cotton) even if you are planning to take a short day hike. Hikers sometimes meet topography head-on, but the rewards of scenic mountain and glacier vistas are many.

A backcountry permit is required for all overnight trips. Camp only at designated campsites or 1 mile from trails and campsites. No camping is permitted on sensitive alpine or subalpine meadows.

Boating: Most of the boating activity on Lake Chelan takes place around the south end of the lake at Chelan. Canoes, kayaks and small craft do travel the lake, but powerful north winds can be dangerous. It is recommended that you keep close to the shore and keep an eye on the weather. Rental boats are available at the North Cascades Lodge in Stehekin.

Sawtooth National Recreation Area

Sawtooth National Recreation Area remains one of the west's last great mountain treasures to be discovered by the traveling public. Though popular with Idahoans, its magnificent snowcapped ranges, alpine lakes and meadows and white water rivers are still relatively unknown as a vacation destination. Within the Sawtooth NRA's 756,000 acres (about the size of Rhode Island) are the Sawtooth Wilderness, the White Cloud and Boulder mountains, more than 90 miles of the Snake River and 5 large lakes. Just south of the NRA boundary is the glamorous winter playground of Sun Valley and Ketchum.

For information, maps and brochures, contact the SNRA Headquarters and Visitor Center, Star Route, Ketchum, ID 83340; phone (208) 726-8291.

Access: You can reach the SNRA on the Sawtooth Scenic Route (Idaho Highway 75) from U.S. 93 (turnoff at **Mile 551** near Twin Falls). See the SAWTOOTH SCENIC ROUTE section for log of Idaho Highway 75.

History: Two million acres in central Idaho was set aside in 1905 by President Theodore Roosevelt to establish the Sawtooth Forest Reserve despite the opposition of cattle, sheep, mining and timber interests. National park bills were introduced in Congress in 1913, 1916, 1935, 1960 and 1966 and all were defeated. Finally, a compromise between landowners and preservationists was achieved in 1972 with the establishment of the Sawtooth National Recreation Area "to assure the preservation and protection of the natural, scenic, historic, pastoral and fish and wildlife values and to provide for the recreational values associated therewith." Some 25,000 acres of the 754,000-acre recreation area remain privately owned and are regulated by the SNRA. The Sawtooth Primitive Area, established by the Forest Service in 1937, was redesignated the Sawtooth Wilderness Area in 1972.

Attractions: The Sawtooth National Recreation Area is a land of exceptional beauty and endless recreational opportunities. You can hike, climb, camp, kayak, waterski, fish, hunt for gold, cross country ski, backpack or ride the rapids. The magnificent scenic wilderness has not been greatly altered by mining, logging or development. Much of the SNRA, including all of the Sawtooth Wilderness and most of the high country of the Boulder and White Cloud mountains, is accessible only on foot or horseback. However, many of the activities in the SNRA are within reach of paved roads. Highway 75, the Sawtooth Scenic Route, is a pleasant introduction to the SNRA. Informational taped tours of the route are available at the Stanley Ranger Station (for north to south trips) and the SNRA Headquarters, 8 miles north of Ketchum (if you are traveling south to north). The tapes point out natural and historical points of interest, what to do in the SNRA and ecological and environmental information.

Accommodations: The Sun Valley resort area is just 9 miles south of the Sawtooth NRA and provides a wide range of services. Reservations and information for a number of

motels and resorts in the area is available through Central Resort Reservations, P.O. Box 979, Sun Valley, ID 83353; phone 1-800-635-4156. Farther north within the SNRA, accommodations are more scarce. Groceries and supplies can be found in Stanley and Obsidian and at Redfish Lake and Smiley Creek resorts. Stanley also has several motels and restaurants.

Two guest ranches and 3 resorts operate in the SNRA during the summer season. The largest of the resorts is Redfish Lake Lodge at the north end of Redfish Lake with cabins and motel units, an RV park, fishing, sailboat rentals and swimming beach, trail rides, pack trips, and a general store and restaurant open to the public.

Hiking: There are hundreds of miles of trails in the SNRA. You can take a leisurely stroll along Pettit Lake or a mountaineering expedition. Most of the trailheads can be reached by car with the exception of 4 trailheads in the Boulders and White Clouds and 3 trailheads in the Sawtooth Wilderness that are only accessible by 4-wheel drive vehicles. Forest Service maps, available at Sawtooth Forest ranger stations and at the SNRA offices, are very useful as road maps to get to the trailheads.

Camping: There are 29 improved campgrounds along the lakes and rivers of the SNRA for a total of 500 campsites. Some have flush toilets and piped water. The most heavily used camps at Redfish, Little Redfish and Alturas lakes fill quickly during the summer. Less crowded are campgrounds along Highway 21, northwest of Stanley. In addition to the developed campgrounds, there are many primitive campsites along the secondary roads of the SNRA. The Sawtooth, Challis and Boise national forests adjoining the SNRA also have a large number of improved and unimproved campgrounds.

Fishing: This is an area famous for its

stream and lake fishing. Good fishing for trout, whitefish and kokanee salmon are still within easy walking or boating distance. However, steelhead and chinook salmon have been adversely affected by overfishing and proliferating dams downstream on the Snake and Columbia rivers. Some of the best native trout fishing can be found in the South Fork of the Payette River near Grandjean, accessible by car. Backcountry fishing in high mountain lakes and streams is within a day hike or pack trip. The eastern brook trout has been very successfully introduced in high country lakes. Native cuttthroat trout are primarily found in the lakes and streams of the White Cloud Peaks.

Idaho state fishing regulations apply and an Idaho license is required. The general trout limit is 6 fish.

Boating and Sailing: Power boating and waterskiing are popular activities on Alturas, Pettit, Redfish and Stanley lakes. Challenging mountain winds are favored by wind surfers and sailboats on the big lakes, especially Alturas and Redfish. Public boat ramps are available at all but Pettit Lake. Rental boats, fuel, paddle boats and canoes can be obtained at Redfish Lodge.

Nonmotorized boats only are allowed on Perkins, Yellow Belly and Little Redfish lakes.

River Rafting: The easiest way to float the turbulent waters of the upper Salmon River is through commercial outfitters operating out of Stanley. Not all of the Salmon River is rough and foaming. Low water levels of late summer tames some parts of the river. Then the stretch from Stanley to Basin Creek can be floated safely in almost anything — from a large raft to an innertube. Keep in mind that Idaho state law requires you wear a life preserver when floating the river.

For information on outfitters operating the river in the SNRA, contact: the Idaho Outfitters and Guides Association, P.O. Box 95, Boise, ID 83701; phone (208) 342-1438.

Winter Activities: During the winter, the Sawtooth National Recreation Area is a beautiful winter wonderland. By early December, snow blankets the mountains and forests of the SNRA. Highways 75 and 21 are plowed and open, but all other roads, buildings and campgrounds are closed to automobiles.

Downhill skiing in Sun Valley draws most winter visitors to the area. The winter season is the busiest time for the resort area, but the SNRA remains peaceful and unpeopled. There is a little downhill skiing in the SNRA (by helicopter), but cross-country skiing is the fastest growing winter sport by far. There are signed and groomed trails laid out by the Forest Service and touring center operators. Forest Service trails are rated by level of difficulty. The North Fork Wood River Trail is a favorite beginners' trail. This 2.5-mile loop trip starts at the north end of the parking lot of the SNRA headquarters building, so it is also easy to find.

Snowmobiling is also a winter activity in the SNRA. The SNRA *Motorized Trail* map, available at the headquarters and at rangers stations, provides information on areas closed to snowmobiles.

A backpacker hikes through a field of lupine in Sawtooth NRA.   (L. Linkhart)

Major Cities

BOISE

Boise (BOY-see), the largest city in Idaho with a population of 110,000, is also the capital and hub of the state's political activity. "The City of Trees" received its name from French fur trappers who, after crossing a hot, sagebrush-covered desert, discovered the Boise River flowing through a wooded valley. The river was named *la riviere boise*, "the wooded river," and when the town was platted in 1863, it was named for the river.

As a fort along the Oregon Trail, Boise soon prospered and in 1864, took the territorial capital status away from Lewiston in northern Idaho. Boise was named the state capital in 1890 when Idaho became a state.

Boise's greenbelt along the river links 6 city parks.

(L.Linkhart)

With excellent transportation routes, Boise soon became a major commerce city in the Northwest. Huge corporate giants sprung from the valley, including Boise Cascade, the J.R. Simplot Co., Albertson's (supermarkets), and construction giant Morrison-Knudsen, all of whom have their world headquarters located here.

Today, the greenbelt of the Boise River still plays a large role in the capital city's identity. Its beautiful parks, golf courses and zoo are all sheltered beneath the trees for which the desert oasis was named.

Boise State University, Idaho's largest with an enrollment of 12,000 students, is itself located in the greenbelt. The school, founded in 1932, now offers 6 schools of instruction with majors in 29 different areas. The university is the site of the Morrison Center for the Performing Arts, where national touring companies come to perform opera, theatre, ballet and music In addition, the BSU Multi-Purpose Pavilion seats 12,500 at sports and entertainment events.

The Broncos, BSU's athletic source of pride, consistently pack the 21,500-seat open-air Bronco Stadium during the football season.

For brochures and travel information, contact the Boise Visitors and Convention Center, P.O. Box 2106, Boise, ID 83701 or call toll free 1-800-635-5240 (out of state).

Attractions

Julia Davis Park, located between the Capitol and the Union Pacific Depot, contains some of Boise's premier attractions, including the Boise City Zoo, the Idaho State Historical Museum and the Boise Gallery of Art. The Boise City Zoo offers a look at more than 100 animal species and a children's section of baby farm animals. The first animal on display at the zoo was a monkey which had escaped from a traveling circus in 1916. Since then, the zoo has collected nearly 250 individual specimens for display. Hours for the zoo are 10 a.m. until 5 p.m. daily (open until 9 p.m. on Thursday in summer). Admission is $2 for adults, $1 for children. Senior citizens and children under age 3 are admitted free. Thursday rates are half price.

The Idaho State Historical Museum has excellent displays of Idaho's yesteryear including the old Overland Saloon; artifacts from the early Chinese miners; and artifacts of the Native Americans who made this region home long before settlement. Admission to the museum is free, but donations are accepted.

Near the museum, the Boise Gallery of Art offers quality Idaho art and prestigious traveling exhibits throughout the year. Behind the gallery is the Memorial Rose Garden, each bush providing a tribute to a loved one.

Other attractions at Julia Davis Park include Big Mike, a 1920 series Mikado locomotive donated by the Union Pacific Railroad; The Fun Spot, with amusement rides and miniature golf; tennis courts; and boat rentals for those wishing to paddle the shallow lagoon system among the ducks and geese.

Old Idaho Penitentiary: At the end of beautiful Warm Springs Avenue is the historic territorial prison, later the early-day state penitentiary. Self-guided tours of this facility are available from noon until 4 p.m. daily. The first inmates moved into the unfinished prison in 1872 and the following year, the prison was completed. As the penitentiary

LANDMARKS

UNION PACIFIC DEPOT is probably the most photographed building in the city. An elegant, mission-style building sitting atop a hill and surrounded by lush Platt Gardens, the depot today is still in use as an Amtrack station.

CAPITOL BUILDING: The city's most impressive public building, Boise's capitol lays claim to being the only state capitol building to be heated with hot water. A smaller version of the nation's capitol in Washington, D.C., construction began in 1905 and was completed in 1920.

grew, virtually all of the expansion work was done by prisoners who quarried the stones on the nearby hills. A member of the Butch Cassidy gang, Butch Meeks, spent time within these walls.

A major riot in the 1970s caused Idaho to construct a new penitentiary (near Gowen Field southeast of town) and the old prison was placed on the National Register of Historic Places in 1974. The self-guided tour allows access to the prison cells and punishment block, referred to as "Siberia" in its time, as well as Death Row and the gallows. The rose garden and grounds are maintained as they were first developed in the early 1900s. On display are pictures of famous inmates and lawmen, stories of escapes and examples of punishment in the early days of Idaho.

Also located at the penitentiary is the Transportation Museum where stagecoaches, buggies and a 1903 steam fire pumper are on display. The nearby Electricity Museum features early generating devices, radios and television sets. Also on the grounds is the Printing Museum containing the original pressroom of the pioneer Idaho newspaper, *Owyhee Nugget.* Scheduled to open in spring 1990 is a botanical garden.

The Old Idaho Penitentiary is open daily (except holidays) and admission is charged.

Capitol Building: The state capitol is Boise's most impressive public building. It was completed in 1920 using native sandstone quarried from nearby Table Rock and marble from Alaska, Georgia and Vermont. A replica of the Winged Victory of Samothrace, a gift from the city of Paris, is of particular interest. Agriculture, timber products and minerals are on display on the lower levels.

The building is located on the corner of Jefferson Street and 8th Street. A 1-hour self-guided tour is offered. The capitol is open from 8 a.m. until 6 p.m., Monday through Saturday. Metered parking is available around the capitol building.

Boise Train Tour is a 1-hour tour aboard open-air cars pulled by a 1890s locomotive replica. The tours depart from Julia Davis Park and travel through the historic neighborhoods, central business district and other sites of interest. Admission for the narrated tour is $4.25 for adults, $3.75 for senior citizens and $2.25 for children age 12 and under. From April through October, the tour train operates from 10 a.m. to 3 p.m. Monday through Thursday, 10 a.m. to 7 p.m. Friday and Saturday and noon to 5 p.m. on Sunday.

Eighth Street Marketplace: While many towns are suffering the affects of aging downtown areas, Boise has countered with the creation of the South 8th Street Marketplace, a renovated portion of the old downtown resembling San Francisco's famed Ghirardelli Square. The converted warehouse district includes galleries, theaters, restaurants and delis and several specialty shops.

Les Bois Park: One of the Boise area's premier attractions during the summer months is the paramutual horse racing at Les Bois Park, located at the Western Idaho Fairgrounds. Horses are running for more than 50 days from May through August.

The Western Idaho Fairgrounds is the site

(L. Linkhart)

The state capitol building is similar in appearance to the nation's capitol.

of year-round sports events, concerts, celebrations and expositions. The Western Idaho Fair begins the last weekend of August.

The Boise River winds right through the town. A greenbelt along the water's edge allows escape to a quiet place without ever leaving the city. Ten miles of paved paths attract joggers, bicyclists, skaters and walkers and link 6 city parks. The river provides many recreational opportunities, including fishing from its banks right in the middle of town. During the summer, tubing the Boise is a favorite diversion. Inner tube rentals and transportation to Barber Park, a popular place to put in, are easily arranged.

Wild Waters Waterslide Theme Park is a 13-acre complex with slides, pools, spas, picnic and children's play area. Open daily, 11 a.m. to 7 p.m. during the summer. Phone (208) 322-1844 for information.

World Center for Birds of Prey: The world's headquarters for The Peregrine Fund (an organization founded to prevent the extinction of the powerful peregrine falcon). Boise was selected, in part, because of its close proximity to the Snake River Birds of Prey Natural Area along the Snake River where the densest population of breeding birds of prey (raptors) exist.

Visitors can see the inner workings of an endangered species program while touring the World Center for Birds of Prey. Large windows look into the monitor, incubator and brooder laboratories. Tours are conducted throughout the year, but are most memorable during the breeding season (March through July) when visitors see the birds courting and feeding chicks (through video monitors), eggs hatching in incubators, and chicks clamoring for food in the brooder laboratory. Visit the center and see rare falcons and eagles from a few feet away. Tours last about 2 hours and are by appointment only. Group size is limited to under 30 people. Special group, student, and children's tours can be arranged. Call (208) 362-3716 for tour information and appointments. Donations to The Peregrine Fund are requested. The center is located at 5666 W. Flying Hawk Lane, Boise, ID 83709. Take Exit 50 off I-84, go south on Cole Road approximately 6 miles to Flying Hawk Lane.

Bogus Basin: Though Idaho may be famous for Sun Valley, Boiseans are rightfully proud of Bogus Basin Ski Area, just 16 miles north of town. The area offers a vertical rise of 1,800 feet with 2,000 acres of skiable terrain. The maximum trail is 1.5 miles and the average midseason snow depth is 8 to 10 feet. There are 6 double-chair lifts (uphill capacity of 6,700 skiers per hour) and 4 rope tows guiding skiers to 44 designated runs.

The area offers 2 lodges, meals, overnight rooms, a ski school, day care for youngsters and cross-country facilities.

Ste. Chapelle Winery. Idaho's wine growing country is on the same latitude as the famed regions of France and local winemakers are producing award-winning vintages on Sunny Slopes above the Snake River. Ste. Chapelle Winery offers free tours and tasting. On Sundays afternoons during the summer there are concerts on the grounds, perfect for an afternoon picnic lunch. The winery is open 7 days a week, Monday to Saturday, 10 a.m. to 6 p.m. and Sunday noon to 5 p.m. Tours are given on the hour and samples of wine are offered for tasting in the retail room. Ste. Chapelle is located off Exit 35 on Interstate 84. Call ahead for tour information and directions at (208) 459-7222.

CALGARY

When Colonel J.F. Macleod built Fort Calgary at the confluence of the Bow and the Elbow rivers in 1874, all of southern Alberta was Indian country occupied only by nomadic bands of buffalo hunters and a few scruffy whiskey traders who came north to exchange their brand of cheap firewater for buffalo robes. The presence of the police put an end to this exchange and established Queen Victoria's law and order in what was then the Northwest Territories. The Indians were quickly settled on reserves and the way was clear for settlement. The grasslands were ideal for cattle, and soon there were huge British-owned ranches in the area. Fort Calgary became the nucleus for a thriving cowboy town.

The Canadian Pacific Railway arrived in 1883 bringing boom times. Settlers, hungry for land poured, into the area and the cowboy town expanded into a city. In 1909 the first oil wells gushed in Pincher Creek and Turner Valley and Calgary experienced a second great building boom: the first skyscraper, the 6-story Grain Exchange Building, sprang up in 1909; the sandstone city hall in 1911. The first oil refinery opened in 1923 and set Calgary on a pattern of dizzying growth that follows the up and down world prices in oil. When oil prices are high, Calgary booms; when it's low, Calgary does not go bust, it just waits quietly for better times.

Today, it's a large cosmopolitan metropolis, full of energy and feisty enthusiasm. Alberta's second largest city, Western Canada's financial centre, it is Canada's undisputed oil capital with more than 450 oil companies headquartered here. Oil brings in far more dollars than the ranching industry, but you can tell where Calgary's heart belongs. Come July, even oil executives wear white Stetson hats as the city remembers its rip-roaring cowboy days in the week-long Calgary Stampede, a tradition since 1912. The whole city seems to go just a little crazy during Stampede week, the second week of July, which attracts a million visitors from all over the world. For information about the Calgary Stampede, call (403) 261-0101 in Canada or toll-free in the U.S., 1-800-661-1260. Or write the Calgary Exhibition and Stampede Tickets, P.O. Box 1060, Calgary, AB, Canada T2P 2K8.

Calgary is Alberta's second largest city and Canada's oil capitol. (L. Linkhart)

Calgary is noted for its abundance of sunshine and for a winter phenomenon called the "chinook," a warm, dry wind that can suddenly substitute shirt-sleeve weather for cold. Summers are warm and winters cold. Average temperatures in Fahrenheit range from the 70s in July to 10°F in January. (In Celsius, that is generally between 17° and -13°.) Average precipitation is 17 inches/423.8 mm.

The city leaps from the surrounding flat prairie, a cluster of high-rise towers surrounded by a sprawl of leafy suburbs. It's easy to get around the city once you have mastered the quadrant system. Each city address has a NE, NW, SE or SW tacked onto it, a handy clue to geographical location. All streets run north/south; all avenues east/west. Both are numbered from the city centre. The main cross-town arteries are called Trails.

If you are driving in the downtown area, parking is easy to come by and, for genuine visitors to the city, absolutely free. You can obtain a free parking pass by calling the Calgary Parking Authority at 262-6174. For pedestrians, the Plus 15 system of covered, elevated pedestrian walkways cross over the streets to connect office towers, shopping centres, hotels and parking facilities. In winter, Calgarians don't have to get their feet in the snow; in summer they can stay cool. There is an electric tram LRT service known as the C-Train which runs conveniently along 7th Avenue where you can get a free ride between City Hall and 10th Street SW.

The city has made the most of its rivers. There are miles of pathways along the banks of the Bow and the Elbow rivers which can be walked or biked and which are popular for joggers. A good place to begin is Prince's Island, within close walking distance of most major hotels, which has a trail circuit of its own. From Prince's Island, paths lead west along both sides of the Bow River to the

Edworthy bridge for a hearty 15 km/9 mile loop. East from the island, the river path leads to some of the tourist attractions of the city — to Fort Calgary, the Pearce Estate, the fish hatchery and the Inglewood bird sanctuary. The Elbow River path also leads south to Stanley Park. Detailed maps of the pathway system are available from the City of Calgary municipal building or from most informations centres. Call 268-5211.

The main Tourist Information office is located at 238-8th Ave. SE, or call 263-8510.

Attractions

Glenbow Museum, located at 130-9th Ave. SE (in the Calgary Convention Centre complex), features the history of western Canada with an emphasis on the Native peoples. It contains superb interpretative displays, Indian and Inuit art and artifacts, and a collection of military arms and armor. Open daily, 10 a.m. to 6 p.m.; admission $2 for adults, $1 for children, free on Saturdays. Phone 264-8300. Also visit the Sarcee People's Museum at 3700 Anderson Road SW with exhibits illustrating the history of the Sarcee tribe, artifacts from early tribal life, a model tepee and traditional clothing. Open weekdays, 8 a.m. to 4 p.m.; admission free. Phone 238-2677.

Heritage Park at 14th Street and Heritage Drive SW, authentically recreates local life in 2 pioneer eras — a prairie railroad town at the turn of the century and the earlier days of trappers, miners and settlers. Visitors can browse through early settlers' homes, ride a steam train or an electric streetcar, or cruise the Glenmore Reservoir aboard the paddle wheeler SS *Moyie.* Open daily 10 a.m. to 6 p.m.; admission is $5 for adults, $3.50 for youths (age 12-17 years) and $2.25 for children. Phone 252-1858.

Stephen Avenue Mall on 8th Avenue

LANDMARKS

between 1st Street SE and 3rd Street SW is the focus of activity during the summer. Outdoor cafes and vendors' carts compete for attention with the historic area's restored Victorian buildings. There is good shopping, good eating and the best concentration of Calgary's historical sandstone buildings. Pull up a bench and plot your day's strategy.

Devonian Gardens is a huge indoor park (between 2nd and 3rd streets and 7th and 8th avenues downtown) under glass amid the skyscrapers, containing 20,000 tropical plants, waterfalls, fountains, pools, bridges, music recitals and quiet places for contemplation. Open daily, 9 a.m. to 9 p.m., admission free. Shops and restaurants are on the floor below.

Fort Calgary is located at 750 9th Ave. SE. Only the outline of the ruined police post remains, but the location (where the Elbow joins the Bow) is great and a fine interpretative centre brings history to life with exhibits and a slide show. Open daily from 9 a.m. to 5 p.m.; free admission. Nearby is the renovated Deane House, built in 1906 for the post commander, with a pleasant tea room. Open daily, noon to 5 p.m. Phone 269-7747.

The Calgary Zoo, located at 1300 Zoo Road NE (off Memorial Drive) on St. George's Island in the Bow River, is Canada's second largest zoo. The zoo displays more than 1,300 wild animals, exotic and Canadian, in enclosures resembling their natural habitats. A prehistoric park with life-sized replicas of prehistoric animals depicts life during the dinosaur age. Botanical gardens, a tropical aviary and conservatory provide an oasis on a winter's day. The zoo is open year-round from 9 a.m. with closing times adjusted seasonally. Admission is $5.50 for adults, $2 for children under 12. Phone 262-8144.

The Science Centre at 701 - 11th Street SW, features interactive and hands-on displays, including holograms, frozen shadows and optical illusions. There are demonstrations of cryogenics, laser magic and bubble science on weekends. Open daily 1:30 to 9 p.m. Admission is $4 for adults, $2 for children. The Centennial Planterium and Aerospace Museum in the same complex features astronomy shows in the planetarium, telescopes for night viewing, laser light shows, vintage aircraft and model rockets. Open daily 1:30 to 9 p.m. The $5 admission includes the Science Centre. Phone 221-3700.

Calaway Park, the grandaddy of all amusement parks, is just outside of town, 6 miles west on Trans Canada Highway 1. It offers western Canada's first major theme park with rides, live shows, food, games and name entertainment. The park is open 7 days a week in July and August, weekends only in May, June, September and October. The $11.95 admission for adults, $8.95 for children includes all rides; park only admission is $6.95. Phone (240-3822).

Bonzai Waterslide on Macleod Trail South and Heritage Drive features 4 giant twister runs, an inner tube river ride and kiddie slides, hot tubs for parents. Open daily 10 a.m. to 9 p.m. Admission is $6.95 for adults, $4.95 for children; $1 extra on the weekends. Phone 278-4012.

THE CALGARY TOWER (266-7171), built in 1967, is a 626-foot/190-m high concrete cousin to the Seattle Space Needle with a high observation terrace and a restaurant which makes a complete revolution every hour for a 360-degree panorama of downtown Calgary. Elevators run from 7:30 a.m. to 11:30 p.m. daily, except Sunday when they stop running at 10:30 p.m. Admission is $3 for adults, $2.25 for youths (age 13-17) and $1.25 for children and seniors. The tower is located at 9th Avenue and Centre Street South.

THE SADDLEDOME is a new addition to the Calgary landscape built for the 1988 Olympics in Stampede Park. The saddle-shaped structure has the world's largest free-span concrete roof, the first to be suspended by cable, which provides enclosure for Calgary's multi-purpose arena. The Saddledome is open for viewing weekdays 11 a.m. to 2 p.m.; admission is free. Guided tours are available. Phone 261-0400.

EDMONTON

Like the Roman god Janus, Edmonton has 2 faces — one looking back while the other looks ahead. Alberta's capital and largest city (pop. 788,000) began as a fur-trading post of the Hudson's Bay Co. Edmonton celebrates its role as "Gateway to the North" during Klondike Days held the third week of July. The historic, traditional face of the city is seen in its magnificent Edwardian legislature buildings, in Fort Edmonton Park, and in walking tours of Old Strathcona. The city sits in the geographic center of the province and at the hub of extensive natural resources. The forward-looking face is reflected in the dramatic glass architecture of Alberta's convention centre and the scale of West Edmonton Mall, the world's largest covered shopping center.

Alberta Legislature Building is surrounded by landscaped gardens. *(Staff)*

Through the city winds the North Saskatchewan River at the bottom of a deep glacially-carved valley. Both sides of this steep valley are the green ribbons of the Capital City Recreation Park, Canada's largest stretch of urban parkland, providing miles of foot and bike trails and public programs for bird-watching, gold panning, campfires and cross-country ski touring. Edmonton is divided by the river like 2 interlocking pieces of a jigsaw puzzle and transportation funnels across the 3 main river bridges. The legislative buildings and the downtown heart lie north of the river. The downtown is reasonably compact and accessible to pedestrians through a system of marked "pedways" or shortcuts. Skywalks and tunnels link department stores and shopping malls, most of which are underground to escape Edmonton's harsh winters. The city has a good light rail transit system and in summer a special tourist bus line, Route 123, links Fort Edmonton Park, the Space Sciences Centre and the Valley Zoo.

The city is known for its large and vital cultural focus; it has 6 theatres with a dozen active production companies, ballet, opera and numerous art galleries. Adding color to the cultural scene are the ethnic traditions of Germany and the Ukraine, homeland of more than 25 percent of Edmontonians. It is also a sports-minded city, home to the Edmonton Oilers hockey team and the Edmonton Eskimos football team.

The main visitor information office is on the main downtown thoroughfare at 9797 Jasper Avenue. It is open daily 8:30 a.m. to 4:30 p.m. Phone (403) 422-5505.

Attractions

West Edmonton Mall. Who hasn't heard of the West Edmonton Mall? It's the world's largest shopping centre, with over 800 stores and services and 100 restaurants. It covers more ground than 115 football fields and it's becoming a northern version of Disneyland with its built-in amusement parks. These include Canada Fantasyland, the world's largest indoor amusement park, with the world's tallest indoor roller coaster, a daring Drop of Doom free-fall experience and other thrilling rides; Deep Sea Adventures, an indoor lake with performing dolphins, rides on submarines and Spanish galleons; World Waterpark, where you can surf the waves, pick up a tan, ride the river rapids waterslides; the Ice Palace, an indoor ice arena (skate rentals available) and Pebble Beach indoor golf course. Nearby, the Fantasyland Hotel features theme rooms depicting several different eras, moods and countries. The mall is located west of town at 8770 170 St. Admission to the complex is free, but there are fees for the various amusements and rides. Open daily, year-round, including all holidays. For up-to-the-minute news on new additions, rates and times, phone (403) 444-5286.

Boardwalk Market, housed in 2 historic buildings joined under a glass Galleria, features arts and crafts, cart vendors, daily live entertainment and cultural exhibits. Located on 102 Avenue, the market is open Monday through Thursday 9 a.m. to 6 p.m.; Fridays until 9 p.m.; Saturdays until 5 p.m. and Sundays 11 a.m. to 5 p.m.

Old Strathcona Historic Area is on 104 Street. The buildings date from 1891 in an area of the city that was once the town of Strathcona. Walking tour maps are available at the Visitor Information Centre or by phoning 433-5866. Nearby on 105 Street the Strathcona Post Office, built in 1913, has been restored to its Victorian splendor and accom-modates interesting retail shops.

The Ukrainian Museum of Canada displays richly embroidered costumes of the various regions, wood carvings, painted Easter eggs and household items. Open June through August, 9 a.m. to 4 p.m. weekdays, Sundays 2-5 p.m. Free admission. The museum is located at 10611 - 110 Ave.; phone (403) 483-5932.

Canada's Aviation Hall of Fame is located at 9797 Jasper Ave. National in scope, this first-class exhibition includes displays of achievements of Canada's top aviators, historic films and a flight-training simulator. Open 9:30 a.m. to 5 p.m. weekdays; 11 a.m. to 5 p.m. weekends and holidays; phone 424-2458.

Edmonton Space Sciences Centre. A world-class attraction, the Edmonton Space Sciences Centre is home to Canada's most advanced planetarium, a giant-screen IMAX theater, and an exhibit gallery full of games to play and buttons to push. Open 10 a.m. to 10 p.m. daily; closed Monday evenings. Admission is free, but charges for shows range from $2 to $7. The centre is located at 11211 142 St.; phone (403) 451-7722.

Fort Edmonton Park. Visitors walk through history in a replica of the Fort Edmonton fur-trading post, then ride a stagecoach, horse-drawn wagon or streetcar to visit the shops and homes of Edmonton as it was in 1885, 1905 and 1920. Summer hours (May through September) are 10 a.m. to 6 p.m. daily. Admission is $4.50 for adults, $3.25 for seniors and youths, $2.25 for children. The park is located at the south end of Quesnell Bridge and Fox Drive. Adjoining

LANDMARKS

The Space Sciences Centre houses an advanced planetarium.

(Staff)

the park is the John Jantzen Nature Centre with exhibits of local plants and animals.

Muttart Conservatory: Inside 3 of the conservatory's striking glass pyramids are plants from the temperate, tropical and arid climates of the world. In the fourth is the Show Pavilion with changing seasonal displays of flowers. Summer hours (June through August) are 10 a.m. to 9 p.m. daily; 11 a.m. to 6 p.m. Thursday through Saturday the rest of the year. Admission is $3 for adults, $1.75 for seniors and youths, $1.25 for children. The conservatory is located at the south side of the river at 98 Avenue and 96A Street; phone (403) 428-2939.

Provincial Museum of Alberta is located at 12845 102 Ave. The panorama of Alberta's natural and human history covers millions of centuries and more than 40,000 square feet of permanent exhibit space. The museum is open 10 a.m. to 8 p.m. daily. Admission is free. For more information phone (403) 427-1730. Next to the museum is Government House, a magnificent sandstone mansion that was once the home of the Vice-Regal Representative. The Government House is known for its impressive collection of Canadian art. Open Sunday only for half-hour tours, 10 a.m. to 4:30 p.m. (May-September), 11 a.m. to 4:30 p.m. (September to November and February to April).

Strathcona Science Park and Archaeological Centre. Located near Edmonton's "Refinery Row" is a 270-acre provincial park where visitors can enjoy a number of recreational activities, see an archaeological dig and explore the Alberta Natural Resources Science Centre. The science centre features 4 buildings filled with hands-on exhibits related to Alberta's natural resources. Among the attractions are a weather station, live animals, tar sands to handle and a bicycle-powered television set. In the Archaeological Centre, excavations of a 5,000-year-old Native site are in progress. Visitors can watch the work and talk with archaeologists. An interpretative centre shows artifacts from the parklands area. During the winter, downhill and cross country skiing and snowshoeing are popular activities. Located on 16th Street between Yellowhead Highway 16 and 16A East, the park is open daily from 7 a.m. to 11 p.m.

THE HIGH LEVEL BRIDGE has been used as the main river crossing since it was built in 1913. In 1980, a man-made waterfall was created to celebrate Alberta's 75th anniversary. The cascade from the bridge operates on Sunday evenings only during holiday weekends and during Klondike Days. The 170 foot/53 m drop makes quite a splash. *(not pictured)*

ALBERTA LEGISLATURE BUILDING AND GOVERNMENT CENTRE, on the site of the original Fort Edmonton, was built in 1907 of carefully worked stone with a classic columnar facade and a large, elegant dome. The grounds have been beautifully landscaped with fountains, reflecting pools, walkways and manicured gardens. At noon, the Centennial Carillon bells chime the hour. A good place just for walking or sitting. Tours available summer from 9 a.m. to 8:30 p.m. weekdays (to 4:30 p.m. weekends). Admission is free. Pedways link the buildings to other government offices.

MUTTART CONSERVATORY is one of the city's most distinctive structures. Three of the 4 glass pyramids house plants from the arid temperate and tropical zones, while the fourth houses special exhibits that change with the season. Located between 98th Avenue and Connors Road on 96A Street.

HELENA

Helena, the Northwest's smallest state capital, enjoys the neighborly attitude of a small town and the conveniences of being the state's political hub. It is a city of contrasts divided into 2 distinct districts: the capital district where most of the state government buildings are located, and historic Last Chance Gulch (or canyon), the old mining district now a pedestrian mall and retail center. Like many frontier towns, Helena owes its existence to the discovery of gold.

The gothic Cathedral of St. Helena, built in 1913, is a Helena landmark. (L. Linkhart)

Four weary and discouraged miners from the South were the first to discover the precious metal in 1864 when they stumbled upon the goldfield they called Last Chance Gulch. The following summer, the strike was legend. The mining camp overflowed with newcomers who dreamed of striking it rich and others who dreamed of getting rich off the strikers. By 1870, Helena had hundreds of businesses and was a major trading center for goods coming by steamboat through Fort Benton on the Missouri River. Helena's importance rose as other Montana mines played out and in 1875, Helena became the territorial capital. The Northern Pacific Railroad provided another boom to Helena's growing population and the economy skyrocketed.

Three times Helena experienced devastating fires and each time the sturdy Montana citizens rebuilt. The fire tower, known as the Guardian of the Gulch, was the only means of notifying the residents of a fire. It still stands over the city today.

The remnants of Helena's golden age (1864-94) when unbridled optimism, an astounding rate of growth and more millionaires per capita than any city in America is embodied in the lavish buildings erected by successful businessmen. Wealthy stockmen and the mining elite even had their own social club, the Montana Club, now open to visitors at the corner of 6th and Fuller. Fire, earthquakes and urban renewal took their toll on many of Helena's historic buildings, but wonderful examples of Victorian, Gothic Revival, Romanesque and French Second Empire architectural styles are still seen along Helena's streets.

The capital city is situated on the eastern side of the Rocky Mountains near the Continental Divide, at the western edge of the rolling Great Plains. Outdoor recreation is at the doorstep for Helena residents: Big game hunting, some of the nation's finest fishing streams, and winter sports.

Residents of Helena are rightfully proud of their place in history, as evidenced by the number and quality of museums, artifacts and displays open to the public. For brochures and visitor information, write the Helena Chamber of Commerce, 201 E. Lyndale Ave., Helena, MT 59601 or phone (406) 442-4120.

Attractions

Montana Historical Society Museum: Across the street from the capitol, at 225 N. Roberts St., is the oldest historical society in the West, incorporated in 1865 by the first territorial legislature. The society's museum features approximately 30,000 objects and artworks acquired in the earliest days of settlement in Montana. The Mackay Gallery of Russell Art has one of the best collections of the "cowboy artist's" oils, watercolors, sketches and bronze statues. The state archives, historical library and the publications office of a Western history magazine produced by the society are also in the building.

The historical society offers tours of the State Capitol Building and the Original Governor's Mansion as well as the society's museum. Information on a self-guided walking or driving tour of Helena's historic district is available. The tour follows the growth of the city and points out the different architectural styles of early citizens' homes and businesses. For tour information or reservations, call (406) 444-2694. The historical society is open from 8 a.m. to 6 p.m., Monday through Friday and 9 a.m. to 6 p.m. on weekends and holidays during the summer; and 9 a.m. to 5 p.m., Monday through Saturday, closed Sunday and holidays the rest of the year.

Governor's Mansion: The Original Governor's Mansion was built in 1888 by William A. Chessman, a wealthy entrepreneur, as a private residence. The unique Queen Anne-style architecture reflected Chessman's wealth and influence. In 1900, after experiencing financial difficulties, Chessman gave the home up to a second private owner, the Larsons, who also passed the home on to another private owner, the Conrads, before the home was acquired by the state of Montana as a governor's mansion in 1913. The home was occupied by Montana's chief executives from 1913 until 1959 when a new mansion was built.

Today, the original mansion is under the administration of the Montana Historical Society with the assistance of the Original Governor's Mansion Restoration Board. The mansion is located at 304 N. Ewing and tours are held from noon until 5 p.m. (beginning on the hour) Tuesday through Sunday, from Memorial Day through Labor Day. The mansion is closed from January through March. For information or group reservations, call the Montana Historical Society, (406) 444-2694.

The new governor's mansion, located at 2 Carson St., is also open to the public. Completed in 1959, the 2-level residence features 11 rooms, constituting 5,700 square feet. The house was built at a cost of $347,000, which concerned the new governor at the time. But, nonetheless, the mansion was built and the executive's quarters were opened to the public for the first time in March 1981. Guided tours are available Memorial Day to Labor Day, Monday through Thursday, 2-4 p.m. Labor Day to Memorial Day by appointment only. For information and reservations, call (406) 444-3111.

Civic Center: The exotic 175-foot Civic Center Tower is the single minaret of the original Algeria Shrine Temple. It is a unique replica of Moorish architecture and was extensively damaged in 1935 during Helena's earthquake. The Shriners sold the building to the city of Helena who converted it to a Civic Center. It now houses most of the department of the municipal government and has a spacious ballroom and auditorium.

Last Chance Gulch Pedestrian Mall: Main Street in downtown Helena has been converted into a pedestrian mall. Many buildings have undergone renovation in an attempt to preserve the historic flavor of this old-time boom town. Many small shops are conveniently located in this district between 6th Street and Wong and are easily accessible.

The water fountain near 6th Street is a replica of Mount Helena. A look up to the west will disclose two stationary observers — a tailor and a seamstress — watching the comings and goings of the mall. At the corner of Last Chance and Broadway is the "women's wall," a tribute to Montana's pioneer women. Across the street is a statue of the Four Georgians, a touch of China, one of the old brothels and an original trolley car which used to make local runs.

The Last Chance Tour Train & London Bus offer a one-hour tour of Helena. Tours leave from the front of the Veteran's and Pioneer Memorial Bldg. 8 times daily. Tickets for the tour are $2 for adults and $1.50 for children age 12 and under.

Cathedral of St. Helena: The handsome Gothic Cathedral of St. Helena is modeled after the Cathedral in Cologne, Germany, and the interior furnishings are of carrara marble, gold leaf and stained glass windows made in Bavaria. The cathedral was built in 1913 at the behest of wealthy miner Tom Cruise. The first mass was celebrated in 1914 on Christmas Day and the church was consecrated as a cathedral in 1924. The church is located at 530 N. Ewing St. and mass is celebrated daily. There is an audio tour of the building provided at no charge. Visitors are welcome.

The Northwest Bank at 350 N. Last Chance Gulch has an excellent collection of gold dust, nuggets, coins and tooled gold which is on display free. The bank is open from 9 a.m. until 4 p.m., Monday through Thursday and until 6 p.m. on Friday.

The Pioneer Cabin (208 S. Park), built in 1864, is the oldest home still standing in Helena. It has been restored and is now a museum open to the public daily 1-4 p.m.

Sapphire Mines: Montana produces 50 percent of the world's sapphires and there are at least 2 mines in the Helena area which allow visitors to dig for their own gems. Yogo sapphire and Montana agates are the state gem stones. El Dorado Sapphire Mine provides the buckets, rental equipment, camping space with RV hookups, groceries and a supply store with a staff who are willing to explain the operation. They are open May 1 through Oct. 1 from dawn to dusk. Write to the El Dorado Sapphire Mine, 6240 Nelson Road, Helena, MT 59601 or call (406) 442-7094.

The French Bar Mine, located 12 miles east of Helena, also offers "dig-your-own" gems. Contact them by writing French Bar Mines, 7032 Canyon Ferry Road, Helena, MT 59601 or call (406) 475-3380 after May 1.

LANDMARKS

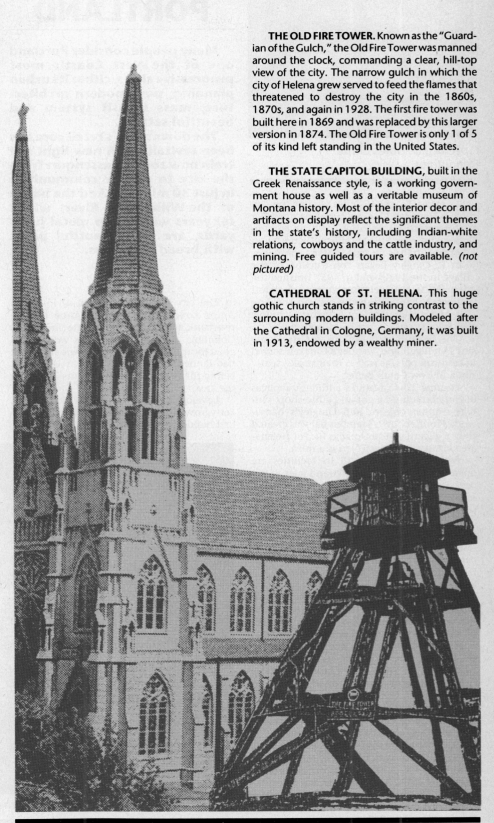

THE OLD FIRE TOWER. Known as the "Guardian of the Gulch," the Old Fire Tower was manned around the clock, commanding a clear, hill-top view of the city. The narrow gulch in which the city of Helena grew served to feed the flames that threatened to destroy the city in the 1860s, 1870s, and again in 1928. The first fire tower was built here in 1869 and was replaced by this larger version in 1874. The Old Fire Tower is only 1 of 5 of its kind left standing in the United States.

THE STATE CAPITOL BUILDING, built in the Greek Renaissance style, is a working government house as well as a veritable museum of Montana history. Most of the interior decor and artifacts on display reflect the significant themes in the state's history, including Indian-white relations, cowboys and the cattle industry, and mining. Free guided tours are available. *(not pictured)*

CATHEDRAL OF ST. HELENA. This huge gothic church stands in striking contrast to the surrounding modern buildings. Modeled after the Cathedral in Cologne, Germany, it was built in 1913, endowed by a wealthy miner.

Spectacular Gates of the Mountains.

(L. Linkhart)

Frontier Town: 15 miles west of the city on U.S. Highway 12 is one of Helena's premier visitor attractions. Frontier Town, an authentic log and rock village built by hand by an eccentric grandson of Montana pioneers. John R. Quigley began construction of the village in the 1940s and in 1957 finished the last building, a chapel complete with choir loft and organ, hand-finished pews and kneeling rails and an altar before a picture window which looks out upon a 75-mile vista.

The restaurant is famous for its Flanagan's Mulligan and Trapper's Chicken served in cast-iron pots, as well as their steaks, spareribs and Cow Camp Buffet.

Frontier Town features authentic replicas of early buildings, a gift and curio shop, vintage frontier objects, and Quigley's handiwork. Frontier Town's famous bar was created from a gigantic 6-ton Douglas fir. For Helena-area visitors, Frontier Town is a must.

Frontier Town and all its facilities are open from 9 a.m. to 10 p.m. (and later, if the occasion warrants, according to the management) from April through October. Admission is charged. Also available is a minimum charge coin at $3 which is fully redeemable in the gift shop, dining room or bar. For reservations of any size, from small parties to banquets for 100, call (406) 442-4560 or write Frontier Town, P.O. Box 836, Helena, MT 59624.

Gates of the Mountains: Gates of the Mountains Wilderness is one of the most spectacular areas of its kind in the Northwest. A charter boat service takes visitors on a 14-mile river cruise through the scenic canyon cut through the limestone terrain. On July 19, 1805, the Lewis and Clark expedition entered this same canyon on their historic journey through the Northwest. Of the canyon, Meriwether Lewis wrote, "this evening we entered much the most remarkable cliffs we have yet seen on our journey. From the singular appearance of this place, I shall call it the Gateway of the Rocky Mountains."

Deer and mountain goats are frequently sighted by cruisers on the river. For information and schedules, contact Gates of the Mountains, P.O. Box 478, Helena, MT 59624. Phone (406) 458-5241.

PORTLAND

Many people consider Portland one of the West Coast's most progressive cities, citing its urban planning, post-modern architecture, mass transit system and beautiful setting.

The downtown's retail core has been revitalized. A new light rail train now zooms passengers from the city to nearby communities in just 30 minutes. And the banks of the Willamette River, which for years were scrap metal junkyards, are now beautiful parks with broad walkways.

The city's history began in 1843, when Amos Lovejoy landed his canoe on the riverbank where the Willamette meets the Columbia. Lovejoy figured this would be a good location for a port city. Lewis and Clark had landed at the same point in 1806, and before them, the Chinook Indians inhabited the area.

Lovejoy and his compatriot, Francis W. Pettygrove, cleared a townsite and erected the first building in 1844 in what was to become Portland. They called it Stumptown because of all the tree stumps created by their construction.

Thankfully, Stumptown was renamed. The final name of Portland was decided by the flip of a coin. Francis Pettygrove was from Portland, Maine, and Amos Lovejoy was from Boston, Massachusetts. Pettygrove won the toss.

Portland, now a major metropolis of the Northwest, is today one of the nation's leaders in the export of wheat and lumber products, and its freshwater port ranks third in ocean-borne shipping on the Pacific Coast.

Portland's moderate climate is ideal for growing roses, hence the nickname, "The City of Roses." Portland boasts an internationally famous rose garden just west of the city.

Part of earlier Portlanders' foresight was leaving plenty of elbow room, with bountiful room set aside for parks. The smallest — which may be the smallest park in the entire country — is Mill Ends Park, a tiny 354 square inches. At the other end of the scale is Forest Park, which sprawls over 4,700 acres, and is the largest urban wilderness within an American city. More than 30 miles of hiking trails, ponds and lakes, and a variety of wildlife in this serene setting are within footsteps of city dwellers.

A green ribbon runs through the city, thanks to the Park Blocks, established in 1852. This urban greenway spans 25 blocks and offers pleasant relief from buildings and asphalt in the midst of the city.

Another favorite Portland retreat is the

The skyline of downtown Portland and the Willamette River.

(© John Barger)

107-acre densely forested park donated to the city by Donald Macleay, who requested that no wheeled vehicles be allowed to enter. The city honored his wishes. Macleay Park remains a haven for hikers, photographers, bird-watchers and other nature lovers.

Portland has long been known for its many lush green parks. But confirmed urbanites are taking notice of the city landscape as well.

Architecturally, Portland is as compelling. Its post-modern city administration building, designed by Michael Graves, is adorned in blue tile and concrete garlands. The building is home to Portlandia, a giant hammered-copper incarnation of the goddess-like figure on Portland's city seal. Next to the Statue of Liberty, this is the largest such sculpture.

But it is not just intriguing new buildings that make downtown Portland an enjoyable city for a stroll. There are bronze drinking fountains, cast-iron street lamp fixtures, floral displays and artwork, cobblestones and brick sidewalks.

Portland is a sports-minded city. The Portland Trail Blazers professional basketball team and the Winter Hawks hockey team make their home at the Memorial Coliseum. One of 2 greyhound race tracks in the Northwest is located near Portland at the Multnomah Kennel Club. Mount Hood, the Cascade Mountains and the accessibility to lakes, streams, rivers and the ocean provide plenty of recreational opportunities for city dwellers and visitors.

Portland is an easy city to explore. The Metropolitan Area Express (MAX) is a sleek light rail train that glides from downtown through neighborhoods on the east side of the city to the growing suburb of Gresham. The light rail departs every 15 minutes for the 15-mile trip. Stops along the way include — Lloyd Center, Oregon's oldest major shopping center (undergoing a $50 million facelift) and the new 500,000 square-foot convention center. Fare for the MAX is $1.15.

Avid walkers find Portland a great city to explore by foot. The blocks are just 200 feet — about half the size of the average city block. There are fountains, parks and street musicians. And if you get tired of walking, Portland's bus system, called Tri-Met, offers an 85¢ all-day fare on line 63 that leaves from S.W. Washington Street at 5th Avenue. The route stops at Washington Park and the International Rose Gardens, Japanese Gardens, Washington Park Zoo, Oregon Museum of Science and Industry (OMSI), the World Forestry Center and Hoyt Arboretum. Tri-Met's information number is (503) 233-3511.

At the river's edge, the Sternwheeler Columbia Gorge offers a variety of excursions on the Willamette River. Phone (503) 223-3928 for more information.

Attractions

The Waterfront. In the past decade, Portland's waterfront has been transformed from a string of dilapidated warehouses and metal salvage yards to a beautiful park-like setting with sidewalk cafes, fountains,

LANDMARKS

THE BRIDGES. The Willamette River runs through Portland, dividing the city east-west. Traffic flows constantly across the Willamette on the 11 bridges that span the river. The Morrison Bridge is illuminated at night and the Portland Light Brigade has plans to light every one of them. The Columbia River borders Portland on the north and 2 bridges cross that river into Washington State. *(not pictured)*

PORTLANDIA. This 34-foot, 6.5-ton hammered copper sculpture depicting the woman on the Portland city seal is second only to the Statue of Liberty in size. She kneels above the entrance of the Portland Building, the controversial post-modern building designed by Michael Graves and built in 1983. Discussion over these additions to the Portland cityscape has brought international attention to the city.

PIONEER COURTHOUSE SQUARE. Situated on one of the most historic blocks in Portland is Pioneer Courthouse Square. The first public school was started here in 1858, and was later the site of the Portland Hotel, which hosted every president from Benjamin Harrison to Franklin Roosevelt.

Today, the square is an urban park with waterfalls, amphitheaters, an open-air market, fountains and over 35,000 bricks bearing the names of local citizens who helped fund its construction. The complex also includes the Pioneer Courthouse, the hotel's original wrought iron gate, an echo chamber, and a series of handmade bronze tiles depicting scenes from the earth's and Portland's past. Visitors see musical performances, exhibits, festivals, debates, poetry readings and other public gatherings. The city's light rail also runs alongside the square, located at 701 - 6th Avenue in downtown Portland. For information call (503) 223-1613. *(not pictured)*

THE OLD CHURCH. Listed on the National Register of Historic Places, the Old Church, built in 1883, is a striking example of Carpenter Gothic architecture. The interior is rich in detail and the exterior is characterized by ornate window traceries, archways, buttresses and spires. Windows of leaded stained and frosted glass reflect several types of glassmaker's art. While on the self-guided tour, note the hand-carved pews, late Victorian furniture and a pipe organ donated by one of the founders. Baroque organ concerts are presented each Wednesday at noon. Admission is free. The church is located at 1422 SW 11th. *(not pictured)*

(L.Linkhart)

Sweeping view of the city from the rose garden at Washington Park.

pleasure boat docks and sidewalks. Called the Tom McCall Waterfront Park, this is now an extensive greenway for joggers and walkers. The Oregon Memorial Marine Park is located here. Front Avenue, which parallels the waterfront park, is the site of Mill Ends Park (which, at 354 square inches, is the world's smallest city park) and the visitor information center (at the foot of Salmon Street).

Pittock Mansion. The French Renaissance-style mansion was built in 1914 by Henry Pittock, founder of the *Daily Oregonian* newspaper. Standing 1,000 feet above the city, the mansion holds many antiques and furnishings, including a grand marble staircase, art from the 17th, 18th and 19th centuries, a Turkish smoking room, Tiffany tiles and a shower of Mr. Pittock's own design. The mansion is the focal point of the Pittock Acres Park, a 46-acre park commanding some of the best views of the city, the Willamette and Columbia rivers and the Cascade Mountains. The mansion and park are open from 1-5 p.m. daily. Admission is $3 for adults, $2.50 for seniors and $1 for children. the Mansion is located at 3229 NW Pittock Drive; phone (503) 248-4469.

The Portland Art Museum houses one of the finest collections of Native American art in the country. It is also known for its outstanding holdings of Asian art, 20th century American and European sculpture, works by Picasso, Degas and Renoir, and Pre-Columbian and West African art. Every Wednesday,

beginning at 5:30 p.m., a live jazz performance takes place in the indoor sculpture court.

The museum is 1 of 3 facilities that make up the Oregon Art Institute, housed in a refurbished complex designed by Pietro Belluschi. Also in the complex is the Northwest Film and Video Center which offers screenings of films you'll likely never see at the neighborhood movie house. Screenings generally are held from Wednesday through Sunday in the Berg Swann Auditorium.

In addition to the museum and the film center, the Art Institute operates the Pacific Northwest College of Art, the first fully accredited school of fine arts on the West Coast.

The Institute is located at 1219 SW Park; phone (503) 226-2811. Hours are Tuesday through Saturday 11 a.m. to 5 p.m. and Sundays from 1 to 5 p.m. The first Thursday of each month, the gallery is open from 11 a.m. to 9 p.m. with free admission from 5 to 9 p.m.

Admission is $3 for adults, $1.50 for students and seniors and 50¢ for children.

The American Advertising Museum at the corner of 2nd and Burnside is one of the first of its kind in the nation. The museum exhibits and preserves the history of advertising with exhibits dedicated to radio, television and print advertising and most memorable ad campaigns. Special exhibits are featured. The museum also produces a quarterly called *It's History* which examines themes and problems in the industry. Open

Wednesday through Sunday. Phone (503) AAM-0000.

Portland Center for the Performing Arts is the heart of Portland's performing arts companies. Dedicated in 1987, the center is made up of 4 theatres, 3 located together at SW Broadway and Main. Together with the Portland Civic Auditorium on SW Clay, the 4 stages offer classic and contemporary theater, music and dance performances attracting top performers. The Oregon Symphony, 2 ballet companies and Portland Center Stage, a resident company of the Oregon Shakespeare Festival, make their permanent home in the arts center. For schedule and ticket information, call (503) 248-4496 or the 24-hour Portland area events hot line at (503) 233-3333.

Several of Portland's most popular attractions, including the a science center, the zoo, 2 international gardens and a forestry center, are located 5 minutes from downtown in one of its most elegant residential areas. Take SW Jefferson Street west to Canyon Road (Highway 26) and follow the signs to the clearly marked exit for Zoo-OMSI.

Oregon Museum of Science and Industry (OMSI). Science comes out of the test tube and into Oregon's leading science center, with interactive exhibits on 4 basic themes; life, earth, space and information sciences. It offers live demonstrations, planetarium and laser light shows, classes, summer camps and special events. Favorite exhibits include a Rube Goldberg-type device called a Gravitram, an active beehive and live reptile exhibits.

During the summer of 1990 (May through September) OMSI will host a dinosaur exhibit featuring more than a half dozen, life-sized, moving replicas. OMSI is also home to the Harry A. Kendall Planetarium, which rotates programs every 3 months. Planetarium shows are presented Monday through Fiday, 1:30 and 3:30 p.m., with additional shows posted daily in the lobby. Light shows are held on Friday and Saturday evenings.

The museum opens daily at 9 a.m. and is open until 5 p.m. during the winter and 7 p.m. during the summer. Fridays, OMSI remains open until 8 p.m. Admission is $4.25 for adults and $2.75 for seniors and children. The OMSI is located off Highway 16 at 4015 SW Canyon Road; phone 222-2828.

Washington Park Zoo. This modest-sized zoo has gained a national reputation for its successful breeding program of the endangered Asian elephant. Since 1962, 24 of the pachyderms have been born, so there's a good chance of a visitor seeing a little one scurrying around with 10 adults in the herd. Another endangered species delightful to watch is the Humboldt penguin. Nearly 25 of these South American birds torpedo at speeds of up to 22 miles per hour in an exhibit that replicates the warm, rocky shoreline of Peru.

In the Cascade exhibit, visitors can see beavers, otters, trout, trillium and many other plants and wild animals native to the Pacific Northwest. Visitors can then travel to the wild remote Alaskan Tundra to see animals that survive in the extreme environment. Other unique exhibits include underwater viewing

Sacajawea statue in Washington Park. (L.Linkhart)

of the polar bears and an insect zoo. The reptile and birds of prey shows, during which visitors can see free-flight demonstrations of eagles and hawks, are free with admission from mid-June to early September. The zoo opens daily at 9:30 a.m.; admission is $3.50 for adults and children over 11. Senior citizens and children are $2. The zoo is located at 4001 SW Canyon Rd.; phone 226-7627.

Railroad buffs and children enjoy the authentic one-fifth-sized steamer train that brings visitors through the zoo, over the wooded hills of Washington Park to the famed International Rose Test and Japanese gardens. From here, visitors have a sweeping view of Portland, the Willamette Valley and majestic Mount Hood. For an added treat, visitors can attend jazz concerts on Wednesday and bluegrass concerts on Thursday evenings throughout the summer. Concerts are free with zoo admission.

Washington Park. This is Portland's oldest park with fantastic vistas of the city and mountains. You may tour the park by car by following the "Scenic Drive" signs or put on walking shoes to walk to the Rose Gardens or Japanese Garden within the park. Also within the park are tennis courts, picnic facilities and Alice Cooper's 1905 sculpture of *Sacajawea.*

The Rose Gardens include more than 400 varieties of roses, most of which are marked at their borders. A Shakespeare Garden with traditional herbs, flowers and shrubs named in Shakespeare's plays, and the Sunken Garden Theatre, which stages summer theatrical performances, are also located in the Rose Gardens.

The Japanese Gardens, a 5.5-acre garden in Washington Park, is regarded as one of the most authentic outside of Japan. The gardens were designed by Professor P. Takuma Tono, an internationally renowned authority on Japanese landscaping. Five traditional gardens and an authentic pavilion recapture the mood of the Orient. Admission is $3.50 for adults and $2 for students and seniors. The gardens are open daily year-round except for Thanksgiving, Christmas and New Years Day. Hours are 10 a.m. to 4 p.m. October through March, 10 a.m. to 6 p.m. April through September.

World Forestry Center. Forest and timber products are the top industry in Oregon and you can see how this business works — from Douglas fir seedling to finished plywood. The self-guided tour through the exhibit hall takes approximately 1 hour. The World Forestry Center itself is a stunning example of wood construction. The landscaped grounds feature a 1890 Shay steam locomotive and a set of high wheels, both used to haul logs. Admission is $3 for adults, $2 for seniors and students. The center is open daily 10 a.m. to 5 p.m. at 4033 SW Canyon Rd.; phone (503) 228-1368.

Powell's Books, at 10th and Burnside, calls itself the "City of Books," and with 30,000 square feet and some 500,000 volumes in stock, the title is appropriate. New and used books, hardbound and paperback books, are shelved by subject in Michael Powell's cavernous bookstore (a store map is available for first-timers). Readings and autograph parties are held in the Anne Hughes coffee room, also a popular gathering place for book lovers, theatre-goers, students and Powell's employees. Powell's is open daily from 9 a.m. to 11 p.m. Monday through Saturday, 9 a.m. to 9 p.m. on Sundays and holidays.

Saturday Market. The 1960s live on at Saturday Market, where handcrafted candles, belts, stained glass and jewelry are hawked in a festive open-air market.

The market is held on W. Burnside, under the Burnside Bridge, in what is considered "Old Town."

The market opens on weekends only from April to Christmas. More than 500 vendors are on the selling list, but only 300 are allowed to sell at any one time. The covered food area has 26 chefs, many of them ethnic specialists. Each weekend, they prepare their own specialty.

The Saturday Market is known for its entertainment, streetside jugglers, dancers, singers and mimes.

Market hours are from 10 a.m. to 5 p.m. on Saturday and 11 a.m. to 4:30 p.m. on Sunday. For more information, call 222-6072.

Yamhill Market Place. This bustling farmers market offering fresh produce, specialty stores and restaurants, is located between First and Second Avenues on Yamhill. Outside and around the market are more shops and restaurants.

Triangle/Pearl District. Art galleries, antique furniture shops, jazz clubs, bookstores, theater companies and microbreweries make up a lively 15-block stretch of renovated warehouses and storefronts just north of downtown and west of the riverfront Old Town.

SEATTLE

On those days when the clouds part and the sun plays on the waters of the Puget Sound and distant snowcapped mountains are etched against the sky, it's hard to imagine a more beautiful city. In the last few years, the skyline and the tempo of the city have changed dramatically as the region has grown rapidly. Seattle is experiencing some growing pains as it adjusts to its major-city status.

Downtown traffic is snarled with the construction of a new underground bus tunnel, and growth management has become a major political issue. Despite the uncomfortable adjustments to growth, the city has retained its air of friendliness and accessibility and has benefited from the sophistication brought by newcomers to the area. There's lots to see and do, good sports teams, terrific restaurants and a thriving cultural life.

Before the discovery of Puget Sound by white explorers, several Indian tribes inhabited the lush green mountains and valleys surrounding Puget Sound. Capt. George Vancouver was the first European to sail into and map Puget Sound in 1792. He described it as "the most lovely country that can be imagined."

The first settlement was by the Denny party in 1851 at Alki Point (now West Seattle). Because of poor weather, northern exposure and shallow water the settlers sought a deeper harbor at Elliott Bay. The first buildings were built on mudflats in what is now Pioneer Square. As Seattle began to grow, it became evident that something had to be done about the steep, impractical streets. After a fire in 1889 destroyed downtown Seattle, the ensuing renovation project included leveling the hills and raising the lower ones to give Seattle a more consistent profile. It was a major undertaking, but it worked and today Seattle continues to benefit from that turn-of-the-century idea.

Seattle is bordered on the west by Puget Sound and on the east by Lake Washington. Lake Union, just north of downtown, and the ship canal that joins Lake Washington and Puget Sound, create something of an obstacle course for the flow of traffic. Two floating bridges connect Seattle to its eastside neighbors. And several bridges, including 2 drawbridges, span the waters that bisect the city. A city map is helpful if you expect to do a lot of driving about the city. If possible, avoid the freeways and floating

View north of Elliott Bay from the Space Needle. *(L.Linkhart)*

bridges during rush hours.

It is relatively easy to get around downtown without a car. The Pike Place Market and the shopping area around Westlake Mall (Fifth Avenue and Pine Street) are only a few blocks apart. You can ride Metro buses for free in the area bordered by the Waterfront, the freeway, Jackson Street to the south and Battery Street (near the Seattle Center) to the north, so it's an easy ride to Pioneer Square. Or hop the Monorail to Seattle Center. Visitors can be surprised by some daunting downtown hills, however.

During the summer of 1990, Seattle and the Puget Sound area will host the Goodwill Games. Hundreds of athletes will compete at various venues around the state. The Goodwill Arts Festival will feature performance and visual arts with attractions such as the Bolshoi Ballet, the Grand Kabuki Theatre of Japan and an exhibit of works by Russian artists and crafts people from the last 5 centuries.

Seafair, a citywide festival that begins in mid-July, has been a summer event since 1950. Seattle's ethnic communities, neighborhoods and suburban communities join in the celebration with parades, milk carton races on Green Lake, salmon bakes and other festivities climaxing with unlimited hydroplane races held on Lake Washington. Another major highlight is the annual Torchlight Parade held the final week of Seafair and featuring the Seafair Pirates.

Attractions

The Pike Place Market, the oldest farmer's market in the U.S., is a favorite place for both visitors and locals. It opened in 1907 as a place where farmers could sell their produce directly to their customers, and by 1927 more than 400 farmers sold produce at the height of the growing season. The market deterio-rated in the years after WWII and almost succumbed to urban renewal in the 1970s. It was saved by a citizen's referendum and today is a bustling, thriving marketplace overlooking Elliott Bay with spectacular views of the water and distant Olympic Mountains.

Shoppers can browse through covered stalls and find local produce, fresh-cut flowers, fresh fish, meats and cheeses and many creations of local artisans and craftsmen. Antique stores, specialty shops, galleries, bakeries and restaurants are also located in the market area. Street musicians, mimes and puppeteers compete for sidewalk space with fishmongers and shopkeepers along the main arcade and enhance the visual delight of the place. Fresh ground coffee and baking cinnamon rolls further tantalize the senses.

The Pike Place Market is located at the end of Pike Street off First Avenue and is open Monday through Saturday. Some stands and stores are open on Sundays. The number and location of vendors changes daily. During the summer, the market is open 7 days a week. On-street parking can be difficult to find, so plan on using one of several parking garages on the perimeter of the market. Do not attempt to drive directly in front of the market. It is crowded, congested and used primarily by pedestrians. It is better to find a parking garage within 2 or 3 blocks and walk in.

Pioneer Square. This is Seattle's birthplace. When Seattle's pioneers abandoned Alki Point (now West Seattle) for a more sheltered site, they came here to start their town. Built on mud and stilts, the whole downtown area was built almost entirely in wood and in 1889, it burned down. A massive rebuilding took place immediately, this time in brick, and the result is an architecturally coherent district. The original Skid Road is here. Yesler Way was once used for skidding logs off the hillside and into the waters of Elliott Bay. The hills were logged off, the city grew and moved north, and the area became run down and the model for the corrupted term "Skid Row." Almost a victim of urban renewal, Pioneer Square was declared a historic district in the 1970s. Today, many of the renovated buildings house art galleries, restaurants, unique shops, bookstores, museums and night spots.

For a narrative and anecdotal history of Seattle's early pioneers, Underground Tours takes you underneath the streets of Seattle. Underground passageways are the result of the rebuilding effort following the Great Seattle Fire in which the streets were raised and sidewalks were built at the second story level. For a while, storekeepers kept their business open on the ground floor, forcing their customers to climb the stairs. This was soon abandoned, and the second stories became street level, leaving underground passageways. The tours begin at Doc Maynards Public House at 610 First Ave. Call 682-4646 for tour times.

The Klondike Gold Rush National Historic Park at 117 S. Main St., phone 442-7220, together with its sister unit in Skagway, AK, is the only site in the national park system which commemorates a major American gold rush. On July 17, 1897, the coastal steamer, *Portland,* arrived in Elliott Bay and unloaded 2 tons of gold. Seemingly overnight, the city became the point of departure for fortune-seekers. The city's boosters successfully promoted Seattle as the gateway to the north, outfitters provisioned those bound for the Klondike, and Seattle became forever linked with Alaska's history. (The Seattle unit interprets the city's role as the dominant West Coast staging area for the Yukon gold rush of 1897-98.)

The park has a visitor center with historic photos and exhibits of hardware, gold mining artifacts, and the mandatory "ton of goods" which miners were required to have before entering the Yukon. Gold panning demonstrations are available. Guided group museum tours are by advance arrangement.

Also in the Pioneer Square district is Elliott Bay Book Company at 101 S. Main, one of the region's best book stores. Its creaky wooden floors and inviting stacks of books make it a wonderful place to browse. There's a cafe downstairs and monthly readings by local and national authors.

The Waterfront. Although Seattle's waterfront has moved south toward Harbor Island, and the downtown waterfront is filled with tourist-oriented shops, restaurants, fish and chip bars and harbor tour operators, it's still worth a visit. You can gaze out into the harbor to watch loaded container ships and ferry boats move across Elliott Bay and imagine the beauty that drew the first settlers here. The waterfront promenade extends from Pier 48 at the foot of Main Street in Pioneer Square north to Pier 70 and Myrtle Edwards Park. If you get tired, you can hop the Waterfront Trolley which runs along Alaskan Way from Main Street to Myrtle Edwards Park with stops in between. A ride costs 60¢ end to end and 1-hour Metro bus transfers are issued and honored.

The Seattle Aquarium (625-4357) on Pier 59 is the waterfront's biggest draw. There are no performing animals here; the Aquarium's

LANDMARKS

innovative displays recreate coastal and inter-tidal habitats. A huge viewing dome shows life underwater in Puget Sound with sharks, eels and octopi swimming in and out of view. A fish hatchery and salmon ladder explain the migration of anadromous fish and playful seal and sea otter tanks can be viewed from above and below. Admission is $3.25 for adults; $1.50 for children. Call 625-4357 for information.

If you've been watching the ferries glide across the water and have been tempted to take a ride, the Washington State Ferry terminal is at Pier 52 at the foot of Marion Street. For some salt air and an easy, short trip, walk on the ferry to Bainbridge Island. The ride takes about 35 minutes one-way and you can either stay on for the round trip or make a stop at the small town of Winslow that is within walking distance of the ferry terminal. The ferries run frequently, call 464-6400 for schedule information.

If you'd prefer a more in-depth look at Seattle's waterfront, several sightseeing companies offer harbor tours at Piers 55 and 56. Tillicum Tours (329-5700) offers a somewhat theatrical Northwest Coast Indian experience on Blake Island. A dance program and cultural displays are capped off with a salmon bake dinner.

A beloved institution, Ye Olde Curiosity Shop at Pier 54, has been a weird and wonderful waterfront store since 1899. It's a sort of combination museum and gift shop that features such odd items as the Lord's Prayer engraved on a grain of rice, a 6-foot mummy, fleas in dresses, the smallest ivory elephants in the world . . . well, you get the idea. There is also a good collection of Indian and Eskimo art and thousands of curios from around the world.

Another Seattle institution, Ivar's Acres of Clams on Pier 54, is famed not so much for its cuisine, but for its founder, the late civic booster and raconteur, Ivar Haglund. Some say the clam nectar isn't what it used to be, but it's a local institution. Outdoor seating makes it a pleasant lunch stop.

BC Stena Lines cruise ships at Pier 69 run daily between Seattle and Victoria. At the waterfront's north end, Myrtle Edwards Park provides a patch of green and a place to picnic and watch lunchtime joggers go by.

The Seattle Center, a legacy of the 1962 World's Fair, is today the cultural, arts and entertainment center of the city. The 74-acre urban park with its landscaped grounds, fountains and hidden sculptures, hosts a number of special events in addition to the restaurants, exhibits, museums and shops open year-round. Three major festivals take place here during the summer that draw tens of thousands of visitors to sample local food, music and crafts. The Folklife Festival opens the summer season during Memorial Day weekend with one of the largest gatherings of musicians and craftspeople of its kind. In July, the city's restaurants entice festival-goers with their favorite culinary delights in a giant food festival called the Bite of Seattle. And Bumbershoot, held during Labor Day weekend, attracts top performers in music, dance and literary arts.

THE SPACE NEEDLE, Seattle's own Eiffel Tower, is a futuristic 650-foot spire built for the 1962 World's Fair which dominates the Seattle skyline. Take the elevator ride to the observation deck on clear days for spectacular views of the city. The ride costs $3.75 for adults, $2.00 for children 5-12 and is free for patrons of the 2 restaurants. *(not pictured)*

THE KINGDOME. Either hailed or scorned for its architectural contribution to the skyline, the 74,000-seat concrete domed structure has none-theless become a visible landmark. It is home to the Mariners baseball and Seahawks football teams. Located just south of the Pioneer Square district, the dome provides a climate-controlled, rain-free environment for sports, entertainment and trade shows. Tours are available during the summer. Call 340-2125.

THE SMITH TOWER. Built in 1914, the Smith Tower (506 Second Avenue) was once the tallest building west of the Mississippi. Now dwarfed by the downtown building boom, you can still take a ride up to the observation area on the 35th floor.

"WAITING FOR THE INTERURBAN." Though this might more appropriately be described as most favorite piece of public art rather than a landmark, this life-size sculpture of patient commuters has a local reputation. It is located at the north end of the Fremont Bridge (N. 34th St.) and fits into the surrounding funky neighborhood. *(not pictured)*

Flowers, food and handicrafts at Pike Place Market. (L.Linkhart)

Though outdoor festivals are popular summer pastimes, the Pacific Science Center at the south end of the Seattle Center is a great place to go with kids on a rainy day. A 5-building complex surrounded by shallow pools and futuristic arches, the Pacific Science Center (443-2001) is nationally recognized for its family-oriented activities and hands-on approach to discovering science and math. There are high-tech simulations, labs and classes, a Starlab Planetarium, environmental exhibits, Sea Monster House, and replica of a Northwest Indian ceremonial house. Admission is $5 for adults, $4 for children and $2 for children under 6.

Also for children is the Children's Museum and Center House Theater, located in the lower level of the Center House. The upper levels are filled with specialty shops, ethnic restaurants and fast food vendors. A few steps from the Center House is Fun Forest, a sort of permanent carnival.

Seattle's Opera House, Playhouse and Bagley Wright Theater on the grounds are home to Seattle's performing arts companies, ballet and symphony. The Seattle Supersonics play in the Coliseum which also hosts rock concerts, trade shows and other event.

The dominant feature of the Seattle Center is, of course, the Space Needle. Two revolving restaurants and an observation deck at the 500-foot level can be reached by a glass-enclosed elevator. The cost ($3.75 for adults, $2 for children) is steep, so make sure the day is clear before going up for the views. The ride is free for restaurant patrons.

Another holdover from the World's Fair is the Monorail that connects the Seattle Center with the Westlake Mall downtown. The trip takes 90 seconds and costs 60¢ one-way. Children under 5 ride free.

The Hiram M. Chittenden Locks (3015 NW 54th Street). The spectacle of watching boats float up and down and the fact it's free make this one of the most-visited spots in Seattle. More than 100,000 commercial and pleasure vessels a year pass through the locks that join freshwater Lake Washington and Lake Union to the saltwater of Puget Sound. The original idea for connecting the navigible waters was developed as early as 1853. The channel between Lake Washington and Lake Union was completed in 1880, and lowered Lake Washington by 8 feet in the process. It was Major Hiram M. Chittenden, a Seattle district engineer for the Corps of Engineers, who was responsible for the design and completion of the locks in 1917.

A popular leisure sport is watching the different kinds of boats that pass through the locks, a trip that takes 10 to 25 minutes. A visitor center at the locks has displays on the history and operation of the locks. The locks are open 7 a.m. to 9 p.m. daily, year-round.

Across the waterway in Commodore Park, the fish ladder provides a unique opportunity to view anadromous salmon and trout fighting their way from the Sound into freshwater spawning grounds. Completed in 1976, the fish ladder has 21 steps leading fish around the spillway dam. An underground viewing area lets visitors watch the fish struggle against the current in their upstream migration. The best time for viewing migrating sockeye salmon is June and July; August for chinook salmon; late September for coho; and January for steelhead.

Around the locks, the Carl S. English, Jr. Ornamental Gardens feature more than a thousand species of trees, shrubs and flowers on a 17-acre site. English spent 34 years cultivating and expanding the garden's exotic plants. This is a fine place to picnic on a summer's day.

Washington Park Arboretum. One of the most beautiful places to walk in Seattle, especially on a spring day when trees and flowers are bursting into bloom, is the Washington Park Arboretum, located just south of the University of Washington. The University maintains a botanical research facility here and you can see more than 5,000 varieties of trees, plants, shrubs and flowers by walking any of the paths that crisscross the park.

Especially popular is the Japanese Garden (684-4725), a secluded garden of pools, waterfalls, rockeries and formal arrangements of Japanese trees, shrubs and flowers. The Japanese Garden is located just off Lake Washington Boulevard East which runs through the Arboretum. A formal tea ceremony is performed in the Japanese teahouse on every third Sunday of the month, April through October. Admission to the Japanese Garden is $1.50 and it is open daily.

There are several trails in the park. Azalea Way winds through azaleas, flowering cherry and dogwood before ending at the Arboretum's visitor center. The Waterfront Trail follows the shore of Lake Washington and connects to Foster Island Nature Walk, a 1.5-mile round-trip walk over marshes and bogs that ends at the Museum of History and Industry parking lot. Plaques along the way describe the interrelationships between marsh plant and animal life. There are benches for sitting and water-gazing along the way.

University of Washington. More than 34,000 students attend the University of Washington (U-Dub) Seattle campus. The University's park-like setting with views of Lake Washington and the mountains, and its fine examples of diverse architectural styles make it a city treasure. The main entrance is located at NE 45th Street and 17th Avenue NE. There you can obtain a map of the campus and park your car to explore the campus on foot.

Notable campus buildings are: the Suzzallo Library, the main research library, with ornate stained glass windows and gothic features; Denny Hall, the oldest building on campus; Drumheller Fountain and Mount Rainier vista; Red Square, an expansive public square surrounded by old and new campus buildings; and the Sylvan Theater, a beautiful hidden natural theater that incorporates 4 columns from the original University building.

The Burke Museum (543-5590) is located at the northwest end of campus. It houses a fine collection of Northwest Coast Indian artifacts and anthropological exhibits. The museum is free, though admission is charged for special exhibits. Soak up some campus atmosphere with espresso and carrot cake in The Boiserie coffeehouse downstairs.

Off-campus, just south of the University, the Museum of History and Museum provides a visual record of Seattle's first 100 years. The main gallery has changing exhibits highlighting Seattle and Pacific Northwest history. Permanent exhibits include a re-created 1880s Seattle street, an aviation wing and information on the development of flight, and a maritime wing with history of water transportation in the Pacific Northwest. Call 324-1125 for information.

Although it has lost some of its bohemian energy in the last few years, The Ave, as it's known (really University Way NE), is the University's shopping, eating, movie theater

Chittenden Locks connect Puget Sound and Lake Washington. (L. Linkhart)

district. The Ave is crowded with ethnic fast-food, espresso and ice cream shops, bakeries, bookstores, boutiques. But smoky coffeehouses can still be found in the University District at The Last Exit (3930 Brooklyn Avenue NE) and Cafe Allegro (4214¹/₂ University Way NE). The University Bookstore (4326 University Way NE) is the largest bookstore on the West Coast; La Tienda Folk Art Gallery (4138 University Way NE) has unusual jewelry, pottery, clothing and crafts from all over the world.

The International District. Once known as Chinatown, the International District is both a collection of distinct Asian cultural and ethnic groups and a cohesive melting pot. The area, growing and vibrant with the influx of new immigrants, is located in the area between S. Weller Street and Washington Street, between Second Avenue S. and 12th Avenue. It's a neighborhood of colorful grocery stores, small shops, cultural centers and museums, and a wonderful variety of restaurants.

The Wing Luke Museum traces the history of Seattle's Asian community since 1860. The museum features Asian folk art and crafts and rotating exhibits. Admission is $1.50 for adults, 50¢ for children and closed Monday. The museum is located at 417 Seventh Ave. S., phone 623-5124.

The Nippon Kan Theater at 6th Avenue S. and Washington Street is a national historic site built in 1910. It is known for its Japanese Performing Arts Series. A tour of the International District starts at the theater and covers the history of Seattle and the Asian immigration experience. Call 624-6342 for tour information.

For a different shopping experience, try Uwajimaya at 519 Sixth Ave. S., a Japanese supermarket/department store/emporium with live fish tanks, toys, clothing, books, cookware and more.

Seattle Art Museum. Volunteer Park sits atop Capitol Hill with sweeping views of the city and Elliott Bay. The Seattle Art Museum is located in the park, but has outgrown its Art Deco building and will be moving into its new downtown location in 1991. The museum has an extensive collection of Oriental art and houses one of the 2 Tiepolo ceilings in America. It also features paintings by members of the Northwest Mystic School of Art, early European, pre-Columbian, Islamic, African and Persian art. A Seattle Art Museum Pavilion at the Seattle Center showcases traveling exhibitions. The museum is open from 10 a.m. until 5 p.m., Tuesday through Saturday and from noon until 5 p.m. on Sunday and holidays. Admission is $2 for adults, $1 for senior citizens and students. Children under 6 are admitted free. For information, write the Seattle Art Museum, 14th Ave. E. and E. Prospect St., Seattle, WA 98112 or call (206) 625-8900. Also in the park is the Volunteer Park Conservatory with flowering plants from tropical and desert climates which makes a warm, steamy retreat on cold, rainy days.

The Museum of Flight. Though not connected with the Boeing Company, it's hard not to think of the aviation giant. The Museum of Flight is located at Boeing Field and the Red Barn, Boeing's first plant, is on site. The 6-story glass and steel complex is as impressive as the collection it houses, with 20 full-sized airplanes suspended from the ceiling. The museum brings to life the rich history of aviation in the Pacific Rim region with priceless photos and artifacts. The museum is open daily from 10 a.m. to 5 p.m. (Thursdays until 9 p.m.); admission is $4 for adults, $3 for children.

The Woodland Park Zoo (624-4500, Ext. 2327) is one of the nation's top 10 zoos. The zoo has strived in the last few years to move animals out of barred cages into life-like representations of their natural habitats. The zoo's newest exhibit, the Asian elephant house, is set among tropical plantings and features a luxurious Thai pagoda-style elephant house. The African Savannah is a 5-acre grassland habitat with water holes, dry creek beds, zebras, giraffes, lions, hippos and patas monkeys. A heavily-planted lowland gorilla habitat is considered one of the best of its kind in the world of this endangered species. The gorillas move about in their forest with a stream, boulders and climbing trees. You can view them at close range from behind a clear barrier. A nocturnal house turns day into night for viewing those creatures we rarely see. And the family farm has a petting zoo for children, an animal nursery and crafts demonstrations. It's a very pleasant way to spend the day.

There are literally thousands of attractions in the Puget Sound area. For specific information, write to the Seattle Convention and Visitors Bureau, 1815 7th Ave., Seattle, WA 98101 or call (206) 447-4240.

SPOKANE

Spokane (pop. 172,700) is the hub of the Inland Empire, an area stretching from the Columbia's Big Bend through Idaho's Bitterroot Mountains, and from Canada to Oregon. Before air freight, UPS and FAX machines, it was the marketing center for all that territory.

Spokane was the center of a world unto itself. Isolated by miles and mountains from other market cities, it developed according to its own needs — farms, industries, electricity, minerals, forest products, medical care and education. In fact it was so perfectly isolated that it became an unofficial test market for America's manufacturers. They rightly figured that a new gadget could be market-tested in Spokane with the scientific control of a sealed test chamber. It followed that Spokanites see more than their share of new cereal boxes, strange soaps and patented widgets.

First were the Indians, of course. And then the missionaries and farmers and ranchers and miners, followed by millers, excited by the ready energy of Spokane's falls. Though leveled by the fire of 1889, Spokane didn't slow up or look back after the rails came, for the railroads were Spokane's vital arteries of commerce for the next half-century.

Where rails went, development followed, and so Spokane's development crowded along its rail lines — orchards, for instance. In the early century, the Spokane Valley's favorite crop was apples. Even today, neighborhoods carry the old apple names — Orchard Prairie, Appleway, Otis Orchards. The list goes on.

But the apple era wound down as competition from Yakima and Wenatchee, the Depression and blight took their toll. The fact of the collapse was written in crumbling fruit warehouses ranged along rail sidings.

Before, during and after the apple era, Spokane's biggest-spending benefactor was the Coeur d'Alene mining district. The miners who made it big spent big on the city and endowed its institutions, established its parks, built its tallest buildings and lined Rockwood Boulevard with their mansions. So much silver, gold, lead and zinc came from the ground to fuel Spokane's economy that the city established its own mining stock exchange to channel the investment fever of its citizens.

All through those years the rails prospered. Spokane's youngsters learned reading and geography from boxcars clacking past at crossings — Chesapeake, Wabash, Atcheson Topeka and Santa Fe.

Landscaped grounds of Duncan Gardens in Manito Park.   (L. Linkhart)

Then came WWII, its warriors and suppliers of war materiel. Spokane jumped into the aluminum business then, thanks to plentiful and cheap power. New plants not only produced the metal, but fabricated aluminum parts for warplanes.

Little Felts Field became a training and jump-off point for new B-25 bombers destined for Russia. A huge new naval ordnance depot was built east of town and a new airfield was laid out on the west side. And the railroads moved even greater loads.

Forest products industries kept a steady work force busy for the half-century ending with the war. But by that time the choice stands of white pine were gone, the city closed around the old mills, and the equipment of newer mills elsewhere had rendered the old-timers obsolete.

By the end of WWII, air travel was an everyday fact, especially among first-class passengers who left rail travel and took to the air. Intercity truck transport also struck at the railroads' customers. Spokane's shippers suddenly found it more convenient to move goods directly to their destinations by truck than to haul them to a rail yard.

For a time, displaced railroad workers found work at Spokane's giant autofreight docks, patterned after the concept of rail yards. That lasted until the trucking industry woke to the fact that point-to-point transport required no great central forwarding docks, and autofreight centers went the way of the rail yards.

The postwar years were difficult ones for the region. The mines slowed, the area's

wheat was diverted to Portland. What the city needed was a miracle — which they found in putting on the 1974 World's Fair.

Spokane. How could an isolated town of 172,000 put on a World Exposition? The prescription involved equal parts of daring and vision. First, the old downtown Great Northern and Milwaukee rail yards were ripped up and the terminals razed to make way for the 100-acre development. And once the nay-sayers saw it actually taking shape, the whole city spruced itself up to welcome world travelers. Expo 74 did happen. It was hugely successful and provided Spokane with its finest attraction, Riverfront Park.

One advantage of Spokane's slow growth is that much of the city's early buildings and old homes have not been destroyed by urbanization. The Spokane County Courthouse (on W. Broadway, north of the river), the City Hall building, and some of the Victorian homes in the area west of downtown are visible reminders of Spokane's past wealth.

Attractions

Riverfront Park. Everyone votes for Riverfront Park as Spokane's top attraction. Present-day visitors may have difficulty imagining Riverfront Park as the site of bustling Expo '74, a full-fledged world's fair. Today Riverfront Park is a place for strolling on the meandering paved paths beside the river and the footbridges leading to Spokane Falls. You can take the Sky Ride gondola over the cascading lower

falls or hop on the 1909 handcarved carrousel. An Imax theater, winter ice skating at the Ice Palace, and the Eastern Washington Science Center are located in the Pavilion. Free concerts, art shows and other events are scheduled throughout the year. Fresh produce and crafts can be found at the Public Market from May through October near the north entrance to the park.

Visit a Museum. Spokane boasts a number of museums and galleries, but 2 deserve special note; The Pacific Northwest Indian Center and the Cheney-Cowles Memorial Museum.

The Northwest Indian Center houses Spokane's Museum of Native American Cultures. The museum and study center have pulled together the most significant collection of Indian artifacts in the West. Twenty-one galleries on 5 floors recreate and display aspects of tribal culture. Dances, performances and demonstrations are held periodically during the summer months.

The Museum of Native Cultures is an easy walk from Spokane's hotels on the edge of Gonzaga University campus at E. 200 Cataldo. It is open Monday through Saturday, 9 a.m. to 5 p.m.

An outstanding record of Spokane's history may be seen at the Cheney-Cowles Memorial Museum, located at 2316 First Ave. Cheney-Cowles, amid the elegant old mansions of Browne's Addition, is Spokane's most extensive museum. An art gallery, natural history collections, dioramas, historical photos and large Indian and frontier displays portray Spokane the way it was.

See Spokane by Air. For an actual overview of the area, take an hour-long charter flight from Felts Field or Geiger Field. Try counting the lakes — they say there are 50 lakes within 50 miles. A scant 22 air miles takes you to Mount Spokane State Park, covering more than 20,000 forested acres with excellent skiing, camping huckleberry-picking and horseback riding.

To the south, your pilot will point out the fertile dust-dunes that support annual bumper crops of Palouse wheat. To the west, you will pass over scabrock country where chunky basalt formations share space with ponds, pine woods and cattle ranching. The 2 consistent features of your aerial tour are beauty and change. This is a landscape that begs to be explored.

Visit Wineries. A good start would be Arbor Crest. Headquartered in a Florentine-style mansion perched on a rock promontory 450 feet above Spokane River, Arbor Crest treats visitors to spectacular views east into Idaho and west of Spokane. Even the tennis courts, pool and gardens press at the brink. Definitely not a stop if you're queasy about heights.

An indicator of Arbor Crest quality is their wines' success in foreign markets where their time-tested varietals are earning respect.

To reach Arbor Crest, drive 1 mile east of Pasadena on Upriver Drive. Signs at the junction with Fruithill Road lead on to the winery.

Latah Creek Wine Cellars occupies an attractive Spanish mission-style winery located off Interstate 90 at the Pines Road exit. Mike Conway, owner and host, believes in the "light-touch" approach to winemaking, intruding as little as possible with the natural processes. It must work, since every bit of wall space is covered with prestigious awards won since opening in 1982.

Founded in 1980, Worden's Winery is the oldest of Spokane's young wineries. Like Latah Creek, Worden's is family-operated. From humble beginnings in a log cabin and storage shed, Jack Worden's winery quickly grew into new quarters and an annual capacity of 20,000 cases per year.

Visitors will find Worden's Winery at Spokane's west end. Turn off Interstate 90 at exit 276 and follow the signs to the tasting room where your host might favor you with a taste of his Gold Medal 1985 Chenin Blanc.

Visit a Nature Park. Among the top choices are Finch Arboretum, Riverside State Park, Turnbull Wildlife Refuge and Walk in the Wild.

Finch Arboretum contains 2,000 specimens in its 65 rolling forested acres. A tumbling stream, quiet trails and many species of birds would make this a gem if only it were easier to find. From city center, go west on Second Avenue to Sunset Highway. Continue on Sunset Highway past Government Way to just before "F" Street. The new entrance to the arboretum is located on the left-hand side of the Sunset Highway.

Turnball Wildlife Refuge deserves attention though it lies some miles out. Located 4 miles south of the town of Cheney (11 miles west of Spokane) on the Badger Lake Road, Turnbull offers unmatched viewing of birds, mainly migratory waterfowl. More than 200 species have been spotted here. Deer, coyote, beaver, raccoon and muskrat abound and are frequently seen from the 5-mile loop road.

Turnbull, a federal reserve, contains more than 120 lakes and ponds in its 7 square miles of scabrock, grassland, and pine and aspen groves. Numerous trails lead to observation blinds where quiet visitors identify wildlife against checklists provided by the management. Best times for visiting are early mornings in spring or fall.

Walk in the Wild is a cageless zoo located on 240 acres overlooking the Spokane River. Exit Interstate 90 at Pines Road (Exit 289) and drive north to Euclid Avenue. Signs lead to the zoo where, for a small fee, visitors follow trails through a variety of habitats. Deer and elk, bison, and elephants, peccaries, eagles and a several northwest species are on display. Children will enjoy the look-and-touch farm animals. Open mid-April to mid-October.

Sports. For the horsey set, Spokane offers expert polo, horse races and mounts to rent for quiet rides through open pine forests.

World-class polo in Spokane? Definitely. The Spokane Polo Club is the undisputed top polo club in the northwest and a perennial contender for national honors. On 80 lush acres east of the top of Sunset Hill, fierce adherents to polo's demanding and dangerous discipline regularly practice and compete.

The Playfair Racetrack, the state's oldest, has long been a civic fixture and a magnet to Spokane's devotees of the "Sport of Kings." For casual visitors, a day at Playfair provides

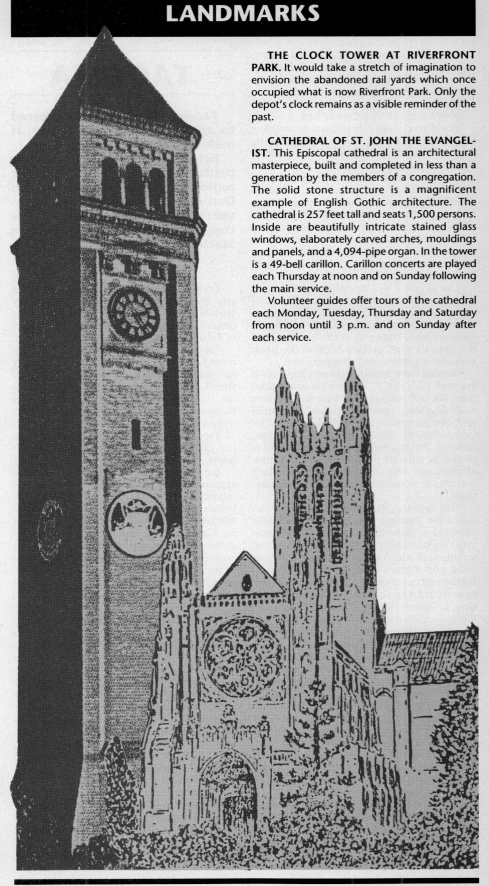

LANDMARKS

THE CLOCK TOWER AT RIVERFRONT PARK. It would take a stretch of imagination to envision the abandoned rail yards which once occupied what is now Riverfront Park. Only the depot's clock remains as a visible reminder of the past.

CATHEDRAL OF ST. JOHN THE EVANGELIST. This Episcopal cathedral is an architectural masterpiece, built and completed in less than a generation by the members of a congregation. The solid stone structure is a magnificent example of English Gothic architecture. The cathedral is 257 feet tall and seats 1,500 persons. Inside are beautifully intricate stained glass windows, elaborately carved arches, mouldings and panels, and a 4,094-pipe organ. In the tower is a 49-bell carillon. Carillon concerts are played each Thursday at noon and on Sunday following the main service.

Volunteer guides offer tours of the cathedral each Monday, Tuesday, Thursday and Saturday from noon until 3 p.m. and on Sunday after each service.

unmatched people-watching. Playfair, like all tracks, is a meeting place for that segment of adult society which dares to be different. How different? One has to experience a race crowd to appreciate it.

Race-goers know Playfair as a "bull-ring," a shorter than normal track. Hemmed in as it is by encroaching industrial parks, it has no room to grow. Still, when Playfair came into existence, it was a big step up from the now-forgotten track around Corbin Park.

But if you're not satisfied unless astride a horse yourself, try the Indian Canyon Riding Corrals at South Assembly and West Drive. The corrals, adjacent to Indian Canyon Park, open onto miles of forested and scenic trails.

Shop the Sky-Walk. How are Spokane's streets like Venetian canals? Answer: One is forever passing under pedestrian bridges. Criss-crossing streets, they connect the second stories of 13 blocks of Spokane's downtown, and up among the bridges, shoppers browse through block after block of shops and eateries.

The Skywalk was downtown's answer to the growing drain on its business by suburban malls. Spokane's planners, unwilling to concede defeat, came up with their truly extraordinary plan. Their plan became reality, and the Skywalk Mall quickly became the heart of Spokane's downtown shopping area.

Manito Park. Manito Park on Grand Blvd. between 17th and 25th Avenues, hosts more than 100,000 visitors each year and features a conservatory, Japanese garden, perennial and rose gardens, and a formal garden. The Conservatory displays tropical foliage, seasonal flowers, houseplant varieties and is of special interest to hobbyists. The center of the dome contains larger tropical plant specimens combined with flowering displays.

The Spokane Nishinomiya Garden, also called the Japanese Garden, is a beautifully designed asymmetrical garden in the park inspiring tranquility and peace in the Japanese tradition. It was completed in the spring of 1974 and named after 1 of Spokane's 2 sister cities in Japan. The Japanese Garden is open from 8 a.m. to dusk from May 1 through Nov. 1. There is no admission fee. The flowering season for the perennial and formal gardens is May through October; the rose garden blooms June through September.

Higher Education. Spokane and its suburbs offer a breadth and depth of education uncommon for cities its size. The lure of the schools' specialities draws students from far away, and many return to make their homes in Spokane. Industry keeps a close watch on Spokane's educated labor market, taking advantage of the resident pool of talent.

Spokane has 5 colleges: Gonzaga University has 3,900 students; Whitworth College, 1,900; Eastern Washington University, 8,000; Spokane Falls Community College, 5,500. To all of this, Washington State University is to add a Spokane campus in the next few years.

Walk the lovely campuses. Visit the colleges' libraries or coffee shops. It is always a vibrant experience to rub shoulders with throngs of intelligent young people who are busy shaping their dreams.

TACOMA

Tacoma, once jokingly referred to as Seattle's ugly stepsister, is making a strong comeback.

Fueled by a sense of strong civic pride, the city has built the region's finest arena (the Tacoma Dome), completed a new convention center, and put a new copper roof on historic Union Station.

Even though this hardworking, blue collar city was sometimes scorned by nearby Seattleites who thought of themselves as urbane and sophisticated, the scenic beauty of Tacoma was never in question.

Tacoma is nestled alongside Commencement Bay, a bustling deep water port. The city has beautiful neighborhoods with tree-lined streets. And the backdrop for the city is the Cascade mountain range, with Mount Rainier towering over the city like a protective parent.

Tacoma, called "The City of Destiny," was the railroad terminus long before tracks reached Seattle 32 miles away.

But long before manifest destiny lured explorers West, the beautiful countryside was inhabited by the Puyallup and Nisqually Indian tribes. It wasn't until 1792 that Captain George Vancouver visited the area. Based on Captain Vancouver's glowing reports about the area's abundant resources, other explorers soon followed including members of the Hudson's Bay Co. In 1885, the company built a fort and trading post 3 miles north of the Nisqually River.

The Wilkes expedition, headed by Capt. Charles Wilkes, began surveying the waters of Puget Sound on the bay around which Tacoma is now built. Wilkes named his starting point Commencement Bay. The artifacts and documents of the Wilkes expedition would later prove to be the initial collection that convinced Congress to establish the Smithsonian Institution.

In 1852, Nicholas Delin became the first settler in what is now downtown Tacoma, building a sawmill and a cabin. Soon after, Job Carr, Tacoma's first mayor, postmaster and election officer, chose a spot for what he hoped would become the terminus for the Northern Pacific Railroad. Others shared his dream, including General M.M. McCarver, who gave the city its first name, Commencement City. In 1869, the settlement's name was set as Tacoma, a derivation of the Indian Tahoma — their name for Mount Rainier, meaning "Mother of Waters."

Tacoma and the surrounding area grew

The statue "Trilogy" in Tacoma's Wright Park. (Tom Barr)

quickly with the completion of the railroad in 1873. Copper-domed Union Station still stands as a reminder of the city's railroad history. Today, Tacoma boasts the sixth busiest port in the U.S., the thriving communities of Fort Lewis and McChord Air Force Base and the seeds of high-tech industries.

Further information on area attractions, activities and points of interest is available from the Tacoma-Pierce County Visitor & Convention Bureau, P.O. Box 1933, Tacoma, WA 98401. Or call (206) 627-2836.

Attractions

Point Defiance Zoo and Aquarium. One of the Northwest's finest parks, 698-acre Point Defiance Park includes trails through forested areas, natural beaches, children's playgrounds, tennis courts, a Japanese Garden and lush rhododendron gardens. Also within the park is a reconstruction of Fort Nisqually (originally built in 1833), a railroad village with a working steam engine and views of the Olympic Mountains, Vashon Island and the Puget Sound. The world-class, 29-acre zoo and aquarium located in the park focuses on Pacific Rim animals. The newest exhibit is the $3.1 million South Pacific Aquarium,

LANDMARKS

comprised of 3 separate tanks, one with 9 varieties of sharks. Admission is $5 for adults; $4.50 seniors; $3.50 youth. The zoo is open from 10 a.m. to 4 p.m., except from Memorial Day to Labor Day, when the zoo stays open until 7 p.m. North or south on I-5, take exit 132 and follow signs that lead to Washington Highway 16 west, toward Gig Harbor; exit on 6th Avenue and follow the signs.

Pantages Center for the Performing Arts. This 1918 vaudeville theater has been painstakingly restored to its original grandeur with a stained glass panel in the ceiling, statues and rich colors. It took an 8-year, $6 million restoration to return the theater to the style of Louis XIV's opera house at Versailles, after which it was originally patterned. The theater, with its strong Baroque architecture and styling, was built by vaudeville entrepreneur Alexander Pantages — the sixth in a series of showcase theaters which, over the years, provided a stage for Stan Laurel and Bob Hope.

After the introduction of movies with sound, the theater was closed and remained unused for 5 decades. Now that it's back to its original splendor, the Center has offered entertainment by such notables as the Joffrey Ballet and the Boston Pops. To find out what's playing, call (206) 591-5894. The theater is located at 901 Broadway at the corner of Commerce & Broadway.

Celebration Meadow Maze. If you've ever wondered what it would be like to be in a maze garden like London's Hampton Court Maze, where you wind through a planted puzzle, here's your chance. Six-foot-high Douglas fir trees have been planted with paths that confound you as you try to find your way through the mile-long course. The maze opened in February 1989 and is open from 10 a.m. to dusk, Wednesday through Saturday, and 9 a.m. to 3 p.m. on Sundays. Cost is $3 for adults and $2.50 for children. The maze is in Gig Harbor, just over the Tacoma Narrows Bridge on Washington Highway 16. The route is well-marked from Harbor View Drive, the main thoroughfare through Gig Harbor. For more information, write Celebration Meadow Maze, 9916 Peacock Hill Ave. NW, Gig Harbor, WA 98335. Phone (206) 851-7930.

Ruston Way. Tacoma's busy port and beautiful setting can be enjoyed on a leisurely walk along the Ruston Way waterfront on the south shore of Commencement Bay. On a clear day, you'll see the wide saltwater bay framed by distant islands, snowcapped mountains of the Olympic and Cascade ranges and towering Mount Rainier. If you get hungry while walking along the 2-mile waterfront promenade, stop at one of the restaurants. Or if you want to savor the view, enjoy one of the parks along the way. Commencement Park at the east end of the waterfront features a large heliochronometer that tells you the time of day by the shadow the sun casts across the numbered bow. An interpretative court surrounding the piece explains the history, geology and other facts of interest about the area.

Pleasure boaters can moor at Old Town Dock, originally built in 1873, or at several other docks along Ruston Way.

TACOMA DOME. Looking something like a huge waylaid spaceship, the Tacoma Dome is 530 feet in diameter and 15 stories high — the largest wood-domed arena in the world. Completed in 1983, this $44 million facility has excellent acoustics and in 1985 was voted the top performing arena by recording artists nationally. The facility is used for concerts, home shows, rodeos, religious crusades and motorcross races. The Tacoma Dome is on Interstate 5 adjacent to the freeway at Exit 133. *(not pictured)*

UNION STATION. Long fallen into disuse and disrepair, Union Station at 1713 Pacific Ave. is being restored. The City of Tacoma purchased this majestic building and has installed a new copper roof. The station opened in 1911 and was the center of activity for nearly 75 years. Listed on the Register of Historic Buildings, Union Station has a style that is reminiscent of the Pantheon in Rome and 16th century Italian Baroque architecture.

THE NARROWS BRIDGE. In the summer of 1940, pious civic leaders stood on the newly-completed Tacoma Narrows bridge and proclaimed: " This bridge will stand for all time. It is the ultimate conquest of nature."

Four months later, the bridge lay at the bottom of the water , a victim of ill-conceived engineering and a violent wind storm. Rebuilt in 1950, the 5,979-foot structure is $187\frac{1}{2}$ feet above water and links Tacoma with the quaint fishing town of Gig Harbor. To get there, take Exit 132 junction with Washington Highway 16 west; continue to bridge.

Old City Hall is one of many historic structures in Tacoma.

(Tom Barr)

Old Town. On a bluff overlooking Ruston Way is Old Town, the original Tacoma settlement area, with many restaurants, galleries and historic buildings, including St. Peter's Episcopal Church. The church is Tacoma's first place of worship, located at North 29th and Starr streets. Built in 1873, the church's ivy-covered bell tower was a prominent landmark in early Tacoma. The original church bell, weighing 965 pounds, was shipped around Cape Horn. Today it is preserved on a mounted display outside the church.

Ruston Way in Old Town is sometimes referred to as "Restaurant Row" because many of Tacoma's best restaurants are here. Each restaurant features a large deck that makes dining alfresco a popular bayside choice. A private company on Dock Street offers harbor tours and the captain relates stories of Tacoma's history; call (206) 572-9858 for more information.

Washington State Historical Museum. One of the largest collections of pioneer, Indian and Alaskan artifacts on the Pacific Coast is located at the Washington State Historical Museum. Located on the bluff above Commencement Bay, the museum is the centerpiece of the Stadium-Seminary Historical District.

The Stadium District is on the National Register of Historic Places due to the broad spectrum of architectural styles and construction methods exhibited within its boundaries: North I, North 10th and North 1st streets. Historic streetlights, brick and cobblestone streets, and stately mansions are preserved within the district.

Points of interest include Annie Wright Seminary, a private school for grades K-12, located at 827 Tacoma Ave., and Stadium High School, located at 111 North E St., which was modeled after a French castle. This chateauesque structure was designed in 1891 as a luxury hotel for the Northern Pacific Railroad. A depression in 1893 halted construction, however, and in 1906 it was adapted for use as a high school.

Stadium Bowl, located behind the high school, was the first stadium built on the Pacific Coast and one of the first built in the country. Constructed in "Old Woman's Gulch," which provided a natural amphitheater for its tiered concrete design, the stadium has hosted such dignitaries as Theodore Roosevelt, Warren Harding, Franklin Roosevelt, Babe Ruth and Jack Dempsey. Guided tours of the district for groups of 10 or more are available by calling (206) 593-2830.

Tacoma Art Museum. During the 1990 Goodwill Games, the Tacoma Art Museum will have an exciting exhibit by Soviet artists — some of which were until recently considered extreme or radical in the Soviet Union. It will require all 3 floors of the museum to house this show called "Between Spring and Summer: Soviet Conceptual Art in the Era of Late Communism." This show will run from June 15 to Sept. 7, 1990.

The rest of the time, the museum will continue to show its permanent collection of American and French paintings including works by Renoir, Pissarro and Degas. A unique collection of jade and imperial robes from China are also on display. Eighteenth century Americana furniture and objects are preserved in a typical living room exhibit.

National and international traveling exhibits are featured in the main gallery, and a children's gallery provides original art exhibitions for young people. The museum is located at the corner of 12th Street and Pacific Avenue and is open 10 a.m. to 4 p.m., Monday through Saturday and noon to 5 p.m. on Sunday. Admission is $2 for adults and $1 for seniors and students.

Wright Park. Tacomans take great pride in their parks and with good reason — a century-old tradition of guarding and preserving open spaces for public use has left Tacoma with a legacy of one of the finest park systems in the country. Wright Park, in the heart of Tacoma (6th and Yakima), offers 27 acres for rest and recreation. Frequently the site for outdoor concerts in the summer, the park also features the Seymour Botanical Conservatory which is on the National Register of Historic Places. The conservatory has an extensive permanent collection of trees, ferns, cacti and orchids. Other activities include lawn bowling, horseshores, putting greens and play areas.

Fireman's Park. Overlooking the Port of Tacoma, Fireman's Park is built on a "lid" over Schuster Parkway. A popular brown bag lunch spot, this downtown park is often the site of outdoor concerts. The park's focal point is a 105-foot-tall totem pole carved by Alaska Indians depicting the legend of the Eagle Tribe.

Rose garden at Point Defiance Park, site of the zoo and aquarium.

(© Ray T. Weisgerber)

VANCOUVER, B.C.

Below the mountains that rise north of Burrard Inlet, Vancouver spreads out like a 3-dimensional map — from Point Grey in the west to the hump of Burnaby Mountain in the east and south to the gleam of the Fraser River. The forested triangle of Stanley Park and the airy thread of the Lions Gate Bridge draw attention to the downtown office towers and high-rise apartments. Behind them, the grid of city streets stretches for 71 square miles, bound by the waters of Burrard Inlet, English Bay and the river.

Visitors enjoy the Vancouver skyline.

(© Ray T. Weisgerber)

In the eyes of history, the glitter and sprawl of today's Vancouver happened overnight. Not much more than 100 years ago, the land between Burrard Inlet and the Fraser River was a thick, virgin forest peopled only with a scattering of Indian villages.

Spanish explorers sailed along the British Columbia coast and anchored briefly off Point Grey in 1791. The following year, Capt. George Vancouver, in search of the elusive Northwest Passage, explored and charted the inlets and took possession of the area for Britain. In 1808, Simon Fraser followed the river (which now bears his name) to the sea, but beat a hasty retreat to the safety of inland fur-trading posts after encounters with the Indians. For the next 50 years, all was quiet.

The Cariboo gold rush of 1858 shattered the peace of the coastal forest as thousands poured into the area from Fort Victoria on their way upriver. Vancouver never became a mining town; when the gold of Cariboo was gone, it was lumber from the thick surrounding forests that was the impetus for settlement.

In 1867, around one of the sawmill communities that had sprung up, "Gassy" Jack Deighton rounded up thirsty volunteers and built a saloon. Deighton House stood at what is now the corner of Water and Carrall streets in Vancouver, and around this jovial center the settlement of Gastown soon grew up. Gastown was officially given the name of Granville in 1870, and with its 3 saloons, 1 hotel, 2 stores and handful of shanties, had a reputation for card-playing, wild drinking and pretty ladies.

Granville continued its brawling ways for the next decade; a period that saw Burrard Inlet become world famous for its fine lumber. There were often as many as 40 ships waiting to load in the inlet. In 1877, 29 million board feet of lumber was exported. Granville flourished. Wooden sidewalks were laid; the false fronts were embellished with gingerbread.

Then the Canadian Pacific Railway (CPR) chose Coal Harbour on Burrard Inlet as the terminus of its trans-Canada line. Granville, just a short distance from Coal Harbour, boomed. By February 1886 there were 100 buildings; in April, a city was incorporated and named for Captain Vancouver; and by June the number of buildings had jumped to 1,000. In the middle of June, however, disaster struck. Twenty minutes of an uncontrolled fire destroyed it all. In the downtown area, only the Regina Hotel was saved.

Within hours of the fire the rebuilding began. When the first CPR passenger train steamed into the city the following year, there was no trace at all of the fire, only a vibrant new city. With a great harbor at its command, the ocean at its feet, forests all around and a vital rail link to western Canada, Vancouver prospered. Her port shipped lumber and prairie grain and off-loaded silk and tea from the great clipper ships from the Orient. Trains brought in hordes of immigrants and took supplies to Interior settlements.

By 1888, Vancouver's population reached more than 8,500. Gold rushes in the Kootenays and the Klondike helped swell her population and bank balance, and soon the city surpassed both Victoria and New Westminster in size and wealth.

Vancouver has never looked back. Fifty-five thousand new residents arrived in 1988, many from Asia. Today it is the third-largest city in Canada, and a sophisticated cosmopolitan center for business, shopping and the arts. Its port is one of North America's busiest for dry and bulk cargo, and its diversified industry supplies the province with its forestry, mining and fishing resources. Vancouver's moderate, year-round climate and spectacular mountain and maritime scenery have made it an attractive place to live and to visit.

Attractions

Stanley Park. On a downtown peninsula, 5 minutes from the business district, is one of the finest and largest natural parks on the continent. Stanley Park was named for Lord Stanley, the governor general of Canada in 1889.

The park is rimmed by beaches, tennis courts, rose gardens and a 6 mile/10 km seawall promenade, a favorite for joggers, walkers and cyclists. Bicycles, even those built for 2, can be rented near the park's main entrance on Georgia Street. Also encircling the park is a 1-way scenic drive that provides access to the various attractions in the park.

Park highlights include: the Vancouver Aquarium, Brockton Point Lighthouse, and the Stanley Park Zoo. The zoo houses mammals, reptiles and birds from all over the world, along with a miniature railway and a children's zoo. Call (604) 682-1118 for information. While many other cities have zoos and golf courses in their parks, few have such stretches of virgin West Coast forest where, if only for a moment, all man-made sounds cease and you can imagine the land as it was 200 years ago.

Vancouver Aquarium. More than 6,000 beautifully displayed marine and freshwater animals make their appearance at the Vancouver Aquarium, including whales, dolphins, turtles, sea otters, sharks, eels, birds and reptiles. This is one of Vancouver's premier attractions.

LANDMARKS

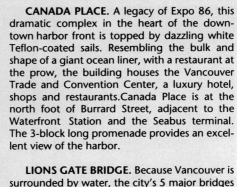

CANADA PLACE. A legacy of Expo 86, this dramatic complex in the heart of the downtown harbor front is topped by dazzling white Teflon-coated sails. Resembling the bulk and shape of a giant ocean liner, with a restaurant at the prow, the building houses the Vancouver Trade and Convention Center, a luxury hotel, shops and restaurants. Canada Place is at the north foot of Burrard Street, adjacent to the Waterfront Station and the Seabus terminal. The 3-block long promenade provides an excellent view of the harbor.

LIONS GATE BRIDGE. Because Vancouver is surrounded by water, the city's 5 major bridges are not only landmarks, they're vital for finding your way around. Most famous is Lions Gate that links the tip of Stanley Park to the North Shore, crossing the First Narrows of Burrard Inlet. This bridge, named for the twin peaks on the North Shore, is as dramatic and pleasant to look at as San Francisco's Golden Gate. This narrow suspension bridge was built by a private company in 1938 and operated for nearly 20 years as a toll bridge. Since Vancouver's centennial celebrations in 1986, the bridge has been illuminated at night. *(not pictured)*

TOTEM POLE, UNIVERSITY OF BRITISH COLUMBIA MUSEUM OF ANTHROPOLOGY. The totem pole is one of the best-known examples of Northwest Coast Indian art. Monumental totem poles once lined the beaches of Northwest coastal Native villages like mythic forests. Often rising to over 30 feet, these massive sculptures represent human, animal, and legendary creatures. This totem pole, carved by a new generation of Haida artists, stands on the museum's grounds as part of a simulated Indian Village. The museum houses one of the largest collections of Northwest Coast art and artifacts in the world.

In the Amazon Gallery, spectators are surrounded by the life and color of the Amazon jungle. Exotic birds, South American crocodilians, piranhas and playful marmosets are on display. The H.R. MacMillan Tropical Gallery features sharks, moray eels, angelfishes, seahorses and more.

The Marine Mammal Complex is one of the most popular features, with killer and beluga whales on display, as well as harbor seals and sea otters. An underwater viewing area is available for spectators to watch as the graceful mammals dive, pitch and roll in their marine habitat.

The British Columbia Hall of Fishes consists of 43 displays of western Canada's saltwater and freshwater sea life. The coast of British Columbia hosts a myriad of sea life species and the province's inland waters are among the most productive in North America.

Killer (Orca) whales, arctic white whales and harbor seals perform daily, and natural history films are shown every afternoon. The Clam Shell Gift Shop specializes in quality, handcrafted Canadian artwork, limited edition prints, and natural history and children's books.

The Vancouver Aquarium is located in Stanley Park at the entrance to Vancouver's harbor. The park is accessible from the downtown area via Georgia Street or from the North Shore, using the park entrance exit off the Lions Gate Bridge. Admission is $5.75 for adults; $4.75 for students and seniors; $3.25 for children.

The Vancouver Aquarium is one of North America's great marine facilities. It is open year-round, 7 days a week. For current hours and showtimes, phone (604) 682-1118.

Gastown. This unique, preserved section of town is located north of Hastings Street between Hamilton Street and Columbia Street. Its brick alleyways, boutiques, art galleries, antique stores and restaurants provide an exciting shopping experience for visitors.

The steam-powered village clock is the only one of its kind in the world. Built by sculptor and horologist Raymond Saunders, it was unveiled and dedicated in 1977. Weighing in at nearly 2 tons, it is a replica of an 1875 vintage design and has a pinwheel escapement that drives a heavy, gold-plated pendulum. A loud steam whistle sounds-off on the hour. Historic Gastown is one of the most visited areas in Vancouver.

Granville Island. Rescued from the blight of industry, this island adjacent to Granville Bridge is now a popular shopping and culture spot. The huge indoor farmer's market beside the False Creek quay is open daily (closed Mondays during fall and winter) and features fresh produce from Vancouver Island and the Okanagan. Imported specialty items, fresh seafood, spices and baked goods can be found. Outside the market along the cobblestone streets are many specialty craft and gift shops, including a glass-blower.

Other attractions on the island include the Kid's Own Market, a brewery, several good restaurants, 2 theatres and a small but elegant hotel. The walkways and parkland surrounding False Creek provide great views of the city center and the multi-tiered condominium complexes that make False Creek an appealing inner city place to live. Access by car is from 4th Avenue just west of the Granville Bridge. Small passenger ferries ply the waters of False Creek between the island and several ports of call, including the Aquatic Centre, the Maritime Museum, the False Creek Yacht Club and B.C. Place. For information, call Granville Island Ferries at (604) 684-7781 or Aquabus at (604) 874-9930.

The Royal Hudson. Train buffs come to Vancouver just for a ride on the Royal Hudson, one of the few operating steam trains in Canada. And what a ride! The 64-km trip along the Howe Sound to Squamish is one of the most scenic on the continent with views along the fjord up to the snow-crowned peaks of the Tantalus Mountains. The Royal Hudson leaves from the B.C. Rail Station at 1311 W. First St. in North Vancouver. You can ride to Squamish on the train and transfer to the cruise ship Britannia for the return trip or do the journey in reverse. Or travel round-trip by train. The Britannia sails from the north foot of Denman near the Stanley Park entrance. This special service runs only from mid-May to September and reservations are recommended. Call (604) 687-9558 or (604) 68-TRAIN for schedules and reservations.

Chinatown. The second largest in North America (San Francisco's is the largest), Vancouver's Chinatown stretches for several blocks between Gore and Carrall Avenues along Pender and Keefer streets. It's a colorful, lively quarter. There are authentic Chinese herbalists, butcher shops with pressed duck and live chickens, strange vegetables spilling their color on streetside stalls, shops selling carved ivory and bamboo, brocade dresses and Chinese pastries, and lots of restaurants and curio shops. The street names are written in Chinese, the phone booths have pagoda roofs — even the McDonald's menu is in Chinese.

The Chinese Cultural Centre displays Chinese art exhibits and behind lies the Dr. Sun Yat-Sen Classical Chinese Gardens. A replica of a Ming Dynasty Pavilion and garden, this $5 million enterprise was built by artisans from the Chinese city of Suzhou using traditional methods and hand tools. Every rock, plant and pool is symbolic and together are designed to create a feeling of complete harmony. The centre is located at 678 Carrall Street; phone (604) 689-7133.

Gardens. This city is crazy about flowers and gardens. Queen Elizabeth Park's quarry garden has colorful carpets of seasonal flowers and great city views. The Bloedel Conservatory, a stunning triodesic dome located in the park, creates a series of mini-climates ranging from tropical to desert with hundreds of flowering and leafy plants, 50 species of birds and a pool with giant carp. The conservatory sits atop Little Mountain and the surrounding Queen Elizabeth Park's lush gardens are a wonderful place to walk. Admission to Bloedel Conservatory is $2.30 for adults, $1.15 for children. Phone (604) 872-5513.

The University of British Columbia

Vancouver's historic buildings have been preserved in Gastown.   (© Ray T. Weisgerber)

Botanical Gardens has 16,000 different plants in special gardens, including alpine, native, physic, food and Asian gardens. Also on campus is a rose garden with 1,000 bushes of 100 varities, and the Nitobe Memorial Garden with traditional Japanese landscaping and an authentic teahouse.

The Van Dusen Botanical Garden at 5251 Oak St. houses different types of gardens, including herb, fragrance, winter, medieval maze, Himalayan, children's garden, and more. For more informaton, phone (604) 266-7194.

Museums. Several museums offer a glimpse into Vancouver's past.

The Museum of Anthropology is known for its stunning modern building designed by Arthur Erickson and its extensive collection of Northwest Indian artifacts. Huge totems and other carvings surround the glass and concrete structure.

A highlight of the museum's contemporary Northwest Coast Indian collection is the massive sculpture carved in yellow cedar, "The Raven and the First Man," by the renowned Haida Indian artist Bill Reid.

This is Canada's largest university museum and visitors may ask at the admissions desk for guided gallery walks, lectures, films, crafts, programs and musical and theatrical events. Short videotapes covering the cultures of the Northwest Coast and other locals are available.

The "Masterpiece Collection" displays small, intricately carved or cast sculpture and Indian objects in silver, gold, argillite, bone and wood.

The museum is located on the university campus at the tip of Point Grey. For information and schedules, write the University of British Columbia, Museum of Anthropology, 6393 NW Marine Dr., Vancouver, BC, Canada V6T 1W5 or call (604) 228-3825 for a taped message or (604) 228-5087 for the business office.

The Vancouver Museum, located at 11 Chestnut St., features Indian art and cultural displays, city history, a trading post, an original Canadian Pacific Railway passenger train and turn-of-the-century rooms. For admission

and schedules, call (604) 736-4431.

At the foot of Cypress Street is the Vancouver Maritime Museum, featuring ship models and displays of artifacts and photographs of the British Columbia coast history. The focus of interest is the *St. Roch,* a restored Royal Canadian Mounted Police patrol boat built in Vancouver in 1928. This short, 2-masted schooner was the first vessel to navigate the Northwest Passage in both directions, the first to make the passage in a single season, and the first to circumnavigate the continent of North America. It can be toured in dry dock, inside a special building. Phone (604) 737-2211. Open daily 10 a.m. to 5 p.m., Wednesdays until 9 p.m.

The H.R. MacMillan Planetarium offers a laser light show on a large dome, as well as astronomy exhibits. The Gordon Southam Observatory, next to the planetarium, offers views of celestial events through a large refractor telescope. This facility is open on clear weekends and holidays only. For information, call (604) 736-4431 or 736-3656.

Views. When the scenery is so splendid, it pays to get up high to see it better. Downtown, the Observation Deck and revolving restaurant at Harbour Centre, 555 W. Hastings St., is the place to start. Glass elevators lift you up 553 feet/167m above the city for a bird's-eye view. Also in town is the Vanterm Container Terminal, 1300 Stewart St.; a viewing area where visitors can watch port operations from an overhead walkway and observation deck. Good views of Burrard Inlet. Phone (604) 666-6129 for information.

Vancouver's mountain skyline dominates the city and 3 of the peaks have ski areas. One of the best viewpoints is the top of Grouse Mountain, accessible by a gondola called Superskyride that goes to the 3,700-foot level for paved walking paths, hiking trails, helicopter tours and 2 restaurants. Call (604) 984-0661 for Skyride rates and times.

For more information on Vancouver and its attractions, write the Vancouver Visitor and Convention Center, 1055 W. Georgia St., Vancouver, BC, Canada V6E 4C8 or call (604) 682-2222.

General Information

Alcoholic Beverages

ALBERTA

The legal age is 18. Packaged liquor, beer and wine are sold in government liquor stores (open daily except Sunday and holidays) and beer (to take out) is also sold in cold beer stores and in some taverns. On Sunday, liquor is served only with food in licensed dining rooms.

BRITISH COLUMBIA

Legal age is 19. Packaged liquor, beer and wine are sold only in government liquor stores (open daily except Sunday and holidays). Children allowed with parents only in the dining rooms of licensed premises. Sunday serving laws in licensed premises vary from community to community.

IDAHO

Legal drinking age is 21 for both beer and liquor. Idaho has an open container law which prohibits the transportation of liquor containers with an open seal. This does not apply to beer and wine.

MONTANA

The legal drinking age is 21. Liquor is sold by package in state liquor stores and by the drink in licensed establishments.

OREGON

The legal drinking age is 21. Transporting open alcoholic beverage containers within vehicle is illegal.

WASHINGTON

Legal drinking age is 21. An open container law is in effect and it is illegal to carry a container of alcohol with a broken seal in your vehicle.

Customs Requirements

ENTRY INTO CANADA
FROM THE UNITED STATES

Your best source of general information on this subject is the Canadian Government Office of Tourism's travel information brochure. For information concerning admission of items not covered, write Revenue Canada, Customs and Excise, Public Relations Branch, Ottawa, ON, Canada K1A 0L5. Here are excerpts from that brochure.

Citizens or permanent residents of the United States can usually cross the U.S.-Canada border either way without difficulty. They do not require passports or visas. However, to assist officers of both countries in speeding the crossing, native-born U.S. citizens should carry some identifying paper that shows their citizenship, just in case they are asked for it. This would include a driver's license, voters registration, passport with photo, or some employment cards with description and photo. Social security cards are not positive identification. Birth certificates of children are sometimes required. Proof of residence may also be required. Permanent residents of the U.S. who are not American citizens are advised to have their Alien Registration Receipt Card (U.S. Form 1-151).

All persons other than U.S. citizens or legal residents, and residents of Greenland, require a valid passport or an acceptable travel document.

Visitors to the U.S. who have a single entry visa to that country should check with an office of the U.S. Immigration and Naturalization Service to make sure that they have all the papers they need to get back into the U.S.

Persons temporarily in the U.S. who would require visas if coming to Canada directly from their countries of origin, should contact the Canadian Embassy, Consulate or Office of Tourism in their home country before departure for the U.S.

Persons under 18 years of age who are not accompanied by an adult should bring a letter with them from a parent or guardian giving them permission to travel into Canada.

Although there is no set standard of monies required for entrance into Canada, the visitor must have sufficient funds to cover his cost of living per day for the planned length of stay. Consideration in assessing "sufficient funds" includes the locale in which the visitor plans to stay and whether he will be staying with a friend or relative. The visitor must also have return transportation fare to his country of origin.

Vehicles: The entry of vehicles and trailers into Canada for touring purposes, for periods up to 12 months, is generally a quick, routine matter, without payment of a customs assessment, and any necessary permits are issued at the port of entry. Rental trailers of the U-haul luggage variety may be subject to a nominal deposit which is refundable on proof of exportation of the trailer. Motor vehicle registration forms should be carried and, if the vehicle is rented from a car rental company, a copy of the rental contract stipulating use in Canada. If a tourist enters Canada using a vehicle not registered in his name, it is suggested that he carry a letter from its registered owner authorizing the use of the vehicle.

United State motorists planning to travel to Canada are advised to obtain a Canadian Nonresident Interprovince Motor Vehicle Liability Insurance Card which provides evidence of financial responsiblity. This card is available only in the U.S. through U.S. insurance agents. All provinces in Canada require visiting motorists to produce evidence of financial responsibility, should they be involved in an accident. Financial responsibility limits vary by province.

All national driver's licenses are valid in Canada.

Trailers: If you plan to leave your vacation trailer in Canada for a season while returning home from time to time, ask Canada customs for a wallet-sized special permit — an E-99. Post the permit inside the trailer so that it can be seen easily from outside. You may not store a vacation trailer in Canada during the off-season.

Entry by private boat: Visitors planning to enter Canada by private boat should contact customs in advance for a list of ports of entry that provide customs facilities and their hours of operation. Immediately upon arrival, visitors must report to customs and complete all documentation. In emergency situations, visitors must report their arrival to the nearest regional customs office or office of the RCMP.

Baggage: The necessary wearing apparel and personal effects in use by the visitor are admitted free of duty. Up to 50 cigars, 200 cigarettes (1 carton) and 2 pounds of manufactured tobacco and up to 40 ounces of spiritous liquor or wine OR 24 12-ounce cans or bottles of beer or ale may be allowed entry in this manner. Additional quantities of alcoholic beverages up to a maximum of 2 gallons may be imported into Canada (except the Northwest Territories) on payment of duty and taxes plus charges for a provincial permit at port of entry. To import tobacco products a person must be 16 years of age or over and to import alcoholic beverages the importer must have reached the legal age established by authorities of the province or territory into which the alcoholic beverages are being entered.

Recreational equipment: Visitors may also bring in sporting outfits and other equipment for their own use by declaring them at entry. These can include fishing tackle, portable boats, outboard motors, snowmobiles, equipment for camping, golf, tennis and other games, radios and portable or table-model TV sets used for the reception of sound broadcasting and TV programs, typewriters and cameras (with a reasonable amount of film and flashbulbs) in their possession on arrival. Although not a requirement, it may facilitate entry if visitors have a list (in duplicate) of each item, including serial numbers when possible. All such articles must be identified and reported when leaving Canada.

Transporting goods through Canada: U.S. citizens from the Lower 49 who wish to transport personally their household or personal effects to Alaska when such goods are not intended for use in Canada, may obtain a temporary admission permit (form E29B) to facilitate the in-transit movements of goods through Canada.

Firearms: Firearms are divided into 3 categories—prohibited, restricted and "long guns."

A nonresident importing a "long gun" or moving in transit through Canada with a "long gun" does not require a Firearms Acquisition Certificate nor a Permit to Transport. A "long gun" means a regular hunting rifle or shotgun as so described by the manufacturer, and which does not fall into the category of a prohibited or restricted firearm.

A prohibited firearm includes any firearm that is capable of firing bullets in rapid succession during one pressure of the trigger, or any firearm adapted from a rifle or shotgun whether by sawing, cutting or other alteration or modification, that as so adapted, has a barrel that is less than 18 inches/46 cm in length, or that is less than 26 inches/66 cm in overall length. Such weapons are not permitted entry into Canada.

A restricted firearm includes any firearm that is not a prohibited weapon, has a barrel less than $18^{1/2}$ inches/47 cm in length and is capable of discharging center-fire ammunition in a semiautomatic manner, or is designed or adapted to be fired when reduced to a length less than 26 inches/66 cm by folding, telescoping or otherwise. Also included would be any firearm designed, altered or intended to be aimed and fired by the action of one hand, such as revolvers and handguns.

Restricted firearms may only enter Canada when accompanied by a Permit to Transport or a Permit to Carry issued by a Canadian Local Registrar of Firearms. These permits are rarely issued.

The following quantities of explosives may enter Canada for personal use by hunters and competitive marksmen without a permit issued by the Explosives Branch of the Dept. of Energy, Mines and Resources: 2,000 safety cartridges; 1,000 primers for safety cartridges; 500 empty primed safety cartridge cases; 4.4 pounds/2 kg smokeless powder (small-arms nitro compound).

Nonresidents arriving at Canada Customs port must declare all their firearms. Anyone who illegally carries a firearm into Canada is subject to a number of penalties, including seizure of the weapon and the vehicle in which it is carried.

Plants, fruit and vegetables: Houseplants may be imported without a permit. Some fruits and vegetables may be restricted entry

Spotted sandpipers on the beach near Grays Harbor, WA.   (© John Barger)

into Canada and all are subject to inspection at the border.

Animals: Dogs and cats (over 3 months of age) from the U.S. must be accompanied by a certificate issued by a licensed veterinarian of Canada or the U.S. certifying that the animal has been vaccinated against rabies during the preceding 36 months; such a certificate shall describe the animal and date of vaccination and shall be initialed by inspectors and returned to the owner.

Up to 2 pet birds per family may be imported into Canada. Birds of the parrot family and accompanied by the owner, may be admitted if found healthy and if the owner certifies in writing that, upon entering the country, the birds have not been in contact with other birds of the parrot family and have been in his possession for 90 days immediately preceding importation. All birds of the parrot family, except "budgies," are on the CITES endangered species list and require an import permit from the Canadian Wildlife Service (and, depending upon species, a U.S. permit) for entry. Contact Canadian Wildlife Service, Ottawa, ON, K1A 0E7, phone (613) 997-1840.

Endangered species: The importation of certain animals and plants that are on the endangered species list is prohibited. This applies to any recognizable by-product made of the fur, skin, feathers, bone, etc., of these creatures. For example, U.S. citizens transporting carved ivory or parts of lynx, otter, brown/grizzly bear or wolf through Canada must first obtain an export and/or transit permit from the U.S. Fish and Wildlife Service. (Permits are available at any U.S. Fish and Wildlife Refuge office.) Many ivory sellers will furnish a permit upon request. To avoid the need for the permit, either mail the items or travel directly back to the Lower 48. Request a list of restricted items

from Convention Administrator, Canadian Wildlife Service, Environment Canada, Ottawa, ON, K1A 0E7.

REENTRY INTO THE UNITED STATES

It is, of course, the responsibility of the traveler to satisfy U.S. immigration authorities of his right to reenter the U.S.

Canadian immigration officers may caution persons entering from the U.S. of any likely reentry problems.

Reentry to the U.S. can be simplified if you list all your purchases before you reach the border, keep sales receipts and invoices handy and pack purchases separately.

Within 48 hours: Residents of the U.S. visiting Canada for less than 48 hours may take back for personal or household use merchandise to the fair retail value of $25, free of U.S. duty and tax. Any or all of the following may be included, as long as the total value does not exceed $25; 50 cigarettes, 10 cigars (non-Cuban in origin), 4 ounces/150 ml of alcoholic beverages or alcoholic perfume.

If any article brought back is subject to duty or tax, or if the total value of all articles exceeds $25, no article may be exempted from duty or tax. Members of a family household are not permitted to combine the value of their purchases under this exception.

Persons crossing the international boundary at one point and reentering the U.S. in order to travel to another part of Canada should inquire at U.S. customs regarding special exemption requirements.

After more than 48 hours: U.S. residents returning from Canada may take back, once every 31 days, merchandise for personal or household use to the value of $400 free of U.S. duty and tax, provided they have

GENERAL INFORMATION

remained in Canada 48 hours. The exemption will be based on the fair retail value of the article acquired and goods must accompany the resident upon arrival in the U.S. Members of a family household traveling together may combine their personal exemptions — thus a family of 5 could be entitled to a total exemption of $2,000. Up to 100 cigars (non-Cuban in origin) per person may be imported into the U.S. by U.S. residents, and up to 200 cigarettes, and 1 liter of alcoholic beverages if the resident has attained the age of 21 years.

Federal wildlife laws affect what U.S. citizens may bring back into the country. The list is extensive and visitors to the North should be particularly aware that the import of the following is restricted except by special permit: products made from seal skin, whalebone and whale and walrus ivory, sea otter, or polar bear, and most wild bird feathers, mounted birds and skins. For a complete list of restricted items and information on import permits, contact the nearest U.S. Fish and Wildlife Service office.

Pets: Domestic dogs, including those taken out of the country and being returned, must have a valid rabies vaccination certificate identifying the dog and date of vaccination and bearing the signature of a licensed veterinarian. A date of expiration should be included. If no date of expiration is specified, the certificate is acceptable if the date of vaccination is no more than 12 months before the date of arrival. Vaccination against rabies is not required for cats.

For further information contact the nearest U.S. customs office or write U.S. Customs Service, Washington, DC 20229.

Driving Information

ALBERTA
Firearms: All rifles and shotguns must be declared at the border (see Customs Requirements). Pistols are prohibited.
Minimum driver's age: 16.
Rest area camping: Permitted.
Right turn on red: Permitted unless otherwise posted.
Riding in towed trailer: Not permitted. Owner's family permitted to ride in pickup camper.
Seat belts: The use of seat belts and child restraint seats is mandatory for all ages. Applies to out-of-state/province drivers.
Studded tires: Permitted.

BRITISH COLUMBIA
Firearms: All rifles and shotguns must be declared at the border (see Customs Requirements). Pistols are prohibited; strictly enforced.
Minimum driver's age: Driver's license divided into 6 classes — 19 for classes 1, 2 and 4; 18 for class 3; 16 for classes 5 and 6.
Rest area camping: Not permitted.
Right turn on red: Permitted after complete stop unless prohibited by signs.
Riding in towed trailer: Prohibited; riding in pickup camper is permitted.

Seat belts: The use of seat belts or child restraint seats is mandatory for all ages. Applies to out-of-state/province drivers.
Studded tires: Legal between Oct. 1 and April 30.

IDAHO
Minimum driver's age: 16; restricted license for age 14 or 15 after completion of approved driver's education course.
Rest area camping: Not permitted.
Right turn on red: Permitted after complete stop unless prohibited by signs.
Riding in towed trailer: Not permitted; riding in pickup camper is permitted.
Seat belts: Mandatory for all front seat occupants in passenger vehicles. Applies to out-of-state drivers. Child restraints mandatory for children under 4. Does not apply to out-of-state drivers.
Studded tires: Legal between Oct. 1 and April 15.

MONTANA
Firearms: A permit must be obtained to carry a concealed weapon. Weapons may be carried in the vehicle if they are in view.
Minimum driver's age: 16; 15 if applicant has passed an approved course in driver's education.
Rest area camping: Permitted where posted.
Right turn on red: Permitted after complete stop unless otherwise posted.
Riding in towed trailer: Not permitted; riding in pickup camper is permitted.
Seat belts: Required. Montana has passed a law requiring seat belts to be worn by all.
Studded tires: Legal Oct. 1 to May 31 unless weather warrants use at other times. Chains are required where posted.

OREGON
Firearms: All weapons must be unloaded and in view. No concealed weapons are permitted.
Minimum driver's age: 16; special conditions permit issued at 14.
Rest area camping: Not permitted.
Right turn on red: Permitted after complete stop unless otherwise posted.
Riding in towed trailer: Not permitted; riding in pickup camper is permitted.
Seat belts: Seat belts are mandatory for driver and passengers. All youngsters under the age of 16 must be seated in a seat restraint or seat belt.
Studded tires: Legal from Nov. 15 to April 30. Chains are required where posted.
NOTE: Self-service gas is not available in Oregon; only full service. Do not attempt to pump your own gas.

WASHINGTON
Firearms: Permits, which are good statewide, are required to carry a concealed weapon. Unloaded shotguns and rifles may be carried in the vehicle.
Minimum driver's age: 16 with driver training course, otherwise 18.
Rest area camping: Not permitted.

Right turn on red: Permitted after complete stop unless otherwise posted.
Riding in towed trailer: Not permitted; riding in pickup camper is permitted.
Seat belts: Washington has a mandatory seat belt law. Drivers are responsible for seeing that all passengers use seat belts.
Studded tires: Legal from Nov. 1 to April 1. Chains required where posted (unless 4-wheel drive with approved traction devices for all 4 wheels).

Fishing Licenses

Following are license requirements for fishing in Alberta, British Columbia, Idaho, Montana, Oregon and Washington. Check with respective state and provincial fish and game authorities for license fees and current regulations.

ALBERTA
Licenses are required of all anglers over 16 years old, except Alberta residents 65 or older, and are valid from April 1 to March 31. Licenses are available at fish and wildlife division offices and from private vendors, usually sporting goods dealers. Trophy lake licenses are required for all anglers on designated trophy lake waters. Angling is permitted year-round, 24 hours per day, subject to specific closures listed in regulations pamphlet. Alberta licenses are valid in provincial parks but invalid in national parks of Canada.

BRITISH COLUMBIA
Fishing resources in British Columbia are under the jurisdiction of both provincial and national governments. Nontidal fishing (fresh water) is managed by the Ministry of Environment, Fisheries Branch, Parliament Bldg., Victoria, BC, V8V 1X5; phone (604) 387-4573. Tidal water (salt water) fishing is managed by the federal Dept. of Fisheries and Oceans, 1090 W. Pender St., Vancouver, BC, V6E 2P1; phone (604) 666-0384.

Freshwater and saltwater fishing licenses are required of all anglers 16 and older. Both licenses are renewable on March 31. Saltwater licenses are available in more than 600 outlets, mostly along the coast, including sporting goods, hardware, resort and marine-related stores. Freshwater permits are available in nearly all sporting goods, resort or hardware stores in the province.

Special permits are required for steelhead and for nonresidents fishing lakes and streams classified as "Special Waters," generally trophy-class fishing opportunities.

A basic general license is required in order to buy a steelhead or special waters supplemental permit. Fishing is generally open in nontidal waters year-round, however, many lakes and streams have temporary closures and a few are permanently closed. Saltwater areas are subject to regional restrictions by season and species of fish. Consult a current copy of the *British Columbia Tidal Waters Sport Fishing Guide* for closures.

The Deschutes River in Oregon is a prime spot for trout fishing.

(© John Barger)

IDAHO

All anglers 14 and older must have a license to fish all Idaho waters. All nonresident children less than 14 must be accompanied by a licensed adult when fishing and their fish must be counted as part of the adult's daily limit.

Resident children under 14 can fish without a license and without an adult. Idaho licenses are also valid when fishing from boats on the boundary waters of the Snake River between Idaho, Oregon and Washington, and Bear Lake which straddles the border with Utah.

Steelhead and salmon fishermen need a general fishing license plus separate steelhead and salmon permits. Children under the age of 14, including nonresidents, are exempt from buying steelhead permits if accompanied by licensed adults. The children's catch, however, must be counted against the adult's bag limit.

Licenses are available at more than 500 sporting goods stores, resorts and marinas and expire Dec. 31.

MONTANA

All anglers 15 and older must have a general fishing license. Nonresidents under 15 don't need a license if they fish with a licensed adult, and the youngster's fish are counted against the licensed angler's limit. Resident anglers between 12 and 14 must have a conservation license to fish. No license under 12.

All anglers must buy a conservation license as a prerequisite to a fishing or hunting license, or special permit. The only supplemental fishing permit required is for paddlefish snagging in the Yellowstone River. All other game fish can be tackled with a general fishing license. State fishing licenses are available at sporting goods stores, resorts and marinas as well as regional MFWP offices. Licenses are valid from March 1 through Feb. 28.

All lakes in the state are open to fishing year-round and rivers are open from the third Saturday in May through November. Free national park fishing permits are issued upon request at the entrance gates to Glacier and Yellowstone national parks. Fishing on Indian reservation land is controlled by the administering tribe.

OREGON

All anglers 14 years old and older need a fishing license for all fish except smelt and shellfish. Licenses *are not* required to dig clams, trap crabs or collect mussels. A fishing license is also not required inside Crater Lake National Park, north of Klamath Falls.

Steelhead and salmon fishermen, regardless of age, are required to have a steelhead/salmon punch card in salt and fresh water, except for daily angler license holders. Both Oregon and Washington licenses are valid when fishing for salmon in the ocean within 5 miles north and south of the Columbia River mouth.

Licenses are available at hundreds of sporting goods outlets, including resorts and charter operations, and directly from the main office of the Oregon Dept. of Fish and Wildlife.

WASHINGTON

When, where and if you need a fishing license in Washington depends on how old you are and what you're fishing for. Fresh- and saltwater license requirements vary with the species of fish and age of the angler. Fishing license are renewable on Jan. 1 except for steelhead punch cards which expire April 30.

A Dept. of Wildlife fishing license is required of all fishermen over the age of 15 while angling in fresh water except in Mount Rainier and Olympic national parks, where unlicensed fishing is allowed. A state fishing license is necessary, however, in North Cascades National Park, and steelhead punch cards are required when steelheading in Olympic National Park.

A fishing license is required to fish in salt water. A Dept. of Fisheries salmon punch card is required for chinook, coho, chum, sockeye and salmon in salt and fresh water. The punch card is free to fishermen inside Olympic National Park and anglers under 16 and over 70. The Dept. of Wildlife requires a general fishing license plus a steelhead punch card, regardless of the angler's age, for steelhead fishing in either salt or fresh water. A fishing license, but no punch card, is required to fish for sea-run cutthroat.

The Dept. of Fisheries requires a license to trap shrimp only in Hood Canal, or dig razor clams on ocean beaches. Licenses are not required to catch saltwater bottom fish, dig hard-shelled clams or trap crabs and non-Hood Canal shrimp. Steelhead fishermen are required to have a Dept. of Wildlife general fishing license plus a steelhead punch card, except in Olympic National Park, where only a punch card is required.

Freshwater fishing licenses, salmon and steelhead punch cards are available in hundreds of sporting goods outlets, bait shops, resorts and charter offices. Quite a few sporting goods stores have quit selling licenses because of the clerical time required, but most can direct you to the nearest license outlet. Regional offices of the Dept. of Wildlife *do not* sell hunting or fishing licenses, although nonresidents may order licenses directly from the Olympia headquarters office.

Most reservation Indian tribes sell fishing permits to anglers fishing reservations waters. Fees vary considerably and are set by each tribe. Some tribes, however, do not permit nontribal sportfishing. A state fishing license does not authorize anglers to fish reservation waters. Inquire at tribal headquarters.

Giardiasis

Purify all surface water that is to be used for drinking or cooking. Northwestern lakes, streams and rivers may be contaminated by the organism *Giardia lamblia* which causes

Silver Falls State Park in western Oregon.

(© John Barger)

a condition known as giardiasis. *Giardia lamblia* is carried in the feces of humans and some domestic and wild animals.

Though the water may appear and taste cool, clear and fresh, *Giardia* cysts may infest it. Many wildlife species are not affected by the disease, so if you see an animal drinking from the stream, do not assume it is safe.

The symptoms of giardiasis (also known as Beaver Fever) include diarrhea, increased gas, loss of appetite, abdominal cramps and bloating. Weight loss may occur from nausea and loss of appetite. These discomforts may appear a few days to a few weeks after ingestion and may last up to 6 weeks. Most people are unknowingly infected and have often returned home from vacation before onset of symptoms. If not treated, the symptoms may resolve on their own, only to recur intermittently over a period of many months. Other diseases have similar symptoms, but if you drank untreated water, you should suspect giardiasis and so inform your doctor. With proper diagnosis, the disease is curable with medication prescribed by a physician.

There are several ways to treat surface water to make it safe, but the most certain is to boil the water for at least 1 minute. For an added margin of safety, boil the water from 3 to 5 minutes.

Chemical disinfectants such as iodine or chlorine tablets or drops are not yet considered as reliable as heat in killing *Giardia*, although these products work well against most waterborne bacteria and viruses that cause disease.

Giardia can be readily transmitted between humans and animals. Dogs, like people, can become infected with *Giardia*. Unless they are carefully controlled, dogs can contaminate water and continue the chain of infection from animals to humans. Feces can contain the organism and should be buried 8 inches deep at least 100 feet from the nearest natural water source.

CAUTION: Swimmers should inquire locally before taking a dip in any gravel pits or roadside lakes. Some of the Northwest's ponds are host to the larvae of schistosomes, which cause "swimmer's itch." Symptoms are redness and itching of the skin, beginning immediately and lasting up to a week. Shower or bathe immediately after being in water you suspect may be infected and dry off well.

Hiking

Trails and trailheads along highways in the Northwest are noted in the individual highway logs. For detailed information on a particular trail, contact the appropriate government agency.

National Park Service (Western Regional Information Office, Fort Mason, Bldg. 201, San Francisco, CA 94123) has general information on hiking in all of the NPS-administered national parks, preserves and monuments.

Hitchhiking

Drivers are warned that picking up hitchhikers is a dangerous and sometimes lethal practice.

ALBERTA
Legal except where posted.

BRITISH COLUMBIA
Legal except where posted.

IDAHO
Law prohibits, but the practice is tolerated. Tolerated only on on-ramps and off-ramps on the interstate highways.

MONTANA
Legal, except where otherwise posted.

OREGON
Permitted, unless otherwise posted.

WASHINGTON
Legal except where posted.

Holidays

	1990	1991
Jan. 1	New Year's Day	Jan. 1
Jan. 15	Martin L. King Day	Jan. 21
Feb. 19	President's Day	Feb. 18
Apr. 13	Good Friday (Canada)	Mar. 29
Apr. 15	Easter Sunday	Mar. 31
Apr. 16	Easter Monday (Canada)	Apr. 1
May 21	Victoria Day (Canada)	May 20
May 28	Memorial Day	May 27
July 1	Canada Day	July 1
July 4	Independence Day	July 4
Aug. 6	Alberta Heritage Day British Columbia Day	Aug. 5
Sept. 3	Labor Day (U.S. & Canada)	Sept. 2
Oct. 8	Thanksgiving Day (Canada)	Oct. 14
Oct. 8	Columbus Day	Oct. 14
Nov. 11	Veterans Day (U.S.)	Nov. 11
Nov. 11	Remembrance Day (Canada)	Nov. 11
Nov. 22	Thanksgiving Day (U.S.)	Nov. 21
Dec. 25	Christmas	Dec. 25
Dec. 26	Boxing Day (Canada)	Dec. 26

Hostels

Youth hostels dot the travel routes through the U.S. and Canada. Hostels are open to anyone possessing a valid membership card (cards are available at any of the hostels).

For information about membership, hostel locations and facilities, opening and closing dates, reservations and special rates for families and groups, contact your national or local hostel office for their respective handbooks. National offices are located in the U.S. at American Youth Hostels, P.O. Box 37613, Washington, DC 20013-7613; phone (202) 783-6161. And in Canada at Canadian Hostelling Assoc., Tower A-3, 333 River Road, Vanier City, ON, Canada K1L 8B9; phone (613) 748-5638.

Information Sources

ALBERTA

Alberta Energy and Natural Resources, Fish & Wildlife Division, 9920 108 St., Main Floor, Edmonton, AB, Canada T5K 2M4; phone (403) 427-3590.

Parks Canada, Western Region, Room 520, P.O. Box 2989, Station M, 220 4th Ave. SE, Calgary, AB, Canada T2P 3H8; phone (403) 292-4401.

Royal Canadian Mounted Police, phone (403) 471-9335 Edmonton for information and help.

Travel Alberta, 14th Floor, 10065 Jasper Ave., Edmonton, AB, Canada T5J 1L8; phone (403) 427-4321, toll free 1-800-661-8888.

South side of Mount Hood rises above coniferous forest.   (© John Barger)

BRITISH COLUMBIA

B.C. Fishing Camp Operators Assoc., Box 3301, Kamloops, BC, Canada V2C 6B9.

British Columbia Ferry Corp., 818 Broughton St., Victoria, BC, Canada V8W 1E4; phone (604) 386-3431. Schedules are available.

Dept. of Fisheries & Oceans, 1090 W. Pender St., Vancouver, BC, Canada V6E 2P1; phone (604) 666-0384.

Ministry of Environment, Fisheries Branch (fresh water), Parliament Bldg., Victoria, BC, Canada V8V 1X5; phone (604) 387-4573.

Ministry of Lands, Parks & Housing, Parks & Outdoor Recreation Division, 1019 Wharf St., Victoria, BC, Canada V8W 2Y9; phone (604) 387-1067.

Royal Canadian Mounted Police, phone (604) 264-3111 for information and help.

Tourism B.C., Parliament Buildings, Victoria, BC, Canada V8V 1X4; phone toll free 1-800-663-6000.

CALIFORNIA

California Dept. of Fish & Game, 1416 9th St., Sacramento, CA 94814; phone (916) 445-3531.

California Highway Patrol. Dial O for operator, ask for Zenith 12000.

California Office of Tourism, 1121 L St., Suite 103, Sacramento, CA 95814; phone 1-800-862-2543 or (916) 322-1397.

California State Parks. For guide to state parks, send $2 to State Parks, P.O. Box 942896, Sacramento, CA 94296-0001. For information, call (916) 445-6477.

California Travel Parks Assoc., 1662 Auburn Ravine Road, Auburn, CA 95603; phone (916) 885-1624.

Campgrounds: Mistix, P.O. Box 85705, San Diego, CA 92138-5705.

National Park Service, Western Regional Information Office, Fort Mason, Bldg. 201, San Francisco, CA 94123; phone (415) 556-4122.

U.S. Forest Service, 630 Sansome St., San Francisco, CA 94111; phone (415) 705-2874.

IDAHO

Highway Information: Idaho Dept. of Transportation, 3311 W. State, Boise, ID 83707; phone (208) 334-3664.

Idaho Campgrounds Owners Assoc., (private) 11101 Fairview Ave., Boise, ID 83704; phone 1-800-635-5240.

Idaho Dept. of Fish & Game, Headquarters, 600 S. Walnut, P.O. Box 25, Boise, ID 83707; phone (208) 334-3700.

Idaho Outfitters & Guides Assoc., P.O. Box 95, Boise, ID 83707; phone (208) 342-1919.

Idaho State Parks and Recreation, State House Mail, Boise, ID 83707; phone (208) 334-2154.

Idaho State Police, 1311 W. State, Boise, ID 83707; phone (208) 334-3850.

Idaho Travel Council, Joe R. Williams Bldg., 2nd Floor, 700 W. State St., Boise, ID 83720; phone (208) 334-3850, toll free 1-800-635-7820.

MONTANA

Montana Campground Assn., Box 215, West Glacier, MT 59936; phone (406) 387-5341.

Montana Dept. of Fish, Wildlife & Parks, Headquarters, 1420 E. 6th Ave., Helena, MT 59620; phone (406) 444-2535.

Montana Outfitters and Guides Assoc., Box 1339, Townsend, MT 59644; phone (406) 449-3578.

Montana Promotion Division, Dept. of Commerce, 1424 9th Ave., Helena, MT 59620; phone toll free 1-800-548-3390.

National Park Service, c/o Grant Kohrs Ranch National Historic Site, P.O. Box 790, Deer Lodge, MT 59722; phone (406) 846-2070.

State Highway Patrol, 303 N. Roberts, Room 162 Scott Hart Bldg., Helena, MT 59620; phone (406) 444-3000.

U.S. Forest Service, Northern Region, P.O. Box 7669, Missoula, MT 59807; phone (406) 329-3711.

OREGON

Crater Lake National Park, P.O. Box 7, Highway 62, Crater Lake, OR 97604; phone (503) 594-2211.

Oregon Dept. of Fish & Wildlife, 506 SW Mill St., Box 59, Portland, OR 97208; phone (503) 229-5551.

Oregon Guides and Packers Assoc., P.O. Box 10841, Eugene, OR 97440; phone (503) 683-9552.

Oregon State Patrol, Information, 107 Public Service Bldg., Salem, OR 97310; phone (503) 378-3071. To report drunk drivers, crime and accidents, toll free 1-800-452-7888.

Oregon Tourism Division Economic Development Dept., 595 Cottage St. NE, Salem, OR 97310; phone (503) 373-1200, toll free 1-800-547-7842.

GENERAL INFORMATION

State Parks & Recreation Division, 525 Trade St. SE, Salem, OR 97310; phone (503) 378-6305.

U.S. Forest Service, 319 SW Pine St., P.O. Box 3623, Portland, OR 97208; phone (503) 221-2877.

WASHINGTON

Dept. of Natural Resources, Public Lands Bldg., Olympia, WA 98504.

Outdoor Recreation Information, National Forest Service/National Parks Service, 1018 1st Ave., Seattle, WA 98104; phone (206) 442-0170 or 442-0181.

Tourism Development Division, Washington State Dept. of Trade & Economic Development, 101 General Administration Bldg., Olympia, WA 98504-0613; phone toll free out of state 1-800-544-1800; in-state phone (206) 586-2088 or (206) 586-2102.

Washington Outfitters & Guides Assoc., P.O. Box 95229, Seattle, WA 98145-2229

Washington Resorts & Private Parks Assoc., 22910 15th Ave. SE, Suite C, Bothell, WA 98021; phone (206) 352-7388.

Washington State Dept. of Fisheries, 115 General Administration Bldg., AX-11, Olympia, WA 98504; phone (206) 753-6600.

Washington State Dept. of Transportation, Public Affairs Office, Transportation Bldg., Olympia, WA 98504; phone (206) 753-2150.

Washington State Dept. of Wildlife, 600 N. Capitol Way, GJ-11, Olympia, WA 98504; phone (206) 753-5700.

Washington State Ferries, Colman Dock, Seattle, WA 98104: 24-hour information — toll free in state 1-800-542-0810 or 1-800-542-7052; out of state (206) 464-6400.

Washington State Parks & Recreation Commission, 7150 Cleanwater Lane, KY-11, Olympia, WA 98504; phone (206) 753-2027. Summers only phone 1-800-562-0990.

Washington State Patrol, General Administration Bldg., Olympia, WA 98501; phone (206) 753-6540.

Metric System

Canada has converted to the metric system. Inches have been replaced with centimeters, feet and yards with meters, miles with kilometers and Fahrenheit with Celsius. Logs of Canadian highways in *NORTHWEST MILEPOSTS®* include metric conversion in the miles, elevations and temperatures. To further assist you with metric configurations, see the accompanying charts.

Pets

Many people travel with their pets and it is generally not a problem. Pet food, pet stores, kennels and veterinarians are available throughout the Northwest.

Keep your dog on a leash, both for his own safety and as a courtesy to other travelers. Pets should be on a leash at government campgrounds; pets are allowed in parks and campgrounds if they are kept under restraint at all times. They are generally not permitted on backcountry trails.

Do have identification on your pet should he get lost. Don't ruin your vacation by losing your pet.

Some hotels and motels allow pets; check their policy on pets when making reservations.

You must have a certificate of rabies vacination for your pet to cross the U.S.-Canada border. See Customs Requirements this section for more information.

LITERS TO GALLONS CONVERSION TABLE

Liters	Gallons	Liters	Gallons
1	0.3	31	8.2
2	0.5	32	8.5
3	0.8	33	8.7
4	1.1	34	9.0
5	1.3	35	9.2
6	1.6	36	9.5
7	1.8	37	9.8
8	2.1	38	10.0
9	2.4	39	10.3
10	2.6	40	10.6
11	2.9	41	10.8
12	3.2	42	11.1
13	3.4	43	11.4
14	3.7	44	11.6
15	4.0	45	11.9
16	4.2	46	12.2
17	4.5	47	12.4
18	4.8	48	12.7
19	5.0	49	12.9
20	5.3	50	13.2
21	5.5	51	13.5
22	5.8	52	13.7
23	6.1	53	14.0
24	6.3	54	14.3
25	6.6	55	14.5
26	6.9	56	14.8
27	7.1	57	15.0
28	7.4	58	15.3
29	7.7	59	15.6
30	7.9	60	15.9

For more precise conversion: 1 liter equals .2642 gallons; 1 gallon equals 3.785 liters.

Pronunciation Guide

The following is a phonetical pronunciation guide for some of the most commonly mispronounced place names in the Northwest.

Agassiz—AG-a-see
Arcata—ar-KAY-ta
Arimo—AIR-i-mo
Boise—BOY-see
Bruneau—BREW-no
Camano—kuh-MAY-no
Cathlamet—kath-LAM-ett
Celilo—se-LIE-lo
Chehalis—che-HAY-liss
Chewelah—che-WEE-la
Cle Elum—clee-ELL-lum
Coeur d'Alene—CORR-duh-LANE
Copalis—Coe-PAY-liss
Coquihalla—COE-kwi-HALL-a
Dubois—DEW-boyce
Enumclaw—EE-num-claw
Galiano—GALL-ee-ANN-o
Hoquiam—HO-kwee-um
Ilwaco—ill-WAU-co
Kalaloch—C'LAY-lock
Kamiah—KAMM-ee-eye
Kananaskis—KANNA-nas-kiss
Keremos—KAIR-e-mose
Kittitas—KITT-i-tass
Kooskia—KOOS-kee
Kootenai—KOOT-nee or KOOT-nay
Lapwai—LAP-way
Lilliwaup—LILL-lih-wop
Lillooet—LIL-Loo-et or Lil-LUTE
Memaloose—MEMM-a-loos
Mukilteo—MUK-il-TEE-o
Multnomah—mult-NO-mah
Naches—nat-CHEESE
Nanaimo—nuh-NEYE-mo
Nespelem—nes-PEE-lem
Nisqually—nih-SQUALL-lee
Okanagan—OH-kuh-NAW-gun
Orovada—ORR-uh-VADD-uh
Osoyoos—oh-SOY-youss
Palouse—puh-LOOS
Pe Ell—pay-ELL
Pend Oreille—Pon-doe-RAY
Pocatello—POKE-a-TELL-o
Puyallup—pew-AL-up
Quilchena—quill-CHEE-na

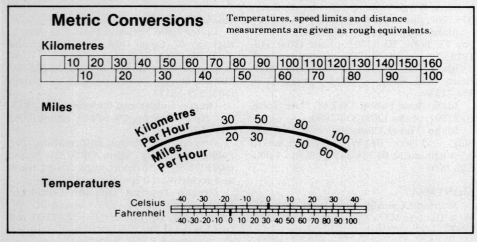

Metric Conversions

Temperatures, speed limits and distance measurements are given as rough equivalents.

Kilometres

	10	20	30	40	50	60	70	80	90	100	110	120	130	140	150	160
		10		20		30		40		50		60		70		80		90		100

Miles

Kilometres Per Hour / Miles Per Hour
30 50 80
20 30 50 60 100

Temperatures

Celsius -40 -30 -20 -10 0 10 20 30 40
Fahrenheit -40 -30 -20 -10 0 10 20 30 40 50 60 70 80 90 100

Quillayute—QUILL-uh-yute
Sappho—SAFF-o
Sekiu—SEE-que
Sequim—SKWIM
Siskiyou—SISS-que or SISS-sk'ewe
Skykomish—Sky-KO-mish
Snoqualmie—snow-KWALL-mee
Stehekin—ste-HEE-kin
Steilacoom—STILL-uh-come
Teanaway—tee-ANN-a-way
Tenino—te-NINE-o
Terrebone—TERR-e-bon
Tete Juane Cache—tee-john-cash
Tofino—tuh-FEE-no
Tonasket—tuh-NASS-kett
Tsawwassen—tuh-WAH-sen
Tualatin—too-AL-i-ton
Tukwila—tuck-WILL-a
Tulalip—too-LAY-lip
Ucluelet—you-CLU-let
Uintah—you-INN-ta
Ukiah—you-KI-ah
Waiilatpu—why-LAT-poo
Walhachin—wall-LAW-chin
Wallowa—wall-LAU-wa
Wenatchee—weh-NATCH-hee
Wetaskiwin—wi-TASS-ke-win
Willamette—will-LAM-met
Willapa—WILL-aw-pa
Wyeth—WHY-eth
Yachats—ya-HOTS
Yakima—YAK-ih-ma
Yaquina—yah-KEE-na
Yreka—why-REE-ka

Railroads

The major rail carrier in the United States is Amtrak. Many of the highways covered in *NORTHWEST MILEPOSTS®* parallel Amtrak service and travelers might enjoy a break from interstate travel by using Amtrak. For information call toll free 1-800-872-7245.

Railroads with passenger service serving Canada include British Columbia Railway, P.O. Box 8770, Vancouver, BC, V6B 4X6; (604) 984-5005. This railroad, operated by the B.C. government, provides passenger service between North Vancouver and Prince George. VIA Rail Canada, a crown corporation, operates passenger trains formerly operated by Canadian National and Canadian Pacific railways. Service between Prince Rupert and Jasper and waypoints, service from Vancouver to Toronto, ON, and points east via Banff and Jasper; and service between Victoria and Courtenay and waypoints. Write VIA Rail Canada, 1150 Station St., Vancouver, BC, V6A 2X7 for information or call 1-800-665-0200.

State Symbols

ALBERTA
  Provincial Bird: Great horned owl
  Provincial Flower: Wild rose

BRITISH COLUMBIA
  Provincial Flower: Dogwood

Provincial Motto: *Splendor Sine Occasu* (Splendor Without Diminishment)

IDAHO
  State Bird: Mountain bluebird
  State Flower: Syringa
  State Motto: *Esto Perpetua* (It Is Perpetual)
  State Song: Here We Have Idaho
  State Tree: White pine

MONTANA
  State Bird: Western meadowlark
  State Flower: Bitterroot
  State Motto: *Oro Y Plata* (Gold and Silver)
  State Song: Montana
  State Tree: Ponderosa pine

OREGON
  State Bird: Western meadowlark
  State Flower: Oregon grape
  State Motto: The Union
  State Song: Oregon, My Oregon
  State Tree: Douglas fir

WASHINGTON
  State Bird: Willow goldfinch
  State Flower: Western rhododendron
  State Motto: Alki (By and By)
  State Song: Washington, My Home
  State Tree: Western hemlock

Time Zones

Utah, Wyoming, southern Idaho (south of the Salmon River), and Montana are in the Mountain time zone. California, Nevada, Oregon, Washington and northern Idaho fall in the Pacific time zone.

British Columbia is on Pacific time and Alberta falls in the Mountain time zone.

All areas covered in *NORTHWEST MILE-POSTS®* observe daylight saving time. (See accompanying map.)

Wildlife

The Northwest is a good place to observe wildlife in its natural habitat. Viewing of wildlife is available in any of the national parks, the many private parks (such as Northwest Trek near Tacoma, WA, or the Sea Lion Caves near Florence, OR), reserves such as the National Bison Range north of Missoula, MT, or alongside the roadways of the prairie lands. Wildlife viewing possibilities are frequently noted throughout the highway logs. Major cities covered in *NORTHWEST MILEPOSTS®* feature excellent zoos for close-up viewing of native and non-native wildlife. See the Major Cities section for details.

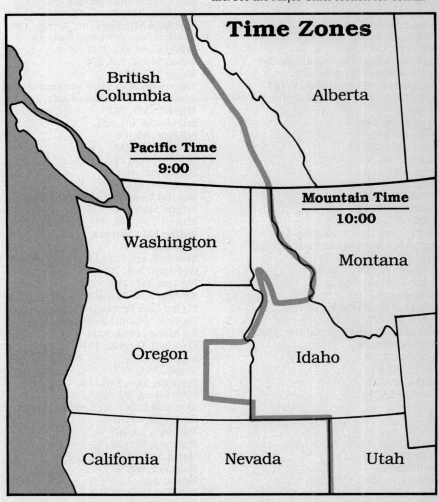

Index

INDEX

Field Editor Report

If, during your travels, you find changes along the highways logged in *NORTHWEST MILEPOSTS®*, pleases let us know by dropping a note to the Editor, *NORTHWEST MILEPOSTS®*, 22026 20th Ave. S.E., Bothell, WA 98041.

We've found that some of our best travel information comes from our readers. So let us know if you find an interesting attraction or new campground not logged in *NORTHWEST MILEPOSTS®*.

Have a fantastic trip . . . and let us know how it goes!   – The Editors

On page_____of *NORTHWEST MILEPOSTS®*, in column _____ (1, 2, 3), we suggest that you make the following change(s):

_____

_____

_____

On page_____of *NORTHWEST MILEPOSTS®*, in column _____ (1, 2, 3), we suggest that you make the following change(s):

_____

_____

_____

On page_____of *NORTHWEST MILEPOSTS®*, in column _____ (1, 2, 3), we suggest that you make the following change(s):

_____

_____

_____

Notes and comments: _____

_____

_____

_____

_____

_____